LET'S GO
India al

■ **Let's Go writers travel o**

"Guides that penetrate the veneer of the holiday brochures and mine the grit of real life."
—*The Economist*

"The writers seem to have experienced every rooster-packed bus and lunar-surfaced mattress about which they write."
—*The New York Times*

"All the dirt, dirt cheap."
—*People*

■ **Great for independent travelers.**

"The guides are aimed not only at young budget travelers but at the independent traveler, a sort of streetwise cookbook for traveling alone."
—*The New York Times*

"Flush with candor and irreverence, chock full of budget travel advice."
—*The Des Moines Register*

"An indispensable resource. *Let's Go*'s practical information can be used by every traveler."
—*The Chattanooga Free Press*

■ **Let's Go is completely revised each year.**

"Only *Let's Go* has the zeal to annually update every title on its list."
—*The Boston Globe*

"Unbeatable: good sight-seeing advice; up-to-date info on restaurants, hotels, and inns; a commitment to money-saving travel; and a wry style that brightens nearly every page."
—*The Washington Post*

■ **All the important information you need.**

"*Let's Go* authors provide a comedic element while still providing concise information and thorough coverage of the country. Anything you need to know about budget traveling is detailed in this book."
—*The Chicago Sun-Times*

"Value-packed, unbeatable, accurate, and comprehensive."
—*Los Angeles Times*

Let's Go Publications

Let's Go: Alaska & the Pacific Northwest 1999
Let's Go: Australia 1999
Let's Go: Austria & Switzerland 1999
Let's Go: Britain & Ireland 1999
Let's Go: California 1999
Let's Go: Central America 1999
Let's Go: Eastern Europe 1999
Let's Go: Ecuador & the Galápagos Islands 1999
Let's Go: Europe 1999
Let's Go: France 1999
Let's Go: Germany 1999
Let's Go: Greece 1999 **New title!**
Let's Go: India & Nepal 1999
Let's Go: Ireland 1999
Let's Go: Israel & Egypt 1999
Let's Go: Italy 1999
Let's Go: London 1999
Let's Go: Mexico 1999
Let's Go: New York City 1999
Let's Go: New Zealand 1999
Let's Go: Paris 1999
Let's Go: Rome 1999
Let's Go: South Africa 1999 **New title!**
Let's Go: Southeast Asia 1999
Let's Go: Spain & Portugal 1999
Let's Go: Turkey 1999 **New title!**
Let's Go: USA 1999
Let's Go: Washington, D.C. 1999

Let's Go Map Guides

Amsterdam	Madrid
Berlin	New Orleans
Boston	New York City
Chicago	Paris
Florence	Rome
London	San Francisco
Los Angeles	Washington, D.C.

Coming Soon: Prague, Seattle

Let's Go
Publications

Let's Go
India and
Nepal
1999

Nate Barksdale
Editor

Bina Gogineni
Associate Editor

Daley Haggar
Associate Editor

Researcher-Writers:

Asbury P. Jones, Jr.	Adam Rzepka
Keith Lee	Tim Santry
Abena Osseo-Asare	Shlomtzion Shaham
Kishan Kumar Putta	Vivek Waglé
Elizabeth Tova Russo	Katarina Wong
Andrew E. Nieland	

St. Martin's Press ⚘ New York

HELPING LET'S GO

If you want to share your discoveries, suggestions, or corrections, please drop us a line. We read every piece of correspondence, whether a postcard, a 10-page email, or a coconut. Please note that mail received after May 1999 may be too late for the 2000 book, but will be kept for future editions. **Address mail to:**

> **Let's Go: India and Nepal**
> **67 Mount Auburn Street**
> **Cambridge, MA 02138**
> **USA**

Visit Let's Go at **http://www.letsgo.com,** or send email to:

> **feedback@letsgo.com**
> **Subject: "Let's Go: India and Nepal"**

In addition to the invaluable travel advice our readers share with us, many are kind enough to offer their services as researchers or editors. Unfortunately, our charter enables us to employ only currently enrolled Harvard-Radcliffe students.

Contents

List of Maps

About Let's Go

THIRTY-NINE YEARS OF WISDOM

Back in 1960, a few students at Harvard University banded together to produce a 20-page pamphlet offering a collection of tips on budget travel in Europe. This modest, mimeographed packet, offered as an extra to passengers on student charter flights to Europe, met with instant popularity. The following year, students traveling to Europe researched the first, full-fledged edition of *Let's Go: Europe,* a pocket-sized book featuring honest, irreverent writing and a decidedly youthful outlook on the world. Throughout the 60s, our guides reflected the times; the 1969 guide to America led off by inviting travelers to "dig the scene" at San Francisco's Haight-Ashbury. During the 70s and 80s, we gradually added regional guides and expanded coverage into the Middle East and Central America. With the addition of our in-depth city guides, handy map guides, and extensive coverage of Asia and Australia, the 90s are also proving to be a time of explosive growth for Let's Go, and there's certainly no end in sight. The maiden edition of *Let's Go: South Africa,* our pioneer guide to sub-Saharan Africa, hits the shelves this year, along with the first editions of *Let's Go: Greece* and *Let's Go: Turkey.*

We've seen a lot in 39 years. *Let's Go: Europe* is now the world's bestselling international guide, translated into seven languages. And our new guides bring Let's Go's total number of titles, with their spirit of adventure and their reputation for honesty, accuracy, and editorial integrity, to 44. But some things never change: our guides are still researched, written, and produced entirely by students who know first-hand how to see the world on the cheap.

HOW WE DO IT

Each guide is completely revised and thoroughly updated every year by a well-traveled set of over 200 students. Every winter, we recruit over 160 researchers and 70 editors to write the books anew. After several months of training, researcher-writers hit the road for seven weeks of exploration, from Anchorage to Adelaide, Estonia to El Salvador, Iceland to Indonesia. Hired for their rare combination of budget travel sense, writing ability, stamina, and courage, these adventurous travelers know that train strikes, stolen luggage, food poisoning, and marriage proposals are all part of a day's work. Back at our offices, editors work from spring to fall, massaging copy written on Himalayan bus rides into witty yet informative prose. A student staff of typesetters, cartographers, publicists, and managers keeps our lively team together. In September, the collected efforts of the summer are delivered to our printer, who turns them into books in record time, so that you have the most up-to-date information available for your vacation. Even as you read this, work on next year's editions is well underway.

WHY WE DO IT

We don't think of budget travel as the last recourse of the destitute; we believe that it's the only way to travel. Living cheaply and simply brings you closer to the people and places you've been saving up to visit. Our books will ease your anxieties and answer your questions about the basics—so you can get off the beaten track and explore. Once you learn the ropes, we encourage you to put *Let's Go* down now and then to strike out on your own. You know as well as we that the best discoveries are often those you make yourself. When you find something worth sharing, please drop us a line. We're Let's Go Publications, 67 Mount Auburn St., Cambridge, MA 02138, USA (email: feedback@letsgo.com). For more info, visit our website, http://www.letsgo.com.

HAPPY TRAVELS!

How to Use This Book

> **Warning: This is a warning box.** Read these for information on how to avoid getting ripped off by jewelry smugglers. Or trampled by angry rhinos. Or both.

BEFORE YOU GO Traveling to India and Nepal, even on a budget, is a costly undertaking that requires a lot of preparation: vaccinations, visas, choosing the right color of backpack, and so on. The **Essentials** section (p. 1) contains all that and more, explaining the logistics of getting there and, once there, the particulars of staying fed, sheltered, clothed, and healthy as you travel.

BACKGROUND INFORMATION Chapters on **India** (p. 73) and **Nepal** (p. 700) trace the two countries' history from ancient civilizations to this year's elections, and provide background on the religious and artistic traditions of South Asia. At the end of the book, there's a **glossary** (p. 814) of common terms used in this book.

LANGUAGES भाषा Most of the city and town names in this book are translated into some local script. Although English and a lot of patience are all the communication tools you really need for most travel in India and Nepal, it never hurts to have the Hindi (or Kannada or Tamil) city name ready to show your bus driver. In the back of the book are **phrasebooks** (p. 807) for the Hindi, Bengali, Tamil, Marathi, Nepali, Gujarati, Kannada, Malayalam, and Telugu languages. Learning even a few words will ease communication and gain you a lot of new friends.

This Is a Graybox

These contain a mix of historical, religious, and cultural topics, such as the design of Mughal tombs, or how to speak Tamil to your cat—not necessarily essential for travel, but amusing and informative nonetheless.

INDIA Our coverage is divided into four regions; in each, coverage spirals out in a roughly clockwise direction from a major city. **North India** begins with **Delhi** (p. 116); **East India** with **Calcutta** (p. 378); **South India** with **Chennai** (Madras; p. 464), and **West India** with **Mumbai** (Bombay; p. 464). Although this quartering follows general Indian regional distinctions, the division is, in places, quite arbitrary.

NEPAL Coverage begins in the **Kathmandu Valley** (p. 717) and moves to the **Western Hills** (p. 765), the lowland **Terai** (p. 782), and the **Eastern Hills** (p. 797), in the shadow of Mt. Everest.

TREKKING The aforementioned **Essentials** section has planning, packing, and health information for trekkers (p. 58). Individual treks are described in the regional write-ups (see **trekking** in the index for a quick list of routes).

A NOTE TO OUR READERS

The information for this book was gathered by *Let's Go*'s researchers from May through August (with the exception of Goa, which was researched in December and July). Each listing is derived from the assigned researcher's opinion based upon his or her visit at a particular time. The opinions are expressed in a candid and forthright manner. Other travelers might disagree. Those traveling at a different time may have different experiences since prices, dates, hours, and conditions are always subject to change. You are urged to check beforehand to avoid inconvenience and surprises. Travel always involves a certain degree of risk, especially in low-cost areas. When traveling, especially on a budget, always take particular care to ensure your safety.

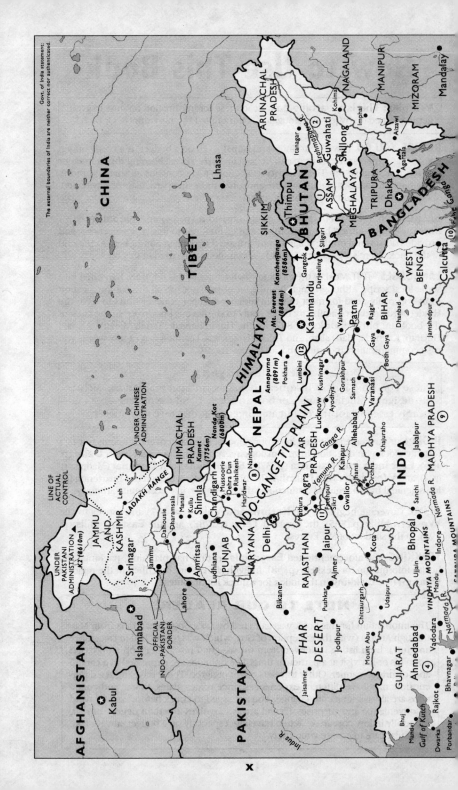

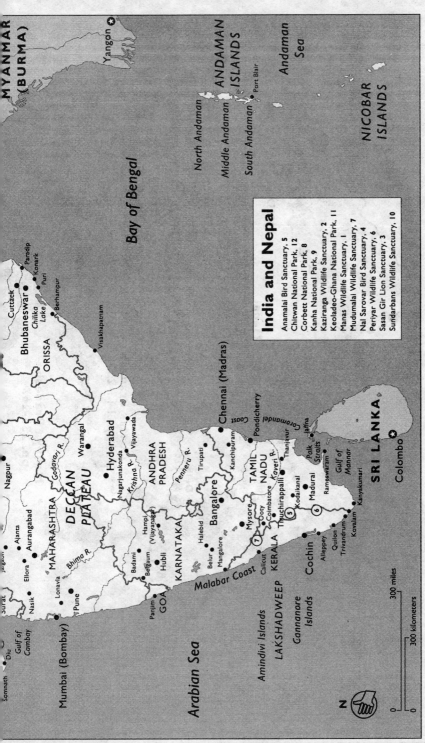

India and Nepal

Anamalai Bird Sanctuary, 5
Chitwan National Park, 12
Corbett National Park, 8
Kanha National Park, 9
Kaziranga Wildlife Sanctuary, 2
Keoladeo-Ghana National Park, 11
Manas Wildlife Sanctuary, 1
Mudumalai Wildlife Sanctuary, 7
Nal Sarovar Bird Sanctuary, 4
Periyar Wildlife Sanctuary, 6
Sasan Gir Lion Sanctuary, 3
Sundarbans Wildlife Sanctuary, 10

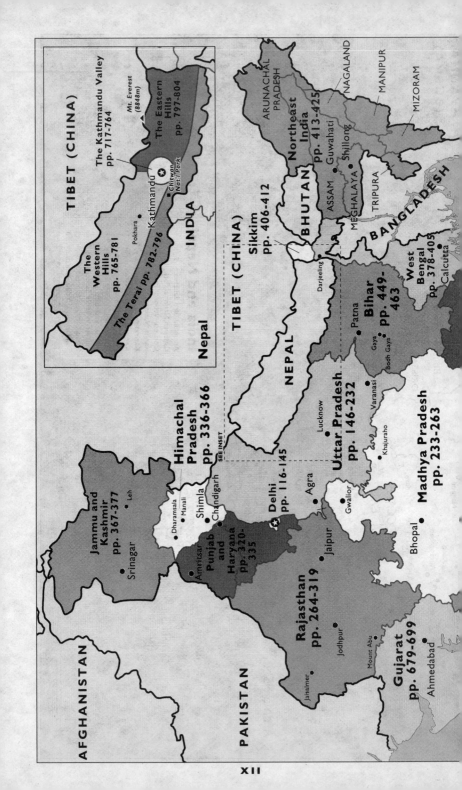

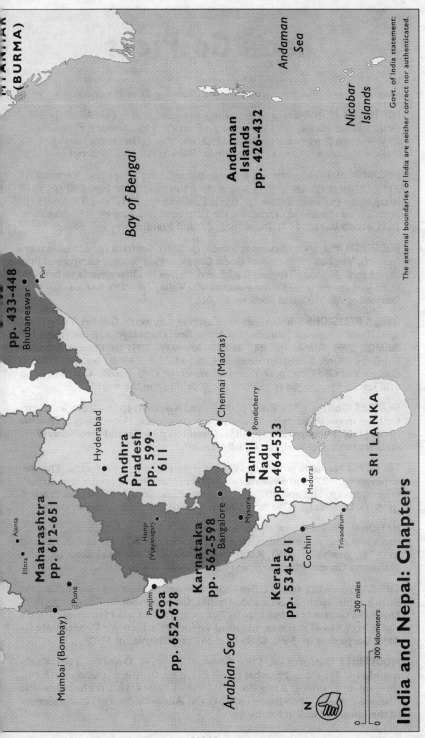

India and Nepal: Chapters

N

300 miles

300 kilometers

Govt. of India statement:

The external boundaries of India are neither correct nor authenticated.

Let's Go Picks

What follows is the best of the best that India and Nepal have to offer, a palatte of sorts to help you plan. For more advice, see **Planning Your Itinerary, p. 3.**

FORTS AND MONUMENTS Among the must-sees: Agra's **Taj Mahal** (p. 193), Delhi's **Jama Masjid** (p. 137) and **Red Fort** (p. 135), Jaipur's **Pink City** (p. 273), Patan's **Durbar Square** (p. 741), Hyderabad's **Golconda Fort** (p. 605), and the abandoned capitals at **Fatehpur Sikri** (p. 198) and **Hampi** (p. 591).

HINDUISM Holy cities abound in India, but none are holier than **Varanasi** (p. 215). Other religious centers and temple towns include **Madurai** (p. 511), **Khajuraho** (p. 249), **Nasik** (p. 634), **Pushkar** (p. 282), and **Tirumala** (p. 609). Those interested in studying the faith head to ashrams in **Rishikesh** (p. 164), **Haridwar** (p. 159), **Pune** (p. 636), and **Pondicherry** (p. 488).

BUDDHISM The ancient ruins at **Sanchi** (p. 238), **Sarnath** (p. 225), **Lumbini** (p. 784), **Vaishali** (p. 460), and **Bodh Gaya** (p. 456) provide glimpses of Buddhism past. Modern **Tibetan Buddhism** thrives in **Dharamsala** (where the Dalai Lama lives; p. 343), the **Kathmandu Valley** (p. 717), **Ladakh** (p. 367), **Darjeeling** (p. 398), and **Sikkim** (p. 406).

OTHER RELIGIONS Sikhism revolves around Amritsar's **Golden Temple** (p. 330). India's greatest **Jain** temples are at **Sravanabelagola** (p. 583) and **Mt. Abu** (p. 296). **Ajmer** (p. 280) and **Lucknow** (p. 203) are centers of Indian Muslim culture. **Christian** structures include the colonial and pre-colonial churches of **Old Goa** (p. 661) and **Chennai** (p. 478). Finally, **Cochin's** beautiful Jewish **synagogue** (p. 555) is the fifth-oldest in the world.

BEACHES Goa (p. 652), **Puri** (p. 440), and **Kovalam** (p. 540) are legendary for their tropical beauty and expatriate party scenes. The strands at **Dwarka** (p. 695), **Mahabalipuram** (p. 483), **Chennai** (p. 465), and **Pondicherry** (p. 488) are more subdued, but equally beautiful.

TREKKING Nepal is where trekking was invented and perfected. The **Annapurna** (p. 777) and **Everest** (p. 797) treks are most popular, but Nepal's other treks (p. 762 and 802) are also incredible. India's **Himachal Pradesh** (p. 364), **Ladakh** (p. 375), and **Sikkim** (p. 410) also have good trekking.

NATIONAL PARKS A few tigers and a whole lot more inhabit South Asia's parks and reserves, including Nepal's **Chitwan** (p. 787) and India's **Corbett** (p. 173), **Kanha** (p. 248), **Keoladeo Ghana** (p. 278), **Kaziranga** (p. 419), **Mahatma Gandhi Marine** (p. 431), and **Sasam Gir** (p. 693).

THE RAJ You can't travel far in India without running into something the British built. Highlights include Delhi's **Government Buildings** (p. 139), Mumbai's **Gateway to India** (p. 627), Calcutta's **Victoria Memorial** (p. 392), and a bevy of **hill stations,** the most famous of which are **Dharamsala** (p. 343), **Darjeeling** (p. 398), **Ooty** (p. 528), and **Shimla** (p. 336).

MODERNITY Calcutta (p. 378), **Chennai** (p. 465), **Delhi** (p. 116), **Kathmandu** (p. 718), and **Mumbai** (p. 612) are South Asia's cosmopolitan centers; up-and-coming **Bangalore** (p. 563) bristles with technology; the planned cities of **Chandigarh** (p. 321) and **Auroville** (p. 495) give a glimpse of the history of Indian futurism.

ESSENTIALS

PLANNING YOUR TRIP

■ When to Go

India and Nepal have both high and low periods for tourism, which correspond with changes in the weather as well as the timing of vacations and festivals. High season brings inflated prices and a flood of people; low season (which coincides with the monsoon in most of the Subcontinent) means reduced services and reduced traffic at reduced prices, and certain tourist towns close down altogether during this time. Specific peak seasons vary by location. It might also be worth timing your trip to enjoy some of the **festivals** that take place every year in India or Nepal; there is almost always a festival happening somewhere. For more information, see **Holidays and Festivals for 1999-2000** (p. 805).

INDIA

In India as in few other places, travelers are truly at the mercy of the weather's whims. Even the best-planned itineraries are no match for monsoons, dust storms, landslides that close roads, and flooding that isolates some regions for entire seasons. Extreme heat and humidity can debilitate even the hardiest travelers. In June 1998, a severe heat wave with temperatures topping 52°C (126°F) killed more than 3000 poor and malnourished people in central India, while a severe cyclone in the West killed another 1000. Because India is so vast, different regions have vastly different weather, even at the same time of year. Northern India has seasons similar to the

State/Union Territory	Average Temp. (°C) Summer	Average Temp. (°C) Winter	Average Monsoon	Best Months to Visit
Andaman Islands	33/22	31/20	May-Oct.	Dec.-Apr.
Andhra Pradesh	41/20	32/13	June-Dec.	Nov.-Mar.
Bihar	47/20	28/4	June-Oct.	Oct.-Mar.
Delhi	45/35	20/7	June-Sept.	Oct.-Mar.
Goa	32/21	32/21	June-Oct.	Oct.-May
Gujarat	41/27	29/14	June-Sept.	Oct.-Mar.
Himachal Pradesh	33/14	15/0	July-Sept.	Apr.-Oct.
Karnataka	35/26	25/14	June-Oct.	Oct.-Apr.
Kashmir	30/10	0/-10	None	Apr.-Oct., Dec.-Jan.
Kerala	35/21	35/21	June-Oct.	Nov.-Apr.
Madhya Pradesh	48/22	23/4	June-Sept.	Oct.-Apr.
Maharashtra	39/22	34/12	June-Oct.	Sept.-Mar.
Northeast States	35/18	26/7	June-Sept.	Oct.-May
Orissa	49/27	16/5	July-Oct.	Oct-Mar.
Punjab	45/35	14/0	July-Sept.	Oct.-Mar.
Rajasthan	45/17	32/7	July-Sept.	Oct.-Mar.
Sikkim	23/22	12/0	June-Sept.	Mar.-May, Sept.-Nov.
Tamil Nadu	43/18	43/18	Oct.-Dec.	Nov.-Mar.
Uttar Pradesh	45/11	32/2	June-Sept.	Oct.-Mar.; May-July (hills).
West Bengal	40/24	26/17	June-Sept.	Oct.-Mar.

northern temperate zones (hot summers, cool winters), while the South, close to the equator, has a year-round tropical climate.

The mountain valleys in the Himalayan foothills have extremely cold winters but are reasonably warm in the summertime. Some mountain roads are only accessible during the summer, which is generally the best time to visit the hills. Northern reaches in Himachal Pradesh and Ladakh are also in rainshadow and get none of the monsoonal torrents. The rest of India, however, is hostage to the mighty monsoon. During the **monsoon**—which refers not to a single event, but to a series of storms—it rains heavily (we're talking downpour) most days, although the afternoon sun will come out for a few hours and steam things up—mountain views, however, remain perpetually obscured. The monsoons can be extraordinarily destructive, inducing mudslides and flooding, cutting communications and transportation lines, and causing irritating power outages. The mountains of northeast India are especially hard hit in July and August, and deadly landslides are not uncommon. The two major monsoons hit the southwestern and northeastern coasts in late May/early June and advance inward over the next two months, dumping deluges of water on most of India except the deep South—Tamil Nadu, southern Andhra Pradesh, and the Andaman Islands get their monsoon lashing in mid-October—and the Himalayan foothills.

The monsoon wanes in September, beginning India's **cool season,** although it takes a few more months for the Deccan plateau to dry up. December and January are cool, and even cold at night. Tropical ovens like Mumbai and Chennai go from being exceedingly and almost intolerably hot to being merely hot, and many travelers head south to beach haunts like Goa. **Winter** is the best time to visit India, although those headed for the Indian hills may find it too chilly—spring and autumn are the most popular times to go. Few good things last forever, though, and by February, heat begins building up across the plains. April, May, and June can be suicidally hot, with temperatures of over 45°C/110°F. After a few weeks of downright unbearable weather (dust and lightening storms are commonplace) the rains come again, and the cycle repeats.

NEPAL

Most tourists visit Nepal in the **autumn** (Oct.-Nov.), when the countryside is fresh, the temperatures are mild, the air is clear, and the mountains are visible. The dry, clean air also makes autumn a great time for trekking. **Spring** is also a good time to visit: flowers are in bloom in the hills, the days are longer, and temperatures are a little warmer than in the autumn. **Winter** is probably the worst time to go to Nepal: snow covers ground over 2000-3000m, and even Kathmandu (although never snowy) gets damp and cold. April to June **(pre-monsoon)** gets hot and dusty, especially in the Terai, although temperatures at higher elevations are more bearable (but the haze hides the mountains from view). The **monsoon** descends from late June to September. While most of the country is cloud-cast and beset with downpours, western Nepal, largely in rainshadow, is drier. Although the land greens visibly during the monsoon, there are also drawbacks: roads wash out, flights get cancelled, and leeches become your closest companions on trekking routes.

■ Information

GOVERNMENT INFORMATION OFFICES

Government of India Tourist Office: Australia: Level 2, Picadilly, 210 Pitt St., Sydney, NSW 2000 (tel. (61) 2 9264 4855; fax (61) 2 9264 4860). **Canada:** 60 Bloor St. West, Suite 1003, Toronto, Ontario M4W 3B8 (tel. (416) 962-3787; fax 962-6279). **U.K.:** 7 Cort St., London W1X 2LN (tel. (0181) 734 6613). **U.S.:** 1270 Avenue of the Americas, Suite 1808, New York, NY 10020 (tel. (212) 586-4901; fax 582-3274). 3550 Wilshire Blvd., Suite 204, Los Angeles, CA 90010 (tel. (213) 380-8855; fax 380-6111).

Nepal tourist offices are located in Nepalese embassies and/or consulates. For more information, see **Diplomatic Missions,** p. 46.

Planning Your Itinerary

Many a traveler arrives in India or Nepal with only an open-ended return ticket and a sense of adventure. For less-adventurous (or more time-conscious) travelers, some level of planning is necessary. Think about where you'd like to go, whether you want an exciting whirlwind trip or a relaxing retreat or a little of both, whether you want to spend most of your time at your destinations, or take long train journeys in order to see the countryside and savor the act of travel. Whatever your whim, charting your own course is often the most exciting and rewarding part of travel in the region. For a brief summary of the best India and Nepal have to offer, see **Let's Go Picks,** p. xiv—pick a few places you'd like to see, and connect the dots. For the less-creative, though, here are a few common routes:

Delhi-Jaipur-Agra. The good news: this route covers the three most touristed cities in North India. The bad news: ditto. Add Varanasi, Khajuraho, and a flight to Kathmandu to complete the standard package-tourist pilgrimage. *(1-3 weeks.)*

Chennai-Pondicherry-Chidambaram-Madurai-Kovalam-Cochin-Mysore-Bangalore. An overview of South India, from Tamil Nadu's temples to Kerala's backwaters, to Karnataka's forts and cyber-pubs. *(3-4 weeks.)*

Goa-Manali-Goa-Manali-Goa... The standard hippie seasonal migratory pattern. For a change of place but not scene, substitute Puri and Hampi. *(Indefinite.)*

Delhi-Agra-Bhopal-Hyderabad-Bangalore-Mysore-Hampi-Mumbai. An epic journey down the spine of India. With overnight train rides, this can be done quite quickly, and offers a great view of India's regional diversity. *(3-5 weeks.)*

Calcutta-Darjeeling-Sikkim. Eastern route covers big cities, resort towns, and gorgeous trekking. Add forays into Assam and Meghalaya if you can. *(1-2 weeks.)*

Kathmandu-Chitwan-Pokhara. Nepal's tourist triangle, covering temple cities, tiger-inhabited jungles, and trekking centers—crowded but good. *(2-3 weeks.)*

Calcutta-Puri-Bodh Gaya-Varanasi-Khajuraho-Gwalior-Agra-Delhi. Winds through the most-populated regions of the country, with stops at Hindu and Buddhist holy cities, spectacular Mughal architecture, placid beaches, and the twin centers of British India. *(2-3 weeks.)*

Mumbai-Ajanta-Ellora-Rajasthan-Delhi. Provides a pleasant *masala* (mixture) of big cities, cave temples, and fort towns. *(2-5 weeks.)*

USEFUL PUBLICATIONS

Travelers can pick up tips on etiquette and plumb the national psyches of India and Nepal with the excellent and useful **Culture Shock!** series, available at bookstores, or from Graphic Arts Center Publishing Company, 3019 NW Yeon Ave., Portland, OR 97210 (tel. (503) 226-2402; fax 223-1410).

Adventurous Traveler Bookstore, P.O. Box 1468, Williston, VT 05495 (tel. (800) 282-3963 or (802) 860-6776; fax (802) 677-1821; email books@atbook.com; http://www.AdventurousTraveler.com). Free 40-page catalogue. Specializes in outdoor adventure travel books, maps, and trekking guides for India and Nepal.

USDA/APHIS Animal and Plant Health Inspection Service, Attn: USDA APHIS PPQ, 4700 River Rd., Unit 130, Riverdale, MD 20737 (tel. (301) 734-7743; fax 734-8434). A division of the USDA, APHIS publishes the *Traveler's Tips* pamphlet, which provides information on which plant and animal products you can safely bring home from other countries. Consult local government phone listings.

Culturgrams, from the Publications Division of the David M. Kennedy Center for International Studies, Brigham Young University, P.O. Box 24538, Provo, UT 84602-4538 (tel. (801) 378-6528; fax 378-5882), are country-specific pamphlets that clue you in on the culture of the country you'll be visiting. The most useful feature is the "Culture and Courtesies" section which helps you avoid giving offense.

Superintendent of Documents, P.O. Box 371954, Pittsburgh, PA 15250-7954 (tel. (202) 512-1530; fax 512-1262; email gpoaccess@gpo.gov; http://www.access.gpo.gov/su-docs). Open M-F 7:30am-4:30pm. Publishes *Your Trip*

Abroad (US$1.25), *Health Information for International Travel* (US$14), and "Background Notes" on all countries (US$1 each). Postage included in the prices.

Transitions Abroad, P.O. Box 1300, 18 Hulst Rd., Amherst, MA 01004-1300 (tel. (800) 293-0373 or (413) 256-3414; fax 256-0373; email trabroad@aol.com; http:// transabroad.com). Invaluable magazine lists publications and resources for overseas study, work, and volunteering (US$25 for 6 issues, single copy $6.25). Also publishes *The Alternative Travel Directory,* a comprehensive guide to living, learning, and working overseas (US$20; postage $4).

Ten Speed Press, P.O. Box 7123, Berkeley, CA 94707 (tel. (800) 841-2665; fax (510) 559-1629; email order@tenspeed.com). *The Packing Book* (US$9) provides various checklists and suggested wardrobes, addresses safety concerns, and imparts packing techniques. Other products include travel journals (US$9-10).

U.S. Customs Service, P.O. Box 7407, Washington, D.C., 20044 (tel. (202) 927-6724; http://www.customs.ustreas.gov). *Know Before You Go* tells everything the international traveler needs to know about customs requirements; *Pocket Hints* summarizes the most important data from *KBYG.*

Wide World Books and Maps, 1911 N. 45th St., Seattle, WA 98103 (tel. (206) 634-3453, toll-free (888) 534-3453; fax (206) 634-0558; email travel@speakeasy.org; http://www.travelbooksandmaps.com/). A good selection of travel guides, travel accessories, and hard-to-find maps for tourists and trekkers.

ONLINE RESOURCES

The Web

Online information about India and Nepal, like the rest of the World Wide Web, ranges from the useful to the incredibly inane, with an unfortunate emphasis on the latter. If you're fine with sifting through pages of random people's vacation photos to find that crucial fact, large-scale search sites like **http://www.hotbot.com** are a good bet. You can also search a large database of India-only web sites at **http:// www.123india.com.** Yahoo offers a more ordered approach to the available info, with detailed indices for India and Nepal (**http://www.yahoo.com/Regional/Countries/India** and **http://www.yahoo.com/Regional/Countries/Nepal).** The Indian and Nepali governments offer collections of cultural, business, and tourism resources at **http://www.indiagov.org** and **http://www.info-nepal.com.** Those in search of the latest current events and culture can read online versions of most of India's major English-language newspapers, including the *Times of India* **(http://www.timesofindia.com)** and the *Hindu* **(http://www.webpage.com/hindu/today).** Many travelers to India register for free Hotmail web-based email accounts **(http://www.hotmail.com).** Most Indians with email use Hotmail, so you'll have no trouble getting quick access.

Usenet

Newsgroup junkies can browse a number of India- and Nepal-themed Usenet groups. The largest and loudest of these is **soc.culture.indian.** Nepalese groups are far fewer; **soc.culture.nepal** remains pretty quiet. For travel advice and info, **rec.travel.asia** has great information and anecdotes, but much of its pan-Asian traffic is irrelevant to India and Nepal. In general, treat any advice you get from a newsgroup or personal website with healthy skepticism. Someone's saying on the net that it's perfectly safe to hitchhike barefoot through Kashmir in the winter doesn't make it so.

■ Documents and Formalities

Apply for travel documents early—processing may take several weeks or even months. Don't fall victim to the inevitable delays and bureaucratic snarls of passport agencies. Before you depart, **photocopy all important documents (plane tickets, passport, visas, etc.) and credit cards;** leave these with someone you can contact easily. **Never carry your passport, travel ticket, identification documents, money, traveler's checks, insurance, and credit cards all together,** or you'll be left high and dry in case of theft or loss.

When you travel in India or Nepal, **always carry your passport on your person,** in addition to another form of ID. Many establishments, especially banks, require several IDs before cashing traveler's checks. A passport combined with a driver's license or birth certificate usually serves as proof of your identity and citizenship. Carry extra passport-size photos that you can attach to the sundry IDs you may acquire. If you plan an extended stay, register your passport with your nearest embassy or consulate.

Discounts for foreign students in India and Nepal are rare, so there's little point in carrying student ID, except for insurance and plane ticket discounts. For more information, see **Youth, Student, & Teacher Identification,** p. 12.

PASSPORTS

Foreign travelers in India and Nepal must have a valid passport. **Photocopy the page of your passport that contains your photograph and identifying information.** Carry this photocopy in a safe place apart from your passport, perhaps with a traveling companion, and leave another copy at home. These measures will help prove your citizenship and facilitate the issuing of a new passport in case of loss or theft. Consulates also recommend that you carry an expired passport or an official copy of your birth certificate in a part of your baggage separate from other documents.

If you lose your passport, immediately notify the local police and the nearest embassy or consulate of your home government. To expedite its replacement, you will need to know all information previously recorded and show identification and proof of citizenship. A replacement often takes weeks to process, and it may be valid only for a limited time. However, some consulates can issue new passports within 24 hours if you give them proof of citizenship. Any visas stamped in your old passport will be irretrievably lost. In an emergency, ask for immediate temporary traveling papers that will permit you to re-enter your home country. Your passport is a public document belonging to your nation's government. You may have to surrender it to a foreign government official at some point, but if you don't get it back in a reasonable amount of time, inform the nearest mission of your home country.

Australia: Citizens must apply for a passport in person at a post office, a passport office, or an Australian diplomatic mission overseas. An appointment may be necessary. Passport offices are located in Adelaide, Brisbane, Canberra City, Darwin, Hobart, Melbourne, Newcastle, Perth, and Sydney. A parent may file an application for a child who is under 18 and unmarried. Adult passports cost AUS$126 (for a 32-page passport) or AUS$188 (64 page), and a child's is AUS$63 (32-page) or AUS$94 (64-page). For more info, call toll-free (only in Australia) 13 12 32.

Canada: Application forms in English and French are available at all passport offices, Canadian missions, many travel agencies, and Northern Stores in northern communities. Citizens may apply in person at any of the 28 regional Passport Offices across Canada. Travel agents can direct applicants to the nearest location. Canadian citizens residing abroad should contact the nearest Canadian embassy or consulate. Children under 16 may be included on a parent's passport. Passports cost CDN$60 (in addition to CDN$25 for consular service), are valid for 5 years, and are not renewable. Processing takes approximately 5 business days for applications in-person; 10 days if by mail. For additional info, contact the Canadian Passport Office, Department of Foreign Affairs and International Trade, Ottawa, ON, K1A 0G3 (tel. (613) 994-3500; http://www.dfait-maeci.gc.ca/passport). In Toronto (416) 973-3251; in Vancouver (604) 775-6250; in Montréal (514) 283-2152.

Ireland: Citizens can apply for a passport by mail to either the Department of Foreign Affairs, Passport Office, Setanta Centre, Molesworth St., Dublin 2 (tel. (01) 671 1633), or the Passport Office, Irish Life Building, 1A South Mall, Cork (tel. (021) 272 525). Obtain an application at a local Garda station or request one from a passport office. The new Passport Express Service, available through post offices, allows citizens to get a passport in 2 weeks for an extra IR£3. Passports cost IR£45 and are valid for 10 years. Citizens under 18 or over 65 can request a 3-year passport that costs IR£10.

New Zealand: Application forms for passports are available in New Zealand from travel agents and Department of Internal Affairs Link Centres in the main cities and towns. Overseas, forms and passport services are provided by New Zealand embassies, high commissions, and consulates. Applications may also be forwarded to the Passport Office, P.O. Box 10526, Wellington, New Zealand (tel. (0800) 22-5050). Standard processing time in New Zealand is 10 working days for correct applications. The fees are adult NZ$80, and child NZ$40. An **urgent passport service** is also available for an extra NZ$80. Different fees apply at overseas post: 9 posts including London, Sydney, and Los Angeles offer both standard and urgent services (adult US$130, child US$65, plus US$130 if urgent). The fee at other posts is adult US$260, child US$195, and a passport will be issued within 3 working days. Children's names can no longer be endorsed on a parent's passport—they must apply for their own, which are valid for up to 5 years. An adult's passport is valid for up to 10 years. More information is available on the internet at http://www.emb.com/nzemb or http://www.undp.org/missions/newzealand.

South Africa: Citizens can apply for a passport at any **Home Affairs Office** or **South African Mission.** Tourist passports, valid for 10 years, cost SAR80. Children under 16 must be issued their own passports, valid for 5 years, which cost SAR60. If a passport is needed in a hurry, an **emergency passport** may be issued for SAR50. An application for a permanent passport must accompany the emergency passport application. Time for the completion of an application is normally 3 months or more from the time of submission. Current passports less than 10 years old (counting from date of issuance) may be **renewed** until December 31, 1999; every citizen whose passport's validity does not extend far beyond this date is urged to renew it as soon as possible to avoid the expected glut of applications as 2000 approaches. Renewal is free, and turnaround time is usually 2 weeks. For further information, contact the nearest Department of Home Affairs Office.

United Kingdom: British subjects, British citizens, British Dependent Territories citizens, British nationals, and British citizens overseas may apply for a **full passport,** valid for 10 years (5 years if under 16). Application forms are available at passport offices, main post offices, many travel agents, and branches of Lloyds Bank and Artac World Choice. Apply in person or by mail to one of the passport offices, located in London, Liverpool, Newport, Peterborough, Glasgow, or Belfast. The fee is UK£31 for adults and UK£11 for children under 16. Processing by mail usually takes 4-6 weeks. Turnaround time for walk-in service is between 5 and 16 working days. The U.K. Passport Agency can be reached by phone at (0990) 21 04 10.

United States: Citizens may apply for a passport at any federal or state **courthouse** or **post office** authorized to accept passport applications, or at a **U.S. Passport Agency,** located in Boston, Chicago, Honolulu, Houston, Los Angeles, Miami, New Orleans, New York, Philadelphia, San Francisco, Seattle, Stamford, West Virginia, or Washington, D.C. Refer to the "U.S. Government, State Department" section of the telephone directory or the local post office for addresses. You must apply in person if this is your first passport, if you're between the ages of 13-16, if your current passport is more than 12 years old or was issued before your 18th birthday, or if your last passport was lost or stolen. Children under 13 need not apply in person. Passports are valid for 10 years (5 years if under 18) and cost US$60 (under 16 US$40). They may be **renewed** by mail or in person for US$40. Processing takes 3-4 weeks; express service (processing within 3 working days) is available for $35 and may require proof of urgent departure. Given proof of citizenship, a U.S. embassy or consulate abroad can usually issue a new passport. Report a passport lost or stolen in the U.S. in writing to Passport Services, 1425 K St., N.W., U.S. Dept. of State, Washington D.C., 20524 or to the nearest passport agency. For more info, call the U.S. Passport Information's **24-hour recorded message** (tel. (202) 647-0518). The **National Passport Information Center** is at (900) 225-5674 and features 24-hour service (35 cents per minute). Live operators are available at (888) 362-8668 M-F between 8am-8pm/EST; each call costs $4.95.

VISAS

A visa is permission for you to stay in a country for a specific purpose and a specific amount of time; it usually must be attached or stamped in your passport. All travelers to India and Nepal (except citizens of India going to Nepal, and vice versa) must have visas. For more information on visa services, see **Diplomatic Missions,** p. 9.

India

Tourist visas are available for three months, six months, or one year and normally allow for multiple entries (important for side-trips to Nepal and other countries). Other options include a one-year visa for students, journalists, or business travelers, or a five-year visa for Indian nationals living abroad. When applying for a visa, make sure your passport is valid six months beyond the date of intended return.

It is always faster to apply through the embassy in the country where you are a citizen. You'll need to fill out an application form and provide your current passport, as well as at least two passport photographs. How much the visa will cost and how long getting it will take varies from country to country, as do other restrictions and regulations governing its procurement and use, so you should check with your country's embassy to be sure. **Australia:** AUS$20 for three months, AUS$42 for six months. **Canada:** CDN$30 for three months, CDN$55 for six months. **Ireland:** IR£14 for three months, IR£27 for six months; non-Irish citizens add IR£10. Irish passport holders should send a stamped, self-addressed envelope to the embassy to get an application. **New Zealand:** NZ$70 for six months (minimum stay). **South Africa:** No fee. Contact the embassy for more information.**U.K.:** UK£13 for three months, UK£26 for six months. Processing takes about three weeks except in the busy tourist season (Nov.-Jan.) when it will take about six weeks. **U.S.:** US$50 for six months, US$70 for one year. Residents should contact the Indian Embassy in Washington or the consulate appropriate for their area (see **Diplomatic Missions,** p. 9).

Special Permits

Certain areas of India require a special permit in addition to an Indian visa. Permits can be issued by Indian diplomatic missions abroad, by the Ministry of Home Affairs in Delhi, or by Foreigners' Registration Offices in various Indian cities. Bear in mind that regional instability is often among the reasons for the extra requirements.

Northeast India: In the words of the Government of India Tourist Department, "Assam, Meghalaya, and Tripura states have been thrown open for tourism." A permit is no longer needed for these three states, but consult your embassy about the political situation there, especially in Assam, before visiting. Due to tribal insurgencies and fears of a conflict with China, the other four states of the northeast— **Arunachal Pradesh, Nagaland, Manipur,** and **Mizoram** require restricted area permits. Almost all requests are granted, but travelers must plan in advance. A minimum of four people are required to travel together, and the group must be sponsored by a government-approved travel agency. Permits generally cost Rs300-400. Permits are good for 15 days and renewable for 15 days at the Foreigners' Registration Office in each state's capital city. Three-day permits to visit Manipur are issued only to groups and are available only through the Ministry of Home Affairs. Restricted area permits can be obtained at the Ministry of Home Affairs, Lok Nayak Bhawan, Khan Market, New Delhi (open M-F 10am-5pm), or at the Foreigners Regional Registration Office (tel. 331 9781 or 331 8179), open M-F 9:30am-1:30pm and 2-4pm. Plan your trip well in advance. Permits take two to 50 days, depending on the state.

West Bengal: Darjeeling and some adjoining areas require a permit (available to individuals or tourists traveling in groups for up to 15 days). Permits can also be obtained through the Home Department of West Bengal.

Sikkim: Sikkim borders China and is treated by the Indian government as a military buffer. Foreigners need a permit to enter Sikkim and can only remain there 15 days per year. Permits are free and readily available in the major Indian cities; the red tape is thickest in Darjeeling, where the process takes an hour; elsewhere it takes only a few moments. Permits allow travel as far north as Phodang and Yuksam. Permits can be extended at the Commissioner's Office in Gangtok in special circumstances, but then only for three to five days, and only once. For North Sikkim, an inner line permit is required. It is only issued through tour companies to groups of four or more. A guide must accompany the group and the minimum charge is US$30-50 per day, including guide. It takes a solid work day to procure such a permit, available only in Gangtok. (Individual tourists are permitted in some areas for periods of up to 15 days.) **See Sikkim,** p. 406.

Andaman and Nicobar Islands: A permit must be obtained in advance before sailing to the Andamans. Leave plenty of time if applying for a permit from the Ministry of Home Affairs or from Indian missions abroad. The Nicobar Islands are off-limits to non-Indian citizens. **See The Andaman Islands,** p. 426.

Lakshadweep: The islands of Bangaran, Suheli, and Tilkam are open to tourists travelling in groups for up to a week. The necessary permit can only be obtained through the Ministry of Foreign Affairs and the Administrator of Lakshadweep.

Bhutan: Though officially an independent country, Bhutan's foreign policy and immigration procedures are controlled by India. The number of visas to Bhutan is limited by a quota system, and those who receive them must be on group tours of at least six and are required to spend *at least US$220 per day.* To apply for a visa, contact the Director of Tourism, Ministry of Finance, Tachichho Dzong, Thimpu, Bhutan or the Bhutan Foreign Mission, Chandra Gupta Marg, New Delhi 110021 (tel. 91 (11) 609217). The odds are similar to the odds of winning the lottery.

Nepal

Anybody with a passport can get a Nepalese visa upon arrival at the airport in Kathmandu or at any of the land border crossings from India; it's really not worth fussing over ahead of time unless you're looking for something to fuss over. The fee is the same either way; at the border it must be paid in U.S. dollars. Any Nepalese consulate or embassy can issue visas for up to 60 days, although this time can be extended once you're in Nepal. The Department of Immigration, Tridevi Marg, Thamel, Kathmandu (tel. (1) 412337, 418573), grants extensions for up to three months. Apply for a visa extension a day or two before you really need it. It costs everyone US$1 per day to extend visas. **Australia/New Zealand:** AUS$40 for 15 days (single entry), AUS$50 for 30 days (single entry), AUS$70 for 30 days (multiple entry), and AUS$100 for 60 days (multiple entry). Submit three passport photos, a passport, and three application forms (available from travel agents) by mail or in person. Visas are processed on the spot for applicants who come in person, or mailed the same day for those who apply by post. **South Africa:** There is no Nepalese embassy in South Africa, which makes getting visa information a little trickier. Contact the Department of Immigration in Kathmandu, Tridevi Marg (tel. 412337, 418573) for more information on how to proceed. South Africans can also simply get their visas on arrival at Kathmandu airport or at a border crossing. **U.K./Ireland:** UK£20 for 30 days (single entry), UK£45 for 60 days (multiple entry). Passport holders from either country should contact the Royal Nepalese Embassy in London for an application. **U.S.:** US$15 for 15 days (single entry), US$25 for 30 days (single entry), US$40 for 30 days (double entry), and US$60 for 60 days (multiple entry). Payment should be a money order, cashier's check or cash. **Canada:** CDN$24 for 15 days (single entry), CDN$40 for 30 days (single entry), CDN$64 for a 30 days (double entry), and CDN$96 for 60 days (multiple entry). Send a stamped, addressed envelope if applying by mail. **Trekking permits** are also required for all trekking areas in Nepal. For more information, see **Trekking,** p. 58.

Surrounding Countries

It isn't easy to travel to many of the countries that surround India and Nepal, nor is it always wise. Myanmar (Burma) and China, in particular, present massive amounts of red tape and restrictions. In addition, a few of these countries are politically unstable, so it is important to check for up-to-date information before embarking. The following general information is intended as a starting point. (See **Border Crossings,** p. 54.)

Bangladesh: All citizens should contact a Bangladeshi embassy or high commission; visa rules change frequently. In any event, 72-hour permits to cross the border are easy to obtain, and they can be validated and upgraded at the Department of Immigration Office in Dhaka. The High Commission's address is 56 Ring Rd., Lajpat Nagar III, Delhi (tel. 91 (11) 683 4668); 9 Circus Ave., Park Circus, Calcutta (tel.

(33) 247 5208); and in Nepal it's located on Chakrapath, Maharajgunj, Kathmandu (tel. (1) 372843; fax 373265).

China: To travel into Tibet from Nepal, a Chinese travel visa is required. Such visas are almost impossible to get at the embassy in Kathmandu. Visas are valid for 30 days and can be extended twice by 15 days per extension. Some travelers have also entered China by signing up for short "mini-tours" advertised all over Thamel, semi-legal group tours that disband soon after crossing the border. Some travelers may, however, get hassled by Chinese police when traveling without the tour. Under this system, travelers can have a two- or three-day taste of Tibet and decide if they want to apply to go back for a longer time. Many travel agents in Kathmandu can arrange mini-tours. The Chinese embassy in India is at 50-D Shantipath, Chanakyapuri, Delhi (tel. 91 (11) 600328) and in Nepal, Baluwatar, Kathmandu (tel. (1) 411740; visa services (1) 419053).

Myanmar (Burma): For a Burmese visa, be prepared to fill out forms, write letters, and show proof that you have already set up a place to stay. Tourist visas last 28 days and barely get you into the country. To go very far beyond Rangoon or Mandalay, more permits or a licensed guide are required. The Burmese embassy in India is located at 3/50-F Nyaya Marg, Chanakyapuri, Delhi (tel. (11) 600 251/2; fax 327204) and in Nepal at Chakupat, Patan City Gate, Kathmandu (P.O Box 2437; tel. (1) 521788, 524788; fax 523402). Note that border crossings into Burma are only in Thailand and China.

Pakistan: The U.S., British, and Australian Departments of State warn their citizens to defer all nonessential travel to Pakistan. Those who do decide to travel to Pakistan need a visa prior to entry. The visa is valid for three months after date of issue, but foreign visitors must register after 30 days at the Foreigners' Registration Office, which has branches in all major cities and towns. In Delhi, 2/50-G Shantipath, Chanakyapuri (tel. (11) 600603), and in Kathmandu, Pani Pokhari (tel. (1) 441421; visa services 415806).

Sri Lanka: A passport and onward/return ticket, as well as proof of sufficient funding (US$15/day), are required to travel to Sri Lanka. Visas are valid for a maximum of 90 days. Visitors staying in private households must register with the local police.

Thailand: Citizens from most European countries and the U.S., Canada, and Australia need not obtain visas if they plan to be in Thailand for less than 30 days and if they have a confirmed ticket as proof of departure. For travelers who wish to spend more time in the country, Thailand issues two main types of visas: **tourist visas** (up to 60 days, US$15) and **non-immigrant visas** for business or employment (up to 90 days, US$20). Every visa is valid for entry up to 90 days from its date of issue. For those who want to pop back to Thailand repeatedly, a **reentry permit** is required to return. Applications should be made at the main Immigration Office well before departure. Make sure to get an exit stamp when you leave Thailand, or face deportation upon your next visit. The Thai embassy in India's address is 56-N Nyaya Marg, Chanakyapuri, Delhi (tel. (11) 6118103; fax 6878103) and in Nepal, Bansbari, Kathmandu (tel. (1) 420411).

DIPLOMATIC MISSIONS

India

U.S.: Visa and passport division for the **southeastern** U.S.: 2536 Massachusetts Ave. NW, Washington, D.C. 20008 (tel. (202) 939-9839); for visas, submit applications M-F 9:30am-12:30pm and pick up visa on the same day, 4-5:30pm. Applications submitted by mail take at least 10 working days to process, and must be paid by money order. **Northeast:** Consulate of India, 3 East 64th St., New York, NY 10021 (tel. (212) 774-0600); submit application M-F 9:15-11am, pick up visa 4:30-5:15pm. **West:** Consulate General of India, 540 Arguello Blvd., San Francisco, CA 94118 (tel. (415) 668-0683; fax 668-9764; http://www.indianconsulate.sf.org); submit visa application 9am-1pm; U.S. passport-holders can pick up visa the same day at 2 or 4:30pm. **Midwest:** Consulate General of India, 455 North City Front Plaza Drive, NBC Tower Building, Suite 850, Chicago, IL 60611 (tel. (312) 595-0405; http://chicago.indianconsulate.com).

Canada: 10 Springfield Rd., **Ottawa,** Ontario K1M 1C9 (tel. (613) 744-3751); submit visa application M-Th 9:30am-12:30pm and pick up visa 3:30-5:15pm. **Consulates:** 2 Bloor St., West, 5th fl., **Toronto,** Ontario M4W 3E2 (tel. (416) 960-0751); 325 House St., Suite 201, **Vancouver,** B.C. VC6 1Z7 (tel. (604) 662-8811); submit application M-F 9:30am-12:30pm and pick up visa next working day 3:30-5pm.

U.K.: India House, Aldwych, **London,** WC2 B4NA (tel. (0171) 836 8484). **Consulates:** 20 Augusta St., Jewellery Quarter, Hockley, **Birmingham** B18 6JL (tel. (0121) 212 2778); submit visa application 9:30am-12:30pm, pick up visa next day 3-4:30pm. Fleming House, 134 Rensrew St., **Glasgow** G3 7ST (tel. (0141) 331 0777); submit application M-F 9:30am-12:30pm, pick up visa 4-5pm.

Ireland: 6 Leeson Park, Dublin 6 (tel. (01) 497 0842); visa services open 9:30am-12:15pm; Irish citizens should allow 2-3 working days for processing.

Australia: 5 Moonah Place, Yarralumla, **Canberra** ACT 2600 (tel. (06) 273 3999; fax 273 1308). **Consulates:** 25, Bligh St., Level 27, **Syndey** NSW 2000 (tel. (02) 9223 9500); open M-F 9am-1pm; visa takes 2-3 days in person. 49 Bennett St., **East Perth**, Western Australia 6004 (tel. (08) 9221 1485); open M-F 9am-1pm; visa takes 5 working days. 15 Munro St., **Coburg,** Victoria 3058 (tel. (03) 9384 0141); open M-F 9am-1pm; visa takes five working days.

New Zealand: 180 Molesworth St., FAI House, Level 10, P.O. Box 4045, Wellington 4045 (tel. (04) 473 6390). Open M-F 9am-5:30pm; visa takes min. 10 days.

South Africa: India House, No. 1 Eton Rd., Park Town, 2193, P.O. Box No. 6805 Johannesburg 2000 (tel. 12 342 5392).

Nepal

Would-be wanderers from Ireland should contact the embassy in London, while New Zealanders are served via the Sydney office. There is no embassy in South Africa. For more information, see **Visas,** p. 6.

U.S.: 2131 Leroy Place NW, Washington, D.C. 20008 (tel. (202) 667-4550; fax 667-5534). **Consulate:** Royal Nepalese Consulate General, 820 Second Ave., Suite 202, New York, NY 10017 (tel. (212) 370-4188; fax 953-2038). Tourist visas available upon entry into Nepal.

Canada: Royal Nepalese Consulate, 200 Bay St., Toronto, Ontario M5J 2J8 (tel. (416) 865-0210; fax 865-0904). Open for walk-in visa service Th 9am-3pm.

U.K.: 12a Kensington Palace Gardens, London W8 4QU (tel. (0171) 229 1594). Submit visa application M-F 10am-12pm; allow 24hr. for processing.

Australia: 48 Mitchell St., McMahons Point, Sydney, NSW 2060 (tel. (06) 958 8815; fax 956 8767).

CUSTOMS: GETTING THERE

India

All personal belongings necessary for your stay can be imported duty-free. You are also allowed an additional Rs2000 of duty-free souvenirs and Rs750 of items intended as gifts. Tourists are allowed the following items duty-free: 200 cigarettes or 50 cigars or 250 grams of tobacco; 1L each of liquor and wine. Expensive electronic items may be noted in your passport to ensure that you take them with you when you leave rather than selling them. The import of gold coins, gold bullion, and silver bullion is illegal. Certain types of weapons are prohibited and all weapons require a license. Indian rupees cannot enter or leave the country. If your baggage was mishandled and you lost any of your belongings, get a certificate from the airline and get it counter-signed by customs officials indicating how much of your duty free allowance you didn't use. Any cash or traveler's checks over US$2500 or equivalent must be declared upon arrival.

Nepal

Duty-free allowance includes 1.15L of alcohol or 12 cans of beer, 200 cigarettes, 50 cigars, one camera and 15 rolls of film, one video camera and 12 video cassettes, one radio, one tape recorder or record player and 10 records/tapes, one sleeping bag, one baby carriage and "one tricycle and one stick." Drugs, arms, and ammo can't enter across under any circumstances. Tourists must obtain a government certificate in order to bring antiques and precious or semi-precious stones in the country. Any money over US$2000 must be declared upon entry and only Indian nationals can import or export Indian rupees.

CUSTOMS: GOING HOME

Upon returning home, you must declare all articles you acquired abroad and pay a **duty** on the value of those articles that exceed the allowance established by your country's customs service. Goods and gifts purchased at **duty-free** shops abroad are not exempt from duty or sales tax at your point of return; you must declare these items as well. "Duty-free" means that you don't pay a tax in the country of purchase.

India: No gold jewelry valued over Rs2000 or other jewelry valued over Rs10,000 (including precious stones) may leave the country. No antiques (defined as anything over 100 years old), animal skins, or animal skin products may be taken out of India. Visitors leaving India after a stay of less than six months are exempt from income tax clearance procedures (in order to prove that you didn't earn any money illegally), but hang on to your exchange receipts nonetheless. Indian rupees may not leave the country. If you are flying to a neighboring country (Nepal, Pakistan, Sri Lanka, or Bangladesh), the **airport tax** is Rs150; to all other countries it is Rs500. Smuggling narcotics is both foolish and dangerous.

Nepal: Gifts and souvenirs may be brought out of Nepal but permission is required from the Department of Archaeology to export antiques. They can be contacted at the National Archive Building, Ran Shah Path, Kathmandu (tel. 977 (1) 215358). In general, nothing over 100 years old can leave the country. Exporting gold, silver, drugs, animals, or animal parts and products is forbidden. There is a **airport tax** of Rs600 for those flying to India and of Rs700 for other countries.

Australia: Citizens may import AUS$400 (under 18 AUS$200) of goods duty-free, and 1.125L alcohol and 250 cigarettes or 250g tobacco. You must be over 18 to import alcohol or tobacco. Amounts of AUS$10,000 or more, or the equivalent in foreign currency, must be reported. All foodstuffs and animal products must be declared on arrival. For information, contact the Regional Director, Australian Customs Service, GPO Box 8, Sydney NSW 2001 (tel. (02) 9213 2000; fax 9213 4000).

Canada: Citizens who remain abroad for more than one week may bring back up to CDN$500 worth of goods duty-free. Citizens or residents who travel for a period between 48 hours and 6 days can bring back up to CDN$200. Both of these exemptions may include tobacco and alcohol. You are permitted to ship goods except tobacco and alcohol home under the CDN$500 exemption as long as you declare them when you arrive. Goods under the CDN$200 exemption, as well as all alcohol and tobacco, must be in your hand or checked luggage. Citizens of legal age (which varies by province) may import in-person up to 200 cigarettes, 50 cigars or cigarillos, 400g loose tobacco, 400 tobacco sticks, 1.14L wine or alcohol, and 24 355mL cans/bottles of beer; the value of these products is included in the CDN$200 or CDN$500. Travelers' Division, Operational Policy and Coordination Directorate, Revenue Canada, Sir Richard Scott Building, Ottawa ON KIA 0L5. (24hr. Automated Customs Information Service tel. (800) 461-9999; fax (613) 954-4570; http://wwwrc.gc.ca.)

Ireland: Citizens must declare everything in excess of IR£142 (IR£73 under 15) obtained outside the EU or duty- and tax-free in the EU above the following allowances: 200 cigarettes, 100 cigarillos, 50 cigars, or 250g tobacco; 1L liquor or 2L wine; 50g perfume; and 250mL toilet water. Goods obtained duty and tax paid in another EU country up to a value of IR£460 (IR£115 under 15) will not be subject to additional customs duties. Travelers under 17 may not import tobacco or alcohol. For more information, contact the Central Revenue Information Office, Cathedral St., Dublin 1 (tel. (01) 873 4555.

New Zealand: Citizens may import NZ$700 worth of goods duty-free if they are intended for personal use or are unsolicited gifts. The concession is 200 cigarettes, 250g tobacco, or 50 cigars, or a combination of all 3 not exceeding 250g. You may also bring in 4.5L of beer or wine and 1.125L of liquor. Only travelers over 17 may import tobacco or alcohol. For more information, contact New Zealand Customs, 50 Anzac Ave., Box 29, Auckland (tel. (09) 377 35 20; fax 309 29 78).

South Africa: Citizens may import duty-free: 400 cigarettes, 50 cigars, 250g tobacco, 2L wine, 1L of spirits, 250mL toilet water, and 50mL perfume, and other consumable items up to a value of SAR500. Goods up to a value of SAR10,000 above this duty-free allowance are dutiable at 20%; such goods are also exempted from payment of VAT. Items acquired abroad and sent to the Republic as unaccompanied baggage do not qualify for any allowances. You may not export or import South African bank notes in excess of SAR2000. For more information, consult the free pamphlet *South African Customs Information,* available in airports or from the Commissioner for Customs and Excise, Private Bag X47, Pretoria 0001 (tel. (12) 314 99 11; fax 328 64 78).

United Kingdom: Citizens or visitors arriving in the U.K. from outside the EU must declare goods in excess of the following allowances: 200 cigarettes, 100 cigarillos, 50 cigars, or 250g tobacco; 2L still table wine; 1L strong liqueurs over 22% volume, or fortified or sparkling wine, 2L other liquors; 60mL perfume; 250mL toilet water; and UK£136 worth of all other goods including gifts and souvenirs. You must be over 17 to import liquor or tobacco. These allowances also apply to duty-free purchases within the EU, except for "other goods," which then has an allowance of UK£71. Goods obtained for personal use within the EU and for which duty and tax have been paid do not require any further customs duty. For more information, contact Her Majesty's Customs and Excise, Custom House, Nettleton Rd., Heathrow Airport, Hounslow, Middlesex TW6 2LA (tel. (0181) 910-3744; fax 910-3765).

United States: Citizens may import US$400 worth of accompanying goods duty-free and must pay a 10% tax on the next US$1000. You must declare all purchases, so have sales slips ready. The US$400 personal exemption covers goods purchased for personal or household use (this includes gifts) and cannot include more than 100 cigars, 200 cigarettes (1 carton), and 1L of wine or liquor. You must be over 21 to bring liquor into the U.S. If you mail home personal goods of U.S. origin, you can avoid duty charges by marking the package "American goods returned." For more information, consult the brochure *Know Before You Go,* available from the U.S. Customs Service, Box 7407, Washington D.C. 20044 (tel. (202) 927-6724).

YOUTH, STUDENT, & TEACHER IDENTIFICATION

The **International Student Identity Card (ISIC)** is useful only for the medical insurance it provides. However, it still may be worth getting for a discount fare on your plane ticket (most travel agencies require an ISIC for student fares). To book special plane fares, you can also call (800) 2-COUNCIL. The card provides basic sickness and accident coverage, as well as emergency evacuation coverage up to $25,000. In addition, cardholders have access to a toll-free 24-hour ISIC helpline whose multilingual staff can provide assistance in medical, legal, and financial emergencies overseas (tel. (800) 626-2427 in the U.S. and Canada; elsewhere call the U.S. collect (713) 267-2525).

Many student travel agencies around the world issue ISICs, including: STA Travel in Australia and New Zealand; Travel CUTS in Canada; USIT in Ireland and Northern Ireland; SASTS in South Africa; Campus Travel and STA Travel in the U.K.; Council Travel, Let's Go Travel, and STA Travel, which have offices in most major US cities; and any of the other organizations under the auspices of the International Student Travel Confederation (ISTC). The card is valid from September to December of the following year and costs US$19 or CDN$15. Applicants must be at least 12 years old and degree-seeking students of a secondary or post-secondary school. Because of the proliferation of phony ISICs, many airlines and some other services require other proof of student identity, such as your school ID card or a signed letter from the registrar attesting to your student status and stamped with the school seal. The US$20 **International Teacher Identity Card (ITIC)** offers the same insurance coverage as the ISIC, and similar but more limited discounts; it is also not particularly useful in South Asia. The ITIC has also recently assumed control of the **GO25 Card,** which offers many of the same benefits as the ISIC (and is also of limited use in South Asia). For more information, consult the organization's web site (http:\\www.istc.org).

INTERNATIONAL DRIVING PERMITS

Few visitors to India attempt to drive cars, as most rental cars come with battle-hardened drivers, and most people value their own lives too much to try their hand at a game of high-speed highway pinball (see **Getting Around,** p. 46). Quite a few visitors, however, rent motor-scooters or motorcycles, both of which require an **International Driving Permit.** These must be issued in your own country before you depart. A valid driver's license from your home country must always accompany the IDP. An application for an IDP usually needs to be accompanied by one or two photos, a current local license, an additional form of identification, and a fee. **Australians** can obtain an IDP for AUS$15 by contacting their local Royal Automobile Club (RAC) (tel. (08) 9421 4271; fax 9221 1887; http://www.rac.com.au) or the National Royal Motorist Association (NRMA) with branches in NSW, the ACT, and many other places (tel. 13 11 22; http://www.hrma.com.au). **Canadian** license holders can obtain an IDP (CDN$10) through any Canadian Automobile Association (CAA) branch office in Canada, or by writing to CAA Central Ontario, 60 Commerce Valley Drive East, Thornhill, Ontario L3T 7P9 (tel. (416) 221-4300). Citizens of **Ireland** should drop into their nearest Automobile Association (AA) office where an IDP can be picked up for IR£4, or phone (1) 283 3555 for a postal application form. In **New Zealand,** contact your local Automobile Association (AA), or their main office at 99 Albert Street, PO Box 5, Auckland (tel. (09) 377 4660; fax 309 4564). IDPs cost NZ$8 plus NZ$2 for return postage. In **South Africa** visit your local Automobile Association of South Africa office, where IDPs can be picked up for SAR25, or for more information phone (011) 466 6641, or write to P.O. Box 596, 2000 Johannesburg. In the **U.K.** IDPs are UK£4 and you can either visit your local AA Shop, or call (01256) 49 39 32 and order a postal application form (allow 2-3 weeks). **U.S.** license holders can obtain an IDP (US$10) at any American Automobile Association (AAA) office or by writing to AAA Florida, Travel Agency Services Department, 1000 AAA Drive (mail stop 28), Heathrow, FL 32746-5080 (tel. (407) 444-4245; fax 444-4247).

■ Money Matters

Once you get there, travel in India or Nepal is unbelievably cheap. The income and the cost of living in these countries are so low that it's not unusual to pay US$2 for a night's accommodation, or less than US$1 for a restaurant meal. Train and bus fares are a pittance when measured in foreign currency. Consequently, two distinct attitudes about money seem to prevail among travelers in South Asia. Some people consider traveling through the Subcontinent an incredible opportunity to live on the very, very cheap. Others seem to revel in the fact that with their dollars or pounds they can afford luxuries that they could never afford at home, like eating lunch at a five-star hotel, or hiring a car and driver for a day. How much money you should bring depends on your style. However, even the most parsimonious of backpackers should budget for emergencies, inevitable exigencies, and the occasional splurge. When thieves strike, illness hits, or you simply get the travel doldrums, money can cushion the shocks.

Avoid exchanging money at luxury hotels and restaurants, which will likely gouge you on both exchange rates and commission rates; the best deal is usually found at major banks. In rural areas, look for branches of banks you recognize from larger cities. In India, the **State Bank of India** is usually the easiest place to change money. Be prepared for long waits. In major cities in India, currency exchange booths controlled by major banks are common. Although commission rates at the booths may be slightly higher, they are convenient and keep longer hours than the banks. It may be wise to keep some U.S. dollars or pounds sterling on hand in case smaller banks and exchange booths refuse to accept other currencies. If you exchange your money at a bank or travel office, get an **encashment certificate** as proof. This is sometimes demanded when paying for plane and train tickets or large hotel bills in rupees.

Remember that unless a commission rate is charged, service charges will eat up a chunk of your money each time you convert. To minimize your losses, exchange large sums of money at once, but never more than you can safely carry. Plan ahead; if caught without local currency in an area with no currency exchange center, you may be forced into a particularly disadvantageous deal, or wind up sleeping on a bus.

Both India and Nepal have recently made their currencies fully convertible and subject to market rates, so there's not much to be gained from changing money on the **black market.** Those who are still willing to risk confiscation of their money for the small premium (and speedier service) must change their money discreetly, with shopkeepers, out of public view, rather than with touts in the street. It is also worth remembering that changing money on the black market contributes to a cycle of illegal transactions, especially the smuggling of gold, gems, and electronic goods, and impedes the government's ability to regulate the economy.

TRAVELER'S CHECKS

Traveler's checks are the safest and least troublesome means of carrying funds. Several agencies and many banks sell them, usually for face value plus a 1% commission. American Express and Thomas Cook are the most widely recognized in India and Nepal. Other major checks are normally exchanged with almost equal ease, although each bank seems to have its own rules about this. Banks in small towns are less likely to accept traveler's checks than banks in cities with large tourist industries. Nonetheless, there will probably be at least one place in most towns where you can exchange them for local currency; just be prepared for a long wait.

Each agency provides refunds if your checks are lost or stolen, and many provide additional services. (Note that you may need a police report verifying the loss or theft of your traveler's checks.) Expect red tape and delay in the event of theft or loss of traveler's checks. To expedite the refund process, keep your check receipts separate from your checks and store them in a safe place or with a traveling companion, leave a list of check numbers with someone at home and record these when you cash them, and ask for a list of refund centers when you buy your checks. American Express and Thomas Cook have offices in Kathmandu and the major cities of India. Keep a separate supply of cash or traveler's checks for emergencies. Never countersign your checks until you're prepared to cash them, and always bring your passport with you when you plan to use the checks.

American Express: In Australia call (800) 230 100 (toll-free numbers may not operate within the Sydney area) or 61 (2) 9271 8666; in New Zealand (64) 9 367 4247; in the U.K. (0800) 52 13 13; in the U.S. and Canada (800) 221-7282, or call (905) 474-9380 collect. Elsewhere, call U.S. collect (801) 964-6665. American Express traveler's checks are available in Australian, British, Canadian, Dutch, French, German, Japanese, Swiss, and U.S. currencies. They are the most widely recognized and the easiest to replace if lost or stolen. Checks can be purchased for a small fee at American Express Travel Service Offices, banks, and American Automobile Association offices (AAA members can buy the checks commission-free). Cardmembers can also purchase checks at American Express Dispensers at Travel Service Offices at airports and by ordering them via phone (tel. (800) ORDER-TC/673-3782). American Express offices cash their checks commission-free, although they often offer slightly worse rates than banks. You can also buy *Cheques for Two* which can be signed by either of two people traveling together. You can also visit their online travel offices (http://www.aexp.com).

Thomas Cook MasterCard: For 24hr. cashing or refund assistance, call (800) 223-9920 in the U.S. and Canada; elsewhere call U.S. collect (609) 987-7300; from the U.K. call (0800) 622 101 free. Offers checks in U.S., Canadian, and Australian dollars, British and Cypriot pounds, French and Swiss francs, German marks, Japanese yen, Dutch guilders, Spanish pesetas, South African rand, and ECUs. Commission rates range between 1-3% for purchases, depending on the individual office.

Visa: Call (800) 227-6811 in the U.S.; in the U.K. (0800) 895 078; from anywhere else in the world call (01733 318 949) and reverse the charges. Any of the above numbers can tell you the location of their nearest office.

CREDIT CARDS

Credit cards are gaining wider acceptance in South Asia, but plastic is by no means the only kind of money you'll need. Cards can, however, be a useful backup to your traveler's checks, and are invaluable in an emergency—an unexpected hospital bill or ticket home or the loss of traveler's checks—which may leave you temporarily without other resources. Additionally, you can use credit cards to purchase domestic airline tickets and train tickets in India.

There is still a great deal of variation in credit card acceptance. A high-class restaurant may refuse credit cards while a home-owned trinket stall accepts every card under the sun. Sometimes a fee is added if you use a credit card, but if you're buying carpets or crafts, using a credit card doesn't mean you can't bargain the price down. Generally, plastic is accepted at major hotels, expensive boutiques, and fine restaurants. **American Express, MasterCard,** and **Visa** are the most commonly accepted. You can often reduce conversion fees by charging a purchase instead of changing traveler's checks.

With credit cards such as American Express, Visa, and MasterCard, a few banks will give you an instant cash advance in local currency as large as your remaining credit line. The nationwide **Bank of Baroda** offers advances in Indian rupees to Visa and MasterCard holders.

American Express (tel. (800) 843-2273) has a hefty annual fee (US$55) but offers a number of services. AmEx cardholders can cash personal checks at AmEx offices outside the U.S. In addition, **U.S. Assist**, a 24-hour hotline offering medical and legal assistance in emergencies, is also available (tel. (800) 554-2639 in U.S. and Canada; from abroad call U.S. collect (301) 214-8228). Cardholders can take advantage of the American Express Travel Service; benefits include assistance in changing airline, hotel, and car rental reservations, baggage loss and flight insurance, sending mailgrams and international cables, and holding your mail at one of the more than 1700 AmEx offices around the world.

MasterCard (tel. (800) 223-9920) and **Visa** (tel. (800) 336-8472) are issued in cooperation with individual banks and some other organizations; ask the issuer about services which go along with the cards.

Credit cards require extra vigilance. Report lost or stolen cards immediately, or you may be held responsible for forged charges. Write down the card cancellation phone numbers for your bank and keep them separate from your cards. Be sure that carbons have been torn to pieces, and ask to watch your card be imprinted.

GETTING MONEY FROM HOME

Having money wired to India or Nepal can be a bureaucratic fuss, subject to long delays; most travelers wisely avoid it. If you really need money from home, it should take about two to three working days. Foreign banks such as CitiBank and ANZ Grindlays are the most reliable; be precise about the bank branch you want the money sent to. **Western Union** (tel. 1 (800) 325 6000 in the U.S.) operates an international money transfer service. The sender must pay in cash at one of their offices; the recipient can pick up the cash at any overseas office (for a fee of about US$30 to send US$250, US$50 to send US$1000).

If you are an American citizen in a **life-or-death situation,** you can have money sent via the State Department's **Overseas Citizens Service, American Citizens Services,** Consular Affairs, Room 4811, U.S. Department of State, Washington, D.C. 20520; open weekdays 8am-10pm, Sa 9am-3pm (tel. (202) 647-5225; after-hours, Su, and holidays (202) 647-4000—ask for the OCS duty officer). Their website is located at http: //travel.state.gov. For a fee of US$20, the State Department will forward money within hours to the nearest consular office, which will then disburse it according to instructions. The quickest way to have the money sent is to cable the State Department through Western Union. Another option is to use a bank wire. Tell your bank that you want to wire the desired amount plus $45 to NationsBank, Department of State Branch, 2201 C St. NW, Washington, D.C. 20520 at (202) 624-4750 via ABA

Number: 054001204; Account Number: 1070603018018; Account Name: PUPID State Department; Special Instructions: Department of State, OCS for benefit of (recipient's name), US Embassy/Consulate (city, country); and include your name and phone number. The check must be made payable to the Department of State and include the recipient's full name and overseas location. Remember that the OCS office only serves Americans in the direst of straits.

Some people also choose to send money abroad in cash via **FedEx** (through the Indian carrier Blue Dart) to avoid transmission fees and taxes. FedEx is reasonably reliable; however, this method may be illegal, it involves an element of risk, and it requires that you remain at a legitimate address for a day or two to wait for the money's arrival. It may be safer to swallow the cost of wire transmission and preserve your peace of mind.

A cheaper and easier way to get money from home is to bring an **American Express** card. AmEx allows green-card holders to draw cash from their checking accounts at any of its major offices and many of its representatives' offices, up to US$1000 every 21 days (no service charge, no interest). There are AmEx offices or representatives in 24 Indian cities and in Kathmandu, Nepal. With someone feeding money into your account at home, you'll be set.

■ Safety and Security

SAFETY

India and Nepal are generally safe countries to travel in; rates of crime, especially violent crime, are extremely low. The sheer mass of population in India means that you will almost always be surrounded by people, and most Indians and Nepalis are well-meaning and will go out of their way to help a foreigner in trouble if they can. There is safety in a crowd; whenever you're around a large group of people, rest assured that they won't just stand back and let someone attack you. What goes on in public is everyone's business, for better or worse.

Blending in

Any would-be attacker knows that tourists carry large amounts of cash and are not as street-savvy as locals, so foreigners are particularly vulnerable to crime. Even if you look South Asian, most people will be able to recognize that you're a foreigner. You won't blend in completely, but it is wise to try not to stand out. Dress modestly—wear local clothes, if possible. Try to look like you know what you're doing; the gawking camera-toter is a more obvious target than the low-profile local look-alike. Do not flaunt your money, or nationality, in public. Try to memorize your map and organize your pack while you're still in your hotel room and if you must do one of these things while outside, step into a shop or restaurant and be casual. Watch out for people who grope in crowds—that goes for both men and women!

Familiarity with the language is important. If you are able to speak even a few words of the local language, this may help you seem confident, and it can gain the confidence of someone who might not help you otherwise. Even if you're communicating only in English, it takes some effort to understand many Indians; not everyone speaks English the same way you do. It is also important to be aware of the laws and customs in the specific area where you are wandering. Be aware of how others are behaving and follow their lead. If no one else has their feet on the table, or is touching the statue, or is jaywalking in a miniskirt, you probably shouldn't be the one to start the trend. For more information, see **Customs and Etiquette, p. 67.**

Find out about unsafe neighborhoods from tourist offices, from the manager of your hotel, or from a local whom you trust. Whenever possible, *Let's Go* warns of unsafe areas, but only your eyes can tell you for sure if you've wandered into one. General desertedness is a bad sign. If you feel uncomfortable, leave as quickly and directly as you can, but don't allow your fear of the new to close off whole worlds to you. Careful, persistent exploration will build confidence and make your stay in an area much more rewarding.

India and Nepal can be more dangerous at night simply because the crowds of people will not be around. When walking at night, stick to main roads and avoid dark alleyways. Unless you are in a neighborhood that is very active at night, it is best not to go out alone. Don't let rickshaws or auto-rickshaws take you down roads you don't know at night. Don't attempt to cross through parks or any other large, deserted areas. A blissfully isolated beach can become unsafe as soon as night falls.

Touts and Con Artists

If you should ever encounter any uncomfortable situations, such as someone following you and asking for something, walk away. Con artists are a major problem in the main tourist centers. You may be "befriended" by someone who ends up pressuring you to smuggle jewels out of the country (don't even think about it) or who wants you to buy silk from his brother's store at outrageous prices. You'll hear sob stories that end with requests for large amounts of money. Be especially alert in these situations. Walk quickly away, and keep a grip on your belongings. Contact the police—or simply threaten to—if a hustler is particularly insistent or aggressive. **It is best to avoid anyone asking you to go somewhere that you haven't asked to go, or to do something you haven't asked to do.**

Be very cautious about accepting food or drinks from a stranger. There have been reports of con men who drug travelers with sleeping pills in tea and rob or rape them. However, remember that offers of food and drink are one of the primary forms of Indian hospitality. A gracious "Doctor told me I shouldn't have that" is a good way to turn down food or drink without offending. Most touts—those young men who mob travelers at bus and train stations, acting as if they want to help—are only after *baksheesh* and don't mean any harm in a violent way, but if you allow them to take you somewhere you could be getting into danger. It's important to be wary of scams, but also remember that many decent Indians and Nepalis will simply want to help you get to wherever you are going, without any strings attached. If you start viewing everyone you meet as somebody who probably wants to hurt or rob you, you'll miss out on a lot of the hospitality and generosity that typify Indian and Nepali culture. Be smart, but don't let yourself become too cynical or paranoid.

Animals

Watch out for stray animals in India and Nepal; rabies is much more prevalent here than in Western countries. The rhesus **monkeys** that hover in the treetops above temples are sometimes aggressive, and they will snatch food and bite. If a stray **dog** growls at you, pick up a stone and act like you're about to throw it—it is truly amazing how South Asian dogs fall for this trick. Even if you can't find a stone, just bending down and pretending to pick one up usually scares dogs away. Also be wary of **rats,** which can be a problem in sketchier hotels; though they're less likely to carry rabies, being bitten by rodents is never fun. Since rats are often attracted to crumbs, keep food away from your bed if you think your hotel is infested. Poisonous **snakes** such as cobras also present a slight danger, even in urban areas. If you've left your shoes outdoors, it never hurts to shake them out before putting them on. Finally, India's larger wildlife, from innocuous **buffalo** to gargantuan **elephants** to (of course) Bengal **tigers** can gore, maul, and trample people. Always be wary and respectful of any animal larger than you are.

Highway Dangers

Be careful of Indian and Nepalese traffic, which is very chaotic. Rickshaws and buses will not stop if you are in the way. *Let's Go* does not recommend hitchhiking, particularly for women. For more information, see **Getting Around** (p. 46).

Political Instability

Political violence is another problem in parts of India and Nepal. Punjab, which was a big problem in the 1980s and early 1990s, appears to have calmed down for now, but the Assam has also become unstable. Threats to foreigners are usually incidental, but in 1995 five western tourists were taken hostage by a militant group in Kashmir. One, a Norwegian, was beheaded. Only that state's eastern regions of Ladakh and Zanskar are completely safe for tourists. Despite the political instability, a small number of tourists opt for package tours of Srinagar in Western Kashmir. **These tours are the only remotely safe way to travel through Srinagar.** For more information, see **Srinagar,** p. 376 Even when there's not a war for secession going on, law and order can be sketchy in remote parts of India and Nepal where political parties or organized thugs rule the countryside. The best place to get advice about unsafe areas is your own country's embassy or high commission, but you should read the newspapers while you're in India or Nepal to keep abreast of what's going on.

For official **United States Department of State** travel advisories, call their 24-hour hotline at (202) 647-5225 or check their website (http://travel.state.gov), which provides travel information and publications. Alternatively, order publications, including a free pamphlet entitled *A Safe Trip Abroad,* by writing to Superintendent of Documents, U.S. Government Printing Office, Washington, DC 20402, or by calling them at (202) 512-1800. Official warnings from the **United Kingdom Foreign and Commonwealth Office** are on-line at http://www.fco.gov.uk; you can also call the office at (0171) 238-4503. The **Canadian Department of Foreign Affairs and International Trade** (DFAIT) offers advisories and travel warnings at its web address (http://www.dfait-maeci.gc.ca) and at its phone number ((613) 944-6788 in Ottawa, (800) 267-6788 elsewhere in Canada). Their free publication, *Bon Voyage, But...,* offers travel tips to Canadian citizens; you can receive a copy by calling them at (613) 944-6788 from Ottawa or abroad, or at (800) 267-6788 from Canada.

Relax and Be Careful

The most important thing to remember when you get to India or Nepal after reading all of the horrible warnings is to relax while staying aware of your environment. No single factor can be as helpful as simply maintaining a watchful eye wherever you go. There is no surefire set of precautions that will protect you from all of the situations you might encounter. A good self-defense course will give you more concrete ways to react to different types of aggression, but it often carries a steep price tag. **Impact, Prepare, Fight Back,** and **Model Mugging** can refer you to local self-defense courses in the United States. They share a national referral hotline (tel. (800) 345-5425). Course prices vary from $50-400. Women's and men's courses are offered. Community colleges also frequently offer inexpensive self-defense courses.

SECURITY

Don't put money in a wallet in your back pocket. Never count your money in public and carry as little as possible. If you carry a purse, consider leaving it at home, or buy a sturdy one with a secure clasp, and carry it crosswise on the side, away from the street with the clasp against you. For your backpack, buy a small combination padlock which slips through the two zippers, securing the pack. A **money belt** is the safest way to carry cash; you can buy one at most camping supply stores or through the Forsyth Travel Library (see **Useful Publications,** p. 3). The best combination of convenience and invulnerability is the nylon, zippered pouch with belt that should sit inside the waist of your pants or skirt. A **neck pouch** is equally safe, though less accessible. Keep a small amount of local cash in your pockets so you don't need to be accessing your secret cash stash every time you want to buy a snack. Do avoid keeping anything precious in a fanny-pack (bum-bag), even if it's worn on your stomach: your valuables will be highly visible and easy to steal. In city crowds and especially on public transportation, pickpockets are amazingly deft at their craft.

Carry a combination padlock with you, as it may be of use in securing hotel room doors while you are out seeing the sights. You will also be able to buy locks of varying sizes and qualities in India and Nepal. Do not under any circumstances trust any strangers with your money, passport, or other valuables. You should carry your **passport, traveler's checks,** and **plane ticket** on you at all times. Make **photocopies** of such important documents and store them separately. This will help you replace them in case they are lost or filched. Keep some money separate from the rest to use in an emergency or in case of theft. It is a good idea to always have US$100 in cash on hand in case of emergencies.

Be watchful of your belongings on **buses and trains,** especially when passengers are getting on and off frequently. Keep everything close to you if you can. On trains, some people use the effective technique of padlocking their bags to luggage racks or bunks. If your bag is going on a bus roof rack, make sure it's tied down securely so someone couldn't jump off with it in a hurry. The best policy is to talk to the other travelers in your seat or compartment and ask them where you can safely put your bag. If you let people help you, they will look out for you.

You might want to leave your luggage at a guest house while you are trekking, but don't leave your valuables there, and make sure what you do leave is locked. Never leave your belongings unlocked and unattended in a hotel. When possible, leave expensive jewelry, valuables, and anything you couldn't bear to part with at home.

If your belongings are stolen in India or Nepal you should go to the police. While there is virtually no chance you'll ever see your camera again, you can at least get an official **police report** which you'll need for an insurance claim. Persistence usually pays off. Dress well and be prepared for unsympathetic, suspicious policemen.

Travel Assistance International by Worldwide Assistance Services, Inc. provides its members with a 24-hour hotline for assistance. Their yearlong frequent traveler package ($235-295) includes medical and travel insurance, financial assistance, and help in replacing lost documents. Call (800) 821-2828, fax (202) 331-1528, or write them at 1133 15th St. NW, Ste. 400, Washington, D.C. 20005-2710. The **American Society of Travel Agents** provides extensive informational resources, both at their website (http://www.astanet.com) and in their free brochure, *Travel Safety.* You can obtain a copy by sending a request and self-addressed, stamped envelope to them at ASTA Fulfillment, 1101 King St., Suite 200, Alexandria, VA 22314. Be sure to indicate which brochure you want.

DRUGS AND ALCOHOL

In the 1960s India and Nepal earned reputations as places where one could go and stare at the mountains or the ocean for days on end while achieving a pot-induced version of *nirvana* or at least a cosmic state of unity with the vegetable kingdom. Many travelers have conveniently adopted one aspect of Shiva worship, smoking *ganja* in groups out of a *chillum,* lighting it with a match and chanting *"bam"* as the flame is lit, then bringing the *chillum* to their foreheads before and after smoking to pay homage to the "third eye." But while marijuana *(ganja)* and hashish *(charas)* are grown throughout the Himalaya and are extremely cheap everywhere in India and Nepal, travelers should understand that these **drugs are illegal** and considered socially unacceptable by most Indians and Nepalis. An exception is made for *sadhus* (Hindu holy men), since *ganja* is associated with Shiva, and a few ethnic groups in the Himalaya use *ganja* and *charas,* although such reports have been exaggerated. In general, drug use is one of those activities that have earned foreign travelers a bad name in India and Nepal—it's better not to get mixed up in it.

India has a 10-year minimum sentence for drug possession or trafficking, but those caught with only a minute amount of *ganja* tend to get off lighter. If charged with drug possession, you are likely to find yourself required to prove your innocence in an often-corrupt justice system whose rules you don't understand. An "out-of-court settlement" with the police officer at the time of arrest is not unheard of, but the police do not go around making drug busts just to get bribes. Those who attempt to "influence" a police officer must do so discreetly and euphemistically. Drug law enforcement in Nepal is a bit more lax, but sentences are still stiff, and you probably don't want to spend any time in a Nepalese prison.

If you get into trouble with the law, contact your country's diplomatic mission. Bear in mind that if you are arrested, diplomats from your country can visit you, provide a list of lawyers, inform family and friends, and lend you a shoulder to cry on, but they cannot get you out of jail.

The more touristy places in India and Nepal, like Kathmandu, Pokhara, and Goa, have an abundance of **alcohol.** Beer is popular. India and Nepal both produce drinkable vodka, gin, rum, whisky and other liquors; in India these are classified as IMFL (Indian-Made Foreign Liquor). Beware of home-brewed concoctions in India and Nepal, however; every year dozens of revelers are killed by bad batches of toddy. The Indian state of Gujarat has been officially dry since 1947, and its prohibitive efforts have recently been copied by Haryana, and Manipur. But illegal, bootlegged alcohol can still be found in so-called "dry" states. Other areas, like Tamil Nadu, Mumbai, and Delhi, have dry days. Liquor permits, available at embassies, consulates, and tourist offices in Delhi, Chennai, Mumbai, and Calcutta, aren't essential but may help you get booze with less difficulty in dry areas. There is no drinking age in India or Nepal.

UNUSUAL LAWS AND REGULATIONS

Every country has its own rules that may not be readily apparent to the visitor. What is most important to remember is that you are a visitor in someone else's country and must respect their culture and customs. If you do not, hassles and potentially much worse may result.

Common throughout India and Nepal is the practice of informal bribery, informally known as **baksheesh.** Those who find themselves in trouble with some aspect of the law may be able to get out of it with some money and a little bit of finesse, depending on the nature of the offense. Contrary to western notions of legality, "smoothing over" problems with a little cash is not only common but even expected in India and Nepal. For such incursions as a traffic offense or a minor customs violation, some find that an offer of money or foreign-made goods may suddenly shed new light on the situation. Some liquor, a shirt, or cash can work equally well depending on the scenario. While bribery is common, and sometimes expected, there are risks involved with it, as with anything illegal. Honest officials may take offense, which would only aggravate problems for the would-be briber. Those who attempt to bribe officials must do so discreetly, with plenty of excuses. It is never wise to call a bribe a bribe.

Visitors to Nepal (especially those who plan to drive) should also be aware that killing a cow is a major offense, punishable by long prison terms. It is also illegal to actively proselytize on behalf of any religion in Nepal, with both the convert and converter eligible for long prison terms (although it is perfectly acceptable to tell others about what you believe and to ask others about their faith).

■ Health

A hectic vacation can take its toll on your health, especially in a tropical climate; India and Nepal often seem like petri dishes for every kind of bug imaginable. Make your health a number one priority: you can almost never be too vigilant. If you are not healthy, you will reap very little from your experience. Keeping your body strong will help ward off serious maladies: eat properly (protein and carbohydrates), drink lots of fluids, get plenty of sleep, and don't overexert yourself. To minimize the effects of jet lag, adjust to the region's schedule as soon as possible—stay in a hotel room with windows so you know when it's night. During the hot season, take precautions against heatstroke and sunburn: drink lots of liquids, wear a hat and sunscreen, and stay inside during midday. That said, if you're too paranoid about your health, you're likely to err on the side of malnourishment, and may wind up getting sick anyway. Take care of your self, but remember that living in fear is no way to spend a vacation.

BEFORE YOU GO

You may want to assemble a **first-aid kit,** including: antiseptic soap, aspirin, decongestant, antihistamine, acetaminophen to lower fever, diarrhea medicine (for the most common medical complaint of travelers in India and Nepal), motion sickness medicine, antibacterial ointment, a thermometer, bandages, insect repellent, hydro-cortisone for when the insect repellent doesn't work, and a Swiss Army knife with tweezers and scissors.

It is a good idea to know your **blood type** and any other essential information about your blood in case an emergency transfusion is necessary. In your passport, write the names of any people to be contacted in case of a medical emergency, and list any allergies or medical conditions to alert foreign doctors.

Bring an up-to-date, detailed copy of any **medical prescriptions** you require (in legible form, stating the medication's trade name, manufacturer, chemical name, and dosage), and carry an ample supply of all medication—matching your prescription with a foreign equivalent is not always economical, easy, or safe. Distribute medication between carry-on and checked baggage in case one goes astray. Travelers with a chronic medical condition requiring regular treatment should consult their doctors before leaving. Bring a statement describing any preexisting medical conditions, especially if you will be bringing insulin, syringes, or any narcotics.

Travelers with **corrective lenses** should bring an extra pair, or at least a copy of their prescription. If you wear contact lenses, carry a pair of glasses in case your eyes are tired or you lose a lens. Bring extra solutions, enzyme tablets, and eyedrops, as prices can be sky-high and availability is restricted to bigger cities. For heat disinfection, you'll need outlet and perhaps voltage adapters; you may want to switch to chemical cleansers, or disposable lenses. Traveling does not always provide sanitary conditions for contact lens care.

Innoculations and Prescriptions

In most cases, no innoculations are required for entry into India or Nepal, but that doesn't mean innoculations are not necessary. Additionally, visitors who have been in Africa, South America, or Trinidad and Tobago within the six days prior to their arrival in India must have a certificate of vaccination against yellow fever. Ask your physican for advice on the shots you'll need; the following is general information that differs from case to case. Most travelers to India or Nepal need shots against Hepatitis A, typhoid, and meningitis. A fairly new **Hepatitis A** vaccine called Havrix is available; though expensive, it lasts up to ten years. The more traditional protection is an immune globulin (IG) injection that is very effective but wears off after only five months. Those who get the IG should wait until right before their departure. **Typhoid** immunity requires either week-long oral vaccine or an injection. The new ViCPS injection requires only one shot, as opposed to the old typhoid vaccination, which involves a protracted series of jabs. Anyway, typhoid innoculations are only 70-90% effective, so continue to practice vigilance in selecting food and water (see p. 26). **Meningitis,** an often fatal disease that causes swelling of the lining around the brain, breaks out now and then in India and Nepal; it is a good idea to be protected. The vaccination is an injection.

It is equally important to make sure you are immune to such diseases as **diphtheria, polio, tetanus, measles, mumps,** and **rubella.** Most people in Western countries are innoculated against these in childhood, but adults need an injectable polio booster called IPOL at some point, and a tetanus booster is necessary every 10 years. Some travelers to India also take mefloquine, an oral inoculation, to guard against the relatively low risk of **malaria** (see p. 27). The general prescription calls for a weekly dose beginning one week prior to departure and continuing four weeks after return. Vaccines are also available for **rabies** (see p. 28) and **cholera** (see p. 26), but neither of these is very effective; the rabies vaccine in particular does not actually prevent rabies, it only reduces the number of shots you need if you get it. Many doctors will not dispense either of these shots, since they can create a false sense of protection.

Useful Organizations

For up-to-date information about recommended vaccinations for India and Nepal, and region-specific health data, there are many resources. The **United States Centers for Disease Control and Prevention** (based in Atlanta, GA), is an excellent source of information for travelers around the world and maintains an international travelers' hotline (tel. (404) 332-4559 or (888) 232-3299; fax 332-4565; http://www.cdc.gov). The CDC publishes the booklet "Health Information for International Travelers" (US$20), an annual global rundown of disease, immunization, and general health advice, including risks in particular countries. This book may be purchased by sending a check or money order to the Superintendent of Documents, U.S. Government Printing Office, P.O. Box 371954, Pittsburgh, PA, 15250-7954. Orders can be made by phone (tel. (202) 512-1800) with a credit card (Visa, Mastercard, Discover). The **United States State Department** compiles Consular Information Sheets on health, entry requirements, and other issues for all countries of the world. For quick information on travel warnings, call the **Overseas Citizens' Services** (tel. (202) 647-5225). To receive the same Consular Information Sheets by fax, dial (202) 647-3000 directly from a fax machine and follow the recorded instructions. The State Department's regional passport agencies in the U.S., field offices of the U.S. Chamber of Commerce, and U.S. embassies and consulates abroad provide the same data, or send a self-addressed, stamped envelope to the Overseas Citizens' Services, Bureau of Consular Affairs, #4811, U.S. Department of State, Washington, D.C. 20520. If you are HIV positive, call (202) 647-1488 for country-specific entry requirements or write to the Bureau of Consular Affairs, #6831, Department of State, Washington, D.C. 20520. For more general health information, contact the **American Red Cross.** The ARC publishes a *First-Aid and Safety Handbook* (US$5) available for purchase. Contact American Red Cross, 285 Columbus Ave., Boston, MA 02116-5114 (tel. (800) 564-1234).

If you are concerned about being able to access medical support while traveling, contact one of these two services: **Global Emergency Medical Services (GEMS)** has products called *MedPass* that provide 24-hour international medical assistance and support coordinated through registered nurses who have on-line access to your medical information, your primary physician, and a worldwide network of screened, credentialed English-speaking doctors and hospital staffs. Subscribers also receive a personal medical record that contains vital information in case of emergencies. For more information call (800) 860-1111, fax (770) 475-0058, or write: 2001 Westside Drive, #120, Alpharetta, GA 30201. The **International Association for Medical Assistance to Travelers (IAMAT)** offers a membership ID card, a directory of English-speaking doctors around the world who treat members for a set fee schedule, and detailed charts on immunization requirements, various tropical diseases, climate, and sanitation. Membership is free, though donations are appreciated and used for further research. Contact chapters in the **U.S.,** 417 Center St., Lewiston, NY 14092 (tel. (716) 754-4883; fax (519) 836-3412; email iamat@sentex.net; http://www.sentex.net/~iamat); **Canada,** 40 Regal Road, Guelph, Ontario, N1K 1B5 (tel. (519) 836-0102) or 1287 St. Clair Avenue West, Toronto, M6E 1B8 (tel. (416) 652-0137; fax (519) 836-3412); or **New Zealand,** P.O. Box 5049, Christchurch 5.

HEALTH WHILE TRAVELING

Pay attention to the warning signals that your body may send you. You may feel fatigue and discomfort, not because of any specific illness, but simply because your body is adapting to a new climate, food, water quality, or pace when you arrive. Once you get going, some of the milder symptoms that you may safely ignore at home may be signs of something more serious; your increased exertion may wear you out and make you more susceptible to illness.

Parasites

Insect bites, particularly from mosquitoes, can plague your visit to India and Nepal. Many (notably mosquitoes) are most active at night, and carry dangerous diseases (malaria and others—see below). Be sure to wear repellent, long sleeves, long pants, and socks. The most you can do for prevention is use an insect repellent containing **DEET** and wear pants and long-sleeved shirts, especially in wet or forested areas or while hiking and camping. The **U.S. Centers for Disease Control** recommends using flying-insect-killing spray in sleeping quarters at night, and, for greater protection, spraying clothing and bedding with **permethrin,** an insect repellent licensed for use on clothing. Few Indian hotels provide mosquito netting, but plug-in aromatic repellants like Good Knight are effective and available at pharmacies. Apply calamine lotion or hydrocortisone to insect bites to soothe the itching. **Tiger balm** is a favorite Chinese method, and is readily available in pharmacies or from street vendors.

A fairly uncommon but irksome affliction is **parasites** (hookworms, tapeworms, etc.). Some can enter your body through your feet, so don't walk around barefoot outside. They can also find their way into your stomach through undercooked meat or dirty vegetables. **Giardia** is a serious parasitic disease contracted by ingesting untreated water from lakes or streams. A stool test from a doctor will uncover these critters, which can be flushed away with the right medicine. Symptoms of general parasitic infections include swollen glands or lymph nodes, fever, rashes, digestive problems, eye problems, and anemia. To avoid parasites, wear shoes, drink purified water, and favor cooked food. Avoid wading in stagnant water and realize that while bathing at ghats or swimming in rivers is risky, you needn't live in fear of puddles.

The Heat and the Cold

Overwhelming heat can stop even the most ambitious adventurers dead in their tracks. It is very important to avoid heat exhaustion and heat stroke. The symptoms of **heat exhaustion** include fatigue, dizziness, headaches, and a feeling of lightness. The cause of heat exhaustion is, not surprisingly, dehydration. If you think you are suffering from heat exhaustion, get out of the sun and sit down in a cool area. Drink cool fluids and avoid physical exertion. **Heat stroke,** which is very serious and sometimes fatal, takes heat exhaustion to a more dangerous level: high temperature, little or no sweating, flushed skin, unbearable headaches, delirium, convulsions, and unconsciousness. It is vital to get the victim of heat stroke to a hospital, but in the meantime, make sure to place wet towels on the victim and place him or her in a cool area; if that is absolutely impossible, at least be sure to continually fan the victim. To prevent **heat exhaustion** or **heat stroke,** drink plenty of fluids; drinking the recommended eight glasses of water per day (minimum) should become second nature. Stay away from diuretics such as alcohol, coffee, and tea, which worsen dehydration.

Less debilitating than heatstroke, but still dangerous, is **sunburn.** Many outdoor wanderers are shocked to find themselves toasted to a crisp despite thick cloud cover. If you're prone to burning, carry sunscreen with you, and apply it liberally and often. Be wary of sunscreens of SPF (sun protection factor) higher than 15 or 20; higher ratings won't be of extra help, but will cost more. Wear a hat and sunglasses and a lightweight long-sleeved shirt. If you do get burned, drink lots of liquids; it'll cool you down and help your skin recover faster.

For some travelers, a visit to India and Nepal will mean an introduction to **prickly heat,** a rash that develops when sweat is trapped under the skin. Men are particularly susceptible to developing this rash in the groin area. To alleviate itch, try showering with mango *neem* soap or sprinkle talcum powder on the affected area just after bathing. Moist, hot weather can irritate the skin in other ways as well. Various **fungal infections** (athlete's foot, jock itch, etc.) can be prevented by washing often and drying thoroughly. Wear loose-fitting clothes made of absorbent fibers like cotton.

Extreme cold is just as dangerous as heat—overexposure to cold brings the risk of **hypothermia.** Warning signs are easy to detect: body temperature drops rapidly, resulting in the failure to produce body heat. You may shiver, have poor coordination, feel exhausted, have slurred speech, feel sleepy, hallucinate, or suffer amnesia. **Do not let hypothermia victims fall asleep** if they are in the advanced stages—their body temperature will drop more and if they lose consciousness they may die. Seek medical help as soon as possible. To avoid hypothermia, keep dry and stay out of the wind. In wet weather, wool and most synthetics, such as pile, will keep you warm but most other fabric, especially cotton, will make you colder. Dress in layers, and watch for **frostbite** when the temperature is below freezing. Look for skin that has turned white, waxy, and cold, and if you find frostbite do not rub the skin. Drink warm beverages, get dry, and slowly warm the area with dry fabric or steady bodily contact. Take serious cases to a doctor as soon as possible.

Travelers to **high altitudes** must allow their bodies a couple of days to adjust to lower oxygen levels in the air before exerting themselves. Also be careful about alcohol, especially if you're used to U.S. standards for beer—many foreign brews and liquors pack more punch, and at high altitudes where the air has less oxygen, any alcohol will do you in quickly.

Water and Food

Don't drink the water! At least not from the tap. Nowhere in India or Nepal is tapwater safe for drinking, and water from streams and wells is just as dangerous. If locals seem to be doing fine, remember that they have built up lifelong immunities. Brushing teeth with tapwater is an acceptable risk for some, but don't swallow. **Drink only boiled or filtered water and avoid ice.**

The most effective method of purification is to **boil** water. Presumably, you won't be carrying a kitchen stove, however, so the simplest tactic is to treat water with **iodine,** either in drops (tincture of iodine) or tablets. Chlorine tablets are also available, but they don't kill abslolutely everything. After treating water with iodine or chlorine wait 20 minutes for the chemical to burn off and for the parasites to die. An easy alternative to boiling and chemical treatments is to buy **mineral water,** which is available almost everywhere in India and Nepal. Beware of unsealed bottles—these have often been refilled with tap water—add iodine drops to a bottle if it seems suspect, and always crush your bottle when you're done, to prevent illicit reuse.

Carbonated drinks ("cold drinks") are also safe—they must be carbonated in factories which use clean water, and they are sealed to keep in the fizz. If a carbonated drink is flat, don't drink it. There have been incidents of "fake" Coca-Cola in India, but if you taste it, you'll know. Remember, however, that caffeine (contained in cola drinks) is a diuretic, and therefore can be bad for rehydration. Fresh lime soda, a mixture of club soda, lime juice, and sugar, is a refreshing, mineral-rich alternative. **Coconut water,** or tender coconut water, sold on street corners all over India, is excellent for replacing fluids and minerals. **Coffee** and **tea,** which are boiled in preparation, are also usually safe, although some of the toughest parasites are not killed by simple boiling. Avoid drinks such as *lassis* or *nimbu pani* (lemonade) except in the best restaurants; these are made with ice-water, and it often isn't purified. **Insist on beverages without ice,** even if that means desert temperatures can only be combatted with lukewarm Thums-Up Cola. The water used to make ice is rarely clean. Many restaurants use "Aquaguard" filters, however, which make their water safe to drink.

Water safety is also seasonal, and it's riskier to drink the water during the **monsoon,** when all the year's crud seeps into the water supply, than during the dry season. If you visit South Asia in the monsoon, be especially careful about water.

Any food that is cooked immediately before serving is safe. To be extra safe, however, avoid food cooked by street vendors, tempting as *chaat* is. Street vendors are rarely sanitary, and their equipment is open to disease-carrying flies. The same is true of juice stands. If possible, eat in restaurants that serve local food and are popular with locals. Indians and Nepalis know what they're doing when they prepare their own cuisine, and busy kitchens are likely to be cleaner. Tourist restaurants that serve shoddy imitations of Western food are often less sanitary than *dhabas* that dish out *dal bhat* to truckers all day. Everything will be much easier, in fact, if you eat at regular times and eat the same sort of foods regularly every day. Eating in different places all the time can be disturbing to your body.

The biggest risk to travelers usually comes from **fruit, vegetables, and dairy products.** With fruit, if you can peel it, you can eat it. If you crave a salad, make sure the restaurant soaks its vegetables in iodine. Take dairy products only from clean-looking establishments. Beware of some juice stands and sugarcane juice stands; their equipment is not always kept clean.

Other than that, the spiciness of the food and the variation in ingredients can also put a strain on your stomach. Adjust to the region's cooking slowly. Have high-

Go For It: Water Snobbery 101

Many budding South Asian gourmands are unnecessarily taken aback by the prospect of choosing the correct bottled water to accompany a Subcontinental menu. But selection is really quite easy, as the following quick-reference list shows:

Chinese: Bottled, purified mineral water.
Continental: Mineral water that has been bottled and purified.
Indian: Purified mineral water, sealed inside a bottle.

Once you've ordered, the water steward will bring you your bottle for inspection. Check the cap to see that it's been sealed with plastic wrap—the mark of refined taste and purity. Also note the computer-printed vintage—recent bottlings are more desirable. Once your glass has been poured, check for clarity. Although dregs might be acceptable in wine, water connoisseurs demand a sediment-free libation. Finally, drink up, being sure to notice your water's characteristic smells or "notes." If your beverage smells like much of anything, send it back!

As your water palate develops, your refined appreciation for different brands of bottled water will grow, and you'll soon be pontificating on the relative merits of Pondicherry and Yes! brands, and discovering why Indian Bisleri is "Pure and Safe," while its Nepali counterpart is "Pure and Refreshing." *Santé!*

energy, non-sugary foods with you to keep your strength up; you'll need plenty of protein and carbohydrates. **Washing your hands before you eat** is a sensible rule that you should not forget while you travel. Bring a few packs of handi-wipes or diaper wipes (or even alcohol pads), since sinks and soap may not always be available.

Diarrhea

Few travelers to India and Nepal get away without at least one bout of **diarrhea.** It has many causes, including parasites, bacteria, food poisoning, viruses, and simply adjusting to new kinds of food. To prevent it, drink safe water, wash your hands before eating, and stay away from street food. **The biggest danger from diarrhea is dehydration. If you get diarrhea, drink liquids constantly in order to keep yourself hydrated.** Water is good for starters, but it is also important to replace the minerals you lose. Adding 60ml (4 Tbsp.) of sugar and 3ml (½ tsp.) of salt to a liter of pure water makes an effective **rehydration drink.** If you can't find these ingredients, prepared mixtures of oral rehydration salts (ORS) are available at all pharmacies. (Electral is the most common brand in India.) Non-caffeinated soft drinks such as Sprite, allowed to go flat, are also good. Down large amounts of these mixtures daily. People with diarrhea should also eat simple, starchy foods like bananas or boiled rice to keep their strength up. Over-the-counter remedies (such as Pepto-Bismol or Immodium) may counteract the problems, but they can also complicate serious infections. Pepto-Bismol alleviates diarrheal discomfort without plugging up the digestive system. Some doctors even recommend taking Pepto daily as a preventative remedy.

Avoid anti-diarrheals if you suspect you have been exposed to contaminated food or water, which puts you at risk for cholera, typhoid fever, and other diseases. Get lots of rest and wait for the illness to run its course. If you develop a fever or your symptoms are particularly severe, consult a doctor. Also consult a doctor if children develop traveler's diarrhea.

Food- and Water-Borne Diseases

Dysentery

One of the most common forms of diarrhea is dysentery, which is caused when bacteria or amoebas infect the mucus lining of the large intestine. The most common symptoms of dysentery are diarrhea (often containing mucus) and gripping abdominal pain. If bacteria is the cause, the dysentery usually comes on suddenly and exhausts itself; amoebas on the other hand cause a long and intermittent illness that will recur if not treated. Pepto-Bismol is ineffective against dysentery, but other drugs can be used to kill the intruders and restore the normal intestinal bacteria. Terramycin (tetracycline) is an antibiotic that kills dysentery bacteria. Metronidazole (known as Flagyl or Metrogyl in India) is commonly used to kill amoebic parasites. Nutrolin B (a combination of *lactobacillus acidophilus* and vitamin B complex) helps restore the intestinal flora, and is essential to take with any antibiotic. It is a good preventitive medicine as well. If you have symptoms of dysentery, see a doctor right away.

Cholera

Cholera is still a perennial problem in India and Nepal, breaking out now and then in deadly local epidemics. Cholera is an acute intestinal bacteria-borne infection that works quickly and with murderous intent. The symptoms—explosive and interminable diarrhea, unstoppable vomiting, dehydration, muscle cramps, and lethargy—come suddenly, and unless quickly treated, prove fatal in a short time. It is vital for the cholera-infected to find a hospital immediately. In the meantime, the patient should guzzle liquids to battle dehydration. Cholera is passed from person to person like wildfire through contaminated food or water, human waste, and unsanitary cooking methods. The best way to prevent cholera is to drink clean water, peel your own fruit, and eat only thoroughly cooked food.

Vaccinations for cholera (and typhoid fever in one shot) are only 50% effective in preventing illness for the first three to six months after vaccination. The CDC recommends vaccination for people with stomach ulcers, those who use anti-acid therapy, and those who will be living in unsanitary conditions in epidemic areas.

Typhoid Fever

Caused by a bacterium, typhoid is spread through contaminated food, water, human waste, and contact with an infected person. Symptoms gradually creep up on the victim. For the first week or so, a fever slowly rises, sometimes accompanied by vomiting and diarrhea. Next, a rash may appear, and delirium and dehydration seize the victim. Headaches, fatigue, appetite loss, and constipation are other symptoms. Untreated, the patient may develop life-threatening pneumonia. As with all dangerous, communicable diseases, it is imperative to seek immediate medical attention.

Typhoid fever is treatable with antibiotics, and a vaccine is available, although it is only 70% effective. The CDC recommends vaccination for those traveling off the beaten tourist paths, that is, those going to small cities or towns, or those staying longer than six weeks. It is also important, of course, to drink only bottled or boiled water and eat only thoroughly cooked food to lower the risk of infection.

Hepatitis

Caused by a virus that attacks the liver, hepatitis is prevalent in India and Nepal. **Hepatitis A,** like typhoid fever, is spread through the contamination of water and food with viruses present in human feces. It is therefore important to be wary of uncooked foods that may have been contaminated during handling, such as fresh fruits and vegetables. It can also be transmitted from direct person-to-person contact. Fatigue, vomiting, nausea, fever, loss of appetite, dark urine, jaundice, light stools, and aches and pains are among the symptoms. At particular risk are travelers, especially those visiting rural areas, coming into close contact with local people, or eating in settings with poor sanitation. Gamma globulin received prior to a trip provides up to six months protection, but is painful and must be repeated for future protection. The hepatitis A vaccine, consisting of two shots, is more costly and must be administered over a course of several months but provides far more long-term protection. **Hepatitis B** is spread through the transfer of bodily fluids, such as blood, semen, and saliva, from one person to another. Its incubation period varies and can be much longer than the 30-day incubation period of hepatitis A. Thus, a person may not begin having symptoms until many years after infection. A vaccination consisting of three shots, which must also be administered over several months, is also recommended. **Check with your doctor, as recommended schedules for vaccines vary from person to person. Hepatitis C,** which is also spread through sexual contact and contact with infected blood, does not always cause serious health problems in the infected person but has the potential to cause severe liver damage. A vaccine has not yet been developed.

Insect-Borne Diseases

Malaria

Malaria is the most serious disease that travelers to India and Nepal are likely to contract. It is caused by a parasite carried by the female *Anopheles* mosquito. The disease is prevalent in most tropical areas of the world. Because the incubation period for the disease varies, it could take up to weeks or months for an infected person to show any symptoms. When the disease does hit, the first symptoms include headaches, chills, general achiness, and fatigue. Next comes a very high fever and sweating. In some cases, vomiting and diarrhea also show up. If you think you may have malaria, go to the nearest hospital immediately and have a blood test. No precautions can fully protect you from contracting malaria. While traveling and for up to a year later, seek medical attention to treat any flu-like symptoms. Malaria can be fatal. Anemia, kidney failure, coma, and death can result if it goes untreated.

Malaria is generally found in heavily forested areas. It is virtually but not entirely impossible to get malaria in big cities and towns. The CDC says that preventative medication against malaria is not necessary if you only visit urban areas; however, as mentioned above, precautions should be taken to avoid being bitten by mosquitoes and to treat flu-like symptoms. Malaria is only found below 1200m in altitude, so the mountainous areas of Nepal and northern India are relatively safe.

Various forms of medication can be taken to prevent malaria (no shots are available). Some doctors may prescribe mefloquine (sold under the name Lariam), taken in a 250mg tablet once a week, one week before leaving until four weeks after leaving. Mefloquine is a drug approved by the Centers for Disease Control, with the reservation that it should not be taken by pregnant women, children under 30 pounds, or people with a history of epilepsy, psychiatric disorder, or a known hypersensitivity to mefloquine. Carrying the drug Fansidar is often recommended, but it should be used only in the case of serious illness and when medical care is not readily available. The best way to combat malaria is to wear insect repellent containing DEET, sleep under bednets, and stay away from uninhabited jungle areas. Also, to combat mosquitoes, you can use mosquito coils or Good Knight, an electric device that cooks little cakes, sending anti-mosquito gases into the air.

Dengue Fever

Mosquitoes can also carry the virus that causes dengue fever, an often-urban malady that exhibits symptoms similar to malaria. Dengue fever has two stages and is characterized by its sudden onset. Stage one lasts from two to four days, and its symptoms include chills, high fever, severe headaches, swollen lymph nodes, muscle aches, and in some instances, a pink rash on the face. The fever subsides temporarily, replaced by profuse sweating, and then reappears along with a rash all over the body. If you think you have contracted dengue fever, see a doctor, drink plenty of liquids, and remain in bed. It is also important to take acetaminophen (Tylenol) or ibuprofen (Advil) for dengue fever; do not take aspirin. Unfortunately, the only prevention for dengue fever is avoiding mosquitoes. Dengue mosquitoes bite during the day, unlike their nocturnal bloodsucking colleagues.

Japanese Encephalitis

The Culex mosquito carries the virus for this nasty ailment, which is most prevalent in rural areas, from July to December. Sufferers experience flu-like symptoms—chills, headache, fever, vomiting, muscle fatigue—and delirium. Symptoms are similar those of malaria, but the fatality rate of Japanese encephalitis is much higher, so it is vital to get medical help as soon as symptoms arise. A vaccine, JE-VAX, is available; you can be vaccinated against this disease with a three-shot series given a week apart or on a longer, safer schedule. The vaccine is effective for about a year. Serious side-effects have been associated with the vaccine, and so travelers should seriously consider whether it is necessary. The CDC claims that there is a very low chance that a traveler will be infected if proper precautions are taken (using mosquito repellents containing DEET, sleeping under nets, etc.).

Other Serious Infectious Diseases

Meningococcal Meningitis

Meningococcal meningitis is an inflammation of the lining surrounding the brain and spinal cord. The bacteria are carried in the nose and throat and so they are often spread through coughs and sneezes. Meningitis is less common in India than in Nepal, where there have been several recent outbreaks. The first symptom of meningitis is a rash, then fever, sensitivity to light, stiffness of the neck, and headache. Consult a doctor immediately if you have these symptoms; meningitis can kill in hours. Fortunately a vaccine exists (see **Innoculations**, p. 21).

Rabies

Transmitted through the saliva of infected animals, and common in India and Nepal, rabies is fatal if not treated. The best policy is to stay away from dogs and monkeys. If you are bitten by an animal, washing the wound thoroughly with soap and water may reduce the chance of infection. If you suspect the animal is rabid, tie it up if you can, and see a doctor immediately. Once you begin having symptoms of rabies (thirst, muscle spasms), the disease is in its terminal stage, so it is absolutely necessary to act quickly. If the animal can be found, tests can ascertain whether the animal does indeed have rabies. You should be admitted to a hospital, where doctors can begin giving you the six shots that will protect you from getting the disease. A rabies vaccine is available but it is only semi-effective; however, if you plan to be in close contact with animals in India or Nepal they are probably a good idea. Three shots are necessary; it takes one year to receive them in series.

Schistosomiasis

Another common infection, schistosomiasis is caused by the larvae of a flatworm that can penetrate the skin. The larvae are found in fresh water, so swimming in fresh water, especially in rural areas, should be avoided. If your skin is exposed to untreated water, the CDC recommends immediate and vigorous rubbing with a towel and/or the application of rubbing alcohol to reduce the risk of infection. If infected, you may notice an itchy localized rash; later symptoms include fever, fatigue, painful urination, diarrhea, loss of appetite, night sweats, and a hive-like rash on the body. Schistosomiasis can be treated with drugs.

AIDS, HIV, AND VENEREAL DISEASES

Because of an active prostitution industry and drug subculture, HIV and AIDS are proliferating at a frightening rate in India and Nepal. The World Health Organization (WHO) estimates that there are two million AIDS cases in India and 5000 in Nepal (although the reported number of cases is minuscule). The governments of India and Nepal are now beginning to recognize AIDS as a problem.

The best advice is to follow all the precautions you would follow at home: avoid sex without a condom and never share needles of any sort. It may not always be easy to buy **condoms** in India or Nepal, and when it is, they may not be of a high quality; it's a good idea to take a supply of good-quality Western-made condoms with you.

Although heterosexual sex is the most common method of HIV transmission in India and Nepal, there are other risks as well. Since many hospitals lack money and resources, they may reuse needles and other instruments without sterilizing them. The risk of obtaining HIV this way is slight, however, so it should never cause you to refuse medical care in an emergency. If you need an injection, make sure the needle has been sterilized; to be extra safe, carry your own **syringes** with you and insist that these be used. Bring a letter from your doctor stating that the syringes are for medicinal purposes. Avoid any other contact with needles (tattooing, piercing, acupuncture, etc.) unless you can be absolutely sure the needles have been sterilized. If you get a shave from a barber make sure he uses a new blade.

For more information on AIDS, call the **U.S. Center for Disease Control's** 24-hour hotline at (800) 342-2437. In Europe, write to the **World Health Organization,** attn: Global Program on AIDS, 20 Avenue Appia, 1211 Geneva 27, Switzerland (tel. (22) 791 2111), for statistical material on AIDS internationally, or write to the **Bureau of Consular Affairs,** #6831, Department of State, Washington, D.C. 20520. A brochure, *Travel Safe: AIDS and International Travel,* is available at all Council Travel offices.

Sexually transmitted diseases (STDs) such as gonorrhea, chlamydia, genital warts, syphilis, and herpes are a lot easier to catch than HIV and can be just as deadly. Condoms may protect you from certain STDs, but oral or even tactile contact can lead to transmission. Warning signs for STDs include: swelling, sores, bumps, or blisters on sex organs, rectum, or mouth; burning and pain during urination and bowel movements; itching around sex organs; swelling or redness in the throat; flu-like symptoms with fever, chills, and aches. If these symptoms develop, see a doctor immediately.

WOMEN'S HEALTH

Women traveling in unsanitary conditions are vulnerable to urinary tract and bladder infections, common and severely uncomfortable bacterial diseases which cause a burning sensation and painful and sometimes frequent urination. Drink tons of vitamin-C-rich juice and clean water, and urinate frequently, especially right after intercourse. Untreated, these infections can lead to kidney infections, sterility, and even death. If symptoms persist, see a doctor. If you often develop vaginal yeast infections, take along enough over-the-counter or prescription medicine; medicine may not be available, and when it is, you cannot buy it over the counter. Women are also susceptible to vaginal thrush and cystitis, two treatable but uncomfortable illnesses that may flare up in hot, humid climates. Wearing loosely fitting trousers or a skirt and cotton underwear may help. Sanitary napkins (pads) and especially tampons are sometimes hard to find in India and Nepal; certainly your preferred brands may not be available, so take supplies along. Refer to the *Handbook for Women Travellers* by Maggie and Gemma Moss (published by Piatkus Books) or to the women's health guide *Our Bodies, Our Selves* (published by the Boston Women's Health Collective) for more extensive information specific to women's health on the road.

GETTING HELP

Tourist centers are full of **pharmacies,** and many pharmacists (called "chemists" in India) speak enough English to understand what you need. Most pharmacies will fill a prescription with a note from a doctor. Few are open 24 hours. In an emergency, head to the nearest major hospital, which is almost certainly open all night and has an in-house pharmacy. Outside the major tourist centers, the going is a bit rougher, although every major town should have at least one pharmacy.

Both India and Nepal suffer from a lack of doctors and medical equipment. In India, there is only one doctor for every 2440 people; in Nepal, only one for every 16,829 people. **Public hospitals** are overcrowded, short on staff and supplies, and rarely have English-speaking staff—they're generally not somewhere you want to be. In many places in India, "hospitals" function essentially as hospices—homes for the dying. In cases of serious medical problems most foreign visitors to India go to more expensive **private hospitals.** These are mainly located in the big cities; elsewhere, they are usually known as **nursing homes.** The best are often run by medical schools or Christian missionary organizations. Small private **clinics,** usually operated by a single physician, are also widely available. In Kathmandu, a number of tourist-oriented clinics offer care up to Western standards. For serious medical problems, however, those who can afford it have themselves evacuated to better facilities in Singapore or Europe (although there are world-class hospitals in Mumbai and Delhi as well).

You can also contact your **diplomatic mission** upon arrival and inquire as to their suggested **list of doctors.** Carry these names around with other medical documents.

To be admitted to many hospitals or nursing homes one must have a doctor who will take your case. If a **blood transfusion** is necessary, inquire as to whether someone from your diplomatic mission can donate blood, or whether family members at home can send blood by air. Also ask whether your diplomatic mission can help arrange emergency evacuation.

Travel insurance (such as that offered with the ISIC and ITIC cards) is enough to cover most **medical expenses** in India or Nepal. Even for long-term stays and major surgery at top hospitals, costs are exponentially lower than what they would be in developed countries. Nevertheless, it is a good idea to carry a credit card for immediate payment. Westerners do not have good reputations for paying their bills fairly and squarely, and many hospitals are hesitant to trust them with outstanding payments.

■ Insurance

Beware of buying unnecessary travel coverage—your regular insurance policies may well extend to many travel-related accidents. **Medical insurance** (especially university policies) often covers costs incurred abroad; check with your provider. Canadians are protected by their home province's health insurance plan for up to 90 days after leaving the country; check with the provincial Ministry of Health or Health Plan Headquarters for details. Australia's national healthcare does not extend to travelers in India or Nepal. Your **homeowners' insurance** (or your family's coverage) often covers theft during travel. Homeowners are generally covered against loss of travel documents (passport, plane ticket, railpass, etc.) up to US$500.

ISIC and **ITIC** provide basic insurance benefits, including US$100 per day of in-hospital sickness for a maximum of 60 days, and US$3000 of accident-related medical reimbursement (see **Youth, Student, & Teacher Identification,** p. 12). Cardholders have access to a toll-free 24-hour helpline whose multilingual staff can provide assistance in medical, legal, and financial emergencies overseas (tel. (800) 626-2427 in the U.S. and Canada; elsewhere call the U.S. collect (713) 267-2525). **Council** and **STA** offer a range of plans that can supplement your basic insurance coverage, with options covering medical treatment and hospitalization, accidents, baggage loss, and even charter flights missed due to illness. Most **American Express** cardholders receive automatic car rental (collision and theft, but not liability) insurance and travel accident coverage (US$100,000 in life insurance) on flight purchases made with the card. Customer Service (tel. (800) 528-4800).

In addition, some credit card companies offer travel-related services as part of their benefits packages. Other companies offering such coverage include **Access America** (tel. (800) 284-8300) and **C.S.A. Travel Protection** (tel. (800) 826-1300. **TripGuard Plus** (tel. (800) 423-3632) also offers a useful informational brochure.

■ Alternatives to Tourism

Opportunities for work, study, or other activities conducive to meeting more than simply hotel owners, auto-rickshaw drivers, and other tourists abound in India and Nepal. Studying at an Indian or Nepalese university, working, or volunteering allows foreigners to meet and get to know Indians and Nepalis on a more intimate level. Foreign tourists often find that what they'd really like is to settle down and get to know one city or village. Many foreigners go to teach English, to study Indian and Nepalese languages, or to volunteer at health clinics and rural development projects. What follows is a list of organized study and work programs and resources for finding out more information. However, don't stop here. India and Nepal are good places to go and just see what happens. A surprising number of alternatives can be arranged informally. Foreigners, who are usually rich compared to Indians and Nepalis, have an advantage because the cost of living is so low. If you're willing to work for room and board, you will find many possibilities open to you (just make sure you have the correct documentation—valid visas, work permits, etc.). We list such out-of-the-way opportunities in the specific city sections when we can, but the best advice is to look and ask around—other foreigners are particularly helpful.

STUDY

Foreign study programs vary tremendously in expense, academic quality, living conditions, degree of contact with local students, and exposure to local culture and languages. There is a plethora of exchange programs for high school students, especially during the summer. Most undergraduates enroll in semester- or year-long programs sponsored by universities, and many colleges have offices that give advice and information on studying abroad. Ask for the names of recent participants in these programs, and get in touch with them in order to judge which program is best for you.

College Semester Abroad, School for International Training, Admissions, Kipling Rd., P.O. Box 676, Brattleboro, VT 05302 (tel. (800) 336-1616 or 258-3267; fax 258-3500). Offers extensive semester- and year-long Study Abroad programs with homestays, intensive language classes, courses in history, politics, arts and humanities, geography, economics, anthropology with field study, and independent study opportunities: in India (US$9300); Nepal (US$9900); and Tibetan Studies (US$11,200). Program costs include international airfare, tuition, room and board, and health insurance. Scholarships are available and federal financial aid is usually transferable from home college or university. Many colleges will transfer credit for work done abroad.

Cornell University, 474 Uris Hall, Ithaca, NY 14853 (tel. (607) 255-6224; fax 255-8700; email cuabroad@cornell.edu; www.einaudi.cornell.edu/cuabroad). Has a program in Kirtipur, Nepal (US$14,200 including tuition, room and board, but not international airfare).

Friends World Program, 239 Montauk Highway, Southampton, NY 11968 (tel. (516) 287-8466; fax 287-8463). Offers a semester- or year-long program in Bangalore that includes language training (in either Hindi, Kannada, or Tamil) and cultural training (approx. US$12,168 per semester, including international airfare, tuition, room and board, and other program costs).

Institute of International Education (IIE), 809 United Nations Plaza, New York, NY 10017-3580 (tel. (212) 984-5413; fax 984-5358). For book orders: IIE Books, Institute of International Education, P.O. Box 371, Annapolis Junction, MD 20701 (tel. (800) 445-0443; fax (301) 953-2838; email iiebooks@iie.org). A nonprofit, international, and cultural exchange agency, IIE's library of study abroad resources is open to the public Tu-Th 11am-3:45pm. Publishes *Academic Year Abroad* (US$43, US$4 postage) and *Vacation Study Abroad* (US$37, US$4 postage). Write for a complete list of publications.

International Schools Services, Educational Staffing Program, 15 Roszel Rd., P.O. Box 5910, Princeton, NJ 08543 (tel. (609) 452-0990; fax 452-2690; email edustaffing@iss.edu; http://www.iss.edu). Recruits teachers and administrators for schools. All instruction in English. Applicants must have a bachelor's degree and 2 years of relevant experience. Nonrefundable US$100 application fee. The *ISS Directory of Overseas Schools* (US$34.95) is also helpful.

Naropa Institute, 2130 Arapahoe Ave., Boulder, CO 80302 (tel. (303) 444 0202; fax 444 0410). Runs a program in Kathmandu; students take classes in art and culture, Buddhist civilization, Nepali, as well as a required meditation class. Open to both undergraduate and graduate students (US$6900 for tuition, room, and board; does not include international airfare).

International Partnership for Service Learning, 815 Second Ave., Ste. 315, New York, NY 10017 (tel. (212) 986-0989; fax 986-5039; http://www.study-abroad.com), offers a 3-week program in Jan. or Aug., and a fall or spring semester (including Jan.) program. Both combine volunteer social work (with terminally ill patients in Missionaries of Charity hospices and in children's rehabilitation centers) with intensive study of language (Bengali) and culture. The cost of the 3-week program is US$4300 (airfare included); the semester-long program is US$7900 (including airfare and intercession). Study is done in Calcutta (in small hotels during 3-week program, homestays during the semester), with stays in Agra and Delhi.

Peterson's Guides, P.O. Box 2123, Princeton, NJ 08543-2123 (tel. (800) 338-3282; fax (609) 243-9150; http://www.petersons.com). Their comprehensive *Study Abroad* (US$30) annual guide lists programs in countries all over the world and provides essential information on the study abroad experience in general. Their new *Learning Adventures Around the World* (US$27) annual guide to "learning vacations" lists volunteer, museum-hopping, study, and travel programs all over the world. Purchase a copy at your local bookstore or call their toll-free number in the U.S. You get 20% off the list price when you order through their online bookstore.

Pitzer College, External Studies, 1050 N. Mills Ave., Claremont, CA 91711-6110 (tel. (909) 621-8104; fax 621-0518; http://www.pitzer.edu/academics/ilcenter/external_studies). Has a semester-long program (fall and spring) for college juniors, emphasizing conversation in a cultural context, with 200 hours of language classes. Different family homestays just outside Kathmandu, with treks in Annapurna Conservation Area and Chitwan National Park. US$14,290 includes airfare, tuition, room and board, and field trip. Financial aid usually transferable.

University of Wisconsin-Madison, 253 Bascom Hall, Madison, WI 53706 (tel. (608) 265-6329; fax 262-6998; http://www.wisc.edu/studyabroad). Has college-year programs in Hyderabad, Madurai, and Varanasi, and a summer performing arts program in Kerala. The college-year programs concentrate on field work, with a yearlong local language class and independently-chosen tutorial as well. One year of local language is required; for an extra US$2750, the program offers a 10-week summer intensive language program (mid-June to mid-Aug.) Fees for the college-year program cover academic expenses, administrative costs, a one-way West Coast to India plane ticket, room, meals, and pocket expenses: US$12,000 for India, US$13,000 for Nepal. Transferable financial aid and travel grants are open to students from other schools.

SPIRITUAL INTERESTS

The birthplace of several major world religions (Hinduism, Buddhism, Jainism, and Sikhism), South Asia remains a land of strong religious beliefs and spirituality. It is no wonder that India and Nepal attract many travelers wishing to throw off their old assumptions and try out other approaches to life's questions. Aside from the mainstream traditions in India and Nepal (see **India: Religion,** p. 91, and **Nepal: Religion,** p. 709), certain religious communities are particularly open to initiates from abroad.

For **Hinduism,** these mostly take the form of ashrams (retreats), many of which are under the leadership of a modern-day guru—those who have attracted many foreign devotees are often referred to as "export gurus." Some of the most famous ashrams in India include that of the late **Sri Aurobindo** in Pondicherry (see p. 488), and the **Osho Commune** in Pune (see p. 636), and **Sai Baba's** Andhra Pradesh ashrams (see p. 572). **Rishikesh** is a major center for gurus and students of yoga (see p. 164). There are literally hundreds of ashrams across India, with bigger and smaller followings. If you have trouble finding a guru to your liking, don't hesitate to talk to other travelers, ask the teacher at the outset what his philosophy is, or simply try a few out. However, what any expert in the world will tell you is that it doesn't matter how many teachers you jump around to, but how much you practice on your own time that counts. Self-fulfillment is a big thing to promise, and while some spiritualists tend to brag about the virtues of their teachings, it really comes down to personal effort. Those who stay in an ashram are normally required to avoid meat, as well as alcohol, tobacco, *paan* (betel), and any drugs, and usually stay clean and quiet.

Since the 1959 Chinese crackdown in Tibet, India and Nepal have also become the most accessible places in the world to study Tibetan Buddhism. **Dharamsala** in India, the home of the Dalai Lama and the Tibetan government-in-exile, is a popular place to study Tibetan Buddhism and learn about Tibetan culture (see p. 343). In Nepal (the Buddha's birthplace), the foremost Tibetan Buddhist center is located at **Boudha** outside of **Kathmandu** (see p. 748). Unlike Tibetan lamas (monks), Western students of Tibetan Buddhism do not usually live in monasteries, although they are expected to live austerely. Public lectures (sometimes in English) and meditation courses are offered at the major Tibetan Buddhist centers. The most thoroughly connected source for information on Tibet is the International Campaign for Tibet, based in Washington, D.C., which provides information about Tibetan organizations in India, Nepal, and worldwide in the International Tibet Resources Directory (US$7). Contact the International Campaign for Tibet, 1820 K St. NW, Ste. 520, Washington, D.C. 20006 (tel. (202) 785-1515; fax 785-4343; http://www.savetibet.org).

Christianity is India's third largest religion, after Hinduism and Islam. There are long traditions of both indigenous faith (Christianity arrived in India in the first century AD) and missionary work. Many hospitals, schools, and NGOs (Non-Government Organizations) are run or supported by local or international Christian organizations; for many travelers to India, volunteerism and faith find confluence at one of these.

VOLUNTEERING

Volunteer jobs are readily available almost everywhere, and the cost of living in India and Nepal is low enough that volunteering is not a great financial setback. You may receive room and board in exchange for your labor; the work can be fascinating (or stultifying). You can sometimes avoid the high application fees charged by the organizations that arrange placement by contacting individual work programs directly; check with the organizations. Listings in Vacation Work Publications's *International Directory of Voluntary Work* (UK£10; postage UK£2.50, £1.50 within U.K.) can be helpful (see above).

Council, Voluntary Services Dept., 205 E. 42nd St., New York, NY 10017 (tel. (888) COUNCIL/268-6245; fax (212) 822-2699; email ivpbrochure@ciee.org; http://www.ciee.org), offers 4-week volunteer programs with local community development projects in India, usually in Uttar Pradesh, during Jan., Feb., Apr., and Oct. The application deadline is 2 months prior to the start of the program. Participants must be at least 18 years of age. US$325 fee (US$275 if you fly through Council Travel) covering placement, room, and board. You are responsible for international airfare, insurance, visas, and immunization costs. This contact information applies to U.S. residents only—others should email the Coordinating Committee of International Voluntary Service at InfoEurope@ciee.org.

Missionaries of Charity, 41 Villiers Road, Southall, Middlesex 3BX UB1, U.K. (tel. 44 (181) 574 1892).

New College of California, 741 Valencia St., San Francisco, CA 94110 (tel. (800) 335-6262 ext. 406, (415) 437-3406; fax 776 7190). Has just started volunteer programs in Nepal (working in Tibetan refugee camps) and India (working in schools and farms in Ladakh); US$300 fee payable to the World Studies Project at New College. Contact Jerry Dekker.

Overseas Service Bureau Program, P.O. Box 350, Fitzroy Vic 3065, Australia (tel. 61 (3) 9279 1788 or toll-free (800) 331-292; fax 9419 4280; email osb@osb.org.au). You must have 2 years work experience and whatever qualifications you have must be generally recognized. For Australian citizens and permanent residents only.

Peace Corps, 1990 K St. NW, Room 8508, Washington, D.C. 20526 (tel. (800) 424-8580; fax (202) 606-4469; email msaucier@peacecorps.gov; http://www.peacecorps.gov). Opportunities available in developing nations in agriculture, business, education, the environment, urban planning, youth development, English-teaching, and health. Volunteers must be U.S. citizens, age 18 and over, and willing to make a 2-year commitment. A bachelor's degree is usually required. Because countries are frequently added and subtracted to the Peace Corps list, check with them for updated information.

Transitions Abroad Publishing, Inc., 18 Hulst Rd., P.O. Box 1300, Amherst, MA 01004-1300 (tel. (800) 293-0373; fax (413) 256-0373; email trabroad@aol.com; http://www.transabroad.com). Has info on volunteer programs in India and Nepal.

Volunteers for Peace, 43 Tiffany Rd., Belmont, VT 05730 (tel. (802) 259-2759; fax 259-2922; email vfp@vfp.org; http://www.vfp.org). A nonprofit organization that arranges speedy placement in 2- to 3-week work programs ("work camps") comprising 10-15 people. They will refer you to specific organizations that have placements in India and Nepal. Most complete and up-to-date listings provided in the annual *International*

Workcamp Directory (US$15). Registration fee US$195. Some work programs are open to those 16 and 17 years old for US$225. Free newsletter.

Voluntary Service Overseas (VSO), 317 Putney Bridge Rd., London, U.K. SW15 2PN (tel. 44 (181) 780 2266; fax 780 7300). For North America: 151 Slater St., Ste. 806, Ottawa, Ontario, Canada K1P 5H3 (tel. (613) 234-1364; fax (613) 234-1444; email: inquiry@vsocan.com; http://www.magi.com/~vsocan/). Must be qualified in your field (carpentry, midwifery, teaching, etc.) and have 2 years post-qualification experience. VSO will pay your airfare; your employer will provide accommodation and local salary; postings are for 2 years.

PAID WORK

There's no better way to immerse yourself in a foreign culture than to become part of its economy. The good news is that it's easy to find a temporary job in India and Nepal; native speakers of English often find that their skills are in high demand. The bad news is that unless you have connections, it will rarely be lucrative or glamorous, and it may not even pay for your airfare. It is also very difficult to get permission to work at all (both India and Nepal are exporters of labor, with many going to earn a living in the Middle East). Officially, you can hold a job in most countries only with a **work permit.** Your employer must obtain this document, usually by demonstrating that you have skills that locals lack—not the easiest of tasks. There are, however, ways to make it easier. Friends in your destination country can help expedite work permits or arrange work-for-accommodations swaps. Many permit-less agricultural workers go untroubled by local authorities. Students can check with their universities' foreign language departments, which may have connections to job openings abroad. Call the Consulate or Embassy of the country in which you wish to work to get more information about work permits (see **Diplomatic Missions,** p. 9).

Many books exist which list work-abroad opportunities. Note especially the excellent guides put out by **Vacation Work.** In order to avoid scams from fraudulent employment agencies which demand large fees and provide no results, educate yourself using publications from the following sources.

Council, publishes *International and Volunteer Projects Directory* (US$20) and *Volunteer! The Comprehensive Guide to Voluntary Service in the U.S. and Abroad* (US$12.95). Write to Council, Marketing Services Dept., 205 E. 42nd St., New York, NY 10017-5706 (tel. (888) 268-6245; fax (212) 822-2699; http://www.ciee.org).

Office of Overseas Schools, A/OS Room 245, SA-29, Dept. of State, Washington, D.C. 20522-2902 (tel. (703) 875-7800; fax 875-7979; email overseas.shools@dos.us-state.gov; http://state.gov/www/about_state/schools/). Keeps a list of schools abroad, including 3 in India, and agencies that place teachers.

Uniworld Business Publications, Inc., 257 Central Park West, 10A, New York, NY 10024-4110 (tel. (212) 496-2448; fax 769-0413; email uniworld@aol.com; http://www.uniworldbp.com). Check your local library for their *The Directory of American Firms Operating in Foreign Countries* (1996; US$220). They also publish regional and country editions of the two Directories (US$29 and up).

■ Specific Concerns

TRAVELING ALONE

There are many benefits to traveling alone in India and Nepal, among them greater independence and challenge. As a lone traveler, you have all the more incentive to meet and interact with natives. This is especially true if you are a woman—women travelers accompanied by white men usually get little opportunity to interact with locals. On the other hand, you may also be a more visible target for robbery and harassment. Lone travelers need to be well-organized and look confident at all times. Try not to stand out as a tourist. Try to maintain regular contact with someone at home who knows your itinerary.

American International Homestays, P.O. Box 1754, Nederland, CO 80466 (tel. (303) 642-3088 or (800) 876-2048). Lodgings with English-speaking host families all over the world.

Connecting: News for Solo Travelers, P.O. Box 29088, 1996 W. Broadway, Vancouver, BC V6J 5C2, Canada (tel. (604) 737-7791 or (800) 557-1757). Bi-monthly newsletter features going solo tips, single-friendly tips, and travel companion ads. Annual directory lists holiday suppliers that avoid single supplement charges. Advice and lodging exchanges facilitated between members. Membership US$25.

A Foxy Old Woman's Guide to Traveling Alone by Jay Ben-Lesser encompasses practically every specific concern, offering anecdotes and tips for anyone interested in solitary adventure. Available in bookstores and from Crossing Press in Freedom, CA (tel. (800) 777-1048), US$11.

Travel Companion Exchange, P.O. Box 833, Amityville, NY 11701 (tel. (516) 454-0880 or (800) 392-1256; fax (516) 454-0170; email travelpals@erols.com; http://whytravelalone.com). Publishes the pamphlet "Foiling Pickpockets & Bag Snatchers" (US$3.95) and Travel Companions, a monthly newsletter for single travelers seeking a travel partner (subscription US$48).

Travelin' Woman, 855 Moraga Dr., #14, Los Angeles, CA 90049 (tel. (800) 871-6409). Monthly newsletter with news, features, and tips. Subscription US$48.

WOMEN TRAVELERS

Due to a general worldwide phenomena of disrespect for women, women exploring on their own face additional safety concerns. A great amount of respect is given to mothers in South Asian culture. On the other hand, South Asian women are seldom given much independence, and are often seen as people to be looked after. Foreign women might notice that the culture of India or Nepal does not allow them the same freedom it would allow a foreign male traveler; at ticket counters, hotel reception desks, and shops, the (mostly male) staff will be puzzled at the fact that women don't have a man with them to arrange everything. This can make it difficult to communicate. Women traveling *with* men often have difficulties as well, for they will seldom get to meet people; any man their companion meets might address himself only to him, ignoring the woman completely.

Incidents of **sexual harassment** are very common, especially in northern India, but seldom more serious than verbal advances or groping. Too many Indian and Nepali men are under the impression that white women are promiscuous. This belief is partly due to the stereotypes from American television and movies, and partly because Western women do certain things (drink alcohol, smoke, travel alone, have premarital sex) that "good" Indian and Nepali women do not. The slightest bit of resistance usually stops such abuse, since most harassers have encountered few foreign women before and are unsure of themselves. On the other hand, sometimes harassment results when women seem to be flaunting their independence, which is associated with promiscuity. Women traveling alone should always stay inconspicuous, and should not set out to overturn the patriarchal social order. If need be, turn to an older woman for help in an uncomfortable situation; her stern rebukes will usually be enough to embarrass the most persistent jerk. Don't hesitate to get the attention of **passersby** if you are being harassed. The crowds are your biggest asset in India and Nepal. People have a strong sense of public morality and will not let anyone hurt someone else in plain view. On the other hand, small-town policemen are sometimes not terribly enlightened about women. They, like other men, may assume that a women traveling alone is looking for sex. Don't hesitate to call the police in an emergency, but don't place all your trust in them, particularly in untouristed areas.

The less you look like a tourist, the better off you'll be. Look as if you know where you're going (even when you don't) and **approach other women** (or couples) if you need help or directions. **Dress conservatively, covering legs and shoulders, and always wear a bra.** Pay attention to different cultural attitudes towards not just the amount of exposed flesh, but to how your body is covered/uncovered. Don't jump to the conclusion that since Indian women wearing saris may reveal their lower backs and stomachs, it's OK to wear shorts—it's most definitely not. And don't automatically assume that a t-shirt, which is considered perfectly modest in the west, and which to Western eyes appears to cover the same vital areas as a sari, if not more, is appropriate. The shape of the breast should be left a mystery—you'll see that most women's chests are covered by more than one layer of clothing. Consider wearing a *salwar kameez,* Indian baggy pants with a loose long-sleeved shirt. However, don't expect that just because you're dressed modestly you won't be harassed.

Also realize that **non-verbal communication** is quite different than in the West. Behavior that would be merely polite back home (making eye contact, responding when asked a question) can easily be interpreted as a come-on by South Asian men.

Always trust your instincts: if you'd feel better somewhere else, move on. Invest in secure accommodations, particularly family-run guest houses with doors that lock from the inside. Stay in central locations and avoid late-night walks. **Hitching** is never safe for solo women, or even for two or more women traveling together. On trains, try to get into a **ladies' compartment.** Train stations often have **ladies' waiting rooms.** On buses, you should be allowed to sit near the front.

All this advice varies from region to region. South India is said to be safer for women than the north, and women travelers here will be treated less invasively and more respectfully. Bihar and eastern Uttar Pradesh, where law and order are lax, are some of the most dangerous areas; there have even been cases of foreign women being raped here. The Himalayan regions, however, from Himachal Pradesh to Nepal to Sikkim, are among the safest areas; attitudes toward women are much more liberal among many mountain ethnic groups. And in the cosmopolitan, Westernized circles in major cities (especially in Mumbai) women can usually feel as comfortable as they would in any other big city.

A **Model Mugging** course will not only prepare you for a potential mugging, but will also raise your level of awareness of your surroundings as well as your confidence (see **Safety and Security**). Women also face additional health concerns when traveling (see **Health**).

For general information, contact the **National Organization for Women (NOW),** which boasts branches across the country that can refer women travelers to rape crisis centers and counseling services and provide lists of feminist events. Main offices include 22 W. 21st St., 7th fl., **New York,** NY 10010 (tel. (212) 260-4422); 1000 16th St. NW, 7th fl., **Washington, D.C.** 20004 (tel. (202) 331-0066); and 3543 18th St., **San Francisco,** CA 94110 (tel. (415) 861-8960; fax 861-8969; email sfnow@sirius.com; http://www.sirius.com/~sfnow/now.html).

Handbook For Women Travellers by Maggie and Gemma Moss (UK£9). Encyclopedic and well-written. Available from Piatkus Books, 5 Windmill St., London W1P 1HF, U.K. (tel. (0171) 631 07 10).

Directory of Women's Media is available from the National Council for Research on Women, 530 Broadway, 10th Fl., New York, NY 10012 (tel. (212) 274-0730; fax 274-0821). The publication lists women's publishers, bookstores, theaters, and news organizations (mail orders, US$30).

A Journey of One's Own, by Thalia Zepatos (US$17). Interesting and full of good advice, with a bibliography of books and resources. **Adventures in Good Company,** on group travel by the same author, costs US$17. Available from The Eighth Mountain Press, 624 Southeast 29th Ave., Portland, OR 97214 (tel. (503) 233-3936; fax 233-0774; email eightmt@aol.com).

Women Travel: Adventures, Advice & Experience by Miranda Davies and Natania Jansz (Penguin, US$13). Info on several foreign countries plus a decent bibliography and resource index. The sequel, *More Women Travel,* costs US$15. Both from Rough Guides, 375 Hudson St. 3rd fl., New York, NY 10014.

Women Going Places is a women's travel and resource guide geared towards lesbians which emphasizes women-owned enterprises. Advice appropriate for all women. US$15 from Inland Book Company, 1436 W. Randolph St. Chicago, IL 60607 (tel. (800) 243-0138; fax (800) 334-3892), or a local bookstore.

OLDER TRAVELERS

Senior citizens are rarely offered discounts in India or Nepal, but prices are low already. Agencies for senior group travel (like **Eldertreks,** 597 Markham St., Toronto, Ontario, Canada M6G 2L7, tel. (416) 588-5000; fax 588-9839; email passages@inforamp.net) are growing in enrollment and popularity.

> **Elderhostel,** 75 Federal St., 3rd fl., Boston, MA 02110-1941 (tel. (617) 426-7788; fax 426-8351; email Cadyg@elderhostel.org; http://www.elderhostel.org). For those 55 or over (spouse of any age). Programs at colleges, universities, and other learning centers in over 70 countries on varied subjects lasting 1-4 weeks.
>
> **No Problem! Worldwise Tips for Mature Adventurers,** by Janice Kenyon. Advice and info on insurance, finances, security, health, and packing. Useful appendices. US$16 from Orca Book Publishers, P.O. Box 468, Custer, WA 98240-0468.

TRAVELERS OF COLOR

For any foreign tourist, travelling in India and Nepal means being in the minority and dealing with often incorrect assumptions about who you are based on what color your skin is. However, in many cases, non-white tourists in South Asia can face a unique set of challenges and prejudices, as much from other travellers (who don't always recognize their fellow Westerners as such) as from locals. India's caste system unofficially associates dark skin with inferiority; such associations are sometimes applied to foreigners as well. But more often than not the worst most non-white travellers experience is a lot of benignly curious, if unceasing, stares and comments.

OVERSEAS SOUTH ASIANS

Persons of South Asian descent face their own particular set of opportunities and challenges while traveling in India or Nepal. Traipsing about alone is a far cry from staying with Grandpa, Auntie, or the cousins. In many cases, South Asians of the diaspora may find themselves the targets of contemptuous glares, insulting wisecracks, or even handicapping discrimination in lines at the bank and post office. While many Indians and Nepalis have somewhat mixed feelings concerning fairskinned tourists, often regarding them with a combination of reverence and resentment, they frequently perceive South Asians who act like foreigners as having "sold out." The result is all too often the worst of both worlds: targeted swindling combined with scorn. Women may have an even tougher time, as they are often viewed as having succumbed to depraved Western moral standards. On the brighter side, however, foreign South Asians are often approached by those curious about life in distant lands. Many Indians and Nepalis view those of their own race as accessible and less-intimidating sources of knowledge. Like anyone else, ethnic South Asian travelers must put up with their share of hassling; once beyond that, however, they are virtually handed the opportunity to interact meaningfully with people whom others must strive to reach.

BISEXUAL, GAY, AND LESBIAN TRAVELERS

Homosexuality is a taboo topic in India and Nepal, and in India, male homosexual sex is illegal. *Hijras* (male eunuchs) form a subculture of prostitutes in the big cites, especially Mumbai and Hyderabad, but this scene is not open to foreigners (see **The Third Sex,** p. 608). Most gays and lesbians in India and Nepal stay closeted. Heterosexual marriage is expected of just about everyone, so occasional sexual encounters are much more common than long-term relationships. However, male friends commonly hold hands or hug in public—these gestures are not construed as sexual.

There are only a handful of specifically gay clubs or cruising areas in India and Nepal, although solo male travelers can expect to be propositioned in public places now and then. Gay organizations tend to stay underground. In the United States, **Aero Travel, Inc.,** 4001 N. 9th St., Ste. 217, Arlington, VA 22203 (tel. (800) 356 1109,

(703) 807 1172), is a travel agency specializing in travel to India *and* travel for gay couples. **Trikone,** a U.S.-based organization for gay and lesbian South Asians, provides a list of gay and lesbian centers in India at http:www.rahul.net/trikone/resources.html. For the latest issue of their magazine, contact Trikone, P.O. Box 21354, San Jose, CA 95151 (tel. (408) 270-8776).

DISABLED TRAVELERS

Most of South Asia is ill-equipped to deal with disabled travelers. Hospitals cannot be relied upon to replace broken braces or prostheses successfully; their orthopedic materials, even in major cities, are faulty at best. Facilities for disabled travelers are generally nonexistent. Public transportation (trains, buses, rickshaws, etc.) is completely inaccessible. While the classier hotels often have elevators (which may not be wheelchair accessible), most budget accommodations don't. Most cities have no sidewalks, let alone ramps, and larger cities are packed with curbs and steps. Many sights require climbing long staircases or hiking.

TRAVELERS WITH CHILDREN

Traveling in India or Nepal with children can be a difficult adventure, as even seasoned adults have difficulty adjusting to the transportation and amenities. However, the friendliness Indians and Nepalis show towards children can often help you meet people and can lead to a more interesting trip. If you are traveling with small children, it is particularly crucial to follow the health advice and protect them from sunburn, excessive heat, insect bites, and especially diarrhea, which can be very dangerous for children. Older children should carry some sort of ID in case of an emergency. Arrange a reunion spot in case of separation when sight-seeing. Children under two generally fly for 10% of the adult airfare on international flights (this does not necessarily include a seat). International fares are usually discounted 25% for children from two to 11. For more information see **Travel with Children** by Maureen Wheeler (US$12, postage US$1.50), published by Lonely Planet Publications (Embarcadero West, 155 Filbert St., #251, Oakland, CA 94607; tel. (800) 275-8555 or (510) 893-8555; also at P.O. Box 617, Hawthorn, Victoria 3122, Australia).

DIETARY CONCERNS

India and Nepal are a paradise for **vegetarians.** The staple foods of a budget-minded connoisseur (rice and *dal*) will meet the most stringent vegetarian standards. Those opposed to consuming any animal products, however, should be warned that *ghee* (clarified butter) is widely used in Indian cooking, and that cheese often appears in otherwise vegetarian entrees. While **kosher** meals are next to nonexistent in India and Nepal, the Muslim presence makes **halal** food a large part of the cuisine.

▓ Pack Light

One of Indian Railways' sternly comic admonitions sums it up: **Less Luggage, More Comfort!** Your backpack or suitcase may be feather-light when you buy it or drag it out of storage, but as soon as the plane lands it will become an uncomfortable nuisance. Before you leave, pack your bag and take it for a walk. Try to convince yourself that you're in Nepal already, sweltering in the high heat and humidity. At the slightest sign of heaviness, curb your vanity and unpack something. As a general rule, pack only what you absolutely need, then take half the clothes and twice the money. That said, it is important to remember to pack the stuff you'll need. Leave the miniskirts and tank tops at home; shorts are a bad idea unless you'll be spending all of your time in a major city. It is considered disrespectful for women and juvenile for men to wear shorts. Even if you're in the middle of nowhere on a trek, shorts are still a bad idea—you don't want to make it easy for insects and leeches to bite. Consider the time of year you are going as well as your regional destination. Also remember that cheap cotton clothing is available all over India and Nepal.

Comfortable **walking shoes** are essential. This is not the place to cut corners, because your feet are going to take a beating. Blisters, corns, and sharp, shooting pains in your feet will be obvious obstacles to your enjoyment of the trip. For most of India and parts of Nepal, **sport-sandals** like Tevas offer a good balance between coolness, support, and durability. You can also buy leather or plastic sandals once there, but thin *chappals* offer next to no support. For heavy-duty trekking, a pair of sturdy lace-up **hiking boots** will help out. A double pair of socks—light polypropylene inside and thick wool outside—will cushion feet and keep them dry. Avoid cotton inner socks, which will cause blisters. Break in your shoes before you go, but if you do get plagued by blisters, moleskin (sold at camping/sporting goods stores) helps protect the tender area. If you only want one pair of shoes, that evolutionary crossbreed, the "sneaker-hiking boot," can serve as well as a hard-core boot for most trekking and may be more comfortable for the rest of your trip's activities. Bring (or buy) a pair of flip-flops for protection against the foliage and fungi that lurk in some hotel showers.

Rain gear is essential in cooler climes. A waterproof jacket and a backpack cover will take care of you and your stuff at a moment's notice, which is often all you'll get. A little more cumbersome, a lightweight poncho will cover your backpack well and serve as a ground cloth. Gore-Tex, that miracle fabric that's both waterproof and breathable, is helpful if you plan on hiking. When the weather's hot and a monsoon storm hits, though, getting drenched is a treat (and raingear won't really help).

LUGGAGE

Backpack: If you plan to cover most of your itinerary by foot or will be riding on a great deal of buses and trains (and you probably will), the unbeatable baggage is a sturdy backpack with several external compartments. Some convert into a more normal-looking suitcase. In general, **internal-frame** packs are easier to carry and more efficient for general traveling purposes. If you'll be doing extensive camping or hiking, you may want to consider an **external-frame** pack, which offers added support, distributes weight better, and allows for a sleeping bag to be strapped on. External-frame packs have been known to get caught and mangled in baggage conveyors; tie down loose parts to minimize risk. In any case, get a pack with a strong, padded hip belt to transfer weight from your shoulders to your legs. Whichever style you choose, avoid excessively low prices—you usually get what you pay for. Quality packs cost anywhere from US$125 to US$400. Packs with several compartments are best, but beware of ones with many outside zippers or flaps that could make a pickpocket's dream come true. An empty **lightweight duffel bag** packed inside your luggage will be useful: once abroad you can fill your luggage with purchases and keep your dirty clothes in the duffel.

Light suitcase/large duffel bag: These are OK if you are going to do your exploring in a large and relatively luxurious city. Those striving for a more casual, unobtrusive look should take a large shoulder bag that closes securely.

Daypack or courier bag: A smaller bag, in addition to your pack, is indispensable for plane flights, sight-seeing, a picnic on the beach, and keeping some of your valuables on you. Make sure it's big enough to hold lunch, a camera, a water bottle, and this book. Get one with secure zippers and closures.

Moneybelt or neck pouch: Guard your money, passport, and other important articles in either one of these, and keep it with you *at all times.* The best combination of convenience and invulnerability is the nylon, zippered pouch with belt that should sit inside the waist of your pants or skirt (though not too inconveniently). Neck pouches should be worn under at least one layer of clothing. Money belts and neck pouches are available at any good camping store. **Avoid the oh-so-popular "fanny pack":** it's an invitation to thieves, even worn in front. Also it screams, "I'm an inexperienced tourist. Try to rip me off." See **Safety and Security,** p. 15.

PACKING LIST

Clothing: Bring lightweight and layerable clothing; avoid jeans in favor of cotton/ linen pants; female travelers find long, lightweight patterned skirts indispensable. Generally, the best clothes you can wear in India and Nepal are the ones you can buy there. Western and local styles are very cheap and well-suited to the climate, so leave those extra clothes behind and go shopping once you arrive. If you're doing hiking or serious **trekking,** pack everything you'll need (see p. 58).

Health and Hygiene: Deodorant, tampons, razors, contact lens fluid, and reliable condoms are often difficult to get in India and Nepal, especially in rural areas. Be sure to bring enough to last your entire trip. Most other hygiene items are available in pharmacies and shops, but they may not have your favorite brands, and women may feel uncomfortable purchasing condoms in India and Nepal. For these, pack as you would to travel in your own country. Bring a small supply of **toilet paper,** enough for the day or two it takes you to get settled and find one of the many pharmacies that sell the sacred parchment. Indians and Nepalis don't use toilet paper (they simply rinse with water and their left hands). Bring sunscreen and a sun hat, moleskin (for blisters), and **insect repellent** with DEET. Keep in mind that fragrant deodorants, shampoos, and soaps attract insects and other unwelcome forest creatures with reckless abandon. Finding non-scented toiletries is your best bet. Be sure to bring more than enough of any prescription drugs you will need; also bring a copy of the prescription in case you need to try to renew it at a pharmacy. Women on the Pill should bring enough to allow for possible loss or extended stays. If you use a diaphragm, be sure that you have a supply of contraceptive jelly as well. To be safe, buy anything you forgot to bring as soon as you arrive, as smaller towns and villages are less likely to have what you need.

Reading and Writing: Bring a notebook and pens, pocket phrasebooks, a **flashlight** (for during power cuts), maps, and some good **books** (for inspiration, see p. 113).

Other Useful Stuff: Carry your own towel and sheets for very cheap hotels and overnight train rides. Also bring a strong padlock (some hotels don't have locks on room doors), a travel alarm clock, good sunglasses, a pocketknife, tweezers, a sturdy plastic water bottle, Ziploc bags (for damp clothes, soap, general organization), a sewing kit, safety pins, rubber bands, electrical tape (for patching tears), earplugs (for loud bus rides and hotels), and a rubber squash ball for plugging hotel sinks to hand-wash your clothes.

■ Electricity

In India and Nepal electricity is 220V AC, enough to fry any North American appliance. Plugs are European round-pin style of various sizes. British, Irish, Australian, New Zealand, and South African plugs will need adaptors, and American and Canadian plugs will require a transformer, too. You might want to consider a circuit breaker (like a power strip) or a voltage stabilizer, especially if you're using something valuable and sensitive, like a laptop computer. Power cuts and surges are quite common, so don't count on electricity, especially in rural areas. Bring a flashlight, and leave the hair dryer and electric razor at home.

GETTING THERE

■ By Air

The **airline industry** attempts to squeeze every dollar from customers; finding a cheap airfare will be easier if you understand the airlines' systems. Call every toll-free number and don't be afraid to ask about discounts; if you don't ask, it's unlikely they'll be volunteered. Have knowledgeable **travel agents** guide you; better yet, have an agent who specializes in the region(s) you will be traveling to guide you. An agent whose clients fly mostly to the Caribbean will not be the best person to hunt down a bargain flight to Mumbai. Travel agents may not want to spend time finding the cheapest fares (for which they receive the lowest commissions), but if you travel often, you should definitely find an agent who will cater to you and your needs, and track down deals in exchange for your frequent business.

Students and others under 26 need never pay full price for a ticket. Seniors can also get great deals; many airlines offer senior traveler clubs or airline passes with few restrictions and discounts for their companions as well. Sunday newspapers often have travel sections that list bargain fares from the local airport. The Sunday travel section of the *New York Times* has advertisements from a number of consolidators. Australians should consult the Saturday travel section of the *Sydney Morning Herald*. Special deals to India and Nepal may also be advertised in publications targeted at immigrants from these countries, or among agents who cater to specific ethnic communities. Outsmart airline reps with the phone-book-sized *Official Airline Guide* (check your local library; at US$359 per year, the tome costs as much as some flights), a monthly guide listing nearly every scheduled flight in the world (with fares, US$479) and toll-free phone numbers for all the airlines which allow you to call in reservations directly. More accessible is Michael McColl's *The Worldwide Guide to Cheap Airfare* (US$15), an incredibly useful guide for finding cheap airfare.

There is also a steadily increasing amount of travel information to be found on the Internet. The *Official Airline Guide* now also has a website (http://www.oag.com) which allows access to flight schedules. (One-time hook-up fee US$25 and a user's fee of 17¢-47¢ per min.). The site also provides information on hotels, cruises, and rail and ferry schedules. **TravelHUB** (http://www.travelhub.com) will help you search for travel agencies on the web. Marc-David Seidel's **Airlines of the Web** (http://www.itn.net/airlines) provides links to pages and 800 numbers for most airlines. The newsgroup **rec.travel.air** is a good source for tips on current bargains.

Most airfares peak between mid-June and early September, as well as during Christmas season. Midweek (M-Th) round-trip flights run about US$40-50 cheaper than on weekends; weekend flights, however, are generally less crowded. Traveling from hub to hub (for example, Los Angeles to Delhi) will win a more competitive fare than from smaller cities. Return-date flexibility is usually not an option for the budget traveler; traveling with an "open return" ticket can be pricier than fixing a return date and paying to change it. Whenever flying internationally, pick up your ticket well in advance of the departure date, have the flight confirmed within 72 hours of departure, and arrive at the airport at least three hours before your flight.

COMMERCIAL AIRLINES

The commercial airlines' lowest regular offer is the **Advance Purchase Excursion Fare (APEX)**; specials advertised in newspapers may be cheaper, but have more restrictions and fewer available seats. APEX fares provide you with confirmed reservations and allow "open-jaw" tickets (landing in and returning from different cities). Generally, reservations must be made seven to 21 days in advance, with seven- to 14-day minimum and up to 90-day maximum stay limits, and hefty cancellation and change penalties. Book APEX fares early during peak season (Nov.-Feb.).

Even if you pay an airline's lowest published fare, you may waste hundreds of dollars. For the adventurous or the bargain-hungry, there are other, perhaps more inconvenient or time-consuming options, but before shopping around it is a good idea to find out the average commercial price in order to measure just how great a "bargain" you are being offered.

BUDGET TRAVEL AGENCIES

Students and people under 26 ("youths") with proper ID qualify for enticing reduced airfares. These are rarely available from airlines or travel agents, but instead from student travel agencies which negotiate special reduced-rate bulk purchase with the airlines, then resell them to the youth market. Return-date change fees also tend to be low (around US$35 per segment through Council or Let's Go Travel). You will usually need an ISIC or GO25 card to purchase your ticket. Most flights are on major airlines, though in peak season some agencies may sell seats on less reliable chartered aircraft. Student travel agencies can also help non-students and people over 26, but probably won't be able to get the same low fares. Students and youths should also check with ticket consolidators (see below), who can often offer better deals than even budget student travel agencies, especially with travel to India and Nepal.

Council Travel (http://www.ciee.org/travel/index.htm; email cts@ciee.org), the travel division of Council, is a full-service travel agency specializing in youth and budget travel. They offer discount airfares on scheduled airlines, railpasses, hosteling cards, low-cost accommodations, guidebooks, budget tours, travel gear, and international student (ISIC), youth (GO25), and teacher (ITIC) identity cards. U.S. offices in: Emory Village, 1561 N. Decatur Rd., **Atlanta,** GA 30307 (tel. (404) 377-9997); 2000 Guadalupe, **Austin,** TX 78705 (tel. (512) 472-4931); 273 Newbury St., **Boston,** MA 02116 (tel. (617) 266-1926); 1153 N. Dearborn, **Chicago,** IL 60610 (tel. (312) 951-0585); 900 Auraria Pkwy., Tivoli Building, **Denver,** CO, 80204 (tel. (303) 571-0630); 28A Poland St. (Oxford Circus), **London,** W1V 3DB (tel. (0171) 287 3337); 10904 Lindbrook Dr., **Los Angeles,** CA 90024 (tel. (310) 208-3551); 1501 University Ave. SE #300, **Minneapolis,** MN 55414 (tel. (612) 379-2323); 205 E. 42nd St., **New York,** NY 10017 (tel. (212) 822-2700); 953 Garnet Ave., **San Diego,** CA 92109 (tel. (619) 270-6401); 530 Bush St., **San Francisco,** CA 94108 (tel. (415) 421-3473); 1314 NE 43rd St. #210, **Seattle,** WA 98105 (tel. (206) 632-2448); 3300 M St. NW, **Washington, D.C.** 20007 (tel. (202) 337-6464). **For U.S. cities not listed,** call 800-2-COUNCIL (226-8624). **For European cities,** call (0171) 28 -3337 (in Europe) or (1071) 437 7766 (worldwide).

Educational Travel Centre (ETC), 438 North Frances St., Madison, WI 53703 (tel. (800) 747-5551; fax (608) 256-5551; email edtrav@execpc.com; http://www.edtrav.com). Flight information, Hosteling International-American Youth Hostels (HI-AYH) cards, Eurail, and regional rail passes. Write for their free pamphlet *Taking Off.* Student and budget airfares.

Students Flights Inc., 5010 East Shea Blvd., #A104, Scottsdale, AZ 85254 (tel. (800) 255-8000 or (602) 951-1177; fax 951-1216; email jost@isecard.com; http://isecard.com). Also sells international student exchange identity cards.

Let's Go Travel, Harvard Student Agencies, 17 Holyoke St., Cambridge, MA 02138 (tel. (800) 5-LETS GO/553-8746 or (617) 495-9649; fax (617) 496-7956; email travel@hsa.net; http://hsa.net/travel). Sells bargain flights, railpasses, HI-AYH memberships, ISICs, ITICs, FIYTO cards, guidebooks (including every *Let's Go*), maps, and budget travel gear. All items available by mail; call or write for a catalogue.

Journeys International, Inc., 4011 Jackson Rd., Ann Arbor, MI 48103 (tel. (800) 255-8735; fax (313) 665-2945; email info@journeys-intl.com; http://www.journeys-intl.com). Offers small-group, guided explorations of 45 different countries in Asia, Africa, the Americas, and the Pacific. Call or email to obtain their free 74-page *Global Expedition Catalogue.*

STA Travel, 6560 Scottsdale Rd. #F100, Scottsdale, AZ 85253 (tel. (800) 777-0112 nationwide; fax (602) 922-0793; http://sta-travel.com). A student and youth travel organization with over 150 offices worldwide offering discount airfares for young travelers, railpasses, accommodations, tours, insurance, and ISICs. Sixteen offices in the U.S. including: 297 Newbury St., **Boston,** MA 02115 (tel. (617) 266-6014); 429 S. Dearborn St., **Chicago,** IL 60605 (tel. (312) 786-9050); 7202 Melrose Ave., **Los Angeles,** CA 90046 (tel. (213) 934-8722); 10 Downing St., Ste. G, **New York,** NY 10003 (tel. (212) 627-3111); 4341 University Way NE, **Seattle,** WA 98105 (tel. (206) 633-5000); 2401 Pennsylvania Ave., **Washington, D.C.** 20037 (tel. (202) 887-0912); 51 Grant Ave., **San Francisco,** CA 94108 (tel. (415) 391-8407). In the U.K.: Priory House, 6 Wrights Ln., **London** W8 6TA (tel. (171) 361 6161). In New Zealand: 90 Cashel St., **Christchurch** (tel. 3 379 9098). In Australia: 222 Faraday St., **Melbourne** VIC 3053 (tel. 61 03 9349 2411).

Travel CUTS (Canadian Universities Travel Services Limited), 187 College St., Toronto, Ont. M5T 1P7 (tel. (416) 979-2406; fax 979-8167; email mail@travelcuts). Canada's national student travel bureau and equivalent of Council, with 40 offices across Canada. Also in the U.K., 295-A Regent St., **London** W1R 7YA (tel. (0171) 637 31 61). Discounted domestic and international airfares open to all; special student fares to all destinations with valid ISIC. Issues ISIC, FIYTO, GO25, and HI-AYH hostel cards, as well as railpasses. Offers free *Student Traveller* magazine, as well as information on the Student Work Abroad Program (SWAP).

Unitravel, 117 North Warson Rd., St. Louis, MO 63132 (tel. (800) 325 2222; fax (314) 569 2503). Offers discounted airfares on major scheduled airlines from the U.S. to Europe, Africa, and Asia.

Usit Youth and Student Travel, 19-21 Aston Quay, O'Connell Bridge, Dublin 2 (tel. (01) 602 1600). In the U.S.: New York Student Center, 895 Amsterdam Ave., New York, NY, 10025 (tel. (212) 663-5435; email usitny@aol.com). Additional offices throughout Ireland. Specializes in youth travel. Offers low-cost tickets and flexible travel arrangements worldwide. Supplies ISIC and FIYTO, GO25 cards in Ireland.

TICKET CONSOLIDATORS

Ticket consolidators resell unsold tickets on commercial and charter airlines at unpublished fares, and are usually the best deals for destinations like India and Nepal. Fares sold by consolidators are generally much cheaper than the airline-published fare; a 30-40% price reduction is not uncommon. There are rarely age constraints or stay limitations, but unlike tickets bought through an airline, you won't be able to use your tickets on another flight if you miss yours, and you will have to go back to the consolidator to get a refund, rather than the airline, although you can usually change your ticket with the airline directly. Keep in mind that these tickets are often for coach seats on connecting (not direct) flights on foreign airlines, and that frequent-flyer miles may not be credited.

Not all consolidators deal with the general public; many only sell tickets through travel agents. **Bucket shops** are retail agencies that specialize in getting cheap tickets. Although ticket prices are marked up slightly, bucket shops generally have access to a larger market than would be available to the public and can also get tickets from wholesale consolidators. Look for bucket shops' tiny ads in the travel section of weekend papers; in the U.S., the Sunday *New York Times* is a good source. In London, a call to the **Air Travel Advisory Bureau** (tel. (0171) 636 50 00) can provide names of reliable consolidators and discount flight specialists. Kelly Monaghan's *Con-*

solidators: Air Travel's Bargain Basement (US$7 plus US$2 shipping) from the Intrepid Traveler, P.O. Box 438, New York, NY 10034 (email intreptrav@aol.com), is an invaluable source for more information and lists of consolidators.

Among the many reputable and trustworthy companies are, unfortunately, some shady wheeler-dealers. Contact the local Better Business Bureau to find out how long the company has been in business and its track record. Although not necessary, it is preferable to deal with consolidators close to home so you can visit in person, if necessary. Ask to receive your tickets as quickly as possible so you have time to fix any problems. Get the company's policy in writing: insist on a **receipt** that gives full details about the tickets, refunds, and restrictions, and record who you talked to and when. It may be worth paying with a credit card (despite the 2-5% fee) so you can stop payment if you never receive your tickets. Beware the "bait and switch" gag: shyster firms will advertise a super-low fare and then tell a caller that it has been sold.

When you call, try to have specific dates and destinations ready, and if you are planning on buying your ticket soon, have the agent check seat availability; some agents will quote you a cheap price on seats that are already sold out. When you make a reservation, note whether your seats are confirmed or whether you are waitlisted and have the agent fax you or mail you a copy of your itinerary. Prices vary greatly depending on the season. October through February is the high season for most travel to India and Nepal. Note that most of the following agents also offer one-way fares that are only slightly more expensive than half the round-trip, and most tickets are valid for three to six months; longer stays merit more expensive tickets.

In North America

Round-trip tickets in low season from New York to Delhi or Mumbai should run you between US$900-1200; high season can cost between US$1100-1500, depending on the airline and the availability. Flying to Calcutta or Chennai is usually about US$100-150 more expensive. Flights from Los Angeles are about US$100-300 more expensive. From the East Coast of the USA, most flights will probably go through Europe and the Persian Gulf states. Aeroflot is usually cheapest, but their service records are close to abysmal; Western European and Gulf airlines tend to be pretty good. From the West Coast, most flights will go through Southeast Asia. Ask your ticket agent about free stops in either Europe or Southeast Asia.

Am-Jet, New York, NY (tel. (800) 414-4147 or (212) 697-5332; fax 949-8081) has cheap flights to all over India and to Kathmandu from all over the USA. They may seem shady at first but they'll pull through. **Hariworld Travel** has offices in New York, NY (tel. (212) 997-3300) and Atlanta, GA (tel. (404) 233-5005) and offers flights to most destinations in India. **Rio Travels,** Staten Island, NY (tel. (718) 667-4497) offers flights to India and Nepal. **NOW Voyager,** 74 Varick St. #307, New York, NY 10013 (tel. (212) 431-1616; fax (212) 334-5243; email info@nowvoyagertravel.com; http://www.nowvoyagertravel.com) acts as a consolidator and books discounted international flights, mostly from New York, as well as courier flights (see **Courier Companies and Freighters,** p. 45), for an annual fee of US$50. **Fly Time,** New York, NY (tel. (212) 760-3737) specializes in South Asian travel and offers flights from all over the USA to all over India and to Kathmandu (free stops in Europe; you can stop in the Pacific for US$200). **Air Brokers International,** San Francisco, CA (tel. (800) 883-3273) will fly you from the West Coast to all over India, with free stops in Southeast Asia. They also offer Round the World tickets. For flights to Delhi and Mumbai from the U.S., try **Airfare Busters** (offices in Washington, D.C. (tel. (202) 776-0478), Boca Raton, FL (tel. (561) 994-9590), and Houston, TX (tel. (800) 232-8783). **Oxford Travel,** Beacon, NY (tel. (888) 425-9958) has flights to Kathmandu. **Travel Avenue,** Chicago, IL (tel. (800) 333-3335; fax (312) 876-1254; http://www.travelavenue.com) will search for the lowest international airfare available, including consolidated prices, and will even give you a 5% rebate on fares over US$350.

In Britain and Ireland

Low-season flights from London to Delhi/Mumbai run between UK£350-500; flights are only a little more expensive to Kathmandu, partly because you'll be flying airlines like Royal Nepal or Aeroflot. High-season flights to Delhi/Mumbai run UK£450-700. Fares to Chennai and smaller Indian cities cost UK£40-100 more. **Global Travel,** 10 Maddox St., London, (tel. (0171) 629 5123) has cheap airfares to all over India, as well as to Kathmandu. **Trailfinders** offers discounted tickets to all over India and to Kathmandu with offices in **London** (42-50 Earls Court Rd. (tel. (0171) 938 3366) and 194 Kensington High St. (tel. (0171) 938 3939), **Manchester** (58 Deansgate (tel. (0161) 839 6969)), **Birmingham** (22-24 Priory Queens Way (tel. (0121) 236 1234), and **Bristol** (48 Corn St. (tel. (0117) 929 9000). Trailfinders also has an office in **Dublin** at 4/5 Dawson St., Dublin 2 (tel. (1) 677 7888). **Travel Bug,** 125A Gloucester Rd., London (tel. (0171) 835 2000) offers flights to India and Kathmandu; they also have an office in Manchester (597 Cheetham Hill Rd. (tel. (0161) 721 4000). **Taprobane Travels,** London, U.K. (tel. (0171) 437 6272) has flights to India via Colombo, Sri Lanka.

In Australia and New Zealand

Peak season is usually from late November to late January, with fares from AUS$1500 to AUS$2000 round-trip from the east coast of Australia to Delhi/Calcutta/Kathmandu. Low season fares run about AUS$1200 to AUS$1500. Flying from Perth is usually about AUS$150 cheaper than flying from the east coast, but not as many airlines fly out of Perth. Most agents fly with the reliable Thai Air, although Air India tends to be cheaper (as much as AUS$300). Many agents also offer free stopovers in either Bangkok or Singapore, depending on the airline, and most tickets are valid for three months. A one-year ticket is usually AUS$100 extra. **Consolidated Travel,** 209 Swanston St., Melbourne 3000 (tel. (03) 9251 5055), has some very cheap fares to Kathmandu and Delhi from the east coast. **Peregrine Travels,** 132 Wickham St., Fortitude Valley, Brisbane (tel. (07) 3854 1022), specializes in treks to Nepal but they also have some flights to Calcutta, Delhi, and Kathmandu, mostly on Thai Air. You can also ask about Air India flights. Peregrine also has an office at 407 Great South Rd., Penrose, Auckland (tel. (09) 525 3074). **Top Deck,** 8th fl., 350 Kent St., Sydney 2000 (tel. (02) 9251 5430), usually does package tours but also sells individual flights. Top Deck has another office at 4 Durham St. East., Auckland (tel. (09) 377 4586). **World Aviation International,** 310 King St., Melbourne (tel. (03) 9679 6860) represents Air Lanka; all flights to India and Nepal go through Sri Lanka, but their rates are good.

COURIER COMPANIES AND FREIGHTERS

Those who travel light should consider flying internationally as a **courier.** The company hiring you will use your checked luggage space for freight; you're only allowed to bring carry-ons. You are responsible for the safe delivery of the baggage claim slips (given to you by a courier company representative) to the representative waiting for you when you arrive—don't screw up or you will be blacklisted as a courier. You will probably never see the cargo you are transporting—the company handles it all—and airport officials know that couriers are not responsible for the baggage checked for them. Restrictions to watch for: you must be over 21 (18 in some cases), have a valid passport, and procure your own visa (if necessary); most flights are round-trip only with short fixed-length stays (usually one week); only single tickets are issued (but a companion may be able to get a next-day flight); and most flights are from New York. Becoming a member of the **Air Courier Association** (tel. (800) 282-1202; http:// www.aircourier.org) is a good way to start; they give you a listing of all reputable courier brokers and the flights they are offering, along with a hefty courier manual and a bimonthly newsletter of updated opportunities (US$30 one-time fee plus US$28 annual dues). For an annual fee of $45, the **International Association of Air Travel Couriers,** 8 South J St., P.O. Box 1349, Lake Worth, FL, 33460 (tel. (561) 582-8320) informs travelers (via computer, fax, and mailings) of courier opportunities worldwide. Steve Lantos publishes a monthly update of courier options in **Travel Unlimited** as well as general information on low-budget travel (write P.O. Box 1058A,

Allston, MA, 02134 for a free sample newsletter; subscription runs US$25 per year). Most flights originate from New York or London. **NOW Voyager** (see above) acts as an agent for many courier flights worldwide, primarily from New York.

You can also go directly through courier companies in New York, or check your bookstore, library, or online at http://www.amazon.com for handbooks such as Air Courier Bargains (US$15 plus $3.50 shipping from the Intrepid Traveler; tel. (212) 569-1081; email info@intrepidtraveler.com; http://intrepidtraveler.com). The Courier Air Travel Handbook (US$10 plus $3.50 shipping) explains how to travel as an air courier and contains names, phone numbers, and contact points of courier companies. It can be ordered directly from Bookmasters, Inc., P.O. Box 2039, Mansfield, OH 44905 (tel. (800) 507-2665).

By Sea

If you really have travel time to spare, **Ford's Travel Guides,** 19448 Londelius St., Northridge, CA 91324 (tel. (818) 701-7414; fax 701-7415) lists **freighter companies** that will take passengers from all over the world to all over the world, including to ports in India. Ask for their *Freighter Travel Guide and Waterways of the World* (US$16, plus $2.50 postage if mailed outside the U.S.).

By Land

Driving a car (or better yet a VW Microbus) across Asia was a classic 1960s hippie expedition. From İstanbul, the route would pass through Turkey and Iran to Kabul, Afghanistan, and from there through Lahore, Pakistan to India. Afghanistan is pretty much off-limits now due to the horrific civil war. The only border crossing open from Pakistan to India is between Lahore and Amritsar. There are no borders open between India and China.

Selling your car in India or Nepal was once a good way to finance a trip, but car import duties have now stolen any hope of profit from such ventures. You must have a *carnet,* an automotive passport, to prove that you'll take your car out with you and not sell it on the black market. Unleaded gas and foreign parts are rare in India.

ONCE THERE

Foreign Diplomatic Missions

Information is listed by region in the book. Most countries have diplomatic missions in **Delhi** (see p. 125). Many have offices in **Mumbai** (see p. 621), and a few in **Calcutta** (see p. 386) and **Chennai** (see p. 471) as well. In Nepal, all foreign diplomatic missions are in **Kathmandu** (see p. 679).

Getting Around

Moving around in India and Nepal can be harder than it looks. You'll be confronted by strange ticket terminology, rigid-sounding departure schedules that get delayed or "improvised" for the strangest reasons, and unfamiliar situations that will test your sense of etiquette. Once you figure out the system, though, you'll be surprised how easy it is to get anywhere, provided you're willing to roll with a few delays.

DOMESTIC FLIGHTS

India and Nepal both have extensive air networks serving every corner of their countries. In the last few years both countries have opened up the skies to private companies, but the government-run Indian Airlines and Royal Nepal Airlines Corporation

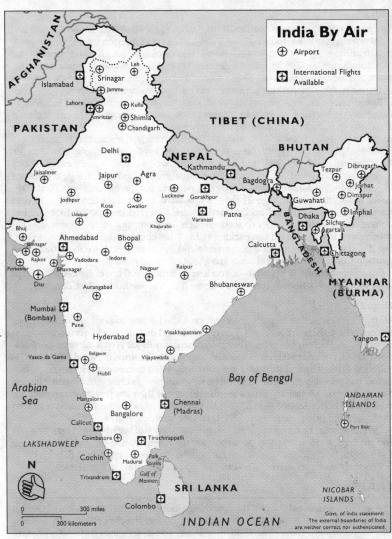

India By Air

⊕ Airport

⊕ International Flights Available

AFGHANISTAN

Islamabad

Leh

Srinagar ⊕

⊕ Jammu

Lahore ⊕ ⊕ Kullu

Amritsar ⊕ ⊕ Shimla

PAKISTAN ⊕ Chandigarh

Delhi ⊕

NEPAL

Kathmandu ⊕

TIBET (CHINA)

BHUTAN

Tezpur ⊕ ⊕ Dibrugarh

Bagdogra ⊕ ⊕ Jorhat

Jaisalmer ⊕ Jaipur ⊕ ⊕ Agra

Jodhpur ⊕ Lucknow ⊕ ⊕ Gorakhpur

Kota ⊕ Gwalior ⊕

Udaipur ⊕ ⊕ Khajuraho

⊕ Patna

⊕ Varanasi

Guwahati ⊕ ⊕ Dimapur

⊕ Imphal

Dhaka ⊕ Silchar ⊕

⊕ Agartala

Bhuj ⊕ Ahmedabad ⊕ Bhopal ⊕

Jamnagar ⊕ Vadodara ⊕ ⊕ Indore

Rajkot ⊕ Bhavnagar ⊕

Porbandar ⊕ ⊕ Diu

Calcutta ⊕

BANGLADESH

Chittagong ⊕

Nagpur ⊕ Raipur ⊕

Aurangabad ⊕ Bhubaneswar ⊕

MYANMAR (BURMA)

Mumbai (Bombay) ⊕

⊕ Pune

Hyderabad ⊕ Visakhapatnam ⊕

Vasco da Gama ⊕ Belgaum ⊕

⊕ Hubli ⊕ Vijayawada

Arabian Sea

Bay of Bengal

Yangon ⊕

ANDAMAN ISLANDS

Mangalore ⊕ Bangalore ⊕ Chennai (Madras) ⊕

Calicut ⊕

Coimbatore ⊕ ⊕ Tiruchirappalli

⊕ Port Blair

LAKSHADWEEP

Cochin ⊕ Madurai ⊕ Palk Straits

N

Trivandrum ⊕ Gulf of Mannar

SRI LANKA

NICOBAR ISLANDS

0   300 miles

0   300 kilometers

Colombo ⊕

INDIAN OCEAN

Govt. of India statement: The external boundaries of India are neither correct nor authenticated.

(RNAC), which had monopolies, still have the most extensive schedules and fly subsidized routes to less popular destinations. However, air travel is much more expensive than surface travel, and it will not always save you time. Waiting in airport-office queues, traveling to and from airports (which are often far from town), and checking in can slow you down, but most of all, Indian and Nepalese airports love to subject passengers to purgatorial delays. It is best to fly only to escape unbearable cross-country bus or train rides. In Nepal, where the roads are so bad—and bus rides therefore interminable—the balance might be shifted slightly in favor of air travel. Air travel is generally safe even though the planes are usually hand-me-downs from European or East Asian airlines, and flights are often bumpy.

India

The government's domestic carrier, Indian Airlines, flies to over 80 cities in India and neighboring countries. India's airline industry has recently been opened up to small private airlines (officially called ATOs, "air taxi operators") such as Jet Airways and Moduluft. Indian Airlines still has the largest fleet and handles about 75% of the traffic, but it is a lumbering dinosaur, losing money heavily. The private airlines are seen as the wave of the future, although several have gone bankrupt recently.

Reservations are essential on almost all flights and must be made well in advance, especially during the peak seasons. Flights almost always sell out. Go to one of the airlines' offices to make a booking, or use a travel agent. If you don't get a seat, put your name on the waiting list and show up at the airport early; miracles can happen.

Indian Airlines offers **youth fares** at a 25% reduction for passengers ages 12 to 30. Children under 12 pay 50%, and infants under two pay 10%. Foreigners must buy their plane tickets with credit cards or foreign currency, and any change is returned in rupees. Indian Airlines offers a traveling package for foreign tourists called **"Discover India"** that provides for 21 days of unlimited air travel for US$750, or 15 days for US$500, provided that no destinations are repeated except the first and last points; only a limited number of seats on each flight are allotted to "Discover India" subscribers. If you plan on jam-packing sights cross-country, this package is perfect, but if you want to glimpse the countryside and ingest more culture than the airport giftshop has to offer, you'll probably have to stick to the ground.

Guard your airline ticket well—if you lose it, airlines and travel agents will accept no responsibility. Check-in time for domestic flights is one hour before departure.

Nepal

Air travel is essential to Nepal's economy, providing access to northern mountainous regions where there are no roads. Travelers will find that air travel is just as important to avoid long, hellish bus rides. The government-run **Royal Nepal Airlines Corporation (RNAC)** operates flights to about 35 airports and airstrips in Nepal. The RNAC is suffering financially and its planes are constantly filled to capacity. However, privatization has recently given birth to three new airlines: Everest Air, Necon Air, and Nepal Airways. All airlines' prices are the same, but the new private companies are said to have better service than RNAC. All foreigners must pay for flights with foreign exchange, and prices range from US$50-160 for domestic flights.

On the whole, air travel in Nepal is unpredictable. Bad weather prevents take-offs and landings, so long delays at the airport are the norm. During the high trekking season it might be difficult to get tickets for popular destinations. It is best to book plane tickets through travel agents, who can give you an idea of what's available.

TRAINS

The Indian rail network, one of the few things Indians will readily thank their British colonial masters for, is incredibly extensive. For budget travelers rail is really the best way to get around India. Due to its mountains and its freedom from colonization, Nepal has no trains except for one that runs across the Indian border to Janakpur.

With over 1.6 million workers on its payroll, **Indian Railways** is the world's largest employer, and trains are generally the best way to cover long distances in India at a reasonable cost. Eleven million passengers are carried over its vast network daily. There is a unique culture on the Indian railways, which is quite a change from India's touristy packaging. From the landscapes rushing outside the window to the storms of clay *chai* cups whizzing inside, you're bound to get a glimpse of Indian India on the train, or at least a glimpse of how India travels. You'll meet locals eager to chat about your country and theirs.

The Indian Railways might not get you there on time, but they will get you there—and "there" is just about anywhere in the country. The only exceptions are the hilly areas, mainly in the North. A few hill stations, such as Darjeeling, Ooty, and Shimla, are reached by **"toy trains,"** narrow-gauge machines that run at a snail's pace. **Express** or **mail** trains are the fast, convenient ones that rush between cities. The

Shatabdi Express, Rajdhani Express, and *Taj Express* are the fastest trains that cover the main lines, such as Delhi-Mumbai and Delhi-Calcutta, and even some smaller ones such as Delhi-Bhopal or Chennai-Mysore. These trains come with full air conditioning and meals, stop only at big cities, and cost at least four times as much as standard second class fares. Below these is a hierarchy of superfast, mail, and express trains, which cost the same but vary in speed. Unless you are headed to an out-of-the-way village it is probably best to avoid local **passenger** trains, which lumber along and stop at every small-town station.

Various classes of comfort are available, from air-conditioned first class, to non-A/C first, to the many avatars of second class. **First class** on an Indian train is three or four times the price of second class, though still not very expensive by Western standards. In first class, you won't be squeezed to your bench by an excessive crowd (which can be half the fun), and your view of the countryside will often be through scratched, amber-tinted windows. Air conditioning is usually unnecessary on trains, even during the summer, because once the train gets moving you'll be cooled off anyway. First-class sleeper cars are divided into compartments, offering more privacy than second-class sleepers, which have rows of berths in the open. **Second class** is probably the best bet on a budget. Though sometimes crowded and dirty, second-class will certainly give you more contact with fellow passengers, and it is possible to get a good night's sleep in second-class **sleepers** (you're guaranteed a vaguely padded berth to yourself). During the day, and for shorter trips, second class is something of a free-for-all, but once you've gotten a seat, it's yours.

For long trips, especially overnight ones, it's necessary to make **reservations** (usually a day or two in advance). It is safest to do this right at the station or booking office. Avoid **travel agents** if you can; they frequently charge hefty commissions and have been known to give false information in order to steer you into the best deal for them. **Computers** in most stations have made bookings systematic, but there are still long, anarchic lineups. A **tourist quota** is often set aside for anyone who can show a foreign passport. A few major stations even have separate queues for tourists and many have ladies' queues or allow women to jump to the front of the line to avoid pushing and shoving. Get a reservation slip from the window, and scribble down the train you want. Each route has a name and a number, information that locals seem to have memorized at birth. For route information, arm yourself with *Trains at a Glance*, Indian Railways' "Abstract Time Table" which contains **schedules** for all mail and express trains (Rs15), although the timetable can be difficult to decipher and does not list every stop each train makes. The fares on Indian Railways correspond to distance and class. If you have trouble finding your way at a station, try the **enquiry counter**—the people at these booths are generally well-informed and speak English.

If you fail to get a reservation, you can still get on the **waiting list** and hope. In an emergency, try to find the **station master.** He will probably be busy and not thrilled to see you, but if anyone can find a seat for you on a "full" train, it's he, and with some patience you might be able to persuade him. As a last resort, *baksheesh* to porters (especially if you're getting on at the beginning of the line) has been known to turn up unreserved berths like nothing else. If you cancel your reservation more than 24 hours before your trip, you can still get a refund but you'll be charged Rs10-50 depending on the class. Up to four hours before, you'll get 75% back, and after that (even sometimes 12 hours after the train has left), you can get still get 50%.

If you have a reservation, you'll be fine getting to the station just a few minutes before the train arrives. If you're leaving from a major station, check the computer-printed list (usually on the platform or attached to the side of each train car) for your name and seat and listen for announcements. If your train is delayed, the **waiting rooms** can be a good place to pass time and avoid stares. It's usually not difficult for foreigners to assume a place in the first class waiting room, regardless of what class they're traveling. The guard probably doesn't speak English, and some travelers pretend not to understand when he or she asks to see tickets. Railway station restaurants are also worth checking out, for their good, cheap, steel-plate *thalis*. Railway retiring rooms are available to anyone with a valid ticket or Indrail pass. These are usually cheaper than budget hotels and can be convenient if you arrive late or have to catch an early-morning train. Retiring rooms operate on a 24-hour basis, and most also rent for 12 hours at a stretch. But check out the noise level first. Women traveling on their own or with children should enquire about **ladies' compartments,** available on most overnight mail and express trains.

Foreign passport holders can buy **Indrail Passes,** which are available for lengths of one-half, one, two, four, seven, 15, 21, 30, 60, or 90 days, in first class A/C, second class A/C, and second class non-A/C. Indrail Passes include all fares, reservation charges, and any supplementary charges, but are not really a bargain. They must be paid for in US dollars or pounds sterling, and prices are high. To spend that much on train tickets in a month you'd have to be constantly on the move. The small advantages of Indrail Passes is that they can save you some hassle: on superfast trains, Indrail pass holders are exempt from reservation fees and extra charges; on shorter journeys, Indrail Pass holders don't need tickets. Reservations are still necessary for longer trips, however.

BUSES

> **Warning:** Poor road conditions and aggressive driving make road travel in India and Nepal dangerous. This is one of the implicit risks of traveling in the region.

Extensive networks of bus routes cover all of India and Nepal. In train-less Nepal, buses are the most popular mode of long-distance transportation. In India they finish a close second to trains. Generally buses are as fast as, or faster than, trains. Buses also go to the hilly areas of India where trains cannot go, and they involve less pre-departure hassle than trains. For short trips, advance bookings are rarely necessary—just show up at the bus stand and climb aboard; you can pay the conductor somewhere along the way. For longer trips (over 10hr.) it might be necessary to book a day in advance. Do this directly at the bus stand rather than through a travel agent.

Bus comfort varies widely by region. Buses in the U.P. Hills are routinely filled to capacity, with people standing in the aisles; in Karnataka, such crowding is rare. The main drawback to most bus travel in India and Nepal is its extreme discomfort. Seats are usually narrower than an adult's shoulder span, with very little cushioning, and they are spaced to allow for absolutely no legroom (and remember you may find yourself assigned to the seat next to a woman carrying two babies in her lap, or a man who keeps nodding off to sleep on your shoulder). For people with long arms and legs, bus travel can be prohibitively uncomfortable. But at least you have a seat—there are often more passengers than seats, and many others make the trip standing up. Buses also tend to make frequent, albeit brief, stops for snacks and *chai,* which slow down the journey, but offer much-needed chances to stretch—however, you may lose your seat if you get up. At scheduled rest stops, women might have a hard time finding a place to use a toilet; they should ask the conductor to wait longer for them as they search. To avoid bumps, stay away from the back seats of the bus. There is also some risk involved in bus travel, as in all road travel in South Asia (see **Getting Around: Cars,** p. 51). Road conditions are usually poor and traffic unpredictable. Most people expect their bus drivers to get from point A to point B as fast as possible—and the driver usually tries to accommodate the wishes of his passengers. Expect to hear much grinding of gears and blaring of horns, and to feel sudden lurches. **Never ride on the roof of a bus,** no matter how cool the breeze or how gorgeous the scenery. This is illegal and terribly dangerous.

Among the different of types of buses available, **tourist buses** or **"superdeluxe" buses** have cushioned seats and more space than other buses; although they are certainly not luxurious by Western standards, they usually seat four passengers abreast rather than five. Tourist buses usually have fans, sometimes air conditioning, but they are usually only available on very popular tourist routes. For other journeys, **express buses** are the norm. Express buses still have padded seats, but they are much more crowded, they stop for anyone who wants to get on, and they don't get there any faster. Nepal and some places in India have special **night buses,** which usually leave for long journeys in the early evening to arrive the next morning, have reclining seats and a bit more legroom, but you shouldn't count on getting any sleep. They stop for *chai* endlessly (just be glad the driver is getting his caffeine). At all costs, avoid **video coaches** unless you like watching old black-and-white Hindi films for five hours (or more) at ear-splitting levels.

Luggage on the roof rack of a bus is usually safe, but bags have been known to disappear at intermediate stops in a flurry of untrackable movement. This is especially a problem at night. Make sure your pack is tied down, and ask if you can put it elsewhere—in a compartment at the back, or at the front of the bus with the driver where you can keep an eye on it. If your luggage goes on the roof, give *baksheesh* to the person who put it up there, so hopefully he'll keep it there.

Local buses in big cities have their destinations inscribed in the local language. In a hurry to wedge themselves into city traffic, bus drivers tend to roll-stop without really coming to rest at all, so you may want to learn the skill of leaping on and off the back entrance stairs. Take notice of the convenient side handle bars. Once safely in, sit or stand until the bus-*wallah,* with his little bus satchel, comes by and clicks a small metal contraption in your face. That means pay-up—ask how many rupees it is to your destination, since ticket prices vary by distance. Women on city buses tend to get preferential seating, so male passengers may be expected to politely give up their seats to female passengers.

In India

Bus travel in India, unlike bus travel in Nepal, is slightly complicated by the existence of both state and private bus companies. In this guide, **bus stands** and **bus stations** are where state (and sometimes private) buses roll in and out; private buses often leave from the particular company's office. State government buses are often crowded, so you may have to buy tickets early; get to the bus stand at least half an hour before departure. Some private bus companies offer excellent service, while others should not hold an operating license; there are so many private operators in the country that it is difficult to know the quality of an operation until you're already on a bus and screaming down the highway. As with train tickets, it is generally unwise to buy bus tickets from random travel agencies, especially for complicated trips that require changing buses; there are endless reports of scams.

In Nepal

Bus travel is widely used in Nepal, although the road conditions are poor and the hilly terrain multiplies travel time. Almost all buses are privately owned, but look out for the government **Sajha** buses which are safer and much more comfortable. For these you'll probably have to book tickets from the bus stand a day in advance. Booking bus tickets can be a pain in Kathmandu or Pokhara, because the bus stands are located far from the tourist center. You might find it easier to have a travel agent make arrangements. Avoid package deals for complex bus journeys, however; these often turn out to be scams. You'll do better buying your second ticket once you arrive.

CARS

Driving a car in India or Nepal is not for the faint of heart. Besides swerving to avoid cars and motorcycles, American travelers have to remember to drive on the left in most places and learn to dodge rickshaws, people, and cows. There is a general disregard for anything resembling traffic regulations. The unwritten rule is that the bigger the vehicle, the greater amount of respect it should be accorded. In the case of an accident, though, it is invariably considered to be the larger vehicle's fault. Drivers are reckless and aggressive, constrained only by the general dilapidation of the roads and their vehicles. Many pedestrians who have just arrived from villages lack a basic traffic sense. Not surprisingly, India and Nepal have high rates of road accidents—although these seem to result in remarkably few fatalities. As with all adversity here, people seem to recover, move on, and clear things up remarkably quickly.

If you get into a traffic accident in India or Nepal, **leave the scene of the accident immediately and go to the nearest police station.** If people are injured or killed, mobs can gather, thirsting for revenge, and you don't want to be caught in one. Also keep in mind that killing one of those omnipresent cows, even by accident, is punishable in Nepal by up to 20 years imprisonment.

A car is entirely unnecessary in a large city; efficient transportation abounds, and taxis are ubiquitous. Also, some rental companies do not offer insurance; a serious accident may mean spending some time in jail or the hospital, and shelling out a large sum of money to cover damages. If you absolutely must have a car, keep your international driver's license handy, as well as a substantial amount of money. Several car rental companies including Budget and Hertz now have offices in major cities. It is also worth inquiring at government tourist offices, which frequently hire cars and drivers. For more information on cars and road conditions in India, contact the **Automobile Association of India,** which has offices in major cities.

The cost of renting a four-door sedan is many times the cost of a night's stay at a guest house. It is more common to hire a car with a **driver,** who looks after petrol costs and repairs, and who will take responsibility for any problems. It is cheaper to hire a taxi for the day or for a specific journey; fares vary by distance. With enough passengers to split the costs, this is usually within the price range of a budget traveler.

Driving in India and Nepal also requires detailed **road maps;** while *Let's Go* includes highways and roads on maps whenever possible, rural roads are sometimes closed or washed-out during monsoon season. *The India and Bangladesh Travel Atlas* published by Lonely Planet Publications contains large-scale maps of Indian highways in a portable package.

Hitchhiking is practically unheard of and unnecessary in most parts of India and Nepal, since public transportation networks are extensive and cheap. In mountain areas like Kumaon and Himachal Pradesh, where traffic is sparse, jeeps and cargo trucks sometimes take on passengers for a small charge. *Let's Go* does not recommend hitchhiking, and women should never hitchhike without a male companion.

BOATS

A ferry service runs between Mumbai and Goa, and ships travel regularly from Calcutta and Chennai to Port Blair. During monsoon, ferries are often the only way to cross certain rivers. Landlocked Nepal has white-water rafting, but that's it.

TAXIS

Taxis are found in the larger cities of India and Nepal; in some cities, such as Mumbai, only taxis and not rickshaws or auto-rickshaws are allowed within the metropolitan limits. India's international airports offer reliable **pre-paid taxi services**—you pay at the official office, and give your receipt to a driver in the waiting queue, who takes you where you need to go. Taxis are supposed to have meters, but these are sometimes out of date, so the driver will add a percentage or wield an official-looking "fare adjustment card" with up-to-date prices. All this varies from city to city; there are no hard-and-fast rules, but in general you should insist on using the meter rather than negotiating a price. Private companies exist to rent out taxis and drivers for longer hours, short trips, or even days; enquire at train stations, airports, or tourist offices. In mountainous regions, **jeeps** (sometimes called Gypsies or Mahindras) function as taxis or mini-buses.

AUTO-RICKSHAWS AND TEMPOS

To some, these podlike three-wheelers are a symbol of the Asian experience; to others, they are diesel fume-belching beasts. Fans argue that they are cheap compared to taxis, more convenient than buses, and small enough to dart through heavy traffic. Much of this, of course, depends upon the driver. Detractors criticize them for the damage they do to the environment and human ears. Auto-rickshaws seat one to three adults (but often up to 10 schoolchildren). Low ceilings, minimal legroom, and narrow seats are part of the adventure.

While the auto-rickshaw-*wallah* will often insist that the meter is "broken," push for its use. Payment will inevitably entail negotiation, haggling, and flat-out struggle. **In most cities, it is illegal for rickshaw-wallahs to overcharge for local, daytime service.** A threat to report them to the police can often do wonders to eke out a fair fare. Avoid pushy drivers, and always scoff at the first price demanded—let a driver come down to about 30-40% of his original price before getting in. Be aware of local specifics: depending on the town, some drivers may add a surcharge to the meter or display a price increase card, because the meters are outdated and the price of fuel has risen. Nighttime fares are generally up to two times the standard meter rate. Many rickshaw-wallahs know surprisingly little about the cities where they work—it isn't uncommon for them to pull over and ask for directions multiple times in a single trip.

Rickshaw-*wallahs* have a habit of getting in commission cahoots with hotels and will inform you that your choice has been shut down or that its staff is on strike. Chances are that the "insider info" is incorrect and your driver simply wants his cut. If a driver taking you home asks if you need a ride the next day, know that if you flippantly agree he will probably sleep in his rickshaw that night waiting for you (many drivers sleep in their rickshaws anyway).

Tempos are larger, seating about six, and some designs resemble elongated auto-rickshaws gone wheelbarrow. Tempos follow fixed routes and have fixed fees; they are of limited use to foreigners, however, because their destinations are never marked.

CYCLE-RICKSHAWS

There are two other kinds of rickshaws in India and Nepal. Calcutta is home to the India's only fleet of **hand-pulled rickshaws,** though even these are rumored to be on their way to extinction. Far more common are **cycle-rickshaws,** where the driver pedals in front while his trusting passengers sit on a cushioned box above the rear axle. Many cycle-rickshaw-*wallahs* have been driving for years, scraping out a living from day to day; few of them own their rickshaws, and most of their earnings go to the machine's owner as rent. They are not always found in metropolitan areas, such as Mumbai, but they are found in the countryside wherever there is flat terrain. In Nepal rickshaws are limited to the Terai and to parts of Kathmandu, where they mainly cater to tourists. The main benefit of riding in a rickshaw is the fresh breeze and the open view; negatives include the longer traveling time and the sorrow of seeing an old man labor away. Pay attention to terrain when hiring cycle-rickshaws. On even the most gentle gradient the *wallah* won't be able to pedal. If he jumps out and starts pushing you up the hill, it's polite to lend a hand. **Make sure your rickshaw-wallah is not intoxicated.** Many rickshaw-wallahs spend the day drunk or stoned; if your driver is unable to follow clear directions, jump out and find a new one.

The worst part about a rickshaw ride is settling the price, which is highly negotiable. Foreigners usually pay about Rs10 per kilometer in India, but rickshaw-*wallahs* in touristy places ask for more, and in villages they ask for less. Haggling can be fierce, and you might have to bluff by walking away repeatedly. Some travelers prefer to settle on a price at the outset to prevent disagreements later. But on the other hand, if you don't ask the fare when you climb on, many rickshaw-wallahs will assume you know the correct fare, and you can just pay what you think it is when you get off.

MOTORCYCLES, MOPEDS, AND SCOOTERS

Motorcycles, mopeds, and scooters are probably more useful for travelers than cars. A motorcycle can liberate you to explore rural roads not accessible by public transportation; although you might get lost, this can lead to memorable adventures. Unfortunately, motorcycles, mopeds, and scooters are very dangerous in India and Nepal. *Let's Go* researchers have consistent track records of two-wheeled misfortune. Helmets are rarely provided, but unless you have a death wish, you shouldn't get on a motorcycle or motorbike without one; traffic fatalities on motorcycles are frighteningly high. As with cars, motorcycle drivers in India and Nepal find themselves dodging new and exciting obstacles, and on motorcycles they have less protection. Remember that larger vehicles have the right of way. Motorcycle rental shops are abundant near major tourist stops. An international driver's permit is legally required for you to rent a scooter or motorcycle, but it is rarely checked. Motorcycle and scooter engines in India and Nepal are usually only 100cc, so they are not very good for long trips. **Mopeds** are easy to operate but dangerous to take into any sort of traffic. **Scooters** have a high center of gravity and small wheels, which make them very dangerous; most scooters are also very difficult to operate and must be manually shifted from gear to gear. A popular alternative for tourists in some areas is to rent Kinetic-Hondas, automatic shifting scooters that are easy to operate and a bit safer on the road. If you are considering renting a motorcycle, keep in mind the disproportionate amount of air pollution they cause.

BICYCLES

Trying to ride a bicycle in the big Indian cities is often an exercise in futility or, worse, a game of human pinball. But on backroads through rural towns, and in much of Nepal, bicycles really become worth the small change they're rented for. Most bikes in India and Nepal don't have gears, so hills are hellish. In many tourist centers like Kathmandu and Pokhara, bikes can be rented very cheaply, usually on a daily basis. Clunky Indian bikes are also cheap to buy and resell.

■ Border Crossings

India-Nepal: There are six overland border crossings between India and Nepal: Mahendranagar, Dhangadi, Nepalganj, Sunauli, Raxaul/Birganj, and Kakarbhitta. Sunauli is a 3hr. bus ride from Gorakhpur in Uttar Pradesh; from there you can catch a 10hr. bus to Pokhara or a 12hr. bus to Kathmandu. Raxaul is a 5hr. bus ride from Patna in Bihar; from Birganj, across the border, it's a 12hr. bus ride to Kathmandu. The Kakarbhitta crossing, at the eastern end of Nepal, is easily accessible from Siliguri, which is a transit point for Darjeeling. It is not necessary to get a Nepalese visa before you arrive at the border, but you must get your Indian visa ahead of time if you're going from Nepal to India. Visitors are also allowed to drive across the border if they possess an international *carnet.* For more information see **Raxaul,** p. 463; **Birganj,** p. 792; **Sunauli,** p. 783; and **Kakarbhitta,** p. 796.

India-Bangladesh: Trains and buses run from Calcutta to Bangaon in West Bengal. From there it is a rickshaw ride across the border to Benapol, Bangladesh, with connections via Khulna or Jessore to Dhaka. The northern border, near Darjeeling, from Jalpaiguri to Haldibari, is only periodically open and requires an exit permit.

India-Burma: No land frontier open.

India-Bhutan: If you are lucky enough to get a Bhutanese visa, you must cross the border at Puntsholing, a 3-4hr. bus ride from Siliguri in West Bengal. Make sure you also have a "transit permit" from the Indian ministry of External Affairs.

India-China: No land frontier open.

India-Pakistan: Due to the Kashmiri-cool relations between India and Pakistan, only one crossing is open along the entire length of the two countries' 2000km border. A daily train runs from Amritsar in the Indian Punjab to Attari, the border town (still in India); from there you catch another train to Lahore in the Pakistani Punjab. For more information see **Pakistan Border,** p. 335.

India-Sri Lanka: The boat service from Rameswaram in Tamil Nadu to Talaimannar in Sri Lanka has been indefinitely suspended due to the war in northern Sri Lanka. Travelers must fly to Colombo, Sri Lanka.

Nepal-China: The Arniko Rajmarg (Kathmandu-Kodari Highway) links Kathmandu with the Tibet Autonomous Region of China via the exit point of Kodari. The border is currently open only to travelers on organized tours. Before crossing into Tibet, check in with your embassy in Kathmandu to make sure that the border situation is stable, as there have occasionally been difficulties for tourists crossing overland into Tibet.

■ Accommodations

Cheap accommodations in India and Nepal are plentiful. You can easily stay here without spending more than US$2 or US$3 per night, as long as you don't mind life without air conditioning. Even posh hotels are much cheaper here than they would be at home. Rates often vary according to the season, however, and in cheaper hotels they're often negotiable. The prices listed in this book represent our best research efforts, but often we cannot predict the frequent ups and downs of Indian and Nepali hotel prices—all prices listed in this book are subject to change.

BUDGET HOTELS

The main travel centers nurture **tourist districts** of shabbily built hotels, which exist to give most budget travelers their first taste of Eastern asceticism—bare concrete cells with hard beds and a ceiling fan on overdrive. They are, nevertheless, all you really need, and compared to hotels in richer countries their rates are unbelievably cheap (with a few notable exceptions). The architects who built them seem to have been blind to the dangers of fire and earthquake, and their structure is often as haphazard as the layout of the city streets around them, squeezing in a range of singles, doubles, and triples, with or without attached bath. Dorm beds are also sometimes available. These hotels often have restaurants, and managers are usually happy to arrange to provide any service rupees can buy. Where tourist districts have developed and most of the clientele is foreign, competition has made hotels much cheaper, cleaner, and more comfortable. It is rarely necessary to make **reservations** at such hotels, except at major peak times (such as festivals). However, it can be difficult to get accommodation in big cities that see few foreign tourists—the hotels may be full of businessmen, or they may lack the paperwork to accept foreigners.

One thing to look out for when choosing a hotel is the **check-out time**—many cheap hotels have a 24-hour rule, which means if you arrive in town in the morning after an overnight train you'll be expected to leave as early when you check out. Above all, don't let touts or rickshaw-*wallahs* make your lodging plans. These shady characters often suck up tourists from train and bus stations and cart them off to whichever hotel is paying the biggest **commission**, which will sooner or later show up on your bill. Touts will fervently insist that the hotel where you wanted to stay is "closed" or "full," and they will continue to lie even as you walk up to the hotel door to learn the truth. For more information, see **Touts, middlemen, and scams** (p. 67).

Many budget travelers prefer to bring their own **padlock** for budget hotels, since the locally made padlocks they provide are often suspect. Sheets (if desired), towels, soap, and **toilet paper** (available at most pharmacies) also need to be carried. It is good to ask about utilities before choosing a hotel. Many have **hot water** only at certain hours of the day, or only in buckets (and for a fee). Since the power supply is erratic everywhere in India, **generators** provide a very noisy solution. **Air-cooling,** a system by which air is blown by a fan over the surface of water, is common.

Prices fluctuate wildly according to the season, and seasons fluctuate wildly according to the destination in question. Most foreign tourists come to India during the winter months (Nov.-Feb.), so places that draw mostly foreigners have "high season" and correspondingly high prices during those months. Indian tourists head for the hill stations during the unbearably hot pre-monsoon months (May-July), causing rates to head higher as well. Towns that see local and foreign tourist traffic often have both high- and mid-seasons, as if all that wasn't confusing enough.

Another important aspect of accommodations in India and Nepal is the existence of a **travelers' scene.** Some hotels in various towns have built reputations as places for foreign travelers to hang out and share stories. This can be an invaluable way of grappling with your travel experiences, and it is something to look out for. Unfortunately, hobnobbing with other travelers too much leads some people to insulate themselves from the locals, as well as from Indian tourists (who often offer great insight into their country). In a particularly sad twist, some budget hotels in India

have even instituted discriminatory **no-Indians policies** in order to create sanitized, foreigners-only environments for their clients.

Nepal's budget lodge scene differs from India's in that it is the result of a very recent boom, and foreign tourists are its main targets. Tourist districts unlike anything in India have grown up in Pokhara and Kathmandu, where fierce competition between neighboring guest houses has led to rock-bottom prices and generally better and friendlier hotels than in India.

Budget hotels frequently have **restaurants** attached, and even Star TV and full-blown air-conditioning in some of the nicer places. One attractive feature of budget hotels in India is **room service,** which usually costs no more than food in the restaurant. If you are a lazy **launderer,** you can surrender your clothes to the local *dhobi* (most hotels have their own, and store-front laundries are pervasive in most places). Your clothes will return cleaner (and thinner) than they ever were back home. Since laundry is charged by the piece, items like underwear and socks can add up, and it could pay to wash some yourself. But on particularly humid days, only the *dhobi*s seem to be able to get your clothes so clean and so dry so quickly.

Youth **hostels** are scattered in various locations throughout India, especially in the far north and south. They are extremely cheap and tend to be popular with foreign visitors, their denizens crowding nearby restaurants in the evenings. YMCAs and YWCAs are only found in the big cities and are usually quite expensive, although YWCA's women-only policy makes them safer for lone women travelers. Hostels in India rarely exclude nonmembers of hosteling organizations, however, nor do they charge nonmembers extra. Hostels in Nepal are, sadly, nonexistent.

In India, the state tourism development corporations have set up large **tourist bungalows** in both popular and less-touristed areas. Combining hotel with tourist office, these places may be convenient, but the slight improvement over budget hotels is seldom worth the price, and the staff can sometimes be unenthusiastic and unhelpful. The overpriced "dining halls" in tourist bungalows are forsaken by cost-conscious Indians, so they can be quiet places to sit and read or write.

UPSCALE HOTELS

Pricier accommodations are certainly available almost anywhere in India, offering such amenities as air conditioning, 24-hour hot water, and televisions, which you won't find in budget hotels. Although these hotels' rates seem exorbitant when compared to those of budget hotels, they are really nothing compared to hotel rates at home. Before you check into a more expensive hotel, however, ask yourself whether you'll really be that much more comfortable. Many mid-range hotels are all show, and upstairs from a spacious, carpeted lobby decorated with hotel logos, the rooms are only marginally better than those in budget hotels. Large, expensive hotels such as the Taj, Sheraton, and Oberoi chains and the ITDC's line of Ashoks are also present in the main cities and tourist centers. In Nepal, more expensive hotels are only available in Kathmandu and Pokhara. Such starry wonders are usually much more affordable in India and Nepal than their counterparts elsewhere, but if a night's stay is out of the question, the bookstores, restaurants, and pools at these places are often a great resource. Nicer hotels offer an escape from the sometimes harsh realities of Indian and Nepalese life; sometimes such an escape is necessary to maintain one's sanity. But tourists who remain in the (somewhat affordable) lap of luxury for their entire stay end up visiting a bunch of hotels, not India or Nepal. Across western and central India, many former **palaces of rajas and maharajas** have now been turned into middle-range hotels, offering travelers the decadence of a bygone era at an affordable price. Palace hotels are sometimes still inhabited by the royal families themselves. Furniture, decorations, and facilities such as libraries give these hotels their character. Larger hotels usually require payment in **foreign exchange;** this rule extends even farther down the price scale in Nepal.

ESSENTIALS

RELIGIOUS REST HOUSES

Traditional rest houses for Hindu pilgrims known as *dharamshalas* are sometimes open to foreign guests as well, providing the most Spartan accommodations free of charge, although it is kind to give a donation. Sikh *gurudwaras* also have a tradition of hospitality. Be on your best behavior if you stay in such religious places. Remember, these places aren't hotels; many have curfews or other restrictions and usually smoking and drinking are not allowed.

HOMESTAYS

Homestays with Indian families provides the paying guest with the opportunity to experience the people, country, and traditions first-hand, and the Government of India Tourist Department is aggressively promoting this concept. The **Paying Guest Scheme** is a relatively new phenomenon in India, but is gaining momentum in a number of states, particularly Tamil Nadu and Rajasthan. The Government of India Tourist Offices publish a comprehensive list of host families and information about the rooms, facilities, and meals that will be provided. Homestays are more expensive than budget hotels, but cheaper than starred hotels. Homestays are rare in Nepal.

■ Trekking

The Himalaya rise majestically from the landscape, and their lofty peaks, including that of Mt. Everest, the world's highest mountain, have a magnetic energy that lately seems to be attracting tourists from around the world, for vacations that appear to be a respite from the ever-quickening pace of modern life. Trekking has become a flourishing industry in Nepal and parts of India, and mountain tourism provides seasonal jobs to skilled guides, porters, cooks, village lodgers, and shop owners.

Trekking is neither mountaineering nor backpacking. Trekking through the Himalaya means walking from destination to destination, following trails, many of which are also used for communication and trade. A trek can be a day, a week, a month, or if it suits you, a lifetime. The trails are often steep and taxing, but the popular routes are well-maintained. Most treks follow trails through populated areas at elevations of 1000m to 3000m, but some extend over 5000m. A typical day's walk lasts from five to seven hours and involves many ascents and descents. You'll be repaid for your efforts with magnificent scenery and aching muscles. You'll meet a lot of people along the way, both Western travelers and Nepali villagers who live in Himalayan hill communities, and who will probably amaze you with their nimble climbing skills (in flip-flops, no less), while you pad your blisters with moleskin and get "acclimatized."

Some trekkers bring medicines such as aspirin to give to villagers along the trail. Such gifts will make you popular and will help people out, but don't give presents too liberally. Some of the main trails in Nepal are now veritable gauntlets of children asking for sweets, pens, and rupees, thanks to the legacy of over-generous trekkers.

WHEN TO GO

The post-monsoon reprieve (Oct.-Nov.) is the favored trekking season for **Nepal's Western** (see p. 777) and **Eastern** (see p. 797) treks. In India, the two main trekking seasons are pre-monsoon (May-June) and post-monsoon (Sept.-Nov.) in the monsoonal hill regions of **Kangra, Kullu** (see p. 355), **Shimla** (see p. 336), **Garhwal** (see p. 170), and **Kumaon** (see p. 176). The areas of **Upper Kinnaur** (see p. 361), **Lahaul** (see p. 356), **Spiti** (see p. 365), and **Ladakh** (see p. 375) are in rain shadow and get none of the monsoon rains. The morning haze gives way to bright sunshine, and crisp, clear air. The temperatures are comfortably warm, even balmy, in October, and you may have more company than you wanted on the more popular trails. From December to February, it may be too cold for trekking at high altitudes in the Himalaya. The temperatures rise in March and April, making trekking more feasible. The the air is usually dusty, dry, and hazy, but rhododendrons, magnolias, and orchids shower magnificent color over the landscape. Come May—the hottest and least predictable of months climatically—the monsoon is just around the corner and most trekking activities taper off, or trekkers retreat to higher regions. Few trekkers choose to endure the cloud-bound, slippery, and leech-beleaguered trail conditions of the monsoon. But for the persistent and enterprising, trekking during the summer season has the benefit of the virtual absence of Western tourists. Remember, however, that extreme weather conditions of all kinds can arise unexpectedly.

PLANNING A TREK

There are two ways of organizing a trek in the Indian or Nepalese Himayala. Trekking independently saves money and allows you to tailor your trek to suit your interests. You set the pace, choose your trekking companions, and plan rest days and side trips of interest in your own personalized adventure. There is a downside to such freedom, however. Arranging your own trek also entails obtaining permits, renting equipment, buying supplies, and hiring porters and guides. If you are blessed with the virtue of patience and the asset of time, then planning an independent trek may be the way to go. Otherwise, a trekking agency can take care of all the preparations for you, minimizing hassle, and their expertise may make it possible to trek through more remote backcountry. The ease and comfort come, of course, with a pricetag.

Trekking Permits and Other Fees

Permits are required for all trekking areas in Nepal and can be obtained in Thamel at the Department of Immigration (tel. 977 (1) 412337). You can complete the process in one day, but at the height of the trekking season, long lines can extend the process to two or even three days. **Always carry your trekking permit on the way to the trek and while on the trek,** so that registering at police posts will be a mere formality, and moving along will be easier. If your trek enters a national park (Everest and Langtang) or the Annapurna conservation area, you will have to pay a fee (for more information see **Kathmandu, Practical Information: Immigration Office,** p. 726).

Except in **North Sikkim** (see p. 411), trekking permits are not required in India. Area permits give access to all trekking areas as well, but no overnight camping is allowed in mountain national parks.

Practical Information

Nepal

Villages along Nepal's most popular trek routes have outdone themselves to accommodate passing foreigners, and are filled with **tea houses,** small lodges that offer food and a place to sleep. There are enough tea houses along the way and enough people who speak passable English for you to do the trek yourself, with the help of a trekking map and a trekking guidebook. For the adventure-seeking and budget-minded, this is the way to trek. Stan Armington's *Trekking in the Nepal Himalaya* (US$14.95, published by Lonely Planet Publications) is the authoritative trekking guidebook for the region. Making an effort to learn about the trek before setting off is helpful—some trekking agencies will offer free advice and information. The officials you come across while securing a trekking permit and paying entry fees will be able to answer additional questions.

On the trek, **use a map** and ask people for directions. The simplest and perhaps the most helpful question to ask is the way to the next village on the map. Every day you need to have an idea of the village where you want to spend the night. A question which causes more confusion is how long it takes to get to the next village. You will get a half-dozen different answers. Ask the people on the paths this question, rather than tea house owners, who have been known to exaggerate distances to trick you into staying at their place. The key for trekking by yourself is going day by day and being flexible. It might rain, you might realize that you aren't as fit as you thought, and of course, you will need time for your body to acclimatize.

In Nepal, English signs advertise **lodging** and **food** at a bargain budget—usually under NRs20—and often an English-speaking manager will greet the guests. Increasingly, private rooms are becoming available along the most popular routes in Nepal, but dormitory-style accommodations predominate in the backcountry and at high-elevations. Many of the tea houses, also called inns, guest houses, or trekking lodges, bustle with activity and noise, and although the physical exertion of trekking can make for sound sleeping, you may want to invest in a pair of earplugs. The tea house social scene can also be an enlivening experience and tea houses are full of potential trekking companions. Many of the lodges have been converted from homes and reveal the behind-the-scenes experience of Nepalese village life. The menu (this, too, is usually in English) may advertise enticing cuisine, which is often permanently unavailable. The staple trekking lodge meal is *dal bhat,* and Tibetan dishes are usually available. Along the most popular routes, you may be able to shovel out a few more rupees for the familiar taste of apple pie and a cold beer to wash it down. The extensive food and lodging industries that enable trekkers to carry minimal equipment are not available everywhere in Nepal, especially in the high mountains above 4500m.

India

Trekking in India requires far more self-sufficiency than does trekking in Nepal. India has no equivalent for the tea houses; in certain areas, there may be the occasional rest house, but they are often out of the way and food supplies en route are unreliable. Tents are essential for shelter, and the stock of supplies and equipment you'll have to carry are considerably greater. Because of the heavier load, porters or horsemen are needed more often than in Nepal—backpacks become a weighty burden on treks longer than a few days. Furthermore, getting lost in the Indian Himalaya is very easy, and often trekkers see no one but their own partners for three or four days at a time. Beginner and expert trekkers alike should be accompanied by someone who knows the specific trails. For more information, see **Packing and Equipment,** p. 59.

Porters and Guides

One variation on individual trekking is to hire your own porters and guides. You'll have a knowledgeable local with you, you won't have to carry as much, and you'll give a boost to the Himalayan economy. **Porters** carry most of your gear, allowing you the comfort of walking with only a small pack with the items you'll need during the day. You will have to constantly make sure that your porter understands what you want him to do and where you want to go each day. There is a small chance that your porter will disappear, leaving you with a heavy bag, or worse still, just the items on your person. Choose your porter carefully.

Guides, who usually speak English, are not necessary for the most well-known routes, where it is easy to find your way. Having someone who knows English and who is relatively educated might prove helpful in negotiations and pre-trek planning, however. A guide can color your experience with his knowledge of the land and culture, and often, guides will take trekkers on unusual side trips to visit friends and family. Guides are generally reluctant to carry anything (that's what porters are for).

In Nepal, porters can often be hired on the spot, even in the most unlikely of places. The trekking service industry in the Indian Himalaya is not as widespread, but you can arrange your own equipment, food, and staff at most hill stations or trailheads. Although porters and guides are easy to find, you'll want to investigate their honesty and experience. Spending some time in choosing a good guide is well worth the effort. Ask to see letters of recommendation from previous employer-trekkers. You can be almost certain to get reputable workers through a guest house or trekking agency. Guides and porters hired through companies are slightly more expensive but are, in most cases, more reliable and better qualified than those that you would find yourself. In the unlikely but still possible event that your guide or porter disappears, you have a company to hold responsible—an insurance that is worth the extra couple of dollars per day. If you do hire your own guides and porters, make sure you know exactly what services are covered in the wage, where you will go, and what supplies you will be obliged to supply along the way. Most agreements stipulate that guides and porters pay for their food and accommodations out of their wages. As a responsible employer, you should make sure that porters and guides are adequately clothed when trekking at high altitudes by outfitting them with good shoes, a parka, sunglasses, mittens, and a sleeping bag. Establish beforehand if you expect them to return anything. The standard salary for a porter carrying 20 kilos is about US$10 per day Nepal, US$5 per day in India; the salary for guides is higher (US$12-20 per day in India). In addition to these fees, you are expected to tip your staff generously at the end of a trek. Trekking in India tends to be a lot cheaper than in Nepal, mostly because tents and sleeping bags replace the cost of trail accommodations.

Organized Trekking

Many tourists do not want to spend their precious vacation time planning their trek, buying equipment, and hiring a porters and guides. You can book through a big international adventure travel company from your home country, in which case everything is organized and arranged before you even touch down in South Asia. If you wait until you arrive, you can book through a local trekking agency, which usually requires one week's advance notice. The agent makes reservations for hotels and transportation well in advance and provides a complete staff—a guide, porters, and cooks—for the trek. While you don't need to worry about arrangements, you must commit to the prearranged itinerary. You may also be trekking alongside people you have never met before. Organized treks can usually veer off from the crowded routes into more remote areas, however. The group carries its own food, which is prepared by cooks skilled in the art of kerosene cuisine. Porters carry tents for the group. Although tents can be colder and more cramped, they do offer a quiet night and the convenience of setting your own bedtime. The comforts of trekking through an agency may also include tables, chairs, dining tents, toilet tents, and other modern luxuries. For all this comfort and convenience, there is a price, which can range from US$15 to US$150 (usually US$40-50) per person per day, and almost none of this money ever reaches the people who live in the trekking region; instead it goes to pad the wallet of the middleman in the city.

PACKING AND EQUIPMENT

What you carry with you on your trek will depend greatly on where you go, the style of trekking you choose, and, if you have arranged a trek through an agency, what they provide. In Nepal, tea house trekking relieves you of having to carry food, cooking supplies, and tents. If you are traveling at high elevations in Nepal, or virtually anywhere in the Indian Himalaya, you will need to take these supplies with you. In addition, if going on a popular trek during high season, there is the possibility that you will not be able to find a bed in a village and will need a sleeping bag.

High-tech gear is not necessary for most trekking. Aim to keep the weight of your luggage to a minimum. Good used and new equipment is available in Nepal, but not in India. In Nepal, the largest number of **rental stores** are in Kathmandu, but rental stores can also be found in Pokhara and stations along the Everest trek such as Lukla and Namche Bazaar. Many rental shops will also sell equipment. If you don't have your own equipment, you'll have to go from shop to shop until you find the size, quality, and to a limited extent, price, you want. Spend a lot of time (an entire day) finding the right gear. In Nepal, most of the gear you will come across was left behind by mountaineering or trekking expeditions, so organized inventories and a huge selection of sizes don't exist. Be sure to inspect clothing and sleeping bags for fleas and broken zippers. Be aware that rental agencies often require a hefty deposit of US$50 or more.

Because it is particularly important to get **footwear that fits** and is comfortable, break in running shoes or boots before you leave. For most treks, running shoes are adequate. However, boots provide ankle protection and have stiffer soles. Boots are necessary wherever there is snow. Clothing should be lightweight and versatile to accommodate the variations in temperature. If you are going on any trek that will take you more than 1km from civilization, you should pack enough equipment to keep you alive should disaster befall. This includes raingear, warm layers (not cotton!), hat and mittens (a must!), a first-aid kit, high energy food, and water. The price of food and bottled drinks rises with the elevation. In much of Nepal, the price of food is fixed by the Annapurna Conservation Area Project, so bargaining is a futile exercise. Souvenir vendors are the people to bargain with.

Clothing	Equipment
boots or running shoes	sleeping bag
camp shoes or thongs	water bottle
socks (polypropylene and wool)	flashlight, batteries
down jacket	insulated mat
wool shirt	backpack
hiking shorts	toilet paper
long pants	matches
poncho or umbrella	sunblock
cotton t-shirts or blouses	towel
thermal underwear	laundry soap
gloves	sewing kit
sunhat	small knife
snow gaiters	first aid kit
snow goggles/sunglasses	

HEALTH AND SAFETY

The three most important things to remember when trekking are to stay warm, stay dry, and stay hydrated. Trekking takes a certain amount of physical exertion, but there is no need for overexertion. Go at a comfortable pace and take rest days when necessary. As you would anywhere in South Asia, make sure your water is safe. Unfortunately, the food and water served at inns and tea houses is not always properly prepared. Lapses in kitchen hygiene increase the risk of stomach illness. Eat in the inns that appear most sanitary. Washing your hands before eating will reduce the chance of contaminating your food. For more information, see **Health,** p. 20.

Knee and ankle strains are common trekking injuries. Knees can become painfully inflamed, especially when carrying a heavy load or walking downhill for long periods of time. If you think you're susceptible to knee injuries, bind them with an ace bandage as a preventive measure, Sprained ankles can be serious and could keep you from walking for hours or days. Good footwear with ankle support is the best prevention. Be sure that boots are broken in. A bad blister will ruin your trek. If you feel a "hot-spot" coming on, cover it with moleskin immediately.

If you are trekking to altitudes above 3500m, you will probably experience mild symptoms of altitude sickness, which can worsen into **Acute Mountain Sickness (AMS).** Serious cases of AMS are rare but can be fatal if left untreated. At high altitudes, there is less oxygen and lower atmospheric pressure, which can take their toll on the body—even the Sherpas aren't immune to elevation changes. It is important to allow time for acclimatization. Most people are capable of adjusting to very high elevations, but the process must be done in stages. Trekkers who fly directly to high altitudes are more likely to be affected by AMS and should be especially careful to acclimatize. Be sure to increase your intake of liquids, eat well, keep warm, get plenty of sleep, and avoid alcohol. Even if you take these precautions, don't panic if you experience headaches, dizziness, insomnia, nausea, loss of appetite, shortness of breath, or swelling of the hands and feet—all minor symptoms of AMS. You shouldn't ascend further until you start feeling better. Those in the know recommend that you sleep at a lower altitude than the greatest height reached during the day. It is also necessary to stop for a few days to acclimatize when you reach 3500m, and again when you reach 4500m. Allow some flexibility in your schedule; it will be easier to turn back or spend a day at one elevation if your plan allows for such contingencies. Also keep in mind that not everyone in your group will acclimatize at the same rate. The group might have to break up or stop entirely in response to the needs of a group member. The minor discomforts of AMS generally abate after a day or so but if they persist or worsen, **the only effective treatment is descent.** Anyone experiencing serious symptoms—vomiting, delirium, lack of coordination and balance, rapid heart rate, breathlessness, bloody phlegm, or blueness in the face—should be taken down-hill immediately. These symptoms can develop within hours, but dramatic recovery can occur with the descent of only a few hundred vertical meters.

Frostbite and **hypothermia** are other altitude-related dangers, because the weather in the Himalaya can be capricious. To prevent exposure, dress warmly and in layers, keep dry, cover any exposed extremities (wear a hat and mittens), eat well, and drink warm liquids. Make for shelter if conditions become severe. A good pair of sunglasses can protect you from snow blindness, a condition which is caused by ultraviolet light reflected from snow or ice. Ultraviolet light is much stronger at higher altitudes, so it is wise to protect against sunburn with sunblock and a sunhat.

Leeches are rampant during monsoon season. Trekkers often get these blood-sucking leeches on their legs or in their boots. Carry salt with you in a small container (a film container works well) for a chemical attack on leeches. Carefully applying a burning cigarette is another effective way of forcing a leech off your skin. Unlike ticks, they do not leave any part of themselves behind, so it is safe to pull them off if you're not too squeamish. Unfortunately, this could leave the bite open to infection. If you feel a leech has entered your shoes, the best thing might be to keep walking until the next village, because stopping will only give other leeches an opportunity to stick to you. A leech bite isn't painful; the effect is more psychological. Leeches are not known to transmit diseases.

Carry a **first-aid kit** for minor injuries. For suggestion on what to include in a first aid kit, see **Health,** p. 20. Cuts to the skin should be cleaned with Dettol, clean water, or Betadine solutions, and covered with a firm bandage. Clean and dress the wound daily. If the wound becomes infected, apply an antibiotic ointment. Broken bones should be realigned, and stabilized with a padded splint. Check frequently to make sure the splint is not cutting off circulation. Compound fractures, where the bone is exposed to the air through the wound, require more urgent medical treatment. Although trekkers do not often need serious medical attention, trekking mishaps do happen. In non-urgent cases, find some kind of animal (horse, pony, yak, crossbreed) to help transport a sick or injured trekker to the nearest hospital or airstrip. If urgent medical attention is needed, **emergency rescue** request messages can be sent by radio at police, army, national park, and other official offices. Helicopter rescue is very expensive (usually US$1000-2000). In Nepal, money must be deposited or guar-anteed in Kathmandu before the helicopter will fly. For people on agency treks, the agency will advance the money. This process is often made easier if you are regis-tered with your national embassy.

Individuals, particularly **women,** are not advised to trek alone. It is better to find a group, either on your own, through noticeboards, or through a trekking agency. For women trekking alone, it might be better to have a porter than a guide. In the few unfortunate cases in the past, many more guides than porters have tried to take advantage of single women trekkers.

Responsible Trekking

Trekking can enhance the local economy, but it can also burden and degrade the environment. Cultivate a respectful relationship with the land on which you tread. The delicate ecological balance in the Himalaya is at risk. Some of the most pressing problems include deforestation, overgrazing, landslides, and sanitation problems. Trekkers can put additional strain on the local wood supplies. When at all possible, eat at teahouses that cook with kerosene or electricity instead of wood. Treat your water with iodine instead of asking innkeepers for boiled water. If trekking with an agency, request that kerosene or gas be used for cooking and heating water. Blazing campfire hearths are taboo where deforestation is a problem. Outfit yourself and your porters with warm clothes so as to reduce your reliance on wood fires for warmth. Limit hot showers to those heated by electricity, solar energy, or back-boilers. Such industrious and innovative shower suppliers deserve encouragement.

Flora and fauna are also threatened in the Himalaya. Trekkers should never cut vegetation or clear new campsites. Loss of vegetation contributes to erosion, which is already widespread because of terraced farming.

Trekkers and their waste also contribute to litter, sanitation, and water pollution problems. The rule to follow is: burn it, bury it, or carry it out. Toilet paper is generally burned, biodegradables such as food wastes are buried, and non-disposables (plastics, aluminum foil, batteries, glass, cans, etc.) are packed up and carried to a suitable waste treatment site. All excrement should be buried in 40cm-deep holes in a spot far away from water sources, religious sites, village compounds, and cropfields. Use biodegradable soap and shampoo, and don't rinse directly in streams. If you can't leave the area clean, don't go. On organized treks, make sure that a person from your team is the last to leave camp; guided tour operators seldom do what they promise about camp garbage disposal. If you hear of a clean trek being organized, jump at the opportunity, or at least write to *Let's Go* about it.

FURTHER SOURCES

Himalayan Rescue Association (HRA) is located near the Department of Immigration in Thamel on the first floor of Hotel Tibicho. P.O. Box 4944, Kathmandu, Nepal (tel. 977 (1) 26; email hra@aidpost.mos.com.np). A voluntary non-profit organization providing information for trekkers on where and how to trek, trekking hazards, altitude sickness, and how to protect the Himalayan environment. During the trekking season (Oct.-Dec. and Mar.-May) they have free talks and slide shows on altitude sickness daily. They also have in-season clinics with volunteer Western doctors during the trekking season in Pheriche on the Everest trek and in Marang on the Annapurna Circuit. Open Su-F 10am-5pm.

Kathmandu Environmental Education Project (KEEP), P.O. Box 9178, Kathmandu (tel. 977 (1) 250070 or 250646). A non-profit organization that promotes "soft trekking," which minimizes impact on the environment and culture. They offer free advice to trekkers and trekking staff. During the trekking season (Oct.-Dec. and Feb.-May) they have a free talk on eco-tourism at their office at 4pm every Friday. Open Su-F 10am-5pm.

Annapurna Conservation Area Project, c/o King Mahendra Trust, P.O. Box 3712, Kathmandu (tel. 977 (1) 526571; fax 526570). ACAP is located in the King Mahendra Trust Office, near Grindlay's bank in Jawalakhel. The most authoritative source of information on the Annapurna region of Nepal, ACAP promotes environmentally sound practices among trekkers. Open M-F 9am-5pm.

Nepal Mountaineering Association (NMA) is located just south of Nag Pokhari in Naxal, in Kathmandu (tel. 977 (1) 411525; fax 416278). The NMA issues permits necessary for climbing Nepal's Himalayan peaks.

Indian Mountaineering Foundation, Benito Juarez Marg, Anand Niketan (tel. 91 (11) 602245 or 671211). Information on treks, especially climbs over 6000m.

■ Keeping in Touch

MAIL

Mail takes about two to three weeks to go between India or Nepal and North America. You can mail your letters at any post office (watch it get postmarked yourself) or have your hotel take care of it for you. **Poste Restante** is like general delivery and it is the best way to get those love letters from home. Have your correspondents mark the date of your arrival on the envelope and emphasize your last name when addressing it. The letters are filed alphabetically at the post office—if you don't see that epistle under your last name, check under your first. Letters should be addressed to you, c/o *Poste Restante*, GPO, and then the city, state and country. Take your passport with you for identification when you go to pick up your mail. **American Express** offices will also hold mail for anyone with an American Express cards or even a single tattered US$20 AmEx Traveller's Check.

Sending a **package** home will involve getting it cleared by customs, taking it to a tailor to get it wrapped in cloth and sealed with wax, going to the post office to fill out the customs forms, buying stamps, and then, finally, seeing it processed and on its way. It may take a couple of months or even a couple of years to get home if you send your booty surface mail—and all packages run the risk of getting x-rayed or searched, so don't try to mail home anything illegal. If you need to receive a package from abroad, it's probably a good idea to have it registered—which will lessen the great likelihood that your Smarties and Spice Girls poster will get stolen.

Aerogrammes, printed sheets that fold into envelopes and travel via airmail, are available at post offices. It helps to mark "airmail" in the appropriate language if possible, though *par avion* is universally understood. Most post offices will charge exorbitant fees or simply refuse to send Aerogrammes with enclosures. Allow *at least* two weeks for mail delivery to or from South Asia. Much depends on the national post office involved.

If regular airmail is too slow, there are a few faster, more expensive, options. Both **FedEx** (tel. 1 (800) 463 3339) and **DHL** (tel. 1 (800) 225 5345) operate throughout South Asia; FedEx operates in India as a joint venture with an Indian company, **Blue Dart.** Federal Express packages from the U.S. to India or Nepal cost about US$58. Delivery takes four business days. **DHL** costs about US$78 to India or Nepal. Delivery takes three to five business days. DHL packages sent from India or Kathmandu to the U.S. cost US$30-40 and take five business days.

Surface mail is by far the cheapest and slowest way to send mail. It is really only appropriate for sending large quantities of items you won't need to see for a while. It is vital, therefore, to distinguish your airmail from surface mail by explicitly labeling "airmail" in the appropriate language. When ordering books and materials from abroad, always include one or two **International Reply Coupons (IRCs)**—a way of providing the postage to cover delivery. IRCs should be available from your local post office as well as abroad (US$1.05).

American Express travel offices throughout the world will act as a mail service for cardholders if you contact them in advance. Under this free **"Client Letter Service,"** they will hold mail for 30 days, forward upon request, and accept telegrams. As with *Poste Restante*, the last name of the person to whom the mail is addressed should be capitalized and underlined. Some offices will offer these services to non-cardholders (especially those who have purchased AmEx Traveller's Cheques), but you must call ahead to make sure. Check the **Practical Information** section of the countries you plan to visit; *Let's Go* lists AmEx office locations for most large cities. A complete list is available free from AmEx (tel. 1 (800) 528-4800) in the booklet *Traveler's Companion* or online at http://www.americanexpress.com/shared/cgi-bin/tsos-erve.cgi@travel/index.

TELEPHONES

Phones are widespread in India and Nepal, and fairly easy to use. The **STD/ISD** sign (Standard Trunk Dialing/International Subscriber Dialing) means that there's a phone nearby. Many towns have 24-hour **Central Telegraph Offices,** which allow free local calls. Many STD/ISD booths are open 24 hours a day, and offer fax services. The **country code** is 91 for India, 977 for Nepal, 1 for the United States and Canada, 44 for the United Kingdom, 353 for Ireland, 61 for Australia, 64 for New Zealand, and 27 for South Africa. **City codes** have between two and four digits. In the listings for this book, city codes are preceded by a zero; when calling internationally, don't dial the 0 in the city code. Calling home from an STD/ISD booth, dial the international access code (00), the country code, the city or area code, and then the number.

English-speaking operators are often available for both local and international assistance, but international collect calls cannot be made from India or Nepal to some countries. It's usually cheaper to find a phone booth and call just long enough to be able to say "call me" and give your number. Discuss this with the booth operator in advance before you try it. The rate for an incoming call should be between nothing and the cost of a local call (or at least a lesser fee). However, many STD/ISD booth operators will not allow incoming return calls because they don't make any money this way. An alternative is to have your friend call you back at your hotel or some other place with a reliable phone. But travelers should budget enough to pay for all overseas calls on the spot if necessary.

A **calling card** is another (often futile) alternative; your local long-distance service provider will have a number for you to dial while traveling (either toll-free or charged as a local call) to connect instantly to an operator in your home country. The calls (plus a small surcharge) are then billed either collect or to the calling card. Many other long distance carriers and phone companies provide such travel information; contact your phone service provider.

Though calling cards can probably work in the major tourist centers of India and Nepal, the ISD booths in many smaller cities and villages do not have access to international operators. And even those cards that potentially work are often disallowed by STD/ISD booth owners, who don't profit on calling card or collect calls.

Rates for international calls from India are the same around the clock, but long-distance calls within India are half-price after 6pm, and one-quarter price after 9pm. When calling home, remember **time zones** (see **Hours and Holidays,** p. 73).

EMAIL AND INTERNET

Hundreds of so-called **cyber-cafes** (most of them serve no coffee—they're just offices with a couple of PCs) are open throughout India, allowing Internet access from most major cities and quite a few small towns for a fixed hourly or half-hourly fee. The easiest way to send email from these places is via **Hotmail,** a free web-based email service that is incredibly popular in India and worldwide (http://www.hotmail.com). In Nepal and in some of India's more mountainous regions without web access, it is often possible (though less private and convenient) to send email from some local entrepreneur's account.

TELEGRAMS AND FAXES

Domestic and international **telegrams** are slower than telephones but faster than post. In India, Central Telegraph Offices (CTOs) in many cities offer telegraph service to Europe or Australasia for Rs2 per word, or to North America for Rs2.50 per word. Central Telegraph Offices also frequently have 24-hour STD/ISD phone services. **Faxes** are available at many STD/ISD booths.

■ Economics and Ethics

For foreigners, the shock of entering a new culture in India or Nepal is often compounded by an equal shock caused by the poverty of those around them. Bony rickshaw-*wallahs* wince as they pedal down flooded roads, cows graze on any available tuft of urban vegetation, and street children roam in tattered clothes. The poverty in these countries is also evident in the poorly paved roads and the piles of household garbage that no one can afford to dispose. Due to their relative wealth, foreigners are mobbed by touts (see p. 67), assailed by armies of beggars, accosted by slippery con men, and often charged more than locals as a matter of official policy. For budget travelers, these shenanigans can be exhausting and infuriating. Inequality does not excuse the lack of respect with which touts and some other people working in the tourism industry treat their customers. After a tout has lied to you about a hotel in order to get you into one that would pay a commission, or after a rickshaw-*wallah* has asked you for five times the real fare in hopes that you might be stupid enough to pay, you may find yourself arguing over small differences in money not because of the amount, but as a matter of principle.

However, Western travelers trying to pinch paise should remember how much their money really means to the people they deal with. Foreigners are wealthy compared to most Indians and Nepalis—no budget travel excuses are acceptable here. Even the most austere budget travelers frequently spend as much in a day as their hotel watchman or rickshaw-*wallah* earns in a month. Budget travelers have also paid for a round-trip plane ticket to India and Nepal, an unimaginable sum of money for most Indians and Nepalis. It is important to accept your status as a privileged outsider and to be prepared to pay more, at least some of the time.

The following sections describe some of the issues foreign travelers in India and Nepal face when they deal with money.

TOUTS, MIDDLEMEN, AND SCAMS

Touts are the scruffy-looking men who surround travelers at bus stands and train stations, or accost them in streets of tourist ghettos, offering deals on transportation, currency exchange, magic from the plant kingdom, or any service rupees can buy. If you have trouble finding something, a tout will probably be able to help you for a little *baksheesh,* but what really distinguishes touts is their unhelpfulness. They are pushy and will try to trap you into paying for something you don't really want. They count on foreigners to be naive enough to follow along.

It is hard to **find a hotel** without a tout getting involved; you'll be approached as soon as you get off the bus or train. Touts (and taxi drivers and rickshaw-*wallahs* too) are paid commissions by hotels to gather tourists, and these commissions are usually added to the hotel bill. The best policy is to be firm. Decide where you want to go and have someone take you there. If the hotel isn't paying commissions, touts will tell you it's full or closed; don't believe it. If no one will take you there, have a driver take you to a general area from where you can hunt for a good place to stay. A traveler wearing a big backpack in a tourist ghetto will attract touts like flies to a rotting mango, so try to find a safe place (often a restaurant) where you can put down your pack while you search.

In major tourist centers you'll often meet people who want you to visit their home or their workplace or to take you for tours. You may be told some story as an excuse for them to take you somewhere to look at jewels, gifts, or other supposedly rare and hard to get export items. Unless you have asked to go somewhere, you are under no obligation to follow them or to pay them for being taken to a place in which you have no interest. Don't give them money when they ask you for it, regardless of what they say they will do for you. This is especially important to remember upon arrival when you will be at your most vulnerable.

Travel agents in the major tourist centers frequently resemble touts with desks and telephones. They are known to give false information, charge hefty commissions, and they even sometimes sell bogus tickets. Unless they have a peon to do it for them, most Indians buy train tickets directly from the station. It's best to do this yourself too. **Eliminating the middleman** will give you more control over your travels, will save you money, and will get you more acquainted with the way things work in the country you're visiting.

Another hassle at many monuments and temples are the unofficial **guides** who won't allow travelers to peacefully enjoy the sights but spew ignorant drivel, later demanding *baksheesh.* Be forceful with these people and they will usually back off—don't hesitate to push your way through. However, some historical sites have sophisticated and informative guides. It is usually better to book a guide through a tourist office or other government organization than to wait to be approached by some strange man.

When ignored, many touts are equipped with a guilt-trip line, tailored to your demographic group, for example: "Excuse me, sir, one question: Why don't you white Americans like to talk to us Indians?" Don't let these attacks on your insecurities get to you. There are better ways of meeting Indians and Nepalis than letting touts cheat you.

BEGGING

From lines of beggars outside temples to children weaving through traffic to beg at car windows, the sad phenomenon of begging is impossible to ignore in India and Nepal. Nothing can prepare a traveler for the all-too-common sight of children and impoverished women holding starving babies while begging for food and money. It is said that some children are even maimed by family members in order to increase sympathy and hence charity. While giving may temporarily ease your conscience, it is not always the best choice. Sometimes a person seen giving charity may be singled out by other beggars and quickly approached. Giving can also encourage a cycle of poverty—some children avoid attending school because they can earn money by begging. But many beggars (lepers, amputees, emaciated mothers) have very obvious needs. When giving to beggars, remember that Rs30 is more than many Indian working people see in a week. **Carry coins and one- or two-rupee bills**—in most cases, these make appropriate donations. For children, offer food instead of money—a gift of biscuits will more likely benefit the child than a cash donation. Finally, if you're staying in a city for very long, ask around to find out which local charities work with the poor, so that you can direct beggars to a source of long-term help.

It is customary to give a little to beggars at pilgrimage sites and to *sadhus,* wandering Hindu holy men who survive by begging (as well as to transvestites on trains! See **The Third Sex,** p. 608). **Don't give** to cute, healthy kids who cheerfully approach tourists with requests for rupees, coins, or pens. These are not beggars, but regular schoolchildren having fun trying their luck to see what they can get from foreigners. This encourages a begging mentality, and their parents usually find this behavior embarrassing. A quick "Begging is bad" or "Don't you have anything better to do?" is a more appropriate response.

BARGAINING

India and Nepal are wonderful places to practice your bargaining skills. Taxi and auto-rickshaw fares (when not metered) and items in outdoor markets are fair game for haggling. Don't bargain on prepared or packaged foods (on the street or in restaurants) or on items marked with a price tag. But in smaller, family-run stores it might not hurt to try. Be prepared to pay what you offer; it is considered outrageous to refuse to purchase something after settling on a price. Start by offering half the stated price and let your charisma do the rest. Bargaining requires patience and cooperation from both parties. If you seem stubborn and grouchy, the vendor is less likely to want to come down. Chat with him or her a little. Strike up a conversation if you have any language in common. You'll find that the personal touch goes a long way. You should feel right to refuse any vendor or rickshaw-*wallah* who bargains rudely.

BAKSHEESH AND TIPPING

The word *baksheesh* is usually translated as a "tip," but the concept really includes a whole range of exchanges, from gifts to outright bribes. Bribing a railway porter to find a seat on a "full" train is *baksheesh;* so is giving small change to beggars. *Baksheesh* can work wonders—Rs20 *baksheesh* given to an Indian traffic policeman has been known to make moving violations disappear forever, and foreigners visiting some Hindu temples have been surprised to be asked for a donation with the phrase *"baksheesh* for God." Small tips are expected for restaurant service, train "coolie" porter service, and unofficial tour guides. There is no need to tip taxi drivers, who often overcharge as it is. Tips depend on your level of satisfaction or gratitude, and usually run between Rs1 and Rs20, not following any particular percentage rule. Alternatively, a pack of cigarettes or some other small gift is often appreciated. In restaurants, leave a few extra rupees in change on the table. Most Indians and Nepalis expect great tips from foreigners, but don't be swayed by groans and protests. If your first offer is met with a quick roll of the head signifying "OK," then you have done well.

■ Environmentally Responsible Tourism

A visit to India or Nepal can be quite a shock for even not-so-environmentally-conscious travelers. From the smog-choked sprawl of Delhi to trailside heaps of trash in Nepal, garbage and pollution are a fact of life in these countries. On the one hand, it is important to limit your own environmental impact on the places you visit, but be wary of adopting a colonialist attitude towards environmental issues. Even Mahatma Gandhi was not successful in his attempts to improve Indian sanitation and environmental consciousness; you'll probably be even less so. As frustrated as you might be, picking a fight with the guy you see throwing trash out a train window isn't going to help anything. The best way to help is to think about the ways your stay is affecting the environment. Most of the trash you generate will end up on the street whether you throw it there or not, so the key is to generate less garbage, period. Fortunately, there's a lot you can do to minimize your own environmental impact as you travel.

The two biggest and often least obvious ways that tourists are prone to waste are the overuse of **water** and **electricity.** Heavily touristed areas, whether large cities or small towns, often have water shortages. When water is available, use it sparingly. Squat toilets and bucket showers may be tough to get used to, but they consume far less water than their Western counterparts. Sending your laundry to a *dhobi* may seem like a luxury, but the professionals use less water than you would in your hotel sink. India and Nepal's frequent power cuts will do a lot of conservation for you, but even when there is electricity, use it sparingly. Always turn off the lights and the air-conditioning when you leave a room, and make sure that the doors and windows are shut when the air conditioning is on. Better yet, stay in a place without air conditioning; most Indians and Nepalis do this their entire lives.

When you're shopping, try not to accept excess packaging, particularly styrofoam boxes as they are not biodegradable. Even using refillable ballpoint pens available at almost all stationery shops will make that small difference. If you are a woman, buy feminine hygiene products with minimal packaging; O.B. brand tampons have no applicator and come in small, discreet boxes. Choose glass soda bottles over drinking boxes, or marginally recyclable aluminum cans. In cities with good tap water, use purifying tablets and your own canteen to avoid having to throw out countless plastic water bottles. Reuse plastic bags. It's hard to convince Indian and Nepali market vendors not to give you three plastic bags where one would suffice, but with a little extra effort, you'll surely succeed.

Beyond these specifics, remember that responsible tourism means understanding the short- and long-term effects of your actions, seriously considering these effects, and realizing you are responsible for them. Only looking at part of the picture does not lead to a responsible decision; often it only fuels unhealthy stereotypes of both Indians and Nepalis and Western tourists.

One of the best ways to undo some of the effects of environmental destruction in India or Nepal and to minimize (or counteract) your own impact is to volunteer for one of the many environmental organizations there (see **Alternatives to Tourism,** p. 30). There remains little information regarding responsible tourism in India and Nepal. Should you happen to uncover a great "ecotourism" operator or have other ideas of how to be a low-impact tourist, we at *Let's Go* would love to hear of them.

■ Customs and Etiquette

CLOTHING

Dress modestly. Clothing can elicit reactions as polarized as a warm welcome or a nasty jeer. While exhibiting sleek, tan shoulders or long, lean legs is a matter of pride and envy in the West, most Indians and Nepalese find it distasteful and even disrespectful. In some areas, a man walking down the street sporting shorts will be giggled at, since only little boys wear shorts and panthood is synonymous with manhood. Similarly, but for different reasons, women should try to keep legs covered, at least to the knee. Try to think of this as much for your own comfort, as a shield from greedy or disapproving eyes, as for cultural sensitivity points. Bare shoulders are another sure sign of immorality (and a quick way to sunburn). Ragged clothes will also draw attention to you. In India, many women will find they are treated more respectfully when they wear a *salwar kameez*. While men's clothing in India is typically more Westernized, men might want to buy a thin cotton *kurta pajama*—these garments will cover you up while keeping you cool. If you are well-dressed, this will certainly affect the way that people respond to you as a foreigner. Like everything in South Asia, these rules vary by region. Clothing taboos are looser in Nepal and throughout the Himalaya, and also in cosmopolitan centers like Mumbai.

FOOD

Most Indian and Nepalis eat with their hands, a skill many foreigners have trouble picking up. While restaurants usually give cutlery to foreigners, you may have to eat with your hands if you are invited to someone's home. The most important thing is to **eat with your right hand only.** The left hand is used for cleaning after defecation, so it is seen as polluted. Keep your left hand in your lap throughout the meal. You can use your left hand to hold a fork or a glass or to pass a dish (and you'll need to do this, because your right hand will get awfully mucky), but it can never touch food or your lips directly. With the tips of the fingers of your right hand held together like a scoop, pick up a bite of food. Lift it up and push it into your mouth with your thumb. Sound easy? If this is done right, in theory, the food should never touch any point higher than the first joint of your fingers.

Any food that comes into contact with one person's saliva is unclean for anyone else. Indians and Nepalis will not usually take bites of each other's food, or drink from the same cup; watch how locals drink from water bottles, pouring the drink in without touching their lips. Besides being culturally correct this is a good rule to follow in South Asia for health reasons.

In Hindu houses, the family **hearth** is sacred, so if food is cooked before you on a fire (as it frequently is in trekking lodges) never play with the fire or throw trash in it.

Meals in India or Nepal begin with a staple dish: usually rice in southern and eastern India, wheat bread in the north. Many foreigners are amazed at the masses of starch consumed. For many people it is the only food they eat on a regular basis. Almost all Jains and many Hindus (especially in South India) are **vegetarian,** and besides, for many non-vegetarians, meat is an expensive luxury. Due to the cow's sacred status in Hinduism, beef is scarce in India and in Nepal. Muslims do not eat pork and are supposed to shun alcohol, although the latter restriction is not always observed. Only the most modernized women of any religion drink alcohol.

HYGIENE

Westerners are often amazed at how Indians and Nepalis can have so many rules about bodily purity while bathing and drinking from rivers filled with garbage and excrement, but such apparent discrepancies testify to the power of cultural customs. All **bodily secretions** and products are considered polluting in South Asian culture, and the people who come into contact with them—laundrymen, barbers, latrine cleaners—have historically formed the lowest ranks of the caste system. The **head** is the most sacred part of the body, and purity decreases all the way to the toes. To **touch something with your feet** is a grave insult, and you should never touch a person with your feet, step over a seated person's outstretched legs, or even point at someone with your foot. Never put your feet on a table, or any other surface used for eating or studying. To touch someone else's feet, on the other hand, is an act of veneration. If you accidentally touch someone else with your foot, touch your forehead and then their knee or foot, whichever is more accessible. The **left hand** is also polluted. Always use your right hand to eat, give, take, or point.

Squat Toilets: A Billion People Can't Be Wrong...

Indian toilets appear to be simple holes in the ground, which can be an unpleasant surprise during those initial attacks of diarrhea. Even worse is discovering that there is no toilet paper. Wait! Don't panic! Placing your feet on either side of the orifice, you squat and push—a simple, elegant process. Many Indian toilets even feature painted footprints to aid the uninitiated; also, the squatting position is less likely to strain your back or to give you a hernia than sitting. Next to the hole, there is generally a cup and a spigot. To clean yourself in the time-honored Indian fashion, fill the cup and—holding it with your RIGHT hand—pour it near the base of your spine while wiping with your LEFT hand. It is remarkably effective and environmentally friendly; think of how much toilet paper you use and multiply that by 950 million—it's a lot of paper and a lot of trees. Two warnings, however: (1) wash both hands carefully afterwards and (2) never, NEVER use the right hand to wipe; this practice is one reason for the stigma associated with the left hand in Indian society. Flushing is usually accomplished by pouring a cup or two of water down the hole. The whole process can be a little stomach-churning at first, but this prejudice soon disappears; independence from toilet paper can simplify your life in India considerably. If—on the other hand—force of habit is too great, most hotels can easily provide you a room with a porcelain throne.

COMMUNICATION AND BODY LANGUAGE

A quick **sideways roll of the head,** similar to shaking one's head but more like a sideways nod, means "OK," or "I understand." Many foreigners are baffled by this gesture, thinking their hosts are answering their most innocent comments and requests with a firm "no." It is actually much easier to get a "yes" from Indians and Nepalis—sometimes too easy. South Asians are often embarrassed to give a negative answer, and will occasionally describe a totally fictional set of directions to the river or the post office rather than admit they don't know the way. Avoid asking yes-or-no questions; phrase questions so that you'll know whether your respondent really knew what he or she was talking about.

When you meet people, be prepared for **questions** about your nationality, age, marital status, family, education, employment, and income. There's nothing threatening about this. None of these are seen as private matters. It's just innocent curiosity. Ask people the same questions back; they'll be glad to chat.

Indian English, especially when written, is full of colorful and antique-sounding phrases. You may be surprised to hear people address you as "madame" or "good gentleman," or to read letters asking you to "kindly do the needful" and signed "your most humble servant."

Many foreigners have trouble adjusting to the constant **stares** they get in India and Nepal. There's no solution but to adjust. Meeting someone's gaze is often tantamount to expressing a desire for further contact. There's no taboo against staring in South Asian culture, and no harm is intended, but be sure not to send mixed signals. Remember that people's curiosity about you is due to the limited chance they have for contact with different people; don't deny them an opportunity. At the same time, realize that at times it is both acceptable and appropriate to ignore attempts at conversation ("Pardon me, which country?" "Hello, what time is it?"). If you don't want to get mired down in a conversation, don't talk to them.

WOMEN AND MEN

Although big city parks are filled with couples courting, nothing ever happens between them in plain view. Displays of **physical affection** between women and men are rare, so stay tame when in public. Some affection is considered completely natural and acceptable, such as that between men. Everywhere, men walk comfortably down the street clasping hands. Except in Westernized circles and among some groups high in the mountains, most Indian and Nepali women appear quite meek and quiet in public. It is difficult for strange men to talk to them, and probably best not to try. Women travelers also might have a hard time meeting Indian and Nepali women, although women should try to find other women to help out in emergencies (see **Women Travelers,** p. 35).

TIME

Nothing runs quite on schedule in India and Nepal as foreigners might expect (although travelers used to other third-world countries may find things surprisingly prompt). Buses leave late, offices open late, dinner parties start late. South Asia operates on a very different conception of time from most Western countries, requiring much patience. The only real solution is to set your clock this way too; if you allow yourself to get annoyed at every delay, you'll be a basket case by the end of your trip. As infuriated as you might want to be, take the time to look around you and enjoy the little things—isn't that what you came for anyway?

In response to your requests in banks, phone booths, and other places you'll commonly be told to **"sit down."** It is assumed you would rather wait and have something done for you rather than doing it yourself, even if you could do it faster.

PLACES OF WORSHIP

Be especially sensitive about etiquette in places of worship. Secular visitors to sacred shrines are expected to follow customs and rituals just as perfectly as believers. **Dress conservatively,** keeping legs and shoulders covered, and **take off your shoes** before entering any mosque, *gurudwara,* or Hindu, Jain, or Buddhist temple. Visitors to Sikh *gurudwaras* must cover their heads as well—handkerchiefs are usually provided. At the entrance to popular temples, shoe-*wallahs* will guard your shoes for a few rupees' *baksheesh.* Ask before taking **photographs** in places of worship. It is normally forbidden to take pictures of images of deities in Hindu temples.

Many Hindu temples, especially those in Kerala, but also in Nepal and in pilgrimage sites such as Puri and Varanasi, ban non-Hindus from entering. In practice this rule excludes anyone who doesn't look sufficiently South Asian. Some Hindu and Jain temples forbid menstruating women to enter.

It is common practice in Hindu temples to partake of offerings of consecrated fruit and/or water called *prasad,* which is received with the right hand over the left (and no one takes seconds). It is protocol to leave a small donation at the entrance to the temple sanctuary, though this can cause some dilemmas when temple priests aggressively force *prasad* into your hands, expecting large amounts of cash in return. Usually a donation of one or two rupees will suffice.

Hinduism and Buddhism consider the right-hand side auspicious and the left-hand side inauspicious; thus it is customary to walk around Hindu temples and Buddhist *stupas* **clockwise,** with your right side toward the shrine. In fact, any circular motion, such as the turning of Tibetan Buddhist prayer wheels, goes in a clockwise direction.

INDIA भारत

On May 11, 1998, India officially joined the world's declared nuclear powers, as Prime Minister Atal Bihari Vajpayee announced the completion of a series of successful nuclear tests beneath the Thar Desert in western Rajasthan. For India, the announcement was a bittersweet coming out. The 51th year of Indian independence, which closed without much fanfare on August 15, 1998, was a time of redefinition for a nation that is at once both young and old: an ancient culture reborn in a post-Imperialist world. India is no single nation at all, and as the world's largest democracy enters middle age, and assumes the responsibilities of a world power, problems old and new cloud the future. The tumultuous 20th century and the promise-filled 21st century provide two equally relevant representations of the nation's divided identity.

For the traveler, India's nuclear stand is actually of very little importance, and pales in comparison to the other challenges of visiting South Asia. Travel in India is both difficult and rewarding, threatening and welcoming. It is not a place to simply observe; India demands reaction. Here the sublime beauty of natural vistas and towering temples and the pungent odors of city gutters and dung-fueled cooking fires are equally likely to bring tears. Some visitors flee India never to return, but many keep coming back, and quite a few never leave.

ESSENTIALS

◼ Money

NRs100=Rs63.93	Rs100=NRs156.42
US$1=Rs42.56	Rs100=US$2.34
CDN$1=Rs27.44	Rs100=CDN$3.64
UK£1=Rs69.77	Rs100=UK£1.43
IR£1=Rs59.33	Rs100=IR£1.69
AUS$1=Rs24.51	Rs100=AUS$4.08
NZ$1=Rs.20.91	Rs100=NZ$4.78
SAR=Rs.6.78	Rs100=SAR14.73

Currency is measured in rupees (Rs) which are divided into 100 paise. Paise come in denominations of 5, 10, 20, 25, and 50, while rupees come in Rs.1, 2, and 5 coins and bills worth Rs.1, 2, 5, 10, 20, 50, 100, and 500. Check all bank notes carefully; ripped bills will be refused by many merchants (although banks will exchange them for new ones). It is common practice for banks to staple bundles of notes together.

The national **State Bank of India** is the most common place to change money, but branches of state banks sometimes have foreign exchange facilities as well; foreign banks, like ANZ Grindlays and Hong Kong Bank, can be more efficient. **Bank of Baroda** offers cash advances on Visa and Mastercard at most of its many locations. Banking hours are short (M-F 10am-2pm, Sa 10am-noon). With the rapid changes in India's economy, inflation is expected in the next year, and all prices in this book could go up by about 8%; on the other hand, the exchange rate is likely to change as well, meaning that prices will probably stay the same in hard currency terms.

◼ Hours and Holidays

Most shops and offices are open from Monday to Friday 10am to 5pm, and some commercial offices and post offices are open Saturday mornings as well. Many government offices confuse things by opening alternate Saturdays. Some of these hours may be extended to as early as 8am and as late as 6pm in major cities like Delhi and in major tourist spots, but don't count on it.

India is 5½ hours ahead of GMT, 4½ hours behind Australian Eastern Standard Time, and 10½ hours ahead of North America's Eastern Standard Time. Summer time puts the northern countries an hour closer to India. India is 15 minutes behind Nepal.

India has many festivals on many different calendar systems, but the Gregorian calendar is used for most official purposes. For more information, see **Holidays and Festivals,** p. 805.

LIFE AND TIMES

■ Geography

Many liken the landscape of India to the colors of its flag: green jungles, white Himalayan snows, orange-red Deccan earth. Poetic as the description may be, to call it an oversimplification would be an understatement. India's landscape is expansive and diverse. One of the most striking features is the arc of the great **Himalayan Range,** the wrinkled wreckage of two continents' slow-motion collision. These mountains' impenetrable heights have historically kept the cultures of South Asia in isolation from those of Central Asia, Tibet, and China. Highest and youngest of the world's mountain ranges, the Himalaya extends over 2000km of almost uninterrupted ups and downs. More accurately described as a series of mountain chains than a single range, the Himalaya's deep nesting valleys fashion the watersheds of the Subcontinent's three major river systems, the **Indus, Ganga,** and **Brahmaputra.** Fed by rainwater and glacial run-off, these rivers' networks of silt-dumping tributaries in turn nourish North India's immense and densely-populated **Indo-Gangetic Plain,** stretching from the state of Rajasthan in the west to West Bengal in the east.

A belt of stepped hills known as the **Vindhyas** separate the Indo-Gangetic Plain from the **Deccan Plateau,** covering swaths of present-day Maharashtra, Karnataka, and Andhra Pradesh. This central, peninsular part of India is considered India's most ancient land surface; the Archean rocks of the Deccan Plateau are 300-500 million years old. Washed by the **Arabian Sea** to the west and the **Bay of Bengal** to the east, peninsular India tapers as it draws south, dipping into the Indian Ocean at its southernmost point, Kanyakumari. Flanking the **Malabar Coast** of Kerala, Karnataka, and Goa, the **Western Ghats** (a north-south chain of mid-sized hills) are separated from the Arabian Sea by a narrow strip of richly forested coastal plain. A broader coastal area stretches between the Bay of Bengal and the **Eastern Ghats.** The southern fringes of the Western and Eastern Ghats converge at the **Nilgiri Hills** of Kerala and Tamil Nadu, the southernmost tip of the Deccan Plateau. The **Lakshadweep Islands,** just off the Malabar coast in the Arabian Sea, and the **Andaman and Nicobar Islands** in the Bay of Bengal, are also Indian territories.

■ People

The 940 million people packed within India's borders represent such diversity that India often seems like a dozen nations packed into one. Six major religions, 18 major languages, and numerous racial and ethnic groups coexist in India, often harmoniously, sometimes not. India's population is primarily agricultural but 25% of the population now lives in urban areas, although the shift of population from rural to urban is slower in India than in most developing countries. Those who remain in villages are largely unaffected by the changes that industrialization has brought to India's huge cities. Population is densest in the valley and delta of the Ganga river and in the extreme south (Tamil Nadu and Kerala). India's four largest cities, Bombay (13 million), Calcutta (12 million), Delhi (9 million), and Madras (6 million) make up only 4%

of the population. India's population is growing at just under 2% per year, which means that India should have one billion people before the year 2000.

The ethnic origins of Indians reflect a mix between the light-skinned **Aryan** people, who still reside mostly in the north, and the darker-skinned **Dravidian** peoples of the south. In fact, although India remains one nation, the south and South Indians are quite different from the north and its inhabitants. India's population also includes numerous "tribal" groups or *adivasis* (aboriginal peoples), many of whose ethnic origins are Tibeto-Burmese or Proto-Australoid. *Adivasis* are concentrated in the northeastern states as well as in Madhya Pradesh, Orissa, and Gujarat. Most Indians (80%) are Hindu, although there is a large minority of Muslims (11%), as well as smaller groups of Christians, Sikhs, Jains, Parsis, Buddhists, and Jews.

■ Language

India is home to an astounding 1600 dialects, varying from state to state and village to village. The languages of North India, such as **Hindi** and **Bengali,** descended from Sanskrit, the language spoken by the Aryan invaders who wandered into the area around 1500 BC. These languages are part of the greater Indo-European family, and it's not unusual to find North Indian words that resemble their counterparts in English or other European languages. **Urdu,** a language widely spoken among Muslims in India, is very similar to Hindi but also contains elements of Persian, having developed as the language of the Mughal empire. The major **South Indian languages,** Kannada, Telugu, Malayalam, and Tamil, all belong to the independent Dravidian family and are unrelated to the North Indian languages. Indo-Aryan and Dravidian languages have inevitably influenced one another, however, and they share some features, such as retroflex consonants, in which the tongue is curled back to touch the palate.

Language has proved to be a difficult issue for independent India. The Indian constitution (written in English) planned for Hindi to be the national language, since it is the most widely-spoken Indian language, used by about 30% of the people. However, most Indians identify strongly with their mother tongue, and linguistic loyalty is often linked to geography. In the 1950s India was reorganized into new states to accommodate various language groups. Eighteen official languages—Assamese, Bengali, Gujarati, Hindi, Kannada, Kashmiri, Konkani, Malayalam, Manipuri, Marathi, Nepali, Oriya, Punjabi, Sanskrit, Sindhi, Tamil, Telugu, and Urdu—are recognized in the Indian constitution. Attempts to spread Hindi have met with resentment; don't be surprised to find some Indians willing to speak anything *but* Hindi, particularly in South India and especially in Tamil Nadu. English holds a controversial place as the nation's *lingua franca*, particularly in commerce, an ironic vestige of British imperialism. English is the first language of many upper-class Indians, and millions more learn English in school. It is easy to get around India with English, although this might make it difficult to have more than simple conversations. For basic Hindi, Bengali, Tamil, Marathi, Gujarati, Telugu, Kannada, Malayalam, and Nepali vocabularies, see the **Phrasebook,** p. 807.

Scripts of India

Devanagari भारत is the most common script in South Asia, used for the Hindi, Marathi, Konkani, Rajasthani, and Nepali languages. Devanagari is based on Sanskrit script, as are **Gurmukhi** ਪੰਜਾਬ, used for Punjabi, **Gujarati** ગુજરાત, **Bengali** পশ্চিম বঙ্গ, and **Oriya** ଓଡ଼ିଶା. In the south, Dravidian languages are spoken, and the scripts used look nothing like their Sanskrit-inspired neighbors to the north. **Tamil** தமிழ் நாடு and **Malayalam** കേരളം share similar scripts, as do **Kannada** ಕರ್ನಾಟಕ and **Telugu** ఆంధ్రదేశ్‌ము. **Urdu** script کشمیر, a stylized form of Arabic writing and Pakistan's national language, is used by Muslims throughout India, and is the state language of Kashmir.

■ History

History, religion, and culture have a peculiar way of blending into one another in India; one story can't really be told without the others. Furthermore, writing a non-controversial history of such a place is impossible; lately, Indian's ancient history has become relevant to modern political controversies (see **Hindu Nationalism,** p. 96). What follows is an exceedingly brief account of thousands of years of history; in general we've eschewed the creative interpretations of political parties and glossy tourist brochures for the more standard academic viewpoint.

Pre-History and the Indus Valley Civilization (400,000-1500 BC)

Tools and stone flakes in India date back 200,000 to 400,000 years, pointing to a long history of human activity. The **geography** of the Subcontinent has always made India hospitable for settlement (see p. 74), and mountain passes at the northwest frontier provided an easy point of entry for foreign invaders into the otherwise isolated Subcontinent. The first known civilization in the Indian Subcontinent arose around 2500 BC, and was located in the valley of the Indus River in what is now Pakistan, where it flourished for nearly a thousand years. The two largest archaeological sites from the Indus civilization are at **Harappa** and **Mohenjo-Daro,** but at least 15 other sites are thought to have been parts of this civilization

The cities of the Indus civilization were planned according to rigid patterns that changed little over their 1000-year history. The streets were laid out in grids and accompanied by strikingly well-designed **drainage systems.** Each city also had a large central bath which probably served some ritual function. The Indus dwellers were skilled farmers and had highly developed systems of irrigation, which allowed them to harvest and keep huge stores of wheat and barley. Each city had a population of about 35,000, and much in their civilization appears to have been regimented. Artifacts indicate that the Indus people traded by land and sea with the civilizations on the Nile, Tigris, and Euphrates Rivers. Despite all of this, little is known about this ancient culture; their script, found on numerous **steatite seals,** remains undecipherable. The multitude of seals left behind by the Indus people depict humans, gods, and animals, and they appear to have worshiped a mother-goddess and a deity who may have been a precursor to the Hindu god **Shiva.** Around 1800 BC, the Indus River apparently changed its course, causing catastrophic flooding, spelling chaos for a civilization that had lasted for 1000 years.

The Aryans (1500-300 BC)

As the Indus civilization waned, a new group entered the Subcontinent. The **Aryans** were a nomadic, light-skinned tribal people who came across the northwest frontier, from the Caucasus mountain region in Central Asia, establishing themselves in India around 1500 BC. They were a warlike people who brought with them a technology and culture that changed the course of the civilizations they encountered. The Aryans belonged to different tribes, each of which was ruled by a *raja* (chieftain or king). With their horses and spoke-wheeled chariots, they were able to spread from the Punjab and northern Indus, where they first arrived, across all of northern India.

Their spoken language was **Sanskrit,** a language related to Latin and Greek, and the root of all the North Indian languages (*arya* means "noble one" in Sanskrit). In their religions, they participated in fire-sacrifices, making oblations to various deities. These sacrifices were performed by the *brahmins*, sages of the priestly caste who chanted the hymns of the **Rig Veda,** a collection of Sanskrit hymns composed between 1500 and 900 BC. These were transmitted orally for several centuries until a script was developed and they were finally written down (see **The Vedas,** p. 92).

Along with their language and religion, the Aryans also established a new social order in India. Aryan society was divided into three classes or *varnas:* the priests, warriors, and commoners, also known as *brahmins, kshatriyas,* and *vaishyas.* This is the basis for what later became the **caste system** (see below, p. 90). As they pressed farther on into new territory, they met the indigenous peoples whom they called *dasas*. Taken as slaves by the Aryans, the *dasas* became a servant class known as the *shudras*. These are thought to be the ancestors of South India's Dravidian people and the remaining survivors of the once-great Indus civilization.

The environment of India altered many of the cultural practices of the Aryans. As they moved into the Doab, the fertile plain of the Ganga and Yamuna rivers, their tribes clumped into kingdoms and the people settled in villages. By the time the Aryans reached what is now Bihar around 1000 BC, they had abandoned bronze for iron. They were superb metallurgists, and the discovery of iron allowed them (for better or for worse) to clear the great forests that then covered the region.

The late 9th century BC is thought to have been the age of the great Sanskrit epics, the **Ramayana** and the **Mahabharata.** It is also the age in which the highly philosophical thought expressed in the **Upanishads** was developed as a rethinking of the meaning behind the sacrifice and vision of the Vedic hymns. The *Mahabharata* is the story of two families, the evil Kurus and their just cousins the Pandavas, five brothers who unfairly lose their kingdom to the Kurus in a dice game and then go to war to win it back. Set in an age of lapsing *dharma* and deteriorating world order, the epic was characteristic of the political and religious climate of the time.

The changes wrought by Aryan culture increasingly alienated the peoples in the lands they had conquered. Many thinkers became dissatisfied with the old Brahmanic religion and its corps of elite priests. A new speculative ascetic movement began around the 8th century BC, which led the establishment of ascetic forest communities, the practice of **yoga,** and belief in the doctrines of **karma, rebirth,** and **moksha** (liberation). The Hindu Upanishads were composed at this time, and in the 6th century two new faiths, Jainism and Buddhism, were founded (also see **Religion,** p. 19).

The Mauryas (300-200 BC)

Although communications and trade had improved in North India by the 6th century BC, the land of the Aryans remained divided into 16 major kingdoms. In 326 BC, Alexander the Great showed up at India's northwest frontier intent on conquering India's riches for himself, but his own mutinous troops forced him to turn back. The Greek invasion seems to have provided both the inspiration and the chaos that allowed another conqueror to take control of India. Shortly thereafter, **Chandragupta Maurya,** an adventurer from eastern India, took control of the kingdom of Magadha, the most powerful Aryan state, located in present-day Bihar. Advised by his brilliant minister Chanakya, who had reportedly met with Alexander, Chandragupta proceeded to conquer the rest of India. The Mauryan Empire, and the first forced unification of India, was a *fait accompli*. From their capital at Pataliputra, at the site of modern **Patna** (see p. 450), the Mauryas would rule for 140 years.

The Mauryan government was strictly regimented, and each village was taxed to pay for a huge bureaucracy and army. The Mauryas' military campaigns soon gave them control of all of South Asia, save the southern tip. But at the height of the empire's power its policies were changed as the result of a bloody battle. The Kalinga kingdom in Orissa put up such resistance to the Mauryas that after conquering them, the Mauryan emperor **Ashoka** (r. 269-232 BC) found he'd lost the stomach for war. He renounced violence, became a Buddhist, and ruled by *dharma*, becoming a righteous emperor as well as a pragmatic one. He organized and spread Buddhism throughout India and dispatched missionaries to the rest of Asia. In India, Ashoka also spread a message of unity. Even though the Mauryan empire collapsed after Ashoka's death, the **pillars** he planted and the edicts he inscribed stand as reminders of a mythical unified past.

Trade and the Growth of Buddhism (200 BC-300 AD)

After the fall of the Mauryas around 200 BC, India found itself politically divided once again. Strong powers such as the **Shakas** and **Kushanas** entered from the north, or like the **Andhras,** rose up in the peninsula, but these kingdoms never expanded beyond the regions in which they originated. In spite of political disarray, however, this was a time of cultural ferment. A system of influential craft guilds reflecting the divisions of the caste system advanced Indian technology, and trade became the main cohesive force in India from the 2nd century BC to the 4th century AD. At the southern tip of the peninsula, it ended the isolation of the **Cheras, Pandyas,** and **Cholas,** three Dravidian kingdoms that had never been part of the Mauryan sphere, giving India commercial links to China and the West, where Roman traders paid richly for Indian cloth, spices, wood, and gems.

This period also witnessed the zenith of **Buddhism** in South Asia. Mahayana Buddhism, a sect that placed less emphasis on monastic life and made Buddhism accessible to the layperson, spread after the 2nd century AD. Hinduism, however, was beginning to de-emphasize the old Brahmanic rituals, and a devotional movement called **bhakti,** stressing personal worship of gods like Vishnu and Shiva, emerged. Competing with Buddhism, *bhakti* Hinduism spread in the south and gradually brought back most of India into the Hindu fold. The **Bhagavad Gita,** a hymn containing the essence of Hindu philosophy, was also composed during the *bhakti* reformations, and integrated into the *Mahabharata* (see p. 97).

Buddhism inspired many artistic and intellectual pursuits, hosted by monasteries and paid for by wealthy guilds. **Sculptors** reached new heights of excellence, carving stone images of the Buddha to be used in worship. At the same time, Indian **medicine** and **astronomy** got going with a push from the Greeks, who had settled down on the northwest frontier after Alexander's campaigns. India's **linguistics** and **mathematics** were already far ahead of those in the West, however; a scientific system for Sanskrit grammar had been developed by Panini as early as the 4th century BC, and Indian mathematicians invented the concept of zero as well as the system of numerals called "Arabic" by Europeans who learned of it from Arab merchants.

The Guptas: A Golden Age (300-500)

In 319 another Chandragupta came to power in the eastern kingdom of Magadha. Though he was not related to his namesake, the founder of the Maurya dynasty, **Chandragupta** openly sought to emulate this conqueror and soon launched an empire of his own. From their base in Pataliputra (Patna), Chandragupta and later his son, **Samudragupta,** expanded up and down the Ganga Valley. By the time of its peak under **Chandragupta II** (r. 375-415), the Gupta Empire encompassed present-day North India.

The Guptas get more credit for the cultural refinements of India's "Golden Age" than for their political endeavors, however. The Guptas were great patrons of the arts and sciences, financed by overseas trade and wealthy craft guilds. India's first stone dams and temples were built, and the sculptures of the caves at **Ajanta** were painstakingly carved out of a sheer cliff face in present-day Maharashtra (see p. 649). **Kalidasa,** the greatest classical Sanskrit poet, was a member of Chandragupta II's court.

The most important difference between the Guptas and the Mauryas, however, was their religion. Though they sponsored the activities of all religions, the Guptas themselves were Hindu. They lavished resources on Hindu theological studies—the **six schools** of Hindu philosophy date from around this time—and on the building of Hindu temples. Their law and institutions reflected an adherence to orthodox Hinduism. Social constructs like patriarchy and the caste system became fixed in North India. The Guptas have become something of a prototype for Hindu monarchs ever since (also see **Hinduism,** p. 91).

Although **South India** was outside of the Gupta empire, it was an active participant in Guptan culture. Northern traders and *brahmin* priests had by this point brought the south into the Hindu world, and even though the south remained politically divided, southern kings were mimicking Aryan political structures. This **Aryanization** catalyzed the south rather than stifling it. Distinct South Indian architectural styles emerged, and Tamil poet-saints (the Vaishnava Alvars and Shaiva Nayanars) and thinkers joined the ranks of the holiest Hindus, leading the *bhakti* devotional movement that overtook the North.

Regionalism (500-1192)

The Gupta Empire slowly disintegrated in the 5th century under pressure from **Huns** attacking from Central Asia. North India broke into small kingdoms again, and except for a fleeting half-century from 606 to 647, when the young conqueror and poet-king **Harsha** built an empire from his capital at **Kannauj** in the Ganga plain, North India remained divided for 700 years. The emergence of strong regional identities and a feudal system measuring wealth in land rather than money only added to people's insularity.

The **Rajputs,** a group of warrior clans who probably originated outside of India but claimed the noble status of *kshatriyas* in the Hindu caste system, became the major force in northwest India after the 8th century. The Rajputs set up several small kingdoms from their base in the Rajasthan desert, creating a culture of chivalry with its own literature and architecture. The Rajput clans warred with one another, however, and they never managed to put together an empire. The strongest kingdom in India at this time was the **Chola** dynasty from Tamil Nadu, which conquered most of the southern peninsula and even sent forces to the Maldives, Sri Lanka, and Malaysia. But the Rajputs would have to contend with the most serious foreign challenge of the age: people from the west with new ideas and the potential to change India. The divided nation was ill-equipped to face them.

The Arrival of Islam (1192-1526)

After its founding in the 7th century (see p. 100), **Islam** spread from Arabia right up to Sindh on the western frontier of India. Muslims traded with India by sea, and a few settled down on the west coast, but Islam made few inroads on the Subcontinent during its first 300 years. This changed with the raids of **Mahmud of Ghazni,** the king of a Turkish dynasty in Afghanistan. Between 997 and 1030 Mahmud's armies swarmed in to loot North India on an almost annual basis. Mahmud never settled in India, content to carry its wealth back into the hills.

By the end of the 12th century, another Turko-Afghan king moved in on India. In 1192 **Muhammad of Ghur** conquered the Ganga Valley and defeated a loose coalition of Rajputs. Though he quickly returned to his home in Afghanistan, he left behind his general, the slave **Qutb-ud-din Aibak,** to govern the conquered lands from Delhi (see **Qutb Minar,** p. 137). When Muhammad died in 1206, Qutb-ud-din seceded, proclaiming the birth of the Delhi Sultanate, India's first Muslim kingdom.

The Sultanate ruled most of North India for 300 years, and by the early 15th century, independent Muslim kingdoms had emerged in Bengal, Gujarat, and central India. Still, the Delhi Sultanate's hold on power was always precarious. The palace was in constant turmoil, chewing up five dynasties in three centuries, and the sultans financed their hedonistic court life with taxes paid by Hindus. The people frequently revolted, as did provincial nobles. In another major setback, the city of Delhi was obliterated by the Central Asian conqueror **Timur** in 1398.

The sultans did not assimilate to India as invaders in the past had often done, nor did India assimilate to them. It was far easier for the invaders to conquer a kingdom than to force its subjects to change religions. Most of those who converted were seeking to gain favor with those in power, or were Untouchables who had nothing to lose. Hindus enjoyed the protected status Islam usually only reserved for Christians and Jews; not converting was an option. But the fact that the new faith accepted Untouchables into its fold only tarnished its image in the eyes of most higher-caste Hindus. In parts of India, Hindu monarchs tried to resist the impact of the Muslim sultans. The Hindu **Vijayanagar kingdom** ruled large parts of South India and the Deccan plateau from 1336 to 1565, building temples vigorously. But it was finally defeated by a coalition of Muslim sultanates from the Deccan.

Many movements attempted to mediate between the two faiths. In the Punjab, **Guru Nanak** was attracting adherents to **Sikhism,** a new religion that took from both Hinduism and Islam (see p. 102). In Bengal, Islam became popular among the masses thanks to wandering **Sufi mystics** and saints, whose religion was similar to devotional movements in Hinduism. But religious fragmentation undermined the centralized political authority of the **Lodis,** the last of the Delhi sultanate's dynasties, and led to many regional problems. Provincial governors seceded in Bihar, Portuguese ships landed in Goa, and in central India the one-eyed, one-armed Rajput leader **Rana Sanaga** called for foreign intervention to vanquish the Delhi Sultanate.

The Mughals (1526-1700)

Rana Sanaga's call was heeded by the Central Asian warlord **Babur** (1483-1530). Babur, descended from both Timur and **Genghis Khan,** was endowed with a warrior's pedigree. In his early years, he gave every indication of following in the blood-soaked footsteps of his ancestors, conquering Samarkand at age 13 and Kabul eight years later. But Babur didn't spend all his time fighting, and when he wasn't boozing it up, found time to compose poetry, indulge in gardening, and craft a wistful autobiography. Recounting his attack on the Delhi Sultanate, Babur wrote: "I placed my foot in the stirrup of resolution, and my palms I placed on the reins of confidence in Allah." His words have a way of obscuring the horrors of combat, and the **Battle of Panipat,** fought outside of Delhi in the spring of 1526, was in fact quite gruesome. But the overmatched Babur prevailed, crushing the Lodi dynasty. There was now some doubt as to what Babur would do. Would his armies occupy and rule South Asia or would they be content to plunder the region and return home? The question was settled in 1530 when Babur's son **Humayun** became sick. According to legend, Babur prayed that the sickness which afflicted his son would be transferred to him—within weeks, Babur was buried in Kabul, and Humayun was proclaimed emperor over territories which stretched from Bihar in the east to Kabul in the west. Sporadic raiding had given way to the Mughal dynasty.

Addicted to opium and dependent on the capricious predictions of his astrologers, Emperor Humayun had difficulty leading his ethnically diverse army, and within a decade his troops were grumbling with disloyalty. In 1540, Humayun was unseated by the Afghan warlord **Sher Shah,** who had carved out a kingdom for himself in eastern India. Humayun was driven into the Sindh desert, where he wandered with a dwindling band of followers. Back in Delhi, Sher Shah secured his position, laying the groundwork for a sophisticated administration and fortifying key cities. But disaster struck in 1545, when he was killed during a siege of a Rajput stronghold. Seizing the moment, Humayun acted aggressively, gaining Persian backing and recapturing Delhi. Only months after his glorious triumphs, however, Humayun slipped down his library stairs. Injuries from the fall killed him (see p. 140), and in 1555, **Akbar,** who had been born in the Sindh desert during Humayun's wanderings, became emperor.

Though Akbar was only 13 when he succeeded his father, he quickly proved his military mettle, quashing rebellions and establishing Mughal hegemony with successful campaigns in Rajasthan, Gujarat, Orissa, Kashmir, and Bengal. As Akbar consolidated his empire through battle, he formulated policies rooted in the assumption that the Mughals' long-term future lay in the south, rather than Central Asia. Akbar created a centralized imperial bureaucracy in order to lend Mughal governance an aura of permanence. Moreover, the emperor and his inner circle devised an efficient revenue collection system so that new territories would not need to be conquered in order to keep the existing empire financially solvent. Most importantly, Akbar concluded that for the Mughals to dominate South Asia they could not rely on brute force and repression indefinitely—the Muslim Mughals would need to earn the trust of Hindus. To give Hindu elites a stake in the success of the Mughal regime, Akbar married a Rajput princess and appointed well-educated Hindus to important government posts; to ingratiate himself to the masses, Akbar denounced the destruction of Hindu temples and eliminated the **jizya,** a widely despised tax levied on non-Muslims.

Akbar's policies encouraged Hindus and Muslims to believe that they would be neighbors in South Asia for centuries, and under Akbar's generous patronage, a sensibility marked by the mingling of Hindu and Muslim elements emerged. **North Indian music** began to assimilate Persian influences, and Hindu painters began to experiment with **miniature painting,** a genre favored by the Mughals. Meanwhile, the **Urdu** language, with its Persian vocabulary and Hindi grammatical structure, gained popularity, and Muslims began the practice of making pilgrimages to the tombs of holy figures. Akbar invited Hindus, Jains, Christians, and Zoroastrians to discuss their faiths in his court and eventually attempted to develop a new religion which incorporated ideas from all the major religious systems of the region. While Akbar's religious esperanto did not outlive him, its pluralistic spirit did, and it was during Akbar's reign that North India made peace with itself culturally.

Akbar's successors **Jahangir** (r. 1605-27) and **Shah Jahan** (r. 1628-57) were content to build on Akbar's work, and their reigns were a golden era for the Mughals; the populace was well-fed, the empire's frontiers were relatively secure, and a series of staggeringly beautiful landmarks—the marble **Taj Mahal** (see p. 193) and the sandstone **Red Fort** (see p. 135)—were erected in Agra and Delhi. Troubles, however, began to make themselves felt in 1657, when Shah Jahan fell ill; soon enough, the emperor's sons were at war with each other, fighting over who would succeed him. The bloody familial fighting sapped the Mughals' strength and left the empire in the hands of the uncompromisingly vicious **Aurangzeb,** who had murdered his older brother, Dara Shikoh, during the succession struggle and who ordered Shah Jahan imprisoned, lest his health improve.

For 48 years, Aurangzeb ruled South Asia as the new Mughal emperor. In some respects, Aurangzeb's reign was successful, and his armies were able to conquer massive tracts of fertile land in southern and eastern India. However, Aurangzeb's imperial policies alienated and angered Hindus, sowing the seeds of Mughal collapse. Deeply pious, Aurangzeb zealously rolled back a century of tolerant social policy, making it difficult for Hindus to advance through the civil service bureaucracy, forbidding the repair of Hindu temples, and re-introducing the discriminatory *jizya* (tax). Aurangzeb's short-sighted radicalism lead ordinary Hindus to turn on the Mughals, and by the time the 88-year-old Aurangzeb died, the Mughal empire had frayed irreparably. Over the next half century, the Mughals would rule in name only, as Delhi was sacked and looted by Persians in 1738 and by Afghans in 1757.

As the Mughal Empire's control over northern India slipped away, others sought to step into the vacuum. The Maratha leader **Shivaji Bhonsle** (see p. 641) posed a serious threat to the Mughals during the reign of Aurangzeb, and the **Maratha Confederacy,** comprised of Maharashtrian "nationalists" of different castes, stood the best chance of taking the Mughals' place in the 18th century. The Marathas' hopes were dashed in 1761, however, when they were dealt a decisive defeat outside Delhi by an invading Afghan army. In the wake of the defeat, the Confederacy splintered. With the Marathas unable to fill the *chappals* of the mighty Mughals, the way was cleared for another empire to play a politically dominant role in South Asia.

The Beginnings of British Rule (1700-57)

Lured by the famed riches of the Orient, European ships sailed the oceans throughout the 15th and 16th centuries, meandering across the globe and happening upon the "New World" in the process. India itself, however, did not witness the arrival of substantial numbers of Europeans until the 17th century, when English, Portuguese, Dutch, and French subjects came to South Asia as agents of government-chartered trading companies. With the gradual ebbing of Portuguese sea power, the Netherlands' decision to concentrate commercial energies on the islands of Southeast Asia, and the settlement which ended the Seven Years' War, the **English East India Company** became the dominant firm in South Asia. From its Indian bases in the south and east—two of which would grow into **Calcutta** (see p. 378) and **Madras** (see **Chennai,** p. 465)—the Company engaged in highly profitable trade, exchanging gold and silver for Indian finished goods, especially hand-crafted textiles.

As the Company carved out a commercial niche during the early 18th century, the Mughal Empire declined, and lawlessness became an increasingly serious problem. From the Company's perspective, banditry was especially troubling—it threatened the network of warehouses storing valuable goods. Seeing rich possibilities in the need to defend its warehouses, the Company recruited small Indian armies and equipped them with comparatively powerful European-made weapons. Often hired out to rival Indian factions; these mercenary armies allowed the Company to became a powerful controlling force in Bengal during the mid-18th century. From Bengal, the Company extended its sphere of domination. Led by the iron-willed **Robert Clive,** it aligned itself with a coalition of Muslims and Hindus and, after a series of battles which culminated with the **Battle of Plassey** in 1757, asserted control over vast areas of Eastern India.

East India Company Government (1757-1857)

As land began to pass under its control, the Company began to behave less like a trading firm and more like an imperial overlord. During the 1774-1793 period, when it was led first by **Warren Hastings** and then by **Lord Cornwallis,** the Company was divided into separate political and commercial units and developed a British-dominated bureaucracy to administer to the Indian territory. Increasingly, land became a more valuable source of revenue than commerce. Territory was parceled out by the Company in accord with the **Permanent Settlement of 1793,** which made the Mughal tax collectors, or *zamindars,* the owners of the lands they had administered. The Settlement created an elite class of powerful Indians who provided a buffer between the Company and the native population. The big losers in the new arrangement were the peasants. Working the land they once owned, they generated the revenue needed by *zamindars* to pay off the Company.

In the wake of the Settlement, the Company gobbled up more and more land. By the 1820s, most of India had become for all practical purposes a post of the British Empire. In the face of this emerging reality, a debate ensued in Britain. On one side were the **conservatives,** represented by leaders like Hastings, who believed that India could be exploited economically but ought to be left alone socially, culturally, and religiously. Opposing the old guard was an informal alliance of **evangelicals,** who sought to spread Christianity to an "idolatrous" India and **liberals,** who believed that progress in India was hampered by "irrational" practices. The liberals were led by **James Mill** and his son **John Stuart Mill.** The elder Mill's massive *History of British India,* which became required reading for all East India Company officers, was written after years of reading and absolutely no travel (he never set foot in India); it made a strong case for Indian inferiority and for the British right to be there. As Britain lurched away from conservatism in the 1820s and 1830s, the evangelicals and the liberals, both of whom spoke glowingly of the "civilizing" power of imperialism, won the day. The process of radically transforming Indian life had begun again.

Between the late 1820s and 1857, the Company was guided by two complementary concerns: eliminating practices they deemed immoral and pressing Indian society into a European mold. In accord with these twin concerns, **railways, textile mills,** and **telegraphs** were introduced into South Asia, and **sati,** the Hindu custom by which widows were burned on their husbands' funeral pyres, and **thugi,** ritual robbery and murder practiced by devotees of the goddess **Kali,** were banned. Moreover, the Company sought to transform India both linguistically and culturally—an 1835 resolution committed Company authorities to "the promotion of European literature and science." To facilitate the realization of this imperialist goal, British authorities changed the official state language from **Persian** to **English,** and funded the development of secondary schools, medical colleges, and universities where knowledge was synonymous with Western knowledge and the language of instruction was English. India was administered by men like **Lord Macaulay,** who claimed that "One shelf of a good English library has more worth than native [Indian] literature in its entirety."

As the cultural agenda of British imperialism undermined traditional ways, millions of Indians became alienated from British rule. This alienation gave way to anger under the pressure of severe and persistent poverty. In the face of seething discontent, British officials extended their authority, inventing an absurd legal fiction, the **Doctrine of Lapse,** which allowed the British to annex any Indian kingdom whose ruler died without a direct male heir. By the 1850s, India had become a powderkeg; it would be ignited by a gun.

INDIA

If You Like Europe, You'll Love This!

The British came to India in part to exploit, and in part to bring their own, Western civilization to the East. To that end, they began what has become a long and glorious tradition of comparing parts of India to the glorious Homeland (and other familiar places as well). With their canals, Srinagar and Alleppey became the twin **Venices** of the East, Catholic Goa became India's **Rome,** and the painted ceiling of the St. Aloysius College Chapel in Mangalore became...why, the **Sistine Chapel** of India, of course. Industrial Ahmedabad won hands-down as the **Manchester** of India, but Coimbatore walked away with the regional title: a tourist brochure names it the **Manchester of South India.** The state of Meghalaya and the city of Kodagu, Kerala, are both India's **Scotland,** with nary a kilted, bagpipin' laddie in sight. The tradition of defining India by the West has continued post-Independence, with pre-Mumbai Bombay Californiaizing itself into **Bollywood,** and Bangalore pulling a similar trick as the **Silicon Valley** of India.

The diversity prize goes hands-down to the holy city of Varanasi, as (depending on who you ask) the **Oxford, Canterbury, Athens, Jerusalem,** and **Mecca** of India. Even uncolonized Nepal has joined in the game: a government brochure proclaims that, besides being the Roof of the World, Nepal is also the **Switzerland of the East** and the **Africa of Asia.**

Mutiny and Aftermath (1857-58)

In 1857, the Company introduced a new rifle for use by its 200,000 sepoys (hired Indian soldiers). Called the **Lee-Enfield,** the rifle's ammunition cartridges were rumored to be lubricated with a mixture of pig and cow fat. Hindus (for whom cows are sacred) and Muslims (for whom pigs are impure) were incensed, especially when they learned that soldiers had to bite the tip off the cartridges with their teeth before loading them. What followed in May of 1857 became known as the **Sepoy Rebellion**, as Indian soldiers raised the Mughal flag over Delhi, indiscriminately massacring Europeans as they reclaimed the city. **Lucknow** (see p. 208) also fell under the control of leaders eager to restore the Mughal Empire. Backed by Sikh regiments, British troops returned the bloody favor four months later, recapturing Delhi and murdering vast numbers of Indians in the process. By March of 1858, the **Mutiny of 1857**, or the **War of Independence,** as Indian nationalists prefer to call it, had been finally and fully suppressed.

After the gory events of the revolt, British attitudes changed radically. An 1858 act of the British Parliament eliminated the governing authority of the Company; within a year, the British crown was directly administering India as a full-fledged colony of the **British Empire.** The Raj had begun. To ensure tight control over India, Crown authorities increased the ratio of British to Indian soldiers stationed in South Asia, forbade Indians from becoming officers of the army, and staffed the upper echelons of the burgeoning **Indian Civil Service** with bureaucrats of British birth. Assuming an attitude marked by increasingly explicit racism, the British also withdrew socially and culturally from Indian society, setting up hill stations remote from major Indian population centers and renouncing their quest to systematically introduce "civilizing" Western learning to South Asia.

Crown Rule and Indian Renewal (1858-1915)

With Britain cracking down, a century-long period of religious revitalization reached its invigorating conclusion as Hindu groups such as the mystical **Ramakrishna Mission** and the reform-minded **Arya Samaj** became exceptionally popular. In turn, this new cultural pride made British political rule seem intolerably invasive. Muslims underwent a similar renewal. Prominent leaders like **Sir Sayyid Ahmed Khan** worked to remove the anti-Muslim aftertaste that the Mutiny had left with India's British rulers. Sir Sayyid shared British liberals' contempt for Indian backwardness, and he sought to remedy this through education, founding the British-style college at **Aligarh** which would produce the bumper crop of Muslim intellectuals instrumental in the creation of Pakistan. With their religious beliefs energized, millions of Hindus and Muslims began to take a newly self-conscious pride in Indian culture.

Demanding reforms which would give Indians more control over their country's affairs, a group of 70 wealthy Indians met in Bombay in 1885 to form a political association, the **Indian National Congress.** As it attracted new members over the next 20 years, controversies rent Congress into two camps, each led by *brahmins.* On the one side were the **moderates,** who advocated reform within the context of the British Empire. Opposing them were the **extremists,** who sought to replace British imperialism with homegrown self-government. The views of the extremists rose to the fore after 1905, when the British viceroy, seeking to simplify administration of the empire (but also to create divisions among Indians), partitioned Bengal into two provinces, one with a Hindu majority, the other with a Muslim majority. The anger and resentment felt by millions of Indians was articulated in 1905 by a man who had once led the moderates, President of Congress **Gopal Krishna Gokhale.** "A cruel wrong has been inflicted on our Bengalee brethren," Gokhale proclaimed. "The scheme of partition ... will always stand as a complete illustration of the worst features of the present system of bureaucratic rule." The ground had shifted, and self-rule became the ultimate objective.

In the decade following the partition of Bengal, Indians from a wide variety of backgrounds did what they could to resist British rule. Disaffected Bengali youth read **Bipin Chandra Pal's** radical journal, *Bande Mataram;* other young people became terrorists. Muslims concerned about Hindu domination of Congress founded the **All-India Muslim League** in 1906; the League threw its support to the cause of self-government in 1913. Men and women of all regions, religions, and ages boycotted British-made textiles, opting instead for the grittier, homespun *swadeshi* cloth, which was worn proudly as a symbol of national self-sufficiency.

Indian nationalist leaders cooperated with the British during the **First World War,** hoping that their loyalty in the British Empire's time of need would be rewarded by greater freedoms after the war. Instead, the British introduced more oppressive measures in 1919, suspending civil liberties and placing India under martial law. When a group of unarmed Indians assembled in **Amritsar** for a peaceful protest, 400 of them were massacred by the British Indian army (see **Jallianwala Bagh,** p. 334).

It was against this backdrop of disaffection that **Mohandas Karamchand Gandhi** (later proclaimed Mahatma—"Great Soul"—by Rabindranath Tagore, the Bengali poet) returned to India in 1915. Born into a Gujarati *vaishya* family in 1869, Gandhi had gone to England to study law. After completing his education, Gandhi spent twenty years in South Africa, where he devoted himself to ending the racist discrimination experienced by Indian South Africans and evolved the idea of **satyagraha.** A kind of non-violent resistance defined by Gandhi in his autobiography as "soul force," the ideal of *satyagraha* would lend the Independence movement moral credibility in the world's eyes for the next three decades.

Toward Independence (1915-47)

Supported by Hindus (for whom he was a true Mahatma), by Muslims (who appreciated his support for the crumbling Ottoman Empire), and by common folk (who were swayed when he renounced his fashionable European clothing for the simple cotton garb of the masses), Gandhi enjoyed amazing popularity throughout the 1920s and 1930s. Gandhi's popularity meant that the leadership of Congress was his; in turn, the once-elite Congress was remade under Gandhi's leadership into a mass party supported by millions of ordinary Indians.

Encouraged by Gandhi's Congress party, millions of Indians participated in non-violent civil disobedience throughout the 1920s. In 1930, however, Gandhi's thunder appeared to have been stolen by **Jawaharlal Nehru,** the young leader of the Congress party's radical wing, who had audaciously declared January 26, 1930 **Indian Independence Day.** Unwilling to be outdone by the radicals, Gandhi embarked on his famous **Salt March** seven weeks after Nehru's declaration. Imperial authorities had declared it illegal for salt to be sold or manufactured except under the auspices of the heavily taxed official monopoly. Pointing to imperial salt policies as a symbol of the broadly deleterious effects of British rule, Gandhi and his supporters marched 380 kilometers through present-day Gujarat, from his **Sabarmati Ashram** in Ahmedabad (see p. 685) to the sea, attracting crowds of supporters and media coverage along the way. Staff in hand and clothing fraying, Gandhi reached the coastal town of **Dandi** on April 6. Wading into the water, Gandhi proceeded to make salt by taking a handful of sea-water and pouring it on dry ground, breaking the salt law.

As Gandhi thumbed his nose at their laws, British authorities cracked down. Over 60,000 Indians were arrested in 1930. But the tide could not be turned back, and the British seemed to know it. In 1932, the army began granting commissions to Indian officers; in 1935, the **Government of India Act,** which granted authority over provincial government to elected Indian representatives, was passed.

Meanwhile, tensions between Congress and the Muslim League were becoming intense. In 1940, leaders of Congress charged that the Muslim League had opportunistically taken advantage of dislocations brought on by the war to gain power for itself. Claiming to speak for India's Muslim communities, leaders such as Muhammad Ali Jinnah retorted that aggressively seizing power was necessary, for Muslim rights could not be guaranteed in the independent, Hindu-dominated India which seemed about to materialize. In 1940, the League declared that the Muslims of India were a separate nation and demanded the creation of an independent Muslim state. The state, the League declared, should be named **Pakistan.**

Sapped by the fight against Nazi Germany and, to a lesser extent, the Japan-allied **Indian National Army,** led by **Subhas Chandra Bose** (see p. 394), British authorities concluded soon after the end of World War II that India could no longer be held as a colony. The vicious religious conflicts which bloodied Calcutta, the Punjab, and the Ganga Valley in 1946 made the division of India into two sovereign states—one Hindu-dominated, the other Muslim-dominated—the only reasonable option. Defying geography, Pakistan was carved out of Muslim-majority areas in both east and west India. Bengal and the Punjab were both rent in two. Independence for India (and existence for the state of Pakistan) officially arrived when the vast territory which had been the "jewel in the crown" of the British Empire was **partitioned.** Pakistan sprang into existence on August 14, 1947. India followed suit 24 hours later, at midnight on the 15th. The last British viceroy, **Lord Mountbatten** would stay in India voluntarily to help in the exchange of power, but the British Raj was over. Hours before independence, Nehru addressed the Constituent Assembly in New Delhi: "At the stroke of the midnight hour, when the world sleeps, India will awaken to life and freedom. A moment comes, which comes but rarely in history, when we step from the old to the new, when an age ends, and when the soul of a nation, long suppressed, finds utterance."

After Independence (1947-64)

Midnight struck, and on **August 15** a nation was born with its own set of hopes and problems. As countries were created, so were refugees: millions of Sikhs and Hindus streamed into India while millions of Muslims headed for Pakistan. The simultaneous and massive migration (probably the largest population movement in human history) touched off stampedes and religious violence on a horrific scale, and more than 500,000 people were killed. Five months later, Mahatma Gandhi was assassinated on his way to evening prayers by **Naturam Godse,** a Hindu extremist angered by Gandhi's attempts to appease the Muslim League (see **Raj Ghat,** p. 137).

The first tasks for **Nehru's government**—forging democratic institutions and establishing a workable administrative structure for the newly free nation—did not meet much opposition. It was quickly decided that India would be ruled as a **federation,** with power shared between state authorities and New Delhi-based national authorities; elections would take place at least once every fifth year, and parliament would be divided between a lower house, the **Lok Sabha,** and an upper house, the **Rajya Sabha** (p. 139). In fulfillment of a pledge Congress had made long before independence, Nehru's government passed the **States Reorganization Act** (1956), which redrew India's internal boundaries; the language of local government now reflected the language of local people.

On the economic front, Nehru's India had many difficulties, the most serious of which were massive poverty and the substantial wealth gap between the urban middle classes on the one hand and the nation's village-dwelling farmers on the other. While the socialist Nehru labored heroically to make India a more prosperous nation, embarking on **five year plans** and successfully soliciting foreign aid, phenomenally rapid population growth (literally) ate up most economic gains—neither per-capita productivity nor per-capita income rose as quickly as they might have. The needs of efficient production of wealth often conflicted with the imperatives of fair distribution. An illuminating example is the case of the **Green Revolution,** which began during the early years of Nehru's administration and which brought high-yield crop strains, high-tech farm machinery, and chemical fertilizers to India. While the Green Revolution greatly increased India's grain production, small farmers who could not afford modern agricultural products could not successfully compete with well-off farmers who could. The result was a surge in share-cropping and tenancy and a wave of migration to the cities.

Other difficult problems encountered by Nehru concerned foreign relations. Under Nehru, India struggled to build constructive relations with Pakistan and to develop a feasible policy regarding Kashmir, a sizable area in the Himalaya approximately 400 miles north of New Delhi. Tensions arose at Independence as Kashmir—where 75% of the population was Muslim but the maharaja was Hindu—considered whether it wanted to be a part of India or Pakistan. Border skirmishes with Pakistan led the maharaja to accede to India, with Nehru promising that the people of Kashmir would eventually be able to decide their own fate by voting. A brief, undeclared war between India and Pakistan ended in 1949 with a U.N.-brokered cease-fire. While the war established a *de facto*—though still disputed—border between Pakistani Kashmir and Indian Kashmir, it did not solve difficult underlying problems. Indeed, Indian Kashmir has been the site of terrible violence since 1989. For more information, see **Jammu and Kashmir** (p. 367). Border troubles weren't limited to Pakistan, though. In 1962, a boundary dispute led to war with **China.**

Indira's India (1964-84)

After Nehru died in 1964, he was succeeded by **Lal Bahadur Shastri,** who died of a heart attack after leading India to victory in a defensive war against Pakistan. Shastri was succeeded by Nehru's soft-spoken daughter, **Indira Gandhi** (no relation to the Mahatma—Indira's last name came from her husband, Feroze Gandhi). During the early years of her rule, it became evident that Mrs. Gandhi's soft-spoken demeanor hid a personality of steel. "My father was a saint who strayed into politics," said Mrs. Gandhi, "I am a tough politician." She feuded with the Congress "old guard," eventually splitting the Congress Party into **Congress (I)**—I for Indira—and the remainder of the old Congress, which disappeared by the 1980s. Mrs. Gandhi also began to move India closer to the **USSR.**

In 1971, **East Pakistan** (the future **Bangladesh**) declared independence, and West Pakistan promptly invaded its eastern wing. Millions of refugees fled into India with stories of Pakistani soldiers committing countless atrocities; it also cost India about US$200 million a month to feed the refugees. India began to arm and train Bengali guerrillas, and in December, Pakistani planes attacked Indian airfields. The next day, Indira Gandhi sent the Indian army into both Pakistan and Bangladesh. Less than two weeks later, Pakistan surrendered; the result was the creation of the independent nation of Bangladesh and, with Pakistan defeated, India emerged as South Asia's dominant power.

In large measure because of Mrs. Gandhi's autocratic tendencies (she rarely attended Parliament, surrounded herself with sycophants, and meddled with state governments), the post-war years were troubled ones for India. After the oil crisis of 1973, India was caught in the twin pincers of runaway inflation and worsening poverty, and millions of Indians slipped toward starvation. Economic troubles rapidly gave way to social and political dislocation, as corruption and nepotism became rife.

In 1975, Mrs. Gandhi was found guilty of election fraud. Rather than step down as the law demanded, she declared a **National Emergency,** "suspending" all civil rights. Mrs. Gandhi endowed herself with dictatorial powers and began to govern even more like a tyrant, imposing sterilization on families with more than two children, aggressively censoring the press, using India's intelligence agencies as her own special police force, and having her political opponents jailed. Her son **Sanjay,** leader of the Youth Congress, became the second most powerful figure in India, and Mrs. Gandhi groomed him as her political heir.

Indira Gandhi ended the state of emergency (she called it "disciplined democracy") in January 1977, believing (incredibly) that she would be re-elected legitimately. She wasn't. The **Janata Dal,** an anti-Indira coalition led by **Morarji Desai,** Mrs. Gandhi's former Finance Minister, came to power two months later. Unable to hold his party together, however, Desai quickly faded and Mrs. Gandhi was re-elected to the prime ministership in 1980. During her second term, the nation was plagued with regional problems. In 1984 she ordered the governor of **Kashmir** to dismiss its popular Chief Minister, **Farooq Abdullah**. A month later she ordered the governor of Andhra Pradesh to remove the popular Chief Minister of that state, N.T. Rama Rao, a former film star who was the leader of a non-Congress regional party and thus a threat to Mrs. Gandhi's majority. She also confronted **Sikh militants,** who had launched a campaign of terror in Punjab and Haryana as a way of pressuring India's national government into creating a sovereign Sikh nation. In 1984, when armed militants seized the **Golden Temple** in Amritsar (see p. 330), the holiest site in Sikhism, Mrs. Gandhi decided to loose the army. The temple was stormed with tragic results—thousands of militants died inside the temple, and hundreds of soldiers and civilians were killed during a four-day battle. The worst was yet to come. By storming the temple, Mrs. Gandhi had effectively desecrated it. On October 31, 1984, two of her Sikh bodyguards assassinated Mrs. Gandhi at her home in New Delhi. Her death touched off massive rioting in the capital, and thousands of Sikhs were massacred by gangs of Hindu thugs while the police looked on or looked away. Indira Gandhi's son **Rajiv Gandhi,** a former Indian Airlines pilot, rushed home to Delhi to succeed her as the next ruler in the Nehru family dynasty (the original heir, Sanjay, had unexpectedly died in a plane crash in 1980).

The Last 14 Years

A "sympathy vote" in the elections following Indira's assassination swept Rajiv Gandhi's Congress (I) party to an impressive majority position, with over 400 of the 500 seats in the Lok Sabha. Many Indians had high hopes that Rajiv's administration would bring about the changes India so badly needed. But Rajiv Gandhi's prime ministership began inauspiciously when a gas leak from the Union Carbide chemical plant in December 1984 tragically killed between two and three thousand people in **Bhopal** (see p. 233). Rajiv's government did not succeed in most of its projects. An agreement with Sikh leaders that would have ended the violence in Punjab by giving the Sikhs the city of Chandigarh was shelved by the government at the last minute. Rajiv's free-enterprise, trickle-down economic policies brought in the imported foreign cars and VCRs that the rich craved, but did little for the poor.

Rajiv also had mixed success with foreign policy, softening India's stance towards the USA without moving away from the Soviet Union, but also making substantial mistakes, particularly in the case of **Sri Lanka.** Located only 35km off the coast of southern India, this island nation is inhabited by a Buddhist Sinhalese-speaking majority, who make up about 70% of the population, and a Hindu Tamil minority, who constitute about 15%. Tamils have felt increasingly alienated since 1956 as successive Sri Lankan governments have instituted policies biased towards the Sinhalese. Since the early 1980s, the **Liberation Tigers of Tamil Eelam** have fought a guerrilla war for a separate Tamil nation in the north of Sri Lanka. The Tigers had been surreptitiously armed and trained in India while Mrs. Gandhi was in power, and by the time Rajiv was at the helm, they were a powerful quasi-army. Under the mantle of the **South Asian Association for Regional Cooperation (SAARC)**, which India had started in 1985 to improve relations with its neighbors, Rajiv Gandhi sent Indian troops to Sri Lanka as "peacekeepers." The Sri Lankan government was happy to get its own troops out of the futile conflict, and India hoped that its **Indian Peace Keeping Force** (IPKF) would soon force the Tigers to the bargaining table. The Tigers, betrayed by their former sponsor, doled out a lashing to the unprepared IPKF; by the time it was forced to withdraw its troops, there were 100 Indian soldiers dead for every Tiger killed.

The 1989 elections transferred power to a fragile coalition led by Prime Minister **V.P. Singh** of the Janata Dal, endorsed by a group of parties including the Hindu nationalist **Bharatiya Janata Party (BJP)**. Even as Singh tried to settle the Punjab crisis, the northern state of Jammu and Kashmir soon eclipsed Punjab as India's most troubled region. Muslim militants, alleged by India to have been trained and armed by Pakistan, fought a guerrilla campaign against Indian authorities (for more information, see p. 367). The state capital of Srinagar, once a popular tourist destination, became a war zone. But other problems would be the cause of the Singh government's downfall. Singh supported a federal commission's recommendation that 60% of university admissions and civil service jobs should be reserved for lower castes and former Untouchables. Young high-caste Hindus, frightened at their eroding status under such a system, took to the streets, and a few even publicly immolated themselves in protest. The final blow to Singh's government came when he arrested L.K. Advani, the leader of the BJP, who was trying to rally support for the building of a Hindu temple on a controversial site in **Ayodhya,** Uttar Pradesh (for more information, see below; for the full story, see p. 210). The BJP withdrew its support for Singh, and the government fell. A new government was formed under Prime Minister **Chandra Shekhar,** lasting only a few months.

The elections of 1991 were basically settled when Rajiv Gandhi, campaigning in Tamil Nadu, was assassinated by a Tamil Tiger suicide bomber. Congress (I) returned to power on yet another sympathy vote, led by the veteran **P.V. Narasimha Rao.** An aging disciple of Nehru, seen by the party as a compromise candidate, Rao surprised everyone with his political wiles. A 1991 financial crisis necessitated the initiation of unpopular **economic reforms** that included cutting government spending and opening India to foreign investment.

Late 1991 brought renewed rumblings of the dispute over the Babri Masjid in Ayodhya. In December 1992, with a BJP government ruling the state of Uttar Pradesh where Ayodhya is located, Hindu nationalist leaders called for volunteers to build a temple on Rama's birthplace. From all over India devotees converged on Ayodhya, bricks in hand, and proceeded to tear down the mosque. **Hindu-Muslim violence** erupted across South Asia, especially in major cities like Bombay. Rao's government banned the Hindu nationalist parties, dismissing the government of Uttar Pradesh and three other states ruled by the BJP.

Although the Rao government visibly weakened, it clung to power and continued with its program of economic liberalization. By 1994 the **Hindu nationalists** had made a complete comeback, winning elections in several states. In 1995 the state of Maharashtra, which includes the industrial powerhouse of Bombay, came under the control of a particularly radical Hindu (some would say fascist) nationalist party, the **Shiv Sena.** Problems in Kashmir continued as well, with the government's handling of the insurgency bringing accusations of human rights violations from around the world. In late 1995, as India headed for another election, a **kickback scandal** tarnished a large number of Rao's ministers.

The **BJP** won more seats than any other party in the May 1996 Lok Sabha **elections,** but it still had a minority, and the government it formed fell to a vote of no-confidence two weeks later. Power passed in June to a makeshift coalition of low-caste, populist, and socialist parties called the **United Front,** which chose **H. D. Deve Gowda** as its candidate for prime minister.

In the meantime, **foreign investment** continued to be the major buzz, as money poured (and is still pouring) into India's energy, telecommunications, and transportation industries. Elections were held in the troubled state of **Kashmir** in May and September 1996, and although some voters were coerced into participating by the Indian Army, most voted freely.

■ This Year's News

Since 1996 parliamentary elections, which left no clear majority in power, India has been ruled by a succession of teetering **coalitions.** Early 1998 saw the final collapse of the United Front coalition and the call for unprecedented mid-term parliamentary elections, in hopes that a recasting of the Lok Sabha would yield a more stable government. These elections, held in February and March, did little to defragment the parliament, but the Hindu-Nationalist **Bharatiya Janata Party (BJP)** gained 67 seats and the leadership of the coalition that emerged from the dust of popular decision. The **Congress (I)** party surprised just about everyone by holding its 141 seats, perhaps a testament to its new leadership by the last of the Nehru dynasty, the Italian-born **Sonia Gandhi.** The BJP and new prime minister were relatively quick to make good its calls for Indian nuclear sovereignty, ordering a series of five **nuclear tests** (including a hydrogen bomb) in May. The international fall-out of this bold move will undoubtedly have negative mid-term effects on the Indian economy. More locally, the nuclear explosions (and Pakistan's counter-tests) have inflamed fears of a regional arms race. The disputed state of Kashmir remains at the center of regional tensions; in July and August, Indian and Pakistani troops exchanged **heavy shelling** across the boarder, killing more than 90 soldiers and civilians.

■ Government and Politics

India's **parliamentary system** is borrowed from Britain, but adapted to suit Indian needs. Its **constitution** (written in English, the least regionally divisive language), adopted in 1950, is the world's longest, with 395 articles. The architects of the constitution created a **federal system** that would reflect India's diversity, but they also wanted a strong central government to handle poverty and religious conflicts. The result has been a highly centralized form of federalism.

At the head of India's government are the president, vice president, and a council of ministers, headed by the prime minister. The president, appointed for a five-year term, is essentially a figurehead. The prime minister, chosen by the majority party in the **Lok Sabha,** the lower house, retains the real executive power. The Lok Sabha (House of the People) and the **Rajya Sabha** (Council of States) together make up the Indian parliament. All but two of the Lok Sabha's 545 seats are elected by general suffrage; members of the Rajya Sabha are chosen by state governments. India's **Supreme Court** is remarkably independent, often asserting its right to make bold decisions on controversial issues the government would rather avoid.

The governments of India's 26 states are organized similarly. **Governors,** chosen by the prime minister's cabinet, act as figureheads, while the real power lies with the **chief minister,** the leader of the party in control of state parliaments. Each state also has a legislative assembly, or *Vidhan Sabha*, whose members are elected for a term of up to five years. Although the state governments depend on the national government for financial support, they have jurisdiction over education, agriculture, welfare, and the police. State governments are divided into local administrations, with the **panchayat** or village council at the lowest level. The central government has the power to dismiss state governments in cases of emergency, and this option of **"President's Rule"** has been abused by central governments—most notoriously by Indira Gandhi's—to attack their opponents.

India may be a working democracy, but its government has been dominated by one family since 1947: Jawaharlal Nehru, his daughter Indira Gandhi, and her son Rajiv Gandhi have all been Prime Ministers; Rajiv's brother Sanjay was one of the most powerful men in India, despite never having been elected to any position; and in 1998 Rajiv's widow, the Italian-born Sonia Gandhi assumed leadership of her mother-in-law's party. The Congress (I) party, which grew out of the Congress that led India to independence, has also dominated Indian politics since 1947. Despite the Congress' tradition of inclusiveness, it has had difficulty incorporating all the disparate interests of ideology, caste, region, and religion. As a result, politics have become more and more regionalized, and state governments are often controlled by regional parties like the **DMK** (in Tamil Nadu), the **Communist Party of India** (in Bengal), and the **Akali Dal** (in Punjab). In the 1996 elections, no single party won a majority of seats in the Lok Sabha, so a group of organizations from the political "left," including populist, lower-caste parties such as the Janata Dal, and parties like the Communist Party of India, ruled as a coalition government with the support of Congress (I). Last year's mid-term elections shifted the balance, with the Hindu nationalist **BJP** emerging as the leader of a somewhat-shaky coalition.

Politics in India are often marred by **corruption** (numerous state and national governments have been brought down by corruption scandals), and violence is used in some regions to intimidate voters, but India's democracy does work smoothly on the whole. Given India's low level of literacy, its high voter participation and political consciousness represent major achievements. Voter participation in rural areas and among women has steadily increased since the 1950s.

Indian politics have been increasingly affected by **caste politics,** as lower castes translate their demographic strength into political clout. Also on the rise is the **BJP,** which is growing more popular and less regional (although it still has not fully penetrated South India). In addition, more and more politicians come from agricultural backgrounds rather than being members of the educated elite.

■ Caste

The ancient codes of *dharma* divided Hindu society into four ranks, each having emerged from a different part of the first person, Manu: the *brahmins,* the priestly and scholarly caste, came from his mouth; the *kshatriyas,* the warrior-ruler caste, emerged from his arms; the *vaishyas,* merchants, came from his thighs; and finally the *shudras,* laborers, came from Manu's feet. These four *varnas,* or colors, form the basis of the Hindu caste system. The rules of the caste system mostly concern notions of "substance" and "purity." Any transaction mixes the "essences" of different people and creates "pollution" between members of different castes. *Brahmins* must be exceptionally pure to perform religious ceremonies, so they do not mix with other castes or accept food cooked by non-*brahmins*. The group formerly known as "Untouchables" comprised people so low (usually toilet-cleaners, leather tanners, undertakers, or anyone associated with substances considered unclean or polluted by Hindus) that they were outside of the caste system. Their mere touch was considered polluting to upper-caste Hindus.

In practice, however, the hierarchy of the caste system has never been clear-cut. More socially important than the *varnas* are **jatis,** subdivisions linked by kinship and usually sharing a very specific occupation (farming, pottery, etc.). There are thousands of these *jatis* in India, some very small and peculiar to a few villages, others numbering in the tens of millions and spread across huge regions. Due to various political and sociological events, such as famines, wars, mass conversions and reconversions, many of these *jatis* have split, joined, risen in status, or descended, regardless of the *varna* they belong to. Some regions of India have politically dominant castes, such as the **Jats** in Rajasthan and Punjab and the **Reddis** in Andhra Pradesh, who were originally very low castes.

The Indian constitution (written by a former Untouchable **Dr. B.R. Ambedkar**) and the demands of life in urban areas have gone a long way towards abolishing the caste system. The notion of Untouchability is on the wane; former Untouchables, now known as "Dalits" (the Oppressed), ride on the same buses and play on the same sports teams as *brahmins*. However, in India's villages (where 70% of the population lives), caste is still extremely important and extremely restrictive. While most Hindus will now eat almost any food, regardless of the caste of the person who prepared it, most Hindu marriages still take place within *jatis,* or at least between *jatis* of equal status (even among educated urbanites).

There is no surefire way to tell someone's caste, although after a while in India you'll recognize some common last names and link them to caste. Occupations are also an indicator, but never certain. In recent years affirmative action programs for lower-caste Hindus have come into effect, with a certain number of university spaces and civil service jobs reserved for scheduled castes. The **President of India**, **K.R. Narayanan,** is a Dalit, the first ever to hold that title. Moreover, lower castes (who make up about 66% of India's population) are beginning to exercise their demographic power through politics, although the sheer size makes of the group makes any kind of internal cohesion almost impossible. Internal differentiation has pitted Untouchables against *shudra* OBCs (Other Backward Castes), who are less low-caste. While many lower-caste parties are in power in many states, the only national vaguely lower-caste party is the Janata Party.

■ Economics

India's economy is overwhelmingly **agricultural,** with about 70% of the people earning a living from agriculture. Staple foods like wheat and rice are the major crops. Cash crops such as tea and cotton are important exports. At the same time, India is a technologically advanced nation. Nuclear reactors, satellites, television sets, and oil rigs are all built in India, although such industries have not yet produced top-quality items for international markets.

This situation was brought about by government planning during the 1950s and 60s. A series of **Five Year Plans,** modeled on the Soviet Union, created huge state-owned industries. Private industries were restricted by licensing, and foreign investment was almost nonexistent. The aim was for India to attain self-sufficiency, in the tradition of the *swadeshi* movement (in which Indians boycotted British imports).

A lack of exports, however, meant that India had to borrow in order to buy from abroad, and in 1991 a **financial crisis** almost forced the country to default on its foreign debt. Under pressure from reformers within India and also from the World Bank and the International Monetary Fund, India made dramatic changes in its economic policies, liberalizing its economy to encourage private investment. The government has eliminated licensing and scrapped quotas on imports. As a result, India has seen rapid industrial development in the past few years. Foreign investment has been pouring in, especially in the areas of communication, electricity, and computer technology. The government has been slower to sell off its money-losing public-sector industries however, because doing so would require massive layoffs.

Big economic reforms have done little so far for the vast majority of Indian people. While there is no way to calculate average incomes in a country where so many people live off the land and pay no taxes, poverty is widespread. In addition, although food production has increased dramatically since Independence and there has not been a famine since 1942, about 25-30% of Indians suffer from malnutrition.

■ Religion

HINDUISM

Known to its many practitioners as **Sanatana Dharma** (Eternal Faith), Hinduism is one of the oldest and most versatile of the world's religions, claiming the largest number of followers in Asia. "Hinduism" was the name given to the religion of the people whom **Alexander the Great** called "Hindus," because they lived across the Indus River. Heavily laden with ritual, this blend of mono- and polytheism is somewhat hard to define and difficult to grasp for most Westerners. Hinduism actually comprises a multitude of local and regional religions, and while it would be wrong to say that Hinduism is a uniform faith, it would be equally wrong to say that the many different strains of Hinduism are not integrated in a way that accommodates them all. All Hindus acknowledge the truths set forth in the books of the four **Vedas.** Beyond that, there is a great deal of variation, with Hindus worshiping a number of gods and goddesses in a variety of ways.

There is general agreement that God, or the Absolute **Brahman,** is one, but Hindus also believe that God takes an infinite number of forms. **Shiva, Vishnu,** and **Durga** (the Goddess) receive the most adulation, but there are many others as well, including local deities, some derived from the Vedic hymns of the Aryans, others from long-lost prehistoric nature cults, and others synthesized from both and then reintegrated as aspects of the major gods. Each deity is surrounded by countless myths which invest him or her with a personality, and each area of the Subcontinent has its own local traditions surrounding the deities.

Hindu worship is usually centered on an image of the deity in question. Contrary to appearances, idols are not what is being worshiped; what is seen is the *form* of the deity. This visible form serves to bring the believer's concentrated devotion fully upon the deity; the "seeing" of the god through its image is called **darshan,** during which the god also has the chance to "see" the worshiper. The most common ritual for Hindus is *puja* (worship), in which flowers, sweets, and other foods are offered to the deity. In Devi (Mother Goddess) temples, especially Kali temples, animals are often sacrificed, even though other Hindu sects have strong vegetarian traditions. **Cows,** however, are considered sacred, and no Hindu will kill a cow.

Philosophy

Hindu philosophy is based on the existence of an absolute unchanging and omnipresent reality called **Brahman,** a universal soul or spirit, and **atman,** the self, which is equated with Brahman. The ultimate goal of existence is to unite *atman* with Brahman in the supreme state of bliss. Unfortunately, the individual self is caught in **samsara,** the cycle of birth, death, and rebirth. Seeking detachment does not mean a denial of life and living. Instead, Hindu thought encourages active living, along with non-attachment to the fruits of life's actions. Realization of *atman,* the first step to **liberation,** can be achieved through any of the four ways of living, the *yogas* described in the *Bhagavad Gita:* action, devotion, knowledge, and psychic exercises.

There are four major goals for a Hindu to follow in his or her life. While *dharma* (duty) and *moksha* (release) remain the ultimate goals in life, there is also room for *kama* (sensual enjoyment) and *artha* (wealth). Hindu thought also divides life into four stages in which to seek these goals. The first twenty-five or so years should be devoted solely to knowledge, the second twenty-five to being a householder, fulfilling the duty to raise a family and future generation. The third stage rounds out the householder life and is a preparatory and slow detachment from worldly connections to enter into the fourth ascetic stage, a complete renunciation of one's life.

Time is cyclical in Hindu thought. Periods called *yugas* constitute one breathing cycle in the life of Lord Brahma and last approximately 314 trillion years. Divided into four parts, a *yuga* begins in a golden era of prosperity and devolves until the *kali yuga* when *dharma* declines and the world is destroyed, to be renewed again in the next *yuga.* Unfortunately but not surprisingly, we are said to be near the tail end of a *kali yuga* at the moment.

The Vedas and Upanishads

The earliest existing religious influences in modern Hinduism came from the Vedic religion of the Aryans and from the religion of the Indus Valley Civilization (see **History,** p. 76). The origins of the Vedic religion are found in books known as the **Vedas** (meaning "knowledge" or "what is known"), collections of poetic hymns in Sanskrit composed between 1200 and 200 BC. These oral texts, regarded as unitary, eternal, and without human origin, were somehow intuited by *rishis* (sages) and addressed to different deities. The **Rig Veda,** the largest hymnal, is a collection of 1028 metrical hymns to all the deities revered in 200 BC. The deities in the Vedas are usually counted as 30 or 33 in number and are associated with certain natural phenomena: **Indra** (the most-mentioned god) appears as the hard-drinking god of war; **Varuna** is the sky god and guardian of *rita* (cosmic order); **Agni** is the sacred fire; **Surya** is the sun; **Soma** is the moon, as well as a hallucinogenic drink; and **Vayu** is the wind. Shiva and Vishnu are only mentioned in passing.

The Vedic religion was characterized by the ritual of **fire-sacrifice,** performed to maintain *rita* (a word replaced in later texts by *dharma*): the Vedas were chanted by the *brahmin* priest who also consumed *soma,* which was then offered to the fire. Those who partook of the *soma* were said to attain a "vision" which would make them immortal. The sacrifices enabled each god to continue his function in the cosmos; any lapse in the sacrifice would result in the dissolution of *rita.* In the Vedas, there is also mention of a mystical essence called **Brahman** which pervades, binds, and maintains the cosmic *rita.* Knowledge and perception of this Brahman brought immortality. *Rishis* transmitted their "vision" in the hymns themselves, which, when heard or spoken, could release the power of their eternal truths.

Beginning with the 8th century BC, the **Upanishads** developed over several centuries, reforming and reassessing the Vedic worldview. The fire-sacrifice, which had formerly been so central to the religion, was displaced by an emphasis on salvation through insight and knowledge, reinterpreted in terms of a personal philosophy of *moksha* (liberation), and the doctrines of *karma* and rebirth. The rituals of the Vedas gave way to emphasis on an inner quest for transcendence, and teachings, previously restricted to priests, became more openly transmitted.

Dharma and the Bhagavad Gita

Similar to *rita,* **dharma** has many different meanings. Most commonly, it simply refers to the continual nature, role, and function of everything that persists in the universe. Thus, the words *sanatana dharma* might also be translated as "the way things eternally are," or "the eternal religion." Another example of *dharma* could be described in the image of a river. Why does a river flow downhill? Because that is its role, its nature, its *dharma.* In the same vein, it is the *dharma* of a *kshatriya* king to eat meat, engage in war, offer food and money to *brahmins,* and rule a kingdom. *Dharma*'s meaning also has connotations of duty. *Dharma* extends to the social order in the form of the *Manusmriti,* the **Laws of Manu,** and in texts called **dharmashastras.** Generally there are three orders one should follow: the first is adherence to the eternal or cosmic *dharma* through religious observances; the second is adherence to one's caste *(jati) dharma;* the third is following one's *svadharma,* a personal moral code. Hindu epics often play on themes of conflict between these various duties; at the end of the *Ramayana,* for example, Rama is torn between his duty as a husband and his duty as a king.

One of the most popular and sacred Hindu scriptures, the **Bhagavad Gita,** makes up the sixth chapter of the great Sanskrit epic, the **Mahabharata,** a dialogue between **Krishna,** an *avatar* (incarnation) of Vishnu, and his disciple **Arjuna.** Heading into a great battle, Arjuna sees many friends, teachers, and elders whom he will be forced to fight. He grows despondent and throws down his weapons in refusal. Krishna (Arjuna's chariot-driver) then gives his disciple a lesson on *dharma.* One of the Gita's central philosophies is that of **karma yoga,** the *yoga* (path) of action. Explaining that one should not be attached to the fruits of one's actions, Krishna declares that He alone is the doer and sustainer of all activity. He tells Arjuna to fulfill his *dharma* as a *kshatriya* (a member of the warrior caste) and fight, allowing himself to be an instrument of the Supreme power and not "the doer."

Gods and Goddesses

No one really knows exactly how many gods and goddesses the Hindu pantheon holds; some put the number at 333 million. From the central trinity of Brahma, Vishnu, and Shiva, many gods and goddesses emerge, each embodying an attribute of the eternal soul. The popularity of all these deities varies from North to South, village to village, and family to family. The largest distinction lies between Vaishnava (worshipers of Vishnu) and Shaiva (worshipers of Shiva) devotees. Strangely unbefitting his role as creator of the human world, **Brahma** is rarely worshiped, and only a single temple in **Pushkar** (see p. 262) is dedicated to him.

One of the most popular gods, especially in the South, **Shiva** is at once terrifying and compassionate. In the Hindu trinity he has the role of destroyer, and he is most commonly depicted as an uncouth ascetic who wears live cobras and leopard skins, wields a trident, rides his bull Nandi, and lives atop Mount Kailasha in the Himalaya with his consort, Parvati, and their two sons, Ganesh and the six-headed Kartikeya (known as Murugan in Tamil Nadu). Yet Shiva also represents the creative and spiritual energy of the universe, and he is worshiped through his *linga,* a simple stone (phallus-shaped) shaft which symbolizes his creative power. Twelve temples around India are sanctified *jyotirlingas* (*lingas* of light) where Shiva, also known as **Mahadev** (Great God), is said to have burst from the earth. He takes on many forms, including **Ardhinarishwara** (half-male, half-female), **Rudra** (the Howler), and **Nataraja** (the Lord of Dance), whose movements, said to have inspired the cosmos, also possess the power to destroy it. Most **sadhus,** Hindu ascetics, are devotees of Shiva.

Vishnu reclines upon a many-headed snake afloat on a sea of milk. As preserver of the cosmos, he has repeatedly stepped in to save the universe from calamity, usually in the form of his ten *avatars,* three of which are very well known. Incarnation number seven is **Rama,** the hero of the *Ramayana.* Rama, a popular deity in North India and the focus of the Ayodhya controversy, represents the ideal son, husband, father, and leader. Vishnu's eighth incarnation is **Krishna,** the focus himself of many myths and a large following. Krishna is both the playful cowherd who cavorts with milkmaids and the philosophical charioteer who sang out the *Bhagavad Gita* in the *Mahabharata;* he is also depicted in households as a fat little baby stealing butter. Vishnu's ninth incarnation is the **Buddha.** The idea that the Enlightened One is an incarnation of Vishnu is obviously disregarded by Buddhists, but it was probably evolved by early proselytizing Hindus in attempts to win them back.

The Ramayana

Arguably the most culturally influential work of literature in India, the *Ramayana* (ra-MAI-yahn) has inspired thousands of dances, paintings, shadow puppet shows, inter-religious riots, and even its own TV mini-series. It is believed that this Hindu epic was written about 500 BC by the sage Valmiki, and is probably based on events that took place between 1000 and 700 BC. Here is a brief synopsis:

The beloved Lord Rama, crown prince of Kosala, was the paragon of beauty, strength, and intelligence. Demonstrating his puissance by breaking a divine bow, Rama won the hand of the beautiful princess Sita. Palace intrigue thrived, however, as Rama's father Dasaratha was tricked by one of his wives into naming *her* son, Bharatha, heir to the throne. Rama, Sita, and Rama's brother Lakshmana were banished to the forest for 14 years. The broken, sorrowful Dasaratha soon died and Bharatha sought out Rama, begging him to return to the throne. Rama refused, claiming that he had a duty to obey his father and king.

Soon enough, the wicked and wily demon Ravana began to eye Sita. Tricking Rama and Lakshmana into leaving her alone, Ravana abducted Sita to his island kingdom of Lanka, where he attempted to win her over. Though temporarily at a loss, Rama and Lakshmana allied with the clever and loyal monkey Hanuman, son of the wind god. Together, they helped the monkey king Sugriva regain his usurped throne. In return, Sugriva sent an army of monkeys and bears to fight against Lanka. As the monkeys formed a simian bridge across the straits, Hanuman led the assault. The terrifying celestial battle culminated with Rama slaying Ravana.

By this time, the period of exile had elapsed, and Rama triumphantly returned to claim his throne, which Bharatha gladly handed over. The capital, Ayodhya, erupted in celebration upon the revelation that Rama was an *avatar* (incarnation) of Vishnu. However, some suspicious subjects questioned Sita's fidelity during her time with Ravana. Subordinating his trust and love of Sita to his princely duty to his people, Rama subjected Sita to a fire ordeal, from which she emerged unscathed and vindicated. Yet rumors persisted, and Rama was forced to banish the then-pregnant Sita to the forest, where she met Valmiki and related her tale. Both Rama and Sita are revered as archetypes of those who staunchly follow their *dharma* (duty or fate) without batting an eyelash.

Besides Shiva and Vishnu, many Hindus worship female deities referred to in general as **Devi** (the Goddess). The many goddesses are recognized as aspects of *shakti,* a single female principle that is the dynamic force behind the universe. The Goddess cult probably predates worship of male gods, although specific goddesses have joined the now-male-dominated pantheon as consorts. **Kali,** however, remains a force to be reckoned with. Although considered a consort of Shiva, she is an independent goddess of destruction in her own right. Her skin is black, her red tongue lolls, she wears a garland of skulls, and she resides in cremation grounds, but she is still worshiped as a "mother goddess." The all-powerful **Durga** was created from the combined power of all of the male deities when none of the male gods could destroy the demon Mahisha. Durga went forth on her tiger, clutching weapons in each of her ten hands, and emerged victorious. One of the most popular festivals in India is **Navratri** (part of Dusshera, which takes place in September), nine nights dedicated to Durga. The other major goddesses are largely benevolent. **Parvati,** Shiva's wife, makes Shiva's power accessible to humans. **Lakshmi,** Vishnu's consort, is the goddess of material and spiritual wealth and luck.

As the remover of obstacles, the elephant-headed god **Ganesh** (also known as Ganapati) is very popular in India and Nepal, and all Hindus come to him at some time or another. Thought to be particularly clever, he can pose obstacles or remove them, and he is often positioned at doorways and gateways. Ganesh's vehicle is a rat, and his huge, fat form is often depicted squashing his poor rodent carrier. Right after his birth, his mother Parvati told him to guard her bathing spot. When Shiva came along and tried to approach his wife, he was stopped by a boy he did not recognize as his son, and in a blind fury, he chopped off the boy's head. When Parvati learned of the incident, she demanded that Ganesh be resurrected, and Shiva replaced the boy's head with the head of the next creature he saw—an elephant.

Hanuman is another lesser deity with a huge popular following. The monkey-god was the faithful servant of Rama in his quest to rescue Sita from Ravana. He is adored for his absolute loyalty; in one story, he tears open his furry chest to reveal the word "Rama" etched millions of times in tiny script across his heart. His shrines are painted orange or red, and recently, Hanuman has been co-opted by the BJP as part of their campaign to milk the *Ramayana* for anything remotely Hindu-Nationalistic.

Bhakti

Of all forms of Hinduism, the most popular today derive from a tradition known as *bhakti.* The *bhakti* movements, which began around the 11th century, were spread by popular poet-saints and characterized by ecstatic religious devotion as a way of realizing the divine. It is said that a true *bhakta* desires not to merge and become one with God, but rather to remain a devotee forever, always praising God. Rebelling against religious orthodoxy and intolerance, *bhakti* worship is filled with songs sung in local dialects and messages delivered to everyone, regardless of caste. One of the most important leaders of the *bhakti* movement in South India was **Ramanuja,** who established the **Sri-Vaishnava** sect. In North India, **Chaitanya** increased the following of Krishna, who is most often worshiped through *bhakti* devotion. Other prominent *bhakti* figures throughout India were **Mirabai, Sur Das, Tukaram,** and **Eknath.** A great devotional figure for both Hindus and Muslims was **Kabir** (1440-1518). Born a Muslim weaver in Varanasi, Kabir spread a message of unity between faiths, insisting that Rama and Allah were the same God.

Modern Hinduism

In the 19th century, Hinduism was reinterpreted by many thinkers, including British and Christian missionaries, who wanted to make it more systematic and "rational." The **Brahmo Samaj,** a group founded by **Ram Mohan Roy** in Bengal in 1828, did away with image-worship and instead held Christian-style services with readings from the *Upanishads.* Another movement, the **Arya Samaj,** also abandoned caste and images, preaching that the Vedas were sufficient for everything in life. A great figure in the 19th-century Hindu revival was **Sri Ramakrishna** (1836-1886), whose message

Swastikas

Visitors to India with memories of the Second World War (inherited or otherwise) may be shocked to see the profusion of swastikas painted on walls and windshields or worked into the architecture. Swastikas go a long way back in South Asia, however, and *swastika* is actually a Sanskrit word, meaning "it is well." The cross with bent arms was a widespread symbol of good luck and power in the ancient world, used by ancient Greeks, Mesopotamians, Chinese, early Christians, Mayans, and Navajos among others. The ancient Indo-Aryans also used the swastika, and it remains one of the most cherished symbols of Hindus, Jains, and Buddhists. The swastika is associated with good luck and the removal of obstacles. With arms pointing clockwise, it is an auspicious solar symbol, since it seems to mimic the sun's path from east to south to west across the sky. The counter-clockwise swastika, however, is a symbol of night, and is considered inauspicious. The Hindu swastika may have originated from a wheel, or from the firesticks in Vedic sacrifices, which were lain on the ground in the form of a cross.

of religious unity left an indelible impression upon modern Hindu thought. Ramakrishna proclaimed the unity of all religions, claiming that the best religion for any person was the one in which they were raised. Describing God as a well, he suggested that each religion was a different path to the well; each found the same substance inside it. A disciple of Ramakrishna, **Swami Vivekananda** (1863-1902) introduced Hinduism and Ramakrishna's philosophy to the West during the World Parliament of Religions at the University of Chicago in 1893. He declared the existence of God in all, and he encouraged self-reliance and a faith in the Self, spreading the lessons of the Vedanta and centuries of Hindu philosophy to a world-wide audience. Proclaiming that God was within, he extended his philosophy to a national level, inspiring Indian patriotism and a belief in the nation's indomitable spirit.

Sri Aurobindo was another reformer and Indian nationalist who, after being imprisoned for sedition by the British in 1908, underwent a series of mystical experiences while practicing yoga in prison. He abandoned his political activities and devoted his life to achieving "Supramental Consciousness" on earth, becoming one of the most prolific writers of poetry and Hindu philosophy in the 20th century. His activities were continued by his associate "The Mother," a French woman "**Mirra Alfassa**, who came to him to assist him in his work. Sri Aurobindo spent the rest of his life in seclusion in Pondicherry, where his ashram remains today (see p. 495).

Hindu Nationalism

The 19th-century Hindu reform movements went hand in hand with a popular desire to revive Indian society by reverting to traditional Hindu values. This sentiment became highly nationalistic in opposition to the British, who viewed Hinduism as an impediment to progress, and also in opposition to the Muslims, whom the Hindu nationalists saw as Hindu turncoats refusing to acknowledge their "true" identity. The freedom fighter **V.D. Savarkar** developed a rallying philosophy for this movement called **Hindutva,** which asserted that all Indians, regardless of religion, must profess a certain "Hinduness" out of loyalty to the nation's primordial culture. The **Rashtriya Swayamsevak Sangh** (National Volunteer Corps), something between a scout club and a paramilitary group founded in Nagpur in 1925, took up this ideology in its quest for a spiritual and cultural regeneration of India. The movement gathered steam until 1948, when a former RSS member, **Nathuram Godse**, assassinated Mahatma Gandhi because of Gandhi's generosity to Muslims. Although many prominent Indians supported Hindu Nationalist political parties through the 50s, 60s, and 70s, the memory of the Mahatma's murder prevented any significant electoral successes.

In 1977, some Hindu nationalists managed to join the short-lived Janata Party coalition government. After it collapsed they founded the **Bharatiya Janata Party (BJP)** in 1980, led by **L.K. Advani**. They have since rocketed from two seats in parliament in 1984 to over 160 in the 1996 elections, more seats than any other party. For two brief weeks, they even formed a minority government before it fell to a no-confidence vote. As a mainstream party, they have had to moderate their most hard-line policies; today the BJP advocates only a cultural nationalism based on Hindu traditions, and they even wheel out a few Muslim members for publicity's sake. But the party maintains strong ties to other radical Hindu organizations like the RSS and the **Vishwa Hindu Parishad (VHP),** which led the campaign to destroy the Babri Masjid in Ayodhya, Uttar Pradesh, in 1992. Not incidentally, the BJP controlled the UP state government at the time, and Advani had essentially begun the recent Ayodhya controversy in 1990 by riding to the temple in a golden chariot, pushed by his followers, intent on destroying the mosque and erecting a temple to Rama. The BJP's following consists mainly of upper-caste North Indian urbanites (especially civil servants and soldiers), but their following in the south and among lower-caste groups is increasing. Their increasing influence threatens to revolutionize India's largely secular politics as well as the generally apolitical nature of Hinduism. Another party, the **Shiv Sena,** led by Bal Thackeray, is a quasi-fascist, Hindu nationalist party based in Maharashtra; the Shiv Sena now controls the state government of Maharashtra, playing a large part in changing the name of Bombay to Mumbai (see p. 620).

JAINISM

Jainism began as a rejection of Brahmanical authority in the 6th century BC, around the same time as the birth of Buddhism. Its founder **Vardhamana,** known as **Mahavira** (Great Hero), was a follower of the ascetic saint **Parshavanatha,** who had lived about 200 years earlier. Mahavira abandoned his hedonistic lifestyle in favor of nudity, chastity, and asceticism, and established a new sect called the **Jains** (from *jina,* "conquerer"). He is venerated as the 24th in a line of **tirthankaras** (crossing-makers) the Jain equivalent to gods (Parshavanatha is the 23rd).

At the center of Jainism is the principle of **jiva,** the belief that all life is sacred and every living being (whether human or animal or plant or insect) possesses an immortal soul. Out of their respect for life, Jains developed the principle of **ahimsa** (non-violence). So as not to harm any animals, Jains practice strict vegetarianism. The most orthodox Jain monks wear a net over their mouths and nostrils to prevent the possibility of killing an insect that might fly in, and walk with a broom, sweeping the path before them so as not to crush any crawling creatures. The occupation of agriculture was avoided, for to pull a plough through the soil would be to murder millions of tiny creatures. As a result, the Jain lay community concentrated on commerce. Liberation from the entanglement of the *karmic* cycle can be achieved when one gives up contact with all matter. This translates into strict ascetic practices, including chastity, renunciation of property, and even nudity. As with most religious orders, the Jains divided into sects—the **Digambara** (Sky-Clad) and the **Shvetambara** (White-Clad). Of these two, the Digambaras have the more austere observances, shunning all material possessions, including clothing.

Ornate Jain temples are found throughout India, but are primarily seen in Western India, in Gujarat and along the west coast. The two most famous sites are at **Palitana** in Gujarat and **Sravanabelagola** in Karnataka (p. 583). Today, there are an estimated four to five million Jains living in India, mostly in Gujarat.

BUDDHISM

In spite of its origins in the Ganga Valley, only traces of Buddhism remain in India today. **Siddhartha Gautama,** who would come to be called the Buddha (Enlightened One), was born around 560 BC in Lumbini, just within the modern borders of Nepal (see p. 784). Gautama was a *kshatriya* prince who stood out the moment he was born from his mother's side (literally—the bouncing baby Buddha-to-be emerged from between his mother's ribs). An astrologer prophesied that Siddhartha would either become a *chakravartin* (universal monarch) or a *buddha* (awakened one). In response, his father prevented young Siddhartha from experiencing the life of a normal man and lavished him with all sorts of comforts in the hope that Siddhartha would appreciate his royal life-style all the more. One day, however, Siddhartha convinced his charioteer to take him around the outside world. On his four outings, he saw a very sick man, a very old man, a corpse, and finally a mendicant. Siddhartha Gautama, unsatisfied with the explanations of worldly suffering given by Hinduism and suddenly taken with the life and attitude of the mendicant, fled his plush life as a prince, leaving behind his wife, child, and kingdom at the age of 29. He wandered around the forests of India as an **ascetic,** joining a band of other ascetics, starving himself, meditating, and practicing other austerities until he was almost a skeleton. He realized that neither abundant wealth nor punishing asceticism were emotionally or philosophically satisfying, and, despite the contempt of the other ascetics, he chose a middle path. He sat and meditated under a **bodhi** tree in Bodh Gaya, Bihar (see p. 456), achieving **nirvana** (enlightenment) and resisting the temptations offered to him by the demon **Mara.** He set off to preach his discoveries about escaping the suffering of the world by overcoming desire, giving his first sermon in a deer park in **Sarnath** (see p. 225), in what has become known as the first turning of the wheel of Buddhist *dharma* or teachings (Buddhist have a somewhat different meaning attached to *dharma* than do Hindus).

The Buddha advocated total detachment from the world. Desires arising for physical and mental things, he said, bring suffering, because they cause one to believe in a self and an individual existence, which are impermanent and fleeting illusions. One's goal should be the end of suffering through the end of desires, thus attaining a state of *nirvana* in which the flame of the self is blown out. At some point on the path to *nirvana,* even the desire for *nirvana* must be abandoned. The Buddha named right understanding, thought, speech, action, livelihood, effort, mindfulness, and concentration (the **Eightfold Path**) as the way to *nirvana.* He rejected all of Hinduism's gods and rituals, but preserved Hinduism's doctrine of *karma* and rebirth, although he rejected the concept of an enduring soul—like a candle flame which lights another candle, an individual's actions give rise to other actions and reactions, but the second candle's flame is not the same flame as that of the first candle, just as the second individual (or soul) is not the same as the first. The Buddha also preached against a caste system, and, as part of the Noble Eightfold Path, Buddhists also became adamant advocates of **ahisma** (non-violence).

This path of abandoning desires and worldly life seemed to put Buddhism out of the reach of most people, however, and the first Buddhists banded together in monastic communities. Lay people supported and contributed to these communities although they did not observe the central tenet of renouncing the world; their practices were more devotional and reverential so that they would gain merit in order to be reborn in a more favorable position for attaining *nirvana.* The Buddhist *dharma,* however, was responsible for the conversion of the Mauryan emperor **Ashoka** in the 3rd century BC, and his state patronage (along with the many edicts regarding proper Buddhist practice he put up on pillars throughout his empire) helped to make Buddhism a mass religion in India and later throughout Asia. Although Buddhism died out in India in the first century AD, about 7 million Buddhist are left in India, mostly at the fringes of the Hindu world in Ladakh and Sikkim, where Buddhism never let go, and in places that have experienced a huge influx of Tibetan refugees, like Dharamsala, the headquarters of the Dalai Lama, the spiritual and political leader of Tibetan Buddhists (for more information on **Tibetan Buddhism,** see p. 711). In 1956, the leader of the Hindu Untouchables, Dr. B.R. Ambedkar, publicly converted to Buddhism as a political protest against caste discrimination; he was followed by another 200,000 Untouchables (mainly in Maharashtra). Though Buddhism is not as widespread as Hinduism and Islam are, sites like Sarnath and Bodh Gaya still attract millions of Buddhist pilgrims from all over the Asia.

CHRISTIANITY

Since Independence, Christianity has become increasingly visible in India, drawing both adherents and political power at a pace so rapid that the **Apostle Thomas** would surely be pleased. In the apocryphal *Acts of the Apostles According to Thomas,* Thomas was chosen to spread the Gospel to India. While he initially disliked the

The Infant Jesus

He's a seven-year-old blue-eyed curly blond-haired boy, clad in European royal garments, and brandishing an orb and scepter. He bestows blessings on all who honor him, and his name is pronounced from the pages of local newspapers and in stickers on the back of auto-rickshaws. He's the Infant Jesus, image of the saviour of the world and an interesting example of the sort of religious syncretism which has typified India throughout its history. The Infant Jesus Church in southeast Bangalore, Karnataka, is a standard Catholic compound, with a meeting-hall sanctuary and daily masses in Tamil, Kannada, and English, where priests and rectors teach the Christian gospel to the faithful and the curious.

Next door to the church, though, is the blue-domed Infant Jesus Shrine, the young saviour does *darshan* with Hindu devotees, who drape garlands of flowers over the statue. They aren't praying, as a Christian would, to Christ in general—offerings and supplications are specifically to the Infant Jesus. Although the priests in charge of the church make efforts to highlight the distinction between the Catholic and Hindu views of images and idols, this difference is lost on or (more likely) ignored by the majority of the Infant Jesus' Hindu devotees.

idea of undertaking so long a trip, Thomas is said to have arrived on the coast of Kerala in 52AD, where he was able to attract some converts. Legend holds that twenty years after his arrival in Kerala, Thomas was killed in Tamil Nadu, his body buried in Mylapore, a suburb of modern Chennai (see p. 478).

Since Thomas, ships carrying missionaries have sailed across the Arabian Sea with some frequency, seeding India's west coast with Christian ideas and values. In the 6th century AD, the **Syrian Church** dispatched missionaries to India, introducing Syrian customs—many of which are still alive—to South Asia. In the 16th century, the Portuguese sought to systematically spread Christianity to India, converting without compunction. Soon after the arrival of the Jesuit Saint Francis Xavier in 1542, Portuguese-ruled Goa became a hotbed of **Catholicism** (see **Goa**, p. 652). During the early years of the East India Company, Protestant Christian missionary work was actively discouraged, lest a gospel of love and service get in the way of Company profit and ruling practices. The latter years of British rule were marked by an increase in missionary work which concentrated on building hospitals and schools. Grand churches were built as well, but these were mainly to serve the spiritual needs of the increasingly withdrawn ruling British.

In the post-colonial period, the diffusion of Christianity in India has been marked by the growth of local, indigenous churches rather than foreign missionary efforts. There are about 25 million Christians in today's India, 50% more than there were in 1970. Most of India's Christians are Protestant; the largest denominations are the Church of South India and the Church of North India, both members of the worldwide Anglican church. There are also sizable Catholic populations in several regions of India, particularly in Goa and the South. Christian worship in India varies from individual congregation to congregation. Even among grass-roots churches, there is a definite (and not unwelcome) influence of British and American Christianity. But Indian Christianity, even in missionary-founded churches, is distinctly Indian—Christians sing devotional songs similar to Hindu *bhajans* and Muslim *qawwalis,* and go to religious retreats at Christian ashrams in the hills.

ZOROASTRIANISM

Founded in Persia between 500 BC and 700 BC by Zarathustra (also known as Zoroaster), **Zoroastrianism** understands the world as starkly divided between pure good (represented by the god **Ahura Mazda**) and pure evil (represented by the god **Angra Mainyu** and his evil minions, *daevas*). According to Zoroastrian belief, Saoshyant, an immaculately conceived messiah, will one day establish Ahura Mazda's reign of goodness on the earth. Zoroastrians believe that burial and cremation are a pollution of the earth, fire, and air, each of which is sacred for its purity; they leave their dead atop specially-designed Towers of Silence, where vultures have easy access.

Zoroastrianism was first brought to India in the middle of the 10th century, when Persian Zoroastrians arrived on the Gujarati coast, fleeing the persecution and dislocation which accompanied the advance of Islam through Iran and Central Asia. Called **Parsis** because of their ancient roots in Persia, today's dwindling numbers of Indian Zoroastrians—about 95,000 are left—are concentrated in western India, especially Bombay. Though few in number, the Parsis are known for their great wealth. One Parsi family, the Tatas, are renowned throughout India for their manufacturing industries (including India's first steel mill, built in 1908) and for their early financial support for India's independence movement.

ISLAM

Approximately 11% of India's population is Muslim, which amounts to about 100 million people, giving India the fourth-largest number of Muslims in the world after Indonesia, Bangladesh, and Pakistan. In fact, India has more Muslims than any two Arab countries put together, and Islam has had a strong influence on Indian culture. Muslims are spread throughout India, forming distinct communities in places like Hyderabad, Lucknow, Kerala, and of course, Kashmir. The questions surrounding their political, religious, and cultural status are the most emotionally charged issues for many Indians today.

History

Islam was founded by the **Prophet Muhammad,** who lived in Mecca (in what is now Saudi Arabia) during the 7th century AD. Between 610 and 622, Muhammad received revelations from the angel Gabriel concerning the true nature of God. His monotheistic teachings incurred the wrath of the **Quaraish,** and he and his followers were driven from Mecca in 622; the **Hijra** (flight) to Medina marks the start of the Muslim calendar. The people of Medina embraced the new faith, and after building up an army, Muhammad returned in triumph to Mecca in 630 and established. After Muhammad's death, the Muslims conquered Arabia and adjacent lands, and by 711 Islam had spread from Spain to Sindh (in eastern Pakistan).

In 661, the community split in a dispute over leadership. A group who followed Muhammad's son-in-law Ali, who was killed trying to maintain his authority as fourth caliph, became known as the **Shi'is.** They recognized only Ali's descendants as legitimate religious leaders, while **Sunnis** accepted the authority of any caliph who was well-versed in the religion and could command obedience. Today, Sunnis comprise the majority of Muslims in India and in the rest of the Muslim world, except in Iran.

Islam trickled into India through Arabian traders, Sufi mystics from Persia, and the armies of Mahmud of Ghazni. Islam's full effect was felt after 1192, however, under the **Delhi Sultanate** and then the **Mughal Empire,** and India was ruled by Muslims for over 500 years (see **The Arrival of Islam,** p. 79). A few Hindus converted to Islam in order to join the new elite, and some low-caste Hindus converted to escape the caste system, but the majority of the population remained Hindu. Large-scale conversion took place only on the eastern and western frontiers of South Asia; these areas became Pakistan and Bangladesh upon Independence, when Muslims suddenly became conscious of their minority status in a new and massively Hindu nation. Before departing in 1947, the British carved out the nation of **Pakistan,** a Muslim nation, with one wing on the west and one wing on the east of India. Millions of people suddenly found themselves on the "wrong" side of the **Partition** line, and millions died in the ensuing migrations in both directions across the border (see p. 85). However, a sizable minority of Muslims also remained in India.

Beliefs

All Muslims believe in one supreme god, **Allah,** and worship him by way of the five "pillars" of Islam: declaration of one's faith ("there is no God but God and Muhammad is his prophet"); praying five times daily; giving alms *(zakat)* to the poor; fasting dur-

Of Mosques and Minarets

Whenever you travel in India, you're bound to encounter a *masjid* (mosque) or two, and whether it's the ruins of the Quwwat-al-Islam mosque in Delhi—the oldest surviving Islamic building in India—or a modern terro-concrete affair, every *masjid* adheres to a simple design. Because the entire congregation will assemble at the mosque during Friday prayers, as well as at other times, there needs to be a courtyard large enough to hold them. While praying, Muslims face towards Mecca (west of India), so the western wall, known as the *qibla,* is often elaborately decorated. A niche in the *qibla,* the *mihrab,* indicates the presence of Allah, and sometimes a light is hung in the niche to represent the Prophet Muhammad. The *minbar,* a kind of raised pulpit, typically with a small staircase attached, may be positioned at the front of the room where everyone can see it. During the Friday service, the *imam* will climb up on the minbar and deliver a sermon. Finally, rising into the sky are the mosque's minarets. Traditionally, a *muezzin* would climb these towers to call the faithful to prayer. Today, loudspeakers attached somewhere on the spire do the job.

ing the month of Ramadan; and making the *haj* (pilgrimage to Mecca) at least once in a lifetime, barring physical or financial hardship. Some Muslims also consider *jihad,* or holy war, a pillar of Islam. A single holy book, the **Qur'an,** is central to Islam and is considered to be the direct word of God as recorded by the prophet. Second in authority after the Qur'an is the **Hadith**, an assemblage of the words and deeds of Muhammad himself.

Friday is the Muslim holy day, when a special prayer is given at the mosque. The ninth month of the Muslim calendar marks the celebration of **Ramadan,** a holiday commemorating the Prophet's receipt of the holy Qur'an from God, during which all Muslims (with the exception of the very young and the very sick) abstain from food and drink during daylight hours. **Muharram** memorializes the death of the Prophet's grandson and is of particular importance to Shi'i Muslims, who observe Muharram with twelve days of singing and prayer.

Indian Islam

Islam considers all humans equal and strongly prohibits any discrimination on the basis of race, but Indianized Islam has, to some extent, succumbed to its own, less rigid version of the caste system. Many Muslim women stay secluded in their homes according to the custom of *purdah,* and after centuries of Muslim rule, this practice has spread among groups of Hindu women as well. Muslims are required by the Qur'an to avoid alcohol, pork, and shellfish; Muslims do, however, eat beef, as long as the cow has been slaughtered according to religious prescription and is thus considered *halal.* At noon on Fridays, men gather for communal prayers at the *masjid;* women usually pray at home. Many Indian Muslims also speak Urdu which, although it uses a Persian script, is linguistically very similar to Hindi.

While the Arab practice of Islam is often seen as being marked by austerity, Indian Islam is much more devotionally and aesthetically oriented, and it has had an influential impact on Indian culture. While orthodox Islam frowns upon the notion of worship, Indian Muslims have a tradition of *pir* (saint) worship, and both Muslims and Hindus make pilgrimages to *pir* shrines to pray for worldly things like children, good grades, and safe passage. Art and architecture flourished under the Mughals, who often ignored the Islamic injunction against painting human figures. Sufi mystics were responsible for the introduction of the **qawwali,** a melancholy devotional song somewhat like the Hindu *bhajan,* and the **ghazal,** another poetic song developed by Persian Muslims in India.

Muslims and Hindus have coexisted in a tense sort of peace for most of their time together, and the problems between them have been no worse than those between other religious faiths. The Mughal Emperor Akbar even tried to bridge the two faiths. Recently, however, **Hindu-Muslim tensions** have flared as Hindu nationalists grow ever popular claiming that India is a fundamentally Hindu country, and unfriendly India-Pakistan relations have aggravated India's Hindu-Muslim domestic relations. In recent years the Mughal legacy of temple-breaking has been flung back at Muslims. The **Babri Masjid** in Ayodhya (see p. 210) has already been destroyed by Hindu nationalists. Meanwhile the riots and massacres that began with the 1947 Partition continue to be Hindus' and Muslims' main way of airing their grievances.

SIKHISM

Guru Nanak (1469-1539), a philosopher-poet born into a *kshatriya* Hindu family in what is today eastern Pakistan, is the venerated founder of Sikhism. After traveling to Mecca, Bengal, and many places in between, Nanak proclaimed a religious faith which brought together elements of Hinduism and Islam: he rejected image-worship just as Islam did, borrowed Hinduism's use of music in worship, and rejected Islam's reliance on a holy book. He also rejected caste distinctions, sex discrimination, and ancestor worship, but he never actually attacked Hinduism or Islam. Nanak proclaimed that the one God was Truth **(Sat),** and he asserted that liberation from *samsara*, the Hindu cycle of life, death, and rebirth, was possible for those who embraced God, known to people through **gurus.** Nanak contended that bathing, donating alms to charity, and, most importantly, meditating, would erode hubris and would clear the way for individuals to accept God's truth.

After Nanak's death in 1539, spiritual leadership over his *sikhs* (disciples) passed to another guru, **Angad.** Guru Angad wrote his and Guru Nanak's hymns in a new script, called **Gurumukhi** (*gurmukh* means "God"), which is still the written script of the Punjabi language. After Angad's death, guru succeeded guru, each adding new tenets to Sikhism. The third guru, **Amar Das** (1509-74), encouraged Sikhs to worship publicly in temples called **gurudwaras;** the fifth guru, **Arjun Dev** (1563-1606), collected more than 5000 of the previous gurus' hymns into a book called the **Adi Granth** and founded the magnificent **Golden Temple** at Amritsar (see p. 330). After Guru Arjun was executed by the Mughal Emperor Jahangir, an extended period of Mughal repression and Mughal-Sikh fighting ensued. By the time the tenth and final guru, Gobind Singh, was assassinated in 1708, raids and skirmishes had become a sad fact of life throughout Punjab, the Siwalik Hills, and other parts of northern India in which large concentrations of Sikhs made their homes.

Under the leadership of the tenth guru, **Guru Gobind Singh** (1666-1708), Sikhism underwent a series of radical changes which gave the faith a more cohesive identity. These changes and the military tradition they imbibed were an attempt to defend Sikhs against persecution suffered at the hands of the ruling Mughals. In 1699, Gobind Singh founded the Khalsa Brotherhood. Sikh men now had to undergo a kind of "baptism," pledge not to smoke tobacco, not to eat *halal* meat, not to have sexual relations with Muslim women, and to renounce their caste names; men took the name **Singh** (Lion) and women took the name **Kaur** (Princess). Moreover, the Khalsa demanded that its members adopt and never go without the **five kakkars:** *kangah* (wooden comb), *kirpan* (sword), *kara* (steel bracelet), *kachch* (short knickers), and *kesh* (uncut hair). Gobind Singh added new hymns to the Adi Granth, re-named it the **Guru Granth Sahib,** and announced that the book was to stand in as the next guru. Since Gobind Singh's death, the Guru Granth Sahib has been Sikhism's spiritual guide and holy book, and Sikhs have become a visible minority, identifiable by the turbans they use to wrap up their uncut hair.

Although Sikhs have a strong military tradition (the British labeled them one of the "Martial races," and there are a disproportionate number of Sikhs in the Indian Army), they also have an equally strong traditions of egalitarianism, hospitality, and community service *(seva).* There are no priests in the Sikh religion, nor are there fixed service times, although congregations often meet in the morning or evenings, and always on the eleventh day of each lunar month, and on the first day of the year. Sikh services include *kirtan,* hymn singing, when verses from the Adi Granth are sung to rhythmic clapping. Following services, Sikhs gather for a communal meal, where all sit at the same level and eat the same food cooked in the *gurudwara's langar* (kitchen). Strong believers in hospitality and kindness, Sikhs offer shelter and food to anyone who comes to their *gurudwaras.*

Since Independence, Sikhism has also been a rallying cry for Punjabi communalism, and even a struggle for an independent Sikh homeland (for more information, see p. 320).

■ The Arts

VISUAL ARTS

India has a very old and rich artistic tradition, fed over the millennia by contact with other civilizations, but which remains distinctly Indian. Indian artists have commonly made their works conform to some ideal, rather than show their subjects naturalistically. There are very few individual portraits in Indian art, and temples were often built in the same style regardless of whether wood or stone was used. The idealism of Indian art comes partly from its religious function—for hundreds of years, most art was used to decorate sacred buildings or to illustrate sacred stories.

Architecture

Because they used wood and brick as building materials, little is known about the architecture of the ancient Indians. The ruins of the Indus Valley Civilization (c. 2500-1800 BC) found in Pakistan consist of functional buildings arranged in planned cities. However, almost nothing remains from this time until the Maurya period (c. 324-184 BC), when builders began to make sparing use of stone. They built fortified cities and monasteries, but the most lasting structures of this time are *stupas,* huge hemispherical mounds of earth that usually contained Buddhist relics. *Stupas* can be elaborately decorated, with the mound sitting atop a terrace and surrounded by stone railings, and often capped by a stone parasol. The **Great Stupa at Sanchi** in Madhya Pradesh (built in the first century BC) is the most famous of these structures (see p. 238).

The next few centuries saw the development of the temple in India, a momentous event for architecture. Early temples (Hindu, Jain, and Buddhist) were still built of wood, but in western India some were carved into the rock of the Western Ghats. These Buddhist **cave-temples,** or *chaityas,* usually had a projecting apse that led to a long, pillared hall, at the end of which was placed a sacred object. The greatest of the cave-temples is found at **Ajanta** in Maharashtra (see p. 649). Cave-monasteries, with each cell hewn into the rock, were also carved at this time. Although these buildings were made of stone, they still imitated wooden forms. A change came around the 4th century AD, with the resurgence of Hinduism and the rise of the Gupta Empire.

The original medieval **Hindu temples** consisted only of a small, dark, square sanctum called the *garbhagriha* (womb chamber), which housed the deity. Soon a tall pyramidal spire, or *shikhara,* was added, symbolizing a connection between heaven and earth. Temples gradually became more and more elaborate, with other buildings acting as gateways for the worshiper. In typical **North Indian style,** a series of up to four rooms leads to the sanctum in a straight line. Each of these outer rooms has its own *shikhara,* growing taller and taller up to the *shikhara* of the sanctum. This row of spires resembles a mountain range, symbolizing the Himalayan peaks inhabited by the gods. Unfortunately, many of the greatest North Indian medieval temples were destroyed by Islamic invaders and rulers from the 12th century onwards, but excellent examples remain in **Orissa** (see p. 434) and in **Khajuraho,** Madhya Pradesh (see p. 249). In **South India,** the temple sanctum was expanded to a larger room and surrounded by four rectangular entrance towers, or *gopurams,* which had *shikharas* of their own topped by barrel-vaults. These *gopurams* eventually became so exaggerated that they dwarfed the central *shikhara.* They marked a sacred area all around, creating great temple-city complexes such as those of **Madurai** (see p. 511) and **Srirangam** (see p. 510) in Tamil Nadu.

The conquest of India by Muslim forces in the 12th century brought the Islamic styles of Persia and Central Asia to India. Since Islam discourages crafting images of human or divine figures, Muslim rulers were glad to put their efforts into architecture, filling India with gorgeous domes, arches, geometric patterns, and calligraphic inscriptions. The most striking monuments to the early years of this Muslim conquest were Delhi's **Quwwat al-Islam Mosque** (see p. 141) and **Qutb Minar** (see p. 137), which were built starting in 1199, using the remains of more than 20 Hindu and Jain temples. The most successful mix of Indian Hindu and Muslim architecture occurred in Gujarat, with the construction of such buildings as the **Jami Masjid** at Ahmedabad (see p. 685). Indian Islamic architecture reached its zenith under the patronage of the Mughal emperors. The pink and red post-and-lintel buildings of **Fatehpur Sikri** in Uttar Pradesh (see p. 198), built between 1569 and 1589, are a testament to the elegance of Mughal architecture. The Mughals also built one of the grandest monuments in the world: Agra's **Taj Mahal,** a white marble mausoleum adorned with calligraphy, studded with turquoise, jade, and coral, and surrounded by gardens laid out in the Persian charbagh style (see p. 193).

With the decline of the Mughals and the coming of European imperial control, Western architectural forms began to appear in India. The 16th-century Portuguese filled their colony in **Goa** with Baroque frills and ripples (see p. 661). In the 19th century the British imported their Neoclassical style to the metropolises of Calcutta, Madras (now Chennai), and Bombay (now Mumbai), where it became fashionable among Indians as well. The British also built in neo-Gothic and neo-Saracenic styles, giving these huge cities a number of massive monuments, such as the **Victoria Memorial** in Calcutta (p. 392). The two great architectural projects of the 20th century in India, the construction of **New Delhi** in the 1920s (see p. 139) and **Chandigarh** (see p. 321) in the 1950s, have both been foreign attempts to find a kind of modern architecture that would suit India.

Sculpture

No museum in India would be complete without a large room containing heaps of poorly labeled sculptures, all of considerable importance to India's artistic traditions.

The peoples of the Indus Valley Civilization created many simple terra-cotta figurines and steatite seals with pictures of animals. As with architecture, however, there is a gap in the history of Indian sculpture until the 3rd century, BC, when the Mauryan emperor **Ashoka** planted stone columns all over India as a symbol of his rule (see **History,** p. 77). Many of these columns were topped with gorgeous sculptures of animals, the greatest of which is probably the **Lion Capitol** found at **Sarnath** in Uttar Pradesh (see p. 225). With its four fierce lions sitting back-to-back on a lotus platform, the sculpture has become one of India's national emblems and appears on all Indian currency. Burnished to a shiny texture, the animals of the Mauryan capitols, which show some Persian influence but which also bear the marks of an emerging Indian artistic style, are naturalistic and muscular, representing the strength of Ashoka's political power.

The first and 2nd centuries BC saw the rise of two-dimensional **bas-relief sculpture,** which appeared frequently on the railings of *stupas,* telling stories from the life of the Buddha or myths about popular gods and goddesses. The Great Stupa at Sanchi in Madhya Pradesh, featuring figures full of energy, emotion, and incredible detail, represents the best of these works. Three-dimensional sculpture continued during this period too. Several great sculptures of *yakshas* and *yakshis* (popular nature deities) were created during the first and 2nd century BC. The beginnings of Indian classical sculpture arrived in the first century AD when artists in **Mathura** (Uttar Pradesh) began to carve images of the Buddha (see p. 200). Unlike the earlier relief sculptures, which were primarily educational, these were sacred images used in worship, a purpose reflected by their strong, sensuous forms. At the same time, in the Punjab (mainly in areas now belonging to Pakistan), the **Gandhara** school of art developed. Strongly influenced by Greek and Roman art, Gandhara artists turned out strikingly naturalistic images of the Buddha, showing intricate folds of clothing and other details. Gandharan art looks like nothing else in Indian art, but it gradually evolved to resemble more idealized forms.

During the Gupta period (4th-6th centuries AD) the sculptural school that began at Mathura reached its full flowering. Spreading throughout North India, the basic form of the Buddha image was adapted for Hindu gods with multiple pairs of arms. The Buddha-figures of this time appear to look inward, toward spiritual contemplation, and they have a more delicate appearance than the Mathura Buddhas. Distinct regional styles spun off from the Mathura style, producing great successes at **Sarnath** (Uttar Pradesh) and in the cave-temples of **Ajanta** (see p. 649) and **Elephanta** (see p. 633) in Maharashtra.

Two separate schools of sculpture emerged during the **medieval period.** In North India, the sensuous and voluminous style gave way to a more elegant and rhythmic look, with more profuse decorations. This style reached its apex around the 10th century, when it was used to adorn the exteriors of the great North Indian medieval temples. In **South India,** a different style of stone sculpture produced the great 7th-century bas-reliefs of **Mahabalipuram** (see p. 483), and the many small, light sculptures used to decorate temples in Tamil Nadu in the 9th century. **Bronze sculpture** in South India also reached a peak during the 9th and 10th centuries. The image of Shiva as Nataraja (King of the Dance) surrounded by a ring of fire is one of South India's greatest contributions to Indian art. Examples of this image are to be found throughout Tamil Nadu, but the best is probably the one still used in worship at the **Brihadishwara Temple** in **Thanjavur** (see p. 503).

Regional traditions also developed at this time in other areas such as Maharashtra, where large, stocky figures were created, conforming to the properties of their material; the best of these are to be found at the **Kailasa Temple** in **Ellora** (see p. 648). Eventually, the emergence of Muslim dynasties whose leaders' religion prohibited the creation of such images, led to a gradual decline in the production of sculpture in the twelfth century.

Painting

The art of painting has ancient roots in India, but due to the humid climate few examples have survived. The only early paintings that remain are those that were sheltered by rock, such as the **wall-paintings** at **Ajanta** in Maharashtra, dating from the 2nd century BC to the 5th century AD (see p. 649). These early paintings are similar to the relief sculpture of the time. In eastern India, miniature paintings on palm leafs were common, though few of these still exist.

The style of Indian painting best known today began in western India during the medieval period. Colorful, cluttered scenes with figures shown in profile were made to illustrate **Jain manuscripts.** The western Indian style gradually spread throughout India and was used for all sorts of religious painting.

The Delhi Sultans and the Mughal Emperors, who began to arrive after the 12th century, brought with them a taste for Persian art and radically changed the course of Indian painting. **Emperor Akbar** (r. 1556-1605), a great patron of the arts, supervised his painters closely while they produced beautiful miniature illustrations for written histories, myths, and fables. Akbar was almost single-handedly responsible for creating the Mughal school of painting. Among other works, his court artists illuminated a magnificent Persian edition of the *Mahabharata,* which is now kept in the City Palace at Jaipur. As the Mughals settled in India, they often disregarded the Islamic injunction against the artistic representation of human form, and during the reign of **Jahangir** (1605-27), artistic emphasis shifted to portraiture, and fewer illustrated books were made. Though not as energetic as the paintings of Akbar's reign, the images of Jahangir's reign are often deeply insightful.

The cool, delicate Mughal style influenced Hindu painting as well. Under the patronage of Hindu Rajput kings in the 16th and 17th centuries, the **Rajasthani School** emerged, combining the abstract forms of the western Indian style with some of the naturalism of the Mughal art. Rajput paintings usually depicted religious subjects, especially myths about Krishna, cavorting with his *gopis* or pining for his number-one maiden Radha.

Both the Mughal and Rajasthani styles had declined by the 18th and 19th centuries, when European art became a major influence. The first Indian attempts to copy European styles, known collectively as the **Company School,** were lifeless engravings and watercolors. In the late 19th and early 20th centuries, however, artists of the Calcutta-based **Bengal School,** led by Rabindranath Tagore, combined older Indian styles with a touch of modern Western art. In the 20th century a few painters such as Jamini Roy and M. F. Hussain have been quite successful at mixing eastern and western influences like this. Indian painting has now become prominent in museums and galleries worldwide.

MUSIC

In the Indian tradition, music is largely considered a spiritual activity. Rather than the musical notes familiar to Westerners, Indian music employs *swaras* differentiated to the most minute frequencies of sound the human ear is capable of discerning. Each *swara* is considered a door behind which stands a god: if the performer, through his or her expression, fulfills the pure dimension of that sound (possible only through devotional surrender), the door will open and the god will appear, blessing both performer and audience with ecstasy and insight. The refined ability to intone minute divisions of sound is considered a mark of spiritual enlightenment.

Modern Indian classical music, divisible between the northern **Hindustani** and the southern **Carnatic** styles, traces its origins to ancient chants. Musical form gained full exposition in the *Bharata-Natyashastra,* considered the textual source of contemporary music. Classical music styles were also introduced by Persians and Turks, whose courts entertained musicians from around the Perso-Arabic world, presenting the song styles of *qawwali, khayal,* and lilting *ghazals.*

Indian classical compositions are based on **ragas** (melodic forms) which combine with specific **talas** (rhythmic cycles). Thousands of *ragas* exist, each associated with a particular moment of the day or season of the year. *Ragas* differ from one another according to the scale each employs (there are full-octave, six-note, and five-note *ragas*), and the *rasa* (mood) the composition explores. Each of the 72 parent scales has rules governing its use, but by permutations, combinations, and subtle changes, thousands of *ragas* are possible. Once the conditions of a *raga* are established and a set of given rules fixed, the artist is free to create and improvise as he or she likes, exploring the *raga*'s potential to be created anew with each performance. Likewise, while the rhythmic cycle of the *tala* repeats itself, between fixed beats there are opportunities for improvisation. *Raga* and *tala* interact expressively with one another, with intonation and inflection converging through regular and off-beat emphases of time. As a creative play, the *raga* unfolds with complexity and subtlety, yet remains as precise and accurate as a computer.

Indian classical musicians have gained a worldwide following. **Ravi Shankar,** who introduced Indian music to western ears in the 1960s and attracted the attention of the Beatles, continues to play the *sitar,* a fretted, 20-stringed instrument with a long teakwood neck fixed to a seasoned gourd. **Ali Akbar Khan** has achieved global acclaim for his enrapturing agility on the *sarod,* a fretless stringed instrument similar to a sitar). **Allah Rakha** and his son, **Zakir Hussain,** mesmerize with their virtuosity on the *tabla,* a two-piece drum capable of producing many tones.

Folk music is linked closely to folk dance and varies from region to region. From Punjabi *bhangra* to Rajasthani *langa,* folk tunes remain close to the hearts and ears of Indians, gaining an even larger audience through the recent international releases of **Ila Arun** and *bhangra*-rap artists in the U.K. A unique genre of Bengali music is *Rabindrasangit,* the poetic words of Rabindranath Tagore set to quasi-classical song.

Popular music ranges from the "filmi" love songs of **Lata Mangeshkar** to the disco-hybrid-pop of divas Made in India to the techno-*bhangra* and *bhangra*-rap played in clubs and blasted from bachelor-filled cars all over India. Subjects run the gamut from the patriotic to the chaotic, from the ecstatic to the erotic, and always make for fantastic sing-alongs. Like their voiceless on-screen counterparts, movie singers are elevated to hallowed ground. Popular singers include the playful and prolific **Kishore Kumar,** whose versatile voice has filled in the melodic blanks for countless actors.

DANCE

The cosmic dance of Nataraja, King of the Dance, reaches into every sphere of human activity in India. Born of particular regions and interwoven with music, India's numerous dance forms, including both classical and folk styles, evolved as acts of worship, dramatizing myths and legends. Technique and philosophy, passed down from gurus to students, have carried the "visual poetry" described in the *Natya Shastra* (dating between the 2nd century BC and the 2nd century AD), into modern times. **Bharat natyam,** the classical dance form which is considered India's most ancient, originated in the temples of Tamil Nadu. It is an intricate, fluid combination of eye movements, facial expressions, exacting hand gestures, and strong, rhythmic, ankle-bell-enhanced steps. The art was originally studied as a form of worship and performed by *devadasis,* women who lived in temples and devoted their lives to the temple's deity. *Bharat natyam* now receives international appreciation. **Kathak,** first performed by *nautch* (dancing courtesans) against the opulent backdrop of North India's Mughal courts, employs dizzying speed and intricacy of footwork and hand gestures. **Kathakali,** an elaborately costumed form of dance-drama unique to Kerala, invents and presents local and mythological stories of heroes, lovers, gods, and battles. Developed from a rigorous system of yoga, the dancers, all male, must study for a minimum of 15 years. A typical study regimen includes strenuous exercise and massage to increase the arch and flexibility of the spine (see p. 557). **Kuchipudi,** a decorative dramatic dance form originated in southern Andhra Pradesh as a means of worshiping Vishnu and Krishna. The old prohibitions against female dancers have since disappeared, and women have come to master the form. **Odissi,** a devotional dance form originating in Orissa, is both lyrical and sensuous. Regional folk dances are also incredibly popular in India, performed at numerous festivals and private celebrations. Folk dancing has become quite common in contemporary India, and most colleges have a folk dance troupe. **Bhangra,** a Punjabi dance, is one of the most popular and is traditionally performed by males dancing with large sticks in a circle while being accompanied by powerful drumming.

LITERATURE

The oldest known Indian literature is the writings of the Aryans, who brought Sanskrit with them to India around 1500 BC. Since the Aryans did not invent a writing system until about 800 BC, many of their tales were transmitted orally, changing from generation to generation. A remarkable exception is found in the **Vedas,** sacred hymns composed about 1400 BC, which were ritually memorized and passed down without a flaw. During the last millennium BC, the greatest of the early Sanskrit stories, the **Mahabharata** and the **Ramayana,** were composed. These epics form an important part of the common cultural discourse; almost every Indian, from the *dhaba-wallah* to the prime minister, knows the stories. The *Mahabharata* (see p. 93), the story of the five Pandava brothers' victory over their treacherous cousins, also encompasses the *Bhagavad Gita*, the divine song with which Krishna heartened the warrior Arjuna. The *Ramayana* (see p. 94) is probably the single best-known story in India; it was even turned into a TV mini-series. Ubiquitously acted out in *Ram lila* pageants, it tells the story of Lord Rama's victory over the Demon King Ravana, and his rescue of his wife Sita from Ravana's clutches. The Ramayana is essentially a morality tale, and millions of Indian men and women look to Rama and Sita as model upholders of *dharma*.

Ancient India also had a secular Sanskrit literary tradition which reached its climax in the work of **Kalidasa,** who probably lived in the 4th century AD. Kalidasa's play *Shakuntala,* about a young girl who becomes the lover of **King Dushyanta,** who, typical male that he is, forgets her when he loses the ring she gave him, has had a tremendous effect on Indian literature.

While Sanskrit flourished in the North, the Tamil-speakers in the South developed their own literature. Anthologies of poetry were collected at great *sangams*—gatherings of bards—beginning in the first century BC, and by the 6th century AD, the

Tamil literary tradition had produced two epics of its own, *Shilappadigaram* and *Manimegalai.*

Muslim dynasties, who consolidated their hold over India in the 13th century, brought the next major infusion of literary influence. The Indian-born Sufi poet **Amir Khusrau** (1253-1325), nicknamed *Tuti-i-Hindi* ("Parrot of India"), wrote the first great Indian literature in the **Persian language.** Indians began to use Persian as both a literary medium and a *lingua franca.* Amir Khusrau also wrote extensively in Hindi, beginning the fusion of Hindu and Muslim traditions. The broad-minded Mughal emperor Akbar was a great patron of literature; his reign produced **Tulsidas,** author of the *Ramcharitmanas,* the Hindi version of the *Ramayana,* which is considered a masterpiece in its language. The **Urdu** language (and its literature of *ghazal* poems) also emerged from the Hindu-Muslim synthesis.

The British invasion cast its greatest intellectual spell on Bengal, where English-language schools prepared Bengalis for service in the East India Company while exposing them to the influence of Western authors like Shakespeare and Milton at the same time. Bankim Chandra Chatterjee combined the European novelistic genre with heady Indian patriotism in *Anandamath* ("The Abbey of Bliss," 1865). The **Bengali Renaissance** also produced **Rabindranath Tagore,** the greatest Indian artistic figure of the 20th century, whose poems, novels, songs and plays captured the Bengali spirit. Tagore's English version of his sublime book *Gitanjali* won him the Nobel prize for literature in 1913, making him the first non-European to receive the honor.

British writers in India during the colonial period left a body of work that makes for a fascinatingly ambiguous memoir of the Raj. The "Bard of the Empire," **Rudyard Kipling,** was born in India and returned there after completing school. The author was responsible for a great deal of *sahib* literature. *Kim* tells the perceptive story of a half-white, half-Indian boy growing up in India. **E.M. Forster** presents a far more conflicted view of colonialism, famously depicting the tragedy of cultural misunderstanding in his novel *A Passage to India* (1924).

The most prominent trends in 20th-century Indian literature have been a shift toward humanistic concerns, a wider use of prose, and the adoption of the English language. Among the most influential writers of the early 20th century was **Mulk Raj Anand,** whose small but powerful novels *Untouchable* (1935) and *Coolie* (1936) railed against the cruelty of the caste system and economic exploitation. The South Indian novelist **R.K. Narayan,** perhaps India's greatest English-language writer of the second half of the 20th century, has become well-known in India and worldwide for such books as *The Man-Eater of Malgudi* (1961) and *The Vendor of Sweets* (1967). Proudly distinct literatures written in the various regional languages of India have also thrived in the 20th century. Indian novelists are increasingly breaking into the contemporary literary scene. The only thread that holds them together as a literary "movement," however, is the fact that many of them live outside India and all of them write in English. **Salman Rushdie**'s masterpiece *Midnight's Children,* written in 1980, set the stage for the world's new interest in "Post-colonial" literature. The famously (and understandably) reclusive Rushdie may be the most well-known contemporary Indian author, but a number of other writers, such as Vikram Seth, Anita Desai, Rohinton Mistry, Vikram Chandra, Kiran Desai, Gita Mehta, Amitav Ghosh, and, most recently of all, Arundhati Roy, are becoming more and more familiar to an international audience.

FILM

She rises from the oasis of green, trim lawns of an Elysian garden, dotted in fuschia and rose. She sings a melodious love song while her curvaceous hips swing energetically to the accompanying beat, all with an air of utterly effortless insouciance. He hears her loving croon and holds her in a passionate embrace against his leather-clad body. Their bliss is interrupted by his drug-smuggling twin brother, separated from him at birth and sent by her society-minded parents to break their love asunder. A brief yet boisterous scuffle ensues, and our hero emerges unscathed to return to the rudely-interrupted embrace. The sun sets on the suddenly mountainous backdrop.

This mythical utopia of otherwise unattainable romance, chivalry, and kitsch is available to the common man in the form of **masala movies.**

Named after the eclectic spice mixture, these popular films contain a piquant pick 'n' mix combination of action, violence, comedy, romance, music, and a dash of the ridiculously impossible. The urban landscape is dominated by various marks of the cinematic genre—strident colors, dramatic gestures, and more than a hint of eroticism. Indian pop music, in the form of **filmi** songs, commands the radio waves. A vast array of film magazines trade on scandal, sex-talk, and, of course, vicious innuendo. Cinemas run regularly at noon, 3, 6, and 9pm to accommodate an average daily audience of 7.5 million. The educated elite may sneer at these puerile "formula" films, but India churns out close to a thousand feature films a year in 23 languages. **Bollywood,** the nickname for the largest movie industry in the world, is based in Mumbai, while the thriving South Indian film industry is based in Chennai.

It all began in 1912, when Dadasaheb Phalke produced the first Indian feature film, *Raja Harishchandra.* The story, drawn from an episode in the ancient *Mahabharata* epic, inaugurated the distinctly Indian genre of film known as the "mythological," which remained a staple of Indian cinema into the 1950s. Sound first invaded the frames in 1931 with *Alam Ara,* directed by **Ardeshir Irani.** The first of the "talkies" was received with thunderous ovations, but the advent of sound technology fragmented audiences into disparate language groups, and subtitles in multiple languages had to be introduced to accommodate them. Hindi, followed by Tamil, emerged as the language with the widest base. Most importantly, sound meant song for Indian cinema. Filmmakers saw song as a way of overcoming the linguistic splintering and tapping into built-in emotional responses to traditional music. The songs became the main attraction of a film and critical to its success. *Indra Sabha* (1932) included nearly 70 songs and the first two decades of talkie film were entirely dominated by "singing stars." The musical numbers were often embellished with dances. In 1935, **P.C. Barua** produced the landmark film *Devdas,* which introduced the popular themes of ineffectual manhood and unrequited love to Indian cinema. In the 1940s, the introduction of pre-recorded songs and playback singing meant that actors no longer had to be singers. The most successful playback singer was **Lata Mangeshkar,** who holds the world record with more than 25,000 recorded songs in her career.

In the 1930s and 1940s, the industry created the **social film** as a more relevant way of addressing the concerns of contemporary life. V. Shantaram's ground-breaking film *Do Aankhen Barah Hath* advocated the rehabilitation of criminals. Shantaram also introduced a preference for loudness—gaudy costumes, flighty and capricious music, exciting choreography, and implied sex—prefiguring the kind of spectacle that has become the hallmark of Bombay film. **Mehboob Khan** (best known for *Mother India*) specialized in Muslim costume dramas and social tragedies, with a sense of the epic and spectacular. In *Andaz* (1949), he established a new norm for Indian film, immortalizing the love triangle and focusing on youth. **Raj Kapoor,** the "founding father" of popular cinema, introduced a more casual attitude toward sex while maintaining the motif of melodramatic love.

Despite moves in the direction of the spectacular, the decade of the 1950s belonged to the serious filmmaker. The first International Film Festival to be held in India was in 1952 and the European neo-realism demonstrated the potential for film to function as a searing political and social document. Nitin Bose and Bimal Roy made films about workers' rights, collective farming and the polarization of classes. In the 1950s and 60s, Tamil film emerged as a vehicle to promote Tamil politics. Script writers like Karunanidhi and Anna Durai were key political figures as well. **N.T. Rama Rao** was a leading actor in Telugu cinema for 40 years before becoming the chief minister of the state of Andhra Pradesh.

This neo-realist trend contributed to the emergent **art cinema,** which reacted against melodrama and cheap romance, using the camera to probe issues of poverty, superstition, caste, and social and economic injustice. **Satyajit Ray,** the leading director of art cinema, is well-known for *Pather Panchali* (1955), in which a diligently composed naturalism focuses on the isolation of rural life. Ray turns his attention to individual relationships in *Pratidwanai* (1970), in which a sensitive young man can't find an answer to the angry and corrupt temper of the time. During the 70s, low-budget filmmakers like Hrishikesh Mukherji and Basu Chatterji portrayed middle-class protagonists that won the hearts of the common viewer. Shyam Benegal, Mrinal Sen, Mani Kaul, and other filmmakers also made inroads in Hindi art cinema.

In the late 70s, popular film widened its mass market with a growing reliance on sex, violence, and action. This was a fertile period for new film talent. Amitabh Bachchan became the new screen hero. His image of an intelligent and rebellious hero seeking justice displaced that of the romantic hero, made popular by the goody-goody, effeminate actor Rajesh Khanna. Hindi film became popular film. In 1975, the movie *Sholay* ran for five years in Bombay, influencing the speech mannerisms of an entire generation, with young men all over India were speaking the catch-phrases of killer bandit Gabbar Singh, played by Amjad Khan.

Following the tradition of art cinema, **Shyam Benegal** has been awarded the unofficial badge of "India's foremost living filmmaker." His film *Manthan,* about the Gujarat Cooperative Milk Marketing Federation, was funded by donations of two rupees each from 500,000 farmers. Works by Gautam Ghose, Saeed Mirza, B.V. Karanth, and Kundan Shah, among others, address social problems of landlord exploitation, urban power, untouchability, corruption, and the oppression of women. Adoor Gopalakrishnan and Aravindan, both directors from Kerala, speak specifically about their own cultures, and the possibility of change.

Contemporary popular films have not relinquished drama, but they have given it a more realistic spin. **Mira Nair**'s *Salaam Bombay!* (1988) explores the lives of Bombay's street children, winning the filmmaker international praise and three awards at Cannes. **Mani Ratnam**'s acclaimed *Bombay* (1995) sets an inter-religious love story against the backdrop of religious riots in the big city.

The arrival of the **VCR** and **cable television** in the 1980s took the wind out of the film industry's sails and put both commercial and art films at risk at the box office. However, the explosion of satellite channels and the use of computer-generated special effects appears to be giving Bollywood a second wind.

THE MEDIA

Several English-language newspapers are printed in India, though their style tends to be a bit stodgy and archaic. Most newspapers are printed simultaneously in several cities. *The Times of India* is the nation's oldest and grandest newspaper, with good coverage of Indian news and a reputation for being pro-government. The *Times* is most popular in Delhi, Gujarat, Bombay, and the rest of Maharashtra. The *Indian Express,* another national paper, is a bit less stuffy and more widely read in South India. The most popular paper in South India is *The Hindu,* a conservative paper which covers South Indian news in more detail. The pro-Congress *Hindustan Times* is the best-selling paper in Delhi while in Calcutta and most of eastern India, *The Statesman* reigns supreme. *India Today* is an excellent fortnightly news magazine with feature articles on Indian politics and society. *Frontline,* published by *The Hindu,* and *Sunday Magazine* are also very good. A number of women's magazines, including *Femina* and *Woman's Era,* are popular in India, although they focus more on glamour than on feminist concerns.

India's national television company, **Doordarshan,** operates two channels. DD1 seems to broadcast endless pictures of hydroelectric projects approaching glorious completion, but it has news in English every night at 7pm. DD2 is a bit more fun, and due to an arrangement with MTV, the channel now broadcasts music videos from 6 to 8 every evening. Also ubiquitous is the Hong Kong-based Star TV satellite network, a package of five channels including "Channel V," TV tycoon Rupert Murdoch's substitute for MTV. A crop of private channels have also opened in the last few years, relaying Hindi dramas by satellite to India and Indian workers in the Gulf states.

Not Quite Cosmo

Boasting the widest circulation of any women's magazine in India, *Women's Era* is of the opinion that a woman's place is most definitely in the home. A quick flip through an issue is at once a culture shock and an entry into time-warp. *Women's Era* is not about baiting a husband; it largely assumes that its readers have gained one already through an arranged marriage. It's not about advancing a career— who needs one when one could be cooking up one of 11 different recipes for vegetable *samosas?* And, unlike the barely-clad beauties gracing the covers of Western women's mags, the figure of the *Women's Era* woman is always soberly restrained, albeit fashionable, in a pastel-flowered *sari* with coordinating high-heeled sandals.

Sports

Cricket isn't a sport in India—it's a national obsession. Despite the long hours, the long sleeves, and the hot sun, Indians turn out in droves both to watch and to play. Like many other former British colonies, India not only revels in the sport but now regularly beats England at its own game. One of the few times that India forgets its internal conflicts and bands together as one nation is when the Indian national cricket team plays their arch-rival **Pakistan.** Test matches are watched avidly by millions of Indians, in upper-middle class homes, and anywhere else that has a TV. If you don't know the names of even the most famous cricket players, you're probably an American, and you'll most likely be taken for a complete imbecile in India. Cricket is played on any available street or open ground, usually by little boys wearing little more than a pair of shorts and using sticks for bats and wickets. India reached the semi-finals of the **1996 World Cup** against Sri Lanka (the eventual winners of the World Cup) but the team was disqualified when "fans" began to throw bottles, rocks, and other assorted missiles onto the field.

India is also a consistent Olympic medal winner in **field hockey.** Involvement with other sports is as much a function of social and regional divisions as anything else in India. Soccer and horse racing are especially popular in the east and in urban areas, while *kabadi,* an indigenous game of tag, enjoys popularity throughout the north. Tennis, polo, squash, and other games brought to India by British imperialism-—except—of course, for cricket–remain the province of the upper classes.

Food and Drink

In the past, protracted Vedic prose prescribed every dash and pinch, every preparation, even every plate placement to provide the therapeutic and medicinal benefits of sustenance in just the right way. Nowadays, the more casual rules of good taste and great variety have taken over India's victuals. Meals vary regionally in taste, color, and texture but universally tend to smell strong and taste spicy. A tour of India can easily become a tour of its many foods. With a myriad of colorful spices and herbs including red chili powder, yellow turmeric, green coriander, and black cumin, a tour of India can easily become a tour of its many foods.

A typical meal in many parts of North India consists of a bread, spicy vegetables, rice, and a lentil curry called *dal.* Breads come in different shapes and sizes: *chapati* is a thin whole wheat frisbee; *paratha* is a bi-layered bread, sometimes stuffed with vegetables; *naan* is a thicker, chewy bread made of white flour and baked in a **tandoor,** a concave clay oven. Some rice dishes come with vegetables—try *biryani* or *pulao.* **Dal makhani,** a thick black lentil soup, is a spicy Punjabi favorite. Needless to say, **vegetarians** are in luck. Meat options consist mostly of chicken and lamb dishes, since beef is off-limits to Hindus and pork is forbidden to Muslims. Some of the best meat dishes are cooked in a *tandoor.* Good Indian cooking also uses *ghee* (clarified butter) as a base, rather than vegetable oils. Meals are often preceded by appetizers and followed by desserts accompanied by *masala chai,* a wonderful spicy tea with

---

Dhabas

If you take a private coach anywhere through India, you're sure to stop at one or two *dhabas,* the 24-hour truckers' stops. Here, the *parathas* and fried rice drip with grease, the *chai* comes with a kick, and a meal guaranteed to leave you sedentary for a while costs about Rs15. Not just for truckers, these dives also cater to the affluent, college set, who come in to refuel after a night of hedonism in dance clubs, or in preparation for an all-night cram session. In the wee hours of the morning, truck drivers catch a few winks on the bamboo cots which functioned earlier in the evening as *sambar*-absorbent tables. Because *dhabas* serve a steady stream of hungry diners round the clock, their food is often left to boil and simmer for hours, killing germs and making *dhabas* a generally safe place to eat. Though *dhabas* originated in Punjab and began serving mainly Punjabi cuisine, truck drivers have disseminated the dives through all of South Asia.

---

milk and lots of sugar. Appetizers and snacks are manifold. Some gems include *samosa,* a spicy, fried potato turnover, and *bhel puri,* a sweet and sour mixture of fresh sprouts, potatoes, and yogurt. Desserts, often made out of boiled milk, tend to be extremely sweet.

South Indian cuisine employs rice and rice flour much more than the north, and rice and rice-based **dosas** (thin pancakes) and **idlis** (thick steamed cakes) take center stage. These are accompanied by vegetable broths like *sambar* (a thick and spicy lentil soup), *rasam* (thinner, with tomatoes and tamarind), and *kozhambu* (sour), which are poured on the rice and mixed with it. *Dosas* are commonly stuffed with spiced potatoes to make *masala dosas.* A thicker *dosa* made with onion is called an *utthapam. Vadais* are doughnut-shaped rice cakes soaked in curd or *sambar.* Less meat is consumed in the south, but seafood dishes abound in coastal areas. A standard South Indian meal comes in the form of a **thali,** a 40cm steel plate filled with *chapati, papadam,* rice, *sambar,* fresh yogurt, *dal,* and vegetable dishes; the restaurant's proprietor walks around ladling *ghee* onto your feast.

Paan is an after-dinner chew and the cause of much of the distasteful crimson-colored spatterings that will surely line every street you traverse. A *paan* leaf is filled with everything from coconut to sweetened rose petals to fennel seeds to flavored betel nut or tobacco. If you decide to try it, ask for a sweet *paan* with no tobacco, and go easy on the *kath-chuna* (a crazy limestone paste). Unsweetened *paan* is an assault for novices. Place the whole thing on one side of your soon-to-be-numb mouth and chew over a period of several minutes, remembering to spit periodically.

Drinks

Sadly, some of India's most delicious drinks have to be avoided because they contain ice cubes made of untreated water. **Lassi,** made with yogurt and sugar, salt or fruit, varies in quality and texture from smooth and scrumptious to watery and bland. Sugarcane juice is sold widely and is another tasty but risky drink. Although India's many varieties of tea are wonderful, coffee is also popular and delicious, especially in South India. Cold coffee with ice cream is an Indian specialty, best tried at restaurants with good ice cream, such as the Kwality chain. Thanks to its pre-1991 protectionist economy, India has also given birth to a bundle of bizarre soft drinks, referred to as "cold drinks." **Thums Up** [sic] is a spicy cola; Teem is a sweet, pungent, lemon-limey drink; Citra has a more subdued citrus flavor. Frooti, a mango drink sold in little green drinking boxes, is excellent when cold.

Drinking **alcohol** is an accepted and encouraged practice in some parts of the country, while it is frowned upon in other regions and may be hard to find (see **Drugs and Alcohol,** p. 19). Popular brands of beer are Taj Mahal and Kingfisher, while the tasty London Pilsner is not common but worth the search. Humorously titled local brews, like Rajasthan's **Godfather** brand, also abound. Liquor is available in many bars and shops (especially in Goa), but chances are you won't get the name brand you ask for. Be careful when ordering difficult or obscure mixed drinks—what gets called Kahlua could taste a bit like fermented Ovaltine and is probably an example of **Indian-Made Foreign Liquor (IMFL).** Imported brands like Smirnoff are available in big cities, and not-so-good domestic wines are available at nicer restaurants. For a glossary featuring all of these tasties and more, see **Food and Drink,** p. 817.

■ Other Sources

BOOKS

General

India, by Stanley Wolpert (1991). An easy-to-follow sampler of Indian culture and history by a well-known historian.

An Introduction to South Asia, by B. H. Farmer (1993). A geography-based description of South Asia, its history, politics, and economics.

Culture Shock! India, by Gitanjali Kolanad (1994). A guide to Indian customs and etiquette aimed at those planning to live and work in India. Contains useful advice for all sorts of social situations and bureaucratic hassles.

Amar Chitra Kathas. A series of educational comic books covering stories ranging from the *Ramayana* to the life of Vivekananda. These are fun to read, as well as being crammed with common-sense knowledge about Indian history and culture.

Ancient Futures: Learning from Ladakh, by Helena Norberg-Hodge (1991). An insightful, provocative account of the effects of modernization on Ladakhi culture.

Travel/Description

An Area of Darkness, by V.S. Naipaul (1964). A somewhat bitter (but accurate) account of Naipaul's first journey around his ancestral homeland. Filled with insights about the country and the author.

India: A Million Mutinies Now, by V. S. Naipaul (1990). A kinder counterpoint to Naipaul's earlier writings on India, examines the subtle rebellions that characterize Indian life in the 90s. Naipaul's prose is excellent, and in his interviews a large cross-section of India is illuminated.

Arrow of the Blue-Skinned God: Retracing the Ramayana though India, by Jonah Blank (1992). A fabulous book comparing the culture of 1990s India to the *dharmic* ideals of Lord Rama, the hero of the epic *Ramayana.*

The Great Railway Bazaar, by Paul Theroux (1975). This travel classic is worth rereading for its descriptions of what it feels like to be a snotty Westerner jammed on a train with hundreds of other people.

Tropical Classical, by Pico Iyer (1997). Essays and articles culled from the last ten years of the journalist's career. Always entertaining, sometimes hollowly so; nevertheless, the history of the Raj is solid, as are the pieces set in Bombay and Nepal.

History

A New History of India, by Stanley Wolpert (1993). An incredibly accessible academic overview of Indian history from time immemorial to the present, with a surprisingly good sense of the author's voice.

A Traveller's History of India, by Sinharaja Tammita-Delgoda (1995). A clear and readable introduction to Indian history for the beginner, with references to historical sites that can be visited today, and invaluable appendices.

The Discovery of India, by Jawaharlal Nehru (1946). Indian history as seen by the founder of modern India—a classic.

An Autobiography, or, the Story of My Experiment with Truth, by Mohandas K. Gandhi (1927). Gandhi's personal account of the development of his beliefs, with surprisingly little commentary on the political events of the time.

Politics and Economics

India: Government and Politics in a Developing Nation, by Robert L. Hardgrave, Jr. and Stanley A. Kochanek (1996). The best summary of recent Indian political issues and the government of modern India.

Operation Bluestar: The True Story, by Lt. Gen. K.S. Brar (1993). An in-depth (albeit slanted) account of the Golden Temple's recent turmoil from the pen of an Indian commando.

India: Economic Development and Social Opportunity, by Jean Drèze and Amartya Sen (1995). Analyzes the economic development of India from a social perspective and with empathy for the underprivileged.

Religion

Banaras: City of Light, by Diana L. Eck (1982). An exploration of the holy city that attempts to "see Kashi through Hindu eyes." A wonderful introduction to the complexities and contradictions of Hinduism in general, and a beautiful description of Varanasi, a city that Eck obviously loves.

Ramayana, by Valmiki, trans. William Buck (1976). An entrancing abridged account of Lord Rama's epic adventure and battle with Ravana. Retold in language that brings the ancient characters to life.

What The Buddha Taught, by Walpola Rahula (1959). A Sri Lankan monk's authoritative and comprehensible explanation of Theravada Buddhist philosophy.

Women's Issues

May You Be the Mother of a Hundred Sons, by Elizabeth Bumiller (1990). A British journalist's exploration of *sati,* sex-selective abortion, and dowry deaths, sometimes a little judgemental, but mostly open-minded. A good introduction to Indian society and politics, with a great chapter on Hindi film actresses.

Unveiling India, by Anees Jung (1987). A journalist who grew up in a family practicing strict Muslim *purdah,* Jung examines the lives of Indian women.

Fiction

Midnight's Children, by Salman Rushdie (1980). Rushdie's masterpiece tells the magical tale of children born at midnight on the eve of India's independence, and how the country's life and theirs evolve together.

Such a Long Journey, by Rohinton Mistry (1992). A humanely written tale of Bombay Parsis (Zoroastrians) who inadvertently become involved in Indira Gandhi's government corruption. A great read that also acquaints its audience with Parsi culture and India in the 1970s.

Karma Cola, by Gita Mehta (1979). A cynical journalistic satire about Westerners in India that offers insight into dark and comic sides of traveler culture.

The God of Small Things, by Arundhati Roy (1997). Roy exquisitely weaves a story of love, betrayal, and tragedy set against the backdrop Kerala's social and political landscape. It deserved the hype.

Red Earth and Pouring Rain, by Vikram Chandra (1995). A melange of stories narrated by a 19th-century Rajput poet-warrior reincarnated as a typewriting monkey and a just-returned-from-California Indian college student. As ambitious projects tend to do, the novel occasionally stumbles, but it's a solid, if eccentric, introduction to India's history and its pantheon of gods and goddesses.

A Passage to India, by E.M. Forster (1924). The oft-cited novel tells the story of the friendship of an Englishman and an Indian during the British Raj. An honest, sensitive account whose observations about culture shock still hold true today.

City of Joy, by Dominique Lapierre (1985). A pulp account of life in a Calcutta slum, that doesn't venture too far beyond the boundary separating documentary and exploitation. The film based on this book is to be avoided, however.

Malgudi Days, R.K Narayan (1986). Centarian Narayan is one of the few English-language Indian writers who lives in India. No post-colonial angst here, just wry, subtle, charming stories set in a fictional village in Tamil Nadu.

The Poison Tree, by Bankim Chandra Chatterjee. Translated from the Bengali. Chatterjee's novellas, set in 19th-century Bengal display a characteristically Calcuttan concern with love, morality, and tragedy.

Poetry

Gitanjali, by Rabindranath Tagore (1913). The Nobel prize-winning work of the great Bengali poet, which uses traditional images from Indian love poetry to discuss a relationship with God.

The Meghaduta, by Kalidasa (4th century AD). The great Sanskrit poet's account of a cloud's journey across India, surveying the landscape and human activity as it carries a message between separated lovers.

Photography

The Ganges, by Raghubir Singh (1992). A compilation of much of the photographer's work, following the course of the Ganga from source to sea, with landscapes and people snapped into amazing configurations.

FILMS

Pather Panchali, by Satyajit Ray (1955). The first and greatest film by the late master of Indian cinema. Produced on weekends with a borrowed camera and unpaid actors, its visuals capture the beauty of the Bengali landscape and the isolation of the village in which Apu and Durga, the hero and heroine, live. The score by Ravi Shankar is brilliantly matched to the picture.

Gandhi, by Richard Attenborough (1981). A grossly romanticized tale of the Mahatma's life and the Indian Independence movement. You've probably seen it already, but take any history lessons with a grain of salt and watch it only for Ben Kingsley's great portrayal of Gandhi.

Salaam Bombay, by Mira Nair (1988). A disturbing tale of Bombay's street children, This fictional story told in documentary style is somewhat exploitative, and the subtitles aren't always accurate, but it's a moving and well-acted film.

God is My Witness (Kuda Gawah), by Mukul S. Anand (1992). Indo-chic is sweeping the West, and this critically acclaimed "curry Western" provides a good introduction to Bollywood's charms and charmers, including Amitabh Bachchan and Sridevi. The first non-pirated *masala* movie to hit American video stores.

Bandit Queen, Shekhar Kapur (1994). The story of Phoolan Devi, a low-caste bandit-turned-politician. A horrifyingly graphic, true-life portrayal of caste oppression in Uttar Pradesh.

Hello Photo, by Nina Davenport (1994). The next best thing to actually traveling in India, this short and visually stunning film shows one woman's experience of looking at India and being looked at.

Delhi दिल्ली

India's capital and third-largest city, Delhi offers both sights to stop your heart and the frenetic energy needed to revive it. Unfortunately, the city needs to be coped with before it can be coddled. All of the contrasts familiar to travelers in India are in full force here: rich and poor, old and new, chaos and control. What distinguishes India's capital from other major cities is the polarity between its government and its people. Delhi maintains a dignified front as national capital, with its official-looking edifices spanning broad green blocks in the city's south-central portion. Nobody sleeps on the lawns between monuments, and the billboards (in English, of course) fervently promote various welfare campaigns. But alongside this facade of control are Delhi's other streets, crammed with the city's legendary slow-churning traffic and threaded by veering auto-rickshaws. It is in these streets that life happens, where the capital's ballyhooed cosmopolitanism is manufactured and displayed, where Punjabi Sikhs, colorfully dressed Rajasthani women, dredlocked *sadhus*, and pavement-dwellers all rub shoulders, sharing space if not conversation. And it is in these streets that North India's heat and humidity (and winter chill) are refracted through layers of filthy, polluted air, acting as a relentless social leveler, forcing the climate-controlled few and the shelterless masses to sweat or shiver together—pressed together, layer upon layer, like the city's history itself.

The history of Delhi begins in 736 AD, with the founding of Lal Kot by the Tomara clan of Rajputs. Their tumultuous and gory rule was neatly ended in 1192 by Muhammad Gauri and his slave general Qutb-ud-din Aibak, who swept in from Central Asia and conquered North India, introducing it to Islam and founding the Delhi Sultanate. For the next 300 years Delhi was wracked by political instability, especially in 1398, when the city was sacked by another Central Asian warlord, Timur. By the early 16th century the Lodi dynasty, the Delhi Sultanate's ruling family, had made its share of enemies in the region. Too meek to challenge the Sultanate on their own, they requested help from Timur's great-grandson, Babur. Babur battled the Lodis into submission and launched the Mughal Empire, which would knit together huge swaths of South Asia for the next two centuries. The Mughals repeatedly shifted their capital between Delhi and Agra, leaving each city with monumental tombs, palaces, and forts. Old Delhi's grandest edifices were built during the 17th century by the Mughal emperor Shah Jahan. In the 18th century, however, Mughal strength waned, and the British jumped into the yawning power void. In 1911, the British imperial capital was moved to Delhi, and the city began to attract the attention of Indian nationalists, who proclaimed that the flag of an Indian republic would one day fly from the Red Fort. With a speech by the Prime Minister delivered from the Red Fort and a tremendous parade in front of the city's most important British buildings, today's Delhi celebrates the vindication of the nationalists' predictions every 15, Independence Day.

As with many cities in the developing world, Delhi's population is growing rapidly; by some counts it has already topped 10 million. Waves of modern fortune-seekers, as well as poor and illiterate rural families seeking relief, have caused Delhi to swell and sprawl. South Delhi, which once seemed downright suburban, has moved to the center of the city's life. This expansion has made Delhi more diffuse and segregated.

🏛 HIGHLIGHTS OF DELHI

- **Old Delhi** bristles with **bazaars** (p. 138) and monuments, including the **Red Fort** (p. 135) and **Jama Masjid** (p. 137), the largest mosque in India.
- South of the city center are the emperor **Humayan's Tomb** (p. 140) and the phenomenal Mughal ruins at the **Qutb Minar complex** (p. 137).
- Delhi's lotus-shaped, garden-ringed **Baha'i Temple** (p. 139) is one of India's most beautiful modern structures.
- The immensely intricate **Jantar Mantar** (p. 141) is an 18th-century astronomical observatory set in stone, complete with massive marble sundials.

■ Practical Information

GETTING THERE AND AWAY

International Flights

> **Warning:** You may be tired from your flight, but keep your wits about you, even in the airport. If you don't understand what's going on, or feel pressured or herded in a particular direction, stop to collect yourself—there's really no hurry. When paying at a counter, **count out your cash as you hand it over.** Switch-the-bill schemes are common. **Never** let a cab driver convince you that the hotel you ask for is full or closed. And remember, **the more assertive someone is with their offers of help, the more likely it is there's something in it for them.** If you need help or have a question, ask someone who hasn't approached you first.

NORTH INDIA

Indira Gandhi International Airport (tel. 565 2011 or 565 2050) serves as the main entry and departure point for international flights. Arrival at the airport is a piece of cake: after passing through customs, you'll proceed to the arrival hall, where across from the various tourist offices is a **State Bank of India** office (open 24hr.). The **Government of India Tourism** and **Delhi Tourism** offices are good places to head for initial questions, taxi-booking, and hotel arrangements. This is also the place to pay for a **pre-paid taxi,** which is the least risky way to get into the center of Delhi. Once you pay, you'll be given a receipt with your destination and a taxi number. People outside the exit will help you find your cab in the queue. Say where you want to go and make them go there (and if it's to the railway station, don't let them take you to a private ticketing agent). Delhi Transport Corporation (DTC), the Ex-Servicemen's Shuttle and EATS (tel. 331 6530) run frequent **buses** to Connaught Place from the airport (Rs30). DTC buses also stop at New Delhi Railway Station and Interstate Bus Terminal (ISBT) at Kashmiri Gate. To get to the airport (international and domestic terminals) pick up the EATS bus near the middle circle on Janpath. Buses leave daily (4, 5:30, 7:30, and 9:30am, 2, 3:30, 6, 7, 10, and 11:30pm, Rs30). **Auto-rickshaws** ferry passengers from the airport to downtown at cheaper rates than taxis, but without the security of the pre-payment system.

    International airlines: Air France, Scindia House, Janpath (tel. 373 8004); **Air India,** Jeevan Bharati Bldg. (tel. 373 6446); **Alitalia,** 16 Barakhamba Rd. (tel. 332 9551); **American Airlines,** Barakhamba Rd. (tel. 332 5876); **Biman Bangladesh,** World Trade Center (tel. 335 4401); **British Airways,** DLF Bldg., Sansad Marg (tel. 332 7428); **Cathay Pacific,** Tolstoy House (tel. 332 3332); **Delta,** DLF Centre, Sansad Marg (tel. 373 0197); **El Al,** Prakash Deep Bldg., Tolstoy Marg (tel. 335 7965); **Emirates,** 18 Barakhamba Rd. (tel. 332 4665); **Gulf Air** G-12, Connaught Pl. (tel. 332 4293); **KLM/Northwest,** Prakash Deep Bldg., Tolstoy Marg (tel. 335 7747); **Kuwait Airlines,** 16 Barakhamba Rd. (tel. 335 4373); **Lufthansa,** 56 Janpath (tel. 332 7268); **Qantas,** Mohan Dev Bldg., Tolstoy Marg (tel. 332 9027); **RNAC (Royal Nepal Airlines),** 44 Janpath (tel. 332 1164); **Singapore Airlines,** Ashoka Estate Bldg., Barakhamba Rd. (tel. 332 9036); **Swissair,** DLF Centre, Sansad Marg (tel. 332 5511); **Thai Airways,** Park Royal Hotel, American Plaza, Nehru Palace (tel. 335 3377); **United Airlines,** 14 K.G. Marg (tel. 335 3377).

Domestic Flights

The **domestic terminal** of Indira Gandhi Airport (tel. 566 5121, or 566 5621) is 5km from the international terminal. Like its sibling, the domestic terminal has **pre-paid taxis, buses,** and **auto-rickshaws** to and from downtown (see above). **Domestic Airlines: Indian Airlines** (tel. 462 0566); **Archana Airways** (tel. 684 2001); **East West** (tel. 375 5167); **Jagson** (tel. 372 1594); **Jet Airways** (tel. 651 7443); **Sahara** (tel. 332 6851). There are many daily flights from Delhi to other cities in India. To: **Agra** (1 per day, 40min., US$50); **Ahmedabad** (4-6 per day, 1½hr., US$120); **Amritsar** (M, W,

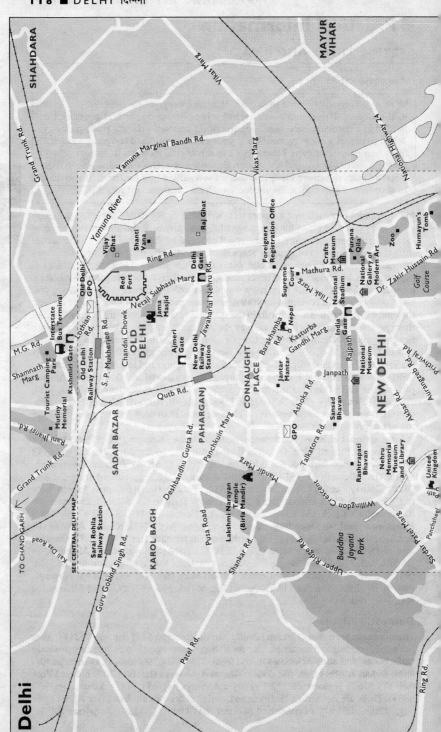

Delhi

SHAHDARA

MAYUR VIHAR

Grand Trunk Rd.

Vikas Marg

National Highway 24

Yamuna Marginal Bandh Rd.

Vikas Marg

Yamuna River

Foreigners Registration Office

Humayun's Tomb

Raj Ghat

Shanti Vana

Crafts Museum

Purana Qila

Zoo

Vijay Ghat

Ring Rd.

Delhi Gate

Mathura Rd.

National Gallery of Modern Art

Dr. Zakir Hussain Rd.

Golf Course

Red Fort

Netaji Subhash Marg

Jawaharlal Nehru Rd.

Supreme Court

Tilak Marg

National Stadium

Old Delhi GPO

Jama Masjid

OLD DELHI

Barakhamba Rd.

Nepal

India Gate

Rothian Rd.

Interstate Bus Terminal

Kashmiri Gate

Old Delhi Railway Station

S. P. Mukherjee Rd.

Chandni Chowk

Ajmeri Gate

New Delhi Railway Station

CONNAUGHT PLACE

Kasturba Gandhi Marg

Rajpath

NEW DELHI

Prithviraj Rd.

Aurangzeb Rd.

Akbar Rd.

M.G. Rd.

Shamnath Marg

Tourist Camping Park

Mutiny Memorial

Qutb Rd.

PAHARGANJ

Jantar Mantar

Janpath

National Museum

Ashoka Rd.

Sansad Bhavan

GPO

Talkatora Rd.

Rani Jhansi Rd.

Grand Trunk Rd.

SADAR BAZAR

Deshbandhu Gupta Rd.

Panchkuin Marg

Rashtrapati Bhavan

Nehru Memorial Museum and Library

United Kingdom

TO CHANDIGARH

Kali Das Road

SEE CENTRAL DELHI MAP

Saral Rohila Railway Station

Guru Gobind Singh Rd.

KAROL BAGH

Pusa Road

Shankar Rd.

Lakshmi Narayan Temple (Birla Mandir)

Mandir Marg

Willingdon Crescent

Buddha Jayanti Park

Upper Ridge Rd.

Sardar Patel Marg

Panchsheel Marg

Patel Rd.

Ring Rd.

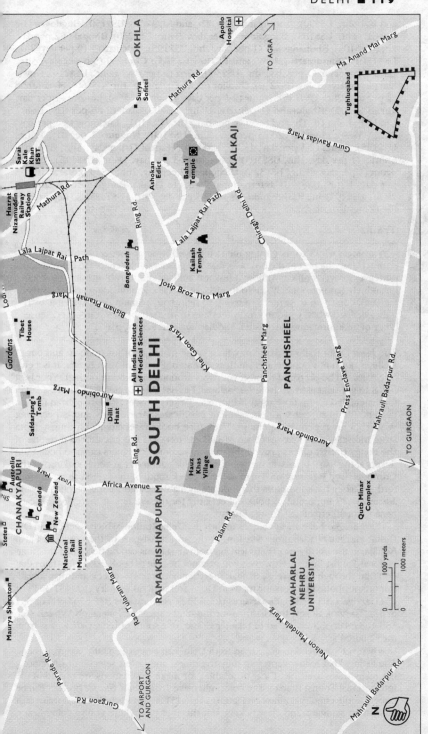

and F, 1½hr., US$90); **Aurangabad** (Tu, Th, and Sa, 3½hr., US$150); **Bagdogra** (1-2 per day, 2hr., US$185); **Bangalore** (7 per day, 2½hr., US$230); **Bhopal** (1-2 per day, 2hr., US$105); **Bhubaneswar** (1 per day, 2hr., US$195); **Calcutta** (7-10 per day, 2hr., US$180); **Chandigarh** (M, W, and F, 1hr., US$65); **Chennai** (5-6 per day, 3hr., US$235); **Cochin** (1 per day, 4hr., US$300); **Goa** (2 per day, 2½hr., US$210); Guwahati (1 per day, 2½hr., US$210); **Gwalior** (M, T, Th, and Sa, 1hr., US$60); **Hyderabad** (2 per day, 2hr., US$185); **Jaipur** (2-3 per day, 45min., US$58); **Jammu** (2 per day, 1hr., US$105); **Khajuraho** (1 per day, 1½hr., US$90); **Kullu** (4-5 per day, 1½hr., US$150); **Leh** (Tu, Th, and Sa-Su, 1 per day, 1hr., US$105); **Lucknow** (3-4 per day, 1hr., US$80); **Mumbai** (20-23 per day, 2hr., US$160); **Nagpur** (1 per day, 1½hr., US$135); **Patna** (2-3 per day, 1½hr., US$130); **Ranchi** (1 per day, 3hr., US$170); **Shimla** (1 per day, 1hr., US$105); **Srinagar** (2-3 per day, 1½hr., US$115); **Trivandrum** (1 per day, 4½hr., US$325); **Udaipur** (1-2 per day, 2hr., US$95); **Varanasi** (2-3 per day, 1-2hr., US$110). International flights to **Dhaka, Bangladesh** (W and Su, 2½hr., US$195) and **Kathmandu, Nepal** (3-5 per day, 3hr., US$142) also depart from the domestic terminal.

Trains

> **Warning:** Delhi's **touts** (young men employed by shop-owners to bring in customers) are the best in the business, and will go incredible lengths to get you into their employer's office. Although few are actually out to rob or hurt you, touts routinely (and elaborately) lie to tourists, using false identification and guilt trips ("Why don't you trust me? I'm trying to help you.") Smiling and walking away may be hard when you don't really feel sure of yourself, but it's your best defense. For more information, see **Touts, Middlemen, and Scams,** p. 67.

The **New Delhi Railway Station,** which is the main depot for trains in and out of Delhi, is north of Connaught Pl., at the east end of Paharganj Main Bazaar. It is a chaotic place, so be prepared to push your way around, and beware of theft. Your best bet is to get tickets from the **International Tourist Bureau** (tel. 373 4164), a large, foreigner-filled room, upstairs at platform 1. Tickets here must be bought in foreign currency or in rupees with encashment certificates. Arrive early and expect long waits (but great people-watching). The office books reservations on tourist-quota seats and sells Indrail passes (open M-Sa 8am-5pm). **Do not get sucked into one of the dodgy tourist offices around the railway station.** Foreigners can also book train tickets at the usual places: at the windows in the station (for general booking) or the **Computerised Reservation Terminal,** one block south of the station along Chelmsford Rd. They have monitors that indicate available seats on popular trains days in advance—it's important to book tickets early for these trains. If there are no seats, head to the International Tourist Bureau.

There are 3 other railway stations in the city: **Delhi Station,** which is actually in Old Delhi; **Hazrat Nizamuddin Station,** in the southeast part of the city; and **Sarai Rohilla,** in the northwest. Trains leaving from all stations can be booked at the International Tourist Bureau. However, you may not be able to book tickets for trains that don't go through Delhi (e.g., Bangalore-Hyderabad trains)—check and plan ahead. Important phone numbers for trains in Delhi are: **general enquiry** (tel. 331 3535 or 131), **arrivals** (tel. 1331), **departures** (tel. 1332), **reservations** (tel. 334 8686 or 334 8787). To book tickets to Rajasthan for the ultra-expensive **Palace on Wheels** (tel. 338 1884; fax 338 2823), go to Bikaner House, due south of India Gate across from the Children's Park.

Wherever you need to go, a train from Delhi can almost certainly take you there. The listings that follow represent only the tiniest and fastest selection from among the many trains available. Clear **timetables** for major destinations are posted in the International Tourist Bureau. The comprehensive *Trains at a Glance* booklet can be bought at the enquiry counter on Platform 1 (Rs15). A/C *Shatabdi Express* trains cost more than standard 2nd class tickets, but they get you where you're going faster, include safe food and comfy seats, and feature nice India Tourism posters to make up for the fact that you won't see much out of the tinted, scratched windows. To: **Ajmer** (2015, 6:15am, 6½hr., Rs480) via **Jaipur** (4½hr., Rs385); **Amritsar** (2013, 4:30pm, 6hr., Rs465); **Bhopal** (2002, 6:15am, 8hr., Rs650) via **Agra** (2hr., Rs305); **Chandigarh** (2005, 5:15pm, 3hr., Rs330); **Dehra Dun** (2017, 7:10am, 5hr., Rs385); **Lucknow** (2004, 6:20am, 6½hr., Rs495) via **Kanpur** (5hr., Rs330). A/C 3-tier *Rajdhani Express* trains run to **Bangalore** (2430, 9:30am, 34hr., Rs1600); **Chennai** (2634, 3:15pm, 29hr., Rs1235); **Mumbai** (2952, 4pm, 16½hr., and 2954, 4:50pm, 17hr., Rs910); **Varanasi** (2302, W-Th and Sa-M, 5:15pm, 9hr., Rs765) via **Allahabad** (7hr., Rs720).

Buses

There are three **interstate bus terminals (ISBTs)** in Delhi. The new **Anand Vihar ISBT** (tel. 214 8097), east of the Yamuna River, runs buses to Lucknow, Ramnagar (for Corbett National Park), Bareilly, Almora, Nainital, Pithoragarh, and Halwandi. **Sarai Kale Khan ISBT** (tel. 469 8343), two blocks east of the Nizamuddin Railway Station, sends buses to Jaipur, Ajmer, Jodphur, Udaipur, and Ghaziabad. **Kashmiri Gate** (tel. 296 0290), north of (Old) Delhi Railway Station, sends buses to most other destinations, including Chandigarh, Amritsar, Jammu, Shimla, Dharamsala, Kullu, Manali, Haridwar, Rishikesh, Dehra Dun, and Mussoorie. There is a pre-paid auto-rickshaw stand at Kashmiri Gate (to Paharganj Rs25, to Connaught Place Rs32).

To obtain bus departure information, it's best to contact the bus company directly. To find out which company serves which destinations call one of the bus stations. Bus companies include: **Himachal Road Transport Company,** 1 Rajpur Rd. (tel. 296 6725); **U.P. Roadways,** Ajmeri Gate (tel. 296 8709 or 214 9089); **Rajasthan Roadways,** Bikaner House (tel. 464 3731); **Punjab Roadways** (tel. 296 7842); **Haryana Roadways** (tel. 252 1262).

Ordinary and deluxe buses leave ISBT Kashmiri Gate. For directions, head to the enquiry counter in the middle of the terminal. **Do not follow any of the touts claiming to offer great rates.** All of the major bus companies have offices on the first floor; if you are led to the third floor to make deluxe bus bookings, something is fishy. Government-run **Delhi Transit Corporation (DTC)** offers deluxe buses to many cities in Northern India. Be sure to shop around if you decide to book a seat on a private bus. Hotels and travel agencies usually charge higher rates, so it's better to go through a reputable agency (see **Budget Travel,** p. 125).

UP Roadways serves: **Almora** (8, 8:30, 9pm, 11hr., Rs125); **Amritsar** (every 30min. 4:30am-10pm, 10hr., Rs150); **Chandigarh** (every 20min. 3:30am-1:30am, 5½hr., Rs80); **Dehra Dun** (every hr. 5:30am-6:30pm, 6½hr., Rs79/145); **Dharamsala** (6 per day, 13hr., Rs160/250); **Faizabad** (every hr. 5:30am-10:30pm, 18hr., Rs145); **Haldwani** (every hr. 3am-9:30pm, 8hr., Rs89/250); **Haridwar** (every 30min. 6am-10pm, 5½hr., Rs65); **Jaipur** (every hr. 7am-9pm, 6hr., Rs80); **Jammu** (8, 9pm, and midnight, 12hr., Rs210); **Jodhpur** (every 30min. 7am-midnight, 16hr., Rs190); **Lucknow** (every hr. 7am-9pm, 13hr., Rs160); **Manali** (10 per day, 15hr., Rs215/450); **Mussoorie** (7am, 8hr., Rs120); **Nainital** (7am and 9:30pm, 9hr., Rs100/173); **Pushkar** (every 30min. 7am-midnight, 10½hr., Rs130) via **Ajmer** (10hr., Rs123); **Ramnagar** (for Corbett National Park, every hr. 5am-9pm, 7hr., Rs75); **Rishikesh** (every 45min. 4am-10pm, 7hr., Rs72); **Shimla** (10 per day, 4:50-9:25pm, 10hr., Rs125/244); and **Udaipur** (9:20am, 17hr., Rs185). Punjab Roadways runs buses to **Amritsar** (every hr. 8am-10pm, 10hr., Rs158/362) and **Chandigarh** (every 10min. all day and night, 5½hr., Rs91/182).

ORIENTATION

Once you get the hang of it, getting around in Delhi is a breeze (and breezes are always a good thing in the smoggy capital). Delhi is situated west of the Yamuna River and runs about 30km from north to south, 10km from east to west. The northern two-thirds of the city are circled by **Ring Road.** The city center, **New Delhi,** spreads geometrically from **Connaught Place,** a circular hub of two-story colonnaded buildings arranged around a similarly circular swath of grass. Connaught Pl. is the

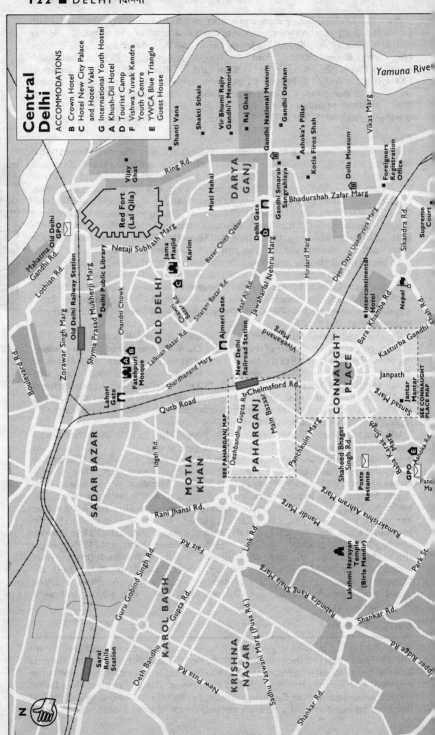

Central Delhi

ACCOMMODATIONS
- **B** Crown Hotel
- **C** Hotel New City Palace and Hotel Vakil
- **G** International Youth Hostel
- **A** Khush-Dil Hotel
- **D** Tourist Camp
- **F** Vishwa Yuvak Kendra Youth Centre
- **E** YWCA Blue Triangle Guest House

Yamuna River

Shakti Sthala

Shanti Vana

Vijay Ghat

Vir Bhumi Rajiv Gandhi's Memorial

Raj Ghat

Gandhi National Museum

Gandhi Darshan

Ashoka's Pillar

Kotla Firoz Shah

Dolls Museum

Foreigners Registration Office

Vikas Marg

Ring Rd.

Moti Mahal

DARYA GANJ

Gandhi Smarak Sangrahalaya

Bhadurshah Zafar Marg

Mahatma Old Delhi Gandhi Rd.

Old Delhi GPO

Red Fort (Lal Qila)

Lothian Rd.

Netaji Subhash Marg

Delhi Public Library

Chandni Chowk

Jama Masjid

Karim

Delhi Gate

Bazar Chitli Qabar

Deen Dayal Upadhyaya Marg

Mirdard Marg

Supreme Court

Sikandra Rd.

Zorawar Singh Marg

Old Delhi Railway Station

Shyama Prasad Mukherji Marg

OLD DELHI

Chawri Rd.

Sitaram Bazar Rd.

Asaf Ali Rd.

Jawaharlal Nehru Marg

Intercontinental Hotel

Bara Khamba Rd.

Nepal

Boulevard Rd.

Lahori Gate

Fatehpuri Mosque

Lalkuan Bazar Rd.

Ajmeri Gate

New Delhi Railroad Station

Vivekanand Marg

CONNAUGHT PLACE

Kasturba Gandhi

SADAR BAZAR

Shardhanand Marg

Qutb Road

Chelmsford Rd.

Deshbandhu Gupta Rd.

Main Bazaar

PAHARGANJ

SEE PAHARGANJ MAP

Janpath

Sansad Marg

Jantar Mantar

SEE CONNAUGHT PLACE MAP

Idgah Rd.

MOTIA KHAN

Panchkuin Marg

Shaheed Bhagat Singh Rd.

Baba Karak Singh Marg

Ashoka Rd.

GPO

Poste Restante

Ramakrishna Ashram Marg

Panc Ma

Rani Jhansi Rd.

Faiz Rd.

Link Rd.

Mandir Marg

Rabindra Rang Shala Marg

Lakshmi Narayan Temple (Birla Mandir)

Guru Gobind Singh Rd.

Gupta Rd.

KAROL BAGH

Desh Bandhu Rd.

New Pusa Rd. (Pusa Rd.)

KRISHNA NAGAR

Sadhu Vaswani Marg

Shankar Rd.

Shankar Rd.

Park St.

Sarai Rohila Station

Upper Ridge Rd.

N

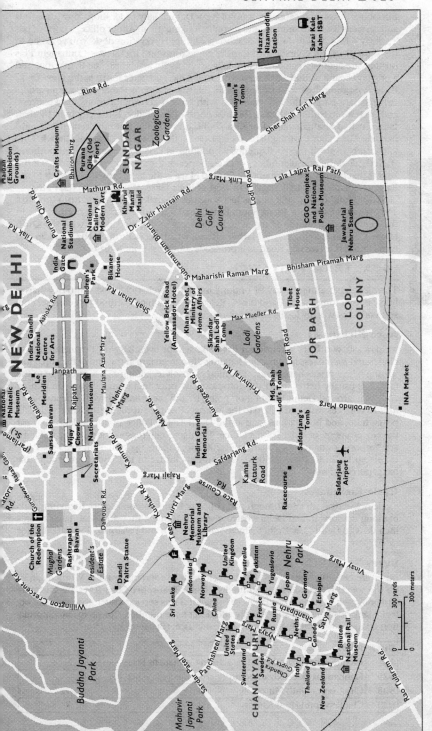

throbbing heart (and capitalist soul) of New Delhi. Many of its shops provide goods and services useful to tourists, and if you're looking for an AmEx office, a copy of last Tuesday's *USA Today,* or the Kazakhstan Airlines reservation desk, you've come to the right place. Of course, with tourists come touts and tricksters—Connaught Pl.'s hustlers are aggressive and exceptionally savvy; as always, a firm "no thank you" and a grin-and-bear-it attitude will serve you well. One kilometer north is the **New Delhi Railway Station.** Just west of New Delhi Railway Station is **Paharganj,** a not-particularly-pleasant part of the city crammed with budget accommodations, backpackers, and even more ruthless cheats. The area north of the station is the city built by Shah Jahan; called Shahjahanabad or **Old Delhi,** it is a delightful tangle of streets and bazaars. The major thoroughfare in Old Delhi is the east-west **Chandni Chowk.** One kilometer south of the parliamentary buildings is **Chanakyapuri,** a neighborhood stuffed full of the consular offices of English-speaking and European countries. Of the streets that break off Connaught Pl., **Sansad Marg** is the most crowded; it leads to the Raj-era parliamentary buildings, 2km west of **India Gate,** straight down **Raj Path.**

South Delhi unofficially begins just south of Chanakyapuri. Aside from Ring Rd. and **Mehrauli Badarpur Road,** South Delhi's major thoroughfares run north-south. In the center is **Aurobindo Marg,** which connects Safdarjang's tomb with the **Qutb Minar Complex;** in the east is **Mathura Road,** which slices through **Nizamuddin** and turns into **Zakir Hussain Road** as it proceeds southeast from India Gate.

LOCAL TRANSPORTATION

Travelers have a huge array of options in Delhi: cycle-rickshaws, auto-rickshaws, horse-drawn tongas, taxis, and buses. Regardless of which method you choose, consult with trustworthy locals about appropriate fares.

Auto-Rickshaws

Auto-rickshaw drivers in particular have a knack for overcharging, driving around in circles and *then* overcharging, or changing the agreed fare at the end of the trip. Fluctuating petrol prices have made most meters obsolete, adding a 75% surcharge to the fare. It is usually better to set the auto-rickshaw price in advance if you don't know your way around Delhi. Insisting on going by the meter can provoke the auto-*wallahs* to unnecessarily add 1-3km to the journey. **Pre-paid autos** are available at the airports, train, and bus stations, and at the Delhi Traffic Police Booth on Janpath, near the Government. of India Tourist Office. The maximum reasonable non-prepaid fares are: Airport-Connaught or Paharganj Rs200-250; Paharganj-Connaught Rs20-30; Paharganj-Old Delhi Railway Rs30-40; Connaught-Old Delhi Rs35-50; Connaught-Chanakyapuri Rs35-40.

Cycle-Rickshaws

Cycle-rickshaws can't go through parts of New Delhi, so don't tempt them into making long detours. In Old Delhi's narrow streets, though, they are ideal. Typical fares include: Old Delhi-New Delhi Railway Station (Rs30) and Paharganj-Connaught Place (Rs5).

Buses

Buses are certainly cheap, but they bring long delays and big crowds. Women can sit on the specially marked seats on the left. **Delhi Transport Corp (DTC)** is currently struggling with private companies to bring local bus service under government control. Many bus lines run sporadically and don't have numbers; for up-to-date information go to the Government of India Tourist Office. (Bus fares Rs1-15.)

Bus #	Route
101	Chandi Chowk/Red Fort-Bus Station-Connaught Place
425	Connaught Place-Nizamuddin
505	City Center-Qutb Minar
620	Chanakyapuri-Haus Khaz

Bicycles

Cycling in Delhi is harrowing but fun. Old Delhi is congested and slow; New Delhi is a bit faster, with broader streets. Exploring by bicycle lets you see more of the main roads, as well as some places tourists don't usually go. **Mehta Cycles** (also known as Aadya Shakti Handicrafts), 2 stores east of the Kesri Hotel on the Main Bazaar, Paharganj (tel. 354 0370) rents bicycles for Rs30 per day, or Rs5 per hr. (plus Rs600 deposit, Rs5 overnight charge; bell and lock included, but no helmets available). Rent long-term, and they may scrap the overnight charge. (Open daily 9am-8pm.)

TOURIST AND FINANCIAL SERVICES

> **Warning:** Delhi is full of "tourist offices" which claim to provide booking assistance, free maps, and other services. Across from the railway are several of these offices—their bookings are likely to be fraudulent, or at least overpriced. Stick to the main government tourist office on Janpath, and for train tickets, to the tourist reservation office in the New Delhi Railway Station, or a government-approved private travel agencies. **Delhi is a haven for subversive activity.** Every rickshaw driver wants to change money, and everyone wants desperately for you to buy their knick-knacks or "dream vacations." Con artists abound, particularly in Paharganj and other tourist hot-beds. If you realize that you've been cheated after the fact, contact the Government of India Tourist Office. They are frequently able to compensate tourists who have been ripped off, even if the exchange in question was ostensibly legal. In general, however, your best tactic is to keep your cool and hone your street smarts.

Tourist Office: Government of India Tourist Office, 88 Janpath (tel. 332 0005 or 332 0008; fax 332 0109), between Tolstoy Marg and Connaught Circus Rd., next to Kapoor Lamps and Delhi Photo Company. The perfect place to begin a trip to Delhi or other parts of India: great city map, helpful staff who won't rip you off, and good brochures on all of India. Open M-F 9am-6pm, Sa 9am-2pm. Closed major holidays. Additional office in the domestic terminal at the airport (tel. 566 5296; open until last flight leaves, around 11pm). Two other government-sponsored agencies providing information and bookings are: **India Tourism Development Corporation** (ITDC, also called India Tourism or Ashok Travels), Connaught Pl. (tel. 332 2336; open 6:30am-10pm), at the corner of Middle Circle and Radial Rd., and **Delhi Tourism** (DTTDC, not to be confused with DTC), Connaught Pl., N-block, Middle Circle (tel. 331 4229 or 331 5322; open 7am-9pm). All three government agencies also have branches in the international terminal at the airport. Delhi has tourist offices for the different states of India, so if you know where you're headed, these are good places to get information. The Chandralok Building, 36 Janpath, south of the government office, is home to the offices for **Uttar Pradesh** (tel. 371 1296 or 332 2251), **Himachal Pradesh** (tel. 332 5320), and **Haryana** (tel. 332 4911). The **Indian Mountaineering Foundation,** on Benito Juarez Marg, Anand Niketan (tel. 602245 or 671211), has information on treks, especially climbs over 6000m. The **Survey of India** has a branch in Delhi (tel. 332 2288) and provides maps of the city and a few trekking maps. Open M-F 9am-1pm and 1:30-5pm.

Tours: See **Sights,** p. 135.

Budget Travel: Travel agencies are a dime a dozen, so, in general, it's best to deal with a government-approved organization. However, there are a few reputable private agencies. For airline reservations and tickets, try **Gagan Travels and Tours,** at the west end of the Paharganj Main Bazaar (tel. 751 0061; fax 753 4093), across from the Hotel Amar. This agency has a reputation for honesty. Open daily 9:30am-7pm. **Bob Tours and Travels** (tel. 355 8788), opposite Sapna Hotel in Paharganj, also provides helpful information. The **ISTC Travels Office** (tel. 332 4789), also adjacent to the Imperial, issues and replaces International Student Identity Cards. Open M-F 9am-1pm and 2-5pm.

Diplomatic Missions: Most are in the Chanakyapuri area in south central Delhi and are open all day. Remember, however, that some services are only available at certain times—call ahead. Most of the listed telephone numbers work 24hr. for emergencies. **Australia,** 1/50G Shantipath (tel. 688 8223; fax 688 7536). Open M-F 8:30am-noon. **Canada,** 7/8 Shantipath (tel. 687 6500; fax 687 6579). Open M-Th 9am-5pm, F 9am-1pm. **European Union** (tel. 611 9513; fax 687 5731). Open M-F 9am-5:30pm. **Ireland,** 230 Jor Bagh (tel. 462 6733; emergency 688 6775; fax 469 7053). Open M-F 9:30am-5pm; visa services open M-F 10am-noon. **Israel,** 3 Aurangzeb Rd. (tel. 301 3238; fax 301 4298). Open M-Th 9am-5pm, F 9am-3pm. **Nepal,** Barakhamba Rd. (tel. 332 7361 or 332 8191; fax 332 6857). Open M-F 9am-3pm. **New Zealand,** 50-N Nyaya Marg (tel. 688 3170; fax 687 2317). Open M-Th 9am-5pm, F 9am-1pm. **Pakistan,** Shantipath (tel. 467 6004; fax 687 2339). Open M, Tu, Th, and F 8:30am-5pm. **South Africa,** B-18 Vasant Marg, Vasant Vihar (tel. 614 9411; fax 611 3505). Open M-F 9am-5pm. **Thailand,** 56-N Nyaya Marg, Vasant Vihar (tel. 611 8103; fax 687 2029). **U.K.,** Shantipath (tel. 687 2161; fax 687 2882). Open M-F 9am-5pm. **U.S.,** Shantipath (tel. 688 9033 or 611 3033). Open M-F 8:30am-5:30pm

Immigration Office: Unfortunately, getting a visa extension is not easy, and the process brings many travelers back to Delhi again and again. For an extension on a simple **tourist visa** (which is *not* lightly given—15 days is usually the maximum, so get your story straight ahead of time!), first head to the **Ministry of Home Affairs Foreigners Division,** in Lok Nayak Bhawan, behind Khan Market, off Subramaniya Bharati Marg around Lodi Estate. They're only open M-F 10am-noon, so arrive early with 4 passport photos and a letter stating your grounds for extension. If they process your application, head over to the **Foreigners Regional Registration Office** (tel. 331 9781, ext. 15), located in Hans Bhawan, near Tilak Bridge. Open M-F 9:30am-1:30pm and 2-4pm. The FRRO is also the office for getting **student visas** (with a bona fide student certificate of a recognized school/university, bank remittance certificate, and an extension application in duplicate with 2 photos), as well as **permits** for restricted areas of India. If you need an **exit visa,** the FRRO can process it in about 20min.

Currency Exchange: American Express: A-block, Connaught Pl. (tel. 371 2513 or 332 4119), is probably the best place to change traveler's checks. They sell, buy, and change AmEx checks, and cash other brands at 1% commission. You can buy Amex checks with rupees and encashment certificates. There's a counter for lost and stolen cards, though the main office for 24hr. check replacement is at Bhasant Lok (tel. 614 2020). The A-block office issues and receives AmEx moneygrams, and offers usual cardmembers' services, including personal check cashing, card replacement, mail holding, and travel services. Open M-Sa 9:30am-6:30pm. After hours, head to a legitimate money changer, such as **S.G. Securities PVT Ltd.,** M-96, Middle Circle, Connaught (tel. 372 3000 or 331 8000). Open M-Sa 9:30am-8:30pm. **Hotel Grand Regency** (tel. 354 0101), in Paharganj, just a block from the New Delhi Railway Station, changes all major currencies 24hr. **Bank of Baroda** (tel. 332 8230) on Sansad Marg in the big, bad building beyond the outer circle, gives cash advances on Visa and MC. Open M-F 10am-2pm, Sa 10am-noon. **Citibank** (tel. 371 2484), around the corner toward Connaught Pl. from the Bank of Baroda, has a **24hr. ATM** (compatible with Cirrus systems.) Open M-F 10am-2pm, Sa 10am-noon. **Bank of America NT&SA,** Hansalaya Bldg., 15 Barakhamba Rd. (tel. 372 2333), also has a tightly guarded **24hr. ATM.** The **State Bank of India** branch at Chandni Chowk (tel. 296 0393), 200m from the east end, changes traveler's checks. Open M-F 10am-2pm, Sa 10am-noon. The main branch is on Sansad Marg, near Connaught Pl., and there is also a 24hr. branch in the international terminal of the airport. For truly desperate situations, there are numerous **illegal money changers** along the Main Bazaar in Paharganj—just ask anyone on the street. They're less likely to change traveler's checks. Don't let them go off with your money promising to return with rupees, even if they leave a "friend" of theirs with you while you wait. **Western Union and Money Transfer** (tel. 331122; 1-800-325-6000) has an office at F-12 Connaught Pl. and charges a 5% commission to transfer money from abroad. Open M-F 9:30am-7pm, Sa 9:30-2pm.

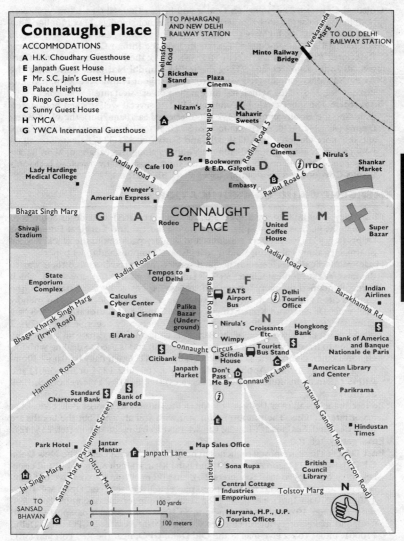

Connaught Place

ACCOMMODATIONS

A H.K. Choudhary Guesthouse
E Janpath Guest House
F Mr. S.C. Jain's Guest House
B Palace Heights
D Ringo Guest House
C Sunny Guest House
H YMCA
G YWCA International Guesthouse

TO PAHARGANJ AND NEW DELHI RAILWAY STATION

TO OLD DELHI RAILWAY STATION

Minto Railway Bridge

Vivekananda Marg

Chelmsford Road

Rickshaw Stand

Plaza Cinema

Nizam's

Radial Road 4

K Mahavir Sweets

Radial Road 5

Odeon Cinema

L Nirula's

H

B Zen

Cafe 100

Bookworm & E.D. Galgotia

C

D

ITDC

Shankar Market

Radial Road 3

Wenger's

American Express

Embassy

Radial Road 6

Lady Hardinge Medical College

Bhagat Singh Marg

CONNAUGHT PLACE

Rodeo

United Coffee House

E M

Shivaji Stadium

G A

Super Bazar

Radial Road 7

Radial Road 2

State Emporium Complex

Tempos to Old Delhi

Radial Road

F EATS Airport Bus

Delhi Tourist Office

Indian Airlines

Bhagat Kharak Singh Marg (Irwin Road)

Calculus Cyber Center

Regal Cinema

Palika Bazar (Underground)

Nirula's

Wimpy

N Croissants Etc.

Hongkong Bank

Barakhamba Rd.

Bank of America and Banque Nationale de Paris

El Arab

Connaught Circus

Citibank

Scindia House

Tourist Bus Stand

American Library and Center

Hanuman Road

Janpath Market

Don't Pass Me By

Connaught Lane

Parikrama

Standard Chartered Bank

Bank of Baroda

Kasturba Gandhi Marg (Curzon Road)

Hindustan Times

Sansad Marg (Parliament Street)

Tolstoy Marg

E

Park Hotel

Jantar Mantar

F Janpath Lane

Map Sales Office

Jai Singh Marg

Janpath

Sona Rupa

British Council Library

TO SANSAD BHAVAN

G

Central Cottage Industries Emporium

Tolstoy Marg

N

0   100 yards

0   100 meters

Haryana, H.P., U.P. Tourist Offices

NORTH INDIA

LOCAL SERVICES

Luggage Storage: Many hotels store luggage at no charge. Ashok Yatra Niwas Hotel has a safe storage room, but charges about Rs4 per day.

Market: See **Shopping**, p. 144.

Library: The **American Center Library**, 24 Kasturba Gandhi Marg (tel. 331 6841; fax 332 9499; email library@usisdel.ernet.in), is large, and their CD-ROM and Internet databases are good for research. This collection includes the embassy's library. Check out up to 4 books with a Rs200 membership. Videotape rentals. Admission Rs10 per day. Open M-Tu and Th-Sa 10am-6pm. The **British Council Library**, 17 Kasturba Gandhi Marg (tel. 371140), up the street on the other side, is less accessible. Check out up to 4 books with a Rs500 membership. Open Tu-Sa 9am-5pm. The **Ramakrishna Mission**, at the west end of Paharganj Main Bazaar, has a library with current periodicals. Rs10 fee, Rs100 deposit. Open Tu-Su 10am-6pm.

Cultural Centers: The American Center and British Council (see **Library,** above), both have regular lectures, film screenings, and minor shindigs. **Max Mueller Bhavan,** 3 Kasturba Gandhi Marg (tel. 332 9506), has a library, and also shows films in Siddhartha Hall. Indian cultural centers include the **Indian Council for Cultural Relations,** Azad Bhavan, 1P Estate (tel. 331 2274); the **India International Centre,** 40 Lodi Estate (tel. 461 9431); the **Indira Gandhi National Centre for the Arts,** C. V. Mess, Janpath (tel. 338 9216); and **Sangeet Natak Akademi,** Rabindra Bhavan (tel. 338 7246), which has information on classical music concerts.

Bookstore: The inner circle of Connaught Pl. has several well-stocked bookstores, including the **Bookworm** (tel. 332 2260; open M-Sa 10am-7pm), the **New Book Depot** (tel. 332 0020; open summer: M-Sa 10:30am-7:30pm, winter: 10am-7pm), and the more cluttered **E.D. Galgotia and Sons** (tel. 371 3227), next door, all on B-block (open M-Sa 10:30am-7:30pm). **Vendors** along the Paharganj Main Bazaar sell second-hand and new books, especially those most read by travelers. **Jackson's Books Corner** has a good supply (open daily 10am-11pm).

EMERGENCY AND COMMUNICATIONS

Pharmacy: The multi-story **Super Bazaar** (tel. 331 0163), outside of M-block of Connaught Pl., has a 24hr. pharmacy. Their **Medical and Surgical Equipment Dept.** (tel. 331476) proffers condoms and sanitary pads round the clock. Several pharmacies along Paharganj Main Bazaar also sell tampons and toilet paper.

Hospital/Medical Services: For hospital service, many travelers find their way to the **East-West Medical Clinic,** 38 Golf Links Rd., Lodi area (tel. 469 9229), which is recommended by many foreign embassies. Expensive by local standards, the clinic is clean and efficient, run by an American-trained Sikh doctor and his friendly Irish wife. Dr. Sharwan Kumar Gupta's **Care Clinic and Laboratory,** 1468 Sangatrashan (tel. 751 7841, home tel. 623 3088, emergency pager 9632 113979), 2 blocks north of the west end of the Bazaar, is convenient to Paharganj and accommodating to travelers; the staff speaks good English and is used to dealing with foreign insurance companies. Recommended by IAMAT. Open daily 8:30am-7:30pm. Other hospitals include **Apollo,** on Mathura Rd. (tel. 682 1254 or 692 5801) and **AIIMS** (All-India Institute for Medical Services) (tel. 661123; emergency tel. 1099 or 102).

Police: Branches all over Delhi—look for Delhi Traffic and Tourist Police kiosks at major intersections. Their motto is "for you with you always," but the booths are often deserted. Stations at Chandni Chowk next to Bahrandi Mandir (tel. 233442).

Emergency: tel. 100.

Post Office: There are postal branches in nearly every part of Delhi. The **New Delhi GPO** (tel. 336 4111), on Ashoka Rd. and Baba Kharak Singh Marg, is big and circular—they offer speed mail (counters 2-4), "hybrid mail" (an inexpensive but cumbersome alternative to fax), and general parcel delivery services. Open M-F 10am-4:30pm, Sa 10am-3pm for express; M-Sa 10am-5:30pm for sale of stamps. *Poste Restante* (counter 19) open M-F 10am-5pm, Sa 10am-2pm. Bring a passport to claim mail, and make sure your loved ones write to *Poste Restante,* GPO, New Delhi, 110001, India. To receive mail at the **Old Delhi GPO,** near the Red Fort and ISBT, use the following address: GPO, Delhi, 110006. Other overnight and express couriers, such as **Overnite Express** (tel. 336 8660; open 24hr.) and **Blue Dart** (incorporated with FedEx; tel. 332 4511, ext. 290; open M-Sa 10am-10pm), are located below the state tourist offices in Kanishka Shopping Plaza, next to Ashok Yatri Niwas Hotel. For **shipping,** the Parcel Packing portion of the Sham Store (tel. 738945), in Paharganj Main Bazaar, has an export license (open daily 10am-8pm). **Belair Travel and Cargo,** 10-B Scindia House (tel. 331 3985), ships bulky luggage and boxes overseas. Open M-F 10am-6pm, Sa 10am-2pm. **Postal Code:** 110001.

Internet: Calculus Cyber Center (tel. 373 4007), next to the Regal Cinema, above Khadi Gramdyog has Web service (Rs150 per hr., Rs100 per 30min., under 15min. Rs50), as does **The Cybercafe,** N-block, Middle Circle (tel. 371 0352). Both open daily 9:30am-8:30pm. **H.K. Choudhary's Guesthouse,** H-block, Middle Circle (tel. 332 2043) offers basic email (Rs100 per hour). **Paharganj's** Internet center is at 1587 Main Bazaar (tel. 752 7744), between Hotel Vishal and Hotel Metropolis

(Rs90 per 30min., Rs40 under 10min.). There is 24hr. access at **Shivam Tour and Travels** (tel. 752 4849), off the main bazaar at the east end, near Hotel Star Palace.
Telephones: Many hotels will let you make local calls or can point you to the nearest office. Paharganj Main Bazaar has dozens of **STD/ISD** offices, which now offer such services as collect and credit card calls abroad, callbacks (usually Rs5 per min., but free at **Hotel Anoop** and at the **Divya Telecom,** off the Paharganj main bazaar, at the east end), fax, and telex. Numerous booths are open 24hr. in Paharganj. In Connaught Pl., head to **Eastern Court,** on Janpath, south of the Government of India Tourist Office, for 24hr. STD, as well as local calls, fax, and postal service. **Telephone Code:** 011.

■ Accommodations

Staying in Delhi can be frustratingly expensive. Prices have been driven up so much that a room under Rs100 is almost invariably a cesspool. Still, bargains can be found in each of three major hotel centers: Paharganj, Connaught Pl., and Old Delhi.

Paharganj (Main Bazaar) is at once hilarious, dangerous, and absurd. Paharganj has adapted to travelers' needs, but still retains its legendary squalor and seediness, and it's important to remember that the area can be dangerous, especially for women traveling alone. Talk to any middle-class Delhi-ite about Paharganj and you're bound to hear stories about passport scams, drugged drinks, rape, and murder. Some of these stories are true, but Paharganj has also become the quintessential New Delhi urban legend. It's important to be a little bit paranoid here—Paharganj is packed with people who cheat tourists for a living. This is no tranquil enclave, but there are dozens of STD/ISD booths, Kashmiri "travel agents" with the gift of gab, hash dealers, money changers, and even occasional elephants walking down the Main Bazaar. It's dirty, it's decadent, and it's unadulterated Delhi. If you've just arrived in India, or are simply not into grime, **Connaught Place** has its own collection of guest houses and hotels, most nicer and more expensive than those in Paharganj. On the other hand, if you really want to put your nose in it, there's always **Old Delhi,** the purist's retreat (no banana pancakes here). Finally, a few budget hotels eke out an existence near **Chanakyapuri's** diplomatic enclaves and sights.

PAHARGANJ

The heart of Paharganj is near the center of the **Main Bazaar,** close to the west end; this is where most restaurants and popular hotels are, so head here if you crave the constant company of other travelers. Hotels nearer to the railway station often offer better deals, however, and the hike to food is not that long. Generators and good rooftop restaurants are key. All of the following directions (right, left) are given from the orientation of someone walking west on Main Bazaar from the train station.

Anoop Hotel, Main Bazaar (tel. 529366 or 521467). Popular, multi-floor backpackers' hotel—disturbing no-Indians policy, though. Rooms (with attached bath) are spacious, and efficiently kept. STD/ISD has free callbacks. Bona fide 24hr. Italian rooftop *ristorante.* Singles Rs180; doubles Rs250, with air-cooling Rs270, with A/C Rs400; extra person Rs50.

Camran Lodge, Main Bazaar (tel. 526053; fax 777 9906), on the right. With the coolest architecture in Paharganj (it's an old mosque), the Camran is a quiet underdog. Not as sterile or as modern as other places, but some rooms are large and airy, with etched designs. Singles Rs75; doubles Rs140, with bath Rs175.

Hotel Vishal, Main Bazaar (tel. 753 2079 or 752 0123), west end, after the Hare Krishna Guesthouse. More mellow than other popular backpacker hang-outs. The security and safety of his clients is the owner's top priority. Great rooftop for relaxation (gaze through the polluted air to the streets below). Check-out noon. Singles Rs100, with bath Rs150; doubles Rs150/200. Air-cooling Rs25-50 extra.

Traveller Guest House, Main Bazaar (tel. 354 4849), left side, not far from the railway station. Rooms are smallish but worth it for black-and-white TV, "disinfected" toilets, and air-cooling. Doubles Rs200; triples Rs250.

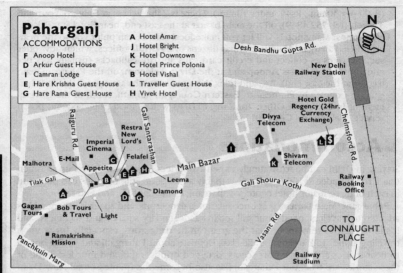

Paharganj
ACCOMMODATIONS

F Anoop Hotel
D Arkur Guest House
I Camran Lodge
E Hare Krishna Guest House
G Hare Rama Guest House

A Hotel Amar
J Hotel Bright
K Hotel Downtown
C Hotel Prince Polonia
B Hotel Vishal
L Traveller Guest House
H Vivek Hotel

Vivek Hotel, 1534 Main Bazaar (tel. 523015 or 753 7102), at the heart of Paharganj. Big, marble hotel with under-used lobby and elevator. Try to get a room overlooking the courtyard. Popular among backpackers. The attached restaurant, Leema, is on the ground floor and the rooftop. Singles with attached bath and air-cooling Rs200, with TV Rs300, with A/C Rs600; doubles Rs250/400/700.

Hotel Downtown, Main Bazaar (tel. 355 5815; fax 752 0033), near the railway station. Next to Hotel Star Palace (which has a sign), set back 10m from Main Bazaar proper, left side. Friendly, clean hotel. Compact rooms have good fans, many have windows. Great staff, rooftop room service 24hr. Check-out noon. Singles Rs125, with bath Rs150; doubles Rs150/200.

Hotel Bright, Main Bazaar (tel. 752 5852), at the east end of the Bazaar, before Camran Lodge. Cheap rooms are relatively clean, if run down. The three buildings comprising this hotel have three different price ranges to match. Check-out noon. Singles Rs60, with bath Rs130; doubles Rs100/150. Air-cooling Rs40 extra.

Hare Rama Guest House, 298 Main Bazaar (tel. 751 8972 or 521413). Entrance 10m back. Always filled with Israelis. Stay away from the attached travel agency. Singles Rs120; doubles Rs170, with bath Rs200, with A/C Rs350.

Hare Krishna Guest House, Main Bazaar (tel. 753 3017 or 592188). Gentle owner not as business-oriented as staff of next-door Anoop. Quieter, clean-enough rooms have tidy, elevated bathrooms, 15cm (thick, not long) mattresses, and a couple have interesting views (such as the legs of people sitting in the Anoop restaurant, to which this hotel is conveniently connected). Check-out 24hr. Singles Rs150, with bath Rs180; doubles Rs190/230.

Ankur Guest House, opposite Hare Rama Guest House. Soft-spoken in shadow of bigger neighbors, but tiny streetside rooftop restaurant draws a consistent crowd. Rooms are ample and have working bathrooms. Singles Rs130; doubles Rs180.

Hotel Amar, Main Bazaar (tel. 354 4849), past Metropolis Hotel, west end of Main Bazaar. Get the single. Dim rooms, but most have TV, air-cooling, and telephone. Singles Rs150, with bath Rs200, with TV and A/C Rs500; doubles Rs250/350/600.

Hotel Prince Polonia, 2326 Tilak Gali (tel. 351 1930; fax 355 7646), make a right at Hotel Metropolis and another right at the next street. Disinfected rooms with satellite TV, water heater, A/C, and a small couch. Singles Rs770; doubles Rs840.

CONNAUGHT PLACE

Some guest lodges long popular among budget travelers have let their boosted egos lead to boosted prices and diminished quality. As a result, Connaught Pl. is better for mid-range and high-end hotels. Still, there are a few exceptions.

Hotel Palace Heights, Radial Rd. 6, D-block (tel. 332 1419), on the top floor. This hotel offers a different rooftop experience for those seeking respite from Paharganj's claustrophobic alleys and backpacking subculture. A good value for Connaught, though the bathrooms could be cleaner. One hole-in-the-wall single Rs150; other singles with air-cooling and common bath Rs250; doubles Rs300-375/660.

Sunny Guest House, Connaught Ln. (tel. 331 2909), past Ringo Guest House. Standard backpacker grotto. Dorms are significantly more spacious than those at Ringo. Dorm beds Rs70; singles Rs150-170; doubles Rs250, with bath Rs350-400.

H.K. Choudhary Guesthouse, H-35/3, Middle Circle (tel. 332 2043; fax 332 6949). Excellent service geared toward business travelers. 24 hr. STD, email (Rs100 per hr.), and computer facilities. Rooms are small but nicely decorated. All rooms have attached baths. Singles Rs300; doubles with air-cooling Rs350, with A/C Rs660.

Ringo Guest House, 17 Scindia House (tel. 331 0605). Off Janpath, outside Outer Circle. A little hideaway beneath the waves of cars and people. Popular among travelers who come to deal with Delhi's bureaucracy—now a backpackers' retreat that's too big for its britches. Ridiculously stuffed dorm rooms, but a relaxed, safe, and happy atmosphere. Food available 24hr. Check-out noon. Dorm beds Rs90; singles Rs125; doubles Rs250, with bath Rs350, with air-cooling Rs400.

Mr. S.C. Jain's Guesthouse, 7 Pratap Singh Bldg., Janpath Ln. (tel. 332 3484). Close to Connaught's services. Women traveling alone might feel safer elsewhere. Well-worn rooms have common baths. Singles Rs150; doubles Rs300-350.

YMCA/YWCA. There are three Y's near Connaught Place, all friendly and reliable, offering pricey, none-too-sleek accommodations (breakfast included, though). **The YWCA Blue Triangle Tourist Hostel,** Ashoka Rd. (tel. 336 1915) is in a peaceful neighborhood and offers the best value of the bunch. Dorm beds Rs250, with A/C Rs325; singles Rs400/550; doubles Rs750/1000. **The YMCA Tourist Hostel,** on Jai Singh Rd. (tel. 336 1915), is a larger operation. Singles Rs375, with bath and A/C Rs735; doubles Rs645/1230. **The YWCA International Guest House,** 10 Sansad Marg (tel. 336 1561 or 336 1662; fax 334 1763) has A/C rooms, higher prices. Singles Rs720; doubles Rs990. All three levy a membership fee (Rs30 per person, valid 30 days). Major foreign currencies accepted; encashment certificates must be presented if rupees are used. Reservations essential and in many cases unobtainable.

OLD DELHI AND TOURIST CAMPS

The few who decide to stay the night in **Old Delhi** get a very different experience than their day-tripping neighbors. For better and for worse, Old Delhi doesn't aspire to impress foreign tourists. While prices are cheaper and people are less likely to try to cheat you, it can be hard to find anyone who speaks English. In addition, stereotypes about Westerners, and Western women in particular, are stronger here than elsewhere in the city: many men will assume that solo female travelers are looking to give sexual favors—women should avoid dressing provocatively or going out alone after dark. Still, if proper precautions are taken, staying in Old Delhi can be an unparalleled experience. Nearby, Delhi's **Tourist Camps** offer a much-better-than-it-sounds outdoors experience unlike anything in the rest of the city.

Hotel New City Palace (tel. 327 9548), west side of Jama Masjid. Superb views of the mosque, complete with loud prayers. Modern rooms have pencil-thin beds, hot water, shower, and balcony and rooftop access. Shops on the streets below cater to late-night mechanics. Great deal on A/C rooms. Dorm beds (men only) with air-cooling Rs60; singles with bath Rs200; doubles Rs250, with A/C Rs400.

Hotel Crown (tel. 237599), just south of Khush-Dil Hotel and Fatehpuri Masjid. Rooms are unusually spacious for Old Delhi; ask for a balcony. Singles Rs60, with bath Rs80, with air-cooling and bath Rs120; doubles Rs140/160/200.

Hotel Vakil, 735 Jama Masjid (tel. 326 9625). On the street west of Jama Masjid, south of New City Palace. Front-side views of the mosque, excellent roof (just don't fall off!), and simple rooms with air-coolers and hot water in attached baths. The halls are dark, and the staff speaks labored English. Check-out 24hr. Doubles with air-cooling, some with bath, Rs150; triples Rs200-250.

Khush-Dil Hotel, Chandni Chowk (tel. 395 2110), at the west end of Chandni Chowk, just south of the Mosque on Fatehpuri Corner. Narrow beds, dank bathrooms, feeble fans, but excellent front-side views of the busy street. Check-out 24hr. Singles Rs80, with bath Rs120; doubles Rs120/150; air-cooling Rs20 extra.

New Delhi Tourist Camp, Jawaharlal Nehru Marg (tel. 327 2898; fax 326 3693), near Delhi Gate, opposite J.P. Narayan (Irwin) Hospital. Excellent location—equidistant from Old Delhi, Paharganj, and Connaught Pl., and far enough away from them all to create its own insular, country atmosphere. Camp outside, or stay in one of the rustic buildings surrounding the garden. Outside restaurant open 7:30am-10pm. The hotel changes money and offers free callbacks. Pitch your own tent Rs50; singles Rs125; doubles Rs180, with attached bath and air-cooling Rs390.

Tourist Camping Park, Qudsia Garden (tel. 252 3121 or 252 2597), across the street and to the right of the ISBT at Kashmiri Gate. Great for crashing after a long bus journey. Smaller and less developed than Tourist Camp, they rent tents and have a great restaurant next door. Check-out noon. Rooms have clean common baths. Tents Rs50 per person; singles Rs110, with air-cooling Rs140; doubles Rs140/170.

CHANAKYAPURI

Vishwa Yuvak Kendra International Youth Centre, Circular Rd., Chanakyapuri (tel. 230 1363). Across from Nehru Planetarium, in a comfortable part of town. Looks and smells uncannily like a typical youth hostel. Popular for conventions. Rooms are big and modern. English books for sale. Singles Rs550; doubles Rs600.

International Youth Hostel (HI), 5 Nyaya Marg (tel. 611 6285 or 467 6349; fax 611 3469), near the Chinese Embassy, a few blocks from the Vishwa Yuvak Kendra Center. Only HI members can stay, but membership is a steal at Rs250, and breakfast is included. The whole place is A/C and wheelchair-accessible. Dorms are gender segregated. Dorm beds Rs400; doubles with bath Rs600.

■ Food and Drink

It's worth shelling out a little cash for some of Delhi's excellent meals. There are countless restaurants in all price ranges, respectable Western-style fast food, superb Chinese and Middle Eastern cuisine, and even a couple of Mexican restaurants. There's plenty of knock-out Indian food as well. For a real splurge—and you have to want this bad—head to one of the 5-star hotels. Those in the Maurya Sheraton (on the road to the airport) and in the Ashok Frontier are considered particularly good—expect to pay up to Rs300-400 for an entree.

PAHARGANJ

This backpackers' district has developed several hot spots for hanging out—and all of them are about five stories up. Just which hotel's rooftop restaurant will draw the crowd on any evening is unclear. None of these places serves particularly good food, though their breakfasts are tolerable. But the rooftops are the place to find Paharganj's backpack-rats sipping tea and munching curd after hours. It's best to get off the Main Bazaar for food, though the strip's joints do offer menus that tantalize foreign tongues. The places near the Railway Station have good tea, but aren't particularly hygienic. Wander the streets north of Paharganj to see where the locals are eating.

Malhotra Restaurant, 1833 Chuna Mandi. Walk west on Main Bazaar, right at Rajguru Rd. at the Metropolis, then take the first left. Tucked down below street level, and often packed with locals. Good, clean, if not always consistent Indian and Chinese fare, with a splash of Continental. A/C branch next door offers the same fare at slightly higher prices. Try the excellent *karhai* chicken (Rs90) and vegetable cutlets (Rs25). Open daily 8:30am-11pm.

Light Restaurant (Sapna Hill Restaurant), Main Bazaar, at the west end. Pronounced "Liggot" by some staff-members. All-veg.: *thalis* are only Rs20, and even better, you can look inside the pots and see which 2 vegetables you want with your *dal*, rice, *chapatis*, and *kheer*. Big bowls of rice pudding Rs8.

Metropolis Restaurant, Main Bazaar, in the Metropolis Hotel. The best restaurant on the block, with subtly prepared Chinese, Japanese, Indian, and Continental dishes. *Palak paneer* Rs60; Julienne of Chicken with "a touch of garlic *demiglace*" Rs150. Subdued setting—inside, or on the rooftop. Open daily 8am-6pm for breakfast and snacks, 11am-11pm for lunch and dinner.

Deluxe Diamond Cafe, Main Bazaar, across from the Hotel Vivek. A narrow little room—good for meeting strangers or people-watching street-side. Decent Indian food, overly ambitious Continental. Veg. *thalis* Rs30, Indian breakfast Rs25, lamb with boiled potato Rs40. Open daily 6:30am-12:30am.

Leema Restaurant, Main Bazaar, in Hotel Vivek. The best budget-hotel restaurant in Paharganj is not on a rooftop, but just above the street. A/C, fresh juices, and excellent veg. sandwiches (Rs15), but the service can be torturously slow. Open daily 6am-midnight.

Felafel, Main Bazaar, next to Hotel Vishal and New Lord's Café. Surprisingly authentic Middle Eastern taste. Fresh pita bread (Rs10) is some of the best in town, with salad or humus Rs30. Open 11am-11pm.

CONNAUGHT PLACE

Like Paharganj, Connaught has a slanted range—here, though, there are one or two good budget spots and several excellent Indian and international restaurants to delight diplomats and executives who long for a taste of home. Fast-food joints such as Pizza Hut and British institutions like Wimpy have started to move in.

Nirula's, L-block (tel. 332 2419). Behemoth multi-restaurant: head to the ice cream bar for smooth mango scoops and shakes, or try Indian flavors like Zafrani Badaam Pista, 21 Love, or Gulabo (Rs25 per scoop). Hit the Potpourri upstairs, with lamburgers (Rs90), a clean, all-you-can-eat salad bar (Rs15), and pizzas (Rs80-120). Eat in their classy "Chinese Room" or sip drinks in one of 2 bars; the popular, pricey, Pegasus Bar is open 11am-midnight. Ice cream and fast food branch near Wimpy's on N-block. Pastry shop open 9am-9pm. Open daily 10:30am-midnight.

Nizam's, H-block, behind Plaza Cinema. Slow service, but worth the wait. The tastiest *biryani* (Rs65) and kebab eggrolls (Rs40) in the city. It's a meat-lover's paradise, but placates the vegetarians with delicious vegetable rolls (Rs25); they have a TV too. Open M-Sa 12:30-11pm, Su 5-11pm.

Don't Pass Me By, 79 Scindia House (tel. 335 2942). Near Ringo and Sunny Guest Houses. Named after the Beatles song. Humble, budget eats are nicely prepared. Two tables inside, more on the outside patio. Cornflakes with fruit and curd Rs30; fried Tibetan bread Rs20; cheese tomato omelette Rs18. Open daily 7am-9pm.

Sona Rupa Restaurant, on Janpath, past the Government of India Tourist Office. Delicious veg. South Indian food at good prices; popular with natives. Buffet (Rs80) and *thalis* (Rs60), *dosa* (Rs30-40), and a la carte options. Self-service system is a little confusing. Open M-Sa 11:30am-10pm, Su 12:30-10pm.

United Coffee House (tel. 332 2075). Quiet, swish setting to act snooty and snotty. Not over-the-top elegant, but not some homey cafe either, 50-year-old restaurant serves "special soup with meatballs and spinach" (Rs55). Veg. and non-veg. Chinese and Continental dishes Rs90. Open daily 9am-midnight.

Rodeo, A-block (tel. 371 3780). Near the AmEx office. For an ol' time American West treat, sidle up to a saddle-stool at the bar. Rope in some Mexican enchiladas and tacos (Rs140). Italian (think Spaghetti Western) and Indian menus, too. Pitchers of draft beer Rs180. Buffet M-Sa noon-7pm (Rs135). Open daily noon-midnight.

Wenger & Co. Pastry Shop, Inner Circle, A-block (tel. 332 4373), next to AmEx office. Western-style treats like chocolate doughnuts (Rs8), strudels, and other scrumptious, if occasionally distorted, versions of European bakery fare. Loaves of whole wheat, sweet, and garlic bread (Rs10-15). Open daily 10am-7:30pm.

Mahavir Sweets, Middle Circle, C-block, has "pure vegetarian sweets," and is also popular for its mixed *thali* (Rs20). Suitable for a quick but filling bite between jaunts to the bank or bookshops. Open M-Sa 8am-8pm.

El Arab, 13 Regal Bldg., Outer Circle, near Gaylord's Restaurant and Regal Cinema, upstairs from The Cellar. Lebanese cuisine: meat-laden buffet (12:30-3:30pm and 6-10pm; Rs190), but a la carte options also available. Open M-Sa 11am-10pm.

Croissants, Etc., 9 Scindia House, Outer Circle. Another recent addition to the fast food frenzy that's storming Delhi. Mild, basic sandwiches refresh on hot days. Ummburgers (Rs30-40), veg. "croissandwich" Rs15, chicken croissant Rs20. Open daily 8:30am-10:30pm.

Zen Restaurant, B-block (tel. 372 4444). Elegant, but can't get its cultures straight—mostly Chinese food, a Japanese name, American 1950s music, all in the middle of India. Still, delicate dishes and gracious service are worth it, particularly if the A/C is on. Veg. and non-veg. dishes Rs70-200. Open 11am-noon for coffee, 12:30-10:30pm for lunch and dinner, 3-7:30 pm for booze and snacks.

Parikrama, Kasturba Gandhi Marg (tel. 372 1616). Delhi's revolving rooftop restaurant takes 1½hr. to go around once, and they won't let your meal finish before that. Good Continental, Chinese, and Indian food. The Chinese soft noodles are a delectable melange of Indian and Chinese spices (Rs130). Come during the day to see more, or at sunset, to see less. Open daily noon-11pm.

Embassy Restaurant, D-block (tel. 332 0480). Good Indian food at not-necessarily-knuckle-busting prices. Brain curry Rs94, cream of asparagus soup Rs45. Open daily 12:45-3:30pm and 7-11pm.

OLD DELHI

Old Delhi offers every class of edible fare—from spices to squawking chickens—and boasts a number of renowned restaurants.

Karim (tel. 326 9880), in a small courtyard off Matya Mahal, about 8 shops down from Jama Masjid (not visible from the road). One of the city's most popular and famous restaurants, Karim is run by descendants of the cooks of Mughal royalty. The menu is full of rich, meat-heavy dishes. Half dishes (at half-price) fit the bill for the budget traveler. Chicken stew Rs76, mutton *burra* Rs90. Try the paper-thin *roomali roti*. Open daily 7am-midnight.

Moti Mahal Restaurant, Netaji Subhash Marg (tel. 327 3611). Outdoor patio or chandeliered dining halls serve delicious Indian, particularly *tandoori* cuisine. Live music (usually singing) happens nightly W-M 8-11:30pm. Meaty menu includes chicken entrees Rs60-200. Mineral water Rs30. Open daily 11am-midnight.

Cosi-e-Cosi (tel. 252 3121), opposite Kashmiri Gate ISBT, next to the Tourist Camping Park. New restaurant knows how to flavor food. *Dal makhni* (Rs30), mixed veg. (Rs35), and South Indian and Chinese dishes as well.

Shree Delhi Gujarati Samaj, 2 Raj Niwash Marg (tel. 252 0369), past Kashmiri Gate ISBT and the Oberoi Hotel (not visible from the street). Excellent restaurant in the middle of a Gujarati apartment building. Fresh *thalis* Rs17, all-you-can-eat Rs28.

NEW DELHI

Village Bistro, Hauz Khas Village (tel. 685 2227). A complete bazaar of restaurants to treat the South Delhi elite. Le Café has Continental fare, Mohalla has spats of live Rajasthani music and an Indian menu; Top of the Village has live jazz nightly.

The Yellow Brick Road, Ambassador Hotel, Sujan Singh Park (tel. 463 2600), 1km south of India Gate. As authentically American as they get in this hemisphere. 1950s photos grace the walls, the decor is bright yellow, and the menu is a bizarre tabloid newspaper. Tiramisu (Rs65), burgers (Rs105-145), Waldorf salad (Rs75), make-your-own sandwiches and pizza (Rs75/125), and Indian fare. Open 24hr.

■ Sights

Like any capital city worth its salt, Delhi boasts a vast number of things to see. There are 1376 monuments, two of which are UNESCO World Heritage sites (Qutb Minar and Humayun's Tomb). If you're spending only a couple of days in Delhi, budget your time wisely! The must-sees are the Qutb Minar Complex and Old Delhi—Lal Qila (Red Fort), Jama Masjid (Friday Mosque), and the bazaars. Round out your time by having a look at Rashtrapati Bhavan, Humayun's Tomb, and if you need respite from the mid-day heat, the National Museum. If you show up first thing in the morning at any of these sights, chances are you'll have the place to yourself. As always, men (and occasionally a woman or two) will linger by the entrance to the various tourist attractions, flashing ID cards (often bogus) and offering their services as guides. While such guides often don't have their facts straight, some are quite knowledgeable. If you hire a guide, be sure to set a price in advance; don't be shy about bargaining. Guides and/ or vehicles can be hired for 4-12 hour stints; contact ITDC or Delhi Tourism (see **Tourist Office**, p. 125). Standard non-A/C taxis cost about Rs310 for 4hr.

Several operations run **guided tours** of Delhi (Rs90-125). These usually hit New Delhi in the morning, stopping at Jantar Mantar, the Lakshmi Narayan Temple, Humayun's Tomb, the Baha'i Temple, driving by the more notable landmarks (such as India Gate), and jaunting south of the city to Qutb Minar. Tours of Old Delhi might include the Red Fort, Raj Ghat, Shanti Vana, and a glimpse of Jama Masjid (Rs90-100). These tours rush through each sight, the guides are not always informed, and a full day of bus riding, even in air-conditioned comfort, is never much of a joy, but these tours are helpful if you've only got a short time in Delhi. Book through ITDC, L-block, Connaught Pl. (tel. 332 0331; open daily 630am-10pm), or at Delhi Tourism and Transportation (open daily 7am-9pm).

OLD DELHI

Red Fort (Lal Qila)
Location: *Enter through Lahore Gate, pass through Chatta Chowk and into the palace area.*
Hours: *Fort open daily 8am-dusk. Museums open Sa-Th 10am-5pm.* **Admission:** *Rs2.*
Other: *English sound and light shows (Rs20): Nov.-Jan. 7:30-8:30pm.; Feb.-Apr. 8:30-9:30pm; May-Aug. 9-10pm; Sept.-Oct. 8:30-9:30pm.*

Shortly after moving the capital from Agra to Delhi, Mughal emperor Shah Jahan embarked on the construction of the Red Fort. Work started on April 16, 1639, and was completed nine years later to the day, at a cost of more than 10 million rupees. Soaring to a height of 33.5m, the fort's red sandstone ramparts ring a 2km perimeter and are surrounded by a moat into which the Yamuna once flowed. Some of its more resplendent features are now gone—the famed Peacock Throne was snatched away in 1739, the gems that adorned the palaces have all been removed, and the canals through which Stream of Paradise once gurgled are now dry. But the Red Fort remains what it has always been—an incredible monument to Mughal power and its splendid architecture, as awe-inspiring to visitors today as it was to citizens then.

The entrance to the fort is toward the middle of its west wall, at the muscular, three-story **Lahore Gate**, through which the Mughal emperors would leave the fort for Jama Masjid. Next to the gate is the spot from which the Prime Minister addresses cheering throngs on Independence Day (Aug. 15). Lahore Gate leads to **Chatta Chowk,** the covered passageway filled with shops which today peddle souvenirs, but which during the Mughal era provided nobles with top-quality silks, precious jewelry, and fine velvets. Chatta Chowk gives way to the rectangular, three-storied **Naubat Khana** (Drum House); five times a day, music was played from this building in tribute to the emperor and his court. The floral-patterned carvings adorning the walls of Naubat Khana were once painted with gold.

Naubat Khana leads into the palace area. Across the mini-courtyard behind the simple, sturdy columns stands **Diwan-i-Am** (Hall of Public Audience), upon which the

---

Divan Dismemberment

As Mughal power declined, so did the glory of the Hall of Private Audience. The precious stones once decorating its interior are gone, its silver ceiling was carted off by the Marathas, and the famed **Peacock Throne** was plundered in 1739 by the Turkish raider Nadir Shah. The throne had been commissioned by Shah Jahan upon his reaching emperorhood; it took seven years for laborers to meet the emperor's ostentatious specifications. The throne's feet were solid gold, its canopy inlaid with diamonds, gems, and pearls, and a parrot carved from a single emerald was nestled behind the emperor's head.

---

early Mughal emperors sat (everyone else stood) for two hours a day, receiving visitors, chatting with nobles, deciding criminal cases, and conducting affairs of state. The throne rested atop the canopied white marble platform now on display. Set to the back of the platform are a series of curious panels adorned with red and green renderings of flowers, birds, trees, and lions. Lording over the entire scene from the central panel is the Greek god Orpheus. Scholars speculate that the panels, which were returned from the British Museum in 1903, were crafted in Florence. The low marble platform in front of the emperor's platform was reserved for the prime minister, who would, within earshot of the emperor, entertain grievances.

Beyond Diwan-i-Am were the private palaces of the Mughal emperor. Of the original six palaces, five remain; each was connected to its neighbor by a canal called the **Nahir-i-Bihisht** (Stream of Paradise). The palaces were set in spacious formal *charbagh* gardens. The southernmost of the palaces (coming from Diwan-i-Am, the palace farthest to the right) is **Mumtaz Mahal** (Palace of Jewels), which originally housed the women of the harem. These days, it houses a museum (see below). North of Mumtaz Mahal is **Rang Mahal** (Palace of Colors), a white marble pavilion where the emperor took his meals. During the Mughal heyday, the ceilings were decorated with silver; other parts of the ceiling are embedded with tiny mirrors that reflected the light from the emperor's candle-lit suppers. Just north of Rang Mahal, **Khas-Mahal** (Private Palace) is a wonder of ostentation; each of the three apartments was lavishly decorated in silk during the Mughal era. The southernmost of these is **Baithak** (Sitting Room), with a scale of justice carved in marble upon the walls. The emperor caught his beauty sleep in the center apartment, known as **Khwabagh** (Sleeping Chamber). Attached to the outer wall of the Khwabagh is a tower called **Muthamman-Burj** (Octagonal Tower), where the emperor would greet his subjects or watch animal fights staged below. King George V and Queen Mary sat on this porch before thousands of Delhi-ites in 1911, when a *durbar* was held and the announcement was made that the Imperial Capital would be moved to Delhi from Calcutta. North of the Khwabagh is **Tasbih Khana** (Chamber for Telling Beads), where the emperor prayed.

Just north of Khas-Mahal is the **Diwan-i-Khas** (Hall of Private Audience), constructed entirely of white marble and replete with arches. Here, the emperor would make crucial political decisions, consult privately with advisers, and speak with special visitors. Attempting to rekindle the old spark, Bahadur Shah II, the last Mughal emperor, held court here during the Mutiny of 1857; in retaliation, the British tried him in the Diwan-i-Am, then exiled him to Burma. North is the **Hammam** (Bath), whose westernmost apartment contained a rosewater fountain. The chambers on either side of its entrance are thought to have been the bathtubs of the emperor's children. West of the Hammam is the delicate **Moti-Masjid** (Pearl Mosque), built in 1662 by Emperor Aurangzeb for his personal use. The black marble outlines on the floor facilitated placement of the *musallas* (prayer mats).

Inside the Red Fort complex are two **museums.** Mumtaz Mahal's is the better of the two, displaying astrolabes, *hookahs,* and weapons. The museum in the Naubat Khana details military developments of the last two centuries.

Jama Masjid

Location: *1km west of the Red Fort.* **Hours:** *Open to tourists 30min. after dawn until 12:20pm (noon on F), 1:45pm until 20min. before prayer call, and again after prayers until 20min. before sunset.* **Admission:** *Rs5.* **Other:** *Camera fee Rs10. Lungi to wrap around bare legs Rs5-10.*

Built between 1650 and 1656 by Emperor Shah Jahan, the imposing Jama Masjid, 1km west of the Red Fort, is the largest active mosque in India. Set on a high platform atop a low hill, Jama Masjid lords over the surrounding streets with its elegant juxtaposition of red sandstone and white marble and its soaring minarets. Its three gateways separate the secular and the sacred. The east gate was reserved for the Mughal emperor and his family; now it is open to all worshippers on Fridays and holidays. Tourists should enter by the north gate. Leave your shoes, but first establish the price with the "shoe guard," as he tends to get carried away. The 900 sq. m courtyard packs in nearly 25,000 worshippers during Friday prayers.

As in most South Asian mosques, a *hauz* (tank) at the center of the courtyard is used for cleansing feet and hands before prayer, and each rectangle designates the space for one worshiper. Prayers are sung from the *imam*'s platform, under the center arch at the westernmost point of the mosque; before amplification systems, the two small posts between this point and the east gate were used by other *imams* who repeated prayers so those in the back could hear. Just west of the mosque is the *imam*'s home; *imams* have lived here since the time of Shah Jahan, and it's still possible to spot them hanging out before prayers. For an extra Rs5 (Rs10 with cameras), the adventurous can climb one of the minarets that rise from the courtyard. While those with a touch of vertigo will want to stay put, the views of Delhi from up top are amazing. Women should keep an arm ready to fend off gropers in the stairwell.

Raj Ghat

Location: *On the west bank of the Yamuna River, 1km east of Delhi Gate and about 2km southeast of the Red Fort.* **Hours:** *Open dawn-dusk.* **Admission:** *Free.*

Here, a perpetually burning flame and a simple black slab set in a grassy courtyard, offers a memorial to Mahatma Gandhi, cremated at this spot after his 1948 assassination by a Hindu extremist. Gandhi's name is notably missing from the monument—the only inscription is of his last words, "He Ram" ("Oh God"). Hundreds of visitors come each day to cast flower petals and contemplate.

Just south of the monument is a park full of trees and flowers planted by numerous dignitaries: flowers from Eisenhower, a pine from Queen Elizabeth II, and a slanted tree planted by Nasser. North of Raj Ghat is **Shanti Vana,** an eerily quiet park (if you can ignore the jillions of squawking birds) where recreational and "domestic" activities are forbidden. Geologically significant rocks are on display alongside memorials to the men and women who have earned a place in India's pantheon of political heroes. The memorial to slain prime minister Rajiv Gandhi is effusive. An adjacent monument to his older brother Sanjay was taken down after critics reminded the government that this Gandhi never served in office or accomplished much at all. After the monument was removed, however, Sanjay's admirers still put flowers at the barren spot, and eventually the monument was re-erected. The humble grassy mound that marks the life and death of Jawaharlal Nehru mentions only his wish to have his ashes thrown in the Ganga.

SOUTH DELHI

Qutb Minar Complex

Location: *At the intersection of Aurobindo Marg and Mehrauli Badarpur Rd., 14km southwest of Connaught Pl.* **Hours:** *Open daily dawn-dusk.* **Admission:** *Rs5.*

Though located in a part of Delhi speckled with crumbling mosques and decaying ramparts, the ruins of the Qutb Minar complex know no rivals. The construction of the complex began in 1199 after the Turkish ex-slave Qutb-ud-din Aibak swept into

Old Delhi: Bazaar or Bizarre?

From Jama Masjid, it's easy to begin an exploration of the dynamic tangle of shops and street vendors that constitute the bazaars of Old Delhi. While the streets surrounding Jama Masjid are cluttered with overpriced tourist-trap crap, walk 200m north, south, or west and you'll be in a part of town rarely visited by tourists, where getting lost is half the fun. Area vendors peddle wholesale paper, high-quality tools, used car parts, and all sorts of other goodies. For **one of the stinkiest places in the universe,** head south from Jama Masjid on a sunny summer afternoon toward the poultry markets, where chickens stacked atop one another in painfully cramped cages are selected by customers and then slaughtered and butchered on the spot, much to the delight of the legions of flies who call the market home. Beware of pickpockets and don't be shy about bargaining.

Ducking into any of the narrow alleys between the shops on the south side of Chandni Chowk leads to another bazaar-o dream world; follow the labyrinthine "street" any which way and stumble upon the aromatic spice market, snag a deal on gems from the jewelers (if you know what you're doing), or float from shop to shop. Don't forget to peek into the mosques and schools that line the way.

North India and defeated the Rajputs. Qutb-ud-din Aibak installed himself at Lal Kot, the site of an old Rajput city, and when his boss, Muhammad Ghuri, was murdered in 1206, he founded the Delhi Sultanate, India's first Muslim kingdom. The events that led to the building of the complex were epoch-making, and the Qutb Minar serves as a 72.5m-high exclamation point.

Qutb-ud-din Aibak began constructing the red sandstone **Qutb Minar** as a celebration of his triumphs in North India and as a milestone marking the eastern frontier of the Muslim world. As one of the tower's inscriptions notes, "the tower was erected to cast the shadow of God over both East and West." Modeled on the brick victory towers of Central Asia, the Qutb Minar also served as the minaret for the Quwwat-ul-Islam Masjid (see below). Before dying, Qutb-ud-din Aibak was able to complete only the first three stories of the tower. His son-in-law Iltutmish added a fourth story, and Firoz Shah Tughluq tacked on a fifth after repairing damage caused by a 1368 lightning strike. The fifth-story cupola erected by Firoz was felled by an 1803 earthquake and replaced by British Major Robert Smith; Smith's Mughal-style cupola now sits in the gardens, having been removed from the Qutb Minar because it was so awkward. Visitors have been forbidden from climbing the minaret since 1981, when more than 30 panicked schoolchildren were trampled to death during a power outage. While most of the calligraphy carved on the minaret is of Arabic passages from the Qur'an, a few Devanagari inscriptions prove at least some Indian influence in its design.

Just north of Qutb Minar is the **Quwwat-ul-Islam Masjid** (Might of Islam Mosque), which is the oldest extant mosque in India aside from those in western Gujarat. Begun in 1192 and completed in 1198 (extensions were added over the next two centuries), the mosque was built from the remains of 21 Hindu and Jain temples destroyed by the fanatically iconoclastic Qutb-ud-din Aibak (according to the inscription over the main entrance). The pillars from the razed temples support the east end of the mosque and are carved with bells, lotuses, and other Hindu and Jain remnants. At the center of the courtyard is the 98% pure iron **Gupta Pillar.** According to the Sanskrit inscription, the pillar was erected in honor of Vishnu and in memory of Chandra, believed to be the Gupta emperor Chandragupta II (r. 375-415 AD). Tradition holds that Anangpal, the founder of Lal Kot, brought the pillar to the area. It is said that anyone who can stand with their back against the pillar and wrap their arms around it is blessed by the gods with superhuman strength.

Just south of Qutb Minar is the domed red sandstone **Ala'i Darwaza,** built in 1311, to serve as the southern entrance to the mosque. Praised for its well-proportioned balance, the building also boasts India's first true arches. Immediately east of Ala'i Darwaza, the domed octagonal tomb with the *jali* decorative screens holds **Imam Zamin,** a Sufi saint who came to India from Central Asia in the early 16th century.

North of the Quwwat-ul-Islam Masjid is a massive, unfinished minaret, **Ala'i Minar.** Expansion had doubled the size of the mosque, and Ala'i Minar was to be twice as tall as Qutb Minar in order to be proportional. After its first 24.5m-high story was completed, construction was stopped and the wildly ambitious project was abandoned. Just south of Ala'i Minar is the **Tomb of Iltutmish,** which the sultan erected himself in 1235, four years after building his son's tomb, 8km from Qutb Minar. While Iltutmish's red sandstone tomb isn't particularly interesting from the outside, have a look at the artfully decorated interior, with its mingling of Hindu and Jain themes (wheels, lotuses, and bells) and Muslim motifs (calligraphic inscriptions, geometric patterns, and the Mecca-facing alcoves built into the west wall). Directly south of Iltutmish's tomb are the ruins of a *madrasa,* an institution of Islamic learning. In keeping with Seljuk Turkish traditions, the tomb of the *madrasa's* founder, Ala-ud-din Khalji, has been placed within it; look for the L-shaped mound of earth and rubble.

Tughluqabad

Atop a lonely, rocky outcrop on the Mehrauli Badarpur Rd., 9km east of the Qutb Minar Complex and 16km southeast of Connaught Place, is **Tughluqabad,** built as a fortified city by Ghiyas-ud-din Tughluq, who ruled the Delhi Sultanate between 1321 and 1325. These days, the abandoned fort has been invaded and conquered by weeds, aggressive monkeys, and a palpable sense of desolation. If you come, have a close look at the absolutely massive 10-15m rubble walls that run along the 6.5km circumference of the fort. Thirteen separate gates lead through the walls, which are topped with husky stone battlements. The **Tomb of Ghiyas-ud-din Tughluq,** a red sandstone and white marble affair, employs the first set of sloping walls to grace a Muslim-made building in India. Shortly after Ghiyas-ud-din Tughluq was murdered, Tughluqabad was abandoned, having been occupied for a grand total of five years.

Baha'i Temple

Location: *4km north of Tughluqabad.* **Hours:** *Open Apr.-Sept. Tu-Su 9am-7pm; Oct.-Mar. 9:30am-5:30pm.* **Admission:** *Free.*

Over the past three decades, members of the Baha'i faith have donated millions of dollars toward the construction of seven Baha'i Temples in locations such as Uganda, Samoa, and the midwestern United States. The latest addition to this series was finished in 1986 and is situated in South Delhi on a 26-acre expanse of cropped grass and elegant pools. The temple, which inevitably draws comparisons to the Sydney Opera House, is built from white marble in the shape of an opening lotus flower. Silence is requested of visitors; there's little to do but settle comfortably onto one of the wood-backed benches, listen to the dull thudding of bare feet, and gaze up at the clean lines of the temple's splendid dome, which soars overhead to a height of 34m.

CENTRAL NEW DELHI

Government Buildings

Of the scores of buildings built by the British when they moved their capital from Calcutta to Delhi in 1911, **Rashtrapati Bhavan** (President's Residence) and **Sansad Bhavan** (Parliament House) are the most impressive. Both were designed by the renowned architect Edwin Lutyens, and their hulking grandeur—a not-so-subtle display of the vast reserves of British power—was intended to communicate Britain's desire to keep India the jewel in the British Crown. The effort backfired—the aesthetic anomaly of European-style buildings in the heart of an Indian city only grated at Indian nationalists, and the buildings became a lightning rod for criticism. In one memorable outburst, Gandhi described them as "architectural piles."

Sansad Bhavan, at the end of Sansad Marg, 1.5km southwest of Connaught Pl., is a massive circular building that looks like a flying saucer. Because India's parliament, the Lok Sabha, meets here (see **Government and Politics,** p. 89), getting near the building can be difficult. To reach **Rashtrapati Bhavan,** head left from the entrance to Parliament and bear right at the statue of Govind Ballabah Pant; or walk due west from India Gate down Rajpath. Once the residence of the Viceroy, the pink Rashtra-pati Bhavan is now the home of India's president. **To get inside the gates of Sansad Bhavan and Rashtrapati Bhavan, you'll need special permission, and possibly a letter from your embassy.** Enquire at the reception at Rashtrapati Bhavan the day before; you may be allowed to enter if no dignitaries are visiting. Meanwhile, you can get a good view from Raisina Hill, the area between the secretariat buildings. Note the sturdy pillars, massive copper dome, and Mughal-style *chhattris* (kiosks). The 145m pillar between the gate and the residence was donated by the Maharaja of Jaipur and is aptly called the **Jaipur Column.** The pillar is capped with a bronze lotus and a six-pointed star, which was then the shape of the Star of India.

Flanking Raisina Hill on its north and south sides are the symmetrical **Secretariats,** which now house government ministries. The buildings are adorned with a variety of imperialism-justifying slogans. For some shade (and fresh air), pass under the slogans and into the Great Hall, an airy room adorned with medallions and crowned by a baroque dome. Try to visit Raisina Hill on a Saturday, when troops parade with precision in front of Rashtrapati Bhavan. (*Ceremonial changing of the guard 10:35-11am in the winter; 8:30-9:15am in the summer.*)

Looking east from the Secretariats, the arch in the distance is **India Gate,** a memorial to Indian soldiers killed in World War I and the Afghan War of 1919. A memorial underneath the arch commemorates the men and women who were killed in the 1971 war with Pakistan. The wide thoroughfare connecting India Gate with Raisina Hill is **Rajpath,** which gets crowded on Sundays, when children frolic in the fountains, and on Republic Day (Jan. 26), when it is the scene of a massive martial parade.

Humayun's Tomb

Location: *2.5km southeast of India Gate.* **Hours:** *Open dawn-dusk.* **Admission:** *Rs5.*

A poem in red sandstone and black-and-white marble, Humayun's Tomb possesses both a blunt beauty and a serene grandeur, set amid carefully laid-out gardens and rows of palm trees. A bellicose drug addict, Humayun was the second Mughal emperor, ruling from 1530 until he was vanquished by Sher Shah in 1540, and again from 1555 until his death in 1556. Humayun's death had all the unimpeachable trappings of piety and scholarship. Walking down the stairs of his library, Humayun heard the *azan* and quickly sat himself down on the nearest step; upon rising, the emperor tripped and slid down the stairs. The injuries incurred in his fall proved fatal, but it wasn't until 1565, nine years after his death, that his tomb was built. In later years, many prominent Mughals were buried at Humayun's Tomb, including Dara Shikoh (Shah Jahan's favorite son), and Bahadur Shah II, the last of the Mughal emperors, who was captured here by the British during the Mutiny of 1857. Humayun's Tomb is located at the center of a rectangular, quartered garden laced with channels and paths (*charbagh*), a type of garden whose development reached its apex with the building of the Taj Mahal. A pioneering work of Mughal architecture, the tomb itself is octagonal and is situated atop a massive pedestal; the tomb's double dome rises to a height of nearly 40m and is home to hordes of squealing bats, birds, and bees.

Hazrat Nizamuddin Dargah

Southwest of Humayun's tomb, on the western end of Lodi Rd. (6km from Connaught Place), is Hazrat Nizamuddin Dargah, one of Sufism's greatest shrines. It was originally erected in 1325, the year its occupant, the great mystic Sheikh Nizamuddin Aulia died, but the present complex was most recently refurbished in the 16th century by Shah Jahan, one of Nizamuddin's many devotees. Its marble verandahs and delicate latticework are especially radiant at dawn and at dusk. Nearby is the grave of the great Urdu poet, Mirza Ghalib. At twilight, bards often gather here to sing *qawali* (Sufi songs of spiritual ecstasy) in homage.

Jantar Mantar
Location: *Sansad Marg, 750m southwest of Connaught Pl.* **Hours:** *Open daily sunrise-sunset.* **Admission:** *Free.*

This Mughal astronomical observatory, feels like an M.C. Escher lithograph rendered as a red-and-white stone diorama, its railless stairs lilting around tight bends and soaring upward to the heavens. Charged by the Mughal emperor Muhammad Shah with the task of revising the Indian calendar to accord with modern astronomical knowledge, Maharaja Jai Singh of Jaipur built Jantar Mantar in 1725 after studying European and Asian science and spending years observing the skies above Delhi. The resulting creation is as scientifically impressive as it is visually striking: the massive sundials and instruments accurately tell time (in Delhi, London, and elsewhere), predict eclipses, and chart the movement of the stars.

Lodi Gardens
Location: *Gate 1, Lodi Rd.* **Hours:** *Open dawn-dusk.* **Admission:** *Free.*

While the sign at the entrance is a bit worrisome—"shooting," it turns out, "is forbidden in the park"—the leafy glories of the **Lodi Gardens** are expertly maintained, and there are nice stone benches. A wide variety of trees and birds make their home here—spread around a handful of crushed Magic Masala potato chips, and you're likely to attract hordes of fluorescent green, hyper-aggressive urban parrots. Along with splendid scenery, the gardens boast a jogging trail (crowded on weekends with upper-class masochists) and a steamy greenhouse. A few ruined buildings scattered throughout the garden rise from the closely cropped grass. Toward the garden's center is the late 15th-century **Bara-Gumbad,** a square tomb of gray, red, and black stones, topped with a massive dome. Scholars have been unable to determine who is buried here. Attached to the tomb is a mosque, built in 1494, whose interior is notable for its dense floral patterns and Qur'anic inscriptions. The square tomb just north of Bara-Gumbad is the early 16th-century **Shish-Gumbad** (Glazed Dome), decorated with the remnants of blue tiles that once completely covered it. Nearly 200m north of Shish-Gumbad is the badly weathered **Sikandar Lodi's Tomb** (1517-18). For views of the park, climb atop the walls that enclose the tomb. Also in the Lodi Gardens, 200m southwest of Bara-Gumbad, is **Muhammad Shah's Tomb,** a high-domed octagonal building constructed in the mid-15th century; 75m east of Sikandar Lodi's Tomb is a 16th-century bridge with seven arches.

West of the Gardens is **Safdarjang's Tomb,** at the end of Lodi Rd. *(Open dawn-dusk. Admission Rs2.)* Built in 1753-54 for the prime minister to the Mughal emperor Muhammad Shah, the tomb is the last great piece of Mughal architecture in Delhi. Built at the center of expansive *charbagh* gardens, the tall, domed edifice was constructed of marble and red sandstone snatched from another local tomb.

Purana Qila (Old Fort)
Location: *Off Mathura Rd., 1km east of India Gate.* **Hours:** *Mosque open daily dawn-dusk.* **Admission:** *Rs2.* **Other:** *Sound and light show Nov.-Jan. 7:30pm; Feb.-Apr. and Sept.-Oct. 8:30pm; May-Aug. 9pm, Admission Rs25.*

The Purana Qila marks a spot continuously inhabited since the Mauryan period (324-184 BC). The discovery of ceramic shards dating back to 1000 BC vindicated bearers of local tradition, who have long contended that the fort was built atop the site of Indraprastha, the capital city of the Pandavas, heroes of the *Mahabharata* (commemorated in a nightly sound and light show). There's never been much doubt as to the 16th-century role of Purana Qila—the massive walls, finely preserved mosque, and ruined library that formed the centerpiece of Humayun's (and later Sher Shah's) Delhi are still standing for all to see. Built in 1541 by Sher Shah, **Qila-i-Kuhna Masjid** (Mosque of the Old Fort) is an ornate tangle of calligraphic inscriptions and red sandstone. Less impressive (and less intact) is the **Sher Mandal,** which Humayun used as a library and observatory after snatching Purana Qila from Sher Shah. A small, free museum on the premises showcases some of the artifacts discovered in and around Purana Qila. The Shunga period (184-72 BC) plaques are particularly good. To get a good sense of the incredible height of the fort's walls, walk the **exercise trail,** which begins just left of the entrance to Purana Qila. The trail winds pleasantly around a small **lake** (dry during the summer) where there are boats for rent.

Next to Purana Qila is the wheelchair-accessible **National Zoologic Park.** *(Open daily April 15-Oct. 15 9am-4pm, Oct. 16-Mar. 9:30am-4pm.)* On sunny Sundays, the expansive zoo teems with delighted Delhi-ites. Check out the three much-raved-about white tigers. The zoo's carefully labeled trees offer little shade; bring extra sunblock.

Birla Mandir

Location: *Mandir Marg, 2km west of Connaught Place.* **Hours:** *Open daily 5am-9pm.*

Built by the wealthy Birlas in honor of Lakshmi, the goddess of material well-being, the Lakshmi Narayan Temple is a marvel of neo-Orissan temple architecture. The room of mirrors at the back of the temple allows you to see yourself together with the infinite reflections of the Krishna statue in the middle. The surrounding gardens delight children (and the young at heart) with ping-pong tables, a brightly colored fountain in the shape of a clump of cobras, gaily painted stone sculptures of tigers and elephants that welcome riders, a plaster cave entered through a gaping lion's mouth, and a sweaty gym where burly boys build bodies by Birla.

MUSEUMS

National Museum

Location: *Janpath, just south of Rajpath.* **Phone:** *301 9538.* **Hours:** *Open Tu-Su 10am-5pm.* **Admission:** *Rs5, students Rs1, Su free.* **Other:** *Camera fee Rs10. Guided tours begin at enquiry counter 10:30, 11:30am, noon, 2, and 3:30pm. Films daily at 11:30am, 2:30pm, weekends and holidays also at 10:30am and 12:30pm.*

The museum's ambitious mission is to provide an overview of Indian life and culture from prehistoric times to the present. Ground-floor galleries showcase some of the museum's most crowd-pleasing items. Other displays trace the international development of Indian scripts, iconography, and coins over the past 16 centuries. (To see the actual coins, head up to the second floor.) An air-conditioned, room-sized vault is the setting for the museum's jewelry collection. Highlights include gaudy gilded earrings, necklaces, and bracelets dating from the first century AD. Another first-rate ground-floor gallery hosts beautiful South Asian paintings, the most striking of which are from Tibet, Nepal, and Rajasthan. Also on display is a hefty collection of Neolithic stone tools (3000-1500 BC). On the second floor, the weapons and armor exhibit includes a colorful, brass-reinforced Rajasthani vest, an 18th-century bejeweled rhino-hide shield of Maharana Sangram Singh II, and the torturously curved and serrated weapons of the Pahari. More pacific pleasures can be found among the galleries of colorful masks and clothing associated with the tribal peoples of the northeastern states. The top-notch collection of musical instruments in the Sharan Rani Gallery, donated in 1980 by renowned *sarod* player Sharan Rani, has unusual breadth, displaying handcrafted Indian instruments such as *sarangis* and *sitars.*

Crafts Museum

Location: *Pragati Bhawan, Bharion Marg, off Mathura Rd.* **Phone:** *337 1641.* **Hours:** *Open Tu-Su 10am-5pm. Outdoor displays closed during monsoon.*

Built in 1991, the mid-sized Crafts Museum is one of the finest in South Asia, and not everything here is stuck in glass cases. The museum is divided into three sections. Entering the museum, you'll pass through an open-air demonstration area where craftspeople wield their art, casting metal for sculptures, stringing jewelry, and weaving baskets from straw. Also outdoors is a village complex, filled with life-sized reproductions of rural huts and houses built by craftspeople brought to Delhi from their native regions. Especially interesting is the vibrantly painted Orissan Gadaha Hut and a spare construction associated with Nagaland's Konyak tribe, where boys are schooled in preparation for life in the community. Inside, displays spotlight the mind-bending diversity of traditional Indian crafts, including 18th-century wood carvings from Karnataka, dazzling storytellers' paintings, and a brightly decorated model of a Bihari wedding chamber.

National Gallery of Modern Art

Location: *Jaipur House, east of India Gate.* **Bus:** *Local #621 and 622.* **Phone:** *338 2835.* **Hours:** *Open Tu-Su 10am-5pm.* **Admission:** *Rs5, students Rs1.*

Once the Delhi mansion of the Maharaja of Jaipur, the Gallery houses a culturally enlightening collection of art produced in India over the last 150 years. The collection's highlights are the paintings by artists associated with the turn-of-the-century Bengal School, which was inspired by South Asian folk art and East Asian high art. For excellent examples, see Abanindranath Tagore's searching water colors, Nandalal Bose's small, sensitive paintings, and landscapes by the poet Rabindranath Tagore. Other highlights include Kunhi Raman's cubist-influenced concrete sculpture "Standing Figure" and two 1986 masterpieces by Kapor Wasim that sardonically depict a society withering into bleakness.

Nehru Museum, Library, and Planetarium

Location: *Teen Murti Bhawan, Teen Murti Rd., north of Chanakyapuri near Murti Marg.* **Hours:** *Open Tu-Su 9am-5:15pm. Planetarium open 11am-5pm.* **Admission:** *Free. Planetarium Rs1.* **Other:** *Planetarium showings Tu-Su 11:30am and 3pm. Admission Rs5.*

Built inside the home of Jawaharlal Nehru, India's first prime minister, the museum reveals as much about the Independence movement as a whole as it does about Nehru. Between voyeuristic peeks into Nehru's study, office, and bathroom, check out the pictures of Nehru as dour youth (with equally somber-looking relatives), as an ambitious student at Harrow and Cambridge, and as the humble, generous leader of India. Newspaper clippings and photographs lead through the turmoil of India's long struggle for self-rule. Adjacent to the Teen Murti Bhavan is the **Nehru Planetarium.** There's a small exhibition hall inside, and whoever can figure out the "human sundial" out front wins a big, big prize.

Other Museums

The **Indira Gandhi Museum,** 1 Safdarjang, features exhibits ranging from blasé (gifts the Gandhis received as prime ministers) to macabre (the bloodstained clothes that Indira and Rajiv were wearing when they were assassinated), all arrayed in Rajiv and Indira's former residence. *(Open Tu-Su 9:30am-4:45pm.)* The **National Rail Museum,** Chanakyapuri (tel. 688 1816 or 688 0939), near Shantipath, has indoor and outdoor exhibits on the history of Indian Railways and a miniature train for the riding. *(Open Apr.-Sept. Tu-Su 9:30am-7:30pm; Oct.-Mar. 9:30am-5:30pm. Admission Rs5. Camera fee Rs100.)* At the Central Bureau of Investigation, in Block 4 of the massive CGO complex, Lodi Rd. (tel. 436 0334), is the **National Police Museum,** replete with crime pictures, bad-ass weapons like the Steel Claw, and other punitive stuff to make you think twice about a life of crime. *(Open M-F 10am-1pm and 2:30-5:50pm.)* You can obtain a pass to the **National Philatelic Museum** (tel. 303 2481) at the reception office in the ground-level parking garage at the oversized post office on Sansad Marg, but only confirmed philatelic phanatics will find much of interest in this postage-stamp-sized museum. *(Open M-F 9am-4pm. Free.)*

■ Entertainment

To find out about other weekly musical and cultural events (as well as other relevant contact information for tourists), buy a copy of the **Delhi Diary** (Rs8), which comes out every Friday.

Dances of India is a nightly performance of Indian dance and music, including Kathak and Manipuri (nightly at 7pm, Parsi, Anjuman Hall, opposite the Ambedkar Football Stadium, Delhi Gate; tel. 331 7831 or 332 0968). There are several **movie theaters** in Delhi, which show Hindi movies. There are also some English-language movie theaters, especially in South Delhi (admission Rs40). Check daily papers for movie listings. Various cultural centers (see **Cultural Centers,** p. 128) screen foreign films and Indian "art" films that are not shown elsewhere.

The Red Fort's nightly **sound and light show,** focusing on the city's Mughal heritage, is unexpectedly entertaining. The fort is surreal at night; the silhouetted sitting halls and mosques invoke the voices of past rulers. A Pink Floyd concert it's not, but it's as good a history lesson as you're likely to get anywhere else in Delhi (see **Lal Qula,** p. 135). The Old Fort also has a nightly sound and light show on the *Mahabharata* (see **Purana Qula,** p. 141).

DISCOS AND NIGHTCLUBS

There's plenty of nightlife in Delhi, but it caters mainly to the city's elite. It seems that every 5-star hotel has its own thriving disco. To the budget traveler, however, the cover charges may seem forbiddingly steep, and the strange world of jeans-clad bodies writhing to an interminable techno beat under flashing lights may seem less appealing than getting wasted with the rooftop backpacker crowd in Paharganj. Still, boogeying the night away can revive the spirits like nothing else, and there are bargains to be found. The key to decoding Delhi's disco scene is understanding why certain places are considered popular and whether that makes them more or less appealing to you.

Mirage, at the Best Western Surya Sofitel (tel. 683 5070). Dance to professionally mixed techno among the sveltest of the svelte. Admission Rs600 per person, Ladies' Night on Wednesdays (women get in free). Open till 4am most nights.

Ghungroo, at the Welcomgroup Maurya Sheraton (tel. 611 2233). Reputed to have the best lighting system in South Asia, Ghungroo gives new meaning to the phrase "sound and light show." Admission Rs400 per couple. Ladies' Night on Saturdays. Open M-Sa 10pm-3:30am.

Wheels, at the Hotel Ambassador (tel. 463200). Popular with foreigners, who come to hear an eclectic mix of Hindi and Western standards. Rs300 per couple. No single admission. Open daily 10:30pm-3am.

Some Place Else, at the Park Hotel (tel. 373 2477). Hear "La Bamba" along with Bob Marley, rap, and Hindi pop. Admission Rs300. Open 10pm-2am.

CJ's, at Le Meridien (tel. 371 0101). Draws a slightly older crowd. Admission Rs300.

My Kind of Place, at Taj Palace (tel. 611 0202). Has two sections, one of which features a positively sublime dry ice cloud to shroud the dancers. Open 9:30pm-2am.

Annabelle's, at Intercontinental, formerly the Hilton (tel. 332 0101). Dance competition in August. Drinks Rs150-250. Couples only. Open 9:30pm-2am.

■ Shopping

Each of **Connaught Place's** blocks is home to booths peddling small curio items, souvenirs, and cold drinks. While prices are better at the **Palika Bazaar** (located beneath the grassy knoll nestled between Radial Rd. 1 and 8), the bazaars of Old Delhi, or even the markets of South Delhi, the Radial Road's stores offer good variety. If you're ready for some bargaining, they offer fairly good value as well. Follow the hordes of Western tourists south along **Radial Road,** which becomes **Janpath,** toward the cheapest souvenir shops in and around Janpath Market, government tourist offices, and the **Central Cottage Industries Emporium** (Jawahar Vyapar Bhavan, Janpath; tel. 331 2373). The Emporium has pricey furniture, clothes, and high-quality knick-knacks from all over India—a good place to stop for gifts en route to the airport. (Open M-Sa 10am-7pm.) Across the way is a good **Tibetan Market,** priced for tourists but with a wide variety of Kashmiri crafts, *chillums,* jewelry, etc., as well as light-weight travel clothes. **Old Delhi** carries it all, starting on **Chandni Chowk** (where *sari* salesmen pull you into various shops "just for looking") and winding into the maze of alleys off to the sides. **Bina Musical Stores,** 781 Nai Sarak (tel. 326 3595), has several *tablas* and *sitars,* as does **A. Godin and Co.** on Sansad Marg, though the latter is a bit overpriced.

NORTH INDIA

Uttar Pradesh उत्तर प्रदेश

Uttar Pradesh, the "Northern State," is India's true heartland. Its parched plains spring to life at the coming of the monsoon, and from its mountains, the Ganga descends to join her sister Yamuna in cutting across the earth. Uttar Pradesh, which has been called "U.P." for short ever since the British carved it out as the United Provinces, is India's most populous state, with 138 million residents in all. The eastern half of U.P. is one of India's most economically depressed areas, while western U.P. has shared in the prosperity of neighboring Delhi. The cradle of Indian civilization from the time of the Aryan chieftains to the reign of the great Mughal emperors, U.P. gave India the *Ramayana*, the Hindi language, and since Independence, eight of its 12 prime ministers. It has also been the focus of bitter communal and inter-caste violence. In 1992 the state's BJP government encouraged the destruction of the Babri Masjid in Ayodhya, leading to thousands of deaths in communal riots across India; the state remains a flashpoint for Hindu-Muslim tensions. Radical affirmative action politics for Dalits (former Untouchables) also have a strong base in U.P. Few people visit India without visiting the U.P., yet there is nothing in U.P. to photograph, slap on a postcard, and declare representative of the state—not its sacred cities of Varanasi, Ayodhya, and Mathura, nor the hill stations and pilgrimage centers in the Himalaya, nor the Taj Mahal in the Mughal capital of Agra, nor the old Muslim city of Lucknow. There is no quintessential U.P. because U.P. is quintessentially Indian.

🖐 HIGHLIGHTS OF UTTAR PRADESH

- **Agra** (p. 187) is home to several of India's most famous and beautiful monuments, including a gem of a royal **fort** (p. 195), the abandoned Mughal capital at **Fatehpur Sikri** (p. 198), and a little marble ditty called the **Taj Mahal** (p. 193).
- Hinduism's holiest city, **Varanasi** (p. 215) draws the living and the dying to her crowded streets and sacred *ghats*.
- *Ashram* towns such as like **Rishikesh** (p. 164) and **Haridwar** (p. 159), pilgrimage centers like **Gangotri** (p. 171) and **Yamnotri** (p. 170), and national reserves like **Corbett** (p. 173) and the **Valley of Flowers** (p. 172) beckon lovers of the natural and the supernatural alike to northern U.P.'s hill districts.

GARHWAL AND KUMAON

Travel in the hills of Uttar Pradesh encompasses the holy, the hilly, and (at times) the downright helly. The neighboring northern regions of Garhwal and Kumaon, with their 7000m peaks and towering *deodar* forests, their chintzy and frenetic alpine hill stations, their roller-coaster roads, their austere ashrams and high-rise temples, their sacred rivers and divine mountains, encompass enough to enthrall, enlighten, amuse, and annoy any tourist, trekker, or pilgrim.

In the 9th century the South Indian saint Shankara came to Garhwal, bringing the local population into the Hindu fold and establishing several important temples. The mountains have kept these areas relatively inaccessible for thousands of years, enabling many local customs to survive. In the early 19th century, Garhwal and Kumaon were overrun by the Nepali commander Amar Singh Thapa. In 1816 these areas came under British control and were later made part of the United Provinces. Recently, many Garhwalis and Kumaonis have agitated for a separate state within India to be called Uttarakhand (Land of the North).

The larger hill stations—Nainital, Almora, Ranikhet, Mussoorie—are more aptly characterized as chaotic Indian cities (with Himalayan views) than as peaceful alpine retreats, and many of the more placid areas, including the major pilgrimage sites, are only open between May and November. Accommodations are provided at dharam-

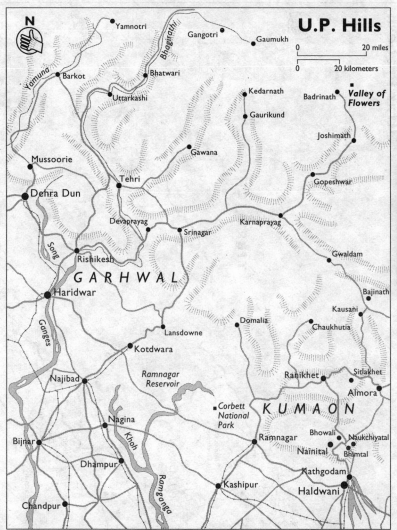

shalas as well as at the hotels of the Garhwal Mandal Vikas Nigam (GMVN), and its sister, Kumaon MVN, hilly subsidiaries of U.P. Tourism. GMVN and KMVN hotels are reliable and clean, offering cheap beds in dormitories or expensive room accommodations, and they should be booked as much as a month in advance in peak pilgrimage season (June-Aug.).

■ Dehra Dun दहरादून

That Dehra Dun has two bus stands—one for Delhi, one for Mussoorie—reveals much about the town's polarized character. On the one hand, the city clearly strives for the capital's modernity, with fuming auto-rickshaws racing past rows of shops filled with *saris*, car parts, and English books. Dehra Dun is the training ground for much of India's elite, who come to learn at the Indian Military Academy, the presti-

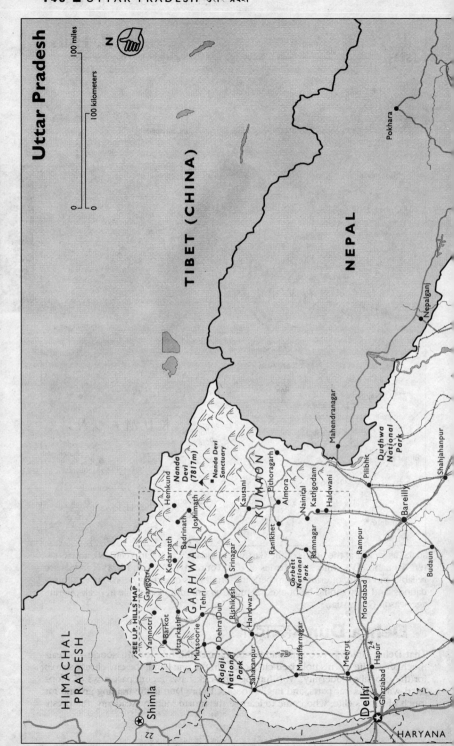

Uttar Pradesh

100 miles

100 kilometers

N

TIBET (CHINA)

NEPAL

Pokhara

Nepalganj

Mahendranagar

HIMACHAL PRADESH

Shimla

Yamnotri
Gangotri
Barkot
Uttarkashi
Mussoorie
Kedarnath
Badrinath
Joshimath
Hemkund
Nanda Devi (7817m)
Nanda Devi Sanctuary

GARHWAL
Tehri
Srinagar
Dehra Dun
Rishikesh
Haridwar
Rajaji National Park
Saharanpur
Muzaffarnagar

KUMAON
Ranikhet
Kausani
Almora
Pithoragarh
Nainital
Kathgodam
Haldwani
Ramnagar
Corbett National Park

SEE U.P. HILLS MAP

Pilibhit
Dudhwa National Park

Shahjahanpur
Bareilly
Budaun
Rampur
Moradabad
Meerut
Hapur
Ghaziabad
Delhi

HARYANA

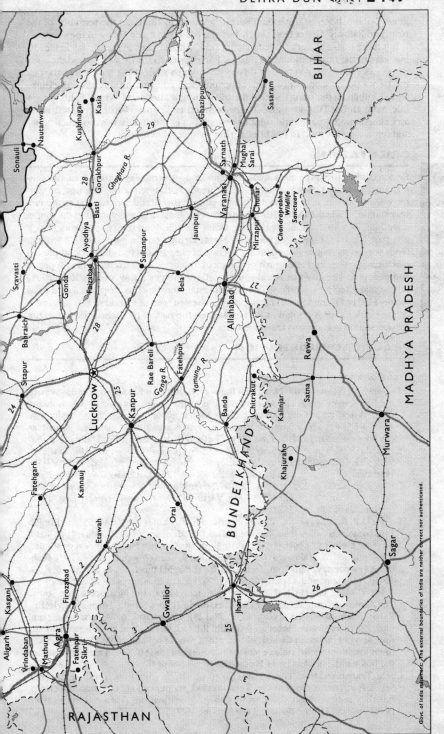

gious Doon School, or the Indian Forest Research Institute. As the terminus of the Northern Railway, Dehra Dun clearly has one eye on its older sibling to the south.

But there is also a gentler side to Dehra Dun, with its heart in the laid-back, life-loving ways of the nearby mountain villages. For as much as the buses race and the auto-rickshaws clamor for room, their drivers do it with a smile. Most travelers to the city use Dehra Dun as a one- or two-day stopover before going to the Shiwaliks (the Himalayan foothills to the north), and to the hill station of Mussoorie, whose lights are visible from Dehra Dun at night. There is much to keep a visitor occupied here, including temples, parks, and sulphur springs, but in the end there's too much "city" and not enough "town" to hold Dehra Dun's visitors down.

ORIENTATION

Understanding the three main areas in Dehra Dun—the **railway station** area, the **central** area, and the **Astley Hall** area—helps greatly with orientation. The first, around the railway station, is to the south; the **Mussoorie Bus Stand** is right next to the railway station, while the **Delhi Bus Stand** (servicing most destinations *not* in the immediate hills) is a 5min. walk away north along **Gandhi Road** (a major thoroughfare), just past the hard-to-miss, tan-colored **Hotel Drona.** Following Gandhi Rd. north feeds you on to **Rajpur Road** and the second central area, which lies around the tall **clock tower.** Gandhi Park, north of the clock tower, is litter-strewn, but still pretty and peaceful. The **city bus stand** is just north of the clock tower along Rajpur Rd., where many services, high-end hotels, and restaurants lie. This strip is referred to as **Astley Hall** or Dilaram Bazaar farther north. The vast web of market streets just south of the clock tower is known as **Paltan Bazaar;** the part of the bazaar nearest to the railway station is known as **Darshani Gate.**

PRACTICAL INFORMATION

Transportation

Trains: As terminus of the **Northern Railway,** Dehra Dun has frequent trains departing for all over India. The enquiry office is in the main terminal; all-class booking office is next door; Computerized Reservation Complex is across the way (open M-Sa 8am-1:50pm and 2-8pm, Su 8am-2pm). Prices are 2nd/1st class. To: **Amritsar** (*Dehradun-Amritsar Fast Pass.* 3297, 7:10pm, 13hr., Rs85/465); **Delhi** (*Shatabdi Exp.* 2018, M-W and F-Su, 5pm, 5½hr., Rs385 A/C chair; *Dehradun-Mumbai Exp.* 9020, 11:45am, 9hr.; *Dehradun-Delhi Exp.* 4042, 9:30pm, 9½hr.; Rs120/398); **Haridwar** (5 per day, 8am-9:30pm, 1½hr., Rs18/125); **Lucknow** (*Dehradun-Varanasi Exp.* 4266, 6:20pm, 13hr., Rs167/564); **Mumbai** (*Dehradun-Mumbai Exp.* 9020, 11:45am, 41hr., Rs267/1209); **Varanasi** (*Dehradun-Varanasi Exp.* 4266, 6:35pm, 24hr., Rs223/757).

Buses: U.P. Roadways (tel. 653797), **Himachal Bus Lines** (tel. 623435), and **Punjab Roadways** run buses from the **Delhi Bus Stand,** next to Hotel Drona. U.P. Roadways to: **Delhi** (32 per day, 5:15am-10:30pm, Rs81/136); **Hardiwar** (every 30min., 5am-7pm, Rs16); **Haldwani** (6:15, 7, 8:30, and 9:30am, 7:30pm, 9hr., Rs110); **Rishikesh** (14 per day, 5am-7pm, 1½hr., Rs16). Himachal Bus Lines to **Shimla** (6, 8:15, 10:30, 11:30am, and 11pm, 10hr., Rs107). Punjab Roadways to **Amritsar** (5:30, 7:30am, 14hr., Rs141). U.P. Roadways also leaves from the **Mussoorie Bus Stand.** To: **Almora** (6am, 12hr., Rs145); **Mussoorie** (every 30min., 6am-8pm, 1½hr., Rs16); **Nainital** (7:15 and 8am, 11hr., Rs125); **Uttarkashi** (6, 8:30, and 10:30am, 9hr., Rs89). **Highway Motors,** 69 Gandhi Rd. (tel. 624211), next to the railway station, serves **Hanuman Chatti** (summer 6am, winter 6:30am, 8½hr., Rs78). Signs in town tout the speedy, **deluxe van** service to Delhi (Rs150-200). **Taxis,** across from the bus stands, head as far as **Mussoorie** (Rs50 per person).

Local Transportation: Local **buses** go to nearby destinations from the City Bus Stand, north of the clock tower. **Tempos** (Rs2 per person) are common and cheap, but they may only get you part-way to your destination. **Auto-rickshaws** from Delhi bus stand to the Botanical Gardens are Rs50.

Tourist and Financial Services

Tourist Office: U.P. Tourist Office (tel. 653217), in Hotel Drona, next to the Delhi Bus Stand. The most helpful tourist office in town, with maps and tips about nearby sights in Dehra Dun and elsewhere in Uttar Pradesh. Open M-Sa 10am-5pm; closed every other Sa. For trekking tips and other information about the Garhwal region, try the government-run **GMVN Headquarters,** Rajpur Rd. (tel. 656817 or 654408), across from Hotel Madhuban. Open M-Sa 10am-5pm.

Trekking Agency: Various private agents, such as **Garhwal Tours and Trekking** (tel. 654774) in Rohini Plaza near Hotel Ambassador, can help with planning treks. Open M-Sa 9:15am-1:30pm.

Currency Exchange: The main branch of the **State Bank of India** (tel. 653240), 1 block east of the clock tower, changes cash, AmEx (U.S., U.K., Canadian, German, and Japanese currencies), and Thomas Cook (U.S. and U.K. currencies) traveler's checks. Commission Rs4 per transaction, Rs25 for encashment certificate. Open M-F 10am-2pm, Sa 10am-noon. **Punjab National Bank** (tel. 656012), Astley Hall, on top of Gandhi Park, changes traveler's checks in U.S., U.K., and German currencies (no commission). Open M-F 10am-2pm.

Bookstore: English Book Depot (tel. 655192), next to Kumar Restaurant. The 75-year-old shop provides a cool and organized browsing environment. Open M-Sa 10am-1:30pm and 2:30-8pm. **The Green Bookshop (Natraj Publishers),** 17 Rajpur Rd. (tel. 653382), has an esteemed nature/ecology section, not to mention the Hardy Boys and Nancy Drew. Open M-Sa 10am-1:30pm and 3-8pm.

Library: Mahatma Khuhiram Public Library and Reading Room, near the Delhi bus stand. Open 8-11am and 5-8pm.

Market: Paltan Bazaar, between the clock tower and railway station, has hundreds of shops, selling everything from *sitars* to *saris* and panties to pineapples.

Emergency and Communications

Hospital: Dr. Diwan (tel. 657660) on Kacheri Rd. is a well-known and respected physician and pediatrician, with his own clinic; he is available 9:30am-2pm and 6-8pm. Consultation Rs80. **Jain Hospital** (tel. 627766 or 621727), open 24hr.

Pharmacy: Many all over town, such as **Fair Deal Chemists,** 14 Darshani Gate (tel. 625252). Open M-Sa 8:30am-9pm, Su 8:30am-2pm.

Police: Dhara Chowki Station, Rajpur Rd. (tel. 653648), south of Hotel Ambassador,

Post Office: Head Post Office, by the clock tower, has *Poste Restante* (M-Sa 10am-6pm) and EMS speed post services (parcels M-F 10am-4pm, Sa 10am-3pm; speed post M-Sa 10am-8pm). **Postal Code:** 248001.

Internet: Computer Base, Rajpur Rd. (tel. 655831), in the Windlass Shopping Center/Hotel Ambassador complex near the clock tower. Connections are iffy, but you'll always shell out Rs100-200. Open M-Sa 10am-8pm, but it's best to call ahead.

Telephones: STD/ISD booths are everywhere. **Telephone Code:** 0135.

ACCOMMODATIONS

Hotels closer to the bus stands or clock tower tend to be either bland high-end boxes or dingy budget dives, but the noise and stink are tolerable if you're only staying a night. Classier hotels line Rajpur, along Astley Hall and beyond.

Hotel White House (tel. 652765). One block east of Rajpur Rd. on Astley Hall. Just far enough out of downtown Dehra Dun, and with relatively presidential panache at a pittance, it's a sound choice for all but those making the briefest of stopovers. Colossal rooms, pleasant gardens, and a kind manager. Check-out noon. Singles Rs165, with bath Rs180; doubles Rs225/245. Air cooling Rs60 extra. AmEx.

Hotel Victoria, one block off of Gandhi Rd., near Pashani Circle. Clean rooms, spacious bathrooms, and fans make this hotel a bargain. Water shuts off during the day, but the management supplies buckets of water. Singles Rs80; doubles Rs160.

Hotel Prince, Gandhi Rd. (tel. 627070), 2 blocks south of the Delhi Bus Stand and 2 blocks east of the Mussoorie Bus Stand. A multi-story business hotel without the high-end price and pretension. Basic, stone-wall rooms have fans, comfortable mattresses, and occasional hot water (but no showers). Great top floor views. Ajay, the lad who comes by nightly to take dinner orders, is nice enough to merit a stay. Singles Rs150; doubles Rs250; deluxe with color TV Rs350; quads Rs450.

Meedo Hotel, 71 Gandhi Rd. (tel. 627088). One block from the railway station. Not to be confused with the expensive Meedo Grand out on Rajpur Rd., which shares this Meedo's incongruous neo-Art Deco architecture. Disappointingly dribbly showers, but the toilets have seats, and the rooms are clean if not sterile. Restaurant attached. Check-out 24hr. after check-in. Singles Rs150-265; doubles Rs265-370.

Osho Resorts, 111 Rajpur Rd. (tel. 749544). About 1km beyond the GMVN Tourist Office. Well-kept rooms, TVs, hot water, and super-guru Osho himself (see p. 641)! Read Osho books, watch Osho TV, or seek enlightenment in the lush meditation center. Rooms range from standard to posh-o "Osho Rajsi" rooms (with A/C, carpets, and all the fixings). All rooms have shower and seat toilet. The attached restaurant, **Heaven's Gate,** serves excellent food in a cool room, if you'll pardon the unsavory cult allusions. Cottage singles Rs390; doubles Rs490. Standard singles Rs490; doubles Rs590. Add 5% luxury tax. Rates Rs100 less off season.

FOOD

Restaurants near Astley Hall and out on Rajpur Rd. are swanker than those in the grime of the bus stand area. The Paltan Bazaar area has good bakers and sweet vendors, plus a row of fruit stands toward the clock tower side. If you're just stopping over, the **Venus** and **Ahuja restaurants** (across from the explosives plant on Gandhi Rd., just east of the railway gate) are open throughout the day. And wherever you are, it's wise to try some of the local specialties. To die for is *kulfi faluda* (Rs17) at the **Kumar Sweet Shop** (next to the clock tower), a luscious log-o'-saffron and pistachio ice cream topped with clear angel-hair noodles.

Kasturi Vaishnav Bhojanalama, Gandhi Rd. (tel. 629049), across from the Venus Restaurant. Extremely popular with locals, this place is crowded at mealtimes. Staff is good-natured, and the atmosphere is homey. Veg. dishes Rs16-20. Breakfast 9am-noon, lunch noon-3pm, and dinner 7-10pm. Closed last Su of the month.

Kumar Foods Restaurant, 15B Rajpur Rd. (tel. 657060), between the post office and Motel Himshri. This, together with the **Kumar Vegetarian Restaurant** (½ block to the north) and aforementioned Sweet Shop, rule the food scene in town. Magically delicious renditions of Indian specialties—*rogan josh* (Rs48), *chicken tikka masala* (Rs85). The service is great, and the ambience is subdued and classy. Open daily 11am-4pm and 7-10:30pm; closed last Tu of the month.

Motimahal Restaurant, Rajpur Rd. (tel. 657307). Across from the Hotel Ambassador. Quality non-veg. food from a large menu in a dim, beige dining room with plush drapes and classical Indian prints. No fewer than 18 fans plus A/C make this the coolest duckaway spot in town. Try the chicken curry (Rs50), the mutton *shahi korma* (Rs48), or the *dal makhani* (Rs24). Open daily 9am-10:30pm.

Daddy's, Rajpur Rd., next to the Hotel President. A wanna-be western-style burger joint that comes through on all but interior design. South Indian and Chinese food accompany a menu of pizza, "thirst aids," and theme burgers—The Great Daddy's Twin (Rs44). Open daily 9:30am-9:30pm.

SIGHTS AND ENTERTAINMENT

Most of what's to be done in Dehra Dun lies outside the city. Buses and tempos leave for all destinations from the City bus stand; taxis and auto-rickshaws charge Rs40-100 for trips to any of the sights, or Rs300-400 for a full day of sight-seeing. If you really want to take your time, pick a destination and make it a full day's excursion. If seeing is more important than staying, however, then a good option is the GMVN day-long package bus trip, **Doon Darshan,** which covers the FRI, Tapkeshwar Temple, Malsi Deer Park, and Sahastra Dhara, for Rs80. The bus stops for 45 to 90 minutes at each place (leaves daily at 10:30am, returns at 5pm). Contact **Drona Travel,** 45 Gandhi Rd. (tel. 654371; open daily 7am-10pm), by the Hotel Drona. Book a day in advance.

Dehra Dun is the proud home of the Indian **Forest Research Institute (FRI).** *(Open M-F 9am-5:30pm.)* Established under British auspices in 1906, and residing in its current location since 1924, the FRI has led the country (and the world) toward a better understanding of the uses and abuses of various aspects of forestry, botany, and biodiversity conservation. The long building is beautifully and incorrigibly colonial, and the vast lawn is reminiscent of a European royal palace. Even if you're not into forestry, there's still quite a bit to do here: there are six museums and a beautiful garden, and the lawn has infinite picnic potential. The best of the museums is the one devoted to pathology, the cataloguing of plant diseases. To see the **Botanical Gardens,** you need a permit from the entrance. The main gate for visitors is at Trevor Rd. Feasting in your own nook of the estate is allowed by permission of the director. There is a canteen for afternoon tea or snacks, and at the far corner of the institute is an **information desk** with free pamphlets about the institute's many functions.

The **Tapkeshwar Temple,** 6km northwest of town (Rs60 for one-way auto-rickshaw, Rs2 by city bus or tempo from the clock tower) isn't far from the FRI, and the two can be easily combined into one action-packed day. *(Open daily 5:30am-9pm.)* Dedicated to Shiva, the temple is the most sacred in the immediate area. Built into a mountainside beside a running stream, the inside is damp, cool, and filled with a curious combination of incense and mist. Note the central *linga* onto which water drips from above. There are actually several shrines around the temple's entrance. The nearby stream also serves as a popular swimming hole for locals and visitors alike. The temple is the site of a large **Shivaratri celebration** (a week of festivities in the last week of March and the first week of April).

Another more natural picnic spot near Dehra Dun is **Robber's Cave,** also called Buchu Pani, located about 8km north of town. Transport leaves you about 100m from the entrance to the "cave," which is actually a 200m long, 15m high chasm. Visitors wade through the stream at the small canyon's bottom, where the water has smoothed the grey rock. At the other end is an opening with large boulders for climbing and even a few little pools for swimming. Wear sandals to Robber's Cave, as the rocks in the stream can be sharp. There's a "real" swimming pool about 100m on the other side from where tour buses stop.

■ Mussoorie मसूरी

The mountain hill station of Mussoorie is chintzy, overpriced, and often overcrowded; however, it's also refreshingly cool, near tranquil forests, and because of (*not* in spite of) its touristy, carnival atmosphere, a hell of a lot of fun. The town certainly isn't for everyone—travelers attempting to shun commercialism in favor of spirituality should stay in nearby Haridwar or Rishikesh, and those hoping for mountain tranquility may be better off in Kumaon. But anyone with an interest in the bizarre subculture of Indian tourists could find no better point of observation.

While today the focal destination for heat-fleeing tourists from Delhi (Mussoorie is the closest hill station to the capital), the town was first settled in 1827 by an Englishman, Captain Young. British officials later developed Mussoorie into a Victorian home-away-from-home-away-from-home, complete with an exclusive club, libraries, and an Anglican Church. The central promenade—the Mall—was made for afternoon strolls and crusty chit-chat, all in full view of the snow-peaked Himalaya to the northeast and the Doon Valley to the south.

Since then, stiff upper-lippers have yielded to middle-class Indians, most of them coming in "peak season" between May and July. "Season" extends from July to October (the foggy monsoon months) and March to May, and prices at these times are mid-range. November through March is distinctly off season, when you're more likely to find solitude, but winter can be pretty chilly.

Warning: There is an Indian Army encampment at **Chakrata,** 82km northwest of Mussoorie. No foreigners are allowed north of the east-west road between Yamuna Bridge and Kalsi without a permit from the army. Foreign tourists heading by road for Shimla or Eastern H.P. must do so via Herbertpur. There have been reports of foreign tourists being arrested traveling north of Kalsi.

NORTH INDIA

ORIENTATION

Mussoorie is about 15km long, stretching around the mountain overlooking Dehra Dun, though the town proper is much more compact. The town has two centers, the **Library Bazaar** and **Kulri Bazaar** areas, connected by a 15-minute walk along the **Mall,** which is lined with murals. Buses from the valley stop near both bazaars. The plaza in front of the library, with a statue of the Mahatma, is called **Gandhi Chowk;** the gate by the library is **Gandhi Gate.** Camel's Back Road runs along the back side of the mountain and connects the two bazaars more circuitously. Even with its large clock tower, Landour Bazaar, to the east, is less kitschy than the rest of town.

PRACTICAL INFORMATION

Trains: No tracks run to Mussoorie, but reservations from Dehra Dun can be made at the **Northern Railways Out Agency,** on the Mall below the post office. Open M-F 9am-1pm and 2-4pm, Sa 9-11am and noon-4pm, Su 9am-2pm.

Buses: U.P. Roadways, leaving from the **Kulri** or **Library Bus Stands** (both below the Mall) and servicing only **Dehra Dun.** From the Library Bus Stand (tel. 632258; every hr. 7am-6pm, 1½hr., Rs16). From the Kulri Bus Stand (tel. 632259; every 30min. 6am-7pm, 1½hr., Rs14). Several signs around town advertise daily direct Dehra Dun-Delhi deluxe service, but you have to get to Dehra Dun yourself. Try **Mussoorie Novelty Store** (tel. 632795), opposite the railway booking office. Non-A/C buses (11am and 10pm, Rs150) and A/C buses (8 and 11am, 10pm, Rs200) depart from the clock tower in Dehra Dun.

Taxis: Booking stands next to both bus stands. To: **Dehra Dun** (Rs60 per seat, Rs300 per car) and **Haridwar** (Rs700 per car).

Tourist Office: (tel. 632863), near the Ropeway, halfway between Kulri and Library Bazaars. Provides a handy color brochure (Rs2) about Mussoorie and local sights, with map. Also has some brochures about nearby treks. Open Apr.-Oct.: daily 8am-8pm; Nov-Mar: M-Sa 10am-5pm.

Budget Travel: GMVN (tel. 631281) offers organized tours of the northern pilgrimage sites, departing from Delhi and Rishikesh. Trips range from a 4-day excursion to Badrinath (Rs2000) to a 12-day voyage to Yamnotri, Gangotri, Kedarnath, and Badrinath (Rs4800). Staff speaks minimal English. Open Apr.-Sep. daily 8am-7pm; Oct.-Mar. 9am-5pm. For sojourns into the hills, either to pilgrimage or nature sites, **Trek Himalaya** (tel. 30491), on the Mall above the ropeway, provides assistance in fluent English, for both organized trips and drop-in consultations. Guides available. Tent rental Rs80-100 per day. Fully planned excursions—you just carry your daypack—for US$50-70. Open daily 10am-8:30pm. May be closed Dec.-Feb.

Currency Exchange: State Bank of India, Kulri Bazaar (tel. 632533), cashes AmEx, Thomas Cook and Citicorp checks in U.S., U.K., and Canadian currencies. Rs4 per check; encashment certificate Rs25. Open M-F 10am-2pm, Sa 10am-noon.

Market: Tibetan Market, along and below the Mall near the library. **Kulri Bazaar** has many stores specializing in curios, woolens, and tourist crap (particularly popular with Indians is the miniature riding whip). Try bargaining.

Library: Tilak Memorial Library, off the Mall in Kulri, is open 9am-noon and 4-8pm. The attractive **Mussoorie Library** is better, but you can't get in without a weeklong application process or an outlandish outpouring of charm.

Bookstore: Several good bookstores along the Mall in Kulri, usually open 8am-8pm, have magazines, fiction, and nonfiction. The **Prabhu Book Depot,** near Banares House Sarees, has a range of popular fiction and Archie Comix.

Pharmacies: These, too, are ubiquitous along the Mall. **P.B. Hamers & Co.** (tel. 632502), up from the Rialto Cinema by President's Restaurant, has a whole lot of everything. Open daily 10am-10pm in June; otherwise 10am-9pm.

Hospital/Medical Services: The **Community Hospital** (tel. 632541) is in Landour 1.5km east of the clock tower. **24hr. emergency care.** For more private treatment, try the **clinic** of Dr. Rana and Dr. Nautiyal (tel. 632594), on the road above the Kulri Mall. Open daily 10am-1pm and 4-7pm.

Police: Above the Mall, just west of the Hotel Mall Queen (tel. 632083). Open 24hr. **Landour police** (tel. 632082). Chief inspector (tel. 632206).

NORTH INDIA

Mussoorie

ACCOMMODATIONS

C Garhwal Terrace
E Hotel Broadway
F Hotel Everest
G Hoel Nishima
A Hotel Prince
D Hotel Saraswati
B PLM Villa

Woodstock School

Landaur Language School

TO DHANOLTI

Sai Baba Temple

The Rink

Camels Back Rd.

State Bank of India

TO DEHRA DUN

Trek Himalaya

Railway Booking Agency

Clock Tower

LANDOUR BAZAAR

SEE INSET MAP

KULRI BAZAAR

The Rink

Sai Baba Temple

Picture Palace Bus Stand

Gun Hill

THE MALL

TO KEMPTY FALLS

Camels Back Rd.

Christ Church

B

Library Bus Stand

Lakshmi Narayan Temple

A

THE MALL

Library

Kempty Bus Stand

CONVENT HILL

TO MUNICIPAL GARDENS AND CLOUD END

TO MUNICIPAL GARDENS AND CLOUD END

N

400 yards
400 meters

0
0

Post Office: Near State Bank of India, above the Mall in Kulri (tel. 632806). Has registered and speed post (via EMS). *Poste Restante* and most services available M-F 9am-1pm and 1:30-5pm, Sa 9am-noon. **Postal Code:** 248179.

Telephones: STD/ISDs are all over, just like you'd expect. **Telephone Code:** 0135.

ACCOMMODATIONS

Mussoorie has so many hotels that one wonders where the locals live. **Kulri Bazaar** has more low-end options than the Library area, and many of Mussoorie's hotels are no better or worse than those listed below. In peak season (May-June), the hotels fill to near capacity. Expect boosted rates at this time, with discounts during mid-season (Mar.-May and July-Oct.) and slashed prices from November to March.

Kulri and Landour

Garhwal Terrace (tel. 632682 or 632683), on the Mall between Kulri and Library Bazaars. Run by GMVN, this hotel has 4-bed and 8-bed dormitories that open up to a lovely veranda overlooking the mountains. Apr. 16-Nov. 15: dorm beds Rs100; rooms Rs1000. Nov. 16-Apr. 15: dorm beds Rs80; rooms Rs500. Try to reserve a bed a couple of days in advance during the in-season.

Hotel Saraswati (tel. 631005), up the ramp from the more visible Hotel Amar, past Hotel Mansarovar. With a hidden location, it's likely to have rooms when all else is full. Rooms are immaculate, staff is gracious, and the surroundings are peaceful relative to the chaos of Mall Rd. Rooms have mirrors, TV, seat toilets, and hot water. May and June: doubles Rs250-600. Off-season: Rs100-300.

Hotel Broadway, Camel's Back Rd. (tel. 632243). Close to the rink, near Kulri Bazaar. A converted English guesthouse, the Broadway retains charm in a peaceful setting, away from all the clamor but that of the roller rink and the nearby mosque. Rooms with balcony have valley view. Food available. Some rooms have seat toilets. May 1- June 15: singles Rs175; doubles Rs250, with valley view Rs300, with hot water Rs400. Off-season: Rs80-150.

Hotel Nishima, Landour Bazaar (tel. 632227), past the clock tower. Popular among language school students, the Nimisha has bunglingly bright rooms and huge hot water buckets. Rest easy behind heavy metal doors, on thickish mattresses. TV in the lobby. Food available, and seat toilets for the lucky few. Rates given are for foreigners—try bargaining with the owners. May-June: doubles Rs150-200.

Hotel Everest, Camel's Back Rd. (tel. 632954), near the rink at the beginning of the road. Massive "lobby," doubles as a parking garage, and rooms (bright to dim) mimic the slightly pricier Hotel Roxy upstairs. TV, tiled floors, and squat toilets. May 25-July 25: doubles Rs300-500. Off-season: Rs150-250.

Library Area

Hotel Prince (tel. 632674), off the Mall, up the ramp from the horse stand—look for the alley access 30m toward Kulri from the library. A magnificent government-designed site, set high above the Mall in a century-old royal summer getaway. Regal halls, huge rooms, high ceilings, and high tea in the drawing room or on the patio. May 15-July 15: doubles Rs400-800, (or sleep in the old servants' quarters for Rs200). Off-season: discount 25-50%.

PLM Villa (tel. 631090), off Camel's Back Rd., a 5-min. walk from the Library. Small garden-fronted place popular with Indian families. The views are spectacular. Food available 7am-10pm. In-season: doubles Rs150, with attached bath Rs200-350. Off-season: 50% discount. Try to book a week in advance.

Outside Mussoorie

Cloud End Forest Resort (tel. 632242; fax 625657), west of the library on the road to the municipal gardens; 7km by jeep. Set amid 2000 acres of unadulterated forest, on the crest of a ridge overlooking the lights of Mussoorie on one side and a lush valley on the other, Cloud End is the opposite of, and for some, the antidote to, the circus throngs downtown. One of the four oldest buildings in Mussoorie, it was built in 1838 by an East India Company tycoon, and the period ambiance has been scrupulously preserved, with old photographs, lush upholstered armchairs, and dark (but clean) wooden beds. The resort harvests rainwater for washing and runs primarily on its own rooftop solar panels. At night, patrons enjoy tea and snacks next to bonfires under sheets of stars. Pony rides to Jwaladevi Temple and wishing well can be arranged a day in advance (4hr. round-trip, Rs60 per hr. or Rs300 per day). The restaurant serves unusually fresh and flavorful food—see if they'll make you some *paneer tikka*. The posh doubles are priced accordingly, but don't despair: spartan 3-tier dorm bunks can get you in cheaply. Another option is camping, either on the front lawn or in the nearby woods, at Rs100 per person or Rs50 if you have your own tent. Reserve at least a day ahead to avoid the Rs150 jeep transport fee from the library. In-season: doubles Rs900; dorm bunks Rs200. Off-season: lop off 50%. Closed Jan.-mid-Mar. MC, Visa, or AmEx Rs100 extra.

FOOD

Mussoorie's residents do their best to make sure the hordes of tourists don't starve; there are fast-food joints, large family restaurants, and restaurant-bars almost everywhere in town. Roasted *masala* corn is sold along the Mall, sweets are scooped up at **Krishna's** in Kulri, and eggy treats are assembled at the **Omelette Specialist,** not far from Picture Palace Cinema (also in Kulri). Food prices listed are in-season.

The Green, Kulri Bazaar (tel. 632226). Delicious veg. fare at reasonable prices, but it's impossible to relax in the afterglow of your scrumptious meal—there are always people in line waiting for your table. For breakfast, try the lewdly buttered *paratha* (Rs16), stuffed with eggs and topped with raisins and cashews. Open May-June: 7am-3:30pm and 7-10pm. Off-season: 8am-3:30pm and 7:30-10:30pm.

Rice Bowl, Kulri Bazaar (tel. 631684). Across from President Restaurant, upstairs. Dining cubicle with street view. Serves Chinese and Tibetan food—a rarity in Mussoorie. Try the special garlic chicken (Rs50), or steamed mutton *momos* (Rs18). Open daily 11am-11:30pm. Off-season: closes 9:30pm.

Jeet Restaurant, right on Gandhi Chowk, next to the library and Jeet Hotel. The ideal place to plan your trek or your next move, since the tables have regional maps built into them. Mostly veg. fare, nothing fancy-schmancy. Attentive service. Cogitate over hot cocoa (Rs20). Open daily 8am-10:30pm.

Le Chef, near the State Bank of India in Kulri. Tries hard to be Western and does a commendable job, with order numbers called over an incomprehensible speaker. Chocolate doughnuts, "All-American Breakfasts" (Rs65), take-out pizza (Rs50), hot dogs (Rs35), "gravy items," and fountain drinks. Needless to say, it's a popular teen hang-out, especially for the after-roller-skating crowd. Open daily 10am-11pm.

Howard Revolving Restaurant, Hotel Howard (tel. 632113), on the Mall between Kulri and Library. The small, cylindrical restaurant makes one noisy, kerklunkety rotation every 9min.—you may not notice that you're rotating, but you'll wonder why the earth is shaking violently. Good cucumber and tomato salad (Rs15), Last rotation starts at 11:21pm! Open daily 7:30-11am, 1-3:30pm, and 9:30-11:30pm.

SIGHTS

There are more things to do than there are to see in Mussoorie, but that doesn't mean the town lacks sights. Keep in mind, however, that any well-known sight is bound to be congested during high season. Not to worry, though—the surrounding mountains and lush vegetation offer solace. Looming directly over the town is **Gun Hill,** its moniker earned through a pre-Independence ritual of firing guns from the top at midday—the townspeople would adjust their watches accordingly. It's possible to walk or to ride rented horses to get to the top, but the best way is via Mussoorie's **Ropeway,** a cable car that zips up the 500m mountainside. *(Open in-season: 8am-10pm; last car up at 8pm. Off-season: 10am-7pm.)* The top of Gun Hill has several lookout points, small food vendors, a surreal and amusing **Laugh House** with a loud laughtrack and bent mirrors to distort your soul (Rs10), and several photo stands that will dress you up in glittery local costume and take a snapshot.

There are several good spots for **walking** around Mussoorie, passing through cool, fragrant pine and *deodar* forests. **Camel's Back Road,** which winds behind the town (3km total), offers keen views of the Himalaya. Points of interest include the **ceme-**

Strange Brew

Though an Englishman founded Mussoorie, it took an unruly Scot to set the tone for the revelry that has outlasted the Brits in the hill station. In the 1880s, a fellow named Mackinnon encountered limestone springs, which were promising for brewing, near present-day Gandhi Chowk. Mackinnon seized the idea and the land and constructed a brewery, turning out Garhwal's first fine domestic beer. From the beginning, Mussoorie was a fun-loving town, and the beer-brewing led to a level of bacchanalian debauchery that wrinkled more than a few official brows. Local lore has it that one English lass, well progressed in the appreciation of the Scotch-Indian brew, stood on a chair on Mall Rd. and sold kisses for Rs5. That spelled trouble for Mackinnon. Since an outright ban on Mackinnon's operation would have been illegal, the authorities shrewdly crippled him by refusing him the right to import barley on the government road.

Shut down but not broken in spirit(s), Mackinnon would not be snubbed—especially by the English. In a daring scheme, he built his own road, about 20km long, fitting it with carts to transport his barley. He even set up a watchtower and tollbooth and ran it as a private highway. Aside from beerstuffs, much of the heavy European furniture in Mussoorie was brought up on "Mr. Buckles Bullock-Cart Train," as the venture was called. And so, Mussoorie had its beer.

To thank his consumers, Mackinnon threw a massive bash, where he cracked a huge wooden cask of new brew. All present were astonished at how truly excellent it was. The rollicking horde polished off most of the keg, noting repeatedly that it tasted better than any beer in the history of brewing. A scream of horror suddenly broke the festivities—for in the dregs of the keg lay a decomposing human body. Apparently, an impatient imbiber had slipped into the cellar, helped himself to a few too many, and fallen in with the hops.

The brew was through. Mackinnon's ruined brewery looms on the Lynndale Estate about 3km west of Mussoorie, but his bullock-cart road now forms 20km of the present road to Rajpur. Fortune indeed favors the bold.

tery (if the main gate is closed, try the side gate), rife with interesting British tombstones; **Camel's Back Rock** itself, which is shaped like you-know-what; and **Chatra (Umbrella) Point,** where you can buy *chai* and snacks and look through a telescope, if it isn't broken. The entire walk takes about 40 minutes. On a clear day, the sunset seen from the road is spectacular.

To the west of town lie **Happy Valley** and the nearby **Municipal Garden** (3km), which has a tiny pool for paddle-boats and much of the carnival stuff you find on Gun Hill or in town—check out the acrobatics of the man operating the ferris wheel. Two kilometers from the garden are the ruins of the old Mackinnon brewery (see **Strange Brew,** p. 158). A more distant destination to the northwest of town is **Kempty Falls,** a popular "retreat," which has sadly gone from pristine, rushing falls and peaceful pools to the same old glitz that pervades Mussoorie. GMVN runs a three-hour bus trip to Kempty falls. *(Apr.-Oct. 9am, noon, and 3pm; off-season 10am and 1pm, Rs40.)* They also run combined daytrips to the orchards and dense *deodar* forest of **Dhanolti** (25km away) to the artificial lake at **Jheel,** which provides boating facilities, and to **Surkanda Devi.** *(35km, Rs120.)* This temple, atop the highest mountain in the area (3300m), provides snow peak views. It's a strenuous 2km walk to the temple from the road head. **Cloud End** (see p. 156), 4km away, is a fairly untouched hiking spot.

At the top of the mountain, above Landour Bazaar, is the **Landour Language School.** Students from around the world come here to learn Subcontinental languages. Founded in 1870 by British missionaries and grammarians, it launched the international academic study of modern Indian languages and offers credit programs in tandem with the University of Chicago and UC Berkeley, among others. Classes are small, with plenty of individual instruction for the school's 80 or so students. Courses offered range from introductory to graduate classes, though sensitive administration may be able to tailor instruction to particular circumstances. A 12-week introductory Hindi class costs Rs18,000. Private lessons cost Rs75 per hr. Students usually stay in private houses (Rs5000 per month) or in one of the two guesthouses near the school (Rs300 per day including food). Contact Principal Chitranjan Datt, Landour Language School, Landour, Mussoorie, U.P., 248179 (tel. 631487; fax 631917).

ENTERTAINMENT

Have no fear of boredom if you feel bound to either of the two bazaar areas in town. The **Basu Cinema,** in the Library area, and the **Rialto Cinema,** in Kulri across from the President's Restaurant, frequently show Hindi movies, and the Rialto shows out-of-date English-language movies. (Movies Sa and Su 11:30am and 4:30pm.) There are also an exceptional number of **video games** (some dating back to the pre-Pac-Man era) in the several parlors clustered in Kulri (Rs2).

There are several discos in the Mussoorie area, but the nightlife merely duplicates the bazaars' numerous restaurants and opportunities for gawking. **Hotel Rockwood,** Kulri Bazaar, rocks 8-11pm every night (Rs150, Rs250 per couple), but only local men seem to go. Outside town, **Residency Manor, Hotel Jaypee** (tel. 631800) has dancing on the weekends (Rs250-375 per person, including dinner at the hotel).

All of these minor amusements are a mere warm-up for the true good-time place in Mussoorie—**The Rink,** in Kulri, India's largest roller skating rink (though seeing it, one wonders what the smallest is like). Guys should don their tightest blue jeans (women should *not* wear skirts) at this strut-your-ball-bearings hangout for the local and vacationing teen crowd. The rink itself dates back 100 years to when British couples experimented with what was all the rage back home. Rent full-shoe "special" skates (Rs50), or those that attach to your own shoes. Shops across the way rent skates, too. Five skating sessions thump to Indian and Western pop music daily (beginners 8:30-10am; open skating 11am-1pm, 3-5pm, 6-7:30pm, and 8-9:30pm; admission with rental Rs35, with your own skates Rs30; "spectators" pay Rs5). Those less inclined to roller-derby glory might appreciate the billiards here (Rs80 per hr.).

■ Haridwar हरिद्वार

The city of Haridwar marks the spot where the Ganga emerges from the mountains to carve its tortuous way across India to the Bay of Bengal. Haridwar is a place of great holiness, especially to Punjabi Hindus. The city's spiritual preeminence is rooted in three distinct Hindu legends: here, the goddess Ganga was persuaded to descend from the heavens to sanctify some poor souls cursed by Rishi Kapila; Vishnu's footprint is said to mark a stone set in the wall of Har-ki-Pairi (Footstep of God), the main *ghat* to the Ganga; most strikingly, Har-ki-Pairi is the site where a divine drop of nectar fell from a pot *(kumbh)* over which the gods and demons had fought for 12 days (see **The Kumbh Mela,** p. 231). The *ghat* became a particularly auspicious spot for a huge communal swim, and during the Kumbh Mela, held once every 12 years, millions rush the Har-ki-Paira *ghat* at a precisely calculated moment. Often, stampedes during the Mela result in mass killings—at Haridwar's most recent Mela in 1986, 50 devotees were trampled or crushed to death.

Hindus take holy Haridwar very seriously, and their reverence isn't limited to Mela years. A steady (albeit less frenzied) stream of pilgrims courses through the city year-round; you'll see them floating flower-boats down the Ganga during the nightly *aarti* ceremony and worshipping at Haridwar's many temples. As a tourist, however, it is not quite so easy to be earnest. Ancient and tacky modern shrines sit side by side, making Haridwar feel much like an amusement park—clean, but somehow unreal.

ORIENTATION

Haridwar runs parallel to and along the River Ganga, which flows from northeast to southwest. Buses and trains arrive at stations near the southwest end of **Railway Road,** the town's main thoroughfare, where most services lie. Walking northeast on Railway Rd., you'll cross **Laltarao Bridge** (over a small stream, not the Ganga) before reaching the post office. Just south of the post office is a barricade that prohibits motor traffic from continuing up Railway Rd. North of this barricade, Railway Rd. becomes **Upper Road.** The main bazaar in town is **Moti Bazaar,** which runs along the streets below Upper Rd., parallel to the river near **Har-ki-Pairi,** which is at the northeast end of Upper Rd. Beyond that is **Broken Bridge,** a broken bridge. A strip of land across the river hosts accommodations and the taxi stand. Haridwar's **temples** lie to the north and south.

PRACTICAL INFORMATION

Trains: Northern Railway Station, next to the bus stand on Railway Rd. Enquiry on the right-hand side, reservation counter on the other. Buy general tickets at **Northern Railway Booking Office,** Railway Rd. (tel. 427724), north of Laltarao Bridge. Fares given are for 2nd class sleeper/1st class. To: **Dehra Dun** (9 per day 5:30am-4:55pm, 2hr., Rs105/155); **Delhi** (*Dehradun-Mumbai Exp.* 9020, 1:45pm, 7hr.; *Dehradun-Delhi Exp.* 4042, 11:15pm, 8hr., Rs103/347; *Shatabdi Exp.* 2018, 6pm, 4½hr., Rs365 A/C chair car); **Lucknow** (*Dehradun-Varanasi Exp.* 4266, 8:25pm, 11hr., Rs152/5311); **Mumbai** (*Dehradun-Mumbai Exp.* 9020, 1:45pm, 48hr. or more, Rs332/1230); **Rishikesh** (5, 8:45am, 5:15pm, Rs76/125); **Varanasi** (*Doon Exp.* 3010, 10:15pm, 20hr., Rs220/766).

Buses: The **bus stand** is across from the railway station, at the southwest end of Railway Rd. **U.P. Roadways** (tel. 427037) runs buses to: **Agra** (2:30, 4:30, 6:30, 7:30, 9pm, 11hr., Rs108; deluxe 7 and 9:15am, Rs173); **Dehra Dun** (every 30min. 5:30am-10:30pm, 1½hr., Rs19); **Delhi** (every 15min. 4:30am-11:30pm, Rs64); **Lucknow** (noon, 3:30, and 7:30pm, 14hr., Rs156); **Rishikesh** (every 30min., 45min., Rs9); **Shimla** (6 and 10am, 5 and 10pm, 12hr., Rs125). **Himachal Roadways** also services distant Shimla (5am and 10pm, 12hr., Rs125).

Local Transportation: Tempos cluster on the east bank of the Shatabdi Bridge; from the railway station to Har-ki-Pairi, Rs2-3; by **auto-rickshaw,** Rs6 or **cycle rickshaw,** Rs5-10.

Tourist Office: GMVN, Railway Rd. (tel. 424240), at Laltarao Bridge. Provides good maps of Haridwar and Rishikesh. Staff knows about nearby treks and has information on pilgrimages. Open M-Sa 10am-5pm. **U.P. Tourism** (tel. 427370), next to Rahi Motel across from railway station, has more regional information. In-season: open M-Sa 10am-5pm. Off-season: M-Sa 10am-5pm.

Budget Travel: Several private agents have information on treks and pilgrimages. **Ashwani Travels,** Railway Rd. (tel. 424581), just south of Laltarao Bridge. Open daily 8am-10pm. **Shivalik Travels,** Upper Rd. (tel. 426855), opposite Goraksh Nath Ashram, specializes in transportation to northern pilgrimage sites. Open daily 7am-3pm and 5-10pm. Pilgrimage destinations are open May-Oct., but the best times to go are May-June and Sept.-Oct.

Currency Exchange: State Bank of India, changes U.S. currency at its branch on Sharwan Nath Nagar. Open M-F 10am-2pm, Sa 10am-noon.

Market: Moti Bazaar, 1 block north along Railway Rd. from Laltarao Bridge, then down 2 blocks. Copious shops selling clothing, wooden crafts, walking sticks, brass pots, and (if you're into red spit and mouth cancer) *paan.*

Bookstore: Most of the bookshops in Moti Bazaar sell religious literature, though some have small selections of fiction and books about Garhwal. **Arjun Singh Bookseller,** Bara Bazaar (tel. 421449). Open daily 9am-9:30pm

Pharmacy: Milap Medical Hall, Railway Rd. (tel. 427193), south of and opposite the post office, has drugs, sunscreen, maxi-pads, and toilet paper. Open M-Sa 8:30am-10pm. **Dr. B.C. Hasaram & Sons,** Railway Rd. (tel. 427860), across from the police station, specializes in ayurvedic medicines. Open daily 8am-9pm.

Hospital/Medical Services: Several private clinics clutter Railway Rd., such as **Dr. Kailash Pande** (tel. 426023; 24hr. **emergency** care 424343—ask for Dr. O.P. Sharma), north of Laltarao Bridge. Open 11:30am-2:30pm and 6:30-9:30pm. **Harmilap District Hospital** (tel. 426060), south of the post office, and **Chain Rai Female Hospital** (tel. 427490), next door, are short on staff and English skills.

Police: Main station (tel. 426200; superintendent of police tel. 425200) at Laltarao Bridge. **Har-ki-Pairi station** (tel. 425160).

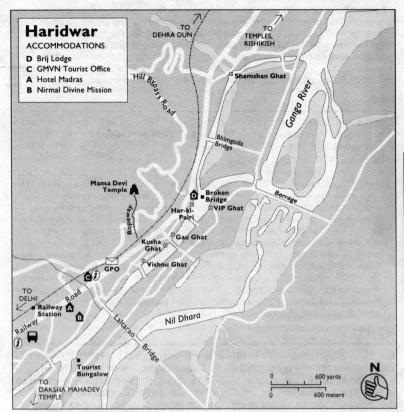

Haridwar
ACCOMMODATIONS
D Brij Lodge
C GMVN Tourist Office
A Hotel Madras
B Nirmal Divine Mission

NORTH INDIA

Post Office: (tel. 427025), on Railway Rd., north of Laltarao Bridge. *Poste Restante*, inter-India speed post services. Open M-Sa 10am-4pm. **Postal Code:** 249401.
Telephones: STD/ISD booths in every nook and cranny. **Telephone Code:** 0133.

ACCOMMODATIONS

Travelers coming to Haridwar for only a short time may want to consider staying in one of the budget hotels near the railway station and the bus stand, or in the railway retiring rooms. Those sticking around longer can get a room closer to the river and Har-ki-Pairi. From November to March prices are 25-50% lower. Unless noted, the prices listed below are for high pilgrimage season.

Nirmal Divine Mission (tel. 423301), off Railway Rd., 2 blocks north of the railway station. Turn right after the Kailash Hotel, go up 3 blocks, and it's on the left. Look for the large Hindi and small English signs. Good fans, erratic water and plumbing, showers, and seat toilets. Cooking facilities and mostly Indian guests make for a neighborly, homey feel. Front rooms have balconies. Singles and doubles Rs70.
Hotel Madras (tel. 426356), off Railway Rd., 2 blocks north of the railway station. Turn right after the Kailash Hotel. A low-end old-timer conveniently close to transport. Rooms built in 1950s have common bath. Decent restaurant. Singles Rs50; doubles Rs80. Off-season: singles Rs30; doubles Rs60.
Brij Lodge (tel. 426872), north of Har-ki-Pairi on the right, near the broken bridge (the name is not visible from the road). Watch the nightly *aarti* ritual from the balcony, which overlooks the Ganga. All rooms have attached bath, no shower, and seat toilets. Doubles Rs250-300; quads Rs600. Off-season: 60-80% discount.

Tourist Bungalow (tel. 426379), across the river from town, toward the railway station end. Buses pass it on the way in, so keep an eye out and ask the driver to stop. Run by U.P. Tourism, it's pricey and far from most sights, but it's the best place for peace and quiet, with its own little lawn, flower garden, and strip of riverbank. All rooms have air-cooling and attached bath with hot water and seat toilet. Restaurant open 6:30am-10:30pm. Check-out noon. Dorm beds Rs100. In-season: air-cooled singles Rs525, with A/C Rs1050; doubles Rs630/1260. Off-season: discount 25%.

FOOD

Purity of diet follows purity of spirit in Haridwar, so alcohol and meat are not available. Most major restaurants are on Railway Rd., midway between the bus stand and Har-ki-Pairi, though some of the little places tucked into the bazaar near Har-ki-Pairi make mean, clean breakfast *puris.*

Ahaar Restaurant (tel. 427601), on "Asli" Railway Rd., near Laltarao Bridge. The Sikh owner presides over guests from his desk as they enjoy exceptional South Indian, Chinese, and Punjabi dishes in a dark, tranquil, wooden chamber below street level. The hefty Punjabi *thali* (Rs50) is not as spicy as many other dishes. Other *thalis* are as low as Rs35; *dosas* run Rs18-30. Open daily 10am-11pm.

New Mysore Kwality Restaurant, Railway Rd. (tel. 426684). On west side of Railway Rd., two-thirds of the way to Har-ki-Pairi. South Indian-run restaurant has an unassuming atmosphere, cool air, and great prices. *Tomato utthapam* Rs14, full *thali* Rs25, *dosas* Rs10-20. Open daily 7am-10pm (closes one hr. earlier in winter).

Swagat Restaurant (tel. 426501), in Hotel Mansarovar on Railway Rd. Typical business-hotel-restaurant. Every table has its own little artificial floral arrangement. Entrees Rs40, veg. chow mein Rs28, plain rice Rs8. Open daily 6am-11pm.

SIGHTS

The most important spot in Haridwar is the sacred *ghat* of **Har-ki-Pairi,** site of Vishnu's footprint and point at which the sacred Ganga flows out onto the plains. It is also the most fascinating place, particularly during the *aarti* ceremony. Although most people bathe at sunrise, you'll see devotees throughout the day—it's a good spot because there are chains to keep bathers from getting swept off to Varanasi by the deceptively fast current. The area is packed with beggars, lepers, *sadhus*, other pilgrims, and several uniformed men who wander the area asking for **donations** for various "trusts." Many of these guys are shysters who pocket their earnings, and you'd do much better to donate via the charity boxes around the area, or at the office of Ganga Sabha, above the temple at the *ghat;* money given there is more likely to go to good works, and they'll give you a box of rice to offer to the gods. Every evening at Har-ki-Pairi is the sublime and spectacular **aarti** ceremony. At sundown, thousands gather to pay tribute to the gods by floating *diyas* (colorful boats made of cupped leaves filled with flower petals and a lit candle) on the river. Sending a *diya* down the river is believed to fulfill one's wish. Arrive early in the high season; the best place to watch is from the bridge on the south end of Har-ki-Pairi or from the strip by the clock tower. You'll have to check your shoes at the stand if you go down to the *ghat*—avoid the 8pm shoe-return stampede.

Within Haridwar's blessed boundaries, wealthy Hindus have erected a number of recent temples. The two most important temples, however, manage to elude the gaudiness that crops up in many of the other new temples. One of these, just above the city, is the **Mansa Devi Temple,** dedicated to Mansa. *(June: open daily 7:30am-7pm; otherwise 8am-6pm.)* To honor the goddess, stand in line for one of the ropeway trolleys (since 1983, more than 20 million folks have made the Rs20 round-trip) to whisk you up and over a garden to the hilltop where views, vendors, and the temple await. You can also avoid a potentially long wait in line by making the 30-minute hike up the hill yourself. The fervor of Hindus offering their coconuts to the shrine is pretty extreme here, so stand back to observe. **Chanda Devi,** 3km from Har-ki-Pairi, is the other exceptionally popular temple, honoring an avatar of the goddess Adishakti

Flashing Eyes, Floating Hair, Holy Dreds

Times were tough for King Bhagiratha: the world had become completely parched, and 60,000 of his ancestors had been burned to a crisp by a disgruntled sage. The King wanted to perform a ceremony to give their souls peace, but to do it he needed holy water, and the parched planet presented no obvious options. A devout man, Bhagiratha took up long ascetic rituals which eventually caught the attention of Brahma, who decided to help him out. Brahma asked the goddess Ganga, who was in the heavens, to descend to earth. However, she was reluctant, for her impact upon landing would pummel the earth to bits. Unwilling to turn the proverbial firehose on earth's sand castle, Brahma realized that only Shiva could soften Ganga's landing. So Bhagiratha practised austerities for many more years until Shiva, Lord of Ascetics (if not of Punctuality), finally arrived. He provided his strands of matted hair as a cushion for Ganga, who consented to descend. A cascade of water touched ground high up in the Himalaya and flowed down in several streams, directed by Shiva's locks. Today these streams flow together as they approach the plains and emerge at Haridwar. In gratitude, King Bhagiratha prayed to Ganga at Gangotri, the source of one such stream. This river is called Bhagirathi to honor a pious man who saved the world from drought and gave India her great watery artery, the Ganga.

Jagdamba. (*Open 8:30am-6pm.*) Ride the ropeway (Rs25) with myriad aging *babas,* or tackle the 45min. hike.

Also in the area are the **Dakseshwara Temple** (also called Daksha Mahadev) and **Sati Kund,** 4km to the south, in Kankhal. The latter marks the spot where King Daksha Prajaputi, Brahma's son and Sati's father, held a *yagya* (public sacrifice), inviting Sati but not her consort Shiva, whom he thought hung around with a bad—nay—demonic, crowd. Sati was so insulted she threw herself on her father's sacrificial fire. (For the end of the story, see **Divine Dismemberment,** p. 418.)

Four kilometers north of town, west of the river, is a small cluster of unusual temples, which are (depending on your viewpoint) either opulent and justly grand, or just chintzy and overdone. Tempo drivers charge Rs150-200 for a three-hour tour of these temples, but it's smarter to let the tempo go once you're at the temples; all are within easy walking distance of each other. The **Pawan Dham Temple,** first along the road from Haridwar, is most representative of the local houses of worship. Its many shrines are made almost entirely of mirrors and stained glass. Shiva and Arjuna ride atop mirror-covered horses; Krishna sees his 100 lovers in 100 different directions. Venture off to the **Sapta Rishi Ashram,** at the north end of the cluster, to pay homage to the seven saints in seven temples.

The **Bharat Mata Mandir,** the six-story shrine to Mother India and its leaders, at the north end of the temple cluster, resembles a modern apartment building with temple domes on top. The top story (reached by elevator for Rs1) houses the Hindu gods, while the floor below hosts the goddesses, including Ganga and Saraswati, goddess of knowledge. Descending floors honor the saints of India's various religions (from Guru Nanak of the Sikhs to the Buddha and Swami Vivekenanda), sisters (including Gandhi's devotees Annie Besant and Sister Nivedita), and fighters for freedom and independence. The second floor has paintings highlighting characteristic features of India's states, and the ground floor has a giant relief model of the country. It's an interesting blend of history and religion. Nearby, **Maa Vaishnodevi Mandir** attempts to simulate the experience of visiting a cave in Kashmir—complete with artificial, fruit-bearing mango trees, a giant Ganga Mata with a crocodile, and a tunnel with knee-deep water, through which visitors duck and wade. **Burma Niketan,** south of Maa Vaishnodevi Mandir, has the added bonus of automation—pay a rupee to enter a room in which robotic representations of Hindu heroes cavort with a giant dinosaur.

ASHRAMS

Hindu pilgrims and *sadhus* flock to Hardiwar for spiritual enrichment, often staying at one of the numerous ashrams located within the city or nearby. Western spiritual seekers, on the other hand, often find themselves more at home in **Rishikesh** (see p. 164), which features more yoga centers and open and accepting ashrams. **Parmath Ashram** (tel. 427099 or 427473) occasionally accepts foreigners. A huge, self-contained community, with its own medical clinic, greenhouse, and a dining patio that serves thousands of meals daily, the Parmath Ashram was founded by Acharya, whose teachings currently reach some 20 million followers worldwide. The famous **Shantikunj** (tel. 424309; fax 423866; email shantikunj.hardwar@sml.sprint-rpg.ems.vsnl.net.in), offers 9-, 30-, and 90-day courses which use meditation, music, and chanting as a means of attaining higher spiritual ends. The 9-day courses begin on the 1st, 11th, and 21st of every month—reserve a space one month in advance. Single or 2-day stays are possible as well. Foreigners are welcome and pay on a donation basis only.

■ Rishikesh ऋषिकेश

Most travelers come to Rishikesh to find *something*—a cure to some deep-rooted ailment, a spiritual leader, or, most often, themselves. Indeed, something about Rishikesh suggests a power to transform—sages first came here to find a splash of holiness along the crashing Ganga before heading north to the region's pilgrimage sites. Every year, thousands turn up for the International Yoga Week (Feb. 2-7), on the banks of the Ganga. Even the Beatles sought a new path here in 1968, under the guidance of the Maharishi Mahesh Yogi (see **Instant Karma**, p. 169). In the end, what travelers find is almost invariably to their liking. Summer is yoga off season; winter has fewer Indian tourists. There are fewer temples in Rishikesh than in Haridwar, but more Westerners, more ashrams, and more *sadhus.*

ORIENTATION

Rishikesh is trisected by the **Ganga** and the **Chandrabhaga** rivers. Northeast of the dry river bed are **Ramjhula,** and farther northeast, **Laxmanjhula,** both of which straddle the Ganga and are connected across it by eponymous footbridges. Most travelers head toward the bridges for accommodations. It's a 5km hike into Rishikesh if you're staying in Laxmanjhula. From the Laxmanjhula Bridge to the road and taxi stand is itself a surprisingly arduous trek.

In town are the **main bus stand** to the south and the **railway station** to the west, as well as the GPO, banks, and tourist office. The main market lines **Laxmanjhula Road,** the main thoroughfare. **Dehradun Road** runs at the northern end of Rishikesh along the Chandrabhaga, intersecting at its east end with Laxmanjhula Road. **Railway Road** reaches west to the rail station along the Chandrabhaga. **Muni Ki Reti** refers to the western part of Ramjhula, and contains **Kailash Gate,** which lies about 1km south of the Ramjhula taxi stand and 1km north of the main market. The east bank of Ramjhula is called **Swargashram.**

PRACTICAL INFORMATION

Trains: Railway Station, at west end of Rishikesh on (surprise!) Railway Rd. Make reservations 8am-2pm. Many connections to major destinations start in Haridwar. To: **Haridwar** (6:40, 7:45am, 2:20, 3:15, and 6:40pm); **Delhi** (6:40am, 10hr., Rs39).

Buses: To confuse travelers, Rishikesh has 2 bus stands. Smog-snorters heading for the **plains** leave from the **U.P. Roadways** bus stand, Agarwal and Bengali Rd. (tel. 430066), on the south side of central Rishikesh. To: **Agra** (8am and 6pm, 12hr., Rs140); **Almora** (9am, 12hr., Rs145); **Chandigarh** (7 and 9am, 6hr., Rs80); **Dehra Dun** (25 per day, 5:30am-8pm, 1hr., Rs13); **Delhi** (every hr. 4am-10:30pm, 6½hr., Rs81); **Haldwani** (8 and 9am, 10hr., Rs100); **Haridwar** (every 30min. 4am-10:30pm, Rs10); **Nainital** (8am, 1hr., Rs120). For buses to the **northern pilgrim-**

Rishikesh
ACCOMMODATIONS

G Bombay Kshetra
F Ganga View Hotel
D Green Hotel
B Hotel Menka
E Hotel Rajdeep
C Yoga Niketan Guest House
A Yoga Study Center

age sites, go to the **Yatra Bus Stand** (tel. 430344), on the northwest end of Rishikesh on Dehra Dun Rd. A rickshaw from the U.P. stand costs Rs10-15. Tickets for Yamnotri, Gangotri, Kedarnath, and Badrinath can be purchased one day in advance. To: **Badrinath** (3:30, 4, and 5am, 12hr., Rs118); **Chamolhi** (7hr., Rs79); **Gangotri** (5:30am, 12hr., Rs112); **Hanuman Chatti** (7am, 12hr., Rs72); **Joshimath** (6am, 10hr., Rs100); **Kedarnath** (3:45 and 5am, 12hr., Rs86); **Srinagar (U.P.)** (every 30min. 4am-3pm, 4hr., Rs42); **Tehri** (every 30min. 3:15am-5:15pm, 3½hr., Rs32); **Uttarkashi** (10 per day, 3:15am-1pm., 7hr., Rs60). Tehri and Uttarkashi serve as launch points for Yamnotri and Gangotri; Srinagar for Kedarnath and Badrinath. **Shared taxis** to Uttarkashi (5hr., Rs1000 per cab, up to 5 seats) congregate outside the bus stand. If you are going to **Uttarkashi** and can't find a cab and can't face the bus, take an auto-rickshaw to **Sharma Travel and News Agency.** Taxis carrying newspapers depart for Uttarkarshi at 5am (Rs125 per seat). Be prepared to be squeezed in, and book your spot the previous day.

Local Transportation: Getting to and from Ramjhula and Laxmanjhula from Rishikesh is best done with one of the **tempos** that run along Laxmanjhula Rd. (Rs2-5). Both bridges must be negotiated by foot—no cross-river traffic, though there are taxis and jeeps in and between the 2 eastern bridge towns. A seat in a taxi to Rishikesh from the Ramjhula Bridge costs Rs20; a rickshaw (all to yourself) from the U.P. bus stand to Laxmanjhula costs Rs40.

Tourist Office: U.P. Tourism, Railway Rd. (tel. 430209), 3 blocks west of the State Bank of India, up an outdoor flight of stairs by a white marble statue. Provides Haridwar and Rishikesh maps (detailed map Rs2, other maps free), and brochures about regional treks, but the staff's English is limited. Open M-Sa 10am-5pm, closed second Sa each month. The helpful staff at the **GMVN Trekking and Mountain-**

eering Office (tel. 430799) at Kailash Gate offer detailed information about treks. May-June, Sept.-Oct.: open eight days a week, 10am-5pm. Off-season: closed Su.

Budget Travel: Several agents are clustered on Laxmanjhula Rd., north of the dry river bed on the way to Ramjhula. **Step Himalayan Adventures** (tel. 432581) organizes treks and rafting trips, offers free advice for those planning their own trips, and rents equipment, including 2-person tents (Rs75 per day) and sleeping bags (Rs25 per day). Virbhadra Rd., (tel. 432851), on the right-hand side on the way out of town, provides information and sets up treks and rafting trips. Open daily 10am-5pm. Closed Su and holidays Nov.-March.

Currency Exchange: The **State Bank of India** (tel. 430114) has offices at Ramjhula and Laxmanjhula but changes foreign currency only at its main Rishikesh office, on the north side of Railway Rd., a 5min. walk from Laxmanjhula Rd. The bank changes U.S., U.K., German, and Japanese cash and traveler's checks from AmEx, Citicorp, and Thomas Cook. Open M-F 10am-2pm, Sa 10am-noon. The smaller branches change only rupee traveler's checks. **Bank of Baroda,** 74 Dehra Dun Rd. (tel. 430653), changes AmEx, Thomas Cook, and Visa traveler's checks in U.S. and U.K. currencies. Open M-F 10am-2pm, Sa 10am-noon.

Market: Main Bazaar in Rishikesh, toward the river from the post office. There's a **didgeridoo** shop near the State Bank of India, Hare Krishna tapes and ceramic *linga* ashtrays in Laxmanjhula, and yoga books and ayurvedic herbs in Ramjhula.

Pharmacy: Dehradun Rd., west of the police office, is peppered with chemists and "medical stores" who'll help you if they can. Some, such as **Asha Medical Agencies** (tel. 432696), across from the Government Hospital, profess to be open 24hr.

Hospital/Medical Services: Government General Hospital (tel. 430402) and **Ladies' Hospital** are in the same, sort of scary, building on Dehradun Rd. Open 24hr. Several **specialist clinics** abut this road. **Dashmesh Hospital** (tel. 431444), between the police station and Yatra Bus Stand, has consultations 10am-2pm.

Police: Main Rishikesh Office, Dehradun Rd. (tel. 430100). There's a branch on the south end of Laxmanjhula (tel. 430228). Both are open 24hr.

Post Office: Main office (tel. 430340), in the center of town east of Laxmanjhula Rd. next to the big Hotel Basera, has EMS and speed post, but only within India. Open M-Sa 10am-5pm. **Ramjhula branch,** Swargashram. Open M-Sa 9am-5pm. **Laxmanjhula branch,** a 5min. walk south from the bridge. Open M-Sa 9am-5pm. All branches have *Poste Restante.* **Postal Code:** 249201.

Internet: Step Himalayan Adventures, Laxmanjhula Rd. **Email** Rs200 per hr. **Blue Hill Travel** (tel. 431865), Swargashram. Web access Rs80 per hr. Open 5am-11pm.

Telephones: Telegraph/fax services are available near the railway station, on the east end of Railway Rd., and in the main post office. **Telephone Code:** 0135.

ACCOMMODATIONS

Where you stay in Rishikesh depends on what you want to do. Searchers for the inner light may want to stay in an ashram, mother nature's sons can stay in one of the guesthouses west of Laxmanjhula, scholars of mellow and quiet punctuated by the revelry of fellow westerners should cross the Laxmanjhula Bridge, and those whose mantra is "wait" might as well stay near the bus stands in Rishikesh.

Hotels and Guesthouses

Bombay Kshetra (Bombay Guest House). In Laxmanjhula, turn left after crossing the bridge, head down 50m, and it will be on the right. Rundown rooms with weak fans, a serene central courtyard, and great roof-space. Come here for the company, not the value. Squat toilets and shower in the back. Bring your own padlock. 8-day max. stay, without manager's approval. Lockout 10pm (summer), 9:30pm (winter). Singles Rs60, with fan Rs70, with 2 beds Rs90; doubles Rs100; triples Rs120.

Green Hotel (tel. 431242), behind Gita Bhavan in Swargashram. Walk away from the bridge along main walkway; after 200m turn left and walk up 50m. Well-run place sails in seas of green (green walls, green beds, etc.). Immaculate rooms, seat toilets, hot showers, good attached restaurant. Yoga classes Rs30 per session (8-9:30am). Singles Rs75; doubles Rs125, with air-cooling Rs200-250.

Ganga Guest House (tel. 433169), 20m south of the Laxmanjhula Bridge. Mellow atmosphere and a fine terrace for *darshans* of either the holy Ganga or the tourists on the bridge. The tranquility is interrupted, though, by the incessant bell-ringing in the attached shrine, starting at 7am. Showers and seat toilets. Riverside singles, Rs100; doubles Rs125. Backside rooms Rs80.

Hotel Rajdeep (tel. 432826), behind Swargashram in Ramjhula. Built in 1996, this upscale facility is pleasantly removed from the bustle of the main road. All rooms have air-cooling and attached bathrooms with hot showers; most have seat toilets. Perks include the 24hr. restaurant, great rooftop views, twice daily yoga classes (Rs50 per hr.), massage (Rs150 per hr.), and trekking reservations. Close to Ramjhula Ashram. Singles Rs150; doubles Rs225; A/C deluxe Rs450-725.

Bhandari Swiss Cottage (tel. 432676), toward Laxmanjhula from Ramjhula (west side), take Bypass Rd., which branches left; 50m later, turn right at the sign for High Bank Peasant's Cottage and take the gravel path. If you haven't slept for weeks, find rest here. Rooms offer valley views, seclusion, and a lovely flower garden. Common bath with cold shower and squat toilets. Neat balconies for contemplating the long hike back to town. Singles Rs80-100.

High Bank Peasant's Cottage (tel. 431167). Before the Bhandari, on the same trail, on the left side. Same virtues as Bhandari (beautiful garden and views), plus a few bonuses: cleaner, bigger rooms, a garrulous owner, and attached tourist services, There are also trained dogs, including Liza, who carries water and newspapers. Prices are higher, although negotiation may be possible. Doubles Rs300-350.

Hotel Menka (tel. 430285), directly opposite Roadways Bus Stand. A safe bet if you're overnighting. Decent mattresses and seat toilets to rest your weary head and bum respectively. Jan.-June: singles Rs125; doubles Rs150. July-Dec.: Rs80/125.

Yoya Niketan Guesthouse, Muniki-Reti, before the taxi stand. Has a well-groomed garden and steps lead down to the Ganga. Spacious rooms are clear and modern, with high-powered fans, white tile floors, seat toilets, and hot water. Convenient location ensures easy access to Rishikesh proper and Swargashram. Join yoga and meditation classes at the nearby Yoga Niketan Ashram for free. For 3 meals at the ashram, add Rs50. Singles Rs200; doubles Rs300.

Ashrams and Yoga

No matter which yoga position you have managed to twist and bend yourself into, an ashram is never out of sight in Rishikesh. Most Westerners head to Ramjhula for ashram stays, which are occasionally combined with yoga and meditation classes. Remember that staying in an ashram isn't like bunking up in a hotel—things are far more spartan, and the meditative atmosphere demands that certain rules be followed. These include total avoidance of meat, eggs, and smelly food (including onions and garlic), abstention from alcohol, tobacco, and drugs of any kind (including *paan*), and adherence to total quiet (no music or late-night talking). Most demand daily bathing and request that menstruating women stay out of the ashram centers, and many have curfews. Some (Swargashram and Parmath Niketan) are set up for pilgrims and Hindu worshippers, and do not allow foreigners.

Yoga Study Centre (tel. 433837), far south end of Laxmanjhula Rd. Nearly outside of town, on the river side of the road. Despite its distance from the bridges, it's a good place to learn *iyengar yoga* if you don't want to stay in an ashram. General, special, and curative classes for those with physical disorders. Three classes per day, alternating days. Rudra, the main instructor, has a good reputation. Winter season course (Feb. 2-24, 1999); summer course (April 4-25); and intensive course (Sept. 2-24). Rs1200 for the month-long courses. Lodging can be arranged Apr.-Aug. and Oct.-Jan. General yoga classes 6:30-8am M-Sa. Pay on donation basis.

Yoga Niketan (tel. 430227). Set in tranquil hills over Ramjhula. 15-night min. stay includes 3 meals, 2 yoga classes, and 2 meditation classes per day. Visible security force keeps the strict rules. Co-ed doubles for married couples only. Otherwise, buildings are single-sex. Guard your valuables. Squat toilets, no showers. Kitchen space in all rooms. Guests help with weekly cleaning. Lockout 9:30pm. Office open 8:30am-12pm and 2-5pm. Rs200 per day.

Omkarananda Ganga Sadan (tel. 431473 or 430763), west side of Ramjhula. Big, sterile building just south of the taxi/rickshaw stand. Yoga instruction daily, Rs200 per week, one lecture/class each evening Oct.-Apr. only. An ashram that feels more like a hospital—clean, dazzling white rooms and bathrooms (some attached; all with squat toilets). Try for a river view. Breakfast (Rs15) and lunch (Rs30) daily. Rooms Rs55 common bath, Rs60 common bath and balcony, Rs80 attached bath, Rs95 attached bath and balcony, Rs30 extra bed; 3-night min. stay (if you bail early, lose a 3-day deposit). Open summer 6am-10pm, winter 7:30am-9:30pm.

Ved Niketan (tel. 433253), south end of Ramjhula's east bank. Caged deities line the entrance to this large bright yellow and orange ashram along the rocky beach of the Ganga. The main guru, now 92, still lives here, but others do the teaching. Day-long yoga fee of Rs50 includes 5:30-7:30am meditation, 9-10:30am lecture, and 6:30-8pm yoga. Gates locked at 10pm. Breakfast Rs10, lunch Rs50, dinner Rs50. Singles Rs60 with common bath only; doubles with attached bath Rs100.

FOOD

If you enjoy vegetarian food, you're in luck, because Rishikesh abounds with yummy vegetarian *thalis*. If you don't then you're emphatically not in luck, because restaurants don't serve meat or alcohol here. So buck up and *dal* with it.

Ganga View Restaurant, opposite Bombay Kshetra in Laxmanjhula. This is where the foreign tourists who snapped up rooms in the Kshestra come together for good conversation, lubed by the Ganga view and comfy rattan chairs. Take pictures of the patrons and create your own *White Album.* Peanut butter toast with honey (Rs10), spaghetti (Rs25), and porridge with milk, nuts, bananas, raisins, and coconut (Rs18). Open daily 7am-9pm. *Thalis* (Rs20) served 6-8pm, but not June-July.

Ganga Darshan, next to Ganga View, closer to the bridge. Inexpensive *thalis* (Rs15-20) are filling, and some special dishes (like "cheese chow mein") provide respite from the spice of most Indian food. Balcony tables are awesome, but the service out there is slower. *Dosas* Rs7-16. Open daily 5am-8:30pm; 5am-8pm winter.

Amrita, in front of Hotel Rajdeep. There's a little library of Western books (Rs100 deposit, Rs5 per day charge). Offers outstanding fresh-baked raisin bread, jars of pure honey (500g, enough for a pie, Rs65), cheddar cheese, lasagna with home-made noodles (Rs50), and banana pancakes (Rs20) and pizza (Rs80). Also, miso soup. Great ambience inside, or sit on the rooftop.

Chotiwala and Chotiwala Restaurant (tel. 430070), in east Ramjhula near the bridge. Impossible to miss. The 2 parts, side by side, were supposedly divided by 2 brothers. You may want to frequent the one on the right, given its lack of a real live painted plump sadhu who waves at tourists (next door). Both Chotiwalas serve similar, standard Indian fare. Very popular among Indians. Chotiwala *thalis* (Rs25-50). Banana *lassi* (Rs12) is short on bananas and sweetness. Open daily 7am-11pm.

Madras Cafe, in Ramjhula rickshaw stand area. Indian food, California-style; emphasis on sprouts and whole wheat. Indian straws meet their match in viscous *lassis.* Himalayan Health *Pullao,* with sprouts, curd, and ayurvedic herbs, Rs40. Hot lemon-ginger-honey tea (yes, you know it's good news: Rs15). In-season: open daily summer 7:30am-10pm. Off-season: 8am-9pm.

SIGHTS AND ENTERTAINMENT

With yoga classes, *chillum* smoking, and requisite chat to keep them busy, most travelers in Rishikesh don't end up doing much more than looking around, round, round. Thus, they can easily forget that the town doesn't offer a ton of other distractions. The **Rama Palace cinema** on Dehradun Road in Rishikesh, screens Hindi movies. **Boats** head across the Ganga at Ramjhula below Sivananda Ashram. *(One way Rs5, round-trip Rs7.)* Another way to go where everything flows is to **shoot the Ganga's rapids.** Outfitters on the north end of Rishikesh, such as **Step Himalayan Adventures** (tel. 432581), run a 15km, 90-minute rafting trip through four "good" and two small rapids. *(Sept.-May. Rs500-900, including all transport.)* GMVN provides accommodations at its rafting camp in Kaudiyalaj, north of Rishikesh. *(Rooms Rs300, tents Rs100. Trips Sept.-May; 3-4hr. Rs350 per person. All-day trip Rs1050.)* After it's all over, settle in for a **massage** at the well-advertised Baba Health and Massage Centre in Rishikesh 100m east of Hotel Shivlok. You can enjoy an ayurvedic, Swedish, Thai, or "general" full-body massage (they even massage your ears) in a dark, cool room with space-age music. *(Open daily 8am-8pm. Rs150 per session.)* They also teach massage in a month-long course with 4 classes a day. *(Rs6000, includes lodgings.)*

The *aarti* ceremony at **Triveni Ghat,** on the south end of Rishikesh, takes place at sundown. The ancient **Laxman Temple,** on the west bank, is easy to find. Look for the engraved "This is the Ancient Temple of Laxman Jhula" over the arch. Sadly, the inside is less thrilling. The two 12- and 13-story mega-temples on the other side of it are also disappointing, with more jewelry shops than shrines as you climb to the top. The view from above is good, however.

Many visitors supplement meditation and vegetation with **music lessons. Sivananda Ramesh Music School** (left at the sign on the far side of the bridge on Laxmanjhula Rd. just after Tehri Rd.) will teach you to make the *didgeridoo* moan, the *tabla* ring, or the *sitar* gently weep. **Hindi lessons** are offered by Mr. Tilak Raj at Ramjhula, Swargashram, behind the Ganga General Store. *(Enquires 9-10am daily. 10-day advanced course Rs1000, includes 1hr. classes for 10 days; 5-day beginner course Rs500, Rs100 per lesson.)*

Instant Karma!

The Beatles came to Rishikesh to study Transcendental Meditation in February, 1968; it was the culmination of several years of Fab Four Indophilia. George Harrison's sitar licks first appeared in "Run For Your Life" (1965); the group attended lectures by the Maharishi Mahesh Yogi in '67, and recorded tracks for "The Inner Light" just before heading for the Himalayan foothills.

In Rishikesh, George, John, Paul, and Ringo embraced the typical ashram experience—they did fewer drugs, meditated more, and mostly just hung out with other Westerners (including Mia and Prudence Farrow, The Beach Boys' Mike Love, and 60s pop anomaly Donovan). They also wrote profusely. Most of *The White Album* and significant portions of *Abbey Road*, (as well as the unreleased "Happy Rishikesh Song") were composed during the group's stay. The most famously Rishikeshan of these is "Dear Prudence," considered an entreaty to the latter Farrow to join in the meditative fun: "The sun is up, the sky is blue/ It's beautiful and so are you/ Dear Prudence won't you come out and play?"

Eventually, though, the blue skies clouded, as the Beatles became disillusioned with the Maharishi. Less than a month after they left Rishikesh, John Lennon and Paul McCartney announced they'd ended their relationship with the guru. The bitterness comes through in the thinly veiled lyrics on *The White Album*'s second disc: "Sexy Sadie what have you done / You made a fool of everyone / ... / However big you think you are / Sexy Sadie oooh you'll get yours yet."

■ Near Rishikesh

Wait until the sun is up and the sky is blue before heading to the temple of **Kunjapuri,** which sits atop a nearby mountain and rewards daytrippers with views of the whole region, including Haridwar and the snow-capped Himalaya. The temple itself is disappointingly modern and small, though the priest is friendly to visitors. To get there, take a bus headed for **Tehri** from the Yatra Bus Stand; tell the driver you want to get off at Hindolakhal (1hr., Rs10). From there, it's a one-hour walk up the mountain along a paved road and up a surreal, narrow stairwell at the very top. Hop on a bus coming from Gangotri or Yamnotri to get back (last one at about 7 or 8pm).

Another destination for a day hike is the temple at **Neel Kanth Mahadev,** a place to which so many pilgrims have brought milk, *ghee,* and Ganga water that the *linga* has eroded down to a few inches. This tradition continues every year in mid-July. The temple and nearby bazaar are too modern and hectic be the sole point of the walk—it's the jungle trail along the way, inhabited by wild elephants, that makes the hike worthwhile. Go early, since it's a four- to five-hour climb with no stops, and the temple is more likely to be peaceful early in the day. Jeeps leave for the trailhead from the Laxmanjhula and Ramjhula taxi stands (12km, Rs35 per person one way, Rs60 round-trip), with great views along the way. Jeeps return to Rishikesh regularly.

About 10km from Rishikesh lies **Mansa Devi,** a temple that provides a wall-less shelter for those souls seeking to get away from town a little. Camp free and in relative isolation. Hindu pilgrims flood the site on the 7-10th of every month (especially Mar., Sept., and Oct.) for Navratna.

■ Northern Pilgrimages and Treks

Until the 1960s, the northern pilgrimage sites could only be reached by foot from the Plains, but new roads have now made them accessible to package-tour pilgrims crammed onto buses from Rishikesh. The resulting development makes it more and more difficult for non-Hindus to enjoy these journeys, but for the true believers, the experience is laced with a holiness that diesel, mud, and litter cannot spoil.

UTTARKASHI उत्तरकाशी

This busy town on the banks of the Bhagirathi River is the administrative center of the Uttarkashi District, as well as the last place to fill a shopping list or catch a Hindi movie before you head out for a trek. It also serves as a transportation hub for the pilgrimage sites to the north. The **tourist office** at the bus stand provides little help for trekking; try **Mt. Support Trekking,** B.D. Nautial Bhawan, Bhatwari Rd. (tel. 2419), about 10 minutes past the bus stand along Gangotri Rd. They also **exchange currency** for a hefty charge. **Buses** head to: **Barkot** (for **Yamnotri,** in season only, Rs45); **Bhatwari** (for treks to Sahasratal and Kedarnath, 1hr., Rs12); **Gangotri** (Rs42-46); **Gaurikund** (12hr., Rs97-102); **Rishikesh** (8hr., Rs60); and **Sayana Chatti** (for Dodital trek, Rs14). Morning taxis to Rishikesh collect at the bus stand. The **District Hospital** (24hr. emergency) lies midway between Gangotri Rd. and the river, near the **post office. Police** roost on Gangotri Rd., 15min. from the bus station on the right. **Telephone Code:** 01374.

Overnighting before an early morning departure can be done at **Bhandari Hotel,** at the bus stand (tel. 2203); there's also a restaurant inside. (In-season doubles Rs600, off-season Rs225.) Other options include **Meghdoot,** main market (tel. 2278). Some rooms have seat toilets and hot water (Rs5 per bucket). (May-June and Sept.: singles Rs100, doubles Rs160. Oct.-Apr. and July: Rs70/100). **GMVN** (tel. 2271) also provides clean rooms with running hot water. Dorms have 6 beds each. (In season: dorm beds Rs60; doubles Rs200, with TV and fancy furniture Rs550. Off-season: Rs60/100/300. For May, June, and Sept., book at least one month in advance.)

YAMNOTRI यमनोत्री

The source of the Yamuna River and the first stop on the Garhwal pilgrimage circuit, Yamnotri attracts 1500 pilgrims every day during tourist season. Yamnotri essentially consists of a temple surrounded by 10 to 15 concrete structures and numerous *dhabas.* The temple remains open from May to November, after which the image from the temple is carried to Kharsoli, a village opposite Janki Chatti. Heavy snows erode the temple so much that it has to be rebuilt every few years, so its architecture is nothing special—a slapdash construction with dressed-up concrete walls and a corrugated metal roof. Yamnotri is accessible only by a 14km trek from the town of Hanuman Chatti. The path angles gently upwards from Hanuman Chatti (2134m) for 8km to Janki Chatti (2676m), then turns steeply uphill until it reaches Yamnotri (3235m). Start early in the morning—there is no shade for the first 10km out of Hanuman Chatti, and by then the higher altitudes and steep path will drain any energy you have left. The path is lined with *chai* and cold drink stands. Sleeping arrangements are available at Janki Chatti. The closest **hospital, post office,** and **communications** system (a wireless only for emergencies) are at Janki Chatti. A seasonal **police** station is set up every year at Yamnotri. Hanuman Chatti is well-connected by buses from Dehra Dun (163km) and Rishikesh (209km). There are **GMVN lodges** at Sayana Chatti, 6km before Hanuman Chatti (Apr.-Nov: rooms Rs250; off-season: Rs150); Hanuman Chatti (dorm beds Rs100, rooms Rs500), and Janki Chatti (dorm beds

Snake-Eating Sadhus of Gangotri

Hashish and tobacco, smoked through a *chillum*, are a big part of the daily intake of most *sadhus*, but really dread-inspiring holy men try something else: a krait (an extremely poisonous snake) is rolled up between two unbaked *rotis* with its tail sticking out. This deadly sandwich is then shoved into the fire. When the *rotis* are fully baked, the *sadhu* removes the preparation from the fire and pulls off the snake's tail, bringing the skin and bones with it. Then, preparing himself, he puts a jug of water by his side. He takes two to three bites of the snake and immediately goes into a coma. Every eight to ten hours the *sadhu* wakes up to drink some water and take another bite, sending himself back into a poisoned stupor. The whole process lasts three to four days. **Warning: requires 30 years of practice—don't try this at home, or anywhere else!**

Rs100, rooms Rs250-450). During the pilgrimage season, many of these accommodations are fully booked for package tours operated by GMVN, so it may be a better idea to stay overnight at Barkot, 40km south, and take an early morning bus or taxi to Hanuman Chatti. Janki Chatti and Barkot have several private hotels as well.

GANGOTRI गंगोत्री

After Bhatwari, the road from Uttarkashi narrows, and the surrounding mountains become more severe, until the shimmering slopes of Mt. Sudarshan (6500m) are finally visible, towering above the small town of Gangotri. At 3140m altitude and 98km northeast of Uttarkashi (here known as the Bhagirathi), and a center for *sadhus* from all over India. The present **temple** at Gangotri was built by the Gorkha commander Amar Singh Thapa in the early 19th century as a replacement for an older structure. Next to the temple is **Bhagiratha Shila,** where King Bhagiratha is said to have prayed for the river to flow (see **Flashing Eyes, Floating Hair, Holy Dreds,** p. 163). Steps here lead down to the *ghat* where pilgrims bathe. A small bridge from the bus stand arches over to Gaurikund, where the Bhagirathi gushes out of the rock into a beautiful pool. Gaumukh (Cow's Mouth), a 17km trek from Gangotri, is the spot where the Bhagirathi emerges from the Gangotri glacier. There are excellent views of the Bhagirathi peaks along the way.

Recent improvements in transportation mean that nearly 2000 pilgrims visit Gangotri every day between April and November, leaving their mark in the form of strewn rubbish and rapidly decreasing forests. To get to Gangotri, take a bus or a shared taxi from **Uttarkashi** (see p. 170). Buildings sit on both sides of the **Bhagirathi River.** The main bridge is just next to Dev Ghat, where the Bhagirathi and the **Kedar Ganga** meet. Two parallel paths run on either side of the Bhagirathi, along which all the *dhabas* and hotels are located. In most accommodations, rooms are unpainted, the plaster is crumbling, and beds are dirty—bring a sleeping bag. Accommodations across the river from the temple are quieter and more secluded. **Manisha Cottage,** near the bus stand, provides small two-bedded rooms (with common bath Rs200, deluxe Rs450). **GMVN Guest House** (tourist lodge), next to Gaurikund and away from the crowded bus stand, is spacious and clean, with a garden and a tasty restaurant. (Dorm beds Rs100, rooms Rs250-550 all year.) Most ashrams in Gangotri do not accept foreign guests. Practical affairs such as currency exchange should be taken care of before coming to Gangotri.

KEDARNATH केदारनाथ

As one of the 12 *jyotirlingas* of Shiva in India, Kedarnath is considered to be one of Shiva's abodes. According to one account, the Kedarnath temple was constructed thousands of years ago when the Pandavas, the heroic brothers of the *Mahabharata*, came here to seek and pray to Shiva. Shiva, who viewed the Pandavas as sinners for having killed their own kin in battle, disguised himself as a bull. When the Pandavas uncovered the ruse, Shiva turned to stone and tried to escape into the ground. But as his front half vanished, one of the Pandavas, Bhima, managed to catch Shiva's rocky rear end. Pleased with the Pandavas' diligence, Shiva appeared in his true form and forgave them. The back half of that stone form is now worshiped at Kedarnath. Shiva's front half is said to have disappeared into the ground, broken off, and reemerged in Nepal, where it is venerated at the Pashupatinath temple (see p. 740). Other parts of Shiva turned up at Tungnath (arm), Rudradnath (face), Madhyama-heshwar (navel), and Kalpleshwar (locks), where together with Kedarnath, they form the **Panch Kedar** (Five Fields) pilgrimage circuit. Many beautiful treks begin at Kedarnath. The town remains open from May until late October. Buses only take pilgrims as far as Gaurikund, 216km from Rishikesh. From there, it's a steep 14km, four-to six-hour trek. It's best to start early in the morning or late in the afternoon to avoid the midday sun.

Many hotel prices are completely discretionary so bargain hard, especially if you turn up after 7pm. Rates are generally Rs100 for a single and Rs200 for a double in season. **GMVN** has two guest houses in Kedarnath, one immediately on your left as you approach the town (tel. (01374) 6210), and a second across the river and below the hillside (tel. (01374) 6228). Many **ashrams** will not accept foreigners, but the **Bharat Seva Ashram** and the **Temple Committee** cave in on occasion.

BADRINATH बद्रीनाथ

The temple town of Badrinath (3133m) is probably the most famous of Garhwal's Hindu pilgrimage sites, attracting the faithful from all across India during its summer season (May-Nov.). Badrinath is the northern *dham* established by the southern saint Shankara in the 9th century. Along with Puri in Orissa, Rameswaram in Tamil Nadu, and Dwarka in Gujarat, it forms the northernmost compass-point in India's sacred geography. Badrinath is located on the Alaknanda River 297km from Rishikesh, not far from the overpowering Nilkanth peak and the Tibetan border. Because it is accessible by road, it attracts growing numbers of pilgrims and secular tourists every year, foregoing the austerity of walking pilgrimage once required in favor of a harrowing bus ride. Badrinath can be reached from Rishikesh via Srinagar, Rudraprayag, and Joshimath. Buses also frequently come here directly from Kedarnath.

The Badrinath **temple** is colorful, with a long main entrance gate (the Singh Dwara) through which worshipers must pass for *darshan* of the meter-high Badrivishal image inside. The temple's architecture is an unusual mixture of Buddhist and Hindu styles, and there is a large debate over whether it was in ancient times a Buddhist temple. Before visiting the temple, worshipers must bathe in the **Tapt Kund** hot spring (45°C), often in preparation for a dip into the icy waters of the Alaknanda.

Accommodations available from numerous *dharamshalas*, at the **Garhwal Hotel**, or at the hotel run by the **GVMN** are very basic. There are numerous *dhabas* around the temple site, but no fancier forms of food. (**Telephone Code:** 01381.)

AULI औली

Sometime in the 1970s, the Indian government realized that the mountains south of Joshimath (253km from Rishikesh) could better be used as a ski resort than a para-military training ground. Chairlifts have replaced airlifts, opening up 550 vertical meters of slopes to skiers. The scenery, particularly eastward toward Nanda Devi (7800m), is spectacular, which keeps Auli open in the summer for sight-seeing rides up the 3km **cable car** from Joshimath. There is a **GMVN lodge** at Auli (Apr.-Nov.: dorm beds Rs60, deluxe rooms Rs750-900; Nov.-Apr.: 100/800-900).

VALLEY OF FLOWERS फूलों की घाटी

The floral splendor of a hidden alpine valley high in the Garhwal Himalayas has been attracting botanists, pilgrims, and nature lovers ever since Frank Smith explored the valley in 1937 and publicized his find to the world as the "Valley of Flowers." Ten kilometers long and 2km wide and enclosed by snow-capped peaks, the valley is bisected by the Pushpawati River. Snow covers the valley floor November to April, rendering the area inaccessible to visitors. In late April, the snow begins to melt, and the onset of spring accelerates in June with the first bloomings. By late July, the valley is aglow in the shades of *androsace*, marsh orchids, and geraniums. In August, the pinks have faded and the yellow flowers of *pedicularis*, *grandiflora*, and *potentillas* predominate. There are over 500 species in the valley; many of them, such as the Himalayan blue poppy, are rare and of great interest to ecologists. However, when the valley was first explored in the late 1930s, the plant species count was 5000. The serious ecological decline of the area has prompted the government to declare it a National Park–no camping and cooking is allowed within the valley. Instead, visitors must trek in on foot for the day and sleep at **Ghanghria**, 4km away, in either a government tourist rest house, or in one of the private lodges (the Sikh Gurudwara has 1000 beds available). From Rishikesh, take a bus to Joshimath (6am, 10hr., Rs100). Govindghat is 19km further by road, and from there, one must trek or ride on the backside of a mule to Ghanghria (13km). To reserve a bed in the dormitory or a room at the tourist rest house, contact the **GMVN Yatra Pilgrimage Tours and Accommodations Office** in Kailash Gate, Rishikesh (tel. (0135) 431783).

■ Corbett National Park कोरबट

Founded in 1936, Corbett was India's first National park, honoring one Jim Corbett (1875-1955), a British gentleman who was renowned as a hunter of tigers and other large felines. Corbett quit killing tigers for sport in the 1920s, but the hunter-conservationist was still called upon to shoot tigers and leopards when they threatened human lives. He became famous for his photographs of tigers and for the books he wrote, including *The Man-Eaters of Kumaon*.

In 1973, the Indian government, with support from the World Wildlife Fund, launched "Project Tiger" to save the country's dwindling tiger population and its supporting ecosystems. Corbett Tiger Reserve (1319 sq. km), formed by the national park and the adjoining Sonandi Wildlife Sanctuary and Reserve Forest, was the first target area of this ambitious preservation project. Currently, there are 138 tigers in the reserve. Sightings of the Bengal beasts can come several times a day, but, even if you don't catch a glimpse of the largest cat on earth, Corbett's other wildlife will not disappoint.

Corbett's other treasures include the endangered gharial crocodile, herds of wild elephants, monkeys, leopards, deer, and over 500 species of birds. The Park's landscape, particularly around Dhikala, is as magnificent as its wildlife. Mountains of *sal* forests surround the Ramganga River and the vast, peaceful swath of plain and jungle.

> **WARNING:** However you decide to enjoy Corbett, do adhere to the park's rules and regulations about treating nature right. Don't throw burning cigarettes around, don't feed the animals, and don't be too noisy. One of the best things about the park is its serenity. Cars aren't even allowed to honk. For your own safety (attacks by tigers are not unheard of), never walk outside the camp perimeter, and be careful at night. Driving after dark is forbidden.

ORIENTATION AND PRACTICAL INFORMATION Corbett has five zones accessible to tourists. These zones are exclusive, which means that one must exit the park (and pay another hefty fee) in order to enter another zone. **Dhikala** is the most popular among tourists, offering a range of accommodations, two restaurants, films and a library. The other four zones—Bijrani, Jhirna, Lohachavr, and Halduparao—offer far more solitude than the Dhikala complex. More specifically, **Lohachavr** is the best place to go bird-watching, and **Bijrani** contains the park's most diverse vegetation. **Jhirna** is an exceptionally beautiful area of the park, and those looking for an especially rugged experience should head to **Halduparao.** Jhirna is accessible to visitors year-round. The rest of the park closes June 15-Nov. 15, during the monsoon. The wildlife viewing is better in the summer (Mar.-June) than in the winter (Nov.-Mar.), although anytime is great for soaking up the park's overall beauty.

From Delhi, **Ramnagar** (through which all park visitors must pass) is reachable by bus (12 per day, 6am-9pm, 7hr., Rs82) and train (11pm, 5½hr., Rs95). The train station is 1.5km south of the bus stand. Ramnagar offers basic services. For last-second **currency exchange,** the **State Bank of India** (tel. (05945) 85337) has a branch a few blocks down and a few blocks left of the bus depot. They change U.S. and U.K. traveler's checks (open M-F 10am-2pm, Sa 10am-noon).

Visitors must stop at **Park Office** (tel. 05975 or 85489), across from the Ramnagar bus stand, to secure a permit (open daily 8am-1pm and 3-5pm). Overnight visitors may visit any of the park's zones, but daytrippers may only visit Dhikala and Bijrani on guided tours (for Dhikala, Rs1200; afternoon tour of Bijrani, Rs600; all prices are for foreigners—Indians pay one-third of these rates). The office books all lodgings for inside the park.

After securing permits (including accommodations) visitors must arrange their own transportation to their site. Now, visitors must shell out Rs500 (plus Rs130 jeep entry fee) for a one-way **jeep** to Dhikala. It is, however, fairly easy to join up with other visitors and split the cost of the ride. To do so, arrive at the office early (around 8am). Jeeps waiting to take visitors to Corbett are parked right outside the office. Those headed to Dhikala can also take one of the **buses** from Ramnagar headed for Ranikhet and ask to be dropped off at Dhangarhi Gate. Then strike a deal with a passing vehicle turning in for Dhikala. Each zone has its own gated park entrance.

Dhangarhi Gate, 16km north of Ramnagar, is the entrance to Dhikala (open 6am-6pm; no one may enter after dark). Here, you'll pay the fees you didn't pay at Ramnagar (first 3 days, foreigners Rs350, Indians Rs30; each additional day, foreigners Rs175, Indians Rs20; car or jeep fee Rs100). There is a small **museum** at the gate, which consists of one room filled with bizarre and morbid exhibits (admission Rs10 for foreigners). Beyond the scale model of the park, there are stuffed specimens of several mammals (with signs documenting how they died), as well as preserved artwork and animal embryos.

Before **leaving** Dhikala, all visitors must obtain a free **clearance certificate,** which should be turned in at Dhangarhi upon leaving. If your next stop is Ranikhet, get off the bus at Dhangarhi and wait by the side of the road for buses headed north (last bus at 2pm, 4hr., Rs33).

ACCOMMODATIONS AND FOOD All lodgings within the park are reserved through the park office in Ramnagar. All private resorts (despite claims to the contrary) lie beyond the park boundaries. At Dhikala, log hut dorms, the tourist hutments, and cabins are available. The **log hut,** one step from the great outdoors, provides austere bunks, stacked three-high, 12 to a room, and lockers (bring your own lock). The squat toilets and showers are in a separate building. **Tourist hutments** (3 beds) and **cabins** (2 or 3 beds) include a bathroom. (Check-out 11am. Log hut bunk Rs100, bedding Rs25; tourist hutment Rs500; cabin Rs900.) Be warned that visitors wishing to extend their stay are often told to wait until the evening to see whether space is available, making it possible to be stuck in Dhikala without accommodation, in which case it will be necessary to hire a jeep out (if one is available) before the night curfew. In short, plan ahead. You'll also need to plan ahead if you want to stay in the hutments or cabins. Call ahead to reserve a space. There are no reservations for the log hut, so if there is no space in the hut the first night, you are almost certainly guaranteed to get a bed the next night. **Tourist rest houses** in other zones are more expensive, ranging from Rs300 to Rs500, depending on location.

Food is only available at Dhikala, which has 2 restaurants—both serving Indian, Chinese, and Continental food for breakfast, lunch, and dinner. The government-run **KMVN Restaurant** (open 7:30-10am, 1-3pm, and 7:30-9:30pm) is more expensive, but has indoor seating (vegetable *korma* Rs36). At the other end of the camp, the privately owned **canteen** serves similar fare for less money. It's next to a pleasant pagoda where you can survey the plain while enjoying your vegetable curry. (Open daily 5am-2pm and 4-10pm.) Visitors to other locations in the park must bring their own food, though staff is on hand to help prepare it in the rest house kitchens. Note

Man Bites Cat

Your elephant conductor from Dhikala may be none other than Subradar Ali, the man one man-eater of Kumaon will remember as the one who bit back. While gathering grass for his elephant Gunti one fine Valentine's Day, 1984, Subradar was attacked from behind by a tiger named Sheroo, who leapt nearly six meters for his target, Subradar's head. As he was being dragged away by the neck, Subradar, taking a lesson from his striped assailant, began biting back. Forcing open the jaws of the beast, he yanked on Sheroo's tongue. This put an end to the dragging, and Sheroo pinned him squarely. Another guide appeared on the scene, distracting the tiger long enough for Subradar to roll down a nearby stream bank. With bleeding gashes on his head and arm, Subradar called his elephant to come and kneel so he could crawl on top. Gunti took him the 3km to Dhikala, and not wanting to disturb his family away in Ramnagar, Subradar cleaned and changed his clothes himself. Both Rajiv and Indira Gandhi visited him in the hospital. Rajiv asked if he wanted fame and fortune—the event has since been the subject of several movies—but Subradar preferred to return to the elephants and tigers of Corbett. In fact, he views the whole experience as having bolstered his confidence, and he admits with a smile he is even more excited to find the tigers than the tourists he guides. His aggressive Valentine's date, Sheroo, has not been seen for years.

that, in observance of a new policy for all national parks, no alcohol is allowed, and only vegetarian food is sold inside the park. A small **kiosk** at Dhangarhi Gate provides bottled water (Rs15) and munchies. These are more expensive inside the park, so you may want to stock up. Though many travelers report drinking the water from the faucets near the station office without problems, this water is not filtered.

If lodgings are not immediately available inside the park, the **Tourist Rest House** (tel. (05945) 85225), next door to the park office in Ramnagar, is more than adequate, with well-kept dormitory rooms and super-deluxe suites, hot water showers, squat toilets, and ceiling fans that whir mightily as long as the power's on. (Check-out noon. Dorm beds Rs60. Doubles Rs315. Deluxe with air cooling Rs420. Extra bed Rs60-80. Extra person Rs30-40.) For Indian, Chinese, and Continental food, head to the **Govind Restaurant**, one block past the bus station from the guest house. The owner is very friendly and the food is delicious. Fruit *lassis* (Rs18) are a treat, as are their famous banana pancakes (Rs25). Open daily 8am-10pm.

SIGHTS There are ways to get down and dirty in Corbett without breaking the rules. By far the best way is to take an **elephant ride.** For Rs100, visitors get a two-hour tour across the prairie and through the jungle, all from a pachyderm's perspective. This is the best way to try to see a tiger, or to come close to wild elephants and other animals. Sign up for a ride at the station office; during the high season, expect to wait up to a few days. However, it is often possible to get a ride if you show up early. Tours depart at sunrise and sunset, approximately 5am and 5pm in the summer and 7am and 3pm in the winter. Both tours have their benefits (cooler weather or more sleep, respectively), and sightings are equally likely at either time. From atop your elephant, marvel at what seems to delight tourists most: yes, those are 3m cannabis plants, acres and acres of them.

You can also hire a **jeep**—up to eight may ride with one or two guides around the Dhikala Station area. The best times for jeep tours are 5am-11am and 4-7pm (Rs450). You cover more ground than on the elephants and can get all the way out to the reservoir where the crocodiles play. While the crocs don't normally encroach on the compound, it's best to adhere to the sign which warns, "NO SWIMMING: Survivors Will Be Prosecuted."

The only excursion **on foot** permitted outside the camp (and then only before sunset) is to the nearby **Gularghati Watchtower,** which offers a good view of the landscape. You can be brought by jeep to one of the other two watchtowers, or *machans,* camouflaged and situated over drinking holes, for a day of observation.

There are free guided **bird tours** (Sa-Su 6-8am and 7-9am; inquire at the office). Every night, free **films** about nature and the park are shown behind the restaurant at around 8pm. Check the office for schedules. To pack your brain with info about what you've encountered, there's a small **library** adjacent to the office. *(Open daily summer 9am-12:30pm and 5:30-8pm, winter 9am-noon and 5:30-7:30pm.)* Maps (Rs10) and other information on the park are available at the Ramnagar office, the library at Dhikala, and the office at Dhangarhi Gate. For those on a tighter budget, it is still possible to experience some of the natural beauty and wildlife from outside the park. One such place is **Sitabani,** which has excellent bird-watching opportunities and a nice rest house—enquire at the Ramnagar office for details.

■ Nainital नेनीताल

When the body of Shiva's consort Sati was chopped into various pieces (see **Divine Dismemberment,** p. 418), one of her eyes, it is said, fell into the hills, and so the stunning emerald lake of Nainital was formed. British colonialists, never ones to pass up a good fallen eyeball, were the first to enjoy and exploit the lake area's beauty. A Mr. P. Barron of Shahjahanpur was the first Brit to come here. He hauled up a yacht and built a "pilgrim cottage," setting in gear what would eventually become a popular British hill station and the summer capital of the United Provinces (which became Uttar Pradesh after Independence). Modern Nainital still serves its "original" purpose as an escape for Indian and foreign tourists fleeing the searing summer sun of the plains. Even with an annual high-season (May-June and Oct.) that pushes the town's capacity way beyond its limits, the lake still radiates an unblinking aura of divine resilience into the cool mountain air. July and August are good months to visit—it's sometimes rainy, but the weather is still warm, and the town is downright peaceful. In the autumn, the view of the Himalayas from the mountains surrounding the lake is clear. As a flashy tourist town in a natural, if carefully controlled, setting, Nainital in high season is an unparalleled destination for those wishing to trade in the chaos of their daily lives for the chaos of a fantasy land.

ORIENTATION

The town of Nainital is split into two major parts—**Tallital** and **Mallital**—which are connected by the **Mall,** a road running along the east side of the lake. Buses arrive at Tallital, which hugs the southern tip of the lake. From there, it's a 20-minute walk along either the Mall or the road on the west side of the lake to Mallital. Most hotels are found along the Mall, while most services are at either end. The **Flats,** a common area used for soccer and field hockey, sprawls between Mallital and the water.

PRACTICAL INFORMATION

Trains: The nearest station is in **Kathgodam.** Trains leave Delhi for Kathgodam at 11pm; trains leave Kathgodam for Delhi at 2:40pm.

Buses: Buses arrive at and depart from the lake front in **Tallital. Haldwani** is the nearest major hub, and nearly every bus goes there first. To: **Almora** (7am, 3hr., Rs31); **Bareilly** (7am, 1:30, and 5:30pm, 4½hr., Rs47); **Bhowali** (every ½hr., 6am-6:30pm, Rs5); **Dehra Dun** (regular 5:30 and 7am, deluxe 8pm, 10hr., Rs131/152); **Delhi** (7 per day, 6am-7:30pm, 9 hr., Rs105); **Kathgodam and Haldwani** (every 15min., 5am-6:30pm, 2hr., Rs16/18); **Ramnagar** (2:30pm, 5hr., Rs35); **Ranikhet** (12:30pm, 3hr., Rs29). Tickets on buses to Dehra Dun and Delhi are often sold to the travel agents that line the Mall. Book ahead, although it's sometimes possible to wait for no-shows and grab a seat at the last second.

Local Transportation: Cycle-rickshaws charge Rs4 to drive the length of the Mall. Traffic is closed to motor vehicles and cycle rickshaws in the early evening.

Tourist Office: (tel. 35337), about two-thirds of the way to Mallital along the Mall. Provides information about the town and region and can help with transport to nearby sights. Open M-Sa 10am-5pm; May-June and Sept.-Oct. Su 10am-5pm.

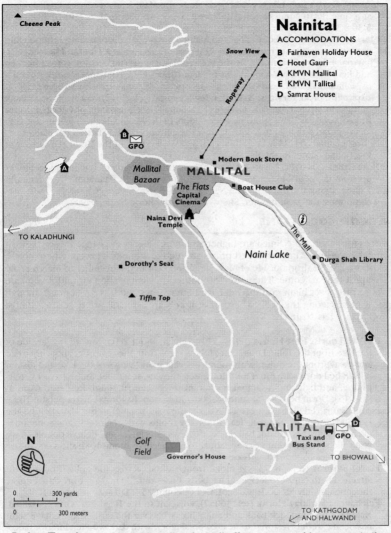

Nainital
ACCOMMODATIONS
B Fairhaven Holiday House
C Hotel Gauri
A KMVN Mallital
E KMVN Tallital
D Samrat House

Cheena Peak

Snow View

Ropeway

GPO

Mallital Bazaar

MALLITAL

Modern Book Store

The Flats

Boat House Club

Capital Cinema

Naina Devi Temple

TO KALADHUNGI

Naini Lake

Dorothy's Seat

The Mall

Durga Shah Library

Tiffin Top

N

Golf Field

Governor's House

TALLITAL

Taxi and Bus Stand

GPO

TO BHOWALI

0   300 yards
0   300 meters

TO KATHGODAM AND HALWANDI

NORTH INDIA

Budget Travel: Several tour agents line the Mall offering comparable tours at similar prices. The tourist office also runs trips. **Shivam Tour and Travel** (tel. 35269), next to Hotel Elphinstone, runs trips to Bhimtal (22km) and Hanumangarhi (3km) and often offers advanced bookings for night buses to Haridwar and Delhi. Avoid daytrips to Corbett as they barely allow any time off the bus. Open daily 7am-9pm.

Currency Exchange: State Bank of India (tel. 35645) has a branch in Mallital just beyond the Flats. Open M-F 10am-2pm, Sat. 10am-noon. An "evening branch" on the Mall near Tallital is open M-F noon-4pm, Sat noon-2pm. Cashes AmEx traveler's checks in US$ and UK£. Many shops take MC and Visa.

Bookstore: Modern Bookstore, on the Mall near the Flats, has textbooks and a modest fiction and self-help section. Open M-Sa 10:30am-9pm, Su 11am-4pm. **Counsel Bookstore**, in Mallital across from Green Restaurant, has a larger fiction section and a substantial science section. Open M-Sa 9:30am-8pm.

Library: Durga Suh Library, lakefront along the Mall, lends readers 1 English book at a time. Rs10 admission, Rs30 deposit. Open Apr.-Sept. M-Sa 7:30-10:30am and 5:30-8:30pm, Oct.-Mar. M-Sa 8:30-10:30am and 4-7pm.

Market: The area west of the Flats in Mallital hosts a largeish market with food and various wares. Scrunched into the west part of this area is a **Tibetan Market.**

Pharmacy: Indra Pharmacy, by the bus stand in Tallital (tel. 35139), is well stocked and keeps long hours. Open M-Sa 6:50am-10pm, Su 6:50am-5pm. Another branch in Mallital, in Bara Bazaar (tel. 35629), is open M-Sa 9am-10pm, Su 3-10pm.

Hospital/Medical Services: B. D. Pandey Hospital (tel 35012) is near the State Bank of India in Mallital. Dr. D.P. Gangola (tel. 35039) is a consulting physician at **Indra Pharmacy** (daily 9am-2pm); he keeps hours in the Mallital branch, 5-9pm. Dr. G.P. Shah operates a clinic (tel. 37001) near the entrance to the Flats on the Mall.

Police: Mallital (tel. 35424), Tallital (tel. 35525), in front of the Hotel Mansarovar at the Tallital end of the Mall.

Post Office: The GPO has its main branch on the north side of Mallital, a few blocks up from the Mall's extension. *Poste Restante* open M-Sa 9am-5pm. The branch in Tallital, facing the bus stop, only sells stamps. **Postal Code:** 263002.

Telephones: Call your mother. She worries. **Telephone Code:** 05942.

ACCOMMODATIONS

Prices for lodging in Nainital are higher and more subject to change by season than anywhere else in Kumaon. Listed prices are high-season rates, except where noted; expect a 25-75% drop outside of May, June, and October. November to March is the cheapest time to come. There are 150 hotels in Nainital; shop around if you can. Those places set higher on the hill have better views and less street noise, though most places along the Mall (where most hotels are) are still pretty sedate. Almost every place has 10am check-out.

KMVN Tourist Rest House (tel. 35570), Tallital, about 200m toward the far side of the lake from the Tallital bus stand; follow signs from the ramp. Set above the road and away from the noise, with rooms offering grand views of the lake and distant hills. 8-bed dorms are often full. Hot water, shower, seat toilet. Suites have TV, telephone, and balcony. Attached restaurant open 7am-10:30pm. In-season (Apr. 1-June 15): Dorm beds Rs75; suites Rs800. Off-season: Rs40/600. Extra person 10%.

Hotel Gauri (tel. 36617), near Tallital, on the road parallel to the Mall, behind the Hotel Mansarovar. Dim halls lead to cheery rooms with chairs, TV, and sometimes even hot showers. Quaint balcony with views. All singles and deluxe doubles have seat toilets; regular doubles have squat toilets. Deluxe rooms have showers. In-season: doubles Rs200-700. Off-season: Rs100-350.

Hotel Samrat (tel. 36273), ½ block from Tallital, across the gully. Rooms with attached bath (squat toilet) and nice beds. Buses outside make for pre-dawn noise, though. May-July Rs500-1000; Sept.-Oct discount 25%. Off-season: discount 50%.

Fairhavens Holiday Home (tel. 36057), adjacent to the Head Post Office, Mallital. Nainital's place to kick back and enjoy life, whatever the cost. This heritage sight has been carefully restored to near-colonial glory, with dark wooden interior balconies and a sitting room that boasts an original London piano. Antique fixtures and clientele, but comfortingly up-to-date attached baths. In-season: doubles Rs1250.

KMVN Mount View Tourist Rest House, Mallital (tel. 35400). The typically clean government-run rest house offers the rare cheap sleep in this hyper-expensive hill station. However, unlike the KMVN Rest House in Tallital, the Mallital rest house has no views of the lake and no charming garden. Restaurant open 7:30am-9pm. In-season: dorm beds Rs75, doubles Rs 550. Off-season: Rs60/415.

FOOD

Whereas most of Nainital's budget hotels are at the Tallital end of the Mall, the Mallital end is grounds for gathering grub. Roasted *masala* corn and similar delectables can be bought along the Mall, and the **market** west of the Flats has several vendors selling cheap, tasty food of questionable quality—eat at your own risk. In Tallital, the main bazaar is lined with little restaurants like **Neera** (6am-9pm) selling *chola bhatura* for Rs8. Many of the hotel restaurants serve decent fare.

Sonam Tibetan Restaurant, next to the Modern Bookstore in Mallital. Meager choices but big servings of Tibetan food. Veg. noodles in broth (Rs25) make for sumptuous sippage—slurp under the Dalai Lama's visage. Open daily 9am-10pm.

Ahar Vihar Restaurant (tel. 35756), upstairs from the well-lit variety stores on the Mall near Mallital. It's a popular low-end restaurant that feels like Mom's kitchen. Gregarious owner assures "every bite a delight." Green peas *masala* Rs18, Rajasthani *thalis* Rs35. Open daily 9:30am-10pm.

Nanak's Restaurant (tel. 35336), between the library and Mallital on the Mall. A would-be Western restaurant serving fast-food veg. burgers (Rs25), "Jughead's trip in life" (a.k.a pizza), milkshakes, and mango sundaes (Rs60) in a dark room aglow with neon lights. Popular with Indian tourists' children. Open daily 9am-9pm.

Green Restaurant (tel. 36522), Bara Bazaar in the heart of Mallital. The maroon interior is lamp-lit and swank. The colorful streamers overhead make up for the uncomfortable chairs and short tables. The Green has *misri roti* (Rs8) and a wide range of Chinese dishes. Open daily 7:30am-11pm.

SIGHTS AND ENTERTAINMENT

The thousands of Indian tourists who migrate annually to Nainital do so primarily to escape the heat of Delhi and the plains, but locals and Mother Nature have made sure they won't be bored once they're here. The first joy is the **lake** itself. To really get out in the middle of Sati's emerald eyeball, **boat rental** is a must. *(Paddleboats Rs30 per hr. for a 2-seater, Rs60 for a 4-seater. Boatman-guided rides, Rs60 for full round of the lake, Rs30 for one trip across.)* You can rent **yachts** from the Nainital Boat Club (Rs60 per hr.), though they might insist you become a member. There are yacht regattas throughout the year, including the **Kingfisher Regatta,** in the third week of June. While cruising around, buy drinks from one of the kids who set up shop under the brush along the water, where only the boat-bound can find them.

In 1880, a disastrous landslide killed 151 people and wiped out the city's largest hotel, but the flattened part of the town was simply turned into the city's best public space. Today the **Flats** are a haunt for snake charmers and musicians and home to tournaments for the field hockey (May-June) and soccer (July-Sept.) clubs. In October, Autumn Festival sponsors sports competitions by day and cultural programs by night. Most underappreciated is the placid, cool walk along the side opposite the Mall, where there are two small temples and a few ledges near the water.

Nainital is replete with nearby peaks that offer views of the city and (if the clouds cooperate) Himalayan peaks as far away as the Tibetan border. The best way to see these (according to the touts) is to rent a horse from one of Mallital's stables and clip-clop to the top. Well, maybe. The ride, often up steep, loose stone trails, can be pretty harrowing. *(Round-trip Rs100, with the guide jogging alongside your steed. Expect to pay more if you want to stop and see the view for more than an hour.)*

The easiest way to get to the top of **Snow View** is to forsake horse and foot altogether and take the **ropeway,** a cable car that leaves from a clearly marked building a steep 30m up from the Mall in Mallital. The low-effort nature of this excursion makes it incredibly popular during high season, so opening time (8am) is the best bet for ensuring tickets and clear views. Last cable car leaves Mallital at 7pm, but last car returns from Snow View at 6pm *(Round-trip Rs35, with an hour stop at the top. (One way Rs20; it's a 2.5km walk down. Binoculars, Rs5. KMVN has a cottage at the top: doubles Rs500 in season.)*

Other viewpoints around Nainital include **Cheena Peak** (2611m), also sometimes called China or Naina Peak, just to keep things interesting. The highest thing around, it's 6km away, one hour by horse or three hours by foot. At the top is a snack shop and a lot of nooks to sit and contemplate the city below or (weather permitting) the peaks of Garhwal, including 7817m Nanda Devi. Watch out for leeches in the gravel, though. You can start in Mallital or have a taxi take you to Tonneleay on Kilbury Rd. to shorten the trip. **Land's End,** on the back side of Tiffin Peak (immediately west of the lake), offers views of the sprawling valley to the west. Farther up Tiffin Peak is **Dorothy's Seat,** a flat, green area near the top, named after a woman who often sat here after her husband died in a crash.

Wandering up the road heading west of Tallital leads to the remarkably British-looking **Governor's House,** then to **Hanumangarh** (a small temple), about 3km away, and the **Observatory** (about 3.5km from Tallital). The observatory can be visited independently; call in advance (tel. 35136).

For evening entertainment, a **stroll along the Mall** becomes less hectic as darkness enshrouds the piles of chintz in the stores. If it's cool, it's a good time to snag a shawl; quality specimens are produced here and in Almora. **Capital Cinema,** near the Flats, runs Hindi movies regularly.

■ Near Nainital

Those in search of lakeside solitude will find that Nainital is just the tip of the regional iceberg where peaceful ponds are concerned. **Bhowali,** 11km to the east of Nainital (buses leave every 30min. from the Tallital bus station) is conveniently close to the lakes, offers much cleaner accommodations, and also serves as a transportation hub for other towns in the region. Buses leave regularly for all Kumaon destinations and larger hubs outside the region. The city itself, however, has nothing to offer besides street muck and bus exhaust. If you find yourself stuck in town, or wish to take an attempt at cheaper accommodations, the KMVN tourist bungalow (tel. (05942) 49062), 1km beyond the city center, has dorm beds at Rs80 and doubles for Rs250.

Of the 3 lakes beyond Nainital, **Sat-Tal** is the least crowded and most lovely. The lake is surrounded by forests of pine and oak trees. It is possible to rent a boat (Rs100 per hr.) on the lake and buy snacks on the lakefront. Otherwise, however, the area surrounding the lake remains undeveloped. The only rest house at Sat-tal is run by KMVN (tel. 47047). Unfortunately, visitors must fork over Rs400-1000 a night in May and June (35% less off season). From Sat-Tal, **Bhimtal** is a 7km hike (10km by road). A much subtler version of Nainital, Bhimtal's large lake and be-shrubbed hills cradle a rather staid town, offering (some) peace without (much) isolation. The **KMVN tourist bungalow** (tel. 47005), on the opposite side of the lake of Bhimtal, is about as quiet and cheap as Bhimtal lakeside hotels come (dorm beds Rs60; tidy doubles with carpets and wood cabinets Rs200). Like treeless Bhimtal, **Naukuchiyatal** offers plenty of solitude but not much shade. The **KMVN tourist bungalow** at Naukuchiyatal (tel. 47138) has a comfortable lounge and a beautiful garden in front (in-season: dorm beds Rs60; doubles Rs400). Dorm beds at the bungalow are Rs60 and doubles start at Rs400 in the on-season. The best time to visit the lakes is in the autumn and winter, when the weather has cooled off, the Indian tourists have gone home, and the rates have come down. No snow covers the ground of the other lakes in January and February.

■ Ranikhet रानीखेत

It's said an ancient queen once settled in the hills of Kumaon. The spot where she stayed, Ranikhet ("Queen's Field"), is hardly the most regal of Indian locales, but a comparatively non-religious, pastoral setting distinguishes Ranikhet from Kumaon's other hill stations. At 2000m, it is the most alpine of Kumaon's centers, and from the town, it's only a short walk up to forests of pine and deodar trees inhabited by *kakar* (barking deer). Those prone to vertigo will undoubtedly note the land's steepness, although the nearby, snowcapped Nanda Devi (7817m) is even steeper. Other than the mountain, the largest presence here is the military, which dates back to British times: the Kumaon Regiment is based in Ranikhet. The army is never far from sight, though it is concentrated in stations above the town. With less traffic noise than the other hill stations, fewer travelers, and markedly less to do, Ranikhet is a prime spot for hikes and relaxation. For true isolation, one should forsake Kumaon's major hill stations altogether in favor of quieter hamlets like Kausani, Sitlakhet, and Binsar. As a local tourist brochure points out, however, "how long Ranikhet can maintain its virginity is a million dollar question." Maybe that's why you now have to pay a Rs2 toll to enter town.

ORIENTATION

Sadar Bazaar, the main road that anchors Ranikhet's meandering geography is in the town center; most services and numerous hotels and restaurants are found here. **Buses** arrive at either end of the bazaar; **UP Roadways** stop at the downhill end, and now buses arrive and depart on the west end. The **mall** area is located above the bazaar and features some of the more expensive hotels. To get to the mall, follow the road next to the **Alka Hotel** (up the mountains and away from the relative chaos). Generally, keep to your left and eventually you will find yourself on the mall road. There is a mural-sized map of Ranikhet across from the **Rajdeep Hotel** that also gives listings to area attractions. Monday is Ranikhet's **business holiday;** most shops are closed then.

PRACTICAL INFORMATION

Trains: The closest stations are in Kathgodam (83km) and Ramnagar (105km).
Buses: U.P. Roadways (tel. 2645) buses run to: **Almora** (5:30am, 2½ hr., Rs27); **Dehra Dun** (8:30am and 3pm, 12hr., Rs150); **Delhi** (4 per day, 3-5pm, 12hr., Rs131); **Haldwani/Kathgodam** (every ½hr., 5:30am-5pm, 4hr., Rs39); **Kausani** (6am, 12:30, and 2pm, 3hr., Rs30); **Nainital** (8am, 3½ hr., Rs27); **Ramnagar** (8:30am and 3pm, 5hr., Rs45). **KMOU** (tel. 2609) has a friendly staff and comfortable buses to: **Almora** (5 buses, 6:30am-2:30pm, 2½ hr., Rs23); **Haldwani/Kathgodam** (7 buses, 7am-2:30pm, 4hr., Rs34); **Kausani** (4 buses, 6am-1:30pm, 3hr., Rs25); **Nainital** (11:30am, 3hr., Rs24); **Ramnagar** (5 buses, 7am-3pm, 4hr., Rs37).
Tourist Office: (tel. 2227). At the east end of the bazaar, just up from the U.P. Roadways bus stand. The man in charge is very helpful and can provide detailed information about Ranikhet and the Larger Kumaon Area. Open M-Sa 10am-5pm.
Currency Exchange: The **State Bank of India** (tel. 2262) is on the road above and parallel to the bazaar. They exchange U.S. and British currencies—only up to $100 or £50 per day—and AmEx and Thomas Cook traveler's checks. Open M-F 10am-2pm, Sa 10am-noon.
Pharmacy: Mayank Medical Hall at the U.P. Roadways end of town (open Tu-Su 8am-8pm, and alternate Mondays).
Medical Assistance: The **clinic** of Dr. Prakash Srivastava (tel. 2101) is located on the bazaar uphill from the Mayank pharmacy. Open daily 9am-5pm.
Emergency: tel. 100. **Police:** tel. 2232.
Post Office: The main branch is along the mall, about 2km from town center, but there's a branch near the tourist office. Open M-F 9am-5pm, Sa 9am-noon.
Telephone: STD/ISDs dot the bazaar. **Telephone Code:** 05966.

ACCOMMODATIONS

Hotels along the bazaar are noisier and less well-kept (but less expensive) than those tucked among the hills along the Mall. To have any chance of hearing birds chirping instead of horns honking, you should stay in the mall area or, for complete isolation from cars and throngs of people, head to **Sitlakhet** (35km away; see p. 182). Room rates in Ranikhet are seasonal. In season (Apr.-Jun.) prices are higher and rooms scarcer. Most hotels don't allow alcohol or afternoon check-out.

KMVN Kalika Tourist Bungalows, Ranikhet (tel. 2893), 5km from the bazaar. Look for the signs along the Mall, beyond the main post office. Running hot water (but no showers). Deluxe rooms have TV. Super-deluxe gets that seat toilet. 10-bed dormitory is dark but spacious. In season: dorms Rs60; deluxe rooms Rs550; super-deluxe Rs800. Off-season: Rs50/415/600. Extra bed 20%. Extra person 10%.
Hotel Rajdeep (tel. 2444), near Midway closer to the west end of the bazaar. Popular among Indian and foreign travelers alike. Resort-caliber views at non-resort prices. The staff speaks English well. Deluxe rooms have attached bath. The hotel restaurant is open 7-10pm and serves tolerable Indian and Chinese fare. In-season: singles Rs175; deluxe Rs500; suites Rs650. Off-season: Rs100/150/200.

Hotel Everest (tel. 2402), above the bazaar. A good bargain. Watch the bazaar from the long balcony. Rooms have mirrors, and common bathrooms are tidy. In-season: singles Rs100, with bath Rs175; doubles Rs125/225. Off-season: Rs60/100/70/90.

Tribhuwan Hotel (tel. 2524), on the west end of town. A mighty beast composed of 3 buildings. Tranquility and higher prices lie further down the hill from the bazaar. Two-sided balconies offer unobstructed views of the valley. Squat toilets and bucket showers. Carpeted rooms are larger and have TV's. Basic rooms Rs250 (Nov.-Jan.), Rs400 (all other times); semi-deluxe Rs350/500; deluxe Rs450/600.

FOOD

Moon Hotel, across from Hotel Rajdeep, has the nicest restaurant in town, with prices to match. The long, airy halls are so elegant they seem out of place along the bazaar. The chicken (particularly the pulled chicken) is outstanding (Rs180). The other food is across the board spicier than the standard regional fare. Butter *naan* (Rs20) goes well with anything. Open 8-10am, 11am-4pm, and 8-10pm.

Milan Restaurant, a few minutes' walk up the bazaar from U.P. Roadways. A simple operation in a pink boxy room. Don't expect lasagna—a *milan* is a mixture, but the fare here is straight-up Indian. *Mutter paneer* Rs30. Open daily 6am-10pm.

Tourist Bungalow has a restaurant that isn't worth a visit from town, but it's good if you happen to be along the Mall. Munch down "fingar chips" (Rs18), or vegetable *pakoras* (eight for Rs18) while sipping tea (Rs5) in front of the TV (free). Chinese fare too (*chow mein* Rs45). Open daily 8-10am, 12-2:30pm, and 4:30-10:30pm.

SIGHTS AND ENTERTAINMENT

Most of the kicks to be found in Ranikhet come from the area behind the town along the Mall. Farthest away (11km) is the most renowned attraction in the area, the **Chaubatia Garden.** *(7 buses head to Chaubatia from the Roadways stand, 8am-6pm, 40min., Rs5. Shared taxi Rs20. Garden open daily 24hr.)* Originally developed as a "Fruit Research Centre," Chaubatia has several orchards and charming gardens. Sneaky travelers sometimes do their own "fruit research" while following one of the trails along the mountainside through the forests of fruit trees. Indian vacationers fill the garden in the high season. Closer to Ranikhet, along the Mall, sits the Hindu temple of **Jhula Devi.** It's small, but the gates around it are covered with bells.

It's possible to walk back toward the Mall from town—and not to have to follow the road. First, visit the impressive new (1994) **Mankameshwar Temple** up from the telephone exchange and across from the Nainital Bank.

For 10 days in June, you can stop in at the **Nar Singh Stadium** (also called the **Nar Singh Ground**) for the evening **Summer Festival.** A homey country fair, it features a ring toss, magicians, kiddie rides, a mini-zoo, 10-rupee gambling, blaring music, and heartburn-inducing Chinese food. Just like home, without the livestock show.

Fortunately, no metal detectors regulate admission to the **Kumaon Regiment Advanced Training Centre and Golf Course,** so bring your irons for one of India's most scenic mountain golf courses. *(Open Tu, Th, and F 7am-6pm; W and Sa 7am-12:30pm.)* It's relatively pricey, but golfers worldwide would fork out a fortune for a chance to see the course's extraordinary views. The links, known as "Upat Kalika," lie a 6km taxi ride (Rs60) or bus-hop from town toward Almora. Foreigners pay Rs200 for nine holes, Rs100 to rent clubs, Rs90 for a ball, and Rs50 for a caddy (plus tip, if he's helpful)—Rs440 total for a chance at a Himalayan hole-in-one.

■ Near Ranikhet: Sitlakhet सितलाखेत

A tiny village with only a few shops, Sitlakhet's main draw is precisely what it lacks. Located 35km from both Ranikhet and Almora, this tiny town allows its few visitors to find a comfortable middle ground between Kumaon's two extremes: wilderness and over-development, with views of Himalayan peaks by day and Almora's lights by night. Sitlakhet's sole hotel is a **KMUN Tourist Bungalow** (tel. 6005; reservations may also be made through the Almora U.P Tourism Office). Surrounded both by orchards on terraced hillsides and alpine forests, guests enjoy clean lodgings, restaurant meals, and (of course) just the right amount of serenity. Rooms should be reserved well in advance. (In-season: dorm beds Rs50; doubles Rs75; deluxe Rs150. Off-season: Rs35/75/150.)

■ Almora अल्मोड़ा

Unlike most of India's hill stations, Almora was developed by Indians. From 1560 to the end of the 18th century, Almora served as the seat of the Chanda dynasty before it was captured by the Gorkhas and then the British. A stroll through the old bazaar evokes those bygone days—the buildings are fading, but colorful facades and cobbled streets speak of centuries past. While its neighboring hill stations pursue the Western gods of finance and leisure, Almora is surrounded by modern and ancient Hindu temples and, off in the distance, by the magnificent natural shrines of the cloud-piercing Himalayan peaks. Almora remains the most mystical of Kumaon's hill stations, having drawn peace-seekers from the likes of Gandhi and Nehru (who used to meet here to talk) to Swami Vivekananda and Timothy Leary. What truly defines the Almora region, though, has not changed in 400 years. The mountains, which offer opportunity for day hikes and exploration, remain oblivious to passing decades and dynasties.

ORIENTATION

Almora wraps around its mountain on only four parallel streets. Buses stop at the **town center** on the **Mall,** the major thoroughfare for traffic and the site of most hotels and services; walking northeast (toward Hotel Shikhar's neon sign) leads to some restaurants and to the road to Kasar Devi. Most other services lie southwest along the Mall. The **Bazaar** is the first major parallel street up from the Mall. It can be steep walking anywhere in Almora, but the Mall is flatter than the Bazaar. Sunday is Almora's **business holiday;** many businesses are closed then.

PRACTICAL INFORMATION

Buses: Almora's bus stand is on the Mall at the center of town. **KMOU** serves **Kausani** and **Bageswar** (11 per day, 6am-5pm, 2½hr., Rs20); **Kathgodam** and **Haldwani** (6:30, 7:30, 9:30am, 1pm, 4½hr., Rs35); **Nainital** and **Bhowali** (6:30am and 3pm, 3hr., Rs28); **Ranikhet** (8, 10, 10:30am, 3 pm, 2½hr., Rs20). **U.P. Roadways** covers short and long hauls: **Bhowali** (every 30min., 5-8am and 1:30-5pm, 2½hr., Rs29); **Delhi** (7am, 3:30, 4:30, and 5pm, 11hr., Rs131/164); **Dehra Dun** (5am, 4pm, 12 hr., Rs160); **Kausani** (7, 9, and 9:30am, 12pm, 2½hr., Rs24); **Nainital** (8am, 3hr., Rs31); **Ranikhet** (6:30am, 1 and 2pm, 2hr., Rs20).

Local Transportation: Taxis clot near the Hotel Shikhar, at the town center.

Tourist Office: The **U.P. Tourist Office** (tel. 30180) is about 800m southwest of the bus stand on the road veering up from the Mall by the post office. They carry information about Almora and Kumaon but hold loose hours—try M-F 10am-5pm. A better bet for information is one of the local **trekking companies,** including **Discover Himalaya** (tel. 31470; fax 31507), across from the post office; **High Adventure** (tel. 31445), on the Mall a bit closer to town center; and **Ridge and Trek** (tel. 30492), on the balcony, first floor, still farther down the Mall. Mr. Shah at the Kailas Hotel is also very knowledgeable about the local sights.

Currency Exchange: State Bank of India, on the Mall (tel. 30048), near the town center. Changes AmEx checks in most currencies and grudgingly cashes Thomas Cook and Citibank checks—be persistent. They don't change foreign cash. Open M-F 10am-2pm, Sa10am-12pm.

Bookstore: Shree Almora Book Depot, next to High Adventure trekking (tel. 30148) carries paperbacks and regional guides. Open M-Sa 9:30am-8pm.

Pharmacy: Several along the Mall and bazaar, including the basic **Himalayan Medical Store,** across from Hotel Trishul. Open daily 8:30am-9pm.

Hospital: Civil Hospital (office tel. 30025, emergency tel. 30064), up a short flight of stairs from the bazaar. Open 8am-2pm, emergency open 24hr. **Base Hospital** (tel. 30012), 3km from town, is cleaner and less crowded. Open daily 8am-2pm.

Post Office: (tel. 30019). On the downside of the Mall about 600m southwest of the bus stand. *Poste Restante* M-Sa 10am-4pm. **Postal Code:** 263601.
Telephones: STD/ISD booths dot the Mall. **Telephone Code:** 05962.

ACCOMMODATIONS

Most of the hotels in town lie along the Mall, with dingier, cheaper places clustered around the center. More relaxed, isolated accommodations, including the unbeatable **Tranquillity Retreat,** dot the surrounding hills (see **Near Almora,** p. 185).

Kailas Hotel (tel. 30624), across from the post office, about 10m above the Mall. This place is the unrivalled sweet spot for foreign budget travelers in Almora. The Kailas is run by the incomparably charming 80-year-old Mr. Shah, who is a marvelous source for all sorts of tales and wisdom about the Almora district and Indian history. The rooms could be cleaner and the mattresses more comfy. Still, the place has a character that many find worth the price. Prices range from Rs65 for a single without bath to Rs365 for an in-season quint. Bargaining is futile.

KMVN Holiday House (tel. 30250), 1km southwest of the bus stand on the descending road. Typically pleasant and clean government accommodation, set apart from the noise of Almora, with its own garden and valley view. Squat toilets for everyone. Dorms have bucket showers. In-season: dorm beds Rs60; doubles Rs300; quads Rs600. Off-season 50/225/450. Extra bed 20%. Extra person 10%.

Trishul Hotel (tel. 30243), a yellow-and-turquoise 3-story building not far down the Mall, opposite the Kailas. Set a bit apart from the rush of the Mall, Trishul offers Himalayan peace—and a great view—in the middle of town. Three-room doubles have double beds, sofas, fireplaces, and quaint sitting rooms. Attached, somewhat tired bathrooms and hot water by the bucket. Lower-floor singles Rs125, upper-floor Rs175; lower-floor doubles Rs150, upper-floor Rs200; triples Rs250.

Hotel Pawan (tel. 30252), across from Trishul, closer to town center. Don't be fooled by the "Enjoy Billiards" sign and the room marked "dining hall"—both are out of service. The good news is you're allowed unlimited access to your own room. Well-kept and sufficient, with bright rooms, large mirrors, and clean bathrooms with squat toilets. Singles Rs100; doubles Rs180; off-season 90/150.

FOOD

A sticker on an Almora *chai*-stand fridge reads: "The secret of longevity is not to eat until one is really hungry." Perhaps the focus on loftier goals explains this city's lack of notable eateries.

Glory Restaurant (tel. 30274), across from Mount View, up the road to the northeast. The second floor, with its short ceilings and red lanterns, lend this vegetarian restaurant an unusual amount of character. Cheese butter *masala* is Rs40. Delicious samosas (Rs8). Open daily 7am-10:30pm.

Hotel Himsagar Restaurant. Decent food at darn cheap prices. Great view, marble wash-sinks, and all-veg. food (*dal makhani* Rs20). Open daily 8am-10:30pm.

Swagat Restaurant, on the side of the Hotel Shikhar, down some steps. An airy, homey place with a commanding view. Don't be fooled by the extensive menu; Swagat often only has *thalis* (Rs30). Open daily 7:30-9:30pm.

Mount View Restaurant, inside Hotel Shikhar, has dependable food an attentive wait staff. *Korma* curry Rs30; curry chicken Rs50. In-season: open daily 6am-11:30pm. Off-season: 6am-10:30pm.

SIGHTS

Almora proper doesn't offer much in the way of sights, but the further from town you go, the more interesting things get. The main attraction nearby is the **Kasar Devi Temple,** near the hamlet of Kasar Devi, about 7km from Almora and reachable by a long hike or by taxi (Rs10 per person 1-way). The temple emits an aura of mysticism, but the visitor's urge to meditate comes mainly from the temple's spectacular setting. On a giant, sloping rock atop a mountain, it has sweeping panoramas of the whole area, marred only slightly by the television antenna that shares the point, emitting an aura of its own. The temple is known as a center of spiritual energy: Swami Vivekananda came here to meditate, as have many soul-searching Americans and Europeans, some of whom still hang around the nearby tea stands today. Follow the trail past the temple through town for the best views of the distant Nanda Devi mountain range. Other temples near Almora are equally noteworthy. Locals go to the locally important **Chitai Temple** to seek justice if they feel they've been wronged. **Katermal** (17km from Almora) boasts an 800-year-old **Sun Temple.** Closer to town is the **Nanda Devi Temple,** which pays homage to the goddess of the distant mountain. The **Nanda Devi Fair** is held here in September.

The **Brighton End Corner** at the south end of town is a popular spot from which to watch the sunsets. Aspiring musicians looking to hang around Almora for a while can seek tutelage at the **Bhadkande College of Music,** which has a branch in town. Almora proper offers other treats. If you are looking to kill time while waiting for the bus to leave, walk across the street to the The small, government-run **G.B. Pant museum** is right in the center of town, across from the bus stand. *(Open Tu-Su, 10:30am-4:30pm; closed second Sun.; Free.)* Pant's museum features not trousers but tools and other artifacts from the Katyuri and Chanda dynasties. Walk past the post office out of town about 750m and head up past the holiday homes to the production center of **Himalaya Woolens,** which makes quality tweeds and shawls. *(Shawls Rs300-2500; jackets Rs850. Open M-Sa 10am-5pm.)* Wander through the **Bazaar** (especially the lower region) and you'll note a lot of pots. Almora is the center of production of *tamta,* a silver-plated copper. **Anokhe Lal** is a good shop for checking these pots out, though they'd be pretty heavy to carry in a backpack.

Tucked between two hills, and far from everything but its own splendor and jaw-dropping views, the **Tranquillity Retreat** is a tiny utopia for the short- or long-term visitor. Now in its third year, Tranquillity has grown to seven rooms, with an organic garden, an apiary (that's bees), its own water source, and a baby. Armelle and Kishan, French ex-patriate and Indian farmer, busily tend the garden, bake bread (7 loaves daily) and steaming scones served with homemade honey, and cook up a vegetarian storm—French and Continental mainstays with the occasional Indian touch—all the while exuding a warmth and compassion that keeps their contented guests from leaving the nest. And why would they, with fried vegetables (Rs35), garlic tomato pizza (Rs25), garden salad with vinaigrette (Rs10), and fresh bread (Rs15) for the taking? Doubles are Rs1500 per month, but food is available 7am-10pm for casual visitors as well as guests. There are 2 paths leading from the road to Kasar Devi to Tranquillity Retreat. If you are walking towards Kasar Devi, look for a blue sign high in a tree on your left-hand side about 10 minutes after passing the Research Institute for Yoga Therapy. If you are walking away from Kasar Devi, there will be a sign on your right-hand side about 15min. down the mountain from the Kasar Devi Temple. For both paths, follow the blue blazes over the ridge. Tranquillity Retreat has no phone as of yet, but reservations can be made by writing and telling when you are coming: Tranquillity Guesthouse c/o Kishan Joshi; 263601 Saria Pina Estate; Almora; V.P.M.

■ Near Almora

North and east of Almora lie many less frequented treasures of the Kumaon region. 124 temples and hundreds of statues make up **Jageswar,** situated 38km from Almora in a valley surrounded by Deodar trees. The temples were built by the rajas of the Chand dynasty and remain an excellent example of the regions architecture. The region's views are more awe-inspiring the higher up in elevation and the closer to the Himalayan peaks you go. There are many such less touristed spots in the Almora and neighboring Pithoragarh districts. Of special note is the **Binsar Sanctuary,** 30km from Almora. Binsar was the summer getaway of the Chand rulers; now Indians and foreigners alike come and stay for immersion in the sanctuary's dense forests. There is a **KMVN Tourist Rest House** but few other hotels and services in the area (in-season: doubles Rs300-600.) For further immersion in Kumaon's natural beauty, consider going on a **trek** to one of the towering glaciers in the Indian Himalayas. The most popular trek in Kumaon is to **Pindari Glacier.** Rest houses line the trail at convenient distances, but the trek's popularity deters many trekkers seeking true stillness. Treks to **Milam Glacier,** via stunning **Munsyari** in the Pithoragarh district, is prime for those hoping to avoid the slow-moving glacial crowds. A good way to find out about trekking in Kumaon is to talk with one of the local trekking agents, such as **Discover Himalaya,** in Almora. Discover Himalaya offers a short four-day trek through the low Himalaya (200-2500m) to the **Barahi Devi Temple** at Devidhura, the site of a stunning ritual during the Rakshabandhan festival, around the third week of August. Two opponents, equipped with baskets as shields, throw rocks at each other. Blood from the ensuing wounds is collected and offered to the virgin goddess. Stand back. This and similar treks cost around Rs800 per day per person.

■ Kausani खुसानी

Though it is possible to glimpse awe-inspiring views of the Himalayan peaks from Ranikhet or Almora, the Himalayan experience can be savored much more fully from the humble town of Kausani. At almost 2000m above sea level, Kausani commands impressive panorama after panorama. Almora is a city and Ranikhet is a bustling town, Kausani is only a bus stop with a few restaurants and quite a few more hotels, a perfect spot for basking in the Himalayan splendor in the company of others of similar mind, but beyond earshot of honking cars and the busy daily life of the larger hill stations. Kausani's strategic location has helped inspire many notable Indians—Hindi poet laureate Sumitra Nandan Pant was born here, and, in 1929, Mohandas Gandhi spent time in the Anashakti Ashram.

ORIENTATION AND PRACTICAL INFORMATION: Buses stop in Kausini's center, the 3-way intersection of the main road and another road which begins to climb up the mountain. The town center is across from a colorful temple. The **tourist office** (open M-F 10am-5pm) and **post office** are located on the main road before the center where the buses stop. The nearest **currency exchange** is in Almora and Bageswar. A couple blocks from the town center, buses stop frequently for Bageswar, Almora, Gwaldam, Ranikhet, Bhowali, and Haldwani. Enquire at the tourist office or ask locals (more than one!) when the buses leave. There are several **STD/ISD** booths on the main road and also on the cement walkway that climbs up the mountain (**telephone code:** 05962). The **Sunil Medical store** is located on this walkway (open daily 8am-8pm). The walkway leads to the road that climbs the mountain. The mountain road continues, leading to the KMVN tourist rest house 2km. away. Take a left instead at the Anashakti Ashram sign to get to many of the town's other hotels.

ACCOMMODATIONS AND FOOD Kausani plays host to a large number of resort hotels advertising their magnificent view of the Himalayas. The good news is that these hotels do not have a monopoly on nature's beauty. The rooms at the **Hotel Uttarakhand,** off the walkway (tel. 45012), have unhindered mountain views, and are far enough away from the town center to offer a modicum of peace and quiet. (May-June, Oct.: doubles Rs100-300. Off-season: Rs50-150.) The attached restaurant (open 6am-11pm) is one of the best in town (veg. fried rice Rs.25). Many of Kausani's nicer hotels in town are located on one strip of road above the town center. **Hotel Prashant** (tel. 45037) has rooftop views and a few cheap rooms. (In-season: singles Rs75, doubles Rs200. Off-season: Rs50/175. Restaurant open 6am-9pm.) A cleaner and quieter bet (no children running around here) is the **Amer Holiday Home** (tel. 45015. Open May-July and Sept.-Dec. In-season: singles Rs150, doubles Rs300-500. Off-season: Rs100/200-350).

On the same row of hotels, is the **Anashakti Ashram** ("the Gandhi ashram"). It is possible to stay in the ashram, though in the high season you may be woken up at daybreak by Indian tourists' children. The ashram's immaculate grounds offer one of the most calming vista points on hotel row. Fees are paid on a donation basis, and the manager stresses that the ashram is for those interested in spiritual living.

KMVN tourist rest houses are always a safe bet in Kumaon, and the one in Kausani (tel. 45006) is no exception. Located 2km from town on a road that hugs the northern face of the mountain, the rest house has dorm beds (Rs60) and doubles (Rs300-800) available (off-season: Rs50/225-600). Book in advance, especially the dormitory. (Attached restaurant open 7am-10pm.)

Unfortunately the variety of good cheap eats is significantly less than cheap sleeps. The **Uttarkhand Restaurant** and the **Kitchen Restaurant,** next to the post office, both offer reliable fare (the latter dishes Rs30 *thalis*). The **Ashoka restaurant,** next to the Bhatt Clinic, serves up local dishes. *Bara dish* (Rs30) is made of ground lentils and looks like falafel. With the local chutney, it is tasty and makes a nice treat after weeks of *dal* and chow mein. Kumaoni dishes take a while to cook, so order early.

SIGHTS As the man in the tourist office says with a smile, the main sights in Kausani are sunrise and sunset. These are also the best times to see the distant mountains when they are enveloped in clouds (summer and monsoon season, Apr.-Aug.). During autumn, when the sky is clear around the clock, the quiet town is still quieter. If gazing at the view and trekking around the area gets tiring after a while, take a day trip to **Bajinath** (16km), a group of ancient temples on the banks of the Gomti River. *(Buses to Bageshwar leave frequently from town center, Rs6.)* If trekking around Kumaon doesn't appeal, try two-wheeling it. **Yogi's Uttarakhand Cycle Tours** (tel. 45012) provides mountain bikes and organizes day and extended trips for one to four people. Tours start from Rs350 per day.

THE U.P. PLAINS

■ Agra आगरा

Over the last decade, the average tourist's stay in Agra has declined from 1.7 days to barely 12 hours. As you travel in North India you'll understand why. At the edges of all the roads and rail lines leading to Agra, the conventional wisdom has left behind a kind of verbal underbrush, and everyone seems to be mumbling the same thing: Agra is a dump. This, however, is not true. While the main budget hotel center, Taj Ganj, is full of aggressive rickshaw-*wallahs* and inlaid marble and rug vendors, the city deserves a chance. In the Cantonment area, for example, there are wide, clean streets, upscale stores, and a string of pocket parks maintained by the local Sheraton, which has a multi-million dollar stake in seeing that Agra puts its best foot forward. But of course, Agra's real draw is the incomparably grand Taj Mahal.

Agra's monuments were all built under the Mughals, who swept into India from Central Asia early in the 16th century. At the Battle of Panipat (1526), the Mughal warrior Babur crushed the ruling Lodi dynasty; as a direct result, the Mughals won a great South Asian empire, which included Agra, the Lodi capital. For the next 150 or so years, the site of the Mughal capital flitted back and forth between Delhi and Agra, leaving both cities with a gaggle of timelessly beautiful landmarks. With the slow decline of Mughal power in North India, Agra fell on hard times, and the new kids on the block—the British—made Calcutta (and later Delhi) their capital, encouraging Allahabad to surpass Agra as the local political powerhouse.

Lately, Agra has worked hard to re-invent itself, recycling the foreign exchange it earns from tourists into industrial development and smoggy economic progress, growing into a city of over 1 million. Even if you're not particularly interested in Agra's modern side, plan to spend some time in and around the city before seeing the Taj Mahal; fleeting glimpses of its sensuous beauty will enhance and intensify your eventual pleasure. Of course, if that doesn't turn you on, you can always be in and out in under 12 hours—you wouldn't be the first.

NORTH INDIA

> **Warning:** Agra, like all major tourist hubs in India, has a number of swindlers who'd love a chunk of that cash you're stashing. First, be aware that rickshaw charges are excessive and the commissions incentive means that they take you to the hotel or restaurant of their (and not your) choice. Insist, at the least, on going to a specific area of town. Ask other drivers and non-driver locals if the price you're quoted seems too high. Also watch out for crafty salesmen who persuade tourists with "parties," tea, and sweet talk to buy rugs to resell back home. Numerous schemes (credit card fraud, false identities, etc.) can stem from this, so don't get lured in. If it seems too good to be true, it is.

ORIENTATION

Agra is a large and diffuse city, most of which sprawls west from the banks of the **Yamuna River,** where the Taj Mahal and Agra Fort lie, separated by 1.5km and the **Shah Jahan Park.** Yamuna Kinara Road runs along the river's western banks from the Taj Mahal to **Belan Ganj,** a bustling neighborhood 1km north of **Agra Fort Railway Station,** where trains from east Rajasthan pull in. Tourist facilities cluster south of the Taj Mahal and Agra Fort. Bargain-basement accommodations are ubiquitous in **Taj Ganj,** a neighborhood just south of the Taj Mahal, while upscale hotels are found up along **Fatehabad Road,** even farther (1km) south of the Taj. **Mahatma Gandhi Road, Gwalior Road,** and **General Cariappa Road** are three major thoroughfares that cross both **the Mall** and **Taj Road.** From the upscale **Sadar Bazaar,** which is nestled between Mahatma Gandhi and Gwalior Rd., it's 2km due west to **Agra Cantonment Railway Station** and its long-distance trains; 2km northwest along Fatehpur Sikri Rd. takes you to the **Idgah Bus Stand.**

PRACTICAL INFORMATION

Transportation

Airport: Agra's **Kheria Airport** is 9km southwest of the city (enquiry tel. 263982 or 301180, ext. 185. Daily flights to: **Delhi** (3:50pm, 40min., US$50); **Varanasi** (1½hr., US$90) via **Khajuraho** (11:05am, 45min., US$80). Book flights at the **Indian Airlines** office (tel. 360948 or 360190; open daily 10am-5:30pm), adjacent to Hotel Clarks-Shiraz, or from **Sita World Travel** (tel. 363013), north side of main shopping bazaar, Sadar Bazaar.

Trains: Agra has several railway stations: **Agra Cantonment, Idgah, Agra Fort, Yamuna Bridge** (across the river), **Agra City** (north of town), and **Raja Ki Mandi** (northwest of Old Agra). Be sure you know in advance where your train arrives or departs. Agra Cantt. Railway Station (enquiry tel. 131 or 133) is the main terminal, southwest of the city and at the west end of the Mall, running toward Taj Ganj. A special window at the computer reservation complex on the south side makes bookings for foreign tourists (as well as for VIPs and freedom fighters—which are you?). Unless noted, fares listed are 2nd/1st class. To: **Bhopal** (*Shatabdi Exp.* 2002, 8:15am, 6hr., Rs495 for A/C chair; *Punjab Mail* 1038, 8:30am, 8hr., Rs102/511); **Delhi** (*Shatabdi Exp.* 2001, 8:18pm, 2hr., Rs305 for A/C chair); **Gwalior** (*Kerala Exp.* 2626, 2:17pm, 1½hr., Rs30/164); **Howrah** (*Udyan Abha Toofan Exp.* 3008, 12:40pm, 29½hr., Rs184/952); **Lucknow** (*Ahmedabad-Gorakhpur Exp.* 5045, 6:50am, 6½hr., Rs135/676); **Mathura** (*G.T. Exp.* 2615, 7:30am, 1hr., Rs18/105); **Mumbai** (*Punjab Mail* 1038, 8:30am, 23hr., Rs191/1000).

Buses: Most leave from **Idgah Bus Terminal,** a short distance northeast of Agra Cantt. Railway Station. To: **Ajmer** (5 per day, 5-10pm, 9hr., Rs100); **Bikaner** (11am, 12hr., Rs170); **Delhi** (every 30min., 4am-9:30pm, 5hr., Rs75); **Gwalior** (every hr., 3½hr., Rs40); **Jaipur** (every 30min., 6am-10pm, 7hr., Rs80) via **Bharatpur** (1½hr., Rs20); **Jhansi** (5am, 10hr., Rs75); **Mathura** (every hr., 6am-8:30pm, 1½hr., Rs25); **Udaipur** (6pm, 14hr., Rs150). Buses to **Varanasi** (5pm, 18hr., Rs210) start at the **Agra Fort Bus Stand,** southwest of the fort. Deluxe buses to Jaipur, Delhi, and elsewhere leave frequently from other places—contact a travel agent in Taj Ganj for daily bookings.

Agra
ACCOMMODATIONS
C Agra Hotel
E Hotel Akbar Inn
G Hotel Kant
A Hotel Ritz
F Hotel Safari
B Pawan/Jalwal Hotel
D Tourist Rest House

Local Transportation: Despite all the rip-offs, **cycle-rickshaws** are still a good way to get around. Pay no more than Rs15-20 for a cycle-rickshaw and no more than Rs20 for an **auto-rickshaw** going between railway or bus stations and Taj Ganj or Agra Fort. Auto-rickshaws can be hired for a day for Rs100-200, depending on your bargaining acumen. Agra is easy to zip around by **bicycle;** there are rental shops all around town, including **Shah Jahan Lodge** in Taj Ganj (Rs25 per day). And if you have some money to spare, hire a **car and driver** from one of the numerous places around the tourist centers (and undoubtedly a few rug and marble shops as well): **R.R. Travels** (tel. 330055), on Fatehabad Rd. in Taj Ganj, charges Rs650 (Rs1100 with A/C) for a 1-day tour that includes Fatehpur Sikri. Open daily 10am-6pm.

Tourist and Financial Services

Tourist Office: Agra boasts 3 different tourist offices. **Government of India Tourist Office,** 191 the Mall (tel. 363959 or 363377), across from the post office. The most convenient and informative tourist office, providing a good map, brochures on Agra and all parts of India, and general guidance. Open M-F 9am-5:30pm, Sa 9am-1pm. **U.P. Government Tourist Office,** 64 Taj Rd. (tel. 360517), near the Clarks-Shiraz. This friendlier but less well-stocked office has brochures on Kumaon, Garhwal, and Varanasi. Open M-Sa 10am-5pm. Their **branch office** for the just-arrived at Agra Cantt. Railway Station is across from the enquiry booth (tel. 368598). Open daily 8am-8pm. Arranges day tours of Fatehpur Sikri, Sikandra, Agra Fort, and the Taj Mahal (includes lunch stop, daily except M 9:30am-6pm, Rs150).
Immigration Office: Foreigners Registration Office, 16 Old Idgah Colony (tel. 269563). Near the bus stand. Register for stays over 3 months.

Currency Exchange: State Bank of India, Fatehabad Rd. (tel. 330449), 1km from Taj Ganj follow the blue "I" signs from the traffic circle at the Shah Jahan park entrance. Cashes currency and traveler's checks up to US$200. Open M-F 10:30am-2pm, Sa 10:30am-noon. **LKP Merchant Financing Ltd.,** Fatehabad Rd. (tel. 330480; fax 331191), in the tourist complex area next to Pizza Hut, buys and sells traveler's checks, and changes major currencies. Open M-Sa 9:30am-8pm. Outside of these hours, many hotel proprietors in the Taj Ganj change money on the **black market;** those who attempt to change money illegally should do so discreetly.

Local Services

Luggage Storage: Available at Agra Cantt. Railway Station (Rs5 for the first 12hr.) and on a short-term basis at many hotels.

Market: For simple shopping needs, **Taj Ganj** has a surprising number of shops off the main strip and a lot of inlaid marble. **Old Agra** is one big bazaar for buying belts, shoes, car parts, or whatever; **Kinari Bazaar,** extending northwest from the fort, is especially stocked. Specialty markets abound, so ask a local to point the way. Resist handicrafts salesmen pulling you into their shops. Shop around and always, always try to bargain (unless a sign claims fixed prices).

Bookstore: The Modern Book Depot (tel. 363133), in Sadar Bazaar, has an extensive selection of books in addition to language dictionaries and Hindi and English magazines. Open W-M 10am-9pm.

Emergency and Communications

Pharmacy: Chemists abound near the major tourist areas. **Shalya Medical Centre,** Fatehabad Rd. (tel. 331106). Well-marked, well-stocked. Open daily 8am-midnight.

Hospital: District Hospital (tel. 364738). **Sarojini Naidu Hospital** (tel. 361318), west of Old Agra near Bageshwarnath Temple and Kali Masjid. **Shanti Manglik** (tel. 330488), on Fatehabad Rd. provides 24hr. emergency assistance.

Emergency: Police, tel. 100 or 361120. **Ambulance,** tel. 102.

Post Office: GPO, the Mall (tel. 363588). Opposite the tourist office. Massive, intimidating, and notoriously inefficient. Speed post and *Poste Restante* available M-Sa 10am-6pm; stamps sold M-Sa 7am-3pm. **Postal Code:** 282001.

Internet: Deepa Tours and Travels, 3/14 Chowk Thana (tel. 330941; email Santan@nda.vsnl.net.in), just west of the hub at the first major crossing. Stable connections from Delhi are rare, but your message will get through eventually. Web access Rs4 per min.; email Rs50 per message. Open daily 10am-11pm.

Telephones: Global Enterprises, Chowk Thana, Taj Ganj (tel. 330932), has Rs3 callbacks. You can also call collect or use your international phone card for Rs3 per min. Open daily 8am-midnight. **Telephone Code:** 0562.

ACCOMMODATIONS

The area immediately to the south of the Taj Mahal testifies to how competition keeps prices in check. Rooms here are surprisingly cheap—there's absolutely no need to pay more than Rs100 for a double. While hectic, dirty, and at times aggravating, this area is closest to the Taj itself. Mid-range and hit-the-roof expensive hotels are mostly to the south of Taj Ganj—from their rooms with a view, the tomb is but a wee thing. The other major centers, near the bus stand, Sadar Bazaar, and Cantonment areas, reward with their convenience and spaciousness. Prices may vary by season; around Christmas, accommodations providers may hike their prices up to 200% above the off-season rates listed below. Most hotels have noon check-out.

Taj Ganj

The best way to orient yourself is to start with the central hub, the rickshaw-cluttered area in front of Joney's Place; Taj Ganj forks to the north (toward the Taj), east, and west. Roads also run along the sides of the Taj Mahal toward the gates.

India Guest House (tel. 330909). On the left side of the street between the hub and the Taj. Stone courtyard with grapevines and pomegranate tree, and welcoming family. Simple, spacious rooms have 2 beds per room, a fan, and ceramic walls. Singles Rs30-50; doubles Rs50-65.

Shahjahan Hotel (tel. 331159). Just west of the hub. Owner loves to do all sorts of business, so he lowers prices to entice guests to eat in his restaurant and buy his marble goods. Adequately comfortable, but quality varies wildly from room to room. Singles Rs40, with bath Rs60; doubles Rs60/80.

Hotel Sheela, East Gate (tel. 33074). Garden and patio in the Taj non-pollution zone, rooftop view of the tomb, many facilities, and generally clean to the extreme. The manager—V.P. of the Hotel and Restaurant Association of Agra—has integrity; there are no commissions or scams here. Check-out 10am. Singles Rs150; doubles with fan Rs200, with air-cooling Rs250.

Hotel Taj Khema (tel. 360140). A short walk east of East Gate, on the left. Run by U.P. Tourism, this place is clean and good for mid-range travelers. Guests get access to the grassy hill (they have the gall to charge non-guests up to Rs25), where there's a nice shot of the Taj. Luggage storage. Bar and restaurant. Singles Rs150, with air-cooling Rs250; doubles Rs200/300, with A/C Rs550.

Hotel Pink, East Gate (tel. 330115). More of an orangish mauve, actually. Hotel Pink has rugs, squat toilets, and nice mattresses in rooms around a classy, florid courtyard. Singles Rs60; doubles Rs80, with air-cooling Rs120; triples Rs150.

Hotel White House (tel. 330907), near Honey's Restaurant, east of the hub. The one room to the right of the entrance wins a gold medal for loft design. The others are average, with squat toilets and air-coolers. Singles Rs80; doubles Rs100.

Shanti Lodge (tel. 330900), on the left side walking east from the hub. The tallest hotel in Taj Ganj, its rooftop restaurant has an unspoiled view of the Taj. Still, the hotel is more geared toward businessmen than backpackers. Check-out 10am. Singles Rs80; doubles Rs100. Rooms with a view Rs150.

Hotel Shyam Palace (tel. 331482), just up the road from the Western gate, next to the Central Bank of India. A quiet oasis on the western edge of Taj Ganj. Leafy courtyard and good view of you-know-what from the roof. Attached baths, hot water. Singles Rs100; doubles Rs150, with air-cooling Rs150.

Beyond Taj Ganj

Tourists Rest House, Kachahari Rd. (tel. 363961; fax 366910), next to Meher Cinema, off Gwalior Rd., northeast of the GPO. Don't confuse it with impostors that go by similar names. Agra's best budget deal, with 2 levels of rooms around a lush courtyard, and many foreigner-friendly facilities, including 24hr. STD/ISD and collect call service. Proprietor speaks English, Japanese, Hebrew, and French and arranges tours to Rajasthan and other hot spots. Singles Rs65; doubles Rs130.

Hotel Safari, Shaheed Nagar Shamsabad Rd. (tel. 360110), opposite Hotel Swagat and near the All India Radio station, this facility provides spotless accommodations, 24hr. STD/ISD service, and free bicycles

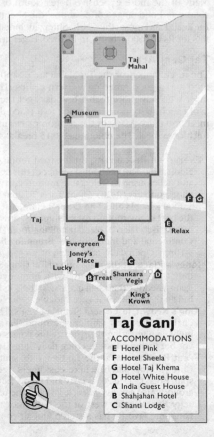

Taj Ganj

ACCOMMODATIONS
E Hotel Pink
F Hotel Sheela
G Hotel Taj Khema
D Hotel White House
A India Guest House
B Shahjahan Hotel
C Shanti Lodge

for those who want to cruise to the Taj (1.5km). Singles Rs150; doubles Rs200, with air-cooling Rs250.

Hotel Akbar Inn, 21 the Mall (tel. 363212), halfway between Taj Ganj and the railway station. On a peaceful, litter-cluttered strip of the Mall's garden, this place oozes tranquility. Stuffy, dim rooms with common bath (and urinal!) Rs40, with bath and spigot shower Rs80, with air-cooling Rs100; doubles Rs150/160.

Agra Hotel, F.M. Cariappa Rd. (tel. 363331). Not far south of Agra Fort, but well outside the city's chaos. Established in 1926 and beginning to show its age, it still has a pleasant garden area. Spacious, airy rooms. Singles Rs150; doubles Rs200; triples Rs350. Air-cooling Rs50 extra.

Pawan/Jaiwal Hotel, 3 Taj Rd., Sadar Bazaar (tel. 363716). The only hotel in the main Sadar strip, with quiet, bright, and cheery rooms, but a bit worn around the edges. All rooms have air-cooling. Singles Rs200; doubles Rs300, with TV Rs400.

Hotel Ritz (tel. 269501). On the road running west of the Idgah Bus Stand. Best of the cheaper places for late-night or early-morning arrivals and departures. Reasonably new and clean. All rooms have attached baths, air-cooling, and TV. Singles and doubles Rs125; triples Rs250.

FOOD

Most of Agra's restaurants—or at least those that are marginally kind to tourists' bellies—cluster in **Taj Ganj, Sadar Bazaar,** and other tourist centers south of the old heart of town. There are a few cheapies near Jama Masjid, and numerous **snacks stalls** around the Red Fort, but most travelers stick to places close to (or inside) their hotels. Many of the more expensive hotels south of Taj Ganj have fancy-schmancy dining rooms and mid-range coffee shops; the Sheraton has a scrumptious breakfast buffet for Rs200 and most (the Clarks-Shiraz included) have elaborate lunch and dinner buffets for Rs400-600—bring an inflated, eager appetite, and prepare to gorge.

Taj Ganj Area

The restaurants near the Taj Mahal are disappointingly similar, offering bland Indian food and a good range of Western dishes. The area is notorious for poor hygiene; most who stay more than a few days get the Agra aches, akin to "Delhi Belly." To avoid such nasty nonsense, stick to a place that treats you right and avoid dubious meat and dairy. Many of the rooftop places are better for a sunset coffee than for a full-blown meal. The ubiquitous Rs15 breakfasts are among North India's best.

Evergreen Restaurant, on the road running along west side of Taj, next to Hotel Siddhartha. The economist owner of this newly conceived place strives for hygiene and deliciousness. Delectable mutton curry (Rs40), flaming banana crepes (Rs15), cheeseburgers (Rs20). Open Tu-Sa 7-10pm.

Shankara Vegis and The Door's Cafe, just east of the hub. Generally known to be the best of the rooftop establishments, now with a pop music cafe downstairs (featuring "Bob Dlen"). Bland-but-filling *thali* (Rs40), yummy *pakora,* and many other Continental and Indian dishes. Brimming beers (Rs50) beam at Happy Hour, from 9-10pm. Open daily 7am-midnight.

Joney's Place, at the main hub of Taj Ganj. Small quaint restaurant that predates its imitation neighbors (many with homonym names like Johnny's, Join-Us, etc.). Renowned for their banana *lassis;* their Rs15 breakfasts are also good, while their Indian dishes (Rs10-30) are variable. Open daily 6am-midnight.

King's Krown, just east of Shankara Vegis. The Krown is crowned with the comfiest chairs and coziest ambience around. Patrons play chess or read under colored bulbs, while eating their hearty breakfasts (Rs25) or *thalis* (Rs45), which lack flavor but include dessert. Open daily 7am-11pm.

Treat Restaurant, at the Taj Ganj hub, south side, kitty-corner from Joney's Place. Cute rooftop patch, where customers perched in wicker chairs watch the hub spin. Breakfast (Rs20) is tasty and filling, but the Rs15 mini-breakfast is the best buy around. Also serves *thalis* (Rs25) and the usual grub. Open daily 6am-10:30pm.

Lucky Restaurant, west of the hub, but east of the road running along west Taj. Longtime favorite has a stereo and air-cooler for a temperate, unassuming atmosphere. The "Danish Farmoon," with coconut, chocolate, banana, and curd is a delight. Israeli food, spaghetti, and mega-*thalis* (Rs40). Open daily 6am-midnight.

Relax Restaurant, Hotel Pink. The famous rooftop joint has a new home. *Thalis* (Rs30-45), crepes (Rs30), and Indian dishes (Rs10-30). Open daily 6am-midnight.

Taj Restaurant (tel. 331344). Immaculate mid-range restaurant west of the Taj's west gate. Highest quality food in the area. Mausoleum-like ambience and sterility. Entomb your own veg. *thali* (Rs70), *masala* peanuts (Rs20), or tandoori chicken (Rs50). Beer Rs80. Nice garden out back. Open daily 7am-10pm.

Beyond Taj Ganj

Sadar Bazaar is the hub of food outside Taj Ganj, though other restaurants dot the Cantonment landscape. In addition to the budget eateries listed here, the Park and Prakash restaurants at the east end of the bazaar have good reputations among locals.

Sonar's, 25 the Mall (tel. 360295). The exquisite Mughlai and Continental cuisine costs as much as your hotel room, but who's counting? *Murgh* (chicken) Mughlai Rs75, sliced lamb with mushroom and garlic sauce Rs104, mega-*thalis* Rs150. Spice and price are determined by looking at you. Open daily 7am-10pm.

Dasaprakash, 1 Gwalior Rd., next to Agra Ashok. Agra's best South Indian (veg.) food, served with deliciously deadly homemade *achar* (pickle). *Masala dosa* Rs50; generous *thali* for two Rs150. Open daily 12:30-3pm and 6-11pm.

Priya Restaurant. There are 2 restaurants by this name, one next to Tourists Rest House north of the Sadar area and the other behind Hotel Ratan Deep, off Fatehabad Rd. The former is popular and not too expensive. The latter has Mughal ambience, a large menu with tasty Indian and Mughlai dishes (Rs40-100), and a *Shah Jahan thali* that will pop your trouser buttons (Rs225). Open daily 7am-midnight.

Zorba the Buddha, Gopi Chand Shivare Rd. (tel. 367767; fax 363757). In the shopping strip stretching north of the main part of Sadar Bazaar. Dreamy new age Oshoism. Float your way through *kofta, paneer,* or "Hawaiian Spree." Most dishes Rs60-120. Open daily noon-3pm and 6-9pm; closed May 1-July 5. Tiny dining room makes reservations necessary for larger groups.

R. Gaylord Bar and Restaurant, 1 Sadar Bazaar (tel. 363558). East end of strip. Lounge about in plush red booths while sipping gin and juice in the new supercooled waterfall room. Roast of grilled chicken, chips, and vegetable (Rs115), *malai kofta* (Rs45), and beer (Rs50). Open daily 11am-11pm.

Garden Restaurant (tel. 361865). In the same eastern bit of Sadar as Lakshmi Vilas, a bit farther down. Inexpensive *dosa*, simple *thali* (Rs25), more elaborate *thali* (Rs45), and veg. snacks and sandwiches. Open daily 7am-11pm.

Petals the Restaurant, 19-A Taj. Rd., Sadar Bazaar (tel. 363807), opposite Agra Stadium. The Italian food is the main attraction here (vegetable lasagna Rs90). Freshwater fried fish with tartar sauce (Rs80). Open daily noon-10pm.

Only Restaurant, 45 Taj Rd. (tel. 364333). American and European travelers flock to this bamboo roofed eatery with live Indian musical performances in the evenings. Bland food prepared especially for "delicate" digestive systems. *Murgh badam* (chicken with almonds) Rs95. Open daily 11am-10pm.

SIGHTS

In Agra, more so than in other tourist hubs, sight-seers seem to share the same set of priorities. First on their list is the Taj Mahal—preferably experienced at dawn or dusk—followed by its next-door neighbor, the Agra Fort. Time permitting, tourists often squeeze in a trip to nearby Fatehpur Sikri and the Itimad-ud-Daulah.

Taj Mahal

Location: *North of Taj Ganj. Enter through the south, east, or west gate. The enclosed Taj complex is approached through the Chowk-i-Jilo-Khana.* **Hours:** *Open dawn to dusk, and full moon nights. Museum open Sa-Th 10am-5pm.* **Admission:** *Rs15; Rs105 between 6 and 8am and 5 and 7pm. Free on Fridays.* **Other:** *Shoe storage Rs5; shoe covers Rs10.*

Even if they've never actually stood before its bulbous white marble domes, many travelers assume that a first visit to the Taj Mahal will provoke feelings of *déja vu*.

After all, pictures of the Taj adorn a great many Indian restaurants, postcards, and tourist trinketry. So why read the book when you've seen the film? Because the Taj's sensuous beauty is so imposing that no amount of overexposure can diminish it. Indeed, for all the interminable hype and silly hoopla, the Taj Mahal is heart-achingly splendid, especially at dawn and dusk, and even the most jaded of globe-trotters often find themselves smiling in joy and wonderment as they stand before it. One of only a handful of constructions with the audacity to deem itself "the most beautiful building in the world," the Taj Mahal is India's ultimate must-see.

The tale of the Taj is a sad, sweet love story. When he became Mughal emperor in 1628, Shah Jahan brought to the throne a great many things—intellect, political acumen, and, not least, a passion for delicately wrought architecture. Three years after becoming emperor, Shah Jahan received news that rent his heart asunder—after 18 years of marriage, his favorite wife, Arjumand Banu Begum, had died giving birth to the couple's 14th child. In his grief, Shah Jahan decided that his beloved should be buried in a tomb of timeless beauty—as the Bengali poet Rabindranath Tagore said, the Taj Mahal was designed as a "tear [that] would hang on the cheek of time."

Work on the Taj began in 1632, one year after the death of Arjumand Banu Begum. Marble was quarried in Makrana, Rajasthan, and precious stones were brought to Agra from Yemen, Russia, China, and Central Asia. Architects were brought from Persia, and French and Italian master craftsmen had a hand in decorating the building; in all, nearly 20,000 people worked continuously on the construction of the Taj. By the time the Taj Mahal was completed in 1653, a great many things had changed—the Mughal capital had been moved from Agra to Delhi, the deceased Arjumand Banu Begum had become popularly known as "Mumtaz Mahal" (Elect of the Palace), and one of Shah Jahan's sons, Aurangzeb, had grown to manhood. In 1658, the severe, reclusive Aurangzeb staged a coup, violently surmounting the opposition of his three brothers and imprisoning Shah Jahan in Agra Fort, where he lived out his days under house arrest, staring out across the Yamuna River at the Taj Mahal. The walk from the fort to the Taj is hardly 2km, but Shah Jahan was never allowed to traverse the distance during his lifetime. Only in death would Shah Jahan and Mumtaz Mahal be reunited. When the deposed emperor passed away in the winter of 1666, his body was interred next to his wife's.

After entering, you'll be just over 100m from the Taj Mahal. The tomb itself is perched atop a large pedestal of white marble. The path to the Taj, from the original entry arch (now the exit) is one of the best-executed architectural approaches in the world. The path of approach shifts from the central axis, paralleling the long reflecting pool and then winding around a central, raised lily pond—this controlled meandering yields sublimely subtle changes of perspective. (Past the pond, photography is forbidden, though in practice few follow this rule.) At the base of the tomb's platform, visitors must pause to remove or cover their shoes. This distraction combines with the shadowy staircase leading up to the top to take your mind off the monument just long enough to make the Taj's reemergence that much more sublime. Close up, the Taj is hardly white at all: precious stones are painstakingly inlaid in the marble to create the meandering floral patterns, framed by elegant Arabic script.

While much of the tomb's interior is off-limits, visitors can enter the dim, echoing chamber that contains the cenotaphs of Shah Jahan and Mumtaz Mahal. The cenotaphs are adorned with detailed inlay work; Mumtaz Mahal's is inlaid with the 99 names of Allah. In keeping with the principles of Mughal tomb design, the cenotaphs merely point the way: the real tombs of Shah Jahan and Mumtaz Mahal lie directly below in a musty, unspectacular room. Outside, the platform affords views of the Taj's **mosque,** to the west, and the **Jawab** (Answer), its architectural mirror, to the east. North is the muddy Yamuna—a popular local myth says that Shah Jahan planned a mirror-Taj, constructed of black marble, across the river from his wife's tomb.

A small **museum** on the west side of the gardens showcases paintings of Shah Jahan and Mumtaz Mahal and architectural renderings of the complex—but few take the time to visit it. If you're in the mood for a massive, ogling crowd, come on Fridays, when admission is free. If you'd prefer a more serene, private audience, show

The Ultimate Kodak Moment

Any visit to the Taj Mahal is accompanied by the clicking of shudders, the whirring of servo motors, and the din of voices shouting "Cheese!" in a dozen languages. People come to the Taj Mahal to photograph it, or rather to be photographed in front of it, and the Taj does not disappoint. Friendly cameramen at the exit gate photograph tour-group after tour-group grinning in front of Shah Jahan's sublime expression of grief. They'll even work the perspective so it looks like you're lifting the tomb from its top, like some oversized onion. "Gardeners" patrol the grounds, eager to show shutterbugs the right spot for that perfect photographic angle, in exchange for a little *baksheesh*. For the ultimate exposure, though, you'll have to go a little further afield—to the other side of the Yamuna. Since there are no bridges near the tomb, this involves a lengthy auto-rickshaw journey (Rs30-40 roundtrip) and a sizeable chunk of time. But if your camera craves that shot of the dome at dawn, reflected in the river, it's worth the trek.

up at dawn, preferably between Monday and Thursday—you'll have the place to yourself, but you'll have to pay extra for the privilege. Also, keep in mind that changing light patterns affect the aesthetic experience of seeing the Taj. On a cloudless day, the Taj exudes a piercingly bright, almost angular white light; in the early morning and toward twilight, the Taj looks softer and grayer—different, but no less beautiful.

Agra Fort

Location: *Between Yamuna Kinara Rd. and Powerhouse Bus Stand, 1.5km upriver from the Taj Mahal.* **Hours:** *Open daily sunrise-sunset.* **Admission:** *Rs12.*

While the Taj Mahal is surely the most magnificent monument raised by the Mughals in Agra, the sprawling, stolid Agra Fort finishes a respectable second, even though much of it is off-limits to visitors. Emperor Akbar initiated construction of the massive fort in 1565. The stronghold was strengthened over the years, and Emperor Aurangzeb completed the fort's 2.5km bulky, red sandstone walls. Of the three outer gates that lead through the walls and into the fort, only the **Amar Singh Gate,** decorated with colorful glazed tiles, is accessible to the public. The gate is named for a Rajasthani maharaja who killed the royal treasurer before the emperor's eyes and jumped the wall here in 1644 to escape the guards.

Due north of the Amar Singh Gate is the breezy **Diwan-i-Am** (Hall of Public Audience), a low three-sided structure that served as Shah Jahan's court while Agra was the Mughal capital. In Agra's Mughal heyday, the Diwan-i-Am was filled with nobles, courtiers, and regal accoutrements, including heavy drapes and lustrous carpets. Shah Jahan sat on his throne, which was perched atop the graceful platform at the east side of the hall. The low marble platform in front of the throne was reserved for his chief minister. The tomb at the courtyard's center belongs to a British officer who was slain here during the Mutiny of 1857.

In the **royal chambers,** which are wedged between the eastern ends of Diwan-i-Am and Agra Fort's ramparts, the emperor slept, prayed, and entertained himself in privacy. From Diwan-i-Am, the first chamber is the expansive **Macchi Bhavan** (Fish Palace), which gets its name from the fish that were dumped into its water channels so that the emperor could amuse himself with rod and reel. The chamber as it now stands is not as elegant as it once was—blocks of mosaic work and huge chunks of the royal bath have been pillaged over the centuries. In the northwest corner (left with your back to Diwan-i-Am) of the Macchi Bhavan is the pleasantly petite **Nagina Masjid** (Gem Mosque) built by Shah Jahan for the women of his *zenana* (harem).

Southeast of Macchi Bhavan is the fabulous **Diwan-i-Khas** (Hall of Private Audience), completed in 1637, where the emperor received VIPs amid gentle breezes off the Yamuna. The **terrace** just east of Diwan-i-Khas offers views of the Yamuna and Taj Mahal. Just south of the terrace is the sturdy, two-storied **Musamman Burj** (Octagonal Tower) with dense inlay work. Legend has it that Shah Jahan lived his final hours here, as an imprisoned man staring out wistfully at his Taj Mahal (mirrors on each

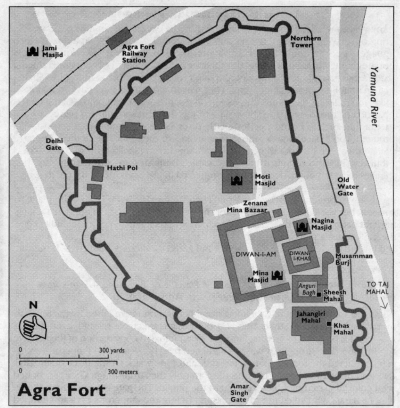

Agra Fort

Map labels: Jami Masjid · Agra Fort Railway Station · Northern Tower · Yamuna River · Delhi Gate · Hathi Pol · Moti Masjid · Old Water Gate · Zenana Mina Bazaar · Nagina Masjid · DIWAN-I-AM · DIWAN-I-KHAS · Musamman Burj · Mina Masjid · Anguri Bagh · Sheesh Mahal · TO TAJ MAHAL · Jahangiri Mahal · Khas Mahal · N · 0 300 yards · 0 300 meters · Amar Singh Gate

wall had a reflection of the Taj). On a grimmer note, the emperor peered with plea-sure at men, tigers, and elephants pitted against one another in the cramped area between the inner and outer walls. Heading south from the tower, it's a hop, skip, and a jump to **Sheesh Mahal** (Palace of Mirrors), where the women of the court bathed. South of Sheesh Mahal is a breezy enclosure that includes the 80m-square **Anguri Bagh** (Vine Garden). On the east side of the garden are three buildings: the **Khas Mahal** (Private Palace) is at the center, flanked by the **Golden Pavilions.** Ren-dered in cool marble, the **Khas Mahal** is reportedly where the emperor slept. The pavilions seem to have been women's bedrooms, with walls that were discreetly packed with hidden jewelry. Note the pavilions' roofs, which were built to look like the roofs of Bengali thatched huts. The **Jahangiri Mahal,** the large sandstone palace to the south, was designed for the Hindu queen Jodhi Bai. The minute etchings and detail in the stone make it look like timber. Once bright gold and blue, the palace's now-faded color is still marvelous. In front of this palace is a large tub, thought to be where Queen Nur Jahan took her rose-scented baths.

Other Sights

The **Jama Masjid** (Friday Mosque) is 100m west of Agra Fort Railway Station. Made mostly of sandstone spliced with ornamental marble, Jama Masjid is Agra's main mosque. Built by Shah Jahan in 1648, the mosque complex was damaged during the Mutiny of 1857, when British forces deemed its main gate a threat to the strategically important Red Fort; the gate was promptly leveled along with some of the front clois-ters of the mosque. For a while, all of Jama Masjid was even held as a sort of hostage-at-gunpoint—the mosque was planted with explosives, and the British authorities loudly proclaimed that if the Mutiny gained a large enough following in Agra, the Jama Masjid would suffer the consequences. The building stayed standing, though it remains in pretty bad shape today.

Across one the four bridges from Agra over the Yamuna are a few other remnants of Mughal days of yore, all of which are open from sunrise to sunset. A small, squat, and entirely exquisite tomb, **Itimad-ud-Daulah** is much less crowded than its cross-river rivals. *(Admission Rs12.)* The tomb was built between 1622 and 1628 for Ghiyas Beg, a Persian diplomat who served as Emperor Jahangir's chief minister and was dubbed Itimad-ud-Daulah (Pillar of Government) for his loyal and exemplary service. Situated in an intimate garden designed by Ghiyas Beg, the tomb itself was built by his daughter Nur Jahan, whom Jahangir married in 1611. The semi-precious stones inlaid throughout the tomb's white marble give it a dense, dazzling beauty. Several of Nur Jahan's relatives were subsequently buried in the central tomb.

One kilometer north of Itimad-ud-Daulah is the **Chini-ka-Rauza** (China Tomb), the decayed burial chamber of Shah Jahan's chief minister, Afzal Khan. Glazed tiles once covered the entire construction—the few that are left are severely weathered. Continuing north, it's 2km to **Ram Bagh,** a garden said to have been designed by Babur. Though there is talk of restoring it, the scruffy-looking garden is overgrown with weeds. The ruins host peacocks and wild flora—but few foreigners come here, and women shouldn't visit alone.

∎ Near Agra: Sikandra सिकांद्रा

A small town just outside Agra, Sikandra is famous as the home of **Akbar's Tomb.** Akbar, who ruled as the Mughal emperor between 1556 and 1605, was a great patron of the visual arts and a respectful admirer of Hinduism. The most impressive of the constructions at the tomb complex is the outlandishly outsized **Buland Darwaza** (Gateway of Magnificence). Embellished with geometric patterns and Qur'anic inscriptions, the gate is a bulky, blocky beauty. The expansive tomb complex is divided into quadrants by unusually wide pathways. Akbar's central mausoleum is sparsely adorned with colonnaded alcoves and marble domes. A ramp on the south side of the mausoleum leads to Akbar's humid, relatively humble crypt. A lonely candle and incense sticks render the final resting place of this greatest of the Mughals reminiscent of a Sufi shrine. One of the many embroidered cloths that cover Akbar's grave was given by Indira Gandhi. Mornings and evening are pleasantly less crowded while on Fridays the joint jumps with the usual mix of hawkers, hustlers, and picnickers. The untended grassy area between the north wall of the mausoleum and the wall that encloses the entire complex is an entertaining place—monkeys, deer, and pea-

---

Mughal Mausolea: What a Way to Go!

The Mughal emperors left a trail of exquisite palaces, impregnable forts, and enormous mosques across India. But the most glorious physical testimony to India's Islamic golden age must be their gorgeous garden tombs. The Taj Mahal, which has set the global standard for architectural elegance since its construction, is only the most celebrated example of a highly developed tradition.

The Taj's "cross-in-a-square" floor plan derives from the Persian pleasure pavilion where the first Mughal emperor, Babur, spent the few idle moments of his youth in Afghanistan and Central Asia. He introduced the design to India when he ordered the construction of four boats shaped like bisected right angles, or short arrows. He had the peculiar vessels lashed together in the middle of the Yamuna River near Delhi to form a floating cross-in-a-square pleasure pavilion.

Babur's son Humayun spent his years of exile in the Persian capital, Isfahan. Perhaps the monumental cityscape there inspired him to employ the hitherto purely sybaritic, secular scheme in his own tomb in Delhi. Like all subsequent rulers, he placed the mausoleum on a platform in the middle of formally-quartered *charbagh* gardens—an allusion to Qur'anic images of paradise.

cocks accentuate the architectural grandeur of Akbar's Tomb. Sikandra is quite accessible: auto-rickshaw-*wallahs* typically charge about Rs75 for a roundtrip journey, and Mathura-bound buses, which can be boarded at the station or along Mathura Rd., all pass Akbar's tomb. (Open dawn-dusk. Admission Rs12, free F.)

■ Fatehpur Sikri फ़ातहपुर सिकरी

Despite having the Mughal universe in the palm of his hand, Emperor Akbar, who ruled from 1556 to 1605, lacked what he most desired: a son to take his place. Although he covered all his bases by keeping three wives—one Hindu, one Muslim, one Christian—Akbar's quest for a successor became so desperate that he ventured out of Agra. Wandering through the village of Sikri, Akbar came across a Sufi mystic named Shaykh Salim Chishti, who consoled the ruler, promising him no fewer than three sons. When, a year later, the first foretold son arrived, Akbar repaid the saint not only by naming his son Salim (later known as Jehangir), but by moving the entire court nearer to the saint's village of Sikri. So, to the disbelief of the whole population of Agra, the palace of Fatehpur Sikri became the new capital of the Mughal empire.

After the hasty construction of an exquisite and original palace, Fatehpur Sikri served as the Mughal center for 15 years before the court shifted back to Agra. Some say that drought forced the Mughals out, while others claim that the death of Shaykh Salim prompted the move. In any case, the abrupt decision left an immaculate ghost-palace in its wake. Still ringing with the decrees of Akbar and the melodies of Miyan Tansen the pristine Fatehpur Sikri casts a haunting spell on visitors, especially at dawn and dusk, when the sun performs colorful dances in the palace courtyards.

ORIENTATION AND PRACTICAL INFORMATION Vehicles drive into Fatehpur Sikri from an access to the east of the palace complex—a fee of Rs5 per passenger is assessed at the entry gate. The deserted city sits atop a hill overlooking the not-so-modern Sikri village, to the south. If arriving by bus or train, it's a five-minute walk up the hill to the city complex. Akbar's city complex is open daily, dawn to dusk.

Most services, including a **bank,** are near the bus stand, though it's difficult to change hard currency or traveler's checks. In desperate cases, ask around at the hotels at the base of the **Buland Darwaza,** the huge gate on the south entrance of **Jama Masjid. Buses** head to: **Agra** (every 30min., 6am-7pm, 1hr., Rs12); **Bharatpur** (5 per day, 1hr., Rs8); and infrequently to **Jaipur.** An **auto-rickshaw** to Bharatpur takes about 30min. (Rs50). **Trains** to Agra leave daily at 5:30, 11am, and 4pm. **(Telephone Code:** 05619.)

ACCOMMODATIONS AND FOOD All hotels in Fatehpur Sikri are within walking distance of the palace. In peak season (Oct.-Mar.) hotels fill up and prices may rise by 25%. The best place to stay is in one of the three rooms at the **Archaeological Survey Rest House** (tel. 882248), just east of Diwan-i-Am in the ruins. For only Rs9 per night, you're within sight of the palace and have access to an inexpensive, old-style dining hall. Rooms must be booked ahead of time at the **ASI office** at 22 the Mall in Agra (tel. (0562) 363506). The **Maurya Rest House** (tel. 882348), down the steps from the base of Buland Darwaza, has spacious, almost tidy rooms off a lovely, tucked-away garden patio. Some rooms are dark, others gorgeous (singles Rs 60-80; doubles with toilet and shower Rs120, with air-cooling Rs150). Down the path to the bus stand right next to the Whiskey Shop, the **Shree Tourist Guest House** (tel. 882276) has roomy rooms (some with attached bath), a pleasant roof area, tiny kitchen, and a common bath off the front balcony (singles Rs80; doubles Rs100, with air-cooling Rs150). East of the Govardhu, about 1km from the monument, U.P. Tourism's **Gulistan Tourist Complex** (tel. 2490) feels like a Mughal palace—though here they have swing sets, cows, and meticulously kept singles and doubles for Rs400-450. (Doubles with A/C Rs700. Beds in 12-bed dorm Rs75 each. Off-season discount 15%.)

Come chow time, indulge in a Rs25 *thali* at Haji Abdali Gani Urf's **Kallu Restaurant,** now managed by the *haji*'s ultra-mellow son. The food is tasty, and the 40-lay-

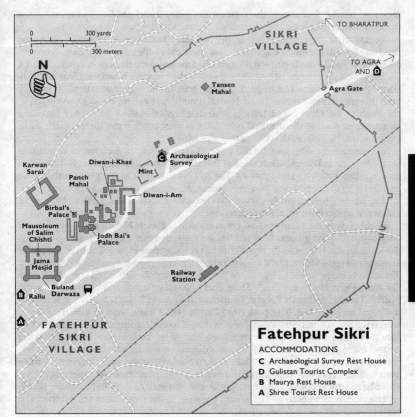

Fatehpur Sikri

0 ——— 300 yards
0 ——— 300 meters

N

TO BHARATPUR

SIKRI VILLAGE

TO AGRA AND D

Tansen Mahal

Agra Gate

Karwan Sarai

Diwan-i-Khas

Panch Mahal

Birbal's Palace

Mausoleum of Salim Chishti

Mint

Archaeological Survey

Diwan-i-Am

Jodh Bai's Palace

Jama Masjid

Railway Station

Buland Darwaza

B Kallu

A

FATEHPUR SIKRI VILLAGE

Fatehpur Sikri
ACCOMMODATIONS
C Archaeological Survey Rest House
D Gulistan Tourist Complex
B Maurya Rest House
A Shree Tourist Rest House

ered *lachcha paratha* (Rs25) traces its origins all the way back to Emperor Akbar (open daily 7am-11pm). For a real feast and classier food, the Gulistan Tourist Complex offers lunch and dinner buffets (Rs200), and Indian dishes (Rs30-70).

SIGHTS Wherever tourists and their buses congregate, so do **guides** eager to offer tours of the deserted palace. Many of these "guides" falsely claim to be licensed; others insist they are students whose "duty" it is to show you around, only afterwards fishing for *baksheesh,* or leading you right into their handicraft shops. Even so, it may be helpful to have someone show you around—just pick someone who speaks good English and don't pay more than Rs40-50.

The base of the **Buland Darwaza** is 13m above street level and its gate stands 40m above that, making it the tallest in Asia. The gate was only added to the complex in 1595, following Akbar's triumph in Gujarat; its style was copied by other Victory Gates around the country. As you pass through the gate, take off your shoes (either deposit them for Rs2 or tote them around). The head of the sprawling **Jama Masjid** is off to the left, facing Mecca. In the middle is the pure white **mausoleum** of **Shaykh Salim Chishti,** the sage who prophesied the birth of Akbar's sons. The core of the tomb is mother of pearl, and visitors who desire the recommendation of Shaykh Salim to God to fulfil their wishes can hang a thread from the marble latticework walls. The story of Shaykh Salim's "summoning" of Akbar's sons brings many son-less women here to pray. The calligraphy on the entrance is typical of Muslim funerary inscription—paradise is for those who do good deeds. Pungent incense burning on the inside and *qawwali* singers on the outside complete the sensory stimuli. It's customary to leave a small donation (Rs5-10) at the tomb itself. Coming out of the mosque, head left through the other main gate, **Badshani Darwaza,** and cross through the parking lot across the palace complex to the east.

Coming from the east, you'll pass the **Naubat Khana** (Drum House), which was used to signal the emperor's arrival, and the ticket office for the palace complex (admission Rs12). Both paths lead into the **Diwan-i-Am,** the court where, from a throne perched between two sandstone slates, the emperor heard the pleas and petitions of common men. The stone ring in the grass to the northeast is thought to have held down either *shamiana* (huge festival tents) or, as a more sinister version has it, the leash of the Elephant of Justice, who determined guilt or innocence by either trampling or sparing the accused men. To the west toward the throne is the main courtyard of the palace (don't forget your ticket).

For orientation's sake, look for the stone plaques in front of each structure. Starting off to the right is **Diwan-i-Khas** (Hall of Private Audience). Here, Akbar is thought to have spoken with VIPs and relatives. The hall is a massive chamber supported in the middle by an overwhelmingly ornate column, meant to represent an opening flower. To the left is a meticulously carved gazebo, thought to be the sitting chamber of either the treasurer or royal astrologer.

Looming over the courtyard on the west side is **Panch Mahal,** a five-story tower with columns—the ground floor has 84, the top only four. You can walk up through the stairs on the west side. Access to the top is sometimes closed, but even the lower levels afford great views. On the south side of the courtyard is a grid tank called **Anup Talao,** the choice venue of legendary Mughal crooner Miyan Tansen (see also **Come On Baby Fight My Fire,** p. 263) More finely carved columns and walls decorate the nearby **Turkish Sultana's Palace.** To the north of Anup Talao stands what served as the royal **banquet hall.** The path from Panch Mahal leads west to **Birbal's Palace,** which housed the minister's daughters or one of Akbar's queens. On the way back to Panch Mahal, a small **garden,** really a lawn, sits off to the left. Legend holds that the bratty young prince Salim, later Jehangir, courted his future wife Nur Jahan here.

Before Panch Mahal, in the middle of the courtyard, is the small **Mariam's Palace** with fading, eerie wall paintings, left over from the palace's more vivid glory days. From here, proceed south and cut right to the entrance of **Jodh Bai's Palace,** which reverberates with Persian voices of days gone by. In the large courtyard, symmetrical patterns and sandstone flowers surround a central fountain (thought to hold *tulsi,* a medicinal plant). The pigeons and green parrots who nest in the dark, urine-stinky chambers add color to the courtyard. Most likely, this complex was used for the harem—apparently a great necessity for a man with only three or four wives. Note the azure-glazed tiles on the roof along the second story. The path out of the palace leads right, and brings you back into the parking lot leading toward the Jama Masjid.

■ Mathura मथुरा

The city of Mathura teems with thousands of temples, where devotees celebrate the birthplace of Krishna. Innumerable Vaishnava pilgrims come each year for Janmashtami, the celebration of Krishna's birth, to pay homage to the blue-skinned hero of Hindu lore. They'll pass the butter pot on Sept. 3, 1999 and Aug. 22, 2000. But even between sessions of worship, the city of nearly 300,000 bustles with a spirited zeal, and though a bit bland and grimy in places, Mathura is a convenient stop on the way into (or out of) Agra.

ORIENTATION

At the heart of Mathura is the bazaar, stretching north from the **Holi Gate,** on the eastern part of town near the Yamuna River. The **old bus stand** is 500m south of the Holi Gate, while the more frequently used **new bus stand** is 1km west and 500m south of the old one. The town's other major landmark is the temple **Shri Krishna Janmasthan (Janmbhoomi),** dedicated to the site of Krishna's birth and 2km northwest of the new bus stand.

PRACTICAL INFORMATION

Trains: The **railway station** is 1.5km south of the new bus stand. Fares listed for 2nd/1st class. To: **Agra** (*Jodhpur-Varanasi Marudhar Exp.* 4864, 8:55pm, 1hr., Rs28/156); **Delhi** (*Punjab Mail* 1037, 5:39pm, 3hr.; *Kerala Exp.* 2625, 12:50pm, 2½hr., Rs34/176); **Gwalior** (*Amritsar-Dadar Exp.* 1458, 11:44pm, 4hr., Rs45/217); **Jhansi** (*Amritsar-Dadar Exp.* 1458, 11:44pm, 6hr., Rs62/312); **Kanpur** (*Jodhpur-Varanasi Marudhar Exp.* 4844, 8:55pm, 6½hr., Rs66/327); **Mumbai** (*Paschim Exp.* 2926, 7:20pm, 20hr., Rs184/952).

Buses: From the **New Bus Stand** to: **Agra** (every 30min. 7am-10pm, 2hr., Rs20); **Bharatpur** (every 30min. 6am-10pm, 1hr., Rs15); **Delhi** (every hr., 6am-9pm, 4hr., Rs45); **Jaipur** (every 30min. 7am-10:30pm, 6hr., Rs80). From the **Old Bus Stand** (tel. 406468), **U.P. Roadways** buses ply to: **Dehra Dun** (5am, 9hr., Rs125); **Haridwar** (10pm, 8hr., Rs125); **Jhansi** (4:30am, 12hr., Rs100); **Varanasi** (2:30pm, 16hr., Rs230); **Vrindaban** (4 per day, 30min., Rs5).

Local Transportation: Stretch **tempos** cruise to Vrindaban (Rs5) and around town, as do **cycle-** (temple to New Bus Stand Rs10) and **auto-rickshaws** (Rs15).

Tourist Office: U.P. Tourism (tel. 405351), north end of the old bus stand, 2nd fl. Campy brochures, no maps, but they know temples. Open M-Sa 10am-5pm.

Currency Exchange: Main Branch, **State Bank of India** (tel. 407647), 1km east of the new bus stand, near the railway, changes cash and traveler's checks.

Market: The **bazaar**, selling everything from chutneys to drums, extends just south and a long way north of Holi Gate. A **fruit market** is next to Jama Masjid.

Hospital: District Hospital (tel. 403006 or 406315), near the old bus stand. **Methodist Hospital,** Jaising Pura, Vrindaban Rd. (tel. 406032).

Post Office: A branch is in the complex next to the temple. **Postal Code:** 281001.

Telephones: STD/ISD booths are packed near Holi Gate. **Telephone Code:** 0565.

ACCOMMODATIONS

Location is probably the most important factor when choosing your digs in Mathura, since the bus stands, Shri Krishna Temple, and the old city are not within easy walking distance of each other. The area near the Holi Gate is the liveliest, noisiest part of town, though Shri Krishna has Hindi pop blaring all day. Mathura has a few **ashrams,** including **Keshvjee Gaudig,** across and up from the old bus stand (Rs50 per room).

International Rest House (tel. 405888), in the complex just east of the entrance to the temple. Inexpensive rooms for pilgrims, as well as a garden where they kick up their feet. Singles Rs30; doubles Rs50, with bath Rs110.

Hotel Brij Raj (tel. 406232), opposite and a bit down the street from the temple. Large lavender rooms set around a plant-filled courtyard have huge beds and clean attached bath. Balcony is unfortunately accessible to the public. Doubles Rs200.

Gaurav Guest House (tel. 406192). Walk 100m south of the Government Museum and turn left in a narrow alley in the neighborhood of Dampler Nagar. Simple rooms have squishy, soft beds, table, and mirror. Common bath is reasonably clean. Owner speaks English and is an enthusiastic pun-ster. Check-out noon. Singles with air-cooling Rs150; doubles Rs225, with bath Rs300, with TV Rs350.

FOOD

The bazaar near the fruit market has inexpensive snacks. Across from the temple, cheap *dhabas,* such as the Prateek and the Madras Cafe, sell good South Indian food.

Hotel Brij Raj Cafe, across from the temple, below and to the side of Hotel Brij Raj. Superb *thali* (Rs25), a variety of Gaylord's ice cream treats, and fresh espresso pressed from the antique machine. Open daily 7:30am-10:30pm.

Brijwasi, across from the temple with another branch near Holi Gate. No eats except for tasty sweets. Open daily 7am-11pm.

Brij-Bhoj Restaurant, inside Hotel Mansarovar Palace, across from State Bank main branch. Chilled, elegant chamber with both meals and snacks—only the non-veg. items are pricey. *Pakora* as they're meant to be, *mutter paneer* (Rs20), cucumber salad (Rs15). Open daily 7am-11pm (snacks served 3-7pm, dinner 7-11pm).

SIGHTS

Most of the sights in Mathura revolve around Krishna, the playful boy-god whose birth put this town on the map. Pay a visit to the **Shri Krishna Janmasthan temple** to see the actual spot of Krishna's "appearance"—the original temple, Kesava Deo, was destroyed by Aurangzeb and replaced with a mosque. *(Open daily 5-11am and 4-9pm.)* The similar histories of the temple here and at Ayodhya, the birthplace of Rama, have made the authorities particularly cautious—visitors must check all belongings (bags, cameras, etc.) in the cloakroom off to the left (Rs2), pass through a metal detector, and undergo an overzealous frisking. Along with the souvenir shops, the complex includes several small shrines. The main shrine, located in the back of the complex to the right as you come in, is a cavernous, dim room marking the site of the birth and representing the prison cell Krishna was born into while the nefarious King Kamsa held his parents captive. Near the rear of the shrine, the heavy-duty barbed wire between the temple and mosque is sharp enough to cut the tension in the air. Nearby **Potara-Kund** is where Baby Krishna's diapers were supposedly washed.

Mathura's other attractions are on the east side of town. Continuing north from the bazaar, the **Dwarkadheesh Temple** is on the left. *(Open daily 5am-1pm and 4-9pm.)* Built in 1814 by pious local merchants, this temple is the main point of worship for local Hindus, and its interior colors are accentuated when the afternoon sun performs shadow dances on the wire-mesh roof. A bit south on the bazaar, the street forks off to the right toward the river and the sacred **Vishram Ghat,** where Krishna came to rest after slaying the menacing King Kamsa, and where many pseudo-priests, would-be guides, and not-so-needy beggars now congregate. Brush off unwanted attention or simply offer a kind "Lord Krishna" greeting and walk away. At the *ghats,* **boats** take visitors on an hour-long tour of the city's shore (Rs40-50), with a prime view of the dilapidated **Sati Bur,** built in 1570 and dedicated to the *sati* of Behari Mal. Sunset boat trips offer a front-row view of the nightly *aarti* ceremony, when priests bring fire to the sacred water amid the sound of gongs. You might be able to talk a few boat-*wallahs* into cruising you down the Yamuna all the way to Agra, a trip that involves an overnight stay (probably in a village barnyard). When negotiating a price, remember that you'll also have to buy food and whisky for the crew.

Back toward the bazaar and farther north is the **Jama Masjid,** the main mosque in town, built by Abo-in Nabir Khan in 1661. The mosque is unusually colorful, its teal domes brightening up the already striking bazaar and fruit market. From its height above street level, voyeurs can observe the goings-on below.

Aside from the mosques, Mathura's only site that is not related to Krishna is the **Government Museum** (tel. 408191), 1km northeast of the new bus stand and 1km west of the old bus stand. *(Open Tu-Su 10:30am-4:30pm. Free; camera fee Rs20.)* Founded in 1874, the museum houses one of the largest collections of ancient Indian sculpture. Its pieces shed light on Mathura's overall religious and cultural significance—for nearly 1200 years, Mathura served as the artistic center for early Indian, Indo-Scythian, and visiting Hellenistic cultures. The museum's true treasures are two Buddha statues from the 4th and 5th centuries which are in pristine condition. Sculptures are placed among the flora outside in the courtyard as well.

■ Vrindaban व्रिंदाबन

While Mathura, the birthplace of Krishna, draws a fair number of devotees, the main religious center of this area is the nearby town of Vrindaban, where a young and frisky Krishna is said to have performed the deeds for which he was later deified: lifting up the hill **Govardhan** (actually at the eponymous town nearby), jamming on his flute, and cavorting with all the *gopi*s (milkmaids) he could find. Legend has it that in order to dance with several maidens at the same time, Krishna would simply multiply himself. Ever since the Bengali teacher Chaitanya discovered the site's importance in Hindu legend, Vrindraban has been a huge draw for Vaishnava pilgrims, including elderly widows, whose ashrams are maintained by wealthy devotees, and the International Society for Krishna Consciousness (Hare Krishnas).

As medieval and rustic as the town feels in places, there are a fair number of con-men and would-be guides (pay no more than Rs30-50 for a tour of the temples). **Buses, trains,** and **tempos** from Mathura arrive south of the heart of town, a labyrinthine and often confusing tangle of narrow streets. There are small restaurants, a few basic hotels, and tea stalls near the major temples for mid-worship munchies. It's also possible to stay at ISKCON (see below).

The **Govind Dev Temple** is a squat, sprawling edifice in the shape of a Greek cross. It lacks the characteristic *gopuram* of most temples and the top four stories were destroyed by Aurangzeb and never replaced. Rhesus monkeys hang out on the meticulously handcarved overhangs outside, while bats crowd the temple on the inside. (Open daily 5:30am-noon and 4-8pm.)

One hundred meters northeast of the Govind Dev is the **Rangnathji Temple,** India's longest. Seth Govind Das combined Rajput and South Indian designs when he built the temple in 1851. The 15m **Dhwaja Stambha,** the central column, is said to be plated in gold. Non-Hindus are not permitted inside, but this rule is laxly enforced. You can also catch a glimpse of the shimmer through either entrance. Photographing the column is not permitted and the *pandits* in the temple take this rule quite seriously. (Temple open 5:30am-1pm and 4-8pm.) In two small galleries next to the entrance gate, twitching robotic puppets dramatize episodes from Lord Krishna's life, including his mellow interaction with the ecstatic *gopis.* (Open daily 5:30am-noon and 4-8pm. Admission Rs1.)

Of the other more notable temples in Vrindaban, the **Madan Mohan Temple,** along the Yamuna near Kali Ghat, has a small shrine in the base of its tall sandstone tower, today sprouting a good amount of flora. Other popular sights include the dilapidated **Radha Ballabh Temple,** dating from 1626, the more modern **glass temple,** east of the Rangnathji Temple, and the popular **Bankey Bihari,** literally "crooked Krishna," named for Krishna's famously bent body. (Open daily 9am-1pm and 6-10pm.)

None of the holy places in Vrindaban draws more foreigners than the **Krishna Balram Temple** (tel. (0565) 442478; open daily 4:30am-8:30pm), the dazzling marble house of worship of **ISKCON,** the International Society for Krishna Consciousness. The founder of the society, Srila Prabhupada, lived and worked here before embarking at the advanced age of 69 on a world tour to spread the word of Krishna consciousness. Next to three shrines and several murals of Krishna's exploits is a life-like mannequin of Prabhupada over his burial site. This part of the temple echoes with chants, drums, and donation requests. Still, the whole place is soul-soothingly placid. In the back is a clean **restaurant** serving great Indian breakfasts (Rs16) with ginger tea and *chiku* milkshakes (Rs8-12). There is also a **guest house** with 45 clean doubles with attached bath for Rs200. Hare Krishnas, who come here from all over the world, are delighted to talk to newcomers. The temple is likely to be full during August, September, and March. An enlightening **museum** dedicated to Prabhupada displays the *swami*'s rooms as he kept them, including books, clothes, jars of vaseline, and other toiletries he used while here. (Open daily 9am-4:30pm. Free.)

■ Lucknow लखनऊ

On the surface, Uttar Pradesh's capital looks much like any big city: political posters are glued everywhere, and government institutions lurk behind many of the city's walls. This facade covers up an older, more cherished Lucknow—a city that was the center of Indian Muslim culture for the century before 1947. Lucknow's citizens are said to have spoken the most poetic Urdu, cultivated fine music and dance, and inspired great architecture.

The city's name is thought to derive from Lakshmana, who reputedly received Lucknow as a fief from his brother, the Hindu god (and king) Rama. Modern Lucknow, however, grew up around a 13th-century fort, and its glory days began after 1775, when it became capital of Avadh (Oudh), one of the small kingdoms born out of the collapsing Mughal Empire. Asaf-ud-Daula and subsequent *nawabs* (rulers) of Avadh made Lucknow a cultural center. They were, however, sorry rulers, more interested in their dancers, *hijras,* and *hookahs* than in their subjects. This made the river town of Lucknow prime picking for the East India Company, which annexed Avadh without a fight in 1856. The annexation and other events led to the following year's rebellion (see **Mutiny and Aftermath,** p. 83).

A pair of fish, the emblem of the *nawabs,* can still be seen all over Lucknow, and traditions such as *chikan* embroidery endure, along with the cherished Urdu language and script. But much has changed since the Partition of India in 1947, when many of the city's Muslims migrated to Pakistan, leaving the city to steer itself into a new era (see **After Independence,** p. 85). Now the fine old Lucknowi brickwork competes with the concrete chaos of a modern Indian city of 1.8 million.

The Shi'a Muslim commemoration of Muharram (also known as Ashoora), the martyrdom of the Prophet Muhammed's son, is the most exciting time to be in Lucknow. Non-Muslims write pathos-laden elegies in honor of the martyrs of Karbala, and join Muslims in the firewalking ceremonies that take place in the *imambaras.* In 1999, the festival falls around April 27; in 2000, April 15.

ORIENTATION

Lucknow occupies the south bank of the **Gomti River** and extends far inland. **Hazratganj** is the center of the city—a stay here makes Lucknow more manageable because of the nearby bookstores, the post office, the police station, and a plentitude of restaurants. The main road in this area is **Mahatma Gandhi (M.G.) Marg,** a wide street with the spiffiest shops and densest concentration of hotels and restaurants. M.G. Marg runs through the city northwest to southeast before sweeping south and out of the city. To the northwest is **Husainabad.** Many of Lucknow's monuments are located on **Husainabad Trust Road.**

The main railway station (and one of the bus stations) is at **Charbagh** in the south. The way from Charbagh to Hazratganj is a major route, going along **Motilal Nehru Marg** and then **Vidhan Sabha Marg** past the state legislature (Vidhan Sabha). **Subhash Road** will take you almost directly from Charbagh to Husainabad, making for a roughly Hazratganj-Husainabad-Charbagh triangle. In the middle of the triangle is **Aminabad,** an old bazaar area.

PRACTICAL INFORMATION

Transportation

Airport: Amousi Airport (tel. 436132 or 436352), 11km from Charbagh. Hire a tempo (Rs15) or auto-rickshaw (Rs100) in front of the main railway station. **Indian Airlines** (tel. 220927) flies to: **Calcutta** (M, W, F, and Su, 2hr., US$140); **Delhi** (7am daily, 8pm M, W, F, Sa, 1hr., US$70); **Patna** (M,W,F, and Su, 1hr., US$90); **Mumbai** (Tu, Th, 2hr., US$225).

Trains: Lucknow Station, Charbagh, 3km from Hazratganj. Tempos follow fixed routes between Station Rd. (100m in front of the station) and Chowk, Aminabad, Kaiserbagh, and Lalbagh/Hazratganj. Fares listed are 2nd/1st class. To: **Allahabad** (*Delhi Bareilly Exp.* 4556, 4:25pm, 5hr., Rs56/266; *Bareilly-Mughalsarai Exp.* 4308, 10pm, 9½hr., Rs56/266); **Ayodhya** (*Farakka Exp.* 3484, Tu, Th-F, and Su 7:20am; *Saryu Yamuna Exp.* 4650, M, W, and Sa 6:10am; 3hr., Rs38/200); **Delhi** (*Shatabdi Exp.* 2003, 3:20pm, 6½hr., Rs450 A/C chair; *Lucknow Mail* 4229, 10pm, 9hr., Rs101/511); **Faizabad** (*Farakka Exp.* 3484, Tu, Th-F, and Su 7:20am, 2½hr., Rs38/200); **Gorakhpur** (*Jammu-Tawi Gorakhpur Exp.* 5088, 3:55pm, 5½hr., Rs65/321); **Kanpur** (*Shatabdi Exp.* 2003, 3:20pm, 1½hr., Rs22/120).

Buses: The **main bus station** is located on Station Rd. From the railway station, walk out the entrance 100m to the main road out front. Take a left; the station is 100m down on the right. Buses are cheap, but be prepared for frequent stops and overcrowding. All timetables are in Hindi. English timetables are difficult to procure, although the men in the office nearest the reservation counter are helpful. To: **Agra** (every hr., 5:30am-10:30pm, Rs125); **Allahabad** (every hr., Rs75); **Ayodhya**

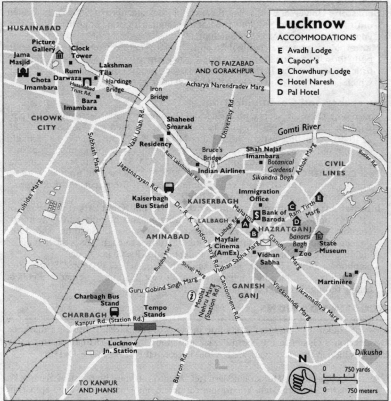

Lucknow

ACCOMMODATIONS

E Avadh Lodge
A Capoor's
B Chowdhury Lodge
C Hotel Naresh
D Pal Hotel

(every hr., Rs46); **Delhi** (every 30min., Rs130); **Gorakhpur** (every hr., Rs90); **Faiz-abad** (every hr., Rs44); **Varanasi** (9 per day, 3am-8pm; Rs90). Another bus station is located in **Kaiserbagh** and services **Kathmandu.** Take a tempo from Station Rd.

Local Transportation: Unmetered **auto-rickshaws** and **tempos** wait outside Lucknow Station—be prepared to haggle. A rickshaw to Hazratganj costs Rs10, but only after much bargaining (a 1hr. ride should be less than Rs30). There are no official tempo stops, although tempos do follow a fixed route. Go to a main road, flag one down, and ask if the driver goes where you're going. Repeat if necessary.

Tourist and Financial Services

Tourist Office: U.P. Government Tourist Reception Centre, Charbagh (tel. 452533). Inside the Lucknow Railway Station. Helpful English-speaking staff. Daily A/C bus tours of the Nawabi Monuments (9am-2pm, Rs50). Call for reservations and English-speaking guides. Open daily 7am-8pm. **U.P. Tourist Office,** 3 Nawal Kishore Rd. (tel. 225165 or 228349), behind Hazratganj post office.

Immigration Office: Jawaharlal Bhavan Marg (tel. 280635). Take a rickshaw from M.G. Rd. (Rs5). Open M-Sa 10am-5pm.

Currency Exchange: State Bank of India (Main Branch), Motimahal Marg (tel. 213074), near Clarks Avadh Hotel. Open M-F 10am-2:30pm and Sa 10:30am-12:30pm. Foreign exchange branch of the **Bank of Baroda,** M.G. Rd. (tel. 215462), several doors down from the State Bank, opposite the British Library. Open M-F 10:30am-2:30pm, Sa 10:30am-12:30pm. **American Express:** M.G. Rd. (tel. 226534 or 212619; fax 212619), Mayfair Cinema Bldg., 2nd floor. Cash advances on AmEx. Cash AmEx traveler's checks with no fee. Open daily 9:30am-6:30pm.

Local Services

Bookstore: Universal Bookseller, 82 M.G. Rd., Hazratganj (tel. 225894). Take a left onto M.G. Rd. from Vidhan Sabha Marg. English fiction, English philosophy, English prices. Open M-Sa 9:30am-8pm.

Market: Main bazaars at **Aminabad** and **Chowk.** Tempos from Station Rd. go to both; those from Hazratganj go only to Chowk. Open daily dawn-dusk. At the main **fruit market** on Ram Tirth Marg (Nahri Bazaar), pick up the delicious mangoes for which Lucknow is known. Open daily dawn-midnight.

Emergency and Communications

Pharmacy: There are several pharmacies in Hazratganj; most open daily 8am-11pm.

Hospital: The main civil hospital is **Balrampur,** located near Kaisarbagh (tel. 224040). A smaller private hospital is **Nishat,** 3 J.C. Bose Marg, Kaisarbagh. Friendly and clean. 24hr. emergency services. Neither staff speaks much English.

Police: Hazratganj Police Station, M.G. Rd. (tel. 222555), opposite Mayfair Cinema.

Post Office: GPO, Vidhan Sabha Marg (tel. 222887). Take a right from M.G. Rd. to Vidhan Sabha. The GPO is a yellow building across the street. *Poste Restante.* Open M-Sa 8am-7pm. **Postal Code:** 226001.

Internet: Instant Communication Centre, 1 Sarojini Naidu Park (tel. 218445 or 219845), opposite Tulsi Petrol Pump near the State Bank of India. Surf away in A/C comfort (Rs60 per 15min.). **Fast Business Centre,** Faridi Building, 2nd floor, Hazratganj (tel. 210592/3). From M.G. Rd. turn down Lalbagh. FBS is the first major building on the right. Private A/C browsing booths (Rs200 per hour).

Telephones: 24hr. STD/ISD, 39/55 Ram Tirth Marg (tel. 275910 or 275948), after the Hotel Naresh. Incoming international calls cost Rs5/min.; international collect calling through AT&T. **Telephone Code:** 0522.

ACCOMMODATIONS

Most of Lucknow's budget hotels line noisy thoroughfares or bustling markets. Decent hotels cluster in the Narhi Bazaar area along the Ram Tirth Marg, and a few bargains hide in the Hazratganj area. Avoid hotels in the disreputable Old City.

Avadh Lodge, 1 Ram Mohan Raj Marg (tel. 282861). 10min. by rickshaw from M.G. Rd. Ask for Sikandra Bagh. The former residence of a Lucknow Raja and aptly (but marginally) pricier than the lodges near M.G. Rd. The most pleasant hotel in town, in a quiet neighborhood far from the action; nights are restful, even sans air-cooler. Spacious, clean rooms with attached baths and fans. Common lounge with color TV. Check-out noon. Singles Rs200, with air-cooling Rs290; doubles Rs300/390.

Chowdhury Lodge, 3 Vidhan Sabha Marg (tel. 221911 or 273135). From the railway station, take a tempo or cycle-rickshaw to Hazratganj. Nestled in an alleyway 20m before Vidhan Sabha Marg intersects M.G. Rd., the Lodge is an oasis in the heart of the city. Clean beds and bathrooms and accommodating staff. Hot water 5:30am-midnight. Bring mosquito repellent during the summer. Singles Rs75, with bath Rs120, with bath and air-cooling Rs180; doubles Rs150/190/230.

Hotel Naresh, Ram Tirth Marg (tel. 275160 or 285298). Walk 2 blocks past the intersection of Vidhan Sabha Marg and M.G. Rd. to the fork and veer right. The hotel is 400m to the left, through the Narhi Bazaar. Rooms available off the street and away from the noisy bazaar. Despite its proximity to the main fruit market, it isn't too buggy. Air-cooled singles Rs120, with TV Rs140; doubles Rs175/195.

Pal Hotel, Ram Tirth Marg (tel. 229476), 50m down Ram Tirth Marg on the right. In the heart of Narhi Bazaar, Mr. Pal runs a tight, no-frills hotel offering clean, basic accommodation. Hot water by the bucket. Room service Rs10-25. Check-out 24hr. Singles Rs90; doubles Rs120, with attached bath Rs160. Air cooler Rs25 extra.

Capoor's, 52 Hazratganj (tel. 223958), opposite the post office. Rooms offer great views of Hazratganj but shield the noise. Capoor's has cable TV, safe deposit box, and taxi service. Clean rooms and attached bath with running hot water. Air-cooled singles Rs300; doubles (with color TV) Rs400.

FOOD

Most good, cheap restaurants are located in the area around M.G. Rd., though *dhabas* and small cafes dot the entire city. Avadhi cuisine (kebabs and such cooked with distinctive spices) is hard to find, but some places offer one or two dishes.

Aahar Restaurant, Lalbagh. Turn left onto Lalbagh after the AmEx office on M.G. Rd. and head to the traffic circle. Walk up from street level into a clean, A/C bistro. Tasty food, especially the Kashmiri dishes, *pullao* (Rs30), and *kofta* (Rs40). Open daily 10am-11pm.

Ranjana, M.G. Rd., past the police station. Attracts a large and diverse clientele, including businessmen, office workers, college students, and families. Inexpensive North Indian (including kebabs for Rs18), and generous portions of South Indian and Chinese cuisines served in a cool, spacious hall decked-out with low plush couches. The staff is friendly but speaks little English. Open daily 10am-10pm.

Sharma Chat House, Lalbagh. From M.G. Rd., take a left onto Lalbagh; it will be on your right before the traffic circle. Famous for cheap *chaat* (Rs15), but not much else on the menu except for the scrumptious *gulab jamun.* Hot mineral water is available, but bring your own cold drinks. Open M-Sa 10am-10pm.

Mini Mahal, Hazratganj, on the right, opposite police station. Best breakfast in town (omelette with toast, Rs16). Crowded after 8pm. Open daily 10am-12:30am.

Falaknuma Restaurant, 9th fl., Clark's Avadh Hotel (tel. 220191). From M.G. Rd., take a 10min. rickshaw ride (Rs10). Overlooking the River Gomti on one side. Serves a full range of lamb and chicken kebabs (starting at Rs180) in a posh, romantic A/C dining room. Beer and cocktails at exorbitant prices (Rs150-300); live classical Indian music starts at 8:30pm. Lunch served noon-3pm, dinner 8-11pm.

SIGHTS

Husainabad

Foremost among Lucknow's buildings are the monuments raised by its decadent *nawabs.* Indian Muslim architecture of the 18th and 19th centuries is considered flamboyant and less perfected than the earlier, Mughal style, but in Lucknow it's the most visible sign of the wealth and power of days gone by. The grandiose decorated archways of the old city are great to drive through while being chauffeured like the *nawab* himself in your rickshaw. The biggest cluster of old buildings is on the northwest side of the city in the Husainabad area.

In 1784 a great famine inspired Nawab Asaf-ud-Daula to cook up the **Bara Imambara** as a food-for-work scheme. *(Open from sunrise to 7pm. Rs10 admission includes bauli, the Rumi Darwaza, and the Picture Gallery.)* An *imambara* is a replica of the tomb of one of the *imams,* descendants of the Prophet Muhammad who are revered by Shi'a Muslims. The Bara Imambara, built in honor of Hasan Ibn Ali, the second *imam,* is noted for sheer size and show (if not for beauty)—domes and arches mark the great blue hall, 50m long, 15m high, and 15m wide, without any internal structural beams. Running through its attic is the **Bhulbhulaiya,** a multilevel labyrinth built as entertainment for the women of the *nawab*'s harem. It might help to hire a guide for the Bhulbhulaiya—they claim to have undergone six months of training. Couples *must* be accompanied by a guide (lest the place's history prove too inspirational). The chaperone rule is an invitation for extortion. To the right of the Bara Imambara is Asaf-ud-Daula's mosque, more imposing than the *imambara,* but closed to non-Muslims. Opposite the mosque is the *bauli,* an old step-well with a five-story tower around it.

Straddling Husainabad Trust Rd. is the **Rumi Darwaza,** another work of Asaf-ud-Daula's. This gate, intended as a copy of the Sublime Port in Istanbul, is covered by a spine of trumpets. Your ticket from the Bara Imambara lets you climb it (or you can sneak in by walking along the wall from the Bara Imambara). There are good views of the River Gomti from the top. The **Picture Gallery** is located just past the 67m clock tower, inside an office building. *(Gallery open M-Sa 7am-7pm. Use your Bara Imambara ticket or purchase the Rs1 pass.)* An American artist supposedly painted the portraits of the *nawabs* pictured here in the late 19th century. It's a dusty and dimly lit gallery, but you get to see what the old boys looked like. Wajid Ali Shah even bares his left nipple to visitors.

Down Husainabad Trust Rd. and around the corner (down the road to the left after the Chota Imambara) is the **Jama Masjid,** whose construction was also initiated by Muhammad Ali Shah. This is Lucknow's largest mosque but is unfortunately closed to non-Muslims, though anyone can approach it and see its painted ceiling of leaf patterns and fruit bowls.

The Residency

Hours: *Open daily 9am-4:30pm.* **Admission:** *Rs2, free on Fridays.*

If the British Raj still governed India, the ruins of Lucknow's **Residency** would be one of its proudest monuments. This complex of scaly brick buildings in a shady park near the center of Lucknow stands much as it was left by the turmoil of 1857 when it was blasted by cannonballs. One of the lengthiest struggles of the great uprising (the Indian "Mutiny" or "Revolt," depending on who's talking) took place when rebelling *sepoys* (Indians enlisted in the East India Company's army) besieged Lucknow's British community from June to November of 1857. The Residency, a mansion for the East India Company's agent in Avadh, was turned into a fortress for the 3000 people who were trapped there. After three months Sir Henry Havelock arrived to relieve the Residency, only to wind up trapped with those he'd planned to liberate. It was another month and a half before Sir Colin Campbell was able to break the siege. Only a third of the original 3000 defenders survived, but it was a miracle that they had kept fighting at all, after four and a half months of hunger, disease, and skillful enemies taking pot-shots through their windows. The defence of the Residency was fashioned into a legend of British bravery. (See also **Mutiny and Aftermath,** p. 83.)

As you enter the complex through the Baillie Gate there are several buildings on the right and left that were used during the siege as hospitals and armories. The Residency building itself is beyond a wide lawn containing a monument to Sir Henry Lawrence, who gathered the British together and organized the Residency's defenses, only to be killed after four days of the siege. One tall tower still stands on the Residency building. A British cemetery is located near the river. There is a miniature version of the complex in the **Model Gallery,** but the model here seems to have endured some worse disaster than the actual buildings did in 1857. Other exhibits include weapons, old prints, and a rather stultified poem by Tennyson. Below the Model Gallery is the basement where many of the British women and children hid. Be careful when walking around the Residency; many shady characters frequent this decaying monument and harass single women or anyone else they find.

Other Sights and Museums

North of the Hazratganj area of downtown Lucknow is another *imambara*, the **Shah Najaf Imambara,** which holds the tomb of Nawab Ghazi-ud-din Haidar (r. 1814-27), and was also the base for the rebels of 1857, consists mainly of one large dome whose inside is painted with leafy patterns and decked with chandeliers. Shi'a Muslims come here to express their devotion to Shah-i Najaf, the first Shi'a *imam* and the spiritual successor of the Prophet, Ali Ibn Abi Talib. On the fifth of Muharram, fire-walking is conducted in the *imambara*'s complex. *(Open daily 6am-7pm.)* The lush **Botanical Gardens** in Sikandra Bagh draw early-morning walkers. *(Open Apr.-Oct. daily 5-8am; Nov.-Mar. 6-9am. Free.)* The plot once included Nawab Wajid Ali Shah's pleasure garden, where the final battle of 1857 for the relief of the Residency took place. Now it is home to the National Botanical Research Institute. The **State Museum** is located in the zoo. *(Open Tu-Su 10:30am-4pm. Zoo open Tu-Sa, 8am-5pm. Admission Rs6)* The collection of *nawab*-era relics is disappointing, and nothing here is particular to Lucknow; the museum also contains (for some unknown reason) an Egyptian mummy.

Finally, to the southeast of Lucknow by the side of the Gomti, is **La Martinière,** a private boys' school, and one of Lucknow's most unique sights. The French adventurer Major-General Claude Martin amassed a fortune in India as soldier and a trader. He decided to settle in Lucknow and designed a palatial home, which upon his death was converted into what became one of British India's most prestigious schools and is still going strong today. The building itself is fabulously eclectic, with curved ramps swooping up to frightened-looking lions and a ballet of classical figures on the roof. Visitors should check in at the principal's office. You may be assigned a servant to show you the festooned chapel and Claude Martin's basement tomb.

Sniffing the Subcontinental Sublime

Mention India and odor in the same sentence and you're likely to get a less-than-positive reaction. Indeed, for many a traveler, India is The Land of Don't-Breathe-Too-Deeply. In Lucknow, though, olfactory observation is more likely to run along the lines of *eau de toilette* than *eau de* toilet: this is a center for production of *attar*, India's finest class of perfumes. For centuries *attar* has remained a pivotal part of Indian aesthetics in both the secular and religious domains. The *attar* oil is extracted from the pre-dawn flower buds and left in a large container of water. As the sun rises, the buds secrete an oily film which is then carefully preserved. There is an *attar* for every season and time of the day: for summer, rose and Indian Jasmine; for winter, musk. The undisputed raja of Lucknow's perfume biz is the Azam Ali-Alam Ali Industry, renowned for its authentic *attars* since Mughal days. Their products are sold all over India, and have been worn by the likes of Empress Nuz Jahan and the late Princess Diana.

ENTERTAINMENT AND SHOPPING

Lucknow isn't renowned for its nightlife, but if you need a drink to take the edge off a nerve-racking day, there are budget **bars** along Station Rd. and pricey drinks (Rs150-300) available in the Falakuzuma Restaurant, at Clark's Avadh Hotel. The only proper bar in Hazratganj is the pine-paneled **Tashna Bar** in the Hotel Gomti. This sports bar—complete with color TV blaring soccer matches—is a hang-out for businessmen and students, but few women. Indian snacks and non-veg. munchies (Rs5-90) available along with premium and regular spirits (Rs50-150). (Open daily 11am-10:30pm.) **Novelty Cinema,** on Lalbagh opposite Aahar's Restaurant, shows English-language movies. For a real treat, try **Mayfair Cinema** on M.G. Rd., which shows Hollywood films dubbed into Hindi (tickets Rs8-30). Lucknow is also home to one of the two major schools of **Kathak Dance.** Check newspapers for performance information.

Aminabad, to the south, is one of Lucknow's old bazaar areas and the best place to shop for Lucknawi crafts. Clothing with *chikan* embroidery comes in a wide variety with prices ranging from Rs50-5000 per piece. An elaborate *chikan* shirt takes five to six months of hand work. Also sold here are tiny bottles of *attar,* alcohol-free perfumes worn by Indian Muslims.

■ Faizabad फ़ैज़ाबाद

Once the capital of the kingdom of Avadh—until the *nawab* moved to more luxurious Lucknow in 1775—Faizabad (also known as Bangla) today pales in the shadow of neighboring Ayodhya. Some monuments of Faizabad's historical heyday remain, including two famous mausolea (Shuja-ud-daula and Bahu Begum), which predate the Avadhi monuments of Lucknow. Travelers headed for Ayodhya should take a train to Faizabad and hop in a tempo at the bus station or in the Chowk region for a 10-minute ride to Ayodhya (Rs10). Ayodhya has some cheap and comfortable accommodations, but Faizabad has a greater number of proper hotels with more amenities and is a pleasant and hospitable small city.

ORIENTATION AND PRACTICAL INFORMATION There are two main roads in Faizabad: **Station Road,** which starts at the railway station, becomes **Civil Lines** and eventually leads to the **Chowk** area where hotels and sights are located; and **National Highway 28,** on the opposite side of town, which has buses going to Ayodhya and

Gorakhpur. Distances are great in Faizabad, but easily traversed by rickshaws, which are readily available at the bus and train stations.

Buses leave for: **Allahabad** (Rs42); **Delhi** (Rs149); **Gorakhpur** (Rs40); **Lucknow** (Rs34); **Varanasi** (Rs49). They do not have a fixed schedule. **Tempos** to Ayodhya leave regularly from Gurdi Bazaar, Chowk, near National Highway 28 (Rs10), as well as the bus station. Take a rickshaw from Chowk (Rs15) or the railway station (Rs5) to the bus station. Prices listed are for 2nd/1st class. **Trains** run to: **Delhi** (*Farakka Exp.* 3483, 4:55pm, 14hr., Rs117/581); **Lucknow** (4 per day, 3hr., Rs31/169); **Varanasi** (*Farakka Exp.* 3484, Tu, Th-F, and Su 10:30am, 4½hr., Rs38/200). **The Regional Tourist Office** (tel. 813214) is located off Civil Lines in an alley. From the railway station, take a right on Station Rd. and take the middle road at the traffic circle. The road turns right and then left at each of the dead ends. After about 600m—past the modern Hotel Krishna Palace—there is a large sign on the left for Tiny Tots School above the Regional Tourist Office placard. Follow the signs into the neighborhood to the poorly marked office. The tourist officer speaks very little English but can be of help in deciphering bus and train schedules, which are all in Hindi. (Open M-Sa 10am-5pm.) The **State Bank of India,** on Civil Lines (tel. 20430 or 22210), is occasionally able to change money. From the railway station, take Station Rd. to the traffic circle and take the middle road at the dead end. The bank is on the left. (Open M-F 10am-2pm, Sa 10am-noon.) The **police** are at Kotwali, Riedganj, Chowk (tel. 812202). Faizabad's **Post office** (tel. 814227) is just off National Highway 28. From the bus stop, walk toward the Chowk. Take the first major street to the left and the post office is #50 on the right. (Open M-Sa, 10am-5pm.) Several **STD/ISDs,** are in the vicinity of the train station (**telephone code:** 05278).

ACCOMMODATIONS AND FOOD There are several cheap, clean hotels in the Chowk area. A few of these have their own restaurants. Otherwise, roadside *dhabas* are the only choice for grub. The well-appointed **Hotel Abha** (tel. 22550 or 22930), in an alley off Bajaja Rd. in Motibagh (5min. from the bus and tempo stops; the rickshaw drivers are familiar with it), is probably the best of the small hotels in this area. All rooms (singles Rs110; air-cooled doubles Rs165) have baths, and quite a few sport balconies. The A/C restaurant downstairs produces delicious South Indian food (open daily 7am-11pm). **Shane Avadh** (tel. 23586 or 27075), Civil Lines, has spacious, clean rooms (singles Rs130; doubles Rs160) with attached bath, cable TV, and same-day laundry service. The restaurant on the first floor, **Mezban,** has good chow mein. The **Tirupati Hotel** (tel. 23231) has the same amenities as its neighbor (air-cooled singles with bath Rs195; doubles Rs245).

■ Ayodhya अयोध्या

The hometown of Rama in the *Ramayana* and one of India's holiest cities, Ayodhya has long been a popular pilgrimage site, with its many beautiful Hindu temples (as well as mosques and Jain temples). But recent years have made it one of India's most famous cities for less-than-peaceful reasons. It began with a mosque—the 16th-century Babri Masjid, which was built by the Mughal Emperor Babur on a site that many Hindus hold to be the birthplace of the god Ram. The mosque became a symbol for the resentment and prejudice many Hindus felt (and still feel) towards Indian Muslims; Hindu Nationalists such as the Vishwa Hindu Parishad (VHP) used the Babri Masjid as a rallying cry, and the mosque was eventually closed due to the controversy.

On December 6, 1992, religious fervor turned to violence when 200,000 VHP-led militant Hindus (most of them from outside Ayodhya) descended on the town, smashing through police barricades to destroy the Babri Masjid and erect a makeshift temple in its place. Thousands were killed in the nationwide riots that followed the destruction of the mosque, and Ayodhya remains a flashpoint for communal violence. A final decision about the holy site has been held in abeyance by the government. Ayodhya makes for an interesting day trip, with its numerous temples, fervent devotees, and allure of controversy. However, festivals (especially Ramnaumi, beginning March 26, 1999 and April 12, 2000) are particularly heady and unpredictable events when travelers should be especially cautious. Its lack of western tourists makes Ayodhya quiet and peaceful under normal conditions and can provide a minuscule glimpse of the unspoiled (or at least un-westernized) heart of India.

ORIENTATION AND PRACTICAL INFORMATION National Highway 28 runs through Ayodhya on its way from Faizabad to Gorakhpur. The **railway station,** tourist bungalow, and some of the major sights (including Hanuman Gardhi and Kanak Bhavan) are all located on either side of the highway, within walking distance of the bus station and tempo stop. Several important temples and *ghats* along the **River Saryu** on the opposite side of town can be reached by rickshaw. To reach the **tourist office** (tel. 32435), turn right from the bus station and walk along National Highway 28. Take the first left after the Birla Dharamsala. Walk 600m straight to the railway station and take a left; the **Tourist Bungalow** is on the left, on Pathik Niwas Saket (open M-Sa 10am-5pm). The office is stocked with brochures, magazines, and a helpful attendant who will give tips on the ever-fluctuating opening times of sights. The tourist office is in the opposite direction from most sights, so if this is your first stop, be prepared for a hike back to the action. The **State Bank of India,** Shrinagar Hat (tel. 2053; open M-F 10am-2pm, Sa 10am-noon) has currency exchange. There is sporadic **train** service in Ayodhya (some stop for a minute or two on the way to or from Faizabad), but it's best to catch trains in Faizabad. Regular **buses** to and from Gorakhpur stop briefly; catch them at the bus station on National Highway 28. **Sri Ram Hospital** (tel. 32100) is near the bus station. The **post office** (tel. 32025) is at Shrinagar Hat (open M-Sa 10am-5pm). **STD/ISD** booths are around of the bus station (**telephone code:** 05276).

ACCOMMODATIONS AND FOOD For lodgings, ashrams seems to be the most popular among the thousands of pilgrims who flock here every year; however, accommodating the throngs of Hindus and non-Hindus has brought them below standard. The nicer ashrams have single rooms (with attached bath and fan) and are concentrated near the bus station. Better bargains can be found near the outskirts of town. Ayodhya's only "proper" hotel—the **Tourist Bungalow,** Pathik Niwas Saket (tel. 352435)—houses the town's only "proper" restaurant. From the railway station turn right and walk 300m to the upscale building on the left. Under new management, and with a fresh coat of paint and copious potted plants, it's a real treat. Rooms (dorm beds Rs40, singles Rs125, doubles with air-cooling Rs200) are spacious and well-maintained. The restaurant is open only in season (Nov.-May) and serves pricey vegetarian food. Across from the bus station, the **Birla Dharamsala** is centrally located in a beautiful compound near the main road. This ashram offers basic doubles (Rs150) with fan and attached bath. The place is fairly clean, but bring your own sheets and a mosquito coil to make yourself a cozier bed.

SIGHTS Faith is serious business in Ayodhya. The city is packed with Hindu, Jain, and Muslim houses of worship, making for a strange mix of sublime experience and sensory overload. Many of the most important temples are within walking distance of the bus and railway stations and the Tourist Bungalow.

The **Babri Masjid** is the contested holy site that led to Hindu-Muslim clashes in 1992 and brought international attention to Ayodhya. *(Open daily 7-10am and 3-5pm.)* It is primarily of interest to the history buff or student of contemporary Indian politics. The mosque, built by the Mughal emperor Babur in the 15th century, was believed by some Hindus to occupy the birthplace of Lord Rama, or Ramjanambhoomi (see **The Ramayana,** p. 94). On December 7, 1992, militants led by the Vishwa Hindu Parishad (VHP) and abetted by Uttar Pradesh's BJP-led Hindu nationalist government razed the mosque to build a temple to Rama. The mosque is now a pile of rubble, and the makeshift Hindu temple erected in its place is nothing more than a tent. The compound is surrounded by high fences, hundreds of armed guards, and a bleak walkway leading to the site. Instead of *bhajans* (devotional songs), visitors hear police walkie-talkies and the injunction to move quickly in line, and the three security checkpoints only leave devotees a five-second *darshan* with the microscopic Ram. Foreigners are often hassled at the entrance and no cameras and few personal belongings are allowed beyond the first checkpoint—you may want to leave your things in your hotel, because the armed guards refuse to take any responsibility for visitors' belongings. The **ghats,** only a couple of blocks from the Rama temple, are as impressive.

The **Birla Mandir,** set in a garden echoing with *bhajans,* is a small but incredibly beautiful marble temple next to the Birla Dharamsala, across the road from the bus station. This *mandir* is a good example of modern temple architecture, with its clean lines, beautifully adorned entrance hall, and Hindi and English passages from the *Gita* lining the walls. To reach the **Jain Temple** at Hanuman Rd., take a right from the railway station, walk 800m, take another right, and the temple will be on the right. Huge, well-maintained grounds with places to sit and relax surround an impressive *mandir,* containing a 9.5m statue of Lord Rishabhadev. It's especially exciting at night, when indirect lighting and legions of monkeys lend the temple a spooky aura.

Hanuman Gardhi is in a white fort to the left of the bus station. The closest thing to nightlife in Ayodhya, this is the place to come if you long for late-night crowds and noise. You are kindly requested to leave your shoes and socks at a roadside *dhaba*—meaning you must climb the 76 steps to the temple, through mud and filth, barefoot. One Ayodhya's most important temples, it honors Hanuman, the monkey god, who is said to have lived here in a cave and protected Rama's birthplace.

■ Gorakhpur गोरखपुर

Founded around 1400 and named for the Hindu saint Gorakhnath, Gorakhpur still houses the temple of the patron saint of the Natha Yogis. At the temple grounds, 4km from the railway station, monkeys and long-earring-wearing *sadhus* sit in solitude. Gorakhpur became an army town under the Mughals and again under the British, who used it as a base for recruiting Gurkha soldiers from Nepal. Because of its location in northeast Uttar Pradesh, the city of Gorakhpur is the major transportation hub between India and Nepal. Buses leave regularly for the border, and the main railway station has trains to major cities in India (Gorakhpur is the headquarters of the North Eastern Railway). Although the city itself has little to offer, there are worse places in India to be stuck waiting to set off on your next jaunt.

ORIENTATION

Most of Gorakhpur lies south of its **railway station.** Many of Gorakhpur's hotels are located on **Station Road,** parallel to the tracks across from the **railway station.** The road that runs perpendicular from the railway station's entrance leads to the **bus stand,** 400m south, before intersecting **Park Road,** which is parallel to Station Rd. Park Rd. marks the beginning of the **Civil Lines** region.

PRACTICAL INFORMATION

Trains: Railway Station, Station Rd. Prices are 2nd/1st class. To: **Allahabad** (*Chauri-Chaura Exp.* 5004, 10:15pm, 10hr., Rs56/274); **Kanpur** (*Kushinagar Exp.* 1016, 7pm, 7½hr., Rs77/390); **Jhansi** (*Kushinagar Exp.* 1016, 7pm, 12½hr., Rs114/521); **Lucknow** (*Kushinagar Exp.* 1016, 7pm, 5½hr., Rs65/321; *Gorakhpur-Secunderabad Exp.* 5090, 5am, 5½hr., Rs65/291); **Varanasi** (*Gorakhpur-Howrah Exp.* 5050, 3:15pm; *Kashi Exp.* 1028, 4:55am; *Gorakhpur-Varanasi Exp.* 5103, 5:10pm; *Krishak Exp.* 5001, 6:30am; 5½ hr., Rs27/153).

Buses: Gorakhpur Bus station, across from the railway station. To: **Sunauli** (frequent, starting at 5am, Rs30). Ask for the next departing bus; just make sure you are getting on a government bus. There are many **private buses** to Sunauli operating from the same area, but they are costly. There are also buses that claim to go straight to **Kathmandu** or **Pokhara** in Nepal, but they do not actually go direct; you will still have to spend several hours at the border arranging your visa and switching buses once in Nepal. For more information, see **Sunauli** (p. 783).

Tourist Office: 7 Park Rd., Civil Lines (tel. 335450), a short rickshaw ride from the railway station (Rs10-20). Not especially informative. Open M-Sa 10am-5pm.

Currency Exchange: State Bank of India, (tel.338497) Bank Rd., Vijay Choraha. Cashes traveler's checks. Open M-F 10am-2pm, Sa 10am-noon.

Post Office: 300m right of the main entrance door of the railway station. Open 10am-3pm. **Postal Code:** 273001.

Telephones: Booths near the rail station offer STD service. **Telephone Code:** 0551.

ACCOMMODATIONS

Budget hotels are located across from the railway station, with the cheapest (and dirtiest) to the left as you exit. Mid-range hotels are located in the center of the city (Rs15 rickshaw ride), and slightly more expensive hotels are located 4km from the railway station, down Station Rd. to the right.

Hotel Elora, L-block, Station Rd. (tel. 200647), across from the railway station. Fairly clean, but the fluorescent lighting makes everything look like it's crawling. Wake up to a hot shower and the sound of military exercises in the back. Rooms have attached baths. Check-out 24hr. Singles Rs90; doubles Rs150; A/C rooms Rs350.

Hotel Siddhartha, Station Rd. (tel. 200976), past Hotel Elora. See your room before you commit—rooms vary. Still, the management is friendly, and some rooms can squeeze in three or four people. Check-out 24hr. Singles Rs90, with air-cooling Rs140, with A/C Rs300; doubles Rs130/180/400.

Hotel Marina, Golghar (tel. 337630), a Rs10 rickshaw ride to the center of town. More upscale with inexpensive, clean singles with common bath. Popular with Indian families. Inconveniently located but quieter (even with the kids around) than the hotels near the bus station Check-out noon. Singles Rs90.

FOOD

Small *dhabas* dish *dal bhat* abound along Station Rd. and the road leading to the bus station. There are a few places that serve more elaborate dishes, Indian snacks, and Western breakfasts.

Hotel Ganges Deluxe Restaurant, Cinema Rd., Golghar (tel. 336330). Offers a cool respite from the nervous bustle of Station Rd. Basic and cheap Indian food (*pulao* Rs25), with some more expensive *tandoori* items. Loud downstairs bar blasts the A/C until midnight (drinks Rs20-50, beer Rs75-100). Restaurant open10am-11pm.

Vardan Restaurant, Station Rd. (tel. 338085), between Hotel Standard and Hotel Elora. The food is standard—omelettes, tomato toast, milkshakes—and the service is slow, but the A/C is super-cold, and the tinted windows shield you from the touts, and them from your sunburned, wrathful self. Open 8am-11pm.

■ Kushinagar कुशीनगर

It's not difficult to see why the Buddha chose Kushinagar as his final resting place. Serene and beautiful, it is one of the four most important holy sites for Buddhists (along with Lumbini, Bodh Gaya, and Sarnath). It is here that the Buddha (before attaining *parinirvana*) delivered his last sermon about the ephemeral nature of life. For many centuries afterwards, the town was patronized by a plethora of religious rulers, the most important being Ashoka, who converted to Buddhism and helped the religion flourish throughout India. With the decline of Buddhism in India after the 12th century, though, Kushinagar lost its widespread importance. In the 19th century, archaeologists working under the auspices of the East India Company excavated this area and found much of what remains in Kushinagar today. Burma, China, Sri Lanka, Japan, and Thailand have all provided financial assistance for the development of Kushinagar, which remains pristine and, for the most part, untouristed. While there isn't much to do in Kushinagar, its appeal lies in the peaceful silence and calm religiosity that its environment exudes. Gentle monks amble along the town's paths, which are curiously devoid of beggars.

ORIENTATION AND PRACTICAL INFORMATION Fifty-one kilometers east of Gorakhpur, Kushinagar is located on **National Highway 28.** All the places of worship, tourist attractions, and accommodations are on Kushinagar's main road, **Buddh Marg,** which is entered through the **Buddha Dwar gate.** Hourly **buses** (6:30am-6:30pm) head to **Allahabad** (Rs100), **Delhi** (Rs250), **Gorakhpur** (Rs17), **Kanpur** (Rs150), **Lucknow** (Rs100), and **Varanasi** (Rs80). The bus station is in the neighboring town of **Kasia,** about 3km from Kushinagar, but most buses from Gorakhpur will drop you right at the Buddha Dwar. The **Regional Tourist Office** is 100m down Buddha Marg, on the right, in front of the Myanmar Temple and next to the Birla Buddhist temple. The tourist office has scads of brochures, maps, and advice to dispense. (Open M-Sa 10am-5pm.) The **Central Bank of India,** National Highway 28 (tel. 71089), a short ride from Buddha Dwar, does not cash traveler's checks. The **post office** (tel. 71029), which doubles as the **police station,** is a small white building opposite the Buddha Dwar on National Highway 28 (open 9am-5pm; **postal code:** 274403). There are 24hr. **STD/ISD** booths on Buddh Marg, next to the Buddha Dwar (**telephone code:** 05563).

ACCOMMODATIONS AND FOOD The cleanest and cheapest accommodations in Kushinagar are at the **Linh-Son Chinese Temple** and the **Myanmar Buddhist Temple and Guest House** (tel. 71035). Both of them are located on Buddh Marg, opposite the tourist office. They are run by friendly Buddhist monks who are willing to answer questions about Kushinagar and their religion. The monks do not, however, speak much English. During the tourist season (Sept.-Mar.), these places give preference to East Asian tourists since most of the money for their construction came from Burma, Thailand, China, and Japan. The facilities run on donations and although the monks will never ask for money, the expected donation is at least Rs50 per day; if you're genuinely out of cash, however, don't sweat it. Mango trees that dot the temple grounds can provide delectable breakfasts. **Hotel Pathik Niwas,** Buddh Marg (tel. 05563 or 71038), about 300m from the tourist office, offers a wide range of accommodations, from dorm beds (Rs100) to A/C deluxe rooms (Rs600). The rooms and bathrooms are clean, and sheets and towels are changed daily. Small, kitchen-equipped "American huts" are Rs550. The staff is friendly and responsive, and the restaurant offers delicious (but pricey) food. Since this is the only hotel in the area that stays open year round, it can be tough to get a room during Buddhist holidays.

The **Yama Kwality Cafe** serves the best food in (and out of) town. It's on Buddh Marg, next to the Myanmar Buddhist Temple. Indian, Burmese, Chinese, Nepalese, Tibetan, and Thai foods are available at reasonable prices—a generous portion of chicken fried rice goes for Rs25. All food is prepared from scratch so don't get restless after 20 minutes. The Burmese *chow soy* is fantastic.

SIGHTS Kushinagar's pervasive Buddhist architectural artifacts create an ambience of serenity and harmony with nature. No matter how boring some *stupas* may seem, the lush gardens that surround them give the entire area a sublime aura. *(Stupas open daily, sunrise to sunset.)* A golden Buddha sits majestically in the **Myanmar Temple,** built in a large water tank opposite the tourist office; in June a fair is held around the tank. On the grounds next to the Myanmar Temple is Kushinagar's holiest site, the **Main Buddha Mahaparinirvana Temple.** Here, the Enlightened One was liberated from the cycles of rebirth and attained the ideal state of *parinirvana.* The discovery of this ancient *stupa* in the 19th century engendered a thriving spiritual community in the midst of the jungle. The *stupa* that was excavated here, which is said by most Buddhists to contain the ashes of the Buddha, rests peacefully under a modern protective *stupa.* In front of it is the 6m **Reclining Buddha,** draped in mustard colored silk and lulled by the rhythmic chanting of his present disciples. The Buddha's expression changes depending on the approaching angle of the beholder. If you turn left when exiting the main temple and go past Hotel Pathik Niwas, staying on the road that veers to the left, you'll find the **Matha Kunwar Temple,** where the Buddha delivered his last sermon. One kilometer away, the **Ramabhar Stupa** commemorates the cremation site of the Buddha. All these *stupas* are surrounded by smaller *stupas* that contain the ashes of devout Buddhist monks.

■ Varanasi वाराणसी

For Hindus, Varanasi (also known as Benares or Benaras) is the holiest place on earth and the chosen residence of Shiva, who abides in every nook and cranny. Hindus claim the whole city is a sacred zone—its power is reputedly so great that it shines out from the earth over the Ganga, hence its other name, Kashi (the Luminous). Everyone who dies in Varanasi is guaranteed *moksha*, or liberation from the cycle of death and rebirth—and everyone here knows it. This otherworldly confidence (and a growing population of 1.2 million) has shaped Varanasi into one of the world's grimiest and most tangled cities.

Amid the cacophony and confusion, it's difficult to discern Varanasi's inspired side. Shiva chose to settle in Kashi with his new bride, Parvati, and he was so awestruck that he vowed never to leave. Nowadays, Varanasi's glory takes time and timing to fully appreciate. At sunrise a quiet band of thousands descends to the riverside *ghats,* flashed head-on by a godlike sun. The water oozes with disease; refuse and even human corpses can be seen bobbing by. But this has no apparent effect on Varanasi's popularity as a place to bathe, nor on the taste of its liberating waters (Let's Go does not recommend drinking from the Ganga—you may be "liberated" sooner than you think). Its houses press up to the waterfront, almost leaning over it for a splash in the sacred river. The Old City is a maze of tortuous lanes, smeared with cow dung and congested with men and beasts. Small boys make fortunes guiding foreigners to the Golden Temple through little-used alleys. Befuddled pallbearers, on their way to Manikarnika Ghat, the most sacred place for cremation, stop mid-chant to ask for hazy directions. Sometimes a dead body, stretched between two bicycles, or tied to the roof of a jeep, is delivered to the pyre amid the traditional chant, *"Ram Nam Sata Hai"* ("Ram is Truth"). On the main street, buses honk madly at stragglers and spew exhaust over strings of shaven-headed pilgrims—the outward sign of earthly loss with only a small catch of hair at the back, just in case the gods decide to snatch them up! The electricity fails almost every night; until the ugly fluorescent lights stutter back to life, the unprepared visitor must navigate the slippery lanes of the City of Light by the teasing flicker of a candle flame.

The physical condition of the city of Varanasi is due in part to five centuries of Muslim levelings, from 1200 to 1700. No building in the city is more than 300 years old. But the attacks never really succeeded—they wiped out the city's temples and images, but not the traditions that have kept Varanasi going from at least as far back as the 6th century BC. In the early days of Aryan settlement in India, Varanasi, one of the world's oldest continuously inhabited cities, sat at the great ford where traders traversing North India would cross the Ganga. It gained fame as a glorious bazaar town, but also as a center for spiritual life. Teachers and ascetics came to mingle with the local deities in the ponds and rivers of the Anandavana (Forest of Bliss) that grew here before the city. The Buddha came to Sarnath, on the outskirts of Kashi, to preach his first sermon. Varanasi's Hindu priests were active in developing their religion through the millennia, and the city itself was soon an object of worship: a holy place, inhabited by holy beings, bound by a holy river.

Neither a military nor a political powerhouse, Varanasi became a sanctuary for Indian culture, renowned for its silk brocades (Benares silk *saris* are still some of the best), its refined Sanskrit and Hindi, and its music. Today Varanasi, especially since the foundation of Benares Hindu University, continues to support a thriving arts culture. But piety and devotion are the main attraction for the millions who come for brief visions of the city, and also for the many who come to settle and die in Varanasi. The living here can frolic knowing this life is their last.

ORIENTATION

Varanasi's city limits are marked by the **Varuna River** in the north and the **Assi River** in the south; hence the hybrid name of Varanasi. The **Panch Koshi Road,** which circles around the city's 16km radius, marks the boundary of the sacred zone of Kashi.

Varanasi is pressed against the west bank of the Ganga at a point where the river flows north. There is nothing on the east bank; it's believed that those who die there will return as donkeys. Varanasi is laid out with such ideas in mind, so it can be a mess to move through as an outsider. But since the geography has so much religious significance locals tend to know it intimately. Banarsis (natives of Varanasi) are great givers of directions, and you'll need them to find your way through the city's twisting lanes, which are often just one cow wide.

Sticking to the river is the best way to navigate Varanasi, and most points of interest are along the waterfront. **Assi Ghat** marks the south end of the riverbank; **Raj Ghat** is farthest north. Trains from the east cross the **Malaviya Bridge,** next to Raj Ghat, to enter Varanasi, and the railway stations are inland from this north part of the city. **Dashaswamedh Ghat** is the city's main *ghat,* easily reached on **Dashaswamedh Road** from **Godaulia Crossing,** a central traffic circle. The surrounding area, known as Godaulia, hoards many of the budget hotels, near the **Vishwanath Temple.** Godaulia is connected to the northern parts of Varanasi by **Chauk Road,** one of the few roads near the *ghats* wide enough for cars.

PRACTICAL INFORMATION

Transportation

Airport: Babatpur Airport (tel. 343275), 22km from Varanasi. **Indian Airlines office,** Cantonment (tel. 343746 or 345959). To: **Agra** (daily 1:30pm, 2hr., US$95); **Delhi** (2-3 per day, 2½hr., US$110); **Kathmandu** (M, W, F, and Su, 12:50pm, 1hr., US$71); **Khajuraho** (daily, 2:40pm, 1hr., US$70); **Lucknow** (T, Th, Sa, and Su, 1:15pm, 45min., US$60); **Mumbai** (T, Th, Sa, and Su, 4hr., US$210).

Trains: Varanasi Junction Railway Station is located at the intersection of the Grand Trunk, Cantonment Station, and Vidyapith Rd. (Rs10 by cycle-rickshaw or Rs20 by auto-rickshaw from Godaulia Crossing). Fares are 2nd/1st class. To: **Allahabad** (*Poorva Exp.* 2381, 8pm, 2hr., Rs46/224); **Ayodhya** (*Farakka Exp.* 3483, 12:30pm, 3½hr., Rs48/238); **Delhi** (*Poorva Exp.* 2381, 8pm, 12hr.; *Shramjeevi Exp.* 2401, 3:20pm, 14hr., Rs155/689; *Patna-New Delhi Rajdhani Exp.* 2309, 11pm, 11hr., Rs1395/2660); **Gorakhpur** (*Howrah-Gorakhpur Exp.* 5049, 3:10pm, 6hr., Rs27/153); **Kanpur** (*Farakka Exp.* 3483, noon, 10hr.; *Poorva Exp.* 2381, 8pm, 5½hr., 13hr., Rs82/405; **Mumbai** (*Mahanagri Exp.* 1094, 11:30am, 28hr., Rs207/116); **Patna** (*Bhiwani-Malda Town Farakka Exp.* 3414/3484, 3:20pm, 5hr., Rs66/269); **Satna** (*Mahanagri Exp.* 1094, 11:30am, 6½hr., Rs57/278, then 4hr. bus to Khajuraho).

Buses: Cantonment Bus Station, 200m to the left on Station Rd., coming out of Varanasi Junction Station. To: **Agra** (7am and 5pm, 15hr., Rs200); **Allahabad** (every 30min., 5am-11pm, 3hr., Rs38); **Delhi** (7pm, 20hr., Rs200); **Gaya** (6:30am, 8hr., Rs62); **Gorakhpur** (10 per day, 4:30am-11pm, 6hr., Rs66); **Kanpur** (6 per day, 5am-11pm, Rs97); **Lucknow** (5am and every hr. 7am-9pm, Rs90); **Sonauli** (3, 5, and 6pm, 8hr., Rs100). Buses to **Chunar** leave from a smaller station at **Pilikothi,** near Varanasi City Railway Station, east of the main Junction Station (every 30min., 6am-8pm, Rs10).

Local Transportation: Auto-rickshaws from Varanasi Junction Station to Godaulia or Cantonment area cost Rs20, or Rs5 in a shared auto-rickshaw (but you may end up sharing a corner of the driver's seat—goats and luggage not allowed). Cycle-rickshaws, whose drivers are notoriously deceptive and belligerent, run between all major points in the city; it helps to know where you are going and to be assertive. **Tempos** run between less touristy spots, like Lanka and Ramnagar Fort (Rs5), and the Civil Court and Sarnath.

Tourist and Financial Services

Tourist Office: Uma Shankar, the branch manager of the **U.P. Regional Tourist Office** (tel. 46370), in the main railway station, is your best friend in Varanasi. If you have the time, he'll give you a frank (though long-winded) survival pep talk. Office open daily 6am-8pm. The staff at the main office in the **Tourist Bungalow,** Parade Kothi, Cantonment (tel. 343413), located in the neighborhood directly in

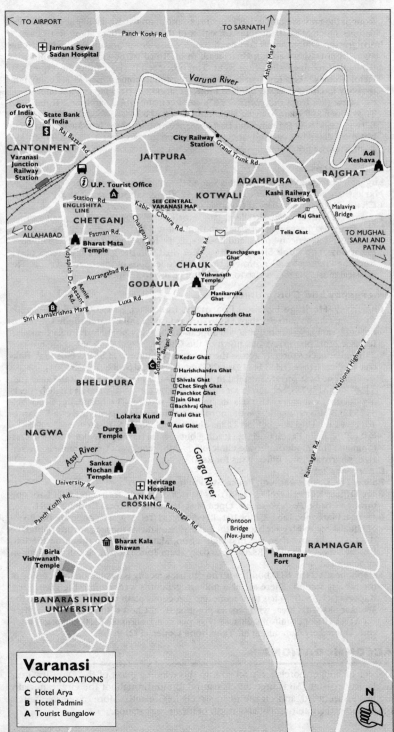

Varanasi

ACCOMMODATIONS

C Hotel Arya
B Hotel Padmini
A Tourist Bungalow

N

front of the railway station, has brochures, and an up-to-date list of guest accommodations. Open M-Sa 10am-5pm. Ask either of the tourist offices about festivals.

Immigration Office: Siddh Giri Bagh (tel. 53968). From Godaulia Crossing, facing away from Dashaswamedh Ghat, walk to the third traffic circle (which includes Godaulia Crossing), then turn right. The office sends visa extension requests to Delhi—it may take a few weeks for the extension to come. Open M-Sa 10am-5pm.

Currency Exchange: State Bank of India, Cantonment (tel. 34345), a 20min. cycle rickshaw ride from the *ghats* (Rs20). Between the Hotel Saryu and Hotel Ideal Tops. Open M-F 10am-5pm, Sa 10am-2pm. **Bank of Baroda,** Godaulia (tel. 321471). Between Godaulia Crossing and Dashaswamedh Ghat, on the left. Most convenient but *only* doles out cash advances on major credit cards for a 1% fee. Open M-F 11am-2pm, Sa noon-1pm.

Local Services

Luggage Storage: Varanasi Junction Station (Rs2 per day). Open 24hr.

Market: Large fruit markets are located at **Vishersarganj** near the GPO and in **Chauk.** Hop in a rickshaw at Godaulia Crossing for the short ride north.

Bookstore: Universal Booksellers, Jangambali (tel. 393042). From Godaulia Crossing, facing Dashaswamedh Ghat, turn right—it will be on the right, 750m up. Sells English and American books, and books specific to Varanasi. Open M-Sa 9am-8pm.

Harmony: The Book Shop, B.1/160, Assi Ghat. On the *ghat* a few doors down from the Pizzeria Vaatika. Browse the travel collections of this peaceful shop. The classical music playing is also for sale. Open daily 10am-5pm.

Emergency and Communications

Pharmacy: Heritage Hospital Pharmacy, Lanka (tel. 313977). From Godaulia Crossing, take an auto-rickshaw (Rs20) toward Lanka and Benares Hindu University in South Varanasi. The hospital will appear on the left, right before Lanka Crossing. It has a 24hr. pharmacy. Just north of the Chowk, down Kabir Rd. there are two 24hr. pharmacies directly across the emergency entrance of **SSPG Hospital: Raksha Medical Store** (tel. 354219) and **Gangaly Medical Store** (tel. 354904).

Hospital: The best private hospital in Varanasi is the **Heritage Hospital,** Lanka (tel. 313977 or 313978). See above for directions. You can usually see an English-speaking doctor right away. Also has an ambulance service. The hospital at **BHU** (tel. 312542) is also reputable. On the north side of town is the **Jamuna Sewa Sadan,** S-15/47, Panch Cosi Rd., behind Thana Shivpur (tel. 383535, residence tel. 383551), just off the main Panch Cosi Rd., leading out toward the airport, 4km from the Cantonment. This modern, private clinic offers 24hr. emergency care, ambulance service, **pharmacy,** and office visits for Rs60.

Emergency: tel. 197.

Police: The **Dashaswamedh Police Station** (tel. 352650).

Post Office: Kotwali (tel. 332090). Rs10 rickshaw ride from Godaulia Crossing through Chauk. *Poste Restante.* Open M-Sa 10am-6pm. **Postal Code:** 221001.

Internet: Matronix, Lane 2, Plot 101, Ravindrapuri (tel. 311721), opposite the Bread of Life Bakery. With your back to the bakery, head down the lane at your right, take the first right, and then the first right again. Matronix is 50m down on the left. Download your email for Rs20. Open daily 10am-7pm. Drop-in, or call ahead for an appointment.

Telephones: A 24hr. STD booth with no call-back facility is located on the left side of the railway station. There are also numerous booths wedged into the *ghats* area. **Kapuria** (tel. 354093) has their name and directions plastered over buildings in the Manikarnika Ghat area, with arrows pointing from Chowk Rd. Collect call service via AT&T (Rs3 per min.), callbacks (Rs3 per min.), and fax (Rs20 per page) available. Open daily 6am-midnight. **Telephone Code:** 0542.

ACCOMMODATIONS

Dozens of budget hotels are packed into the winding maze of the Old City, near Godaulia Crossing. Mid-range hotels can be found throughout the city, especially along Vidyapith Rd. and on the main streets in Godaulia. More expensive hotels tower above the Cantonment area north of the railway station.

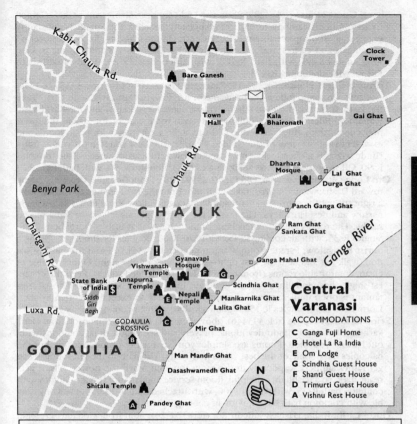

Warning: Rickshaw-*wallahs* in Varanasi often collect commissions from hoteliers for delivering guests. Be firm about where you want to go, or find a mellow rickshaw-*wallah* who won't harass you. Don't believe your rickshaw-*wallah* if he tells you that the hotel you asked for is "full" or "closed."

Vishnu Rest House, D24/17, Pandey Ghat (tel. 329206), at Dashaswamedh Ghat, facing the Ganga, walk right along the shore until you see "Pandey" written above the ghats. Not to be confused with the Vishnu Guest House or Old Vishnu Rest House. Plant-laden terrace transforms the hottest of winds into cool zephyrs. Clean sheets cover comfortable mattresses. The Rest House pays no commissions, so rickshaw-*wallahs* often claim it's closed. Restaurant open daily 7am-2pm and 6-9:30pm. Dorm beds Rs35; singles Rs60; doubles with attached bath Rs70.

Hotel Padmini, Sigra Rd., Mahmoor Ganj (tel. 222274). From the railway station go 1km to Sigra crossing, turn right, and walk 500m to Mahmoor Ganj (Rs10 by rickshaw). The clean, friendly atmosphere and downstairs restaurant, Malika, are bound to please. Extras include marble floor and staircase, paintings on the walls, and prompt laundry service. Singles Rs350, with A/C Rs470; doubles Rs400/575.

Ganga Fuji Home, D. 7/21 Sakarkand Gali, Old City (tel. 327333). Near Golden Temple, Main Ghat, and Dashaswamedh Rd. The owner is more host than hotelier: he has a doctorate in Ayurvedic medicine and palmistry. Bedsheets and bathrooms are extremely clean; the gates are locked most of the day to keep riff-raff out; the kitchen is spotless; and the water is filtered (the *lassis* and lime water are relatively safe). No attached baths (yet). Singles Rs80; doubles Rs120. Air-cooling Rs20 extra.

Shanti Guest House (tel. 322568), in the Old City near Manikarnika Ghat. Gorged by its popularity among foreigners (especially Israelis), the Shanti is constantly expanding. Rooftop restaurant is Party Central in the Old City. Exchanges over 47 currencies and cashes AmEx traveler's checks. Clean sheets and soft mattresses, too. Singles Rs60, with bath Rs100, with air-cooling Rs125; doubles with bath Rs150, with air-cooling Rs175.

Trimurti Guest House, CK. 35/12, Saraswati Phatak, Old City (tel. 323554). From Godaulia Crossing, follow Dashaswamedh Rd. toward Dashaswamedh Ghat. Take the last left before the *ghat* (there will be signs for Trimurti and for Kashi Vishwanath (Golden) Temple). Follow this small road straight for 200m; the guest house is on the right. One of the Old City's largest hotels, with basic rooms and excellent rooftop view of the Golden Temple (the best you'll get if you're not a Hindu). Draws a chemically enlightened crowd. In-season: singles Rs60; doubles Rs90. Off-season: dorm beds Rs30; singles Rs45; doubles Rs90, with bath Rs130.

Om Lodge, Bansphatak area, Old City (tel. 392728). From Godaulia Crossing, facing toward Dashaswamedh Ghat, take a left turn onto the road leading to Chauk. Take a right turn at the signs for Shanti and Om Lodge. Follow these down increasingly narrow and desolate alleys. The owner is a jolly, sagacious fellow—a Santa turned *sadhu*. The rooms are extremely basic, although A/C is available. Dorm beds Rs20. Singles Rs35, with air-cooling Rs45, with A/C Rs60; doubles Rs50/60.

Tourist Bungalow, Parade Kothi, Cantonment (tel. 343413). From the railway station, walk left and take the first right—it's set back on the right. Offers a range of clean, comfortable rooms (from dorm beds to full-fledged suites). Even the cheapest singles have satellite TV; some also have big, beautiful bathrooms. The A/C restaurant is open until 2am, and the tourist office has an exceedingly friendly staff. Dorm beds Rs40; singles Rs150; doubles Rs200, with air-cooling Rs250/325.

Scindhia Guest House (tel. 393446), above Scindhia Ghat, up the beach from Manikarnika Ghat. Hear Hindu devotional prayers and see Hindu ritual ablutions without leaving your bed. Rooms are simple: you pay for the prime location, but the balconies have some of the best views in the city. The path to the guest house can get rather slippery, especially in the monsoon, and when the power fails, it gets really dark, so a flashlight is helpful. Room service and laundry service. Singles with common bath Rs75, with view Rs100, with attached bath Rs125/150; balcony double with common bath Rs125, with air-cooling Rs250.

Hotel La-Ra India, Dashaswamedh Rd. (tel. 320323), 30m from Godaulia crossing on the right as you head toward the *ghats*. Hotel in the heart of the action offers hot running water, TV, safe deposit, and a travel desk. A/C restaurant open till 11pm. Singles Rs175; doubles Rs225; air-cooling Rs75 extra; A/C rooms Rs350/450.

Hotel Arya, Sonar Pura (tel. 313869), 1km from Godaulia Crossing on the main road to Assi Ghat. More sane than some, this hotel is just far enough removed to allow you to catch your breath, but still only minutes from a plunge back into the thick of things. Hot running water, international collect calling, and roof-top restaurant. Singles Rs100-150; doubles Rs200; deluxe with TV and air-cooling Rs250.

FOOD

Keshari Restaurant, on a side street between Godaulia and Dashaswamedh Ghat. Popular among upper-middle-class Indians, this cool dark veg. restaurant serves some of the best *thalis* around, including a special house *thali* with cheese, cauliflower, potato, brown *dal, raita,* and fruit salad (Rs75, feeds 2 easily). The staff is friendly. Open daily 10am-10:30pm.

Malika, in Hotel Padmini. Serves delicious veg. and non-veg. food at a reasonable price (veg. *biryani* Rs50) in surroundings reminiscent of some Maharaja's dining compartment in a palatial train. The friendly waiters and prompt service makes Malika ideal for a quick dinner.

Shanti Guest House Rooftop Restaurant, Shanti Guest House, near Manikarnika Ghat. The 24hr. rooftop restaurant offers the only nightlife in the Old City, unless sacred-cow-tipping's your thing. Guests exchange uproarious stories of the day's adventures late into the night. Things quiet down around 2am, when you can sit and enjoy the fine view of the Ganga. The food itself (Rs15-40) is bland but tasty, and the service is slow, especially when the place is packed. The gate of the Shanti Guest House closes at midnight, but you can knock loudly for entry.

Restaurant at Trimurti Guest House, CK. 35/12, Saraswati Phatak (tel. 323554). From Godaulia Crossing, with your back to Dashaswamedh Ghat, take the last left before the *ghat*, go straight for 2.5km. Popular with tourists, the Trimurti Restaurant offers bland standard fare. Well-lit, with a small library, it's a great place to chat or read. Open daily 7:30am-10:30pm.

Yelchico Bar and Restaurant (tel. 323248), near Godaulia Crossing. From Godaulia Crossing, with your back to Dashaswamedh Ghat, it's 1 block up on your left, inside a mall and down a flight of stairs. It's difficult to believe that such a casually cool and quiet bar exists just a few steps away from the noisiest and most irksome part of Varanasi. Drinks at standard prices (beer Rs70) and some excellent snacks (entrees Rs25-60). Open 11:30am-10:30pm.

Bread of Life Bakery and Western Restaurant, B3/322, Shivala (tel. 313912), on the main road between Assi Ghat and Godaulia. The managers also proudly serve American pancakes with maple syrup (Rs55), chicken salad (Rs85), and baked potatoes (Rs55). A luscious loaf of wheat goes for Rs10, and fresh oatmeal and peanut butter cookies are Rs5 a pop. Open M-Sa 8am-3pm and 6-8pm. Closed May and June; bakery open M-Sa, 8am-noon and 5-9pm.

Pizzeria Vaatika (tel. 313208), on Assi Ghat. Relax in the garden overlooking the Ganga while you enjoy scrumptious pizza (Rs35-40) or pasta (Rs25). Fruit, muesli, and yogurt (Rs22) for breakfast or apple pie (Rs15) for a snack will bring a smile to your face. The brick oven is fired up daily 7am-10pm.

SIGHTS

Pilgrims come to this holy city to experience *darshan,* the sacred seeing of gods through images. Those to whom this practice is foreign can still roam the city and look, but they might not see what pilgrims see. Some religious imagination is needed to bring Varanasi—its temples, its tanks, and especially its **ghats**—to life.

The holy Ganga is the main attraction in Varanasi, and a series of *ghats* (steps) lead down to the river. Thousands come at dawn to bathe in and make offerings to the heavenly water. But the *ghats* are not reserved for sacred activities. While matted-haired *sadhus* roam around, teenagers dive bravely from the steps, and others wash their clothes and tend to their goats and cows. The Ganga draws all sorts of life, and death as well, for in Varanasi, Hindu pollution beliefs are reversed so that cremation grounds are wholly auspicious. **Cremations** take place right on the *ghats,* rather than out of town on inauspicious soil as in most cities. The bodies of those who can't afford cremation, as well as holy men and babies, are consigned to the river and can sometimes be seen floating along. Let's Go does not recommend bathing in the Ganga, except for those with exceptionally good *karma.*

The steps themselves are huge, usually numbering over 100 from top to bottom, though some are hidden when the water is high. Each *ghat* has its name painted in large black-and-yellow letters both in Hindi and English. Many *ghats* are named after princely states, whose rulers donated money to pave them.

Assi Ghat to Dashaswamedh Ghat

The south end of Varanasi's riverfront begins with **Assi Ghat.** This first *ghat* is a broad clay bank, much like they all were in the beginning, at the confluence of the Ganga and Assi River. The Assi has recently shifted south into a *nala* (stream), but Assi Ghat is still considered the south edge of Varanasi and is a busy religious center. Along with *Shivalingams* it has an array of shops and cold drink stands.

Inland from Assi Ghat are some of Varanasi's more important temples. The **Sankat Mochan** temple, dedicated to Hanuman, has orange *sindur* smears that attest to its popularity. *(Open daily 4am-noon and 4-10pm.)* Up the road is the **Tulsi Manas Temple,** a modern Vishnu temple erected in honor of Tulsi Das, the premier poet of the Hindi language, who wrote the Hindi version of the Sanskrit epic *Ramayana. (Open daily 6am-noon and 4-10pm; admission Rs1.)* Built of white marble and flanked by palm trees, the Tulsi Manas Temple looks like a five-star hotel from the front. The walls inside are inscribed with Tulsi Das's verses, and on the second floor at the back, Hindu religious images have entered a magical dimension: a spinning small world of figures that would make Disney proud to act out Rama's life. It's extremely popular with pilgrims. The walls inside the temple are also adorned with paintings, the most notable of which is one depicting brotherly love: Bharat, Rama's step-brother worships Rama's wooden sandals for the 14 years of Rama's exile (see **The Ramayana,** p. 94). Close to the Tulsi Manas Temple is the ornate, red-and-white **Durga Temple,** a focal point of fairs in July and August. *(Open 24hr.)* Also close is a tank where the goddess is said to have rested after she defeated the demon Mahishura and saved the world.

Tulsi Ghat is the next significant *ghat* after Assi; it was here that Tulsi Das lived in the 17th century. His house is at the top of the *ghat,* and you may be able to find your way in. Back from the water above Tulsi Ghat is one of Varanasi's most ancient sacred spots, the **Lolarka Kund.** Sunk precariously in the ground, this tank was at one time the site where early Hindus worshiped Surya, the sun god; now the tank is cherished only once a year, in August or September, when couples come to pray for sons.

Tulsi Ghat is followed by the city water intake, but the *ghats* resume further north. **Chet Singh Ghat** is topped by the palace of Maharaja Chet Singh, who rebelled against the British in 1781. Stacks of firewood and groups of solemn people distinguish the next major *ghat* from the others—**Harishchandra Ghat** is Varanasi's second most important cremation ground. It's an old and sacred site, though less renowned than Manikarnika Ghat up north. **Photography is strictly prohibited** at both cremation *ghats.* The *ghat* with the red-and-white painted circus stripes is **Kedar Ghat.** The Kedar Temple is one of Varanasi's oldest and most important Shiva temples. Kedar means "field," and this is the field where liberation is said to grow. **Chauki Ghat** has a fierce collection of *nagas,* early aquatic snake-gods, around a central tree. From this point on, a long stretch of *ghats* is used for laundry, with a collage of colorful *saris* and *lungis* stretched out to dry.

Dashaswamedh Ghat, the next major bathing spot, is the most crowded *ghat* in Varanasi, the place boatmen call the "Main Ghat." The wide approaching road lures buses filled with pilgrims. Bamboo parasols heighten Dashaswamedh's beach-like atmosphere, and kids clamber up and down the steps selling flowers for offerings. Here, the creator god Brahma is said to have performed 10 royal horse-sacrifices for the mythical King Divodasa, making the waters auspicious. The area up Dashaswamedh Rd. is known as Godaulia, after a stream that once flowed into the Ganga here. Just south of Dashaswamedh Ghat, the "cold" goddess of smallpox and other diseases, Shitala, is still loved and appeased, as seen in the colorful paint and tinsel that adorns the square white **Shitala Temple** and heard in the distorted music that blares in stereo. This maverick goddess' temple is more popular than any of the *lingas* of Dashaswamedh. Also on the *ghat* is **Brahmeshwar,** the *linga* that Brahma is supposed to have established.

The Vishwanath (Golden Temple) Area

Go up Dashaswamedh Rd. and turn right through a temple-like archway (braving the drug pushers), and signs will lead you to the center of Varanasi's religious geography: the temple of Shiva as **Vishwanath** (Lord of All). Nicknamed the **Golden Temple,** the Vishweshwar *linga* it contains is claimed to have been the first one on earth; it is one of India's 12 *jyotirlingas,* which are said to have shot up from the ground as shafts of light. All of Varanasi is measured in circles around Vishwanath, and it is the most important place for pilgrims. The temple is closed to non-Hindus, but shopkeepers across the road are glad to charge visitors for the view from their rooftops (about Rs5). One can gaze at the gilded spire of the Golden Temple and listen to the bells inside. Within the main temple are many smaller temples of other deities and *pandits* sitting in front of each of them, asking for outrageous donations—you can ignore them. It is, however, customary to take flower garlands into the temple. The present temple is relatively recent, dating from 1777, but many versions stood here before.

The carpeted corridor to the right of the temple leads to the **Gyanavapi** (Well of Wisdom), which is protected under columns and a roof. The well's opening is thoroughly sealed off, but its sacred waters of wisdom, said to have been tapped from the earth by Shiva, are ladled out daily under police supervision. The police are nervous about the Gyanavapi because it sits between the Vishwanath Temple and the **Gyanavapi Mosque,** which the Mughal emperor Aurangzeb built in 1669 from the rubble of an earlier Vishwanath Temple he supposedly destroyed. The mosque is now ringed with barbed wire and only open at prayer times, a precaution against Hindu communalist threats to knock it down.

The most important goddess temple in Varanasi is dedicated to Shakti (power or energy), Shiva's consort, in the form of **Annapurna.** It is across from Vishwanath, just down the lane, and it, too, is closed to non-Hindus. Annapurna is a provider of food, armed with spoons and saucepans. A "Mountain of Food" festival occurs here in late October or early November.

The next *ghat* on the river from Dashaswamedh is **Man Mandir Ghat,** topped by one of the observatories built by Maharaja Jai Singh of Jaipur in the 18th century. Climb up on the right side of the building to see an arsenal of astronomical scales made of stone. Above **Mir Ghat** and **Lalita Ghat** are a few important temples. The **Vishalakshi Temple** belongs to a "Wide-Eyed" local goddess, but it is also a *Shakti pitha;* the eye of the goddess Sati (or by some accounts her earring) is said to have landed here when she was chopped apart in the heavens (see **Divine Dismemberment,** p. 418). Nearby, a deep well, the **Dharma Kup,** marks the site where Yama, the god of death, paid homage to Shiva.

Manikarnika Ghat

An axis of holiness runs between the Vishwanath Temple and the next *ghat,* **Manikarnika Ghat.** This is the most sacred of the *ghats* and the last stop pilgrims make on the river. Manikarnika's holiness is such that the area just south of it has become the city's **prime cremation ground.** Boats full of wood are moored here and the pyres emit a campfire-like smoke 24 hours a day, consuming the corpses of those liberated in Kashi. Bodies are carried down on stretchers and dipped in the Ganga, then burned for three hours on fires lit from an eternal flame on the *ghat.* Members of the formerly Untouchable Dom caste manage the ceremony. When the burning is complete, the eldest son of the deceased throws a pot of Ganga water onto the fire, and the ashes are sprinkled in the river. Local commentators will tell you that the shoulder bones of men (because of their strong hearts) and the pelvic bones of women (because of their strong wombs) will not burn; these are thrown in the river along with the ashes. Above the *ghat* are hospices where the dying come to wait their turn.

Visitors can watch the cremations from boats or from buildings above the *ghat,* but mourners and workers get annoyed (it is, after all, a cremation, not a side show) with anyone who lingers on the *ghat.* **Photographing the cremations is not permitted.**

Manikarnika Ghat takes its name from **Manikarnika Kund,** the small white-painted tank just past the cremation grounds, which Vishnu is said to have dug out at the beginning of time and filled with his sweat. This first pool of water so delighted Shiva that he dropped his jeweled earring *(manikarnika)* in it. Vishnu's footprints have been installed nearby under a circular shelter. People don't just come to Manikarnika Ghat to die; bathing here and worshiping at Vishwanath is a daily pattern for many Banarsis, and an essential part of any pilgrimage.

Sankata Ghat and Beyond

One next approaches **Sankata Ghat,** above which is the baby-blue temple of **Sankata Devi,** a powerful mother-goddess. But the next important *ghat* at which to bathe is **Panchganga Ghat.** Here five rivers are said to converge: the Ganga, Yamuna, and Saraswati, which flow together from Allahabad upstream, and two old rivulets, the Dhutapapa and Kirana, which have now disappeared. Vishnu chose this place as the greatest spot in Kashi, and his creaky painted temple of **Bindu Madhava** sits above the *ghat.* During the month of Karthika (Oct.-Nov.) the temple and the *ghat* are decked with lamps at night. The rest of the year the most prominent feature of Panchganga Ghat is the tall **Dharhara Mosque** perched at the top. Emperor Aurangzeb built this on the ruins of an earlier Bindu Madhava temple, and now it dominates a section of the riverbank skyline. It is closed to visitors because of threats from Hindu communalists to "take it back."

A statue of a sacred cow at **Gai Ghat** watches over an array of *Shivalingams*. Close to this is **Trilochan Ghat,** with the popular temple of the "Three-Eyed" Shiva. **Varanasi Devi,** the city-goddess of Varanasi, also inhabits this temple.

North from this point, the *ghats* begin to thin out, both in construction and population. This is the oldest part of the city, but it was also the part Muslims settled in, and many ancient Hindu spots now lie forgotten. The next *ghat* of visible importance is **Raj Ghat,** the last before the Malaviya Bridge. This is the crossing-point where, since ancient times, traders have forded the Ganga or ferried across it.

The temple of **Adi Keshava** (Original Vishnu) sits on a high, lonely bank to the north of the bridge. Vishnu supposedly washed his feet here at the confluence of the Ganga and Varuna rivers, but the confluence is also sacred as the northern city limit of Varanasi. Vishnu's tall temple here predates the city of Varanasi.

Inside the City

In general, the farther one is from the water in Varanasi, the less there is to see. One exception is the temple of **Kala Bhaironath,** up Chauk Rd. from Godaulia, near its intersection with Kabir Chaura Rd. *(Open daily 6am-1pm and 3-9pm.)* Once an angry and sinful form of Shiva, Kala Bhaironath (also known as Bhairava) chopped off one of the heads of the god Brahma. As punishment, the rotting head stuck to his hand, and for years Bhairava had to wander in fits of remorse. It was not until he got to Varanasi that the head (which was just a skull by this point) miraculously dropped off his hand. After this he became the mustachioed police chief of the holy city, in charge of making sure that the citizens of Varanasi live righteously. Not too far away, on the other side of the Chauk-Kabir Chaura Rd. crossing, is the temple of **Bare Ganesh,** the central Ganesh shrine in Varanasi.

A spirit of urbane and modernized Hinduism can be seen in the **Bharat Mata Temple,** on the city's western outskirts south of the Cantonment. Mahatma Gandhi inaugurated this temple, which has a swimming-pool-sized marble relief map of India in place of a deity. There's a good view from the upper balconies (camera fee Rs5.)

Varanasi's other sights are outside the city proper. Across Panch Koshi Rd. at the south end is **Benares Hindu University (BHU).** Founded in 1916 by the reformer Madan Mohan Malaviya, it was designed to merge modern ideas with the best traditions of Hindu learning. For those not stopping to study Indian languages or philosophy here, there are two places suited to shorter visits. One is the **Birla Vishwanath Temple,** the largest temple in the city, with its tasteful white spire meant to replicate the one knocked down by Aurangzeb in 1669. *(Open daily 6am-1pm and 3-9pm.)* It contains Shiva's *linga,* adorned with flowers and quenching its thirst with the drops of Ganga water which fall from the copper bucket hanging above. Most afternoons, the temple echoes with the melodious voice of Ram Naresh, a blind devotee of Shiva, singing *bhajans* in classical Hindustani *ragas.* The second sight on campus is the **Bharat Kala Bhawan,** the BHU museum. *(Open July-April M-Sa 11am-4:30pm, May-June M-Sa 7:30am-12:30pm. Admission Rs5.)* Its collection of paintings, artifacts, and sculptures is extensive and comes from a great range of styles, even if they appear a bit neglected. The second floor boasts the sculptures and paintings of Alice Boner, the renowned Indophile who claimed she could understand India on its own terms. There is plenty here from Varanasi too, from 19th-century etchings of *ghats* to a great statue of Krishna lifting Mt. Govardhana.

The barren expanse of the east shore of the Ganga holds one point of interest, the **Ramnagar Fort.** This is the castle of Varanasi's maharaja, located in the village of Ramnagar, approximately opposite BHU at the south end of the city. The river can be crossed on a pontoon bridge in winter or a ferry in summer. The fort contains a royal museum with plenty of sedan chairs and swords from the royal family's past, though all of the exhibits are quite dilapidated. Ramnagar is probably not worth the detour unless it's for the **Ramlila,** the festive *Ramayana* pageant. *(Sept. 24-Oct. 23, 1999; Sept. 12-Oct. 12, 2000.)*

SHOPPING

Varanasi is famous for its silk, and the touts will never let your forget it. There are seven silk shops in Varanasi which have fixed prices and government-enforced quality control. Three of these are located on Vishwanath Gali in the Old City, on the same road as the Golden Temple: **Mohan Silk Stores,** 5/54 Vishwanath Gali (tel. 322354); **Bhagwan Stores,** D 10/32 Vishwanath Gali (tel. 322365); and **J.R. Ivory Arts and Curios,** D 20 Vishwanath Gali (tel. 321772). Two others are at Sindhu Nagar, off Aurangabad Rd. near the intersection of Aurangabad and Vidyapith: **M/S Bhagwanlila Exports,** 41 Sindhu Nagar Colony, Sigra (tel. 357003), and **Mahalakshmi Saree House,** 16 Sindhu Nagar, Sigra (tel. 356607). The other two are **Chowdhary Brothers,** Thatheri Bazaar (tel. 320469), opposite the police station, and **Mehrotra Silk Factory,** S.C. 21/22 Englishia Line, Cantonment (tel. 345289), off Cantonment Station Rd. just before it intersects with Vidyapith. Mehrotra has also opened a small branch in the Vishnu Rest House for your shopping convenience. It's a good idea to visit these shops to get a sense of the prices of top-quality silk before bargaining in the Chauk or Old City, where you might get a great deal. (Shops open daily 10am-9pm.)

MUSIC

Varanasi is well-known as a bastion of Indian classical music. Many Westerners come to Varanasi to learn how to play the *sitar* or *tabla*. The best resource in this respect is the music school at **Benares Hindu University (BHU),** located near Lanka Gate, south of Godaulia (tel. 310290, ext. 241). Though the school itself only offers degree courses in both Hindi and English (which require one year's attendance and cost Rs6000 per year, including mandatory dorm rental), the faculty offer **private lessons** and can refer students to other teachers. Another good place to learn *sitar* or *tabla* is the **Triveni Music Centre** (tel. 328074), on Keval Gali in Godaulia, not far from Baba Restaurant. Instructor Nandu and his father are particularly recommended, but instructors and fees must be negotiated face-to-face. The **International Music Centre,** near Dashaswamedh Ghat, offers private *sitar* and *tabla* lessons for Rs60 per hour. From Godaulia Crossing, walk toward Dashaswamedh Ghat. When the road splits, go right, and at the sign for the Kali Temple, go right again. The path swings to the left. Take the first right, the next left, walk straight, and the school will be on your left.

Buying musical instruments can be a tricky business. *Sitar* and *tabla* stores abound in the Old City area. There is one *sitar* store recommended by the faculty at BHU, located near the Jangambali Post Office; the proprietor, Mr. Nitai Chandra Nath, is a sage of string instruments and a true artisan. From Godaulia Crossing, facing Dashaswamedh, turn right, go straight, turn into the third lane on your left (1km from Godaulia Crossing); the Jangambali (Beagalitola) Post Office will appear immediately on your left, and the unmarked *sitar* store is several doors down on the left. *Sitars* range from Rs2000 to Rs5000. One *tabla* shop comes highly recommended by Mr. Nath: **Imtiyaz Ali,** Siddh Giri Bagh. From Godaulia Crossing: facing away from Dashaswamedh Ghat, walk or take a rickshaw to the third big intersection (including Godaulia Crossing), take a right turn, and after 1km the small shop appears on the left. Tablas range from Rs1500 (brass drums) to Rs2000 (copper drums).

■ Sarnath सरनथ

In the wooded suburbs north of Varanasi lies Sarnath, the site of Gautama Buddha's first and, some say, last sermon (since subsequent teachings were in the form of dialogues, like those of Socrates). After the Buddha attained enlightenment in Bodh Gaya, the Awakened One walked 200km to Sarnath, lotuses blooming where his feet touched the ground. He gathered his former companions, and here, among the deer and peacocks, revealed the Noble Eightfold Path. In later years he occasionally returned to this quiet grove to meditate amid the lush vegetation.

In the 3rd century BC, under the rule of the Mauryas, *stupas* were built to commemorate the visits of the Buddha. This construction continued in force until the 4th century AD, when the Hindu Guptas rose to power and Buddhist influence began to wane. It was at this point, however, that Sarnath became famous for its sandstone images of Buddha. Sarnath's prestige as a center of Buddhism came to an abrupt end in the 12th century when it was demolished by Qutb-ud-din Aibak. Although Sarnath's Deer Park is dotted with the foundations of many small and large *stupas,* only one monument, the Dhamekh Stupa, remains intact. Nevertheless, simply by walking around the sites, it is possible to get some sense of the breadth, if not the depth, of Sarnath's devotion to Buddhism. Thousands of Buddhist pilgrims from South and Southeast Asia come here on pilgrimage; and reaching back further still, it is possible to imagine the Buddha himself walking these same paths. For more information on **Buddhism,** see p. 97.

ORIENTATION AND PRACTICAL INFORMATION Ashok Marg, which runs north from Varanasi, turns into **Dharmapal Road.** As you enter Sarnath, the **Archaeological Museum** is on the right as you round the bend toward the official entrance to the sites, 500m down on the left. The **bus stand** is 500m away at a small intersection. A small **railway station** lies 1km from the bus stand on Dharmapal Rd., but few trains stop here. Try local **buses** instead, which go to Lanka/BHU and the Varanasi Railway Station (every 5min., 7am-5pm, 15min., Rs5). **Tempos** go to the Civil Court, Cantonment, Varanasi (Rs20). **Auto-rickshaws** putter where you please (Rs50 for Varanasi). There's a small **government hospital** in a yellow building across from the Tourist Bungalow. The **post office** (tel. 385013; open M-Sa 8:30am-4:30pm) and **Tourist Bungalow** are located opposite each other on a side road near the bus stand. From the bus stand, facing toward the sites, turn left onto a small road, and they're 200m down on the left. There's a small information counter in the bungalow, which gives out maps of the sites (open M-Sa 10am-5pm). STD/ISD **telephone** booths are located nearby on Dharmapal Rd.

ACCOMMODATIONS AND FOOD Most tourists don't spend the night, but it's possible to stay in some of the monasteries for a small donation. The **Tourist Bungalow** (tel. 386965) has rooms with bath, air-cooling, lockers, and soft mattress (dorm beds Rs35; doubles Rs225). The large dining room (open daily 7am-10pm) serves breakfast items and standard Indian and Chinese dishes (Rs30-60). The other restaurant worth mentioning is **Rangoli Garden Restaurant** (tel. 381725), 1km after the Tourist Bungalow on the left. Dishes are prepared fresh, so be prepared to wait—the taste is worth it. Garlic chicken (Rs50) or spring rolls (Rs50) make for a darn good lunch.

SIGHTS Sightseeing in Sarnath is more like *site*-seeing. Most points of interest are piles of rubble, only recently excavated. The first stop, however, is completely intact. From the bus stand, walk 100m along Dharmapal Rd., turn right under the arch, and walk 200m toward the sandstone spires of the modern Buddhist temple **Mulgandha Kuti Vihar.** *(Open daily 4-11:30am and 1:30-7pm.)* The interior is decorated with wall paintings by the Japanese artist Kosetsu Nosi, inspired by the *Buddhacarita (The Acts of the Buddha).* The *pipal* tree growing in the shrine is purportedly a close relative of the tree under which Buddha achieved enlightenment. A book stall sells Buddhist pamphlets and a bilingual edition of the *Buddhacarita.*

Leaving the temple, walk right along a clay path to **Dhamekh Stupa,** the only ancient structure left intact by Qutb-ud-din's armies. It commemorates the spot where the Buddha delivered his first sermon. Built in either the 5th or 6th century, in the twilight of Buddhist predominance in North India, it remains unfinished. The bottom is made of elaborately decorated stone, with eight niches in eight directions, all of which once held images of the Buddha. The top is composed of small bricks, made from the clay abundant in the area.

Straight ahead are the foundational bricks of the **Dharmarajika Stupa.** The breadth of the foundation indicates a massive structure. It was built by the Mauryan emperor Ashoka in the 3rd century BC to house the relics of Buddha which, these days, are displayed at the Buddha Purnima festival in May. Unlike other structures at this site, the Dharmarajika Stupa was destroyed only recently (1794) by greedy treasure-hounds.

To the rear of the *stupa* are the remains of the **Main Shrine,** also built by Ashoka, to commemorate the place where Buddha meditated. To the left down a shallow well is the bottom portion of **Ashoka's column.** The column is engraved with Buddhist edicts in Brahmi script, admonishing Buddhist monks and nuns against creating schisms among the followers of the Buddha (the advice wasn't taken). When Ashoka converted from a warlord's life to the path of *dharma,* he advertised his new beliefs in edicts on many such columns. The capitol has also been preserved and can be viewed in the Archaeological Museum.

Walking back from the Main Shrine, or taking a roundabout clay path which starts to the left of Ashoka's column, you arrive at the high fence which guards the deer sanctuary, known today as **Deer Park,** although, historically, this name belongs to all of Sarnath. Peacocks cavort with long-horn stags, as they are said to have done in the Anandavana (Forest of Bliss), the ancient forest which covered southern Varanasi. Now the animals' un-self-conscious play is broken by the bewildering "deer calls" of young touts jockeying for *baksheesh.*

Exiting through the official entrance in front of the Dharmarajika Stupa, cross the street to the **Archaeological Museum.** *(Open Sa-Th 10am-5pm. Admission Rs2.)* Inside the museum, the splendidly engraved capitol from Ashoka's column, with four roaring lions seated back to back, is one of the great masterpieces of early Indian art. It was adopted as the emblem of the Indian republic and appears on all Indian currency. The museum displays at its entrance a first-century standing Buddha from Mathura. With his broad shoulders and strong arms, this Buddha looks more like a warrior than a wandering ascetic. Other pieces of note include a perfectly wrought teaching Buddha from the Gupta period, who sits, serenely contemplative, holding forth on some *topos* of the Eight-Fold Path.

One kilometer from the Archaeological Museum, on the road parallel to the Rangoli Garden Restaurant road, is the magnificent melange of Buddhist-Mughal architecture, the **Chaukhandi Stupa.** The rectangular Gupta-period foundation commemorating the site where the Buddha met his five disciples, is graced by a crowning Mughal-style tower built by either Emperor Akbar or Raja Govandhan, the local ruler, to mark the site where Emperor Humayun once spent a summer night.

■ Allahabad इलाहाबाद

Allahabad (ee-LA-ha-bad) is the sacred city on the Sangam, the confluence of the Ganga and Yamuna rivers, as well as the mythical Saraswati, the river of wisdom. Lord Brahma called this spot Tirth Raj—king of pilgrimage sites—and all devout Hindus try to bathe in its waters once in their lives. For thousands of years, the city reaching back from the river bank was called Prayag (Confluence). While this name is still sometimes used, more common is Allahabad, the Persio-Arabic name meaning "Place of God" given to the city by the Mughal emperors. The British would later claim Allahabad as the capital of the United Provinces (Uttar Pradesh's precursor) after 1901. The Indian Independence movement was strongly rooted here due to the work of the Nehrus, the Allahabad family that would forge a political dynasty after Independence. Now Allahabad is a rather quiet city of one million people. This very un-Indian city, with its wide avenues and British buildings, becomes Indian-ized every 12 years when it hosts the Maha Kumbh Mela, the greatest Hindu festival of all, during which millions of pilgrims converge at the Sangam.

ORIENTATION

Allahabad is divided both in body and spirit by the **railway.** North of the tracks is the shady British-built **Civil Lines** area, with all of its roads in a grid; south is the congested and gritty **Chauk** area. Both of these stretch east-west along the tracks. Not only do Chauk and Civil Lines look different, it is actually hard to get from one side to the other since only a few roads go over or under the tracks. At the center of town the two sides are completely divided. On the south side of Allahabad is the **Yamuna River,** and on the east side is the **Ganga,** but apart from the spiritual importance of the Sangam, the city is not very river-oriented.

In Civil Lines, **Mahatma Gandhi (M.G.) Road,** with a lineup of hotels, restaurants, and ice cream stands, is the road to stick to for orientation; its tall statues make memorable landmarks. **Kamla Nehru Road** turns up from M.G. Rd. toward Allahabad University. **Leader Road** runs alongside the tracks on the Chauk side, while the **Grand Trunk Road** takes you through the heart of Chauk. Turning onto Triveni Rd. from the Grand Trunk Rd. you can reach the **Sangam.** Many cheap hotels dot **Dr. Katiu Road,** close to the train station between Leader Rd. and the Grand Trunk Rd.

PRACTICAL INFORMATION

Trains: Allahabad Junction Railway Station, Leader Rd. A 30min. walk from the Civil Lines Bus Stand on M.G. Rd. With your back to the bus stand, walk left 6 blocks west until you hit the All Saints' Cathedral, then take a left turn and walk 3 blocks to the train station. Fares 2nd/1st class. To: **Agra** (*Udyan Abha Toofan Exp.* 3007, 4:30am, 11hr., Rs94/470); **Delhi** (*Howrah-New Delhi Poorva Exp.* 2381, 10:50pm, 10hr.; *Puri-New Delhi Exp.* 2381, 7:25am, 9hr; *Puri-New Delhi Purshottam Exp.* 2801, 7:05pm, 9½hr., Rs124/620); **Gorakhpur** (*Chauri-Chaura Exp.* 5003, 9:15pm, 9hr., Rs56/274); **Gwalior** (*Howrah-Gwalior Chambal Exp.* 1159, M, Tu, Th, and F 6:10am, 11½hr., Rs101/511); **Kanpur** (*Poorva Exp.* 2381, 10:50pm, 2½hr.; *Muzaffarpur-Delhi Exp.* 5205, 6:25pm, 2½hr., Rs48/239); **Lucknow** (*Triveni Exp.* 4269, 4:10am, 5hr.; *Mughalsarai Bareilly Exp.* 4307, 10:30pm, 7½hr., Rs44/180); **Satna** (*Varanasi-Chennai Ganga Kaveri* 6040, 7:55pm, 3hr., Rs49/246, then a 4hr. bus trip from Satna to Khajuraho).

Buses: There are 3 main bus stations: Civil Lines Bus Stand, around the corner from the Tourist Bungalow on M.G. Rd.; Leader Rd. Bus Stand, behind the main Allahabad Junction Railway Station; and Zero Rd. Bus Stand, north of Chauk. From **Leader Rd.,** buses leave for **Agra** and **Delhi** (every hr., 6am-8pm, 2hr., Rs15). From **Civil Lines** to: **Ayodhya** (9am, Rs60); **Gorakhpur** (9am, Rs50); **Lucknow** (2:30pm, Rs65); and **Varanasi** (every 30min., Rs35). All schedule inquiries should be directed to the drivers standing in front of their respective buses.

Local Transportation: Cycle-rickshaws are the most common mode of transportation (Rs10 from the Allahabad Junction Railway Station to the Tourist Bungalow on M.G. Rd.). Drivers are less cut-throat than those in big tourist cities. There are no auto-rickshaws. **Tempos** wait at the bus or railway stations. To reach the Sangam, take a tempo to Daraganj Railway Station and walk south from the tracks.

Tourist Office: Tourist Bungalow, M.G. Rd. (tel. 601873). Just around the corner from the Civil Lines Bus Stand. A Rs10 rickshaw ride from Allahabad Junction. Has a cluttered city map inside a UP Tourism brochure (Rs2). Open M-Sa 10am-5pm.

Currency Exchange: State Bank of India, 4 Kacheri Rd. (tel. 608224), near District Court. Take a cycle-rickshaw up Kamla Nehru Rd.; take the 4th left after Allahabad Museum. Open M-F 10am-2pm, Sa 10am-noon.

Market: There's a large fruit market at **Khuldabad Mandi Bazaar** near the clock tower, at the intersection of Dr. Katiu and Grand Trunk Rd.

Bookstore: M/S A. H. Wheeler Book Shop, 19 M.G. Rd. (tel. 624106) is one of the best in U.P. Facing away from the Tourist Bungalow, walk 5 blocks to the left. On the left side, to the right of the Palace Cinema. Has excellent travel guides and literary selections. 10% discount with university affiliation. Open M-Sa 10am-7pm.

Pharmacy/Hospital: Nazareth Hospital, 13/A Kamla Nehru Rd. (tel. 600430). From the intersection of M.G. and Kamla Nehru Rd., it's 1km to the northeast, on the left side, marked by a red cross and the name of the hospital in Hindi. The best private hospital in town, with a fully stocked pharmacy.

Emergency: tel. 652000.

Post Office: GPO, Queen's Rd. Go left at the Tourist Bungalow until All Saints' Cathedral, then right for 1 block. Open M-Sa 9am-5pm. *Poste Restante* operates on the same hours: enquire at the desk at the back right corner of the sorting hall opposite the main hall. **Postal Code:** 211001.

Internet: Vivek Internet World, 12 Johnstonganj (tel. 402627), in the PCO booth attached to Hotel Vivek. Surf in A/C comfort for Rs25 per 10min. Open daily 9am-11pm. **Pioneer PCO,** M.G. Marg (tel. 624383), across from the Palace Cinema. Small, cramped, noisy A/C booth (Rs25 per 10min.). Open daily 10am-10pm.

Telephone: STD/ISD booths are as common as dirt here. **Telephone Code:** 0532.

NORTH INDIA

Allahabad

ACCOMMODATIONS

B Hotel Continental
A Hotel Kohinoor
C Hotel Vivek
D Tourist Bungalow

Ganga River

Sangam

TO VARANASI

TO VARANASI

Hanuman Temple

Daraganj R.S.

Prayagghat R.S.

Beni Bandh Road

Bandh Road

Prayag Railway Station

TO LUCKNOW

State Bank of India

Immigration Office

Anand Bhawan

Jawaharlal Nehru Marg

Fort

Fort Road

Grand Trunk Road (NH2)

Trivani Road

Yamuna Bank Road

Saraswati Ghat

Minto Park

Yamuna River

University and Archaeological Museum

Motilal Nehru Road

St. Joseph's Cathedral

Allahabad Museum

Pannalal Road

Maharaja Marg

Lala Sitaram Road

City Railroad Station

Nazareth Hospital

Kamla Nehru Road

Kasturba Gandhi Marg

Lauder Road

Yamuna Road

Yamuna Bridge

Tejbahadur Sapru Road

CIVIL LINES

Sardar Patel Marg

Civil Lines Bus Stand

Smith Road

Swami Vivekanand Marg

Zero Rd. Bus Station

Zero Rd.

CHAUK

Tilak Road

Muir Road

Clive Road

Indian Airlines

Tashkent Marg

Lal Bahadur Shastri Marg

Nawab Yusuf Road

Colvin Rd.

Leader Road

N.S.C. Road

A.P. Banerji Road

Shaukat Ali Marg

Maharshi Dayanand Marg

Naidu Marg

Sarojini Marg

GPO

All Saints' Cathedral

Allahabad Junction

Dr. Katju Rd.

Clock Tower

Khuldabad Mandi Bazaar

Nirula Road

Purushottamdas Tandon Marg

Leader Rd. Bus Stand

Khusrau Bagh

Grand Trunk Road (NH2)

Carlappa Road

TO KANPUR

TO KANPUR

N

ACCOMMODATIONS

Civil Lines lends luxury to the hotel scene. Quiet, less pricey hotels are located along M.G. Rd. More cheapies are concentrated around Leader Rd., near the bus stand.

Tourist Bungalow, M.G. Rd. (tel. 601440), near Civil Lines Bus Stand. From the bus stand, walk left—it will be on the left. A Rs10 rickshaw ride from Allahabad Junction. For some reason, the locks are outside the windows. Extremely clean, with hard foam rubber mattresses. Downstairs restaurant open daily 6am-10pm. Bar serves liquor (Rs25-50) and beer (Rs60-100) daily noon-10pm. Check-out noon. Dorm beds Rs30; singles with bath Rs150, with air-cooling Rs225, with A/C Rs400; doubles Rs200/275/450.

Hotel Continental, Dr. Katiu Rd. (tel. 652058). From Allahabad Junction Railway Station, walk to Leader Rd., make a right on Leader, then an immediate left onto Dr. Katiu Rd. In a noisy, congested area. Clean, soft beds and limited room service. STD/ISD service, hot water (in winter), and check-out are all 24hr. Singles with bath Rs140, with air-cooling Rs180, with A/C Rs400; doubles Rs180/240/450.

Hotel Kohinoor, 10 Noorulla Rd. (tel. 602031). From Allahabad Junction, take a right onto Leader Rd. and a left onto Noorulla; the hotel is 300m down the road on the left. Tastefully decorated accommodations, situated around lush gardens. Peach-colored restrooms, comfy leather chairs in every room, and room service. Singles Rs200; doubles Rs250, with air-cooling Rs300/400.

Hotel Vivek, 12 Johnstonganj (tel. 400033). From the Tourist Bungalow, take a right and then another right onto P.D. Tandon Park Crossing, then go 500m—Hotel Vivek is on the right. All rooms have attached bathroom and air-cooling. Singles Rs70; doubles with attached bathroom and air-cooling Rs110.

FOOD

Dining outside is *de rigueur* along M.G. Rd. Crowded benches surround fast food stalls serving Indian snacks, cold drinks, and imitation American junk food. More traditional Indian restaurants curry favor in Chauk, especially along Dr. Katiu Rd. and Nirula Rd., while some gloomy bars border Leader Rd.

Tandoor, 40 M.G. Rd. (tel. 623436). Take a left from the Tourist Bungalow and go past the Bose statue at the intersection; Tandoor is in the shopping center on the left. The tempting array of food at this friendly, family-oriented restaurant includes cheese *masala dosa* (Rs15) and Karhai chicken (Rs60).

El Chico Restaurant, M.G. Rd. (tel. 420753). Take a left from the Tourist Bungalow, and El Chico is on the right after the four-way crossing. No enchiladas here, just a classy, unpretentious restaurant. The Continental and Indian entrees are tasty but expensive. The prices are better for the salads, which are washed with filtered water. Open daily 10am-10:30pm.

Hot Stuff, Sardar Patel Marg. From the Tourist Bungalow take a left and a right onto Sardar Patel Marg at the four-way crossing. Allahabad's coolest fast food joint ("fast food" Indian style—12min.). The selection of ice cream, pizzas, and lamb-burgers draws crowds of hip, English-speaking college students. "Boyish Burger" Rs25.

Hotel Bridges, 22 Sardar Patel Marg (tel. 622878). From the Tourist Bungalow take a left and then a right onto Sardar Patel Marg at the four-way crossing. The hotel is 800m down on the left in Hotel Vilas-Bridges. The best Chinese food in town. Crisp noodle chow mein goes for Rs120. Open daily 11am-11pm.

SIGHTS

Allahabad's chief attraction for millions of Hindu pilgrims is the **Triveni Sangam,** the confluence of the rivers Ganga, Yamuna, and Saraswati, and the site of the dodecennial Kumbh Mela. The Yamuna skirts the south side of Allahabad, and the Ganga rushes along the east. The mythical Saraswati, the river of wisdom, is said to flow underground. For a negotiable fee (no more than Rs20) boats will take visitors from the riverboat by the fort to the meeting place of the rivers, although the different colors of the Ganga and Yamuna's waters are clearly visible from the shore. Sharing a boat

The Kumbh Mela

The Maha (Great) Kumbh Mela at Allahabad in 1989 set the record for the world's largest human gathering. Thirteen million people are estimated to have come for this Hindu festival, the holiest time to bathe in the Sangam. Every 12 years, at one precisely calculated moment, all the pilgrims splash into the water, an act which is believed to undo lifetimes of sin. Columns of charging *sadhus*, often naked and smeared with ash, are among the most zealous bathers.

The story behind the Kumbh Mela concerns a *kumbh* (pot) said to have contained an immortality-bestowing nectar. The demons battled the gods for this pot in a struggle that lasted 12 days, during which time four drops of nectar were spilled. One landed at **Haridwar** (see p. 159), one at **Nasik** (see p. 634), one at **Ujjain** (see p. 244), and one at **Allahabad.** The mythical 12-day fight translates to 12 human years, the length of the festival's rotation between cities. Every three years a Kumbh Mela is held in one of the four cities in January or February. The Maha Kumbh Mela, held at Allahabad every 12th year, is the greatest of all. Smaller *melas,* known as Magh Melas, are held in Allahabad in off-years during the month of Magh (Jan.-Feb.). In the sixth year, midway between Maha Kumbh Melas, an Ardh (Half) Kumbh Mela is held. The next Kumbh Mela is scheduled to occur in Allahabad in 2001.

with pilgrims costs much less and is much more interesting. The water is warm and shallow in summer; sometimes it's possible to walk to the Sangam over the floodplains that spread out from the city. Millions of pilgrims camp here during the Kumbh Mela. At other times, especially at dusk, the sand around the Sangam is ideal for meditation.

Alongside the road approaching the Sangam is the **fort** built by Emperor Akbar in 1583. The Indian army still finds the confluence strategically important, so the fort is full of soldiers, and visitors are not allowed entrance, except to a small courtyard in the east side of the fort. Beneath the dirt here is the **Patalpuri Underground Temple** and its weird toybox of gods and goddesses illuminated through ceiling grates.

In the shadow of the fort's outer wall facing the Sangam side is the **Hanuman Temple,** dedicated to the monkey god. *(Open daily 6am-2pm and 5-10pm.)* What looks like an orange King Kong lies buried in flowers in the basement; it is rare to see Hanuman lying down like this. The temple itself is only a shed, but a very popular one (not to be confused with the multi-storied affair grinning out over the trees—that's the Shankar Viman Mandapam). The floodwaters are said to pour over Hanuman's feet each year before they recede.

To reach the other side of the fort, it is necessary to take either a boat ride or detour through the fenced-off military installation behind the fort. Beyond the fort, on the bank of the Yamuna, is **Saraswati Ghat,** where boats dock and evening ceremony lamps are floated down to the confluence. Follow Yamuna Bank Rd. away from the fort to reach **Minto Park** on the right, where Lord Canning in 1858 proclaimed that India would be ruled by the Queen of England. Independent India has reclaimed the historic site by renaming the park for Madan Mohan Malaviya (an Independence figure and critic of the caste system) and erecting a part-Mauryan, part-Italian monument. Allahabad's teenagers have had the last word, however, with their graffiti.

At the northeast corner of the city, close to the Civil Lines, is **Anand Bhawan** (tel. 600476), once the mansion of the **Nehru family,** now a museum devoted to their memory. *(Open Tu-Su 9:30am-5pm. Admission Rs2.)* Independence leader Motilal Nehru, his son Prime Minister Jawaharlal Nehru, and Jawaharlal's daughter and future Prime Minister Indira Gandhi all lived and worked here, hosting meetings of the Independence movement. The Mahatma even had a room and working area here. The surprisingly modest Nehru showcase exhibits the family's passion for books; their bookshelves are stacked with everything from Roman Law to Tagore, all of which can be peered at through glass panels. There's also a **bookstore** at Anand Bhawan, as well as a **planetarium.** *(Shows daily at 11am, noon, 2, 3, and 4pm; admission Rs8.)* And if you just can't get enough of the Gandhis, then head next door to the **Swaraj Bhawan Museum,** the home of the patriarch Motilal Nehru. *(Open T-Su 9:30am-5pm.)* This well-preserved mansion has an excellent Hindi sound and light show (Rs5) which takes you through the house while walking you through the independence movement.

The **Allahabad Museum** (tel. 600834) is on Kamla Nehru Marg. *(Open Tu-Su 10am-5pm; Rs2.)* It houses numerous sculptures including many terra-cotta figures from Kausambi, the ancient city and Buddhist center 60km from Allahabad. There's also a room with photographs and a few mementos of Jawaharlal Nehru.

The boldest reminder of the British in Allahabad is in Civil Lines, at the intersection of Mahatma Gandhi Rd. and Sarojini Naidu Marg (incidentally, both roads' namesakes were strong Independence leaders). **All Saints' Cathedral** waits in the middle of the traffic circle here as if it were on a coaster. *(Open daily 10am-5pm. Services Su 8am.)* The Gothic edifice, with its stained-glass windows, was designed by Sir William Emerson, the same architect who drew up the Victoria Memorial in Calcutta.

Just as All Saints' is the most British remnant in Allahabad, **Khusrau Bagh,** in the Chauk area across the railway lines, is the most Mughal. These gardens hold the speckled tombs of Khusrau (a son of Emperor Jahangir), Khusrau's Rajput mother (who committed suicide), his sister, and his faithful *paan-wallah.* Following Mughal family tradition, Khusrau plotted against his father and was subsequently murdered by his brother, the future emperor Shah Jahan, in 1615. Fruit is grown in the gardens, where would-be civil servants sit and study for examinations.

■ Kanpur कानपुर

This bustling business and transportation center has little to offer the tourist, unless you're into macabre murder scenes. With 2.5 million inhabitants, Kanpur is the largest city in UP. This strategically located merchants' hub, situated near major rail and river routes, is surrounded by an outer ring of factories and chemical plants and an inner circle of tall, dingy apartment buildings. The city spreads out for miles and miles from the **Ganga River.** For the most part, everything is situated around the **Mall Road.** area, with the **Kanpur Central Railway Station** located 3km to the south, connected to Mall Rd. by the busy **Birhana Road.**

The **State Bank of India,** Mall Rd. (tel. 311448), 2km from the intersection with Birhana Rd., heading toward the bus stations, cashes traveler's checks and foreign currency (open M-F 10am-2pm). **Trains** leave from **Kanpur Central Railway Station.** to just about everywhere. **Chunmniganj Bus Stand,** Mall Rd. (tel. 210646; reservations open 6am-10pm) serves most points west; **Collectorganj Bus Stand,** 1km up Bhiranch Rd. from the rail station, serves Eastern U.P. **Leela Mani Memorial Hospital,** 14/116-C, Civil Lines (tel. 210022 or 210219), 500m directly behind the Landmark Hotel, has a 24-hour **pharmacy.** Kanpur's **GPO,** Mall Rd., is 1km further toward the bus stations. **Postal Code: 208001. Telephone Code: 0512.**

For just a few hours' sleep, the **dorm beds** on the second floor of the **railway station** are clean, and a good value (Rs80 for 12hr.). If you're uneasy about this prospect, a number of hotels offer fairly good deals. **Central Hotel** (tel. 328996), directly across from the railway station, has worn but spacious rooms, some with balconies overlooking the bazaar (dorm beds Rs35; singles Rs75; doubles Rs130, with air-cooling Rs200). **Hotel Ashoka,** 24/16 Birhana Rd. (tel. 312742), in an alley at the first crossing on the left from Mall Rd., has clean, well-appointed rooms (singles Rs160, with air-cooling Rs200; doubles Rs250). Most of Kanpur's hotels have attached **restaurants.** There are also coffee shops, bars, and fast-food and ice-cream joints lining Mall Rd.

The few sights in Kanpur are spread out throughout the city and require time and money to visit. Several, however, are noteworthy. About 4km down Mall Rd. is the infamous **Satichawra Ghat,** also known as **Murder Ghat,** where the English general Sir Hugh Wheeler and over a hundred other captives were hacked to death at the hands of Prince Nawa Sahib. After being captured and promised passage to Allahabad, the English were brought here to ostensibly board the boats only to be brutally murdered and have their remains thrown in a well. Later, the atrocity was returned in kind by General Sir James Neill. Before *his* prisoners were massacred, Neill forced the Hindus to eat beef and told them they were to be buried; Muslims were force-fed pork and told they were to be cremated.

Madhya Pradesh मध्य प्रदेश

True to its name, Madhya Pradesh ("Middle State") stretches across the belly of the country. Although Madhya Pradesh covers a larger area than any other state, its population numbers less than 80 million, thanks to an often arid and inhospitable climate. Aside from the Narmada River Valley's heavily populated and fertile farmland, scrubby hills and ravines cover much of the state, making travel difficult and providing refuge for *dacoits* (bandits) and tigers, as well as a home for Gond and Bhil tribals. This difficult terrain has sheltered natural and historical treasures which might otherwise have disappeared. The forests conceal the ruined cities of Mandu and Orchha, where palaces and creepers fight it out under tourists' gazes, as well as the infamous temples of Khajuraho, whose erotic carvings of cavorting kings keep visitors riveted.

Historical remains in Madhya Pradesh date back to the 3rd century BC, when the Emperor Ashoka founded Sanchi as a religious center. A succession of Buddhist and Hindu dynasties gave way to Muslim marauders from the north, all of whom inscribed their identity onto the terrain. The Mughal emperors eventually lost control of the region to the Marathas, whose leading families ruled until Independence. Today, although 93% of its population is Hindu, and its politics are dominated by the BJP, the landscape of Madyha Pradesh—from commercial centers to Buddhist pilgrimage sites to dramatic ruins—represents its multi-layered and multi-faceted past.

🖐 HIGHLIGHTS OF MADHYA PRADESH

- Madhya Pradesh has India's largest tiger population—and **Kanha National Park** (p. 248, of *Jungle Book* fame, is the best place to see them.
- The northern village of **Khajuraho** (p. 249) is home to some of the world's most exquisite erotic sculpture.
- Sublime **Bhopal** (below) provides a unique look at Muslim culture in Northern India. The city's **Bharat Bhavan** (p. 236) is one of the country's best museums.
- India is full of **forts,** but the **Gwalior's** (p. 261) is one of the most impressive.

▌ Bhopal भोपाल

With 1.2 million inhabitants, a thriving arts community, and a lively Muslim bazaar quarter, the state capital of Bhopal serves up a rich, eclectic slice of North Indian culture. The sequence of enlightened women rulers who embarked on a program of civic improvements during the 19th century have left the city interspersed with lakes and parks and punctuated with the minarets of massive mosques. Bhopal remains a good staging point for visits to the nearby Buddhist ruins at Sanchi and other sights in the state, but it is also a pleasant city in its own right. Mention Bhopal today, though, and many people pale, remembering the city as the site of the worst industrial accident in history: in the middle of the night on December 2, 1984, a cloud of lethal methylisocyanate gas leaked from the Union Carbide fertilizer factory in the north of the city. By morning, 2000 people in Bhopal had died and thousands more had been crippled for life. The plant is long closed, and though the effects of the tragedy will be felt here for years to come, Bhopal moves forward with beauty and pride, rewarding those who do visit with beautiful sights and cool lakeside breezes.

ORIENTATION

The huge **Upper Lake** and smaller **Lower Lake** separate Old Bhopal in the northwest from the **New Town** in the southeast. **Hamidia Road** runs from near the Taj-ul-Masjid (the city's largest mosque) on the western fringes of the old town, past the bus stand to the railway station in the east. There, amid many cheap hotels and restaurants, it turns right and runs south toward the new town and the government center. The

MPTDC, Indian Airlines office, and the rare State Bank with foreign exchange facilities reside in **T.T. Nagar,** one of the many neighborhoods in the diffuse colonial area.

PRACTICAL INFORMATION

Airport: Agra Rd. (tel. 521789), 12km from city center. **Indian Airlines** (tel. 550480), next door to the Gangotri Building in T.T. Nagar, about 100m on the left past the Rang Mahal cinema. Open M-Sa 10am-1pm and 2-5pm. To: **Delhi** (1 per day, US$105) via **Gwalior** (M, W, and F, 45min., US$50); **Mumbai** (1 per day, US$115) via **Indore** (30min., US$70).

Trains: The **railway station** (tel. 536827) is down the street that leads off the bend in Hamidia Rd., 1km east of the bus station. Reservation office outside platform 1, on the far right as you face the station. Open M-Sa 8am-2pm and 2:15-8pm, Su 8am-2pm. Prices listed are for 2nd class. To: **Agra** (*Shatabdi Exp.* 2001, 2:40pm, 5½hr., Rs122); **Delhi** (*Shatabdi Exp.* 2001, 2:40pm, 10hr., Rs152); **Gwalior** (*Shatabdi Exp.* 2001, 2:40pm, 4½hr., Rs96); **Hyderabad** (*Dakshin Exp.* 7022, 9:20am, 15hr., Rs67); **Indore** (*Narmada Exp.* 8234, 6:20am, 7hr., Rs65); **Jabalpur** (*Narmada Exp.* 8233, 11pm, 7hr., Rs79/388 1st class); **Jalgaon** (*Pushpak Exp.* 2134, 5:40am, 3½hr., R95); **Jhansi** (*Shatabdi Exp.* 2001, 2:40pm, 3hr., Rs67); **Mumbai** (*Pushpak Exp.* 2134, 5:40am, 15½hr., Rs223).

Buses: The **Nadra Bus Stand,** Hamidia Rd. (tel. 540841), west of the train station, 1km on the right. Frequent departures for **Sanchi** (every hr. 6am-6pm, 1½hr., Rs15); **Indore** (every 10min., 6am-6:30pm, 5hr., Rs58); and other cities around the state. For longer distances, private operators nearby offer more luxurious vehicles.

Local Transportation: Metered **auto-rickshaws** will take you anywhere, including the airport (Rs80-100), but **minibuses** (usually with helpful conductors) will whisk you almost as far for much less (about Rs2 a pop). Minibus #9 goes from the railway station to T.T. Nagar, and #7 and 11 go by Sultania Rd.

Tourist Office: MPTDC main office, 4th fl., Gangotri Building, T.T. Nagar, New Town (tel. 764397), just past the Rang Mahal movie theater. Staff can reserve rooms at all MPTDC hotels in the state. Open M-Sa 10am-5pm. Another office occupies a corner booth in the railway station lobby.

Currency Exchange: State Bank of India, Main Branch, Parcharad Building, New Market Rd., T.T. Nagar (tel. 551804 or 556299). Foreign exchange upstairs. Open M-F 10:30am-2:30pm.

Market: The wholesale **fruit and vegetable market,** which stretches to the left off Hamidia Rd. and into the bazaars as you go from the railway to bus stations, is among India's best. It gets started at about 4am and lasts into the night

Bookstore: Books World, 33 Bhadbhada Rd., T.T. Nagar (tel. 462003) stands out for its quirky selection and perilous shelving system. Open daily 10:30am-9pm.

Hospital: Hamidia Hospital (tel. 540222), Sultania Rd., near Taj-ul-Masjid, also houses a **24hr. pharmacy.**

Emergency: tel. 511446.

Police: SPO, Sultania Rd., Jehangirabad (tel. 555911), between T.T. Nagar and the railway station.

Post Office: GPO, Sultania Rd., near Taj-ul-Masjid. For *Poste Restante* ask at the enquiry counter (#1). Open M-Sa 10am-7pm.

Telephone Code: 0755.

ACCOMMODATIONS

Hotels in Bhopal cater mainly to business travelers, leaving few real cheapies. To add insult to injury, they all levy taxes and service charges of up to 20%. This does mean, though, that most rooms have luxuries like TVs, telephones, and attached bathrooms.

Hotel Sonali, 3 Hamidia Rd. (tel. 533880 or 533990), down the small alley to the right of Hotel Raijit and around to the right. Their letterhead claims the hotel is one of the highlights of modern civilization—maybe not, but it is quiet, comfortable, and quite popular. Singles Rs185, with air-cooling Rs400; doubles Rs250/415.

Hotel Taj, 52 Hamidia Rd. (tel. 533162 or 536379), opposite the Ranjit. Though rates run up to Rs1100, even those in the cheapest rooms enjoy the attentions of

Madhya Pradesh

(SEE INSET MAP AT UPPER LEFT)

NORTH INDIA

the bellboys, bearers, and cleaners. The atrium design insulates guests from the Hamidia hullabaloo. Check-out noon. Standard singles Rs150; doubles Rs300.

Hotel Ranjit, 3 Hamidia Rd. (tel. 533511 or 535211), between the bus and train stations, on the right, about 200m before the road turns. The diminutive rooms share a building with Bhopal's busiest restaurant and bar. High customer turnover allows the management to keep the room prices down. Singles Rs150; doubles Rs200.

Hotel Meghdoot, Hamidia Rd. (tel. 534093), on the leg of the street south of the train station, on the right about 200m before the turn. One of the cheapest deals in Bhopal, it has all the standard facilities, but in a noisy, mostly male, betel-stained atmosphere. Check-out 24hr. Singles Rs100; doubles Rs150.

FOOD

NORTH INDIA

Manohar Dairy and Restaurant, 6 Hamidia Rd., across from the Hotel Taj. Good, cheap, South Indian fare. The evening scene is lively, turnover is fast, and children won't hesitate to ask where you're from. Try *shahi dosa* (Rs22), *dahi* or *challa samosa* (Rs11), and a wide selection of desserts (Rs5-20). Open daily 8am-11pm.

Ranjit, 3 Hamidia Rd., inside Hotel Ranjit. Bhopal's most popular dinner joint features many dimly lit levels of bar and restaurant. Big portions of Indian chicken or mutton go for Rs60, while veg. fare ranges up to Rs55 for *kaju* (cashew) curry. Subcontinental Chinese costs Rs30-50. Open daily 11:30am-11pm.

Hotel Surya, Hamidia Rd. (tel. 536925 or 536926), on the southern branch. About 200m before the turn on the right as you approach the railway station. Surya's motto: "for those who value class." Classy dim lighting turns the trip to the table into a spelunking expedition. Mostly men munch chicken dishes (Rs35) and *paneer masala* (Rs34). Beer Rs65. Open daily 10am-midnight

Indian Coffee House (tel. 532895), next to Sangam Cinema off Hamidia Rd. and on New Market Rd. The unruffled waiters in their ruffled headgear serve delightful South Indian snacks to their delighted guests. Special *dosa* or *utthapam* Rs13. Delicious sugarless coffee Rs4. Open daily 7am-10pm.

New Inn, 28 Badbhada Rd., New Market, T.T. Nagar (tel. 532895). Leaving M.P. Tourism, turn right, cross the intersection, and continue past the bookstores. As close to an old-school diner as you'll find: clean, airy, and relaxed. Veg., chicken, or mutton burgers (Rs15-18), Indian and Chinese cuisine. Open daily 7am-10pm.

SIGHTS

Bharat Bhavan

Location: *On the shores of Upper Lake, in the new town.* **Transport:** *Auto-rickshaws from downtown Rs20.* **Hours:** *Open Tu-Su 2-8pm.* **Admission:** *Rs2.*

A cultural center encompassing theater, music, poetry, and the fine arts, the Bharat Bhawan is one of Bhopal's premier sights. Its modern architect created a multi-layered, courtyard-intensive, and altogether charming public space. The three oddly shaped and more oddly decorated protuberances are skylights that illuminate subterranean galleries where choice artifacts from the center's collections of modern tribal and non-tribal art are displayed. At the lakeside, open-air atrium and modern indoor auditorium, a repertory company performs throughout the year. Past seasons have featured works by Jean-Paul Sartre and Samuel Beckett (*Gouda la Dekhat Han,* a Chattisgarhi dialect version of *Waiting for Godot,* premiered here in 1997). The Bhavan also hosts classical music concerts and poetry readings; check at the ticket office for schedules. A small library and a cafe (featuring "French Tries") complete a culture vulture's holiday.

Old Town

Bhopal's status as an independent Muslim-ruled princely state until 1952 has endowed the city with a strong Muslim character and a wealth of impressive mosques. The old Muslim bazaar quarter, or **Chowk,** wedged in the crook of Hamidia Rd., has the strongest Islamic flavor. Although most of the area's old buildings have disappeared, skull-capped men returning from pilgrimages to Mecca and women in

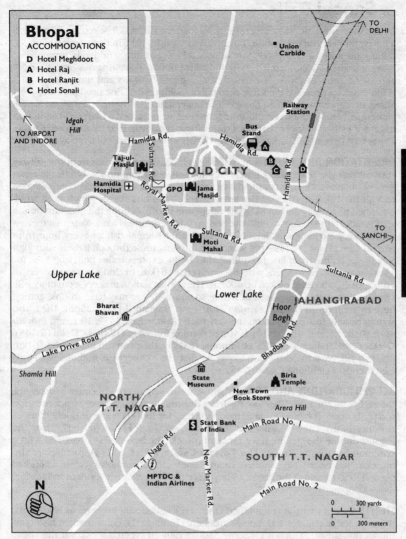

Bhopal

ACCOMMODATIONS

- **D** Hotel Meghdoot
- **A** Hotel Raj
- **B** Hotel Ranjit
- **C** Hotel Sonali

chadors continue Bhopal's Muslim traditions. Compounded with the narrow, twisting streets full of goats browsing in central gutters, Chowk is a fascinating scene.

The **Taj-ul-Masjid,** Bhopal's biggest mosque, is a more spectacular illustration of Bhopal's tradition of Islam. *(Open dawn-dusk. Free.)* The plans of the Victorian Nawab Shajehar Begum were so grandiose that they have not been completed to this day. The 18-story minarets, the vast, hot courtyard, and the three huge domes over the prayer hall filled with Qur'anic students create a grand impression. Despite the huge staircase on Sultania Rd., the mosque can only be approached from Royal Market Rd.

Other interesting mosques dot the old town. The **Jama Masjid,** built by Kudsia Begum in 1837, struts its stuff with gold-spiked minarets. The **Moti Mahal,** constructed in 1860 by Kudsia Begum's daughter, Sikander Jehan, continues the Mughal tradition of small-scale, elegant, "personal" mosques. Although less opulent than its counterparts in Agra or Delhi, this mosque lifts many features (including striped domes) from the most magnificent Indian mosque of all, the Jama Masjid in Delhi.

■ Sanchi सांची

In the 3rd century BC, the emperor Ashoka founded the Buddhist retreat at Sanchi as a haven for peaceful meditation. Twenty-two centuries have not succeeded in undermining his purpose. However, Sanchi only reemerged into worldwide prominence when a British officer, roaming about India in search of a civilizing mission, stumbled across the ruins in 1818. The deserted complex of *stupas* and monasteries on a remote hilltop preserve the same meditative quietude that first prompted the great Mauryan emperor to build on the site. The huge, white hemispherical *stupas,* and the subsequent encrustations of exquisite sculpture, were named a UNESCO World Heritage site in 1989. Sanchi remains a tiny village, now sustained by the tourist trade. The added fame lures tourists chiefly on daytrips from Bhopal, 50km away.

ORIENTATION AND PRACTICAL INFORMATION One road leads from the **railway station,** past the few budget hotels and the **police station,** up the hill to the **main gate** of the ruins. The road to Bhopal crosses this street at a right angle, continuing on to Vidisha, 10km northeast. The **small market** and **bus stand,** which hold an ill-equipped **pharmacy** and an STD/ISD **telephone** booth, occupy the quadrant on the station side of the main road and the Bhopal side of the cross road. Note that there is **no currency exchange** in Sanchi. **Buses** leave for **Bhopal** at least every hour from 6am to 6pm (1½hr., Rs14)—but some take the slow route through Raisen. Although Sanchi sits on the main line from Bhopal to Delhi, express **trains** only stop here for 1st class or A/C passengers who have traveled 161km, or 2nd class journeyers in groups of 10 who have racked up 400km. The Bhopal station masters seem more officious in this matter than those at Sanchi so although you may have trouble getting here by train (from Bhopal: *Punjab Mail* 1038, 9:05am; 1457, 2:25pm, 1hr.), you should be able to snag a seat on the way back (*Dadar Exp.* 1457, 10:15am; *Punjab Mail* 1038, 3:40pm, 1hr., Rs16). If you're coming from **Agra** (Rs104), **Delhi** (Rs145), **Gwalior** (Rs92), **Iatarsi** (Rs72), or **Mumbai** (Rs171), then you can invoke the 161km clause if you have the extra cash to pay for first class. Otherwise, find nine well-traveled friends. **Telephone Code:** 07482.

ACCOMMODATIONS AND FOOD If you want to stay overnight (most visitors see the sights in 2hr.), the **Railway Retiring Rooms** come complete with a dressing room, showerless bathroom, and mosquito nets for Rs100 (single or double; prices rise after 24hr.). The **Sri Lanka Mahabodhi Society Guest House** (tel. 62739), on the left just outside the station, has a range of rooms. The best deal is a bare cell with a common bathroom (Rs40). **The Tourist Cafeteria** (tel. 81243), just before the museum, has bright, airy, spotless rooms (singles Rs200; doubles Rs250; additional tax and Rs50 for use of the cooler). They serve food in a pleasant, modern hall (dishes Rs12-90; open daily 7am-9pm).

SIGHTS Except that the Enlightened One never visited Sanchi (as far as is known), the complex of temples and monasteries here chronicle the entire ancient history of Indian Buddhism. Mauryan Emperor Ashoka himself erected a pillar at the Great Stupa, while sculptures dating from the end of the Buddhist period begin to morph into deities from the Hindu pantheon. Surprisingly, even though Sanchi was an active Buddhist site for over 1000 years, only a few scattered references to Sanchi have been identified in the vast corpus of Buddhist literature. Thus, archaeology provides the only hints about the hilltop ruins' history. When the ruins were first unearthed, archaeologists wasted no time in unlocking their secrets—they nearly destroyed the Great Stupa in their search for valuable artifacts, before discovering that there was no treasure inside—the *stupa* was solid throughout. It was later restored, and today, along with its amazingly well-preserved gateways, the Great Stupa reigns over the rest of the crumbling edifices which surround it on the hill.

A small **museum,** just past the Tourist Cafeteria, holds a modest collection of statues unearthed at Sanchi, including some impressive lion-headed Ashokan pillar capitols. A kiosk in front sells tickets (Rs5; free on F when the museum is closed) good for entry both to the exhibit inside and to the hilltop ruins, as well as an informative guidebook (Rs12). A motor road loops circuitously up the hill, but on foot, the steep staircase leading off to the right is the more direct route to the ruins.

At the top of hill, the **Great Stupa** dominates the scene. *(Open dawn-dusk. Admission Rs5; free on F).* The **south gate** once constituted the main entrance, as evidenced by the stump of the pillar erected by Ashoka (a local *zamindar,* or landlord, broke off the rest to use in a sugarcane press) and the staircases leading to the raised balcony. The Satavahanas, in the first century BC, tacked on Sanchi's richest addition: the four monumental **gateways** facing the the cardinal directions. So detailed is the sculpture that archaeologists attribute it to ivory carvers accustomed to making maximum use of minimum surface—a theory borne out by a Pali inscription on the south gate.

Since all the sculpture save the four **seated Buddhas** inside each gate dates from the Theravada period, no direct depictions of the Buddha appear on the gates; he is referred to obliquely with symbols such as the lotus flowers (for his birth), the *pipal* tree (for his enlightenment), and the wheel (for his sermons). Figures commonly depicted include six *manushis*—Buddha's predecessors who appear as *stupas* or trees, each of a different species. *Jatakas* (tales from the Buddha's previous lives) such as the **Chhadarta Jakata** in which the Buddha, as an elephant, helps a hunter saw off his tusks, and stories from the subsequent history of Buddhism, particularly those detailing the distribution of the Buddha's relics, are also illustrated here. The middle rung of the **south gateway** shows one of the latter: Ashoka's army has arrived (on the right) at the last of the eight original *stupas* containing the Buddha's relics at Ramagrama. But he is prevented from carting off the loot (as he had at the other seven) by the army of snake people to the left. On the inside, the middle rung depicts the Chhadarta Jataka, with the Buddha as the six-tusked elephant, while above this scene are the trees and *stupas* of the *manushi* buddhas. The bottom rung shows the siege of **Kushinagar** (see p. 213), a historical nod to Buddhist non-violence wherein eight armies' imminent clash over those sought-after relics was averted by equitable distribution.

The front face of the **west gateway** features (from top to bottom) more *manushis,* the Buddha's first sermon (note the wheel) and more scenes of Chhadarta. Inside, the top two rungs show more wrangling over relics, while the bottom reveals the Buddha achieving enlightenment despite the distracting demons sent by Mara. On the south pillar of this gate, the **Mahakapi Jataka** shows the Buddha as a monkey turning himself into a bridge so that his brethren could escape to safety over a river.

The **north gateway,** which has been less scarred by the ravages of time than its counterparts, shows the **Vessarkara Jataka,** around both sides of the bottom rung in which the Buddha gives away successively a magic elephant, his horse and chariot (on the front), and his children and wife, before being reinstated to his princedom (on the rear). While the upper registers of the **east gateway** repeat earlier scenes, the south pillar below depicts the Buddha walking on water on the outside and facing, unhurt, a fearsome cobra on the inside. Below this scene, the villagers try to make a sacrificial fire in thanksgiving—but the wood won't burn without the Buddha's permission.

■ Indore इंदौर

With a population of 1.2 million, Indore is the Mammon of Madhya Pradesh. More people pack its cityscape, more businesses clutter its buildings, more industries sear its escarpments, and more money flows through its coffers than any other city in the state. Its bustling markets and hustling marketeers are unavoidable, so much so that other hotel guests might greet you by asking, "Are you an exporter?" The old-town market will reward travelers who wander its warrens long enough, but most hurry to jump the next bus to Mandu or Ujjain.

ORIENTATION

Indore is bisected by **Station Road,** which leads south from the railway station to the **Sarawate Bus Stand** about 500m away. In the market to the west, narrow streets lined with stalls predominate; to the east, workshops and businessmen's hotels occupy new and unremarkable concrete row houses. **Mahatma Gandhi Road** is the main east-west artery; **Maharuja Yeshwant Hospital Road** leads southeast from the station area to the GPO and the bank.

PRACTICAL INFORMATION

Airport: 10km west of town center along M.G. Rd. (auto-rickshaw Rs40). To: **Bhopal** (1 per day, US$50); **Delhi** (1 per day, via Bhopal, US$120); **Mumbai** (1 per day, US$80). The **Indian Airlines** office (tel. 431595 or 431596) is on Dr. R.S. Bhadari Marg, 1 block north of M.G. Rd., 2 blocks east of R.N. Tagore Rd. Open daily 10:05am-1:15pm and 2:15-5pm. **Private airlines** also fly to various cities.

Trains: The **railway station** is on Station Rd. Despite being a commercial hub, Indore sits astride one of the Western Railway's most antiquated and inefficient lines, which demands time-consuming changes and recouplings when joining the main routes. Prices given are for sleeper car. To: **Delhi** (*Malwa Exp.* 9367, 3:05pm, Rs248); **Mumbai** (5:45pm, 15hr., Rs230); **Udaipur** (4:10pm, 12hr., Rs130).

Buses: **Sarawate Bus Station** at intersection of M.Y. Hospital and Station Rd. To: **Bhopal** (every 30min., 5am-midnight, 5hr., Rs47/57); **Jalgaon** (5am and 8:30pm, 10hr., Rs107); **Maheshwar** (6:45pm and 8:45pm, 4hr., Rs38); and **Omkareshwar** (frequent morning departures, 3hr., Rs25). **Gangawal Bus Stand** serves **Mandu** via **Dhar** (frequent, 6am-6pm, Rs25).

Local Transportation: English street signs are rare, and the old part of town is a labyrinth. Take advantage of the ubiquitous, metered **auto-rickshaws.** Base fare Rs5; most destinations in town can be reached for Rs10-20.

Tourist Office: MPTDC, R.N. Tagore Rd. (tel. 528653 or 521818), behind Ravindra Natya Graha Hall, ½ block south of M.G. Rd. Lethargic staff sells maps of Madhya Pradesh (Rs15) and offers free brochures. Open daily 10am-5pm.

Currency Exchange: State Bank of India, Main Office, Agra-Bombay Rd., south of M.Y. Hospital Rd. on the left. Foreign exchange on the 1st fl. Open M-F 10:30am-2:30pm, Sa 10:30am-12:30pm.

Bookstore: Shri Indore Book Depot, 504 M.G. Rd., (tel. 432479), 2 blocks before the Indian Coffee House and across the street, has lots of used books.

Hospital: M.Y. Hospital, M.Y. Hospital Rd. Sketchy and intimidating. Private physicians, however, are listed in English in the telephone directory.

Pharmacy: Medico Corner, (tel. 467691), one block to the right when exiting Sarawate bus station. Open M-Sa 8am-10pm, Su 8am-6pm.

Police: in the blue booth (tel. 464488) in Sarawate Bus Station, under the staircase in front of the booking office.

Post Office: GPO, Agra-Bombay Rd., between the State Bank of India and the museum, on the left just south of M.Y. Hospital Rd. Open M-Sa 10am-6pm, Su 10am-1pm. **Postal Code:** 452001.

Telephones: STD/ISD booths infest the bus station area. **Telephone Code:** 0731.

ACCOMMODATIONS

Hotels in Indore fill up fast with itinerant businessmen, especially at the start of the month. The relatively cheap places behind the Sarawate Bus Station offer modest accommodations for the middle class Indian entrepreneur, including check-out a full 24 hours after you arrive. Normally, rooms with grandiose descriptions yield only extra knick-knacks and thin carpeting.

Hotel Payal, 38 Chhoti Gwaltoli (tel. 463202 or 478460), in the row of hotels hidden behind the Patel flyover, just around the corner from Sarawate. The extravagantly stingy might want to consider the subterranean rows of dorm beds before succumbing to the TV'd, toileted rooms above ground. Dorm beds Rs20; singles Rs110; doubles Rs155.

Hotel Ashoka, 14 Nasia Rd. (tel. 465991 or 475496), opposite Sarawate Bus Station, 100m to the right as you exit. Rooms feature the standard-issue TV, phone, and bathroom with hot water. Upgrade yourself from the basic rooms to get a quieter room in the back away from bus stand bustle. Singles Rs125, doubles Rs175; with A/C Rs200/300; with air-cooling Rs250/350.

Hotel Dayal (tel. 462865 or 462866), next door to Sant Plaza. This cheapie has a bewildering array of rooms featuring intimidatingly hardy coolers. Singles Rs80, with air-cooling Rs130; doubles Rs100/160.

FOOD

Siddharth Restaurant, opposite Sarawate Bus Station, on the left as you emerge from the flyover. The bar battles nature's purest form with a tree trunk enclosed within the dining room. A bit dark and slightly eerie. The veg. menu features tasty yellow *dal* fry (Rs14) and butter *paneer masala* (Rs25) as well as cold beers (Rs52-65). Open daily 9am-11:30pm.

Indian Coffee House, M.G. Rd., on the left inside a courtyard (look for the Deadend Jeans sign on the archway), as you head away from the city center about 100m past the Central Hotel. Part of an India-wide chain, trusty old ICH serves tasty *masala dosas* (Rs13) and *sada dosas* (Rs11). The real highlight is, as always, the unsweetened coffee (Rs9). A second location, opposite the M.Y. Hospital, features outdoor tables in a small park. Open daily 7:30am-10pm.

Woodlands Restaurant, Hotel President, 163 R.N. Tagore Rd., next to the Nehru statue. The ritzy crystal dining room features the usual fare (Rs25-40) for lunch (noon-3pm) and dinner (7-10:30pm), and an all-day menu of tasty South Indian snacks (Rs8-22).

SIGHTS

For most pilgrims, Indore is little more than a waystation. After pausing to change their mode of transportation, they are off to the next *yatra*. If stuck with time to kill in Indore, however, you can choose between getting lost on the market side of town or checking out an official "sight," two of which stand out.

Travelers generally stop in for a look at **Lal Bagh Palace,** a full-blown British manor house built by the Holkar Maharajas beginning in the 1870s. *(Open Tu-Su 10am-5:30pm. Admission Rs2. English/Hindi guidebooks Rs2.50.)* Conveniently located on the road that runs from the bus and train stations in town to the Gaugawal bus stand, the buildings and grounds of Lal Bagh can be gone over with the proverbial fine-toothed comb in under an hour. Designed by an English architect keen on Italian and Baroque style it could just as well be a lordly (but not particularly remarkable) pile set above a Cotswald village.

Along with the usual stuffed wildcats and crystal chandeliers, the house features a state-of-the-art suspension system for the ballroom dance floor and an underground tunnel connecting the main house with the kitchens on the opposite side of the river. Don't jump out of your *chappal*s when a statue of a stern Queen Victoria greets you at the exit. Farther down the street than the GPO on Agra-Bombay Rd., Indore's tatty **Central Museum** presents religious sculpture from Madhya Pradesh and exhibits on the area's prehistory. Although several works are beautiful, the drab presentation and poor info-cards detract. *(Open Tu-Su 9am-5pm. Free.)*

■ Near Indore

■ Maheshwar महेश्वर

Both the *Ramayana* and the *Mahabharata* mention **Meheshwari,** the capital of King Arjuna Kartavirya's domain around 200 BC. Not much was heard of Maheshwar for about two millennia, until the late 18th century when the Holkar Queen Ahalyabai made it her capital, building a fortified palace and a pair of richly carved temples along the Narmada River. Known today as Maheshwar, it remains a small and somewhat out-of-the-loop town whose name is famous throughout India because of the fine, hand-loomed *saris* made there. Maheshwar has found more recent fame in the form of Sabrina, a young Holkar princess-turned-fashion model.

A four-hour bus ride from either Indore (Rs38) or Mandu (Rs20) will deposit you at the **station.** To reach the sights, clustered inside the **fort,** head due south through the village. You'll pass several **STD/ISD telephone** booths. Exchange currency at the **State Bank of India** (tel. 42229), just before the fork on your right (open M-Sa 11am-3:30pm). The left at the fork in the road ascends to the fort's gates. **Buses** return to Indore every hour and leave for Mandu in the early morning and afternoon.

There are no tourist accommodations in Maheshwar, but when evening comes, the folks at the **Ahilya Trust Guest House,** located behind the museum at the top of the stairs that lead down to the temples, may let you crash on one of the clean mats laid out under the eaves of the open courtyard. Alongside the bus station, hawkers peddle street food; if you won't eat what they offer (*samosas* and *dal*), you won't eat.

The fort's bulbous battlements dwarf the houses in the village below; past the main gate, a smaller gate leads into the palace grounds, where a two-room museum contains a jumble of broken statuary and Holkar dynasty paraphernalia. The gate to the left of the museum leads to steps down to the *sari* workshop and the temples and *ghats* below. The workshop at the top of the stairs, run by the Rehwa Society (established in 1978 to preserve Maheshwar's silk-cotton *sari*-weaving tradition), is set up for the benefit of tourists. (Open W-M 10am-5pm. Free.) In a dark, low historic building lit by fluorescent tubes, workers, most of them women, spin and weave material in a stunning array of colors and designs. The manager, who sits just inside the door, will call someone to show you around. *Saris* are most vehemently *not* sold on the premises, although they are available in town beginning around Rs900.

Past the *sari* workshop, at the bottom of the stairs, Maheshwar's **temples** are pressed into small courtyards that make them seem larger than they really are. They tower over the *ghats* below, the *sati* stones sunk in the quay, and the pilgrims bathing in the sacred Narmada. Sadly, tour buses have left their mark here—children scramble after you screaming for blood, pens, and chocolate.

■ Omkareshwar ओम्करेश्वर

Omkareshwar derives its name from its remarkable likeness to the holiest of all Hindu symbols, the "Om" (ॐ). Omkareshwar is therefore regarded by the scores of pilgrims who flock to it at all times of the year as a sacred place. Still, mediating the confluence of the Narmada and Kaveri Rivers, Omkareshwar emerges as an impressive and beautiful product of nature with genteel vistas, unspoiled landscapes, and Jain and Hindu temples gracing jagged cliffs, like candles in a chocolate sea.

Omkareshwar can be reached directly by bus from Indore (5-6 per day, 3hr., Rs25) or Ujjain (1 per day, 5hr., Rs37). Trains from Indore stop at the Khandhwa/Omkareshwar Rd. **railroad station,** 12km from Omkareshwar's **bus station.** The **police station** (tel. 344015; open daily 9am-5pm), the **post office** (tel. 71222; open M-Sa 9am-5pm), and the only tourist accommodations in town, the **Yatrika Guest House** (tel. 71308; singles Rs100-150), cluster around the bus station. There is no place in town to change currency.

From the bus station that lies at the edge of town, a three-minute walk through the village reveals the **Government Hospital** on your right (open daily 8am-noon and 5-6pm) and the **pharmacy** on your left (open daily 7:30am-9:30pm). The only **STD/ISD** telephone booth lies just beyond the pharmacy (**telephone code:** 07280).

To reach the temple, just continue to walk through the village until you reach the newly constructed bridge ascending above the deep gully that divides the island. The view from the bridge reveals the city's two major temples: the exceptionally detailed **Shri Omkar Mandhara,** home to one of only 12 *Jyotirlingas* in India; and **Siddhnath Temple,** an early Medieval Brahmanic temple.

If you're stuck for cash on your travels, don't panic. Millions of people trust Western Union to transfer money in minutes to 153 countries and over 45,000 locations worldwide. Our record of safety and reliability is second to none. So when you need money in a hurry, call Western Union.

WESTERN UNION | MONEY TRANSFER®

The fastest way to send money worldwide.®

MCI Spoken Here

Worldwide Calling Made Simple

For more information or to apply for a Card call: **1-800-955-0925**

Outside the U.S., call MCI collect (reverse charge) at: **1-916-567-5151**

International Calling As Easy As Possible.

Calling Card

123 456 7890 1234
J.D. SMITH

WorldPhone

The MCI Card with WorldPhone Service is designed specifically to keep you in touch with the people that matter the most to you.

The MCI Card with WorldPhone Service....

- Provides access to the US and other countries worldwide.

- Gives you customer service 24 hours a day

- Connects you to operators who speak your language

- Provides you with MCI's low rates and no sign-up fees

For more information or to apply for a Card call:
1-800-955-0925

Outside the U.S., call MCI collect (reverse charge) at:
1-916-567-5151

Pick Up the Phone, Pick Up the Miles.

You earn frequent flyer miles when you travel internationally, why not when you call internationally? Callers can earn frequent flyer miles if they sign up with one of MCI's airline partners:

- American Airlines
- Continental Airlines
- Delta Airlines
- Hawaiian Airlines
- Midwest Express Airlines
- Northwest Airlines
- Southwest Airlines
- United Airlines
- USAirways

Your MCI Worldphone Access Numbers

COUNTRY	WORLDPHONE TOLL-FREE ACCESS #
#Singapore	8000-112-112
#Slovak Republic (CC)	00421-00112
#Slovenia	080-8808
#South Africa (CC)	0800-99-0011
#Spain (CC)	900-99-0014
#Sri Lanka (Outside of Colombo, dial 01 first)	440100
#St. Lucia ⊹	1-800-888-8000
#St. Vincent	1-800-888-8000
#Sweden (CC) ◆	020-795-922
#Switzerland (CC) ◆	0800-89-0222
#Syria	0800
#Taiwan (CC) ◆	0080-13-4567
#Thailand ★	001-999-1-2001
#Trinidad & Tobago ⊹	1-800-888-8000
#Turkey (CC) ◆	00-8001-1177
#Turks and Caicos ⊹	1-800-888-8000
#Ukraine (CC) ⊹	8▼10-013
#United Arab Emirates ◆	800-111
#United Kingdom (CC) To call using BT ■	0800-89-0222
To call using C&W ■	0500-89-0222
#United States (CC)	1-800-888-8000
#Uruguay	000-412
#U.S. Virgin Islands (CC)	1-800-888-8000
#Vatican City (CC)	172-1022
#Venezuela (CC) ⊹ ◆	800-1114-0
Vietnam ●	1201-1022
Yemen	008-00-102

#	Automation available from most locations.
(CC)	Country-to-country calling available to/from most international locations.
⊹	Limited availability.
▶	Wait for second dial tone.
■	When calling from public phones, use phones marked LADATEL.
★	International communications carrier.
●	Not available from public pay phones.
◆	Public phones may require deposit of coin or phone card for dial tone.
▲	Local service fee in U.S. currency required to complete call. Regulation does not permit Intra-Japan calls.
⊹	Available from most major cities

And, it's simple to call home.

1. Dial the WorldPhone toll-free access number of the country you're calling from (listed inside).

2. Follow the voice instructions in your language of choice or hold for a WorldPhone operator.
   - Enter or give the operator your MCI Card number or call collect.

3. Enter or give the WorldPhone operator your home number.

4. Share your adventures with your family!

The MCI Card with WorldPhone Service...
The easy way to call when traveling worldwide.

MCI ★ Calling Card
123 456 7890 1234
J.D. SMITH
WorldPhone

COUNTRY	WORLDPHONE TOLL-FREE ACCESS #
American Samoa	633-2MCI (633-2624)
#Antigua	1-800-888-8000
(available from public card phones only)	#2
#Argentina (CC) ◆	0800-5-1002
#Aruba ÷	800-888-8
#Australia (CC) ◆ To call using OPTUS ■	1-800-551-111
To call using TELSTRA ■	1-800-881-100
#Austria (CC) ◆	022-903-012
#Bahamas	1-800-888-8000
#Barbados	800.000
#Belarus (CC) From Brest, Vitebsk, Grodno, Minsk	8-800-103
From Gomel and Mogilev	8-10-800-103
#Belgium (CC) ◆	0800-10012
#Belize From Hotels	557
From Payphones	815
#Bermuda ÷	1-800-888-8000
#Bolivia (CC) ◆	0-800-2222
#Brazil (CC)	000-8012
#British Virgin Islands ÷	1-800-888-8000
#Brunei	800-0011
#Bulgaria	00800-0001
#Canada (CC)	1-800-888-8000
#Cayman Islands	1-800-888-8000
#Chile (CC) To call using CTC ■	800-207-300
To call using ENTEL ■	800-360-180
#China ✦ For a Mandarin-speaking Operator	108-17
#Colombia (CC) Collect Access in Spanish	980-16-0001
#Costa Rica ◆	0800-012-2222
#Cote D'Ivoire	0800-99-9100 (?)
#Croatia (CC) ✷	0800-22-0112
#Cyprus (CC) ◆	080-90000
#Czech Republic (CC) ◆	00-42-000112
#Denmark (CC) ◆	8001-0022
#Dominica	1-800-888-8000
#Dominican Republic Collect Access	1-800-888-8000
Collect Access in Spanish	1121
#Ecuador (CC) ÷	999-170
#Egypt (CC) ◆ (Outside of Cairo, dial 02 first)	355-5770
El Salvador	800-1767

— FOLD —

COUNTRY	WORLDPHONE TOLL-FREE ACCESS #
#Federated States of Micronesia	624
#Fiji	004-890-1002
#Finland (CC) ◆	08001-102-80
#France (CC) ◆	0800-99-0019
#French Antilles (CC) (includes Martinique, Guadeloupe)	0800-99-0019
#French Guiana (CC)	0-800-99-0019
#Gabon	00-1-99
#Gambia	00-1-99
#Germany (CC)	0-800-888-8000
#Greece (CC) ◆	00-800-1211
#Grenada ÷	1-800-888-8000
#Guam (CC)	950-1022
#Guatemala (CC) ◆	99-99-189
Guyana	177
#Haiti ÷ Collect Access in French/Creole	193
	190
#Honduras ÷	800-122
#Hong Kong (CC)	800-96-1121
#Hungary (CC) ◆	00800-01411
#Iceland (CC) ◆	800-9002
#India (CC) ◆ Collect Access	000-127
	000-126
#Indonesia (CC) ◆	001-801-11
#Iran ÷ (SPECIAL PHONES ONLY)	
#Ireland (CC)	1-800-55-1001
#Israel (CC)	1-800-940-2727
#Italy (CC) ◆	172-1022
#Jamaica ÷	1-800-888-8000
#Japan (CC) ◆ (From public phones) To call using KDD ■	00539-121▶
	0066-55-121
To call using IDC ■	0044-11-121
To call using ITJ ■	18-800-001
#Jordan	8-800-131-4321
#Kazakhstan (CC)	080011
#Kenya ✦ (From Special Hotels only)	00309-14
#Korea (CC) To call using KT ■	00309-12
To call using DACOM ■	00369-14
To call using ONSE	
Phone Booths■ Press red button, 03, then ✶	
Military Bases	550-2255
#Kuwait	800-MCI (800-624)

— FOLD —

COUNTRY	WORLDPHONE TOLL-FREE ACCESS #
Lebanon Collect Access	600-MCI (600-624)
#Liechtenstein (CC) ◆	0800-89-0222
#Luxembourg (CC)	0800-0112
#Macao	0800-131
#Macedonia (CC) ◆	99800-4288
#Malaysia (CC) ◆	1-800-80-0012
#Malta	0800-89-0120
#Marshall Islands	1-800-888-8000
#Mexico Avantel	01-800-021-8000
Telmex ▲	001-800-674-7000
Collect Access in Spanish	01-800-021-1000
#Monaco (CC) ◆	800-90-019
#Montserrat	1-800-888-8000
#Morocco	00-211-0012
#Netherlands (CC) ◆	0800-022-9122
#Netherlands Antilles (CC) ÷	001-800-888-8000
#New Zealand (CC)	000-912
#Nicaragua (CC) Collect Access in Spanish (Outside of Managua, dial 02 first)	166
From any public payphone	✷2
#Norway (CC) ◆	800-19912
#Pakistan	00-800-12-001
#Panama	108
#Papua New Guinea (CC)	05-07-19140
#Paraguay ✦	00-812-800
#Peru	0-800-500-10
#Philippines (CC) ◆ To call using PLDT ■	105-14
To call using PHILCOM ■	1026-14
Collect Access via PLDT in Filipino	105-15
Collect Access via ICC in Filipino	1237-77
	00-800-111-21-22
#Poland (CC) ÷	00-811-1234
#Portugal (CC) ◆	05-017-1234
#Puerto Rico (CC)	1-800-888-8000
#Qatar ✦	0800-012-77
#Romania (CC) ◆	01-800-1800
#Russia (CC) ◆ ÷ To call using ROSTELCOM ■	747-3322
To call using SOVINTEL ■	747-3320
(For Russian speaking operator)	960-2222
To call using SOVINTEL ■	960-2222
#Saipan (CC) ÷	950-1022
#San Marino (CC) ◆	172-1022
#Saudi Arabia (CC) ÷	1-800-11

■ Mandu मंडु

If the past is a country we can never visit, Mandu allows us a glimpse over the border fence. Stretched out atop a narrow plateau in the Vindhya range, the city was fortified as long ago as the 6th century. Mandu's golden age lasted from 1401 to 1526, when the Muslim rulers of the kingdom of Malusa called it their home, building mosques, palaces, and pleasure domes in stone and marble across the length of the plateau. Five centuries later their monuments still stand, dramatically abandoned, in the midst of a tranquil, underpopulated mountain region. Set against a backdrop of great natural beauty, Mandu is a breathtaking oasis in the midst of modern India.

ORIENTATION AND PRACTICAL INFORMATION The road to Mandu enters the once-great kingdom from the north. After passing through a series of precariously narrow gates, vehicles pause at a toll booth to pay the Rs1 per person entry fee (included in the price of a bus ticket). Once atop the plateau, the **main road** runs south through the village, past the **market square** and **Jama Masjid,** and ends at the **Rewa Kund** group of ruins at the far end of town. All the hotels, as well as the **post office** (tel. 63222; open M-Sa 9am-5pm), **police station** (tel. 63223), and eating establishments, are on the main road. The sights around town are well-marked, and signs in English and Hindi direct visitors to the ruins. There is no tourist office in Mandu, but the **MPTDC** in Indore can help with hotel reservations (recommended in winter). **Buses** leave from the market square to: **Dhar** (3-4 per day, Rs15); **Indore** (4-5 per day, Rs25); **Maheshwar** (1 per day, Rs25). You can rent **bicycles** in the market square or from a family living on the main road just north of the square. (Rs2 per hr. or Rs25 per day). **STD/ISD** calls can be placed from a booth in the market square (open daily 8am-9pm), or from the Roopmati Hotel. Power outages are frequent, and phone lines are often down during the monsoon. **Telephone Code:** 07292.

ACCOMMODATIONS AND FOOD SADA runs a tourist rest house (tel. 63234), at the corner of the main square across the side street from the Jama Masjid. Dank cement bunkers, complete with squat toilets, cost Rs125 per double. **MPTDC** has two excellent but pricey hotels in Mandu. The **Travelers' Lodge** (tel. 63221), 1km north of the square on the main road, has lovely views over the eastern ravine from its comfortable, seat toilet-equipped double rooms. The **MPTDC Tourist Cottages,** on the main road 2km south of the square (tel. 63235), has nicer rooms in small cottages, but no views. Prices are the same at both places (singles Rs290; doubles Rs375; additional 10% luxury tax, 25% discount in May and June), and reservations can be made at any MPTDC office. Both have restaurants (cottages outdoor, lodge indoor), with the standard MPTDC menu of snacks (veg. sandwiches Rs15, way-inland fish fingers Rs40), Continental dishes (fish and chips Rs45), veg. (*paneer shahi korma* Rs30), and non-veg. (chicken *masala* Rs40). MPTDC restaurants are open daily 6:30am-11pm. The only other game in town is the **Roopmati Hotel** (tel. 63270), which recently finished building its own motel-esque block just north of the Travelers' Lodge on the main road. Singles start at Rs300. The original Roopmati restaurant is a better deal: veg. dishes in its open-air pavilion, overlooking a landscaped lawn, run Rs15-45, while non-veg. dishes cost as much as Rs120 for a whole butter chicken. Beer is available at Rs50. (Open daily 7am-10pm.)

SIGHTS Ruins punctuate Mandu's entire landscape, from the arched gateways you pass through on the way into town to the mosque and tomb in the market square, the crumbling houses sprinkled liberally along the sides of the main street, and the palace at the very tip of the plateau. Historical figures appear and reappear, while modern villagers appear in sub-plots of their own, plowing the fields behind the ruined palace, scrambling over the old city walls with water vessels balanced on their heads. As you explore Mandu, you add your own story to theirs; don't limit yourself to the celebrated spots—there's as much craft and pathos in the remote, nameless ruins as in the palace at Roopmati.

The big attractions fall into three main areas: the **Royal Enclave** in the north, the **central group,** and the **Rewa Kund complex** in the south. The central group, in the middle of both the plateau and the village, includes Mandu's beautiful **Jama Masjid.** Like the other monuments here, it typifies the austere style of architecture imported from Afghanistan by Hoshang Shah. Reputedly designed after the mosque in Damascus, and completed in 1454, the scale and simplicity of the Jama Masjid still impress.

Behind the Jama Masjid, Hoshang Shah's son built a white marble **mausoleum** for his father in the mid-15th century. The structure so inspired Shah Jahan that he sent his architects to study it before they began work on the Taj Mahal. Opposite the Jama Masjid, the over-ambitious and underachieving **Ashrafi Mahal** proves, by contrast, the patience and skill that went into Mandu's other monuments. In the 15th century Mahud Shah Khilji tried to slap together a huge tomb and seven-story victory tower so quickly and carelessly that most of it has subsequently collapsed, leaving only the remains of a *madrasa* (theological college) complete with students' cells.

The road next to Hoshang Shah's tomb continues to the Royal Enclave. Just inside the gateway, the Sybaritic Sultan Ghiyas Shah constructed the huge **Jahaz Mahal** to house his equally large harem. The long, narrow floorplan (120m by 10m) and the two artificial lakes to either side help the building live up to its nickname of "Ship Palace," especially during the rainy season when water runs through the complex system of once-tinkling pools and conduits. With its cool breezes and wide-open views, it evokes images of the Love Boat it once was. Behind stands the **Hindola Mahal,** so named because its chunky, sloping buttresses are supposed to look like they are swinging out at an angle. Ghiyas Shah also had a ramp built so that he could ride to the upper floor without going through all the hassle of getting off his elephant. Among the many other nearby ruins is the **Taveli Mahal,** with a worthwhile **Archaeological Museum,** where an informative booklet with a good map is available for Rs11. (Open Sa-Th 9:30am-5:30pm.)

At the southern end of the village, a fork leads right (west) from the main road to the **Nil Kanth Temple,** 3km away. The building was originally a Mughal pleasure pavilion, complete with water flowing over ribbed stones and in front of candles to create visual effects. Today, the Shaivas have taken over. From this inspirational spot perched just below the clifftop on the valley slopes, they worship an incarnation of Shiva whose throat turned blue when he drank poison.

The main road ends at the **Rewa Kund** complex, named after the tank which used to supply water to the nearby palaces. The last independent ruler of Mandu, Baz Bahadur, built his eponymous **palace** in the 16th century as a quiet retreat with views of the surrounding greenery. But even this tranquil spot would not satisfy the stunning Roopmati, the sultan's favorite dancer. Life on the plateau made this plains-dweller homesick. As legend has it, Roopmati demanded that Baz Bahadur build her a pavilion on the crest of a hill, from which she could see her former village in the Narmada Valley far below. No sooner had the dutiful sultan completed **Roopmati's Pavilion** than the jealous Akbar marched on Mandu in order to seize the renowned dancer. Baz Bahadur fled, Roopmati swallowed poison, and Akbar, after a brief stay, let his testosterone guide him to the next desirable dancing girl (see **Orchha,** p. 250) leaving Mandu desolate. The unparalleled view over the plains from the palace is sobering—villages, trees, and fields recede in a patchwork haze to where the silver smudge of the Narmada River shakes along the horizon.

■ Ujjain उज्जैन

Ujjain has had a long and eclectic history. In the 3rd-century BC, the city was the imperial seat of Ashoka, Buddhism's seminal patron. It would later serve as the capital of at least two other empires as well as a development center for Indian mathematical astronomy; long before the prime meridian, Hindu stargazers made Ujjain India's Greenwich. An 18th-century observatory on the southwestern side of town is still in use today. Ujjain is also among the holiest of holy Hindu cities; every twelve years during the festival of **Kumbh Mela** Ujjain attracts devotees by the millions with the promise of a hard-earned, elbow-bruising space along the city *ghats* for a dip in the sacred River Shipra (see p. 231). Ujjain's temples, however, don't inspire; the time to come is during the Mela, if you can handle the crush of millions of pilgrims. Ujjain impresses not with the quality of its attractions but rather with the pressing quantity of modern religiosity here.

ORIENTATION

Delineated by the **River Shipra** to the west and the **railroad tracks** to the south, Ujjain's **old city** charms with many small shops and narrow lanes that frustrate the most modest navigation tools. There are no street signs, few landmarks, and countless non-linear byways. The temples and *ghats* can be reached easily on foot, but other destinations require a rickshaw ride. Thankfully, the railway station, bus stand, GPO, and most tourist hotels cluster together around one intersection.

PRACTICAL INFORMATION

Trains: The **railway station** is on Subash Rd., 100m west of the bus station. Prices listed are for 2nd class. To: **Bhopal** (several per day, 4hr., Rs50); **Delhi** (*Mahwa Exp.* 4667, 7:15pm, 17hr., Rs228); **Gwalior** (*Ahmedabad-Gorakhpur Exp.* 5045, M only, 9:50am, Rs151); **Mumbai** (*Indore-Bandra Avantika Exp.* 2692, 5:20pm, 10hr., Rs216). To reach **Orchha,** change trains in Ahmedabad.

Buses: Mahakal Bus Stand, on the corner east of the train station. To: Bhopal (8 per day, 5hr., Rs58, night service Rs66); Indore (every 30min., 6am-6:30pm, Rs14).

Local Transportation: The sights in Ujjain are diffuse and most **auto-rickshaw** drivers refuse to use meters. Try to talk them down; the longest ride should cost no more than Rs25-30.

Tourist Office: MPTDC Hotel Shipra, Vishva Vidhyalaya Rd. (tel. 551495 or 551496). Exiting the railway station on the right, make your first right (the bus station should now be on your left). Follow the bend in the road, cross the pedestrian flyover on the right, turn 180 degrees, make your first left, and the hotel is 200m on the right. Although there's no tourist office per se, the staff at the reception desk can provide a large map of Ujjain (Rs2).

Currency Exchange: The hard-to-find but indispensable **State Bank of India,** Budhwara St. (tel. 550154). Exiting the railway station, turn left, take the 2nd right, and walk 20min.; turn right at the water tower, and the bank is on the left, past the Nirmala Sagar Theatre. Open M-F 11am-3pm.

Pharmacy: Vishwanwani Medical Store (tel. 560353), exiting train station 75 meters beyond Mahakal Bus Stand on the opposite side of the street. Open M-Sa 7:30am-9:30pm, Su 8am-6pm.

Hospital: Civil Hospital, (tel. 550088) Ager Rd., 15 meters beyond pharmacy. Open daily 8:30am-12:30pm and 5pm-7pm. For private medical assistance contact Dr. Bishi and Dr. Rita Shinde anytime (tel. 555067).

Police: tel. 552140.

Post Office: GPO (tel. 551024), behind the bus stand, at the 2nd gate on the left. Open M-Sa 7-8pm, Su 10am-4pm. **Postal Code:** 456001.

Telephones: STD/ISD booths are as common as electrons. **Telephone Code:** 0734.

ACCOMMODATIONS

Nearly all the budget hotels are located across the street from the railway station. Prices listed do not include state taxes (5-10%).

Hotel Rama Krishna (tel. 553017), across from the train station to the left. A sign above the door warns that no meat is allowed on the premises. The staff is friendly, and as long as you're not a huge sausage fan, it's a good choice. Avoid the stuffy interior rooms. Attached bathrooms. 24-hour check-out. Singles Rs110-150, with air-cooling Rs350; doubles Rs200-220, with air-cooling Rs450.

Hotel Chandragupta (tel. 561600), next to the Rama Krishna, is slightly cheaper and slightly less clean. Hot water is available in buckets. The reception is up 1 flight of stairs; the ground floor holds a decent veg. restaurant. Attached bathrooms with squat toilets and wall faucets. Singles Rs100-140; doubles Rs130-170.

Hotel Surya (tel. 560747), across from the railway station, has many rooms, small but sufficient attached bathrooms, and bucket hot water. Rooms Rs85-130.

Hotel Shipra, Vishva Vidhyalaya Rd. (tel. 551496), behind the railway station. Ujjain's lap of luxury, run by the state tourism bureau. The clean, high-ceilinged rooms have big windows and desks, and the service caters to the neo-imperialist in you. Attached bathrooms. Singles Rs300-590; doubles Rs350-690. MC/V accepted.

FOOD

Sudama Restaurant, across from the railway station, next to Hotel Chandragupta. Contemplate the fascinating cut-mirror decor while chowing down on *paneer korma* (Rs22) and other veg. fare. Dinner only after 7pm, but snacks (Rs10-15) and good veg. fried rice (Rs28) all day. Open daily 11m-11pm.

Chanakya Restaurant, on the ground floor of Hotel Chandragupta. The whole extended family can fit into one of the giant booths—which are cooled by a profusion of ceiling fans—and throw back something from the large selection of beer and spirits (Rs40-58). Don't miss the pseudo-erotic sculpture on the walls. All veg. dishes run Rs14-25. Open daily 8am-11pm.

Navratna Restaurant, inside Hotel Shipra. The standard M.P. Tourism menu, including scrambled eggs and toast (Rs25), decent coffee (Rs10), and a range of both veg. and non-veg. Indian dishes (Rs15-40). Beer (Rs20) must be consumed in the separate bar. Open daily noon-3pm, 7-10:30pm.

SIGHTS

True pilgrims don't need maps, but if you picked one up from M.P. Tourism you might as well start praying now—it's hard to find anything in Ujjain without aid from above. The largest temples and *ghats*, however, are not far from the railway station. After strolling along the narrow street in front of the bus station for about 10min., you'll catch a glimpse of the pinkish spire of the main building at **Mahakaleshwar Mandir,** down one of the biggest side streets to the left. Check your shoes at the stand on the right side of the entrance ramp descending into a series of long, narrow tunnels that eventually lead to an underground room containing the **Shivalingam,** one of twelve *jyotirlingams* (manifestations of Shiva as brilliant columns of light). It's too crowded to move, but people seem truly glad you're here and will even let you snap a few pictures if you ask politely. Moving on, the passage disgorges you into a spacious, well-swept courtyard where several smaller shrines and temples await.

When you've got your shoes back on, take the road that passes by the side of the temple complex into and over the buffalo-grazed marsh beyond. When you hit dry land again, you've reached **Harsiddhi Mandir,** the large temple complex behind high white walls just to the right. This is the focal point of Devi worship; it marks the spot where, when Shiva pulled Parvati from her *sati* pyre, her arm was severed (see **Divine Dismemberment,** p. 418). Enter on any of the four sides.

The streets and paths that continue on behind the Mandir all lead to the **Ram Ghat,** the largest, although not always busiest, of the long row of *ghats* lining both sides of the river. Near the north end of the row, the **Bhartirihari Caves** are home to the hoop-earringed Kanphata *yogis*.

Back in the center of town, in a busy market square where vendors display the season's most sought-after devotional paraphernalia, the **Gopal Mandir** (or Ganesh Temple) sits behind a high, onion-domed, and whitewashed fortification. Inside, pilgrims lounge or nap under the arched platforms that circle the complex's perimeter, while in the lush, sumptuous main hall, a figure of Ganesh sits obediently between figures of his parents, Shiva and Parvati.

Seeing the other sights requires booster shots of patience and fortitude (not to mention energy). On a road leading southwest from the back of the railway station, the impressive instruments of the **Vedha Shala** sit in a compound behind a gate with a sign reading Shree Jiwagi Observatory. The mathematically-inclined will wonder at the precision of doo-dads like the parallel sundials on either end of a 1m cylinder. Each side tells the time for exactly half the year. Although set atop a hill looking out over the river and fields beyond, the observatory rattles with non-stop truck traffic just outside the gate—the world of machines and modernity is never far away.

■ Jabalpur जबलपुर

The Madhya Pradesh tourism office tries to promote protracted sojourns in this dusty town of just over 1 million people (it seems like 100,000) on the basis of some scenic white cliffs nearby. In other words, there is nothing to see in Jabalpur, and as far as most tourists are concerned, the city is merely a staging point for Kanha and Bandhavgarh National Parks.

ORIENTATION

Collectorate Road curves around from the rear of the **railway station** past the hospital and Gothic High Court to the **clock tower** marking the beginning of the **bazaar area** 1.5km away. **Station Road,** outside platform 1, leads left toward **Residency Road** and right to the center of town. Two hundred meters before Empire Cinema, the street to the right leads under the railroad tracks to **Russel Chowk,** the center of the city. A fork to the right just beyond the underpass passes the State Bank of India on its way to Collectorate Rd. From Russel Chowk, the main drag heads north to the bazaars over the **Navdra Bridge,** while another leads west, past the museum, the **tempo stand** for the Marble Rocks, and a bridge to the **bus station.**

PRACTICAL INFORMATION

Trains: The **railway station** (tel. 320378) is a Rs15 rickshaw ride to the east of Russel Chowk. The A/C reservation office is open M-Sa 8am-8pm, Su 8am-2pm. Window #3 serves tourists. Prices listed are for 2nd/1st class. To: **Bhopal** (*Narmada Exp.* 8234, 10:15pm, 7hr., Rs79/388); **Calcutta** (*Mumbai-Howrah Mail* 3004, 2:05pm, 23hr., Rs182/952); **Delhi** (*Gondwana Exp.* 2411, 3pm, 23hr., Rs147/746); **Jalgaon** (for Ajanta Caves, *Ajanta Exp.* 3417/5214, 5:30pm; *Mahangawi Exp.* 1094, 7:15am, 11hr., Rs144/574); **Patna** (*Patna Exp.* 5213/3418, 3:45pm, 16hr., Rs185/883; **Satna** (for Khajuraho, *Pawan Exp.* 4257, 4:10am; *Howrah Mail* 3004, 2:05pm, 3hr., Rs53/238); **Varanasi** (*Mehanagri Exp.* 1093, 4:35pm, 10hr., Rs152/766); **Umaria** (for Bandhavgarh National Park, *Narmada Exp.* 8233, 6:30am, 6hr., Rs26).

Buses: The chaotic **bus stand** has both public (MPSRTC) and private sections. For any but the short regional trips, shop around for the comfiest private service—or better yet, take the train. For **Kanha National Park,** go to Kisli (7 and 11am, Rs50). To reach **Mukki,** go to Baihar (Rs35) and cover the remaining 12km by taxi (Rs25-30). For **Bandhavgarh,** take the train to Umaria and switch to the Bandhavgarh bus there (4 per day, 1hr., Rs10). To: **Khajuraho** (9am, 10hr., Rs100).

Local Transportation: Auto-rickshaws and **cycle-rickshaws** are unmetered. **Tempos** run from the museum to the White Rocks for Rs8.

Tourist Office: MPTDC (tel. 322111), inside the railway station , makes reservations at MPTDC facilities at Kanha and Bardavgarh. In season (Dec.-Mar.) bookings for accommodations in parks should be made at least 72hr. in advance from this or any other MPTDC office; 100% payment required. Open daily 6am-10pm.

Currency Exchange: State Bank of India (tel. 322259), opposite Hotel Rishi Regency, near the railway underpass. The international banking division lives upstairs, past a pair of botanically lush murals. Open M-F 10:30am-2:30pm.

Hospital: Medical College, Nagpur Rd. (tel. 322117), 8km south of the bus stand, also has a 24hr. **pharmacy.**

Police: Collectorate Rd., Civil Lines (tel. 325420), in front of the clock tower.

Post Office: GPO, Residency Rd. Out of the station, turn left on Station Rd. and then right on the next main road. The GPO is about 500m down on the left. *Poste Restante* at counter 6. Open M-Sa 10am-6pm. **Postal Code:** 482002.

Telephones: 24hr. STD/ISD booth at the railway station. **Telephone Code:** 0761.

ACCOMMODATIONS

Anywhere decent slaps on 15-20% tax—check to discover what the total price will be. Check-out at most places is 24hr.

Hotel Natraj (tel. 310931), near Karamchand Chowk. Heading north (away from Russel Chowk), take the right fork after crossing the Navdra bridge and take the first major right when you see the JFK quote ("Ask not what your country can do for you..."). It's on the left, opposite the Indian Coffee House. Rooms with attached baths have TV, air-cooling, and hand-held showers. Singles Rs80 with bath Rs120.

Hotel Utsav, Surya Commercial Complex, Russel Chowk (tel. 26038 or 23538), where the roads meet. Economy rooms have all the amenities, including A/C. Singles Rs200; doubles Rs250.

Hotel Swayau (tel. 325377), opposite Jyoti Talkies, Navdra Bridge. In a noisy part of town. Rooms have attached baths and TVs. Singles Rs50; doubles Rs88.

FOOD

Indian Coffee House, Malaviya Marg, near Karamchand Chowk, opposite Hotel Natraj. The mothership of the ICH chain. Sky-high ceilings, rock-solid tables, deep wicker chairs, and vintage advertisements make this one a true classic. The usual *dosas* and *utthapams* (Rs12) as well as other snacks and great, unsugared coffee (Rs3). Open daily 7am-9:30pm.

Hotel Republic Bar (tel. 310017), just over Navdra Bridge, on the right. Rows of tall straight-backed chairs and the no-nonsense Sikh owner behind the bar give the Republic a wild west feel. Butter chicken (Rs65) is their speciality, but they have veg. dishes (from Rs18) and a full range of booze. Open daily 10am-11:30pm.

Hotel Kalchuri (tel. 320491), across from the GPO. Comfort and reassurance await the Madhya Pradesh traveler at this MP Tourism hotel, which features the standard MPT menu, prepared by an above-average MPT chef. Open daily 7:30am-10:30pm.

Project Tiger

Faced by a shocking drop in the tiger population due to hunting and India's industrialization, Indira Gandhi inaugurated a drastic initiative to save tigers in 1973. Named **"Project Tiger,"** it set aside nine areas of tiger territory as national parks and hired a staff of armed guards to patrol the areas and thwart poachers. The plan was initially successful, and the tiger population grew from several hundred to several thousand. Ten more national parks were set aside. Lately, however, poaching has increased (tiger products fetch incredibly high prices), and the armed guards are less formidable than they were in the beginning. The tiger remains an endangered species and some fear it could face extinction soon. The best places in India to try to catch a glimpse of the beasts are **Corbett National Park** (see p. 173) and at Kahna.

SIGHTS

On the road from Russell Chowk to the bus stand sits the local **museum** (open Tu-Su 10am-5pm; free) which houses temple sculpture from the region. About 20km from the city, the Narmada River passes through the white-cliffed gorge so beloved by the MPTDC. For Rs7 per person, you can view the rocks from a rowboat. The White Rocks receive full illumination by night to maximize tourist viewing hours. On the way, tempos (Rs12) pass the old grand fortress of **Madan Mahal.**

■ Kanha National Park कंहा

Gorgeous Kanha has a counterintuitive history. The same Brits who cantered across the continent with their rifles, driving game to the brink of extinction, also set aside Kanha as a hunting preserve. This doubtlessly saved it from the encroachment of local population until Kanha became a wildlife reserve in 1933 (hunting continued until 1955). The result is nearly 2000 square kilometers of bona fide *Jungle Book* jungle—Rudyard Kipling set many of his stories here. Many tourists make the arduous 175km trip from Jabalpur with visions of Mowgli and Baloo dancing in their heads. They are not far off—with over 100 tigers as well as leopards, deer, sambar, wild boar, bears, pythons, and porcupines, there are enough animals for everyone to run with. Although the tiger population is thought to be declining again due to poaching, your chances of seeing one here are better than anywhere else in India.

The park itself is open only for morning and evening excursions from November 1 through June 30; it closes completely during the monsoon months. Each **entry** costs Rs50 per six-person vehicle. The park has two main gates—at **Kisli** in the northwest and **Mukki** in the center on the west side. **Buses** for Kanha National Park depart from Jabalpur to **Kisli** (7 and 11am, Rs50) or **Mukki** (9am, Rs75). For more information, see **Jabalpur: Practical Information,** p. 247. Both Kilsi and Mukki have visitor centers run with the assistance of the U.S. National Park Service, as does Kanha village in the middle of the park's core area. These centers have informative displays and sell brochures and postcards and show films (open daily 9am-noon and 6:30-8pm).

Except for the **MPTDC hotels,** all accommodation is outside the park, concentrated at Khatia near Kisli. The MPTDC operates **Baghira Log Huts** (singles Rs590; doubles Rs690), a **Tourist Hostel** (dorm beds with full board Rs240) near Kisli, and the **Kanha Safari Lodge** (singles Rs390; doubles Rs490) near Mukki. (Prices do not include 10% state tax.) For information or reservations for these hotels, contact one of the MPTDC offices in major Madhya Pradesh cities or Mumbai, Calcutta, or Delhi. The head office is in Bhopal (tel. (0755) 764397). Book MPTDC hotel rooms in advance during high season. The MPTDC hotels also function as a staging point for **jeep trips** into the park. Consult the managers for a seat in one of the six-person vehicles. The rate usually works out to about Rs9 per km, or Rs400 for a whole session between six. Book these berths as soon as you arrive—they are understandably popular as the only means of visiting the park. Elephant safaris have been discontinued, and jungle walks are both dangerous and **illegal.**

■ Khajuraho खजुराहो

The seemingly unremarkable village of Khajuraho, in northern Madhya Pradesh, wouldn't appear to inspire uninhibited erotic passion. But nowhere else in India are so many couples shown prominently copulating in every position and direction. Each explicit detail is chipped into sandstone temple facades, leaving nothing to the imagination but the question of what might have inspired such a holy peep show. Visitors come to this town as much for titillation as for art appreciation, and no one bothers to hide it. The name "Khajuraho"—which in fact refers to the village's date palm trees—has now become so linked to hedonism that it graces the label of a cheap Indian beer. However, the sculptures that started all the fuss are not merely pornographic; they are imbued with a sincere and tender exuberance for life and a luxuriant sensuality (and a UNESCO World Heritage certification to boot).

All of Khajuraho's temples date between 900 and 1100 AD. Medieval craftsmen fashioned classic examples of North Indian temple architecture from pink and yellow sandstone, and draped them with inspired sculpture. The reigning Chandela dynasty, ruled by a Rajput clan claiming to be descended from the moon god, sponsored the construction. When Chandela power waned, however, the temples were forgotten and lay hidden in jungled obscurity for 700 years before the outside world (in the form of the British officer T.S. Burt) stumbled across them in 1838. (See **Sex in Khajuraho,** p. 253). Of an original 85 temples, 25 still stand today.

Tourism has transformed this Indian village into a traveler's mecca with all the trappings. A "new village," consisting entirely of hotels, handicraft shops, and STD/ISD booths, has sprung up around the temples. To the locals, tourists are the main attraction, and they get their share in this boomtown. Even though there is no railway within 100km, the government has built an airport here. The biggest event in Khajuraho is the annual Festival of Dance in March, for which the government flies in some of India's best classical dancers to perform in front of the temples.

ORIENTATION

Khajuraho has just one **main road,** running from the airport in the south, past several luxury hotels, to the **Western Group of Temples** (known simply as the Western Group) in the new village and beyond. Just opposite are the police stand, the tourist office, and many cheap hotels and restaurants. From here, **Jain Temple Road** leads east past more hotels to (surprise!) some Jain temples. A fork to the left at the Plaza Hotel leads to the Old Village and several temples in the **Eastern Group.** The bus stand stands on the grandiosely designated **Link Road Number Two,** about a 10-minute walk down the main road toward the airport, and then eastward.

PRACTICAL INFORMATION

Airport: Khajuraho Civil Aerodrome, 6km south of the Western Group. **Indian Airlines,** Main Rd. (tel. 2035; airport 2036), next door to the Clarks Bundela Hotel. Open daily 10am-1:15pm and 2-5pm. To: **Agra** (daily, 45min., US$70); **Delhi** (daily, 1½hr., US$90); **Varanasi** (daily, 45min., US$70). Off-season (May-July) flights operate only on Tu, Th, Sa, and Su. Year-round, advance reservations are essential.

Buses: Apart from flying, buses are the only way to get to Khajuraho. The station is clean and has English schedules posted. Frequent departures for the nearest railheads at Satna, Mahoba, and Jhansi. To: **Agra** (9am, 12hr., Rs135); **Bhopal** (6 and 7:30pm, 10hr., Rs150); **Gwalior** (9 and 11:15am, 6hr., Rs90); **Jabalpur** (7:30am, 12hr., Rs100); **Jhansi** (9am, 4hr., Rs60); **Mahoba** (10:15am, 2:30 and 6:30pm, 3hr., Rs30, for trains to Varanasi); and **Satna** (7:30, 8:30, 9:30am, 2:30 and 3:30pm, 3½hr., Rs30, for trains to Varanasi). **MPTC** runs a "luxury" coach that coordinates with the *Shatabdi Exp.,* leaving Khajuraho at 4pm (Rs85) and continuing to Gwalior. The 9am Jhansi bus continues to Gwalior and Agra. The last bus to Khajuraho leaves Satna at 3:30pm, Jhansi at 1:15pm, and Mahoba at 5pm.

Local Transportation: Bicycles can be rented at hotels or stands in the square for about Rs15 per day. The few **auto-rickshaws** are overpriced. A **cycle-rickshaw** trip should cost between Rs5-10. Fortunately, everything apart from the Chaturbhuj Temple is manageable **on foot.**

Tourist Office: Main Rd., opposite the Western Group (tel. 42347). Hands out maps and brochures, and helps arrange sight-seeing with one of its 50 licensed guides (English, French, German, Italian, Japanese, or Spanish) for Rs230 (up to 4 people) per half-day, Rs350 for a full day. Also suggests various jeep excursions to nearby waterfalls and wildlife parks. Open M-F 9am-5:30pm, Sa 9am-1pm. There is also an **MP Tourist Information Center** (tel. 2163) at the bus stand. Open M-Sa 9am-6pm.

Currency Exchange: State Bank of India, Main Rd., opposite the Western Group, cashes traveler's checks and changes over 20 currencies. Open M-F 10:45am-2:45pm, Sa 10:45am-12:45pm.

Hospital: 500m down the road in front of the Western Group, on the left side, are 2 small clinics and a **pharmacy.** Open daily 8am-noon and 5-9pm. Dr. R.K. Khare (clinic tel. 2177, residence tel. 24374) is recommended by local luxury hotels. His clinic is located in the strip mall beside the bus station. Open M-Sa, 8am-noon and 5-9pm. Medical facilities are limited; serious cases are sent to Jhansi or Satna.

Police: (tel. 2032), in the booth opposite the Western Group and by the bus stand.

Post Office: Opposite bus stand. Open M-Sa 10am-6pm. **Postal Code:** 471606.

Telephones: STD/ISD booths are many, but lines are few. **Telephone Code:** 07686.

ACCOMMODATIONS

Prices vary enormously with the season. There is a mini boom in July and August, but between April and June rates usually drop. The major boom runs from November to March, when most, if not all, hoteliers inflate their prices to their heart's content; a Rs50 room will go for Rs200, leaving you no option but to fork out the money, as most hotels really are full. Book in advance at peak times. Check-out time is noon.

Yogi Lodge, Main Sq. (tel. 2158). Down a narrow alley by the Terazza Restaurant, on the left side of the square with your back to the Western Group. Simple, clean rooms with bathrooms, hot running water, and air-cooling available. The owner is

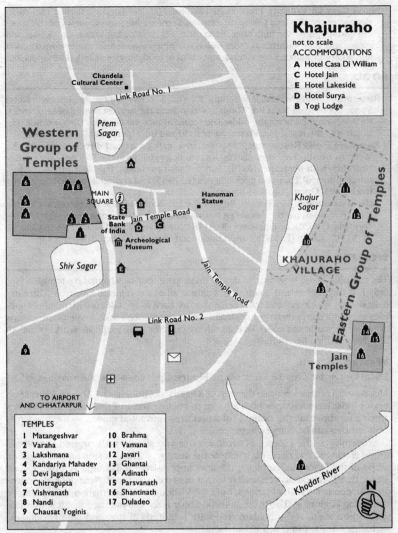

Khajuraho
not to scale
ACCOMMODATIONS
A Hotel Casa Di William
C Hotel Jain
E Hotel Lakeside
D Hotel Surya
B Yogi Lodge

TEMPLES

1	Matangeshvar	10	Brahma
2	Varaha	11	Vamana
3	Lakshmana	12	Javari
4	Kandariya Mahadev	13	Ghantai
5	Devi Jagadami	14	Adinath
6	Chitragupta	15	Parsvanath
7	Vishvanath	16	Shantinath
8	Nandi	17	Duladeo
9	Chausat Yoginis		

an established yoga instructor and offers his services free of charge. Singles Rs60 and up; doubles Rs100; triples Rs120 and up. Discount 20% off-season.

Hotel Surya, Jain Temple Rd. (tel. 42341). On the right about 200m from the main road, opposite Ristorante Mediterraneo. Spotless, friendly place offers uncluttered rooms with squat toilets and balconied, air-cooled rooms. They also have a spacious lawn and reasonable veg. food (*thali* Rs30-40). In-season: singles Rs200, deluxe Rs350; doubles Rs200/300. Off-season: singles Rs90; doubles Rs100/125.

Hotel Jain, Jain Temple Rd. (tel. 2052). Next door to the Surya. This popular spot run by a friendly family offers cramped but clean rooms around a central courtyard. Attached veg. restaurant (*thalis* Rs35) closes in the summer. In-season: singles Rs90, with air-cooling Rs150; doubles Rs125/175. Discount 10% off-season.

Hotel Lakeside, Main Rd., opposite Shiv Sagar Park, next door to the museum (tel. 2120). Another simple, clean spot with a wide terrace with great views, and common bath. Off-season: dorm beds Rs30; singles Rs80, with attached bath Rs125; doubles with bath Rs200, with air-cooling Rs250. Prices jump 20-100% in season.

Hotel Casa Di William, Prem Sagar Lake Rd. (tel. 2244). The 1st road that turns right after the Western Group of temples. Terrace offers scenic views of the Western Group, justify the high rates. Each room has running hot water, air-cooling, and clean, spacious bathrooms (seat toilets). A new restaurant is under construction and will offer Italian, Continental, and Chinese food. Singles Rs250; doubles Rs300.

FOOD

Ristorante Mediterraneo, Jain Temple Rd. (tel. 378009). On the left, opposite Hotel Surya, 200m from Main Rd. About 1000km from the nearest source of mozzarella, the Mediterraneo beats the odds. The *fettucini alla malanzana* (Rs65) tastes startlingly like the real thing. Pizzas, pasta Rs50 and up. Open daily 7:30am-10pm.

Raja Café Swiss Restaurant, Main Rd. In a leafy courtyard directly opposite the Western Group. The Swiss sisters, Joy and Betty, who run the Raja not only proffer pancakes with bechamel (Rs75), but will also exchange temple ashtrays for anything imported! They also pack lunches (Rs40-55) and arrange tours to their nearby treehouses. Open daily 8am-10pm.

Safari Restaurant, Jain Temple Rd. On the left 20m from the intersection with the Main Rd. No-nonsense breakfasts of pancakes (Rs30), banana porridge (Rs20), cornflakes (Rs20), or omelettes (Rs10-18). Also standard Indian (Rs20-40), Chinese (Rs30-70), Italian (Rs30-75), and Continental (Rs40-80). Open daily 6am-10pm.

SIGHTS

The morning is the best time of day to make your tour of Khajuraho's temples. Not only is it the coolest and quietest, but almost all of the temples face east. The early light reveals sculptures and relief detail that are hard to see later on. Khajuraho's temples are divided into three groups mainly for convenience's sake. Some of the groups are more thematic and cohesive than others, but they're all exquisite works of art. All temples are open from sunrise to sunset.

Western Group

Location: *Across from the tourist village.* **Hours:** *Open dawn-dusk.* **Admission:** *Rs5.*

The western temples contain the best of Khajuraho's bunch. The Archaeological Survey of India has mercifully built a fence to enclose most of the group and charges admission; above all, this brings protection from unwanted guides, so these magnificent temples can be enjoyed in peace.

According to the custom of *pradakshina* you should walk around the whole group clockwise and circle each temple the same way. The first stop on your *pradakshina* of the fenced-in temples is the least impressive: the Lakshmi Temple, a small shrine that 19th-century repairs left with a jagged cement roof. Next door, the open-air 10th-century **Varaha Mandap,** built for Vishnu's boar incarnation, offers a more promising beginning. The huge sandstone boar is so well-polished that it shines like glazed porcelain, and it is blanketed with hundreds of tiny gods and goddesses, including Ganga, Yamuna, and Saraswati.

The **Lakshmana Temple,** across from the Lakshmi and Varaha temples, is also magnificent. Dating from 941 AD, it is one of the largest of Khajuraho's temples and one of the most famous. A trip around the base of the temple (clockwise, please!) reveals a stream of carvings of a military procession, which wanders here and there into bizarre erotica. Soldiers get into somewhat unprofessional relationships with their steeds, while lusty women ease martial monotony. The temple itself has four halls leading up to its *shikhara,* and subsidiary shrines at the four corners of its platform. A band of hulking elephants in the stonework supports the temple, and the higher carvings have plenty of sex and many scantily clad women. High up on the west side one figure arches her back away from the viewer, her clothes dripping wet as she leaves her bath. Two-thirds of the way around clockwise, a winsome, limber maiden picks a thorn from her foot, a common Khajuraho theme. The interior of the temple has columns as if it were an audience hall for the presiding Vishnu, and there's an inner passage for circumnavigating the inner sanctum.

Sex in Khajuraho

The sculptor had at times allowed his subject to grow rather warmer than there was any absolute necessity for his doing; indeed, some of the sculptures here were extremely indecent and offensive.
—T. S. Burt, describing Khajuraho, 1838

Ever since a Victorian officer was guided to Khajuraho, art historians and religious scholars have wracked their brains to figure out why so much sex has been carved onto the walls of the temples. Some have suggested that the sculptures were used for sex education or for a study of the art of lovemaking, others that they were offerings to voyeuristic gods, especially Indra, the lord of lightning, who had to be entertained, lest he destroy the temples.

A more plausible recent theory gives deeper significance to the sculptures with the explanation that Tantric cults conceived of sexual intercourse as symbolic of male and female elements in the universe uniting to make the world go round, and may have used the temples for ritualized sex. More mainstream Hindus hold that much of the sculpture in Khajuraho can be read as part of the wedding myth of Shiva and Parvati. The posing women, who seem to have been caught unawares looking in the mirror or pulling up their pants, have stopped whatever they were doing in order to watch the wedding procession. All the other gods are here as guests. And of course, finally, the wedding is consummated—in a great lovemaking session that lasts 1000 god-years. Of course not all the sculptures fit into the story, and some of the more bizarre scenes can only be attributed to the private jokes of the craftsmen.

Straight ahead at the far end of the park, three temples stand together on the same plinth. Built between 1025 and 1050 and dedicated to Shiva, the **Kandariya Mahadev Temple,** on the left, is the tallest temple in Khajuraho and the most architecturally perfect. Rows of ornamental pots pour down over the perforated stone, while the lower walls are endlessly indented, projected, articulated, refracted, and retracted to create an intricate 3-D stage. On the south side, a sex scene delights many gawkers, but the complexity of these kinky calisthenics pales in comparison with the orchestration of the temple's overall design. Circular *amlakas* sit like spinning gears atop square mini-*shikharas,* and lower down, angular pieces form lids to off-set the human figures. The Kandariya Temple's beauty is heightened because it hasn't blackened with age as the other temples have. Over the doorway is a stone garland of flowers, and in the sanctum is a *linga.*

Next to the Kandariya Temple on the same platform is the **Mahadev Shrine,** with no sacred image, but only a statue of a lion grappling with a human figure of indeterminate gender. It has no religious significance, so it is thought to be a Chandela symbol. The same pair of figures can be found all over Khajuraho. On the other side of the Mahadev Shrine is the **Devi Jagadami Temple.** This temple is smaller than the Lakshmana and Kandariya temples, but it has good sculpture, notably its directional guardians, who are stationed between boldly flirting women and delicate erotic scenes. The image inside is of Kali, but this was once a Vishnu temple, as the sculptures of Vishnu all over the outside and inside attest.

The overall shape of the **Chitragupta Temple** is identical to that of Jagadami, but this is Khajuraho's only temple to Surya, the sun god. A small band of processions runs low around the temple, and higher up are many large amorous couples, but much of the wall and roof are broken and have been repaired with concrete. Most of the statues inside the temple have had their heads bashed off, but the main image of Surya, driving his chariot across the sky, is missing only his arms.

Continuing around the circuit you'll come to the small and damaged **Parvati Temple.** It is overshadowed by the more spectacular **Vishvanath Temple** next to it, a large Shiva temple dated to 1002 by the inscription inside. Notice the elephant guardians as you approach the stairs to the temple: the *mahout* on the right side has fallen asleep. The erotic sculptures on the Vishvanath Temple are perhaps the best of all: whole dramatic scenes appear in which the couples' attendants also get caught up in the action. There are fascinating sculptures of posing women here—look for the one on the south side twisting her hair to dry, and the one on the ceiling inside holding a tiny baby. Plenty of soapstone onlookers, stealthily eyeing the unions, are so finely sculpted that attention has even been paid to their cuticles. The Vishvanath Temple originally had a shrine at each corner of its foundation, like the Lakshmana Temple, but only two remain. This loss is compensated for by the **Nandi Mandap** in front of the temple, an open shrine where Shiva's bull Nandi sits and looks into the temple.

The two members of the Western group that stray outside the fence are older and noticeably different from the others. Just over the fence from the Lakshmana Temple is the **Matangeshvar Temple.** Built around 900, it is still in use, unlike Khajuraho's other temples. More people come here to worship than to look at the architecture. It is a rather plain temple, with only thin stripes of sculpture, but it has a 2.5m *linga* inside which sits on a huge platform that you must circle before climbing on it (the platform, not the *linga*).

Following the main road south from the square one comes to the **Shiv Sagar tank,** a small "lake" used for bathing and laundry; it's fenced off, apparently to keep out cows. Along the south side of it a tree-lined path leads off the main road and out to the temple of **Chausat Yoginis** (Sixty-Four Goddesses). The high building is made of crudely cut blocks of granite, piled together like sandbags. Around the top is a gallery of empty shrines—there were once 64 of these little windows, but now only 35 remain. The Chandelas used this temple for worship early in their reign; it is Khajuraho's oldest, dating from the 9th century.

Across the street from the Western Group enclosure, the **Archaeological Museum** houses sculptures separated from their temples. A large dancing Ganesh undulates at the entrance, but perhaps the most interesting piece is in the center of the Miscellaneous Gallery on the right. A stout king and queen sit together making an offering; this is possibly a portrait of the sculptor's Chandela patrons. Also note the unfinished amorous couple whose small noses have been left stuck together in a gooey thread. *(Open Sa-Th 10am-5pm. Admission free with Western Group ticket.)*

Eastern Group

The Eastern Group is scattered in and around Khajuraho village, and the temples are not as stunning as those in the Western Group. Nevertheless, the Eastern Group is still amazing. On the way to the Eastern Group, you will come across a **Hanuman Shrine** on the left of Jain Temple Rd. The large monkey is smeared with orange *sindur* and is one of Khajuraho's oldest sculptures, dating from the 9th century. Crossing the bypass road and entering Khajuraho village, the path veers to the left along the side of a seasonal pond called the **Khajur Sagar.** Not far along it on the left is the small **Brahma Temple,** misnamed by 19th-century art historians. A four-faced Shiva *linga* sits in the sanctuary and Vishnu is carved on the lintel above the door. The **Vamana Temple** is at the end of this lakeside path. It is as large as some of the western temples but is distinguished by its single, non-multiplying *shikhara*. By the time this temple was built, between 1050 and 1075, Khajuraho's sculptors seem to have toned down their erotic fantasies. The outer porch has collapsed, giving the temple an appearance that often gets described as "stunted," which seems only fitting since Vamana was Vishnu's dwarf avatar.

A section of the Eastern Group consists of Jain temples, walled into a Jain monastery complex on the far side of Khajuraho village. The old temples here are mixed in with new ones, and this mixture is embodied in the **Shantinath Temple,** which was built recently but has heavy pillars and doorways taken from old temples. The inside has a collection of photographs and posters of Jain pilgrimage sites; if your interests lie in another direction, it also contains plenty of sculptures of naked Jain monks.

Over to the left of the Shantinath Temple is the best of the **Jain temples,** the **Parsvanath Temple.** Architecturally it is noted for its simple plan (there are no balconies) and the small shrine at the back. In addition to Jain *tirthankaras* (saints), the sculptures on the outside include just about every Hindu deity, so it's thought that this was once a Hindu temple. Some of the most famous posing women in Khajuraho are here, including one putting on ankle-bells and another using *kohl*. On the other side of a big mango tree is the **Adinath Temple,** whose porch has been reconstructed with concrete. The temple has some very flexible female figures. Both temples have shiny black images of their respective *tirthankaras*.

Southern Group

The Southern Group isn't really a group at all, just two temples further from one another than from the other groups. A paved road off to the right of Jain Temple Rd. marked Dhulade leads to the **Duladeo Temple.** This temple's *mahamandapa* room, wide with a great rotunda ceiling, has an elaborate star shape. The top of the *shikhara* has been broken and the blocks used to repair it give a sense of its underlying shape. By 1100, when this temple was built, sculptors were getting carried away with ornaments and jewelry on their human figures and the sculptures themselves are not very good. The *linga* inside the Duladeo Temple looks oddly scaly because it is carved with innumerable replicas of itself.

   Chaturbhuj Temple is a few kilometers south of Khajuraho. It's a trip best made in the late afternoon, for Chaturbhuj is the only big temple in Khajuraho that faces west. The light shines warmly on its 2.7m *dakshinamurti* statue: one stone, but three deities. This huge image is thought to be a combination of Shiva, Vishnu, and Krishna, but archaeologists have been unsure what to make of the symbolism here. The sculptures around the outside include another interesting hybrid: on the south side, an image of Ardhanarishvara (half-Shiva, half-Parvati) split down the middle.

▓ Jhansi झाँसी

Jhansi exemplifies strip-development, Indian style. Endless greasy, single-story garages vie for space along dusty, jarring streets, punctuated by intermittent cinemas and permit rooms. Trucks roar, crowds mill, rickshaws riot, urbanism sprawls, and tempers fray. As enticing as all this sounds, Jhansi draws tourists due to its proximity to Orchha and its status as a railhead for Khajuraho. Although Jhansi is actually located in a peninsula of Uttar Pradesh, it is almost entirely surrounded by and absorbed into Madhya Pradesh. Schedules may conspire to detain you here, in which case you can while away the hours in rapt contemplation of Maharani Lakshmi Bai's last stand at the city's otherwise uninspiring fort. A celebrated revolutionary, she joined the anti-British sepoys in the Mutiny of 1857. As the British recaptured the region, Jhansi was one of the last rebel holdouts. Dressed as a man, her guns blazing, the *maharani* rode out into battle to meet her final demise 180 km from Jhansi (yes, even she had to get out).

ORIENTATION AND PRACTICAL INFORMATION Downtown Jhansi covers a 5km span from the **railway station** in the west to the **bus stand** in the east. About 1km north of the station, **Shivpuri Road** runs straight-ish all the way across town. The **U.P. Tourism Main Office** is in Hotel Veerangana on **Sipri Road** (tel. 441267). To get there, take a left on **Station Road,** go straight to Sipri Crossing, and take a right. The hotel is on the left: not much literature, or even a map, but plenty of helpful advice from the friendly tourist office staff. Open daily 8am-6pm. The **MPTDC** booth (tel. 442622; open daily 6am-11pm), on platform 1 of the railway station, makes reservations for the 11am deluxe bus to **Khajuraho** (4½hr., Rs85). The regular 6 and 7am **buses** (Rs65) also leave from the railway station, while the 11:45am and 1:15pm services depart from the bus stand. The best train to **Delhi** (4hr., Rs435), **Agra** (2hr., Rs245), and **Gwalior** (1hr., Rs165) is the superfast, A/C *Shatabdi Exp.* 2001 at 5:45pm. The *Shatabdi Exp.* 2002 heads in the other direction to **Bhopal** (10:45am, 3hr., Rs375), and the *Mahakosal Exp.* 1450 to **Jabalpur** (10:45pm, 12hr., Rs111/554). The **Reservations Office** (on the left as you face the station) opens M-Sa 8am-2pm and 2:15-8pm, Su 8am-2pm. Rapacious **rickshaws** abound on the main streets while tempos for Orchha (Rs10) leave directly from the bus stand. The **State Bank of India** (tel. 440534), Jhokar Bagh Rd. at the center of town, near Elite Crossing, changes traveler's checks (open M-F 10am-2pm, Sa 10am-noon). The **telegraph office** sits opposite Hotel Pujan on Gwalior Rd. (open M-Sa 10am-5pm). Mani Chowk, the market at the base of the fort, houses the government **hospital** (tel. 440521), while the **police station** is located on the Main Rd. (tel. 440538). A 24-hour STD/ISD booth sits on platform 6 at the railway station. **Postal Code:** 284001. **Telephone Code:** 0517.

ACCOMMODATIONS AND FOOD Travelers coming to see Orchha are better off staying in Orchha itself. If you cannot, **The Prakash Guest House,** Sardarilal Lal Market, Civil Lines (tel. 330133 or 330226), just south of the fort, offers pleasant mid-range lodgings. The air-cooled rooms feature wall-to-wall carpeting, elliptical blue bath tubs, and two beds (Rs250, with A/C Rs425). The nearby **Hotel Pujan,** Gwalior Rd. (tel. 330037), opposite the telegraph office, exacts a plunge in comfort for a modest reduction in prices (*paan*-stained singles Rs80, with air-cooling Rs125; doubles with headless showers Rs150/200). **Hotel Veerangana,** (tel. 441262), run by U.P. Tourism, has clean dormitories (beds Rs50) and single air-cooled rooms with bathrooms (Rs250). The dingy restaurant serves up a limited menu of bland Indian and Chinese eats at decent prices (Rs30-60) daily from 6am-10pm. For a really good night's sleep, visit the A/C bar (open daily noon-11pm) with its thumping pop music, liquor shots (Rs25-50), and beer (Rs75-100).

   Hotel Sita, Shrivpuri Rd. (tel. 444690; open daily 6:30am-10pm) dishes out pricey food (*dal makhni* Rs35), that might be a good consolation prize for climbing the fort steps only to get a superb view of Jhansi's latest plague: satellite dishes. The Prakash Guest House features a restaurant and bar called **Sagar.** Businessmen tuck in to rich chicken dishes (Rs50) or butter *masala* (Rs40) in the dim, mirrored interior typical of any classy Indian eatery. Brave souls might sample the *paneer pasendida,* "stuffed with sultans," for Rs35 (open daily 6:30am-11pm).

SIGHTS Jhansi Fort has little to offer but a sequence of curiously proportioned equestrian statues and lackluster views. *(Open 10am-5pm. Admission 25paise.)* The fort abounds in anachronisms, uniting new and old in a sort of uniform ugliness. The silver lining is a life-sized model of a battle from the Indian Mutiny below the Southern Wall. Local mailmen proved their resemblance to other dashing uniformed types by converting old letterboxes into weapons. Mailbox cannons appear to have inflicted mortal wounds on several Brits, much to the satisfaction of Indian onlookers. This stirring scene may quicken the pulse, but the nearby **museum** is sure to induce catatonia. *(Open July-April 15 Tu-Su 10:30am-4:30pm; April 16-June Tu-Su 7:30am-12:30pm.)*

■ Orchha ओरछा

A sense of wistfulness characterizes the ruins speckling the small town of Orchha, located on a loop in the Betwa river 16km from Jhansi. An abandoned 17th-century city shoots up out of the hills and trees, its tumbledown towers still assertively grasping the rocky terrain. Orchha was the capital of a small Bundela kingdom during its heyday in the 16th and 17th centuries, but had to be abandoned in 1783 after too many attacks by Mughals and Marathas. Raja Rudra Pratap Bundela chose Orchha as his capital in 1531, and the Bundelas' fortunes grew as they kept the Mughal Empire at bay. Raja Bir Singh Deo (r. 1605-27), the greatest Bundela king, befriended the emperor Jahangir and even had him visit Orchha. Under Bir Singh Deo the Bundelas expanded to control the whole region of Bundelkhand, which still uses their name. Later Bundela rulers succeeded in annoying the Mughals, however, and the emperor Shah Jahan attacked Orchha, initiating a long, slow decline.

   The Bundelas left a landscape filled with palaces and temples, and nothing has interfered with them for 200 years but the forces of nature. This seems fitting in Orchha—the name means "hidden," and when human rulers gave up the attempt to conceal the city from invaders, nature took up the challenge. Vines hang over cracked walls, and cow dung is strewn over palace floors.

ORIENTATION AND PRACTICAL INFORMATION Tempos sputter to Orchha from Jhansi (Rs10) and from the intersection of **Orchha Road** with the highway running from Jhansi to Khajuraho, spitting out their passengers just south of the village's only **crossroads.** South past the bus and tempo stand lies the pricey MPTDC Betwa Cottages, as well as some royal cenotaphs and the new 5-star Orchha Resort along the banks of the **Betwa River.** The right-hand (eastern) crossroad, heading up from the bus station, leads to the bridge connecting the main palace complex to the village. You'll first pass the **Post Office** (don't send any mail if you want it to reach its destination). Towering over the village are Orchha's best-preserved sights, the enormous **Jehangir Mahal** and the decorated **Raj Mahal.** From the crosswords in the other direction lies the MPTDC's second property, the Marsarovar Hotel, more stalls, the Chaturbhuj and Ram Raja temples, and the Palki Mahal Hotel, on the way to the Lakshminarayan Temple at the western edge. **Police:** tel. 52622 (only within the village). There are two **STD/ISD telephone** booths near the crossroads, but all other needs will have to be taken care of in Jhansi—justification for its existence.

ACCOMMODATIONS AND FOOD The MPTDC has converted an 18th-century palace in the middle of Orchha's ruins into the moderately priced **Sheesh Mahal Hotel** (tel. 52624). If this is your only chance for a dream night in a palace, you might want to take the plunge in this generous, peaceful setting. Be warned, however, that only the suites are palatial on the inside, which means little more than carpeting in any event. (In-season: singles with bath Rs390, with air-cooling Rs440; doubles Rs490/560. Suites with air-cooling Rs1890. Off-season: 25% discount.) Be prepared to shell out Rs2390 for the maharaja treatment. The hotel's **restaurant,** open to guests and non-guests, features standard entrees (Rs25-50), as well as breakfast and snacks. (Open daily 7am-10pm.) Try to book at an MPTDC office up to a month in advance. The local SADA runs three budget lodges: the **Palki Mahal** inside the Phool Bagh Palace (next door to the Ram Raja temple) combines dorm beds (Rs25) with history, while the **Mansarovar** by the crossroads mixes threadbare sheets with banal modernity. (Singles Rs50; doubles Rs75.) The final SADA offering is the **Pryatak Guest House,** in which your cement cottage is complemented by a cement courtyard. All rooms are Rs75 with attached bath. There are also five rooms in the **Ram Mandir Lodge,** main market (tel. 522660), across from the Mansarovar. These clean second-story rooms face the bazaar, but the hot shower in the common bath will compensate for the noise. Two rooms have air-cooling and cost Rs100.

There are plenty of *dhabas* in the market, but the Maharaja would likely be more comfortable at the **Orchha Resort** (and he'll need to bring his treasure chest along if he wants to stay there). The all-veg. restaurant serves a breakfast buffet (daily 8-10am; Rs150), and lunch and dinner buffets (noon-3pm and 7:30-9:30pm; Rs350) in a plush dining room. *A la carte* items with rich sauces go for the rich price of Rs50-150.

SIGHTS The ruins of Orchha are scattered just about everywhere around this bend in the Betwa, and they spill across from the main "island" to the modern town and beyond. (*All locations open 8am-5pm. Admission free.*) Nothing has happened in the last 200 years to clear them away, so many old buildings still linger all over the landscape, poked by trees and unsure of their purpose. There are many more slumping towers and gateways—all unnamed landmarks. Hotel Sheesh Mahal offers a **walkman tour** (2hr., Rs50, Rs500 deposit) that covers the three main palaces. Although the voiceovers frequently degenerate into hackneyed "picture-the-scene" sequences (complete with cheap sound effects), it's quite informative about Orchha's history.

The two biggest palaces face each other across a quadrangle which has for a third side the whitewashed palace of the Sheesh Mahal Hotel. The **Raj Mahal,** on the left side as you face the hotel, is the same building that looks like a perforated concrete curtain from the town across the river. Lacking any ornamental features, it's one of the earlier buildings in Orchha. This was the king's usual residence and has a room for his private audiences as well as several chambers for his harem. The building is quite blocky but some of the ceilings inside are painted with botanical patterns and mythical scenes. The top windows offer a good view of the town.

The steps to the right of the Raj Mahal take you down to the **public audience hall,** after which the path veers down and to the right through numerous ruins. The next complete palace is the **Rai Praveen Mahal,** which was built for Raja Indramani's favorite dancing concubine. This palace was intended to be level with the treetops in the Anand Mahal gardens behind it, which can be viewed from the second floor, each shrub sticking out of its octagonal berth in the concrete.

Continuing along the same path that brought you to the Rai Praveen Mahal will take you to a Royal Gate. If you walk through the arch and head up the hill to the right (you'll pass the camel stables), you should be able to enter the main door of the stunning **Jahangir Mahal** palace. If the door is locked try scrambling around the stone apron to the left of the building to the entrance opposite the Raj Mahal; the less game will have to retrace their steps all the way. The Bundelas built a better palace for their imperial guest than they ever did for themselves. Two happy concrete elephants rang bells at the outer entrance to welcome Emperor Jahangir on his visit to Orchha in 1606. The Jahangir Mahal is filled with balconies, walkways, and railings. Traces of Islamic style are visible in the stone screens and decorated domes; the Bundelas evidently aimed to please. The views to the east from the third-floor balconies are Orchha's best: the Betwa river can be seen curling past all the little palaces, and it is easy to get an overall sense of the area. The carvings of peacocks, parrots, and snakes throughout the palace have been carried off with finesse.

The north end of Orchha's island is reached by turning left after passing through the Royal Gate, then passing through another archway in a wall. This is a good place to fight back the thornbushes and explore—it's dotted with **old temples** that have largely been neglected and are now besieged by small wheat farms. People dip into the ancient wells for their drinking water here, and, in some cases, the temples have become toolsheds and kitchens.

An arching granite bridge over a small stream takes you back to the town of Orchha. The best Bundela temples are in the town, and the two most prominent ones have an interconnected history. The devout Raja Madhukar Shah carried an image of Lord Rama all the way to Orchha from Rama's hometown, Ayodhya. He meant to install it in the **Chaturbhuj Temple,** but first he put it down in his own palace, from whence it refused to move. The palace had to become the **Ram Raja Temple,** where, in keeping with the setting, Rama is worshiped in his role as a king. (*Open daily 8am-1pm and 8-10pm.*) Ram Raja is now a popular temple, painted pink and yellow, and overlooks a cobbled square. The Chhaturbhuj Temple, however, is defunct, and it is left with a great arching assembly hall and several large spires. Spiral staircases at each corner of the cross-shaped floorplan lead to high lookout points.

The **Lakshminarayan Temple** is a short walk west of town, at the crest of a hill. (*Open daily 10am-5pm.*) Its location seems like the place for a fort, and the temple is built like one, with four high walls and turrets at the corners. The temple is guarded by the two mighty lions, Shardulas. The best painted ceilings in Orchha are inside the temple—some of them date from the 19th century, including one fabulous scene of British soldiers swarming around an Indian fort. The jocund relationship between Radha and Krishna is played out on all levels of the temple. The lookout above the entrance offers a breathtaking view of the entire scene of town, temples, and palaces.

The boxlike Bundela **royal chhattris** (cenotaphs) cluster on the bank of the Betwa south of town. (*Open daily 10am-5pm.*) Even though the Bundelas burned their dead, they borrowed the Mughal custom of mausoleum-building. The *chhattris'* river-bank location is peaceful. The other side of the river is covered with forest, and from there you can see them reflected in the water.

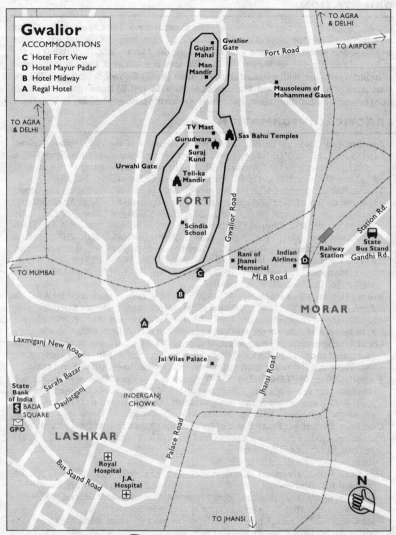

NORTH INDIA

Map labels:
- TO AGRA & DELHI
- TO AIRPORT
- Fort Road
- Gujari Mahal
- Gwalior Gate
- Man Mandir
- Mausoleum of Mohammed Gaus
- TO AGRA & DELHI
- TV Mast
- Gurudwara
- Sas Bahu Temples
- Suraj Kund
- Urwahi Gate
- Teli-ka Mandir
- FORT
- Gwalior Road
- Station Rd.
- State Bus Stand
- Railway Station
- Gandhi Rd.
- Scindia School
- Rani of Jhansi Memorial
- Indian Airlines
- TO MUMBAI
- MLB Road
- MORAR
- Laxmiganj New Road
- Jai Vilas Palace
- Jhansi Road
- Sarafa Bazar
- State Bank of India
- Daulatganj
- INDERGANJ CHOWK
- BADA SQUARE
- GPO
- LASHKAR
- Palace Road
- Bus Stand Road
- Royal Hospital
- J.A. Hospital
- TO JHANSI
- N

Gwalior
ACCOMMODATIONS
C Hotel Fort View
D Hotel Mayur Padar
B Hotel Midway
A Regal Hotel

■ Gwalior ग्वालियर

"Ruins" are a common trope throughout India, but few in the Subcontinent rival those in Gwalior, the largest city in northern Madhya Pradesh (pop. 800,000). Whether for its musical *maestri*, or for its majestic, floating hilltop bastion, which Emperor Babur called "the pearl amongst the fortresses of Hind," Gwalior has remained legendary for centuries. Whole genealogies of conquerors brought their business here, from Rajputs and Marathas to the Mughals and the British to the Scindia family, who still dominate local politics. During the Raj, the Maharaja of Gwalior earned one of the five 21-gun salutes accorded Indian potentates by the British, thanks to his loyalty during the Mutiny—a stark contrast with nearby Jhansi's Maharani Lakshmi Bai (see p. 255). The Scindia royal family is still the focus of civic pride: their palace, a 19th-century shrine to tastelessness, preserves a glimpse into history almost as fascinating as the aforementioned hilltop bastion.

ORIENTATION

Gwalior is spread out, and it can take a while to get around. The city wraps itself in an asymmetric "U" shape around the fort. The **Old Town,** home of the **railway station** and state **bus stand,** lies to the east of the fort; the **Morar** area, dominated by the gaudy **palace,** is to the southeast; the **Lashkar** area is southwest. Lashkar is the heart of modern Gwalior, with a bazaar area and **Bada (Jiyaji) Chowk,** where the GPO and State Bank of India are located. **Maharani Lakshmi Bai (MLB) Road** runs across town from northeast, near the station, to Lashkar. Gwalior's **business holiday** is Tuesday.

PRACTICAL INFORMATION

Airport: (tel. 368272), on Bhind Rd., 10km northeast of the city. **Indian Airlines** (tel. 326872) is on MLB Rd., opposite Shelter Hotel. Open daily 10am-5pm. Flights on M, T, Th, and Sa to: **Bhopal** (5:30pm, 1hr., US$50); **Bombay** (5:30pm, 3hr., US$108); **Delhi** (9:50am, 45min., US$45); **Indore** (5:30pm, 2hr., US$70).

Trains: Railway Station, MLB Rd., Morar (tel. 341344 or 340306). Reservation office is at the far left of the building. Open M-Sa 8am-8pm, Su 8am-2pm. *Shatabdi Exp.* fares are A/C chair-car; others are 2nd/1st class. To: **Agra** (*Shatabdi Exp.* 2001, 7pm, 1hr., Rs185); **Bhopal** (*Shatabdi Exp.* 2002, 9:30am, 4hr., Rs420); **Delhi** (*Shatabdi Exp.* 2001, 7pm, 3½hr., Rs385); **Jhansi** (*Shatabdi Exp.* 2002, 9:30am, 1hr., Rs165); **Kanpur** (*Ahmedabad-Gorakhpur Exp.* 5045, Tu, 4:15am, 7½hr., Rs49/246); **Lucknow** (*Ahmedabad-Gorakhpur Exp.* 5045, 4:15am, 9hr., Rs 48/239); **Mathura** (*Punjab Mail* 1037, 3pm, 2½hr., Rs45/217); **Mumbai** (*Punjab Mail* 1038, 11:10am, 10hr., Rs70/310).

Buses: The **state bus stand** (tel. 340192) is near the railway station off MLB Rd. To: **Agra** (8 per day, 3hr., Rs42); **Bhopal** (8am, 16hr., Rs131); **Delhi** (2 per day, 8hr., Rs120); **Jhansi** (6 per day, 3hr., Rs34); **Khajuraho** (1 per day, 8hr., Rs85). The **private bus stand** inhabits the wilds of Lashkar, not too far from Bada Chowk.

Local Transportation: Tempos cruise down MLB Rd. from one side of town to the other. Hail them, and check the destination before climbing in. Fares are typically Rs2. There are also unmetered but reasonably-rated **auto-rickshaws** and **taxis.**

Tourist Office: MPTDC (tel. 345379), platform 1 of the railway station. Friendly officer metes out maps and pamphlets about M.P., arranges city tours (9:30am-2pm, Rs40), and provides bus transportation (daily, 6:30pm, Rs25) for the fort's sound and light show (Rs20 for Indians, Rs50 for foreigners). Open M-Sa 8am-7pm.

Currency Exchange: State Bank of India, Bada Chowk (tel. 422968), 1st fl., main building. Cashes traveler's checks and foreign currency. Open M-F 10:30am-2:30pm, Sa 10:30am-12:30pm.

Police: Jayendra Ganj (tel. 26268).

Hospital: Royal Hospital, Kampoo (tel. 332711), near Roxy Cinema. Recommended private hospital with doctors available 24hr. and ambulance service. Attached **pharmacy** open daily 8am-11pm. **Kasturba Medical Stores,** 6 Kasturba Market (tel. 322183), is located 1km away and is open 24hr.

Post Office: GPO, Bada Chowk. Ask the postmaster for *Poste Restante.* Open M-Sa 8am-8pm, Su 10am-6pm. **Postal Code:** 474001.

Internet: Bhargava Computers, Sanjay Complex, Jayendraganj (tel. 429884), 4km from the train station down MLB Rd. in the back of the office. Call for an appointment. Web access Rs150 per hr. Open daily 9:30am-9:30pm.

Telephone Code: 0751.

ACCOMMODATIONS

Cheap, acceptable hotels—all with 24-hour check-out—line the market in front of the railway station. From the station, walk down the road connecting it to the market.

Hotel Mayur, Paday (tel. 325559). From the railway station, turn right after the flyover at the Lal Bahadur Shastri statue, take the first right onto the service road, and the first left onto Green Hotel Colony Rd. Lockers, and 24hr. hot water. Spotless dorms have air-cooling. Dorm beds Rs55. Singles Rs120; doubles with bath Rs150.

Hotel Midway, MLB Rd. (tel. 424392), 2½km from the rail station, opposite the *gurudwara*. A sterile complex with clean sheets and towels. Rooms have TVs, telephones, and running hot water. All rooms with air-cooling Rs250. A/C singles Rs350; A/C doubles Rs425.

Hotel Fort View, MLB Rd. (tel. 423409). Views not only of the fort's fearsome walls, but also of the locals climbing up the fort slopes for their morning *toilette*. Rooms in this mid-range, midtown hotel improve in value as their descriptions (executive, deluxe, etc.) get less grandiose. Rooms are clean and livable. Attached bar and restaurant. Check-out noon. Rooms Rs175-225.

Regal Hotel, Shinde Ki Chhawanii, MLB Rd. (tel. 334469). A whole range of rooms, with the best value at the bottom end. The standard doubles, off the pleasant rooftop terrace, have clean common bathrooms and are one of Gwalior's few good deals. Noisy on busy bar nights. Doubles Rs120.

FOOD

Indian Coffee House, Station Rd. From the station, turn right, then head left at the traffic circle. Two low-ceilinged, pokey rooms attract the same middle-class clientele as always. (*Dosa* and *utthapam* Rs20; coffee Rs5). Open daily 7am-8pm.

Kwality Restaurant, Deendayal Market, MLB Rd. (tel. 423243). Chalk up another one for the dim, nondescript, A/C chain with a spelling problem. A standard range of north Indian veg. (Rs18-50), chicken (Rs45), and mutton (Rs40) dishes. Open daily 11:30am-11pm.

Volga Restaurant, inside Hotel Surya, Tayendra Ganj (tel. 321092). The *malai-de-la-malai* of Gwalior society frequent this chandeliered, A/C bastion of the *bourzhaozya*. Rich, delicious chicken *tikka masala* (Rs50) and *dal makhani* (Rs18) that gleefully swims in *ghee*. Open daily 11am-2pm and 7-11pm.

Usha Kiran Palace, Jayendraganj, Lashkar (tel. 323993). Its proximity to the Jai Vilas Palace has proved contagious—the delicacies here are debaucherous, sending customers into the bygone eras when raja left no recipe unturned in order to enthrall their guests. Decadent prices to match (entrees about Rs100-250).

SIGHTS

Gwalior Fort

Hours: *Open daily 8am-6:30pm. English Sound and Light Show 8:30pm.* **Museum:** *open Tu-Su 10am-5pm.* **Admission:** *Free. Palace museum Rs2. Sound and Light Show Rs50 for foreigners, Rs20 for Indians.*

Gwalior's amazing fort, almost 3km long and at points 1km wide, presides over the city from a height of 90m, behind 10m-high walls. It has been the center of control for this region for longer than history has recorded. According to legend, it was built in the first century AD by a king named Suraj, who was cured of leprosy here by a saint named Gwalipa. Out of gratitude Suraj named the fort Gwalior. Later, the fort came to be ruled by all of the region's succeeding dynasties: Rajputs, Delhi Sultans, Mughals, Marathas, and the British. Since 1886, the fort has belonged to the Scindias, Gwalior's present royal family. The fort has collected palaces and temples through the ages, and more recently a prestigious boys' school, a TV relay station, and two post offices. Long roads swirl around a plateau traversed only by motorcycle and moped riders willing to brave the heights.

There are two entrances to the fort, **Gwalior Gate** on the northeast side, adjacent to the Old Town, and **Urwahi Gate** on the southwest, which is approached through a long gorge. Both have long, steep ramps which must be climbed on foot, although cars and taxis (but not auto-rickshaws) can enter through Urwahi Gate. It's worth entering at Gwalior Gate for the view of the Man Mandir Palace's picture-postcard towers above as you climb. At the base of the hill just inside Gwalior Gate is the **Gujari Mahal Palace**, built by Man Singh Tomar for his favorite queen. The sunny courtyard has an **Archaeological Museum** with a mixed bag of sculptures and paintings from the region. The curator keeps a Salabhanjika miniature sculpture of the tree-goddess Gyraspur—a priceless piece of art history—locked up, but he will show it to those with a good reason to see it.

The northeastern ramp continues up through a series of archways past Jain and Hindu shrines. Looming overhead are the blue-splotched towers of the **Man Mandir Palace.** As you pass through the Elephant Gate (there was once a big stone elephant here) into the fort itself, Raja Man Singh Tomar's creation on your right becomes livelier, with blue, green, and yellow tiles forming pictures of plants and ducks. Inside the palace are many small rooms split by lattices carved in the shape of animals and dancers. These elaborate, perforated screens with a *dandia-ras* motif bear witness to the *purdah,* or veiling system, pervasive among certain groups of Hindus. The "noble" women would sit behind the screens and watch their male relatives (and husbands) drool over their courtesans. A flashlight can lead the way down to the bat-infested dungeon complex, where in the 17th century, the Mughal emperor Aurangzeb had his brother Murad chained up and slowly killed through starvation and intoxication, feeding him nothing but boiled and mashed-up poppies. Near the Man Mandir Palace is another **museum,** this one run by the Archaeological Survey of India. It's not as impressive as the one at the bottom of the hill, but it is free, and the staff sells cold drinks. *(Open Sa-Th 10am-5pm.)* On the other side of the Elephant Gate from the Man Mandir Palace are seats for the nightly **sound and light show.**

To reach the north end of the fort pass through the gate on your right as you exit the Man Mandir Palace. This area is a barren landscape where ruined palaces and dried-out tanks cling to the edge of the hill. There are four palaces here, two built by the Tomar Rajputs and two by the Mughals. The huge **Jauhar Tank** next to them is remembered for the *jauhar* (mass suicide) of Rajput queens that took place here in 1232 when Sultan Iltutmish of Delhi was on the verge of capturing the fort.

Other points of interest are at the south end of the hilltop. About midway along the eastern edge are the **Sas Bahu** temples, built in 1093. One temple's spire has fallen, but its assembly hall, still standing, has a beautiful stack of skewed false stories. The edge of the fort here offers a drab view of the city, although the big brown dome of Muhammad Gaus's tomb is visible. The west side of the fort affords better views of the spreading city and its craggy landscape.

The nearby **Bandi Chhor Gurudwara** is a Sikh pilgrimage site that marks the spot where the sixth Sikh guru, Hargobind, was imprisoned for two years under Emperor Jahangir. Ritual cleansing is required for entry and cloths are provided for you to cover your head before entering the *gurudwara.* Inside, young men sit and chant Sikh scriptures above a sunken silver chamber marking the guru's jail.

The **Teli-ka Mandir** (Oilman's Temple) is a tall building, though it doesn't rival the nearby TV mast. The roof rolls up into a cylindrical shape, commonly but incorrectly said to be a South Indian design—this is actually a very early northern style. The Mandir dates from the 9th century. It was once a Vishnu temple, but when the British occupied the fort in the 19th century, they turned it into a soda-water factory. The sculpture on the outside is excellent, erotic, and eroded. The southwestern entrance passes through the long Urwahi Gorge, a natural split in the hillside. Its walls are adorned with rows of **Jain sculptures** from the 7th to 15th centuries. These figures of *tirthankaras* still stand impassively above the road, despite the efforts of Mughal conqueror Babur, who smashed many of their faces and genitals. One statue, an image of Adhinath, is 19m tall. More of these carvings are on the southeast side of the fort, including one still used as a Jain shrine.

Jai Vilas Palace

Hours: *Open Tu-Su 10am-5pm.* **Admission:** *Rs160 for foreigners. Keep your ticket stub for entry to both wings.*

Maharaja Jiyaji Rao Scindia commissioned a British architect to erect this great white whale of a complex to impress the Prince of Wales (later Edward VII) on his state visit in 1875. Generations of Scindias filled it with the most outrageous *objets d'art* and kitsch; now part of it is open as a museum (the rest is still the *maharaja*'s residence). Furniture from Versailles, silly old prints, toys: the flamboyance goes on and on, roomful after roomful like reflections in mirrors placed opposite each other; of course there are plenty of mirrors too. Tatty stuffed tigers fill up the "Natural History Gallery;" from the gilded ceiling of Durbar Hall hang two enormous Belgian chandeliers, each weighing 3.5 tons, and below them is the largest handmade carpet in Asia. Downstairs (down a crystal staircase), the dining table has tracks for a silver toy train that once wheeled around after-dinner brandy and cigars.

The City

To the east of the fort in the Old Town is the **Mausoleum of Sheik Muhammad Ghaus,** a Muslim saint who helped the Mughal emperor Babur capture Gwalior Fort. (*Open daily sunrise-sunset.*) The walls of this fine early-Mughal monument are composed of cut-stone screens with entrancingly rhythmic geometric patterns. The **Tomb of Tansen** in the same graveyard evokes a different kind of rhythm: the 16th-century *raga*-singer was one of the greatest musicians in Indian history. A prestigious classical music festival takes place here in November or December. Chewing the leaves of the tamarind tree near the tomb is supposed to make your voice as sweet as Tansen's, although it won't sweeten your palate. In the Lashkar area, **Bada Square** is one of the most scenic parts of Gwalior. Palm trees and benches are ringed around the Henry VIII-like figure of Maharaja Jiyaji Rao Scindia. The architecture in this busy circle features frilly arches and a clock tower. Gwalior's newest big thing is its **Sun Temple,** in the Morar area. (*Open daily 6am-noon and 2-7pm.*) Built by the philanthropic Birla family, it is a scaled-down knock-off of the Sun Temple in **Konark** (see p. 445).

Come On Baby, Fight My Fire

Legend has it that Akbar's greatest court singer, Miyan Tansen, learned the powerful *raga dipak* after having seen a twig spontaneously catch fire in a songbird's beak. The *raga,* when performed with the full intensity, supposedly turns the practitioner's vocal chords into ashes. When Tansen's jealous rivals challenged him to sing *dipak* for the emperor, he welcomed the opportunity. Little did the baddies know that the savvy musician had trained his wife in the rain-inducing *raga mahar* to offset *dipak*'s fiery impact. When the crooner began to ignite, his wife was called in, and the subsequent duet of fire and water so impressed Akbar that he aided Tansen's ascendancy in the emperor's court.

Rajasthan राजस्थान

When enemies faced down Rajput foes, they would first see a cloud of dust on the horizon, followed by the fierce defenders of this Land of Kings, charging into an unwinnable battle, outnumbered and outgunned. In the cliff-top fortresses of the Thar Desert, Rajput women and children would follow their men in honorable death, choosing mass immolation *(jauhar)* over surrender. Perhaps it was the stark desert and the unforgiving heat that bred this intensity, for the stubborn loyalty and pride of Rajasthan's people prevails to this day.

Rajasthan's maharajas were so obstinately concerned with their own independence that Rajasthan dissolved into a mess of uncooperative kingdoms, easily overthrown by the powerful and united Mughal Empire. However, the Mughals quickly realized that granting the Rajputs some power in their ruling hierarchy was more effective than engaging in punishing battles with unwavering foes. Even when the British overthrew the Mughals, the maharajas collaborated with the Raj; in return they were given license to live in utter decadence, depleting the state's resources and arresting its social and economic development. Their subjects, however, stuck by their nobles, and the unequivocal pride and piercing poetry of traditional village artisans still mingles naturally with the lavish palaces, *havelis,* temples, and pavilions that blanket the state. The close relationship between maharaja and subject, often one of *noblesse oblige,* has continued well into the late 20th century, with royal families entering the politics of democratic India and being elected by their loyal citizens.

Rajasthan can be geographically divided into three regions. The flat lands of the eastern part of the state feature a combination of rich national parks and cosmopolitan centers like Jaipur, the state's capital and part of the Delhi-Agra-Jaipur "Golden Triangle" of tourism. To the west, in the "Marwar" region, the plains gradually yield to the arid lands of the Thar Desert and its imposing forts. In the south, the majestic Aravali Mountains of the "Mewar" region decorate the landscape with lush valleys and mountain lakes. While some Rajputs have traded in their swords for cell-phones, you'll catch, amid all the development, glimpses of the glorious past: the colored *bandhani* cloth of Jaipur's markets, the fortress at Chittaurgarh, the hardened shepherds in the hills, the camels in Pushkar, and Udaipur's opulent palaces.

HIGHLIGHTS OF RAJASTHAN

- **Jaipur** (below) is Rajasthan's most popular destination. Its **City Palace** (p. 273), **Hawa Mahal** (p. 275), and **Amber Fort** (p. 275) are worth the hype.
- **Udaipur's lake palaces** (p. 294) have long been a draw for honeymooners and secret agents alike—one glimpse of the sunrise city and you'll see why.
- Peaceful **Pushkar** (p. 282) is a quiet oasis in the frenetic desert of Rajasthani tourism, soothing pilgrims and travelers 360 days a year. The other four, which make up the **Pushkar Fair** (p. 285) in early November, are another story entirely.
- Rajasthan's only hill station, **Mt. Abu** (p. 296) resembles a fantasy golf course; the city's **Jain Temples** temper the fun with some serious beauty (p. 299).

Jaipur जयपुर

Rajasthan's prosperous capital is a city to be savored. Although many of Jaipur's tourists only stay long enough to have their pictures snapped in front of all the major attractions, don't be surprised if you stay for weeks–tasting a bit of the city each day, sampling its easy-going cosmopolitan spirit, enjoying its effortlessly elegant architecture, and being lulled by its deliciously dry heat into sweaty afternoon naps.

To an unusual extent, the story of Jaipur is the story of one man, Maharaja Sawai Jai Singh II. By all accounts, Jai Singh possessed rare erudition and a ferocious curiosity for the sciences. However, he had little time for scholarship during the early years of his reign, when his kingdom was threatened by both the Marathas and the Mughals. Fortune favored the maharaja: his intelligence won him the Mughal emperor Aurangzeb as an ally, and the might of his Rajput forces dealt crushing blows to the Marathas. By the mid-1720s, Jai Singh was ready to settle down, and he set about designing a city for himself, with help from the renowned Vidyadhar Bhatcharya, a Bengali *brahmin*. The magnificent walled city of Jaipur was born.

In laying out Jaipur, Jai Singh and Vidyadhar Bhatcharya made the city both beautiful and functional. The city's walls provided solid defense, and Jaipur's wide sidewalks and streets were designed to allow easy movement of pedestrian traffic. Underground aqueducts delivered ample drinking water, and the entrances to stores and homes were placed on side streets so that the Maharaja's massive royal processions could pass without disturbing the daily habits of Jaipur's residents.

Time wrought inevitable changes on the Maharaja's city. The most striking came in 1853, when the city painted itself pink in honor of a visit by Prince Albert; newsman Stanley Reed dubbed Jaipur the "Pink City," and the name stuck. While modern Jaipur with its population of 1.7 million has sprawled outside the walls of Reed's Pink City, Jaipur's heart and soul remains within this old world enclave, replete with extraordinary museums, forts, temples, and palaces, as well as the crowds and animals that make up India at its hectic best and worst.

Warning: Tourists in Jaipur's old city bazaars are almost inevitably accosted by oh-so-friendly locals interested in chatting about tourism, education, the city, and life abroad. Having thus established themselves as "friends," they offer travelers their hospitality: "You're a guest in my country. The least I can do is invite you to my place for some food." Nine times out of ten, their "place" is a **jewelry or gems shop.** Eventually, travelers are offered the opportunity to carry anywhere from US$500 to US$10,000 worth of jewelry abroad to be handed over to an "overseas partner" (who, despite "evidence" to the contrary, is usually a fictional character). In return, these dealers offer a 100% commission. The rationale is straightforward. Export laws impose a 250% tariff on gems and jewelry. Foreigners with tourist visas are allowed to carry a certain amount of gems and jewelry out of the country. So, by having tourists do their exporting for them at 100% commission, gem dealers save a lot of money. The gem dealers call it "couriering," and insist that it's done all the time. **The Indian government calls it smuggling, and punishes it with long prison terms.** Generally, export schemes of any kind sound too good to be true because they are. Stay away from these offers. If you ever start to feel uncomfortable in a store, just leave, even if it seems rude or awkward. If you're interested in buying gems and jewelry for yourself, try to go with a local whom you trust so such issues won't come up in the bargaining process.

ORIENTATION

Though Jaipur is a good-sized city, getting around isn't particularly difficult (mostly because of its wide, straight streets), provided you can keep track of street name changes. The walled **Pink City,** encompassing most of the sights, is in the northeast; the **new city** sprawls south and west. The most important roads in the new city are **Mizra Ismail (M.I.) Road, Railway Station Road,** and **Sansar Chandra Road,** which interconnect and in whose vicinities lie the **railway station,** the **Central Bus Station,** the GPO, and most budget hotels and restaurants. M.I. Rd., which is Jaipur's main east-west thoroughfare, becomes **Agra Marg** after it skirts the three gates that lead into the heart of the Pink City: **Ajmeri Gate, New Gate,** and **Sanganeri Gate.** From Ajmeri Gate, **Kishanpol Bazaar** (which becomes **Gangauri Bazaar**) leads north into the Pink City and **Sawai Ram Singh Road** leads south to the new city. From Sanganeri Gate, **Johari Bazaar** (which becomes **Hawa Mahal Bazaar**) runs nearly 2km north. Just south of New Gate and beyond the **Ram Niwas Gardens, Jawaharlal Nehru Marg** runs south for nearly 2km before changing names and continues past the Birla

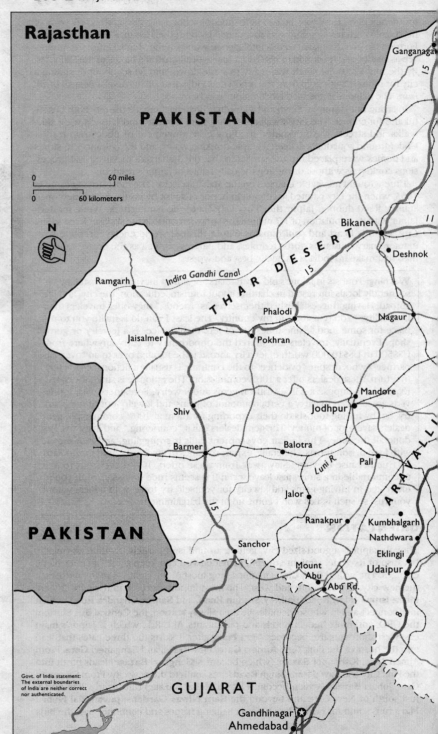

Rajasthan

PAKISTAN

0 ——— 60 miles

0 ——— 60 kilometers

N

Ganganagar

15

Bikaner

11

Deshnok

THAR DESERT

15

Indira Gandhi Canal

Ramgarh

Phalodi

Nagaur

Jaisalmer

Pokhran

Mandore

Shiv

Jodhpur

ARAVALLI

Barmer

Balotra

Luni R.

Pali

Jalor

PAKISTAN

Ranakpur

Kumbhalgarh

Nathdwara

Sanchor

Eklingji

Mount
Abu

Udaipur

Abu Rd.

8

Govt. of India statement:
The external boundaries
of India are neither correct
nor authenticated.

GUJARAT

Gandhinagar

Ahmedabad

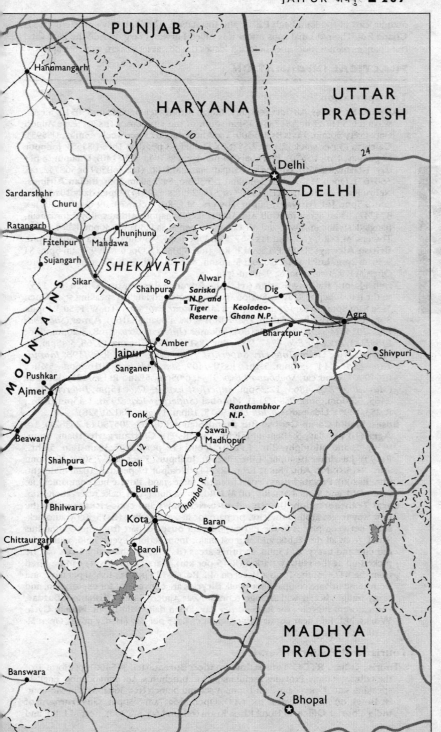

Mandir, east of the Ram Bagh Palace and the station. The Pink City's western gate is **Chand Pol.** The road that runs under it is called **Nirwan Marg** outside the Pink City, but changes names four times before it leaves the city at its eastern gate, **Suraj Pol.**

PRACTICAL INFORMATION

Transportation

Airport: Sanganer Airport (enquiry: Indian Airlines tel. 550222 or 550519; Jet Airways tel. 551729 or 551733), 15km south of the city. Buses (Rs20) leave Ajmeri Gate every 30min. Taxis Rs200-300. To: **Ahmedabad** (3 per week, 45min., US$95); **Calcutta** (3 per week, 2½hr., US$180); **Delhi** (2-3 per day, 1hr., US$55); **Jodhpur** (2 per day, 1hr., US$70); **Mumbai** (2-4 per day, 1½-3½hr., US$140); **Udaipur** (3 per day, 1-1½hr., US$70). **Air India,** Ganpati Plaza, M.I. Rd. (tel. 368569 or 368742; fax 360767). Open M-F 9:30am-1pm and 2-5:30pm, Sa 9:30am-2pm. **Indian Airlines,** Nehru Place, Tonk Rd. (tel. 514407 or 515324; fax 510344). Open daily 10am-1pm and 2-5pm. **Jet Airways,** Jaipur Towers, M.I. Rd. (tel. 370509 or 375430; fax 374242), is an agent for Gulf Air, Air France, Singapore Airlines, Royal Jordanian, Bangladesh Biman, TWA, and Air Canada. Open M-Sa 9:30am-5:30pm. **KLM,** Jaipur Towers, M.I. Rd. (tel. and fax 367772). Open M-F 9:30am-6pm, Sa 9:30am-2pm. **British Airways,** Usha Plaza, M.I. Rd. (tel. 370374). Open M-F 9:30am-6pm, Sa 9:30am-2pm. **Lufthansa,** Saraogi Mansion, M.I. Rd. (tel. 562822), near New Gate. Open M-F 9:30am-6pm, Sa 9:30am-2pm.

Trains: Jaipur Railway Station (tel. 131). **Advance Reservation Office** (tel. 135), to the left of Jaipur Railway Station. Tourist quota and English-speaking staff. Open M-Sa 8am-8pm, Su 8am-2pm. To: **Agra** (*Marudhar Exp.* 4864, Tu, W, F, Su 3:15pm, 5hr., Rs60/465); **Ahmedabad** (*Delhi Mail* 9106, 4:30am, Rs160); **Ajmer** (*Shatabdi Exp.* 2015, M-Sa, 10:40am, Rs180); **Bikaner** (*Intercity Exp.* 2468, 3:20pm, 7hr., Rs89/243; *Bikaner Exp.* 4737, 9pm, 9hr., Rs119/492); **Chennai** (9768, 3:45pm, Tu only, Rs410); **Delhi** (*Intercity Superfast* 9759, 6am, 5½hr., Rs89/198; *Jammu Tawi Exp.* 2414, 4:30pm, 5½hr., Rs109/409; *Shatabdi Exp.* 2016, 6pm, 5½hr., Rs440 A/C chair car; *Shekhavati Exp.* 9734, 6:05pm, 5½hr., Rs133/421); **Jodhpur** (*Marudhar Exp.* 4863, 12:25pm; *Superfast Exp.* 2307, 4:15pm; *Intercity Exp.* 2465, 5:30pm, 5hr., Rs89/214); **Mumbai** (*Superfast Exp.* 2956, 1:45pm, 18hr., Rs253/1095); **Udaipur** (*Chetak Exp.* 9615, 10pm, 11½hr., Rs120/528).

Buses: Sindhi Camp Central Bus Stand, Station Rd. (tel. 205790 or 205621). To: **Agra** (10 per day, 5:30am-midnight, 5hr., Rs93); **Chittaurgarh** (10am, noon, 9:30pm, and midnight, 8hr., Rs140); **Delhi** (12 per day, 5:30am-1am, 5½hr., Rs190); **Jaisalmer** (9:40pm, 13hr., Rs240); **Jodhpur** (5 per day, 7:30am-10:45pm, 7hr., Rs158); **Mt. Abu** (8pm, 12hr., Rs244); **Udaipur** (7 per day, 10am-midnight, 9hr., Rs200). **Private buses** depart from the same stand. Private bus companies line Station Rd. and Motilal Atal Rd., off M.I. Rd.; most hotels can make reservations too.

Local Transportation: Unmetered **auto-rickshaws** and **cycle-rickshaws** are the best way to get around the city; prepare for heavy haggling (Rs15-30 by auto-rickshaw between places in the old city). **Local buses** depart from the Central Bus Stand, from all the sights, and at most major intersections every 5min. within the old city and every 10-15min. in other areas (Rs5-10). Ambassador **taxis** can be picked up at the railway station (Rs15 per km). **Cars** (with driver) can be hired from the RTDC at the Tourist Hotel on M.I. Rd. (Rs125 per hr., Rs650 per day), and from some private companies as well. **Bicycles** are convenient for exploration, and many budget hotels will arrange rentals. Near Ajmeri Gate in **Kishanpol Bazaar,** you can rent bicycles for Rs25-30 per day. Open daily 8am-10pm. **Mohan Cycle Works,** M.I. Rd., near Jaipur Tower, charges Rs25 per day (10-day min.). Open M-Sa 10:30am-8pm.

Tourist and Financial Services

Tourist Office: RTDC Tourist Information Bureau (tel. 315466), platform 1 of the railway station. Provides useful maps and brochures. Accommodating, English-speaking staff. Open daily 7am-10pm. A second branch (tel. 360238) is in the Tourist Hotel, off M.I. Rd., near the GPO. Open M-Sa 7am-5:30pm. **Government of India Tourist Office,** in Hotel Khasi Kothi (tel. and fax 372200), near M.I. Rd. and

Station Rd. intersection. Open M-F 9am-6pm, Sa 9am-1:30pm. The monthly publication *Jaipur Vision,* available at most bookstores for Rs25, has lots of useful tourist information as well.

Tours: RTDC offers full-day and evening **city tours,** which jam the Pink City into a compact, unimaginative, and uncomfortable drive-by (Rs60-130). Arrange all tours through the Tourist Information Bureau at the railway station. Both the RTDC and the Government of India Tourist Office can arrange government-approved private **guides** (half-day Rs200-300). For more information about private guides, contact the **Guide Room** at Ranbagh Palace Hotel (tel. 381919). If you want to avoid paying inflated prices at the appointed RTDC lunch spot, pack your own lunch.

Budget Travel: Tours and Travels, Rambagh Palace Hotel (tel. 381668; fax 381784). Open daily 7:30am-6pm. **Tourist Guide Service,** M.I. Rd., near Panch Bhati (tel. 367735; fax 367760). Open daily 9am-6pm. **Priti Travels and Tours,** 180 Guru Nanak Pura (tel. 566806; fax 561492), in Raja Park outside Hotel Meru Palace. Open daily 8am-8pm.

Immigration Office: Foreigners Registration Office (tel. 49391), behind Rajasthan Police Headquarters near Jantar Mantar. Contact at least 1 week before visa expiration date. Open M-Sa 10am-5pm. Closed 2nd Sa.

Currency Exchange: State Bank of India (tel. 561163; fax 564597), off M.I. Rd., near Sanganeri Gate. Currency and traveler's checks. Open M-F 10am-5pm, Sa 10am-2pm. **Andhra Bank,** M.I. Rd. (tel. 374529; fax 365094), near Panch Batti. Currency exchange, traveler's checks, credit card advances. Service charge Rs20 per transaction. Open M-F 10am-2pm, Sa 10am-noon. **Thomas Cook** (tel. 360940; fax 360974), in Jaipur Tower, near the intersection of Station and M.I. Rd. Currency exchange, traveler's checks, and money wiring. Service charge is Rs20 per transaction for everything except encashment of Thomas Cook traveler's checks. Open M-Sa 9:30am-6pm. **American Express:** M.I. Rd. (tel. 367735; fax 367760), in the Tourist Guide Service near Panch Batti, can cash, but not issue, traveler's checks. Open daily 9am-6pm.

Local Services

Library: Radhakrishnan Public Library, Jawaharlal Nehru Marg (tel. 516694). Tourists aren't allowed to check out books, but they may browse. Open W-M 7am-7pm.

Luggage Storage: Jaipur Railway Station, Rs3 per item for the first 24hr., Rs5 for the second, Rs6 for additional 24hr. Open 24hr.

Bookstore: Books Corner, M.I. Rd. (tel. 366323; fax 366313), near Niro's Restaurant. Good collection of English books and international newspapers and magazines. **The Book Shop** (tel. 381430), in Rambagh Palace Hotel, off Bhawani Singh Marg, offers an expansive, expensive selection of books about India. **Usha Book Agency,** Chaura Rasta (tel. 312034), across from Premprakash Cinema. Jaipur's oldest book shop (est. 1949). Open daily 7-9am and 10am-8pm.

Market: Food and vegetable stalls abound in the old city, most notably near Chand Pol and along M.I. Rd. Most bazaars open dawn-dusk, closed Su; Bapu Bazaar is open Su, closed M.

Emergency and Communications

Pharmacy: Pharmacies cluster around hospitals. There is also one in Shiv Marg, across from Jaipur Inn. Most open daily 8am-10pm.

Hospital/Medical Services: Sawai Mansingh Hospital, Sawai Ram Singh Rd. (tel. 560291). Government-run, large, efficient, organized, and English-speaking. Among Jaipur's bevy of **private hospitals,** the best (English-speaking, clean, 24hr.) include **Santokba Durlabhji Memorial Hospital,** Bhawani Singh Marg (tel. 566251 or 566258), and **Soni Hospital,** Kahota Bagh (tel. 571122 or 571123; fax 564392), off Jawaharlal Nehru Marg.

Police: Main Police Station (tel. 565555), in King Edward Memorial Bldg., near Ajmeri Gate. Branches are abundant—look for the red-and-blue diagonal pattern.

Emergency: Police, tel. 100. **Fire,** tel. 101. **Ambulance,** tel. 102.

Post Office: GPO, M.I. Rd. (tel. 368740). Contains a museum filled with old stamps and weapons carried by mail runners of yore. Open for *Poste Restante* M-Sa 10am-

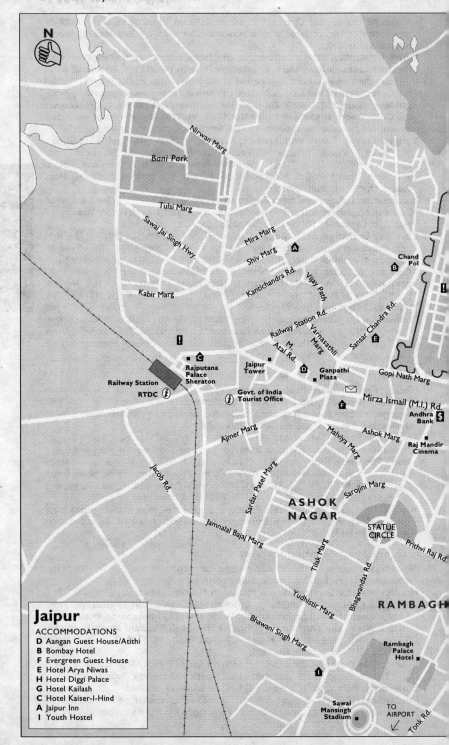

Jaipur

ACCOMMODATIONS

D Aangan Guest House/Atithi
B Bombay Hotel
F Evergreen Guest House
E Hotel Arya Niwas
H Hotel Diggi Palace
G Hotel Kailash
C Hotel Kaiser-I-Hind
A Jaipur Inn
I Youth Hostel

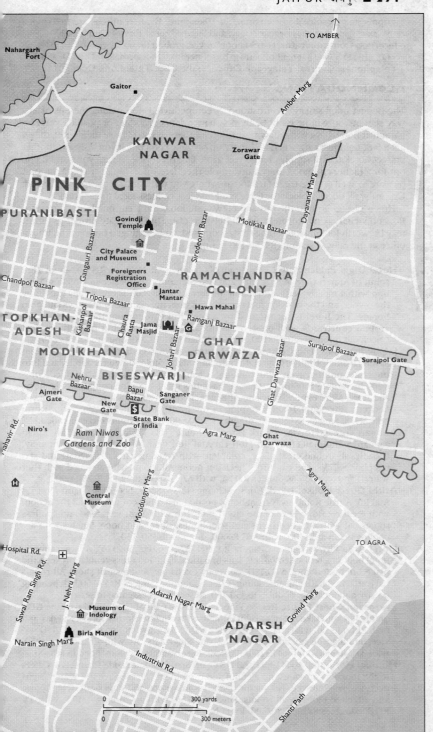

TO AMBER

Nahargarh
Fort

Gaitor

KANWAR
NAGAR

Zorawar
Gate

Amber Marg

PINK CITY

PURANIBASTI

Govindji
Temple

City Palace
and Museum

Foreigners
Registration
Office

Gangauri Bazaar

Siredeorti Bazaar

Motikala Bazaar

Dayanand Marg

Chandpol Bazaar

RAMACHANDRA
COLONY

Tripola Bazaar

Jantar
Mantar

Kishanpol Bazaar

Hawa Mahal

Ramganj Bazaar

TOPKHAN-
ADESH

Chaura
Rasta

Jama
Masjid

Johari Bazaar

GHAT
DARWAZA

MODIKHANA

Surajpol Bazaar

Surajpol Gate

Nehru
Bazaar

BISESWARJI

Ajmeri
Gate

Bapu
Bazaar

New
Gate

Sanganer
Gate

State Bank
of India

Ghat Darwaza Bazaar

Niro's

Ram Niwas
Gardens and Zoo

Agra Marg

GHAT
DARWAZA

Mahavir Rd.

Moridungri Marg

Central
Museum

Agra Marg

TO AGRA

Hospital Rd.

Sawai Ram Singh Rd.

J. Nehru Marg

Museum of
Indology

Adarsh Nagar Marg

Govind Marg

Birla Mandir

ADARSH
NAGAR

Narain Singh Marg

Industrial Rd.

Shanti Path

0   300 yards

0   300 meters

6pm. Stamps sold M-Sa 5am-8pm, Su 10am-6pm. **Branch offices** are in Tripolia Bazaar, Bapu Bazaar, Jawahar Nagar, and Shastri Nagar. **Postal Code:** 302001.

Internet: Communicator, G-4/5 Jaipur Tower, ground floor (tel. 368061 or 204100; fax (1041) 374413; email pravin@jp1.vsnl.net.in). Offers **email, ISD/STD,** and **fax.**

Telephones: Central Telegraph Office, in the GPO. **Telephone Code:** 0141.

ACCOMMODATIONS

The budget hotel situation is frustratingly competitive. Upon exiting the bus or railway station you will be mobbed by rickshaw drivers prodding or pushing you to a particular hotel. It's a win-win-win situation for them: if you choose their hotel, they'll get a 50% commission, which will show up on your hotel bill; if you insist on another budget hotel, they'll simply charge you triple fare (or refuse to take you); and if you opt for a higher-end hotel, they'll quadruple their fare since you're "rich." Your best bets are to shell out the triple fare and go where you want. It'll be cheaper in the end. Or, just walk down a block (or three) and find less ruthless local transportation.

Hotels cluster around the bus and railway stations, and a fair number occupy M.I. Rd. and vicinity. Unfortunately, few hotels can claim the Pink City proper as turf. It may be worth looking into home-stay accommodations, arranged through the tourist office at the railway station (Rs150-400 per night).

Hotel Diggi Palace, Sawai Ram Singh Marg (tel. 373091; fax 370359), about 1km south of Ajmeri Gate. A spacious, 200-year-old converted palace in a mellow location with a mellow staff. All food in the terrace restaurant is organically grown by the owner, and the cooking fuel is produced from the manure of his cows and polo horses. The hotel is surrounded by a beautiful garden, and the rooms are set around courtyards with outdoor sitting areas. Unreliable but friendly service. Check-out noon. Singles Rs100, with attached bath Rs200; doubles Rs150/250.

Jaipur Inn, Shiv Marg (tel./fax 201121; http://anymac.com/jaipur_inn.htm). From Sawai Jai Singh Highway, go right onto Shiv Marg, 5min. down the circle, and into the large, unoffensively pink building. Clean, well-illuminated, plant-filled corridors. Incredible roof-top restaurant. Facilities include a ping-pong table, laundry, and store. More expensive rooms offer attached baths, air-cooling, and great views. Lockers. Check-out 10am. Camping in the front garden Rs50 per person. Dorm beds Rs75. Singles Rs120-400; doubles Rs200-500. Reservations recommended.

Aangan Guest House, 4 Park House Scheme (tel. 373449; fax 364596; email aangan25@hotmail.com), off Moti Lal Atal Rd., near All India Radio. A homely, friendly, all-around great place, complete with relaxing garden. STD/ISD and fax, telephones, TVs, and car hire. Check-out noon. All rooms with attached bath (hot water!) and air-cooling. Singles Rs175, with A/C Rs500; doubles Rs250/600.

Atithi Guest House, 1 Park House Scheme (tel. 378679; fax 379496), off Moti Lal Atal Rd. A true home-away-from-home nestled in a quiet corner near all the action, with great rooftop views of the city. Family-run with great veg. food and spotless rooms, all with attached baths and telephones. Check-out noon. Singles with air-cooling begin at Rs300, with A/C Rs600; doubles Rs350/750.

Hotel Arya Niwas, Sansar Chandra Rd. (tel. 372456; fax 364376). A large, simple, hotel built in a renovated *haveli.* Lots of natural light and cross-ventilation keep the place bright and cool. STD/ISD, currency exchange, and a small shop. All rooms have attached bath and air-cooling. Check-out noon. Singles Rs350-600, depending on size and location; doubles Rs450-750. Reservations essential in season.

Evergreen Guest House (tel. 363446; fax 371934), off M.I. Rd. Head past the GPO on the left, and take the next right. Mingle with countless other tourists all day and night. Rooms (all with attached bath) are rather bare. Swimming pool, STD/ISD service, and luggage storage. Check-out 10am. Singles Rs150, with air-cooling Rs250, with A/C Rs450; doubles Rs200/300/550. Reservations recommended in season.

Mumbai Hotel (tel. 304412; fax 304181), off Station Rd., outside Chand Pol. Caters to the morally-conscious: no alcohol and prominent "Please Save the Water" signs everywhere. Pure-veg. restaurant, 24hr. room service and check-out, telephones, and attached baths in all rooms. Singles Rs150, with air-cooling Rs175, with TV Rs180; doubles Rs200/250/300. Extra bed Rs40.

Youth Hostel (HI/AYH), Bhagwandas Rd., near the intersection of Bhawani Singh Rd. Clean common baths, curfew 10pm, liquor and drugs prohibited. 5-day max. stay. Check-in 7-11am and 4-9pm. Check-out noon. Linen charge Rs10 per week. Dorm beds Rs40, Rs35 for nonmembers. Singles Rs60/100; doubles Rs 80/100.

Hotel Kailash, Johari Bazaar. One of the lucky few located in the heart of the Pink City proper. Sure, it's noisy, but it's in the middle of the action. Adequate rooms, with central air-cooling, black and white TV, and hot water in season. Check-out 24hr. Singles with common bath Rs125, with attached bath Rs150-250; doubles Rs115-150/175-315. Reservations recommended.

Gangaur RTDC Hotel, M.I. Rd. Lacks character, but it's the best of RTDC's offerings. Attached restaurant and bar. Singles Rs350; doubles Rs500-700.

FOOD

Jaipur doesn't have its own renowned specialties, but you'll find a range of Rajasthani classics. For cheap quickies, the *bhojnalyas* on Station Rd. and in the old city are where the locals go, and if the sweet tooth calls, know that the *mishri, mawas,* and *ghevars* of Jaipur are the best in the state. And for the truly (home)sick: Baskin Robbins and Pizza Hut await on M.I. Rd., in Ganpati Plaza.

Shri Shanker Bhojnalya, Station Rd., outside Chand Pol. Perhaps the most popular *bhojnalya* in town. Cheap, quality food—excellent *thalis* (Rs26) and tandoori. Open daily 8am-11pm.

Surya Mahal, M.I. Rd. (tel. 369840), next to Niro's and Books Corner. Popular with locals and tourists alike. Specializes in South Indian, Chinese, and pizza. A/C sweet shop in the back. Most entrees under Rs60. Open daily 8am-11pm.

Bismallah, Chand Pol. Notoriously non-veg. Persian cafe. Stuff yourself with *kebabs* (Rs40). Open daily 7am-11pm.

Niro's, M.I. Rd., near Panch Batti. Their card justly claims "quiet grandeur, warm hearted courtesy, personalized service." Add A/C to get the best non-veg. dining experience in town. Expect a crowd. The melange of Indian, Chinese, and Continental dishes comes at a hefty-but-worth-it Rs100-150. Open daily 10am-midnight.

LMB, Johari Bazaar. Incredible veg. food in a quirky A/C environment. Dishes a range of Subcontinental specialties (Rs30-60). Open daily 8am-11:30pm.

Hanuman Dhaba, near where Govind Marg turns into Industrial Rd. This is where locals go to get quality veg. food at cheaper prices (Rs20-40). Street-side seating with views of the busy kitchen. Open daily 9:30am-11pm.

Milky Way, off Bhagwandas Marg. Midway between M.I. Rd. and Statue Circle, on a side street to the left. The best ice cream in town—*gelato,* thick shakes, fountain sodas. Unique "Herbonic Shake" Rs25. Open daily 9am-midnight.

Suvarna Mahal (tel. 381919), in Rambagh Palace. If you're gonna splurge, you might as well do it in style: beautiful, A/C dining room, dim lights, live Indian classical music, excellent service, and superb Indian, Chinese, and Continental cuisines. Entrees Rs130-365; dessert Rs95-150. 10% gratuity. Open daily 7am-11pm.

Old Green Tandoori Dhaba, off M.I. Rd., near Indian Panch Batti. Locals come here for quality non-veg. food at great prices. Tandoori oven heats up the street along with delicious *rotis* and chicken (Rs30-60) served hot until midnight.

SIGHTS

City Palace

Location: *In the center of the Pink City, flanked by Gangauri Bazaar to the west and Siredeori Bazaar to the east.* **Hours:** *Open daily 9:30am-4:45pm.* **Admission:** *Rs40; students with ID and children Rs25.* **Other:** *Camera fee Rs50. No photography inside the galleries. Government-authorized guides Rs100.*

Built between 1729 and 1732 by Jai Singh as a home for himself and his successors, the **City Palace** encompasses nearly 15% of the Pink City's total area. As the home of the current maharaja, Sawai Bhawani Singh, much of the palace is off-limits, but what you can see is delightful. Architecturally, the palace has changed little since it was

Meeting the Maharaja

The current maharaja of Jaipur, Sawai Bhawani Singh, is a man of refinement and verve. Paying him a visit is about the coolest thing you can do in Jaipur. An old military man, the maharaja is an avid polo player who enjoys driving top-of-the-line cars, and who talks with real excitement about computers and ham radio.

The maharaja typically grants **private audiences** to visitors on weekdays. Appointments are necessary. To make an appointment, ask at the main entrance of the City Palace for the ADC (Aide de Camp) Office. Be persistent in confirming the date and time of the appointment. There you can speak with the PPS (Principal Private Secretary), who organizes the maharaja's schedule. It's best to give the PPS a couple of days' advance notice. Throughout the process, modest, respectful clothing and behavior are expected.

built, but its character and the culture it has accommodated have changed substantially. Until the decline of the Rajputs during middle and late 19th century, the maharaja of Jaipur was the most important ruler in what is now eastern Rajasthan. Early maharajas filled the palace with scientific and artistic treasures. Others concentrated on public affairs. Those interested more in pleasure than business cultivated a lively palace harem, which, it is said, held over 1000 women into the 20th century. Lately, the palace has taken on a fresh aspect: it opened to tourists in the 1950s, and over 400 films—including *North by Northwest* and the Errol Flynn version of Rudyard Kipling's *Kim*—had scenes shot within its walls.

After paying your admission fee, you'll find yourself in a large courtyard enclosed by red-and-yellow mortar walls with decaying arches and balconies. At the center of the courtyard is an attractive, albeit monotonous, building, adorned with the usual carved patterns, marble pillars, and arched balconies. This once served as a secretariat, containing the offices used by the maharaja for state business. These days, the ground floor houses the offices of the director of the palace, a museum complex, and a library—accessible only with the permission of the director. The library holds nearly 90,000 items, including centuries-old manuscripts collected by the maharajas, photo albums, and recent periodicals. The second floor of the building holds a **Textile Museum,** with collections of cloth and costumes, including the massive robes of the notorious "Fat Maharaja," Sawai Madho Singh I, who was 2.15m tall and is said to have weighed over 250kg. Also noteworthy are the harem mock-up and 19th-century prints produced in the nearby village of Sanganer, made by a traditional wood-block process still used there.

Up the stairs in the northwest corner of the courtyard is the **Arms and Weapons Museum.** Of its excellent collection, best are the displays just to the right of the entrance, which showcase daggers whose large hilts contain secret chambers and gunpowder holders made of seashells. The ceilings are expertly decorated with mirrors, paintings of women, and dense floral patterns. The museum also offers hokey pleasures—keep your eyes peeled as you enter and exit for a somewhat disturbing "WELCOME" and "GOODBY" spelled out in daggers and pistols respectively.

Exiting the courtyard, you'll pass through an elaborate gate with massive brass doors flanked by two marble elephants. Centering the next courtyard is the **Hall of Private Audience,** where two *gangajalis,* silver urns built to contain incredible quantities of Ganga River water, are on display. A sign notes that each urn holds 9000 liters of water, and weighs 345kg, giving them the *Guinness*-certified distinction of being the largest pieces of silver in the world. In the corner of the courtyard is the **Hall of Public Audience,** housing the **Art Museum,** which displays a hodge-podge of terrific objects collected by the maharajas over the centuries. The walls are lined with massive Persian-style carpets. A large collection of manuscripts demonstrates the maharajas' traditional patronage of learning and provides excellent opportunity to see examples of old Tamil and 16th-century Assamese scripts. The collection of works on astronomy boasts a 16th-century translated edition of Aristotle's scientific writings. A highlight of the museum is its outstanding collection of vibrantly rendered miniature paintings. Particularly interesting is the **Well of Mercury,** a painting of a beautiful woman in front of flowing water that has caused something of a controversy among scholars. While the painting can be understood strictly as an illustration of a Hindu myth, some argue that it is a coded visual explanation of how to extract mercury from the earth.

Exit the courtyard and you'll find yourself in a smaller one, surrounded by four gates, each representing a different season. Lording over the courtyard is the **Chandra Mahal,** the maharaja's residence. Parts of the first floor are open to the public.

Hawa Mahal (Palace of Winds)

Location: *On the east wall of the City Palace, facing Siredeori Bazaar.* **Hours:** *Open daily 10am-5pm.* **Admission:** *Rs2.* **Other:** *Camera fee Rs30.*

Jaipur's most recognizable landmark, the Hawa Mahal's five-story pink sandstone edifice was built in 1799. The Palace was the brainchild of Maharaja Sawai Pratap Singh, who wanted a comfortable place where he could compose his devotional songs to Krishna, some of which are still sung in the nearby Govindji Temple. Designed to catch the breeze, the Hawa Mahal takes its name from the many brass wind vanes that adorned it until the 1960s, each set at different levels to point in a variety of directions as they caught different zephyrs. Spacious underground tunnels connected the palace to the harem. Behind the Hawa Mahal sits the ornately sculpted **Govindji Temple,** perhaps the most popular Hindu temple in town, dedicated to Krishna.

Jantar Mantar

Location: *Next to the City Palace entrance.* **Hours:** *Open Sa-Th 9:30am-4:30pm.* **Admission:** *Rs80, free M.* **Other:** *Camera fee Rs50. Guides available, Rs80.*

Jaipur's Jantar Mantar is one of the massive astronomical observatories built by Maharaja Jai Singh (there are similar installations in Delhi, Ujjain, and Varanasi). Before building, Jai Singh sent emissaries to the East and West; they returned with cutting-edge technical manuals, including a copy of La Hire's "Tables," which the maharaja had coveted. Ironically, after building the Jantar Mantar, Jai Singh found that it produced readings 20 seconds more accurate than those reported by La Hire. The observatory features 18 large instruments, including a 30m sundial—impressive, but incomprehensible without a guide or an astute knowledge of astronomy.

Amber Fort

Location: *11km north of Jaipur.* **Bus:** *Leaves from the front of the Hawa Mahal, every 15min., Rs8.* **Hours:** *Open daily 9am-4:30pm.* **Admission:** *Rs8; children under 7 free.* **Other:** *Camera fee Rs50.*

Standing sentinel over the Pink City below, the three Garland Forts dominate the northern horizon. Foremost among these is Amber Fort, locally known as Amber. Amber today is a reflection of the quasi-legendary Kachhwaha dynasty, a Rajput clan that dominated the area from the 12th to 18th centuries. Constructed in 1592 by Raja Man Singh, Amber Fort is a blend of Hindu and Islamic architecture. Solidly built, with defense as its top priority (evidenced by its hilltop location, winding roads, and multitudinous gates), the fort nonetheless smoothly integrates artwork and creature comforts.

From the main road, half the fun is getting up to the fort itself. Walking up the steep, curvy road takes 15 minutes, with beautiful views of the surrounding valleys. Other means include jeep (Rs15) or elephant rides (a whopping Rs250 for up to 4 people). To the side of this courtyard is the **Shri Sila Devi Temple,** dedicated to the goddess of strength. *(Closed noon-4pm.)* Entry through the majestic silver doors leads to a black marble idol of the deity. From the main courtyard, a flight of stairs leads to **Diwan-i-Am** (Hall of Public Audience), a pillared, latticed meeting gallery. Opposite is the magnificently frescoed, mosaic-tiled **Ganesh Pol,** which marks the entrance to what used to be the maharaja's apartments. Wandering around here is almost as much fun as getting lost among numerous corridors, courtyards, balconies, terraces, and rooms—some threadbare, others adorned with blinding mirrorwork and beautiful coloring, such as the famous **Jai Mandir** (Hall of Victory). Other attractions include the **Sheesh Mahal**, the original private chambers of the maharaja, whose walls and ceilings are completely covered with colored glass and mirrors, and the **Sukh Mahal** (Pleasure Palace). The lake below the fort offers paddle-boat rental. (*Boats Rs40 per 30min., up to 4 people.*)

Jaigarh Fort

Location: *500m southwest of Amber.* **Rickshaws:** *From Amber, Rs40.* **Hours:** *Open daily 9am-4:30pm.* **Admission:** *Rs10; students Rs5.* **Other:** *Camera fee Rs20.*

From the Amber Fort balconies, you can see the stocky Jaigarh Fort, second of the Garland Forts, perched on a nearby hilltop. Its chambers and courtyards are hardly as elaborate as Amber's, but it does possess the gigantic **Jaivana**, the biggest cannon on wheels in the world. It could fire a shot 35km. The main courtyard contains three enormous underground water tanks: one was used by prisoners for bathing; one held the gold and jewels that financed Jaipur's founding; and the largest contained...nothing, as the Indian government discovered when they ransacked it in 1976 in a futile attempt to locate legendary treasure. Jaigarh's museum contains the expected armory and bland relics. The view of Amber Fort and Jaipur from the ramparts is breathtaking. The fort can be reached by vehicle or with a long climb from Amber.

Nahargarh Fort

Location: *A shadeless 20min. walk uphill from the road leading from Amber to Jaigarh.* **Hours:** *Open daily 10am-5pm.* **Admission:** *Rs4, guides Rs50.* **Other:** *Camera fee Rs30.*

Nahargarh Fort, the third Garland Fort, also known as the Tiger Fort, is solitary and romantic, with its labyrinth of chambers, painted with bright floral patterns. The Fort's view of the nearby valleys is stunning. A shady, open cafeteria next to the fort provides overpriced food and drink.

South of the Pink City

As Chaura Rasta leaves the Pink City via New Gate, it becomes Jawaharlal Nehru Marg, a thoroughfare dotted with successive diversions. **Ram Niwas Gardens**, 50m south of New Gate, shelters at its center Jaipur's **Central Museum**, often called **Albert Hall.** (*Open Sa-Th 10am-5pm. Admission Rs30, M free. Photography prohibited.*) The museum complex is a mixture of pillars, arches, and courtyards adorned with murals. The ground floor of the museum offers informative displays of various facets of Rajasthani culture and history, including miniature paintings and ivory carvings, shields depicting scenes from Hindu epics, costumed mannequins, and stone sculptures.

About 2km south of the Central Museum, just off Nehru Marg, is the eccentric, encyclopedic, privately funded **Museum of Indology,** featuring the troves of Vyakul—poet, painter, and super-nice guy who has been collecting stuff since he was 13 and can't bear to part with any of it—knick-knacks, curio pieces, and, yes, real treasures. (*Open daily 10am-5pm. Admission, with guide, Rs35.*) The museum holds a massive collection of textiles, architectural drawings, and 20,000 buttons. In one room, the marriage contract of the last Mughal emperor vies for attention with a grain of rice on which a full-color map of India has been drawn.

Three kilometers farther south on Nehru Marg, the **Lakshmi Narayan Mandir** is rapidly becoming one of Jaipur's most beloved buildings. (*Open daily 6am-9pm. Free guide available 8-11am and 4-7pm. Prayers are said at 6, 8, 10:30am, 7, and 8:30pm.*) Commonly called the **Birla Mandir,** the white marble temple was built by the wealthy Birla family. Designed as an expression of the Birla's multi-denominational approach to religion, the temple has three domes, each styled according to a different type of religious architecture. Pressing the theme of pluralism at subtler levels, the artwork in the *parikarima* was done by a Muslim, and the pillars flanking the temple include carvings of Hindu deities as well as depictions of Moses, Christ, Zarathustra, and many others, including Socrates. On the hill overlooking the temple are the crumbling remains of **Motidungri Fort,** owned but not maintained by the maharaja. The fort complex encloses a **Shiva temple** and is open to the public only once a year, on Shivaratri in the first week of March.

Off Agra Rd. is the pilgrimage destination of **Galta (Monkey Temple).** A series of temples and pavilions hidden in a gorge surround a natural spring considered holy. The nearby **Sun Temple** offers a great view of the city and provides for a popular picnic spot. Buses leave for Galta from Badi Chopar (Rs2). A round-trip auto-rickshaw ride (Rs100-200) provides a more scenic route through the mountains.

SHOPPING

Jaipur is essentially a series of interconnected bazaars. Shopping here means heavy bargaining and constant harassment—it can be draining, but the effort is well worth it. You'll find a huge assortment of handicrafts, clothing, textiles, jewelry, and perfumes. Unique local specialties include *meenakari* (enamel work on silver and gold) and blue pottery. The jewelry and gemwork of Jaipur is world-famous and remarkably inexpensive, but unless you know your stuff you'll have to be on the lookout for scams galore. Remember, you are under no obligation to buy anything, no matter how kindly you are treated. In the Pink City, **Johari Bazaar** and two lanes off it— **Gopalj ka Rasta** and **Haldiyon ka Rasta**—contain a barrage of jewelry and gem stores and gold and silver smiths. Parts of the bazaar are closed on Sunday. Connecting the Ajmeri, New, and Sanganeri Gates are **Nehru Bazaar** and **Bapu Bazaar.** These specialize in textiles, unique perfumes, camel-skin shoes, and *mojiris* (a type of sandal). These bazaars are closed on Sundays and Mondays respectively. **Tripolia Bazaar** and **Charra Rasta,** closed Sundays, have a variety of stores selling lacework, ironwork, miscellaneous wooden and ivory relics, and local trinkets. Watch master carpet-makers at work in **Siredeori Bazaar,** and find exquisite marble sculpture and carvings in **Chandpol Bazaar.** Several **government emporiums** offer solace from the bazaars' commotion, but with higher fixed prices, they're a little dull.

ENTERTAINMENT

Cultural Activities

Although any time's a good time to see Jaipur, **festivals** are especially fun. The **Gangaur Fair,** dedicated to the goddess Gauri, celebrates women and lasts for the 18 days after Holi (beginning Mar. 20-21, 1999). The festival is accompanied by singing, dancing, and parades with incredible costumes and decorations. The **Elephant Festival** — featuring fast-paced elephant polo and a tug-of-war pitting man against beast—is slated for March 1, 1999. The **Teej Fair** (Festival of Swings) celebrates the monsoon (Aug. 14-15, 1999). Decorated swings are hung from trees, and the city goes wild.

For authentic, traditional Rajasthani **dance and music,** the **Panghat Theater** (tel. 381919), in Rambagh Palace, off Bhawani Singh Rd., offers in-season nightly performances in high-class surroundings for Rs300 per person. Shows are generally 7-9pm. Call in advance. **Ravindra Manch** (tel. 49061), in Ram Nivas Gardens, offers evening performances of Rajasthani dance, music, and plays, usually for Rs20 or less. Occasional films and fashion shows can be more expensive. The Modern Art Gallery upstairs (tel. 48531) is open daily 10am to 5pm and is free. **Jawahar Kala Kendra** (tel. 510501), on Jawarharlal Nehru Marg, offers regular in-season performances of traditional and contemporary Rajasthani dance and music as well as plays in Hindi and Rajasthani. Performances in the indoor theater are Rs5 and performances in the open-air theater are free. There is also an extensive arts library.

For a glimpse of "authentic" village life, **Chauki Dhani,** 20km south of the city, promises a night of wild entertainment. Camel and ox rides, parrot astrology, palmistry, snake charming, *mendhi* hand-art, puppet shows, acrobatics, and tribal music, all in traditional style, are available in this replica of village living. The highlight of the evening is the over-spiced dinner, served on leaf plates in a large mud hut. (Open daily 8pm-midnight. Auto-rickshaw Rs250 round-trip.)

Bars and Nightclubs

Due to a strange prohibition law that's been in effect for years, only hotels can legally serve alcohol stronger than beer. Of course, some restaurants take this restriction with a grain of salt, but in general, if you're looking for the **bar scene,** hotels are it. For air-conditioned, high-class boozing, try the popular **Polo Bar** (tel. 381919) in Rambagh Palace, off Bhawani Singh Rd. (open daily 11am-11:30pm). **Rana Sanga Roof Top Bar** (tel. 378771, ext. 2677), in Mansingh Palace, off Sansar Chandra Road is open daily noon to 3pm and 6:30 to 11pm with a 24hr. coffee shop on the ground floor. The **Sheesh Mahal** (tel. 360011, ext. 1713) in the Welcomgroup Rajputana Palace Sheraton, near the railway station, is open daily 11am to 11pm. Getting sloshed at cheaper prices with locals and budget tourists is better accomplished at the **Talab Bar** (tel. 200594), in Swagatam Tourist Bungalow (open noon-3pm and 6-11pm). Other cheap bars include **Amrapali Bar,** in Chandragupt Hotel, across from Sindhi Camp Bus Stand (open daily 11am-11pm), and **Dubki Bar,** in Hotel Sangam, near the Ganpati Complex (open daily 10am-11:30pm).

Other Diversions

Jaipur's 16 **cinemas** are packed with people at every showing. Regardless of your interest in or comprehension of Hindi films, worth experiencing is the plush, luxurious, world-renowned **Raj Mandir Cinema** (tel. 374694), off M.I. Rd. The four daily showings are *always* sold out; arrive *at least* 1 hour in advance to get tickets. ("Diamond box seats" Rs50, "Emerald" Rs40, "Ruby" Rs30, or "Pearl" Rs20.) Look for the tourist/student queue. **Swimming pools** abound in the hotels and stadiums of Jaipur. The **Evergreen Guest House** (tel. 36446), off M.I. Rd., lets outsiders use their pool (Rs75). **Monsingh Palace** (tel. 378771; fax 377582), off Sensor Chandra Rd., also allows swimming (Rs200; 7am-8pm).

▩ Sariska Tiger Reserve and National Park

Nestled in the dry, temple-studded Aravali Mountains, 108km northeast of Jaipur and 200km west of Delhi, the 866 sq. km Sariska Tiger Reserve and National Park (tel. (0144) 41333), features a rich population of wildlife: *nilgai* (blue bulls), *sambar* (large deer), spotted deer, wild boar, common langur, rhesus monkeys, leopards, hyenas, wild dogs, peafowl. Unfortunately, the number of tigers sadly continues to decline because of poaching. Most tours visit **Hanuman Mandir** and the **Pandu Pole Temple,** where pilgrims go to wash away their sins in the jungle pools and streams. (Open daily Oct.-Mar. 7am-4pm; Apr.-Sept. 6am-4:30pm; gates close at dusk. Admission Rs100 per person, Rs150 per jeep. Rs200 video camera fee.) Tickets can be bought from the booking office across from Hotel Sariska Palace. **Buses** for three-hour tours of the reserve leave from Alwar (every 30min. dawn-midnight, 1hr., Rs14). Buses from Jaipur are equally frequent (regular until 7pm, 2hr., Rs40). You can also rent a **jeep** that seats up to five people (Rs600).

Accommodations include the popular **Hotel Tiger Den** (tel. 41342), next to the park entrance. (In-season: singles Rs550, with A/C Rs700; doubles Rs600/825. Off-season: singles Rs350, with A/C Rs550; doubles Rs450/600). The **Forest Lodge Rest House** (tel. 41333), across the road from the super-posh Sariska Palace, offers no-frills accommodation and a small, cheap restaurant (singles Rs100, with air-cooling and attached bath Rs200; doubles Rs200/400; extra bed Rs100).

▩ Bharatpur भारतपुर

A convenient stop on the popular tourist route between Agra (56km) and Jaipur (172km), Bharatpur merits attention in its own right for its spectacular Keoladeo-Ghana National Park, one of the premier bird sanctuaries in India and the world. Founded by Badan Singh in 1733 as a princely state, Bharatpur soon became known for the fierce armies of Suraj Mal, who plundered Delhi in 1753 and occupied Agra from 1761 to 1774. The state of Bharatpur was recognized as autonomous by the Mughals, and it successfully resisted two attacks by the British before being captured by Lord Combermere in 1826. After Independence, it became a part of Rajasthan. But history isn't what draws thousands of migrating birds and foreign travelers each winter; the pull is the rich ecosystem of the well-maintained park.

ORIENTATION AND PRACTICAL INFORMATION Both the bird sanctuary and the adjacent hotels are a few kilometers southeast of the center of town. **Buses** coming from Jaipur drop passengers off on the west side. **Rickshaws** (Rs15-20) make the journey to the hotel areas. At the core of town lie the ruins of the old fort. The area between **Jama Masjid** and the **Old Laxman Temple** functions as a sort of downtown, and here you'll find the densest population of services. Nearer to the sanctuary, **Hotel Saras** serves as a good starting point for looking for rooms, as it's right in the center of the intersection of the road leading to Fatehpur Sikri.

Trains leave from the station north of town (enquiry tel. 131) and chug to **Mathura** (*Paschim Exp.* 2925, 6:30am; *Golden Temple Mail* 2903, 3:35; *Mumbai-Debra Dun Exp.* 9019, 1:55am; *Mumbai-Firozpur Janata Exp.* 9023, 8:15am; *Indore-Nizamuddin Exp.* 4005, 2:45am) en route to **Delhi** (*Mumbai-Debra Dun Exp.* 9019, 1:55am; *Mumbai-Firozpur Janata Exp.* 9023, 8:15am; 4hr., Rs46/224). **Buses** leave from the main bus stand (enquiry tel. 23434) on the southwest side of town, but most, particularly those heading toward Agra, can be waved down near the Hotel Saras. Buses go to: **Agra** (every 45min. 1hr., Rs23); **Delhi** (every 30min., 4:30am-10pm, 5hr., Rs57); **Fatehpur Sikri** (every 30min. 7:30am-6pm, 1hr., Rs10); and **Mathura** (every 30min. 5am-9pm, 1hr., Rs15). The bus stand also has government or private transport to **Jaipur** (every 30min. 5am-12:30am, 3½hr., Rs60) and a few direct buses to **Ajmer, Bikaner,** and **Udaipur.** You can rent **bicycles** at several hotels near the sanctuary (Rs30-50 per day). The **RTDC Tourist Reception Centre** (tel. 22542) is adjacent to the Hotel Saras and has basic booklets about the area and Keoladeo (open M-F 10am-5pm). The **State Bank** (tel. 22441), near Binarayan Gate, northwest of Birdland, exchanges currencies and traveler's checks, but has a US$100 limit (open M-F 10am-5pm, Sa 10am-2pm). **Pharmacies** are common throughout the city, except near the bird sanctuary. **Lokesh Medicos** (tel. 26879), near the **General Hospital** (23633) is open 24hr. The **post office** is across from Jama Masjid to the east. **Faujdar ISD** (tel. 27022), next to Pratap Palace Hotel on the road leading to the sanctuary, is open 24 hours with collect calling, callbacks, and credit card calling available (Rs3 per min.). **Emergency:** tel. 22451. **Police:** tel. 22526. **Postal Code:** 321001. **Telephone Code:** 05644.

ACCOMMODATIONS AND FOOD The road to the park has everything from camping plots and dorm beds to full-blown hotel rooms. Many hotels rent bicycles, binoculars, and birding books. Room prices soar in the high bird season (Oct.-Mar.), particularly around Christmas; unless noted, prices listed here are off-season. If you're looking to go low-end, try the popular **Tourist Lodge** (tel. 23742), near Mathura Gate 2km from the railway station (singles Rs50, with attached bath Rs80, with air-cooling Rs100; doubles Rs80/125/150).

Prices are much higher inside the park. The **Ashok Forest Lodge** (tel. 22722) and **Forest Lodge** (tel. 22760) charge a whopping Rs2395 for a room. When they are not available, park officials sometimes make their few boarding house rooms available (Rs300 per person). For camping, try the **Wilderness Camp,** next to the Annexy Hotel; a plot between eucalyptus trees costs Rs30-50.

The **Saras Tourist Bungalow** (tel. 23700) is a well-run but uninspiring RTDC hotel. Still, it has a great garden and restaurant, plus clean rooms with chairs, sinks, and mirrors. (Dorm beds Rs50; singles Rs300, with air-cooling Rs350; doubles Rs350/400, with A/C and TV Rs550; extra bed Rs75.) Up the road toward the park, **Hotel Sunbird** (tel. 25147) has clean, spacious rooms with attached baths and air-cooling (doubles Rs350-550). Closer to the sanctuary, **Hotel Pelican** (tel. 24221) is efficiently run, and the owner (also owner of the Tourist Lodge in town) is a chatty naturalist (singles Rs50; doubles Rs80, with attached bath and hot water, Rs80/150).

Most of the hotels have attached restaurants, some with rooftops for sunset, binoc-ular-aided birding. The **Spoonbill** has Mughlai, South Indian, Chinese, and Continen-tal dishes (veg. and non-veg. entrees Rs25-40). The **Krishna Restaurant,** in Pratap Palace, has pricier veg. and non-veg. dishes (Rs30-80). The **Pelican** offers ultra-rich *lassis* and many delicious dishes, and they'll pack you a lunch (with tea or coffee in a thermos) to take to the park (Rs25-60).

SIGHTS The main reason foreigners flock to Bharatpur is to go cuckoo for the hordes of birds at Keoladeo Ghana National Park (see below). Still, if you're in town and are sick of binoculars, check out the town's 18th-century **Lohagarh Fort,** near Nehru Park, north of the center of town. The fort was built by Maharaja Suraj Mal and has been notoriously resistant to attack; heavy British armaments are said to have bounced off the walls. The **museum** here features two large galleries of ancient Jain sculpture, and a gallery of the fort's artifacts, including gaudy vases, photographs of weapons, and stuffed miniature bears. *(Open Sa-Th 10am-4:30pm. Admission Rs3.)*

Bharatpur's 29 sq. km of pride and joy, the **Keoladeo Ghana National Park** (tel. 22777) annually plays host to one of the world's most impressive assemblages of feathered friends. *(Open daily sunrise to sunset in the high season; 6am-6pm during the mon-soon. Admission Rs100 for non-Indians; with cycle additional Rs3; with video camera additional Rs200.)* The marshes, woodlands, and grassy pastures draw hundreds of bird species each year, including VIBs (Very Important Birds) such as the rare Siberian crane, the painted stork, shoveller, widgeon, and grey, purple, and night herons. Along with the birds, there are pythons, spotted deer, jackals, and other reptiles and mammals. Iron-ically, the local maharaja originally set aside the land as an elaborate hunting ground, and the bloodsport didn't end until 1972.

Visitors must rent a **bicycle** or **cycle-rickshaw** to explore the grounds because motor vehicles are not allowed past Keoladeo's only entrance. The **main office** at the gate rents bicycles for Rs20 (deposit your passport or Rs1000), and many local hotels do the same for Rs30-50. Only rickshaws that wear a special "yellow plate" have paid their dues and are certified to enter. Inside the office, a small visitors center features nests, eggs, and stuffed specimens, as well as a color map of the park. Tongas (Rs20) and cycle-rickshaws (Rs5) leave from the gate on tours through the park. Some rick-shaw drivers know enough to serve as guides, but while your wallet is open, it might be better to hire one of the certified naturalist **guides** from the office (Rs35 per hour)—they have keen eyes for spotting and identifying birds.

Inside the park you can hire a **boat** in season for up to six people (1hr., Rs60-120), or follow one of the **walking tours** suggested in the guidebook (Rs3), available at the office. A reference book with all the English, Hindi, and scientific names of the vari-ous species is available for Rs10. The park has strict rules against smoking, noise-mak-ing, and other polluting activities in order to preserve the tranquility of the park. Early morning and dusk are particularly beautiful and bountiful.

■ Ajmer अजमेर

The bustling town of Ajmer, 132km west of Jaipur in the heart of the Aravali Moun-tains, is hailed among tourists more for its proximity to Pushkar than for its own sights. Nonetheless, Ajmer is remembered as the final resting place of Khwaja Muin-ud-din Chishti, founder of India's premier Sufi order, and as a result, thousands upon thousands of Muslims and Hindus make a yearly pilgrimage to Ajmer during the Urs Ajmer Sharif (Oct. 11-16, 1999; Sept. 9-14, 2000). During this time, the town bursts at its seams with people and festivities. The annual Pushkar Camel Fair induces even wilder crowds.

ORIENTATION AND PRACTICAL INFORMATION Ajmer is a small town, only about 3km long, and if you wander around for a bit its geography becomes clear. If, however, wandering is not your thing, all of the standard modes of transport apply. For Rs10-25, **cycle-rickshaws** and **auto-rickshaws** will get you anywhere. Crowded tempos charge Rs2. Popular in Ajmer are motorized **tongas,** which charge Rs5-10 to get around town. **Station Road** runs north-south in front of the **railway station** (tel. 331), whose reservation office (tel. 431965) is on the second floor above the main entrance (open M-Sa 8am-8pm, Su 8am-2pm). Trains head for **Delhi** (*Shatabdi Exp.* 2016, 3:10pm, 7hr., Rs580 A/C chair only; *Ahmedabad-Delhi Mail* 9105, 7:15pm, 9hr., Rs142/511), **Jaipur** (*Shatabdi Exp.* 2016, 3:50pm, 2hr., Rs290 A/C chair only; *Ahmedabad-Delhi Mail* 9105, 7:15pm, 3hr., Rs69/185), and **Udaipur** (*Chetak Exp.* 9615, 1:50am, 8hr., Rs105/350). Adjacent to the station is a small **Tourist Information Center** (tel. 52426). There is another branch on the west side of town, next to the Hotel Khadin. (Both open M-Sa 8am-noon and 3-6pm.) From the railway station, points of interest are straight ahead in **Diggi Bazaar,** the main commercial area, and to the right toward the **GPO,** which has *Poste Restante* services (tel. 432145; open daily 10am-6pm). **Postal Code:** 305001. **Telephone Code:** 0145.

From the intersection near the GPO, **Kutchery Road** darts southeast, joining **Jaipur Road,** before passing the **Main Bus Stand** (tel. 429398), which is 2km southeast of the railway station. Buses lurch toward **Ahmedabad** (6 per day, 5:45am-12:30am, 13hr., Rs154); **Abu Road** (4 per day, 7:30am-3:30pm, 8hr., Rs90); **Bikaner** (13 per day, 5am-1:30pm, Rs90); **Chittaurgarh** (18 per day, 6am-11pm, 5hr., Rs58); **Jaipur** (every 15min., 8am-10pm, 3hr., Rs40); **Jaisalmer** (8am, 10hr., Rs125); **Jodhpur** (every 30min. 6am-11pm, 5hr., Rs62); and **Udaipur** (every hr. 5am-10pm, 9hr., Rs87). The **Pushkar Bus Stand,** near the Station-Kutchery Rd. junction, sends buses to (surprise!) Pushkar every 15 minutes (5am-midnight, 30min., Rs7). **Private bus** companies line Kutchery Rd. and have deluxe buses to most destinations. Most will pick up in Pushkar if needed; check in advance.

Bicycles can be rented through the Tourist Information Bureau, near the Main Bus Stand, for Rs1 per hour. For currency exchange, the **State Bank of India** is north of the Main Bus Stand. Dr. Yadava's **Pratap Memorial Hospital,** Kutchery Rd. (tel. 426406), is the best private hospital. The **Main Police Office** (tel. 425080) is opposite the railway station.

ACCOMMODATIONS AND FOOD Hotels in Ajmer aren't bad, but few offer anything special. Most tourists head to Pushkar for a better selection of accommodations, visiting Ajmer as a daytrip. Across from the railway station is a noisy bunch of no-frills, dirt-cheap hotels. Prithviraj Marg and Kutchery Rd. host similar congregations of hotels. The **City View Paying Guest House,** Nalla Bazaar (tel. 426747), is a tiny, family-run hotel on a narrow, winding street in the old city. The rooms (singles Rs50-100, with attached bath Rs100-150; doubles Rs200-250) are very basic but spacious, and the rooftop offers spectacular views. The best of the cheapies is **Bhola Hotel,** Agra Gate (tel. 432844), with simple, well-decorated rooms (singles Rs100; doubles Rs150; extra bed Rs50; air-cooling Rs50). The **Hotel Nagpal,** Station Rd. (tel. 429503; fax 429521), features clean rooms with phones and attached baths (singles Rs125, with TV and air-cooling Rs250, with A/C Rs500; doubles Rs400/600; extra person Rs150; check-out 24hr.). Hotels are booked heavily, so call in advance. Prices skyrocket during the Urs Ajmer Sharif and the Pushkar Camel Fair.

There aren't many **restaurants** in Ajmer, but the few you'll find are decent. For a quick bite, jet over to the snack, juice, and egg (Rs12 for 5 hard-boiled) stalls around Delhi Gate. For non-veg. Persian food and great street views, the **Madeena Hotel,** Station Rd., opposite the railway station, is cheap (Rs40 or less) and friendly (open daily 5:30am-11pm). **Rasma,** Prithviraj Marg (tel. 432646), has pure veg. food (entrees Rs20-40) served in underground A/C bliss. For the best of both worlds, the **Honeydew Restaurant,** Station Rd. (tel. 32498), offers Continental, Chinese, and Indian cuisines (entrees around Rs45; open daily 8am-11pm). The enticingly-named **Fun-n-Food,** Hospital Rd., in Azad Park, is every toddler's dream come true—a small but popular shop offering Indian snacks and a wide selection of ice cream, almost everything under Rs25 (open daily 9am-10pm). The nearby swimming pool (Rs10 per hr.; open daily 6-11:30am and 4-9pm), playground, and fire station allow patrons to regress to their hearts' content.

SIGHTS When thousands of devotees flock to Ajmer during the Urs Ajmer Sharif, **Dargah** is their destination. On the north side of town in the old city, the tomb of the Sufi saint **Khwaja Muin-ud-din Chishti** looms above the surrounding bazaars at the foot of a hill on the left side of Dargah Bazaar. Originally a simple brick cenotaph, Dargah has expanded to an elaborate marble complex as rich rulers have paid tribute. A tall, elaborate gateway leads to the first courtyard, where two massive cauldrons called *degs* are filled with rice that is then sold to devotees as *tabarukh*, a sanctified food. Akbar's mosque is to the right, and the exquisitely grand mosque of Shah Jahan is farther inside. The tomb of the saint himself is in a central marble mosque, encircled by silver railings. Respectful behavior and a small donation is expected at Dargah—at the very least buy flowers for the grave site.

Continuing on the road past Dargah about 500m takes you to the **Adhai-din-Ka-jhonpra** (Mosque of Two-and-a-Half Days) named for the time the legendary Muhammad of Ghur took to build it in 1193. Giant pillars loom behind the facade, whose seven arches are decorated in elaborate Persian calligraphy.

On the northeast side of town is the 11th-century artificial lake **Ana Sagar.** It's a nice spot for a stroll or picnic, and the **Dault Bagh** gardens along the banks boast marble pavillions built by Shah Jahan. Boats can be rented from the newly built Luvkush Gardens (Rs30 per 30min). In the bazaars near Agra Gate, the magnificent rich red of the **Nasiyan Temple** may lure you. The temple houses a museum where the Jain conception of the universe is illustrated with golden models. *(Open daily 8am-5pm; admission Rs2. Photography prohibited.)*

■ Pushkar पुष्कर

Legend holds that at the beginning of time Lord Brahma dropped a *pushkara*, or lotus flower, into the desert. Where the flower fell, a holy lake sprung up, a place where pilgrims could be cleansed of all their sins. The lake is now the central attraction of the calm town of Pushkar, the site of the only Brahma temple in all of India. Some Hindu pilgrims consider Pushkar the final stop on their pilgrimages. A dip in the waters completes the circuit of redemption. Besides spiritual enlightenment, Pushkar offers a respite from the hassles and hustles of the bigger cities. The noisy auto-rickshaws that plague other cities are delightfully absent in Pushkar; a stroll around the 1km long city is peaceful and relaxed. This serenity is transformed into a beehive of activity in November for the annual Pushkar Fair (Nov. 20-23, 1999; Nov. 9-11, 2000), but otherwise the mellow mood prevails.

> **Warning:** Given its religious and cultural roots, Pushkar is a purely vegetarian town, with strict prohibition of alcohol and drug use (the drug and alcohol scene in this quasi-hippie town is entirely underground). Although Pushkar's policies may clash with many Western conceptions of a good time, please be respectful of the heritage and traditions of the town.

ORIENTATION

Pushkar runs less than 1km in each direction, so getting lost is hardly an issue. Most travelers arrive from Ajmer at the **Ajmer Bus Stand,** on **Ajmer Road** in the southeast side of town. In town, Ajmer Rd. becomes **Chhoti Basti (Small Bazaar),** the main thoroughfare, which follows the north shore of **Pushkar Lake.** Chhoti Basti becomes **Bodi Basti (Main Bazaar),** winding south and ending on the west side of town, near **Brahma Mandir.** A right turn on one of the meandering side streets off Chhoti Basti leads to the road that marks the northern boundary of the town and hosts the GPO, the **Marwar Bus Stand,** and the government hospital.

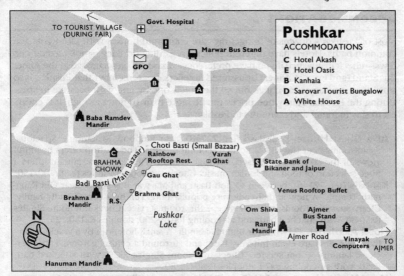

To Tourist Village (During Fair)
Govt. Hospital
Marwar Bus Stand
GPO

Pushkar
ACCOMMODATIONS
C Hotel Akash
E Hotel Oasis
B Kanhaia
D Sarovar Tourist Bungalow
A White House

Baba Ramdev Mandir

BRAHMA CHOWK

Choti Basti (Small Bazaar)
Rainbow Rooftop Rest.
Varah Ghat

Badi Basti (Main Bazaar)
Gau Ghat

Brahma Mandir
R.S.
Brahma Ghat

State Bank of Bikaner and Jaipur

Venus Rooftop Buffet

Pushkar Lake

Om Shiva
Ajmer Bus Stand
Rangji Mandir
Ajmer Road
Vinayak Computers
TO AJMER

N

Hanuman Mandir

PRACTICAL INFORMATION

Buses: Ajmer Bus Stand, Ajmer Rd. To Ajmer (every 15min., 6am-8:30pm, 30min., Rs5). All other destinations can be reached through the **Main Bus Stand** (tel. 429398) in Ajmer. **Private buses** companies line Chhoti Basti and the area around Marwar Bus Stand. For most destinations, they provide free jeep transportation to Ajmer, where their main offices are located and where most of their buses depart from. Daily buses going direct to **Jaisalmer, Jodhpur, Udaipur, Mumbai,** and **Delhi** leave from the Marwar Bus Stand. **Ekta Travels** is the only government-recognized agency in Pushkar. Most hotels make private and government bus and train arrangements for guests.

Local Transportation: Most visitors travel everywhere on foot. **Bicycles** can be rented from several shops near the Ajmer Bus Stand (Rs3 per hr., Rs25 per day).

Tourist Office: Ajmer's Tourist Information Bureau (tel. 52426) has information about Pushkar (open M-Sa 8am-noon and 3-6pm). During the Pushkar Fair, the RTDC-run **Tourist Village** (tel. 72074) provides a wealth of information. **Ekta Travels** main office (tel. 72131; fax 72921), near the Marwar Bus Stand, also provides brochures and maps. Open daily 7am-10pm.

Currency Exchange: State Bank of Bikaner and Jaipur, Chhoti Basti, opposite Varah Ghat. Exchanges foreign currency and traveler's checks. No service charges. Open M-F 10am-2pm, Sa 10am-noon.

Bookstore: Lalchand Ranchand Company, Chhoti Basti (tel. 72082), has a decent new and used paperback collection. **British Book World,** next door, has a good selection of (yes) British books. Both open daily 9am-11pm.

Pharmacy: Most pharmacies line the northern side of town near the hospitals and Marwar Bus Stand, but several dot Chhoti Basti as well. Most open daily 8am-11pm.

Hospital: Government Community Hospital (tel. 72029), near Marwar Bus Stand. English-speaking, reputable, and open 24hr. for emergencies. Open for consultations Oct.-Mar. 9am-1pm and 4-6pm; Apr.-Sept. 8am-noon and 5:30-7pm.

Police: Main Police Station (tel. 72046), next to Government Hospital. Tourist-friendly and English-speaking. Open 24hr.

Post Office: GPO (tel. 720222), on the north side of town near the police station. *Poste Restante*. A branch office is on Chhoti Basti. Both are open M-Sa 9am-5pm, 9am-2pm for parcel post and registered mail. **Postal Code:** 305022.

Internet: Vinayak Computers (tel. 72760), next to the Hotel Oasis.

Telephones: The **R.S. Restaurant** (tel. 72060), near Brahma Mandir, has free call-backs. Open daily 7am-11pm. **Telephone Code:** 0145.

ACCOMMODATIONS

Most of Pushkar's dozens of budget digs are converted houses with clean cots and common baths. Hotels have different policies regarding drinking, smoking, and curfews—check in advance if you have preferences. Expect to get harassed at the Ajmer Bus Stand (and even in Ajmer) by assorted hoteliers. But remember that Pushkar is so small that you can safely check out all the hotels one by one with baggage in arms. During the Pushkar Fair, when prices can be more than 10 times as high, it is cheapest to stay in Ajmer and commute to Pushkar.

Alka Guest House, Bodi Basti (tel. 72738), near Rainbow Restaurant. Spacious, clean rooms near the lake. Excellent common baths. The rooftop offers beautiful views of the lake and the desert. Luggage storage. The terrace restaurant offers a huge selection of food and Indian music. Check-out noon. Doubles Rs80/100/150.

Kanhaia (tel. 72146), between Chhoti Basti and Marwar Bus Stand, near Old Rangnath Temple. A new and already very popular hotel run by a very friendly family. Clean, spacious rooms, travel service, 24hr. room service. Check-out noon. Singles Rs50-80, with attached bath and air-cooling Rs100-200; doubles Rs150-225.

Hotel Akash (tel. 72498), near Brahma Mandir. A small hotel run by a gracious family. The rooms are clean but very basic and surround a central garden. Travel services, laundry, room service. Check-out noon. Singles Rs20, with attached bath Rs50, with air-cooling Rs70; doubles Rs40/70/80.

Hotel White House (tel. 72147; fax 72950), between Chhoti Basti and Marwar Bus Stand. Spacious, spotless rooms around an airy, open shaft. Gardens all around. Rooftop restaurant with sweet views and sweeter mango tea. 24hr. room service. Check-out 10am. Singles Rs60-80, with attached bath and air-cooling Rs100-150; doubles Rs100-150/200-350. Rooftop dorm beds Rs30, in-season only.

Hotel Oasis, Ajmer Bus Stand (tel. 72100). Large, simple rooms, all with attached baths, some with balconies. Room service 24hr., swimming pool. Check-out noon. Singles Rs100, with air-cooling Rs200, with A/C Rs450; doubles Rs150/250/550.

Sarovar Tourist Bungalow, Ajmer Rd., 100m west of the Ajmer Bus Stand. A government building with character. RTDC-run establishment has nice, cool rooms and a pool. Singles Rs150; doubles with air-cooling Rs350. Apr.-Sept.: Rs75/175.

FOOD

While Pushkar has its share of good Indian cuisine, most travelers indulge in the local interpretations of Western food. For quick snacks and sweets, a stroll down Chhoti Basti should fix most cravings.

Rainbow Rooftop Restaurant (tel. 72044), near Brahma Temple. Delightful, well-prepared Indian and Western dishes and a menu as stunning as the rooftop view. Homemade peanut butter, *falafel*, pizza, banana fritters, real cappuccino, and the best lemon soda in town. Open daily 8am-11pm.

R.S. (tel. 72060), opposite Brahma Temple. Great Indian dishes, as well as spaghetti and macaroni (around Rs25). Garden and terrace seating. STD/ISD service with free callbacks. Popular among locals. Fresh juice (Rs20). Open daily 7am-11pm.

Venus Rooftop Restaurant, Chhoti Basti (tel. 72323). Another multi-cuisine restaurant, but with particularly tasty Indian dishes, fresh juice, and a rooftop view of the lake and city. Limited *thalis* Rs25. Open daily 7am-10:30pm.

Om Shiva Buffet, Chhoti Basti (tel. 72647), opposite the State Bank of India. The best buffets in town (Rs35)—their breakfasts are especially popular. Open daily 7am-12:30pm, 1-4pm, and 5-10pm.

SIGHTS

Most of Pushkar's 540 **temples** were rebuilt after assorted raids and pillages by the Mughal emperor Aurangzeb in the 17th century. A few of the temples are only open to Hindus. The most visited temple is the **Brahma Mandir,** which has the surprising distinction of being the only temple in India dedicated to Brahma, the Hindu creator-god. The temple has a red minaret with a blue-and-green base and smaller shrines flanking the sides. Expect to be mobbed by eager guides; their services are hardly necessary to view the temple. On the way out is a **handicrafts store.**

There are two major hillside temples in Pushkar, offering superb panoramic vistas of the town and valley, especially at sunset and sunrise. Named for two of Brahma's wives, **Savithri Mandir** and **Gayatri Mandir** crown hills on the east and west side of town (each a 1½hr. climb). Other temples of interest include **Rangji Mandir** with its white stone facade, the **Hanuman Mandir,** a colorful tower depicting Hanuman's exploits, and the turquoise-green **Baba Ramdev Mandir.** Encircling Pushkar Lake are broad **ghats,** connecting the temples and the holy waters. Of Pushkar's 52 *ghats,* the most important are the **Gau Ghat,** where an assortment of politicians, ministers, and VIPs have paid their respects, **Brahma Ghat,** which Brahma himself is said to have used, and the central **Varah Ghat,** where Vishnu is said to have cameoed in the form of a boar. Signs in almost every hotel instruct visitors to remove their shoes 50m from the lake, and to refrain from smoking and taking photographs while at the *ghats.* Pilgrims and tourists at the *ghats* request local priests to perform a Pushkar *puja,* a ceremony of scripture-reading and rose-petal-scattering for a donation which usually goes to the temple, but occasionally to the priest. Do not feel pressured into donating the exorbitant amounts that the priests insist are "standard." After the *puja,* your patronage is officially recognized with a red wrist-band—the "Pushkar Passport"—giving you the freedom to visit *ghat*s and stroll around town without priestly harassment.

ENTERTAINMENT AND SHOPPING

The annual **Pushkar Fair** is an event of colossal numbers, crowding 200,000 people from all over the world into one square kilometer. Thousands of pilgrims bathe in the lake's holy waters seeking redemption for their sins. Concurrently, an enormous camel fair brings in over 50,000 camels, who excite the masses in races, auctions, contests, parades, and, of course, safaris. Stalls selling handicrafts from all over India saturate the streets, punctuated by performers at every corner. And it wouldn't be a fair without food—specialty cuisines abound as well. At night, the air is filled with the sounds of bells and songs, and with scented smoke from campfires at the edge of town. The dates vary each year with the lunar calendar (Nov. 20-23, 1999; Nov. 9-11, 2000). Make hotel reservations well in advance. Expect prices to at least quadruple.

If you come during one of the other 361 days of the year, though, Pushkar is just a wonderful place to relax. Most visitors enjoy meandering along the tiny streets, visiting the temples and *ghats,* and perhaps hiking up to a nearby hill for the views. **Camel safaris** into the desert are becoming increasingly popular in Pushkar, along with **camel treks** across the desert to Jaisalmer, Jodhpur, or Bikaner. Most hotels and travel agents can make these arrangements for you; expect to pay around Rs350 per day for a good camel safari. If you don't have enough time for a safari or trek but want to make friends with a hump-back, go for a **camel ride**—loops around the city cost Rs50 per hour. The **shopping scene** is exciting but expensive, especially during the Fair. Nonetheless, it's fun to stroll down Chhoti Basti, visiting clothing, music, and handicrafts shops, bargaining all the way.

■ Chittaurgarh चित्तौड़गढ़

Rajasthan is full of picturesque cities with looming forts; few, though, loom with Chittaurgarh's tragic nostalgia. Perched on a prominent plateau 115km northeast of Udaipur, the Chittaurgarh Fort's prime location has made it a point of contention for centuries, painting it as the proverbial poster-child for the Rajput ideal of death before dishonor. In 1303, the Delhi Sultan Ala-ud-din Khilji besieged the city in an attempt to capture the beautiful Padmini, wife of Maharaja Ratan Singh. The odds were overwhelmingly against the starved Chittaurgarh people. In an act of sacrifice, 13,000 women declared *jauhar* (self-immolation), jumping onto a burning funeral pyre to save themselves from the conquerors, while 7000 warriors donned orange robes and went forth into battle certain of defeat and death. Barely two centuries later, in 1535, the Gujarati Sultan Bahadur Shah attacked by surprise, annihilating another generation of Rajput warriors even as their wives self-immolated. Then in 1568, the Mughal emperor Akbar laid siege to the city, killing over 30,000 inhabitants; again, the women committed *jauhar*. The people of Chittaurgarh remember their turbulent history proudly, although the town has been a bit quieter of late; the tourist hordes pursue their photographic plunder at other looming forts in other picturesque cities, leaving Chittaurgarh relaxed and marvelously untouristed.

ORIENTATION

Chittaurgarh (or "Chittore") is too diffuse to navigate by foot. The **railway station** is on the west side of town. The major street to the right of **Station Road,** which runs straight north out to Ajmer, is **City Road.** The GPO and General Hospital are near this junction. City Rd. passes the **Roadways Bus Stand** before crossing the Gambheri River and proceeding to the base of the Fort, where it turns into **Fort Road.** The main commercial area and the **new city** are here. Fort Rd. zig-zags steeply up to the **Fort,** which sprawls 7km across the plateau. One main road loops around inside the Fort and leads to all of Chittaurgarh's major sights.

PRACTICAL INFORMATION

Trains: Railway Station, Station Rd. (tel. 131). Reservation office open daily 10am-5pm. To: **Ahmedabad** (*Ajmer-Ahmedabad Mail* 9943, 1:50pm, 15hr., Rs46/633); **Ajmer** (*Meenakshi Exp.* 9770, 5:15am, 4½hr.; *Ahmedabad-Ajmer Mail* 9944, 1:30pm, 5½hr.; *Poorna-Ajmer Passenger* 582, 3pm, 7hr., Rs26/388; *Chetek Exp.* 9616, 9:40pm, 4hr., Rs48/388); **Jaipur** (*Meenakshi Exp.* 9770, 5:15am; *Chetak Exp.* 9616, 9:40pm; 7½hr., Rs74/933). **Udaipur** (*Chetak Exp.* 9615, 6:30am, 3hr., Rs31/310; *Ajmer-Ahmedabad Mail* 9943, 1:50pm, 3½hr., Rs21/310).

Buses: Roadways Bus Stand (tel. 3166). To: **Abu Road** (7 and 1am, 10hr., Rs96); **Ajmer** (all buses to Jaipur stop at Ajmer, 5hr., Rs57/66); **Jaipur** (18 per day, 5:15am-1am, 8hr., Rs93/120); **Jodhpur** (7 per day, 5am-10:30pm, 8hr., Rs96/120); **Kota** (11 per day, 6:30am-1am, deluxe at 8:30am and 4:30pm, 7hr., Rs64/70); **Udaipur** (9 per day, 7:30am-7pm, deluxe at 5:30pm, 2½hr., Rs34/40). A few **private bus** companies located on Station Rd. operate to most destinations.

Local Transportation: Unmetered **auto-rickshaws** and horse-drawn **tongas** are the most common modes of transport. An auto-rickshaw to the Fort costs Rs20; tongas won't make the climb. Many autos operate tempo-style—cramming people in and charging Rs10 to get up to the Fort. A round-trip up to the Fort and around all the sights should cost Rs100, Rs70 off season. **Bicycles** can be rented (Rs15 per day) from shops near the railway station. You'll have to walk the bike up to the Fort, but the cruise down is thrilling.

Tourist Office: The **Tourist Reception Centre,** Station Rd. (tel. 41089), provides maps and travel information. Open M-Sa 10am-1:30pm and 2-5pm. Daily **RTDC** tours (tel. 3238) leave from Hotel Rama (8am and 3pm, 3hr., Rs25).

Currency Exchange: State Bank of Bikaner and Jaipur, Station Rd. (tel. 40933). Exchanges traveler's checks. **Bank of Baroda** (tel. 3198), off Fort Rd., on the 2nd big side street to the right after crossing the river. Exchanges hard cash and traveler's checks. Both open M-F 10am-2pm and Sa 10am-noon.

Market: The main market area for food, provisions, and crafts is around Fort Rd., across the river from Roadways Bus Stand. Most stores open daily 9am-11pm.

Pharmacy: Chittaurgarh Cooperative (tel. 41276), on the campus of the General Hospital, is the only 24hr. pharmacy. Other pharmacies cluster near the hospital.

Hospital: General Hospital, Station Rd. (tel. 41102). English-speaking, large, efficient. Open 24hr. Private hospitals abound but lack the former's facilities.

Police: Main Police Station (tel. 41060), opposite the bus stand. Open 24hr.

Emergency: Fire, tel. 41101. **Ambulance,** tel. 41102.

Post Office: GPO, Station Rd. (tel. 41159), near the railroad crossing. *Poste Restante.* Open M-Sa 7-10:30am and 2:30-6pm. **Postal Code:** 312001.

Telephones: STD/ISD booths dot Station and City Rd. **Telephone Code:** 01472.

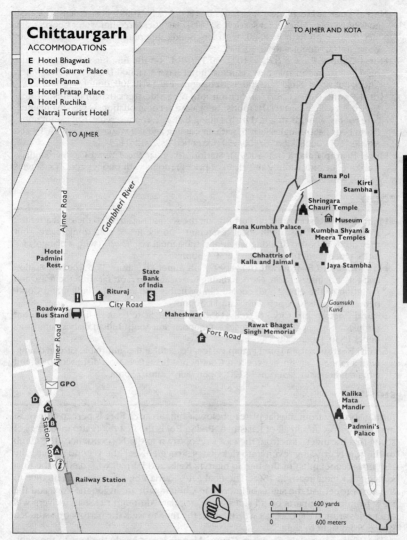

Chittaurgarh
ACCOMMODATIONS
E Hotel Bhagwati
F Hotel Gaurav Palace
D Hotel Panna
B Hotel Pratap Palace
A Hotel Ruchika
C Natraj Tourist Hotel

TO AJMER AND KOTA

TO AJMER

Ajmer Road

Gambheri River

Rama Pol
Kirti Stambha
Shringara Chauri Temple
Museum
Rana Kumbha Palace
Kumbha Shyam & Meera Temples
Chhattris of Kalla and Jaimal
Jaya Stambha

Hotel Padmini Rest.

State Bank of India

Rituraj
City Road
Maheshwari
Gaumukh Kund

Roadways Bus Stand

Ajmer Road

Fort Road
Rawat Bhagat Singh Memorial

GPO

Kalika Mata Mandir

Padmini's Palace

Station Road

Railway Station

N

0   600 yards
0   600 meters

NORTH INDIA

ACCOMMODATIONS

Hotels in Chittaurgarh cluster near the railway station along City Rd., and on Fort Rd. as it passes the bus stand and crosses the river into the old city. Rickshaw-*wallahs* operate on commission; Rs2 rides to hotels aren't the best deal in the long run.

Hotel Ruchika (tel. 40419), near the railway station. Follow the signs for Hotel Meera. A delightful small hotel run by a very friendly man and his sons. Rooms are basic but clean. 24hr. room service, hot water buckets Rs3. Singles Rs80, with attached bath, air-cooling and TV Rs125; doubles Rs100/175. Extra bed Rs25.

Hotel Bhagwati, Fort Rd. (tel. 3226), across the bridge from the Roadways Bus Stand, near the old city. Clean, spacious rooms with attached baths around a tiled courtyard. 24hr. room service and a *bhojnalya* downstairs that dishes Rs20 *thalis*. Check-out 24hr. Singles Rs60, with air-cooling and hot water Rs100; doubles Rs100/150. TV Rs20 per person. Extra bed Rs30.

Natraj Tourist Hotel, near Roadways Bus Stand (tel. 41009). Conveniently located, no-frills rooms, 24hr. room service, STD/ISD facilities. Free hot water buckets. Singles Rs30, with bath Rs50-60, with air-cooling, telephone, TV, and running hot water Rs100; doubles Rs50/90/175.

Hotel Gaurav Palace (tel. 43107), off Fort Rd., on the first big side street to the right. All rooms in this new, modern hotel have attached baths with hot water. Check-out noon. Singles Rs200, with balcony and TV Rs300; doubles Rs300/350.

Hotel Panna (tel. 41238), off Station Rd., on a sidestreet that branches off near Nehru Park. Standard RTDC tourist bungalow accommodations—well-maintained, bare rooms, all with attached bath. Dining hall, bar, room service. Check-out noon. Dorm beds Rs50. Singles Rs125, with air-cooling and hot water Rs225, with TV and A/C Rs450; doubles Rs175/300/550. Extra bed Rs75/125/175.

Hotel Pratap Palace (tel. 40099), Station Rd., near the Tourist Centre. English-speaking. Beautiful lobby and clean (if pricey) rooms with phones and TVs. Singles Rs550, with A/C Rs625.

FOOD

Maheshwari Restaurant, off Fort Rd., on the second big street to the right after the river crossing. A decidedly local restaurant—no menus or cold drinks here—but they do have boiled drinking water and substantial veg. *thalis* (with a mango!) for Rs25. Open daily 10am-3pm and 6:30-9:30pm.

Hotel Padmini Restaurant (tel. 41997), off Ajmer Rd., about 3km from the Station and City Rd. intersection. Garden dining in a beautiful resort far from the noise and pollution of the city. An air-cooled dining hall is also available. Indian and Continental dishes Rs30. Open daily 7am-11:30pm.

Rituraj Restaurant, City Rd. (tel. 41450), near the State Bank of India. A small but popular shop specializing in snacks, tandoori, and South Indian dishes, almost all under Rs30. Open daily 7am-11pm.

Shakti Restaurant, in Hotel Pratap Palace. Peaceful and comfortable garden dining, with a range of cuisines. Excellent Continental breakfast. Most dishes Rs30-40, but a full tandoori chicken runs Rs120. Open daily 7am-10:30pm.

SIGHTS

Jutting abruptly from the flat plateau below, Chittaurgarh's **Fort** is perhaps the most impressive structure in all of Rajasthan. **Padan Pol** is the first *pol* (gate) in a series of seven that meander 1km from the east side of town to the Fort entrance. The climb to the top is grueling; even auto-rickshaws struggle. Near the second *pol* are the *chhattris* (cenotaphs) of the heroic martyrs **Kalla** and **Jaimal,** who died in the final sacking of Chittaurgarh in 1568. The final gate, **Rama Pol,** serves as the entrance to the Fort proper. All the sights of interest in Chittaurgarh are inside the Fort, and the view from the ramparts on all sides is spectacular. Although rickshaw drivers will offer rides around the Fort, it's worth taking the time to walk the narrow tree-studded streets from sight to sight.

The 15th-century Jain **Shingara Chauri Mandir** is just inside the Fort to the right. The temple's elaborate decoration indicates Hindu influences. Just ahead is the quasi-ruined **Rana Kumbha Palace,** where the third *jauhar* of Chittaurgarh supposedly took place in an underground cellar, but after the siege of the city, only stables and a Shiva temple remain. Also nearby are the towered **Kumbha Shyam Mandir** and the elegant **Meera Mandir,** which honors the Jodhpuri mystic poetess Mirabai.

Following the shady Fort Rd. south leads to the **Jaya Stambha** (Tower of Victory), which adorns every brochure and postcard of Chittaurgarh and much RTDC literature. The sandstone tower boasts Chittaurgarh's story and glory from an imposing 37m. Elaborate multi-denominational sculptures grace the exterior. The tower's construction began in 1458 to commemorate an important victory in 1440, and took 10 years to complete. You can climb its nine stories (Rs2); if you don't knock yourself unconscious on the low ceilings, the view is breathtaking. The ramparts around the tower are a popular hang-out as well. The **Sammidheshwar Mandir** is nearby on the hill, as is the chilling **Mahasati** with its thousands of *sati* marks (handprints of women who self-immolated on the funeral pyres of their husbands).

Off the main road a bit further south is the **Gaumukh Kund** (Cow's Mouth Tank), featuring a carved cow who fills the tank with water. Continue down the main road to **Padmini's Palace,** a dainty but run-down palace sitting in a shallow pool. According to legend, Ala-ud-din-Khilji saw beautiful Padmini's reflection in a palace mirror, and setting his sight on her (and his might on Chittaurgarh), he staged the first siege of Chittaurgarh that led to the terrifying acts of *jauhar.* The **Kalika Mata Mandir** is directly opposite. It was originally dedicated to the sun god Surya in the 8th century, but now pays tribute to the goddess Kali.

The road continues down south for a while, looping past the often-empty **Deer Park,** the quiet **Bhimlat Tank,** and a small crack-in-the wall where traitors and political prisoners were thrown to their deaths below. The road then turns north again past **Suraj Pol,** the eastern gate of the Fort, and the **Kirti Stambha** (Tower of Fame). Built by a wealthy Jain merchant, the tower features decorative images of the Jain pantheon, particularly that of Adinath, the first *tirthankara,* to whom the tower is dedicated.

■ Near Chittaurgarh

Forty kilometers south of Chittaurgarh is **Bijaipur,** an unspectacular village with a spectacular 200-year-old palace. The palace is now **Hotel Castle Bijaipur** (tel. 76222). The palace hotel offers fancy rooms, excellent dinners (Rs250), and blissful solitude, along with jungle trekking and safaris of the horse and village variety. (Check-out noon. Singles Rs750; doubles Rs800.) **Morcha Restaurant,** run by Chittaurgarh's Pratap Palace, has cheaper eats and a pleasant garden setting (Rs50 and under).

■ Udaipur उदयपुर

Udaipur, City of Sunrise, epitomizes Rajasthan's romantic allure; countless visitors who plan to tour the sights in a few days end up staying for weeks in this refreshing oasis. The old city overlooks the green Lake Pichola, whose postcard perfection is removed from the industrialization farther out. Modernization has taken hold; logging barons have left the once luscious valleys barren, and crowds and chaos fill the new urban center outside the old city walls. Still, Udaipur's architectural offerings are surpassed only by Jaipur's, and Udaipur's lakeside languor is surpassed by none.

Maharaja Udai Singh II founded Udaipur when he fled after Chittaurgarh's final siege in 1568. Four years later, Udai's son and his troops successfully defended Udaipur against invasion by Akbar's fierce forces. The next 150 years were peaceful and the city grew in opulènce. Miniature painting became a specialty, and architects peppered the town with majestic palaces. In 1736 the city was crippled by the mighty Marathas, but bounced back with British aid, somehow remaining firmly independent. Since then, the city's arts have continued to flourish, James Bond films notwithstanding (yes, *Octapussy* was filmed here). The Mewar Festival (March 20-21, 1999; April 7-8, 2000) brings in dexterous dances, masterful music, fabulous fireworks, and a brilliant lake parade.

ORIENTATION

Situated 113km southwest of Chittaurgarh and 270km south of Ajmer, Udaipur rolls gently with the green hills of the surrounding Aravali mountains. The **Old City** straddles the northeast bank of Lake Pichola; the **New City** expands to the north, east, and south. The **Udaipur City Railway Station** sits to the southeast of town along **City Station Road.** From the station, it's a 2km hike north to the **bus stand,** opposite **Udai Pol** (Gate), one of the four main entrances to the Old City. Following the same main road leads to **Suraj Pol,** another city entrance, which also opens onto the two main shopping streets, **Bapu Bazaar** and **Bara Bazaar.** Bapu Bazaar runs parallel to **Town Hall Road,** home to many banks, and leads north to **Delhi Gate.** From Delhi Gate, a left leads west down Ashwani Rd. and **Hathi Pol,** on the north end of the Old City. A right leads to **Shastri Circle,** which includes the Tourist Bungalow, the GPO, and the General Hospital. **Chetak Circle** is about 1km down Hospital Rd. to the left.

Hathi Pol affords the easiest access to the **City Palace** and **Jagdish Mandir,** by way of the **clock tower.** From the clock tower, the right fork uphill leads southwest toward the Mandir and a left leads east down Bara Bazar to Suraj Pol. From Jagdish Mandir, **Bhatiyani Chohotta (B.C.)** leads south, eventually swinging east and becoming **Lake Palace Road** before dead ending in Bapu Bazaar. Heading north on B.C. takes you past the palaces and the ghats to the Chand Pol and west and north over bridges to the beautiful but less regal **Fateh Sagar Lake.**

PRACTICAL INFORMATION

Airport: Dabok Airport (tel. 655453), 25km east of Udaipur (taxi Rs200). **Indian Airlines,** Delhi Gate (tel. 410999). Open daily 10am-1:15pm and 2-5pm. **U.P. Air** (tel. 527919; fax 527919), near the GPO. Open M-F 9am-1pm and 2-5:30pm, Sa 9am-noon. To: **Aurangabad** (3 per wk., 1hr., US$90); **Delhi** (1-3 per day, 2hr., US$65); **Jaipur** (1-3 per day, 1hr., US$45-60); **Mumbai** (1-3 per day, 1-2hr., US$95).

Trains: Udaipur City Railway Station (tel. 131). Reservation office open M-Sa 8am-8pm, Su 8am-2pm. Fares listed are 2nd/1st class. To: **Ajmer** (3 per day, including *Chetak Exp.* 9616, 6pm, 8hr., Rs118/375); **Ahmedabad** (*Mewar Fast Passenger* 931, 9am, 12hr., Rs118/315); **Chittaurgarh** (frequent, 4hr., Rs81/184); **Delhi** (*Chetak Exp.* 9616, 6pm, 20hr., Rs203/708); **Jaipur** (*Chetak Exp.* 9616, 6pm, 12hr., Rs158/495); and **Jodhpur** (2 per day, including *Passenger* 222, 6am, 11hr. with transfer at Marwar Junction, Rs75/340).

Buses: Main Bus Stand (tel. 484191). Regular/deluxe to: **Ahmedabad** (16 per day 5am-10:30pm, 7hr., Rs74/90); **Ajmer** (buses to Jaipur pass through, 7hr., Rs75); **Bikaner** (4:30pm, 15hr., Rs67); **Chittaurgarh** (every hr. 5am-9pm, 3hr., Rs31); **Delhi** (2 per day, 15hr., Rs204); **Jaipur** (20 per day, 5am-10:30pm, 10hr., Rs128/ 174); **Jodhpur** (8 per day, 7hr., Rs80/118); **Mt. Abu** (5 per day, 7hr., Rs70); and **Ranakpur** (buses to Jodhpur pass through, 2½ hr., Rs 30/35). Between the lot of **private bus companies,** there are hourly departures to all major cities (see **Budget Travel,** below). For trips under 5hr., **private buses** are best, but for long trips deluxe buses are better.

Local Transportation: The best way to get around is by **bicycle. Vijay Cycles,** B.C. Rd. (tel. 411274), next to Raj Palace Hotel, rents cycles for Rs20 per day, and scooters for Rs150, Rs25 per hr. **Auto-rickshaws,** though unmetered, are not exorbitant. **Taxis** can be hired from most travel agents (Rs3-5 per km, min. 200km).

Tourist Office: Tourist Reception Centre, Suraj Pol (tel. 411535). Current maps and brochures are available. Open M-Sa 10am-5pm. **Tourist Information Bureau** (tel. 412984), at the railway station, has a smaller collection of information. Open M-Sa 8-11am and 4-7pm, closed 2nd Sa. A small information counter (tel. 655433) is at Dabok Airport. Open M-Sa 8am-1pm and 4-7pm.

Budget Travel: Dozens of agents line City Station Rd. and the Jagdish Mandir area, and there are more around Delhi Gate and Chetak Circle. Most hotels double as agencies. Travel agencies book train, bus, and plane tickets; city tours by car (Rs350-450); airport taxis (Rs200); camel, horse, and elephant safaris (from Rs500 per day); and bus tours. Prices are virtually equal due to competition. Reputable agencies include **Shrinath Travels,** Udai Pol (tel. 422201; fax 422206), near the bus stand, and **Rajasthan Tours,** Lake Palace Rd. (tel. 525777; fax 414283). Most agencies open daily 8am-5pm, but **Ajanta Travels,** off B.C. Rd., is open until 10pm.

Currency Exchange: Andhra Bank, Shakti Nagar Rd. (tel. 410699), advances cash on credit cards (no service charge), as does the **Bank of Baroda,** near Delhi Gate. **State Bank of Bikaner and Jaipur,** Chetak Circle (tel. 527087; fax 525066), wires money. Both exchange foreign currency and cash traveler's checks. Open M-F 10am-2pm, Sa 10am-noon.

Bookstore: Mayur Book Paradise, 60 B.C. (tel. 410316; fax 412160), opposite Hotel Shakti Palace. Wide multi-lingual paperback selection and some international 'zines. Open daily noon-7pm. The **book stall** at the railway station has an unusually good collection of English novels. Open daily 5-10am and 4-8pm.

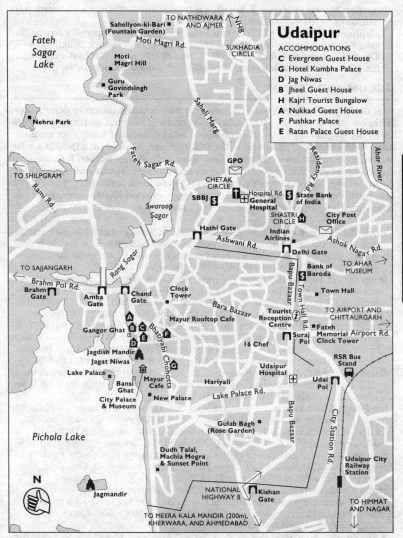

Udaipur

ACCOMMODATIONS
- **C** Evergreen Guest House
- **G** Hotel Kumbha Palace
- **D** Jag Niwas
- **B** Jheel Guest House
- **H** Kajri Tourist Bungalow
- **A** Nukkad Guest House
- **F** Pushkar Palace
- **E** Ratan Palace Guest House

Market: In addition to Bara Bazaar and Bapu Bazaar, market areas, food stores, and food stalls are located around Jagdish Mandir, the clock tower, Chetak Circle, and all of the gates. Most open daily 7am-11pm.

Emergency: Police, tel. 100. **Fire,** tel. 101. **Ambulance,** tel. 102.

Police: A major police station is at every gate. The biggest are at **Delhi Gate** and **Udai Pol.** There are also stations near the bus and railway stations. Police superintendent (tel. 413949). Police control room (tel. 23000).

Pharmacy: Hospital Rd. and Udai Pol are filled with pharmacies. Most open daily 7am-9:30pm. **Udaipur Hospital** (tel. 421900) has a well-stocked, 24hr. pharmacy.

Hospital: RNT General Hospital, Hospital Rd. (tel. 528811). Government-run. **Udaipur Hospital,** Bapu Bazaar (tel. 420322), near Udai Pol, is an excellent ultra-modern private hospital with pharmacy. Both English-speaking and open 24hr.

Post Office: GPO, Chetak Circle (tel. 528622). Open M-F 10am-6pm, Sa 10am-1pm. **Shastri Circle** has *Poste Restante.* Open M-Sa 6am-6pm. **Postal Code:** 313001.

Internet: Mewar Internet & Email, Raj Palace Hotel, Bhatiyani Chohatta (tel. 410364 or 52702; fax 410364).

Telephones: A number of STD/ISD booths are open 24hr., especially around the Lake Palace Rd./Jagdish Mandir area. Many offer fax and call-back facilities as well. **Central Telegraph Office** (tel. 520275; fax 529922), in the GPO, offers STD/ISD, fax, telex, and telegraph services. Open 24hr. **Telephone Code:** 0294.

ACCOMMODATIONS

Most of Udaipur's 200-plus hotels commission auto-rickshaw drivers to deposit way-farers on their doorsteps. The system is the norm in Udaipur, and complaining is futile, but you can ask to be dropped at one hotel or area and easily check out the many others nearby. The hotels on the beautiful **east bank** of Lake Pichola are far preferable to any others in the city. Those along **Lake Palace Rd.** and **B.C.** are solid runners-up. Hotels in the **new city** are noisy and graceless. **Home-stay** accommodation is an alternative. Currently more than 200 families participate. The Tourist Reception Centre (tel. 411535) makes arrangements (Rs150-400 per night). Most hotels listed below have laundry, travel, and 24-hour room service.

Hotel Raj Palace, B.C. Rd. (tel. 410364 or 410395), between Jagdish Mandir and the City Palace. Great location, good service, and food. And then there are the rooms: stained-glass windows, alcoves, fancy mirrors, spotless bathrooms, and garden views. Check-out 10am. All doubles Rs300-500, w/A/C Rs750.

Jheel Guest House and **Paying Guest House,** 56 and 52 Gangaur Ghat (tel. 421352; fax 520008). On the edge of the lake. Big, well-kept rooms. All baths have hot water. Check-out 10am. Singles Rs50-80, with attached bath Rs100-200; doubles Rs80-100/150-300. Deluxe rooms with balconies onto lake Rs500-550.

Evergreen Guest House, 32 Lal Ghat (tel. 421585). Set in an area with lots of Westerners, this one's popular with its cool, basic rooms and good views. Painting shop below offers free lessons. Luggage storage and free 24hr. hot water buckets. Check-out 10am. Singles Rs50, with attached bath Rs100; doubles Rs125/175.

Ratan Palace Paying Guest House, 21 Lal Ghat (tel. 561153). A family-run place with clean, well-decorated rooms, attached baths and hot showers. Check-out 10am. Singles Rs200-450; doubles Rs350-450.

Jag Niwas Guest House, 21 Gangaur Marg (tel. 422067), near Jagdish Mandir. No longer owned by the Maharaja; still, it exudes style. Big rooms with attached baths. Check-out noon. Singles Rs60; doubles Rs100-120, with air-cooling Rs250-350.

Pushkar Palace, 93 B.C. (tel. 417685), near Asha Pala Temple. Family-run "palace" offers huge, well-maintained rooms around impressive courtyards. Funky bed-spreads, too. Common baths are even nicer than the private ones. Check-out 10am. Singles Rs50; doubles with attached bath Rs100.

Hotel Kumbha Palace, 104 B.C. (tel. 422702). The central garden borders the city walls. Distinctive rooms have colorful stained-glass windows and decorations from the Jaisalmeri desert, as well as attached baths and air-coolers. Check-out 10am. Singles Rs80-100; doubles Rs150-200.

Kajri Tourist Bungalow (tel. 410501; fax 411950), near Shastri Circle. Good-size rooms with attached baths. Set around lush gardens and decaying tennis courts. Starting point for RTDC tours. Check-out noon. Dorm beds Rs50. Singles Rs200, with air-cooling Rs350, with A/C Rs550; doubles Rs275/450/750. Apr.-Sept. discount 50% after the first night.

FOOD

Udaipur has a fairly good range of restaurants to choose from, many of which offer (you guessed it) continuous screenings of *Octopussy*. Most are hotel rooftop eateries, but quality stand-alones are growing in number.

Mayur Café, Jagdish Mandir (tel. 412368). Quality food, quick service and an A/C dining hall make the Mayur a local haunt. Especially popular are the Indian *thalis* and snacks, and Western favorites, all under Rs40. Open daily 8am-10pm.

The 16 Chef Restaurant, 16 Gyah Marg (tel. 561771), near Suraj Pol. A huge red sign showing a bear hugging the number 16 invites you into a spectacular garden restaurant inaugurated by the Maharana of Mewar himself. Indian, Continental, and Chinese food galore, all (even tandoori!) for under Rs35. Open daily 8am-11:30pm.

The Red Herring Restaurant, Chand Pol (tel. 529269). The chef's fingers are golden at this lakeside garden restaurant run by a gracious family. Indian, Italian and Swiss dishes. The view is fabulous, and the garden is lush. Closed off season.

Gayitri Dosa Centre, Lake Palace Rd. (tel. 520053). Bond with locals as you queue up for scrumptious *dosas* at this quasi-stall eatery. Open daily 7am-11pm.

Sai Niwas, Hotel Sai Niwas, 75 Nav Ghat (tel. 524909). Deciding what to order will be Moore fun than you're used to, and you'll owe it all to the pictorial menu with elaborate descriptions of the entrees. The food is family-cooked and lives up to the menu descriptions (veg. entrees Rs45-50). Open daily 6am-11pm.

Mayur Roof Café, Shakti Palace Hotel, 76 B.C. (tel. 410453 or 42240). The best of the "rooftop" restaurants, with views to kill for. Groove to the Hindi film music that plays in the background. Good Indian selection, and some Continental and Chinese (veg. generally less than Rs30, non-veg. Rs30-50). Open daily 7am-11pm.

Hariyali Restaurant, off Lake Palace Rd. (tel. 561678). Specialty veg. South Indian cuisine; Continental and Chinese also available. Secluded atmosphere saves the lush garden for your eyes only. Most entrees Rs30-40. Open daily 9am-11pm.

Jagat Niwas Palace Hotel. Head down to the lake from the Jagdish Temple for affordable, lake-view dining luxury at this renovated palace. The rooms here are expensive, but dinner is not (entrees start at Rs60-110; beer Rs70). Have a romantic meal for two in the center alcove on the balcony. Attentive service.

SIGHTS

The visual highlights of Udaipur may be the elegant palaces rising from the deep green of Lake Pichola, but the historical focal points are the **City Palace** and **Jagdish Mandir,** to the west of the old city. A good way to take in the sights in a quick daytrip is with a five-hour RTDC city tour. *(8am-1pm, departure from Kajri, Shastri Circle, Rs50.)*

City Palace

Location: *West of the city.* **Hours:** *Open daily 10am-5pm.* **Admission:** *Rs20.* **Other:** *Camera fee Rs50. Tours Rs70.*

Despite its worn beige exterior, the grand palace, begun in 1559 by **Udai Singh,** the proud Mewar migrant and founder of the city, is a culmination of the combined architectural efforts of more than 20 kings. The City Palace is currently part museum, part royal residence, and part luxury hotel. Before entering the museum, note the two large paved stone indentions—they were once elephant beds. The museum opens into the **Raja Angan Chauk** surrounded by rooms of Udaipuri miniature paintings, one of which appears in three dimensions when viewed at a distance. This vast court-yard was once a Holi playground.

The palace is filled with tributes to Rana Pratap, Udai Singh's heroic progeny. Among them are an eerie, larger-than-life marble bust and 400-year-old armor that once graced his equally valorous Arabian stallion, Chetak (see **A Helluva Horse,** p. 295). The palace is best-known for the **Mor Chauk** with its blue and green inlaid glass peacocks and convex mirrors. **Krishna-vilas,** a small room with walls completely covered by miniature paintings, is dedicated to a 16-year-old princess, Krishna Kumari, who was betrothed to two princes and chose suicide to avoid an almost sure war for her hand. The **Zenana Mahal,** the women's quarters, is disappointingly ill-maintained and houses little more than Maharaja Bhopal Singh's 1922 Rolls-Royce.

Jagdish Mandir

Location: *Down the steep hill from the City Palace.* **Hours:** *Open daily 5am-2pm and 4-10:30pm. Winter: 5:30am-2pm and 4-10pm.*

A 17th-century temple built by Maharaja Jagat Singh and dedicated to Vishnu as Jagannath, whose black marble image resides in the sanctum, the Jagdish Mandir is smack in the heart of the old city, this *mandir* sees many worshippers daily. Legend has it that Jagat Singh received the inspiration for the temple in a dream. The outer structure rises in a pyramid-like *shikhara* of worn stone decorated with rows of elephants and *apsaras,* along with figures from Mewari mythology. The entrance is guarded by a large bronze Garuda, Vishnu's mount. The cornerstone at the left base of the stairs supposedly bestows good luck on anyone who rubs it seven times. The central dome teems with mythological figures while a huge silver bed meant for the gods' rests in front of the sanctuary entrance.

Jag Niwas (Lake Palace)

Once the royal summer palace, the **Jag Niwas** seems to float lightly on the gentle waters of Lake Pichola; not far away, on another island, is the **Jag Mandir,** a domed pavilion famous for the safety it provided to the exiled Shah Jahan (then a prince leading a revolt against his father Jahangir), and later to English women and children during the Mutiny of 1857. The Lake Palace (now a luxury hotel; tel. 527961) is well worth the buffet dinner (Rs500; reserve in advance) that comes with short boat rides from **Bansi Ghat.** The palace grounds and open-air courtyard cafes, with white marble inlay and corner towers and turrets, are stunning. Jag Mandir can be visited on non-dinner cruises as well: hour-long jaunts around the lake leave from Bansi Ghat. *(Daily 10am-8pm, Rs125.)*

Bharatiya Lok Kala Mandal Folk Museum

Phone: *529296.* **Hours:** *Open daily 9am-6pm. Dance performances daily 6-7pm.* **Admission:** *Rs10.* **Performances Rs30.** **Other:** *Camera fee Rs10; video fee Rs50.*

A large complex intended as a center for the preservation and distribution of tribal folk arts, the museum has several rooms off one main hall, each containing a variety of items ranging from colorfully painted caricature masks used in dance dramas to clay figure dioramas depicting local festivals to a rather dusty collection of life-sized models of local tribals. The museum's highlight is the collection of traditional Rajasthani **puppets** called *kathpurli*—wide-eyed wooden string puppets dressed in bright, traditional costumes. A **minimalist puppet show** is put on every 20 to 25 minutes in the puppet theater—music accompanies the shimmying hips of wooden dancing girls. The puppets are expertly, and a little obscenely, manipulated. The Lok Mandal also puts on dance performances.

Shilpigram

Location: *West of Udaipur off Lake Fateh Sagar.* **Transit:** *Rickshaws around Rs50 each way. Bicycles are a cheaper option.* **Phone:** *560304.* **Hours:** *Open daily noon-8pm.* **Admission:** *Rs10.* **Other:** *1-2hr. cultural programs daily, 7pm, Rs60.*

A self-dubbed "rural arts and crafts complex," Shilpigram's spacious cleared paths lead to model homes from specific rural and tribal communities of Rajasthan, Gujarat, Maharashtra, and Goa, from the circular, white stone, clay-roofed homes of the Meghwal Bahni to the thatched-roofed square home of a Kohlapuri shoe maker. The village redeems itself with tents of rural crafts sold by potters and cloth makers and lively performances by musicians and dancers from the various rural communities who live in the village for short periods of time. The village is something of a cultural petting zoo, but it does provide a fun, brief glimpse into the richness of folk culture.

Gardens

Udaipur is known for its gardens as well as its palaces. Nehru Park, Saheliyon-ki-Bari, and Sajjan Niwas are the best maintained, but also the most tourist-trampled. **Nehru Park,** built in part as a public works project to create jobs during a famine, sits pretty in Fateh Sagar (open daily 8am-7pm; admission Rs5). It is spread over fairly open and fountain-dotted grounds, with beige domed cupolas, swaying palm trees, and bright bushes of bougainvillea. Small, crowded boats leave the banks of Fateh Sagar every 20 minutes for the island park. They offer funny, if slightly harrowing, adventure. It is also possible to take a 30-minute tour around the lake for Rs40.

A Helluva Horse

The cow might be an object of worship for Hindus, but the Rajputs of Rajasthan have a special place in their hearts for a certain white stallion named Chetak. Indeed, his name lives on in Udaipur's main circle and graces the main express train in Rajasthan. Chetak, whose statues abound in Udaipur, was the loyal battle companion of Rana Pratap. At the famous bloodbath of Hathigari in 1532, Chetak's leg was cut by an enemy elephant wielding a machete in its trunk; Pratap was also wounded. Though hobbled, Chetak bravely carried his master from the battlefield through a narrow passage, leaping over a 3m crevice before finally coming to rest under a tree 6km away. There, poor Chetak breathed his last, having saved his master's life. Many tours of the area surrounding Udaipur stop at Hathigari to pay respects at Chetak's tomb and hear the tale of his valiant death.

The 18th-century **Saheliyon-ki-Bari** (Garden of the Maids of Honor) lies 2km to the north of town and was built by Maharana Sangram Singh for the maharani and her corps of friends and servants. The luscious garden, with its palm-lined walks and lotus pool is more a tourist sight than the refuge it was once meant to be. During the monsoon rains the pool is spectacular (open daily 8am-7:30pm; admission Rs2).

Sajjan Niwas, set on Lake Palace Rd., and the nearby **Gulab Bagh** (Rose Garden) are sprawling, thickly vegetated dream gardens. The former's wide paths are lined with local flora, including giant umbrella *neem* trees. The garden is popular with local cyclers and provides several smaller wooded paths for the die-hard garden-goer.

For a mind-blowing view of the city and valley, head to **Sajjangarh (Monsoon) Palace** (closed to visitors) perched on a steep hill 5km west of Udaipur. Good luck getting up by bike; even auto-rickshaws sputter (Rs150 round-trip). **The Dudh Talal and Sunset Point** off of Lake Palace Rd. offers more solitary, serene lake views.

ENTERTAINMENT AND SHOPPING

Udaipur's wonders don't end at lakesides palaces and museums, though. Traditional **Rajasthani folk dances** and music performances, involving a dazzling blend of earthy tribal trances and circus-like balancing feats, are held Monday through Saturday from 7-8pm at **Meera Kala Mandir** (tel. 583176), near the Pars Theater in Sector 11. Tickets to the show cost Rs60; a rickshaw ride from the old city costs Rs25-30. For information about **puppet shows** at the Bharatiya Lok Kala Folk Museum and **folk dances,** see **Shilpgram,** p. 294). **Shopping** here can be an addictive diversion. Around Jagdish Mandir, Lake Palace Rd., Bara Bazaar, and Bapu Bazaar are countless clothing, jewelry, textile, and handicrafts shops featuring wares from all over Rajasthan at inflated but negotiable prices. **Miniature painting** is an Udaipuri speciality, and Lake Palace Rd. has a series of shops where skilled artists can be watched at work without any obligation (despite extortion) to buy. In general, it's best to explore shopping areas on your own. "Guides" will offer to take you to the best textile, handicrafts, and jewelry stores, but they receive a 20% commission.

■ Near Udaipur: Eklingi इकलिंगी and Nathdwara नथद्वारा

Twenty-two kilometers north of Udaipur in the heart of marble-producing territory is the inspiring village of **Eklingi,** home to a magnificent temple of Shiva. The temple itself is vanilla-colored marble and encloses a four-faced solid black image of Shiva. Silver doors, silver lamps, silver parcels, and a solid silver bull adorn the interior, and the exterior and surrounding shrines are decorated with impressive stonework. (Open daily 4:30-6:30am, 10:30am-1:30pm, and 5:30-6:45pm. Photography is not permitted.) Many tours stop at Eklingi, which is also accessible by bus from Udaipur (Rs18).

Forty-eight kilometers north of Udaipur is the important Vaishnava pilgrimage site of **Nathdwara,** built entirely around its incredible **Nathji Mandir,** dedicated to Krishna as Sri Nathji. Legend maintains that in the 17th century a chariot en route from Mathura to Udaipur, bearing Krishna's image, inexplicably became trapped in the mud; the bearers interpreted the situation as a divine signal and built the temple at the spot. The image of Sri Nathji, with blazing diamond-studded eyes and Mughal dress, is found on decorative items in households all over India. The stalls outside the temple have commercialized the image—the assortment of Krishna paraphernalia is intense, and prices are high. Although the temple's architecture is visually stunning, far more interesting are the daily 5pm ceremonies attended by many and revolving around a prescribed schedule of feeding, bathing, and resting the image. Viewing the image is only possible at certain times of the day, and after 3pm the temple only re-opens at 4:45 for fifteen minutes of viewing. The mad rush that ensues is not for the claustrophobic, but its serves pick-pockets well—guard your belongings. Photography is strictly prohibited in the temple. Nathdwara is a stop on many tours and is accessible by bus from Udaipur (Rs24). The RTDC runs a bus (Rs85 per person) to Hathigari, Eklingi, and Nathdwara leaving every weekday at 2pm from the Kajri Tourist Bungalow in Chauk Circle and returning at 7pm.

▣ Ranakpur रनकपुर

Eighty kilometers northwest of Udaipur, roads zig-zag through the verdant Aravali mountain's valleys to Ranakpur's complex of superb Jain temples rivaling Mt. Abu's Dilwara complex. The main white marble **Chaumukha Temple,** was built in 1439 and dedicated to Adinath, the first *tirthankara.* The three-tiered entry facade is delicately crenulated and punctuated by squashed spires along both sides. Inside, each of the 29 halls, 80 domes, and 1444 pillars (no two of them alike) is intricately carved and sculpted—every last bead on a dancer's earring is rendered meticulously. The temple's most intricate carvings surround a four-faced image of Adinath in the inner-most sanctum. Within the complex are smaller shrines to Parshvanath and Neminath, with similarly impressive architecture, and a Hindu temple to Surya; its sculpture and latticework is striking, although a bit weathered. (Temple open to non-Jains daily noon-5pm. Camera fee Rs25. A rickshaw to the temple should cost about Rs35; retain the driver if you can because other forms of return transportation can be expensive.)

Most **buses** from Udaipur to Jodhpur stop at Ranakpur; check in advance (see **Udaipur,** p. 289). Private bus companies in Udaipur and Mt. Abu arrange frequent departures and tours to Ranakpur as well. From Ranakpur, private buses leave to Jodhpur, Jaipur, and Udaipur throughout the day, about every two hours. There is an **STD/ISD** booth on the temple grounds (open daily 7am-8pm), and another at the Roopam Restaurant, as well as a **post office** in Shilpi Tourist Bungalow (open M-Sa noon-5pm). **Telephone Code:** 02934.

There are only two accommodation options in Ranakpur proper. The **dharam-shala** (tel. 3619) offers simple lodgings (Rs5 per bed, additional donations appreciated) and basic but plentiful veg. lunches and dinners (Rs15). Alcohol and smoking are prohibited, and lights-out is at 10pm. The **Shilpi Tourist Bungalow** (tel. 3674) has reasonably clean rooms and an expensive restaurant. All rooms have attached baths. (Singles Rs200, with air-cooling Rs250; doubles Rs200/300; extra bed Rs25.) **Drinks and snacks** are available at a small restaurant at the bus stand. The **Roopam Restaurant** (tel. 3921), 2km past the tourist bungalow, is an open-air establishment set among several forest villages. (Most entrees Rs30-50. Open daily 7am-11pm.)

▣ Mount Abu आबु

Situated 1220m above sea level on a temperate plateau, with lush vegetation and bearable temperatures year round, Mt. Abu is a popular destination for Indian (mainly Gujarati) families and honeymooners. Once part of the kingdom of the Chauhan Rajputs, Mt. Abu is now an important pilgrimage site. Thought to be the home of the sage Vashishta whose sacrificial fire gave rise to the 5 Rajput clans, Mt. Abu also boasts Nakki Lake whose holy waters are held to be as purifying as those of the Ganga. However, Hindus are not the only pilgrims to Mt. Abu; Jains pay homage at

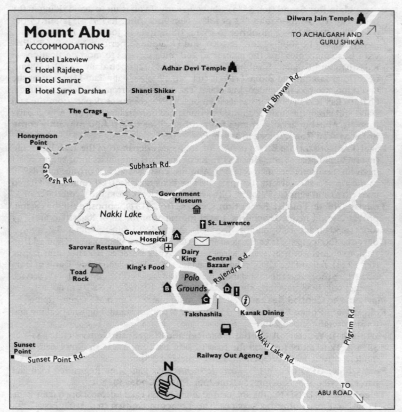

Mount Abu
ACCOMMODATIONS
A Hotel Lakeview
C Hotel Rajdeep
D Hotel Samrat
B Hotel Surya Darshan

Dilwara Jain Temple
TO ACHALGARH AND GURU SHIKAR

Adhar Devi Temple

Shanti Shikar

Raj Bhavan Rd.

The Crags

Honeymoon Point

Subhash Rd.

Ganesh Rd.

Nakki Lake

Government Museum

St. Lawrence

Government Hospital

Sarovar Restaurant

Dairy King

Central Bazaar

Rajendra Rd.

King's Food

Toad Rock

Polo Grounds

Takshashila

Kanak Dining

Sunset Point

Sunset Point Rd.

Railway Out Agency

Nakki Lake Rd.

Pilgrim Rd.

N

TO ABU ROAD

NORTH INDIA

the architecturally breathtaking Dilwara temples. The religious atmosphere does not inhibit frolicking honeymooners from enjoying their holidays. During the Summer Festival, held annually June 1-3, tourists nearby head here to cavort amid tribal dances and folk music. With its ubiquitous palm trees and sunsets over the rock-ridged lake, this desert oasis (the only hill station in Rajasthan) approaches utopia.

ORIENTATION

The railhead at **Abu Road,** 27km downhill, serves Mt. Abu. The small town can be traversed in 25min., and buses will drop you off within walking distance of several hotels, but too far from the lake. The main drag, **Nakki Lake Road,** leads into town from Abu Rd., passing the Railway Out Agency, Tourist Reception Centre, **Main Bus Stand,** and police station. A left after the police station takes you past the taxi stand; the road curves around the **Polo Grounds** and, continuing along the right fork, reunites with Nakki Lake Rd., which then continues onto the **Central Bazaar.** A right takes you past the **hospital,** the **GPO, St. Lawrence Church,** and, much further on, the **Dilwara Temples.** Veering left from the Central Bazaar takes you to **Nakki Lake.**

PRACTICAL INFORMATION

Trains: Trains depart from the **Abu Road Railway Station** (tel. 22222), 27km away. Abu Rd. is 1hr. from Mt. Abu (see **Local Transportation**). **Railway Out Agency,** Nakki Lake Rd. (tel. 3353), near the petrol pump, handles reservations. Open M-Sa 9am-1pm and 2-4pm. To: **Ahmedabad** (*Ahmedabad Mail* 9106, 2pm, 5hr., Rs88/367) and **Jaipur** (*Ahmedabad Mail* 9105, 12:35pm, 7½ hr., Rs146/640).

Buses: Main Bus Stand (tel. 3434). Show up early if you want to avoid riding in the back seat. To: **Ahmedabad** (12 per day, 6am-9pm, 6hr., Rs55/75); **Jaipur** (3 per day, 12hr., Rs138/184); **Jaisalmer** (6:15am, 10hr., Rs117); **Jodhpur** (12:30pm, 8hr., Rs90); **Surat** (12:30pm, 12hr., Rs100); and **Udaipur** (4 per day, 6hr., Rs62). **Private bus** companies line the main road and offer services to most destinations in Rajasthan and Gujarat. **Shobha Travels** (tel. 38302; open daily 7am-10:30pm), near Hotel Samrat, and **Baba Travels** (tel. 38747; open daily 7am-11pm), near the taxi stand, are recommended, but **Najat Travels,** across from the Telecom Office, charges Rs5 less because it has its own buses. **Private buses** depart from the taxi stand and along the main road. All bus transportation arranged in Mt. Abu departs from Mt. Abu, but **arrangements from other cities to Mt. Abu may only come as far as Abu Road.** Check in advance.

Local Transportation: Buses to Abu Rd. frequently depart from the Main Bus Stand (every 30min., 6am-9pm, 1hr., Rs15). Jeeps and vans serving as local **taxis** depart from the taxi stand. A shared taxi to Abu Rd. costs Rs15-25, a private taxi Rs200 roundtrip. To the Dilwara Temples, private taxis cost Rs50-60 roundtrip. Shared taxis (Rs3) and vans (Rs5) to the Dilwara Temples leave from the Central Bazaar.

Tourist Office: Tourist Reception Centre, (tel. 3151), opposite the bus stand, provides good maps, brochures, travel information for all of Rajasthan and city tours (8:30am and 1:30pm, 5hr., Rs35-40). Open M-Sa 10am-1:30pm and 2-5pm.

Currency Exchange: State Bank of India (tel. 3136; fax 38882), near General Hospital, exchanges currency and wires money. **State Bank of Bikaner and Jaipur** (tel. 3224), behind the GPO, changes traveler's checks and currency. **Bank of Baroda** (tel. 3166), near the taxi stand, gives cash advances on credit cards (1% service charge; sells BOB traveler's checks). All open M-F 10am-2pm, Sa 10am-noon.

Market: The **Central Bazaar** is Mt. Abu's main market. Open M-Sa 9am-10pm.

Police: Main Police Station (tel. 3333), near Main Bus Stand. English-speaking and tourist-friendly. Open 24hr.

Hospital: J. Watumull Global Hospital and Research Centre (tel. 3347 or 38348), 1km out of town on the road to Dilwara Temples, is an ultra-clean, ultra-modern private facility. Open M-Sa 9am-1pm and 3-5pm.

Post Office: GPO (tel. 3017). *Poste Restante* M-Sa 9am-5pm. Registered mail and parcel service M-F 9am-3pm, Sa 9am-2pm. **Postal Code:** 307501.

Telephones: STD/ISD booths are located along Nakki Lake Rd. Most open daily 8am-11pm, and many offer fax services. The **Telecom Centre** (tel. 3107; fax 3729), near the taxi stand, offers STD/ISD, fax, telex, and telegraph services. Open M-Sa 8am-8pm, Su 10am-5pm. **Telephone Code:** 02974.

ACCOMMODATIONS

Most of the hotels in Mt. Abu cater to the honeymoon crowd, so doubles are the norm. Some hotels offer honeymoon suites, often booked weeks in advance. Visitors arrive here in droves from April to June and September to December, and especially around **Diwali** (Nov. 7, 1999; Oct. 26, 2000). Prices of accommodations at least triple during these peak times, and reservations are essential. As in most tourist locales, touts will accost you at the bus and taxi stands. The dozens of "youth hostels" around town are intended for students at Mt. Abu private schools. Most hotels have travel, laundry, and room service, and 9am check-out.

Shree Ganesh Hotel (tel. 3591), near Nakki Lake on the road up to the Maharaja of Jaipur's summer palace. Popular because of its separation from the main clusters and relative value. The rooms are sparse, but they have TVs and attached baths. Garrulous owner. Doubles Rs50-120; triples and quads Rs300-400. Extra bed Rs25.

Hotel Surya Darshan (tel. 3165; fax 38900). The best value of the western Polo Grounds group. Rooms are big and clean, with attached baths. Singles Rs150, with color TV and views of the Polo Grounds Rs200; doubles Rs200/250.

Hotel Rajdeep (tel. 3525), opposite the bus stand. The arched building that houses this hotel has seen better days. Still, the rooms here are clean and large and the lawn is a nice place to relax. Attached baths and hot water buckets (Rs5). Doubles Rs90-150; 20% discount for singles.

Hotel Lakeview, Nakki Lake (tel. 38659). An odd, irregularly leveled, whitish build-ing with a step-garden in front. Big, well-lit rooms with tie-dye bed spreads and attached baths. Lakeside balconies have swings and excellent views. Singles Rs100-200; doubles Rs300-400; luxurious lakeside rooms Rs500-700.

Hotel Samrat International (tel. 3173 or 3153), on the main road opposite the Polo Field. Ordinary rooms are simple, clean, and comfortable. The honeymoon and VIP suites have arched wood beds, swings, and mild erotica on the bathroom tiles. Singles Rs70; singles and doubles with attached bath and TV Rs130/200; hon-eymoon suites Rs450. VIP suites Rs450, with A/C Rs700.

FOOD

Restaurants in Mt. Abu serve both Gujarati and Rajasthani cuisines, and many offer Punjabi and Chinese dishes as well. Between the Central Bazaar and the main bus stand, *dhabas* offer quick service and roadside seating.

Hilltone Hotel, near the Main Bus Stand. There are two excellent restaurants and a bar in this large, luxurious hotel. The **Handi Restaurant** is veg. and offers indoor or garden seating. The food is superb and most entrees are Rs40-60. Both open daily 7-11pm. The **Kalali Bar** is also in the hotel, with domestic and imported drinks. Open daily 11am-11pm.

Takshashila Restaurant (tel. 3173 or 3153), in Hotel Samrat. The best veg. food in town, according to the locals. The restaurant is elegantly decorated with covered wooden chairs, marble floors, and red and white tablecloths. Indian, Chinese, and Continental entrees (Rs40-60), and Aquaguard water! Open daily 7am-11pm.

Karak Dining Hall (tel. 38305), near the Main Bus Stand. Come around lunchtime to see the stainless steel fly in this spacious, undecorated dining hall. Crowds swarm around the excellent Gujarati *thalis* (Rs40). Open daily 7am-10pm.

Chennai Cafe, Nakki Rd., opposite the Bank of Baroda. Good, fast meal/snack joint, specializing in South Indian food. Not as fast as King's Food, but more sanitary.

Dairy King (tel. 3328), opposite King's food. The best of the many ice cream joints around Mt. Abu. Try the stupendous mango and pineapple shakes (Rs35) or the floats, ice cream, and sundaes, all in many flavors. Order, pay, then join the hordes waiting to get their goodies, but watch out for the flies. Open daily 8am-11pm.

Sarovar Restaurant, Nakki Lake. The RTDC finally gets creative—a fake plaster boat jutting into Nakki Lake houses this little snack-bar. The view is beautiful, with lakes up front and gardens to the rear. Occasionally, fishermen try their luck on the deck as well. Snacks Rs20-40. Open daily 8am-10pm.

SIGHTS AND ENTERTAINMENT

Dilwara Jain Temple
Location: *3km northeast of town.* **Hours:** *Open to non-Jains noon-6pm.* **Admission:** *Free.* **Other:** *Photography, and leather items prohibited.*

The cluster of marble Jain temples houses within its worn grey simple stone exterior some of the country's most amazing marble sculpture. The main temple, an 11th-cen-tury construction by Vimal Shah, Chief Minister to the Solanki King, is dedicated to the first *tirthankara* (crossing-maker) Adinath. Devotees of art and Adinath alike flock to Dilwara to see the immaculately carved pillars of dancers and spiralling lotus domes which adorn the halls that house 57 smaller *tirthankara* statues. The ceiling depicts different myths, one playfully illustrating Krishna and his *gopis.* Other domes depict various goddesses soaring overhead, detailed down to the fingernails.

The central dome is alive with more dancing and a triumphant marble elephant overhead turning up his smooth white trunk in homage to Adinath. Sarnavasaian workers toiled on this colossal achievement for 14 years, supposedly being paid in amounts corresponding to the weight of marble removed, inspiring them to create the finest, most intricate carvings. The balconies to either side of the main sanctuary, built by two brothers, are almost identically decorated save the last figure on the left, who is bent in due respect to the work of the elder.

A step into the outer sanctuary leaves the pomp and design far behind. The dome and walls are uncarved so as to not disturb meditation. The statue of Adinath is modeled on a 3500-year-old granite statue housed in the back corner of the temple; according to legend, Vimal Shah discovered the statue on this very spot under a sweet-smelling champa tree revealed to him in one of his dreams.

Even more intricate are the curling arches of the second largest temple, dedicated to the 22nd *tirthankara,* Neminath, also the cousin of Krishna. Its breathtaking tiered lotus dome was carved from a single marble stone. Both temples house marble memorials to their patrons, seated atop models of the elephants who faithfully transported the building materials. There are three other temples in the complex, including a 16th-century dedication to Mahavira and another tribute to Adinath Rishabdeo. Another is a memorial to the gifted workers, constructed of many types of stone and dedicated to *tirthankara* Parshvanath. Menstruating women are forbidden to enter. Unofficial guides give tours and appreciate a tip or a donation to the temple.

Other Sights

Visiting **Nakki Lake,** where most of Mt. Abu's activity is focused, is a bit like visiting a carnival—crowding the short street to the lake are small shops alongside popcorn sellers, fast-food restaurants, rather conspicuous photo stalls, and brightly decorated ponies. *(Pony rides Rs20 per 30min.)* A mob constantly clamors for the paddleboats or rowboats, available from the dock from competing agencies (Rs50 per 30min.). The festive ambience tends to obscure the religious significance of this lake, thought to contain holy waters, having been dug out with merely the *nakh* (nails) of a god. To experience the lake more placidly, take a scenic walk along the left bank leading past the small **Ragunath Temple** to the quiet bank opposite, lined with its huge estates and stately homes. Keep your eyes open for the many bizarre granite rock formations that overlook the lake.

Sunset Point lies along the left fork from the main road past the taxi stand. Although once it surely offered a beautiful cliff view of the setting sun, the constant rabble of tourists here has made it is much more of a people-watching spot. A similar fate has befallen **Honeymoon Point,** off the road leading northwest behind **Nakki Lake.** Though the view from here is also superlative, the name has drawn truculent newlyweds by the dozen. More remote viewpoints are **The Crags,** beyond Honeymoon Point, the remote **Shanti Shikar,** east of the Crags, and the surprising **Summer Palace** of the maharaja of Jaipur, sitting on the hill south of Nakki Lake. If you choose to explore these areas, it's best not to do so alone.

A left off the northeast road to Dilwara leads to the base of what can easily prove to be a good 30-minute heart-pumper. Three hundred and sixty steps make their way up the mountainside to the **Adhar Devi Temple,** dedicated to the patron goddess of Mt. Abu. The "temple" is actually a natural cleft in the rocky mountaintop that can only be entered by crawling, and offers a spectacular view of the green valleys below.

Back in town across from the GPO is the bizarre **Government Museum,** displaying a huge collection of stone chunks and slabs from assorted archaeological hunts. Most of it dates from the 8th through 12th centuries and comes from Jain temples. *(Open Sa-Th 10am-4:30pm. Admission Rs3, Rs1 for students, free on M.)*

■ Near Mount Abu

Eight kilometers past Dilwara is **Achalgarh,** where a small 9th-century temple to Achaleshwar Mahadev, an incarnation of Shiva, stands amid the heavy, sweet scent of the plentiful *champa* trees. The temple marks a small, supposedly bottomless crater that was created by the impact of Shiva's big toe. The temple also contains a 4320kg Nandi statue of silver, brass, gold, copper, and tin. Outside the temple is a tank which, according to legend, was once filled with *ghee.* Lard-loving demons, dressed as buffalo, attempted to lap up the grease, but the king, ever-vigilant when it came to clarified butter, killed them. The three stone buffalo flanking the tank are the beasts' remains. Another five minutes up this same road is **Guru Shikar,** the highest point in Rajasthan (1721m). It is marked by a small Vishnu temple. The long climb up will make you appreciate the cold drinks stand back down at the bottom.

■ Jodhpur जोधपुर

Once the capital of the state of Marwar (literally, "Land of Death") and home to the warrior clans of Rathore, Jodhpur (pop. 720,000) has a past rife with royalty and valor. In the 18th century the city was overrun by the Mughals, and Maharaja Ajit Singh was exiled to Afghanistan and then murdered. The Mughals tried to legitimize their rule by claiming that there was no one left to take the throne of Jodhpur. Thirty years later, Maharaja Ajit Singh II—kidnapped as an infant and brought up secretly in a tiny Himalayan village—rode through the city gates at the head of an enormous army and drove out the Mughals, who never returned.

Jodhpur cultivates such legends, and even the modern city is engulfed by their spirit. As the sun rises on the eastern edge of the Thar Desert, the elaborate towers of Jodhpur's ancient buildings poke into the daylight; they remind us of a vivid history of maharajas, princesses, caravans crossing sand dunes, and walls protecting the city from the beasts and bandits of the desert night. As daylight penetrates the canopy of centuries-old stone houses, Rajasthan's second-largest city comes to life, and the fairytales mix with the realities of industry, grime, and poverty. Jodhpur, however, remains vibrant and its people resilient. The city is awash with color, from the deep reds and blues of *bandhani* cloth to the bright fuchsia of hanging bougainvillea, from the brilliant yellow of the scorching desert sun, to the sea-blue walls of the old city houses.

ORIENTATION

Jodhpur's **sher,** or old city, is enclosed by a stone wall with eight entrance gates, of which **Jalori Gate** and **Sojati Gate,** on the south side of town, are the most important—the busiest commercial centers surround them. The **new city** expands to the south and east of the *sher.* **Jodhpur Railway Station** lies to the southwest of Sojati Gate along **Station Road.** Outside the station, three main roads fan out from a statue of a horseman. **Olympic Cinema Road,** to the far left, leads to the **telegraph office.** The road directly ahead of the statue, leads to Jalori Gate, the best way into the old city. Station Rd., leading off to the right toward Sojati Gate, is lined with cheap hotels and restaurants. **High Court Road** is the main east-west avenue, running from Sojati Gate past the **Umaid Gardens** and the **Tourist Reception Centre** to the distant **Raika Bagh Railway Station,** just opposite the **bus stand,** where it bends north toward **Paota Circle.**

Nai Sarak, or New Road, leads through Sojati Gate to the old city's biggest shopping thoroughfare and then to the market area, **Sadar Bazaar,** at the base of the **clock tower** that marks the center of Jodhpur. The magnificent **Meherangarh Fort** (way up there), and **Jaswant Thada** can be seen from almost everywhere. Both can be reached by a short auto-rickshaw ride up a winding mountain road. From the base of the **clock tower,** the **Umaid Bhawan Palace** sits alone in the distance to the southwest. The **airport** is a 15-minute drive south.

PRACTICAL INFORMATION

Transportation

Airport: Jodhpur Airport (tel. 142 or 630617). 6km from the city center, down Airport Rd. 15min. from town by auto-rickshaw (Rs40) or taxi (Rs90). To: **Delhi** (6 per week, 2hr., US$135); **Jaipur** (3 per week, 45min., US$70); **Mumbai** (6 per week, US$120); **Udaipur** (3 per week, 45min., US$55). **Indian Airlines,** Airport Rd., (tel. 636757 or 636758). Open daily 10am-1:15pm and 2-4:30pm.

Trains: Jodhpur Railway Station, Railway Station Rd. (tel. 131 or 132). Prices are 2nd/1st class. To: **Ahmedabad** (*Marwar Express,* 3:25 and 9:05pm, 8hr., Rs135/532); **Bikaner** (Jammu Exp. 4806, 8:10pm, 5hr., Rs72/500); **Delhi** (*Mandore Exp.* 4862, 7:30pm, 12hr., Rs140/866); **Jaipur** (*Intercity Exp.* 2466, 6am, 5hr., Rs89/252); **Jaisalmer** (*Jaisalmer Exp.* 4810, 11pm, 7hr., Rs72/518); **Udaipur** (10:15am and 10pm, 12hr., Rs47/307). Reserve at the **Advance Reservation Office,** Station

Rd. (tel. 636407), located to the right of the GPO. A tourist quota line is available, but all lines are unbelievably slow; plan to be there at least an hour. Reservations for long trips should be made several days in advance, especially in 1st class. Open M-F 8am-1:45pm and 2-8pm, Su 8am-1:45pm. **Raika Bagh Railway Station,** High Court Rd. Down High Court Rd. under a bridge, near the bus station. East-bound trains stop at this station after departing from the main station.

Buses: Main Bus Station, High Court Rd. (tel. 544686 or 544989). Features a retiring room and a disorganized ticket-purchasing system. To: **Ahmedabad** (8 per day, 5:30am-10pm, 12hr., Rs181); **Agra** (7am, 4 and 8:45pm, 12hr., Rs221); **Bikaner** (12 per day, 5am-10:30pm, 6hr., Rs101); **Delhi** (6 per day, 9am-8:15pm, 13hr., Rs232; deluxe at 4pm, 11hr., Rs347); **Jaipur** (every hr., 5:15am-10:15pm, 8hr., Rs129; 5 deluxe per day, 11am-11:30pm, 7hr., Rs158); **Jaisalmer** (1:30pm, 7hr., Rs89; deluxe at 5:30am, 6hr., Rs133); **Osian** (every 30min., 5:30am-9pm, 3hr., Rs25); **Udaipur** (5 per day, 7:30am-10pm, 9hr., Rs105; deluxe 5:30am, noon, 3, and 10:30pm, Rs129). **Private bus companies** number in the dozens; most are located along High Court Rd. Their fares are generally lower than the government bus fares, but their departure times are even less rigid. Tickets can be booked through the Tourist Reception Centre on High Court Rd. **Solanki Tours,** Station Rd., located opposite the railway station, rents buses to tourists (min. Rs6 per km).

Local Transportation: Small, convenient local **buses** (every 2-10min, Rs1-3) run by the railway stations, the bus stand, and along all major roads. A/C **taxis** lurk at all the major sights and in front of the tourist bungalow. Fares are at least Rs3 per km, min. Rs60. Smaller side streets are inaccessible by taxi, particularly in the old city. **Car hire** (Rs3-6 per km) is available from the Tourist Reception Centre and private travel agencies. **Auto-rickshaws,** the best way to maneuver through the small streets of the old city, congregate around all the major sights and stations. You should be able to get anywhere in the city center for Rs10-30. Rates are unmetered and negotiable. **Tempos** (Rs1-5), though less common than auto-rickshaws, can be found all over the city. **Bicycles** are a chaotic but fun way to explore the city. **Hanif Cycle Store,** in front of a wall opposite the railway station's statue of Maharaja Umed Singh, charges Rs2 per hr., Rs25 per day.

Tourist and Financial Services

Tourist Office: Government of Rajasthan Tourist Reception Centre, High Court Rd. (tel. 545083). From the railway station, up Station Rd. past Sojati Gate to High Court Rd., past the Umaid Gardens, on the left. Helpful, English-speaking staff provides maps, train and bus schedules, and reservations. **Sight-seeing tours** operate daily in season (off-season: M-Sa) 9am-1pm and 2-6pm, Rs60 per person (min. 4), plus Rs40 in entry fees. Open daily Apr.-Sept. 8am-7pm.

Currency Exchange: State Bank of India (tel. 544247 or 544169). Near Paota Circle on campus of Rajasthan High Court. Change currency and traveler's checks with no service charge. Also offers money-wiring and telex services. **Bank of Baroda,** Sojati Gate (tel. 636539), just below Hotel Arun. Traveler's checks and cash advance with major credit cards. Both open M-F 10am-2pm, Sa 10am-noon. Many banks and hotels also exchange currency but don't cash traveler's checks.

Local Services

Pharmacy: Chemists exist in particularly dense concentrations near hospitals, around Sojati and Jalori Gates and along Nai Sarak. Most open daily 8am-11pm.

Market: High Court Rd., Nai Sarak, and Sadar Bazaar are the main shopping areas. Fresh fruit and vegetable stalls and stores are found in Sadar Bazar and along Station Rd. Most stores open daily 8am-10pm, closed one weekday near the end of each month. Stores near Sojati Gate market occasionally close on Su and M.

Bookstore: Rathi's Media Centre, Ratanada Rd. (tel. 634580). On the bridge over the railroad tracks. Has a large collection of assorted paperbacks, children's books, reference works, and current best-sellers, plus newspapers and international magazines (including *Time, The Economist,* and *Vogue*). Open daily 8am-9pm.

Library: Sumer Public Library, High Court Rd., in Umaid Gardens, has a small collection of English books and newspapers. No check-out fee. Open daily 6am-8pm.

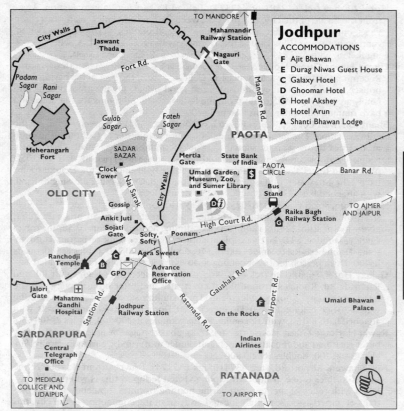

Luggage Storage: Jodhpur Railway Station, in the cloakroom. Rs3 for first day, Rs5 for the second, and Rs6 per additional day. Store at your own risk.

Emergency and Communications

Police: Ratanada Rd. (tel 633700). English-speaking, particularly helpful to tourists. **Ladies' police station** (tel. 641001) in Sadar Bazaar.

Emergency: Police, tel. 100. **Fire,** tel. 101. **Ambulance,** tel. 102 or 103.

Hospital: Mahatma Gandhi Hospital, Mahatma Gandhi Hospital Rd. (tel. 636437), between Sojati and Jalori Gates, also accessible from the Station Rd. side. English-speaking staff. Open 24hr. **Private hospitals** abound. The best are **Goyal Hospital,** Residency Rd. (tel. 32144) and **Jodhpur Hospital,** Shastri Nagar (tel. 48100), both near the Medical College; **Sun City Hospital** is in Paota Circle.

Post Office: Jodhpur Head Post Office, Station Rd. (enquiries tel. 636695, postmaster tel. 636746). Large building on Railway Station Rd., near the main Railway Station toward Sojati Gate. Enter on the left side, closest to the rail station. *Poste Restante* available. Open daily 10am-5pm. **Postal Code:** 342001.

Telephones: Dial 197 for directory assistance. **Telephone Code:** 0291.

ACCOMMODATIONS

Budget hotels thrive near the Jodhpur Railway Station and along Nai Sarak. Travelers staying in these central locations will feel the heart of the city lub-dubbing around them. Hotels on Airport Rd. and near Raika Bagh Railway Station offer quieter but less enticing accommodations. The Tourist Reception Centre will set up tourists with local families for Rs200-500 per night.

Hotel Akshey (tel. 612481 or 437327). Behind Raika Bagh Railway Station. Away from the bustle of the city, this place is sweetly serene and immaculate. Travel services, currency exchange, room service, TVs and phones, STD/ISD at reception, running hot water. Check-out 24hr. Dorm beds Rs50. Singles Rs175, with air-cooling Rs250, with A/C Rs400; doubles Rs225/325/550. Extra beds Rs50.

Durag Niwas Guest House, 1st Old Public Park (tel. 639092). South of Tourist Reception Centre, near K.M. Hall Girls' College. One of the best of the paying guest houses, provides a homey atmosphere at good prices. Owner "Mr. Desert" and family are very knowledgeable about the Jodhpur area. All rooms are air-cooled and have running hot water 24hr. Rooms Rs200-500.

Shanti Bhawan Lodge, Station Rd. (tel. 621689; fax 639211). Directly opposite the railway station. The former residence of the prime minister of Jodhpur—the enormous front doors were designed to repel elephant attacks. Small, clean, basic rooms overlook a noisy main road and open courtyards. Friendly staff. STD/ISD phone and travel agency. Midtown Restaurant is right underneath. Deluxe rooms have 24hr. hot water; others get buckets of the stuff. Check-out 24hr. Singles Rs80, with attached bath Rs140; doubles Rs250; deluxe Rs700.

Hotel Arun, Sojati Gate (tel. 620238; fax 543019). Opposite Sojati Gate. Moderately sized rooms with great vantages of the crazy streets below. Surprisingly quiet, given its location. 24hr. room service, dining hall open 6am-10:30pm, travel agency, laundry, STD/ISD, fax, photocopier, massage. Bank of Baroda is downstairs. Dorm beds Rs80. Singles Rs120-170; doubles Rs170-250; triples Rs300; quads Rs400. Extra person Rs40. Air-cooling Rs40 extra. Reservations recommended.

Galaxy Hotel, Sojati Gate (tel. 620796). At the intersection of High Court Rd. and Ratanada Rd. Rooms surround florid courtyards and offer intimate views of the heart of the city. Room service 6am-11pm, laundry services, 24hr. hot running water. 20-bed hall for Rs1500; kitchens Rs500. Dorm beds Rs60. Singles Rs80, with attached bath Rs150, with air-cooling Rs195; doubles Rs200-500; triples Rs300-550.

Rawla Heritage Guest House (tel. 649092), Shastri Nagar. A little out of the way, but a great bed and breakfast (lunch and dinner too!) run by a friendly family. Singles Rs400-700; doubles Rs500-800.

Ajit Bhawan, Airport Rd. (tel. 437410; fax 637774). Down Airport Rd. before the Indian Airlines office. If Rudyard Kipling visited Jodhpur, this is where he'd stay. Filled with relics of the Raj—hunkering hunting trophies, opulently framed portraits of imperialists. Peacefully located away from the commotion of the city, this hotel features individually decorated cottages around a lush garden and swimming pool you won't forget. Fantastic restaurant. Not cheap, but Rudyard was no miser. Half-day village safaris Rs450. Singles Rs1200; doubles Rs1550. Extra bed Rs350. Off-season (Apr.-Sept.): singles Rs1200; doubles Rs1600.

Ghoomar Hotel, High Court Rd. (tel. 544010 or 548010). Abuts the Tourist Reception Centre. Crafts shop, restaurant, travel agency, doctor, and folk music on call. Three-day max. stay. Telephones in all rooms, and running hot water. Large, simply decorated rooms. Check-out noon. Dorm beds Rs60. Singles Rs200, with air-cooling Rs400, with A/C Rs600; doubles Rs300/475/700. 50% discount in July.

FOOD

Jodhpuri dishes such as *kabuli* (rice preparation) and *chakki-ka sagh* (spongy wheat dish) should definitely be savored, preferably over a refreshing *mousmi* (orange drink) or a cold glass of famous saffron-flavored *makhania lassi.* Along Nai Sarak and near Sojati and Jalani Gates you'll find a wide assortment of small **fast-food restaurants** and **stalls** selling drinks, fresh fruits and vegetables, and snack foods.

Midtown Restaurant (tel. 637001), in the Shanti Bhawan Lodge. A great introduction to Rajasthani cuisine, this veg. restaurant features a host of local specialties, including *kabuli* and *chakki-ka sagh* (Rs40 each), as well as the ubiquitous Continental and Chinese dishes—181 dishes in all. The *Rajasthani maharaja thali* (Rs70) samples many Jodhpuri specialties. Open daily 7am-11pm.

On the Rocks, Ajit Bhawan (tel. 611410), adjacent to Ajit Bhawan Hotel, on Airport Rd. Free live Indian classical music presentation every Sa and Su. Well-stocked bar, and nearby coffee shop. Excellent Indian, Chinese, and Continental food. Entrees Rs80-120. Open daily 11am-midnight.

Poonam Restaurant (tel. 547036), High Court Rd., near the intersection with Nai Sarak. Choose from over 200 dishes and sit under fans in dark wood-panelled rooms with mirrors. All-Jain food (pure veg. and nothing that grows underground). Almost everything is Rs10-30. Open daily 11am-4pm and 6-11pm.

Gossip Restaurant, 32 Nai Sarak, in the City Palace Hotel. A much less shameful indulgence than its namesake. Excellent North and South Indian, Chinese, Continental, and Rajasthani veg. food. The dark, cool, **Classic Bar** downstairs takes music requests. Entrees Rs60-80. Open daily 7am-10:30pm.

Kalinga Restaurant, Station Rd. (tel. 627338), in the Adarsh Niwas Hotel. Indian, Continental, Chinese, Italian—a veritable, if typical, potpourri. Be sure to try items from their "Marwari Food Festival" menu, featuring regional specialties for Rs40-70. Their package specialty deals—the *Marwari thali* and *shahi thali,* for Rs50 and Rs80, are particularly excellent. Open daily 11am-3pm and 6-10pm.

Ajit Bhawan Palace Hotel Restaurant (tel. 20409). Off Airport Rd., before the Indian Airlines office. In the florid main courtyard of the hotel, overlooking the swimming pool. Buffet dinner has superb food and live Rajasthani folk music and dance, all for Rs275. Explore the majestic grounds while you're here. Open daily 9am-11pm. Reservations recommended 2hr. in advance.

Agra Sweets, Sojati Gate (tel. 615260). Located directly opposite Sojati Gate. The oldest shop in Jodhpur, where mobs descend on the best *makhania lassi* in town at Rs10 a hit (*Gourmet Magazine* once wanted the recipe). Try *mava kachori,* and *ras-malai* (the shop's specialty). A wide range of sweets and Rajhasthani snacks are also available. Open daily 8am-8pm.

Softy Softy (Janta Sweet Home), 3 Nai Sarak, across from Priya Hotel. The best ice cream joint in town. The slushies are an excellent cure for the homesick. Enjoy juice, sundaes, ice cream, and milkshakes in A/C comfort. Open daily 10am-11pm.

SIGHTS

Meherangarh Fort

Hours: *Open daily 8am-5pm.* **Admission:** *Rs30.* **Other:** *Camera fee Rs50, video fee Rs100. Government-guided tours Rs60.*

Rising magnificently above Jodhpur, Meherangarh dominates the city's landscape. The fort is a blend of well-designed defense systems and amazing artistry. Eight *pols* (gates) mark the entrances to various parts of the fort. The formidable **Jayapol** is the main entrance commemorating Maharaja Man Singh's military achievements, and the impressive **Fatehpol** (Victory Gate), created by Maharaja Ajit Singh after his return from exile, marks the original entrance into the fort. The **Lohapol** (Iron Gate), where 15 handprints mark the *sati* sacrifice of Maharaja Man Singh's widows, is particularly dramatic. Despite modern anti-*sati* sentiment, Jodhpuris pay tribute at this gate daily. The final gigantic **Surajpol** marks the entrance to the tiny **Fort Museum,** located in the sculpted red sandstone palace. Features of the museum include extravagant *howdahs* (elephant mounts), exquisite wood and ivory artifacts (including assorted boxes, pipes, toys, and carpet-holders), a weapons room, the royal dumbbells of the maharani, a beautifully woven 250-year-old tent canopy, 150 types of cannon (so they say), fancy baby cradles, musical instruments, paintings, and a 300-piece turban collection. Of particular interest is the **Phool Mahal** (Flower Palace), an elaborately mirrored dining hall. Turn off the flash on your camera here or risk blinding everyone in the room. The **Moti Mahal** (Pearl Palace), a conference room with a glass and gold ceiling, is ostentatious yet serene. The nearby **Chamunda Temple** is less interesting, but check out the view of the blue city from the temple before leaving. Don't bother taking the lift—the view is better if you walk. As you exit, noisy "traditional" musicians will surround you, demanding *baksheesh*. Ten minutes from the fort by foot down a windy road is the **Jaswant Thada,** a pillared marble memorial to the beloved Maharaja Jaswant Singh II, erected by his wife after his death. (*Open daily 8am-5pm. Free. Photography not allowed inside.*) Locals liken it to a miniature Taj Mahal; the structures are quite similar, as are the legends explaining their constructions. Smaller marble cenotaphs are nearby. The view of the city from here is splendid in its own right.

The City

The **Umaid Bhawan Palace** is a majestic marble-and-sandstone palace, the eminent edifice of the eastern part of the city. *(Open daily 8am-5pm. Admission Rs40, including tour. Cameras strictly prohibited.)* The palace offers well-kept, picnic-perfect gardens. A grandiose hotel and restaurant consume half the palace, while an eccentric museum containing traditional art, models, weapons, trophies, and miscellaneous relics—all belonging to the maharaja—occupies the rest.

Back in the center of the city, the **Clock Tower** stalwartly marks the center of the *sher* and the splenetic Sadar Bazar. Along High Court Rd. lie Jalori Gate and Sojati Gate, large, simply carved structures more interesting for their adjoining commercial centers than as sights, and the **Umaid Gardens** near the Tourist Bungalow. *(Open Sa-Th 9am-noon, 3-6pm. Free.)* The gardens make for pleasant strolling, and they contain the Sumer Library, a rudimentary "zoo," and a rather dull museum.

ENTERTAINMENT

What little nightlife Jodhpur has is geared to foreign tourists. **On the Rocks** and **City Palace Hotel** both have popular bars. There are **Hindi cinemas** everywhere; two of the most popular are Girdhar Mandir Cinema on Nai Sarak and Olympic Cinema near the Railway Station.

The annual **Marwar Festival** (Oct. 23-24, 1999; Oct. 12-13, 2000) showcases local culture, history, dance, music, art, and most of all, food. All restaurants load their menus with high-priced regional specialties. Less theme-oriented than other Rajasthani festivals, the Marwar Festival is intended mostly as a rollicking good time.

SHOPPING

The **Sojati Gate** and **Nai Sarak** areas, especially **Sadar Bazar** by the Clock Tower, are constellations of stalls, markets, emporia, and department stores. Everything can be found here, from craft works to stereo equipment. Haggling is expected nearly everywhere, and the best deals await those who are willing to brave the cacophonous bazaar scene. However, there are also fixed-price shops that offer high quality Rajasthani crafts at good prices. For gold and silver jewelry, utensils, and decorations, try **Saraswati Jewels** (tel. 622526), next to Sojati Gate (open Tu-Su noon-9pm).

Handicrafts are one of Jodhpur's largest industries, and excellent art shops abound. Two of the best are **Rajasthan Arts and Crafts** (tel. 639220 or 639420; open 9am-7:30pm) and **Ajay Art Emporium** (tel. 624636; open daily 9am-8pm), both near Circuit House on Umaid Bhawan Palace Road. They offer a huge selection of items in wood, brass, marble, iron, clay, *papier mâché*, and textiles—all hand-made in Rajasthan. For more prudent prices and a more intimate atmosphere, try the **Emporium Merustholy**, High Court Road (tel. 547684). Also available are the beautiful and fabulously colorful cloths and *saris* of Rajasthan, including the traditional *bhandani saris*, which are tie-dyed. On Nai Sarak, the **National Handloom Corporation** (tel. 623096 or 620734; open daily 10am-9pm), Rajasthan's largest department store, sells *saris*, carpets, and cotton cloth, with prices starting at Rs95. **Lovely Silk Palace,** Railway Station Rd. (tel. 621590; open M-Sa 9:30am-9pm), and **Lucky Silk Stores,** Sojati Gate (tel. 622221 or 624221; open daily 10:30am-9pm), both sell cloth and hand-made *saris* from all over India.

VILLAGE SAFARIS

Guided tours of the villages in the desert around Jodhpur allow visitors to witness and participate in carpet-making, weaving, spinning, foraging, indigenous medicine, and cooking. In particular, the villages of the **Bishnoi** leave visitors feeling enlightened and environmentally conscious: their religion, which originated in the 15th century, is devoted to environmental protection and conservation. Maharaj Swaroop Singh (not the maharaja himself but a member of the big guy's family) sometimes personally leads tours, arranged through the Ajit Bhawan Hotel (tel. 637410; Rs400 per person, 5hr., 8am, including lunch). Mr. Parbat Singh arranges tours and cross-desert camel

Turban Legends

Once upon a time, no one wore turbans in India; the idea of wrapping 7 to 10 meters of cotton cloth around the head had simply never entered popular imagination. This changed forever one day in 1526, when the beturbanned Mughals poured into northern India and conquered it. The invasion sent shock waves through the world of South Asian fashion, and the repercussions are still with us today. Originally worn as a sign of respect when appearing before a Mughal official, they soon became an indicator of status among high-caste Hindus and a symbol of the Sikh religion.

In Rajasthan, turban colors and styles vary according to region; the turbans of Jaipur are different than those of Jaisalmer, which will never be the same as those of Udaipur. In Bikaner, *brahmins* wear a yellow turban except when mourning, when they cut their hair off and switch to white headwear. Bikaner Rajputs, a *kshatriya* caste, wear brightly colored, striped, or *bandhani* (tie-dyed) turbans wrapped around one ear with a long tail in the back. Jats and Bishnois, the farming castes, wear enormous white turbans called *safas. Vaishya* castes wear small turbans called *pagoris.* Untouchables and *shudras* are not allowed to wrap their heads at all. Because of the headgear's religious and social significance, turbans can show shame as well as status. Debtors and criminals often have their turbans forcibly removed in public—a popular form of mob justice.

safaris (as far as Jaisalmer and Bikaner, Rs500-900 per person, per day). Contact him at Meherangarh Fort (tel. 548790). The **Ghoomar Tourist Bungalow** also offers tours (5hr. tour Rs700 per 2 people, day-long tour Rs485 per person).

■ Near Jodhpur

Once the capital of Marwar, the town of **Mandore,** 9km north of Jodhpur still houses the cenotaphs (tombs) of the Rathore maharajas, including that of Ajit Singh. Near the tidy garden where the cenotaphs stand is the **Hall of Heroes,** a series of 15 colorful, life-size statues of Hindu gods and Rajput warriors carved out of one large rock wall. Also nearby is the **Shrine of the 330 Million Gods,** a polytheistic site of celebration and triumph. Mandore is accessible from Jodhpur by local buses (Rs2-3).

The ancient town of **Osian,** 65km north of Jodhpur, reachable by bus, and surrounded by sand dunes, is home to 16 sculpted Jain and Hindu temples from the 8th-11th centuries. Osian is accessible by regular buses from Jodhpur (see **Practical Information,** p. 301).

For beautiful picnic spots, try **Kailana Lake,** about 11km from town on Jaisalmer road, or **Balsamand Lake and Palace,** about 7km from town (Rs75-100 by auto-rickshaw). Both are man-made tanks. Balsamand Lake is surrounded by 12th-century mango, guava, papaya, and date groves.

■ Jaisalmer जैसलमेर

In the heart of the Thar Desert, 285km west of Jodhpur and 100km from the Pakistan border, lies the "Golden City" of Jaisalmer. While other spots in Rajasthan have been inundated by grosser—and to the Western eye, more visible—incarnations of consumerism, such as garish billboards and splenetic traffic, Jaisalmer markets itself much more charmingly. Most of Jaisalmer's old city is still contained within the remains of its city walls, and its winding, gritty streets are crowded (more by pedestrian creatures than motorized ones). Exploring these streets is like walking into a fairy tale—the city can subtly cajole the hardest of backpackers to succumb to its enigmatic and innocent charm. Although the city is flooded with tourists during the winter, and though tourism is its major industry, the local people's traditional, conservative way of life preserves the city's identity and keeps it from seeming like some sort of giant amusement park with cows.

Built originally as a strategic fort, Jaisalmer was twice sacked and conquered by Muslim invaders before becoming a prosperous trade center for camel caravans in the 17th century. Maritime trade under the British eclipsed the desert trade routes, and Partition in 1947 cut them off altogether, diminishing Jaisalmer's wealth and importance. With the Indo-Pakistan tensions of the 1960s, however, Jaisalmer became a military outpost, and the army presence is now a source of income second only to the booming tourism industry. Now, Jaisalmer primarily offers camel safaris amid Jain temples, desert craftwork and cuisine, and peerless *havelis* (royal mansions) that retain sandstorm-sculpted memories of the city's golden years.

ORIENTATION

Hanuman Circle is just outside **Amar Sagar Pol,** the main entrance to the old city. Littered with jeeps, buses, and taxis for hire, adjacent to a market, Hanuman Circle is easily identified by a bizarrely placed jet fighter, a relic from a war with Pakistan. The **local bus stand** is north of this circle. **Sam Road** heads east from the circle into the city. Just inside Amar Sagar Pol is **Gandhi Chauk,** the main market area. The entrance to **Badal Mahal,** the old royal palace, is just inside the gate area on the right. This same road leads narrowly through the market to the **fort.** The road continues to the north of the fort to the **Gopa Chauk** market before winding its way to **Gadi Sagar Pol,** the east gate of the city. From here the road becomes **Gadi Sagar Road** and ends at Lake Gadisan, or Gadi Sagar. A left turn just outside of Gadi Sagar Pol leads to the remote **Main Bus Stand** and **Railway Station.**

PRACTICAL INFORMATION

Trains: Jaisalmer Railway Station (tel. 52354; enquiry 51301). Out of Gadi Sagar Pol, bear left, 10min. away on your left. Reservation counter open daily 8am-8pm. Platforms are open to passengers 1hr. before the departure of each train. Passenger trains leave for **Jodhpur** (2JPJ, 7:30am; *Exp.* 4809, 10:30pm, 8hr., Rs124/336). The night train is much cooler and faster.

Buses: Main Bus Stand (tel. 51541), near the Railway Station. Open daily 5am-11pm. To: **Ahmedabad** (6pm, 12hr., Rs173); **Bhuj** (2:15pm, 16hr., Rs198); **Bikaner** (8 per day, 7-9hr., Rs84-120); **Jaipur** (7am, 15hr., Rs198; deluxe 5:30pm, 12hr., Rs290); **Jodhpur** (7am, 6hr., Rs69; deluxe 5:30pm, 6hr., Rs131); **Mt. Abu** (5:30 and 8:30am, 11hr., Rs177). All buses leave 30min. earlier from the **Local Bus Stand** in Hanuman Circle. Tickets for express buses can be purchased at the local bus stand; there is advance booking for deluxe buses at Hanuman Circle. Tickets for all classes are available at the Main Bus Stand. **Private buses** leave frequently, but departure times are less strict. All hotels and all travel agents can arrange both government and private bus reservations.

Local Transportation: By foot, it takes only 15-20min. to cross the city. **Auto-rickshaws** are unmetered and ubiquitous. You can find them almost anywhere in town except in the Fort during peak tourist hours (8am-noon and 4-7pm), when they are not permitted to enter. Most charge Rs10-15. **Bicycles** are a convenient means of touring Jaisalmer. Try shops inside Amar Sagar Pol, and near the fort gate (Rs2-3 per hr., Rs10-15 per day). Be careful—the roads are hilly. **Jeeps** are needed to get to places outside of the city. Expect to pay Rs3 per km for routes over 80km or Rs6 per km for shorter routes. Travel agents and hotels can rent out their own jeeps at cheaper rates for fixed tours.

Tourist Office: Government of Rajasthan Tourist Reception Centre (tel. 52406). Exit Gadi Sagar Pol and turn right at the first intersection. The tourist bureau is on your right after a 3min. walk. Helpful, English-speaking staff provide bus, train, plane, and camel safari information, maps of Jaisalmer (Rs2), and hotel reservations. Offers tours to Sam to see the sunset (4-5pm, Rs100). Open M-Sa 10am-5pm. The **Moomal Tourist Bungalow** (tel. 52392; fax 52545), on the other side of town, off of Sam Rd., provides basic information. You can also track down **Mr. Nanda Vyas** at either the train station or the RTDC centre; ask for him by name, and he will answer all of your questions.

NORTH INDIA

Jaisalmer

ACCOMMODATIONS

F Deepak Rest House
A Hotel Anurag
E Hotel Nachana Haveli
G Hotel Paradise
B Hotel Pleasure
D Hotel Renuka
C Hotel Swastika

Gadi Sagar
(Lake Gadisan)

TO BIKANER
AND JODHPUR

TO BARMER

Railway Station

Main Bus Stand

Barmer Rd.

Kishanghat Pol

City Walls

Gadi Sagar Pol

Gadi Sagar Rd.

Tilon-ki-Pol and Jaisalmer Folklore Museum

Govt. of Rajasthan

Jama Masjid

Kanchan Shree

Midtown

Salim Singh-ki-Haveli

GOPA CHAUK

Monica

Patwon-ki-Haveli

Sahara Travels

Nathmalji-ki-Haveli

Chainpura St.

Malka Pol

Kalpana

Man Bhavan

FORT

Palace

Jain Temples

Jaisal Castle

City Walls

C
B
D
A
E
GANDHI CHAUK

Trio

Badal Mahal/Mandir Palace

Amar Sagar Pol

Local Bus Stand

HANUMAN CIRCLE

GPO

Sam Rd.

Rampgarh Rd.

Bara Bagh

Moomal Tourist Bungalow

Government Museum

Jawahar Niwas Palace

TO AIRPORT, AMAR SAGAR, AND SAM

Budget Travel: Safari Tours, near Amar Sagar Pol (tel./fax 51058). An excellent source of information on everything in and around Jaisalmer. Open daily 8am-8pm. For more information, see **Camel Safaris,** p. 313.

Currency Exchange: Bank of Baroda, Amar Sagar (tel. 52402), just inside Amar Sagar Pol on the right. Currency exchange, traveler's checks, credit card cash advance. Open M-F 10am-2pm, Sa 10-11am.

Bookstore: Bhatia News Agency, Gandhi Chauk (tel. 52671), on the right past Nachana Haveli, coming from Amar Sagar Pol. A smart, pithy, and generally attractive selection of English, French, Italian, German, and Hindi books, magazines, and newspapers, new and used. Open daily 8am-8pm.

Market: Gandhi Chauk is the main commercial center. **Hanuman Circle** and the **Fort Gate area (Gopa Chauk)** are also shopping districts. Fresh fruit and vegetables are sold from stalls mainly in Gopa Chauk—just remember to wash and/or cook what you buy. Most stores open daily 8am-10pm.

Pharmacy: The **Government Pharmacy** outside Shri Jawahar Hospital is open 24hr.

Hospital: Sri Maheswari Hospital (tel. 50024; direct to doctors 52721), on the left of Sam Rd. after the government hospital past Hanuman Circle. Private, extremely modern, and clean with helpful, English-speaking staff. **Sri Jawahar Government Hospital** (tel. 52343), in the large pillared building on the right of Sam Rd. past Hanuman Circle, before Amar Sagar Pol. Not particularly clean.

Police: Main Police Office, Ramgarh Rd. (tel. 52322, emergency 100). South of Hanuman Circle (on the right when walking south on Ramgarh Rd.). English-speaking and very helpful to tourists.

Post Office: GPO (tel. 52407 or 51377), south of the police station, 5min. from Amar Sagar Pol. Branch offices around the city. All open M-Sa 9am-5pm. **Jaisalmer District Telegraph Office** (tel. 52308 or 52708), on the right going north from Hanuman Circle. Open M-Sa 7am-8pm, Su 8am-3:30pm. **Postal Code:** 345001.

Telephones: STD/ISDs (some with fax service) abound. **Telephone Code:** 02992.

ACCOMMODATIONS

Jaisalmer bristles with budget hotels. New ones pop up by the month as tourism takes over more and more of the city. Large clusters of hotels are found in the fort area and outside the city walls along Sam Rd. All hotels without exception offer **camel safaris** (see p. 313 for more information on the insanely competitive safari situation), as well as other travel services. Expect rates to at least double during the Desert Festival. (Jan 29-31, 1999; Feb. 17-19, 2000. See **Entertainment,** p. 313.)

Hotel Pleasure, Gandhi Chauk (tel. 52323), in Amar Sagar Pol to the left. The Holy Grail of the budget traveler. The rooms are simple, tiled, and of decent size. The owners (two brothers) speak excellent English. Breakfast room service available. Free luggage storage while on camel safari (even if you are on a competitor's safari), free incoming ISD calls, refrigerator/freezer, and free washing machine (bring your own soap). All rooms have air-cooling. Check-out noon. Singles Rs50-60, with bath Rs80-90; doubles Rs120/140. Camel safaris Rs350 per day.

Deepak Rest House (tel. 52665 or 52070; fax 52070). In the Fort near the Jain temple. The best budget hotel in the Fort, with fantastic desert views from clean, modest rooms in the fort wall, some of which occupy large, windowed circular bastions. The labyrinth of hallways and staircases is run by a friendly family fluent in English. Dorm beds Rs20; singles Rs40-50, with attached bath Rs60-80; doubles Rs50-80/100-350. Excellent camel safaris for Rs250-500 per day.

Hotel Renuka, Chainpura St. (tel. 52757; fax 51414). Enter Amar Sagar Pol, left on Chainpura, 5min. down on the left. Familial and clean. 24hr. room service from rooftop veg. restaurant. For Rs500 per hr., the owners can arrange to have folk dancing and music performed on the rooftop. Check-out 10am. Rs250/750 per day for 2½-day jeep/camel safari. Singles Rs50, with bath Rs70; doubles Rs60/90-110. Reservations recommended.

Hotel Swastika, Chainpura St. (tel. 52483). Similar to Hotel Renuka. Well-run, well-decorated, decent-sized rooms around a sunlit courtyard. No restaurant, but they'll prepare bread, jam, and tea for breakfast. Check-out 9am. Singles Rs80, with attached bath Rs120; doubles Rs150/180. 50% discount May-Jun. Camel safaris Rs300 per day. Reservations recommended.

Hotel Paradise (tel. 52674). In the fort to the left. Once a part of the Diwanon ki Haveli, now simply a cool, 400-year-old building. Bask on the rooftop in the glorious sunset panoramas. Carpeted rooms around a central garden. 24hr. room service. Check-out 10:30am. Traditional music and dance in rooftop restaurant at sunset; no flat fee, but tips are expected. Singles Rs80, with bath Rs150, with balcony Rs400; doubles Rs120-250, with bath Rs300-450. Suite with double balcony Rs650. Award-winning camel safaris Rs250-300 per day.

Hotel Anurag, Gandhi Chauk (tel. 57206). A small family hotel with rough-and-ready accommodations for very low rates. Rooms are clean and the atmosphere is very informal. Singles Rs30, with bath Rs40; doubles with bath Rs60. Camel safaris are Rs350 per day and there is a rooftop snack shop in season.

Hotel Jaisal Castle (tel. 52362; fax 52101), in the Fort. Every room has windows and a balcony in this former Maharaja's palace, and the bathrooms are absolutely spotless. Added bonuses include a gracious staff, huge, hand-carved beds, a beautifully tended courtyard, and a rooftop from which to see the most splendiferous sunset in town. Singles Rs500; doubles Rs650; triples Rs850. Extra bed Rs200.

Hotel Nachana Haveli, Gandhi Chauk (tel. 52110; fax 52778). Inside Amar Sagar Pol to the right. Imperial relatives provide royal treatment that doesn't cost a king's ransom. A renovated *haveli* with room decor that includes bear skins and spears. Large, spotless rooms with air-cooling and attached bathrooms; deluxe rooms have bathtubs. Extremely competent staff. Check-out noon. Singles Rs550; deluxe Rs950; doubles Rs650/1150. 50% discount May-Jun.

FOOD

The main reason to eat at restaurants here is the rooftop view, but Jaisalmer also has an earthy desert cuisine not found elsewhere. While every restaurant features Continental and Chinese food, local specialties are basic and savory. Be sure to experience *ker sangri,* a mix of desert capers and beans (it looks like a bundle of gravied twigs); *gatte,* a *garam* flour preparation; and *kadi pakoras,* a yogurt-based appetizer.

Trio Restaurant, Amar Sagar Pol (tel. 52733), next to the Badal Mahal, in Gandhi Chauk. Considered by many to be the best restaurant in Jaisalmer, Trio (tr-EYE-oh) features first-class service, well-prepared specialties, and traditional Rajasthani music at a very reasonable price. The view is great, and a backup generator keeps things humming during power outages. Entrees Rs30-60. Open daily 7am-10:30pm. Reservations recommended in season.

Midtown Restaurant (tel. 50242), Gopa Chauk. Dim red lamps give it an atmosphere as intimate as the view of the Fort. Chockfull of Westerners. The menu contains the usual items, as well as some unusual desserts—the homemade Dutch apple pie is delicious. Rajasthani *thalis* Rs40. Open daily 7am-11pm.

Monica Restaurant (tel. 51586), Gopa Chauk, left of the fort gate. A local favorite with a range of cuisines. Every night, local musicians perform just a betel-spit from the fort. Beer Rs65-75. Entrees Rs30-60. Open daily 8am-2pm and 6:30-10:30pm.

Kalpana Restaurant, Gandhi Chauk (tel. 52469). Located in the heart of Gandhi Chauk, Kalpana offers a rooftop view, specialty *tandoor* cuisine, and one of the best bars in the city. This place is very popular, and not just among tourists. Prices are reasonable at Rs30-35 per entree. Open daily 7am-11pm.

Natraj Restaurant, Salim-Singh-ki-Haveli (tel. 52667). Good food for slightly higher than average prices. Decorated with flags from around the world and surrealist paintings, this place is the only A/C dining room in the city. Standard range of dishes, all well-prepared. Entrees Rs30-50. Open daily 8am-11pm.

Kanchan Shree Restaurant, in Jaganipura near Gopi Chauk Market. Refreshing replenishment central, with juices, ice cream, homemade peanut butter, and 18 flavors of *lassi* to cool parched palates. Open daily 6am-10pm.

Man Bhavan, at the base of the fort, slightly hidden. Local joint serves South Indian and Bengali food for under Rs30. Open 7am-11pm.

Chandan Shree Hotel, Amar Sagar Pol. Cheap, filling *thalis* (Rs12) served by friendly youths. Open 9am-11pm.

SIGHTS

Jaisalmer should truly be appreciated as a whole experience and not just as a sum of its tourist spots. Camel safaris, rolling dunes, and the sand-dusted fort of the old city all contribute to Jaisalmer's unique, mysterious medieval glory.

Jaisalmer Fort

Hours: *Open daily 10am-5pm.* **Admission:** *Rs5.* **Other:** *Video fee Rs10.*

Jaisalmer's **fort,** founded in 1156 by Maharaja Jaisal, a king of the Bhatti clan of Rajputs, overlooks the city from the south. Its 99 circular bastions surround a labyrinthine world of small homes and shops along narrow gullies that wind around the old palace. Enter from Gopa Chauk, the commercial square outside the fort's main gate. The **city palace,** just inside the fort, is open to visitors and is composed of five smaller palaces, one of which has a dancing hall decorated with blue Chinese tiles and green screens from the Netherlands. The old stone rooms are half-preserved; some even remain closed by their original locks, while others store decaying elephant *howdahs* (saddles). A climb to the windy ramparts affords a great view of the fort and old city. It is said that the fort does not have a single cemented joint in its foundation but is constructed stone upon stone from the ground up.

Jain Temples

Hours: *Open daily 8am-noon.* **Admission:** *Free.* **Other:** *Camera fee Rs25, video fee Rs50. Menstruating women prohibited. Library open daily 10-11am or by request, especially if accompanied by an offering of Rs5 or more.*

A cluster of seven interconnected **Jain Temples** lies within the fort, a short walk from the entrance to the palace along the second road to the right. Built on a raised platform, the temples' low archways and tiny halls display amazing sculpture, with not a visible inch spared. A winding staircase leads to a circular balcony with an open view of the sanctuary and the temples' domes below. A magnificent **library** with ancient relics is still farther below.

Old City Havelis

Hours: *Open M-Sa 10am-5pm.* **Admission:** *Free.*

Any walk through the old city will inevitably bring you to one of the three large *havelis,* or mansions. **Patwon-ki-Haveli,** the most impressive of the three, is composed of five joint *havelis* built in the early 1900s by a family of wealthy merchants. The single golden facade rises four dramatic stories, each fitted with stone balconies topped by arched stone umbrellas and exquisite lattice-work windows. While parts of the *haveli* are now occupied by shops selling jewelry and embroidered cloth, two doors still open to reveal stairs up to the building's towering rooftop view of the surrounding sand-brick street. **Nathmalji-ki-Haveli** is another architectural monument built by two rather stubborn brothers, who each took one half of the building's face. The divergent, intricate carvings on the left and right sides of the main door belie this sibling rivalry. This *haveli* can only be seen from outside, since lucky (and hopefully less contentious) families currently live here. **Salim Singh-ki-Haveli,** with peacock buttresses adorning its exterior, was built by the infamous prime minister Salim Singh Mohta around 1800. Considered a tyrant for his crippling taxes, Salim Singh impoverished the populace while securing his power through bribery and crafty legislation. He is said to have attempted to construct two additional levels on his own *haveli* in order to make his home taller than the maharaja's, but the maharaja had the additional levels torn down. Ultimately, Salim Singh's audacity drove the maharaja to have him assassinated.

Other Sights

Lake Gadi Sagar, an artificial reservoir constructed in 1367, was once Jaisalmer's only source of water. Today, it is frequented by bathers, *dhobis,* and visitors who come to view the **Folklore Museum,** which contains quirky paintings and carvings.

(Open daily Aug.-Mar. 8am-6:30pm, Apr.-Jul. 4:30-7:30pm. Admission Rs10.) Gadi Sagar's other attraction is a yellow sandstone gateway, the **Tilon-ki-Pol.** With its grand arched windows, this portal once held beautifully carved windowed rooms in which the royal family stayed during the monsoon. Said to have been built by the king's chief courtesan, the gate was once a source of great controversy for the town's citizens, who refused to allow their womenfolk to walk beneath the "tainted" creation. As a compromise, a smaller entrance to the lake was built to the right side. The lake is now decorated with a few royal stone *chhattris* (cenotaphs).

ENTERTAINMENT

Jaisalmer has little nightlife, but plenty to keep you occupied: the wildest time to come to Jaisalmer is for the annual **Desert Festival** (Jan 29-31, 1999; Feb. 17-19, 2000). Prices double (at least), and tourists mob the place, but you'll still be able to enjoy traditional music and folk dance, camel races, camel polo, camel dances, puppeteers, moustache contests, and more—all consummated by the crowning of Mr. Desert, who is then featured in ads and tourist posters as the unofficial king of Jaisalmer. RTDC sets up a special tourist tent-village for accommodations. The affair is a definite tourist trap—but it's enjoyable nonetheless.

Other diversions include **swimming** in Lake Gadi Sagar (free) or at the indoor pool at Narayan Niwas Palace (near Patwon ki Haveli; Rs150 per hr.). Film fans can indulge at Hindi **cinemas,** including **Ramesh Talkies** (tel. 52242), near Patwon-ki-Haveli.

SHOPPING

Jaisalmer is a haven for **crafts,** including embroidery, patchwork, leather goods, and mirrorwork, as well as stonecarving, silver, and pottery. Bargain hard, and don't attempt to shop during the Desert Festival. **Gandhi Chauk** and the main road past the fort to Gadi Sagar Pol are the main commercial areas. Among fixed-priced shops, government shops tend to be cheaper than private ones, the drawback being that you must arrange shipping yourself. The **Rajasthani Government Emporium** (tel. 52461), just outside Amar Sagar Pol, south of Sam Rd., offers a vast selection of Rajasthani desert handicrafts in brass, silver, wood, and textiles, as well as carpets and paintings. Prices start at Rs50. (Open daily 10am-8pm.) The tailors of **Pansari Bazaar** are skilled, fair, and friendly, particularly Mr. Dunga Ram ("The Tourist Tailor").

CAMEL SAFARIS

Camel safaris are the heart and soul of Jaisalmer's tourist economy, and are a wonderful way to experience the Thar Desert. The camel safari business has become ruthlessly competitive. Every hotel offers camel safaris, as do several independent agencies. But few hotels actually have their own camels; most safaris operate through independent agencies. Hotels pay the agencies about Rs100 per day just for the camels, with food and equipment costs added. For the hotels to make a profit, they must charge at least Rs200 per day. **Indeed, the tourist office recommends spending at least Rs350 per day on safaris.** Deluxe safaris with tents, quality food, portable bars, dancing, music, and other goodies can cost over Rs2000 per day.

If you take the train or bus to Jaisalmer from Jodhpur, expect to be hassled by hotel agents en route. You will be offered incredible deals such as Rs10 hotel rooms, provided you go on that hotel's safari. When you arrive in Jaisalmer, you will be mobbed by touts offering similar deals. All will offer free transportation to the hotel in question. If you express interest in another hotel, touts will pull out the business card of that hotel, claiming that they are authorized to transport patrons. Most touts carry a full deck of Jaisalmer hotel business cards. They will then give you a story about that hotel being closed or full, and take you to their hotel. However, some hotels do provide free transportation without hassle. **Look for hotel banners, not business cards.**

Also, lookout for hotel scams. At some hotels, **if you go on another hotel's or agency's safari, you will be kicked out. Hotel agents will follow you around town** making sure you don't visit other places. If you go on your own hotel's safari, **you may be kicked out the next day as more tourists arrive.**

Once you've chosen a safari, still be wary. Cheap safaris often have **hidden costs,** such as Rs50 or more for bottles of mineral water in the desert heat. They also often skimp on basic amenities such as blankets (it gets very cold in the desert at night) and English-speaking guides. Furthermore, several scams exist to steal your possessions on the return trip. **Never accept offers to watch your luggage** while you explore a sight.

Of course, not all hotels run scams. Many hotels have honest, decent, and inexpensive safaris. The most reliable camel safaris are booked through independent agents. **Safari Tours** (tel. 51508; fax 51414), just inside Amar Sagar Pol, is excellent for general tourist information and safari specialties (open daily 9:30am-7pm). Basic safaris cost Rs450 per day, and deluxe safaris start at Rs1000 per day. Safari Tours is one of the few that genuinely tries to keep the desert clean. Other reputable agencies are **Royal Safari** (tel. 52538), in Nachana Haveli, basic Rs450 per day, deluxe Rs1000 per day; **Caravan Safari** (tel. 51330), in Gandhi Chauk, basic Rs350 per day, deluxe Rs2000 per day; and **Sahara Travels** (tel. 52609), near the Fort Gate, basic Rs250 per day, deluxe Rs550 per day. Ask safari agents to specify all food and equipment; "deluxe" and "basic" can mean many things.

Camel safaris often head to the spectacular Sam sand dunes, stopping at nearby villages and sights along the way. A round-trip takes 4½ days. All hotels and agents offer shorter jeep/camel combos for assorted prices, but you might not get the chance to sleep under the stars in the Thar Desert. Longer cross-desert safaris to Bikaner, Pushkar, or Jodhpur are also available from all of the safari companies listed above.

■ Near Jaisalmer

The areas surrounding Jaisalmer are as interesting as the city proper. Camel and hybrid camel/jeep safaris stop at many of these locales on their way to the sand dunes and are the best means of introduction to them. They are, however, accessible by bus, jeep, and even bicycle. The area 45km west of Jaisalmer is restricted because of border disputes, and special permission is required from the **District Magistrate Office,** near the police station. Permission is never granted for tourist reasons.

About 5km north of Jaisalmer is **Bada Bagh,** where a 500-year-old barrage of sculpted sandstone tombs stands next to the 300-year-old mango trees of the royal garden. An old dam and plush foliage make for a popular picnic spot and sunset watch. Another well-known tiffin spot is **Amar Sagar,** 5km northwest of Jaisalmer, where a beautifully carved Jain temple in a perpetual state of renovation guards an often-dry lake and fertile gardens.

Once the capital of the region, **Lodurva** now lies in ruins 15km north of Jaisalmer. Rebuilt Jain temples are the only remnant of the town's former splendor. An amazing 1000-year-old archway from the original temple still stands in the courtyard of the new one. A cobra occasionally emerges from a small hole in the temple; glimpsing the snake is deemed auspicious. (Open 24hr. Free, camera fee Rs25, video fee Rs50.)

One way or another, most camel safaris end up in **Sam,** an expanse of rippling, desert 42km west of Jaisalmer. The dunes are beautiful at any time, but especially at sunrise and sunset, when the scenery eclipses the growing piles of litter on the overtouristed dunes. Most safaris spend the night on the dunes, sleeping under the stars or in a tent. The RTDC-run Hotel Sam Dhani is also available. Camel rides are available (Rs50-60 per 30min.). There are two daily buses from Jaisalmer, one in the late morning or early afternoon and one in the early evening.

■ Bikaner बीकानेर

The fourth largest city of Rajasthan, Bikaner has been trying to pull in tourists, but its remote location and more spectacular neighbors (Jaisalmer to the west and Jodhpur to the south) have meant tough going for the RTDC in this desert city. Those who trek here, though, are rewarded with Jain temples, an enchanting fort, and (this is, after all, Rajasthan) lots of camels. Moreover, for those weary of the tourist infestation in the rest of the state, Bikaner offers an unvisited feel. The fact that modern, industrial Bikaner doesn't depend on your money is a welcome change, but it also means that there is little tourist infrastructure, making services harder to come by.

Founded in 1488 by Rao Bika, Bikaner was a stop on the Silk Route as well as an important camel breeding ground. In the 16th century, its maharaja, Rei Singh, became one of the most successful generals in Emperor Akbar's well-nigh invincible army; by the 18th century, Bikaner was a power to be reckoned with, a mortal enemy of Jodhpur, and the home of the legendary Bikaner Camel Corps. Since Independence, the city has been almost exclusively concerned with its own economic advancement, and as such has become increasingly industrialized, commercialized, and well-connected to the rest of India. Only recently has Bikaner looked to tourism as another possibility for expansion and economic development; this new desire reaches its peak during the annual Camel Festival (Jan. 1-2, 1999; Jan. 20-21, 2000), a celebration of food, music, and all things camel: races, contests, parades, trading, and safaris aplenty. Prices of everything double (at least) as Bikaner fills with tourists.

ORIENTATION

Bikaner lies in the center of the hot **Thar Desert,** 240km northeast of Jodhpur. The layout is pretty straightforward outside the old city. Noisy **Station Road** is the hotel strip and runs parallel to the tracks in front of the **railway station.** To the right of the station, Station Rd. intersects the main commercial throughfare, **KEM Road,** and then continues to the **Junagarh Fort** and the GPO. Left on KEM Rd. leads to **Kote Gate,** the main entrance to the walled **old city;** right on KEM Rd. leads to the front side of the fort, where you'll find the **State Bank of Bikaner and Jaipur** and the **Central Telegraph Office.** Back at the railway station, a left on Station Rd. leads past the **Clock Tower** through two intersections. Left at the second intersection leads to Ambedkar Circle. From the circle, the right road is the **PBM Road,** home of the aptly named **PBM Hospital.** PBM Rd. ends in **Major Puran Singh Circle,** close to the **Golden Jubilee Museum.** Going left at the circle takes you back to KEM Rd.

PRACTICAL INFORMATION

Trains: Bikaner Railway Station (tel. 131 or 132). A Rs30 auto-rickshaw ride from anywhere in the city. Prices are for 2nd/1st class. To: **Delhi** (*Bikaner Exp.* 4790, 8:35am, 10½hr., Rs99/586; *Bikaner-Delhi Link Exp.* 4710, 5:50pm, 11hr., Rs137/416; *Bikaner Mail* 4792, 7:45pm, 8½hr., Rs137/562); **Jaipur** (*Intercity Exp.* 2467, 5am, 7hr., Rs180/500; *Bikaner Exp.* 4738, 8:25pm, 10½hr., Rs128/497); **Jodhpur** (5:45am and 8:25pm, 6½hr., Rs65/477). **Advance Reservation Office** (tel. 523132), next to the railway station. Open M-Sa 8am-8pm, Su 8am-2pm.

Buses: Central Bus Stand (tel. 523800), 3km north of the city, across from Lalgarh Palace. To: **Ahmedabad** (1:30pm, 10hr., Rs249); **Ajmer** (11 per day, 6am-11:30pm, 7hr., Rs106); **Delhi** (6 per day, 5:45am-7:15pm, 11hr., Rs175); **Jaipur** (13 per day, 4:30am-10:30pm, 7hr., Rs137); **Jaisalmer** (4 per day, 5am-10:30pm, 7½hr., Rs133); **Jodhpur** (every 30min., 5am-1:30am, 5½hr., Rs101); **Udaipur** (6:30pm, 12hr., Rs172). **Private buses** can be arranged through hotels, excursion agents, and the bus agencies that congregate around Goga Gate, south of Kote Gate, and behind the fort. Private buses leave frequently for all major cities from the Central Bus Stand.

Local Transportation: Auto-rickshaws are unmetered and will take you anywhere around the city for Rs15-20. **Bicycles** can be rented from cycle stores opposite the police station on Station Rd. **GNP Cycle Store** and **Baba Cycle Store** both charge Rs2 per hr. Both open daily 8am-9pm. **Jeeps** can be found near the railway station and across from the Fort's front entrance. They can be rented for Rs3-5 per km.

Tourist Office: Tourist Reception Centre, Hotel Dhola Maru Complex (tel. 544125). From PBM Rd., turn right at Major Puran Singh Circle. Dhola Maru is on your left. Helpful English-speaking staff. Open M-Sa 10am-5pm.

Budget Travel: Desert Tours (tel. 521967; fax 525150), behind the GPO, provides a wealth of tourist information. Mr. Kamal Saxena organizes tours of the city and its surrounds: half day Rs95, full day Rs175, camel tour Rs350. Open daily 8am-8pm.

Currency Exchange: Bank of Baroda, opposite the railway station, changes currency and traveler's checks. Open M-F 10am-2pm, Sa 10am-noon.

Luggage Storage: Railway Station Cloak Room, Rs3 per item for the first 24hr., Rs5 for the second, Rs6 thereafter.

Bookstore: Nauyug Giranth Kuteer (tel. 520836), inside Kote Gate, on the right. Books, international magazines, and newspapers. Open daily 9am-9pm.

Market: Most of Bikaner's pervasive stores and bazaars are open daily 8am-9pm.

Pharmacy: PBM Hospital and M.N. Hospital both operate 24hr. pharmacies. Others pepper the areas around the hospitals and Kote gate.

Hospital: M.N. Hospital near Kerni Singh Stadium and the **Desert Winds Hospital** (tel. 523563) and **Sethelik Hospital** (tel. 544122), inside Jessusar Gate, are all clean and modern and have English-speaking staff.

Police: Main office (tel. 61840), next to the railway station. Open 24hr. The Superintendent of Police (tel. 61173) speaks English. Open M-F 9am-5pm.

Post Office: GPO (tel. 524185), behind Junagarh Fort. *Poste Restante.* Open M-Sa 10am-6pm. **Branches** near PBM Hospital, inside Kote Gate, and near State Bank of Bikaner and Jaipur. **Postal Code:** 334001.

Telephones: Central Telegraph Office (tel. 523144), near State Bank of Bikaner and Jaipur. Open M-Sa 8am-8pm, Su 8am-3:30pm. **Telephone Code:** 0151.

ACCOMMODATIONS

Most of Bikaner's budget dives are clustered on the noisy Station Rd., and all are pretty much the same. Hotels are being established near Junagarh Fort and in other areas, though, so choices should rapidly increase. Home-stays with local families can be arranged through the tourist office (Rs150-500 per night).

Hotel Amit, Station Rd. (tel. 54451), on a side street near the Evergreen Hotel. Basic but clean, cramped rooms, all with attached baths. Rooms have black-and-white TVs. Hot water buckets Rs3 each. Check-out 24hr. Singles Rs75, with air-cooling Rs100; doubles Rs100/125. Extra bed Rs25.

Hotel Joshi, Station Rd. (tel. 527700; fax 52123), across from the police station. Modern and centrally located, the Joshi offers a pleasant escape from the heat, dust, and noise of Bikaner. Good veg. restaurant, elevator, STD/ISD, currency exchange, and laundry services. All rooms have attached bath and TV. Check-out 24hr. Singles with air-cooling Rs300, with A/C Rs575; doubles Rs375/675. Enormous A/C deluxe double Rs775. Reservations recommended in season.

Thar Hotel, PBM Hospital Rd. (tel. 543050; fax52150), next to Ambedkar Circle. Good-sized, quiet rooms. Room service, puppet show, folk music, TVs, excellent restaurant. Camel safaris Rs600-900 per day. All rooms have attached bath. Singles with air-cooling Rs517, with A/C Rs700; doubles Rs660/850. Extra bed Rs150.

Bhairon Vilas (tel. 544751), next to the fort, opposite the GPO, a few minutes from the bus stand. Not cheap, but a great deal for the money. *Haveli*-hotel provides gorgeous, plush rooms. Stay in the same posh suite that Lord Mountbatten did for less than Rs1000 off season. Luxurious baths with tubs to melt away heat exhaustion. Delicious (if pricey) meals served in attached restaurant. Save up for this one.

FOOD

Kastori Kanar, Jaisalmer Rd. (tel. 71892). Features the normal range of Chinese, Continental, and Indian dishes for very reasonable prices (most entrees under Rs30). Eat outside in the beautiful garden and then go swimming in the huge, clean pool. Open daily 5pm-midnight. Pool hours 6-10am and 5-10pm, and by request. Rs100 per person for 2hr. of watery bliss.

Moomal Restaurant, Panch Sebi Circle (tel. 521719). Worth the 20min. walk. A large, dark, air-cooled veg. restaurant presenting standard Chinese, Continental, and Indian cuisine. Fast service. Expect to pay Rs70-100 for a hearty dinner. Open daily 6am-3pm and 6-10pm.

Metro Bar and Restaurant (tel. 528986), at the front of the Fort, near Sadul Singh Circle. Air-cooled restaurant with plush booths on 3 levels and standard entrees (Rs20-40). Beer Rs50-60. Open daily 8am-10:30pm.

Hotel Sagar, Lalgarh Palace (tel. 520677). Near the road in front of the palace. Features a wide range of entrees, most for less than Rs50, and some unusual items like deep pan pizza and apple onion soup. Open daily 6am-10:30pm.

Tripti Restaurant, opposite Thar Hotel. Great interior and cheap veg. *thalis* Rs25.

SIGHTS

Junagarh Fort

Hours: *Open daily 10am-4:30pm.* **Admission:** *Rs50.* **Other:** *Camera fee Rs30, video fee Rs100. Group tours free. Authorized government guides cost about Rs100.*

Bikaner's most prominent and famous attraction, the fort was built in 1589 by Rai Singh and is distinguished as one of the few in the country that has never been conquered. The fort is a solid, densely packed, ground-level structure with a 986m-long wall capped with 37 bastions, surrounded by a 9m-wide moat. It looks pretty damn impregnable. The Fort is entered from the east side through a succession of gates. Near the second, **Daulat Pol,** are 24 dramatic handmarks of women who performed a *sati* self-sacrifice after their husbands had perished in a successful attempt to prevent a siege. The Fort's main entrance is the **Suraj Pol** (Sun Gate), a large iron-spiked door flanked by two stone mangy elephants.

The Fort is an intricate complex of palaces, courtyards, pavilions, and temples—37 in all—each added to the original structure by successive rulers. Each new addition was built to connect harmoniously to the previous structures, so that there appears to be one elaborate but continuous palace. The **Karan Mahal,** constructed after an important victory over the Mughal army of Emperor Aurangzeb, features gold-leaf paintings and the silver throne of Lord Karan Singh. The **Chandra Mahal** (Moon Palace) is a beautifully painted *puja* room adorned with Hindu gods and goddesses. To the side is the **Sheesh Mahal** (Mirror Palace), a room studded with mirrors that provide a magnificent glitter—light a match or shine a flashlight and enjoy the dazzle. **Shardaw Miwas** was the music room of the Fort; it features old instruments and an ancient system of air-cooling. **Hanuman Temple** is filled with arrays of swords, saws, spears, and nails, which are danced upon by *fakirs* from neighboring villages every January. The **Ganga Singh Hall,** the last portion of the Fort, houses the **museum,** with a collection of weapons and various relics, including a WWI biplane.

Jain Temples

Hours: *Open daily 6am-9pm in season.* **Admission:** *Free.* **Other:** *Camera fee Rs10 at Bhandeshwar. All temples require the removal of shoes. Sandeshwar and Laxminath do not allow socks, umbrellas, watches, cameras, or leather goods.*

Following the main road through Kote Gate will eventually lead you to the base of the old city, where two extraordinary Jain temples, built by merchant brothers in the 16th century, can be found. The **Bhandeshwar Temple,** one of the most spectacular in India, is adorned with gilded floral motifs painted by Persian artists from Emperor Akbar's court. Fifty years, 500 laborers, and 40,000kg of *ghee* went into its construction (the *ghee* was used in place of water to make the temple's cement foundation). On hot days, the temple's base is said to ooze the clarified butter. The **Sandeshwar Temple** also features intricate gold-leaf painting and is decorated with sculpted marble rows of popular saints. **Laxminath Temple,** next door, is a masterfully carved stone temple with superb views of the desert and city.

Lalgarh Palace

Location: *3km north of the city, across from the Main Bus Stand.* **Phone:** *543815.*
Hours: *Museum open Th-Tu 10am-5pm.* **Admission:** *Rs50.*

Three kilometers north of the city, across from the Main Bus Stand, is the large, multi-tiered **Lalgarh Palace,** made of red sandstone. It was designed for Maharaja Ganga Singh in 1902, in an attempt to combine European opulence, "Oriental" majesty, and Rajasthani tradition—unfortunately, it stops short of all of those goals. The royal family of Bikaner lives in part of it, a luxury hotel takes up some more space, and the **Sri Sadul Museum** occupies the rest. The museum houses every remaining personal item of Maharaja Ganga Singh and his son, Maharaja Kerni Singh. It seems endless, but it becomes more and more interesting, containing relics such as a picture of Ganga Singh signing the Treaty of Versailles and Kerni Singh's rifle from the 1960 Olympics, where he was a silver medalist...in diving!

ENTERTAINMENT

Although nowhere near Jaisalmeric proportions, **camel safaris** have recently become quite popular in Bikaner. Most of these begin with a tour of the city and nearby sights, followed by a trek through the desert, with frequent stops at rarely touristed traditional villages where you can witness local handicrafts and desert lifestyles. Also common are **intercity safaris** to Jaisalmer and Jodhpur. As in Jaisalmer, the safaris can often involve combinations of jeep, horse, and camel travel. Few hotels offer safaris, and those that do operate exclusively through independent agencies. **Vinod Travels** (tel. 204485), near Gopeshur Temple, organizes camel safaris for two to 13 days at Rs300-600 per day. The agency is run by a group of musicians, teachers, and social workers who use the revenue to fund classes in basic literacy, English, math, history, geography, and crafts in the slums of Bikaner. (Open daily 8am-5pm.) **Desert Tours** (tel. 521967), located behind the Fort near the GPO, offers a wide range of safaris for Rs400-800 per day. **Rajasthani Safaris & Treks** (tel. 543738; fax 520321), in BASSAI House near Jungarh Fort, organizes camel and jeep safaris. (Rs1200-1600 per day. Open M-Sa 10am-5pm.)

SHOPPING

Unsurprisingly, Bikaner is a haven for desert **handicrafts.** The primary commercial areas are **KEM Road** and almost all of the **old city.** Just inside Kote Gate on the left are cloth and textile stores and a fruit market. Leather and other craft stores congregate near the Jain temples. The government-approved **Abhi Byakti** (tel. 522139), located just inside the Fort, sells high-quality wares from 115 villages around the city. Shop hassle-free and rest assured that proceeds go directly to the artisans and projects that promote primary health care, basic literacy, and women's rights.

■ Near Bikaner

Devi Kund Sagar, 8km west of Bikaner, contains the marble and red sandstone royal *chhattris* (cenotaphs) of Bikaner rulers and their wives and mistresses, whose handprints commemorate their self-sacrifice. There is a *sati* temple where the spirits of the women who immolated themselves here are worshiped. It all surrounds a tranquil lake inhabited by pigeons and peacocks.

The **Camel Breeding Farm,** 10km south of the city, is the largest in Asia, breeding 50% of India's bred camels. In the early evening hundreds of camels of all ages return here from the desert. During World War II, the British Imperial Army's Camel Corps was pulled from this farm. Of course, during the Camel Festival, this place goes ballistic. The farm can be reached by auto-rickshaw. (Round-trip Rs80. Open M-Sa 3-5pm. Admission free. Photography permitted outside only.)

Gajner Wildlife Sanctuary, 32km west of Bikaner, was once the location of the royal hunting grounds. It then became a resort for important visiting dignitaries and now stands as a sanctuary for antelopes, black bucks, gazelles, and assorted birds.

Famous Siberian imperial sand grouse migrate here every winter. The elegant palace on the lake has been converted into the high-end Gajner Palace Hotel. The sanctuary is accessible from Bikaner (buses depart the Central Bus Stand every 30min., Rs10 one way).

Rats! Spoiled Again!

At the Karni Mata Temple in Deshnok, 30km from Bikaner, thousands of holy rats called *kabas* run rampant at the feet of thronging worshipers, who consider it auspicious to have the *kabas* run over their feet. The temple is not for the faint of heart, but it is worth visiting the temple for the magnificent solid silver gate donated by Maharaja Ganga Singh, and for its ornate stone carvings. Those lucky enough to see a white rat can consider themselves blessed. These rodent rapscallions eat and drink massive quantities of grain and milk and play all day to work it off. According to regional legend, the Bikaner patron deity, Karni Mata, was once asked to resurrect her drowned beloved nephew. She called up the god of death, Yama, who told her the boy had already been reborn as a rat, and that all her male descendants would first be born as rats in her temple at Deshnok. The *kabas* are fed *prasad* every morning—what's left is given to worshipers, who eat it without compunction, as the *prasad* anointed with the animals' spit is also considered auspicious. The best time to visit is during the Navratri festival in March, when the temple is swamped with devotees. The temple is accessible by taxi (about Rs200 round-trip) and by buses from Bikaner (every 30min., Rs8-12), and is a stop on the city tours. Capture the scene for a lifetime for a mere Rs10 camera fee.

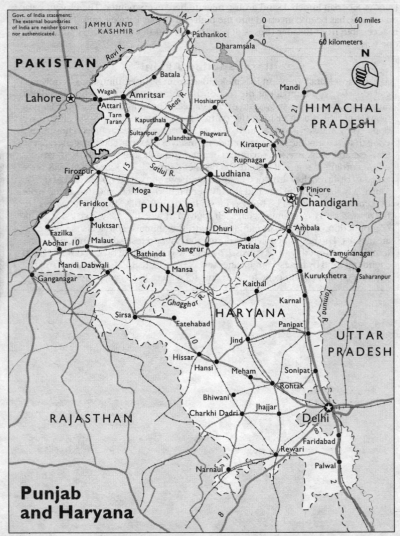

Govt. of India statement:
The external boundaries
of India are neither correct
nor authenticated.

**Punjab
and Haryana**

Punjab ਪੰਜਾਬ and Haryana हरियाणा

When the 1947 Partition divided the northwestern state of Punjab between India and Pakistan, only two of the five rivers to which the Persian *punj aab* refers still lay within India's borders. Nineteen years later, what was left of the Indian Punjab was again divided, this time along linguistic lines (between Punjabi and Hindi), forming the states of Punjab and Haryana. Despite linguistic differences, Haryana and Punjab share a capital (Chandigarh), a fertile geography, and the pride of overcoming a long and turbulent history to become one of India's most prosperous regions. Combined, the two states produce more than half of India's wheat and rice supply.

Punjab has long been the foyer through which aggressive guests have entered the Subcontinent—and stayed. The Aryans' arrival here in 1500 BC brought about the birth of the *Vedas* and the *Mahabharata*. The 1526 Battle of Panipat inaugurated the Mughal's political and cultural sweep of India, which began its swift decline with British viceroys in the Punjab in 1739 and 1761. Not content simply to be the screen door of South Asia, the Punjab has also exerted strong cultural influences on India, primarily through the Sikh religion, founded in the 15th century by Guru Nanak. Although Nanak's religion spread throughout India, the majority of Sikhs—and their holy city of Amritsar—are in Punjab. (For more on **Sikhism,** see p. 102.)

But prosperity and peace have not gone hand in hand, and there has long been friction in Punjab between moderates and Sikh militants demanding the formation of an independent Sikh nation, Khalistan ('Land of the Pure'). Things came to a head in 1983-84, with Sikh-militant mass-murders of Hindus and a subsequent army raid on the militants' headquarters in Amritsar's Golden Temple. The siege of the holy site led to Sikh army desertions, mutinies, and, eventually, the murder of Indira Gandhi by two of her Sikh bodyguards. Subsequent Hindu rioting, in which thousands of Sikhs were slaughtered, meant an increase in support for the Khalistan movement that has only recently begun to dwindle. Although separatist groups continue to demand independence, they lack popular support and pose no threat to travelers.

🦅 HIGHLIGHTS OF PUNJAB AND HARYANA

- Amritsar's **Golden Temple** (p. 330), the most sacred site of the Sikh religion, offers visitors an incredible combination of beauty, holiness, and hospitality.
- Modern **Chandigarh's** pre-planned sectors and structures offer a history of Indian futurism, set in pre-poured concrete (below).

■ Chandigarh चंडीगढ़ ਚੰਡੀਗੜ੍ਹ

Chandigarh was born of the starry-eyed optimism of India's newly independent government. The Punjab (including present-day Haryana) had been partitioned, and its capital, Lahore, was now inconveniently across the border in Pakistan. A new capital was needed; Nehru's government chose the present site of Chandigarh for its scenic and fertile location, and chose a team of crack Western architects for their modernist bent and willingness to work for *paise.* One of these architects, Le Corbusier (the artist formerly known as M. Charles Jeanneret), soon made it clear that Chandigarh was going to be his baby. Le Corbusier's plan for a functionally and symbolically laid-out human habitat meshed well with the designs of fellow modernist Nehru for a planned city that would rise above India's chaotic urban past. The result was a huge grid of broad, gardened avenues and functional "sectors."

Today, Le Corbusier's California dream of "sun, space and silence" means different things to the squatters who cluster in derelict lots, the affluent businessmen of Sector 17's gigantic concrete market, and the cycle-rickshaw-*wallahs* panting through the glaring heat of endless, identical avenues. Being expansive and quasi-modern also means that Chandigarh is without many of India's typical tourist attractions, but its museums, gardens, and lake are pleasant, and a stay here feels like a vacation from the furious swirl of other Indian cities.

ORIENTATION

No one can say that Chandigarh is illogical. The whole city is a massive grid that would make disorientation impossible, but for the house-of-mirrors effect afforded by the near-identical appearance of its avenues. Each of Chandigarh's 50 "sectors," or blocks, was designed to be self-sufficient, with its own marketplaces and shopping centers. **Sector I** is to the north, where the main government buildings, **Sukhna Lake,** and the **Rock Garden** are situated. The rest are numbered from west to east, then east to west, in rows proceeding to the south. Buses stop at the south end of **Sector 17,** where most services are located. (Sector 17 is the primary "downtown" zone.) **Sector 22,** immediately south, comes in a close second with its many hotels and restaurants. Stray from the main avenues into the heart of any of the other 47 sectors for a taste of Chandigarh's trademark affluence and tranquility.

PRACTICAL INFORMATION

Transportation

Airport: Chandigarh's airport is 11km out of town, a Rs80-120 auto-rickshaw ride. **Indian Airlines** (tel. 704539) accepts credit cards to book flights. To: **Amritsar** (M, W, and F, 12:30pm, 35min., US$55); **Delhi** (M, W, and F, 12:30pm, 40min., US$65); **Leh** (Tu, 9am, 55min., US$70). Book two months early to guarantee a ticket to Leh.

Trains: Chandigarh's **railway station** is an annoying 8km to the southeast of town. Local bus #37 connects the railway station with the bus stand (20min., Rs5). On the third floor of the bus stand there's a **Railway Reservation Office** (tel. 704382), open M-Sa 9am-1pm and 1:30-4pm, Su 9am-2pm. To: **Delhi** (*Shatabdi Exp.* 2006, 2012, 6:50am and 12:20pm, 3hr., Rs330, A/C chair only; 5:30pm and 1am, 5-6hr., Rs72/181); **Shimla** (5:30, 7, and 11:40am, 4-6hr., Rs97 for A/C chair); and **Jammu** (10:15pm, 12hr., Rs137). **Amritsar** and **Rishikesh** can be reached by catching a train first from Chandigarh to **Ambala** (several daily, 1hr., Rs42) and getting a connection from there.

Buses: Inter-State Bus Terminal, on the southwest side of Sector 17, across from the hotels in Sector 22. Buses depart for **Amritsar** (every 20min., 4:30am-11pm, 5hr., Rs63/127); **Dehra Dun** (every 10min., 4:30am-11pm, 5½ hr., Rs87; deluxe every hr., 4:30am-11pm, Rs174); **Dharamsala** (6 daily, 6:50am-10:30pm, 8hr., Rs94; deluxe at 11pm, Rs122); **Jaipur** (7:30, 9, and 9:30am, 12hr., Rs190; deluxe at 4pm, Rs364); **Jammu** (4:30am, 11hr., Rs90); **Manali** (12 daily, 4am-11:30pm, 11hr., Rs152); **Shimla** (10 daily, 4:50am-1:30pm, 4½hr., Rs 49/59/240 for day/ night/deluxe); **Rishikesh** (10:30am, 8:30, and 11:30pm, 8hr., Rs8). **Dalhousie** can be reached by a train to **Banikhat,** then a 10min. bus ride.

Local Transportation: Chandigarh is so sprawling that even the toughest **cycle-rick-shaw-wallahs** break a sweat after a block or two. Blue **auto-rickshaws** may charge Rs15-25 for a 2-sector trip. Starting from the local bus stand (west of the interstate bus terminal), **buses** go to the Rock Garden (Sector 1, Bus #13, 15min., Rs5), and the railway station (Bus #37, 20min., Rs5).

Tourist and Financial Services

Tourist Office: CITCO. The Chandigarh Industrial and Tourism Development Corp. has offices upstairs in the bus stand (tel. 703839) and at the railway station (tel. 658005), both of which offer various out-of-date brochures about the city. The bus stand office is open daily 10am-5pm; the railway office is open during arrivals. The squalid but amiable **Punjab Government Tourist Information Centre** (tel. 711878) is also in the bus stand (open M-F 9am-1:30pm and 2-5pm), as are the **U.P.** (tel. 707649) and **Himachal Pradesh** (tel. 708569 or 707267) offices. The **Haryana** office is in the main shopping complex of Sector 17 (tel. 702955 or 702956).

Budget Travel: Indian Airlines (tel. 704539), in the center of Sector 17, accepts credit cards to book flights.

Immigration Office: Foreigners Registration Office (tel. 44064 or 44074, ext. 382), in SSP, Police Headquarters, across from Sector 9. Foreigners can register for long-term stays here if they've taken an HIV test. This office also infrequently extends visas. Open M-F 9am-5pm and Sa-Su 10am-noon.

Currency Exchange: Many banks are clustered in Bank Square, the central and northern parts of Sector 17. **State Bank of India** (tel. 708359), changes AmEx and Thomas Cook traveler's checks, as well as major currencies. There is also a 24hr. **ATM** here that gives cash advances on Visa and Mastercard. Open M-F 10am-2pm, Sa 10am-noon. **Tradewings Ltd.,** 1068 Sector 22 (tel. 709666), located upstairs on the southeast side of Sector 22, also changes traveler's checks, and stays open longer. Rs4 service fee. Open M-Sa 9:30am-5:30pm.

NORTH INDIA

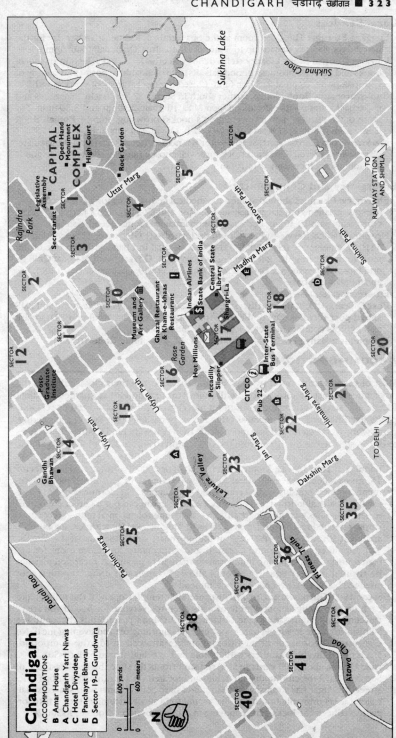

Chandigarh

ACCOMMODATIONS

B Amar House
A Chandigarh Yatri Niwas
C Hotel Divyadeep
E Panchayat Bhawan
D Sector 19-D Gurudwara

Sukhna Lake

Sukhna Choa

Rajindra Park

CAPITAL COMPLEX
Legislative Assembly
Secretariat
Open Hand Monument
High Court
Rock Garden

Uttar Marg

SECTOR 1
SECTOR 2
SECTOR 3
SECTOR 4
SECTOR 5
SECTOR 6
SECTOR 7
SECTOR 8
SECTOR 9
SECTOR 10
SECTOR 11
SECTOR 12
SECTOR 14
SECTOR 15
SECTOR 16
SECTOR 17
SECTOR 18
SECTOR 19
SECTOR 20
SECTOR 21
SECTOR 22
SECTOR 23
SECTOR 24
SECTOR 25
SECTOR 35
SECTOR 36
SECTOR 37
SECTOR 38
SECTOR 40
SECTOR 41
SECTOR 42

Madhya Marg
Sarovar Path
Sukhna Path

Post-Graduate Institute
Gandhi Bhawan

Museum and Art Gallery
Ghazal Restaurant & Khana-e-khaas Restaurant
Indian Airlines
State Bank of India
Central State Library
Shangri-La
Hot Millions
Rose Garden
Piccadilly Slipper
Inter-State Bus Terminal
CITCO
Pub 22

Vidya Path
Udyan Path

Leisure Valley
Fitness Trails

Jan Marg
Himalaya Marg
Dakshin Marg
Paschim Marg

Patiali Rao
Atawa Choa

TO RAILWAY STATION AND SHIMLA
TO DELHI

0 600 yards
0 600 meters

N

Local Services

Luggage Storage: The cloak room at the bus terminal. Rs2 per item per day for the first 2 days, Rs3 per day for up to 3 months thereafter. Open daily 9am-5pm.

Library: Central State Library (tel. 702565), Sector 17. Good selection of Indian books and eclectic business periodicals. Rs100 refundable deposit (plus a copy of your passport). Open M-Sa 11am-6pm. Closed the last Saturday of every month.

Bookstore: Asia Book House, farther south in Sector 17, has trashy magazines and paperbacks among its offerings. Open M-Sa 10:30am-2:30pm and 3:30-8pm. For more outlandish (as in Marxist children's books) browsing, stop by **Punjab Book Centre,** on the southeast side of Sector 22-B. Open M-Sa 9am-4pm.

Market: Arora Confections, SCF3, Sector 8-B market (tel. 782264). An immaculate, obsessively ordered little shop stocking a well-chosen range of Western-style goods and toiletries. Open daily 9am-10pm.

Emergency and Communications

Pharmacy: Chemists abound around the medical center in Sector 17. In Sector 22-C are several late-night pharmacies, such as **Anil and Co.,** Bayshop #42 (tel. 777565). Open daily 8am-10:30pm. Both hospital pharmacies require membership.

Hospital/Medical Services: Post Graduate Institute (PGI), Sector 12 (reception tel. 541018, emergency tel. 541005). The best hospital in Chandigarh and one of the most reputable in India. 24hr. emergency services. **Government Medical College and Hospital,** Sector 32, Dakshin Marg (tel. 665545-49, emergency ext. 1200), has an ambulance service.

Emergency: tel. 100.

Post Office: GPO, at the northwest corner of Sector 17, has *Poste Restante* and EMS **speed post** services. Open M-F 9am-4pm, night post office until 6pm. There are also express couriers in Sector 17. **Postal Code:** 160017.

Telephones: Many STD/ISD booths in Sector 22. **Telephone Code:** 0172.

ACCOMMODATIONS

Most of Chandigarh's hotel owners assume that because their city is affluent, the city's guests must be too. No one will point you to a hotel that charges less than Rs200, and staying at cheaper (but often nicer) government-subsidized or religious places like **Bhawans** or **gurudwaras** often means persisting in the face of a glowering, paperwork-averse clerk. If this is more hassle than you want (and if you've got rupees to burn), step across the street from the bus station to Sector 22 for lodgings galore.

Chandigarh Yatri Niwas, Sector 24 (tel. 706038 or 700050). Just across from Sector 15. An excellent, peaceful retreat for a few relaxing days. Part hotel, part government complex housing civil servants and bureaucrats. The dorm rooms are possibly the best deal in town, but are only available if you can put together a group of 8. The place has a comfortingly airy feel, and some rooms open onto grassy courtyards. Attached restaurant. Dorm beds Rs50. Doubles Rs450, with A/C Rs600.

Panchayat Bhawan (tel. 780701), on the northeast side of Sector 18. Enormous, well-appointed rooms around a pristine and empty courtyard. Extra forms for foreign tourists and a booming Indian tourist trade here mean that reception may not be thrilled to meet you. No alcohol allowed. Check-out noon. Doubles with attached bath Rs80. Reservations recommended.

Sector 19-D Gurudwara. *Gurudwaras* are Sikh temples open to the public, and each one has a large room with floor mats open to everyone for free. If you aren't traveling on to Amritsar and the Golden Temple, don't pass up this chance to see Sikhism from the inside. Private room includes morning tea and evening meal. No cigarettes, alcohol, or other intoxicants are allowed inside the compound. Decrepit but livable chambers with double bed, fan, and shared bath (Rs50).

Amar House, about 200 yards behind the storefronts that line the northeast side of Sector 22. Off-the-cuff, under the table, and located on a soothing suburban side-street, the Amar has a ramshackle handful of bare-bones rooms with shared squat-toilet. Caters primarily to Indian tourists, but for a small price hike, they'll take foreigners. Check the locks before moving in. Check-out noon. Doubles Rs200-280.

Jullundur Hotel, Sector 22 (tel. 706777 or 701121). Opposite the Interstate Bus Terminal, next to Sunbeam. The best bet for close-to-the-middle, spare-your-wallet rooms. Courteous staff, running hot water, and attached restaurant. Check-out noon. Air-cooled singles Rs280; doubles with TV Rs375.

Hotel Divyadeep, 1090-91, Sector 22-B (tel. 705191). On the northeast side of Sector 22, adjacent to Bhol Restaurant. Immaculate, spacious, old-style, wood-paneled rooms with seat toilets. Room service (veg. only) 6am-10pm, doctor on call. Check-out 24hr. Singles Rs200, with A/C Rs400; doubles Rs250/Rs450.

FOOD

There's no dearth of restaurants in wealthy Chandigarh. Fast-food joints abound in Sector 17, as do classier "special night out" places, many of which have attached banquet halls. To escape the glitz and sample the local *thalis, samosas,* and "sweets," simply wander through the markets of any Sector besides 17 or 22.

Ghazal Restaurant and Pub, SCO 189, Sector 17-C (tel. 704448). Elegant, doorman-type place specializing in Mughlai and tandoori cuisine. Watch Chandigarh's business elite at play in the light of a giant red and blue stained-glass wall. Draft beer Rs20 "regular," Rs30 "strong." Meaty menu includes *methi* chicken with fine, fine *fenugeek* (Rs105). Mushroom *mattar* (Rs70). Open daily 11am-11pm.

Khana-e-khaas Restaurant, Sector 17 (tel. 703061). Across from the Ghazal and similar to it but not quite as stuffy, although the waiters wear bow ties. *Rogan josh* Rs75, mutton *korma* Rs80. Open daily 10:30am-11pm.

Shangri-La, SCO 96, Sector 17-C (tel. 702026). Unlike most of the Chinese restaurants in India, the best joint for Chinese chow in Chandigarh is actually run by a Chinese person. Shangri-La's elegance is a bit cramped, but a new free delivery service means you don't even have to see it. *Szechuan* lamb Rs75, "Vegetable Manchurian" Rs52. Open daily 10:30am-11pm, delivery noon-11pm.

Pub 22, Sector 22 (tel. 706439). Downstairs from Nirankari Restaurant in the strip across from the bus stand. A fun place to waste away in absurd, dim blue cocktail lighting. Draft beer Rs20, status-quo Indian dishes Rs10-60. Open daily 9am-1am.

Hot Millions, Sector 17 (tel. 777287, 776944). Hot Millions now has 3 branches in Sector 17 (and promises millions more). All serve quick-n'-greasy Indian, Chinese, and Continental food. Chicken burger Rs38, pizza Rs45-80. Delivery service (free with orders over Rs100, Rs10 extra otherwise). Open daily 11:30am-2:30pm.

Nanak's Sweets Shop, Sector 19-D, next to the 19-D *Gurudwara.* Brave palates will be rewarded with chalky, dough-based splendor. The shop is an homage to dad run by three friendly Sikh brothers—beware the strength of their whiskey-and-beer *aperitif.* Chocolate, coconut, and pineapple *barfis* Rs80.

Sindhi Cake Shop, Sector 8, across from Panchayat Bhawan. An extensive array of Indian and Continental cakes, pastries, and vegetarian amalgamations, marshaled behind fly-proof glass. Vegetarian burgers Rs20; cake Rs15. Open daily 9am-9pm.

SIGHTS

Rock Garden

Location: Sector 1, near the Capital Complex. **Hours:** Open daily Apr.-Sep. 9am-7pm, Oct.-Mar. daily 9am-6pm. **Admission:** Rs1. **Other:** Appointments with Nek Chand, the garden's creator, occasionally available. Inquire at the ticket window.

Chandigarh's inception as a government-supervised golden child has given it a fixed set of pleasant but standard museums, gardens, and parks, all in various states of cleanliness or disrepair. One garden, however, sits well beyond the ken of the government and most other earthlings. Visit Nek Chand's Rock Garden, and you'll never look at Indian concrete the same way again. Former road-construction worker Chand has brought this humble material, and even some road trash, into a state of grace, assembling an escapist wonderland that now meanders through 40 surreal acres. Highlights of the journey through the garden (set aside at least an hour) include waterfalls, ponds with kiddie boats (Rs10), giant chain swings, and a miniature army of primitivist villagers and livestock who blithely see you off back into the lower realms of Chandigarh. Sometimes there's a camel out front for quick rides (Rs20, negotiable). Purchase your ticket to the garden at the tiny, mock-bureaucratic window facing the driveway. One rock garden regular is local tourist saint Narinder Singh, an elderly Sikh in a blue turban who frequents the cafeteria, as well as the bus stand. Look for him if cheap accommodations elude you—he's one of a handful of folks in Chandigarh whose hotel and city tour is entirely (incredibly) benevolent.

Other Sights

Sector 1 plays host to other notable attractions. The **Capital Complex,** with its monumental, concrete buildings, was Le Corbusier's way of staging the functions of government in symbolic and geometric relation to one another and to the rest of the city (as "head" to "body"—the parks were to be the "lungs"). Visit the **High Court** and **Open Hand Monument** if you come here—they are more accessible than the **Legislative Assembly** and heavily-guarded **Secretariat.**

Also in the north is **Sukhna Lake,** a small reservoir which CITCO has neatly turned into a tourist site with cafeteria, pub, mini-amusement park, and paddle boats. *(2-seater Rs25 per 30min., 4-seater Rs50 per 30min.)* Come at sunset, hop in one of the swan boats if possible, and float over to the mangrove alcoves across the lake. There is also the semi-exclusive **Lake Club,** where, for a hefty fee, you can indulge in a round of golf or tennis.

Leisure Valley is the term Le Corbusier used for the long parkland stretching through the heart of Chandigarh. It is meant to provide "care for the body and spirit." The highlight of this public park is the Dr. Zakir Hussain **Rose Garden,** supposedly the largest in Asia, off Jan Marg in Sector 16. There are spritzy fountains to the north and many species of roses; try to visit in spring when they are in bloom, or in February, for the giant Rose Festival.

NIGHTLIFE AND ENTERTAINMENT

In a city full of government administrators and bureaucrats, it isn't surprising that opportunities for debauchery are kept to a minimum (or at least kept private and out of sight). Chandigarh's streets are abandoned by 10pm, and pubs close at midnight. Still, there are a few options for revelry-seekers. **Piccadilly Sipper,** Sector 17-E, (tel. 703338; look for the neon martini glass) has a well-stocked bar with plush, intimate booths (beer Rs60, Scotch Rs85-140, whisky Rs30-50). Open 11am-11pm. **The Galaxy Bar,** SCO 325-28, Sector 35-B (tel. 600546), at the Hotel Maya Palace, features live Indian music. For some discotheque action, head to **Las Vegas Den,** SCO 915, Kulka Highway (tel. 554487), where you can dance your heart out to a curious blend of Indian and Western beats (couples Rs150, single women Rs50, single men often not allowed). The **Shri Ram Theatre** has regular cultural performances—check the local paper for listings. The **Neelam Theatre,** in the middle of Sector 17, shows Bollywood favorites and (occasionally) films in English, in a giant decorated movie hall. Floor seats Rs15, balcony Rs25. "Popcorn" Rs5. Shows daily at 3, 6, and 9pm.

■ Amritsar ਅੰਮ੍ਰਿਤਸਰ

Perhaps it is because Guru Nanak, the founder of Sikhism, had traveled so widely through India and even the Middle East that the city of Amritsar, founded later in the century by subsequent Sikh gurus, is particularly hospitable to modern backpackers. Amritsar, named for the sacred tank or "pool of immortal nectar" at the city's heart, is the largest city in Punjab and the focal point of Sikhism. An awe-inspiring monument to the Sikh faith, Amritsar's Golden Temple is a must-see for Sikhs, travelers, and tourists alike. Guru Ram Das initiated the construction of the temple in 1579, but the city did not begin to form around it until the fifth guru, Arjun, enshrined the Sikh holy book, the Granth Sahib, here. Centuries of Mughal invasions led to a continuous cycle of destruction and reconstruction of the Golden Temple, but had minimal impact on the growth of the population, which now numbers 800,000. Amritsar today is a thriv-

Amritsar

ACCOMMODATIONS

B Chinar Hotel
D Grand Hotel
C Hotel Palace/Pegasus
G Hotel Sita Niwas
A Mohan Int'l Hotel
F Sharma Guest House
E Tourist Guest House

ing industrial center which has expanded far beyond the 20 gates still surrounding the old part of the city. Unfortunately, Amritsar is famous for a violent past, including the Mughal invasions and the Jallianwala Bagh massacre in 1919, when British Brigadier General R.E.H. Dyer fired on unarmed Indians in a closed compound; Partition riots; and recent violence between the Indian government and Sikh extremists. Despite this history of warfare, the city opens its arms to visitors without the usual follow-up offer of dubious business. An added attraction is Amritsar's proximity to the Pakistan border, where each evening an elaborate military ceremony accompanies the closing of the border gates.

ORIENTATION

Amritsar's **railroad tracks** divide the city into north and south sections. The major vehicle conduit in the very center of town is the **Bhandari Bridge,** which runs over the tracks and over a hill, and which taxes cycle-rickshaw drivers to no end. The older, livelier section of the city jams beyond the gates to the south of the railway; several bazaars (52 markets total in Amritsar!) and the Golden Temple draw in locals and visitors. Be sure to take at least one walk through the tiny side-streets in this part of town—you'll find a wider (and weirder) variety of shops, and, as always, less hassle. Northeast of the temple across the tracks is the **bus stand,** and west of that is the newer part of town, sprawling around the **railway station** to the north. Here, gardens and posher hotels spread themselves along **Mall Road** and **Lawrence Road,** the two major thoroughfares.

PRACTICAL INFORMATION

Transportation

Airport: Raja Sanhsi Airport, 12km northwest of town, has a small tourist office and other basic services. Flights to: **Delhi** (M, W, and F, 1:30pm, 2hr., US$90). Book from the **Indian Airlines** offices, located in the Mohan International Hotel on Albert Rd. (tel. 226970) and on Green Ave. (tel. 503780).

Trains: The **computer reservation** complex is on the south end of the railway station; walk over the platforms on the bridge (tel.562811 or 562812). Open M-Sa 8am-1:30pm and 2-8pm, Su 8am-2pm. Fares are given for 2nd/1st class. To: **Agra** (*Amritsar-Nanded Exp. 2716*, 5:55am, 11hr., Rs210/532); **Delhi** (*Shatabdi Exp. 2014*, 5:10am, 5hr., Rs365; *Flying Mail Exp. 4648*, 2:25pm, 8hr., Rs150/365); Haridwar (3:30am and 9pm, 12hr., Rs87/160); **Lahore, Pakistan** (*Lahore Exp. 4607*, M and Th 9:30am, Rs98/140); **Lucknow** (*Amritsar-Howrah Exp.*, 5:45pm, 19hr., Rs417/737); **Mumbai** (*Paschim Exp. 2926*, 8am, 21hr., *Golden Temple Mail 2904*, 9:30pm, 32hr., Rs105/193); and **Patna** (*Amritsar-Howrah Exp.*, 5:45pm, 30hr., Rs591/1062).

Buses: Enquiry office (tel. 551734). To: **Chandigarh** (hourly, 4:50am-4:10pm, 5hr., Rs.63; deluxe 5:20, 6:17, and 7:45am, Rs63); **Dehra Dun** (5:12 and 7:02am, 10hr., Rs79); **Delhi** (several daily, 5:20am-6:50pm, 10hr., Rs123; deluxe 10:08am, Rs150); **Dharamsala** (noon, 7hr., Rs68); **Rishikesh** (7:45am, 11hr., Rs142); **Shimla** (5:50 and 7:20am, 10hr., Rs116); and the Pakistan border at **Wagah** (every 15min., 7:10am-6pm, 1½hr., Rs18). Explore the boards at the bus terminal for other destinations and times. Times and prices tend to change frequently.

Local Transportation: Bicycle rental available at a couple of the bike shops across the street north of the bus stand. **Sigma Cycles** charges Rs20 per day on top of a hefty Rs1000 deposit. Open M-Sa 9am-8pm. **Rickshaws** of all shapes and sizes populate Amritsar. Cycle-rickshaws from the railway area go to the bus stand (Rs10-15) and Golden Temple (Rs10-15) but can be frustrating, especially if you're toting luggage, since they make you get out and walk over the Bhandari Bridge.

Tourist and Financial Services

Tourist Office: Punjab Government Tourist Office, Railway Rd. (tel. 231452), 1km east of the bus stand. Ask the rickshaw driver for Mall Mandi and look to your left for the building with the map plastered on its facade, set back 20m from the road. Affable staff knows a lot about Sikh gurus and nearby towns. Open M-Sa 9am-5pm. There is also a helpful **Information Centre** at the Golden Temple (see p. 330).

Foreigner Registration Office: The sometimes-elusive Police Superintendent performs the duties of the Foreigner Registration officer. Inquire at the Royal Police Force Office at the Railway Station (tel. 565976) if you need a visa extension.

Currency Exchange: Most major banks have branches in both the north and south parts of the city. **Bank of Punjab** (tel. 554895) has a branch at the Golden Temple's north side and exchanges major currencies and traveler's checks for a nominal service charge. Open M-F 10am-5pm, Sa 10am-2pm. **R.K. Traders** (tel. 212701), at the base of Mehra Hotel, across from the railway station, changes traveler's checks after hours. The railway area also has several offices that change **Pakistani Rupees.**

Local Services

Luggage Storage: The cloakroom at the railway station—Rs5 for 1st 24hr., Rs6 thereafter. Some hotels also offer this service upon request.

Market: The **bazaar** immediately in front of the main entrance to the Golden Temple carries a wide selection of merchandise, from Rajasthani shoes to Sikh daggers and swords. The steel bracelets *(kara)* worn by all Sikhs, symbolizing strength of will and determination, are available here. Be discriminating—*kara* that are not made of stainless steel will certainly erode after a few months of wear. For **fresh fruit,** check out the market between Gandhi Gate and the Bhandari Bridge.

Library: Sri Guru Ram Das Library, next to the Sri Guru Ram Das Niwas Gurudwara at the Golden Temple, has a small collection of English-language books about Sikhism and the temple, as well as daily periodicals. Open summer M-Sa 7:30am-5:30pm; winter 8am-5pm (sometimes slow to open).

Bookstore: Booklover's Retreat, on Hall Bazaar, south of Gandhi Gate (tel. 545666). Teetering stacks of new and used books include everything from *Sex, Scotch, and Scholarship* to Shakespeare. Open M-Sa 9am-8pm.

Emergency and Communications

Pharmacy: Although they can be found all over town, several chemists are clustered on Cooper Rd., around the corner from Crystal Restaurant and several blocks northeast of the railway station. Among these, **Amritsar Medicare** (tel. 212320), carries tampons and is otherwise well-stocked. Open daily 8am-9pm.

Hospital: Kakkar Hospital, Green Ave. (tel. 210964; emergency tel. 62018). Near Mall Rd., northwest of the railway. The most reputable hospital in town, enough people know the name to point the way. **24hr. Emergency Room** on Mahna Singh Rd., in the Golden Temple area.

Post Office: On Court Rd. (tel. 566032). Northwest of the railway station. Offers *Poste Restante* (c/o Post Marshall) and EMS speed post. Open M-Sa 9am-5pm. The **Golden Temple Post Office** sells stamps (open M-Sa 9am-6:30pm). **Postal Code:** 143001 for main GPO, 143006 for Golden Temple area.

Telephones: STD/ISD booths near Golden Temple, railway station, and one block east of Tourist Guest House. **Telephone Code:** 0183.

ACCOMMODATIONS

Amritsar has hotels to suit nearly every price range. They are clustered in three parts of the city: the bus station, railway station, and Golden Temple areas. Though undoubtedly the cheapest are near the bus station, these are neither sanitary nor safe—over the years the bus station area has become a red-light district where rooms are rented out by the hour. A number of decent, reasonably-priced hotels directly opposite the railway station await travelers arriving by train. Admittedly, hotels near the temple are more scarce, but the temple area is the most vibrant (and hectic) part of the city. The best place to stay, of course, is in the temple compound itself, although this can become taxing after a few days.

Railway Area (North of Bhandari Bridge)

Tourist Guest House, G.T. Rd., Hide Market (tel. 553830). On the road from the bus stand to the railway station; ask the rickshaw driver for Nandan Cinema, which is on a nearby side-street. Foreigners funnel in here for peaceful, homey rooms and tranquil evenings on the front deck of the owner's family home. Singles Rs100-120; doubles with attached bath Rs150-200, with A/C and TV Rs175-250.

Hotel Palace/Pegasus (tel. 565111), opposite the railway station. Convenient location and ultra-friendly owners more than make up for the aged feel of the place. In-house travel agency, STD/ISD, wake-up calls, and a complimentary newspaper. Most rooms have attached bath with seat toilets and towels, and cable TV. Hot water available during the winter 6:30-11:30am, at other times upon request. Check-out noon. Singles Rs150-200, with A/C Rs400; doubles Rs250-300/600.

Grand Hotel (tel. 562424), directly opposite the railway station. Well-kept rooms that surround a pleasant courtyard with a garden and lawn chairs. All rooms have attached baths with seat toilets, running hot water, and color TV. Room service 5am-11pm. Check-out noon. Singles Rs395, with A/C Rs600; doubles Rs500/700. 10% surcharge.

Chinar Hotel, Railway Links Rd. (tel. 54655). A half-block up from the railway station. Spotlessly clean, with huge front-side rooms. Room service 6am-midnight. Check-out noon. Doubles Rs150, with attached bath Rs350, with A/C Rs450.

Golden Temple Area

Sharma Guest House, Mahna Singh Rd. (tel. 551757), directly above Sharma Dhaba, one block north and one-half block east of the Golden Temple. Follow the well-placed signs. Clean rooms with a partial view of Jallianwala Bagh. All rooms have air cooling, seat toilets, cable TV, and phone. Room service 6am-11pm. 24hr. check-out. Doubles Rs200-250; deluxe Rs300-350. Reservations recommended.

Hotel Sita Niwas, Sarai Guru Ram Das (tel. 543092). Southeast of the temple. Plentiful signs make this place easy to find. Friendly family-owned enterprise offering rooms to suit every need, from cramped singles with common bath to palatial deluxe A/C suites. Travel bookings, STD/ISD, doctor on call 24hr. Veg. and non-veg. room service 6am-11pm. 24hr. check-out. Singles Rs150; suites Rs750.

Shri Gujrati Lodge and Guest House (tel. 557870), tucked into an alley between Jallianwala Bagh and several music stores, 1 block in front of the main Golden Temple gate. Look for the sign on the second floor. Beautiful, marble-floored dorm-room overlooks Jallianwala Bagh and has equal access to the airy second-floor lobby and tiny balcony. Doubles have phone and seat toilet. TV and food in the lobby. Owners prohibit alcohol on the premises. Doubles with common bath Rs130, with A/C Rs150; with attached bath Rs160/175. No reservations accepted.

Inside the Golden Temple

Sri Guru Ram Das Niwas Gurudwara, outside the east gate of the temple past the community kitchen. As the main Golden Temple housing complex the set-up is basic. All guests are entitled to use the washing spouts and showers as well as the dank line of toilets. Foreign guests are banished to a set of floor mats in an open-ceiling bunker. Prohibition on smoking and drinking certainly make it a mellow place. Despite the nighttime heat and the periodic prayers broadcast through the courtyard, the overall experience is fun. It's free, although donations at the charity box out front are appreciated. The door is guarded 24hr., but don't leave any valu-ables—mug shots of convicted robbers at the *gurudwara*'s entrance explain why.

Sri Guru Hargobind Niwas (temple manager tel. 553953, Hargobind Niwas ext. 323), 100m south of Ram Das Niwas Gurudwara. If the free digs are a bit too free for your tastes, pay a token tariff for a sparkling new, marble-covered double with attached bath. No drinking or smoking. Doubles with bath Rs50.

FOOD

Eat at least one meal in the Golden Temple itself—the *dal* may surprise you and bring you back for more. If not, ask a local about a favorite *dhaba;* everyone generally knows which are clean enough for Western stomachs. **Bubby Vaishno Dhaba,** directly across from the main access to the Golden Temple, has good pre-temple-tour breakfasts. For air-conditioning, head to one of the ominous tinted-windowed places on Lawrence Rd.

Manbhavan, inside the Mohan International Hotel on Albert Rd. Proffering a "murmur-ling experience," the Manbhavan dishes out delectable Punjabi delights to Amritsar's well-to-do. Try the *murg saagwala* (chicken cooked with spinach and ginger Rs90). **Madira,** the equally ritzy bar next door, is an ideal place for an after-dinner drink. Cock-tails Rs100, beer Rs65-80. Open daily 10:30am-4pm and 7-11:30pm.

Bharawanda Dhaba (tel. 552275). Across from Town Hall and next door to Punjab National Bank. Well-known, well-endowed, well-lit cafeteria with superb *thalis* (Rs30). Speedy service and foreigner friendly. Open daily 8am-11pm.

Neelam's (tel. 556353), a few doors down from the entrance to Jallianwala Bagh. Cush booths and A/C makes it the most comfortable *dhaba* in the Temple neigh-borhood. Don't miss the *masala dosa* (Rs15). Open daily 10am-11pm.

Sindhi Coffee House, Lawrence Rd. (tel. 566039). Across from Ram Bagh Gardens. A dim but tasteful cave of a place, serving good ice cream and standard Indian/Chi-nese dishes. "Cock rolls" (spring rolls) Rs30-50. Open daily 9am-10pm.

Burger King, 1-A Lawrence Rd. (tel. 225033). A short block north of Jallianwala Bagh. No Whoppers here, just franchise-free Indian pizzas (Rs40-55), Chinese burg-ers (Rs30-40), sundaes (Rs35), and ice cream sodas (Rs25). Open daily 10am-11pm.

SIGHTS

The Golden Temple

Location: *Golden Temple Information Centre is on the northeast side of the complex.* **Phone:** *553954.* **Hours:** *Complex Open daily, 24hr. Information Centre open daily Apr.-Aug. 8am-8pm, Sep.-Mar. 8am-7pm.* **Admission:** *Free.* **Other:** *No tobacco, alcohol, or narcotics of any kind are allowed in the temple complex. Visitors may deposit cigarettes a*

Headless Heroism

In 1761, the Mughal Ahmad Shah Abdali blew up the Golden Temple and filled the sacred tank with refuse. As a result, Baba Deep Singh, an understandably miffed Sikh leader, began an attack on the desecrated temple from 10km outside Amritsar. Baba Deep had sworn to reach the temple, but halfway through he had his head cut off by a Muslim soldier. Disembodied head in hand, the Sikh leader supposedly trudged on, eventually crossing the temple's gates and plopping his noggin in the water before finally expiring. On the road to Tarn Taran is a large shrine to Baba Deep Singh. All passing vehicles stop here to offer a prayer of appreciation for the man's spectacular exploits. The shrine is built on the spot where Baba Deep is thought to have started his zealous shuffle.

block away from the temple's entrance. Shoes, socks, and umbrellas must be left at free depositories at each of the main entrances or at the tourist information center. Visitors must rinse their feet in the tanks in front of the entrances. Photography is allowed inside the temple complex, but not inside the temple itself. Head-coverings are required at all times inside the Temple. They are available for free at the Information Centre and for sale (Rs5-7) outside the Temple, but any scarf, hat, or towel will suffice.

No matter what you choose to call it—the Golden Temple, Hari Mandir, or Darbar Sahib (as it's known in Punjabi)—Amritsar's focal monument is awesomely beautiful and hauntingly serene, oblivious to the grind and grime only a few feet outside its walls. The Golden Temple's tranquility is especially impressive given the tumultuous history of the Sikhs and that of the temple itself. The nearly 400 years of the temple's existence have been marked by incessant destruction and desecration from outsiders. All Sikhs (and quite a few members of other religions) try to make a pilgrimage here at least once in their lifetime.

History

Although Guru Nanak, the founder of Sikhism, once lived near the modern tank, it was **Guru Ram Das** who sparked the growth of a religious center when he began building the pool in 1574. That task was completed under Guru Arjun 15 years later, when the area was named Amritsar. Guru Arjun built the **Hari Mandir** in the tank's center and placed the **Guru Granth Sahib,** the Sikh holy book, inside it.

A series of destructive Mughal invasions followed the 1601 completion of the temple. The temple fell alternatively under Mughal and Sikh control until Ahmad Shah Abdali took the temple and, taking no chances, blew it to smithereens. Finally, under British rule and auspices, the Sikhs reclaimed the site. Punjabi ruler **Maharaja Ranjit Singh** rebuilt the complex, beautified parts with marble and copper, and coated the newly built Hari Mandir with gold leaf. Several years thereafter the British assumed less-than-reverent management of the temple. It wasn't until the 1920s that the practice of pure Sikhism was restored within the temple's walls.

Sadly, the Temple's insistent status as a site of violence extends almost to the present. The 1980's saw the rise of a vocal Sikh militant group, which called (and, in small factions, continues to call) for the creation of an independent Sikh nation. Tensions began to peak in 1983, when the movement's leader, Sant Bhindranwale, sequestered himself in the Golden Temple and incited acts of violence against Hindus. With over 350 Hindus killed by the summer of 1984, Indira Gandhi ordered the national army to storm the temple—a plan dubbed **Operation Bluestar.** But what was intended as a commando raid spiraled into a three-day siege. When the smoke had cleared, more the 750 people were dead, including Bhindranwale and 83 soldiers. Tour guides and brochures are hush-hush about this latter-day violence, emphasizing instead historically distant bloodbaths and the site's current state of peace.

Inside the Golden Temple

The best time to visit is probably around sunset, when the gilded *Hari Mandir* (the central shrine) turns a stupendous orange. The main entrance to the Golden Temple is on the north side, beneath the **clock tower.** This side also has the main shoe depository, several tourist stands, and the **tourist information centre,** which conducts hourly tours in English. The staff here provides informative brochures about the temple and Sikh gurus, and also conducts hourly tours (in English).

The clock tower leads to the **Parikrama,** the 12m wide marble promenade encircling the tank. The four entrances to the temple and the complex symbolize an openness to friendly visitors from all sides—both geographically and metaphorically in terms of caste and creed. Guru Arjun once exclaimed, "My faith is for people of all castes and all creeds from whichever direction they come and to whichever direction they bow."

Traffic moves clockwise around the Parikrama. Here, the **68 Holy Places** represent the 68 holiest Hindu sites in India—to merely walk along this northern edge, Guru Arjun declared, is to attain the holiness a Hindu takes a lifetime to acquire. The small tree at the northeast corner of the tank is said to have been the site of a miracle healing of a cripple; healthy, wealthy, crippled, and destitute alike indulge in the tank's mysterious powers at the adjoining **bathing ghats.** Just next to the *ghats* along the tank is one of four booths in which priests read from the Guru Granth Sahib. **Ongoing readings** are meant to ensure the continuation of Sikh beliefs; with each priest reciting for three hours, a complete reading takes about 50 hours. The eerie tranquility of the temple is enhanced by other speakers perpetually piping *kirtans* (devotional songs) from inside the Hari Mandir.

On the other side of the Parikrama are the **Ramgarhia Minars,** two brick towers that were damaged when tanks plowed through this entrance in 1984 (see **History,** p. 331). This access leads to the Guru-ka-Langar, the communal kitchen, and the *gurudwaras,* the housing for temple pilgrims (see **Accommodations,** p. 329).

The south side of the tank has a shrine to **Baba Deep Singh,** whose headless exploits made him a Sikh hero (see **Headless Heroism,** p. 331). The west end of the tank has several notable structures. First on a clockwise revolution is the window where devotees collect *prasad,* the sweet lumps of cornmeal used as an offering inside the *Hari Mandir.* Farther on, across from the entrance to the Hari Mandir, is the **Akal Takhat,** the second-holiest place here. Guru Hargobind, the sixth Sikh guru, built the Akal Takhat in 1609 as a decision-making center. Many weapons, fine pieces of jewelry, and other Sikh artifacts are stored here.

The two towering flagstaffs next to the Akal Takhat represent the religious and political facets of Sikhism; the two are joined by the **double swords of Hargobind,** reflecting how intertwined these aspects of Sikhism are. Illuminated at the very top, the poles are intended as beacons for pilgrims heading into Amritsar. Near the flagstaffs is the shrine to the last and most militant guru, Gobind Singh.

The last noteworthy spot along the Parikrama, other than the Hari Mandir itself, is the wizened 450-year old **jujube** tree. Baba Buddhaja, the temple's first priest, is thought to have hung around here, though it is unlikely that the umbrella of braces which today support the tree's haggard limbs were needed then. Still, even in its old age, the tree is thought to bring fertility for those who touch it.

Seemingly floating in the middle of the tank, the **Hari Mandir** is the holiest part of the complex. Photography is not allowed past the gate to the temple walkway. The architecture of the Golden Temple incorporates Hindu and Muslim styles—this is most noticeable in the synthesis of the rectangular form of the Hindu temple with the domes and minarets of the Muslim mosque. The three stories of the Hari Mandir, capped by an inverted-lotus dome, are made of marble, copper, and about 100kg of pure gold leaf. Inside the temple on the ground floor, the chief priest and his musicians perform the *gurbani* (hymns) from the Guru Granth Sahib. Devotees sit around the center and toss flowers and money toward the jewel-studded canopy, where the silk-enshrouded Guru Granth Sahib lies.

The holy book is brought to the temple from the Akal Takhat each day and returned at night. The morning ceremony takes place at 4am in the summer, 5am in the winter. At the nighttime ceremony (10pm in winter, 11pm in summer) the temple complex becomes even more serene. The lights that reflect off the blackened

Gataka: 400 Years of Cool Weapons

The Sikhs' success in resisting centuries of oppression is in part attributable to their skill as warriors. Through countless battles, the group developed a martial art known as *gataka*. Today, young would-be warriors practice *gataka* on the roof of the Guru-ka-Langar (daily, 8:30-11pm). They enjoy having visitors watch as they deftly wield the *neja* (spears), swords, bamboo sticks, and other ancient weapons and practice *talwar baji* (fencing), or as it's more bluntly known, *kirpan* (the art of stabbing). The most impressive weapon is the *chakkar*, a wooden ring with stone spheres dangling off it by 4-foot strings. The warrior stands in the middle and spins the ring, the whirling balls forming a barrier around him, then tosses it up into the air (still spinning) for someone nearby to catch. Watching the nightly spectacle is exciting, but participating is even better—the warriors will often let you try the weapons out. To really indulge in *gataka,* they recommend heading out to Raia, 50km outside of Amritsar, where Baba Bakala, the training center for the most hard-core students, is located on G.T. Rd.

NORTH INDIA

tank and the lanterns that illuminate the causeway enhance the temple's vivid colors. Arrive about an hour early to observe the ceremony. Hymns echo through the building before the book is finally revealed and the priest takes over the prayers and chants, folds the book in gold leaf and more silk, and finally places it on the golden *palanquin.* Head downstairs at this point, and you may end up in the line of devotees waiting to shoulder the book as it is carried out of the temple. Although allowed this privilege, non-Sikhs often decline. Finally, a blaring serpentine horn and communal drum beating signal a final prayer that puts the book to bed, near the flagstaff. The entire ceremony lasts about an hour and a half.

Step outside to the left (north) side, onto the *pradakhina,* the **marble path** leading around the temple. On this north side is a stairwell leading to the second floor, where flowers, animals, and hymns ornament the walls and where you can catch a good look at the procession and Adi Granth below. On the east side of this floor is a small *shish mahal* (hall of mirrors). Once occupied by the gurus, the halls now reverberate with the voices of modern-day priests engaged in the *akhand path,* the ongoing reading of the holy book. On the ground floor on the east (back) side of the temple is the **Har-ki-Pari** (Steps of God), which allow visitors easy access to the holy water at this most sacred section of the tank.

No visit to the Golden Temple is complete without a meal at the **Guru-ka-Langar,** the enormous **community kitchen** which is characteristic of all Sikh temples. Sikh founder Guru Nanak instituted the custom of *pangat* (dining together) to reinforce the idea of equality. *Pangat* continues in the dining hall here, where basic meals are dished out daily to 20,000 people who sit in unifying rows, regardless of wealth or caste. As one group eats, the next gathering waits by the door out front in an ongoing cycle. The meal itself begins only after all have been seated along one of the mats and a prayer has been sung—tempting as it is to dive into that *dal,* wait until those around you have started. After that, it's all-you-can-eat *dal-chapatis;* simply hold out cupped hands as the *chapati* chap walks by and he'll toss you more. Afterwards, kindly leave a donation in one of the charity boxes, since this ongoing charity is largely funded by such contributions. A glimpse of the kitchen reveals the heaps of *chapatis* that are flipped nimbly on flaming woodstoves and a gigantic cauldron of simmering *dal.*

The **Central Sikh Museum,** or Gallery of Martyrs, is housed in the northern part of the temple complex; the entrance is on the right of the main gate. *(Open daily 7am-7pm. Free.)* There are portraits of renowned Sikhs, including Baba Deep Singh and Sevapanthi Bhai Mansha Singh, who swam across the tank amid gunfire to keep the temple's light lit. The display of heavy duty arms includes everything from spears to blunderbusses. Paintings of martyred bodies that were boiled or sawed at Chandni Chowk in Old Delhi and photographs of slain Sikh martyrs with pop-eyed, bloody faces spare no detail and are not for the faint of heart.

Just beyond the more modern Hargobind *guruudwara* to the south is the nine-story **Tower of Baba Atal Rai.** According to legend, the tower is named after the son of Guru Hargobind, who perturbed his father with his precociousness, performing a miracle at age nine. In shame, the young *baba* came to this spot and died. On the first floor are some detailed miniatures depicting episodes from Guru Nanak's life and a *nagarah* (drum) for your beating pleasure. The other floors are empty, but you can climb past them to the top for the unsurpassed view of Amritsar, the Golden Temple, and the tank of Kamalsar to the south.

Other Sights

Although the Golden Temple taps most of Amritsar's touristic energies, the city does have other interesting sights. About two blocks north of the temple's main entrance is **Jallianwala Bagh,** the site of one of the most inhumane and horrific moments in colonial—and world—history. On April 13, 1919, crowds filled Jallianwala Bagh to peacefully protest a law which allowed the British to imprison Indians without trial. British Brigadier-General Reginald E.H. Dyer was brought in to quell the disturbance. Dyer stood behind 150 troops in front of the main alley, the only entrance and exit to the compound and ordered his men to open fire without warning on the 10,000 men, women, and children who had gathered there. The shooting continued for an estimated 6 to 15 minutes. People were shot as they perched to jump over walls; others drowned after diving into wells. Dyer's troops had fired 1650 rounds, and nearly all of them found their mark. In all, about 400 people died, while 1500 were wounded. The massacre sparked a rallying cry for Indian insurgence. The Bengali poet Rabindranath Tagore, who had been knighted after winning the Nobel Prize for Literature in 1913, returned his knighthood after the massacre. Dyer was reprimanded and relieved of his duties but never charged with any crime. In 1997, Queen Elizabeth II visited Jallianwala Bagh. Although no official apology was made during her controversial visit, the British Monarch remarked on the regrettability of the massacre, and laid a wreath at the memorial to the victims.

Today Jallianwala Bagh is a calm garden, populated with squatters, college kids, and *bidi*-smoking retirees. The stone well is a monument to the drowned Indians who jumped in attempting to flee and the **Martyr's Gallery** features portraits of heroes related to the event. *(Open summer daily 9am-5pm, winter daily 10am-1pm and 3-7pm.)*

The high profile of the Golden Temple overshadows the existence of the tiny Hindu shrines tucked into alleyways in the immediate vicinity, as well as the more impressive **Durgiana Mandir.** This temple, set back from the busy street four blocks northwest of the Golden Temple, honors the goddess Durga. The exterior is surprisingly like the Hari Mandir, set on a platform in a medium-sized tank.

In the northern part of Amritsar, **Ram Bagh** is a park between Mall and Queens Rd., northeast of the railway station. On the northwest corner of the park stands a menacing statue of Maharaja Ranjit Singh, the Sikh responsible for the early 19th-century restoration of the Golden Temple. Ram Bagh served as his summer residence between 1818 and 1837, and the central building now houses the **Ranijit Singh Museum,** containing oil paintings, weapons, manuscripts, and miniatures from the maharaja's era. *(Open Tu-Su 10am-4:45pm. Admission Rs5.)* The tourist office's pamphlet *Amritsar: Spiritual Centre of Punjab* is a good guide to the museum. Across the street from Ram Bagh on Lawrence Rd., east of the Sindhi Coffee House, the **Indian Academy of Fine Arts** has a small but interesting gallery featuring 20th-century Indian art. *(Open summer daily 8-11am and 4-8pm, winter daily 10am-1pm and 3-7pm. Admission Rs1.)* Amritsar also has an active theater group; consult the local English paper for showings.

■ Near Amritsar

■ Tarn Taran ਟਰਨ ਟਰਨ

Once the Hari Mandir has whetted your appetite for shiny, golden Sikh temples, head 22km south to the town of Tarn Taran. Buses leave every half-hour from the main stand (Rs18). From the Tarn Taran bus stand, it's a 5-minute walk through the narrow alley of the bazaar up to the local *gurudwara.* Its founder, Guru Arjun Dev, built the temple in 1768 to commemorate Guru Ram Das, who, in an act of selfless concern, slept side-by-side with a leper. Though local clinicians don't provide any evidence for the common belief that the water here cures leprosy, they do attest to its curative effects on several minor skin conditions. The architectural style here resembles that of the Amritsar complex. With the long marble *parikrama* and still water reflecting the blazing sun above, it has a serenity all its own. The *gurudwara* in Tarn Taran has free accommodations and a community kitchen that dishes out Amritsar-style *dal.*

■ Pakistan Border

> **WARNING:** If you want to cross into Pakistan, **make sure you have your Pakistani visa and that your Indian visa allows multiple entries.** Stepping across the line isn't easy. For more information, please see **Border Crossings,** p. 46.

Amritsar is the first or last stop in India for travelers heading to or from Pakistan; the *only* border crossing between the two countries is at **Wagah,** 32km from Amritsar, although trains cross at the town of **Attari,** 25km away. Attari Road is the main route to Wagah. On Attari Rd., on the way out of town, keep an eye out on the right side for the impressive edifices of Khalsa College. (The college grounds are open to visitors and its residents are friendly, although there isn't much to see.)

The border is open daily 9am-4pm. There is a **Punjab Tourism** information center (open 9am-5pm), a **State Bank of India** branch for currency exchange (open-Sa 10am-5pm), and a post office for last second send-offs. Those leaving India must declare currency and pass through customs, although tourists need to obtain an export certificate. Also at the border are several eager and friendly cold drink and food vendors. If you're looking for a basic restaurant or a place to crash, head to the **Neem Chameli Tourist Complex,** which has huge, fresh rooms with showers, and a garden. (Singles with fan Rs150; doubles Rs200.)

Border Ballet

A few people go to Wagah to *cross* the border, but a crowd shows up to watch the border closing. A half-hour before sunset (approximately 7pm in the summer), an elaborate nightly ritual accompanies the Indo-Pakistani border's closing and the lowering of the neighboring nations' flags. Tourists crowd around the spiked gate on either side and jostle for the best views. Right on schedule, with a near-farcical dose of solemnity, the ceremony unfolds. As one officer barks an order and another follows with furious stomping and wild high-stepping, the audiences on both sides break into raucous applause. After some machismo-packed face-offs and lengthy siren-like yells, the respective flags are lowered, the lights go bright, the bugles blare, and the visitors mob the gate for a glimpse of the faces on the other side—or for a chance to toe one of the world's most famous white lines.

Himachal Pradesh
हिमाचल प्रदेश

To travel through Himachal Pradesh (Lap of Snow) is to experience a feeling of remoteness unfamiliar to much of India. You'll walk through apple orchards and paddy fields and cross rivers swollen with glacial run-off. The mountain passes will leave you breathless with their beauty and altitude. Different worlds exist side by side in Himachal. Cross the Rohtang Pass and the rain-drenched forests of Manali suddenly give way to the rock, ice, and harsh winds of Lahaul and the vast emptiness and harsh heat of Spiti. Travel from Shimla to Kaza, and you'll see Hindu temples gradually replaced by Buddhist prayer flags and *gompas*. If you take the road from Manali to Leh, in Kashmir, you'll see beauty and feel exhilaration too intense to fully describe.

Himachal is not all serenity and remoteness, however. With the deteriorating political situation in Kashmir, Himachal has been "discovered" by tourists, and the three main tourist towns in H.P. act as oft-packed gateways to the worlds beyond. Dharamsala, which somehow manages to remain peaceful, has a Tibetan population and is the starting point for treks into the Dhauladars and the Pir Panchal, while Manali and Shimla are favorites with both Indian and foreign travelers. The less touristed rainshadow areas—Lahaul, Spiti, and Upper Kinnaur—can be reached from Manali via the Rohtang Pass or from Shimla via Kalpa and Kaza. Road maintenance is difficult in these places, and routes that are theoretically open from June to September can be closed down at any time. Although the tourist season in most of Himachal Pradesh is from May to June and September to October, winter—when roads to Shimla, Manali, Dharamsala, and from Shimla to Chango remain open—is also an ideal time to visit H.P. Prices are lower, and the snow crowns the land's stunning natural beauty.

🖐 HIGHLIGHTS OF HIMACHAL PRADESH

- **Manali** (p. 356) and **Dharamshala** (p. 343) are the alpine stomping grounds where the mythic East (*sadhus*, picture-postcard scenery, and the Dalai Lama) meets and mixes with the equally mythic West (hippies, addicts, and pop stars).
- From the green forests to the isolated, icy mountain-tops, H.P offers some of the most beautiful **trekking** in India, particularly in **Kinnaur and Spiti** (p. 361).

■ Shimla सिमला

During the summer months, Shimla's allure—as the British realized over a century ago—is its weather. Everyone who migrates to this preeminent hill station is set on escaping the sweltering heat that oppresses the rest of the country. The bus window view of what looks like a landslide of tin and concrete turns most foreigners off before they even arrive. But the mix of rickety colonial architecture, cool fog, and gleeful bourgeois Indian holiday antics gives Shimla a surreal grace that merits a longer stay. At an altitude of 2206m, Shimla affords magnificent views of the Shivalik foothills and, off season, when the streets are less crowded and everything is blanketed with snow, the place attains a soul-smoothing serenity. In winter, the nearby resorts at Kufri and Norkanda become skier's heaven.

The modern period of Shimla's history began in the 19th-century, when persistent Gorkha raiders ravaged the small village with fearful efficiency. Local rulers appealed to the British for military aid; the British, seeing a chance to extend their power into the Sutlej River area, obliged, defeating the Gorkhas in 1815. Over the next half-century, British civil servants and injured soldiers flocked to Shimla each summer seeking rest from the rigors of administration. In 1864, imperial authorities made the summer haul to Shimla official, declaring that it would serve as a seasonal capital for the Raj.

NORTH INDIA

Shimla

ACCOMMODATIONS

C Hotel Diplomat
B Hotel Grace
F Hotel Mehman
E Hotel Ridge View
D YMCA
A YWCA

Kaithu Bazaar

TO NARKANDA, RAMPUR, & KINNAUR

TO AIRPORT (21 km)

Indira Gandhi Medical College

TO KUFRI & WILDFLOWER HALL (13 km)

Jakhu Hill (2455m)

Jakhu Temple

LAKKHAR BAZAAR

Daulat Ram Complex

Ladies Park

Lower Mall Rd.

Lift

Tibetan Refugee Shop

THE RIDGE

Circular Rd.

SCANDAL CORNER

Cart Rd.

SEE INSET

Additional Divisional Magistrate's Office

Punjab National Bank

Telegraph Office

The Mall

THE MALL

Main Bus Stand

Kali Bari Temple

Shimla Rail Station

State Bank of India

Cart Rd.

N

Taradevi Rail Station

Kennedy House (Tourist Reception Center)

TO STATE MUSEUM, OBSERVATORY HILL (Rashtrapati Niwas & The Institute for Advanced Studies, 1km), SUMMER HILL (5km), CHADWICK FALLS (7km)

TO ZOO (4km, Turkandi), PROSPECT HILL (5km), KALKA, CHANDIGARH, & DELHI

125 yards
125 meters

INSET

Christ Church

The Mall

Local Bus Stand (Rivoli)

THE RIDGE

Town Hall

ANZ Grindlays Bank

GPO

The Mall

SCANDAL CORNER

Jama Masjid

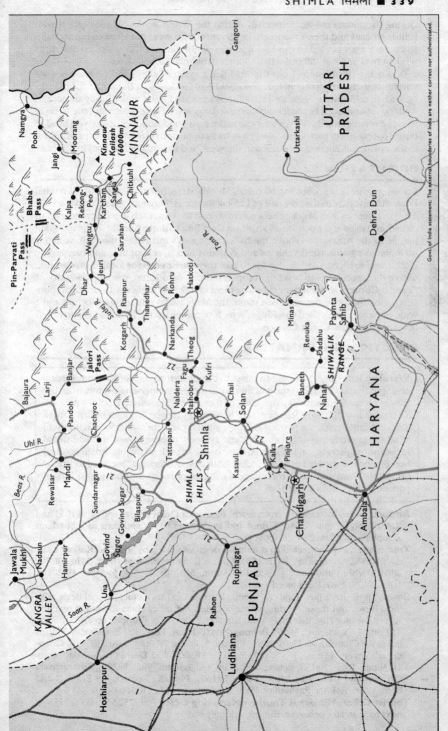

Govt of India statement: The external boundaries of India are neither correct nor authenticated.

During the summers—and especially during the World Wars—Shimla bustled with British officials and their entourages of servants (who were not allowed in the Mall). Keep your eyes peeled in the Mall and you might glimpse the aging, tweedy Brits who "stayed on" and still make their homes in Shimla, 50 years later.

Down any of the steps from the Mall lies a maze of alleys and crushed houses where, as Rudyard Kipling noted, you could stay hidden from the police for months on end. In mid-winter, Shimla's 110,000 residents are buried under heavy snow, and walking around town becomes difficult and dangerous. There is actually little to do in Shimla except enjoy the views, so it can make for a good stopover before you head to busier (or rougher) parts of the state: it is well-connected by road to Kullu and Lahaul in the north, to Kangra and Chamba in the west, and to Kinnaur and Spiti in the east.

ORIENTATION

Set on a large, crescent-shaped ridge, Shimla stretches from west of Himachal Pradesh University to the area east of **Lakkar Bazaar,** where many of the town's 5000 Tibetan refugees live. Major streets run from east to west, each at a different level of elevation. Trains and many buses arrive on **Cart Road.** Above Cart Rd. is the crowded jumble of the bazaar, and above the bazaar is Shimla's main drag, **the Mall,** which is off-limits to all motorized vehicles and contains hotels, restaurants, and banks. The easiest way to ascend and descend is to take the **tourist elevator** located on Cart Rd., where the street starts to bend right (open summer 6am-10pm, winter 7am-9pm). At **Scandal Corner** (so named for the elopement of a British soldier with an Indian princess), directly above the main bus stand, the Mall divides into a lower section and a wide upper section called **the Ridge,** which becomes Lakkar Bazaar as it curves left beyond the yellow **Christ Church.**

PRACTICAL INFORMATION

Warning: Foreigners planning to travel to the eastern regions of Kinnaur, Lahaul, and Spiti (including Tabo) must obtain an all-inclusive **inner-line permit** from the sub-divisional (or assistant) magistrate, as these areas are sensitive border regions. There are also offices in Rampur, Peo, Kaza, and Chamba. Though Indian nationals don't require special permission, they should carry their passports with them at all times while passing through these regions. In Shimla, see the **additional assistant magistrate,** on the second floor of the left side of the big, green colonial building below the Mall near the Indian Coffee House. Bring a "recommendation" (available from any local travel agent), 2 passport-sized photos, and lots of patience. Open M-Sa 10am-5pm.

Airport: Jubbarhatti, 30km from town. Flights to **Delhi** (daily, 1hr., US$105) and **Kullu** (daily, 30min., US$67). Book **Indian Airlines** flights and taxis to Jubbarhatti at Ambassador Travels (see above).

Trains: Shimla is connected to a number of cities via a "toy train" to **Kalka** (4 per day, 10:55am-6pm, 4hr., Rs16/114). Connections to: **Bikaner** (8am, 11hr., Rs70/200); **Delhi** (3 and 6am, 4:15 and 11:30pm, 6hr., Rs45/150); **Jodhpur** (9:20am, 10hr., Rs75/230). Fares listed are 2nd/1st class.

Buses: There are 2 bus stands in Shimla: the one next to Victory Tunnel deals with local buses and those heading to major cities; the other abuts Rivoli Cinema and serves Rampur (the gateway to the Kinnaur Valley). To: **Rampur** (every hr., 4am-4:30pm, 7:45pm, 3hr., Rs65); **Rekong-Peo** (6:10am, 12hr., Rs120). Victory Tunnel buses to: **Chamba** via **Dalhousie** (4:15am, 5, 6, and 7:10pm, 14hr., Rs200); **Chandigarh** (every 15min., 6:30am-9pm, 10hr., Rs60); and **Delhi** (10 per day, 6am-10:30pm, 10hr., Rs158; deluxe at 8:25am and 7:30pm, 9hr., Rs290); **Dharamsala** (15 per day, 4:15am-10:15pm, 10hr., Rs160); **Manali** (5 per day, 8-11am, 7 and 8pm, 10hr., Rs170); **Pathankot** (5am and 6:30pm, 11hr., Rs180).

Tourist Office: Himachal Tourism Marketing Office (tel. 252561; fax 252557), next to Scandal Corner, on the left. Friendly staff.

Budget Travel: There are travel offices on every corner, all offering transport and trekking assistance. **Ambassador Travels,** the Mall (tel 258014; fax 211139) is reliable. **Transmount Adventures,** on the 2nd floor of the Daulat Ram Complex in Lakkar Bazaar, specializes in adventure travel.

Currency Exchange: Punjab National Bank, ANZ Grindlays, and the **State Bank of India,** all on the Mall. All open M-F 10am-2pm. ANZ Grindlays offers cash advances on MC and Visa.

Bookstore: see **shopping,** p. 343

Police: Foreign tourists should contact the **Control Room** in the Mall (tel. 212322).

Hospital/Medical Services: Himachal Pradesh Civil Hospital, Lakkar Bazaar. **Private doctors** are more helpful. Ask your hotel manager to contact one, or call the **Nehru Clinic,** on the Mall (tel. 201596), in a side alley. Open M-Sa 10am-2pm and 4:30-6pm. Consultation fee Rs40. You can also call the **Shri Ram Medical Centre,** just off the Mall (tel. 205300). Open 9:30am-2pm and 3-7:30pm. For emergencies, call **Indira Gandhi Medical College** (tel. 203073). **Ambulance** (tel. 252102).

Pharmacy: There are a number along the Mall. The pharmacy inside the **Indira Gandhi Medical College** complex on Circular Rd. (tel. 203073) is open 24hr.

Post Office: GPO, just above Scandal Corner. Speed post and *Poste Restante* available. Open M-Sa 10am-7pm. **Postal Code:** 171001.

Telephone Code: 0177.

ACCOMMODATIONS

Prices skyrocket from May-June and September-October, when thousands ascend from the steaming plains, and decent rooms run about Rs500. The really cheap places near Victory Tunnel and the bus station are congested dumps with common baths (Rs200-250 in season). Nicer hotels are up the Mall. Expect discounts of up to 50% off season, unless otherwise indicated. Most hotels levy an additional 10% tax.

YMCA (tel. 204085 or 252375; fax 211016), up the stairs behind Christ Church. Not just for men, and quite possibly the last affordable, truly worthwhile place to stay in Shimla. Colonial grandeur melds seamlessly with kitsch. Rooms are standard but clean, and the rec rooms have TV, billiards, and other diversions. Arranges treks and jeep safaris to Kinnaur, Spiti, Leh, and the Kullu Valley. Breakfast included. Prices stay the same year round. Running hot water 7pm-9am. Doubles Rs210, with attached bath Rs280. Membership fee Rs40. Extra person Rs125 per day.

Hotel Mehman, Daisy Bank Estate (tel. 252604 or 204390). All rooms have plush wall-to-wall carpets, color TV, and attached baths with 24hr. running hot water, and heating in the winter. The lap of luxury. Check-out noon. Doubles Rs550-1100.

YWCA (tel. 203081), opposite the Main Telegraph Office. The rooms are in the third-oldest building in town and they retain a tattered colonial ambience. The garden lends a sense of space rare in most Shimla hotels. Attached baths. Open to men and women. Offers beautician and textile design courses. Hot water and quilt Rs3. Check-out noon. Rooms Rs150-250. Membership fee Rs10.

Hotel Ridge View, Ridge Rd. (tel. 255002), near the Ritz Cinema. The more expensive rooms come with a TV and hot water. Room and laundry services available. Check-out noon. Doubles with attached bath Rs250-500.

Hotel Diplomat, Lakkar Bazaar, The Ridge (tel. 252001 or 257754), in the middle of the bazaar and impossible to miss. Rooms are clean and carpeted (though they have a sickly cast), with attached baths with 24hr. running hot water. Cable TV. Check-out noon. Doubles Rs440, with a view Rs650, with balcony Rs660. Extra person Rs125. MC, Visa.

Hotel Grace. The 10min. walk northeast of the Mall (down through Lakkar Bazaar) makes a noticeable difference in terms of peace and quiet. All rooms have attached marble bathrooms, color TV, and 24hr. room service. Doubles Rs450-800.

FOOD

Though Himachali cuisine is as distinctive and varied as its regions, don't expect to find any restaurants serving regional specialties here. Most menus feature everything from South Indian to Italian to Thai and Chinese. In addition, an impressive array of snack stalls line the Ridge.

The Solitaire, the Mall (tel. 257329). Part lounge with plush sofas, part restaurant with delectable eats, The Solitaire makes for pleasant dining, even if you're alone. The window seats offer splendid views of the valley below. *Malai* mushroom Rs80. Open daily noon-10pm.

Park Cafe, on the slope between the Mall and the Ridge. The bamboo-plastered interior holds Western regulars in thrall with up-to-date pop music, English newspapers, and well-executed foreign standards. The wait can be long, but the pizza (Rs35) and the superb milkshakes (Rs20-30) are worth it. Open daily 8am-10pm

Alfa (tel. 25715), on the Ridge. A nice place to sit and feed after a stroll along the Ridge. Clean and cozy atmosphere. Serves Continental, Chinese, Thai, and Mughali entrees Rs30-90. Open daily 11am-10pm.

Indian Coffee House, on the Mall. A favorite hang-out with locals and tourists alike, ICH is always packed, and finding a table during lunch hours is a pain. Good coffee; even better is the old Indian Coffee Workers' Union Propaganda on the walls. South Indian food (Rs20-30) and snacks. Open daily 8:30am-9:30pm.

SIGHTS

Himachal Pradesh State Museum

Location: *Walk west along the Mall until you reach a concrete ramp labeled "Museum," directly next to the Ambedkar Chowk sub-post office.* **Hours:** *Tu-Su 10am-1:30pm and 2-5pm.* **Admission:** *Free.*

Although the walk is long, the two-story museum has a wide-ranging collection and informative placards explaining the sights. A collection of vibrantly colored **Pahari miniature paintings** is the cream of the museum's crop; additional works by H.P. artists can be found on the second floor. If you plan to hike up to the Jakhu Temple (see below), the precisely rendered "Hanuman Adoring Rama" is worth a special look. A collection of coins discovered in H.P. includes some well-preserved specimens of 2nd-century BC Indo-Greek coins, while a collection of dressed-up mannequins and dolls showcases India's splendid sartorial diversity.

Viceregal Lodge (Rashtrapati Nivas),

Location: *Pass the entrance to the state museum and walk west along the Mall for 15 minutes.* **Hours:** *Daily 10am-1pm and 2-4:30pm.* **Admission:** *Free.* **Other:** *Guided tours Rs5. Aviary open Tu-Su 10am-5pm. Admission Rs5.*

The Lodge, which houses the fellows of the **Indian Institute of Advanced Study,** was built between 1884 and 1888. This unabashedly grand building nestled amid well-manicured gardens was the summer headquarters of the Raj. The lodge was designed to impress: it was the first government building in British India equipped with electricity. Next to the entrance to the Indian Institute of Advanced Study is the **Himalayan Aviary,** opened in August 1994. The small, chain-link enclosed aviary houses red jungle fowl, perky pheasants, and some magnificent peacocks. With white feathers filling the air, the aviary can feel like the inside of a pillow.

Jakhu Temple

Location: *At the east end of the city, with the trail beginning just left of Christ Church.*

The temple sits atop a 2455m hill, and the 20-minute walk to the top is a steep huffer and puffer, especially if you've been smoking too many *bidis*. The red-and-yellow temple on top of the hill is architecturally uninspiring, but inside are what some believe to be the footprints of the monkey god Hanuman. Hordes of pesky, aggressive monkeys revel in their heritage and in the snacks tourists feed them. The temple also has a canteen, swing, and, in the morning, a view of the mountains. Two networks of paths lead back toward town. While both cut through magnificent, lush forests, the sinuous paths directly to the right of the temple afford better opportunities for seeing pristine forests and taking pleasant detours. Neither set of paths is marked, but they all eventually lead down. Allow 45 minutes to an hour to reach town on the way down from Jakhu; expect to emerge from the forest near Lakkar Bazaar, 15 minutes or so from Scandal Corner.

ENTERTAINMENT

Most visitors are content to simply stroll along the Mall or the Ridge, where the breezes are cool, the architecture is pretty, and the company is friendly. Diverting pit-stops abound. The Mall has a number of book shops, as well as stores selling ice cream, nuts, and candy, making the street a snacker's paradise. The Mall is also home to a dismal second-story **billiard hall** and numerous small **video arcades** for those who really need a Super Mario Bros. fix. For sudsy diversions, there are a few **pubs. Himani's** serves drinks at inflated prices (beer Rs60-70) until 9 or 10pm. Other options for booze are the bar at **Rendezvous,** just next to the statue of Lalalajpatrai (beer Rs40), and **The English Wine Shop,** which sells bottled alcohol from a spot on just below Christ Church.

For **movies** in English, head to **Rivoli** or **Ritz.** Rivoli usually shows its English-language flicks at 5pm (buy tickets by 4:30pm); it's down the ramp nestled between ANZ Grindlays Bank and Rendezvous. Ritz usually screens sexy English-language films at 5:30 and 9pm; it's just east of Christ Church, on the ramp leading up to the YMCA Guesthouse. Just below Rivoli is an **ice-skating rink,** which rents skates, and typically opens for the season in January.

SHOPPING

Himachal's geographical isolation has allowed a tradition of out-of-the-ordinary hand-icrafts to evolve; in Shimla, the tradition assaults travelers in the form of stores selling fine woodwork, leather embroidery, engraved metalwork, patterned carpets, and traditional woolen shawls. Check out any of the stores that crowd the Mall and Lakkar Bazaar. **Kashmir Craft Emporium,** 92 The Mall, has a particularly breathtaking collection of shawls (Rs100-5000) and silk *saris* (Rs250-4000).

While it was the British who bequeathed upon Shimla the delightful habit of mingling business with pleasure, it is Rajiv Sud who has perfected the practice. Sud is the soft-spoken and affable owner of **Maria Brothers,** 78 The Mall (just below the church), a store specializing in bizarre and beautiful old books. Prices aren't cheap, but Sud is as nice to browsers as he is to buyers. (Open daily 10:30am-1pm and 3-8pm.)

■ Dharamsala धर्मशाला

After China's invasion of Tibet in 1959, the 14th Dalai Lama and his Buddhist government were given asylum in Dharamsala, a former British hill station. Since then, a steady stream of Tibetan exiles has relocated here, some of them walking across the winter Himalayas to escape oppression and to be near the man they regard as their religious and political leader. Today, Upper Dharamsala, also called McLeod Ganj (named after David McLeod, a former governor of the Punjab), attracts tourists, students, and devotees of Buddhism to its temples, monasteries, nunneries, meditation centers, and Tibetan shops. A rapid rise in the global popularity of the Tibetan cause over the past few years has increasingly given the refugee community the feel of a crowded international crossroads. Many *dharma*-seekers are perturbed to find their spiritual vacation marred by other tourists and nightly taxi jams, and many young Tibetans here have had to invent new ways of presenting themselves—and their cause—to the growing number of foreigners.

The city perhaps best known as "Little Lhasa" is one of the most beautiful places in India. Nestled against the craggy Dhauladar mountains amidst pine and deodar forests, Dharamsala offers fantastic views of Himalayan peaks and the Kangra Valley. Several easy hikes from McLeod Ganj take you into the Dhauladhars within a few hours. During July and August, however, Dharamsala is wet—really wet—so bring flip-flops to navigate the muddied streets, as well as a jacket for the evenings.

ORIENTATION

The town is divided into two sections with a 500m difference in altitude. Its geography is the result of a massive earthquake in 1905, which destroyed all of the buildings and killed 900 people in the Kangra Valley. Alarmed at the destruction atop the hill, the British administration established **Lower Dharamsala,** which now holds mostly offices and houses, as well as the tourist office and the major banks. **Upper Dharamsala (McLeod Ganj)** attracts far more tourist attention. Seven roads branch off the main bus circle in McLeod Ganj. First is **Cantonment Road,** the route used by the bus to travel to and from Lower Dharamsala. Going clockwise, the next road is the **Taxi Stand Road,** which leads to the Tibetan Children's Village. Next is a steep road to Dharamkot. The fourth road is the **TIPA Road,** which also leads to Dharamkot but passes the Tibetan Institute of Performing Arts on its way. Next is **Bhagsu Road,** which leads to Bhagsu Nag (a 20min. walk) after passing many restaurants and hotels. The sixth road is **Jogibara Road,** chock full of restaurants and guest houses. Finally, **Temple Road** leads to the Dalai Lama's residence, Tsuglagkhang Temple, and Namgyal Monastery. A steep 30min. walk down either Jogibara or Temple Rd. lands you in Gangchen Kyishong, the Tibetan government-in-exile complex and home of the Library of Tibetan Works and Archives.

PRACTICAL INFORMATION

Buses: Non-local ordinary **buses** usually arrive at and depart from the **New Bus Stand** in Lower Dharamsala. Booking Office open daily 8am-noon and 2-8pm. To: **Amritsar** (5am, 6hr., Rs73); **Dalhousie** (8:30am, 7hr., Rs65); **Delhi** (5, 6, 7:20am, 2 and 8:30pm, 14hr., Rs160; semi-deluxe 8:30pm, 13hr., Rs295); **Manali** (5 per day, 4am-8:30pm, 11hr., Rs180); **Pathankot** (9 per day, 7:40am-5pm, 3½hr., Rs40); **Shimla** (7 per day, 5am-9:30pm, 10hr., Rs110-198; semi-deluxe 7am, 11hr., Rs160). **Deluxe buses** can be booked in McLeod Ganj; be sure to check where they depart from. To: **Delhi** (5pm, 13hr., Rs390) and **Manali** (9am, 9hr., Rs225). Buses to and from Manali and Dalhousie are sporadic during monsoon and snow seasons due to blocked roads and mudslides.

Local Transportation: Buses run between the New Bus Stand and McLeod Ganj every hr. 4am-6:30am and every 30min. 6:30am-8:30pm (Rs5). Faster but even more cramped are the shared jeeps, which run between Kotwali Bazaar and McLeod Ganj (Rs5). If they're all already full, try catching one 50-100m down from Kotwali. Once in McLeod Ganj, you can walk anywhere. The **Taxi Union Stand** beside the bus circle has pricey fixed rates to most destinations—they're generally only worth it if you're heading up to Dharamkot at night.

Tourist Office: Himachal Tourism Marketing Office (tel. and fax 24212), in Lower Dharamsala. Tries to help out with local sight-seeing, books expensive Himachal Tourism-run hotels, and disseminates leaflets. Open daily 8am-8pm.

Budget Travel: Most agencies in McLeod Ganj organize **treks** in the Pir Panchal and Dhauladhar ranges (Rs700-1000 per person per day) and provide guides and porters for non-organized treks. **Yeti Trekking,** in the Yeti Guest House on the steep road to Dharamkot, is well-established and offers comprehensive trekking services and advice. For computerized airline, train, and deluxe bus bookings, Pradeep at **Dhauladar Travel,** on Temple Rd., is helpful and accepts Visa, MC, and AmEx for charges above Rs500. Open daily 9am-1pm and 2-6pm.

Currency Exchange: State Bank of India, between Jogibara and Temple Rd., McLeod Ganj, and on the main road in Lower Dharamsala. Both branches exchange cash and traveler's checks. Open M-F 10:30am-1:30pm, Sa 10:30-11:30am. **Bank of**

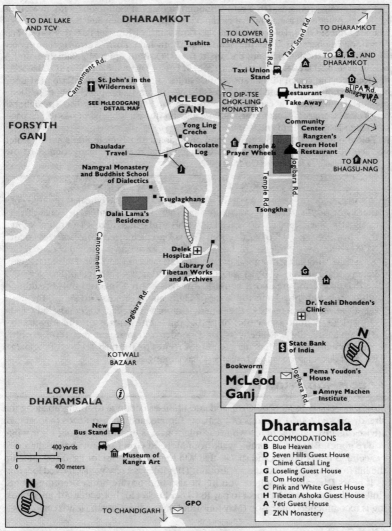

Dharamsala

ACCOMMODATIONS
B Blue Heaven
D Seven Hills Guest House
I Chimé Gatsal Ling
G Loseling Guest House
E Om Hotel
C Pink and White Guest House
H Tibetan Ashoka Guest House
A Yeti Guest House
F ZKN Monastery

Baroda, Lower Dharamsala, gives overnight Visa and MC cash advances (Rs100 plus 1% service charge). Open M-F 10am-2pm, Sa 10am-noon.

Bookstore: Bookworm, Temple Rd. At the fork, follow the sign to Hotel Bhagsu; Bookworm will be 10m on the right. Loads of wonderful books are watched over by Lhasang Tsering, owner of the store, co-founder of the Amnye Machen Institute (see below, **Sights**), and friend of the Beastie Boys. Open daily summer 9am-6:30pm; winter 10am-5pm. **Information Office Bookshop** on Jogibara Rd., near the prayer wheels, has political books and magazines. Open Tu-Su 9am-1pm and 2-6pm.

Police: The closest station (tel. 21483) is in Forsyth Ganj, west of McLeod Ganj.

Hospital: Himachal Government Hospital, McLeod Ganj (tel. 22189). The Tibetan **Delek Hospital,** on Jogibara Rd. just before Gangchen Kyishong (tel. 22053), has a good walk-in clinic, a small lab, and an **Ambulance Service** (tel. 23118). For minor or chronic problems, **Dr. Yeshi Dhonden** (tel. 21461), off Jogibara Rd. in McLeod Ganj, practices Tibetan herbal medicine (see p. 346). Open Su-F 8am-noon.

Post Office: GPO, Lower Dharamsala, 1km south of Kotwali Bazaar. **Post Office,** along Jogibara Rd., past the State Bank. Both have *Poste Restante.* Letters not addressed to McLeod Ganj end up at the GPO. Both open M-F 9am-2pm and 3-5pm. **Postal Code:** McLeod Ganj 176219, Lower Dharamsala (GPO) 176215.

Internet: The Green Restaurant on Bhagsu Rd., now runs a **Cyber Cafe** next door, where you can send email and access the Web from 10am-3pm (Rs50 per hr., Rs13 for 15min.). Stop by early to get a spot on the lengthy waiting list. The **Tibetan Youth Congress Computer Section,** also on Bhagsu Rd., charges Rs40 per page. Open M-Sa 9am-1pm and 2-7pm.

Telephones: STD/ISD booths abound on Jogibara and Temple Rd., some of which stay open until 1am. Himachal Travel on Jogibara Rd. is particularly friendly to low-charge calls. **Telephone Code:** 01892.

"Tell Me Where It Hurts, Your Holiness."

Not many doctors besides Yeshi Dhonden can claim to have healed the body of the divine *bodhisattva* of compassion. But then Yeshi Dhonden, personal physician to the Dalai Lama for 20 years, knows his stuff—and there's a lot to know. At the most precise level of distinction, Tibetan medicine recognizes no less than 84,000 different disorders. The bad news is that each one is ultimately caused by a specific "afflictive emotion." "In the Tibetan system," says Dr. Dhonden, "we believe that basically all of us are sick." The good news is that each disorder can be diagnosed and treated. Diagnosis involves a three-fingered pulse reading, which tells the physician the state of eight major organs and six bodily elements—even (upon request) the patient's future with regard to friends, kids, and evil spirits. A huge repertoire of herbal pills gently heads off the unwanted (though karmically just) ill effects. Dr. Dhonden will treat you, too, 100% earthly being though you are. His clinic (tel. 21461) is just off the busy section of Jogibara Rd., and consultation is free (open Su-F 8am-noon).

ACCOMMODATIONS

Most tourists stay in McLeod Ganj, and guest houses continue to spring up along the already packed tourist sections of Jogibara, Temple, and Bhagsu Roads (a local joke advises against parking here—your car might have a guest house built on it while you're gone). **Bhagsu,** a 20min. walk from McLeod Ganj but only marginally more peaceful, is full of houses and shacks that will rent you a room for Rs50-100; hike up the hill from the main road and ask around. TIPA Rd. has a few well-removed lodgings as it nears **Dharamkot,** where you might also find private houses renting rooms. Unless otherwise stated, expect to pay Rs10 per bucket for hot water. Advance booking is recommended in season (May-June) and during the Tibetan New Year.

Yeti Guest House (tel. 21032), 75m from McLeod Ganj bus circle up the steeper road to Dharamkot. Enjoy views of the valley and a game of frisbee on the lawn. Age has left the rooms and common bathroom a bit decrepit. Check-out noon. Blankets Rs2 per day, quilts Rs5 per day. Doubles Rs65-85.

Chimé Gatsal Ling (tel. 21340). Head 10min. down Temple Rd., then left up the driveway across from the School of Dialectics—the big orange building is on the left after 75m. Part housing for Nyingmapa-sect monks, part hidden hotel. Spotless, carpeted rooms have plenty of space. Roof is perfect for watching the sun set on the Dhauladars. Doubles Rs75, with attached bath (shower and seat toilet) Rs125.

Om Hotel (tel. 21313), in McLeod Ganj, just down the paved path to the right of Temple Rd. from the bust stand. Travelers from other hotels flock to the balcony restaurant for a peaceful early morning *chai* or for the awesome sunset view. The upscale rooms are large and well-appointed, and the attached bathrooms have seat toilets and hot water. In-season: doubles Rs225-250, depending on the view. Off-season: Rs200.

Tibetan Ashoka Guest House (tel. 21763), off Jogibara Rd., on the left about 75m from the bus circle. With over 37 rooms, this place is likely to have a spot for you during high-season. The common squat-toilets are clean, and some rooms have valley-side balconies. Small, sterile doubles in the concrete abode begin at Rs55, and prices climb to Rs330 as your room gets a view or a bathroom and water heater.

Blue Heaven (tel. 21005), just below Dharamkot. A steep but enjoyable 20min. walk up TIPA Rd. brings you to this quiet, luxurious guest house. Blue Heaven's rooms have sitting areas, fully equipped private baths, and balconies overlooking both serene terraces. Attached restaurant serves Italian pasta (Rs55) and other goodies. In-season: doubles Rs200-250. Off-season: Rs150.

Zilnan Kagyeling Nyingmapa (ZKN) Monastery, up the driveway just past Last Chance Tibetan Restaurant, 15min. up Bhagsu Rd. Dim, spare rooms line the sides of this shiny new (and fully functional) monastery. A few steps out your door take you to the meditative courtyard and its temple architecture. All rooms have common baths. Singles Rs50; doubles Rs70.

Seven Hills Guest House (tel. 21580), in McLeod Ganj, on the left side of TIPA Rd., 100m from the bus circle. Second-story rooms don't catch the noise pollution from the bus circle area. Make friends on the large balcony. Spacious and clean, all rooms have 2 single beds. White-tiled common baths with squat toilets sparkle (hot showers Rs10). Singles Rs50; doubles Rs90, with bath and hot water Rs150, with private balcony Rs250 (negotiable). All rooms 50% off in snowy Jan.-Feb.

Loseling Guest House, Jogibara Rd., McLeod Ganj (tel. 21072), 60m from the bus circle on your left. A favorite with visiting Tibetan monks. Rooms are so clean you could eat off the floor. Private bathrooms with hot water pass the same test. Checkout noon, lockout midnight. No alcohol. Doubles with private bath Rs150-250, depending on hot shower and balcony.

Pink and White Guest House, up the hill from the center of Bhagsu, next to German Bakery. An array of faux-luxury rooms barely set apart from busy Bhagsu. Room service 6am-11pm; entrees Rs20-35. Rooms have private bath and 24hr. hot water. In-season: singles Rs200; doubles 350-500. Off-season: discount 40%.

FOOD

In McLeod Ganj, the appearance of heavy, flat noodles and hunks of mutton reminds you that you're in Tibetan culinary territory. Dharamsala also offers a few local twists on the tired "Chinese-Indian-Continental" menu: muesli, pancakes, *lassis*, and *thalis* all enjoy a rare level of imaginative experimentation. Head for the smaller, monk-filled *dhabas*, where the *momos* are authentic and the conversation spirited and spiritual.

Tsongkha Restaurant, Jogibara Rd., across from the Loseling Hotel. Monks hang out and chat beneath motivational posters of mountain scenes and galloping horses. Probably the best veg. *momo* soup in town (Rs16), as well as 16 styles of pancakes and sublime honey and curd muesli (Rs25). Open daily 7:30am-10:30pm.

Green Hotel and Restaurant, Bhagsu Rd. A favorite among foreigners for carrot cake (Rs15) and coffee (Rs10). The "farmer's breakfast" is a massive omelette packed with veggies (Rs25). Open daily 7:30am-10pm.

Lhasa Restaurant and Beer Bar, McLeod Ganj, on the bus circle. Enjoy a tasty meal and a beer (Rs65) with images of Gandhi and the Dalai Lama gazing over you. Popular with young Tibetans and monks out on the town. Open daily 8am-9pm.

Rangzen's, next to the Green Shop. Smack your lips on tasty garlic potato *momos* (Rs20) or fit them around one of the stacked Tibetan brown bread sandwiches (Rs15-20). Close quarters make for good conversation. Open daily 7am-10pm.

Take Away, Bhagsu Rd., next to Hotel Tibet. One of the most popular bakeries in town. Fresh croissants, "chocolate chocolate cake," and an array of breads (Rs10-15) laid out daily at 12:30pm. Open daily 8am-10pm.

Chocolate Log, 70m past the Post Office on Jogibara Rd. The corrugated tin building is actually shaped and colored to resemble a giant log of chocolate. Inside, a case displays a small range of confections with densities nature never intended—the chocolate balls make a good snack at Rs5 a piece. Open daily 7am-8pm.

Welfare Café, inside the Community Center on Bhagsu Rd. Grab a book from the library across the hall, peruse the latest postings, and listen to the jangling folk-guitar posse out on the balcony (for as long as you can take it). This roomy awareness-enclave stocks a basic all-veg. menu and decent coffee (Rs10). Open M-Sa 9am-10pm (later on "jam session" nights).

SIGHTS

Gangchen Kyishong

Location: *Halfway between McLeod Ganj and Lower Dharamsala on Jogibara Rd.—turn left through the archway.* **Phone:** *2467.* **Hours:** *Open M-Sa 9am-1pm and 2-5pm, closed 2nd and 4th Sa.* **Admission:** *Free.* **Other:** *Library reading membership Rs15 per month, lending membership Rs150 per month. Nine-month courses in Buddhist philosophy Rs50 registration fee plus Rs100 per month. Classes M-Sa at 9 and 11am, except 2nd and 4th Sa. Tibetan language courses Rs200 per month.*

Gangchen Kyishong is the site of the administrative offices of the **Tibetan government-in-exile.** The information office here answers questions about the Tibetan political situation. The **Library of Tibetan Works and Archives,** at the far end of Gangchen Kyishong, has documents, periodicals, and books in Tibetan and English. Language and philosophy courses are offered as well; you can attend a session or two for free, although the Tibetan government would no doubt appreciate the registration fee. Remember to behave respectfully during your class: remove your shoes before entering the study hall and, for philosophy sessions, don't stand up until the lama has left. The **museum** upstairs has beautiful *thankas,* Tibetan coins, and a model mandala.

Other Sights

Tsuglagkhang Temple sits behind the Buddhist School of Dialectics, a 10-minute walk from the bus circle in McLeod Ganj. *(Open daily sunrise to sunset.)* The temple houses images of the Buddha, Padmasambhava, and Avalokiteshvara ("Chenresig" in Tibetan). This last image, of the *bodhisattva* of whom the Dalai Lama is an incarnation, was rescued from the Tokhang Temple in Lhasa and brought here during the massive destruction wrought by the Chinese Cultural Revolution. Monks from the School of Dialectics come to debate in the temple's courtyard in the afternoons, snapping, clapping, and shouting at each other. Each highly stylized snap, clap, and stomp corresponds to a specific moment in the argument being advanced by the standing member of the debating pair. The debate proceeds via an immensely complex system of logic, one of the defining features of the Gelugpa sect's teachings.

The **Tibetan Children's Handicraft and Vocational Centre,** a 45-minute walk up the hill from the taxi stand in McLeod Ganj, instructs refugees in the arts of *thanka* painting, carpet weaving, and good old-fashioned capitalist marketing. Another 10-minute walk up the hill and you'll pass Dal Lake before you see the **Tibetan Children's Village School (TCV)** on the right. The TCV has been housing, caring for, and educating more than 2400 orphaned Tibetan children under the patronage of the Dalai Lama since 1960. Foreigners are welcome to visit the school (M-F 9am-4pm), and staff will show you around. If you show up on a Saturday or Sunday, you'll likely end up shooting hoops with the kids or helping them practice their English. You can sponsor a child (US$30 per month). Any donations are needed and accepted.

The **Tibetan Institute of Performing Arts (TIPA),** a 10-minute walk up TIPA Rd. toward Dharamkot, has cultural shows and performs a Tibetan opera for the New Year. Stop in for more details. *(Open M-Sa 8:30am-4:30pm, closed 2nd and 4th Sa).*

The **Bhagsu-Nag Temple,** at the north end of Bhagsu, rests beside several cool *kunds* (pools) in which devout Hindus and rowdy kids bathe. According to legend, 9035 years ago, there was a drought in the kingdom of Ajmer, in present-day Rajasthan. In order to save his realm, King Bhagsu headed near here, to a peak 5400m high, where he discovered two lakes and trapped their waters in his bowl. But as the king lay down to sleep, Nag, the cobra who owned the lakes, challenged him to a fight.

Politics, Tibetan Style

Being a political leader, Nobel Peace Laureate, and world religious figure is a tall order for anyone. But the Dalai Lama's job description is even broader—it includes, for example, interviewing a man temporarily possessed by the Nechung oracle (which gives him the superhuman strength to leap around in an 50kg costume) on a regular basis in order to make political decisions. Other tools of statecraft include hiding fortune-cookie-type slips of paper in dough balls, rolling them in a bowl until one pops out, and reading the verdict. Meanwhile, His Holiness has to make decisions regarding 1000-year-old politico-religious quarrels and then travels internationally, lecturing on Tibet's position in global politics—not exactly the easiest job in the world. Even divinity, it seems, has its difficulties.

Although the weary king was mortally wounded, he made a dying wish that the people of Ajmer be rid of the drought. Impressed by Bhagsu's devotion to his people, Nag granted him his wish. The result of the battle is today known as the **Indira Gandhi Canal,** which irrigates most of Rajasthan. The temple at Bhagsu-Nag marks the event and the snake-god's respect for the king. The Vadilal Ice Cream depot next to the *kunds* irrigates tourists and locals with excellent milkshakes (Rs25). A 20-minute walk beyond the temple (step through the chink in the wall to reach the path) is the **Bhagsu Waterfall,** which cascades up to 30 spectacular feet during the monsoon season. There are small open-air cafes above and below the falls. The lower one has cold drinks, crackers, and a crowd of Indian bathers strutting around in their underwear (but only in the summer). The upper one, Shiva Café, has hot meals, chessboards, and opium-inspired rock paintings.

St. John's in the Wilderness, a 15-minute walk downhill toward Lower Dharamsala, is a functioning relic of the bygone British era. *(Open daily 9am-5pm. Sunday services are held in English at 11:30am. Christmas candle-light services.)* The kind pastor will happily converse with you about your country or his. Lord Elgin, an ex-Viceroy of India, is buried in the church cemetery, where dusk fog swirls around grave stones.

Well worth the journey is the **Norbu Lingka,** 30km from McLeod Ganj in the Kangra Valley, a haven and learning center for the master artists of Tibet and their pupils. *(Open M-Sa 9am-1pm and 2-5pm, closed 2nd and 4th Sa. Free.)* You can stroll through the compound, talk to top-notch wood carvers, *thanka* painters, and iron workers, and pick up a handicraft or two for the folks back home. To get to Norbu Lingka, take the public bus from Dharamsala toward Palampur (Rs10) and hop off at Norbu Lingka, or shell out Rs250 for a round-trip taxi from McLeod Ganj.

Dip-Tse-Chok-Ling Monastery, home to a small (and largely young) community of monks, is a 10-minute walk from the bus circle down a stone path that begins just past Om Hotel. Seek out a lama to help you decipher the frescoes, butler sculptures, and (seasonal) sand *mandala* for which the temple is known, but be sure to leave a generous donation. Rooms can be rented here for Rs80, if you don't mind the hike.

A perfect day-hike from Dharamkot takes you to the rolling, grassy ridgetop of **Triund** (just below the Dhauladar peaks in the view from McLeod Ganj). There's a small, sporadically functional resthouse here, as well as a comfortable cave 50m uphill. A second basic resthouse can be found 5km up the trail, where you can see the peaks in their massive entirety. Resist the urge to climb higher unless you've gotten good, detailed advice and have some mountaineering experience—it's an all-day endeavor even from here, and clouds rush up from the valley in the afternoon.

ENTERTAINMENT

The market section of Jogibara Rd. is home to two hole-in-the-wall **movie houses,** which show a seemingly random mix of surprisingly recent American blockbusters and bizarre low-grade flicks. The wooden benches are only slightly more comfortable than an ordinary bus, but the biggish TV screens have good reception. Movie times are generally 5 and 9pm (Rs10). **Mullo's** third-floor bar (on the bus circle), with its Hawaiian decor and endlessly looped Beatles cassettes, makes for a surreal place to swill. Young, unemployed Tibetans gather here to mingle with and vent to the mobs of Westerners. Occasional **dance parties** start at 11pm and go until the 95% male dance floor clears (cover Rs50).

VOLUNTEER OPPORTUNITIES

The Tibetan community has decided that the ability to speak English is a necessity in its struggle for freedom, and English teachers and simple conversationalists are highly appreciated. The enthusiastic monks and Tibetan students who frequent McLeod Ganj's cafes will often agree to exchange regular language lessons with foreigners. The **Earthville Institute,** at the Khana Nirvana Restaurant on Temple Rd., serves as a community center, non-profit educational society, and clearing house for information about volunteer opportunities in and around Dharamsala. The Khana Nirvana Restaurant has an Interfaith Shabbat on Fridays; most meals run Rs60. Earthville has a current database of all of Dharamsala's needs and staffers who will happily direct you. (Open W-M noon-9:30pm. Tel. and fax 21733; email mandala@del2.vsnl.net.in; or write to Mandala, Dalai Lama Temple Rd., McLeod Ganj, Dharamsala (HP) 176219.) The official **Community Center,** near Rangzen's on Bhagsu Rd., has postings on local events and opportunities and serves as the headquarters of the local **recycling program,** started two years ago by Tibetan Welfare Officer Dawa Tsering and Dutch coordinator Jan Willem Den Besten. The program employs a dedicated squad of seven "green workers" in collecting plastic, bottles, and paper from McLeod Ganj for recycling at Pathankot and Kangra, but volunteers (minimum 6 months) are accepted from time to time—coordinator Tsering Kya is especially in need of anyone with a solid background in recycling theory or environmental science. You can contact him c/o the Tibetan Welfare Office, Upper Dharamsala 176215, H.P. (tel. 21059; email tcrc@dsala.tibetnet.ernet.in). Even if you don't volunteer, you can do your part by filling up your empty water bottles (Rs5) at the Community Center.

Before volunteering, decide realistically on the length of time you want to commit—and stick to that commitment. Those interested in short-term or day projects should consider the **Yong Ling Creche,** across from the nunnery on Jogibara Rd., where anyone can drop in for a day of conversation with the students. The **Tibetan Welfare Office's Environmental Division** sometimes offers easy but essential volunteer opportunities as well. You can spend a day crushing bottles, making and posting flyers, or doing whatever else comes up. Contact the Green Shop for information.

Those interested in long-term opportunities can **teach English** to the nuns or monks at any of the many monasteries in Dharamsala. Keep in mind that same-sex teachers are essential for reasons of modesty. There may also be opportunities available at the **Tibetan Centre for Human Rights and Democracy** (tel. and fax 23363) and at the **Tibetan Medical Institute** (tel. 22618). The **Tibetan Women's Association** may have filing, proof-reading, or teaching positions available. You can write to them at P.O. McLeod Ganj, 176219, Dharamsala Dist. Kangra (tel. 21527 or 21198; fax 21528; email twa@del2.vsnl.net.in). The **Tibetan Children's Village** is always interested in committed, long-term English, math, and science teachers. Write to Tibetan Children's Village, Dharamsala Cantt. 176216 Dist. Kangra (HP), or call him at 3pm at 21528. Finally, the Tibetan Youth Congress, on Bhagsu Rd., produces publications that may need English-speaking proofreaders. The **Amnye Machen Institute,** just before the Yong Ling Creche on Jogibara Rd., is a Tibetan literary organization with a wide range of projects (including the translation of works like Thomas Paine's *Common Sense* into Tibetan). You may be able to help out (long-term only) with editing, proof-reading, or other paperwork, especially if you know some Tibetan.

MEDITATION

Yoga courses, ranging from risky to respectable, abound in McLeod Ganj—check the postings at the Community Center or in most restaurants. Nestled in a forest down a secluded road, the **Tushita Meditation Centre,** in Dharamkot, 20 minutes from the bus circle, specializes in meditation through complete silence. (Dorms Rs40. Singles

So You Think You're Richard Gere ...

To schedule a private audience with His Holiness the Dalai Lama, send your request 4 months in advance and start praying. Private audiences are hard to come by, but not unheard of if your reason is truly specific to the Dalai Lama. You can write to the Office of His Holiness the Dalai Lama, Thekchen Choeling, McLeod Ganj, 176219, H.P., Dharamsala; fax (01892) 21813; or email ohhdl@cta.unv.ernet.in. Much more likely is a public audience of 300 or so people, held once or twice a month for foreigners and recent arrivals from Tibet. At the public audience, the crowd files slowly past His Holiness, who takes time to speak and laugh with each person (despite his aides' attempts to speed things up). Check with the security branch office near Hotel Tibet on Bhagsu Road to see when the Dalai Lama will next be in town.

Rs60, with bath Rs75; doubles Rs50/65.) Expect to pay a facilities fee of Rs100, as well as take three meals a day (all veg. but not vegan) for Rs100. Contact the office with questions. (Open M-Sa 9:30am-12:30pm and 1-4:30pm; register M-Sa 1:30-3:30pm.) If Tushita doesn't suit your needs, try **Vipassana Meditation Centre** (tel. 21309; fax 21578), also in Dharamkot. (Information sessions M-Sa 4-5pm).

■ Dalhousie डलहौज़ी

Built around 5 ridges along the edge of the Dhauladar mountain range, Dalhousie was named after Lord James Ramsey, Marquis of Dalhousie, who became the Governor General of India in 1848. The hill station was founded in 1854, when the British rented the land from the largely autonomous Chamba *raja* in order to expand vacation options for their increasingly beleaguered colonial administrators. Today, Dalhousie rarely finds its way onto most Western tourists' itineraries, but throngs of Indian honeymooners, older couples celebrating anniversaries, and Sikh families escaping the Punjabi swelter flock here between April and July. Some Tibetans have settled here as well. In the 1940s, Subhas Chandra Bose came here to secretly strategize for the Indian National Army, and today the nearby cantonment offers glimpses of Indian soldiers in all their finery. Except in August, when the fog rolls in, Dalhousie also offers magnificent views of the Pir Panchal mountains and the valleys below.

ORIENTATION AND PRACTICAL INFORMATION Almost everything you'll need in Dalhousie is within a 15-minute walk from the **bus stand,** including **Subhash Chowk** and **Gandhi Chowk.** Slightly to the south of Subhash Chowk is **Sadar Bazaar,** where most locals live. Well-paved roads and circular paths connect these places.

The **Tourist Marketing Office,** near the main bus stand, organizes and conducts tours, books buses, and hands out leaflets (in-season: open daily 9am-6pm; off-season: 10am-5pm). **Punjab National Bank,** next to Aroma 'n' Claire Hotel on the loop road off Subhash Chowk, is the only place in town to change money (open M-Tu and Th-F 10am-2pm, Sa 10am-noon). Regular and semi-deluxe **buses** depart from the main bus stand. If roads are blocked during the monsoon or snow season and you are attempting to go westward, consider going to Pathankot first (but know that Pathankot is one of the nastier towns in India). Buses from Dalhousie run to: **Amritsar** (9:10 and 9:45am, 8hr., Rs60); **Chamba** via **Khajjiar** (about 1 per hour, 7-10:30am and 3:30-4:45pm, 2½hr., Rs28); **Dharamsala** (8:30am, 8hr., Rs65); **Pathankot** (1 per hour, 6:30am-1:45pm, and at 4:30pm, 3hr., Rs32); **Shimla** (12:45pm, 12hr., Rs185). **Local buses** shuttle between the main bus stand and Gandhi Chowk (Rs4). **Taxis** are expensive and unnecessary. **Mules** will haul you around for the day (Rs50) or to your hotel from Gandhi Chowk (Rs20). If you fall on (or off) your ass, the **Civil Hospital,** near Aroma 'n' Claire, has bare-bones facilities. **St. Joseph's Clinic,** just up the road, is a little better (open daily 9am-4pm). The **police** at the station across from Aroma 'n' Claire speak very little English. The **Sub Post Office,** at Gandhi Chowk, has *Poste Restante* (open M-Sa 9am-5pm). **STD/ISD booths** cluster at the two Chowks. **Postal Code:** 176304. **Telephone Code:** 01899.

ACCOMMODATIONS AND FOOD There are plenty of hotels in Dalhousie, and off season, you can get a sizeable room with a view and private bath for about Rs200. In season, prices can quadruple. As in most of Himachal Pradesh, the official season runs from April 15 to July 15 and from September 15 to November 15; each hotel registers a fixed set of prices with the government for these dates, along with off-season discounts. If you want to be sure you're getting a fair shake, **Treks 'n Travels** (tel. 40277, fax 40476) books rooms at the government-approved rates. There is often a charge of Rs100 per day for a space heater during the winter, and some hotels levy fines (as much as Rs100) if you wash your clothes in your room rather than using their *dhobi*. The serene **Hotel Crags** (tel. 42124), on Garam Road, is a five-minute walk from Subhash Chowk. Sit in plush comfort on the massive patio as you watch the sun rise over the magnificent valley. The pricier rooms have carpets, armoires, wood-framed beds, and squat toilets perched atop a throne-like cement stand. (In-season: Rs250-400. Off-season: Rs125-200.) **Shivali Hotel,** (tel. 42299), 10m from Subhash Chowk, also has massive patios with views over the cantonment area. Its oddly shaped rooms have carpets, TVs, and huge beds. (In-season: Rs650. Off-season: Rs250.) Near Gandhi Chowk is **Mehar's Hotel** (tel. 42179), touted as the "Biggest Hotel in Dalhousie." Mehar's offers an attached restaurant and cabin-like accommodations in 4 colonial-style bungalows with views of the Pir Panchal range. The rooms are cozy, with attached bathrooms and arched ceilings (doubles Rs450, with cable TV and carpeting Rs650; "service tax" 10%; off-season discount 30%). If you have a Youth Hostel membership, the **hostel** in Dalhousie (tel. 42189) is undoubtedly the best deal in town. Take the road uphill just across from the bus stand and follow it about 200 meters. The hostel's well-kept dorm-style beds are Rs20—double your money and they'll throw in morning tea, breakfast, and an all-you-can-eat dinner, too. Lockout is from 10am to 5pm. No drinkin', smokin', or clothes-washin'.

Dalhousie's plentiful eateries churn out the same bland food popular in many Indian-tourist weekend vacation spots. Try the **Moti Mahal Beer Bar,** at Subhash Chowk (beer Rs60; open daily 10am-10pm). Fresh fruit and vegetables can be purchased at Sadar Bazaar and in the tunnel-like "Tibetan Refugee Union Market" just off Chandi Chowk. In season, restaurants stay open as late as the tourists desire.

SIGHTS One of the most pleasant things to do in Dalhousie is simply to stroll between the chowks on roads lined with oak, *deodar* cedar, and pine trees. The Garam Rd. walk between Subhash and Gandhi Chowks is especially nice because no cars are allowed on the road and Tibetan refugees have painted reliefs of Padmasambhava, Chenresig (of whom the Dalai Lama is an incarnation), and other Tibetan deities on the stone cliffs beside the road. Panch Pulla Rd., off Gandhi Chowk, leads to the **fresh water spring**. This is the spot where Ajit Singh, a supporter of Subhash Chandra Bose, died on Independence Day. **Dainkunt Peak,** a beautiful 9km uphill walk from Gandhi Chowk, is the town where all the major rivers of the area—the Chenab, the Beas, and the Ravi—can be seen on a clear day. **Khajjiar,** a pristine meadow 22km from Dalhousie, is trumpeted by the local tourist industry as "the Switzerland of the East." In Khajjiar, **Hotel Devdar** (tel. 36333) has 12 rooms (in-season: Rs650-750) and dorm beds (Rs50).

■ Chamba चामबा

A precipitous 56km bus ride from Dalhousie, Chamba spills up the ridge from the Ravi River in a medieval maze of porticoed shacks, school-houses, and hidden temples. The town was founded in 940 A.D. as the new capital of an older princely state administered from Bharmaur for 400 years. Isolation, attitude, and wily diplomacy has kept the Chamba Valley prodigiously independent ever since. Even the British seem to have left little more than a hydro-electric plant. The result is a rich and unique local culture; Chamba and the surrounding area have developed trademark styles of cooking, politics, handicrafts, religious art, and even a literary dialect (Chambali). Town spirit is in full force in early August when residents throw a riotous week-long harvest festival called Minjar. Best of all, many of Chamba's hospitable residents have no qualms about expounding on all of this to you personally.

ORIENTATION AND PRACTICAL INFORMATION Most of the government business and tourist bustle in Chamba centers around **Court Rd.,** which runs from the crowded bus stand area in the south of town along the eastern side of the **Chaugan,** Chamba's wide, grassy mall. **Court Road** continues beyond the Chaugan past shops and markets as **Hospital Road,** then loops back through chicken-shacks and liquor counters as **Museum Road.** From this hair-pin road, the tight alleys of residential Chamba climb steeply up the ridge.

The **Tourism Development Office** (tel. 24002), next to the Hotel Iravati on Court Rd., offers H.P. tourist brochures and a friendly lesson in small-town bureaucracy (open M-Sa 10am-5pm; closed 2nd Sa of the month). Two doors down the Chaugan is the **post office,** which has *Poste Restante* (open M-F 9:30am-5:30pm). Further down, on Hospital Rd., **Punjab National Bank** changes traveler's checks, but not currency (open M-F 10am-2pm, Sa 10am-noon). **Buses** leave for **Bharmour** (5, 6:30, and 8:30am, 3½hr., Rs32); **Dalhousie** (every hr. 7am-9:30pm, 2½hr., Rs28); **Dharamsala** (6 and 11:30am, 4 and 9:30pm, 9hr., Rs68); **Manali** via **Kullu** (11:30am, 14hr., Rs235); and **Pathankot** (3:45am and every hr. 6:30am-4:30pm, Rs51). The **taxi stand** is in front of the Post Office, but fares run high, and taxis are generally unnecessary. Medical facilities in Chamba are not first-rate, but there is a **District Hospital** (tel. 22392) on—you guessed it—Hospital Rd., with a few private clinics a couple of doors down. **Pharmacies** also line Hospital Rd., including **Shrikanth Chowfla and Sons** (tel 22735), which proudly announces that it's also "Licensed to Deal Arms and Ammunition" (open 9am-8pm, M-Sa). The **police station** is on Hospital Rd. (tel. 22736), but reports vary as to its willingness to help foreigners. **STD/ISD** booths are scattered along Court Rd. and Hospital Rd. **Postal Code:** 176310. **Telephone Code:** 01899.

ACCOMMODATIONS AND FOOD Chamba's budget hotel scene isn't spectacular, but there are some comfortable places to stay apart from the prominent and pricey Hotel Iravati. Hotels here can fill up fast in season (Apr. 15-July 1 and Sept. 15 -Nov. 15), especially if there's a heatwave in Punjab. Off-season discounts are less common here than in Dalhousie, so bargain hard. **Jimmy's Inn** (tel. 24748) is the first place you'll see after stepping off the bus, and its standard rooms (all with attached bath) and shady courtyard make for a pleasant and convenient place to crash. (Doubles Rs150-250. Check-out noon.) The HPTDC runs the **Hotel Champak** (tel. 22774), 50m behind the Tourist Development Office. The dim but carpeted dorm room (Rs50) is your best bet here—the private rooms don't offer much more. (Doubles with common bathroom Rs200, with attached bath Rs250. Check-out noon). Up **Temple Rd.** from Hospital Rd., **Rishi Hotel and Restaurant** crams in plain but clean rooms, all with attached bath, some of which overlook the **Laxmi Narayan Temple** across the street. (Singles Rs110; doubles Rs165; "triple plus" Rs275.)

Finding Chamba's local cuisine can take some looking (and some legwork). If they're serving their full menu, the **Olive Green Restaurant** on Temple Rd. will make you the Chamba valley specialty *madhara* (kidney beans and curd cooked in *ghee*)—perhaps one of the densest foods in the universe (Rs25). Chamba is equally well-known for its sweet but fiery chili sauce (*chukh*), which the brave of stomach can sample on gloriously deep-fried chicken at shops on Museum Rd. A good fruit and vegetable market spills out of Temple Rd. onto Hospital Rd.

If you're planning to stay in the Chamba valley for more than a night, don't miss the eco-friendly charms of the **Orchard Hut,** a serene wood and clay guest house 12km from Chamba up the Sal River valley. From tea and organic plums in the morning to home-cooked local gourmet (powerful *madhara*, tasty pickled ferns, and *pakoras*) and folk-dances at night, this place may convince you to stay for months. Owner Prakash Dhami and his family can—and will—tell you everything you ever wanted to know about all things Chambali, eco-tourism in India, and orchard agriculture (samples included). Call ahead and Prakash will pick you up at the bus stand and guide you through town before taking you home. One night is Rs250. Contact the family-owned **Mani Mahesh Travels** (tel. 22507; fax 25333), a few doors down from the entrance to Laxmi Naryan Temple. Mani Mahesh also organizes treks all over Himachal Pradesh, including one six-day trip from the Orchard Hut to Dharamsala.

SIGHTS For a sense of Chamba's royal and military past, head to the north end of Museum Rd. and into the **Bhuri Singh Museum.** (*Open Tu-Su, 10am-5pm. Free.*) Named for Raja Bhuri Singh, who ruled Chamba district from 1904-1919, the museum displays his collection of small weaponry, giant doors, musical instruments, *rumals* (a form of silk embroidery native to the valley), and other regal relics. Some of the carved stone slabs on display mark the sites of hidden springs in the hills.

Chamba has enough temples to reward almost any climb through town—those higher up the hill are marked by yellow and green-railed staircases. The largest temple complex is that of the **Laxmi Naryan Temple,** up Temple Rd. and around the corner opposite Rishi Hotel. (*Open daily 6am-12:30pm and 2:30-8:30pm.*) The various temples in the complex vary in age from the 19th to the 10th century, when Chamba's founder commissioned the Laxmi Naryan Temple (opposite the entrance) and the statue of Laxmi Naryan (a.k.a. Vishnu) it houses. The elaborate stonework covering each temple combines classical convention with Chamba's own highly developed local style. The best time to visit the complex is in the early morning or the evening. No shoes are allowed.

A steep walk along the outskirts of town will take you past several other important holy sites. From the bus stand, a short climb south and east leads to the long staircase up to **Chamunda Devi Temple.** Chamunda Devi is the goddess Durga in her wrathful aspect, but the brass bells (meant to clear your head of worldly scheming) and stupendous view ensure that you'll leave in a peaceful one. Further on, as the road starts to turn west into the Sal River Valley, sits the ancient and removed temple of **Vajresh-wari** (Durga as the goddess of lightning). Tradition holds that the temple originated as a thank-you note from Raja Sahil Varman to the family who donated the land for Chamba town. Although a number of stone carvings have been looted from the sides of the main shrine, finely crafted images of Durga, Undavi (the goddess of food), and other deities still gaze out from its walls. Look for the Tibetan-style demonic faces on the rear of the main shrine—their presence here remains a minor mystery. As always, the stone lions out front are the divine mode of transportation (not for hire).

When they weren't propitiating at the temples, Chamba's 18th- and 19th-century ruling elite retired to the Mughal-style corridors of the **Rang Mahal** ("Old Palace"). Dominating the upper center of Chamba, the palace currently houses the **Himachal Emporium,** a one-room shop selling *rumals*, hand-woven shawls, candleholders, and molded brass plates. Ask the shopkeeper about the workshop upstairs, where you can see some of these items being crafted.

■ Near Chamba: Bharmour भारमौर

Bharmour, the capital of the Chamba valley kingdom from the 6th century to 920A.D., is 65km outside of Chamba town. Its temple square encloses 84 separate shrines, some of them 1100 years old. If you stop by in the summer, you're likely to meet some of the rowdy **gaddis,** nomadic shepherds who make seasonal migrations up and down the valley. In mid-August Bharmour is the launching point for the **Manimahesh Yatra,** a devotional procession that winds its way 34km up to the high-altitude lake at Manimahesh to worship and bathe in its icy waters.

The quiet farming village of **Saho** is a bumpy 1½hr. bus ride from Chamba up the Sal River valley. Its temple houses an ancient Shiva *linga*, said to have once been subject to rapid and inexplicable growth—a hole had to be cut into the temple's stone ceiling to accommodate the linga's skyward ambitions before a visiting priest was able to return it to a reasonable size. Today devotees crawl through the (removed) holy ceiling-piece for luck and strength. Opposite the *linga* is a particularly fine stone sculpture of the ubiquitous smiling bull, Nandi. Though only one piece of stone was used in its production, this Nandi's neck bell actually produces a muffled tone.

■ Kullu कुल्लू

Kullu is tucked between two lush mountains at the southern end of the Kullu Valley. At first glance, the city itself does not have much to offer besides shawl shops and a bus station that can connect you to more restful and majestic places. Given the in-season tourist glut in nearby Naggar and Manali, however, Kullu makes for a relaxing stopover and a good chance to get a look at small-town life in Himachal. Every year in early October, tourists and Indians crowd Kullu for Dussehra, a massive, vibrant, festival celebrating the gods of this glorious valley. An ideal daytrip from Kullu takes you up to the **Bijli Mahadev** (God of Electricity) **Temple** where, legend has it, lightning strikes each year and breaks the massive *lingam*, which is painstakingly reassembled by a priest. Take a bus from town (Rs6) to the Chan Sari stop; from there, you'll have to hike 3km uphill to the temple, which affords fantastic views and a terrific opportunity for Indian-pilgrim-watching.

The main **bus station** is in the north end of town, next to the river. Across the Beas River footbridge (west of the bus station), up the hill and 750m to the left is the **tourist information office** (tel. 24605), in a white building just off the **maidan** (square). The **State Bank of India**, 2km from the center of town, is currently the nearest place to change cash and traveler's checks (open M-F 10am-2pm). **Buses** leave for: **Amritsar** (4 and 5:30pm, 14hr., Rs195); **Delhi** (4 and 6am, 3:30 and 4pm, 16hr., Rs195; semi-deluxe 6pm, 16hr., Rs275; deluxe 6:30pm, 13hr., Rs418); **Dharamsala** (7:15, 7:45, 9:45am, and 5pm, Rs110; 8pm, Rs140); **Manali** (every 30min. 4am-7pm, 2hr., Rs20); **Naggar** (every 30min. 4am-7pm, 1hr., Rs12); and **Shimla** (4, 7:45, 8:30am, and 7:45pm, 9hr., Rs110-145). **Deluxe buses** can be booked through **Harrison Travel** on the maidan to: **Delhi** (6:15pm, 12hr., Rs420); **Dharamsala** (9pm, 8hr., Rs250); **Leh** (5am, 2 days, Rs900); and **Shimla** (9pm, 8hr., Rs250). **Taxis** at the maidan can be hired to: **Chandigarh** (Rs2500); **Delhi** (Rs4400); **Dharamsala** (Rs1900); **Haridwar** (Rs4600); **Leh** (Rs10,000); and **Bhuntar Airport** (Rs100), 10km to the south. The **post office** (open M-Sa 9:30am-5pm), 200m south of the maidan, has EMS and *Poste Restante*. There are a number of **STD/ISD booths** near the footbridge and at the maidan. **Postal Code:** 175101. **Telephone code:** 01902.

To the left of the bus station and over the footbridge you'll find the immaculate **Madhu Chandrika Guest House** (tel. 24395), where spacious balconies look out over the town and onto the mountains. (Dorm beds Rs40; doubles Rs150, with TV and attached bath Rs200.) The bird-and-flower-filled courtyard of the **Hotel Ekrant** (tel. 22756) is at the end of a narrow street, 100m behind the tourist office (doubles Rs150-Rs375). Just off the maidan, closer to the tourist office, **Hotel Bijleshwar** (tel. 22857) lounges around a pleasant garden and patio restaurant which look south down the valley (doubles Rs350). Turn right at the top of the pedestrian market (toward the post office) to find the sickly yellow facade of **Baba Guest House** (tel. 22821). Inside, you'll find an intelligent, friendly owner and tiny rooms with eagle's-nest views (Rs50-60), as well as a free kitchen—budget backpacker paradise.

Most of the food in Kullu takes the form of large, raw vegetables, or small, ambitiously deep-fried ones. If you've still got a hankering for road-stall *samosas*, *pakoras*, and "sweets," you can kill it at the pedestrian **market street** across the river from the bus stand. Those feeling lucky can try **Hotel Bijleshwar's** trout curry (Rs45) and pizza (Rs40). In any case, be sure to stop by for a beer (Rs75) at **Shobla Restaurant** off the maidan; the view is astonishing, especially after a potent Kingfisher.

■ Naggar नागगर

Halfway between Kullu and Manali on the eastern side of the Beas River rests the quiet hillside village of Naggar, blissfully blanketed by pine forests, apple orchards, and fields of cannabis. Naggar was the regional capital until the mid-1800s, but it is now a serene little town with slate-shingled roofs and delicate temples.

ORIENTATION AND PRACTICAL INFORMATION Buses arrive and depart by the shops on the highway running along the east side of the Beas River. Most buses run on the west-side highway; to reach Naggar from here, get off at Patilkuhl and take a taxi across the river. From the east-side highway, it's a 1km walk up the hill to Naggar's 500-year-old **castle.** There is a small **hospital** across from Hotel Alliance. The tiny **post office** has *Poste Restante* and is on the road just before the castle (open M-Sa 9:30am-5pm). **Postal Code:** 175130. **Telephone code:** 01902.

ACCOMMODATIONS AND FOOD Naggar is an ideal place to stay and simply relax. **Hotel Alliance** (tel. 47763) lies 2km from the highway up the hill toward the Roerich Gallery and has an attached restaurant and common bathrooms with squat toilets and 24-hour hot water. (Singles Rs60; doubles Rs130, with bath Rs150.) One kilometer on the road up from the highway lies **Ragini Hotel** (tel. 47855), which has large rooms, bath-tubbed bathrooms with 24-hour hot water, balconies, and a rooftop garden (doubles Rs300; off-season: Rs200). Foreigners intrigued at the prospect of living in a castle stay at the **HPTDC Castle Hotel** (tel. 47855), 1km up the hill from the highway, but you may want to consider just taking tea or dinner in its outdoor restaurant, rather than staying in pricey rooms (Rs500-900). If you've got the bucks, the honeymoon suite, with its 270° panorama, will blow your mind (Rs1000). A 25% discount is offered off season. There are also **private cottages** to be rented, 50m up the hill from the Castle. They come complete with a fully equipped kitchen and private apple orchard, two balconies, a living room, double bedroom, and bathroom with seat toilets (Rs1000; off-season: Rs650).

The food at Ragini's **rooftop restaurant** will set you back Rs100, while the **Castle Restaurant** is a little pricier but worth it for the ambience. The communal feel, shady pines, and hearty dishes at the **Hotel Alliance** make it worth the walk if you're not staying there. Naggar proudly joins the likes of New York and Paris with a **Hard Rock Cafe** by the bus stand, which serves **La Purezza**'s respectable pasta dishes (Rs50-70).

SIGHTS Naggar's somewhat diminutive 504-year-old castle hangs out in the stiff breeze 1km up from the highway, and houses a sacred slab of stone called Jagti Patt. The most striking local theory concerning the slab is that the valley's gods "transformed into honey bees endowed with great strength" to cut the hefty block and fly it up. Up the hill past the Castle Hotel, the **Tripuri Sundri temple,** with its 3-tiered pagoda roof, is the site of a local *mela* in mid-May. Further up the pine-lined road stands the **Nicholas Roerich Art Gallery.** Here, the Russian artist Roerich and his family thrived during the early part of the century; their home now displays his paintings, as well as his 1930s Dodge convertible (look in the upstairs window). Sitting 200m farther up the hill, through 6 ft. cannabis plants, the **Himalayan Folk and Tribal Art Gallery** holds fine examples of traditional northern Indian dress and metalwork. The gallery upstairs has more pseudo-mystic Roerich-scapes, as well as a handful of contemporary Indian paintings ranging from banal to brilliant to just plain bizarre. *(Both galleries open M-Sa 9am-1pm and 2-5pm. Rs10 ticket covers both.)*

▓ Manali मनाली

Cradled between majestic mountains, Manali is a mellow favorite of hashish-seeking hippies, newlywed Indian couples, and travelers looking to rest before heading out on treks into the Himalaya. Once serene and remote, Manali's apple orchards and pine forests are now peppered with wooden guest houses and concrete hotels, a result of the precarious situation in Kashmir that has sent tourists flocking to Himachal Pradesh in search of a sublime substitute. The Mall is a center of tourist commercialism, although it remains relatively hassle-free. Despite Manali's increasingly crowded feel, there are still choice hotels to be found, glorious hikes to challenge you, kind locals to converse with, and some of the most phenomenal scenery in all of India to behold.

Warning: Manali, where cannabis grows wild, has been touted as the cool place to hang out and smoke hash, but stories of local use have been blown out of proportion. The drug is used by locals only at times of extreme hard work or in cold weather. Recently, harder drugs such as LSD and cocaine have hit Manali, and many predict that drug-related crimes and arrests will soon become a problem here. It may not seem so, but **hashish is illegal, even in Manali.** If you've got it, *don't* flaunt it.

ORIENTATION

Manali is structured roughly in the shape of a Y. **The Mall** constitutes the trunk of the Y, where you'll find a **bus station** and most services and offices. Off either side are alleys full of gift shops, *dhabas,* and provision stores; these get increasingly dense in the area just behind and north of the bus stand. Following the left fork at the Nehru Statue leads you uphill 1km on the **Old Manali Road** to **Old Manali,** just across the bridge. From here, Old Manali spreads out along the uphill road to your left. Taking the right fork at the statue sends you over another bridge to the eastern bank of the Beas River. Going 3km farther north from here will lead you to **Vishisht.**

PRACTICAL INFORMATION

Airport: The nearest airport is in **Bhuntar,** 52km from Manali. Flights on **Jagson Airlines** can be booked at the office across from the HPTDC Marketing Office. To: **Delhi** (daily 11am, US$150) and **Shimla** (daily, 7:15am, US$67).

Buses: The bus stand is smack dab in the center of the Mall. To: **Amritsar** (2pm, 14hr., Rs222); **Chamba** via **Dalhousie** (2:55pm, 15hr., Rs240); **Delhi** (11:30am, 2:35 and 5pm, 16hr., Rs240-265; deluxe 4:30, 5, and 7pm, 14hr., Rs454); **Dharamsala** (5:30 and 8:20am, 10hr., Rs131); **Kullu** (every 15min. 5am-6:30pm, 2hr., Rs20); **Leh** (7am, 2 days, Rs500, plus Rs200 to sleep in the communal tent midjourney); **Naggar** (every 30min. 5am-6:30pm, Rs10); **Shimla** (7am, 10hr., Rs135; deluxe 6am, 6pm, 9hr., Rs174). Other **deluxe buses** can be booked at the Himachal Tourism Marketing Office on the Mall or at any travel agency in town. The deluxe bus stand for these buses is at the southern end of town, a short walk from the center. Be sure to confirm just where your bus departs from. To: **Delhi** (5pm, 15hr., Rs450); **Dharamsala** (9am, 9hr., Rs275); **Leh** (6am, on alternating days, 2 days, Rs450, Rs1000 with food and tent rental); **Shimla** (8am, 10hr., Rs275).

Local Transportation: Expensive **auto-rickshaws** abound in Manali, Old Manali, and Vishisht. Expect to pay Rs20 for a trip to and from Old Manali. **Taxis** can be arranged at any tourist office or in front of Hotel Kanzam.

Tourist Office: Government of India Tourist Office (tel. 52175), on the Mall next to Hotel Kunzam, has copious brochures, maps, and information. Open daily 10am-5pm. **HPTDC Marketing Office** (tel. 52116), on the Mall in a large white building on your right with your back to the bus stand, books HPTDC hotels and deluxe buses. Open daily 10am-7pm.

Budget Travel: A million of Manali's zillions of travel agents offer treks (US$30 per person per day, all inclusive) and rafting (Rs850 and up per day). Two reliable companies are **Dragon Tours** (tel.52790; fax 52769), opposite the bus stand, and **Himalayan Journeys** (tel. 52365; fax 53065), just past the bus stand.

Currency Exchange: State Bank of India, on the Old Manali Rd., just past the Mall. Accepts Thomas Cook and AmEx traveler's checks. Open M-F 10am-1:30pm, Sa 10-11:30am. Get there early to avoid the daily rush.

Bookstore: Bookworm (tel. 52920), in the New Market, behind the bus stand.

Hospital: Mission Hospital (tel. 52379) is down the alley which begins across the street from Hotel Kanzam. **Civil Hospital** is next to the deluxe bus stand.

Police: The station (tel. 52326) is next to the deluxe bus stand.

Post Office: Sub Post Office. Down the alley to the right of Monal Himalayan Travels. EMS available. They hold *Poste Restante* for up to a month. Open M-Sa 9am-5pm. **Postal Code:** 175131.

Telephones: STD/ISD booths close by 11pm. **Telephone Code:** 01902.

ACCOMMODATIONS

One of the keys to having an enjoyable stay in Manali is deciding which type of environment you want your hotel to be in. In **Model Town,** along the Mall, you'll find concrete high rises which offer TV, carpeting, attached bathrooms, a mostly Indian clientele, and a price range from Rs200 to Rs600, depending on the season. British-built guesthouses overlooking gardens and apple orchards line the stretch of road between the Mall and Old Manali. In **Old Manali,** accommodations cluster along the river, or up the hill to the left of the bridge where the Hendrix/acid crew resides. To find real solitude, head past the end of the road on the hill in Old Manali, where a number of houses post "room for rent" signs. Rooms are generally Rs50-100. "In season" is considered to be May 15-July 15, when rich Indians escape the heat of the plains, and ragged travelers flee Goa. A second season runs from September 15-November 15. Unless a set off-season price is given, bargain hard.

> **Sunshine** (tel. 52320), halfway between the Mall and Old Manali. For colonial Brits who couldn't make the Shimla cut, this was The Place. Each room has a private dressing room and bathroom, as well as a verandah overlooking the valley. The gardens and apple orchards provide solace. Restaurant is an old-style dining room with a massive wooden table next to the fireplace. Rooms Rs350.
>
> **Hotel River Bank** (tel. 53004 or 52968), to the right of the bridge in Old Manali. A pretty typical concrete luxury complex. You'll feel like you're at a ski resort as you sip tea and recline in red velvet chairs on plush blue carpets. All rooms are spacious and clean with attached seat toilets and hot water. In-season: doubles Rs500, but bargain away. Off-season: Rs250.
>
> **Hotel Splendour**. Head up the hill in Old Manali and keep your eyes peeled for the signs on your right. Five minutes down a side path takes you past several other guest houses to Splendour. Gorgeous views. Each room has its own hot water heater and seat toilet. Attached restaurant and kitchen. In-season: all rooms Rs250. Off-season: singles Rs150; doubles Rs200. You can also pitch your own tent (Rs75) or rent one for two people (Rs200).
>
> **John Banon's Guest House** (tel. 52335 or 52388; fax 52392), a 5min. walk from the Mall up Old Manali Rd. One of the oldest hotels in Manali, it was opened in 1960 on what was the edge of town, nestled in its own private apple orchard. Spacious rooms with huge windows and working fireplaces. Doubles Rs550. Reservations recommended one month in advance in season.
>
> **Rishi Guest House,** 600m south of Jagat Suk on the Naggar Highway, on the east bank of the Beas River. Take a public bus (Rs5) from Manali, or ask the driver to stop on the way from Kullu. Comfy rooms with private kitchens and a white tile bathroom (squat toilet). Rooms Rs200. Off-season: Rs125.
>
> **Wildlife Information, Education, and Awareness Center,** on your right as you head from the Mall toward Old Manali. Serves as both the information center for the Great Himalayan National Park and a hotel. Comfortable but dim dorm accommodations. Common bathrooms with squat toilets and 24hr. hot water. Ask to see wildlife films on Saturday, or get a map of the park so you can meander through the forest. Check-in 10am-5pm. Dorm beds Rs50. One musty double Rs125.

Vishisht

Comparatively quiet Vishisht and its semi-temporary foreign residents bliss out by the river, 3km north of Manali, and small guesthouses are packed tightly next to one another. Most have basic, clean rooms with baths (Rs100 off season), but be wary of staying too close to Prachi Restaurant, which blasts techno into the wee hours. The **Dharma Guest House** is farther up the hill and to the right. Its common bathrooms are clean, and some rooms have a sizable loft (Rs100). Even farther up the hill, **Deve Guest House** has rooms for Rs60.

FOOD

There's at least one *dhaba* down almost every alley off the Mall near the bus station. Check the cleanliness of the place before you dive into your food. Most of the guest houses in Old Manali also have restaurants. Along the hill road to the left of the bridge

NORTH INDIA

Manu Temple

TO OLD MANALI VILLAGE, **A**, AND **B**

Vashisht Temple

Vashisht Bath

TO **C** & **D**

B

Club House

Manalsu River

Great Himalayan National Park

E

F

Old Manali Road

Hadimba Devi Temple

G

State Bank of India $

The Mall

HPTDC Marketing Office

Mission Hospital ✚

Peter's Cafe

Himalayan Journeys

New Market

Bookworm

Dragon Tours

Tibetan Market

Bees River

H

Jagat Sukh

The Mall

0   200 yards
0   200 meters

Manali

ACCOMMODATIONS
C Deve Guest House
D Dharma Guest House
B Hotel River Bank
A Hotel Splendor
F John Banon's Guest House
H Rishi Guest House
E Sunshine
G Wildlife Information, Education, and Awareness Center

Delux Bus Stand

N

in Old Manali, you'll find a dozen cafes, all with the same menu but varying degrees of popularity, depending on the owners' leniency toward *chillum* smoking.

Peter's Cafe, down a small, dingy lane, in a small garden, near State Bank. Serve yourself quiche (Rs10) or pie (Rs15), or wait a few minutes for cheddar omelettes (Rs20) and garlic toast. A loaf of fresh bread (Rs15) and homemade preserves (Rs35) will spare you from *chow mein* for days. The owner has a razor-sharp wit and a collection of classical records, and he'll treat you to both. Open 8am-8pm.

Ristorante Italiano (tel. 53111), 20m up Hadimba Temple Rd., between the Mall and Old Manali. Gabriele, the proprietor, makes Italian cheese, which he sprinkles on home-made *taglielle* (Rs60-100). *Secondi piatti* of meat will run you Rs80, although a pasta dish is plenty of food. Fresh bread and olive oil comfort you while you wait. Top off your meal with cappuccino (Rs15).

Tibetan Kitchen, beneath the Hotel River View in Old Manali. A vegetarian vacation: fresh veg. *momos* (Rs20) and a sizzling veg. platter (Rs35) will tempt you more than once. The Tibetan bread (Rs4) goes well with your meal, or with butter and jam for breakfast (Rs20). Open daily 8am-11pm.

Sher-e-Punjab, south of HPTDC, across the street. Authentic Punjabi food for those tired of Italian food and *momos.* Decently priced (entrees Rs30-55) and a favorite with Indians. They'll make *makki-ki-roti* if you ask nicely (Rs110). Open daily 9am-11pm.

Moondance Garden Restaurant, up the Old Manali hill. It's the psychedelic shack of choice for Enfield-less hipsters who can't make it to Pete's. Hefty Italian food and enchiladas (Rs45).

SIGHTS

The four-tiered **Hadimba Devi Temple,** with a pagoda-shaped roof, is dedicated to the demoness-turned-goddess Hadimba, wife of Bhima. Valley residents lay claim to the story of the king's rewarding the temple's builder by cutting off his right hand to prevent duplication. Undaunted by the amputation, the builder trained his left hand and constructed a more elaborate temple at Tritoknath. This time, he lost his head. To get to the temple, walk along Old Manali Rd., take a left after five minutes, and follow the signs.

The **Manu Temple,** a pleasant 30-minute walk up the hill in Old Manali, is claimed to be the spot where Manu stepped onto the earth after a great flood. Manu (the first man to possess knowledge) and his wife Shatrupa had a series of thoughtful children who purportedly developed the world's religions. Vaulted ceilings, elaborate woodwork, and marble floors distinguish the temple, which was rebuilt in 1992. The townspeople who live near the temple appreciate foreigners who make the effort to show respect by dressing appropriately and displaying reverence at the temple.

The Himachal Tourism-run **Club House** (tel. 52141), to the right of the bridge in Old Manali, offers sundry activities, not to mention a fully-stocked bar (beer Rs75). *(Open daily 10am-10pm.)* Try your hand at billiards (Rs100 per hr.), *carom* (Rs40 per hr.), or badminton (Rs60 per hr.), or just kick back in the plush lounge with one of the books from the library.

Entrance to the **Great Himalayan National Park** is well worth the Rs2 fee, if only to see what the towering pine forests might have looked like before the modern architectural invasion. *(Open daily 10am-5pm.)* The entrance is at the Wildlife Information, Education, and Awareness Center, on the Old Manali Rd. Moji, the manager, can arrange showings of nature videos on Saturday afternoons.

If you all else fails, go **shopping.** In addition to the plethora of shawl shops on the Mall and on Old Manali Rd., the **Tibetan Market,** at the southern end of town, affords the opportunity for some hard bargaining. *(Open daily 8am-10pm.)* Watch out for cheap, machine-made imitation wool shawls. As always, if something is surprisingly cheap, it's probably of shoddy quality.

■ Near Manali

Getting stinky? The temple in Vishisht has free **hot baths,** separated for men and women (open daily 5am-9pm). Himachal Tourism runs a **Hot Bath Complex,** which has clean, private, tiled rooms with hot spring baths (Rs40 per person, Rs50 for 2).

The **Mountaineering Institute** (tel. 52342 or 53789; fax 53509) is 2km south of the bridge over the Beas River. Courses in mountaineering, skiing, and water sports are offered throughout the year, with fees ranging from US$190 (skiing) to US$250 (a 4-week mountaineering course). Although some courses allow women, most are limited to men. The institute can also organize trips for larger groups. For more information, write to Mountaineering Institute, H.P. 175131.

Further south is **Jagat Suk** and its glorious wood-and-stone Shiva temple. Beside this 5000-year-old site, men play *carom* while women crush rocks to make gravel. The regular bus from Manali (every 15min., 5am-6:30pm, 30min., Rs3) will drop you in Jagat Suk, where you can check out the temple and take a *chai* with the locals.

Rohtang Pass (3998m) is open erratically between June and September and is the only motorable way into the Lahaul-Spiti area from Manali (see **Kinnaur-Spiti Road,** below). Nowadays, it's best described as a polar dump; the place is a complete *mela* of tea tents, with debris scattered all around. But Rohtang can make for a decent trip if you're looking for high-altitude scenery without the exercise. Buses, as well as HPTDC tours, will take you here, and you can rent fabulous fur coats on the way. Check out the creative H.P.P.W.D. road advice on the way up, including slogans like "Divorce speed" and "Peep, peep, don't go to sleep."

■ The Kinnaur-Spiti Road

One of the most incredible routes in the world, the road from Shimla cuts through mountains of solid rock and traverses all of Kinnaur, Spiti, and Lahaul, eventually crossing the Rohtang Pass and descending into Manali. Its construction was a feat in and of itself: Gorkha workers were hung by their feet and lowered along mountainsides with live dynamite to blast out space for the road. The ride can be harrowing—the river often leaps and crashes hundreds of feet below the road, and you'll see the locals sitting next to you literally praying that the bus doesn't do the same.

For some of the route, the only accommodations options are Public Works Department (PWD) or Irrigation and Public Health (IPH) **resthouses.** Permits for them are extremely difficult to secure, and even with a permit you may be booted out if a VIP shows up. Your options will be much greater if you bring a tent and sleeping bag—there are plenty of **camping** spots along the way.

The **Shimla-Kaza Road** is open virtually year round, although it is often blocked on the Shimla-Peo stretch. Blockages usually occur in the form of a fast-flowing current of water caused by snow melting at higher elevations. Don't take any unnecessary risks; chances are that the water will go down in a day or two. If traveling by bus, it's sometimes possible to get off, cross the obstacle on foot, hike to the next town, and catch an ongoing bus from there. This option is feasible only if it is still relatively early in the day and you've scoped out the distance to the next town. Don't chance getting stranded here at night; the region is a desert, and virtually all traffic stops after nightfall due to the hazardous roads. Foreigners going past Jangi on the Shimla-Kaza road must obtain an **inner-line permit** (available from the sub-divisional magistrates in Shimla, Rampur, Peo, Kaza, Chamba, Keylong, and the home office in Delhi, but supposedly only to groups with four or more people and a guide (though this rule is rarely enforced). For more info, see **Permits,** p. 340. The **Kaza-Manali Road** is theoretically open from mid-June to mid-September, but weather makes it unreliable. In 1998, this stretch did not open until mid-August due to glacier and boulder blockages. **Foreigners should keep in mind that there are no banks that exchange foreign currency along the route and shoud plan accordingly.**

From Shimla, the road climbs to rainy **Narkanda** (60km, 2½hr. by bus), and then descends steeply to **Rampur** (120km, 3½hr. by bus), the first major town on the route. A dirty old town, Rampur has no decent hotels or restaurants, and entry into

the spectacular Padam Palace is prohibited. Twenty-three kilometers farther is **Jeuri.**
Buses depart from Jeuri for the 17km ride to **Sarahan** (buses at noon, 4:30, 1½hr.,
Rs40), the site of the amazing **Bhima-Kali Temple.** The temple was the site of human
sacrifice until this practice was banned by the British. About 40km past Sarahan, you
can catch a bus up into the splendid **Sangla Valley** (see **Treks Around Kalpa,** p. 364).
The road from Jeuri continues along the banks of the wild **Sutlej River** to **Rekong-
Peo,** 70km from Jeuri, the district headquarters of Kinnaur (see p. 363).

From Peo, elements of Buddhist culture start creeping in, and by the time you
reach **Pooh,** the town 50km (3hr.) down, most people you see are Buddhists. The
change in beliefs seems to mirror the transformation from greenery to rainshadow;
from Pooh onwards, the land is dry, and sand, stone, ice, and burning sun seem to
dominate everything. Mud houses are bleached by the sun, prayer flags are strung up
across hills and on high ridges, and a splash of color in the *gompas* marks the beginning of Buddhist country.

Seventy kilometers (5hr. by bus) from Peo, at **Khab** (or Kabo), the confluence of
the Spiti and Sutlej Rivers, the road turns left and starts climbing to the plateau above.
In the middle of this brown plain is a splash of green—the village of **Kah.** Further
down, in **Yangthang,** you can branch off to see the beautiful lake in **Nako** (7km from
Yangthang). Bus service from Yangthang to Nako is erratic, but it's only a three-hour
trek each way. There are two **guesthouses** at Nako, but none in Yangthang. **Chango,**
100km (3½hr.) from Peo, is one of the most prosperous villages in the region. Check
out the Chinese shop in the center and the 13th-century temple, which was said to
have been hewn out of a single stone in one day. Chango also has a PWD rest house.
From Chango the bus proceeds in fits and starts, stopping at **Shalkar,** at the check-
post at **Sumdo** (the Spiti boundary), and then at **Tabo,** made famous by its millennium celebrations in 1996, when the *kalachakra* ceremony was performed here by
the Dalai Lama. The monastery at Tabo lies on a hot plain 47km from Kaza. Tabo has
a PWD resthouse. There are also excellent rooms in the *gompa,* and in some village
houses.

After Sumdo, the responsibility for road maintenance passes from an army organization to the Public Works Department, and the transfer in authority shows. Beyond
Tabo, road quality begins to decline, and the ride is incredibly bumpy. On the way to
Kaza (66km from Tabo) a detour from Shichling (38km) takes you to Dankar *gompa.*
The sheer power of the *gompa*'s location—precariously perched on towers of shale
and mud—is worth the drive. If you have walked up, or want to stay the night, the
small *gompa* next to the road has accommodations, but it's advisable to bring your
own food. Donations are expected and appreciated (Rs50-100). The last big town on
the way to Manali is **Kaza** (see p. 365).

From Kaza, the road takes another turn for the bumpier as it winds its way 50km
up to the village of Losar (5hr.). Losar has two small guesthouses and serves as the
final launching point for the Kunzum Pass (4500m) and the road through the spectacular Lahaul Valley. The pass is 18km (1½hr.) from Losar, after which the road drops
steeply to the four or five houses and single *dhaba* comprising **Batal.** There are resthouses at **Chottha Dara** (18km) and **Chattru** (17km) before the journey takes you
back to a main road at **Gramphoo** (17km). From here it's a rough but beautiful ride
over the Rohtang Pass to **Manali** (64km).

Warning: A PWD road sign on the Rohtang Pass reads, "no one is a gamma in the
land of the lamas: take it easy." The Kinnaur-Spiti Road, especially the section
between Tabo and Gramphoo, reaches altitudes of more than 4500m, and has no
facilities for dealing with **Acute Mountain Sickness.** Try not to spend the night
more than 500m higher than where you spent the night before. If you start experiencing symptoms (irregular breathing, headaches, nausea, irritability, and poor
judgement), **don't go any higher.** If the symptoms persist, **go back down.** This
isn't the place to push yourself. Above all, drink as much water as you can.

■ Rekong-Peo रिकोंग पेव

Halfway between Shimla and Tabo, Peo serves as the district headquarters of Kinnaur and is also the first noticeably Buddhist town on the way up through the mountains. Just off the main road, the town is a small collection of concrete structures, friendly *dhabas* and market stalls, and woe-ridden donkeys braying late into the night. A bus to Kalpa offers escape from the cloud of bureaucracy that seems to hang over Peo. The views of Kinnaur Kailash are beautiful on the journey to Kalpa, but bus service is erratic; if you are only stopping overnight, it's best to stay in Peo. There is one main road along the **market.** The large concrete **Fairlyland Hotel** is just above it to the left. One end of the market continues onto a dirt side-road, which becomes a small footpath leading uphill beyond the *dhabas* to the bus stand and the **Shivling View Guest House.** The closest place to get help arranging treks is the **Timberline Tent Colony** in Kalpa (see above). The **bus stand** is just above the town (a 10min. walk). The buses which come from Rampur or Tapri are quite crowded by the time they reach Peo, so try to take a bus which originates at Kalpa or Peo for your onward journey. To: **Chandigarh** (5:30am, 17hr., Rs180); **Chitkul** (9:15am, 2hr., Rs35); **Delhi** (10:30am, 21hr., Rs280); **Kalpa** (7:30 and 9:15am, 1, 3:15, and 5:15pm, ½hr., Rs5); **Kaza** (7:30am, 13hr., Rs105); **Manali** (4:30am, 14hr., Rs155); **Rampur** (2pm, 7hr., Rs55); and **Shimla** (4, 7:30, and 8:30am, 10hr., Rs120). To get an **inner-line permit** for the road between Jangi and Kaza (which goes through Tabo), see the **sub-divisional magistrate** in Peo's administrative complex near the market (open M-F 9am-5pm). The **police station** is near the market. For **medical assistance,** the district hospital is 2km above the town, on the way to Kalpa (open 24hr.). The **post office** is next to the bus stand (open M-F 9am-1pm and 2-5pm). There are 5 **STD/ISD** booth in Peo market (open daily 6am-9pm). **Postal Code:** 172107. **Telephone Code:** 017852.

Some hotels have attached restaurants, and there are a couple of *dhabas* serving Tibetan food along the road between the bus stand and the market. **Try A** liquor store sells "English" wine and beer in the market. The **Shivling View Guest House** (tel. 22421), near the main bus stand, has only 5 rooms (doubles Rs200). Running hot water, an attached restaurant, and clean rooms offer respite after 12 hours spent munching dust in a smoke-spewing bus (although at night the thin walls can seem like a giant PA system). The **Fairlyland Hotel** (tel. 2477), above the market, has a restaurant and daily bus service to Kaza and Shimla. The rooms (doubles Rs250) are clean but spare, so bring a sleeping bag.

Rekong-Peo is famous in Kinnaur for its *chilgoza* forests; flora-enthusiasts need only take a 10-minute walk from the center of town to witness this rare spectacle. If you are fortunate enough to be here in November, the age-old **Lavi Fair** is not to be missed. A variety of goods, including the highly prized Pashmina wool, dried fruits, and horses, are traded. The fair takes place each year during the first week of November on the grounds near the District Commissioner's office.

The **gompa** with the massive statue of Buddha is 20 minutes uphill from Peo. It is the site of a *kalachakra* ceremony performed by the Dalai Lama in 1992.

Pining Away

In Kinnaur, the *chilgoza* pine (*rbi*) enjoys an honor not often conferred on vegetable matter. Botanists have noted the tree's rarity (it only grows here and in Afghanistan), while locals say that its tasty seeds provide an ayurvedic kick. As a display of their importance, *chilgoza* clippings are perched on long poles by villagers. The totem-like memorials dot roads as far up as Lahaul.

■ Kalpa कल्पा

The small village of Kalpa, or Chini-Gaon (Chinese Village), offers numerous long walks and breathtaking views of the Kailash range. Simply point your camera southward, and the picture promises to be postcard-worthy. A stay in Kalpa offers more than picturesque settings; it affords a rare glimpse into Kinnauri village life. Men and women here don traditional clothing, everyone eats locally grown food, and age-old festivals synthesizing elements of Hinduism, Buddhism, and various mountain cults dominate the calendar. Kalpa is also a good place to hone your ethical tourism skills before heading up the valley to more remote spots. The relative isolation of Lapa and Tabo make them seem unlikely candidates to become the next Manali or Shimla, but remember that those hill stations seemed just as secluded not so long ago.

Kalpa piles its central handful of stone houses, shrines (often displaying bizarre local touches), and lanes onto a jutting point overlooking the valley. The rest of the village spreads up the ridge, and getting around can be a small trek in itself. Kalpa shares most of its official facilities with **Peo**, although there is a **sub-post office** and a few small supply stores. Five **buses** per day head to **Peo** (8, 9:45, and 11:30am, 2 and 5:45pm, Rs5). There are also daily buses to **Chandigarh** (5am, 18hr., Rs180) and **Shimla** (6am, 12hr., Rs120). Buses to **Tabo** and **Kaza** leave only from Peo (daily, 7:30am). Expect a **taxi** from Kalpa to Peo to run about Rs150; it is also possible to hike the 8km through the forests. **Kinnaur Villa** (tel. 26006), a steep 15-minute walk from the bus stand, has spacious rooms, bucket hot water, thick blankets for chilly nights, and food cooked to order (doubles Rs200, with attached bath Rs400-600). The **Timberline Trekking Camps** are on the same road, a little farther down—about a 10-minute walk from the bus stand. Pleasant tents have two beds, chairs, a table, and attached bath for an inexplicable Rs950. The price includes three gourmet meals a day. They can also arrange regional treks with porters and guides. (Open Apr.-Oct.) Make reservations at 206/207 Allied House, 1 Local Shopping Centre, Mandangir, Delhi, 110062 (tel. 6982903 or 6984049; fax 6980746). **Food** is available at hotels or in basic *dhabas* in the center of town. If you're only stopping overnight on your way somewhere else, it's best to stay in Peo (see below). Kalpa has the same **postal** and **telephone codes** as Peo.

■ Treks Around Kalpa

The most popular trek within Kalpa itself is to **Chaka,** a plateau above the village that makes an ideal place for camping or a picnic. It's only a two-hour hike each way. In addition to the many short hikes possible in this area, Kalpa can also serve as a starting point for longer treks into the Sangla Valley. The much-famed **Parikrama trek** begins at **Thangi** (60km from Kalpa, approachable by road) and takes about five days. From Thangi it's a one-day hike to **Kunnu** (3375m) and another day to **Lalanti** (4421m). From Lalanti the trail descends to **Chitkul** (3450m), where a road connection again becomes available. By far the most difficult route in this region, and one that should only be attempted by seasoned trekkers, is the trail leading up **Kinnaur Kailash** (6050m). The base of the mountain is in **Powari**, 20km from Kalpa. Expect the trek to take two days each way.

In Chitkul there is a PWD resthouse as well as another **Timberline Tent Colony.** From here it is worthwhile to take a one-day diversion (14km) and hike to the massive glacier that forms the source of the Baspa River. The Parikrama continues from Chitkul to Sangla (27km). Midway between them is the tiny **Rupin River View Guest House** (doubles with attached bath, Rs200), which also has a restaurant. The Parikrama ends at **Sangla,** about 50km from Kalpa. The luxurious tent colony of **Banjara Camps** specializes in arranging treks throughout the entire region (tent with double bed, all meals included, Rs990). Reservations can be made through **Transmount Adventures** in Shimla (tel. (0177) 252561; fax 252557). From Sangla, it's two hours by bus back to Kalpa, or, alternately, a two-day trek. For more information about planning treks, see **Trekking, p. 58.**

■ Tabo ताबो

Everything in Tabo suggests a place where faith has run deep for centuries. In fact, one suspects that faith alone has sustained the people in this barren hinterland for so long. The tiny hamlet is home to some 350 people. The town's mud huts (and their residents) cluster around the **Tabo gompa,** a few hundred yards from the river on one side, and enormous, smooth ridges on the other. Tabo remained in virtual isolation until the Sino-Indian border disputes of the 1950s, when the geo-political importance of this region once again took center stage. Today the area is home to a number of Indian military outposts, and **foreigners must obtain a permit before visiting.**

Tabo's **Primary Health Center** (tel. 33325; open M-Sa 9am-1pm and 3-5pm) is at the edge of town. Treatment and medicine are free, but donations are appreciated. For any sort of **police** assistance, one must travel to Sumdo, 32km away. There is one **STD/ISD** booth (**telephone code:** 01906) in the center of town (open daily 6am-10pm), and the **post office** is a little ways off the highway toward the *gompa* (open M-F, 9am-1pm and 3-5pm, Sa 10am-2pm; **postal code:** 172113). If the postmaster isn't there (most of the time he isn't), ask around for his whereabouts; you can usually find him having tea in one of the nearby *dhaba*s.

After the much ballyhooed *kalachakra* ceremony performed by the Dalai Lama here in 1996 (celebrating the 1000th birthday of the Tabo *gompa*), life in Tabo has at last returned to normal, and the extensive accommodations that were available then for tourists have since vanished. Happily, the *gompa* itself continues to rent out excellent rooms in its meditative and boundlessly friendly confines (dorm beds Rs40; doubles Rs100-250) and has an attached restaurant and multi-lingual library. To enjoy this area in its pristine (if pricey) surroundings, stay at **Banjara Camps,** located 4km outside Tabo in the village of Kurith. Tented accommodations have double beds (Rs980, all meals included) and common baths with buckets of hot water upon request. Befriend the manager Dhiraj and he might even give you a personal tour of the monastery. Reservations can be made at Transmount Adventures in Shimla (see above). Within Tabo itself there is a **PWD Guest House** (tel. 33310), with five well-maintained doubles with attached bath (3 with seat toilets and running hot water). All rooms Rs109, Rs284 for foreigners. For food, try any of the Tibetan *dhaba*s around town; the one attached to the monastery serves decent *thukpa*s (Rs14).

One of the holiest shrines of trans-Himalayan Buddhism, the **Tabo Monastery** is the largest, and most sacred, monastic complex in Spiti. Based on an obscure inscription, 996 is accepted as the year of its construction. It is comprised of nine temples, 23 *chortens,* a monks' chamber, and an extension that houses the nuns' chamber. Each temple contains a wealth of wall paintings and stucco images, many of which are barely visible due to poor maintenance. It's worth taking a look at some of the library's books on Tibetan art first; ask if you can borrow one for an hour or two. At the core of the complex lies the Temple of Enlightened Gods, otherwise known as the **Assembly Hall.** Light incense here and leave a donation. To the right of the Assembly Hall is the **Bodhisattva Maitreya Temple,** in which stands an impressive image of the Bodhisattva Maitreya, over 6m high. Those who wish to attend morning prayer should plan to be at the monastery by 6am. Above the complex on the sheer cliff-face overlooking the town, are a series of **caves** which were once used as monk dwellings. Here again, there are dim traces of the paintings that once adorned these walls. Bring a flashlight.

■ Kaza काज़ा

From Tabo, the road winds up the Sutlej Valley, and the ride becomes bumpier, as sizable streams begin to flow over the road. Dust floats through the windows until everybody starts looking like a worker in a cement factory. When you think you've just about had it, the valley broadens, and the vast pea fields and sandy plains of Kaza appear in the distance. Traditionally an important trade center, today's Kaza is an important government post and the first big town on the Manali-Shimla route.

Both **Old Kaza** and **New Kaza** lie between the **main road** and the **river.** A small, often dry, **stream** separates the new (shining tin roofs) from the old (mud houses and thatched roofs). The **bazaar** and eateries are all in Old Kaza while the **hospital, police station,** and government administrative buildings have come up in the newer part of town. The **bus stand** is just off the main road. Heading west, Kaza is the first town where you'll be able to get semi-reliable information on road conditions at Kunzum-La and in the Lahaul Valley, although even as far as Losar, most people are still just guessing. Bus service to **Manali** begins sometime after July 1 (6:30am, 12hr., Rs135). Buses leave daily for **Tabo** (7am, 3hr., Rs35), **Peo** (8:30am, 12hr., Rs102) and **Shimla**

(10am, 22hr, Rs250). The **hospital** (tel. 22218), in a big shed in New Kaza, runs an **ambulance** service. The **police** station is in New Kaza. The **post office** in Old Kaza, two minutes from the road, sells stamps (open M-F 9:30am-5:30pm; **postal code:** 172114). The **STD/ISD** booth is located near the market in Old Kaza (open daily 6am-10pm; **telephone code:** 01906).

Lodging in Kaza is available from April to November. **Sakya's Abode,** New Kaza (tel. 22213) is probably the best place to stay in Kaza. The rooms are clean, with attached baths and cold running water. The garden, views, and dining make this place a favorite. The owner will give useful advice about Kunzum and beyond (Check-out noon. Dorm beds Rs50-500.) The hulking yellow **Zumbala Hotel** (tel. 22396), in Old Kaza, is five minutes from the road and has basic rooms (dorm beds Rs35; doubles Rs150), a dining hall, and kitchen. The **Karma Bakery,** 100m from the bus stand, makes tasty biscuits and breads.

The **Kyi Monastery,** 18km from Kaza, is one of the most impressive monasteries in Spiti. Small mud houses containing the remains of dead lamas sit on an eroded cliff, which rises high above the sand plains near Kaza but is dwarfed by the mountainside opposite. The monastery houses 1000 living lamas and an exquisite collection of *thankas,* which is now kept locked up after reports of theft or purchase by wealthy tourists in other places. As the projected site of the Dalai Lama's *kalachakra* ceremony for the year 2000, Kyi is receiving a subtle face-lift: prayer flags now have to be sure not to steal the sun from the brand-new solar panels. Kyi is connected to Kaza by two morning **buses** (7 and 9am, Rs10). It's also possible to stop off on the way back from Kibber or take a **taxi** (Rs200 round-trip), which you can catch in the market in Old Kaza, near the bus stand.

A link road from Kaza leads to **Kibber,** which at 4250m is reputed to be the highest village in the world reachable by motor vehicle. The bus from Kaza leaves early in the morning (7am) for the 28km ride to Kibber and returns after only 15 minutes there. If that isn't enough time, it is possible to walk back to Kaza, although the four-hour hike is hot and dusty.

■ Kunzum Pass and Lahaul

Once you cross the Kunzum, the landscape is dominated by glaciers, towering cliffs, icefalls, and scrubby greenery. There are no villages of more than three or four huts until you reach **Gramphoo,** but each of them has a guesthouse (usually PWD). The road is brutal here, but it's possible to walk the valley in July if buses aren't running yet. A snow-clearing truck runs from **Batal** to **Losar** (30km) and back daily (ask Tashi Chopal at Sarchu *dhaba* in Losar). From Batal, it's an all-day (32km) hike to **Chhatru** with a lunch stop at **Chhota Dhara.** Another 17km will take you to Gramphoo and the main road. If the Lahaul road is closed, chances are you'll find yourself clomping over glacier ice, through streams, or around piles of boulders for part of the way. Remember that there is no medical assistance or transport nearby, so plan carefully when crossing these obstacles. Gramphoo's two *dhabas* rent **rooms** for Rs50 per person. Expect to be joined in bed by shepherds or family members at any time. **Buses** headed for **Keylong, Leh,** or **Manali** stop on the main road starting at 9:30am.

Stiff Demons

After repeatedly banging their heads on small door frames in Kinnaur, Spiti, and Lahaul, many travelers begin to wonder (provided they can still think at all) why many entrances and exits seem to be booby-trapped. It's to hinder the progress of evil spirits. The spirits are as tall as humans but cannot bend, so small doors bar their way (and the way of absent-minded travelers).

Labels within map:
AFGHANISTAN
CHINA

Disteghil Sar 7785m
Rakaposhi 7788m
K2 8611m

UNDER PAKISTANI ADMINISTRATION
Gilgit
Masherbrum 7821m
BALTISTAN

Nanga Parbat 8126m

UNDER CHINESE ADMINISTRATION

LINE OF ACTUAL CONTROL
Kargil
Mulbekh
Shyok River
LADAKH

Baramula
Sonamarg
Dras
Lamayuru
Spituk
Leh
Gulmarg
Srinagar
Alchi
Tikse
LADAKH RANGE
TIBET (CHINA)
Khilanmarg
Pahalgam
VALE OF KASHMIR
Nun Kun 7135m
Hemis
Anantnag
ZANSKAR
Jhelum River
PIRPANJAL RANGE
Kishtwar
Padum
ZANSKAR RANGE
Indus River
Taglang La Pass
RUPSHU
Batoti
Chenab River
Kud
Jammu
Chamba
Kathua
Keylong
Manali
OFFICIAL INDO-PAKISTANI BORDER
UNDER CHINESE ADMINISTRATION
PAKISTAN
HIMACHAL PRADESH

Govt. of India statement:
The external boundaries of India are neither correct nor authenticated.

PUNJAB
Jammu and Kashmir

N

Jammu जम्मु and Kashmir كشمير

The northernmost state in India, Jammu and Kashmir rolls across 222,000 sq. km of mountains, valleys, and plateaus, only two-thirds of which are in fact controlled by India. The northwest and northeast portions of the state are ruled by Pakistan and China respectively. Kashmir is India's most volatile region, and travelers are advised not to visit the western part of the state, which is currently the site of an armed insurgency. The beautiful capital of Srinagar is overrun with army encampments and considered too risky to visit by most foreign state departments. Western Kashmir, described by visitors and natives alike as the most beautiful place on earth, has been destroyed economically by war. However, the violence has so far been confined to the western half of the state, which includes the predominately Muslim Kashmir Valley, and the region of Jammu, populated by Dogra Hindus. The eastern part of the state, comprised of the Tibetan Buddhist regions of Ladakh and Zanskar, remains free from violence. Beautiful Leh in Ladakh has replaced Srinagar as a major tourist destination.

Kashmir's troubles began when India was partitioned along religious lines in 1947. Although the population of Kashmir was predominantly Muslim, the Hindu raja did not want to let his kingdom become part of Pakistan *or* India—and most Kashmiri Muslim leaders agreed with him. In late 1947, however, thousands of Pathan tribesmen, supplied with arms by Pakistan, crossed the border in an attempt to force Kashmir into Pakistan. Desperate, the maharaja turned his state over to India in exchange for military help. The Indian government accepted the offer, promising that a plebiscite would be held to determine whether the Kashmiri people, and not just the maharaja, wanted to join India. When the shooting stopped, however, Pakistan held a large chunk of Kashmir, and in 1962, China annexed the area of the state now known as Aksai Chin. India and Pakistan went to war over Kashmir again in 1965, although no territory changed hands. The 1948 cease-fire line remains the de facto India-Pakistan border, and the plebiscite promised by India was never held.

Politically, Kashmir is important to both India and Pakistan. As the only state with a a Muslim majority, Kashmir is a vindication of India's tolerant secularism. The desire to control the state is also a literal extension of Pakistan's founding theoretical precept that all of South Asia's Muslims belong in a separate homeland. (Both claims seem to fall apart when force is needed to control the state.) Within Kashmir arguments have been made for remaining part of India, joining Pakistan, and becoming a totally independent nation.

Since the 1947 conflict, both India and Pakistan have worked to integrate their respective slices of Kashmir into their nations. During the 1950s and 60s, the Indian portion of Kashmir remained somewhat autonomous, with a special status in India's constitution. But during the 1970s and 80s, the prominent Kashmiri leader Sheikh Abdullah, who had at times leaned toward independence, and his son Farooq Abdullah, who succeeded him, moved closer to Delhi. Kashmiri fears of absorption into India led to an outbreak of violence in 1989. Since that time, the western half of Indian-held Kashmir has been battered by the Jammu and Kashmir Liberation Front (JKLF), fighting for total independence; by various Islamic groups fighting for a merger with Pakistan; and by the Indian army which now occupies the state. While India accuses Pakistan of supplying arms to the rebels, human rights groups accuse the Indian army of torturing and summarily executing its opponents. Meanwhile, Kashmir's main sources of income (fruit exports and tourism) have been smothered by civil war. In 1995, five foreign tourists were taken hostage in Kashmir; one of them was executed. Since then, Kashmir has shakily come under India's control, and elections were held in the state in May and September 1996, with decent voter turnout. Many see this as a sign that the government has regained control, and that the insurrection is slowly dying. But recent cross-border shelling between Pakistani and Indian troops, as well as terrorist massacres on Hindu villagers in outlying regions—most recently in the summer of 1998—have kept Kashmir's future uncertain.

🖐 HIGHLIGHTS OF JAMMU AND KASHMIR

- **Ladakh,** in eastern Kashmir, draws tourists with bleak Himalayan vistas, serene treks, pocket-size villages, and the high-altitude expat party that is **Leh** (p. 369).
- Smack-dab in center of the Vale of Kashmir, **Srinagar** (p. 376) is the most beautiful place in the world you probably shouldn't visit.

■ The Manali-Leh Road

Two roads connect Leh to the rest of the world. Both are two-day hauls and involve crossing several passes well over 5000m. These roads are supposed to be open from mid-June to mid-September, but in the last few years intense rain and heavy snowfall have led to massive mud and rock slides that have closed the road for weeks on end (if you're on a tight schedule and can get a confirmed seat, take a flight to Leh).

The **Manali-Leh Road** is perhaps one of the most beautiful overland journeys on the planet, as well as the world's second-highest motorable road. It crosses the Rohtang Pass (3980m) to reach the rainshadow and then the Baralacha La (4892m) and Tanglang La (5325m) before descending to Upshi and following the Indus River to Leh. The journey lasts about 20 hours, and the landscape changes constantly. The lush, green valleys of Manali give way to rugged gorges and the barren edge of the

Tibetan Plateau, which in turn give way to towering, snow-capped Himalayan peaks and sandstone cliffs raw from erosion, which finally yield to Astroturf-green valleys speckled with herds of goats. When all is said and done, though, successful completion of the Manali-Leh route depends almost totally on the **weather.** Many travelers have made it through by **bus** (local Rs500, deluxe Rs1000) in the budgeted two days (with one night at a tent camp at Sarchu, Rs200). Others, however, have been stranded for up to a week due to **mudslides.** Sometimes the roads are even impassable by foot. Often, however, one can take a bus up to the landslide, walk over the mangled ground, and snag a bus continuing on in your direction. If the two buses are run by the same company, you probably won't have to pay twice; otherwise, you'll have to fork out more money for the fare from the mudslide to your destination. If you've hired a **jeep** (Rs10,000) to make the trip, the changeover becomes expensive, although you can sometimes swap jeeps with travelers going the other way, as long as you're not past the halfway mark.

There are *chai* stalls along the route (with very high prices), but you should stock up on food before beginning your journey. It can get below freezing point on the high mountain passes, so **bring warm clothes.** If you end up having to walk across landslides, both you and your bag will get soaked, so put anything you want to keep dry in a plastic bag.

The journey is exhilarating no matter what kind of weather you have, although the thrill can wear off after 20 hours on a hot, crowded bus or after hiking 3km across a mudslide. Most travelers are all the more excited to see the crumbling palace, the prayer flags high above town, and an old man turning a giant prayer wheel—all signs that they have finally reached Leh.

> **Warning: The Srinagar-Leh Road is dangerous** due to the precarious political situation in Kashmir (last year, one bus ride was rudely interrupted by a shell detonating 30 feet away). Nonetheless, many travelers made the trip safely in 1998.

▨ Leh

The capital of the vast former kingdom of Ladakh, Leh is remarkably different from cities further south in Kashmir. Its location at the corner of a 3500m desert plateau, surrounded by tremendous mountain ranges has made it a vibrant meeting-place for Tibetan Buddhist culture from the east and Islamic influences from the west. But Leh has accommodated the newer ideals of the tourist trade with even greater rapidity—a source of some controversy. In the summer, its streets ring with Kashmiri hawkers and STD phones as well as Muslim prayer calls and amplified Buddhist chants. At its worst, Leh becomes a frothing pit of embittered hipsters. The overwhelming number of peak-season visitors drives many away from the open-air bars, travel agents, bakeries, and *gompas* of Leh itself to the world-class trekking routes that begin nearby. Some of these follow the same routes used for centuries by traders hauling goods from Western Tibet over the Chang-La (5547m) or Kardung-La (5602m) to Leh's bustling bazaar. These days, however, the main traders are to be found on the Goa-Manali-Leh tourist route.

> **Warning: When arriving by road, carry your passport with you at all times** since this is a border region in an unstable state. The routes to Leh come close to areas under Pakistani control. **When arriving by plane,** remember that Leh is 3505m above sea level. **Rest for at least one day** (that means not even walking around and definitely not consuming alcohol) before undertaking anything strenuous, and **watch for any signs of acute mountain sickness (AMS).** The symptoms—headaches, breathlessness and nausea—normally develop during the first 36 hours (see **Trekking: Health and Safety,** p. 62). Leh has an emergency facility for dealing with AMS (tel. 52012, 52113, 24hr. tel. 52014; daily 10am-4pm).

ORIENTATION

The **main bazaar** is a wide street of shops that marks the western edge of the **Old City.** Running west from the center of the main bazaar is **Fort Road,** which has the highest density of restaurants, travel agents, and carpet shops. **Zangsty Road** begins at the north end of the main bazaar, connects to Fort Rd. via **Library Road,** and then runs north where it forks: the left branch is the long, windy **Changspa Lane,** which leads past the smaller guesthouses. Local **buses** leave from the Old Bus Stand, 5 minutes south of the bazaar. Other buses generally leave from the New Bus Stand, another five minutes down on **Airport Road.**

PRACTICAL INFORMATION

Airport: (tel. 52098), 4km from Leh (Rs80 by taxi). **Indian Airlines,** in the Tushita Office, a 10min. walk from town down Fort Rd., has an inconvenient monopoly on flights in and out of Leh. During the summer, book your ticket several months in advance; flights are packed. Flights are often delayed or cancelled due to bad weather. If you have trouble getting a confirmed flight, talk to one of the more reputable tour agencies in town—their agents can work wonders and sometimes convince Indian Airlines to send extra planes to clear out stranded tour groups. To: **Chandigarh** (Tu 7:30am, 1hr., US$70); **Delhi** (Tu, Th, Sa, and Su, 1½hr., US$105); **Jammu** (Th and Su, 7:30am, 1hr., US$65); **Srinagar** (Sa 7:30am, 1hr., US$55). **Batteries and lighters are not allowed in carry-on luggage flown out of Leh. Bags are checked at least twice.**

Buses: Depending on weather and road conditions, schedules change frequently; it's best to check the day before departure. The Tourist Information Office by the taxi stand has up-to-date schedules and prices. **Deluxe buses** to: **Manali** (Rs800 plus Rs200 for overnight tent at Sarchu) and **Srinagar** (Rs400). For more information on the beautiful, dangerous drives out of Leh, see p. 368.

Local Transportation: The **taxi** union is in the center of town, near the top of Fort Rd. There are fixed rates for all destinations during the season (July-Aug.). Bargain with the driver off season. Tourist season rates are about Rs10 per km for a round-trip fare, Rs15 per km for one way. The best way around town is on **foot.**

Tourist Office: Tourist Information Centre (tel. 52297). The main office is inconveniently located 2km from town on Airport Rd. **The Tourist Information Office,** in the State Bank of India compound on Fort Rd., has information on treks, local bus schedules, and festivals. Open M-Sa 10am-4pm, 8am-7pm in-season. You can pick up a copy of Gypsy World's map at the airport or at their office on Fort Rd.

Trekking Agents: There is a travel agent every 2m in Leh, and all kinds of excursions are offered, from river-rafting to mountaineering. Although all travel agents are registered, not all are qualified to handle high-risk activities. Ask around to find out whom to trust. **Snow Leopard Trails,** Fort Rd., P.O. Box 46 (tel. 52074; fax 52355); and **Ibex Tours and Travels** (tel. 52661) are well-reputed agencies that handle trekking and rafting. **Gypsy's World Treks and Tours,** in the White House complex on Fort Rd., is friendly, well-run, and handles all kinds of treks. Yak Hotel also rents equipment.

Currency Exchange: State Bank of India has an exchange counter in the same building as the tourist office, just off Fort Rd. Open M-F 10:30am-1:30pm, Sa 10:30am-noon. **Hotel Khangri,** a bit further down and just off the opposite side of the road, gives lower exchange rates but is less crowded. Open M-Sa 10:30am-1:30pm.

Bookstore: Book Worm, just off Fort Rd., near Zangsty Rd., sells second-hand books. Exorbitant prices, but the shop buys back at half the cost. **Artou's** (Zangsty Rd.) has books on Ladakh. Open daily 10am-1pm, 2-4pm, and 5-8pm.

Library: The only library is in the **Ecology Development Centre,** around the corner from Mona Lisa Restaurant, just off upper Zangsty Rd. Collection focuses on Ecological Development and Buddhism. Open M-Sa 10:30am-4:30pm.

Meditation Centers: Mahabodi Society. Head up Changspa Rd. and watch for signs on the left. Meditation meetings M-Sa at 5pm (guided for 20-30min., but you medi-

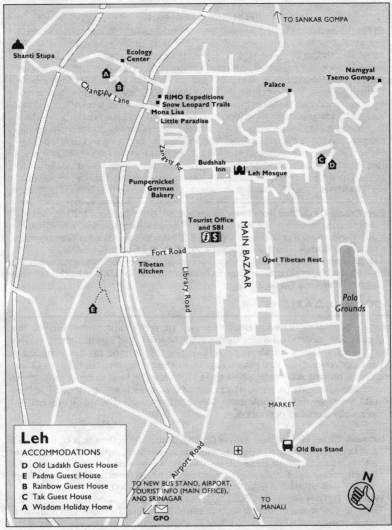

NORTH INDIA

Leh
ACCOMMODATIONS
D Old Ladakh Guest House
E Padma Guest House
B Rainbow Guest House
C Tak Guest House
A Wisdom Holiday Home

tate until 7pm). For more extensive meditation retreats, contact **Milarepa Medita-tion Centre** (tel. 44025), in Davachan, Choglamsar, on the Tikse Road.

Laundry: All the runoff from laundry, done individually or by hotels, eventually finds its way into the river, and can be extremely polluting because of the use of non-bio-degradable detergents. An eco-friendly women's organization runs **DZOMSA,** which protects the river by using a desert pit away from Leh. The service is highly recommended. Shirts and trousers Rs13, underwear Rs7, ironing Rs3. Open M-Sa 8am-8pm, Su 8am-11am and 5-8pm.

Hospital: SNM Hospital (tel. 52360), just before the bus station. Well-maintained, with 2 ambulances and a quicker, more reliable special tourist wing.

Police: The station (tel. 52018) is halfway up Zangsty Rd.

Internet Access: Gypsy's World (email matin.chunka@gems.vsnl.net.in), in the White House complex on Fort Rd., between town and the Indian Airlines office. Rs100 per page to send, Rs60 per page to receive messages. Open daily 9am-10pm.

Strange Medicine

Sniffly? Rheumatic? Plagued by vindictive demons? Ladakhi *lhamos* (faith healers) can treat all of these afflictions and more simply by sucking the appropriate vile liquid directly through your skin! A *lhamo* typically begins her therapeutic career when her socially problematic excess energy is recognized as a possession by spirits. She is then taught how to control the powers that possess her and to apply them to patients. The upshot for the ill (or haunted) is that the *lhamo*, after entering a furious trance, is able to locate the afflicting agent in the form of internal fluids or objects and draw them out with her mouth without breaking the skin. Reports of these nasty substances (which the *lhamo* repeatedly spits out during the process) cover everything from "red and lumpy" or "black and tarry" to "pebble" or "small, moving, salamander thing." *Lhamos* legit and licentious still practice in Ladakh. Ask around, but be warned—sessions can get violent to the point of slaps on the head with the flat of a sword. Remember, too, that you should only see a *lhamo* if you have a serious, long-term problem.

Post Office: GPO, 2km from town on Airport Rd. *Poste Restante,* but tell your buddies to send letters c/o the Pumpernickel German Bakery in town, where you can pick them up with greater ease. Open M-F 9:30am-5:30pm. The itsy-bitsy branch in town sells stamps. Open M-F 9:30am-4:30pm. **Postal Code:** 194101.

Telephones: Leh has 4 outgoing phone lines, and hundreds of outgoing tourist calls, so, if possible, avoid calling home from here. Most **STD/ISD** booths close by midnight. **Telephone Code:** 01982.

ACCOMMODATIONS

Most of the mud-plaster guest houses in town are very similar, and where you stay will most likely depend on where there's available space. Old Town, with its winding mud lanes and loudly broadcast prayers ringing through the air, has a handful of decent, conveniently located places. Karzoo, a neighborhood just uphill from Changspa Ln., is blessed with rolling hills and valley views. A long string of basic guesthouses line Changspa Ln. itself, while most of the bigger hotels are located on busy Fort Rd. Prices are more flexible during June and from the end of August onward. Hot water usually costs Rs5 per bucket.

Lakrook Guest House, near Sankar Gompa, 20min. from the town center; you'll find Lakrook resting in a remote, massive organic garden, replete with streams and a terraced patio. Fresh meals (Rs40-50) and solar-powered hot water. Common bathrooms are squat or Ladakhi style, where waste becomes fertilizer after it drops down a well-maintained hole. Singles Rs100; doubles Rs200.

Wisdom Holiday Home (tel. 52427), in Karzoo. Continue along the road from the Ecology Centre and follow the signs to either Wisdom or Rainbow. This brand-new guest house, in a wheat patch, offers views of a bleached-white *chorten* and the rugged cliffs behind it. Large doubles with picture windows and sparkling common bath (seat toilet) Rs150, with private bath Rs250, with balcony Rs350.

Rainbow Guest House (tel. 52332), in Karzoo. A 10min. walk from the center of town; follow the signs as you head past the Ecology Centre. Lounge in wicker chairs in a well-maintained garden or in the clean, carpeted rooms with views over green fields and rising ridges. Common squat toilet. Rooms Rs100-170.

Old Ladakh Guest House (tel. 52951), in Old Town. From the main bazaar road, follow signs for the guest house (near the palace). The oldest guest house in Leh (est. 1976), and one of a handful open year-round. Small alleys lead up to the mud and wood building and its traditional Ladakhi rooms. Shaded courtyard is perfect for postcard-writing. Single Rs80, with private bath Rs200; doubles Rs150/350.

Tak Guest House, across from the Old Ladakh Guest House, Old Town. A generous Ladakhi family runs this quaint little place. Common baths have squat toilets. The rooms are clean and quiet, but the beds in singles sag; put your mattress on the floor if you have back problems. Singles Rs80; doubles (with firm beds) Rs150.

Padma Guest House (tel. 52630), down a path off Fort Rd., 200m before Indian Airlines. A traditional Ladakhi home converted into a guest house, with spacious, clean rooms, bamboo-and-wood ceilings, and its own solar-heated water. The rooftop patio has spectacular views, and the kind owners let you eat in their kitchen. Doubles Rs200, with seat toilet and bathtub Rs350.

FOOD

> **Warning: Absolutely do not drink the water in Leh.** There is no sewage system and no clean water except in bottles. DZOMSA, on Zangsty Rd., offers pressure-boiled, safe drinking water (Rs7). **Meat can also be unsafe to eat here.** Ask if your dinner was killed here in Leh or if it's imported (in the latter case, it has most likely spent several days in an unrefrigerated truck).

Leh's food industry has grown to accommodate the tourists, with Italian restaurants, morning pancakes instead of *parathas,* and more German bakeries than you can shake a strudel at. You can also step into one of the many Tibetan restaurants along the main bazaar road, or ask your hotel manager to cook up something Ladakhi.

Üpel Tibetan Restaurant, upstairs on the southeast side of the main bazaar. An enormous range of Tibetan and Chinese dishes done by a cook who knows his stuff. Eggplant with hot garlic sauce (Rs30). Open daily 10am-10pm.

Little Paradise, Zangsty Rd., next to the Mona Lisa Restaurant. This candle-lit bistro (and its fanatically enthusiastic *maître d')* serve up homemade *tagliatelle,* roast chicken, and full breakfasts. Topped with garlands of garlic, fresh tomatoes, and a neon-red sauce, the *napoletano* (Rs40) is almost authentic. Try the great coffee (Rs7), but avoid the thin apple pie. Open daily 7am-9:30pm.

Budshah Inn Restaurant, upstairs in the block of buildings just to the left of the mosque (street-side). The only place in Ladakh to get addicted to Kashmir Valley food. Meat-eaters can risk the *rista* (Rs70), but there are veg. options too. Open daily 8am-10pm.

Pumpernickel German Bakery, between Fort Rd. and Zangsty Rd. Not quite the only German bakery in town, but as much an ex pat community center as an eatery, with a board for notices about taxis to Manali and treks that need more people; the staff will even hold your mail. Desserts (Rs25-30) and an excellent Yak-cheese and tomato sandwich (Rs28), and huge breakfasts (Rs50). Open daily 7:30am-9pm.

Tibetan Kitchen, further down Fort Rd. and impossible to miss. The same food you've seen all over North India, but cooked right, and with care. Elegant decor, patio dining, and daily specials add class. The soups (Rs35-40) are done well, as are the *momos* (Rs60).

Summer Harvest, Fort Rd., next to Dreamland. A central location, a decent breakfast, and a menu with North Indian delicacies and the standard *momo* chow mein set. One of the few places in Leh where one can find standard Delhi *dhaba* food like mixed vegetables (Rs30). Open 9am-11pm.

Mona Lisa Restaurant, up the right-hand fork off Zangsty Rd. Chilled-out open air bar and restaurant. *Falafel* and *hummus* (Rs40) make a good showing. Liquor is served, but the beer is lousy. A good place to leave notices for trek partners.

SIGHTS

Sengge Namgyal's nine-story **palace,** above the Old Town (but clearly visible from every house in Leh), a site built in 1553 to emphasize Leh's ascendancy over Shey as the Ladakhi capital, is said to have inspired the Potala Palace in Lhasa. *(Open daily 7am-5pm. Admission Rs5.)* The opening of the East Gate here used to be ostentatiously marked by the roar of a caged lion. The palace contains 1000-year-old *thankas,* gold statues, and swords. The palace was badly damaged during a war and today only a small temple on the first floor is accessible to visitors. Nestled high above the palace, the red **Namgyal Tsemo Gompa** contains the amazing two-story statue of Chamba in meditation. *(Open daily 7am-9pm. Admission Rs5.)* Ask a monk to open the door. A long line of prayer flags flutter in the wind, connecting the granite tops above the **Old Leh Castle** and the *gompa*. Toil up from the Chamba statue for another 10 minutes and you will reach a blue sign that announces your arrival at the "Castle," which is in a state of utter disrepair. The main reason to hike up here is for the excellent views of Leh and the Stok-Kangri range.

Referred to by locals as the **Japan Stupa,** the **Shanti Stupa** in Changspa village, 3km west of the bazaar (walk to Changspa and then follow a direct line to the *stupa*), is at the top of 560 steps. When you've stopped panting and puffing, feast your eyes on the legacy of Fujii Guraji, a Japanese Buddhist who moved to India in 1931. *(Open daily 5am-7pm.)* One of many built in India by Japanese Buddhists, this Peace Pagoda was built in 1983 and features gilt panels depicting episodes from the Buddha's life.

Walk along the footpath across the fields from the Ecological Centre to get to the **Sankar Gompa,** the official local residence of the reformist Gelug-pa (Yellow Hat) sect. *(Open daily 7-10am and 5-7pm. Admission Rs10.)* The main deity is the hundred-headed, thousand-armed Avalokitesvara.

Muslim influence is also strong here. The reading of the *namaz* can be heard throughout Leh five times each day from the large **Leh Mosque** at one end of the main market. Built in 1555, the large and imposing *masjid* displays Turkish and Iranian architecture at its best.

VOLUNTEER OPPORTUNITIES

Travelers wishing to do volunteer work in Leh with either the Leh Women's Alliance or the Ecology Centre, or travelers wanting to arrange a homestay at a Ladakhi farm (1 month minimum) should contact the following organizations: the **International Society for Ecology and Culture (ISEC),** 850 Talbot Street, Albany, CA 94706, USA (tel. and fax (510) 527-3873); or **Apple Barn,** Week, Dartington, Devon TQ9 6JP, U.K. (tel. (44 1803) 868650; fax 868651). The **Ecological Development Centre,** left from the Zangsty-T in Leh, is a brave attempt to examine conventional notions of development and to rethink policy prescriptions for Ladakh (open M-Sa 10:30am-4:30pm). The center screens a video on Ladakh at 4:30pm on Monday, Wednesday, and Friday off season and everyday in season, and distributes a pamphlet on dos and don'ts for tourists in Ladakh. The center has ongoing projects which need volunteers from time to time, and can refer would-be volunteers to other local organizations.

SHOPPING

There are plenty of opportunities to shop (and get suckered) in Leh. Masks, carpets, jewelry, shawls, and so-called "antiques" abound in the shops around the main market, but prices are often significantly higher than those in Delhi, Shimla, or Dharamsala, and most of the traders are Kashmiris who come to Leh only during the tourist season. The **Tibetan Children's Village Handicrafts Centre,** on the road towards Choglamsar, has crafts made at the Tibetan Children's Village (open M-Sa 9:30am-5pm). The **Tibetan Handicraft Emporium,** in the main market, is approved by the Dalai Lama (open M-Sa 9am-1pm and 2-7pm). You can drop in at the Ecology Centre's handicraft store for local Ladakhi goods (open M-Sa 10:30am-4:30pm). The **Co-operative store,** in the Galdan hotel complex just off Fort Rd., sells similar things. These places support the local community (rather than the transient one) and have fixed prices. **Cashmere Ladakh Arts,** on Zangsty Rd., is a private shop that prides itself on fixed prices and no-hassle salesmanship. Shopping elsewhere resembles a sophisticated mugging.

■ Near Leh

Sixteen kilometers from Leh is **Shey,** the summer palace built by Deldun Namgyal, son of the famous builder Sengge Namgyal. Walk up to the *gompa* (admission Rs5) to see the three-story-high **Shakyamuni Buddha,** built in 1633. Just to the left of the *gompa* is a victory *stupa*, crowned with pure gold.

Built by the intrepid Sengge Namgyal, the expansive *gompa* at **Thikse** (19km southeast of Leh) is accentuated by an open courtyard decorated with murals and a giant prayer flag. The Du-Khang, up a steep flight of stairs, houses an ancient Buddha image and scriptures. Once a year, at the time of the **Thikse Gustor Festival** (Oct. 27-28, 1999), giant *thankas* are unraveled and displayed. Climb up to the roof of the old Kali temple and library for incredible views of the Indus Valley plains around Leh and the Stok-Kaupri range. (*Gompa* admission Rs15.) Buses leave every hour from the bus stand in Leh (Rs10).

Forty-two kilometers from Leh is the Ladakh's largest and richest monastery, **Hemis.** The ideal time to come here is during the **Hemic Setchu Festival** (June 23-24, 1999), when people from all over Ladakh trek down for a few days of rituals and festivities. Old, old villagers wearing *lams* (shoes made of yak skin and wool) and twirling prayer wheels mingle with camera-carrying foreigners to watch the unraveling of the immense *thanka*—said to be the largest in the world—which is hung for two hours from the side of the palace. The monastery itself is a wide and sprawling mud-brick building with several chambers built by Sengge Namgyal in 1620. The presiding deity is a Buddha inlaid with precious stones. (Open daily 7am-6pm.) You can get here by bus (one in the morning—not too reliable); it drops you off at the main road, from where you have to walk 3km to the monastery. Walk back down to the road to catch the bus back to Leh. You can also take a taxi (Rs825 round-trip from Leh).

My Two Dads

Life in a mountainous desert at 4500m isn't easy, especially when your livelihood depends on agriculture. The effort to make such a life livable is reflected in every aspect of Ladakhi life, including family structure. In traditional Ladakhi (and Tibetan) villages, the need to maintain the precarious balance of land and labor resulted in a system of polyandry, in which younger sons automatically married the eldest son's bride. Generally, this only added up to two "dads" in the new family (judiciously called "big dad" and "little dad" by the children). Other sons were often sent to monasteries or, to make matters even more complex, into a marriage with the daughter (and younger sisters) of a son-less family. All this creative shuffling ultimately served to save the family farm from being divided up into unmanageable small pieces with insufficient labor, and kept the population down in the process. Although the Indian government has outlawed the practice, large, happy polyandrous families can still be found in the more remote villages of Ladakh.

■ Trekking Around Leh

Trekkers from around the world flock to Leh, the starting point for some of the most phenomenal treks in the Himalaya. Most book their trek through agents back home, but here in Leh, **RIMO Expeditions,** on Zangsty Rd. (tel. 53348), organizes safe, conscientious treks (US$45 per person per day; 5-person min.) and can help you set up shorter, lesser-known routes (mostly out of Stok). You can contact the managing director, Chewing Motup, at http://www.atrav.com/rimo or in Delhi (tel. (11) 6136568).

The **Lez-Kaza** route is a beautiful but extremely demanding trek that passes the 23km Tsomoriri Lake at 4480m. It's a one-day drive to Tso Moriri, where lush pastures are used by *changpas* (nomads) to graze yaks and goats. The trek crosses the Parang-La at 5490m and then descends down to Kibber and Kaza (9 days). On the fourth day, you'll cross the Phirsta Phu, a river that usually flows from Tibet to Tso Moriri, but seasonally, when the water levels change, reverses flow. The Leh-Kaza trek can only be done between July 20 and September 30.

The **Nubra Valley** is reached by crossing the highest motorable pass in the world—the Khardung-La (5602m). The Nubra Valley is famous for the double-humped camels that were used in earlier days for transport along the ancient silk route. The trek usually goes through Khaphang Meditation Center and finishes at Khalsen (9 days), but starting the trek in Khalsen allows you to acclimatize better, and

NORTH INDIA

you'll cross the Khardung-La pass at the end of your trek, rather than on the second day. The trek takes 7 days and is best done before mid-July or in September.

The **Stok-Hemis** trek (via Markha Valley) is a classic trek that takes you through a village every day so self-sufficiency is not necessary. It can be cut short after crossing the Stok-La by coming down to Runbak (3 days). The full route crosses the Stok-La (4900m) to Yurutse and continues on to Maukha village and Hemis (8 days, with plenty of acclimatization required before crossing the Stok-La). Consider starting at Spituk and doing the trek in reverse. The visits to *gompas* are separated by enough trekking days to avoid cultural overload. Because the trek is quite easy—passing the grazing grounds of local herds with 3000m mountains as a backdrop—most trekkers organize the journey themselves. Make sure that your pony man knows the route and that you have ropes for fording any rivers swollen with glacial melt.

For travelers with less time, the **Lamayuru-Alchi** trek (5 days) is ideal. With villages along the way, trekkers need not carry too many provisions. There are no large mountain passes to scale, so altitude sickness can be avoided. Both Lamayuru and Alchi have phenomenal monasteries which boast beautiful wall paintings. You can also continue on to Stok from Alchi, expanding the trek to 10 days.

The **Lamayuru-Darcha** trek (20 days), is one of the most arduous. You must be very well-equipped, **and a guide is essential**. The demanding experience leads you into Zankskar, an area of India that is completely cut off from the outside world for eight months of the year, when snow and ice make this region inaccessible.

Rightfully labeled by trekking agents as "strenuous and demanding," the trek from **Hemis** to the **Manali-Leh Road** at **Sarchu** (18 days) cannot be attempted before the end of August because the rivers along the way are too full and fording them is impossible. Trekking at an average height of 4000m, you must be entirely self-sufficient (including kerosene for cooking). Besides shepherds, you'll see few people on this trek leading toward the Tibetan Plateau. **A guide is necessary for this trek as well.**

■ Srinagar سرينجر

> **Warning:** Despite the easing of tensions in 1996-98, travel to the western half of Jammu and Kashmir (including the Kashmir Valley) is risky. **Foreign tourists have been the targets of acts of extreme violence as recently as 1995.** Border skirmishes between India and Pakistan continue, and militant activity is widespread in rural areas. Travelers are strongly advised to stay within the limits of Srinigar city, where a prominent Indian Army presence mitigates the risk somewhat.

From Goa to Delhi to Leh, you are bound to meet at least one zealously friendly Kashmiri who's convinced that his houseboat in Srinigar is the place for you. For about eight years (between 1989-1997), this was an invitation to probable disaster: kidnappings, bomb blasts, and random gunfire in the streets made the once-idyllic Vale of Kashmir off-limits to Western tourists. Recently, however, such vacation plans have been upgraded from impossible to dangerous-but-doable. Srinagar has begun to settle down and open up, and a growing (if still small) number of intrepid houseboaters are visiting the city. While *Let's Go* is neither smarter nor better-connected than your embassy (which will most likely advise against traveling to Western Kashmir), we offer a few suggestions if you decide to go.

You can avoid a great deal of hassle by **pre-booking** your trip in Delhi or Goa, provided the travel agent isn't charging you a commission. Rather than accepting desperate offers from **touts**, ask at the tourist office for a reliable **travel agent** who books accommodations in Srinigar (most agents book for only one houseboat or group of houseboats). Ask to see pictures of the same houseboat you'll be staying on and decide on a reasonable fixed price. **Houseboats** come in 5 classes with government-set rates (deluxe Rs1500, A Rs1000, B Rs700, C Rs600, and D Rs200 per double room). However, the decimated tourist trade makes it possible for you to demand half-price (and sometimes less). The more expensive boats are definitely worth the extra money. It is also possible to hire a *shikara* (canvas-roofed canoe) at **Dal Lake** and shop around. The land-locked **hotels** in Srinagar are often pricier than house-boats, and many are still occupied by the good-time boys of the Indian Army. **Swan Houseboats,** just off Dal Lake, comprises a luxurious, well-maintained group of boats run by an honest, exuberant family and their staff. Reservations can be made at **Mer-rygo Travels** (tel. 3347364; fax 3347365; email travels.merrygo@axcess.net.in), on Connaught Place in Delhi, or directly (tel. (0091) 194 475038). Rates are 50% of gov-ernment rates, in addition to a Rs50 per night discount for *Let's Go* users.

Despite the decreased political tensions in Srinagar proper, it's still better to fly in and out rather than taking the risky **bus** ride through the still-hazardous outlying areas. It's also much easier to get a seat on a Srinagar-Leh flight than on a Delhi-Leh flight. **Indian Airlines** flies to Srinagar from **Delhi** (daily, US$155). Srinagar's **airport** is currently operating out of a military airbase, so the baggage claim is a free-for-all com-ing in, but security is extremely tight going out. All your worst suspicions about mili-tary police will be confirmed, but at least you'll feel safe in the knowledge that your socks have been checked for hidden explosives.

Once on the houseboat, you'll probably be offered a **meal-and-tour package.** These can be extremely expensive (up to US$300 for 4 or 5 days), but it's not a bad idea to have someone to accompany you around the city. A few tourists wander the streets alone, but this is dangerous. Even riskier is trekking alone in this part of the state. A guide can improve your chances against would-be abductors. The treks out-side Srinagar are indeed spectacular, but **a recent and marked increase in militant activity in outlying areas of the Kashmir Valley makes trekking foolhardy at best.**

Although many visitors are happy just cruising the lotus gardens and waterways, life on land in Srinagar is also beginning to pick up after 9 years of relative stagnation. Incredible Kashmiri dishes can be sniffed out in parts of the city. **Adhoo's** refined din-ing hall has superb Srinagar standards in the Rs50-100 range, and **Mughal Darbar,** offering food at the same prices, has a well-deserved local following. **Lhasa Restau-rant,** which serves upscale Tibetan and Chinese food, is another (pricier) favorite.

Srinagar's world-renowned **Mughal Gardens** are in a state of disrepair, due in large part to the military government's refusal to fund their maintenance. **Shalimar Gar-den** is open, but its central line of fountains has been entirely dismantled for renova-tions. The awe-inspiring **Nishat Garden** is in full working order.

No one escapes Srinagar without some exposure to high-intensity Kashmiri sales-manship—whether it's carpets, papier mâché, silver, or shawls, you'll be tempted to drop some serious rupees. Prices on Kashmiri **handicrafts** here are better than any-where else, and most salesmen aren't working for a commission. Try to buy from family-owned or collective outfits. **Honey** is one of the least expensive and most enjoyable specialties available here. **The Oriental Apiary,** between Dal and Nagin Lakes, has been producing a wide variety for 45 years.

West Bengal পশ্চিম বঙ্গ

The mighty Ganga begins its sweeping turn toward the sea in West Bengal, creating the world's largest delta. Nestled among various streams and tributaries lies a patchwork of farms and plantations that provide the agricultural base to support India's most densely populated state. Nourishing (to some degree) almost 800 people per square kilometer, West Bengal has stretched its resources to new limits, owing to the dominant Communist Party's skillful management of the land. Despite the fact that two-thirds of the land in the state is used for farming, however, all is not terraces and paddies in West Bengal. Nature can be cruel, often ravaging coastal areas with cyclones. The landscape varies enormously and often abruptly, from the misty hill station of Darjeeling peeking out over the Himalaya, to the Sundarbans, the world's largest mangrove swamp, spilling into the Bay of Bengal and home to voracious crocodiles and Bengal tigers. Tucked away in a peaceful corner, Santiniketan's university—the beloved and famed brainchild of the poet Rabindranath Tagore—continues to maintain the Bengali traditions of intellectualism and respect for high culture. And in the middle of it all—as much as this strangely shaped state can be said to have a middle—lies Calcutta, a choked, crowded, and captivating city representing both the glories of the past and the hopes for the future.

West Bengal's position at the mouth of the Ganga made it a rich agricultural and commercial region, attracting European plunderers in the 17th and 18th centuries. After the Battle of Plassey in 1757, when Robert Clive defeated Nawab Siraj-ud-Daula and the French, claiming Bengal for Britain, the province rose to prominence in the Raj. Although the British made Calcutta their capital and sought to use Bengal as a base for expansion, they found themselves unable to eradicate the region's tenacious cultural identity. For hundreds of years, Bengalis had spoken their own language and maintained unique religious traditions, often centering around the Mother Goddess Devi (worshipped as the terrifying Kali, or Durga). Islam has long been a presence in Bengal as well, and even after the state was partitioned along religious lines, 22 percent of the "Hindu" Western half remained Muslim. In the 19th century, Bengal was also the center of the revival of Indian culture, and Calcutta still lays claim to being the artistic and intellectual capital of India. West Bengal also revels in its enlightened Marxist traditions; the Communist Party of India has held power since the 1960s. Today, even many middle-class Bengalis display an admirable social conscience, funneling much of their earned income into charities, while the state as a whole has avoided the communal violence that has plagued other areas of the country.

🏛 HIGHLIGHTS OF WEST BENGAL

- India's most famous hill station, **Darjeeling** (p. 398) entices heat-weary travellers with tea plantations, toy trains, and superb Himalayan views.
- **Calcutta's** temples, monuments, museums and parks (p. 391) are upstaged only by the unchecked exhuberance of the city's citizens.

■ Calcutta কলিকাতা

Eastern India's greatest urban center and a city of over 12 million people, Calcutta draws passionate reactions from almost every visitor, even those who are already aware of its poverty and suffering. The sidewalks are jigsawed apart and teem with bookstands, beggars, and men selling squeaky toys. One can't just walk down the street in Calcutta—one must step into, over, and around it, breathing in layers of snotblackening soot. Old men trot through the traffic by day, hauling the world's last fleet of hand-pulled rickshaws; families by the thousands sleep on the pavement at night. Calcutta sometimes seems like a human cyclone. Yet the same Calcuttans who lament their city's overpopulation and pollution also sing of their hometown as a

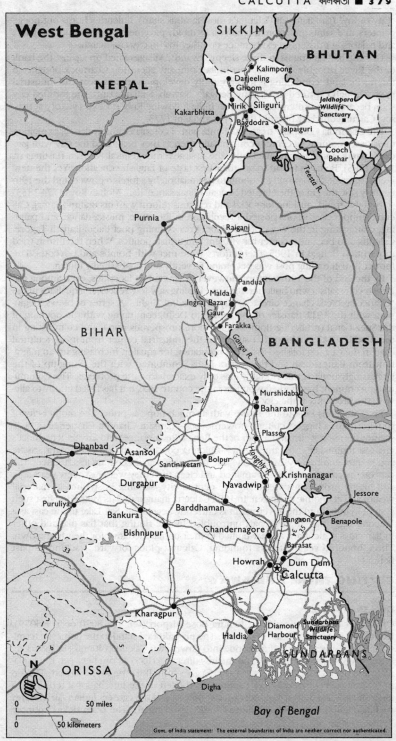

West Bengal

SIKKIM

BHUTAN

NEPAL

Kalimpong
Darjeeling
Ghoom
Mirik
Kakarbhitta
Bagdodra
Siliguri
Jalpaiguri

Jaldhapara
Wildlife
Sanctuary

Cooch
Behar

Teesta R.

Purnia

Raiganj

34

Pandua

Malda
Ingraj Bazar
Gaur
Farakka

Ganga R.

BIHAR

BANGLADESH

Murshidabad
Baharampur

Plassey

Dhanbad
Asansol
Santiniketan
Bolpur

Hoogly R.

Durgapur
Navadwip
Krishnanagar

Jessore

Puruliya
Bankura
Barddhaman
Chandernagore
Bangaon
Benapole

Bishnupur

2

34
33

Barasat

33

Howrah
Dum Dum
Calcutta

6

4

Kharagpur

Diamond
Harbour

Sundarbans
Wildlife
Sanctuary

Haldia

ORISSA

SUNDARBANS

N

0   50 miles
0   50 kilometers

Digha

Bay of Bengal

EAST INDIA

Govt. of India statement: The external boundaries of India are neither correct nor authenticated.

"City of Joy" (the name of Calcutta's most famous slum). Calcutta churns out poets, painters, and saints and, from the rain on its moldy pavement to its magnificent parks and palaces, it musters an exuberance no other Indian city can match.

The city had its origins in three sleepy, swampy villages lined up against the bank of the River Hooghly. In 1690, East India Company agent Job Charnock bought up the fertile land, combining it into a rapidly developing trading-post and industrial base. Though captured in 1756 by Bengal's Nawab, Siraj-ud-Daula, the fortified city soon became the centerpiece of British India following Robert Clive's victory at Plassey. Calcutta officially became the Raj's capital in 1773.

The East India Company treated Calcutta with a colonialist ambivalence, exploiting their new commercial center economically even as they beautified the city with gardens, parks, and monuments. Under the first governor-general, Warren Hastings (r. 1774-1785), Bengalis began to get their first taste of English education. Yet the new literati remained too proud to submit to assimilation by a foreign power, and the 19th century saw the era of the elite-led Bengali Renaissance. Ram Mohan Roy (1774-1833) started this trend, pushing for social and religious reform with his Brahmo Samaj. Calcutta's upper-class salons hosted a revolution in literature, music, dance, and painting, culminating in the work of the Nobel Prize-winning poet Rabindranath Tagore. Calcutta also became a center for virulent anti-British politics. When the British tried to partition Bengal in 1905, their efforts were met with bombs and boycotts. The former British trading post was becoming fervently and unabashedly Indian.

By the end of the 19th century, however, Calcutta had its critics, even among the British colonialists who built her. Rudyard Kipling saw few redeeming qualities in the "chance-erected, chance-directed, city of Dreadful Night." A series of blows, beginning with the 1911 transfer of the capital to Delhi, continuing with the opening of the Suez Canal (rendering Bombay a far more prosperous port), and culminating in the bloody 1947 Partition that sundered the industrial center from its agricultural base in the east, established the city's reputation for squalor. Increasing urban migration from Bangladesh and the rest of India, combined with the silting-up of the increasingly unnavigable Hooghly, has only exacerbated the problems. The Communist government has worked wonders in the countryside, but has failed utterly to alleviate the problems in the city.

Yet Calcuttans look to the future with as much hope as pride. The mother-city of some of India's biggest cultural powerhouses—Bankim Chandra Chatterjee (a civil-servant turned novelist and leader of the Bengal Renaissance) and Satyajit Ray (India's greatest filmmaker), to name a few—Calcutta continues to house a vibrant artistic and literary community. Meanwhile, the power cuts are becoming less frequent, the cars on the roads are more streamlined and clean than they were just a few years ago, and highly prosperous areas ring the central city, sending in streams of material wealth and economic optimism. In 1984 Calcutta inaugurated its Metro, the first such system in India, and the government is currently developing Salt Lake to the east as a "second Calcutta." In large part untroubled by the rioting that has plagued other Indian cities, Calcuttans appear unified in their unmatched love for their hometown. Three hundred years after its founding, Calcutta plods forward, tracking its past behind it.

GETTING THERE AND AWAY

Dum Dum Airport

Officially called Netaji Subhas Chandra Bose Airport (tel. 511 8070 or 511 8079), Dum Dum is 2km northeast of the city. The **prepaid taxi** stand in the domestic terminal is the best bet for an efficient ride into downtown Calcutta (40min., Rs135). City buses #303, 46, and 510 (Rs2) and the less direct E3 (Rs5) all run between the Esplanade and the airport. Minibus #151 (Rs15) goes from BBD Bag to the airport. The airport has a **currency exchange counter** (to the left in the international terminal), a **post office,** West Bengal and India **tourist offices,** and the carriers **Indian Airlines, Jet Airlines,** and **Sahara India Airlines** (domestic terminal). The **train ticket counter** serves Delhi, Bombay, and Madras only. With proof of a layover of under 24 hours, the airport manager in the Domestic Terminal can arrange beds for tired travelers. There is a counter at the domestic terminal where you can make hotel reservations, but most budget accommodations aren't on their list.

International Flights

All carriers have offices at the airport as well as in Calcutta proper. **International Airlines: AeroFlot,** 58 Chowringhee Rd. (tel. 249831 or 243765). Open M-F 10am-1pm, 2-5:30pm, Sa 10am-1pm. **Air France,** 41 Chowringhee Rd. (tel. 226616). Open M-Sa 9am-5:30pm. **Air India,** 50 Chowringhee Rd. (tel. 242 2356 or 242 1187). Open daily 9:30am-5:30pm. **Alitalia,** 228A AJC Bose Rd. (tel. 247 1777 or 247 5794). Open daily 9:30am-5:30pm. **American Airlines,** 2-7 Sarat Bose Rd. (tel. 745091 or 745093). Open M-F 9am-1pm and 1:30-5:30pm, Sa 9am-1:30pm. **Air Canada, Gulf Air,** and **TWA,** 230A AJC Bose Rd. (tel. 247 2526 or 247 5576). Open M-F 9am-1pm and 1:30-5:30pm, Sa 9am-1:30pm. **Bangladesh Biman,** 30C Chowringhee Rd. (tel. 226 3453 or 246 9161). **British Airways,** 41 Chowringhee Road (tel. 226 3453 or 246 9161). Open M-Sa 9:30am-5:30pm. **Canadian, SAS, South African,** and **United Airlines,** 2-7 Sarat Bose Rd. (tel. 747622 or 745370). Open M-F 9:30am-1pm and 2-5:30pm, Sa 9:30am-1pm. **Cathay Pacific,** 1 Middleton St. (tel. 240 3211). Open M-F 9:30am-1pm and 2-5:30pm, Sa 9:30am-1:30pm. **Delta,** 13D Russell St. (tel. 246 3873 or 246 3826). Open M-F 9am-5:30pm. **Japan Airlines,** 35A Chowringhee Rd. (tel. 298370). Open M-F 9am-1pm and 1:30-5:30pm, Sa 9am-1pm. **KLM and Northwest,** 1 Middleton St., Jeevan Deep (tel. 240 4452, airport branch tel. 511 8329). Open M-F 9am-5pm, Sa 9am-1pm. **Lufthansa,** 30A/B Chowringhee Rd. (tel. 246 9365, fax 246 4010). Open M-F 9am-1pm and 1:30-5:30pm. **RNAC,** 41 Chowringhee Rd. (tel. 298534). Open M-F 9am-1pm and 2-4pm, Sa 9am-1pm. **Thai Airways,** 18G Park St. (tel. 299 8464). Open daily 24hr.; tourist window (#12) open M-F 9am-1pm and 2-5pm.

Domestic Flights

Domestic Airlines: Indian Airlines, 39 Chittaranjan Ave. (tel. 266869 or 262548 or 264433; fax 262415). Open 24hr.; tourist window (#12) open daily 9am-7pm. Hotel Hindustan branch, 235/1 AJC Bose Rd. (tel. 247 6606). Open M-Sa 10am-1:15pm and 2:30-6:30pm. Great Eastern Hotel branch, 1-3 Old Court House St., 2nd fl. (tel. 248 0073 or 248 8009). Open M-Sa 10am-1:30pm and 2-5pm. **Jet Airways,** 18D Park St. (tel. 292214). Open daily 9am-7pm. **Sahara,** 2A Shakespeare Sarani (tel. 242 8969 or 242 7686). Open M-Sa 10:30am-5pm.

To: **Agartala** (1 per day, 50min., US$50); **Ahmedabad** (Tu-Su, 2½hr., US$205); **Aizwal** (M-Sa, 2hr., US$90); **Bagdogra** (1-2 per day, 1hr., US$80); **Bangalore** (1 per day, 3½hr., US$240); **Bhubaneswar** (M-Sa, 1 per day, 1hr., US$75); **Chennai (Madras)** (2 per day, 2hr., US$200); **Delhi** (3 per day, 2hr., US$180); **Dibugarh** (4 per week, 1½hr., US$95); **Dimapur** (4 per week, 2½hr., US$90); **Guwahati** (2-3 per day, 1hr., US$70); **Hyderabad** (1-2 per day, 2hr., US$190); **Imphal** (1 per day, 2hr., US$80); **Jaipur** (1 per day, 2½hr., US$200); **Jorhat** (4 per week, 1½hr., US$90); **Lucknow** (M, W, and F, 2½hr., US$140); **Mumbai (Bombay)** (5-6 per day, 3hr., US$205); **Nagpur** (3 per week, 1½hr., US$150); **Patna** (F-W, 1½hr., US$90); **Port Blair** (4 per week, 2hr., US$195); **Dhaka, Bangladesh** (2-4 per day, 1hr., US$66); **Kathmandu, Nepal** (Th-Tu, 1½hr., US$96).

Trains

Calcutta has two stations, **Sealdah Station,** northeast on AJC Bose Rd., with trains going north, and **Howrah Station,** across the Hooghly River from Calcutta, with trains going to the rest of India. The best way to get to or from Howrah Station is by **bus.** If you're going to the Sudder St. area, take a bus to the Esplanade (Rs1.50) and it's a 5-minute walk. There is a **prepaid taxi** stand at the station (Rs40 to downtown Calcutta), but the Howrah Bridge is notoriously congested. The **West Bengal Tourist Office** here is open M-Sa 7am-1am, Su 7am-12:30pm. Tickets can be purchased at the **Railway Booking Office,** 6 Fairlie Pl. (tel. 220 3496), near BBD Bag. The **Foreign Tourist Office,** on the 1st floor, has a helpful staff and A/C, but expect long lines.

There are other train offices scattered around the city but this is the only one that sells from the tourist quota. You can pay in foreign currency or rupees with encashment certificate. Open 9am-1pm and 1:30-4pm.

Fares listed are 2nd class sleeper/A/C 3-tier. From **Sealdah Station** to: **New Jalpaiguri** (*Darjeeling Mail* 3143, 7:15pm, 13hr.; *Kanchenjunga Exp.* 5657, 6:25am, 12hr., Rs187/910); **Patna** (*Lal Quila Exp.* 3111, 8:15pm, 10hr., Rs167/776). From **Howrah Station** to: **Bhubaneswar** (*Rajdhani Exp.* 2422, 8hr., Rs283/860); **Chennai (Madras)** (*Coromandal Exp.* 2841, 2pm, 27½hr., Rs327/863; *Madras Mail* 6003, 8:15pm, 32hr., Rs317); **Delhi** (*Rajdhani Exp.* 2305, 1:45pm, 20hr., Rs1145, A/C 3-tier only; *Rajdhani Exp.* 2301, 5pm, 18hr., Rs1120, A/C 3-tier only; *Poorva Exp.* 2381, 9:15am, 23hr., Rs309/791); **Mumbai (Bombay)** (*Howrah-Mumbai Mail* 8002, 7:20pm, 36hr.; *Howrah-Mumbai Mail* 3003, 8pm, 40hr.; *Geetanjali Exp.* 2860, 12:25pm, 32hr., Rs350/964); **Patna** (*Rajdhani Exp.* 2305, 1:45pm, 7hr., Rs685, A/C 3 tier only); **Puri** (*Howrah-Puri Exp.* 8007, 10pm, 10½hr.; *Sri Jagannath Exp.* 8409, 7:20pm, 11hr., Rs159); **Varanasi** (*Howrah-Amritsar Mail* 3005, 7:20pm, 15hr., Rs213).

Buses

Private buses go to Siliguri (12hr.), a departure point for Darjeeling and Jalpaiguri. The most direct bus is run by West Bengal Tourism, departing Calcutta at 6pm, reaching **Siliguri** at 6am and **Jalpaiguri** at 6:15am (Rs170). Buses also run to **Dingha** (7am, 6hr., Rs40) and **Jaigon** (6pm, 19hr., Rs210). Tickets must be purchased in advance at the booth at the Esplanade; turn left off Chowringhee Rd. on S.N. Banerjee Rd. and the booth is on the right just before the tram tracks. Other private bus company booths are located to the left (follow the tracks).

Boats

Two to three ships sail to **Port Blair** in the Andaman Islands each month, but their schedule is subject to the weather. Tickets and a tentative schedule for the month are available at the **Shipping Corporation Office,** 13 Strand Rd. (tel. 246 2354; open M-F 10:30am-1pm). The office is two blocks south of the Railway Booking Office; enter through the mail entrance, go through the back door and up one floor. Arrivals and departures are also announced on the radio and in local daily newspapers one week in advance. Ticket sales commence seven days before scheduled departure and often sell out in the first couple of days. Bring three passport photos to purchase tickets (Rs955/1725/2852 for bunk/2nd class/1st class; food costs an additional Rs50 per day for bunk, Rs100 per day for 1st and 2nd class). The trip takes 3-4 days. The **Silver Jet,** located just opposite the Shipping Corporation Office on the river bank, is a catamaran service between Calcutta and Haldia. Boats leave Calcutta at 7:45am and return at 5:30pm (2hr., Rs400-1000).

GETTING AROUND

Local Buses

Tourist fears of Calcutta's city buses are largely unfounded. Buses are cheap, ubiquitous, and will put you into close, close contact with locals. However, it's important to let go of the "bus stop" concept: you can get on just about anywhere, and buses seldom actually stop. Just put your hand out and the driver will slow down for you. If it's moving too fast for you to feel comfortable running alongside and jumping aboard, politely shout *"asthe!"* The key to finding your bus is identifying a major destination (like Esplanade, BBD Bag, Howrah Station, etc.) that's in the same direction. Destinations are not always written in English, but not to worry: the sole occupation of one man on the bus is to shout the highlights of its journey. If you're not sure whether a bus is going to your destination, he's the *wallah* to ask. Women can always find a designated "Ladies" seat, and even if you can't get to an official one, most men are happy to stand if asked. When the ticket-*wallah* comes, tell him where you're going—he'll tell you how much you owe and, if you ask, and when to get off. Make sure you get a ticket or he may ask you to pay again. Fares are Rs1-3.

EAST INDIA

River Ferries

Ferries run on the Hooghly River from Howrah Station to Fairlie Place (train reservation office) to Babu (Chandpal) Ghat (every 10min. 8am-8pm, Rs2). Though not as efficient as buses, they are a calm and scenic way of crossing the Hooghly.

Metro

India's first subway extends in a virtually straight line from Tollygunge, up Chowringhee Rd., to Dum Dum Station. From this station, a taxi or auto-rickshaw to the airport takes 45min. with traffic (Rs70). The metro is relatively uncrowded and rapid (Rs2-5; open M-Sa 8am-8:30pm, Su 2-8:30pm).

Taxis

Though expensive and isolating, cabs are the most convenient way to cover long distances in Calcutta. Name your destination and only get into the cab if the driver recognizes it. Don't ask about the price. If the driver states a charge and refuses to use the meter, get out of the cab; it's an argument you can't win. The meter begins at Rs5, and the fare is double the displayed fare to take into account the rising cost of petrol. The prepaid taxi counters at the airport may have long lines, but are worth waiting for. The fare is Rs135 to the center of the city.

Rickshaws and Auto-Rickshaws

Calcutta's **hand-pulled rickshaws** fight for space on the congested roads. In most cases, you can walk faster than they can pull. **Auto-rickshaws** can be quite efficient, but leave you open to breathe all the exhaust fumes. They are cheaper than taxis, but they aren't metered. Negotiate beforehand.

Trams

Trams depart from the central Esplanade to major destinations throughout South Calcutta and to Sealdah and Howrah Bridges (Rs1-2). They are slow and sometimes crowded. A list of routes can be purchased at any bookstand.

ORIENTATION

Though the city is expansive and sprawling, Calcutta's layout is relatively straightforward, and a little while in the city should be enough to get one's bearings. The **River Hooghly** cuts through town, separating Calcutta proper from **Howrah;** these areas are linked by the record-setting **Howrah Bridge** and, farther south, the **Second Hooghly Bridge.** Flanking the river's east bank is the sizable **Maidan,** a grass-topped field cut through by streets and sprinkled with monuments. The central city hugs the Maidan, while **Strand Rd.** cuts between it and the river. At the Maidan's northeast corner is the **Esplanade** (rhymes with lemonade), the central bus and train terminus. A couple of blocks north is **BBD Bag** (formerly Dalhousie Square), around which one may find the tourist office, GPO, railway and shipping companies, and banks. On BBD Bag's eastern side is **Old Court House Rd.,** which continues northward to become Netaji Subhas Rd. Together with Chittaranjan Ave. to its east, it is the major thoroughfare leading to North Calcutta.

Running up the Maidan's east side is **Chowringhee Rd.** (renamed Jawaharlal Nehru Rd.) Several smaller streets wend eastward from Chowringhee: these include Park St., with fancier restaurants, hotels, and shopping areas, and (two blocks north of Park St.) **Sudder Street,** home to the vast majority of budget accommodations. At Sudder's St.'s eastern end is the north-south **Free School St.** (now Mazra Ghalib St.), with a range of eating and shopping facilities. Even farther east is **AJC Bose Rd.,** which used to circle the city—to the south it curves back westward in a semicircular pattern and leads to St. Paul's Cathedral and Victoria Memorial, which are at the Maidan's southeast corner. East of it all is the clean and efficient **Eastern Metropolitan Bypass.** This is the route taxi drivers should take to bring you into town.

In the south, Chowringhee Rd. becomes Ashutosh Mukherjee Rd., which continues directly into southern Calcutta. To the west is the posh residential area of **Alipur,**

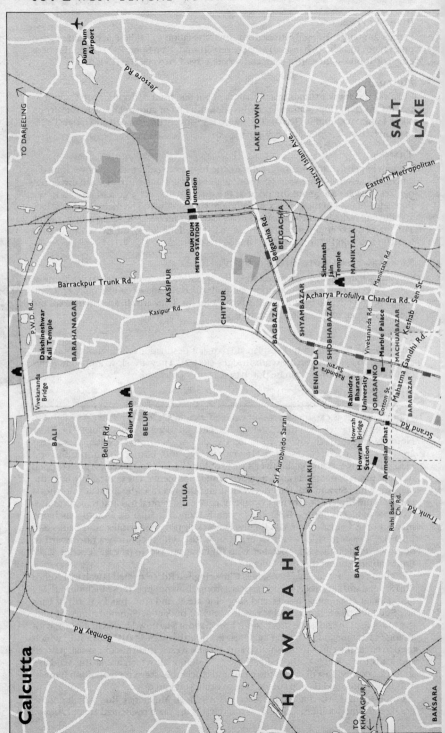

Calcutta

TO DARJEELING

Dum Dum
Airport

Jessore Rd.

SALT
LAKE

Eastern Metropolitan

Dum Dum
Junction

Nazrul Islam Ave.

LAKE TOWN

DUM DUM
METRO STATION
DUM DUM STATION

Belgachia Rd.

BELGACHIA

MANIKTALA

Sitalanath
Jain
Temple

Barrackpur Trunk Rd.

KASIPUR

Maniktala Rd.

CHITPUR

Acharya Profullya Chandra Rd.

Kasipur Rd.

SHYAMBAZAR

Sen St.

P.W.D. Rd.

BAGBAZAR

SHOBHABAZAR

Vivekananda Rd.

Keshab

Dakshineshwar
Kali Temple

BARAHANAGAR

Marble Palace

MACHUABAZAR

Gandhi Rd.

BENIATOLA

Rabindra
Sarani

Mahatma

BARABAZAR

Strand Rd.

Vivekananda
Bridge

Belur Rd.

Belur Math

BELUR

Rabindra
Bharati
University

JORASANKO

Cotton St.

BALI

Sri Aurobindo Sarani

SHALKIA

Howrah
Bridge

Armenian Ghat

Howrah
Station

LILUA

Rishi Bankim
Ch. Rd.

Trunk Rd.

H O W R A H

BANTRA

Bombay Rd.

TO
KHARAGPUR

BAKSARA

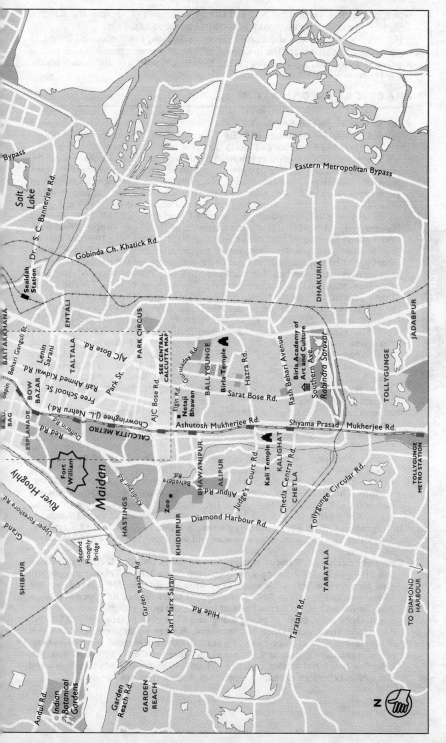

Bypass

Salt
Lake

Dr. S. C. Bannerjee Rd.

Gobinda Ch. Khatick Rd.

Eastern Metropolitan Bypass

Sealdah
Station

ENTALI

BAITAKKHANA

Jepin

Behari Ganguli St.

Lenin
Sarani

Rafi Ahmed Kidwai Rd.

Free School St.

Park St.

A/C Bose Rd.

TALTALA

PARK CIRCUS

SEE CENTRAL
CALCUTTA MAP

Gurusaday Rd.

Birla Temple

BALLYGUNGE

Hazra Rd.

DHAKURIA

Birla Academy of
Art and Culture

Rash Behari Avenue

Southern Ave.

Rabindra Sarovar

TOLLYGUNGE

JADABPUR

BOW
BAZAR

B.B.D.
BAG

ESPLANADE

Red Rd.

Dufferin Rd.

Chowringhee (J.L. Nehru Rd.)

A/C Bose Rd.

Elgin Rd.

Netaji
Bhawan

Sarat Bose Rd.

Ashutosh Mukherjee Rd.

Shyama Prasad Mukherjee Rd.

CALCUTTA METRO

Fort
William

Maidan

HASTINGS

Khidirpur Rd.

BHAWANIPUR

ALIPUR

Belvedere
Rd.

Judge's Court Rd.

Kali Temple

KALIGHAT

Chetla Central Rd.

CHETLA

Tollygunge Circular Rd.

TOLLYGUNGE
METRO STATION

River Hooghly

Grand

Upper Foreshore Rd.

Second
Hooghly
Bridge

Zoo

Alipur Rd.

Diamond Harbour Rd.

KHIDIRPUR

Garden Reach Rd.

SHIBPUR

Karl Marx Sarani

Hide Rd.

TARATALA

Taratala Rd.

TO DIAMOND
HARBOUR

Andul Rd.

Indian
Botanical
Gardens

Garden
Reach Rd.

GARDEN
REACH

N

which houses the zoo and the National Library; just south of Alipur is the Kalighat Temple, beyond which most travelers don't feel the need to sojourn.

Howrah's centerpiece is the frenetic **Howrah Station,** easily accessed from Calcutta by the Howrah Bridge. The main road in Howrah, running parallel to the river is the **Grand Trunk Rd.,** which connects the **Botanical Gardens** in the south with the **Belur Math** up north.

PRACTICAL INFORMATION

Tourist and Financial Services

Tourist Office: Government of India Tourist Office, 4 Shakespeare Sarani (tel. 242 1402 or 242 5318; fax 242 3521). The best source of information, this office provides customized computer printouts for desired locations in India. Ask for the map of Calcutta and the free pamphlet of cultural events, *Calcutta This Fortnight. Calcutta: Gateway to the East* (Rs25), published by the West Bengal Chamber of Commerce, a smart, honest, comprehensive introduction to the city and its sights. The office also provides a list of host families and *dharamshalas* if you're looking for alternative accommodations. Open M-F 9am-6pm, Sa 9am-1pm. **Airport Branch** (tel. 511 8299) in the domestic terminal of Dum Dum Airport. **West Bengal Tourist Bureau,** 3/2 BBD Bag E. (tel. 248 8271). Open M-Sa 10:30am-1pm, Su and holidays 7am-1pm. Provides tours of the city (full day, Rs75), information and tours for all of West Bengal, and passes for wildlife parks and the Marble Palace. Has counters at airport and Howrah Station (tel. 660 2518). Both open daily 7am-1pm. Less plush and well organized is the **Government of India Tourist Office. State Tourist Offices: Andaman and Nicobar Islands,** 3A Auckland Pl. (tel. 247 5084), in the CMDA Bldg. Open M-F 10am-6pm. **Arunachal Pradesh,** 4B Chowringhee Pl. (tel. 228 6500). Open M-F 10am-4pm. **Assam,** 8 Russell St. (tel. 295094). Open M-F 10am-4:30pm. **Manipur,** 25 Ashutosh Shastri Rd. (tel. 747937). **Mizoram,** 24 Old Ballygunge Rd. (tel. 475 7034). Open M-F 9am-5pm. **Nagaland,** 13 Shakespeare Sarani (tel. 242 5269). **Sikkim,** 5/2 Russell St., Poonam Bldg., 4th fl. (tel. 246 8986). Open M-F 10:30am-4pm. **Tripura,** 1 Pretoria St. **Orissa,** 55 Lenin Sarani (tel. 244 3653). Open M-F 10:30am-4pm. **Bihar,** 26B Camac St. (tel. 247 0821), upstairs. Open M-F 9am-4pm. **Meghalaya,** 9/10 Russell St. (tel. 290707). Open M-F 10am-5:30pm.

Budget Travel: Every street corner seems to have a travel agent. Thomas Cook and AmEx also provide full service to members (see below).

Diplomatic Missions: Bangladesh, 9 Circus Ave. (tel. 247 5208). **Bhutan,** contact **Bhutan Tourism,** 35A Chowringhee Rd. (tel. 298363). Open M-F 10am-5pm. **Nepal,** 19 National Library Ave. (tel. 479 1003). One photo needed for visa (visas also available at the border and in Kathmandu). Open M-F 9:30am-12:30pm and 1:30-4:30pm. **Sri Lanka,** Nicco House, 2 Hare St. (tel. 285102). Open M-F 10am-5:30pm. **Thailand,** 18B Mandville Gardens (tel. 407836 or 760836). Open M-F 9am-noon. **U.K.,** 1 Ho Chi Minh Sarani (tel. 242 5171). Open M-F 9am-noon. **U.S.,** 5/1 Ho Chi Minh Sarani (tel. 242 3611). Open M-F 8:30am-12:30pm and 2-4pm.

Immigration Office: Foreigners Registration Office, 237 AJC Bose Rd. (tel. 247 3301). Provides long-term visa extensions and work visas only. Open M-F 9am-1pm and 2-4pm.

Currency Exchange: Banque National de Paris, 4A BBD Bag E. (tel. 248 2166 or 248 0197). Open M-F 10am-5pm, Sa 10am-2pm. Has a 24hr. **ATM** that accepts MC, Visa, Cirrus, Pulse/Plus. **Citibank,** 43 Chowringhee Rd. (tel. 249 2484). Open M-F 10am-2pm, Sa 10am-noon. **ANZ Grindlays,** 41 Chowringhee Rd. Open M-F 10am-3pm, Sa 10am-12:30pm. **State Bank of India,** Dum Dum Airport, international terminal. Open 24hr. **Bank of Hong Kong and Shanghai,** 8 Netaji Subhas Rd. (tel. 248 6363). Holds mail. Open M-F 9am-4pm. **American Express,** 21 Old Court House St. (tel. 248 2133 or 248 9555; fax 248 8096). Has travel services and currency exchange. Open M-Sa 9:30am-6:30pm. **Thomas Cook,** 230A AJC Bose Rd., Chitrakut Bldg., 2nd fl., side entrance (tel. 247 4560; fax 247 5854). Offers travel services and currency exchange. Open M-Sa 9:30am-1pm and 1:45-6pm.

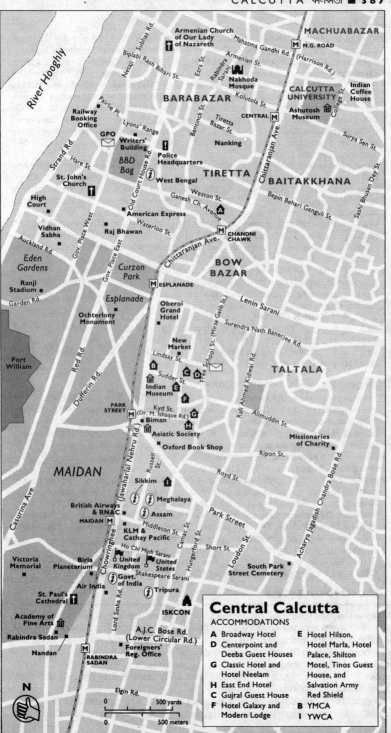

Central Calcutta

ACCOMMODATIONS

A Broadway Hotel
D Centerpoint and
   Deeba Guest Houses
G Classic Hotel and
   Hotel Neelam
H East End Hotel
C Gujral Guest House
F Hotel Galaxy and
   Modern Lodge

E Hotel Hilson,
   Hotel Marla, Hotel
   Palace, Shilton
   Motel, Tinos Guest
   House, and
   Salvation Army
   Red Shield
B YMCA
I YWCA

0   500 yards
0   500 meters

Local Services

Luggage Storage: Howrah Station cloak room, track 12. Rs5-8 per day. Luggage must be locked. Note "Beware of Rats" sign. Most **hotels** also store guests' luggage.

Bookstore: Oxford Book Store, Park St. (tel. 297662). Carries everything from Clive Cussler to James Joyce. Open M-F 10am-8pm, Sa 10am-1pm. **The Modern Book Depot,** 15A Chowringhee Rd. (tel. 249 3102), just west of New Market across the street from Light House cinemas at the entrance to Shreeram Arcade. Open M-F 10am-7:30pm, Sa 10am-4:30pm. **College Street** is lined with book stalls and shops offering a bazaar atmosphere minus the bargaining. **Maps: Survey of India Map Sales Office,** 13 Wood St. Sign in; the guard will point the way. Many maps are restricted, but there's a good selection of trekking maps. Open M-F 10:30am-1pm and 2:30-5pm.

Library: National Library, Alipur Rd. near the zoo. India's largest library with 2 million books in all of the official languages. Ask for access as a casual visitor. Open M-Sa 9am-8pm, Su 10am-6pm. **Asiatic Society of Bengal,** 1 Park St. A Calcutta institution dating back to 1784 and the best place to go to study Persian manuscripts and 19th-century academic tomes. The adjacent museum contains paintings by Rubens and Reynolds. Open M-F 10am-6pm. **British Council,** 5 Shakespeare Sarani (tel. 282 5378 or 282 9108; fax 282 4804). Membership Rs400. Open Tu-Sa 10:30am-6:30pm. **United States Information Service (USIS),** 38A Chowringhee Rd. (tel. 245 1211 or 245 1216). Open M-F 10am-6pm.

English Media: *The Statesman* and *The Telegraph* (both daily) focus on Calcutta. Nationwide English publications can be found in newstands. *The Asian Age* (daily) has informative entertainment and sports sections.

Cultural Centers: Alliance Française, 24 Park Mansions, Park St. (tel. 298793; fax 242 2863). **British Council,** 5 Shakespeare Sarani (tel. 242 5378 or 242 5380; fax 242 4804). Open Tu-Sa 10:30am-6:30pm. **USIS,** 38A Chowringhee Rd. (tel. 245 1211 or 245 1215). Open M-F 10am-6pm. **Academy of Fine Arts,** Cathedral Rd. (tel. 248 4302). **Rabindra Sadan,** corner of Cathedral Rd. and AJC Bose Rd. **Birla Academy of Art and Culture,** Southern Rd.

Emergency and Communications

Pharmacy: Common throughout the city. **Dey's Medical Store, Ltd.,** 6A Nell Sengupta Sarani (tel. 249 9810), on the left where Madge St. intersects New Market. Particularly large and well-stocked. Open M-F 8:30am-9pm, Sa 8:30am-5pm.

Hospital: Kothari Medical Centre, 8/3 Alipur Rd. (tel. 479 2557). Highly recommended English-speaking doctors. Ambulance service available.

Police: Police Headquarters (tel. 255900 or 255915), Lal Bazaar .

Emergency: Police, tel. 100 or 215 5000.

Post Office: The **GPO,** BBD Bag (tel. 248 2574), has *Poste Restante.* Let the people outside in the "guide" booths help you avoid lines. Open M-Sa 7am-8:30pm. **Branch post offices:** Airport, Russell St., Park St., and Mirza Ghalib St. **New Market Post Office** is opposite Sudder St. on Free School St. **Postal Code:** 700001.

Internet: Hotel Palace, 13 Chowringhee Rd. (email palace@cal.usnl.net.in, http://www.intwebservice.cybercafe). Open daily 9am-8pm.

Telephones: Most STD/ISD booths throughout the city have fax services. Don't let them charge you more than Rs3 per min. for callbacks. **Central Telegraph Office,** 8 Red Cross Pl. Free callbacks. Open 24hr. **Telephone Code:** 033.

ACCOMMODATIONS

Prices in Calcutta tend to be on the high side. The vast majority of budget accommodations in town are concentrated around the Sudder St. area. The location is central and the prices are reasonable, but the hotels are a little shabby, and you'll sleep, eat, and shower with all the other budget travelers in the city. A few other cheap hotels are located off Chittaranjan Rd., south of the Indian Airlines office, and to the northeast of New Market. Hotels are generally open 24 hours, but they often fill up before noon. Most have a noon check-out policy.

Contact the Government of India Tourist Office for a comprehensive list of host families who are willing to take in **paying guests** (Rs200-400 a night, including breakfast). The office can also supply a list of *dharamshalas* that accept foreign visitors for free, or for a small donation.

Modern Lodge, 1 Stuart Ln. (tel. 244 4960). From the east end of Sudder St., across from Astoria Hotel and down a small street on the left, upstairs. Popular with Missionaries of Charity volunteers. The manager, Mr. Dasu, washes the entire establishment daily, ensuring that his guests enjoy the immaculate bathrooms and breezy terrace. Rooms are not large, but come with desks and tables. Lockers Rs2 per day. Check-out 10am. Singles Rs70; doubles with attached bath Rs90-270.

Hotel Maria, 5/1 Sudder St. (tel. 245 0860). Enter through the green gate. Spartan, congenial, and often very crowded. Rooms are a bit cramped and the green color-scheme is...different, but there's a great breeze floating through the place. No alcohol. 11pm curfew. STD/ISD and fax. Dorm beds Rs60; singles with bath Rs180; doubles Rs180, with bath Rs250; triples Rs350. No reservations during high season.

Gujral Guest House, Lindsay St. (tel. 244 0392 or 245 6066). Circle around the right side of Lindsay Hotel and turn left on an alley behind the hotel. Enormous, comfortable rooms await on the third floor. Potted plants, nature paintings, tables, and telephones. Common TV room, tea, and breakfast available. Singles Rs200; doubles with bath Rs450-650 (some with TV).

Salvation Army Red Shield Guest House, 2 Sudder St. (tel. 245 0599). Right in the middle of the Sudder St. scene, it's one of the most popular with the backpacker set. The large dorm rooms are a little grungy, and the bathrooms are not exactly gleaming, but the lounge is spacious and the staff friendly. Small lockers Rs2 per day; luggage storage Rs5 per article per day. Lights out at 10pm; gate closes at midnight. The bathrooms are a bit leaky. Check-out 10am. Dorm rooms Rs55. Doubles with bath Rs100-280. Reservations not accepted.

East End Hotel, Kyd St. (tel. 298921), right off Mirza Ghalib, 2 blocks off Sudder St. The rooms are large and clean, but the bathrooms are stuffy and prone to invasion by cockroach and cricket. Still, TV's, desks, and strong fans make for a good deal. Check-out 24hr. Singles Rs180-250; doubles Rs350.

Centerpoint Guest House, 20 Mirza Ghalib St. (tel. 244 3928 or 244 8184; fax 244 2876). The singles and doubles are an okay deal, but the barracks-style dormitory on the top floor is bright and convivial. Clean common showers in the open air on the terrace above. A mix of foreigners and Indian guests. TV room and free luggage storage. Dorm beds Rs65; doubles Rs200, with A/C Rs350.

Shilton Hotel, 5A Sudder St. (tel. 245 1512 or 245 1527). Set back away from the bustle. Absolutely enormous rooms, all with spotless bathrooms. Dark but friendly TV room. Singles Rs190; doubles Rs275; triples 325.

Broadway Hotel, 27A Ganesh Chandra Ave. (tel. 263930 or 263931; fax 264151; email broadway@giasc101.vsnl.net.in). One block west of Chittaranjan Ave. from the Indian Airlines office and directly across the street from the Mission Café. A little out of the way, but a pleasant location and clean, comfortable rooms. Singles Rs230, with bath Rs285; doubles with bath Rs385; triples with bath Rs475.

Deeba Guest House, 18 Mirza Ghalib St. (tel. 244 9415). Next to the Centerpoint. Rooms are a bit warm, and the bathrooms are a bit cramped, but the place is clean as a whistle. Laundry, room service, and TV room. Singles Rs130; doubles Rs200.

Hotel Palace, 13 Chowringhee Rd. (tel. 244 6214), next to Blue Sky Café on Sudder St., midway down on the south side. The tiny corridors lead to decent-sized rooms with clean, medium-sized bathrooms. All rooms with desks, TV's, and attached baths. Singles Rs150; doubles Rs250.

Times Guest House, 3 Sudder St. (tel. 245 1796). Upstairs near the Blue Sky Café. Rooms are dark and small, but well-ventilated. Singles Rs100; doubles Rs200.

Hotel Neelam, 11 Kyd St. (tel. 226 9198), across the street from East End Hotel in the architecturally aberrant orange house. Relatively spacious rooms with carpeting and clean seat toilets. ISD and fax available. Singles Rs150-175; doubles Rs275, with color TV Rs325, with A/C Rs350.

Classic Hotel, 6/1A Kyd St. (tel. 290256), just off Mirza Ghalib St., next to Mehfil restaurant. Copious marble cools you down. Generator in case of power cuts. Room service. Singles Rs150; doubles with bath Rs260, with bath and A/C Rs550.

YWCA, 1 Middleton Rd. (tel. 297033; fax 292494), right off Park St. Simple but spacious and clean rooms. Meals are included in the price, as is access to badminton and tennis tables (lawn tennis requires an extra Rs20 court fee). The staff is quite friendly and keeps the place safe and secure. Singles Rs305, with bath Rs555; doubles Rs510/760. Call at least a week in advance to reserve rooms.

YMCA, 25 Chowringhee Rd. (tel. 249 2192; fax 249 2234). From Sudder St., turn right on Chowringhee Rd.; the YMCA is immediately on the right. Despite the telegraph address (MANHOOD), it's a non-threatening place with enormous, clean rooms, all with spacious attached bathrooms. Breakfast is included in the price. Church service is held on Sunday mornings, and no drinking or gambling (including card playing) is allowed. Dorm beds Rs110, with dinner Rs220. Singles Rs325, with A/C Rs565; doubles Rs460/730. Best to call 10 days in advance.

Hotel Galaxy, 3 Stuart Ln. (tel. 246 4565). Right opposite the Modern Lodge. When Calcutta starts to get to you, come here to get away from it. The staff is very friendly, and will bend over backwards to accommodate you. Huge rooms have color TV, A/C, and wood furniture. The clean bathrooms are on the same scale. You're paying for the quality, though. Singles Rs400; doubles Rs500.

Hotel Hilson, 4 Sudder St. (tel. 249 0864). Noisy and less-than-secure, but it's as central as you can get. The large doubles are a much better value than the sweltering, Lilliputian singles. Desks, chairs, and telephones in each room. Singles Rs150; doubles Rs200, with bath Rs250-300.

FOOD

Good food is not difficult to find in Calcutta. In addition to the Chinese and standard Indian fare that most restaurants serve, **Bengali cuisine** is hot on the scene with its mix of mustard-seasoned rice and fish. For the newly arrived, the difference might be difficult to distinguish. Those whose stomachs are strong enough for street food may want to peruse the stands that dot the city, particularly on **Park St.** The highest concentration of restaurants is also here, many dating back to the jazz scene of the 1960s and '70s. Most restaurants close around 10 or 11pm, and reopen 12 hours later or even sooner if they serve breakfast. For excellent, cheap, and authentic Chinese food, jump in a cab and head to **Tangra,** about 20 minutes west of the city center. Pick any restaurant there, but watch your pockets. Bengalis adore their government, but gentle Marxism doesn't come free—watch for taxes of up to 30%.

Abdul Khalique and Sons Restaurant, 32 Marique Amir St. One block south of Sudder St. near the Jamuna Movie Theatre. You can watch your food being cooked at this popular, hectic eatery. Find a place on a bench and enjoy local flavors that are satisfying but not subtle. Beef stew Rs7, mutton *masala* Rs13, fish curry Rs8. Open daily 5am-11:30pm.

Anand Vegetarian Restaurant, 19 Chittaranjan Ave., located between the Indian Airlines office and Chowringhee Rd. Excellent South and North Indian food on two floors behind tinted glass. Popular with bourgeois Calcuttans for post-cinema jaunts. Entrees Rs15-34.

Khalsa Restaurant, Madge Ln., just north of the Salvation Army Guest House, serves the best economy meals around. Thick *dal* Rs10. Open daily 4:30am-10pm.

Mehfil Restaurant, 54 Mirza Ghalib St, 2 blocks south of Sudder St. on the right. The sunken room at the corner is a popular for Bengali food served fast. Mutton *kofta* Rs17, Lucknow chicken Rs22. Open daily 6am-11:30pm.

Indian Coffee House, 15 Bankim Chatterjee St., 1st fl., just off College St. near Calcutta University. Let the din of voices pummel you into your seat at this popular haunt for students and Calcutta's intelligentsia. A portrait of Rabindranath Tagore presides over the scene. Chicken *bakka* Rs20.

How Hua, Mirza Ghalib St. (tel. 226 7819). Across from Hotel Paramount, south of Sudder St. People from northern China lovingly prepare northern Chinese cuisine in a classy, quiet, and dark A/C dining hall. Their specialty is *chimney* soup, which can be made with chicken, crab, or bean curd. A bowl for 8 costs Rs175, a bowl for 3-4 costs Rs155. Open W-M 11am-11pm.

Bar B-Q, 43/47 Park St. (tel. 299916). An open, airy restaurant with extensive Chinese and Indian (dinner only) menus. Almost-fresh flowers almost match the red tables. Szechuan chili chicken Rs63. Lunch noon-3pm, dinner 7-10:30pm. Major credit cards accepted. Make reservations on weekends.

Flurys, 18 Park St. Large white building on the corner. A Calcutta tradition. Relaxed cafe has a large pastry and sweets shop. Ask for a pastry assortment (Rs8.50) with your tea while you decide what to take home. Open daily 6:30am-8pm.

Nizam's, 22/25 New Market (tel. 245 2663). Northeast of New Market, just southwest of the large red municipal building. Ask for directions—everyone knows where it is. The "pioneer of kabob rolls in India" sells their specialty in chicken, mutton, and beef for Rs13-15. Delivery available.

Mission Café, Ganesh Chandra Ave., across the street from the Broadway Hotel. Pizza, *kulcha channa,* chow mein, tandoori, and South Indian items, all available in fast food format: stand at counters inside or get take-out in a box. Entrees Rs11-30. Espresso Rs8. Open daily 9:30am-9:30pm.

Tulika's Ice Cream Parlor, Russell St., next to the post office across the street from the Royal Calcutta Turf Club. Possibly the best ice cream in Calcutta. Feel like a kid on 2ft. tall butterscotch and chocolate benches. Snacks, *idlis, dosas,* pizzas, Rs30-60. Popular with the office crowd for its sweet lunches. Open daily 8am-11pm.

Hare Krishna Bakery, at the corner of Russell and Middleton St., 2 blocks west of the U.S. consulate. Toned down a little bit recently, the bakery no longer features *sadhus* and shaved heads; only the background music serves as a reminder that the profits go (theoretically) to ISKCON, the International Society for Krishna Consciousness. All the food—breads, pastries, *samosas* (Rs10-15)—is *prasad* (blessed). Open daily 10:30am-8pm.

Haldiram Bhujiawala, AJC Bose Rd. at the corner of Chowringhee Rd. next to the AeroFlot office. A neon sign advertises this sweet and snack shop that's popular with the Calcutta middle class. The *kulfi* (Rs15), which comes with *faluda,* is famous. No seats, though.

Kwality, 17 Park St. (tel. 297849 or 297681), next to Park Hotel. Kwality has long been a popular spot among well-to-do Calcuttans and foreigners for its rich North Indian cuisine. It prides itself on its well-deserved reputation for attentive, courteous service. Avoid the Continental items. Entrees Rs40-75. Major credit cards accepted. Open 11am-11:30pm. Reservations recommended.

Zaranj and **Seville,** 26 Chowringhee Rd. (tel. 249 5572), right at Sudder St. Twin restaurants, one Indian, one Continental, serve up some of the best cuisine in town. Entrees (Rs150-250) might break the bank, but a taste of the fabulous *biryani* or the lamb chops might make the prospect of a night on the street a little more palatable. Open daily 10am-11pm. Major credit cards accepted.

SIGHTS

Calcutta's sights are beautiful and plentiful, but the city distinguishes itself because the monuments are not simply monuments but a fundamental part of the city. The best introduction is to take one of West Bengal Tourism's day tours (Rs75). While they rush you around the city, cramming as much as possible into ten hours, it is a good way to catch a glimpse of everything and decide what you want to return to.

The Maidan and Shahid Minar

Unquestionably the best spot for a taste of public life in Calcutta, the Maidan is a vast field cleared by Robert Clive to give his soldiers a clear shot. The old cannons that dot the ground hint at the Maidan's military past; unfortunately its *raison d'etre,* **Fort William,** is strictly closed to the public. While during the Raj period, the Maidan was the site of a posh, year-round whites-only cocktail party/cricket-pitch hybrid, these days it belongs to the masses. Aging Krishna devotees do their morning meditations, young courting couples whisper to each other, exuberant children kick soccer balls around, and hardened herdsmen parade their skinny cattle. Tram and bus lines run straight through the Maidan, while community rallies take place daily. At the northwest corner of the Maidan, near the river, lie the **Eden Gardens,** site of soccer and *kabaddi* matches; these take place in the shadow of the enormous **Ranji Stadium,** which has a capacity of over 100,000. The Maidan is often the site of local festivals and parades.

Near the Maidan's northern edge is the Shahid Minar (Martyrs' Tower), built by the British in 1817 and named **Ochterlony Monument.** Originally designed as a tribute to David Ochterlony, who led royal forces against Nepal in 1814-16, the obelisk—renamed in 1969—is now a symbol of fierce Bengali pride. To climb its 224 steps, you have to obtain a free permit from the police headquarters in Lal Bazaar (near BBD Bag). No one is allowed in after dusk.

BBD Bag Area

Most of Calcutta's historic buildings are located near its center, north of the Maidan. **BBD Bag,** the hub of this area, previously known as Dalhousie Sq., was renamed for Benoy, Badal, and Dinesh, three freedom fighters hanged by the British during protests following the 1905 partition of Bengal. The misty Lal Digha (Red Tank), a big square of water, sits in the center. Spanning the north side is the prickly red-brick caterpillar of the **Writers' Building.** No great literary figures toiled here other than the clerks of the East India Company, for whom it was built in 1780. It's now the lair of the West Bengal government, containing Kafkaesque tunnels of bureaucracy. Up Netaji Subhas Rd. to the left side of the Writers' Building is Calcutta's financial district. On **Lyons Range** *bakda-wallahs* sell stocks in the street, but only Indians can buy.

On the west side of BBD Bag is the silver-domed **GPO,** which rises over the site of the 1756 Black Hole of Calcutta, where, purportedly (it's now a matter of debate), Siraj-ud-Daula's men stuffed 146 English prisoners into a chamber with no ventilation; many had suffocated by the next morning. Down Government Place W (to the left if you're facing the GPO) is **St. John's Church,** the oldest British church in Calcutta, with its clumsy-looking spire. *(Open M-F 9am-noon and 5-6pm. Sunday services 8am. Morning prayer 9am weekdays.)* The octagonal mausoleum of Job Charnock, founder of Calcutta, is tucked away in St. John's grumpy yard. Through the trees you'll also find the British Indians' monument, which previously stood out on BBD Bag, to their martyrs in the Black Hole incident. Some personal belongings of Warren Hastings, the first governor-general of India, are kept inside the church.

Diagonally opposite St. John's is one tip of the vast grounds of **Raj Bhawan** (Government House), the West Bengal governor's residence, formerly home to British governors-general and viceroys. The furnishings inside are suitably palatial, but it's not open to the public, so enjoy the walk in the shade of the barbed wire. Nearby, on the other side of Government Place W, are the State Legislature and the cheerful tricolor Gothic **High Court.**

Victoria Memorial

Hours: *Open Tu-Su 10am-5pm Mar.-Oct.; 10am-4pm Nov.-Feb.* **Admission:** *Rs2.* **Sound and Light Show:** *Tu-Su 8:15pm. Admission Rs10.* **Cathedral:** *Open M-Sa 9am-noon and 3-6pm; services Su 7:30, 8:30, 11am, and 6pm.* **Academy of Fine Arts:** *Permanent Collection open Tu-Sa noon-6:45pm. Admission Rs2. Local Artists' Exhibition open daily 3-8pm. Free.*

The south end of the Maidan is the domain of the **Victoria Memorial,** Calcutta's greatest flower of imperialism. The British spent 15 years (1906-21) building this, a tombless Taj Mahal for their beloved queen. Four minarets surround a central dome of white marble, lugged at great expense from the same Rajasthani quarries that furnished the material for Shah Jahan's project. But unlike Agra's great white monument, the "V.M." is shaped by the angles and spheres of the Italian Renaissance, with a bronze winged statue of Victory on top of the memorial. A statue of an aging Queen Victoria waits at the entrance to the complex, greeting the crowds who come to wander through her gardens and pools. A much younger Victoria stands inside the building, which has become a museum chock full of British war memorabilia and state portraits. Several of the colonialist paintings and finery on display still evoke resentment among Bengali tourists, yet their malice doesn't extend to the ever-popular queen, whose name has remained affixed to the building despite decades of political efforts to change it. The most impressive exhibit is undoubtedly the air-conditioned **Calcutta Gallery,** a timeline chronicling the city's history and featuring examples of artwork, literature, and craftsmanship by leading Bengali figures.

At the south end of Chowringhee, on Cathedral Rd., opposite the Victoria Memorial, is **St. Paul's Cathedral,** the cavernous and friendly center of Anglican metropolitan Calcutta. The British moved their center of worship to this white Gothic building in 1847. The **Academy of Fine Arts** next door, part of Calcutta's ongoing cultural buzz, holds exhibitions of local artists' work. The permanent collection here features many works by Rabindranath Tagore and the Bengal School of painters

South Park Street Cemetery

Location: *Southeast end of Cemetary Rd., near AJC Bose Rd.* **Hours:** *Open daily 7am-4pm.* **Admission:** *Free.*

The final resting place of British colonialists since 1767, the cemetery is one of the city's most sublime spots. Pillars, vaults, and stone chambers lie overgrown with weeds, and the desolate area allows for hours of meditative solitude. The encircling walls block out most of the street noise, ensuring that you are only disturbed by the scores of crows in the trees above. If the gate is staffed, ask for the guidebook (Rs30).

Indian Museum

Location: *Corner of Sudder St. and Chowringhee Rd.* **Hours:** *Open Mar.-Nov., Tu-Sa 10am-5pm; Dec.-Feb., Tu-Sa 10am-4:30pm.* **Admission:** *Rs3.*

The nation's largest and oldest museum, this Italian-style building houses an impressive collection of sculpture from around India. Many of the greatest works of Indian art have been transported here, including several Mauryan and Shunga capitals and a large section of railing from the *stupa* at Bharhut in Madhya Pradesh. The geology, history, and archaeology sections require a bit more patience, as their displays are poorly labeled and hidden away in dusty glass cases. Don't miss out on the anthropology gallery or the creepy Egyptian mummies. The painting collection upstairs is usually closed to visitors, but persuasion and a little *baksheesh* can work wonders.

Parasnath Jain Temple

Hours: *Open daily 6am-noon and 3-7pm.* **Admission:** *Free.*

Built by a jeweller in 1867, this exquisite, shiny palace is dedicated to Sithalnath, the tenth Jain *tirthankara* (Jain spiritual leader). It's worth the cab fare to view the garden of European statues. The building itself features colored glass and mirrors everywhere, set with intricate designs that warrant close inspection. In one corner is an "ethereal lamp" that has been burning since the temple's founding. Chandeliers from the likes of Belgium and the Czech Republic adorn the ceiling.

Dakshineshwar Temple

Location: *10km from the city center.* **Bus:** *#32 from the Esplanade, Rs3.* **Hours:** *Open daily 6am-9pm.* **Admission:** *Free.* **Other:** *Non-Hindus are welcome anywhere in the complex.*

It was here that the Hindu spiritual leader Sri Ramakrishna had his vision of the unity of all religions. One day, a brash, urbane young agnostic walked into the compound and asked for proof of God. Promising revelation, Ramakrishna led him into an adjacent chamber, where the young fop was shown God—in his heart. Later, that man became known as Swami Vivekananda, and traveled around the world spreading the message of spiritual unity. The temple consists of three parts. The smallest chamber is devoted to Vishnu, and nearby is the more impressive building dedicated to Shakti, adjacent to the sacrificial platform. Directly opposite are five domes built in the traditional Bengali style, each of which houses a *shivalinga*.

Belur Math

Location: *Across the river in Howrah.* **Transportation:** *taxis Rs40 from BBD Bag.* **Hours:** *Open Apr.-Sept., Tu-Su 6:30-11:30am and 4-7pm; Oct.-Mar.: 8:30-11am and 4-6pm.* **Admission:** *Free.*

As the center of the movement founded in 1897 by Ramakrishna's disciple Vivekananda, Belur Math features several shrines devoted to Hindu saints and their wives. While the soaring temple of all religions dominates the grounds, the most eerily peaceful spot on the compound is at the end of the field, in a small cottage. This is where Vivekananda spent his dying days, and his bedroom has been preserved (thankfully without him in it). An attached museum contains some of his belongings.

Kali Temple at Kalighat

Hours: *Open daily 6am-10pm.* **Admission:** *Free.*

Probably Calcutta's most important temple, Kalighat is where the goddess Sati's little toe is said to have fallen to earth after being hacked off by Vishnu (see **Divine Dismemberment,** p. 418). Though pilgrims have streamed in and out of the structure since its construction in 1809, authorities have recently decided to close it to foreigners. Nevertheless, a bit of charisma and *baksheesh* might be enough to get you into the impressive building, built in the medieval Bengali style. Inside you can gaze into the goddess's wise and terrifying red eyes, which are reproduced on dashboards and refrigerators all over West Bengal. During Durga Puja and Kali Puja, goats are sacrificed on the compound.

Marble Palace

Location: *Muktaram Babu Dr., off Chittaranjan Ave.* **Hours:** *Open Tu-W and F-Su 10am-4pm.* **Admission:** *Free.*

Built in 1835 as a mansion for the *zamindar* Raja Rajendro Mullick Bahadur, the Marble Palace features works by Rubens and Titian, as well as many displays of pseudo-Mughal lavishness. Regrettably, poor maintenance has taken its toll on some of the exhibits. The Mullick family still lives here but they hide while you see their stuff. A pass from the West Bengal Tourist Office on BBD Bag or the Government of India Tourism Office on Shakespeare Sarani is necessary to visit the Marble Palace, but *baksheesh* works just as well, and you're as likely to feel watched by the garden statuary as by the guards.

Rabindra Bharati University

Location: *Dwarakanath Tagore Ln., near the Marble Palace.* **Hours:** *Museum open M-F 10am-5pm, Sa 10am-1:30pm.* **Admission:** *Free.*

The grounds of one of several universities founded by the most famous Tagore, this one is the site of his lifetime home. The old mansion of the prolific Tagore family has been expanded and turned into an arts college, and the house itself has been preserved as the **Rabindra Bharati Museum.** Beginning with the room where Rabindranath Tagore died, the museum traces the story of the Tagores and the Bengal Renaissance with a large collection of art and memorabilia. There is an entire section devoted to paintings by Rabindranath himself.

Netaji Bhawan

Location: *Elgin St., near Chowringhee.* **Hours:** *Open Tu-Sa noon-4pm.* **Admission:** *Rs2.*

For many, the non-violent tactics of Gandhi are seen as an anathema to real progress. Their hero is Subhas Chandra Bose, erstwhile leader of the Indian National Army, which sought to wrest control of the country from the British by force. Netaji Bhawan is the home of Bose, who led his troops against the British during the Second World War. It features a museum with Bose's belongings (including several letters) and a history of his achievements. Every January 23, his birthday is celebrated here.

Botanical Gardens

Location: *West bank of the Hooghly.* **Transportation:** *20min. by taxi from Howrah Station. Ferries from Armenian Ghat Rs3.* **Hours:** *Open dusk-dawn.* **Admission:** *Free.*

One of Calcutta's more relaxing spots—if you go during the week, you'll have few companions other than the storks, cranes, and insects that populate the Gardens' astonishing array of flora. There is a section for plants from every region of India and every continent. Don't miss out on a picnic underneath the **Great Banyan Tree,** claimed to be the largest in the world. A series of storms destroyed the trunk decades ago; however, its standing roots survive and flourish under the expansive canopy.

ENTERTAINMENT

Calcutta supports a thriving tradition of **performing arts.** Bengali music, dance, and drama are staged at several venues throughout the city. The Drama Theater at the back of the **Academy of Fine Arts** (tel. 223 4302) has shows daily at 6:30pm and Saturday at 10am and 3pm (admission Rs10-25). On the corner of Cathedral Rd. and AJC Bose Rd. sits **Rabindra Sadan,** an important concert hall dedicated to Tagore and mobbed by well-to-do Calcuttans in the evenings.

Although Calcutta is home to India's artsiest **film** industry, its cinemas, such as **Globe Theater** on the corner of Madge and Lindsay St., typically show Indian and Western bilge. The gigantic New Empire and Light House Cinema movie theaters, located side by side just west of New Market, both favor recent Western hits. For less carnal and more celestial viewing, head to the **Birla Planetarium,** a *stupa*-esque edifice next to St. Paul's Cathedral. (English shows at 6:30pm. Admission Rs10.) For popular current films, the **Nandan Theater,** just south of the Academy of Fine Arts, has both English and Bengali productions. Films are typically shown at 2, 4, and 6pm; admission is Rs5-12. Check newspapers for listings and go early for tickets. The **Calcutta Information Centre** (tel. 248 1451) is in the same complex as the Nandan and provides information on theater and film showings and other cultural events (open M-F 1-8pm).

Although Calcutta has numerous bars, most of the city's **nightlife** is not particularly welcoming to foreigners, especially women. All of the 5-star hotels feature nightclubs, but most are open only to guests. Those that are more welcoming are often ludicrously expensive. Your best bet is probably **Someplace Else,** at the Park Hotel on Park St. (Open Th-Sa 7pm-2am; Rs250 cover.)

SHOPPING

The greatest treasure at the **Treasure Island** complex north of Sudder St. is the air-conditioning (open M 1-8pm, Tu-Sa 10am-8pm). Other not-so-valuable discoveries at this mall include an overpriced food store in the basement. For real shopping, step into the enclosed, labyrinthine **New Market,** north of Lindsay St. (open dawn-dusk). There is a little of everything—Kashmiri carvings, *filmi* cassettes, food, clothes, animals—and a lot of chaos. Runners attempt to entice passersby to their shops, which are often nowhere in the vicinity. Don't bother trying to shrug off the clingy porters—they're an inevitable part of the New Market experience. Every morning (except for Sunday) from about 8 to 11am, a huge outdoor **flower market** sets up just before Howrah bridge on the left side.

VOLUNTEER OPPORTUNITIES

Even after her passing, Mother Teresa's organization continues to care for the destitute and dying. Now headed by Sister Nirmala, the **Sisters of Charity** have bases around the city. Their **Mother House** on 54AJC Bose Rd. is the place to go if you're interested in learning more about volunteering. While the Sisters always welcome those willing to help, they expect a certain degree of dedication, commitment, and fortitude. They are also notoriously difficult to get a hold of—go late in the afternoon, before 6pm, for the best chance of talking to someone in charge.

■ Near Calcutta: Santiniketan শান্তিনিকেতন

Santiniketan is a star in the troubled skies of Indian education and the living legacy of India's foremost poet and intellectual, Rabindranath Tagore. The city was originally the site of an **ashram,** founded by Tagore's father. Tagore founded the school, **Visva Bharati,** to respond to the roteness and rigidity of his own primary education with a model of creative expression and spontaneity and to promote scholarship on Indian and Eastern civilizations. At the peaceful, sprawling campus outside Bolpur, circles of saffron *kurta*'d children sit beneath trees to learn and discuss their daily lessons in their mother tongue, Bengali doctoral students on bicycles debate Indian philosophy, and musicians tune up their *sitars* and *tablas.*

The **museum** inside **Rabindranath Bhavan** (on the right side of the main Campus Rd.) is a small but terrific tribute to Tagore. With pictures and paraphernalia, the museum tells Tagore's inspiring story: his childhood, his art, his experiments in education, his engagement in politics, his work in rural development, and his vision for a prouder, freer India and a better relationship with the West. (Museum open Th-M 10:30am-1pm and 2-4:30pm, Tu 10:30am-1pm. Admission Rs3, students Rs1.) Most of the guides roaming around, including the "authorized" ones outside of Rabindra Bhavan, are a rip-off. If you would like to sit in on lectures (the university is English medium) or meet with professors, the staff in Rabindranath Bhavan can direct you to the appropriate department. The university kitchen serves basic, wash-your-*thali*-afterward meals for Rs11. Ask to reserve **accommodations** at the West Bengal Tourism Office on BBD Bag.

Visva Bharati offers a one-year **Foreigner Casual Course,** which can be taken in any subject: painting, Indian philosophy, music, and Indian languages are the most popular. Currently, fees are negligible (Rs15 per month), but they are likely to rise in the near future. Inquiries should be addressed to Pritam Ray, Advisor to Foreign Students, Visva Bharati University, Santiniketan, WB. 731235 (tel. (03463) 52751, ext. 362; fax (03463) 52672; email pritam@vbharat.ernet.in).

Santiniketan is accessible from Calcutta by **train** to Bolpur (*Rampurhat Exp.,* 6:45am; *Santiniketan Exp.,* 9:55am, 3hr., Rs63 reserved 2nd class). From Bolpur train station, it's a Rs20 cycle-rickshaw ride to Santiniketan's campus. The *Rampurhat Express* returns to Calcutta in the evening, stopping at Bolpur at 6:30pm.

Rabindranath Tagore

The Bengali poet Rabindranath Tagore (1861-1941) towers over modern Indian literature and Bengali life. The youngest son in the large family of the prominent *zamindar* and Brahmo Samaj leader Debendranath Tagore, Rabindranath dropped out of school at an early age to educate himself in English and Sanskrit. Rabindranath began writing poetry while still a boy, and before long his poems broke new ground, introducing English forms previously unknown in Bengali. He traveled around Bengal looking after his family's estates; many of his poems and stories concern the lives of villagers in Bengal, and his songs draw from the melodies of Bengali folk music.

Tagore translated many of his verses into rhythmic English prose, catching the attention of Western readers. In 1913 he received the Nobel Prize for *Gitanjali* (Song Offerings), a collection of poems expressing his wish to merge with God. Tagore was knighted by the British in 1915, but renounced his title following the 1919 Jallianwala Bagh massacre in Amritsar. In his later years Tagore experimented with novels, plays, and elaborate songs; near the end of his life he took up painting as well. Gandhi and other political leaders considered Tagore an inspiration and frequently visited him at Santiniketan, the school he founded in 1901. Verses by Tagore now constitute the national anthems of both India and Bangladesh. His plays are widely produced, and his songs, known as *Rabindrasangit,* have become a genre of their own, and the filmmaker Satyajit Ray has produced interpretations of several of Tagore's novels.

■ Siliguri শিলিগুড়ি and New Jalpaiguri

Siliguri is a brash, young town, confident in its unavoidability as a transit point to Nepal, Sikkim, and the Northeast, and as such it makes few concessions to the traveler. The city's Marxist government, though vastly improving the plight of surrounding rural communities, has been unable to keep up with Siliguri's rapid industrialization. The result is unreliable power and water supplies, and roads that can barely cope with city traffic. Travelers usually move quickly between New Jalpaiguri Railway Station and Siliguri's bus terminal; few stay long enough to see what Siliguri and NJP don't have to offer.

ORIENTATION

The bustling termini of these conjoined cities are Siliguri's **Tenzing Norgay Bus Terminus** (named for Edmund Hillary's Everest-climbing partner) and, 6km south (cyclerickshaw Rs20), the **New Jalpaiguri Railway Station.** They're connected by **Hill Cart Road,** also known as **Tenzing Norgay Road,** a wide, buzzing lifeline that runs northsouth. There are two useful landmarks: the now-defunct **Siliguri Town Station,** where trains cross Hill Cart Rd., and the **bridge** farther north. Most of the shops and bazaars are around the town station area, while budget accommodations cluster north of the bridge, near the bus terminal.

PRACTICAL INFORMATION

Airport: Bagdogra Airport, 12km west of Siliguri. Take the Hill Cart Rd. bus, which starts at NJP Station, stopping in front of Tenzing Norgay Bus Terminal before arriving in Bagdogra (Rs3); then hop on a rickshaw to the airport (Rs10). The trip takes 1hr. To: **Calcutta** (1 per day, 1hr., US$80); **Delhi** (1-2 per day, 3hr., US$185); **Guwahati** (3 per week., 45min., US$50). Check schedules and make reservations at **Indian Airlines,** 2nd fl., Mainak Hotel, Hill Cart Rd. (tel. 431495), a 5min. walk north from the bus station. Open M-F 10am-4:30pm.

Trains: All trains to this area stop at **New Jalpaiguri Station,** 7km south of the bus station on Hill Cart Rd. The **Central Rail Booking Office** (tel. 423333; reservations tel. 431493), near the police traffic booth north of Siliguri Town Station, immediately on the right. Open daily 8am-8pm. Fares are 12t/2nd class. To: **Calcutta-Sealdah** (*Darjeeling Mail* 3144, 6:45pm; *Teesta Torsha Exp.* 3142, 3:45pm; *Kanchan Jungha Exp.* 5658, 8am, Rs176/490); **Calcutta-Howrah** (*Kamrup Exp.* 5660, 4:45pm, Rs172/480); **Delhi** (*Mahananda Exp.* 4083, 12:15pm, Rs290/790; *Brahmaputra Mail* 4055, 10:50pm, Rs340/887; *Rajdhani Exp.* 2424, 3 per week, 12:40pm, Rs1225 for A/C 3-tier).

Buses: The **Tenzing Norgay Bus Terminal,** next to the dilapidated Siliguri Junction Station at the north end of Siliguri. Private buses congregate on Hill Cart Rd. next to the main bus station and are slightly more expensive, more frequent, and faster than their public counterparts. Fares listed are for private coaches and change frequently. To: **Calcutta** (3 per day, 12hr., Rs170); **Darjeeling** (every 30min., 6:30am-10:30pm, 3½hr., Rs45); **Kalimpong** (every 30min., 6:15am-4:35pm, Rs40); **Kurseong** (every hr., 7am-5pm, 1hr., Rs30); **Mirik** (every hr., 7am-4pm, 3hr., Rs45). **Sikkim Nation Transportation (SNT) Centre** is located on Hill Cart Rd. From the bus station, it's a 2min. walk south. To: **Gangtok** (every ½hr., 7am-3pm, 4hr., Rs47/Rs80 deluxe); **Mangan** (1pm, 5hr; Rs60); **Pelling** (1pm, 5hr., Rs60). Buses for **Kathmandu** leave from Kakarbhitta, Nepal. Take a city bus north along Hill Cart Rd. to the Nepali border town of Panitanki (1hr., Rs6), where cycle-rickshaws cross the border to Kakarbhitta (Rs10). **Private jeeps,** which fit 7-9 passengers and leave from Tenzing Norgay Bus Terminal, are the most expensive and fastest means of transportation. To: **Darjeeling** (every 20min., 5:40am-4pm, 3hr., Rs50) and **Kurseong** (every hr., 7am-5pm, 1hr., Rs40).

Tourist Office: West Bengal Tourism (tel. 431974), just beyond the 2nd police box at the major intersection north of Siliguri Town Station, tucked away in an alley on the right. Open M-F 10am-5pm. There's a smaller branch at the NJP Railway Station. **Sikkim Tourist Office** (tel. 432646), Sikkim Nation Transportation Center

(SNT), across from the bus station. Information and free **permits** (bring a passport-sized photo) for those seeking Sikkim. In a rush, the 24hr. permit process can be trimmed down to 1hr. Open M-Sa 10am-4pm, closed 2nd Saturday of the month.

Currency Exchange: State Bank of India, next to the West Bengal Tourism Office on Hill Cart Rd. Open M-F 10am-2pm, Sa 10am-noon. Numerous other banks and hotels along Hill Cart Rd. will gladly sate your money-changing urge.

Market: Hong Kong Market, a 5min. walk north of the West Bengal Tourism Office, is where locals gander at local produce, Indian-made goods, and the latest in Nepalese exports, including cameras, calculators, and fake name-brands.

Luggage Storage: Tenzing Norgay Bus Terminal: on the right as you enter; **NJP Station:** track 4. Both Rs3 per day.

Pharmacy: Medical booths dot the city. Ask around. Or just look around.

Emergency: Police: tel. 100.

Post Office: GPO (tel. 421 965) turn right at first police traffic booth north of Siliguri Town Station, then up Hospital Rd. on the right. *Poste Restante.* Open M-Sa 7am-7pm.

Telephones: Most STD/ISD booths close by 11pm. **Telephone Code:** 0353.

ACCOMMODATIONS AND FOOD

The 11-room **Siliguri Lodge** (tel. 533290), across the main street from the bus station and set back to the right, has a spacious garden, bright art on the walls, and a gregarious owner. (Singles Rs100; doubles Rs130; quads Rs200, with bath Rs350. Check-out noon. Reservations recommended.) Nearby, the friendly **Hotel Mount View,** Hill Cart Rd. (tel. 425919), lets large, institutional rooms, and has a good attached restaurant. (Singles Rs175-250; doubles Rs250-350. Accepts MC, V. Check-out noon. Reservations recommended.) The **Rajasthan Guest House** (tel. 525163) 50m north of Siliguri Town Station, off Hill Cart Rd. on the left., offers spacious—albeit grim—accommodation. (Singles Rs65, with bath Rs80; doubles Rs110/140; triples Rs200; quads Rs250. Check-out 24hr.)

There are **fruit markets** at each of the railway stations, but locals prefer the **Hong Kong Market,** where the fruit is cheaper and cleaner. **Ranjit Hotel** (tel. 431758), on Hill Cart Rd., a few minutes south of the West Bengal Tourist Office, is popular with locals and serves pan-Indian and quasi-Continental cuisine (entrees Rs24-120; open daily 9am-11pm). Inexpensive and authentic **Sikkimese cuisine** is cooked up at the canteen across from the Sikkim Tourist Office (entrees Rs12-25).

■ Darjeeling দার্জিলিং দারজিলিঙ

As the road from Siliguri winds up through forested hills, the temperature drops sharply, signs in Bengali begin to disappear, and the people begin to take on a distinctly Nepalese look. This is Gorkhaland, a semi-autonomous area within West Bengal, whose proud and kind inhabitants waged a long battle for independence. Their urban center throbs with an electric pulse worthy of the name Darjeeling—the place of the thunderbolt.

Though justifiably famous for its tea leaves, Darjeeling is popular with tourists from the plains and abroad for its cool climate and majestic mountain views. When the British chanced upon this wooded ridge in 1828, they were so enraptured by the location that they cornered the king of Sikkim into letting them use it as a health resort. Darjeeling's popularity with heatstruck colonials grew and grew, and by 1861 Sikkim was forced to cede this great playground of colonial India. In present times, Darjeelingites have taken advantage of the town's popularity, and Darjeeling's infrastructure strains to meet the demand for electricity, water, and transportation.

As a getaway from the plains, Darjeeling is certainly a success—narrow roads tangled around hillsides keep out motor vehicles, the air is cool and windy, and during the monsoon, the town is engulfed by clouds. The region's Gorkha inhabitants, most of whom were brought over from Nepal as laborers, never abandoned their language, dress, or blend of Hinduism and Buddhism. The Gorkha National Liberation Front's

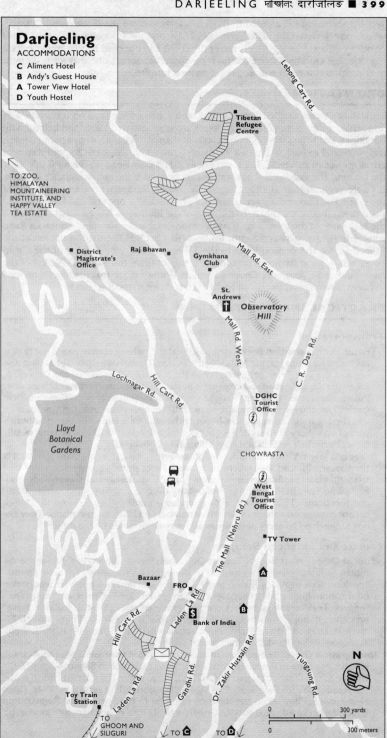

Darjeeling
ACCOMMODATIONS

C Aliment Hotel
B Andy's Guest House
A Tower View Hotel
D Youth Hostel

Lebong Cart Rd.

Tibetan Refugee Centre

TO ZOO, HIMALAYAN MOUNTAINEERING INSTITUTE, AND HAPPY VALLEY TEA ESTATE

District Magistrate's Office

Raj Bhavan

Gymkhana Club

Mall Rd. East

St. Andrews

Observatory Hill

Mall Rd. West

C. R. Das Rd.

Lochnagar Rd.

Hill Cart Rd.

DGHC Tourist Office

Lloyd Botanical Gardens

CHOWRASTA

West Bengal Tourist Office

The Mall (Nehru Rd.)

TV Tower

A

Bazaar

FRO

Laden La Rd.

B

Bank of India

Hill Cart Rd.

Dr. Zakir Hussain Rd.

Tungsung Rd.

N

Laden La Rd.

Gandhi Rd.

Toy Train Station

TO GHOOM AND SILIGURI

TO C

TO D

0   300 yards

0   300 meters

war for secession culminated in the 1958 formation of the Gorkha Hill Council, which now governs the area. Tensions persist, and the Council occasionally holds *bandhs* (strikes), during which the entire town and the road to Siliguri close for a day. Though Gorkhas have a fearful reputation, the same pride that leads them to seek political autonomy manifests itself in their hospitality.

ORIENTATION

Darjeeling's steep, tangled streets, alleys, and stairways are hard on both your legs and sense of direction. Fortunately, locals are very knowledgeable and helpful with directions. Darjeeling was built on a crescent-shaped ridge with its tips pointed north and south and its back to the east. Few streets are within range of cars, and staircases are as important as streets. The town's belly is **Hill Cart Road** on the west side, near the bottom. The **railway** and **bus stations** are here, as is the motor entrance to town. It's a steep climb from Hill Cart Rd. to **Chowrasta,** the town center near the top of the ridge. The Chowrasta intersection has a bandstand at one end and a fountain and the tourist office at the other. To the right of the fountain is **Nehru Road** (also called the **Mall**), one of the town's main avenues for shops and restaurants. **Laden La Road** runs right below, between Nehru Rd. and Hill Cart Rd. The road to the left of the fountain (past the ponies) leads to the TV tower area, where many of the cheap hotels are. A good landmark on the north side of town (on Mall Rd. W., left of the bandstand) is **St. Andrew's Church,** a yellow Gothic edifice that sits where the road to Chowrasta meets the series of roads leading down to the bus stand.

PRACTICAL INFORMATION

Transportation

Trains: The **Reservation Booth** (tel. 52555) at the **railway station** issues quota tickets for major trains leaving NJP (Siliguri) Station. Open 10am-4pm. The station also services the **Toy Train,** which traverses the route between Siliguri and Darjeeling, following the main road and crossing it nearly 100 times, at every switchback in its 90km, 9hr. route. The train's steam engines now pull only 3 cars on the 60cm tracks. The time-saving alternative to the full 9hr. circuit is to ride the Toy Train for the 1hr. leg from Darjeeling to Ghoom (although that's said to be the most boring part of an otherwise beautiful journey). Operation is sporadic—the train usually leaves Darjeeling 8:25am and leaves Siliguri at 9:30am.

Buses and Jeeps: Virtually all rides out of Darjeeling leave from the main bus stand at the Bazaar, Hill Cart Rd., where there are a lot of private companies. Jeeps cost Rs15-20. Buses to: **Siliguri** (many, 6am-5pm, 3½hr., Rs40) and **Gangtok** (8:30am and noon, 5hr., Rs75). Jeeps to: **Kalimpong** (frequent, 7am-4:30pm, 2½hr., Rs50) and **Jorethane** (1½hr., Rs40), where service is available to points north. Do not accept passage on vehicles with white numbers on black license plates. **They are not authorized to carry passengers** and may be detained by the police.

Tourist and Financial Services

Tourist Office: West Bengal Tourist Office (tel. 54050), Chowrasta. Just above the Indian Airlines office; enter around to the right, up the ramp. Friendly, English-speaking staff provides hiking maps, luggage storage, and good transportation information. Runs a bus to Bagdogra Airport (3½hr., Rs65) if there are enough passengers. **Trekkers** should check out the revamped and helpful "Himalayan Treks" brochure. Reports from trekkers written in tourist logs at the Youth Hostel, Aliment Hotel, and Tower View Lodge are also helpful. Open M-F 10am-4:30pm. Transport desk open daily during tourist season.

Immigration Office: The process of securing a **Sikkim permit** is simple, but will take hours owing to bureaucracy (it's quicker at the office in **Siliguri**—see p. 397). First go to the **District Magistrate's Office,** 7min. down Hill Cart Rd., north of the bus stands; look for the Sikkim Pass sign. Office on 1st fl. of central building. Open M-Sa 10am-4:30pm. With the stamped form, go to the **Foreigners' Registration Office,** Laden La Rd., next to ANZ Grindlays Bank, for a police signature (or stamp).

Then return to the District Magistrate's Office for the official permit. For all this effort, at least the permit is free and valid for 15 days.
Currency Exchange: ANZ Grindlays Bank, Laden La Rd. (tel. 54551), just down from the Nehru Rd. intersection. Accepts traveler's checks, cash, and Visa. Open M-F 10am-3pm, Sa 10am-12:30pm. **Bank of India,** Laden La Rd. Travelers' checks exchanged M-Sa 10am-1pm, Rs100 fee. Open M-F 10am-2pm, Sa 9am-noon.

Local Services
Bookstore: Oxford Bookshop, Chowrasta (tel. 543225), overlooking town. Excellent collection of fiction and nonfiction with an emphasis on regional topics. Open M-F 9:30am-7pm, Sa 9:30am-2:30pm, Su in season.
Cultural Center: The **Manjushree Center of Tibetan Culture,** 8 Busdwan Rd., organizes intensive language courses in 3-, 6-, and 9–month chunks. It also holds seminars, lectures, and cultural programs concerning Tibetan culture and Tibetan Buddhism. Contact Norbu Dekevas (tel. 54159; fax 53298).
Luggage Storage: Free at the tourist office, most hotels, and trekking companies.

Emergency and Communications
Pharmacy: Economic Pharmacy, Laden La Rd., across the street from the GPO, at the bend. Open daily 7:30am-8pm.
Hospital: tel. 54077. Above the main bus stand. **Emergency:** tel. 100.
Post Office: GPO, Laden La Rd., halfway down, just after sharp bend. Open M-F 9am-3pm, Sa 9am-noon. **Postal Code:** 734101.
Internet: Udayan Communication, 37 Laden La Rd. About 300m south of the GPO, upstairs in the Hotel Red Rose. Send (Rs20 per page) and receive (Rs10 per page) email. Open daily 7am-10pm.
Telephones: Most STD/ISD booths close around 11pm. **Telephone Code:** 0354.

ACCOMMODATIONS

Darjeeling's abundance of hotels ensures year-round low prices. The least expensive of these lodgings are on the stairs directly uphill from the GPO, between Gandhi and Laden La Rd. Off-season (mid-June to Aug.) discounts of up to 40% are often available; in season, you may have to hunt a bit for a room.

Aliment, 40 Dr. Zakir Hussain Rd. (tel. 55068). From Chowrasta, take the road to the left of the Indian Airlines office and bear right at the intersection; at the next intersection, by the TV tower, turn left. An unassuming, expertly run hotel with an excellent restaurant. The owner and tourist log are helpful in planning treks. Laundry service. Hot water Rs5 extra. Dorm beds Rs35; singles Rs60-70; doubles Rs100.
Tower View, Dr. Zakir Hussain Rd. (tel. 54452; fax 54330). Near the TV tower; follow the signs. The outgoing owner caters to foreigners, sharing his regional knowledge; the tourist log has good trekking tips. Great backpacking scene in the restaurant. Rooms look out over Kanchenjunga. STD phones available for guests' use. Dorm beds Rs35. Singles Rs40, with bath Rs70; doubles Rs100-120.
Guest House Andy's, 102 Dr. Zakir Hussain Rd. (tel. 53125). Close to Chowrasta, 150m past the *puri* stalls. Huge doubles with great views; those facing out back are discounted 33%. Quiet and spotlessly clean, with large seat toilets (don't fall in!). Running hot water Rs5 extra. Doubles Rs150-300.

FOOD

Restaurants abound in Darjeeling. **Aliment** is the best of the hotel restaurants. Numerous quasi-fast food joints are located on the Chowrasta and along Nehru Rd.

Greenwood, Dr. Zakir Hussain Rd. (tel. 52663), just before Aliment. Dinesh and Sarita prepare exquisite Nepalese and Tibetan cuisine. The cooking is so personalized that it must be ordered in advance. Choose between a 5-dish Nepalese meal, 2 kinds of traditional Tibetan meals, and the organic green and fruit salads. Rs60 per meal. They also offer a discounted STD/ISD rate. Open daily 7am-1pm.

EAST INDIA

Nimto Snacks, at the intersection of Nehru and Laden La Rd., across from the police booth. The snacks and sweets are clean, cheap, and yummy. No meat. Excellent Tibetan *momo* (4 pieces with hot soup Rs6).

Wali's Bakery and Confectionery, Hill Cart Rd. Rapid turnover and wide array of breads and cakes make it the ideal stock-up spot for any trek. Open daily 7am-7pm.

Dekevas, Nehru Rd., across the street from Kev's. Excellent food and classy venue. Serves traditional Tibetan dishes like *thukpa* (veg. noodle soup) and Tibetan bread, as well as Indian, Continental, Chinese food, and, of course, Darjeeling tea. Service is slow when crowded, but they keep a fire going in the winter. Entrees Rs30-50.

Stardust (tel. 54136), Chowrasta. Packed with tourists, Stardust's makes for prime people-watching. All-veg. Indian and Chinese entrees Rs15-75.

SIGHTS AND ENTERTAINMENT

Darjeeling's most popular sight is **Kanchenjunga,** the world's third-highest mountain. Located on the border between Nepal and Sikkim, some 70km from Darjeeling, its 8586m cone can be seen on a clear day. In addition to mountain views, **Observatory Hill** has a shrine to Shiva as Mahakali. Colorful Buddhist prayer flags flap around the temple complex; monkeys like to hang on the flags' strings—beware their bite.

Below the Gymkhana Club is the **Bengal Natural History Museum,** which has an extensive (if crowded) collection of stuffed creatures, particularly birds. *(Open F-W 10am-4pm. Admission Rs2.)*

Below the bus stand are the **Lloyd Botanical Gardens,** which specialize in alpine foliage. Farther north on Hill Cart Rd., past the District Magistrate's Office, a rocky road drops to the **Happy Valley Tea Estate,** the best place to see a Darjeeling tea plantation. *(Open Tu-Sa 8am-4pm, Su 8:30am-noon.)* Pickers work through the shrubs on the hills around you, and the "factory" is open to visitors. Except during off season (late June-Aug.), a worker will guide you through four days in the life of a tea leaf as it is processed by various machines (don't forget to give him a small tip).

At the north end of Darjeeling's ridge (about a 20min. walk from Chowrasta, straight along the road to the left of the bandstand) is Darjeeling's zoo, the **Padmaja Naidu Himalayan Zoological Park.** *(Open F-W 8am-4pm; admission Rs3; camera fee Rs5.)* Though small, this zoo gives its animals much leafier spaces than most Indian zoos, and it has species rarely seen elsewhere, such as Siberian tigers and red pandas. Nevertheless, animal-lovers have been upset by the conditions. A few restless snow leopards are being coaxed into breeding in a separate section on the other side of the hill, where visitors are equally welcome. Above the Siberian tigers is the cenotaph of **Tenzing Norgay,** the Darjeelingite who conquered Everest with Sir Edmund Hillary in 1953. Tenzing was the long-time director of the **Himalayan Mountaineering Institute** (HMI), which is adjacent to the zoo. HMI offers climbing courses to Indians only; its main function is to instruct Indian Army soldiers. Darjeeling has had a long connection with mountaineering; when Nepal was a closed country, the earliest Everest trips took off from Darjeeling. HMI's **Everest Museum** is full of relics. The displays in the **Mountaineering Museum** connected to it range from butterflies to icepicks to relief models of the Himalaya. *(Open daily 9am-1pm and 2-4:30pm. Everest Museum free. Mountaineering Museum Rs3.)* Around the corner a telescope is set up to catch views of Kanchenjunga; it was given to one of Nepal's Rana prime ministers by Adolf Hitler.

Clockwise around the ridge from the HMI is the starting point for the **Rangeet Valley Passenger Ropeway.** *(Open M-F 9am-noon and 12:30-4pm. 4 person min. Round-trip Rs45.)* The cablecar no longer makes the full trip to Singla Bazaar north of Darjeeling, but it does go for a scenic ½-hour dip over the tea shrubs.

The **Ghoom Monastery** in Ghoom, 8km south of Darjeeling, makes an easy excursion; the Toy Train runs here twice a day. Don't be confused by the Samten Choling Ghoom Monastery, a new and not terribly interesting Buddhist monastery below the road to Ghoom. The original (and the region's most famous) monastery, Yiga Choling Ghoom, is above the road, close to the railway station. Founded in 1850, its large shrine contains a 5m golden statue of the Maitreya Buddha (the future Buddha). The murals inside have just been refurbished and stand beautifully reborn.

Simian Sanitation

In India, despite a lack of planning and organization, things always seem somehow to work out. Such is the case on the tree-lined streets of Darjeeling, where every afternoon dozens of women sweep the roads as part of an effort to maintain the hill station's otherworldly aura. But the forested area to the sides is not cleaned, and despite prohibitory ordinances, tourists insists on tossing their drained Frooti cartons and empty biscuit wrappings into the grass. Enter the monkeys. High above the tree-cover, these Rhesus rapscallions lurk awaiting the discarding of such treats. Upon seeing a wrapper, they rush down and use hands and teeth to get at whatever crumbs or sweet droplets remain. When their snack is finished, the monkeys in turn discard *their* leftovers—back into the road, where all is swept up by the laboring street cleaners.

For Kanchenjunga views, nothing beats sunrise on **Tiger Hill,** which has become something of a pilgrimage site for Indian tourists. Jeeps leave Darjeeling for the hill (11km away) at 4am on clear days (Rs50). An observation tower on top of the 2590m rise offers views stretching from the flood plains of the Ganga delta to the snowcaps of the Himalaya, each peak lighting up in turn as the sunlight inches west. Everest and its neighbors are often visible. Beginning in June, however, such views become elusive, and you may end up taking pictures of fellow backpackers among the clouds. There's nowhere to stay on the hill unless you camp, and most sunrise spectators come right back down once it gets bright.

Below Observatory Hill on the town side, close to St. Andrew's Church, is the **Gymkhana Club,** a Raj-era relic with yawning, hauntingly empty rooms. A day-member charge allows visitors to tour the cane furniture and tiled fireplaces of the regime. *(Open 7am-8pm. Day membership Rs30. 1-week membership Rs150. Additional activities Rs10.)* The **Gorkha Hill Council** holds cultural programs almost every evening in season. They also conduct **rafting expeditions.** Contact their tourist office, a few meters from Chowrasta to the left, past the bandstand, for more information.

SHOPPING

Darjeeling's main product is its excellent **tea,** available in shops and stalls all over town. For the best stuff, head for Nehru Rd., which is lined with tea shops. **Hayden Hall,** Laden La Rd. (tel. 53228), across from the Bank of India, is a women's cooperative that sells locally made handmade blankets, rugs, bags, and sweaters. Proceeds go to needy women in Darjeeling (open M-Sa 9am-5pm). A larger collection of handmade goods is available at the **Tibetan Refugee Self-Help Centre,** located beyond and below Observatory Hill. Follow Mall Rd. to the left of the bandstand and around to the other side of the hill. The Centre is down the path and steps. Established by Tibetans who fled here in 1959, the workshop produces carpets, sweaters, woodcarvings, and other crafts (open to visitors M-Sa 9am-4pm).

■ Trekking Around Darjeeling

Trekking is the ideal way to get around the Darjeeling region and Western Sikkim from October to early December and from March to early June. Treks consists of day hikes of six or seven hours between villages, where small hotels (usually Rs35) and simple food are available. On the trail itself, water and snacks are usually unavailable and should be packed, along with a sleeping bag, warm clothes, and rain gear. If you bring your own purification system, you can drink stream water. The routes are often old jeep roads with trails bypassing large sections of the winding road. For the most recent and detailed information, consult **West Bengal Tourism** (see **Practical Information**) and the tourist logs at the Youth Hostel, Tower View, and Aliment Hotel.

Rimbik is the most common starting and finishing point for treks and has the best accommodations, food, and transportation. **Buses** run from Darjeeling to Rimbik (7am, 12:30, and 1pm; Rs42) and back (6am and noon). A popular loop is from Rimbik to Gorkhey, Phalut, Sandakphu, and back to Rimbik—each leg takes a day. The direct trail from Sandakphu to Rimbik has many bifurcations and it's easy to get lost; it's better to go from Sandakphu to Rimbik via Gurdum and Srikola, which has a nice trekkers' hut. For a longer trek, it's best to start in Manabhanjan (bus from Darjeeling, 7am, 12:30pm, and 1pm, 1½hr., Rs18) and hike north up the Singalila Ridge, pass through Sandakphu and Phalut, and end in Rimbik. North of Phalut, the ridge forms the border between Nepal and Sikkim and leads up to the peak of Kanchenjunga.

■ Kalimpong কালিম্পং কালিম্পোড়

An aura of tension and transition pervades the growing city of Kalimpong. The early-morning mist gradually dissipates to reveal signs and walls covered with slogans proclaiming the imminent triumph of the Gorkhaland National Liberation Front and the realization of a new nation. Meanwhile, the people of the town begin going about their daily business, seemingly certain that despite inspiring rhetoric, Kalimpong's future lies in its past—as a crossroads between kingdoms. With Sikkim increasingly open to tourism and rumors of new connections with the formerly impenetrable Tibet, Kalimpong no longer seems content to play second-fiddle to its much-visited-sibling Darjeeling. The close of this century just might offer travelers one last chance to savor Kalimpong's salubrious cool climate and relaxed pace before the city is reborn as a bustling metropolis.

ORIENTATION

The **bus stand** consumes most of **Central Square,** which is in the center of town. On the east of Central Square is Hotel Cosy Nook, on the west is a corrugated roofed building. **Sikkim Nation Transport (SNT)** is located just to the left of the corrugated building and the Himilashee Lodge to the right. Just south of Central Square is the old **football stadium,** also known as the **Mela Grounds. Ongen Road** crosses the square at the west end. Parallel to Ongen Rd. is **Main Road,** extending from **Gompu's Restaurant** and the central bank to the post office, telephone exchange, police station, and Foreigners Registration Office (all just beyond the south end of the football field). On either end, Main Rd. becomes **Rishi Rd.,** which to the north leads to Deki Lodge and to the south passes Hotel Silver Oaks.

PRACTICAL INFORMATION

Trains: The closest station is NJP (Siliguri), but there is a **booking office** (tel. 55643), 2nd alley on the right as you exit Central Square toward Gompu's. Quota seats are available on major trains, but reservations must be made a few days in advance. Open M-Sa 10am-1pm and 4-5pm, Su 10am-1pm.

Buses: Buses depart from Central Square, with booking offices along the perimeter, particularly by the football field. To: **Darjeeling** (noon and 12:30pm, 2hr., Rs35); **Gangtok** (7:30 and 8am, 3hr., Rs37); **Siliguri** (every hr. 7am-4:30pm, 2hr., Rs30). **Sikkim Nation Transport (SNT)** runs a crowded bus to Gangtok (8:30am, 3½hr., Rs37). Reserve 1 day in advance. Open daily 7:30am-2pm.

Tourist Information: The best information is found at the hotels. The **Deki Lodge** has maps and information about the area (see **Accommodations,** below).

Budget Travel: Mintri Transport, Main Rd. (tel. 55741 or 55697), books airline tickets and runs daily buses to Bagdogra Airport (Rs100) and NJP Station (Rs45). Open daily 8am-7:30pm. **Shangri-La Services,** Rishi Rd. (tel. 55109), is an authorized agent for Jet Airways, Blue Dart Express, and Sita World Travels. It also rents cars. Open daily 8am-5pm.

Currency Exchange: None of Kalimpong's banks change currency. **Silver Oaks Hotel,** Rishi Rd., on the left after the post office, changes currency for guests and will sometimes assist others, as will Mintri Transport. Hotel open daily 9am-9pm.

Immigration Office: Because Kalimpong is so close to the Chinese border, foreigners are required to register their arrival and departure at the **Foreigners Registration Office,** next to post office. No visa extensions given here.

Pharmacy: Shree Tibet Stores, Main Rd. (tel. 55459), across from Snow White Fashion near Gompu's Restaurant. Open M-Sa 8am-9pm, Su 9am-9pm; if it's an after-hours emergency, knock loudly on the door. Doctor available 9am-6pm.

Post Office: GPO, Main Rd., at the end of the football field. Open M-Sa 9am-5:30pm. *Poste Restante* available. **Postal Code:** 734301.

Telephones: Most STD/ISD booths are open 6am-11pm. **Telephone Code:** 03552.

ACCOMMODATIONS

Himalshree Lodge (tel. 55070), Central Square, just to the right of the corrugated building. It's worth the walk up several flights of stairs. The 5 rooms are often full, but no reservations are taken. Cozy, but the noise outside starts early. Meals available on advance order. Singles Rs60; doubles Rs120. Lock-out 9pm.

Deki Lodge, Tripai Rd. (tel. 55095). Take a right at Gompu's Restaurant and go up the hill to Rishi Rd. Branch left off Rishi Rd.; it's just up the hill on the left. Peaceful location, perpetually smiling staff, and a relaxed backpacker atmosphere set Deki apart. Sleep in the spacious rooms, enjoy hot showers, and set off armed with the owner's extensive local knowledge. Singles Rs100; doubles with bath Rs150-350.

Cosy Nook (tel. 55541), Central Square. The *betel*-chewing owner offers advice on seeing the sights. Rooms are small and basic, but all have attached bath (bucket hot water Rs4). Singles Rs150; doubles Rs250.

Bethlehem Lodge, Rishi Rd. (tel. 55185). Just beyond the movie theater on the right. Large, immaculate rooms and bathrooms. The location is peaceful, yet convenient to Central Square. Singles Rs100; doubles Rs200. Service charge 10%.

Gompu's Hotel (tel. 55818), just west of Central Square. A good location for catching morning breakfast and transport. The rooms are small for the price; the newer ones in the back have better views. All have baths. Singles Rs150; doubles Rs300.

FOOD

Kalimpong has never been known as a great culinary destination, but a collection of good Chinese eateries has popped up around the Central Square, while Main Rd. is lined with several veggie snack stalls.

Kelsang Restaurant, by the football stadium. Follow the path towards the field, then go down some steps into a kind Tibetan family's home. No menus, but cheap, non-veg. Tibetan food—all you have to do is ask. *Momos* Rs10; beef chow mein Rs22. Open daily 7am-7:30pm.

Gompu's Restaurant, Main Rd., west of Central Square. Central and bustling. Chinese entrees Rs25-40, chicken entrees Rs50-60, beer Rs50. Order ahead for particularly large and well-prepared *momos.* Dim lighting but fast service.

SIGHTS AND ENTERTAINMENT

Kalimpong offers a bountiful bouquet of orchids, amaryllises, roses, gladiolus, and dahlias, most impressive from March to June. **Ganesh Mani Pradhan Nursery,** 12th Mile Rishi Rd., past the monastery, specializes in orchids (Open daily 9am-5pm). Off D.M. Moktan Rd., which connects Tripai Rd. and Rishi Rd., is **Tharpa Choling Gompa Monastery,** a 40-minute walk uphill east of town beyond the Deki Lodge. This Gelug-pa (Yellow Hat) monastery was founded in 1892 and is now undergoing renovations. Visitors are likely to see wood-carvers and other artisans at work. Further up Deolo Hill is the complex of **Dr. Graham's Home,** built in 1900, when a Scottish minister set up a home for six orphaned students. The school eventually acquired the whole hilltop and became largely self-sufficient. It now has over 900 students and is the model for many schools for poor and handicapped children. At the bottom of the hill is the brilliant yellow **Bhutanese Monastery,** also called Thongsa Gompa, established in 1692. The **Kanchan Cinema Hall,** on Rishi Rd. between Tripai Rd. and Central Square, often shows somewhat stale Hollywood films (11am, 2pm, and 5:30pm; admission Rs4-12).

Govt. of India statement:
The external boundaries
of India are neither correct
nor authenticated.

Sikkim सिक्किम

Sikkim is a drop-dead gorgeous traveler destination, and its inhabitants know it. Nestled between Nepal, Tibet, Bhutan, and West Bengal, the proud state encompasses some of the most inspiring natural scenery in the world: a countryside full of sheep, lush hills, leaping waterfalls, thundering rivers, and placid lakes. Maintaining an un-Indian tradition of communal intermingling, the people of Sikkim remain among the most peaceful in the world (indeed, the state once appeared in the *Guinness Book of World Records* for going 10 years without a single criminal case).

The earliest known inhabitants of Sikkim were the Lepchas, who arrived in the 13th century. In the 15th and 16th centuries, following conflicts between Buddhist sects in Tibet, many Tibetans emigrated to North India. The first *chogyal* (king) of Sikkim was appointed in the 17th century. Under the British protectorate, which began in 1861, Hindu Nepalese were brought to Sikkim by the British to work on tea plantations; they soon outnumbered the Lepchas and Tibetans. When India became independent in 1947, Sikkim was made a semi-independent Indian protectorate. In 1975, 97% of the Sikkim's electorate voted to join India and became India's 22nd state. It is easy to romanticize the hard rural life of Sikkim's countryside-dwellers, but it must be remembered that each tourist rupee helps to improve their standard of living.

In Sikkim, people from the flatlands to the south are "Indian" while those who grew up in the mountains identify themselves according to their ancestry: Nepalese, Bhutanese, Tibetan, or Lepcha. The Hindu Nepalese currently represent 75% of the population, although Sikkim is historically a Buddhist kingdom, closely linked to Tibet and home to over 250 monasteries. Now Sikkim is being forced into the late 20th century and the era of TV, AIDS, rapid transit, and mass tourism, and its cities and towns have come to resemble, in many ways, the rest of urban India.

The best times to visit Sikkim are from late March to May, when the flowers are in bloom, and October to November, when clear views are guaranteed. Visitors to Sikkim must first get permits. For more information, see **Special Permits**, p. 7 and **Trekking in Western Sikkim**, p. 411

👐 HIGHLIGHTS OF SIKKIM

- **Western Sikkim's treks** (p. 411) spread out from **Geyzing and Pelling** (p. 410), wind through clouded hills, past Buddhist monasteries and pristine lakes.

■ Gangtok गांतोक

Gangtok is not a pretty town. Perennially choked with well-off Bengali tourists, the urban hillside blotch lacks reasonable prices and any soothing area of *shanti*. The mighty tourist infrastructure dominates activity—it's hard to stroll a few meters without tripping over a travel agency. Furthermore, in order to extend Sikkim permits or obtain the appropriate documentation for trekking north of Yuksam or Phodong, travelers must deal with red tape and a Delhi-esque bureaucracy

But Gangtok's people have yet to sell their souls to tourism, and several worthwhile sights remain tucked away in the surrounding hills. And as the capital of Sikkim, Gangtok is your best bet for store-bought goods and supplies, as well as practical services. The patient, laid-back traveler might well find a few pricey days in Gangtok worthwhile. But most will find it nothing more than a hub for the rest of Sikkim.

ORIENTATION

Gangtok spreads itself out along the **National Highway**, which cuts up the hill slope diagonally northeast, with roads branching off horizontally above and below. The **SNT Bus Terminal** is 100m off the highway at the northern and upper end of town. **Mahatma Gandhi (M.G.) Road** branches up off the highway 30m south of the intersection that leads to the SNT Terminal. The tourist center dominates this intersection. M.G. Rd. becomes **Naya Bazaar** farther south. Below Naya Bazaar, on the Highway, is **Lal Bazaar**, where shared jeeps and private buses await.

PRACTICAL INFORMATION

Airline Office: The nearest airport is **Bagdogra,** near Siliguri. **Josse and Josse,** M.G. Rd. (tel. 24682), next to Raj Enterprise, are authorized agents for Jet Airways, Sahara, and Skyline NEPC. Open daily 9am-7pm. The proprietor of the **Green Hotel,** M.G. Road (tel. 24049; fax 23354), just beyond the tourist center, is a sub-agent for Indian Airlines and Jet Airways.

Trains: The **railway reservations window,** at the far end of the SNT Bus Terminal, has quota tickets on major trains that leave New Jalpaiguri Station. Open daily 8am-noon and 12:30-5pm.

Buses: Sikkim Nation Transport (SNT) Bus Terminal is located down from the National Highway at the north end of town. Book tickets early at the left-most window (open daily 6:30am-3pm). The crowded, subsidized buses are the cheapest and slowest mode of transport. To: **Darjeeling** (7am, 5hr., Rs75); **Geyzing** (7am and 1pm, 5hr., Rs46); **Jorethang** (7am and 1:30pm, 2½hr., Rs38); **Kalimpong** (7am and 2pm, 3hr., Rs37); **Mangan** (8am and 4pm, 5hr., Rs44); **Namchi** (7am and 2pm, 5hr., Rs46); **Rumtek** (4pm, 1hr., Rs11); **Siliguri** (6 per day, 6am-2pm, 4hr., Rs47-80). **Private buses** gather along the National Highway, around Naya Bazaar. **Shared Jeeps,** available below Lal Bazaar, just below the National Highway, are faster and costlier than SNT buses (to Siliguri, Rs80). Make sure you are sharing a jeep and not paying for the whole thing (over Rs1000).

EAST INDIA

Tourist Office: National Tourist Centre (tel. 23425), on the corner of M.G. Rd. and the National Highway. Useful maps of Gangtok and Sikkim. Open daily 9am-7pm Mar. 15-June 15 and Sep. 15-Nov. 30; otherwise, M-Sa 10am-4pm.

Tours: Tour companies provide comprehensive trek services, including permits, guides, and equipment. Tours are expensive (upwards of US$25 per day) but, because of the permit system, necessary for any trek beyond Yuksam. **Modern Central Hotel,** Tibet Rd. (tel. 24670), is on the affordable side, as are agencies closer to the trails, like **Bumchu Tours and Travels,** Tashiding Bazaar, P.O. Sinek, West Sikkim 737111. **River rafting** in the Teesta river is increasingly popular. Tour agencies (including several along M.G. Rd.) organize trips. Overnight adventures go for about US$40 per person, less if the group is large.

Currency Exchange: State Bank of India, National Highway (tel. 23326), behind the tourist center. Located on 1st fl.; enter on the right through the side entrance. Traveler's checks accepted. Open M-F 10am-2pm, Sa 10am-noon.

Local Transportation: Taxis ply the National Highway. Prices are negotiated pre-trip. It shouldn't cost more than Rs15 for the length of the city.

Pharmacy: Many along M.G. Rd. and Naya Bazaar. Locals like **Chiranjilal Lalchand Pharmacy,** M.G. Rd., across from the Green Hotel. Open daily 8am-8pm.

Hospital: Sir Thutab Namgyal Memorial Hospital (STNM) (tel. 22059), located above the National Highway above the tourist center.

Police: tel. 22033 or 22042.

Post Office: Halfway up the street from SNT Terminal and National Highway. On the left as you descend. Open M-Sa 9-11am and 2-5pm.

Internet Access: Sikkim Tours and Tracks, Church St., down the stairs from the Highway near the Tourist Center and around the bend at the bottom. **Email** Rs30 per message. Open daily 7:30am-7pm.

Telephones: STD/ISD booths are in tourist offices along the road on which the GPO stands. Most open until 11pm. **Telephone Code:** 03592.

ACCOMMODATIONS

Many of Gangtok's hotels are sparkling new, but most are oriented toward wealthier Indian tourists. The few places that have kept their prices low are always crowded. Always ask for a discount—many managers take pity on well-behaved travelers. Consider staying near the **Rumtek Monastery** (see p. 409), 24km across the river valley.

Green Hotel, M.G. Rd. (tel. 24049; fax 23354). On the right just beyond the tourist center. The clean rooms in this popular and established hotel are usually full. Restaurant on main floor. STD and fax machine on premises; the proprietor also runs a travel agency. Singles Rs150; doubles Rs250-450. Off-season: discount up to 50%.

Modern Central Hotel, Tibet Rd. (tel. 24670), up the hill off M.G. Rd. at the tourist center, and left on Tibet Rd.; it's around the bend. TV room upstairs. Common bath has a delightfully hot shower. Dorm beds Rs40; doubles with bath Rs120-200.

Travel Lodge, Tibet Rd. (tel. 23858), a block from Modern Central, closer to M.G. Road. Worth the added expense. Huge rooms have balconies and hot showers. Star TV in deluxe rooms. Doubles Rs300-350. Off-season: discount 20%.

FOOD

Food, like everything else, is expensive in Gangtok. Bulk foods for hiking are available along Naya Bazaar, which offers the best selection in Sikkim. The restaurant in the **Green Hotel** (entrees Rs20-40) is popular with locals.

Sagar, Daigha, and **Laxmi Sweets,** M.G. Rd., across from the Green Hotel and to the south. A popular trio of side-by-side snack shops. Open daily 6:30am-8:30pm.

Hungry Jack Restaurant, National Highway, south of the lower taxi/private bus stand, just beyond the gas pumps. Clean, spacious, Westernized restaurant and bar. North Indian, Chinese, and sandwiches, Rs35-65 plus 10% service charge. Sikkim-brewed Dansberg beer Rs33. Open daily 7am-9pm.

Tripti's Bakery Confectionery, National Highway, below Hungry Jack; enter from highway side. Mouth-watering assortment of desserts, breads, and ice cream. The aroma alone should last you at least half a trek. Open daily 6:30am-7pm.

SIGHTS AND SHOPPING

Though not much of a destination *qua* destination, Gangtok is surrounded by an assortment of lakes, parks and gardens that make for worthwhile daytrips. Sikkim Tourism's sight-seeing trips (Rs250-500) are the easiest way to take in everything. Contact the Tourist Department for more information. A 40-minute hike from Gangtok, the **Enchey Monastery** is perched on the landing spot of Lama Druptob Karpo, who is said to have flown over from Maenam Hill over 200 years ago. The building itself dates from 1909 and has beautiful views of Kanchenjunga. Farther south and closer to town is the **Tsuglakhang,** or Royal Chapel. Its inside walls are covered with murals, and the chapel holds huge collections of scriptures. In theory, both are closed to tourists, but you may be able to charm your way in as long as you're not toting a camera or an especially large gun.

The **Research Institute of Tibetology** (tel. 22525, 24822), 1km south and downhill from Naya Bazaar along a large road, was founded by the Dalai Lama in 1957 and now holds approximately 30,000 volumes of old Tibetan documents (mostly wooden boards called xylographs). *(Open M-Sa 10am-4pm. Admission Rs2.)* The collection of ornate *thankas* is impressive. Though it is billed as the world's foremost center for Tibetology, there are now only a small number of researchers here.

The **Government Institute of Cottage Industries** is 20 minutes north of the tourist center on the National Highway, on the left. It serves as a "factory" for handicrafts and furniture, and a display center where colorful crafts are sold. *(Open M-F 9:30am-4pm, Sa 10am-2pm, Su 9:30am-2pm.)* For additional shopping, the **Kunphenling Tibetan Cooperative Society Handicraft Emporium** is located just below the National Highway on the way to the SNT Terminal. *(Open M-Sa 9am-6pm.)*

■ Near Gangtok: Rumtek रुम्तेक

Only 24km from Gangtok (Rs30 in a shared jeep, 40min.), Rumtek is the head of the Karma-pa (Black Hat) sect of the Kargyu-pa order of Tibetan Buddhism. The **Rumtek Monastery,** built in the 1960s, is modeled on the main Kargyu-pa monastery in Chhofuk, Tibet. Located in a back room is an impressive collection of golden statues of the 16th Gwalpa who fled Tibet when China invaded. Turn on the charm, and a monk might let you have a peek. A 45-minute walk downhill is the impressive **Old Monastery,** which is visible from behind the Kunga Delek; ask a young monk to show you the path. The not-to-miss sight here is the collection of sometimes-uplifting, sometimes-horrifying (think disembowelment) wall paintings. Two days before Losar, the Tibetan New Year (February), and on the 10th day of the 5th month of the Tibetan calendar (in July), Rumtek is the site of celebratory dances called *chaams.*

Accommodations in Rumtek are a high-season alternative to the crowds and high prices of Gangtok. The **Sangay Hotel** is located just up the hill beyond the checkpoint for the monastery. A friendly family runs the hotel and serves good, cheap food. (Singles Rs50; doubles Rs75-100.) **Kunga Delek** is farther up the hill, close to the monastery. All rooms have great views and attached baths with hot-water showers. If your wallet can take it, head for the **Sun-gay Guest House,** near the checkpoint. Beautiful, spacious rooms (with attached bath) are a great value. (Singles Rs100; doubles Rs120.) If you plan to return to Gangtok in the evening, consider hiring a taxi from the city (Rs250 round-trip), as jeeps leave Rumtek only in the morning.

WESTERN SIKKIM

Everything seems bigger in Western Sikkim—except the prices and crowds. The hills are more rugged, the lakes more expansive, and the monasteries truly exhilarating. The ancient soul of Sikkim remains in the West—the first Sikkimese capital was at Yuksam, in the north of Western Sikkim, and the ruins of the second palace of Sikkim's *chogyals* (kings) lies near Pemayangtse Monastery. To this day, the people exhibit a pride in their land and culture that they are eager to share with visitors.

The ideal way to enter Western Sikkim is by making the one- or two-day journey by foot from Gorkhey to Dentam, where there is an Alpine Hut. Ask in Dentam or Gorkhey for explicit directions; you'll need a passport and a permit. Once in Western Sikkim, most towns are a five- to six-hour hike from one another. Always schedule a few extra days in case of cloudy weather—the views are too spectacular to miss. Western Sikkim is also accessible from Gangtok and from the south through Jorethang, Sikkim's second-largest town. Although there's little to attract tourists to this unpretentious place, those who do end up spending the night meet with good food and friendly people. From Jorethang there are jeeps to Darjeeling on a regular basis (starting at 7am, Rs55) and buses and jeeps to Siliguri (Rs60). From Jorethang, buses to Pelling and Geyzing cost Rs25 or less; the trip takes under 2½ hours.

■ Geyzing गेज़िना and Pelling पेल्लिना

Sitting up in the clouds, Geyzing should be peaceful and relaxing. Yet as a bustling marketplace and transportation hub, it proves less than ideal for those wishing to get away from it all. Pelling, a hamlet above Geyzing (30min. by jeep), is a good stopover on the way to peace and relaxation. Geared towards foreign trekkers, its accommodations are excellent sources for hiking information, and its location is convenient to the shortcut paths to Yuksam, Tashiding, and Khechopalri Lake. It is also within easy walking distance of **Pemayangtse Monastery** (25min.) and numerous other sacred spots (inquire at any of the hotels).

Geyzing's **SNT Bus Terminal** is down the main road from the central square at the bend in the road. Buses ply to **Gangtok** (9am and 1pm, 5hr., Rs50), **Jorethang** (8, 10, 11am, and 4pm, Rs20), **Pelling** (M-Sa 2:30 and 3:30pm, Su 2:30pm, Rs5; the 2:30pm bus continues on to Khechopalri Lake), **Siliguri** (7am, 5hr., Rs50), **Tashiding** (2pm, Rs15), and **Yuksam** (Rs25). Jeeps run frequently to **Pelling** (Rs15; 30min.) from the small gazebo next to the field near the bus station. Jeeps are available in season, but more difficult to find off season. Given the irregularities in the transportation schedule, walking from town to town is often more convenient than taking buses or jeeps. **Currency exchange** is not available. The **post office** is located on the side of the **Sikkim Tourist Centre** building in Pelling (open M-F 9am-5pm, Sa 9am-2pm). The service window and sign are all that are visible. **STD/ISD** services are available in the booth next to the No Name Hotel in the Geyzing central square (open 6am-9pm) and at **Hotel Window Park**, next to Hotel Garuda in Pelling (**telephone code:** 03595).

The **accommodations** scene in Geyzing is limited, and Pelling, the small village 9km (take a jeep) from Geyzing, is much more accommodating. Most hotels are in the central square and actually have higher off-season (May-Sept.) rates. You'll get a nice bed and clean bathrooms, but don't expect any favors from the hassled staff. The **No Name Hotel and Restaurant** (tel. 50722 or 50768) also has beds. (In-season: dorm bed Rs30; triple Rs100. Off-season: Rs40/120.)

Pelling, on the other hand, is budding with new accommodations, but the majority are expensive. A few places maintain low prices, but don't expect the cleanest or most bug-free rooms. The family at **Hotel Garuda** (tel. 50614), right in front of the jeep stand (look for the sign), gives out a helpful map of Pelling and surrounding areas and keeps a tourist log with extensive firsthand information on trekking. They allow luggage storage and will even make you a bag lunch. (Off-season: dorm beds Rs30; singles Rs60. In-season: dorm beds Rs60; singles Rs100.) If they're full, the owner will direct you to the nearby and nearly identical **Sister Guest House**. **Hotel Kabur** (tel. 50685), just uphill from the Sikkim Tourist Centre, has similar offerings. One of the children there might join you for a walk to Pemayangtse. (Dorm beds Rs50; singles Rs200; doubles Rs350. Discount 40% during Jan.-Feb. and June-Sept.) Both Kabur and Garuda serve meals.

■ Near Geyzing: Pemayangtse पमयानाट्से

Founded in 1705 during the reign of Chadov Namgyal, the third king of Sikkim, the *gompa* of **Pemayangtse** (The Sublime Perfect Lotus) is currently the principal Nyingma-pa (Red Hat) monastery, with over 100 monks. In the top room at the monastery is the **Sang Thog Palri**, a massive wooden representation of Maha Guru's Paradise. Despite the Crayola/Legoland feel of the brightly-colored, intricate figures, the explicit sex scenes and gruesome depictions of Hell banish any childlike thoughts. You may have to wait for a young monk to retrieve a key before showing you the way. Behind the white Buddhist *stupa* at the first bend in the road up to the monastery is the **Cheshay Gang**—an old seat for the three-trunked tree. (Monastery open M-Sa 7-10am and 2-4pm, Su 2-4pm. Admission Rs10.)

The **Rangdentse Palace ruins** are located past the entrance to Pemayangtse towards Geyzing. From the main road, take a left onto a small path just before the 3km marker. The path crosses a small meadow before it climbs to the main ruins. Sikkim's second king, Tensung Namgyal, built the palace in 1670, shifting the capital from Yuksam. On the right as you climb through the ruins are the remnants of the stable and military headquarters; on the left is the site of the main throne. The view from here captures the holiest areas of Western Sikkim, including Yuksam and Tashiding.

The Monastery also runs the **Denjong Padma Choeling Academy,** a 30-minute walk from Pelling toward Pemayangtse and Geyzing—take the stairs on the right. A school for destitute Sikkimese children, the Academy lets foreign tourists stay for a small fee (Rs20-40 per person). Visitors here find few comforts, but get a chance to bond with the schoolchildren, who are eager to practice their English. The children are all from Sikkimese families, and some are orphans. Donations and volunteer services are welcome.

■ Trekking in Western Sikkim

The best way to take in the culture and natural beauty of Western Sikkim is on foot. Though the most popular sites, such as **Khechopalri Lake, Yuksam,** and **Tashiding,** are connected by road, the more enjoyable and challenging routes are the trails called "short-cuts," which locals nimbly ascend and descend in slippers while travelers struggle in hiking boots. The trails are unmarked and have many branches, but there are plenty of farmers around who will help you find your way. *"Namaste"* is a polite greeting, after which you can ask for the "short-cut *rasta*" to your destination.

One popular loop starts in **Gorkhey** and goes to **Dentam,** Pelling, Khechopalri Lake, Yuksam, Tashiding, and then back to Pelling, Dentam, and Gorkhey. Each leg of the loop takes a day. A shorter version is Pelling-Khechopalri-Yuksam-Tashiding-Pelling. Serious trekkers may want to head for **Dzongri** (4550m altitude) from Yuksam; the trek takes 6-9 days to get there and back. Trekking per-day rates range from US$15 (really roughing it) to US$80 (bring your hair-dryer). Planning with a tour agency in Gangtok is necessary: parties must have at least four people and a permit. Tour agencies are plentiful in Gangtok. Gangtok and Darjeeling are the last stops with substantial shopping services before Western Sikkim. Though trekkers can always find a place to eat dinner and a place to sleep, lunch is rarely available on the trails.

KHECHOPALRI LAKE

Located 30km from Pelling, Khechopalri is the holiest lake in Sikkim (make your wish wisely), and legend has it that a sacred bird removes the leaves from its surface as soon as they land in the water. No swimming is allowed. There is a festival here on

> ### The Search for the Extreme ... Rhododendron?
>
> Recently, adventure tourism has come to Sikkim, luring thrill-seekers with prom-
> ises of exciting whitewater rafting and rock-climbing opportunities. But inquire a
> little further, and guides will tell you in proud, hushed tones of the true wealth of
> Sikkim. Steep drops and terrifying chasms are all well and good, but the Sikkimese
> are most proud of the region's wildlife. Agents are surprised and thrilled when
> asked about Sikkimese flora and fauna, and many will offer to take travelers on (far
> less-expensive) tours that emphasize nature-watching. The people of Gangtok are
> most fired-up about the dazzling variety of orchids and rhododendrons that flower
> around town. In addition, the region boasts several indigenous species that are
> sure to awe even the most experienced feather-gazer.

the 15th and 16th of the first month of the lunar calendar (Dec./Jan.). Just before the
monastery, on the left side, there is a privatized trekkers' hut with beds for Rs50.
Home-cooked meals and biscuits for the next day's lunch are available. There is also a
pilgrims' hut at the monastery (Rs40; the only toilet is the public one outside). Basic
food is available at nearby stalls.

YUKSAM

The historic town of Yuksam is a three-hour bus ride or six-hour walk (via shortcut)
from Pelling, and slightly shorter from Khechopalri Lake. According to some
accounts, Yuksam became the first capital of Sikkim when, in 1641, its king was consecrated by three Tibetan Lamas—hence the name Yuksam, "three Lamas" in the Lepcha language. The white stone throne in front of the monastery is called Norbugang
Chorten. The **Dubdi Monastery,** the oldest in Sikkim, is a one-hour walk up the hill.
Founded by Gyalwa Lhabchen Chenpo in 1701, it currently houses about 60 monks.

   Permits for the **forest lodge** (above the road on the left side; follow the sign) must
be obtained from the Forestry Department in Gangtok (Rs60 per person). The **Wild
Orchid,** on the right side of the road just before the town's bazaar, has information on
the area and home-cooked meals for Rs20. (In-season: singles Rs75; doubles Rs100.
Off-season: Rs40/80. Hot water by the bucket, Rs5.) There are also accommodations
in the village, which is composed mostly of Bhutanese farmers. Treks to Dzongri
leave from here, but the tour companies in town are of little use to foreigners, who
must process their paperwork in Gangtok.

TASHIDING MONASTERY

An unreliable two-hour bus ride or a three-hour walk (via shortcut) from Yuksam, the
Tashiding Monastery is located on a *stupa*-dotted hill between the Rangeet and Ral-
hong Rivers, up from the main town. The monastery dates from 1716 and now
houses about 50 monks and the **Bhumchu,** a sacred water vase, and the center of a
local festival (March). Climbing up the hill, the path to the cave is on the left just
before the first major *stupa*. The **Hotel Blue Bird,** on the right side of the road as you
walk into Tashiding Bazaar, is simple but familial (Rs25 per person).

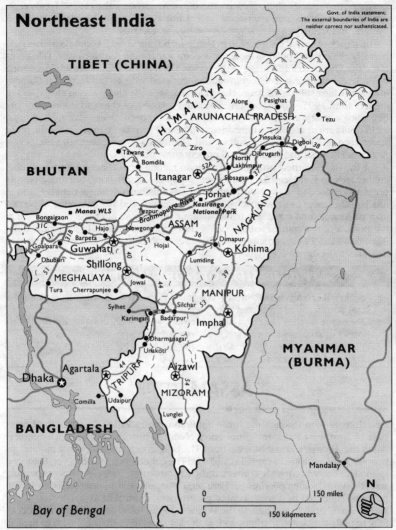

Northeast India

TIBET (CHINA)

HIMALAYA

ARUNACHAL PRADESH

Along · Pasighat

Tezu

Tinsukia

BHUTAN

Tawang · Ziro · Digboi 38

Bomdila · North Dibrugarh

Itanagar · 52A · Lakhimpur · 37

Sibsagar

Manas WLS · Tezpur · Brahmaputra River · Jorhat

Bongaigaon · Kaziranga National Park · NAGALAND

31C · Hajo · Nowgong · ASSAM

Goalpara · 31B · Barpeta · 37 · 36 · Dimapur

Dhuburi · Guwahati · Hojai · Kohima

51 · Shillong · 40 · Lumding

MEGHALAYA · Jowai · 39

Tura · Cherrapunjee · 44 · MANIPUR

Sylhet · Silchar · 53

Karimganj · Badarpur · Imphal

Dharmanagar

Dhaka · Unakoti · MYANMAR (BURMA)

Agartala · Aizawl

TRIPURA · 54

Comilla · Udaipur · MIZORAM

Lunglei

BANGLADESH

Mandalay

N

Bay of Bengal

0 _____ 150 miles
0 _____ 150 kilometers

Northeast India

Northeast India consists of seven states connected to the rest of the country by a narrow isthmus of land and an even narrower thread of cultural similarity. Forming the heart of the region is the Brahmaputra valley state of Assam, which until recently encompassed the entire region. Surrounding Assam are Arunachal Pradesh, Nagaland, Manipur, Mizoram, Tripura, and Meghalaya, all of which comprise the hilly regions bordering China, Burma, and Bangladesh. The Northeast is largely inhabited by *adivasis* (tribal peoples) whose culture has had little or no exposure to modernization. In 1963, these diverse tribes' struggles for autonomy led to the splintering of Assam and the creation of six new states. Turmoil and bureaucratic difficulties accompanied the changes, and to this day instability threatens many areas. The capital of Assam (formerly Shillong) was officially moved to Guwahati in 1974, two years *after* Meghalaya became a separate state. Until 1981, Assam, Nagaland, Manipur, Tripura, and Meghalaya were administered by one governor.

The legacy of armed insurrection in Mizoram, Nagaland, and Assam continues only partially abated, and political violence is common around the Northeast. Dissidents claim that India takes advantage of the region's rich natural resources while ignoring its underdevelopment. Political instability, coupled with Indian fears of a Chinese invasion (China still claims Arunachal Pradesh), kept the entire region closed to foreigners until 1995. However, long-promised relaxing of the restrictions is finally becoming a reality, and travel in the region has never been easier. Assam, Meghalaya, and Tripura are now open to unrestricted tourism. **Permits** are required for the other states (see p. 7). Of these, Manipur and Mizoram are the easiest to visit, while Arunachal Pradesh and Nagaland still present some obstacles.

For the traveler, the Northeast offers virgin natural beauty and a glimpse of tribal culture. Assam and Meghalaya are the most popular destinations, offering a cosmopolitan introduction to the Northeast, as well as a mellower climate than is found in much of the rest of India. Arunachal Pradesh, Nagaland, and Mizoram remain spectacular, pristine natural paradises, while Manipur and Tripura offer less exotic scenery but boast a proud cultural legacy. Finally, not entirely unrelated to its appeal is the Northeast's lack of infrastructure, which makes exploration that much more exciting and, alas, more expensive.

HIGHLIGHTS OF NORTHEAST INDIA

- Assam's **Kaziranga National Park** (p. 419) teems with wildlife, including a large population of protected rhinos.
- One of the wettest places on earth, **Meghalaya** (p. 420) showers visitors with hospitality, sublime scenery, and well-watered greenery.
- Less-traveled states like **Manipur** (p. 425) and **Mizoram** (p. 425) are renowned for their natural beauty and cultural singularity.

ASSAM অসম

Stretching 800km through the low-lying Brahmaputra Valley, Assam is the largest state in Northeast India. It did not enter recorded history until the 13th century, when the Ahoms, a Buddhist tribe from Thailand, conquered the area's indigenous peoples and established a capital at Sibsagar. The cultural victory, however, belonged to the Hindus, who quickly converted their conquerors. Today, Assamese-speaking and East-Asian-looking pilgrims perform *puja* alongside Hindi-speaking Aryan Indian pilgrims. Hindered by a weak central government, control of Assam shifted in the 19th century from the Ahoms to the Burmese to the British, each trying unsuccessfully to unite the dissolute tribes, and, in the last case, to assimilate Assam to Bengal. The British built huge tea plantations (Assam now grows over half of India's tea) and Asia's first oil refinery at Digboi. But Assam's resources and economy have languished since the British left.

Until recently, the Brahmaputra Valley was one of the few places in South Asia with a surplus of agricultural land. An influx of migrants from West Bengal and illegal immigrants from Bangladesh has added a substantial Muslim, Bengali-speaking population to Assam and led to tension between the new arrivals and the indigenous tribes. Anti-Bengali sentiment brought the now-entrenched Ahom Gana Parishad (AGP) party to power in the early 1980s. Bengali-Assamese tensions, which have never taken on the dimensions of a religious war, have supposedly improved in recent years. Yet frustration over the poor economy, the increasing illegal immigration of Bangladeshis, and the central government's neglect have led to the formation of Assamese separatist organizations such as the United Liberation Front of Assam (ULFA), whose tactics include train bombings and kidnappings.

Fed by rains from the Bay of Bengal, Assam is heavily forested and boasts two major wildlife preserves, one of which is closed indefinitely due to political violence. Assam's capital, Guwahati, is an inescapable gateway to the other northeastern states because of its air and rail connections. Bumpy rides on rickety buses lead from Guwahati to outlying towns rich in tribal culture. At Majuli, the largest river island in the world, tourists can visit *satras* (monasteries) to see traditional Assamese drama, art, music, and dance. Majuli is accessible by ferry from Jorhat, 314km from Guwahati.

Warning: For the past couple of years, there have been occasional terrorist attacks on trains and buses in Assam. In June 1998, explosions temporarily severed all road and rail links between the Northeast and West Bengal. Travelers are advised to keep abreast of the news and to avoid traveling at night.

■ Guwahati ওয়াহাটি

Although initially appearing sporadically in ancient Indian texts as Pragjyotishpur—City of Astrology—Guwahati (pop. 632,000) today represents a much more earthy existence. Its major market area, Paltan Bazaar, is a sweltering mess of mud, dung, and aggressive merchants. Even nearby Fancy Bazaar, with its posh hotels and A/C showrooms, cannot escape the grimness, as poverty-stricken families refuse to abandon their sidewalk homes. For a smallish (by Indian standards) town, Guwahati is remarkably unfriendly—visitors are often treated to scornful glares from the well-dressed middle-class and suspicious stares from the ubiquitous rifle-toting soldiers.

EAST INDIA

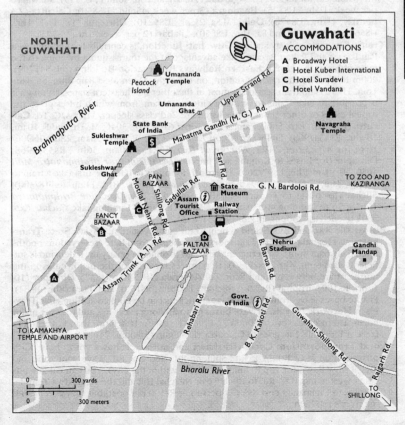

A few interesting sights, including the Kamakhya Temple, line the edges of the modern city. In the west, Nilachal Hill foreshadows the mountainous regions to the north and south of Assam and casts its shadow over the Brahmaputra River. Still, there's nothing to hold one's interest for long, and most find Guwahati nothing more than a stopover en route to more felicitous climes.

ORIENTATION

The center of the city is small. The bazaars, bus and railway stations, and important public offices are within walking distance of one another. The **Guwahati Junction railway station** and the **Kacheri Bus Stand** are adjacent; **Paltan Bazaar** is just behind these, to the south. **Pan Bazaar** (with more expensive lodgings) and **Fancy Bazaar** are a 15-minute walk to the northwest. **Mahatma Gandhi (M.G.) Road** runs behind Pan Bazaar along the river's edge; government buses ply this route to the Kamakhya Temple, 8km to the west, and the Navagraha Temple, 1km to the east.

PRACTICAL INFORMATION

Transportation

Airport: Judge Field (tel. 84223), 24km from town. **Buses** (every 2hr.) go from Judge Field, adjacent to Nehru Park, to VIP Point, 2km from the airport, where you can snap up an auto-rickshaw (Rs10-20). To get to Judge Field from the front of the railway station, take a rickshaw (Rs5), city bus, or walk straight through 2 major traffic circles. You can share a cab directly to the airport (Rs60 per person) or hire the whole car for Rs300. To: **Agartala** (Tu, Th, and Su, 40min., US$45); **Aizwal** (6 per week, 1½hr., US$75); **Bagdogra** (3 per week, 45min., US$50); **Calcutta** (2-3 per day, 1¼hr., US$70); **Delhi** (M-Sa, 2½hr., US$210); **Dimapur** (Tu, Th-F, 1hr., US$60); **Imphal** (Tu and Sa, 1hr., US$50); **Lilabari** (2 per week, 1hr., US$75).

Trains: The main railway station, **Guwahati Junction,** is centrally located between Pan Bazaar and Paltan Bazaar. Take advantage of the tourist quota by going to the main office at the **North Eastern Railways Reservation Building** (tel. 541799), 200m in front of the railway station, on the right. Open M-Sa 8am-8pm, Su 8am-1pm. There is no train service to most of the other northeastern states, although it is possible to take trains to outlying cities in Assam, from which buses go to the capital cities of other states. Fares listed are 2nd class sleeper/3-tier A/C. To: **Calcutta** (*Kamrup Exp.* 5660, 7am, 24hr.; *Sarai Ghat Exp.* 3046, M, Th, and F, 10am, 18½hr., Rs334/968); **Delhi** (*Rajdhani Exp.* 2423, M, W, and F, 6am, 28hr., Rs906/1644 for A/C 3-tier/2-tier; *Northeast Exp.* 5621, 4:30am, 36hr., Rs334/968; **Dimapur** (for buses to Kohima and Imphal, *Delhi-Dimapur Brahmaputra Mail* 4050, 10:30am, 7hr., Rs97/260); **Harmoti** (for buses to Itanagar, first take a train to Rangia, 7am, 3hr., Rs21/109, then take *Arunachal Exp.* 5813, 11am, Rs118/300); **Silchar** (for buses to Tripura and Mizoram; take *Delhi-Dimapur Brahmaputra Mail* 4056 to Lamding, 10:30am, 4hr., Rs47/185; from Lamding take *Cachar Exp.* 5801 to Silchar, 7:30pm, 11½hr., Rs134/613).

Buses: The **Kacheri Bus Stand** is behind the railway station; **Assam State Transport** and **Meghalaya State Transport** buses depart from here (reservations booths open daily 6am-4pm). Government buses go to Shillong (every hr. if demand is sufficient, 4am-6pm, 4hr., Rs29/39). Departures for each of the major cities in the northeast are between 6 and 8am. To: **Agartala** (18-20hr., Rs237); **Dimapur** (10-12hr., Rs100); **Imphal** (Rs220); **Silchar** (14-15hr., Rs150); and **Tura** (8hr., Rs84). Private buses leave from **Paltan Bazaar;** tickets can be booked at **Blue Hills Travels** or **Network Travels. Private buses** go to **Shillong** every hr., and to other major northeastern cities (every 30min., 6-8pm). Fares are 10% more than government fares. A Blue Hills bus goes to **Calcutta** via Siliguri (5:30pm, 24hr., Rs250).

Local Transportation: Cycle-rickshaws and **auto-rickshaws** whiz about. **City buses** run on M.G. Rd., A.T. Rd., Shillong Rd., and G.S. Rd. Wave your hand and they'll slow down for you to jump on (Rs1-3 within the city). You can catch a bus going west along M.G. Rd. to the base of Nilachal Hill and the Kamakhya Temple. **Ferries** to Umananda cost Rs5 per person or Rs100 per boat, but they don't run if the river's too high.

Tourist and Financial Services

Tourist Office: Government of India Tourist Office, Dr. B.K. Kakoti Rd., Ulubari (tel. 547407). Turn right at a police point onto B.K. Kakoti Rd. The office is a little ways in on the right, through a little gate. Open M-F 9:30am-5pm, Sa 10am-1:30pm. **Assam State Tourist Office,** inside the tourist lodge on the left side of the road leading to the front of the railway station. Open daily 10am-5pm, closed 2nd and 4th Sa of each month.

Immigration Office: Superintendent of Police (tel. 544475), near District Court. This is where to apply for visa extensions. Open M-Sa 10am-4:30pm.

Currency Exchange: State Bank of India, M.G. Rd. (tel. 544264), near District Court. Open M-F 10am-2pm, Sa 10am-noon.

Emergency and Communications

Police: Stations in Pan Bazaar (tel. 543104) and Paltan Bazaar (tel. 540126).

Hospital: Guwahati Medical College (GMC), G.S. Rd., Bhangagarh (tel. 569161 or 562521), specializes in trauma and common gastro-intestinal complaints. **Downtown Hospital,** Dispur (tel. 560824, 562741), near Capitol Complex, with fluent English speakers on staff, is ideal for extended stays, if that's your thing.

Post Office: GPO, Meghdoot Bhawan (tel. 541294), near Pan Bazaar. Open M-Sa 10am-6pm. **Postal code:** 781001.

Telephones: Central Telegraph Office (CTO), Pan Bazaar (tel. 540209), allows free call-backs. Open 24hr. **Telephone Code:** 0361.

ACCOMMODATIONS

In general, Guwahati's accommodations are either cheap and extremely unsanitary or expensive and luxurious. Either way, most are overpriced. The proximity of Paltan Bazaar to the railway and bus stations may not make up for its nastiness. There are good options in Pan Bazaar, Fancy Bazaar, and near the riverside. Guwahati's hotels fill up quickly, so book in advance; if you arrive late, you may have to spend a night in one of the more expensive hotels in Pan Bazaar or Paltan Bazaar.

Hotel Suradevi, Motilal Nehru Rd., Pan Bazaar (tel. 545050). A Rs10 rickshaw ride from the station. Large rooms with desks. Lots of young Indian couples stay here, chillin' on the breezy balconies. The beds are soft and the attached bathrooms clean. Good neighborhood restaurant on the ground floor. Dorm beds Rs60; singles Rs85; doubles Rs150. Often full, but no reservations are accepted.

Broadway, M.G. Rd., Machkhowa, Riverside (tel. 548604). From the railway station, a Rs15 rickshaw ride to the river. Combines the lowest prices in Guwahati with a serene riverside location. Airy rooms with attached baths with shower and mosquito nets. Restaurant inside. Call in advance, but be patient—management speaks little English. Curfew 10pm; check-out noon. Singles Rs70; doubles Rs100-120.

Hotel Kuber International, Ham Baruah Rd., Fancy Bazaar (tel. 520807). A 3-star hotel with some rooms that are a great value. Walk through the garlanded entrance, ride the modern elevator, and glimpse the Indian bourgeoisie. TVs, desks, and a few bugs. A little run-down, but still relatively luxurious considering the competition. Astrologer on premises. Singles with bath Rs200; doubles Rs300. 10% service charge. Major credit cards accepted.

Hotel Vandana, G.S. Rd., Paltan Bazaar (tel. 543475). From the back of the railway station, turn right onto G.S. Rd. The hotel is set back on the left, before the Mayur Hotel. The rarely-full Vandana has a large lobby-lounge area and an STD/ISD booth operating until midnight. The rooms are large, and the foam rubber mattresses are surprisingly pliant. Singles Rs60, with bath Rs80; doubles Rs80/110.

FOOD

Only one restaurant in all of Guwahati serves genuine Assamese cuisine, which consists of fish, rice, and heavy mustard seasoning. Chinese food is plentiful and good— some of the restaurants along Rajgarh Rd., far to the east near the Gandhi Memorial, are run by Chinese immigrants who dish up correspondingly Chinese cuisine.

Paradise, Moniram Dewan Rd., Silpukuri (tel. 546904). From the front of the railway station, take a rickshaw or city bus toward Silpukuri. Excellent Assamese dishes in a soothing environment. The *thali* (Rs40) has 9 different samples, including fried fish and chili chicken; the veg. version (Rs35) is equally eclectic. Beer served. Open daily 10am-3:30pm and 6-9:30pm.

Madras Cabin, G.S. Rd., Paltan Bazaar. From the back of the railway station, turn right and the Cabin is on the left, by the Vandana Hotel. Popular with locals for (what else?) South Indian snacks. *Masala dosa* Rs13. Open daily 5am-10:30pm.

Divine Dismemberment

Legend has it that the beautiful goddess Sati fell in love with an uncouth ascetic who had the gall to marry her. Her disapproving father, Daksha, decided to hold a sacrifice and invite every god except for the vagabond bridegroom, Shiva. Incensed by this snub of her husband, Sati flung herself on the sacrificial pyre (incidentally lighting the way for generations of Indian women to commit ritual suicide, a practice banned by the British). When Shiva learned of his wife's demise, he tenderly lifted up her blackened body and began to sob convulsively, perilously shaking the entire universe. In the interest of saving the cosmos, Vishnu stepped in and began hacking off bits of the charred corpse with his *chakra* (discus-like weapon). Strangely enough, this action seemed to soothe Shiva, who ceased his sobbing. The places where fragments of Sati's body fell to earth became *shakti pithas.* These sacred sites, which number 4, 51, or 108 by various accounts, began as independent goddess shrines, but the myth of Sati's dismemberment provides a unifying thread. The most important *shakti pithas* are those which came from the most potent parts of Sati—which is why the Kamakhya Temple in Guwahati is the greatest of all.

SIGHTS

The mighty **Brahmaputra** (Son of Brahma) surges past the city in the north, often overrunning its banks in the rainy season and drowning the riverside settlements. From its banks, or from any of the adjacent hills, the river looks sluggish or serene, but its undercurrents are swift. The river's vast hydroelectric potential has not yet been exploited—building dams in an earthquake-prone area is extremely costly—but engineers have claimed that the Brahmaputra could satisfy 30% of India's energy needs. Ferries run regularly from Umananda Ghat, near the Brahmaputra Ashok Hotel, to the **Umananda Temple,** which sits on a small island in the middle of the river. The temple is unimpressive, but it offers the best possible view of the river.

From M.G. Rd., it's a 5km bus ride west to the **Kamakhya Temple** on Nilachal Hill. Devout pilgrims approach the temple from the footpaths leading up from the road. The Kamakhya Temple is one of the most sacred *shakti pithas* in Hinduism—it is said that the goddess Sati's *yoni* (vulva) fell on this spot when she was cut into pieces by Vishnu (see **Divine Dismemberment,** below). After it was burned down by a brahmin priest who converted to Islam, the temple, with its beehive-shaped spire, was rebuilt in 1665 by King Naranarayana. Naranarayana is said to have inaugurated the temple by offering the goddess Kamakhya 140 human heads. Inside, the Mother-Goddess is worshipped in the form of a crevice in a rock, rather than as a sculpted image. The ancient stone bleachers that rise up from the base of the temple seat spectators eager to see animal sacrifices—male goats tied to the posts at the main temple gate each morning are decapitated by evening. The shrine inside the temple is open to non-Hindus, but hour-long queues are normal.

Navagraha (Nine Planets), a small temple located on a hill in east Guwahati, is a reminder that Guwahati was once a great center of astronomy and astrology. An echo chamber holds nine *lingas* dedicated to the nine heavenly bodies that ancient Indians identified without the aid of astronomical equipment—the sun, the moon, the ascending and descending nodes of the moon, Mercury, Venus, Mars, Jupiter, and Saturn. The dark, dank temple now seems more abandoned than mysterious.

The **Assam State Museum,** Dighali Pukhi, next to the library and across from the lake, has a relatively new section on Assamese tribal culture. *(Open in summer Tu-Sa 10am-5pm, in winter 10am-4:15pm, closed 2nd and 4th Sa. Admission Rs2.)* The best way to take in all the sights is with **Assam Tourism's** full-day tour (Rs70).

■ Kaziranga National Park

Since its inception in 1908 as a conservation park, the Kaziranga National Park, located in tea country 217km from Guwahati, has been wildly successful. The rhinoceros population, the park's main concern, has increased threefold since 1966, although poaching still occurs (rhino horns are much-coveted aphrodisiacs). A visit to the park practically guarantees sightings of docile one-horned rhinos munching marsh grass. Their horns may look lethal, but they use them primarily to root around in the mud. Your chances of seeing a tiger are close to nil, but wild buffalo, equipped with mammoth horns, abound. Various kinds of deer and occasional wild elephants can also be seen. For bird lovers, the treetops call out with the cries of fishing eagles and grey-headed pelicans. A jeep ride or view from an observation deck at Sohola or Foliumare (located along the major road routes through the sanctuary) takes in a great swath of Kaziranga in all its vegetative splendor and variety.

The 430sq. km sanctuary, only a small part of which is open to human traffic, is a hodge-podge of habitats. Swampland gives way to jungle, which rises up to deciduous forests and finally to the evergreen slopes of the Karbi Anglong Hills. The best way to see the animals is on the back of an elephant—which seats up to four humans—since jeeps tend to scare animals. The sanctuary is open from late October to late April. During the monsoon, animals flee the flooded marshland for the muddy roads, making passage through the park dangerous or impossible.

ORIENTATION AND PRACTICAL INFORMATION Kaziranga is 217km from Guwahati and 96km from Jorhat, the closest airport. The most common way to visit the park is on the ATDC's **package tour,** a two-day trip including transportation in a luxury coach, one night's accommodation, and a one-hour elephant ride into the park on the morning of the second day. The bus departs from the **Assam Tourist Office,** located just down the road from the railway station in Guwahati, and the whole package costs Rs530. Unfortunately, this two-day tour involves a lot of waiting around and a very short amount of time in the park. While it is possible to arrange a more economical and more exciting tour on your own or with a small group, eastern Assam is unstable and a guided tour brings some peace of mind. During the monsoon, the Wild Grass Hotel sponsors excursions to choice vantage points on the edge of the preserve, but these are expensive.

Local buses and the tourist bus roll up at **Kohora,** a small collection of tea stalls and government lodges at the edge of the sanctuary. It is necessary to register at the **Directorate of Tourism** in the mid-range priced **Bonani Lodge.** The road into the park diverges into three main routes: Kaziranga Range, Western Range, and Eastern Range. Details and maps of each can be obtained at the Directorate of Tourism. The Eastern Range passes near an observation tower from which it is possible to get a bird's eye view of wallowing rhinos. Five kilometers from Kohora is a small village called Bokakhad, and National Highway 37 continues on to Jorhat and Sibsagar.

A one-hour **jeep ride** in the park, booked at the Forest Department, costs Rs300. **Guided elephants** can be rented at the Directorate of Tourism (Rs50 per person per hr.). Rides leave at 5, 6:30am, and 3:30pm. Exchange all **currency** in Guwahati. Government **buses** to Kaziranga depart from the main bus station next to Guwahati Junction Station between 6 and 10am (5hr., Rs60). Buses back to Guwahati pass through in the morning from 6 to 8am. **Jeeps** go to Guwahati for Rs800.

ACCOMMODATIONS AND FOOD Most travelers eat where they sleep, although anyone can mix and match. The **Aranya Tourist Lodge** has expensive rooms (singles Rs350, doubles Rs450; add Rs100 for A/C) and a Continental restaurant-bar. **Bonani** has slightly less expensive rooms (singles Rs175) and a restaurant. **Bonoshree** has basic doubles with attached bath for Rs170. The best bargain is the dormitory in **Kunjuban** (beds Rs30).

MEGHALAYA

Travelers who take the hilly roads into Meghalaya from Assam soon discover why the region is named "Adobe of Clouds." The state's seven ranges of hills seem perpetually swaddled in a cool, cumulonimbus mist, which occasionally bursts into violent action, dousing the valley areas and swelling the Brahmaputra. Meghalaya is home to Cherrapunjee and Mawsyn, two of the wettest places on earth, and the state sports an amazing assortment of flora and fauna.

The politically sensitive region was only opened to unrestricted tourism in 1995 and has seen few foreign tourists. Two distinct ethnic groups inhabit the state: the Proto-Australoid Hynniewtrep people, found mainly in the east; and the Tibeto-Burmese Achiks, or Garos, in the Garo Hills to the West. Welsh missionaries settled in the region during the 19th century, bringing Christianity to the population (75% of whom remain Christian). Less concerned about the indigenous population, British government officials found Meghalaya reminiscent of St. Andrews, Scotland, so they built an 18-hole, very wet golf course in Shillong and made it the capital of Assam. They also frowned upon human sacrifice and discouraged the practice. To this day, Meghalayans remember the Welsh with fondness, while they resent Britain.

Meghalaya became India's 21st state in 1972, but many of its tribal traditions have been very liberal for a long time. Democracy, for one, has old roots here. Regional *syiem* (kings) have long allowed and encouraged popular self-government through public discourse and referendums. Gender egalitarianism, too, is long-standing, sustained in part by a maternal system of lineage and property inheritance. But most people come to Meghalaya to simply savor the cool weather of Shillong and neighboring spots in the Khasi Hills. Several wildlife sanctuaries in West Meghalaya are approached by bad roads from Shillong and better ones from Guwahati.

▓ Shillong

The Meghalayan capital is many things that its Assamese cousin Guwahati is not. Cool, relaxed, and friendly, the hill-town radiates a sense of prosperity and well-being. Although its name derives from an incarnation of the Khasi Creator, Shillong rose to prominence as the erstwhile capital of British Assam. To this day, black-and-yellow cabs dominate the streets, and English is the town's *lingua franca*. Fast-paced development has kept Shillongites at the forefront of fashion, and the hip Van Heusen-clad, leather-purse-sportin' inhabitants are anything but stodgy.

The town does exhibit a few disturbing signs of modern fraying around the edges. Signs everywhere warn against the dangers of AIDS, drugs, and extortion, while scattered graffiti manifests ominously repressed anger and frustration ("Khasi by birth, Indian by accident"). Still, Shillong displays an exuberance and exhilarating energy that extends from its fanciest shops to the bustling, tangled, rancid Bara Bazaar.

ORIENTATION

A map of Shillong resembles a network of varicose veins. Many tiny, nameless roads snake out near the MTC bus stand in the **Police Bazaar. Guwahati-Shillong (G.S.) Road,** lined with many budget hotels, twists westward, eventually leading to **Bara Bazaar** (Big Bazaar), a web of narrow lanes littered with pineapple tops and animal fat. **M.E. Road** (Kacheri Rd.) twists away from Police Bazaar to the southeast, with many government offices. Along this wide, tree-lined boulevard you'll find the Shillong Club, State Bank of India, and at its southern tip, the State Museum. Aside from **Ward Lake,** adjacent to one curve of IGP Point, most of Shillong's natural wonders—waterfalls and parks—are located on the outskirts of or even kilometers outside the city. The only way to reach them is by taxi from Bara Bazaar or Police Bazaar.

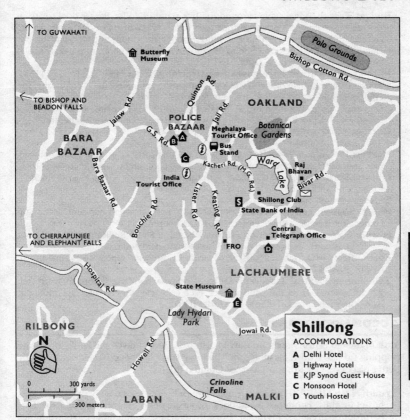

↑ TO GUWAHATI

Polo Grounds

Butterfly Museum

Bishop Cotton Rd.

← TO BISHOP AND BEADON FALLS

OAKLAND

Quinton Rd.

Jaiaw Rd.

Jail Rd.

POLICE BAZAAR

G.S. Rd.

Meghalaya Tourist Office

Botanical Gardens

BARA BAZAAR

Bara Bazaar Rd.

Bus Stand

Kacheri Rd. (M.G. Rd.)

Ward Lake

Raj Bhavan

Bivar Rd.

India Tourist Office

Lister Rd.

Keating Rd.

Shillong Club

State Bank of India

Bouchier Rd.

← TO CHERRAPUNJEE AND ELEPHANT FALLS

Central Telegraph Office

FRO

D

LACHAUMIERE

Hospital Rd.

State Museum

RILBONG

N

Lady Hydari Park

Jowai Rd.

E

0   300 yards
0   300 meters

Howell Rd.

Crinoline Falls

LABAN

MALKI

Shillong
ACCOMMODATIONS

A Delhi Hotel
B Highway Hotel
E KJP Synod Guest House
C Monsoon Hotel
D Youth Hostel

PRACTICAL INFORMATION

Trains: Shillong has no train service, but reservations for trains elsewhere can be made at the booth in the MTC building. Tickets for trains leaving Guwahati are hard to get; try to plan a week in advance. For specific trains see **Guwahati**, p. 415. Tourist quota tickets not available. Open daily 8am-1:30pm and 2-5pm.

Buses: Government buses depart from the **MTC bus stand** in Police Bazaar; tickets can be purchased and reserved in the MTC building. To: **Guwahati** (every hr., 6am-5pm, 4hr., Rs30/40); **Siliguri** (8am and 3pm, Rs150); **Tura** and **Williamnagar Wildlife Preserve** (7am and 7pm, 10hr., Rs89/129). Government buses also leave for **Ranikor;** you can jump off en route and then walk 2km on a side road to **Mawsyn.** If you want to go to **Cherrapunjee,** the MTDC tour is the only practical way to go (see **Sights,** p. 423). **Private buses** to cities in other northeastern states leave from the Polo Ground, a Rs10 cab ride from Police Bazaar. Tickets can be booked at any of the travel agents near the MTC bus stand. Many buses go to Silchar (7pm-midnight, 10hr., Rs150); from there, buses go to **Agartala, Aizawl,** and **Imphal.** For all three cities, buses leave throughout the morning (10hr., Rs150).

Local Transportation: Shared taxis, at Rs5 per head, barrel through the city streets, without even coming to a complete stop to pick up passengers. Try to flag down a taxi that already has passengers, or the driver might think you want it all to yourself. Watch how much the other passengers pay. For about twice the normal rate, whole taxis can be hired for trips to more remote tourist spots.

Tourist Office: Government of India Tourist Office, G.S. Rd. (tel. 225632), near Police Bazaar. Friendly staff. Open M-F 9:30am-5:30pm, Sa 9:30am-2pm. Less helpful is **Meghalaya Tourist Information** (tel. 226220), at the bus stand, Police Bazaar, right across from the MTC building. Open M-Sa 10am-5pm.

Budget Travel: Travel agents around the bus stand in Police Bazaar book seats on private buses going to other northeastern states. **Network Travels,** Quinton Rd. (tel. 221863), just down from the central police point and not far from the bus stand. Open daily 6am-8pm. **Sheba Travels,** by the police point, runs a daily bus to Guwahati Airport (Rs120). Open M-Sa 10am-5pm.

Immigration Office: Foreigners Registration Office, M.G. Rd. (tel. 224137). Across from the main office of the YMCA, near the State Museum. Technically, foreigners should report their arrival and departure. Open M-F 10am-5pm. Visa extension applications (rarely granted) can be filed at the **Secretariat,** a big white sore thumb (with a clock tower) 2 doors down to the right. Open M-F 10am-5pm.

Currency Exchange: State Bank of India, M.G. Rd. (tel. 223520) Open M-F 10am-2pm, Sa 10am-noon.

Market: The outdoor **Bara Bazaar** in West Shillong carries everything from pineapples and star fruit to cow hooves and electronic equipment. Open daily 9am-9pm.

Library: State Library, M.G. Rd., next to the State Museum. Open M-Sa 11am-5pm. Closed 2nd and 4th Sa.

Emergency: tel. 100.

Police: Superintendent's Office (tel. 224400), is on IGP Rd., adjacent to the Foreigners Registration Office. Open M-Sa 10am-4:30pm.

Hospital: Woodlands Nursing Home, Dhanketi, South Shillong (tel. 225240 or 224885), is a private hospital with the most up-to-date equipment.

Post Office: GPO, (tel. 222768), across from Raj Bhawan. Open M-Sa 7am-7pm, Su 4-7pm. **Postal Code:** 793001.

Telephones: Central Telegraph Office, Vivekananda Marg, European Ward (tel. 226288), across from the youth hostel. Free callbacks. Open daily 7am-midnight, 8am-6pm on holidays. **Telephone Code:** 0364.

ACCOMMODATIONS

Most of the old British hotels are now in disrepair. Budget dives and family hotels are popping up like toadstools along the shadowy lanes in Police Bazaar, with slightly better places on G.S. Rd. and Thana or Quinton Rd. (on the way to Cherrapunjee).

Youth Hostel (HI-AYH), Vivekananda Marg (tel. 222246). Possibly the least hostile hostel in India. Enormous 6-bed dorm rooms, wonderfully spotless and spacious bathrooms. Breakfast included. Dorm beds Rs40, nonmembers Rs60; doubles Rs160. Discounts for extended stays.

KJP Synod Guest House (tel. 228611), right across from the State Museum and Library (on M.G. Rd.). Run by a tiny little Khasi woman called "Auntie." Comfortable dorm beds in spacious rooms with fireplaces. Common kitchen and complimentary breakfast, but little English is spoken. It's a Christian establishment: weekly services are held in a central chapel, and most of the guests are Christians from Mizoram and Manipur. Check-out noon. Dorm beds Rs75; triples Rs120.

Highway Hotel, G.S. Rd. (tel. 223681). The wood of the furniture and paneling in the lobby gives off a pleasant smell in humid Shillong, as the predominantly male clientele sits around watching TV. Moderately-sized rooms and lots of common bathrooms. Singles Rs 60; doubles Rs130.

Shillong Club, Kacheri Rd. (tel. 225533; fax 221740). The club has suffered a little bit since the British pulled out, but it's still pretty classy. The rooms are huge, with TVs, fireplaces, phones, and a few bugs. "Temporary membership" (Rs10) includes access to the club's billiard tables and library. Singles Rs230; doubles Rs425. Rooms must be booked in advance. Call or write to Shillong Club Ltd., Residential, P.O. Box 45, Shillong 793001.

Delhi Hotel, A.C. Ln., Police Bazaar (tel. 223562). From G.S. Rd., past Broadway Hotel on the right; turn right onto A.C. Ln. The rooms are a bit grimy and damp. Common bath. Check-out noon. Singles Rs40; slightly bigger doubles Rs70-100.

Monsoon Hotel, G.S. Rd. (tel. 223316), across from Govt. of India Tourist Office. The least claustrophobic of the G.S. Rd. hotels, with both male and female clientele. Broad halls lead to vast rooms with wooden furniture. The mattresses are somewhat hard and the bathrooms run-down, but the new management is planning renovations. Singles with bath Rs125-150; doubles Rs225-275.

The Cook, The Thief, His Wife, and Their Visitor

All of the lips, teeth, and gums in Meghalaya are stained orange. Everyone—men, women, children—chews *paan*. Here, it is made not from the processed, shredded *supari* of the plains, but from the unadulterated betel nut that is grown locally. A Meghalayan myth connects the ingredients of *paan* with the characters of a dastardly drama, steeping the spittle of *paan* in social significance.

The story goes that a poor couple found themselves with a guest but without any food to offer him. Unable to bear the shame, the husband and wife said, "Please sit down, just a moment," went into the kitchen, and killed themselves. The guest, after waiting and waiting, became alarmed and wandered into the kitchen to find his friends bloody and dead. Realizing he had been the cause, he killed himself as well. Soon afterward, a robber showed up and was shocked to find, instead of loot, three dead bodies. Overcome with panic, he mopped up the blood and hid in the house.

Now, *paan* consists of three parts: *kwai* (betel nut), *shun* (lime paste), and *tympew* (leaf). *Kwai* is masculine, and represents the husband. *Paan*-eaters chew *kwai* first, just as it was the husband's blood that was first shed. *Shun* is feminine and represents the wife. *Tympew*, again masculine, stands for the guest, whose arrival wraps the house in disaster. The robber, finally, is represented by the masculine *dumasha*, or tobacco leaf, which Khasi women use to wipe the red stains from their teeth. It is said that Meghalayan hosts will never again have to commit suicide because even the poorest can afford to offer their guests *kwai tympew shun*. *Paan* exceeds even *chai* as the standard offering in Meghalayan households. If your host tempts you to orange your mouth, please, sit down—Meghalayan *paan* has a kick that'll float the unaccustomed sky-high.

FOOD

Decent Chinese food can be found in Police Bazaar and Khasi food at many small shops in Bara Bazaar, though one glance at the meat market might dissuade you.

Abba Restaurant, G.S. Rd., by Monsoon Hotel (a larger branch is in South Shillong). Authentic Chinese food (a rarity in India) including veg. chow mein Rs50. Open daily 10am-7:30pm.

Trattoria, Police Bazaar (tel. 225345). With your back to the bus stand and the MTDC office on your right, walk straight for 100m, take the first sharp right; Trattoria is on the right. A small, hygienic stall serving Khasi food in the center of Shillong's posh shopping district. Entrees Rs20-40. Open daily 9:30am-7:30pm.

Pizza, Jail Rd., Police Bazaar (tel. 221617). On the right before the bus stand. American food with Indian touches that make it better than the original. Veggie burger (Rs20) is fat, filling, and flavorful. Popular with locals. Open daily 10am-8:30pm.

SIGHTS

The cheapest and most convenient way to see the city's major tourist attractions is to join the MTDC's half-day tour, which includes **Shillong Peak, Elephant Falls,** and **Bishop Beadon Falls.** The tour leaves at 8:30am and costs Rs70 (book tickets at the MTDC office across from the bus stand). **Sweet Falls,** 8km from Police Bazaar, has unspectacular cascades, but there are plenty of paths to explore and plenty of room for picnics. **Crinoline Falls,** near Lady Hydari Park within the city limits, has a pool for swimming (take a city bus toward IGP Point, Rs2).

Beetle (if not Beatle) fans will love the **Butterfly Museum** (tel. 223411), on G.S. Rd., walk past the Grand Hotel (on your right); take the first right (but not a sharp right) onto Umsohsun Rd. When this forks, go left and follow the curving residential street 500m. The museum is on the right and the sign is difficult to see, so ask locals. This vast collection of butterflies and exotic bugs includes 30cm-long poisonous stick bugs and what is claimed to be the world's heaviest beetle. (*Open M-F 10:30am-4pm, Sa 10:30am-1pm.Admission Rs5.*) Started by a Mr. Wankhar in the 1930s, the collection was passed down to his son in the 1960s, and now *his* son is being groomed for the job of caretaker.

■ Near Shillong

Until recently, the town of **Cherrapunjee,** 56km south of Shillong, held the record for the greatest rainfall within a 24-hour period. Unbelievably, 104cm of rain fell here on June 16, 1876. The only real way to see Cherrapunjee, which has no local transportation and no accommodations, is by guided tour. One rickety bus goes to Cherrapunjee from Shillong in the morning, leaving from the MTDC office at 8am and returning at 4:30pm. Tickets (Rs90) are available at the MTDC office. Cherrapunjee's watery sights are spread out over several kilometers on the outskirts, but the MTDC tour is decent and covers all the major spots, stopping first at the **Nohkalikai Falls,** India's second-highest waterfall, which plummets into a lush valley. On a clear day, the deserted flood plains of Bangladesh are visible. The next stop is **Mawsmai Caves,** which are (surprise!) flooded during the monsoon; more adventurous guides will let you strip down and wade through to the jungle on the other side. At around 1pm, the bus pulls up to the cusp of a deep valley and stops at the Tourist Bungalow for lunch and a view of the **Seven Sisters Falls.**

Many **tribal festivals** are held in Meghalaya, such as the festival celebrated by the Jaintas in the town of **Jowai** during July, when hordes of people dance in a pool of muddy water to stomp out epidemics and pray for a healthy crop. Jowai is 64km from Shillong. **Buses** (Rs40) and **jeeps** (Rs50 per person or Rs350 to rent the whole jeep) leave from the private bus stand across from Anjalee Cinema Hall, near Bara Bazaar. For more information on festivals, contact the Government of India Tourist office, Shillong branch, or the MTDC.

Meghalaya is also a haven for **spelunking.** The best information and tours are provided by the hardy members of the Meghalaya Adventurers Association in Shillong. Their office is near the Synod Complex in Mission Compound (tel. 243059). (Contact B.O. Kharpran Daly (general secretary), c/o Hotel Centre Point, Police Bazaar, Shillong.) MTDC also has out a brochure called *Discover the Caves of Meghalaya.*

TRIPURA

Tiny Tripura comprises a finger of land poking into Bangladesh. As the southwestern corner of Northeast India, the region has a very different feel from its neighboring states. Tripura was a princely state until 1949, when it acceded to the Indian Union. While several ethnic groups continue to inhabit the state, Bengalis constitute the majority of the population; ethnic demography is a point of contention for such insurgent groups as the National Liberation Front of Tripura and the Tripura Resurrection Army. Although the Manikya, historical rulers of Tripura, submitted to the Mughals, they regained and retained direct control of the state throughout the Raj. While Tripura has its share of forests and wildlife sanctuaries, development is threatening what was once an impressive ecologists's paradise. Today the few who visit Tripura go mainly for its cultural attractions, which are all in close proximity to one another.

Diminutive **Agartala** is the sleepy capital of Tripura. While there's little to do in this administrative center, some travelers have been charmed by the soporific pace of life here, and a few have been known to stay for weeks. The town is dominated by the **Ujjayant Palace** at its center. The sprawling white structure was built in 1901 by Radhakishore Manikya; it now houses the state legislature. Go around to the back for the **Tripura Tourist Office** (tel. 225930 or 223893; fax 224013; open M-Sa 10am-4pm). This is the place for inquiries regarding accommodations and food. They will also direct you to money-exchange facilities and the Bangladesh Visa office. Buses connect Agartala with Silchar in Assam. There are also a few buses that run directly to Guwahati. For safety, consider flying directly to the city, which is connected directly with Calcutta and Guwahati. You can also reach the town by bus from **Dhaka,** Bangladesh (6hr.). **Telephone code:** 381.

The famed **Water Palace** at Neermahal lies 53km south of Agartala. Constructed as a summer resort in 1930 for Bir Bikram Kishore Manikya, it serves as a beautiful example of Indo-Saracenic architecture. The red-and-white structure lies in the middle of a large lake, whose shores feature a **tourist lodge** and a few restaurants, leaving the area blissfully deserted at night. Neermahal is about 1km from **Melaghar,** which is connected by bus to Agartala (2hr., Rs50).

MIZORAM

The southernmost state of this corner of India, Mizoram is known for its lush hill stations and valleys as well as the hospitality of its people. Bound by a code of ethics known as *tlawmgaina,* the Mizos tend to be very welcoming and have traditionally not discriminated on the basis of class or sex. Originally from northwestern China, the Mizos fought a 21-year war of independence before finally acceding to the Indian Union in 1987. Today, they remain overwhelmingly Christian, and maintain one of the highest literacy rates in India.

Although Mizoram continues to attract tourists because of its natural splendor, its ecological story sadly parallels that of much of the region. Mizos practice "*jhum* cultivation," known less romantically as slash-and-burn agriculture. Politically troubled and superficially prosperous, the state is under constant threat of resource depletion. In addition, the Indian government considers Mizoram a strategically important region, and foreign tourists are required to band together in groups of at least four and obtain a Restricted Area Permit to visit, while Indians must obtain an Inner Line Permit. Fortunately, these are relatively easy to procure and should not deter travelers in the least.

Cool and placid **Aizwal** (EYES-wall) is perched over 1000m above sea level. To the east of the ridge on which it hangs flows the river Tuiral; on the west is the Tlawang River. The scenery from the city is nothing short of overwhelming, and travelers often find themselves dumbstruck when trying to describe the beauty of the location. Despite supporting a tiny population of about 200,000, Aizwal has its share of parks, gardens, and museums. Information regarding these and accommodations can be obtained from the **Mizoram Tourist Office** (tel. 21226). Aizwal is connected by **bus** to **Silchar** (6hr.) in Assam and **Shillong** in Meghalaya. It is also accessible by **air** from Calcutta and Guwahati. **Telephone code:** 389.

MANIPUR

Despite a long history of foreign invasions and domestic insurgency, Manipur has only recently begun to break away from its "at least we're not as boring as Tripura" tourism campaign. Indeed, the strongly Hindu state is home to Moirnag, the site of yearly folk festivals, and **Loktak Lake,** the largest body of fresh water in the Northeast and home to the world's only **floating national park.** Manipuri martial arts and dances, including the Jagoi form of dance, are known throughout India, and the state claims to be the birthplace of modern polo. Nevertheless, Manipur has never been a popular tourist destination, and its infrastructure is correspondingly underdeveloped.

The principal inhabitants of Manipur are the Meities; other tribal groups include the Naga and Kuki-Chin-Mizo. While these people have lived together peacefully for centuries, recent times have seen friction build to the point of violence. Travelers are advised to contact the Government of India tourist office for the latest details.

While Indians do not need permits to visit Manipur, those arriving by road must obtain an Inner Line Permit to pass through Nagaland. Foreigners need **Restricted Area Permits** (see p. 7).

At 790m above sea level, **Imphal** isn't the highest of capitals, yet it offers hills and lakes aplenty for the traveler. As in many other northeastern states, wildlife and foliage are main attractions—but the town has its share of monuments and temples. Most prominent is the Vaishnavite **Shree Govindjee Temple,** whose significance is more religious than architectural. Mainpur's struggle against the British is immortalized in the **Shaheed Minar** and **War Cemetery.** For information on these sights, as well as excursions to nearby destinations and accommodations in Manipur, contact **Manipur Tourism** (tel. 224603). There's also a small branch at the airport. **Flights** serve Imphal from Calcutta and Guwahati. You can also take a **bus** from Guwahati or Shillong. **Telephone code:** 385.

NAGALAND

Historically, one of India's least accessible regions, Nagaland is slowly opening up to tourism. The eastern slice of the region, Nagaland's precarious position between Assam and Burma has often resulted in crackdowns by the India Army on Naga nationalists, who to this day struggle for increased autonomy (as they enjoyed under the British) or even independence. The fiercest fighting was incited by the Nagaland National Council, with support from China. One of the largest factions of these militants laid down their arms in 1974, bringing a degree of peace to the region.

Today, Nagaland promotes itself as a nature destination. There is good trekking in the Dzukou Valley, 30km from the capital, Kohima, and around Mt. Saramati, 269km from **Kohima.** The best way to experience the region is probably to arrange a guided tour or trek with **Naga Tourism,** in Kohima (tel. 22214, 21607; open M-F 10am-4pm). **Telephone code:** 370.

Dimapur is home to impressive monoliths and the state's only **airport.** Kohima is connected to Dimapur by road (3hr., Rs70). Foreigners must travel in groups of four or more and have a **Restricted Area Permit** (see p. 7); Indians need an Inner Line Permit. Both of these are considerably more difficult to obtain than permits to visit other states.

The Andaman Islands
अंदमान द्वीप-समूह

Beautiful isolated beaches, luscious rainforests, mangrove swamps, and unique marine and bird life come together in the Andaman Islands, which were recently opened to tourism. The *Ramayana* identifies the monkey-god Hanuman (from which "Andaman" is derived) as the first visitor to the islands—he used them as stepping stones to hop across to Burma. If the story is true, Hanuman was also the first to trample on the territorial rights of the islands' indigenous inhabitants. In turn, the British would arrive to build a penal colony to imprison agitators for Indian Independence. Since Independence, the Indian government has tempered further efforts to colonize the islands with an anthropological interest in the island tribes, but natives have still been forced to watch their land succumb to settlement and deforestation, the source of much tension.

Port Blair, on South Andaman, is the main transportation hub, connected to Chennai and Calcutta by boat and plane. The islands have very poor commercial and transportation infrastructures, and getting around (or getting what you need) requires a lot of energy and patience. The neighboring Nicobar Islands are currently off-limits to tourists altogether. Your exertion will be rewarded, however, with some of the most secluded beaches in the world. The temperature remains tropical throughout the year, although a lot of rain (sometimes accompanied by cyclones) falls from June to mid-September and from November to December.

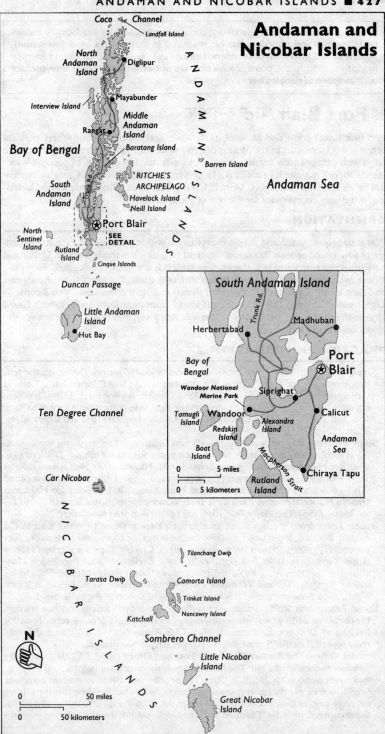

Andaman and Nicobar Islands

Coco Channel
Landfall Island
North Andaman Island
Diglipur
Interview Island
Mayabunder
Middle Andaman Island
Rangat
Baratang Island
Barren Island
Bay of Bengal
South Andaman Island
RITCHIE'S ARCHIPELAGO
Havelock Island
Neill Island
Andaman Sea
North Sentinel Island
Port Blair
SEE DETAIL
Rutland Island
Cinque Islands
Duncan Passage
Little Andaman Island
Hut Bay
Ten Degree Channel
Car Nicobar
Tilanchang Dwip
Tarasa Dwip
Camorta Island
Trinkat Island
Nancowry Island
Katchall
Sombrero Channel
Little Nicobar Island
Great Nicobar Island

ANDAMAN ISLANDS

NICOBAR ISLANDS

N

0   50 miles
0   50 kilometers

Detail: Port Blair area

South Andaman Island
Herbertabad
Trunk Rd.
Madhuban
Bay of Bengal
Wandoor National Marine Park
Siprighat
Port Blair
Tamugli Island
Wandoor
Alexandra Island
Calicut
Redskin Island
Boat Island
Macpherson Strait
Andaman Sea
Rutland Island
Chiraya Tapu

0   5 miles
0   5 kilometers

EAST INDIA

> **Warning:** The relationship between the Andaman and Nicobar Islands' indigenous peoples and outsiders has been soured in many cases by deforestation, poaching, and government blunders. Understandably, some tribes are unfriendly to visitors, even to the point of violence. **Do not attempt to come into contact with indigenous peoples here.**

▒ Port Blair पोर्ट ब्लैअर

Port Blair hasn't come that far since its days as a British penal colony where political activists who took part in the Mutiny of 1857 were sent. Although its hilly streets are filled with exceptionally friendly people, mopeds, and lots and lots of coconut water stands, there's not much to see or do. However, this is the Andamans' major city, central for air and water transport. As such, it has good tourist offices and plentiful hotels, and is the only access point for the rest of the islands.

ORIENTATION

Port Blair is quite small, and almost everything is within walking distance. At the center of town is **Aberdeen Bazaar,** at one end of which sits the **bus stand.** Uphill and east from the bus stand is a **clocktower** which is a common landmark. From the clocktower, the road to the youth hostel and, eventually, **Corbyn's Cove,** heads east and then south. If you walk in the other direction from the bus stand, you'll come to **Lighthouse Cinema.** The road straight ahead from here leads to Jagganath Guest House; the road to the right leads to **Phoenix Bay Jetty;** and uphill to the left sits the Andaman Islands' tourist office.

PRACTICAL INFORMATION

Airport: Junglighat Rd., past the Government of India Tourism Office, on the left. Public buses leave every 30min. from the bus stand (5am-8:30pm, Rs2). Taxis to the airport run from downtown (3km, Rs50). **Indian Airlines** (tel. 33744) is downhill from the Andaman tourism office, on the right side of the road. Open M-Sa 9am-1pm and 2-4pm. Flights to **Calcutta** (Tu, Th, Sa, and Su, US$195) and **Chennai** (M, W, and F, US$195).

Ships: Phoenix Bay Jetty is a 5min. walk past Lighthouse Cinema going north. Tickets available 1 day in advance. Booth open 9am-noon. Ships sail for: **Diglipur** (Tu, 4pm; via **Mayabunder,** F 6:30am; 16hr., Rs62); **Havelock** via **Neil Island** (M and Th, 6:15am, 4hr., Rs13); **Rangat** (Tu, W, F, and Sa 6:15am, 9hr., Rs30); **Ross Island** (Th-Tu 8:30am, 10:30am, 12:30pm, and 2pm, 20min., Rs13). Boats for **Mahatma Gandhi National Marine Park** leave from Wandoor Jetty, 30km from the city (Tu-Su, 10am, Rs55). The *Daily Telegraph* has updates on ship schedules.

Buses: Leave from the bus stand in Aberdeen Bazaar. Don't trust the man in the enquiry booth; ask the ticket-*wallahs* on the buses for route information. To: **Airport** (every 30min., 5am-8:30pm, 10min., Rs2); **Chiriya Tapu** via **Corbyn's Cove** (approximately every hr. 5am-6pm, 1½hr., Rs6); **Diglipur** (6am, 12hr., Rs63); **Mayabunder** (5:30am, 8hr., Rs57; deluxe 5am, Rs1000); **Rangat** (6am, 5hr., Rs40; deluxe 5am, Rs100); and **Wandoor** (5, 5:30, and 8:30am, noon, 3, 5, 6, 8:30pm, 1½hr., Rs6). Buses returning from northern towns depart at the same times.

Local Transport: Most distances are walkable but hilly. **Taxis** do not use meters. **Motorbikes** and **cycles** are popular. **Jagganath Guest House** rents both for Rs120 and Rs30 per day (respectively). **TSG Autos** (tel. 32787), Junglighat Rd., rents motorbikes (Rs75 per ½day, Rs120 per day, Rs500 deposit).

Tourist Office: The **Andaman Islands Tourism Office** (tel. 32747) is a tall, spiffy building at the top of a hill. The information is thorough and helpful, and they can make reservations for Dolphin Guest House, the only place to stay on Havelock Island, as well as other government-run hotels further north. Their bus trips, however, are pricier than public buses. Open M-F 8:30am-4:45pm, Sa 8:30am-12:30pm. **Government of India Tourism Office,** Junglighat Rd., on the left side, towards

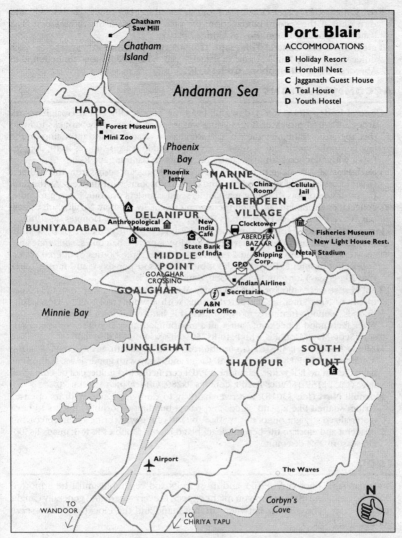

Port Blair

ACCOMMODATIONS

B Holiday Resort
E Hornbill Nest
C Jagganath Guest House
A Teal House
D Youth Hostel

Andaman Sea

Chatham
Saw Mill

*Chatham
Island*

HADDO

■ Forest Museum
■ Mini Zoo

*Phoenix
Bay*

Phoenix
Jetty

MARINE
HILL

China
Room

Cellular
Jail

ABERDEEN
VILLAGE

DELANIPUR

Anthropological
Museum

New
India
Café

Clocktower

ABERDEEN
BAZAAR

Fisheries Museum
New Light House Rest.

BUNIYADABAD

State Bank
of India

Shipping
Corp.

Netaji Stadium

MIDDLE
POINT

GOALGHAR
CROSSING

GOALGHAR

GPO

Indian Airlines

Secretariat

A&N
Tourist Office

Minnie Bay

JUNGLIGHAT

SHADIPUR

SOUTH
POINT

Airport

The Waves

TO
WANDOOR

TO
CHIRIYA TAPU

*Corbyn's
Cove*

N

the airport. The office is smaller, more out of the way, and has less information. Port Blair's newspaper, the *Daily Telegraph,* has a "Today for Tourists" section.

Currency Exchange: State Bank of India is across from the bus stand, but takes forever and sometimes won't change money at all. **Island Travels** (tel. 33358), 110m east of the clocktower, is a better bet (in-season: open daily 9am-6:30pm; off-season: 3-4pm).

Library: Post Office Rd., next to the Telegraph Office. Open M-Sa 12:30-7:45pm. Closed 2nd Sa. There's a decent library upstairs in the **Zonal Anthropological Museum,** but you'll have to convince the head office (on the left, 100m down Junglighat Jetty on the left) that you're a "researcher."

Pharmacy: Devraj Medical Store, Hospital Rd. (tel. 34344), in the bazaar across from the stadium, is trustworthy. Open daily 8am-1pm and 2-8pm.

Hospital: G.B. Panth Hospital has ambulance service (tel. 100).

Post Office: GPO, Post Office Rd. From the local tourism office, go downhill and turn right at the second intersection; the post office is on the right. Open M-Sa 9am-12:30pm and 1-5pm. **Postal Code:** 744101.

Telephones: The **Central Telegraph Office** is on Post Office Rd., next to the post office. Open M-Sa 7am-9:30pm, Su 8am-3:30pm. **STD/ISD** booths can be found in Aberdeen Bazaar. **Telephone Code:** 03192.

ACCOMMODATIONS

Central Lodge (tel. 33632), downhill from the Tourist Office near Goalghar—ask around. Retired professor R.K. Sharma was inspired by his army barracks to build this, the ultimate budget guest house. Rooms are basic but pleasant. Camp on the lawn or in the jungle-like "garden." Can be packed in season. Singles Rs40; doubles Rs60, with attached bath Rs80. Extra person Rs20. Camping fee Rs20.

Youth Hostel, Aberdeen Bazaar (tel. 32459), by the ocean, across from the stadium. Great location, floral surroundings, and clean bathrooms with showers. As the temporary home of lots of young mainlanders and islanders on tour, it has a friendly, collegial environment, although there aren't too many women. No alcohol. Checkout 10am. Dorm beds: HI members Rs20, nonmembers Rs40. Doubles: Rs40/80.

Jagganath Guest House, Moulana Azad Rd. (tel. 32148). Well-kept by a kind, thoughtful manager. Rooms have two windows, private balconies, sometimes-hot showers, tiled bathrooms, and 24hr. running water. Free bottles of filtered water. Snorkel equipment (Rs40 per day), bicycles (Rs30 per day), and motor bikes (Rs120 per day) for rent. Singles Rs80; doubles Rs125.

Teal House (tel. 34060 or 340611), down Moulana Azad Rd., away from the center of town. Nice smelling, carpeted rooms with a wonderful hilltop view. Telephones, bamboo furniture, mosquito nets, big bathrooms with hot showers—this place feels good. Check-out 7am. Call a month in advance if you're coming in season (Sept.-May). Doubles with bath Rs250. Off-season: 25% discount.

Holiday Resort (tel. 30516). Go up the road from Jagganath, veer to the left at the junction, and Holiday is on the right. Clean and classy with good views. Bathrooms have tile but no hot water. Samudra, a PADI certified scuba guide, can be contacted here (tel. 21159). Singles Rs200; doubles Rs280. Off-season: discount 20%.

Hornbill Nest (tel. 33018), just over halfway to Corbyn's Cave. With its open-air atrium shaped like a giant spider and pastel buildings, Hornbill appears to have materialized straight out of the 1950s. A bit out of the way (bring a motorbike), but peaceful and close to the beach. Clean, bland rooms. Doubles Rs170; quads Rs300. Off-season: 25% discount.

FOOD

Andaman soil is not very fertile, and most fruits and vegetables must be imported from the mainland. Seafood, as you might expect, is everywhere and generally caught the same day. The *dhabas* between the bus stand and the clocktower also serve good, filling food.

Lighthouse Restaurant. The youth hostel's canteen has simple, delicious, and cheap food. The atmosphere is brotherly and, at times, a little raucous. Veg. and non-veg. *thalis* Rs10-15. Open daily 5:30am-9:30pm.

China Room (tel. 30759), on Marine Hill. From the bus stand, walk north about 1km and turn right up the hill; the restaurant, lit with a red sign, will be on the left. A dizzying selection of gourmet seafood—daily specials include cashew prawns (Rs100) and barracuda fillet (Rs80). With a day's notice, roast duck (Rs250) or *szechuan* lobster (Rs300) are available. Open daily noon-2pm and 5:30-10:30pm.

New India Cafe, beneath Hotel Jai Mathi, 20m from Jagganath Guest House. A surf-style cafeteria with heart, delicious, no-frills dishes and excellent *naan*. Fish *thali* (Rs20) and prawn coconut curry (Rs40).

The Waves, at Corbyn's Cove, across the street from the beach. Lounge around in bamboo chairs in front of the ocean. Snacks (sandwiches, *prapad*) Rs5-12, prawn *pakora* Rs50, beer Rs63. Open daily 6am-10pm.

Ananda, Aberdeen Bazaar, below Kavita hotel. Walk from the bus stand to the clock-tower and turn right; the restaurant is on the left. A wide variety of Indian dishes available, and the chicken is served in a million different ways. Popular with locals. Eat in A/C comfort for Rs1 extra. Snacks Rs7-13, chicken coconut Rs40.

New Light House, by the Fisheries Museum, 1km east of the clocktower. Tiny restaurant consists of a kitchen with take-out windows and a small patio. Lobster, squid, crab, tiger prawns, and cuttlefish are priced by size, and you can have them raw! "Fish 65" is a tasty fish-fry (Rs40), while "Fish 555" is a *masala* dish (Rs50).

SIGHTS

With their unending capacity to divide and conquer, the British used the Andamans until Independence as a prison site for freedom fighters, lest the righteous rile up fellow prisoners on the mainland. The **Cellular Jail** (tel. 30117), which once held rebels, is a monument to India's freedom struggle. *(Jail open daily 9am-5pm. Sound and light show Tu-Su 7:15pm.)* From the clock tower, go down toward the ocean and bear left and uphill. The **museum**'s two ground floor galleries chart the history and inhumanity of the prison and document the broad base of Indian resistance to colonialism. *(Museum open Tu-Su 9am-noon and 2-5pm.)* One upstairs room is devoted to the life and work of Subhas Chandra Bose, who was imprisoned here. The **Zonal Anthropological Museum** is one of the few places on the Andamans where you can find photos and relics of the islands' indigenous peoples. Unfortunately, there isn't a great deal of information displayed. A beautiful, 15-minute coastal bike ride takes you to **Corbyn's Cove,** a pretty, white sand beach surrounded by green palms that'll ease you into the stupendous beauty before you explore the Andamans further. From the clocktower, go downhill, turn right, and follow the road and the coastline.

■ Near Port Blair

Ross Island, on the northeast side of South Andaman, houses the leftover buildings of the British penal colony for which it was once the center of operations. It's a great (and surreal) place to wander around for the day. **Ferries** leave about every two hours from Port Blair and take two hours. The last ferry back to Port Blair is at 5:30pm. **Viper Island,** like Ross Island, features the hauntingly overgrown ruins of the British penal project. You can reach Viper as part of a general Harbour Cruise, which leaves daily from Phoenix Bay Jetty (3pm, 2hr., Rs20). **Chiriya Tapu** is a tiny village on the south end of South Andaman, 30km from Port Blair. The road is rough at times, but the long beach here has excellent camping and decent snorkeling.

■ Mahatma Gandhi National Marine Park

The water at Mahatma Gandhi National Marine Park is a world of mysterious, sometimes pulsating **coral** structures that provide a home for millions of wildly colored, elegantly and oddly shaped, social and competitive marine life, including angelfish, clown fish, starfish, silver jacks, yellow butterfly fish, green parrotfish, and sea anemones. The 8:30am bus to Wandoor from the Port Blair bus stand connects with the 10am boat to either **Jolly Buoy** or **Red Skin Island** (Rs55). A park permit is Rs15 and snorkel rental is Rs50, but equipment gets scarce during season—you should bring your own or rent from it from a Port Blair hotel. The boat will take you to a glass-bottomed boat, where you can catch glimpses of the beauty underneath. To get the real McCoy, however, explore the under-water-world on your own. **Coral and shell collecting is forbidden. Bharat Hotel,** a shack 50m from the boat dock, rents snorkels for Rs50 and serves excellent fish curry (Rs6) and *chapati* (Rs2), and may rent you one of its tiny rooms (Rs50-80). The road leads a few kilometers past the boat dock to a beautiful beach with drift-logs perfect for setting up a tarp. Beer (Rs65) and basic food can be had at the government-run restaurant a few yards away.

■ Ritchie's Archipelago

Havelock Island is the most popular tourist getaway, and for good reason. The **beaches** are beautiful and isolated and the way of life quiet and peaceful. Boats leave from Phoenix Jetty (M-Sa, 6:15am, 4hr., Rs13). The only places to stay are the **Dolphin Guest House** and the **Tent Colony.** Reservations must be made at the Andaman Islands Tourist Office in Port Blair. Rooms cost Rs150-250.

   Neil Island, Long Island, and **North Passage** are all open for overnight stays (camping is probably the best option), although most visitors find better beaches on South Andaman or Havelock. Ships leaving Phoenix Bay Jetty stop at Neil (M, W, Th, and F, 6:15am, Rs7) and Long (W and F, 6:15am, Rs13).

■ Middle and North Andaman

Baratang, Middle Andaman, and **North Andaman** can be reached by buses heading up the Grand Trunk Road or by ferry from Phoenix Bay. Because the road has been stubbornly built through reserves set aside for the indigenous Jarawas, travel on it is generally limited to government buses (which carry armed guards to deter attacks). The only places to stay on Middle and North Andaman are the main towns of **Mayabunder** (Middle) and **Diglipur** (North). The Tourism Office has recently opened **Swiftlet Nest** in Mayabunder (doubles Rs250) and **Turtle Nest** in Diglipur (doubles Rs300). Reservations must be made at the Tourism Office in Port Blair.

Tribals of the Andaman and Nicobar Islands

Outside of the cloggy bustle of Port Blair, the Andamans seem beautifully, peacefully underpopulated. But there are a sizable (though still precariously small) number of unseen indigenous inhabitants here, and their recent history has been far from peaceful. Troubles began with the British penal colony established on Viper Island. Western diseases, deforestation, and armed skirmishes (spears vs. rifles) initiated a decimation of the Andaman and Nicobar tribal populations that only began to level off in the 1980s. By then, the Andamanese, who have now been relegated to Strait Island, numbered a mere 28. With the exception of the Nicobarese, who have been largely "integrated" through government development programs, other tribes have suffered the same dramatic decline.

   Since Independence, the Indian government has shifted its tribal policy from colonize-or-bust to colonize-with-scientific-curiosity, and has set aside indigenous reserves. Still, understandably, some tribes have opted for zero communication with the disastrously bungling invaders. The Sentinelese, who occupy North Sentinel Island (64km southwest of Port Blair), have been a target of government anthropological excursions since 1967. Government boats would pull up to the island, leave gifts of plastic buckets, roast pigs, and sacks of coconuts, and attempt contact. The Sentinelese would take the gifts—and then fire arrows at the anthropologists. The Jawarese, who occupy much of the busier Middle Andaman, have had a more contentious time of it, and many have been shot while trying to deter poachers and loggers (in one case by chopping off the offenders' hands). Buses plying the Trunk Road, which runs directly through "reserve" land, now carry armed guards—an arrow or two still occasionally crashes through the windows.

   For more information on the Andaman and Nicobar tribes, stop by the Zonal Anthropological Museum (see p. 429).

(see p. 429).

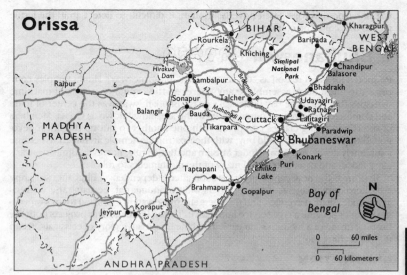

Orissa ଓଡ଼ିଶ

The sea has had a major influence on Orissan history and continues to dominate the lives of almost everyone who lives here. The Bay of Bengal licks the state's coastline for 482km, nearly all of Orissa's urban residents live within rock-throwing distance of the Mahanadi River Delta, and most of its rural population toils in half-submerged rice paddies. Right after dawn, fishing fleets set out from the beach at Puri in their narrow wooden boats; watching as hundreds of these small crafts fight the pounding surf calls up images of the power that the Kalingas and other local dynasties once wielded over the high seas, sending colonists as far as Java. In the backcountry, thick forest cover has allowed *adivasis* (tribal peoples) to survive relatively undisturbed, although they suffer from a mix of poverty, prejudice, and disenfranchisement. As urban India races ahead, they are likely to be left behind.

Although unequivocally a part of modern India, Orissans have defended their independence for thousands of years. The Kalingas held out against the expanding Mauryan Empire in the 3rd century BC, capitulating only after a battle so bloody that it convinced the emperor Ashoka to renounce violence and convert to Buddhism. Orissa also withstood Muslim rule until 1568, almost 400 years after surrounding regions had been conquered. Orissa's contained cultural continuity led to the development of the distinctive artistic forms for which it is hailed, including its style of Hindu temple architecture (one of India's finest), and the Odissi form of dance.

Today Orissa is one of India's most uniformly Hindu states, with over 95% professing the religion (and worshiping first and foremost Lord Jagannath, a local version of Krishna). It is also one of India's poorest, prone to cyclones and heavy monsoons that

🗣 HIGHLIGHTS OF ORISSA

- Edged by the Bay of Bengal, **Puri** (p. 440) gracefully juggles dual roles as religious center and beach-side resort.
- Temple-packed **Bhubaneswar** (below) showcases the unique beauty of the region's varied and intricate Hindu architecture.
- The Buddhist ruins at **Ratnagiri, Udayagiri,** and **Lalitagiri** (p. 448) provide glimpses of both ancient and modern Orissan rural life.

wreak havoc on crops. Such poverty, though, is difficult to detect amid the fertile greens that color the countryside.

■ Bhubaneswar ଭୁବଚନେଶ୍ବର

Promoted for good reason as "the temple city," Bhubaneswar's Hindu temples comprise the finest such assemblage anywhere. As the capital of powerful maritime dynasties that ruled the Bay of Bengal's coast, Bhubaneswar was the center of trade and commerce for over a thousand years in the area now known as Orissa. Members of the Hindu ruling classes competed with one another to put up the finest devotional structures money could buy; with their patronage, temple architecture became a sublimely developed form. Under Muslim and British rule, however, Bhubaneswar's glory faded, and neglect reduced many of the monuments to rubble.

Reborn as the new capital of Orissa soon after Independence, Bhubaneswar grew a modern appendage as urban planners built monumental, bureaucratic warrens along wide, shaded avenues, and the energetic preservation of the old town's remaining temples became a civil service imperative. Today, Bhubaneswar projects both the bustling image of a modern state capital and the imaginative glory of classical Orissan temple architecture.

ORIENTATION

Bhubaneswar is really two cities: the well-planned and spaced-out **New Town** to the north, and the temple-crowded **Old Town** to the south. Large roads like the north-south **Jan Path** and **Sachivalaya Marg** and the east-west **Raj Path** cut the New Town into neat squares called **units**, or **nagars**. As units these squares have numbers; as *nagars* they have names. There is no clear city center, but the closest approximation is **Station Square,** in front of the **railway station,** with a huge horse statue in its roundabout. To the north and west of Station Square are **Ashok Nagar** (Unit 3) and **Kharavela Nagar,** containing many shops and services. Many hotels are located around Station Sq., but the cheaper ones are at **Kalpana Square,** located at the junction of **Cuttack Road** and Raj Path, to the south. The railroad runs along the eastern edge of town, and Cuttack Rd. runs north-south just east of it. The rear exit of the railway station leads to a small street that intersects Cuttack Rd. To the right, the road forks left and, after passing the Old Town, continues on to Puri. The haphazardly laid out Old Town has no main roads but has many conspicuous landmarks; the tank known as **Bindu Sagar** sits in the center and the tall **Lingaraj Temple,** just south of it, is visible from a distance.

PRACTICAL INFORMATION

Airport: (tel. 406472 or 401084). Northwest of the temples in the Old Town. Cycle- and auto-rickshaws Rs50. **Indian Airlines** (tel. 400533 or 400544), across the street from Capital Market. Open daily 10am-1pm and 2-4:30pm. Flights to: **Calcutta** (6 per week, 1hr., US$75); **Chennai** (Tu, Th, Sa, 2hr., US$180); **Delhi** (1 per day, 2hr., US$195); **Hyderabad** (M, W, and F, 2hr., US$145); **Mumbai** (M, W, and F, 2hr., US$225);

Trains: Bhubaneswar Railway Station, Station Sq. (reservations tel. 504042). Make enquiries at 2nd class booking counter (tel. 402233). Tourist quota available. Fares listed are 2nd/1st class. To: **Calcutta** (*Dhauli Exp.* 2822, 2:10pm; *Puri-Howrah Exp.* 8008, 8:45pm, Rs209/1043; *Sri Jagannath Exp.* 8410, 11pm; 9hr., Rs90/490); **Chennai** (*Coromandel Exp.* 2841, 9:30pm, 20hr., Rs339; *Chennai Mail* 6003, 4:30am, 25hr., Rs285); **Delhi** (*Purshottam Exp.* 2801, 9:45pm, 31½hr., Rs157/767); **Hyderabad** (*East Coast Exp.* 8045, 7:40pm; *Falaknuma Exp.* 7003, Tu, F, and Su, 3:40pm, 19hr., Rs263/960). Regular trains run to **Puri** (1½hr.).

Buses: Baramunda New Bus Station, NH5 (tel. 470695), 9km from Raj Mahal Sq. Buses to: **Balasore** (every 10min., 4:30am-10pm, Rs51); **Berhampur** (6 per day, 5-11am and 3pm, 4hr., Rs40/54 for regular/deluxe); **Calcutta** (4:15, 6, and 6:30pm, 3hr., Rs120); **Cuttack** (every 15min., 45min., Rs5); **Konark** (every 30min., 6am-

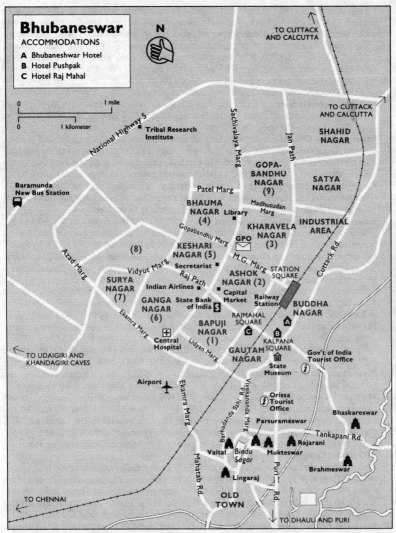

Bhubaneswar
ACCOMMODATIONS
A Bhubaneshwar Hotel
B Hotel Pushpak
C Hotel Raj Mahal

N

TO CUTTACK
AND CALCUTTA

0 _____ 1 mile
0 _____ 1 kilometer

TO CUTTACK
AND CALCUTTA

National Highway 5

Tribal Research
Institute

Sachivalaya Marg

Jan Path

SHAHID
NAGAR

GOPA-
BANDHU
NAGAR
(9)

SATYA
NAGAR

Baramunda
New Bus Station

Patel Marg

BHAUMA
NAGAR
(4)

Library

Madhusudan
Marg

KHARAVELA
NAGAR
(3)

INDUSTRIAL
AREA

Gopabandhu Marg

GPO

Azad Marg

(8)

KESHARI
NAGAR
(5)

M.G. Marg

Vidyut Marg

Secretariat

SURYA
NAGAR
(7)

Raj Path

Indian Airlines

ASHOK
NAGAR (2)

STATION
SQUARE

Cuttack Rd.

GANGA
NAGAR
(6)

State Bank
of India

Capital
Market

Railway
Station

BUDDHA
NAGAR

Ekamra Marg

BAPUJI
NAGAR
(1)

RAJMAHAL
SQUARE

A

B

KALPANA
SQUARE

EAST INDIA

TO UDAIGIRI AND
KHANDAGIRI CAVES

Central
Hospital

Udyan Marg

GAUTAM
NAGAR

C

State
Museum

Gov't of India
Tourist Office

Airport

Ekamra Marg

Barhadanda Sahi Path

Vivekananda Marg

Orissa
Tourist
Office

Parsuramésvar

Bhaskaresvar

Tankapani Rd.

Vaital

Bindu
Sagar

Mukteswár

Rajarani

Mahatab Rd.

Lingaraj

Puri Rd.

Brahmeswar

TO CHENNAI

OLD
TOWN

TO DHAULI AND PURI

5pm, 2hr., Rs15); **Puri** (every 15min., 1½hr., Rs13/14 for regular/express). Buses to most of these destinations can also be boarded near **Kalpana Sq.**, on Puri Rd., just beyond the state museum.

Local Transportation: Minibuses cover all the major streets (Rs2-3). A useful route runs from the front of the Kalinga Ashok Hotel to the Baramunda Bus Stand, passing the bank and airline office on the way. Like a plague of locusts, **cycle-rickshaws** harass indiscriminately; most will settle for 50% of the price first quoted. **Auto-rickshaws** will grudgingly take Rs5 per km if only you could get them to gauge distances realistically—there are no meters here. **Taxis** are worst of all, demanding as much a Rs25 per km in town. They congregate in front of larger hotels and the OTDC office.

Tourist Office: Government of Orissa Tourist Office, 5 Jayadev Nagar (tel. 431299). Head south down Puri Rd. and turn right. The tourist office is 50m down the street on the left. The helpful, patient staff shares their wealth of pamphlets—be sure to ask for a brochure listing the Buddhist relics of Orissa. Open M-Sa 10am-

5pm. Counters at the airport (tel. 404006) and railway station (tel. 404715) open 24hr. **OTDC** (tel. 431515), on the corner of Puri Rd. and Jayadev Nagar, behind the Panthanivas Tourist Bungalow, arranges cheap, rushed tours of Bhubaneswar, Puri, and Konark. Contact Transport Unit Panthanivas (tel. 431515). **Government of India Tourist Office,** B-21 Kalpana Area (tel. 432203). From the railway station, take the last left before the fork that leads to Puri Rd.; the office is on a side road 750m on the right. Friendly staff provides a plethora of information on other parts of the country from a slightly out-of-date computer database. Open M-F 10am-5pm.

Budget Travel: Swosti Travels, 103 Jan Path (tel. 508738; fax 520796; email swost@cal.vsnl.net.in). Next to the Hotel Swosti. From Station Sq., walk north on Jan Path. Reputable and professional. Open M-Sa 9:30am-6pm.

Immigration Office: Foreigners Registration Office, District Intelligence Bureau, Sahid Nagar (tel. 403399). From Station Sq. take a rickshaw 3km north on Jan Path to the Jan Path-NH5 intersection. On the left is the FRO, inside the building of the Superintendent of Police. Head to Delhi for visa extensions. Open M-Sa 10am-5pm.

Currency Exchange: State Bank of India, Main Branch, Raj Path (foreign exchange tel. 403810). A short walk from Raj Mahal Sq., on Raj Path, across from Capital Market. No commission. Open M-F 10am-2pm, Sa 10am-noon.

Bookstore: Modern Book Depot (tel. 502373), on the right side of Station Sq. Well-stocked and presided over by a knowledgeable, avuncular owner. Maps and a section on Orissan history and culture. Open M-Sa 9:30am-1:30pm and 4:30-9pm.

Library: Harekrishna Mahtab State Library and **Bhubaneswar Public Library,** Sachivalaya Marg (tel. 404315). From Station Sq., head northwest on Mahatma Gandhi Marg until you reach Sachivalaya Marg. Turn right; the library complex is 300m on the left, across from Keshari Talkies. To even enter the research facilities and reading room, written permission must be obtained from the librarian, who sits down the hall to the right. Open M-F and alternate Sa 8am-8pm.

Market: Capital Market, Unit 2, Raj Path, across from the Indian Airlines office. High-quality market selling handicrafts, clothing, and fresh fruit and vegetables. Open Tu-Su 9am-8pm. Inspiration and other necessities available at the **Mom and Pop** store, ½ block past Panthanivas, on the right. Open daily 7am-10:30pm.

Pharmacy: Iswar Medical, Ashok Nagar (tel. 400359), half a block north of Raj Mahal Sq. Open daily 8am-10:30pm. Capital Hospital's pharmacy is open 24hr.

Hospital: Capital Hospital, Unit 6 (tel. 400688). From Raj Mahal Sq., proceed south on Jan Path. After 1 long block, turn right and head west on Udyan Marg, past the intersection of Udyan Marg and Sachivalaya Marg. A wee bit to the left is the 24hr. **government hospital.** English-speaking staff. **Ayurvedic Hospital,** Malisha Sq. (tel. 432347). A short distance to the east of Vivekananda Marg, across from the Rameswar temple.

Emergency: Police, Control Room (tel. 53377). **Ambulance,** tel. 400076.

Post Office: GPO, PMG Sq. (tel. 454387), on the corner of Mahatma Gandhi Marg and Sachivalaya Marg. From the big horse statue in Station Sq., cross Jan Path and walk to the end corner of Mahatma Gandhi Marg. Inside the courtyard, on the right. *Poste Restante* at window 6. Open daily 10am-5pm. **Postal Code:** 751001.

Internet: Com-Cyber Tech, Ashoka Market (tel. 425180), on the southeast corner of Station Sq. Internet access (Rs5 per min.) and email (send only, Rs20 per page). Open M-Sa 9am-7:30pm, Su 2-7:30pm.

Telephones: The railway station's **STD/ISD** booth is open 4am-midnight. **Central Telegraph Office,** inside the GPO. Open daily 8am-8pm. **Telephone Code:** 0674.

ACCOMMODATIONS

Bhubaneswar—along with Orissa in general—has become a hip destination, and hotels have evolved to meet the demands of foreign travelers with large-ish wallets.

Hotel Raj Mahal, Raj Mahal Sq. (tel. 402448), at the corner of Jan Path and Raj Path. Airy hallways, clean, cool rooms, balconies, a new restaurant, a central location. All rooms have attached baths. Singles Rs100; doubles Rs150. Extra person Rs20.

Hotel Swagat, Cuttack Rd. (tel. 416686 or 425879). Exit the east side of the railway station (not the main exit facing Station Sq.), turn right, and walk 5min. Clean rooms, affordable prices. Restaurant inside. No visitors after 10pm. Singles Rs125; doubles with bath Rs160, with TV Rs225, with A/C Rs475; quads Rs160.

Hotel Pushpak, Kalpana Sq. (tel. 415545 or 415943). At the corner of Raj Path and Cuttack Rd. When Happy Hour begins, the party spills out into the hallway, even though the rooms are large, clean, and well-ventilated. Restaurant and full bar downstairs, complete with color TV screaming Hindi hits (11am-11pm). Room service will bring the drinks until midnight, and even later if you're buying. Singles with bath Rs100; doubles with bath Rs150, with A/C and TV Rs350.

Bhubaneswar Hotel, Cuttack Rd. (tel. 416977). Just past Swagat. Small, cubical rooms and a troupe of persistent rickshaw-*wallahs* outside. Attached restaurant and travel counter (rail and air reservations). Singles with bath Rs125, with bath and TV Rs150; doubles Rs175/200.

FOOD

Traditional Orissan cuisine, served in small *ginas* arranged on a large *thali,* is lightly spiced. Bhubaneswar is also the perfect place to sample this toned-down version of South Indian food. The entirety of Jan Path and Raj Path, culminating in the Kalpana Sq. area, offers delicious vegetarian and non-vegetarian choices for under Rs50.

Cook's Kitchen/Restaurant, 260 Bapuji Nagar. From Station Sq., turn left, travel south on Jan Path, and take the third left past Raj Mahal Sq. Take advantage of the street-side "take away" kitchen offering well-endowed curries (Rs18 and up), or be initiated into Cook's vividly clean and A/C restaurant, on the first floor of the Blue Heaven Hotel. Here, the savory Navaratna Curry (Rs25) melts in your mouth, and the "Cook's specials" are special indeed. Open daily 10:30am-10:30pm.

Hotel Suruchi, Raj Path. Several blocks northwest of Raj Mahal Sq., across from the State Bank of India. Steep your senses in its spacious atmosphere and stuff your stomach with the suggested Rs24 Suruchi Special, simply a scoop of rice with *puri* and *ginas* swimming in spicy, strictly veg. South Indian sauces. Speedy service. Swarming with local families. Open daily 7am-10:30pm.

Hare Krishna Restaurant, Lalch and Market Complex, Master Canteen. Directly across from Hotel Jajati. From the railway station, walk up to Station Sq. and turn right onto Master Canteen. A/C dining room. No meat or alcohol allowed. Open daily 11am-3pm and 7-10:30pm.

Shanti Restaurant, 50 Ashok Nagar (tel. 418041), one flight up. A quiet A/C family restaurant as peaceful as the name implies. A huge menu with a variety of soups (Rs15-30), *dal* fry (Rs8), and tasty kebabs (from Rs55), as well as Chinese and Continental. Open daily 11am-11pm.

SIGHTS

Hindu Temples

Location: *Old Town, south of the Railway Station. Most of the major temples are in the area around the Bindu Sagar.* **Hours:** *All temples open dawn-dusk.*

It is said that there are more ancient temples in Orissa than in the rest of North India put together. Although more monumental and more famous individual temples stand in Puri and Konark, Bhubaneswar has Orissa's fullest collection. The sculptures on its temples, carved between the 7th and 12th centuries under several Hindu dynasties, tell the story of Hinduism's resurgence. Purportedly, the figure of a lion pouncing on an elephant represents Hinduism's triumph over Buddhism. Lakulisa, a 5th-century Shaiva saint who converted many Orissans, also appears often. Most of Bhubaneswar's temples are dedicated to Shiva, whose cult remains an important part of the lives of most men in the region. The densest concentration of temples, around the center of the Old Town, can be covered in a few hours. **Guides** roam the temple circuit soliciting customers, but they are of little use. Watch out for the guys with a "temple register" listing contributions made by foreign visitors—it's a scam. Certified guides can be hired from the state tourism office.

EAST INDIA

An obvious landmark, the large green tank at the foot of Vivekananda Marg plays a central religious role. The waters of the **Bindu Sagar** (Ocean-Drop Tank) supposedly contain drops from all the holy pools and streams of India. Early-morning bathers take advantage of the blessings the waters bestow (when the tank isn't bone dry on account of a tardy monsoon), and an image of Lord Tribhubaneswar takes a dip in the tank during the local Cart Festival in March or April.

The oldest and best-preserved of the early group of Orissan temples can be reached by turning down the road to the left just before the tank as you approach from the New Town. Not far on the left is the boxy 7th-century **Parsurameswar Temple,** which has many of the common features of early temples, including a small, squat *shikhara* and an uncarved roof over the porch. The window-like shapes that frame many of its sculptures derive from an even earlier artistic touch used in Buddhist temples. At the back, on the left side of the rear entrance, a *linga,* with 1000 tiny *lingas* carved on it, stands sentinel.

The **Mukteswar Temple,** a short walk down the road from the Parsurameswar Temple, was built 300 years later. Here, in contrast to the Parsurameswar's single building, a whole landscape of small monuments rises from the complex, which has a bold, U-shaped archway in front and a lotus carved into the porch's ceiling. The Mukteswar is considered one of the finest Orissan temples, both for its carvings and its well-preserved state. From the Mukteswar Temple, turn left past the trinket stands and cold drink shops to reach the whitewashed and very active **Kedareswar Temple.** To reach the **Rajarani Temple** (11th century), go up the road behind the Mukteswar Temple, then turn right on the large Tankapani Rd. After a five-minute walk, you will see the temple on the right, at the back of a rectangular park. Originally dedicated to a raja and rani now long out of power, the defunct temple is an Archaeological Survey-administered monument. The *shikhara* is multiplied in the *shekhari* style, with miniature *shikharas* projecting from it on all sides. Though common in other parts of India, this type of tower is rare in Orissa. The carvings of the *dikpalas,* the guardians of the eight points of the compass, are the best around. These ancient Vedic gods stand stiffly with flags, thunderbolts, and nooses.

The chunky, cement-splotched **Bhaskareswar Temple,** a short rickshaw ride farther down Tankapani Rd. past the sewage canal, is no artistic triumph, but it contains a 3m *linga* encased in what is thought to be a 3rd-century BC Ashokan column. Wander down a cow-trampled lane to the right after the Bhaskareswar Temple to the 9th-century **Brahmeswar Temple,** which is unfortunately closed to non-Hindus. The temple has smaller Shiva shrines at the four corners of its compound. Some of the carvings illustrate temple dancers who were "married" to the deity here and worked in the temple, often having to perform "favors" for local men in exchange for "contributions" to the temple.

Bhubaneswar's biggest bouquet of flags flies atop the **Lingaraj Temple,** to the south of the Bindu Sagar. The Lingaraj is one of Orissa's great temples, notable especially for the balanced placement of sculpture on its 45m spire. Built around 1100 AD, it has the full four-roomed structure: a sanctum (under the spire), a porch, a dance hall, and an offering hall. Shiva is worshipped here in the form of Tribhubaneswar, "Lord of Three Worlds," from whom Bhubaneswar takes its name. The temple is known as Lingaraj, however, derived from an earlier name for Shiva. The temple compound contains a jungle of ornate stonework—more than 50 smaller temples are strewn around the main one. The second-largest temple in the compound, in front of the main temple to the right, is devoted to Shiva's consort Parvati. The entire temple compound is closed to non-Hindus, but the British smugly built a **viewing platform** right next to the wall, which still stands to provide tourists their token look.

The **Vaital Temple,** sunk in the ground at a crossroads on the western side of the Bindu Sagar, differs from the other temples. Its oblong, rounded *shikhara* is from a very old style, adapted from Buddhist temple design and obsolete by the time Bhubaneswar's other temples were built. Take a flashlight with you to illuminate the gory carvings inside the temple, depicting scenes of human sacrifice and the skull-clad goddess Chamunda with her attendant owl and jackal. Chamunda is a popular form

Orissan Temple Architecture

Until 1568, the Kalinga kings were able to stave off temple-razing Muslim invasions, allowing Orissa to develop a distinctive architectural style and more beautiful examples of old stone Hindu temples than any other region of northern India.

The most important part of a temple was the *deul* (inner sanctum), which housed an image of the deity. The *deul* was usually small, dark, and square, but on top of it rose a huge, pyramidal, and elaborately carved *shikhara* (spire). The *shikhara* was built with vertical ridges; early designs had three on each side, but later ones had five, seven, or even nine bands. Atop the *shikhara* hovered a lotus-shaped stone called an *amlaka*. Above that was a small pot, and finally the deity's weapon: a trident on Shiva temples and a discus for Vishnu.

Adjoining the *deul* was a rectangular *jagamohana* (assembly hall). These "porches" had simpler roofs than the *shikharas* of sanctums, signaling lesser importance. Yet in time they too grew spires, made of flat stones arching into a steep pyramid. Bigger temples added more rooms in single file behind the *jagamohana*: first a *nata mandir* (dance hall), then a *bhoga mandir* (offering hall).

The sculpture that decorated the architecture was equally complex. Aside from the consecrated images in the sanctum, there were symbols relevant to the temple itself (such as guardian figures) and illustrations of legends. Early temples had only their outsides lavishly ornamented; later, the interiors were embellished. Orissan sculptures tend to be rounder and deeper than those in other parts of India. Since so much sculpture had to be produced to cover the walls of huge temples, much of it appears amateurish, but the authentic wonders, such as the Jagannath Temple in Puri and the Sun Temple in Konark, were obviously the result of some inspired chiseling.

of Durga nowadays, but in the 8th century when the Vaital Temple was built she was worshipped by Tantric cults. Beside the Vaital Temple is the **Sisireswar Temple,** at first sight a small replica of Vaital, but in fact, a near-duplicate of the nearby **Markandeswar Temple.** In both twin temples, the images in niches were carved directly into the temple walls, a practice later discontinued.

Museums

The **State Museum,** on Puri Rd., a short walk from Kalpana Sq., displays a small collection of wonderfully illuminated palm leaf manuscripts, a roomful of traditional Orissan musical instruments and ethnographic exhibits on the region's tribal people, and heaps of orphaned temple sculptures and friezes. *(Open Tu-Su 10am-1pm and 2-5pm; admission Rs1.)* At the **Tribal Research Institute** (tel. 403649), National Highway 5, 2km east of the Baramunda Bus Station, rooms full of bureaucrats sort papers in the front building, while in the jungly garden behind, *adivasi* experts put the finishing touches on replicas of traditional tribal buildings. *(Open M-Sa 10am-5pm; free.)*

▧ Near Bhubaneswar

■ Dhauli ଧଉଳି

The hill of Dhauli, 8km south of Bhubaneswar on the Puri road, marks Orissa's claim to fame in world history. The Mauryan emperor Ashoka the Terrible defeated the Kalingas in a horrific battle here in 261 BC, and he was so appalled by the bloodshed that he converted to nonviolent Buddhism, becoming Ashoka the Righteous. A long-winded **rock edict** in Brahmi script at the foot of Dhauli Hill explains Ashoka's theory of government by *dharma* (an English translation is posted near these inscriptions). Coming out of the rock above is a gentle and elegantly sculpted head and forepart of an **elephant,** one of the earliest stone carvings of embryonic Buddhist India. On the summit of Dhauli hill, which affords fantastic views of Bhubaneswar and the sandy River Durga, sits the **Shanti Stupa** (Peace Pagoda), built by Japanese Buddhists who had erected a similar structure in Rajgir, Bihar. Auto-rickshaws will make the round-trip to Dhauli from Bhubaneswar (Rs100). Buses (Rs5) deposit passengers 3km short of the hill. Alternatively, Dhauli is on the guided bus tour itinerary (see Tourist Office). The sites at Dhauli are open daily from 5am to 8pm and are free.

■ Udaigiri ଉଦୟଗିରି and Khandagiri Caves ଖଣ୍ଡଗିରି

More vestiges of antiquity can be found at the Udaigiri and Khandagiri Caves, 6km west of Bhubaneswar, less than 1km off National Highway 5 past Baramunda Bus Station. These twin hills contain 33 small niches cut into rock which served as sacred retreats for Jain ascetics in the first and 2nd centuries BC. A road now divides the Udaigiri caves (on the right) from the Khandagiri caves (on the left). Artisans decorated these caves with sculptures large and small. Of those that remain, the best sculptures are in and around Cave 1 at Udaigiri, the two-storied **Rani Gumpha** (Queen's Cave), with its faceless guardians. Cave 12 is carved as the gaping mouth of a tiger. Cave 14, the **Hathi Gumpha** (Elephant Cave), has an inscription on its ceiling from King Kharavela of the Chedi Dynasty, perhaps the greatest of Kalinga kings and the patron of the caves. Jain legends, mythology, and iconography linger in **Rani Nur** and **Ganesh Gumpha** (Cave 10). The top of the hill, directly above this cave, has the foundation of an old building that was probably a Jain hall of worship. The caves of Khandagiri are not as well-carved, though an active **Jain temple** sits at the top of the hill. From it, there's a great view of Bhubaneswar, including the Lingaraj Temple and Dhauli Hill in the distance. The best preserved carvings at Khandagiri are in **Cave 3.**

The caves are open daily from 6am to 6pm (Rs2 for both sites), and can be reached from Bhubaneswar by **auto-rickshaw** (Rs80). If you don't bring peanuts, be prepared to face down the tiny, hungry baby monkeys.

■ Puri ପୁରୀ

To travel to Puri is to experience healing, be it through rest, religion, or recreational drugs. A seaside resort whose cleansing Bay of Bengal waters soothe the weariness of traveling souls, Puri is also a sacred Hindu pilgrimage site and a center for *chillum*-smoking *sadhus* and *sadhu*-wannabes. The city has been dominated since the 12th century by the powerful temple of Lord Jagannath, which rises above the crowded old town.

Three varieties of visitors come here—international travelers, tourists from other parts of India, and pilgrims from various aspects of Hindudom. Most foreign travelers typically escape to the eastern edge of town, where the relative calm and simplicity of day-to-day beach life and hotels and restaurants devoted to pampering them make for a comfortable holiday, while groups of extroverted middle-class Bengalis travel in jam-packed, frenetic tour buses for a harried and often hurried (but thorough) vacation of resort rest, *dharma* duty, and temple touring. The third contingent consists of the thousands of focused Jagannath worshipers who fill the eight *dharamshalas* that line the busy Grand Ave., leading directly to the temple.

Puri is a good place to relax from the travails of Indian travel, to walk sandy beaches and temples, or to practice your religious duties and devotions. It is not a town that many pass through; most come to Puri very deliberately and, in one way or another, find themselves moved by its healing intensity.

ORIENTATION

Puri's busiest area is on **Grand Avenue,** which runs east-west through the northern (inland) part of town, arching southwest near the **Jagannath Temple** to become **Swargardwar Road.** On its southern side, Puri is washed by the Bay of Bengal. Along the shore runs **Chakratirtha (C.T.) Road,** concentrated with budget hotels. As it moves west, C.T. Rd. becomes **VIP Road** and then **Marine Parade Road.**

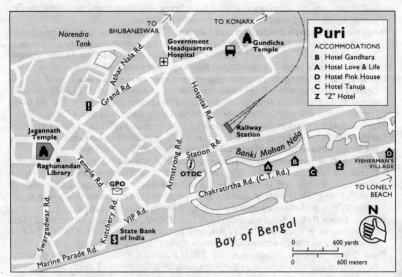

PRACTICAL INFORMATION

Trains: Puri Railway Station, Station Rd. At the junction of Hospital Rd. and Station Rd. Regular trains run from Puri to Bhubaneswar, though the bus is more convenient. To: **Calcutta** (*Puri-Howrah Exp.* 8008, 6:30pm; *Jagannath Exp.* 8410, 9:05pm, 11hr., Rs112/546 for 2nd/1st class) and **Delhi** (*Purushottam Exp.* 2801, 8:10pm, 33hr., Rs249 for 2nd class). The 2nd class booking office is open 24hr. Ask about the tourist quota at the reservation counter. Open M-Sa 8am-8pm, Su 8am-1pm. Foreign non-reserved tickets sold at window 7.

Buses: New Bus Stand, Grand Rd. At the eastern corner of Grand Rd., past Canara Bank. Buses to **Konark** (every 15min., 6am-7pm, 30min., Rs8). Numerous **private companies** (arranged from tour agencies or hotel desks) operate interstate buses. To: **Bhubaneswar** (every 5min., 1½hr., Rs13); **Calcutta** (1:30pm, 12hr., Rs140); **Cuttack** (frequent, 2hr., Rs20).

Local Transportation: Cycle- and auto-rickshaws ride from one corner of Puri to another for not more than Rs20—the going Indian price is Rs5 per km; foreigners are charged more. Unmetered **taxis** can be arranged by your hotel or travel agent. Though they are cheap (fares under Rs5), **local buses** rarely run properly, if at all.

Cycle Rental: For those who wish to take their transport (and life) into their own hands, a plethora of **bicycle, scooter,** and **motorcycle** rentals await. **Aju's,** east on C.T. Rd. across from the Holiday Home, has bicycles (Rs15 per day), Sunys (Rs150-200 per day), medium-sized motorcycles (Rs250 per day), and attractive Enfield Bullets for the motorcycle-experienced (Rs250 per day). Driver's license and passport required for all rentals. Open daily 6am-8pm.

Tourist Office: Government of Orissa Tourist Office, Station Rd. (tel. 22664). From the railway station, follow Station Rd. west 500m. The office is on the right just before VIP Rd. Upstairs, a tiny branch of the State Museum displays local handicrafts and photos of the Rath Yatra. Both open M-Sa 10am-5pm.

Budget Travel: Om Travels, C.T. Rd. Ashram/travel agency/religious bookshop offers standard Orissa Tourism-run tours of the area. Open daily 6am-10pm. Accepts MC, Visa. **Gandhara International** (tel. 24623; fax 25909), in front of Hotel Gandhara, provides a wide variety of services including rail and international flight booking. Open daily 8am-8pm. AmEx, MC, Visa.

Currency Exchange: State Bank of India, VIP Rd. (tel. 23995 or 23682). From the railway station, head west on Station Rd., turn left onto Armstrong Rd. and left again onto VIP Rd. and follow it south past the Bose statue. No commission. Open

M-F 10am-2pm, Sa 10am-noon. **Hotel Gandhara** will change any traveler's check, but at slightly less favorable rates. Open daily 8am-8pm.

Bookstore: Loknath Bookshop and Library, C.T. Rd., toward the fisherman's village. Next door to Raju's Restaurant. Books can be rented (Rs10 per day, with a Rs300 deposit) or purchased (Rs800). Passport photos (Rs15 for 3) and stamps sold. Open daily Sept.-Apr. 9am-9pm; May-Aug. 8am-noon and 3-8pm.

Library: Puri Library, Temple Rd., above the Government of Orissa Tourist Office. Open Tu-Su 11am-6pm. **Raghunandan Library,** Grand Rd. (tel. 22252), straight across from Jagannath Temple. Historically a monastery and library, the 1st floor houses books and palmleaf manuscripts. Open daily 8am-noon and 4-7pm.

Market: Laxmi Market, west on Grand Rd. The best and priciest of Puri's markets sells fresh fruits and vegetables, fish, and more. A bit farther east on Grand Rd. is the smaller **Municipality Market.** Both open daily 6:30am-10:30pm.

Hospital: Government Headquarters Hospital, Grand Rd. (tel. 22124). From Jagannath Temple, go 1.5km east on Grand Rd., past Om Services and the Hotel Shreeram. To the left is the GHH, an old and dilapidated facility that is best avoided. English is barely spoken and the best aspect about this place is its decently run **ambulance service** (tel. 102). **Emergency:** tel. 22094.

Police: Town Police Station, Grand Rd. (tel. 22039), near Jagannath Temple. The control room is open 24hr. **C.T. Rd.** area police station (tel. 23485). **If a beach emergency occurs, contact City Beach Police** (tel. 22025, emergency tel. 100).

Post Office: GPO, Kutchery Rd. (tel. 22051). From C.T. Rd., walk west past the Bose statue and turn right after the State Bank of India. Proceed north on Kutchery Rd. The GPO will be visible down the first street to the left. *Poste Restante* available. Stamps sold M-Sa 9am-6pm, Su 3-5:30pm. Other enquiries M-Sa 10am-6pm, Su 3-5:30pm. **Postal Code:** 752001.

Telephones: Most **STD/ISD** booths are open 24hr. in season. **Telegraph Office,** Chandan Hazuri Ln. (tel. 22806), across from the Ramakrishna Mission. Open M-Sa 7am-10pm, Su 8am-3:30pm. **Telephone Code:** 06752.

ACCOMMODATIONS

Budget accommodations are concentrated around **C.T. Rd.,** a small stretch of beach accessed most conveniently by the rickshaw-*wallahs* who scamper to attract every weary soul who stumbles off the bus from Bhubaneswar. They play a commission game with some hotel owners who kick back up to 50% of the rent—whatever you do, don't pay for more than one night in advance. When approached by such a *wallah*, announce confidently that you want to go to C.T. Rd.

Hotel Love & Life, C.T. Rd. (tel. 24433; fax 26093). On the town end of C.T. Rd., across the street from a path to the beach. A perennial favorite of travelers. Whether a bed in the comfortably small dormitory (Rs30), the comfortably small rooms in the 3-story building, or the cozy cottages out back, the place promises sweet dreams. Singles Rs80-125; doubles Rs100-250; cottages (double occupancy) Rs200-250, with A/C Rs450-600.

Hotel Gandhara, C.T. Rd. (tel. 24117; fax 25909), next to Hotel Love & Life. In front, an early 19th-century colonial bungalow contains dormitory and budget rooms; behind, a new 5-story building houses fancier people in pricier accommodations. Dobermans Sakura and Limca are part of the hotel and the family. All rooms have attached bath. Check-out 9am. Dorm beds Rs30. Singles Rs110; doubles Rs100-550, with A/C Rs750. AmEx, MC, Visa.

"Z" Hotel, C.T. Rd. (tel. 22554). Walk east of Hotel Gandhara past Restaurant Peace. Once home to a maharaja of Puri, this enormous open-air old structure draws many a tourist with its seaview rooms, the serenity of its multicolored garden, and its direct beach access. "Z" (pronounced "zed" by everyone but the Americans) comes complete with an excellent cook, continual room service, and friendly, accommodating staff. Mosquito nets. Dorm beds (women only) Rs50. Singles with bath Rs150; doubles Rs200, with bath Rs400.

Hotel Pink House, C.T. Rd. (tel. 22253), 5min. south of C.T. Rd. A bit run down from constant sea winds, this ultra-budget cottage offers the open Bay of Bengal for next to nothing. Rooms open directly onto the beach, the spirit of which pervades every nook and cranny, including the straw-roofed restaurant. Road-weary Suny cycles lounge around awaiting rental (Rs125-200). Mosquito nets, coils, and bug spray available. Doubles Rs150, with bath; triples Rs225.

Hotel Tanuja, C.T. Rd. (tel. 24823 or 24974). Across from Harry's Cafe and the Mickey Mouse Restaurant. Alcohol, smoking, and visitors are allowed in the rooms. A common TV room, laundry service, and in-house postal service complete the offerings. The attendant Tanuja Tribe Tour agency provides extensive and affordable trips and more costly wild adventure tours. Mosquito nets. Singles Rs50; doubles Rs60, with bath Rs150.

FOOD

"Z" Hotel Restaurant, C.T. Rd. The kitchen staff does a superlative job with local seafood, cooking up a spicy fish curry (Rs30) with the day's catch. The veg. *navratnan* (Rs25) and *aloo dum* (Rs12) stand out, and the beer (Rs60) is always chilled. Open daily 7am-3pm and 6-10pm.

Chung Wah, VIP Rd. (tel. 23397), walk west on C.T. Rd. and take a right on VIP Rd. Less than 1km farther, on the left side of the street. One of the cleanest and coolest spots in Puri. Sink into the squishy chairs and choose from an array of authentic flavors of the Middle Kingdom. Veg. dishes (Rs20-25). Garlic fish (Rs52) available on special request. Open daily 7-10am, 11:30am-3pm, 4:30-6pm, and 6:30-10:30pm.

Mickey Mouse Restaurant, C.T. Rd. (tel. 24146), diagonally across the street from the "Z" Hotel. A reggae-playin', international-copyright-violatin' hippy holdover. Try 6 different *lassi*s (Rs12), 18 custard varieties (Rs10-25), or one of 30 pancake permutations. Coffee and honey combo (Rs12) is a must. Complete *thalis* Rs14. Alcohol not sold here but may be brought in. Open daily 6am-11pm.

Harry's Cafe, C.T. Rd. (tel. 23852). near the "Z" Hotel. Six huge green picnic tables sit coolly amidst swirls of incense, coconut milkshakes (Rs15) and chocolate (Rs20) pancakes. No alcohol served. Open daily 8am-10pm.

Wild Grass, VIP Rd. (tel. 23656), around the corner from Chung Wah. An open-air courtyard restaurant inspired by the indigenous people's movement. Serves local food at non-local prices (*thalis* Rs40). Thatched roofs and tribal drawings evoke Orissa's "primitives." The restaurant hypes itself as "eco-friendly." What does that mean? "It means we provide a natural environment for eating," says the manager, but waiters have few qualms about tossing bottle caps into the garden. Open daily 11:30am-2:30pm and 7-10:30pm.

SIGHTS

Junagadh Temple

Every pilgrim's entrance into Puri is initiated by a short devotional stop in front of the main *simhadwara* (lion gate), the eastern and most important entrance to the spectacular Jagannath Temple, which rises to 65m. It's *the* feature of the Puri skyline, and it's obvious that this pilgrimage town is ruled by the "Lord of the Universe," the charcoal-faced Jagannath. Constructed in the early 12th century by the Ganga king Anantavaram Chodaganga, the temple illustrates the might of Orissan temple architecture.

The temple is closed to non-Hindus. Don't take offense—Prime Minister Indira Gandhi herself was denied access because of her marriage to a Parsi. A comprehensive view of the eastern gate, the Jagannath Temple, and the surrounding smaller temples can be had atop the roof of the **Raghunandan Library,** across the street, where travelers are ushered by a palmleaf manuscript expert and a gregarious and capricious congregation of temple monkeys. *(Open daily 8am-noon and 4-7pm.)*

The three roughly hewn but divine inhabitants of the temple look almost abstract: dense, rectangular wooden blocks represent the bodies of **Jagannath,** his brother **Balabhadra,** and his sister **Subhadra.** Tiny arms extend from stumpy legless abdomens and enormous, unblinking eyes glare out from disproportionately-sized and perfectly circular heads. It is said that Lord Jagannath doesn't have eyelids because he wishes to continually look after the well-being of the world. Some say he never

Gods on Wheels

Sweating, singing, shouting, and praying, exuberant crowds move en masse to enact an event of cosmic proportion. The **Rath Yatra** (Cart Festival) of Puri is celebrated two days after the new moon in the month of Ashadh (June-July). The festival day begins with the Gajapati (the King of Puri) making a gesture of *chhera paharna,* ritually "sweeping" the *rathas* (chariots) to symbolize humanity humbling itself in preparation for the mercy and goodwill of Jagannath. As the mesmerizing chants of the *sadhus* and the ecstatic shouts of "Jai Jagannath" fill the frenzied air, Jagannath arrives on the scene to take the yellow-and-red draped seat of pomp in his 13m, 18-wheeled, gold-domed chariot, otherwise known as Nandigosha. Once Balabhadra and Subhadra, the other members of the divine family, are placed in their respective chariots, movement can begin.

On the day of the festival, each of the three deities are pulled by some 4000 devotees from the main gate of the temple east on Grand Ave. As if propelled by divine force, the *ratha* carriers proceed forward on a 3km journey, dragging the newly constructed chariots. The three gods spend a nine-day outing at **Gundicha Ghar** (Garden House), where they eat specially prepared rice cakes and are dressed anew each day. Their symbolic tour of the universe, as erratic and intensely delirious as the trip to the Gundicha Ghar, is completed with a repeat processional performance back to the temple. Nineteenth-century British observers reported that ecstatic devotees would sometimes throw themselves under the wheels of the carts to obtain instant *moksha.* The word "juggernaut" (meaning an object that crushes everything in its path) comes from the god's name.

sleeps. His small arms project outwards in a gesture of unconditional love for his devotees. *Yatripandas* (pilgrimage priests) and other temple priests cite ancient myths to explain the peculiarly shaped forms while many academics suggest that the deities' forms have tribal origins.

Patterned on the same architectural principles as the older Lingaraj Temple in Bhubaneswar, the abode of Jagannath is structurally aligned from east to west. The *bhoga mandir* (offering hall) and *nata mandir* (dance hall) lie nearest to the entrance and were 15th- and 16th-century additions to the original *jagamohana* (assembly hall). The *deul* (inner sanctuary), crowned by a 65m pyramidal roof, signifies the presence of the divine family trio. Surrounded by a 6m wall, the massive temple compound hosts action-packed days of *darshan* and treats worshippers to devotionals and sacred dances at night. The complex employs approximately 6000 temple servants—specially trained temple priests who care to the daily needs of the deity (waking, cleaning, feeding, and dressing), artist communities who produce ritual materials, and thousands who work throughout the days to prepare *prasad* for Jagannath himself. The kitchen to the left of the temple serves meals to 10,000 people daily and up to 25,000 during festival times, such as the Rath Yatra.

ENTERTAINMENT

Warning: The beaches of Puri are generally free of violent crime, but locals still advise against going to the beach alone at night.

Puri's **beaches** are all the entertainment most travelers need. Since much of the water is now filtered with chemical protectants, the beaches are becoming more populated, and unfortunately, are often ravaged by tourists. If you go to **Lonely Beach,** the eastern beach past the fishermen's village, take only lotions and drinking water. Leave valuables in your hotel if it seems trustworthy. If you rent a cycle, take it with you to the water, or you may be hitching a ride back and paying big bucks later.

In a pilgrim city like Puri, there is an abundance of **festivals** during the year, although most locals don't always make them well-known. The grand-daddy of these is the **Rama Yatra Fetsival,** when Lord Jaganath, his brother Balabhadra, and his sister Subhadra are paraded through Puri on large chariots (see above). Puri's **Beach Festival** (held at the end of Janunary), showcases the best of Orissan folk dancing, music and handicrafts. The Government of Orissa Tourist Office also arranges **dance and theatrical programs.** Check their bulletin board for up-to-date information. You can even take an evening stroll along Marine Parade through the Swargadwar area and the **night market** in western Puri. *Saris* color the market landscape, and the bright lights from Puri's burning *ghats* glow in the distance.

■ Konark ଚକାଶାର୍କ

Konark, named for the god who was "sun of the corner," sits along an isolated stretch of the coast. While little is known about the town's ancient history, its Sun Temple is hailed throughout India as one of the country's greatest architectural marvels. Even in ruins, the Sun Temple is magnificent, and since the temple's excavation and restoration in the early 20th century, Konark has become a much-frequented tourist spot. Small hotels have sprung up nearby, and con men and pushy salesmen abound, but Konark and its deserted beaches still manage to make an even quieter and more peaceful retreat than neighboring Puri.

ORIENTATION AND PRACTICAL INFORMATION Konark's streets resemble a "Z." The diagonal stroke is the main street with the temple entrance and a bevy of small shops and eateries; the top stroke is the road to Bhubaneswar; the bottom stroke is the road to Puri, passing beautiful deserted beaches along the way. The **Orissa State Tourism Office** (tel. 35820) is inside Yatri Nivas hotel, around the far side of the temple grounds (open M-Sa 6am-10pm). The **New Bus Stand,** down a side road leading off the intersection just before Yatri Nivas, is not yet completed, so **buses** leave from the middle of that intersection, heading to **Bhubaneswar** (every hr., 5am-6pm, 2hr., Rs15) and **Puri** (every 15min., 5am-8pm, 1hr., Rs9). Labanya Lodge rents **mopeds,** and the tourist office arranges **taxis.** The **post office** is just past the Archaeological Museum, on the right (open M-Sa 9:30am-5pm). Labanya Lodge has a **24hr. STD/ISD** facility. **Canara Bank** (tel. 35828), just past the post office, changes cash and traveler's checks (open M-F 10am-2pm, Sa 10am-noon). **Police:** tel. 35825. **Post Code:** 75211. **Telephone Code:** 06758.

ACCOMMODATIONS AND FOOD Labanya Lodge (tel. 35824), a few minutes out of town on the right side of the road to Puri, is a tasteful salmon block framed by palm trees (singles Rs60; doubles with bath Rs75-150; extra person Rs10). The **Yatri Nivas** (tel. 35820), next to the Archaeological Museum on the road to Bhubaneswar, is a state-run hotel with small, clean rooms around green courtyards (doubles Rs100, with A/C Rs250; quads Rs120). The **Pantha Nivas** (tel. 35831), across from the main entrance to the temple, has less light and a colder feel (doubles Rs160, with A/C Rs450; 20% discount off-season). **Konark Lodge,** on the right just as you enter town from Puri, has dark, basic, not-overclean rooms. It's cheap, though: doubles with bath go for Rs70. Konark's food isn't much to write home about. However, the **Geetanjali Restaurant,** next to the Pantha Nivas and set back in the trees, has great breakfasts (scrambled eggs Rs15, french toast Rs15; open daily 6am-10pm). The **Sun Temple Hotel** (tel. 35876) on the right, just past Pantha Nivas, has the longest, most wide-ranging menu in town, but achingly slow service (open daily 8am-10pm).

SIGHTS Konark's **Sun Temple,** dedicated to Surya, the sun god, once stood along the shore and was used as a navigational aid by European sailors on the way to Calcutta who called it the "Black Temple" to distinguish it from the "White Pagoda," the Jagannath Temple at Puri. *(Admission Rs5, free on Fridays. Temple open daily from dawn to dusk.)* An earlier Surya temple existed at Konark as long ago as the 9th century, but most of the existing structure dates from about 400 years later. Over time, the shoreline has moved more than 3km out to sea, and today, tall pines in the barrens that stretch to the beach conceal the Sun Temple from sea-going vessels, but even though worn and, in places, collapsed, it remains the central feature in the geographic—and economic—landscape of the area. Half the town, it seems, freelances as "guides" to the temple's racy iconography, while the other half aggressively hawks trinkets from streetside stalls which line the street to the **temple entrance,** a gate set in an ancient wall. The ticket booth is up to the left of this gate. Another entrance to the grounds, the next left after the Archaeological Museum, brings you to the outer wall at the complex, but you still have to walk around to the booth to pay.

Whatever your angle of approach, the **jagamohana** (porch, or audience hall), a step pyramid rising up in the middle of the compound, is the most prominent feature of the ruined temple. Originally, the eastward-facing door would catch the light of the morning sun and transmit it to the sanctuary, which stood behind the porch and contained a giant statue of Surya. The sanctuary is now in ruins, and the doorway and interior of the porch have been filled in to support the crumbling structure.

The sanctuary and the porch are mounted on an ornate **platform** carved with 24 giant wheels and, at the front, seven horses: the temple represents Surya's chariot riding across the sky. The spokes of the chariot wheels symbolize the hours of the day, like a clock, and in some cases the images carved on them follow this logic. On one wheel, toward the front of the porch on the south side, the first six spokes are decorated with images of a woman bathing and performing housework, while the last six spokes—the nighttime hours—show her making love to her husband.

The **porch** itself is also carved with erotic images, some tiny and intricate, other clunky and larger-than-life. Behind the porch, steps lead up to three images of Surya in chlorite stone on the south, north, and west sides. Two modern staircases lead from the three statues to the remains of the sanctuary itself. Before the temple was ruined, the sanctuary could only be reached through the porch. Since the porch was filled in, engineers have created this alternate route.

Considering the breathtaking appearance of the Sun Temple overall, the **sanctuary** is rather plain. The statue that once presided here is no more, and archaeologists can only speculate about its design. Some tour guides claim that the statue floated in the air, suspended by powerful magnets lodged in each corner of the sanctuary. It is more likely that it rested on the highly ornate **pedestal** still extant. The frieze on the east side of the pedestal shows King Narasimha, the temple's patron, and his queen. The north and south faces depict the retinues of the queen and king, respectively.

Behind the sanctuary to the southwest are the remains of a temple popularly known as the **Mayadevi Temple.** Formerly thought to be dedicated to one of Surya's wives, it is now believed to be an older Surya temple. The temple is decorated with erotic images. In front of the porch and main sanctuary is a huge **platform** with four thick columns rising up in the corners, enhanced with carvings. Some say it was a dancing hall, but it was more likely used for ritual banquets in honor of the deity.

Various **sculptures** from the temple have been scattered about the site by plunderers and collectors. Some of the finest fragments from the temple, cleaned and polished, now reside in the **Archaeological Museum** (tel. 35822), on the road to Bhubaneswar, down the road from Yatri Nivas. *(Open Sa-Th 10am-5pm.)* Still others are in the Indian Museum in Calcutta and the Victoria and Albert Museum in London. Konark's small **museum,** well worth a visit, sells the Archaeological Survey's informative guide to the Sun Temple for Rs13.

▓ Cuttack କଟକ

Cuttack occupies the top of the Mahanadi River Delta. Here, the inland waters fan out before making their way to the Bay of Bengal. Not much else happens in this crowded metropolis of a quarter-million people. Cuttack had an inauspicious beginning—not long after King Anangabhima Deva III of the Ganga dynasty founded the city, Muslim invaders sacked it. The Marathas and British eventually joined in the fun, but Cuttack's most recent sacker has been Cuttack itself. In 1950, overcrowding and urban frenzy prompted Orissa's leaders to move the state capital from Cuttack to Bhubaneswar, 35km away. Still, Cuttack is bursting with character, for visitors who are willing to make the effort to discover it.

ORIENTATION AND PRACTICAL INFORMATION Cuttack is crammed on to a skinny finger of a peninsula that points northwest. **National Highway 5** and the railway line cut across the southeast; the fort-like **railway station,** complete with battlements, lies east of the **Badambadi Bus Stand.** The main **bazaars** occupy the center of town, the fort and **dock** for boats to Dhabaleshwar lie in the less crowded northwest.

The **Tourist Office,** Link Rd. (tel. 612225), is 1km down from the bus stand, at the left front of the U-shaped Arunodag Market complex (open M-Sa 10am-5pm), and has an outpost at the railway station (open daily 10am-5pm). The **State Bank of India** (tel. 618235), west of Choudhury Bazaar, is next to the High Court; foreign exchange is upstairs (open M-F 10am-2pm, Sa 10am-noon). Passenger **trains** run to **Bhubaneswar** (1:54pm, 1½hr., Rs14); **Calcutta** (3 per day, 8hr., Rs95/471 for 2nd/1st class); and **Puri** (8am, 4:35, and 7:30pm, 4hr., Rs30). You could also hop one of the many trains on the Calcutta-Chennai line that swing by the coast, but you'll pay more (Rs81 for 2nd class to Puri or Bhubaneswar). **Buses** run to **Bhubaneswar** (every hr., 1hr., Rs56 and **Puri** (9pm, 2½hr., Rs20). Private buses leaving from the many private stands nearby are more frequent. **Cycle-rickshaws** will go almost anywhere for under Rs10, and harder-to-find **auto-rickshaws** charge about twice that. The **GPO** (tel. 620799) is 50m off the main intersection in Buxi Bazaar (open M-Sa 10am-5pm, Su 11am-2pm). The **Cuttack Medical College Hospital** (tel. 614499 or 614622) is 20min. down the road past the GPO; its **pharmacy** is open 24 hours. The **STD/ISD booth** in the railway station, opposite the tourist office, is open 5am-11pm. **Police:** Control room (tel. 621477). **Postal Code:** 753001. **Telephone Code:** 0671.

ACCOMMODATIONS AND FOOD A crowd of seedy hotels surrounds the bus stations, and few more hide away in the bazaars. **Hotel Adarsh,** Choudhury Bazaar (tel. 619898), halfway between the mosque and the jewelers, has tiny cubicles, ceiling fans, and hot water in the winter months (singles Rs40, with bath Rs50; doubles with bath Rs60). That famous smile greets you at the **Hotel Mona Lisa** (tel. 621109), rising high over Badambadi Bus Stand. The hotel has hot water buckets and 24hr. checkout. The courtyard decorations reminiscent of I.M. Pei's are the closest you'll get to the Louvre in Cuttack (singles Rs120; doubles Rs150, with A/C Rs300). **Panthanivas** (tel. 621916), in the middle of Buxi Bazaar, is Orissa Tourism's clean, well-maintained hotel with the largest rooms in town, overlooking a courtyard. The 8am check-out, however, is slightly obscene. (Rooms Rs250, with A/C Rs400.)

Cuttack's residents obviously aren't keen on eating out; most restaurants come attached to hotels. The A/C **Panthanivas Hotel Restaurant** (tel. 621916), inside the hotel, dishes a thick, rich Rs20 vegetable *korma* (open daily 7am-10:30pm). **Hotel City Light,** across from the GPO, is popular with the youngsters. City Light makes its rolls (veg. Rs6, chicken Rs9) in the open window to entice passersby. Sit back in the crowded, stylin' dining room and watch the cows come home, which, in this country, may happen sooner than you think. (Open daily 4pm-midnight.)

SIGHTS Even the tourist office admits that Cuttack's blessings do not include world-shaking historical monuments or spectacular natural wonders. **Dhabaleshwar,** the most prominent feature in the State Tourism's pitch, lies across the Mahanadi River. A Shiva temple, a state-run hotel, and an excuse to get out of the house make it a popular outing for locals. Take a town bus to Bidanasi, where small private launches at Cuttack Ghat cross the river to Dhabaleshwar. The road to the *ghat* passes a small, leafy Deer Park, where a sizeable herd of spotted deer munch lazily on local vegetation. Back in town, **Barbati Fort,** near a park in the northwest of town, was reduced to ruins when the British came crashing in. Only a small pile of stones, marred by graffiti, remains.

■ Near Cuttack: Lalitagiri ଲଳିତଗିରି, Udayagiri ଉଦୟଗିରି, and Ratnagiri ରତ୍ନଗିରି

While the towering temples of Bhubaneswar, Konark, and Puri highlight Orissa's rich Hindu past and shape its so-called "Golden Triangle of Tourism," Orissa boasts a fascinating Buddhist heritage as well. Forming their own triangle of sorts, Udayagiri, Lalitagiri, and Ratnagiri stand as remarkable ancient monuments to a culture steeped in art and learning. **Lalitagiri's** first-century ruins include a large brick monastery, several stupas, and various other artifacts in various stages of discovery and recovery. The ruins at **Udayagiri** are a good several centuries younger than their counterparts in Ratnagiri and Lalitagiri, and comprise Orissa's largest Buddhist site, replete with stupa, brick monastery, and stone step-well, as well as some splendid hilltop Bodhisattva and Dhyani Buddha sculptures. Like its be-*giri*'d neighbors, **Ratnagiri** too features monasteries, stupas, shrines, sculpture and a sizeable Siddhartha statue. The university had its origins as a center of Mahayana Buddhism, but in the 9th century shifted its focus to Buddhism's Tantric form. Since all three locations are still active excavation sites, they provide great opportunities to view ancient relics *au naturel.*

All three sights can be seen in a day. From the private bus yard behind Cuttack's Government Bus Stand, take the 43km (1hr.) ride to **Chandikol,** 7, 9, and 12km respectively from Lalitagiri, Udayagiri, and Ratnagiri. Tempos by the bus stand make the journey to Ratnagiri and stop at Udayagiri on the way back (Rs200 round-trip). To add Lalitagiri, add an additional Rs50-100. A cheaper (but more time-consuming) method involves boarding tempos ferrying locals to villages near the sites, which can decrease costs dramatically (the entire circuit can be completed for under Rs20). The surrounding countryside is some of the most beautiful in India. However you travel, bring plenty of water—*dhabas* are ubiquitous in Chandikol, but mineral water is scarce. All sites are open daily dawn to dusk. Admission is free.

Forgotten Gandhi

After his assassination in Delhi on January 30, 1948, Mohandas K. Gandhi was cremated on a pyre there next to the Yamuna River. His ashes were divided into about two dozen lots, and sealed in as many ceremonial wooden coffins. These were then sent to India's holiest places, where they were scattered over the most sacred rivers and revered *ghats.* Incredibly, someone overlooked one batch of Gandhi's ashes, and for nearly 50 years the remains remained locked up in a safe deposit box at the State Bank of India office in Cuttack, Orissa. No one knows how the ashes were forgotten—the transfer of the Orissan capital from Cuttack to Bhubaneswar in 1950 may have had something to do with it, but more likely, bureaucratic inertia is to blame. Word of the lost ashes began to circulate in the early 90s. One of Gandhi's great-grandchildren attempted to claim them, but without a receipt State Bank officials were unwilling to give up the goods. After drawn-out legal proceedings, the Supreme Court in 1996 affirmed the authenticity of the ashes and ordered that they be turned over to the Gandhi family. Bank officials, still fretting over the missing receipt, dug the ashes out of the vault and turned them over to a heavily armed military unit for delivery by rail to Allahabad, where Gandhi's great-grandson poured them into the Ganga.

Bihar बिहार

Bihar is justly proud of its past. Some of India's most formative events took place in its once-thick forests. The Ganga Valley's eastern region get its name from the word *vihara* (monastery), referring to the secluded centers of Buddhist learning that flourished here during the first millennium. The Buddha gained enlightenment under a

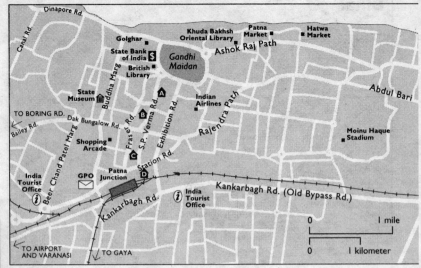

tree in Bodh Gaya, and the Mauryan and Gupta empires both grew from the city of Pataliputra (modern-day Patna).

Few tangible traces are left of Bihar's past glories, however. Bihar is now the least urbanized and poorest state in India. Bihari politics have seen an unending stream of controversy and periodic outbreaks of caste-based violence. In July 1997, Bihar's Chief Minister, Laloo Prasad Yadav, stepped down as a result of another corruption scandal; in his place, he appointed his illiterate wife. Much of the Bihari countryside is effectively ruled by *goondas* with under-the-table connections to politicians, and *dacoits* (bandits) are still part of Bihari life. Partly as a result of this lawlessness, Bihar draws few Western tourists, though travelers pass through on their way to Nepal.

⚜ HIGHLIGHTS OF BIHAR

- The so-called **Lotus Circuit** traces the Buddha's steps through eight of Bihar's towns—**Bodh Gaya** (p. 456), where the Buddha achieved enlightenment; **Rajgir** (p. 461), where his teachings were compiled; **Nalanda** (p. 463), where he studied philosophy; **Vaishali** (p. 460), where some of his ashes are interred; and **Patna** (p. 450), which was a bloated transit hub even then.
- The border town of **Raxaul** (p. 463) is one of the nastiest in India, but it leads to a great country: **Nepal** (p. 792).

■ Patna पटना

Most travelers visit Patna, the capital of the much-maligned Bihar, on their way to or from Nepal or while they're on the Buddhist pilgrim circuit. Despite the city's off-beat attractions and rowdy markets, many find its essence captured in the name of one of its major streets—Boring Road. All this is in spite of Patna's illustrious past—Patna was, in a way, the first capital city of India. The Mauryan Empire was seated here, and the Guptas, too, made it their capital. But Pataliputra, as it was called in antiquity, was abandoned after the decline of the Guptas and only refounded, as Patna, in 1541 by Sher Shah Suri, rival of the Mughals. Patna became a regional center for the Mughals and the British—the East India Company's largest opium warehouses are here, now converted (vice for vice) into a state government printing office.

ORIENTATION

Patna stretches along the south bank of the mighty Ganga, and getting from east to west is a road trip in itself. **Ashok Raj Path** is the main thoroughfare, sticking close to the river the whole way, while **Kankar Bagh Road (Old Bypass Road)** covers the same distance on the southern side of the city, just south of the railroad tracks. The east end of town is Old Patna, with many small, creaky lanes. Most trains stop at the west end's **Patna Junction Station. Fraser Road,** where Patna's hotels, restaurants, and other conveniences are concentrated, runs straight north from the station. The **Gandhi Maidan,** a large park north of Fraser Rd. (touching Ashok Raj Path), is a major landmark and local transportation hub. Next to the railway station, **Station Road** leads west to the **bus station** and various government buildings.

PRACTICAL INFORMATION

Airport: Patna Airport, 6km from the railway station (Rs150 by taxi, Rs50 by auto-rickshaw, and Rs25 by cycle-rickshaw). To: **Calcutta** (6 per week, 1hr., US$90); **Delhi** (2-3 per day, 2-3hr., US$130); **Lucknow** (M, W, F, and Sa, 1hr., US$90); **Mumbai** (3 per week, 3hr., US$195); **Varanasi** (1 per day, 45min., US$40). Occasional winter flights to **Kathmandu** (1½hr., US$140). **Indian Airlines,** S. Gandhi Maidan (tel. 222554).

Trains: Patna Junction Station is a major hub. Fares are 2nd/1st class. To: **Calcutta** (*Howrah Exp.* 5050, Th, 1:40am, 10hr.; *Rajdhani Exp.* 2306, 5:30am, 7½hr.; *Poorva Exp.* 2304, 7:45am, 8½hr., Rs125/611); **Gaya** (many, including *Palamau Exp.* 3348, 8:15pm, 2hr., Rs32/173); **Gorakhpur** (*Kashi Exp.* 1027, 1:20pm, 6hr.; *Chauri-Chaura Exp.* 5003, 11:50pm, 6hr.; Rs94/274, connect for trains to Gorakhpur at Varanasi); **Lucknow** (*Amritsar Mail* 3005, 5:02am, 11hr., Rs117/574); **New Jalpaiguri** (*Mahananda Exp./A Link Exp.* 4084, 1am, 14hr.; *Rajdhani Exp.* 2424, 5:17am, 8½hr.; *Northeast Exp.* 5622, 10pm, 12hr., Rs113/556); **Varanasi** (*Amritsar Mail* 3005, 5:02am, 5hr.; *Himgiri Exp.* 3073, W and Sa-Su 10:25am, 4hr.; *Howrah Exp.* 5049, F 10:25am, 4hr.; *Shramjeevi Exp.* 2401, 11:20am, 3hr., Rs62/313).

Buses: The bus stand is 500m west of Patna Junction on Station Rd. To: **Hajipur** (frequent, 6am-6pm, Rs8.50; connect for buses to **Vaishali** and **Sonepur** at Hajipur); **Ranchi** (every hr. 7-10pm, 12hr., Rs139); **Raxaul** (noon, 1pm, and every 30min. 7pm-midnight, 6hr., Rs70); **Siliguri** (1 bus per day from Gandhi Maidan, 4:30pm, Rs139).

Local Transportation: The major hub for **tempos** is Patna Junction; from there you can get tempos to many other places in the city. **Auto-rickshaws** are unmetered and typically shared. Try to bargain or find a group of people going your way.

Tourist Office: State Government Tourist Office, Fraser Rd. (tel. 225295), on the right above the "Grand Hotel" sign, sells maps of Bihar. Open M-Sa 10am-5pm. There's a branch office (tel. 221093) at the entrance to the railway station. Open 24hr. **Government of India Tourist Office,** Sudama Palace Complex, 5th fl., Kankarbagh Rd. (tel. 345776). From the railway station, take a tempo or rickshaw to Kankarbagh Rd., which runs behind the railway station. Located in a 6-story building on the right side near the Jaisarmil Hotel; there is no sign on the street, only on the balcony of the 5th fl. office. Open M-F 9am-6pm, Sa 9am-1pm.

Budget Travel: Royal Nepal Airlines, Dunlop Compound, Fraser Rd. (tel. 231946), just before it makes a right hook. Ultra-knowledgeable staff applies its expertise to all manner of tourist queries and quandaries. If all else fails, they, and they alone, may be able to get you where you need to go.

Currency Exchange: State Bank of India, Gandhi Maidan (tel. 226134). From the railway station, take a tempo (Rs3) to Gandhi Maidan. The bank, a low white concrete bunker at the very beginning of the circle, will be on your left. Open M-F 10:30am-2:30pm, Sa 10:30am-12:30pm.

Luggage Storage: On the right as you exit the railway station. Rs5 the first day, in increasing increments up to one month.

Market: Maurya Lok, Dak Bungalow Rd., is a major shopping center, with clothing stores, hair salons, and fast-food joints.There are several **fruit markets,** including **New Patna Market,** in front of the railway station, and **Patna** and **Hatwa Markets,** on Ashok Raj Path near Gandhi Maidan and the Ganga.

Library: British Library, Bank Rd. (tel. 24198), the street to the left of State Bank of India. One-month membership required, Rs300. Open Tu-Sa 10:30am-6:30pm.

Bookstore: Tricel, Fraser Rd. (tel. 221412), just before Rajasthan Hotel. Small but varied selection. Open M-Sa 10am-8:30pm, Su 4-8:30pm.

Pharmacy: Popular Pharmacy (tel. 226393), on the left of the railway station, across from the mosque. Open 9am-10pm.

Hospital: Raj Lakshmi Nursing Home, Kankarbagh Rd. (tel. 352225 or 354320), 4km east of the Government of India Tourist Office.

Police: Control Room (tel. 223131), on Gandhi Maidan N., next to the white-domed Shri Krishna Memorial Hall.

Emergency: tel. 111.

Post Office: GPO, Station Rd. (tel. 225019 or 224150), near the railway station. Open M-Sa 10am-4:30pm, Su 10am-3pm (stamps only). **Postal Code:** 800001.

Internet: can be accessed from the **British Library** (see above). Rs100 for 30min, Rs50 for members.

Telephones: STD/ISD booth at the GPO is open 24hr. **Telephone Code:** 0612.

ACCOMMODATIONS

When it comes to hotels, everything in Patna conspires against the budget traveler. Many of Patna's cheaper hotels don't have the paperwork necessary to register foreigners, and mid-range hotels are often booked. Still, it is possible to find bargains in the **Fraser Road** area. There is a cluster of budget lodgings on Hotel Ln., a dirty alley that slinks away from Fraser Rd. opposite the bank.

Ruby Hotel, S.P. Verma Rd. A little hard to find; take a rickshaw up to S.P. Verma Rd. The hotel is on the left side before the 2nd big intersection. Extremely laid-back, quiet place. Comfortable beds; some rooms have tiny balconies, although others get stuffy and the fluorescent lighting is a bit harsh. Check-out noon. All rooms have attached bath. Singles Rs50; doubles Rs80.

Hotel Anand Lok, Station Rd. (tel. 223960), is a large white edifice towering over the railway station. A gate by the luggage office leads right to the door. Built for function, not form, and plagued by maintenance problems, the Anand Lok is nonetheless ideally situated for train hoppers. All rooms are spacious and have attached bath. Singles Rs215; doubles Rs295.

Hotel Prakash, Hotel Ln. (tel. 224013 or 223168), off Fraser Rd. The entrance to the alley is near Dilal and Sons, across from the Samrat International on Fraser Rd. There's not much to recommend this place except its proximity to the railway station and its price. Check-out 24hr. All rooms have attached bath. Singles Rs90; doubles Rs140.

Patna Youth Hostel, Fraser Rd., after it jogs right, then left. If you have your own linens, the best bargain in town by far, with beds in 2- and 4-person rooms with attached baths. Kitchen under construction. Max. 7-day stay. Open 24hr. Rooms Rs40; Rs20 for HI members.

Hotel Mayur, (tel. 224142). From the railway station, walk 500m up Fraser Rd.; it's on the right side. Attached baths. Singles Rs200; doubles Rs240.

FOOD

Most of the good restaurants are concentrated on Fraser Rd. A couple of fast food places can be found at the hip shopping arcade at Maurya Lok.

Rajasthan Hotel Restaurant, Fraser Rd., north of the intersection of Fraser and Dak Bungalow Rd. If the consistent consumption of Indian food has waged war on your mouth (not to mention your stomach), these subtly spiced, if predictable, veg. dishes and soups are perfect. Almond soup (Rs36) and special *naan* (stuffed with nuts and vegetables Rs15) are particularly pleasing. Open daily 8am-10:30pm.

Bansi Vihar, Fraser Rd., not far from the railway station, on the left. The intoxicating smell of South Indian food surrounds you, recirculated by the powerful A/C. Add some of their very good ice cream to complete the Frigidaire effect. The *masala dosas*, with cashews and raisins (Rs35), are amazing. Open daily 8am-10:30pm.

Mayfair Ice Cream Parlor and Restaurant, Fraser Rd., across from the Bansi Vihar, 5min. from the railway station. Every hour seems like Happy Hour here. In the evening it's packed with young people enjoying ice cream (flavors include vanilla, strawberry, and blind love). Lengthy veg. (Rs18-42) and non-veg. (Rs22-60) menus too. Open daily 8:30am-10:30pm.

Mamta Restaurant and Bar, Fraser Rd., next to Mayfair Ice Cream Parlor. At the end of a long day, slip into the Mamta and relax amidst its colorful decor and fancy dishes. The butter *naan* (Rs12) melts in your mouth and the *kashmiri korma* (Rs40) is a dish to write home about. Open daily 10:30am-10:30pm.

SIGHTS

Although archaeologists have unearthed bits of Patna's past, most of the city's history remains concealed beneath its flaking concrete and dirt. A few places of historical interest, scattered around the city, await the dedicated sightseer. In the twisting lanes of Old Patna is **Har Mandir,** a Sikh *gurudwara* marking the birthplace of the 10th and last Sikh guru, Gobind Singh (born 1666). The second-most important throne of the Sikh religion (after the Golden Temple in Amritsar), Har Mandir is set in an echoing blue enclave reached through a tunnel of shops. Visitors must remove shoes and cover their heads to enter (scarves are provided). The present building was constructed after a 1954 earthquake destroyed the original temple. Inside, young men chant the verses of the Guru Granth Sahib, the Sikh holy book. Upstairs, a museum honoring Gobind Singh holds a few relics and lots of bad pictures.

One of Patna's most bizarre but popular landmarks is the **Golghar,** an egg-shaped grain storage bin near Gandhi Maidan. Built by the British in 1786 to avert famine, it was actually never needed. Two staircases spiral 29m above the street—a quick climb. The blue corners of the city and the brown Ganga can be seen from the top.

The prize piece in the **Patna Museum,** located on Buddha Marg in a fortress-like building guarded by cannons, is a voluptuous stone Mauryan *yakshi* from the 3rd century BC, which stands in the middle of the first-floor halls. (*Open Tu-Su10:30am-4:30pm. Admission free Sa-Th; F Rs2.*) Many less interesting sculptures surround the *yakshi,* but upstairs in glass cases there are good terra-cotta figures and heads, especially from the Mauryan era. There's also a substantial collection of *thankas* and other Tibetan artifacts collected by Rahula Sankrityayana in the 1930s.

The **Khuda Bakhsh Oriental Library,** located on Ashok Raj Path, houses a vast but esoteric collection of Islamic literature and relics. *(Open Sa-Th 9:30am-5pm.)* In the lobby, display cases show off beautiful, illuminated manuscripts hundreds of years old, 19th-century astronomical and astrological equipment, and some very delicate wooden models of ships and mosques crafted by the library's assistant librarian.

ENTERTAINMENT

There is a burgeoning bar scene in Patna, mostly along Fraser Rd. The most impressive of the lot is the **Daawat Bar** (tel. 239410), on the right side of Fraser Rd., near the railway station. The whole bar is designed according to a submarine theme: the bar itself is a large tank, filled with exotic tropical fish. The drinks are reasonably priced (beer Rs60), and the bar is open daily 11am to 10:15pm. Bars at the Maurya and Chanakya Hotels are also popular.

■ Gaya गया

According to folklore, the name Gaya derives from the demon Gayasura, who purified himself through rigorous yoga and received as a reward this sacred tract of land along the River Phalgu. As a further reward, Gaya was imbued with the power to absolve ancestral sins—it is said that one *shraddha* (funeral rite) in Gaya is equivalent to 11 *shraddhas* at any other place. Hindu pilgrims visit each of the 45 shrines in Gaya (including the Bodhi tree in Bodh Gaya), offering up prayers for the dead and rupees for the *gayaval* (attending priest). The high season comes in September when the Phalgu swells up with monsoon rains and thousands of pilgrims descend the *ghats* to perform their ritual ablutions. Gaya is as important to devout Hindus as its sister city is to Buddhists. Thirty-six kilometers north are the **Barabar Caves,** rock-hewn temples which starred as the Marabar Caves in E.M. Forster's *A Passage to India.*

ORIENTATION

Gaya's boundaries are marked by the **railway station** in the northwest bank of the **River Phalgu** in the northeast, and the base of **Brahmyoni Hill** in the southwest. **Station Road** goes right from the railway station and then takes a sharp left turning into **Civil Lines,** the administrative center of the city where the post office, police station, bus stands, and banks are located. Continuing east, the broad lanes of Civil Lines dissolve into the cluttered streets of the **Kacheri Road Bazaar,** which approach the river and disperse north and south into narrow brick paths, dotted with shrines and small shops. The spiritual center of the city is built around the **Vishnupad Temple** and the Phalgu *ghats.*

PRACTICAL INFORMATION

Trains: Trains leave from **Gaya Junction Station.** Fares are 2nd/1st class. To: **Bela** (10 per day, 1hr., Rs17 for 2nd class; from Bela to Barabar Caves, 12km ride in tempo or tonga and 5km walk to caves); **Calcutta** (*Rajdhani Exp.* 2302, 4:41am, 6hr., Rs411/717; *New Delhi-Howrah Poorva Exp.* 2382, 8:56am, 7½hr., Rs104/510); **Patna** (*Palamau Exp.* 3347, 4:22am, 2hr; *Hatia-Patna Exp.* 8626, 2:15pm, 2hr., Rs31/161); **Varanasi** (*Doon Exp.* 3010, 5:32am, 5hr., Rs61/294).

Buses: There are 5 major bus stands in Gaya. **Panchayati Akara Bus Stand,** 4km from Gaya Junction near Ram Shila Hill, has buses to numerous locations in southern Bihar. **Bihar State Road Transport** is located near Gandhi Maidan, a Rs5 rickshaw ride from Gaya Junction. To: **Jamshedpur** (5 per day, 11hr., Rs102); **Ranchi** (every hr., 5:30am-10:30pm, 7hr., Rs65). The **Manpur Bus Stand** is across the Phalgu River near the bridge and has buses to **Nalanda** and **Rajgir** (every hr., 6am-6pm, 2hr., Rs18). The **Zila School Bus Stand** is near the Kachahari area and has buses to **Bodh Gaya** (every 30min., 5:30am-6:30pm, Rs4). Buses to Varanasi leave from Bodh Gaya. Buses leave from **Gaya Junction,** in front of the train station, to **Calcutta** (2:30pm, 12hr.) and **Patna** (8am and 3pm, 4hr., Rs30).

Local Transportation: Rickshaws charge Rs7 to go to the Zila School Bus Stand, where there are buses and tempos to Bodh Gaya; Rs10 to the Vishnupad Temple or Shaktipith near the Phalgu River. These rates apply to rickshaws carrying at least 4 people; single travelers pay triple.

Tourist Office: inside the railway station. Features a wall map of Gaya. Open M-Sa 6am-10pm; 24hr. in Sept.

Currency Exchange: Bank of Baroda (tel. 22884) won't change cash, but will advance up to Rs2000 on major credit cards. Take Station Rd. right, go left at the bend, make the first right, and it's on the left.

Luggage Storage: Platform 1, Gaya Junction Station. Rs5 per day. Open 24hr.

Market: A large **fruit market** is located at **Purani Godam,** Tekari Rd., Chauk, between Gaya Junction and the Phalgu River.

Pharmacy: Many pharmacies are located along Station Rd. Most are open 8am-9pm.

Hospital: The **Magadh Medical College** (tel. 22410) is a government hospital. Bihar's government services being what they are, Gaya is an awful place to be sick.

Police: Control Room tel. 223131 or 223132.

Emergency: tel. 20999.

Post Office: GPO, Kachahari Rd. (tel. 20660). Rs20 rickshaw ride from railway station, right along Station Rd., and then left through the main fruit market. Open M-Sa 7am-6pm. **Postal Code:** 823001.

Telephones: A 24hr. **STD/ISD** booth is located inside the railway station. The **telegraph office** is attached to GPO. Open daily 8am-4pm. **Telephone Code:** 0631.

ACCOMMODATIONS

Cheap hotels have accumulated across from the railway station and to the right along Station Rd. These tend to be quite noisy. Off-season (May-Aug.) rates are negotiable.

Hotel Buddha, Laxman Sahay Ln. (tel. 23428), straight back from the railway station, at the end of a long road perpendicular to Station Rd. Much quieter than the hotels along Station Rd. Smallish, sunny doubles are clean, with comfortable mattresses and attached baths with good showers. Singles Rs125; doubles Rs160.

Station View Hotel, Station Rd. (tel. 20512), several hundred meters to the right of the station, past the Ajatsatru Hotel, on the left side of the street. Don't be misled by the hotel's name: among its assets is the *lack* of a station view. Often filled to capacity, even off season. Spacious restaurant with some private booths. Staff is friendly and laid-back. All rooms have attached bath. Singles Rs45; doubles Rs55.

Ajatsatru Hotel, Station Rd. (tel. 21514 or 23714), across from the railway station on the left side. Among the largest hotels on this strip. Air-cooled doubles are spacious and fairly clean with comfortable mattresses. Attached restaurant is open till 11:30pm. Room service 24hr. All rooms have attached bath. Singles Rs150; doubles Rs195. Suite with kitchen Rs540.

FOOD

Most hotel restaurants on Station Rd. are narrow, fly-infested holes. There are a few exceptions, including one good but expensive restaurant in the Siddharth International. *Dal*-and-rice *dhabas* abound en route to the Vishnupad Temple.

Station View Hotel Restaurant, Station Rd. (tel. 20512), 300m to the right of the railway station, on the left side. The best of the budget hotel restaurants, its former garage is now an airy dining room with some small curtained booths for privacy. Veg. and non-veg. cuisine (*dal* Rs2; veg. *pulao* Rs15*).* Open daily 6:30am-11pm.

Siddharth International Restaurant, Station Rd. (tel. 436243, 436252). From the railway station, walk right 500m; it's on the left. A/C restaurant serves the usual. Veg. food starts at Rs30; chicken starts at Rs80. Continental soups and salads are cheaper, but still nourishing and delicious. Open daily 7am-11:30pm.

Sujata Restaurant (tel. 23714), inside Ajatsatru Hotel, Station Rd. A loud, rough-and-tumble, testosterone-rich environment, with plenty of beer (Rs60), veg. dishes (Rs13), chicken galore (Rs25), and breakfast until 10am. Open daily 7am-11:30pm.

SIGHTS

Gaya is one of Hinduism's seven sacred cities, but its temples are not nearly as spectacular as those in large pilgrimage centers such as Varanasi, and non-Hindus may not enter the main shrine, **Vishnupad.** Towering over the bank of the Phalgu River, this golden-spired temple is said to house the 2m footprint of Vishnu in the form of Buddha, enshrined in a silver basin. Non-Hindus can get a closer look at the sanctum (but not the print) by climbing the stairs at the back of the first shop to the left of the temple entrance.

One kilometer east is a rather mundane **Durga temple,** where non-Hindus can observe and even participate in the *shraddha*. Pilgrims who wish to perform the *shraddha* at Gaya must first circle their own village five times. Once in Gaya, a *gayaval* (priest trained in the *shraddha*) guides them in a complicated ritual involving Sanskrit prayers and offerings of *pinda* (water and rice kneaded into a ball). The pilgrims usually repay the *gayaval* for his services with a hefty donation. Two steps away lies **Shaktipith,** where Sati's breast is said to have fallen after she was cut to pieces (see **Divine Dismemberment,** p. 418). Images of the goddess are housed in a squat, cavernous mausoleum, inscribed on the front with the epic verse of Sati's destruction. *(Open daily 6am-noon and 1pm-midnight.)*

One kilometer southwest of the Vishnupad Temple is the entrance to the **Brahmyoni Hill.** Climb 1000 stone steps to Shiv Mandir, where cool winds whip across the top and views of Gaya (on the right) and Bodh Gaya (on the left) impress the impressionable. There is also a small goddess temple with an image of Shiva's foot at the door. The hill is sacred to Buddhists, as it is associated with Gayasirsan (the Head of Gaya), the mountain where Buddha is said to have delivered several important sermons. Guides will try to tell you that Shiva's footprint is Buddha's, and even that the images of the goddess are statues of the Enlightened One.

■ Bodh Gaya बोध गया

Strangely enough, the little village of Bodh Gaya, 14km south of Gaya, is the center of the Buddhist universe. It was here in the 6th century BC that Prince Siddhartha Gautama gained enlightenment under a *pipal* (Bodhi) tree, launching his career as the Buddha. During the winter months, pilgrims from all over the world (the Dalai Lama included) come to this most powerful of places, where many Buddhists believe that the Buddha of the future, Maitreya, will also attain enlightenment. Some expect him soon—in about a hundred years. To welcome him, devotees plan to erect an enormous Maitreya statue in a field on the edge of town. The Buddhist presence in Bodh Gaya, whose population is primarily Hindu, is quite new and mostly foreign. Although Buddhist monasteries thrived here long ago, they were left to sink into the mud after Buddhism faded out of India in the 12th century. Not until the 19th century, when Sri Lankan and Burmese monks led the campaign to restore the Mahabodhi Temple, was Bodh Gaya revived as a religious center.

During Bodh Gaya's season (Dec.-Feb.), the monasteries quietly fill up, visiting teachers (many of them Westerners) offer meditation courses, and scads of tent restaurants appear. Monks from several Buddhist nations intone *sutras* in monasteries built in their own national styles. By April, however, the crowd has thinned out and Bodh Gaya takes on a quietude appropriate to its status as a world religious center.

ORIENTATION

The road from Gaya meanders into town, turning right at the **market square** and running past the high walls encircling the **Mahabodhi Temple** on the left and the Sri Lankan and Tibetan Gelug-pa compounds on the right. It turns left in front of the **Chinese temple,** passing the **museum** and the **Thai Temple,** on either side of which roads run back to the other monasteries behind. Continuing out of town, the road passes turn-offs for the Root Institute and the planned Maitreya Statue.

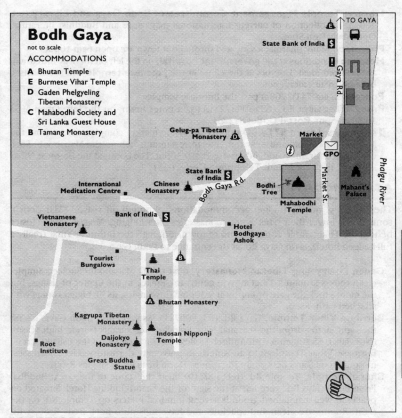

Bodh Gaya
not to scale

ACCOMMODATIONS

A Bhutan Temple
E Burmese Vihar Temple
D Gaden Phelgyeling
   Tibetan Monastery
C Mahabodhi Society and
   Sri Lanka Guest House
B Tamang Monastery

EAST INDIA

PRACTICAL INFORMATION

Buses: Buses leave for **Gaya** from the stand near the Burmese Temple (every 30min., 5am-6pm, Rs4), with the bus stopping every 10m for passengers to embark, disembark, and sometimes just bark. The shared **tempos** are well worth the extra, and nominal, expense (see **Local Transportation,** below). Two buses per day depart from the Tourist Bungalows to **Patna,** (7am and 2pm, Rs35, 4hr.), and a bus to **Varanasi** stops in front of the Mahabodhi Society (on the right side after the market complex) at 5:30am (Rs54).

Local Transportation: Autorickshaws charge Rs10 from one side of town to the other. **Tongas** are also available. They make the trip to Gaya for as little as Rs50, shared among as many people as can cram in, strap-hang, or squat top-side.

Tourist Office: Market Complex. Located across from the Mahabodhi Temple, in a small shopping center. Open M-Sa 10am-5pm.

Budget Travel: Middle Way Travels (tel. 400561), just before the main temple, next to Weston Shoes. Shahab, the proprietor, an expert on T.S. Eliot and Buddhism, will trade quotes from *The Waste Land* and the *Tripitaka* with you while waiting for his man to fetch your train ticket from Gaya. Also offers Buddhist-oriented tours of Bihar. Major credit cards accepted. Open daily 9am-9pm.

Currency Exchange: State Bank of India, Gaya Rd. (tel. 400746). Entering Mahabodhi Temple, walk to the left for 3min., and the bank is to your right. **Bank of India** (tel. 400750), on a path leading to the International Meditation Centre. From the Mahabodhi Temple, walk 10min. to the far side of town; turn right at the sign. Both banks open M-F 10:30am-2:30pm, Sa 10:30am-12:30pm.

Market: At the intersection of Gaya and Bodh Gaya Rd., a small lane to the left leads to a bazaar where you can buy fruit, handicrafts, and umbrellas.

Library: Temple Management Committee of Bodh Gaya and Library (tel. 400735). Collection of current international magazines and Buddhist literature. Open daily 9am-5pm.

Pharmacy: Many pharmacies located throughout town are open 6am-10pm.

Hospital: Conditions at the **government hospital,** on the left on the way into town, are far from ideal. Doctors at the clinic in the **Japanese temple** will see tourists, but only in an emergency.

Police: (tel. 400741), 200m past the Burmese temple.

Post Office: Gaya Rd. (tel. 400472). As you enter town, on the left. Open M-Sa 10:30am-5pm. **Postal Code:** 842231.

Telephones: Lots of **STD/ISD** booths are at the market complex across from the Mahabodhi Temple and near the Tibetan restaurants behind the Mahabodhi Society. Open 24hr. in season; otherwise 7am-9:30pm. The booth at the Burmese Vihar is open 24hr. year-round. **Telephone Code:** 0631.

ACCOMMODATIONS

There are few quality budget accommodations, although off season (Mar.-Sept.), some hotels lower their rates. Some monasteries offer lodging. Most of these cluster behind the Thai temple at the far end of town, although the Burmese Vihar (really a full-fledged hotel), is on Gaya Rd. at the entrance to Bodh Gaya.

Gaden Phelgyeling Tibetan Monastery, next to the Mahabodhi Society. Simple, clean rooms around a Tibetan-style courtyard. Smack in the center of things, but the monks lock the gate promptly at 9:30pm. Tiny singles, Rs30; bigger rooms with attached bath, Rs80.

Burmese Vihar Temple, Gaya Rd. (tel. 400721). As you enter Bodh Gaya, it's on the right, across from the seasonal New Pole-Pole restaurant. During high season (Nov.-Jan.), 35 students with Antioch College in Ohio transform the usually serene Burmese Vihar Temple into an American university dormitory. Flat mattresses, mosquito coils, and nets equip the rooms. Dorm beds Rs40; singles Rs60.

Bhutan Temple, Temple Rd. (tel. 400710), near the statue of the Great Buddha. From Bodh Gaya Rd., turn left at the sign for the Shanti Buddha Hotel. Situated on peaceful, well-maintained grounds several hundred meters up Temple Rd. on the right. Rooms are clean and spacious and have mosquito nets. Beds Rs60, with attached bath Rs100; Royal Suite Rs400. Off-season: Rs40/80/250.

Tamang Monastery, Bodh Gaya Rd. (tel. 400802). On the left side of the main road, after the Archaeological Museum, down the dirt path across from the International Meditation Centre. Clean, cramped rooms fill this charming little temple. Advance booking is essential in season. Bed Rs100, with bath Rs150. Off-season: Rs40/100.

Mahabodhi Society and Sri Lanka Guest House (tel. 400742). Set back from the road across the street from the Mahabodhi Temple. Large dormitories with comfortable beds, but no mosquito nets or coils. Clean, almost sterile conditions throughout; the water pressure is positively explosive. Check-out 24hr. Dorm beds Rs50. Doubles with bath Rs300 per person.

FOOD

Restaurants are highly seasonal. The gourmand can stray from the middle path and pick from a smorgasbord of international cuisine. Winter raves include the chocolate chip cookies at the **Original Pole-Pole,** across from the Burmese Temple, and **Ginza,** on the opposite side of town, across from the Thai Temple.

Sujata Restaurant (tel. 400761), inside Hotel Bodh Gaya Ashok, next to the Museum. Bihari food like *aloo jeera* (Rs40), and other veg. dishes from Rs40, soups from Rs30, and breakfast (Rs20-100). When you're ready to ditch asceticism, the Sujata offers an all-you-can-eat lunch and dinner buffet (Rs300) in season.

Aahar Restaurant (tel. 400799), just across from the Tamang Monastery. Start your day with a savory mushroom omelette (Rs25) or treat your tummy to a lightly spiced vegetable *jhal frazi* (Rs35). Open daily 7am-10pm.

SIGHTS

Mahabodhi Temple
Hours: *Open daily 5am-9pm.* **Admission:** *Free.* **Other:** *Camera fee Rs5.*

The main point of interest in Bodh Gaya is the Mahabodhi Temple, referred to as "the *stupa*" by most Buddhists. The tall, thin *shikhara*, which is covered with a jigsaw-puzzle-like pattern, towers over the many *chaityas* and other shrines in its courtyard. The temple is right next to the actual site of enlightenment, while some of the other shrines are linked to different stages in the Buddha's meditations. Emperor Ashoka built the first temple on this site in the 3rd century BC. The present temple, which has been through layers and layers of restorations, dates from the 6th century AD. Much of the rescue work was initiated in 1882 by Burmese monks who found the temple neglected and overrun by squatters. Over the last 30 years, many statues have been stolen from the temple's circular niches. The oldest structure left on the site is a stone railing built in the first century AD to keep out wild animals; however, a quarter of it has been whisked away to museums in London and Calcutta.

At the back of the temple is the sacred **Bodhi Tree,** a grandchild of the tree under which the Buddha attained enlightenment. The platform between the tree and the temple is thought to be exactly where the Buddha sat. It is called the **Vajrasana** or "diamond throne," and some believe that an enormous diamond buried beneath the earth here fuels the site's spiritual power. It is said that Emperor Ashoka killed the original Bodhi tree prior to his conversion to Buddhism. After he converted, however, Ashoka sent his son, Mahinda, on a mission to Sri Lanka carrying an offshoot from the tree. This tree still lives on in Anuradhapura, Sri Lanka; the Bodhi tree at Bodh Gaya has grown from one of its saplings. It's considered to be almost as good as the real thing, and it is surrounded by its own fence. *(Open 6 to 8am and 6 to 8pm.)*

A large gold Buddha is kept behind glass in the temple, and another is on the first floor, which is only open in the evenings for meditation. A part of the first floor is permanently closed off, due to one man's recent attempt to saw off a branch of the sacred tree as a souvenir.

Other Temples and Monasteries
Hours: *Most temples open daily dawn-noon and 2pm-dusk.*

The **Thai Temple,** Bodh Gaya's second-most prominent landmark, is located 500m after the main road takes a sharp left. A large *wat* with the classic clawlike tips on its orange roof, it opened in 1957. Its eclectic interior includes Thai tourism posters. Side-roads branch off the main road on either side of the Thai Temple. To the left are the **Bhutan Monastery** and the Japanese **Indosan Nipponji Temple.** The Indosan Nipponji's peace bell rings with a swinging cadence throughout the morning. The lane on the right side of the Thai Temple leads to the **Kagyu-pa Tibetan Monastery,** which contains Disneyesque, larger-than-life murals depicting the life of the Buddha. Next door is the **Daijokyo Temple,** another Japanese construction with an oppressive modern concrete exterior. Just up the road from the Daijokyo Temple, the 25m **Giant Buddha Statue,** which was built by Japanese monks and inaugurated by the Dalai Lama in 1989, sits on a lotus, the Buddha's robe rippling out of the red sandstone blocks. The **Gelug-pa Tibetan Monastery,** right next to the Mahabodhi Society near the center of town, is accustomed to sightseers. Its second-floor chapel has walls painted with *thanka*-style clouds, wheels, and *bodhisattvas*. Visitors are invited to turn the massive silo of a prayer wheel downstairs. And don't neglect the **Mahant's Palace,** on the left just before you reach the center of town. Now a working Hindu temple, its rear views of the Neranghana River and the Sujata Mountain beyond make it a great spot for meditation, contemplation, or just plain chillin' out.

BUDDHISM AND COMMUNITY SERVICE

During the high season, meditation courses are a major industry in Bodh Gaya. Teachers from all over the world jet (or rickshaw) in to provide training to Buddhists and aspiring Buddhists in the *karma*-rich atmosphere of temple town. A few permanent institutions in Bodh Gaya dedicated to spreading the Buddha-word also conduct lessons. **The Root Institute for Wisdom Culture** (tel. 400714), located at the edge of town, down a dirt path to the left, offers 10-day courses during the winter months with guest lamas in a quiet, intimate setting. The fee for a double runs Rs190-400, depending on quality of room, number of meals, and hours of instruction. Room and board (veg., of course) is also available for non-meditators, and although they don't provide instruction off-season, any and all comers are welcomed year-round for retreat or other purposes. **The International Meditation Center,** across from the Thai monastery, offers courses in the Vipassana Method year-round. The 10-day course is free, but a donation of Rs75-100 per day will defray costs to the monastery, including a dorm bed in doubles or triples, as well as three meals. The **Vipassana Meditation Center,** behind the university, has 10-day courses from October to February. They will also house and feed you for no charge—but, again, donations are appreciated. A branch of **Goenha,** the **Dhamana Bodhi Meditation Center** (tel. 400437), one kilometer past the big Japanese Buddha, also holds classes in season, as does the **Burmese Vihar** (see **Accommodations,** above).

There are a number of licensed charitable organizations in Bodh Gaya. The Root Institute is always looking for volunteers (and donations). They sponsor tree planting during the monsoon and in January toward the end of tourist season, in addition to all-year Leprosy and Polio Projects and the Destitute House. Many charitable organizations pop up during peak season—avoid anything that looks like a hit-and-run operation. Additional information is available at the Mahabodhi Society.

This Doesn't Bodh Well...

Though most of the Buddhists in Bodh Gaya hail from countries elsewhere in Asia, a few Indian Buddhists also live here. Recently, Indian Buddhists began a campaign to wrest control of the trust that oversees Bodh Gaya's religious matters from the Hindus who dominate its board of directors. Local Hindus, it is said, protest that they too are Buddhists (and thus entitled to Bodh Gaya's administration), as they worship Buddha as an incarnation of Vishnu. Indian Buddhists counter that, except for at Bodh Gaya's temples, images of the Enlightened One are not a fixture at Hindu temples. Given Bihar's often hysterical political scene and Bodh Gaya's international presence, the dispute may have worldwide consequences.

■ Vaishali वैशाली

A mellow hamlet two hours by bus from Patna, Vaishali's diverse claims to fame touch on Buddhism, Hinduism, and Jainism. Around the 6thcentury BC, Vaishali was the capital of the Vajjian confederacy, a republic governed by a parliament elected under universal suffrage and kept in line by a system of checks and balances. Birthplace and hometown of Mahavira, the founder of Jainism, Vaishali also figures prominently in the life of the Buddha: it was here that he announced his impending *parinirvana;* afterwards, his relics were first en-*stupa*-ed and his followers held the second Buddhist council at Vaishali. Of course, these are small potatoes compared to the Hindu story: the *Ramayana* says Vaishali is where the gods and demons pow-wowed before churning the oceans. Popular with backpackers from Japan, Korea, and others, the town attracts more with its quiet than its relics.

Direct **buses** to Vaishali leave the main bus stand in Patna at 5:30, 10:30, and 11:30am (2hr., Rs20). Alternatively, after crossing the M.G. Bridge to **Hajipur** on one of the frequent buses (Rs9), switch to a bus to Lalgang (Rs8), where many shared taxis (Rs8) ply the road passing through Vaishali. Ask to be let off when you see the government's **Tourist Lodge.** A gate on the left just past the lodge leads back 1km to the large **Coronation Tank.** The **Japanese temple** and new *stupa* (consecrated in October 1996) occupy the south side, while the **museum** and the rest of the tourist accommodations are in the north. A side road leads off the north side, by the water tower, passing the **stupa** supposed to be the first to hold the Buddha's ashes, and continuing through several villages to the **Ashokan Pillar** and **Monkey Tank** 4km away. Follow the fat paved road—eventually you'll see the pillar on your left. Continue on to the next village, where a bridge over the stream sends you back towards the entrance to the site. To return to Patna, hop a direct bus in front of the lodge (7, 9am, 12:30, and 3:30pm), or jump a taxi to Lalgang, where connections are frequent.

Vaishali is a tiny village; the state runs all the tourist facilities. At the **Tourist Lodge,** on the main road, singles run Rs52 and doubles Rs77. All rooms have king-sized bathrooms, and a restaurant operates in season (Oct.-Feb.). By the tank, a friendly government **Youth Hostel** offers simple doubles (Rs77) as well as dorm beds (Rs20) in triples. Again, the restaurant—and here the running water, too—operate only in season, but the manager enthusiastically helps to arrange your feeding, as well as other expediencies. There's also a colonial-style government **Guest House** for VIPs, if you qualify. Off season, *dhabas* on the main road may be your only dining option.

A big pile of rubble in the fields behind the Tourist Lodge, off to the left, is all that remains of the **Raga Vishal Ka Garh,** a great Vajjian assembly hall. After the republic's demise, it served as a palace and then a fort before crumbling into the cow pasture. The **Coronation Tank** was used to anoint the town's leaders during inaugural ceremonies—today it's the local laundromat. A small, unremarkable **museum** next to the tank showcases some of the stone and terra-cotta pieces dug from the earth nearby. (Open Sa-Th 10am-5pm. Free.) The *stupa* behind the museum, **Stupa 1,** covered with a conical tin roof, occupies a small garden adjoining the Archaeological Survey office. It is believed that this *stupa* contains a portion of the Buddha's ashes.

The other noteworthy attractions, in a fenced-in compound 4km farther down the road, are best reached by rickshaw or bicycle. (Ruins open daily 8am-5pm. Admission Rs2.) The road cuts through rice paddies and several villages. At the site, a **pillar,** thought by some to be Ashokan, stands sentinel over another *stupa* **(Stupa 2),** excavated only recently. The pillar differs from other Ashokan pillars in many respects: it is square, thick, and squat, not round and slender, and the lion leaves a little too much to the imagination.

■ Rajgir राजगृह

Rajgir (once known as Rajagriha, "House of Kings") is nestled in a lush valley between the Ratnagiri mountains. During the Buddha's time, it was capital of the kingdom of Magadh, whose rulers built grandly—the faintest outlines of their palaces and the great 40km wall they constructed around their city, destroyed by Muslim marauders in the 13th century, lie in the middle of a well-trodden tourist path. Because Rajgir figured prominently in Buddha's life, Buddhist pilgrims from Asia flock here during the winter months. You'll see them taking the chairlift to Gridhrakuta, or "Vulture's Peak," a secluded mountain retreat where the Buddha gathered his disciples to unfold the Four Noble Truths. The first Buddhist Council took place at Rajgir, and the extensive nearby ruins of the university at Nalanda convey a sense of the success and scale of Buddhist learning that thrived here for nearly a thousand years.

Jain influence in Rajgir was also strong, and Jain temples dot the low hills around the city center, commemorating the 14 seasons that Mahavira spent in this tranquil valley. Hindus are omnipresent (of course), and they celebrate the Magh Mas (Excessive Month) every 33rd month. For 30 days the entire Hindu pantheon of 330 million gods purportedly makes merry in the streets. Equally rowdy are the flocks of peasants from outlying villages, who leave the place a complete wreck.

ORIENTATION AND PRACTICAL INFORMATION The road from Bihar Sharif passes Nalanda and then, 15km later, arrives at the **bus stand** in Rajgir. From here, **buses** go to **Gaya** (every 30min., 5:30am-6pm, 3hr., Rs18), **Nalanda** (every 20min.,

Rs3), and **Patna** (3 and 6pm, Rs30, 4hr.) from the central bus stand. The road contin-ues as a new by-pass but the left turn just before the bus stand leads through the old part of town—the markets, GPO, hospital, telephone exchange, and the Burmese and Bengali temples—after which it reunites with the bypass just before the complex containing the tourist office. Even farther on, a well-marked road to the left leads to the base of Mt. Ratnagiri and the lift to the top.

The state-run **tourist office** (open M-Sa 10am-5pm) has a detailed (and imaginative) map on its walls. Rajgir's **railway station** is set back 1km on the left from the main intersection on the way to Nalanda. **Passenger trains** leave for **Patna** (Rs16) at 5:50am and 4:30pm. **Rickshaws** and **tongas** charge around Rajgir. The carriages are a better and faster deal for the ride to Mt. Ratnagiri (Rs30 round-trip). **New Popular Pharmacy,** next to the GPO, has a decent stock of medicines (open daily 6am-8pm). The **police station** (tel. 5228) is 200m past the **GPO,** which is in the old town's cen-tral square (open 24hr. a day). A little shack next to the tourist office sells stamps. The **STD/ISD** booth in the telephone exchange is open until midnight. Be advised of the dearth of **currency exchange. Postal code:** 803116. **Telephone code:** 06119.

ACCOMMODATIONS AND FOOD The tourist industry in Rajgir is set up to serve busloads of pilgrims. The **Burmese Buddhist Temple** (tel. 5024), on the old road just before it reunites with the bypass, feeds, houses, and entertains Buddhists from back home, thanks to the generosity of generations of gentle Burmese Buddhists, whose names adorn everything from the fridge to the ceiling fans to the crockery. The tem-ple has comfortable mosquito-netted beds and a large dining hall (doubles and triples with common bath, or cargo-hold sized dorm rooms for a donation, usually Rs50 per person per night). The **Bengali Buddhist Society Temple,** next to the Burmese tem-ple, also has many rooms for a donation. The rooms in the brand new complex are funded by Calcutta Buddhists, and more rooms and a restaurant should be ready by October, 1998. Although not as welcoming as the Burmese next door, the Bengalis provide clean, comfortable surroundings. The wholly secular **Hotel Gautam Vihar** (tel. 5273), also known as Government Bungalow #1, on the main road between the bus stand and the railway station, has large, high-ceilinged rooms. (Dorm beds Rs50. Doubles Rs250. Off-season: Rs25/100. All A/C rooms are Rs500.)

Restaurants are highly seasonal. Most visitors to Rajgir come on high-volume pack-age tours and eat where they live. *Dhabas* and basic hotel restaurants around the bus stand feed locals. **Green Hotel Restaurant** (tel. 5352), at the other end of the shop-ping strip containing the tourist office, has a wide selection of cheap, unremarkable fare (Rs15-40; open daily 7am-10pm).

SIGHTS The sights on and around **Mt. Ratnagiri** constitute the main draw. Running along the side of the mountain, the access road reaches **Gridhrakuta,** once the Bud-dha's retreat. Above two natural caves recognized as sites of the Buddha's sermons are the remains of a monastery from the Gupta period. Backtracking a bit, a path leads up to the new Japanese golden *stupa,* **Viswa Shanti,** which sits atop a colossal sandstone dome and is dedicated to world peace. Around the dome are four images of the Buddha, representing his birth, enlightenment, teaching, and death. To avoid the climb, take the chairlift to the *stupa* and catch Gridhrakuta on the way down. *(Open 8am-5pm, Rs15.)* Just outside of town on the Vaibhara Hill is the **Saptaparni Cave,** where the first Buddhist Council was held after the Buddha's death, when 500 monks gathered to compile in written form the Buddha's teachings. Nearby, **Pippala Cave,** a natural rectangular rock once used as a watch tower, remains a revered abode of hermits. At the foot of Vaibhara Hill, the Buddha and his disciples once cavorted in the half-dozen **hot springs** that were later incorporated into the design of a Hindu temple, known as **Lakshmi Narim.** Today, locals crowd the baths to perform ablutions—or just have a warm wash in the lower pools. Although it's part of a tem-ple, non-Hindus are welcome to cavort and cleanse. Be on guard for "priests" looking for "contributions." Mornings are busiest. Some of the springs, directed through the temple sculptures, gush from the mouths of lions.

■ Near Rajgir: Nalanda नलन्दा

Nalanda is the site of one of the oldest universities in the world, built by the Guptas in the 5th century. Its reputation as a center of learning dates back even further to the first millennium BC. The Buddha first came here to study philosophy with local gurus, later attracting his own disciples. Another famous Buddhist philosopher, Nagarjuna, began his studies at Nalanda in the 3rd century, but the university itself wasn't inaugurated until two centuries later. Scholars at Nalanda pursued studies in both Buddhist and Vedic philosophy, logic, and medicine. In subsequent centuries as Nalanda's fame increased exponentially, so did its size. New buildings soared to the height of nine stories, and with the aid of King Harsha of Kannauj, Nalanda amassed a **library** of over nine million manuscripts. By the 13th century, successive waves of Muslim invaders had chased out all the students and reduced the library collection to cinders. It is now possible to walk among the remains of nearly a dozen monasteries, which housed 3000 students and teachers but are now home only to meandering goats and nesting birds. The remains of an impressively tall **main temple** are at the south entrance. Climbing to the top, the view extends northward where the monasteries on the right face the temples on the left. A **smaller temple** to the right of the monasteries is sheathed in 6th-century wall-paintings. A **museum** there houses excavated relics, including Buddha images. (Open Sa-Th 10am-5pm. Admission Rs2). **Minibuses** leave for Nalanda every 10 minutes from the bus stand at Rajgir (Rs3). From the bus stand in Nalanda, you can take a tonga (Rs5 per seat, Rs25 to rent the whole vehicle) or walk the 2km (stay to the right) to the site.

■ Raxaul रक्सौल

> **Warning:** Crossing the border into Nepal requires four steps: Indian Immigration, Indian Customs, Nepali Immigration, and Nepali Customs. You'll need at least US$15 to pay for your visa and a photo. **No other currencies are accepted, and there are no currency exchange facilities at the border.** Exact change is best, and the closest place to buy dollars is Patna. Also, remember to **get your passport stamped** to say that you left India, or you'll have trouble entering Nepal. The Indian **immigration office** is easy to miss; some rickshaw-*wallahs* don't know where it is since Indians and Nepalis don't have to go there.

With all the dirt but none of the charm you'll find elsewhere in India, Raxaul, 206km north of Patna, is a pitstop for travelers on their way from India to Nepal or vice-versa. Luckily, transportation is easy to come by, whether it's a rickshaw to the Nepalese border town of **Birganj** (less unpleasant than Raxaul; see p. 792) or a bus to Patna, with its train connections to Calcutta and Delhi.

Raxaul's main street leads right over the Nepalese border, cutting through the market area, a tangle of alleyways to the east and west. Coming from Nepal, you'll have to stop at Indian **customs,** right after the bridge, then at the **immigration office** (open daily 5am-8pm), a little farther down the road on the right. There are no facilities for **changing money** in Raxaul—Birganj and Patna are the closest places to do so. **STD/ISD telephones** line the main road. Between 7pm and 7am, **buses** leave from the **bus park** on the north side of town, just off the main road, near the railway tracks. During the day, buses leave from **Laxmipur,** 3km south of Raxaul (IRs10 by rickshaw). Buses to **Patna** leave approximately every hour (5-6hr., IRs70). **Pharmacies** can be found along the main street. The **post office** is on the west side of the main street and is open M-Sa 9am-4pm. **Postal Code:** 845305. **Telephone Code:** 06255.

If you're stuck here overnight, we're sorry. Try the **Hotel Ajanta,** Ashram Rd. (tel. 61019), down a lane east of the main road, close to the border. The dreary rooms all have fans, but only the rooms with attached baths (cold water only) have mosquito nets. The hotel has its own generator, and there's an attached **restaurant.** (Doubles Rs90, with bath Rs125, with bath and air-cooling Rs300; additional 3-7% tax.)

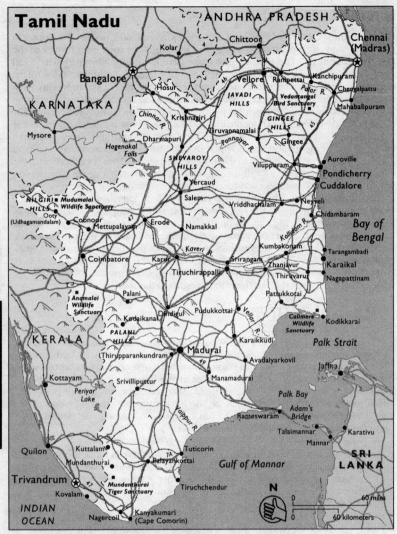

Tamil Nadu தமிழ் நாடு

The southernmost state in mainland India, Tamil Nadu is the heartland of Dravidian culture and is a bastion of conservative Hinduism. Some of the finest temple architecture in India can be found here; *gopurams* (gateway towers) can be seen towering over huge temple-city complexes with streets spiraling around an active central shrine. Tamil Nadu is also home to the sounds of Carnatic music and to *bharat natyam,* India's most popular classical dance form. Since at least the first century, the state has nurtured South India's oldest literary tradition, in its mother tongue, Tamil.

The Mauryan Empire, which controlled virtually all of India during the 3rd century BC, never made it this far south. During the last few centuries BC, Tamil Nadu was ruled by three rival dynasties, the Cholas, Pandyas, and Cheras. By the 4th century AD the Pallava kingdom had ascended, only to be stopped in the 9th century by the long-standing Cholas, who grew to rule all of South India. Not until the 14th-century growth of the Vijayanagar Empire was the present-day area of Tamil Nadu ruled by a kingdom based outside its borders. Under the British, Tamil Nadu was part of the Chennai Presidency, which included parts of present-day Andhra Pradesh, Kerala, and Karnataka; this entity was divided according to language groups in the 1950s. Most people in Tamil Nadu speak at least a smattering of English, since fierce cultural pride has caused them to resent the introduction of Hindi.

Tamil Nadu can be divided into the eastern plains along the Coromandel Coast and the northern and western hills, culminating in the Nilgiris, where the Eastern and Western Ghats meet. These hills were developed into tea and coffee plantations by the British. Tamil Nadu's only perennial river, the Kaveri, flows into the state from Karnatak; it has been dammed heavily and is now a mere trickle in places. The plains are home to paddy fields where the harvest festival of Pongal takes place every year in January. At Kanyakumari, the southern tip of the Indian peninsula is marked by sea-breeze, orange sunsets, and vast stretches of rocky beach.

🏵 HIGHLIGHTS OF TAMIL NADU

- "We'll always have **Pondy**"—a fascinating cultural mix distinguishing **Pondicherry** (p. 488), the former capital of French India, now home to the famously surreal **Aurobindo Ashram** (p. 493).
- Thousands flock to the **Meenakshi Amman Temple** in **Madurai** (p. 511), where some 30 million sculptures provide an artistic counterpoint to a lively, fun city.
- **Ooty** (p. 528), in the Nilgiri hills of Western Tamil Nadu, features the standard Hill Station amusements, set against some of India's finest film-grade scenery.

■ Chennai (Madras) சென்னை

SOUTH INDIA

India's fourth-largest city and South India's preeminent commercial center, Chennai (officially named Madras until 1996) has less of the pollution, overcrowding, and general chaos that plague its urban counterparts in the North. The city is remarkably well-planned, and patches of greenery throughout the town provide a sense of openness and tranquility that few other metropolises of this size can. But in terms of tourist interest, Chennai loses to the magnificent temples and lush countryside that are so accessible from it. Still, tourists who stay are rewarded: Chennai boasts excellent restaurants, beautiful beach-strolls, and quality cultural offerings.

Madras was founded by Francis Day, an official of the British East India Company in 1639 as a "factory," or trading outpost, near the fishing village of Madraspatnam, on land granted by the local raja. Soon, Day's venture burgeoned—a fort and church were built, and an Indian weaver's colony called Chennaipatnam grew north of the fort. To accommodate the new arrivals, East India Company agents purchased great swaths of land around the fort and Chennaipatnam, eventually fusing them into an important metropolis. Unfortunately for the British, what one empire built another coveted, and in 1746 French forces stormed, seized, and sacked the city. Though a treaty returned the territory to British control two years later, the city's vulnerability had been exposed, and Calcutta moved to the forefront as the center of imperial administration. While Madras ceased to be a place where crucial political decisions were made, it became a thriving economic center, and the city's sprawling factories produced thousands of tons of export-grade cotton clothing throughout the late 19th and early 20th centuries. After Independence, the city once again swelled (its population is now pushing 6 million) and began to assert power beyond its stretching city limits, this time as a center of Tamil culture and the capital of Tamil Nadu.

Recently, Chennai has been swept up in India's wave of politically motivated name changes. Many of the town's major thoroughfares have been stripped of their colonial names and re-christened in honor of Tamil leaders. In 1996, "Madras" was officially replaced by "Chennai," a Tamil name that invokes the original Indian settlement

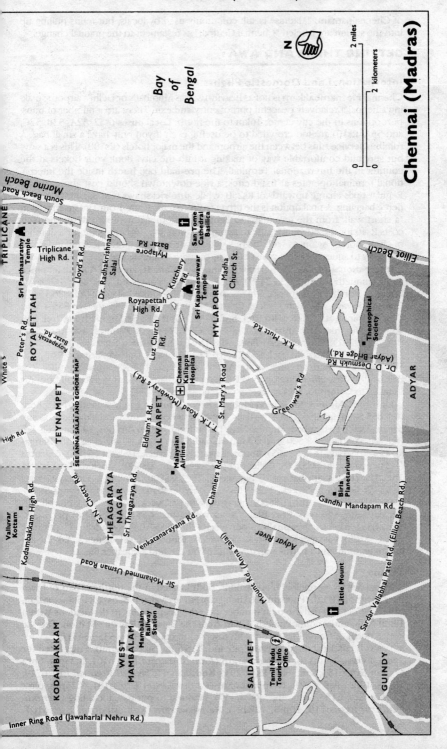

Chennai (Madras)

Bay of Bengal

2 miles

2 kilometers

N

Marina Beach

South Beach Road

TRIPLICANE

Sri Parthasarathy Temple

Triplicane High Rd.

Lloyd's Rd.

Dr. Radhakrishnan Salai

Mylapore Bazar Rd.

San Tome Cathedral Basilica

ROYAPETTAH

Peter's Rd.

Royapettah Bazar Rd.

Royapettah High Rd.

Kutchery Rd.

Sri Kapaleeswarar Temple

MYLAPORE

Madha Church St.

White's

High Rd.

TEYNAMPET

Luz Church Rd.

Chennai Kailappa Hospital

St. Mary's Road

R.K. Mutt Rd.

Dr. D. Desmukh Rd. (Adyar Bridge Rd.)

Theosophical Society

ADYAR

Elliot Beach

SEE ANNA SALAI AND EGMORE MAP

Eldham's Rd.

ALWARPET

Malaysian Airlines

T.T.K. Road (Mowbray's Rd.)

Chamiers Rd.

Greenway's Rd.

G.N. Chetty Rd.

Valluvar Kottam

Kodambakkam High Rd.

THEAGARAYA NAGAR

Sri Theagaraya Rd.

Venkatanarayana Rd.

Adyar River

Birla Planetarium

Gandhi Mandapam Rd.

Sardar Vallabhai Patel Rd. (Elliot Beach Rd.)

KODAMBAKKAM

Sir Mohammed Usman Road

WEST MAMBALAM

Mambalam Railway Station

Mount Rd. (Anna Salai)

Little Mount

SAIDAPET

Tamil Nadu Tourist Info Office

GUINDY

Inner Ring Road (Jawaharlal Nehru Rd.)

of Chennaipatnam. "Madras" is still commonly used by locals, but trains pulling up into the station are labeled "Chennai Central," as testament to the gradual change.

GETTING THERE AND AWAY

International and Domestic Flights

Chennai Meenambakkam is not as heavily used as Mumbai's or Delhi's airports, making Chennai a relatively peaceful port of entry and exit. There are a number of transport options to the city center 16km to the north. **Local buses** (#52, 52A, 52B, 52C, and 55A; Rs10) are too crowded to be useful, even if you only have a small bag. A **minibus service** runs between the airport and the major hotels (Rs100). This is a slow but sure and comfortable way of making it into the city. Book your tickets at the counter in the International Terminal. The **pre-paid taxi booth** inside the international terminal operates at fixed rates; a ride downtown should cost about Rs140. Regular **taxis** charge upwards of Rs250, while **auto-rickshaws** cost Rs100 with some fierce haggling. A final option is the urban **train** system; it runs from Tirusulam station (a short walk from the terminals) to Egmore and other downtown destinations. It costs Rs40 for the 40-minute ride to Egmore Station, the drop-off point for a number of cheap hotels. Again, as with the bus station, you may get quite a few unkind stares if you try to squeeze onto a crowded train car with a bulging pack.

International Airlines: American Airlines, Air Canada, and **TWA** share an office at 50 Montieth Rd. (tel. 826 2409); **Air France,** 47 White's Rd. (tel. 855 4894); **Air India,** 19 Marshalls Rd. (tel. 827 4477); **Air Lanka,** 76 Cathedral Road (tel. 826 1537); **British Airways,** Alsa Mall Khaleeli Centre, Montieth Rd. (tel. 855 4680 or 855 4767); **Delta Airlines,** 47 White's Rd. (tel. 852 5755); **Gulf Air,** 52 Montieth Rd. (tel. 855 4398); **Lufthansa,** 167 Anna Salai (tel. 852 5095); **Malaysia Airlines,** 498 Anna Salai (tel. 434 9291); **Singapore Airlines,** 108 Dr. Radhakrishnan Salai (tel. 852 2871); **Swiss Air,** 47 Whites Rd. (tel. 857 1128). **Thai Airways, United Airlines, SAS,** and **Varig Airlines** share an office at the Malavikas Centre, 144 Kodambakkam Rd. (tel. 822 6149). Most offices are open M-F 9am-6pm, Sa 9am-1pm. Air Lanka and both Air India fly to **Colombo, Sri Lanka** (4-5 per day, 1½hr., US$90).

Domestic Airlines: Jet Airways India, Thaper House, 43-44 Montieth Rd., Egmore (tel. 855 5353; fax 855 5109) has daily flights between Chennai and Bangalore, Coimbatore, Delhi, Hyderabad, Mumbai, and Trivandrum. **Indian Airlines,** 19 Marshalls Rd. (tel. 855 0640 or 855 5204). To: **Ahmedabad** (3 per week, 3½hr., US$220); **Bangalore** (3-4 per day, 1hr., US$65); **Bhubaneswar** (3 per week, 1½hr., US$180); **Calcutta** (1-2 per day, 2hr., US$200); **Calicut** (4 per week, 1hr., US$80); **Cochin** (4 per week, 1hr., US$105); **Coimbatore** (3 per week, 1hr., US$80); **Delhi** (2 per day, 2½hr., US$235); **Goa** (4 per week, 2½hr., US$125); **Hyderabad** (2–3 per day, 1hr., US$95); **Madurai** (1 per day, 1hr., US$80); **Mangalore** (4 per week, 2hr., US$95); **Mumbai** (3 per day, 2hr., US$145); **Port Blair** (3 per week, 2hr., US$195); **Pune** (5 per week, 3hr., US$155); **Tiruchirappalli** (3 per week, 1hr., US$70); **Trivandrum** (1 per day, 2hr, US$105). Cheaper fares can sometimes be found at travel agencies. Ask the airline to recommend a partner agency where you can find a cheaper flight.

Trains

Chennai has two principal train stations, both located in the northern part of town near Periyar EVR Rd. (Poonamalee High Rd.). For **arrival and departure information,** call 535 7583 and dial the train number after the beep. Trains to destinations within Tamil Nadu and Andhra Pradesh depart from the **Egmore Railway Station.** The station is north of Gandhi Irwin Rd. The reservation counter (tel. 535 3545) is to your left as you enter (open M-Sa 8am-2pm and 2:15-6pm, Su 8am-2pm). Fares listed for 2nd/1st class. Trains to: **Chidambaram** (*Rameshwaram Exp.* 6101, 8:25pm, 6hr.; *Cholan Exp.* 6153, 9am, 6hr., Rs32/293); **Kodaikanal** (*Chennai-Madurai Exp.* 6719, 10pm, 12hr., Rs97/480); **Kumbakonam** (*Rameswaram Exp.* 6101, 8:25pm, 6hr.; *Cholan Exp.* 6153, 9am, 8hr., Rs74/357); **Madurai** (6 per day, including *Chennai-Madurai Exp.* 6719, 10pm, 12½hr.); **Rameswaram** (*Rameswaram Exp.* 6101,

8:25pm, 18hr., Rs176/574); **Thanjavur (Tanjore)** (*Rameswaram Exp.* 6101, 8:25pm, 9hr.; *Thanjavur Fast Passenger* 628, 5:25am, 6hr., Rs76/343); **Tiruchirappalli** (15 per day, including *Pallavan Exp.* 2605, 3:35pm, 6½hr., Rs76/343).

Chennai Central, where most long-distance trains arrive and depart, is in George Town near the Buckingham Canal, also fairly close to the hotels of Gandhi Irwin Rd. The reservation counter is located upstairs in the administrative building, the 10-story, yellow concrete structure to the left of the huge red station (open M-Sa 8am-2pm and 2:15-6pm, Su 8am-2pm). A special desk attends to tourists. General inquiries tel. 135. Fares listed for 2nd/1st class. To: **Ahmedabad** (*Navjivan Exp.* 6046, 9:35am, 35hr., Rs231/1213); **Bangalore** (*Brindavan Exp.* 2639, 7:15am, 6hr.; *Bangalore Exp.* 6023, 1pm, 7hr.; *Chennai-Bangalore Mail* 6007, 10pm, 7hr., Rs145/450); **Calcutta** (*Coromandel Exp.* 2842, 9:05am, 28hr.; *Howrah Mail* 6004, 10:30pm, 32hr., Rs218/1116); **Coimbatore** (4 per day, 7hr., Rs192/556); **Delhi** (*Tamil Nadu Exp.* 2621, 9pm, 34hr.; *Grand Trunk Exp.* 2615, 10:15pm, 37½hr., Rs416/1984); **Hyderabad** (*Charminar Exp.* 7059, 6:10pm; *Hyderabad Exp.* 7053, 4pm, 15hr., Rs221/720); **Mangalore** (*Mangalore Mail* 6601, 7pm, 18hr., Rs248/813); **Mumbai (Mumbai)** (*Chennai-Mumbai Mail* 6012, 11:45am, 28hr., Rs377/1280); **Tirupati** (*Tirupati Exp.* 6053, 1:50pm, 3hr., Rs61/176); **Trivandrum** (*Trivandrum Mail* 6319, 6:55pm, 18hr., Rs225/830); **Varanasi** (*Ganga Kaveri Exp.* 6039, M and Sa, 3:30pm, 39hr., Rs393/1543).

Buses

Most buses to tourist destinations leave from the **State Express Transport Corporation Bus Stand,** on the south side of George Town (in an area officially known as Park Town; tel. 534 1835; open daily 7am-9pm). After you go upstairs to the reservations area, first stop in the small room on the right to pick up the required reservation form (Rs0.25). A kiosk in the corner lists bus routes and departure times. TTC runs to: **Bangalore** via **Kanchipuram** or **Vellore** (#628, 831, 21 per day, 9hr., Rs84); **Chidambaram** (#300, 8 per day, 5hr., Rs42); **Coimbatore** (#460, 883, 9 per day, 12hr., Rs90); **Kanyakumari** (#282, 8 per day, 18hr., Rs115); **Kodaikanal** (#461, 5:45pm, 14hr., Rs87); **Kumbakonam** (#303, 33 per day, 7hr., Rs64); **Madurai** (#135, 137, every hr., 10hr., Rs76); **Mysore** (#863, 5, 6 and 8pm, 11hr., Rs137); **Ooty** (#468S, 7pm; #860, 6pm, 14hr., Rs94-120); **Pondicherry** (#803, every 30min., 4hr., Rs30); **Rameswaram** (#166, 5:45pm, 14hr., Rs93); **Thanjavur (Tanjore)** (#323, 9hr., Rs57); **Tiruchirappalli** (#123, 124, 6hr., Rs70); **Tirupati** (#902, 911, every hr., 4hr., Rs46).

Broadway Terminal, across the street from State Express stand, is somewhat nightmarish, and necessary only for travelers headed to **Kanchipuram** (#76, 79, 130, every 30min., 3hr., Rs12) or **Mahabalipuram** (#19C, 119, 188, 189, every ½hr., Rs10).

Boats

Adventurous travelers might consider the long (3 per month, 56hr.) boat ride to the Andaman Islands. Fares are Rs960 for a bunk, Rs2243 for a 2nd class cabin (with common bath), Rs2854 for 1st class (with attached bath), and Rs3450 for a deluxe cabin. Meals are available at the on-board restaurant. To purchase tickets, foreigners need four passport photos (get them at one of the shops on Anna Salai). For more information, contact the Deputy Director of Shipping Services, Andaman & Nicobar Administration, 6 Rajaji Salai (tel. 532 1401 or 522 6873).

GETTING AROUND

Auto-Rickshaws

Like those of most Indian cities, the streets of Chennai are infested with buzzing swarms of auto-rickshaws. These yellow and black creatures are probably the best way to navigate the city. Though the minimum charge is Rs7, plus Rs1 per km, many drivers tamper with the meters or ask for more money. This is technically illegal, except at night. Be prepared to be taken for a ride if you hop in without any sense of direction. If possible, know the route beforehand, and bark at the driver if he, in hopes of upping his profits, strays from it. Rs25 is a typical fare between two downtown destinations. Always insist that your driver use the meter; if for some reason it's "broken," find another. From the airport and railway station, take pre-paid rickshaws.

Most rickshaw-*wallahs* will happily agree to meet you at your hotel in the morning or will take you around town for the day—simply discuss your plans beforehand and agree on a lump sum. Many drivers will refuse to indulge your laziness when asked to drive a walkable distance—it's not worth the hassle for them. If you have serious trouble with a driver, threaten to take down his number (located on the back of the vehicle or on a black pin worn on his shirt) and report him to the police.

Taxis

Taxis are much less common and about twice as expensive as auto-rickshaws. One advantage, however, is that taxis will allow you to cram in up to five passengers. While most have meters, it's probably best to confirm a price range beforehand. Expect to pay at least Rs100 from the railway stations to Anna Salai or to Triplicane.

Local Buses

The mere idea of boarding an Indian bus deters many, but the bus system in Chennai is efficient, frequent, and (marginally) less crowded than those of Mumbai, Delhi, and Calcutta. Many public buses are green and have their final destination printed on the side. Before boarding ask locals to make sure you can get where you need to go. Bus stands are located every few blocks throughout the city—if there's no awning, seek out the throngs of locals. Try to avoid rush hour (7:30-10:30am and 5:30-7pm).

Buses are boarded from the rear. Inform the conductor of your destination and pay up (usually Rs2-3). Note that many buses are unofficially segregated by gender—women on one side, men on the other. Married couples are an exception to this rule. Nevertheless, out of respect for custom (and women's safety—women are frequently sexually harassed on buses) it's best to follow the locals' lead.

Bus #	Route
22, 27, 27B, 29A	Egmore-Triplicane
40, 40A, 23C, PP23C	Egmore-Anna Salai-Adyar Depot
M4	Egmore-Central
17D, 17K, 9, 9A, 10, 7E	Broadway-Egmore
A18, B18, 18A, 52B, DD18, 60, 60A, 52B	Broadway-Guindy National Park-Airport
9, 10	Parry's Corner-Central-Egmore
9A, 17D	Parry's Corner-Nungambakkan
60A, 18A, A18, 52B, 60	Parry's Corner-Anna Salai-Airport
21G, 17A, 11D, 18K, 18E, 19M, 5, 5C	High Court-Adyar-Guindy National Park-Airport
11A, 11B, 18	Parry's Corner-Anna Salai
4, 23C, PP23C	Anna Salai-Besant Nagar (Adyar)
21, 1A, 19M, 3A, 5	Anna Salai-Mylapore
17A, 17G, 25E, 25B	Anna Salai-Nungambakkan
40, 27A, 27L, 25B, 25E	Anna Salai-Triplicane-Egmore
5, 23C	Adyar Bus Depot-Anna Salai
23A, 23B, 23C, PP23C	Adyar Bus Depot-Anna Salai-Egmore

Cars

Since most tourists lack the gumption to brave the streets of Chennai on their own, many car rental agencies offer battle-worn drivers along with their vehicles. Try **Wheels Rent-a-car,** 281 Precision Plaza, Anna Salai (tel. 433918). (Uniformed, trained drivers, and 24hr. service. Major credit cards accepted.) For 24hrs. or 150km Rs2300/2100, depending on car model. **Bala Tourist Service,** 132A K.H. Rd., Nungambakkam (tel. 822 4444), is also open 24 hours. For local use, cars are Rs1050 per 100km (with A/C). Non-A/C local use Rs700; non-local destinations are Rs9/5.50 per km.

Mopeds

You need an international license to rent a moped (Rs75 per day). If you're craving your own pair of wheels, check out **U-Rent Services Ltd.,** 36 II Main Rd. (tel. 491 0838), in the Gandhi Nagar district in the southern part of town, past the Adyar river.

ORIENTATION

Chennai is a massive sprawl of a city, extending more than 15km along the western shores of the **Bay of Bengal.** While the city feels like a conglomeration of several small neighborhoods, it can be divided into three sections. The northernmost is **George Town,** an area of long, straight streets which run south to **Fort Saint George** and the **Central Railway Station.** George Town's major east-west artery is **NSC Bose Road,** which ends at its intersection with **Rajaji Road (North Beach Road)** and runs north-south close to the shore and parallel to **Prakasam Road (Broadway). Parry's Corner,** at the intersection of NSC Bose and Rajaji Rd., is the wheeling, dealing locus of market area, the city's **bus terminals,** and many rickshaws.

The southernmost of Chennai's three sections is 10km south of George Town and stretches from **Mylapore** in the north to the residential areas south of the **Adyar River.** This section is pleasant, but there is little of tourist interest except for the **Guindy National Park,** south of Adyar in the city's nether regions.

Wedged between George Town and Mylapore is Chennai's pounding heart, which includes **Egmore** and **Anna Salai (Mount Rd.),** Chennai's longest, busiest street. Anna Salai runs northeast to southeast and houses many tourist services. North of Anna Salai lies the congested Egmore area, full of cheap, convenient hotels. Egmore's northern boundary is **Egmore Railway Station,** just off hotel-saturated **Gandhi Irwin Road. Pantheon Road** runs parallel to Gandhi Irwin Rd. Two kilometers south of Egmore Railway Station is the **Cooum River,** which skirts just north of Anna Salai. **Triplicane** is an energetic neighborhood, just south of Anna Salai, near the coast.

PRACTICAL INFORMATION

For the most up-to-date information, tourists should pick up a copy of **Hallo! Madras,** which details everything from practical information to sights and shopping.

Tourist and Financial Services

Tourist Office: Government of India Tourist Office, 154 Anna Salai (tel. 852 4295; fax 852 2139), at the corner of Clubhouse Rd. The best place to start collecting information on Chennai, Tamil Nadu, or the country. Helpful, English-speaking staff. Open M-F 9:15am-5:45pm, Sa 9am-1pm. There's also a 24hr. **GOI information counter** in the domestic airport (tel. 234 0386 or 234 5801). **Tamil Tourism Development Corporation (TTDC) Office,** has moved to a new location near Chennai Central RW Station (tel. 535 3351). Staff dishes out an assortment of brochures, reserves hotels, and books TTDC tours. Open daily 6am-8pm. **TTDC information counter** at the airport's domestic terminal (tel. 234 0569; open daily 8am-8:30pm) and at the international terminal (open 10pm-6am and often in the morning). **Kerala Government Tourist Information Office,** 28 C-in-C Rd. (tel. 827 9862). Open M-Sa 10am-5pm (closed second Sa of each month).

Budget Travel: TTDC (see above) has reasonable excursions to nearby cities. Daytrips to Kanchipuram and Mahabalipuram start at Rs160; to Tirupati Rs260. Government-approved **Sita Travel,** 26 C-in-C Rd. (tel. 882 78861 or 827 0985; email sitamaa@sita.sprintrpg.ems.vsnl.net.in), just past Hotel Connemera, north of Anna Salai Airline ticketing, currency exchange, and Western Union. Open M-F 9:30am-6pm, Sa 9:30am-1:30pm.

Diplomatic Missions: Australia, 114 Nungambakkan High Rd. (tel. 827 6036). Open M-F 10am-12:30pm. **France,** 202 Prestige Point Bldg., 16 Haddows Rd. (tel. 826 6561). Open M-F 10am-3pm. **Germany,** 22 Ethiraj Salai (tel. 827 1747). Open M-F 9am-noon. **Indonesia,** 5 North Leith Castle Rd., Santhome (tel. 234 1095). Open M-F 10:30am-12:30pm. **Japan,** 11 4th St. (tel. 827 6694). **Malaysia,** Asst. High Commissioner, 6 Sri Ram Nagar, North St. (tel. 434 3048). Open M-F 9-11:30am. **Netherlands,** Catholic Center, 64 Armenian St. (tel. 584894). Open M-F 10am-4pm.

Philippines, 86 Radhakrishnan Salai (tel. 235 1016). Open M-F 10am-4pm. **Sri Lanka,** 9D Nawab Habibullab Ave. (tel. 827 0831). Open M-F 9am-5:15pm. **U.K.,** 24 Anderson Rd. (tel. 827 3136). Open M-F 8:30am-4pm. **U.S.,** 220 Anna Salai (tel. 827 3040), at Cathedral Rd. Open M-F 9:30am-6pm.

Immigration Office: Foreigners Registration Office, Sastri Bhavan Annex, 26 Haddows Rd. (tel. 827 8210), off Nungambakkam High Rd. Three-month visa extensions take about 2 working days and cost Rs900. Take 3 passport-size photographs. The office also issues special permits for restricted areas. Open M-F 9:30am-12:30pm and 2:30-3pm.

Currency Exchange: Surly-looking men along Anna Salai will offer to exchange your money. If you wish to avoid the black market, try **Bank of America,** 748 Anna Salai (tel. 852 2386), 2 blocks west of the tourist office and across the street. Open daily 10am-7pm. **CitiBank,** 768 Anna Salai (tel. 852 2151), diagonally to the left from the government tourist office. Open M-F 10am-2pm and Sa 10am-noon. **State Bank of India,** at the international airport. Open for exchange M-F 10am-2pm, Sa 10am-noon. **Thomas Cook,** Eldorado Building, 112 N.H. Rd. (tel. 827 2610). Extra charge for non-Thomas Cook traveler's checks. The private **Forexpress,** 1 Prestige Point, 16 Haddows Road (tel. 827 6597), guarantees 5min. exchange. Open daily 9am-7pm. **American Express** (tel. 852 3628), on the 1st fl. of the Spencer Plaza Mall, across from the government tourist office, Anna Salai. Currency exchange, travel, and cardmember services. Open M-Sa 9:30am-6:30pm.

Local Services

Markets: Merchants at **Parry's Corner,** NSC Bose Rd., in George Town, northeast of city center, vend everything and anything. The nearby **Burma Bazaar** carries imported goods. **Foodworld,** 769 Anna Salai, in Spencer Plaza Mall, provides a more bourgeois shopping experience. Open M-Sa 9am-6pm.

Libraries: Connemera Public Library, Pantheon Rd. (tel. 826 1151). No membership required. Open M-F 9am-7:30pm, Sa 9:30am-6pm, Su 9:30am-6pm. **American Library,** U.S. consulate building (see **Diplomatic Missions,** above). Day membership Rs30. Open M-Sa 9:30am-6pm. **British Council,** 737 Anna Salai (tel. 852 5002). Month membership Rs100. Open Tu-Sa 11am-7pm.

Cultural Centers: Max Mueller Bhavan, 13 K.N. Khan Rd. (tel. 826 1341). Screens German movies and has a collection of German books. Open M-F 9am-6:45pm, Sa 11am-6:30pm. **Alliance Française,** 40 College Rd., Nungambakkam (tel. 827 1477). Brings that neo-imperialist *je ne sais quois* to Chennai. **Soviet Culture Center,** 27 Kasturi Ranga Rd. (tel. 499 0050). For more information on Tamil cultural events, see **Entertainment,** below.

Bookstore: Landmark, Apex Plaza, 3 Nungambakkam High Rd., a busy, bookstore with a huge selection. **Higginbothams,** 814 Anna Salai (tel. 831841). Open M-Sa 9am-7pm. **Fountainhead,** Laxmi Towers, 27 Dr. Radhakrishnan Salai (tel. 828 0867). Open Tu-Su 9:30am-8:30pm.

Pharmacy: Emsons Medicals, 105 Poonamalee Rd. (tel. 825 5232). Open daily 8am-10pm. **Spencer & Co.,** Spencer Plaza, Anna Salai (tel. 826 3611). Open M-Sa 8am-7pm. **Apollo Pharmacy,** 21 Greams Ln. (tel. 824 0200), off Greams Rd., has branches across town.

Hospital: Apollo Hospital, 21 Greams Rd. (tel. 827 7447). **K.J. Hospital,** 496 Periyar EVR Rd. (tel. 641 1513). **Malar Hospital,** 52 1st Main Rd. (tel. 491 4023), near Adyar Bridge, Gandhi Nagar. Excellent lab facilities and specialists. Open 24hr.

Emergency and Communications

Police: Stations in **Mylapore** (tel. 498 0100), **Adyar** (tel. 491 3552), **Guindy** (tel. 234 1539), **Kodambakkam** (tel. 483 8902), **Thyagaraja Nagar** (tel. 852 1720), **Anna Salai** (tel. 852 1720), and **Egmore** (tel. 825 0952).

Emergency: Police, tel. 100. **Fire,** tel. 101. **Ambulance,** tel. 102. English understood, but speak calmly and slowly.

Post Office: GPO, Rajaji Salai (tel. 524 4338, enquiries tel. 514289). **Mount Road Head Post Office** (tel. 852 1947) Egmore, Kennet Ln. Convenient *Poste Restante:* Anna Salai Head Post Office, Madras 60002. Open M-F 10am-4pm, Sa 10am-2pm. **Postal Code:** 400001-400069.

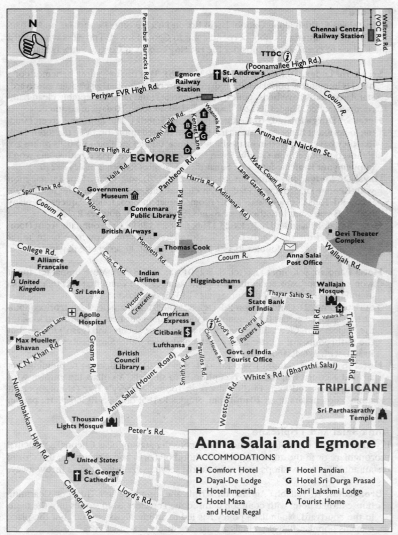

Anna Salai and Egmore

ACCOMMODATIONS

H	Comfort Hotel	F	Hotel Pandian
D	Dayal-De Lodge	G	Hotel Sri Durga Prasad
E	Hotel Imperial	B	Shri Lakshmi Lodge
C	Hotel Masa	A	Tourist Home
	and Hotel Regal		

Internet: netcafé@india.com (tel. 822 3286), just off of Cathedral Rd. next to the Music Academy. You can't miss the neon-yellow signboard. Web-browsing and email (Rs50-60 for 30min.), as well as snacks and coffee (Rs20-65). Open daily 7am-11pm. **World Link,** Apex Plaza (tel. 822 7388), above Landmark Books. Cheaper (Rs75 per hr.), but connections are less reliable. In Egmore, check out **Web Surf,** #6 Gandhi Irwin Rd., Hotel Imperial Complex (tel. 825 4908 or 825 5965). Open daily 10am-10pm (Rs75 per hr.).

Telephones: STD/ISD booths are everywhere; many offer **fax** service as well. **Directory Assistance:** 197. **Telephone Code:** 44.

ACCOMMODATIONS

Hotels in Chennai cater to virtually every budget, but this is a big city, and travelers scraping the dregs of the barrel may find Chennai pricey. Budget hotels have infiltrated Gandhi Irwin Rd. (just south of the railway station), but decent deals can be found almost anywhere. Reserve in advance. Most hotels have a 24hr. check-out.

Egmore

Budget dives flourish along Gandhi Irwin Rd. and trickle onto Kennet Ln. and Whannels Rd., both running roughly perpendicular to Gandhi Irwin. Travelers who need a quick place to crash should consider the **retiring rooms** at Central Railway Station.

Sri Laxmi Lodge, 16 Kennet Ln. (tel. 825 4576). This canary-yellow behemoth of a hotel is immensely popular with Indian wayfarers. Set around a spacious courtyard, standard rooms have beds, tables, chairs, mirrors, and fans. Acceptably clean bathrooms attached. Singles Rs120; doubles Rs180. Reserve 10 days in advance.

Hotel Sri Durga Prasad, 10 Kennet Ln. (tel. 825 3881). The imposing green building looks like it has seen some years; the men fixated upon the TV in the lobby look like they haven't moved in just as long. Popular budget lodging—no-frills rooms are removed enough from Gandhi Irwin for a quiet night. Attached bathrooms won't impugn your hygienic integrity. Squat toilets. Singles Rs150; doubles Rs240.

Dayal-De Lodge, 486 Pantheon Rd. (tel. 822 7328), just west of the intersection with Kennet Ln. Driveway leads to an elegant villa removed from the hectic Pantheon Rd. Fans cool ample (if aged) rooms. Squat and seat toilets. Squeeze as many bodies as you want into the larger rooms. Singles Rs185; doubles Rs240.

Hotel Regal, 15 Kennet Ln. (tel. 823 1766; fax 825 1261). Get your daily fix of Doordarshan TV from the comfy beds. Squat toilets, but would you have it any other way? Singles Rs258; doubles Rs330, with A/C Rs480. Reserve one day in advance. Visa, MC, Amex.

Hotel Pandian, 9 Kennet Ln. (tel. 825 2901; fax 825 8459). More upmarket, but it won't bust your bank account. Indulge in some cable TV and that seat toilet. Perks include email and on-call doctor. Singles Rs375; doubles Rs550.

Tourist Home, 21 Gandhi Irwin Rd. (tel. 825 0079). A shamelessly overpriced tourist trap situated across from Egmore Station; crane your neck upward and look for the English sign. Clean, airy rooms with telephones, sheets, and (gasp!) towels, but the bathrooms are a little grimy. Attached restaurant. Singles Rs330; doubles Rs360, with A/C Rs450/540.

Hotel Imperial, 6 Gandhi Irwin Rd. (tel. 825 0376). A collection of buildings set around a courtyard; the A/C reception is to the left. A collapsing empire with sunken sinks and beds in dim, decrepit rooms. **Sherry's Bar** (ahem, "permit room") downstairs open 10am-10pm. Singles Rs185; doubles Rs360. Extra person Rs50.

Anna Salai and Triplicane

If you're looking for a piece of the action, consider staying near Chennai's principal thoroughfare or in the adjoining neighborhood of Triplicane. From here, the chi-chi restaurants, highbrow shops, and most tourist services are but a stone's throw away.

Broadlands, 16 Vallabha Agraharam, Triplicane, opposite Star Theaters. Charming house-turned-hotel with common bathrooms. Travelers swap stories into the night in the courtyard. No-Indians policy has led to an unofficial boycott, but the place remains popular. Bicycle rentals and free callbacks. Rooms Rs175-340.

Hotel Comfort, 22 Vallabha Agraharam (tel. 858 7661; fax 854 9671), at Triplicane High Rd., down the street from Broadlands. A great deal. Smallish rooms have hot water, TVs, and A/C. Some rooms have squat toilets, others have seats, so peek at the potty beforehand. Singles Rs250; doubles Rs350, with A/C Rs485.

FOOD

Dining in Chennai constitutes many travelers' first exposure to South Indian food and its rice-based dishes: *dosas,* thin rice pancakes in a variety of forms; *idlis,* steamed patties of rice flour; and *sambar,* lentil curry doused on rice. It's hard to find meat here, but proximity to the coast makes seafood a popular item on menus around town.

Egmore

Budget dining in Egmore is a strictly proletarian experience. So roll up those sleeves, wash your hands at the basin, and plunge into that *thali* with your fingers.

Vasanta Bhavan, at the corner of Gandhi Irwin and Kennet Ln. Not to be confused with the hundreds of restaurants in Tamil Nadu that share its name (and ambience and menu). A pantheon of fattening Indian sweets are sold in front. Nice second-floor view of Kennet Ln. Basic *thali* Rs18. Open daily 8am-late.

Bhoopathy Cafe, on Gandhi Irwin, directly across from the main entrance to Egmore Station. Could pass as Vasanta Bhavan's stunt double: purchase fresh juices or snowball-sized *ladus* from the front counter before joining travel-weary Indians in back. Refreshingly cool atmosphere. South Indian *thali* Rs18.

Ceylon Restaurant, 15 Kennet Ln., in front of Hotel Mass. A cross between the whirring *thali*-joint and hotel restaurant, Ceylon is calmer than its brethren across from the railway station. Fresh food is popular with Indians and foreigners. Veg. and non-veg. options Rs20-40. Open daily 7am-11:30pm.

Raj, 9 Kennet Ln., attached to the Hotel Pandian. A prototypical hotel restaurant, with the A/C humming away, and virtually no decor. (Any color would spoil the perfectly institutionalized atmosphere.) Tandoori and Chinese supplement the usual Indian fare. Entrees Rs30-50. Open daily 6:30am-11pm.

Anna Salai and Triplicane

Some of the city's classiest restaurants sit along its main thoroughfare. With prime location and extra pampering, however, come prices more inflated than an Indian politician's ego. Still, bargains can be found.

House of Dasaprakash, 806 Anna Salai (tel. 825 5111), in a white cottage somewhat removed from the street. Although best known for its ice creams, Dasa also serves up safe salads (Rs125) and light veg. Indian entrees that send your salivary glands into overdrive. Open daily noon-3pm and 7pm-midnight.

Buhari's, 83 Anna Salai, across from the Tarapore Towers, near where Anna Salai veers slightly to the right. The speciality is decadent tandoori cooking (7pm-midnight). Locals wolf down chicken *biryani* (Rs28) in the cool, crowded dining hall. At night, take in the cityscape from the terrace. Open daily 8am-midnight.

Hotel Maharaja, Triplicane High Rd., at the Wallajah end (tel. 854 9079). *Thali* restaurant is peppered (or, rather, salted) with a sampling of foreigners. Food is pretty tasty, including veg. tandoori fare (Rs15-30). Open daily 7am-11pm.

Southern Chinese Restaurant, 683 Anna Salai (tel. 852 2515). Small and romantic, with red decor and tables for two. Delicious food and attentive service. Non-veg. options include beef dishes (Rs55-70). Open daily 11:30am-3pm and 6-10:30pm.

Annalakshmi, 804 Anna Salai (tel. 852 5109), next to the House of Dasaprakash Restaurant. Two-floor dining area provides an elegant setting for enjoying traditional, set-price veg. menu (Rs200-300) or a la carte items. Open daily 11am-3pm.

Aavin, on Anna Salai, between the GOI and Tamil Nadu tourist offices. Get to know the name of this ice-cream/flavored-milk bar now, since you'll be seeing its blue-and-white stalls all across the city. Rich dairy goodies like mango ice cream (Rs12). Open daily 10am-7pm.

Cakes 'N' Bakes, 22 Nungambakkam High Rd. (tel. 827 7075), off Anna Salai's southern end. Try a piece of the black forest cake or some good ol' apple pie. Tasty milkshakes wash down the heavy desserts (Rs20-35). Open daily 10am-10pm.

Fruit Shop on Greams Road, 11 Greams Rd. (tel. 823 3548), north of Anna Salai. A cool, colorful oasis from the blistering heat. Fruit punch and fruit cocktails made before your eyes with mineral water. Sit upstairs and try the "sheikh shake" (Rs25), or the "Jughead Special." Open daily 10am-midnight.

Mylapore

Woodlands, 72/75 Dr. Radhakrishnan Salai (tel. 827 3111), attached to the New Woodlands Hotel. Efficient service in cool surroundings. South India *thali* (Rs45), *idli, vadai,* and *dosa* served promptly, if abruptly. Open daily 7-10am and 3-11pm.

Snofield, Amaravati Complex, 1 Cathedral Rd. (tel. 827 4467), just off Anna Salai. Opposite Music Academy. Your source for vaguely erotic sundaes—"One exciting night," "Sweet Dreams," "Playmate," and yes, "Stimulator" (Rs48-60). Open daily 10am-1am. Tuck in *bhel puri, pani puri,* and *aloo chaat* at **Nala's,** next door.

Coastline, Kaaraikudi, Dessert Storm, and **Shogun,** at the Kaaraikudi Complex, #84 Dr. Radhakrishna Salai. Seafood, North Indian, ice cream, and pan-Asian.

Gem Restaurant, Peter's Rd. Candlelight, gilded swans, and exquisite cuisine make this place a true gem. Succulent Reshni *kebab* (Rs70), non-veg. selections (Rs30-100), and fruit drinks (Rs30). Open 11am-3pm and 7pm-midnight.

Chungking, 67/2 Anna Salai (tel. 857 0134), adjacent to Buharis. A popular, classic Chinese restaurant. The decor isn't all that enticing, but the food is fast and delicious. Szechuan chicken Rs65. Open daily noon-3pm and 6-10:30pm.

SIGHTS

For a city of six million, the sightseeing pickings in Chennai are surprisingly slim. If you're in town for a day, avoid overdosing on unimpressive monuments—instead, head for Marina Beach and the city's sumptuous shores (see **Entertainment,** p. 478). If you do anything, climb up St. Thomas Mount for the city views (see p. 478).

Fort St. George

Location: *500m south of Parry's corner; 3km east of Egmore. Tell your rickshaw driver to take you to the Secretariat (SECK-reh-tree).* **Hours:** *Fort open daily 9am-5pm. Museum open Sa-Th 10am-5pm. St. Mary's open daily 9am-5pm. Services Su 9am.* **Admission:** *Rs2.*

Foremost among the city's traditional attractions is Fort St. George, a massive construction standing vigil over the Bay of Bengal. Supervised by Francis Day, construction of the fort began in 1654 and ended later that year on St. George's Day, April 23. Many of the original buildings were damaged or destroyed during mid-18th century French attacks, though some remain. These days, the fort complex is home to Tamil Nadu's state government. Most of it has been converted into government offices, and buildings that are of no use to the administration have fallen into disrepair. The government's occupation of the complex has diminished its appeal as a tourist attraction.

Amid the everyday workings of the Tamil Nadu Legislative Assembly and Council, the ghost of the fort's colonial past lingers. To get a sense of what Fort St. George used to be like, head for the **Fort Museum,** housed in the fort complex's Exchange Building. The museum displays an eclectic assortment of items from British Madras, including old uniforms, coins, and weapons from the Raj. On the upper floors, you can browse through a superb collection of lithographs from colonial times—the images subtly betray the British view of things. Also on display are original writings by Robert Clive, an adventurer of that era who laid the foundation for British rule.

South of the museum, on the opposite side of the gray and white Fort House, sits the modest and rather schizophrenic **St. Mary's Church,** the oldest Anglican church east of the Suez. Consecrated in 1679, the church was built with a vaulted, bomb-proof ceiling to withstand the frequent attacks on the fort. The shuttered windows and wicker pews are distinctively Indian. The interior of the church, however, is cluttered with assorted memorabilia and plaques commemorating British colonists and their descendants. The altar is tastefully simple, graced by a solemn painting of *The Last Supper.* Finally, the fort complex houses the wholly unimpressive homes of Robert Clive and Elihu Yale, the founder of Yale University and governor of Madras.

Not far from the fort, on the southern edge of George Town, rise the minarets of the **High Court** and the **Law College,** both constructed in an Indo-Saracenic style. Both buildings, erected in the mid-19th century, are still in use today, and men in black judicial robes traverse the busy streets surrounding the edifices.

Marina Beach

Extending south from Fort St. George, the 12km strand is one of the longest in the world. The beach is spectacular at dusk, when the setting sun casts an iridescent glow across the skies. In the evening, peddlers hawk everything from roasted peanuts to balloons to ice cream, and hundreds of Chennai residents amble away their worries along the shore. On isolated patches of sand, fortune tellers and palm readers lure customers, soothsaying with the aid of seashells and tarot cards. Most youngsters seem caught up in the carnivalesque air-gun booths that are strangely popular here.

Despite the heat, few locals use the beach for all-out swimming, in part because of the dangerously strong tides, and in part because of the social current—wearing a swimsuit in public is seriously frowned upon. Instead, residents are content to wade along the shore, or simply sit on the beach and drink in the atmosphere. Near the beach are **Anna Park** and the antenna-like **MGR Samadhi,** memorials to former Tamil Nadu Chief Ministers C.N. Annadurai and M.G. Ramachandran. There is also a slimy aquarium and several decrepit swimming pools which are best avoided.

Government Museum

Location: *Pantheon Rd., south of Egmore Station.* **Hours:** *Sa-Th 10am-5pm; ticket booth closes at 4:30pm.* **Admission:** *Rs3.* **Other:** *Camera fee Rs10. Free tours at 10am, noon, 2 and 4pm.*

An archipelago of six buildings in varying states of dilapidation, the Government Museum was established in 1857 by British imperial authorities. Its collection boldly seeks to cover everything from archaeology to ethnology to modern art. But most of the museum's holdings cannot compare to its *pièce de résistance:* the world's finest collection of South Asian bronze sculpture. The high point of the museum is the free-standing bronze gallery, west of the ethnology galleries. This unparalleled collection of Chola bronzes includes a complete set of characters from the *Ramayana* and a succession of excellent 11th-century renderings of Shiva in the guise of Nataraja (King of Dance).

West of the bronze gallery is the less-than-thrilling **Children's Museum,** graced with a much-photographed pair of dinosaurs out front. Next door is the **National Art Gallery,** housed in a splendid Indo-Saracenic edifice, built in 1906. With such an elaborate exterior, the collection inside is somewhat anticlimactic. Finally, the **Museum of Contemporary Art** contains, well, a collection of contemporary art, which varies tremendously in quality.

Sri Parthasarathy Temple

Location: *Triplicane, west of South Beach Rd.* **Hours:** *Open daily 7am-noon and 4-8pm.*

Originally raised by the Pallavas in the 8th century, then renovated by the Cholas and the Vijayanagar kings, the temple is dedicated to Krishna, who served as the chariot driver (Sarathy) to Arjuna (Partha) in the *Mahabharata*. The distinguishing feature of this temple is that it contains the images of four *avatars* of Vishnu: Varaha (boar incarnation), Narasimha (lion incarnation), Rama, and Lord Venkatakrishna. The principal image of Lord Venkatakrishna is constructed of black granite.

Sri Kapaleeswarar Temple

Location: *Mylapore, off Kutchery Rd.* **Hours:** *Open daily 7am-noon and 4-8pm.*

Built after an earlier temple on the same site was destroyed by the Portuguese, this temple has a magnificent 40m *gopuram* (gateway) adorned with a colorful array of gods and goddesses. The great saint Thirugnanasambandar is supposed to have sung the glory of the temple in his hymn. In the same temple, he is said to have brought back to life a girl who died of a snake bite—a shrine and statue commemorate this sacred event. The name of the temple is derived from a story involving Brahma and Shiva. At a meeting on Mount Kailas, Brahma did not proffer the due respects and courtesies to Shiva. An angry Shiva plucked off one of Brahma's *kapalams* (heads), and in an act of regretful penance, Brahma came to Mylapore and installed the *linga* himself. Non-Hindus are only allowed in the outer courtyard, which houses a shrine to Parvati in peacock form.

San Tome Cathedral Basilica

Location: *Eastern Mylapore, 6km south of Egmore.* **Hours:** *Open daily 7am-7pm. Museum open M-F 9am-noon and 3-6pm.*

The Basilica is an important pilgrimage site built over the tomb of the apostle St. Thomas. It is believed that Thomas arrived in India from Palestine in 52 AD and was killed

26 years later. About 1000 years later, Thomas's remains were moved inland and a new church was built, likely by Madras's Persian Christian community. In 1606, the church was refurbished and made into a cathedral, and in 1896 it was rebuilt as a basilica. San Tome is more interesting historically than aesthetically, although the church is pleasant and peaceful, and bears a large stained glass window depicting the apostle's life. A museum on the premises contains a 16th-century map of South Asia.

Little Mount and St. Thomas Mount

Location: *Little Mount is 10km south of the city center. St. Thomas Mount is 5km further.*
Transportation: *Auto-rickshaws from downtown Rs30-40.*

About 6km southwest of the Basilica and just south of the Adyar River is **Little Mount,** a complex of caves where St. Thomas the Apostle led the life of an ascetic, occasionally offering prayers and sermons from his rocky pulpit. Today, the cave once inhabited by St. Thomas bears only a small cross. According to local legend, the impressions in the caves are St. Thomas's handprints. Little Mount has two churches, both of which attract plenty of pilgrims. The older church was built in 1551 by the Portuguese while the newer, Our Lady of Health, was constructed in 1971. About 5km southwest of Little Mount, 160 steps allow pilgrims to ascend the 95m-high **Saint Thomas Mount (Great Mount),** where Thomas is said to have been killed after fleeing his home at Little Mount. The Portuguese-built church atop the Mount was raised in 1523 on the site of a church that had been constructed nearly 1000 years before by Armenian traders. It is said that the current church's altar is built on the very spot where Thomas died, and that the paintings over the altar were done by St. Luke. The cross, which is claimed to have bled in 1558, is said to have been hand-carved by Thomas. The gorgeous view makes you realize just how much green space there really is in Chennai.

Other Sights

One kilometer south of Little Mount is **Guindy National Park,** a peaceful, though increasingly scruffy, expanse. *(Park open daily 8:30am-5:30pm.)* Popular with families, the park is home to some deer and the occasional jackal, mongoose, and monkey. Also on the premises is the popular **Snake Park,** with the usual representation of rep-tiles—king cobras, adders, pythons, vipers, and crocodiles. Hourly demonstrations start at 10am. Eastern Adyar is home to the headquarters of the **Theosophical Society** (tel. 491 7198), a spiritual movement formed by a pair of Americans in the late 19th century. *(Open Tu-Sa 8:30-10:30am and 2-4pm.)* The mansion is surrounded by elabo-rate gardens, perhaps the best in the city.

ENTERTAINMENT

Movies and Cultural Shows

Chennai is home to India's second-largest film industry, so if you have time, take in a Tamil talkie, too. Language barriers won't prevent you from understanding the show—*masala* is *masala* the whole country through. Many cinemas screen English-language movies. **Sathyam,** 8 Thurni Vika Rd., off Peters Rd., near New College, **Woodlands,** Royapettah High Rd. (tel. 852 7355), and **Devi,** Anna Salai (tel. 855 5660), all show four films per day. You might want to prop your feet up on the seat in front of you—rats enjoy the theater's cool darkness. Unfortunately, so do some of the male movie-goers looking to cop a feel, so women should beware. Sound is also an on-again/off-again phenomenon. *The Hindu* has listings of films, special screen-ings, cultural events, and more.

There are music performances and dance dramas at the city's various music and dance academies. The Carnatic Music and Dance Festival takes place annually, from Dec. 2 to Jan. 15. Scout newspapers, like *The Hindu,* to find out what's going on at these places.

I'm Not a Politician, But I Play One in Real Life

Residents of Tamil Nadu, in a trend that can only be termed eerily Californian, have of late developed a penchant for electing members of the immensely popular local film industry to positions of power. In 1977, the film star M.G. Ramachandran ("MGR") won a landslide victory on behalf of the All India Anna Dravidia Munnetra (AIADMK), a breakaway faction of the ruling DMK. That was only the beginning. In 1990, the most (in)famous of AIADMK's leaders, Sri Jayalalitha Jayaram came to power. The former actress and dancer quickly became embroiled in a veritable mini-series of corruption and scandal. She was forced to make a hasty exit in 1995 as her unfolding political drama was too much for her fans (or was it voters?) to handle. Her successor, the DMK-backed N. Karunanidhi, is the bald, sunglasses-wearing character whose unflattering mug is immortalized in statues and billboards in every town in the state. A former screenwriter for Tamil films, Karunanidhi is often depicted alongside Rajinkant, a feather-haired, mustachioed actor who is deeply concerned, of course, in a variety of social causes. For now, Karunanidhi runs a fairly clean ship (of state), but locals jokingly wonder what sort of high-stakes *filmi* scandal this writer will dream up.

Bars and Clubs

Tamil Nadu only recently repealed its prohibition laws, and alcohol consumption is still stigmatized. Most bars have heavily tinted windows and doors, as if to obscure the shameful goings-on inside; many alco-halls bear the moniker "permit room," a relic from Chennai's dry days, when the sale of alcohol required endless bureaucatic hassles. Nearly every hotel three stars or above has its own permit room. But don't expect to find your quaff of choice, since most permit rooms are stocked with just about any IMFL the owners can get their hands on. Near Egmore, decent bars are attached to the Hotel Imperial **(Sherry's)** and the Hotel Chandra Towers **(Bon Santé).** Both are open from 11am to 11pm.

For the serious action, posh hotels are the venues to look into, as young, designer-jean-clad Chennaiis are apt to know. Only the trendiest name brands converge upon **Socko,** Ambassador Pallava, 53 Montieth Rd., Egmore (tel. 855 4476), a popular disco that plays Indian pop for collegiate types (Rs300 per couple; open 11pm on).

SHOPPING

Before you bust out your wallet, take a moment to reflect on your itinerary. Many crafts and silks can be had for considerably less in smaller towns, where you can purchase goods directly from the artisans. Still, **street shopping** can be rewarding since hawkers are common and often offer good deals. The best place for shirts is **Pondy Bazaar,** Theagaraya Nagar, southwest of city center; take Anna Salai westward. Dozens of makeshift shops also line the streets in **Luz** (directly south of city center in **Alivarpet).** **Radha Silk House (RASI),** 1 Sannadhi St., Mylapore (tel. 494 0528), next to the Kapaleeswarar Temple, is a hot favorite among foreigners, with silk *saris,* silk material, silk ties—a profusion of colors. Open M-Sa 9am-9pm. The basement boasts an excellent selection of gift items, wooden carved boxes inlaid with ivory, brassware, and paintings. An art collector's paradise, **Victoria Technical Institute (VTI),** 765 Anna Salai (tel. 852 3141), is one of the best places to pick up paintings, woodwork, exquisite sculpture, brassware, and pottery. The proceeds of this state-run shop go to charity. Open M-F 9:30am-6pm, Sa 9:30am-1:30pm.

SOUTH INDIA

■ Kanchipuram காஞ்சீபுரம்

From the dusty streets to the towering *gopurams*, Kanchi is a city of temples, "the Varanasi of the South." Counted among Hinduism's seven sacred cities (although, of course, there are many more than seven), Kanchi derives its name from the words Ka (another name for Brahma, the creator) and *anchi* (worship). Brahma is said to have worshiped Vishnu and the goddess Kamakshi here, and the magnificent temples constructed by the Pallava kings (4th-8th centuries A.D.) in their capital city reinforce the story. Kanchi was also the episcopal seat of the guru Shankara (780-820), and has been a center of philosophy and learning ever since. Officially, Kanchi is divided into two parts: Little Kanchi houses the important Vishnu temples and Big Kanchi has 1008 temples (by some accounts) dedicated to Shiva.

Modern Kanchipuram is a place where the smell of *chakra pongal,* the sound of temple bells, and the sight of a dazzling array of silks at every store front conspire to launch a sensory assault. When in town, look out for these elegant threads worn by Tamil women—Kanchipuram silk *saris* are famous all over India.

ORIENTATION

The **bus stand** has one main entrance on the east side of **Kamarajar Street** (also known as Kossa St.), which runs north-south through the center of town; most shops and eating places are here, on **Nellukkara Street** (which runs east-west at the northern terminus of Kamarajar St., approximately 200m north of the bus stand entrance), and on **Gandhi Road,** which runs parallel to Nellukkara St., some distance to the south. One block east of the Nellukkara-Kamarajar intersection, **East Raja Veethi** shoots northward, leading out of town. The bus stand has another entrance just south of where Nellukkara and E. Raja Veethi meet.

PRACTICAL INFORMATION

Trains: The **railway station** (tel. 23149), on Station Rd., is east of the Vaikuntha Perumal Temple. Take E. Raja Veethi north and follow the signs. 2nd class only to: **Chennai** via **Chengalpattu** (7 am, 8:40am, noon, 6:10pm, Rs7).

Buses: The chaotic **bus stand,** hidden behind storefronts at the intersection of Kamarajar and Nellukkara St., can be accessed from either thoroughfare. State-run buses run to **Chennai** (#76B, every 30min., 2½hr., Rs17); **Mahabalipuram** (#212A, 212H, 7 per day, 3hr., Rs13); **Vellore** (every 30min., 2hr., Rs10). You can also get on a bus to the transport hub of **Chengalpattu** (#118, every 30min., 1½hr., Rs7) and catch the frequent buses to **Mahabalipuram** and **Pondicherry.** For departures to Chennai, it may be possible to catch a **point-to-point** buses, which will significantly reduce travel time. You must reserve a seat 15min. before departure (Rs2).

Local Transportation: Auto rickshaws can be flagged down on Kamarajar St. or Gandhi Rd., or picked up next to the bus stand. For taxi trips to other cities, consult one of the tourist agencies on Nellukkara St.

Bicycle Rental: Cycles are the easiest way to navigate Kanchi. Rent from the shop outside Perumal Temple or from the stall near the railway station (Rs10 per day).

Tourist Office: While there is no official tourist office, some basic information and advice can be gleaned from the **TTDC Headquarters** (tel. 22553 or 22554) at the Hotel Tamil Nadu on Railway Station Rd. Follow E. Raja Veethi north from the bus station. Turn right at the sign, and follow this street to its end at Railway Station Rd. Turn right again and the main entrance is just ahead.

Currency Exchange: State Bank of India, 16 Gandhi Rd. (tel. 22821). Only changes State Bank of India traveler's checks, so you'll have to head back to Chennai if you want rupees for anything else. Open M-F 10am-2pm, Sa 10am-noon.

Market: Rajaji Market, at the intersection of Railway and Gandhi Rd.

Pharmacy: Tamil Nadu Medicals, (tel. 22285), 25 Nellukkara St., west of the intersection with Kamarajar St. Open M-Sa 8am-11:30pm.

Hospital: Government Hospital, Railway Rd. (tel. 22307). A number of **private hospitals** can be found on E. Raja Veethi.

Police: Police Control Room, Kamarajar St. (tel. 22000).

Post Office: Railway Rd. Open M-F 9am-5pm. **Postal Code:** 631502.

Telephone Code: 04112.

ACCOMMODATIONS

Most of Kanchipuram's budget hotels are noisy and full, clustering near the bus station, close to the intersection of Kamarajar and Nellukkara St.

Hotel Abirami & Lodge, 109B Kamarajar St. (tel. 20797), upstairs from the eponymous restaurant (open daily 5:30am-10:30pm; meals Rs15). Tile floors and bathrooms worthy of a mother's approval. Phones in the rooms, but no windows or sheets. Seat and squat toilets available. Padlocks. Doubles Rs120; deluxe Rs145.

Rajam Lodge, 9 Kamarajar St. (tel. 22519), south of the bus stand entrance. Forget the temples—the colorful, mosaic-tiled floors here are works of art themselves. Serviceably clean rooms. Squat toilets. Better lighting than many of its neighbors. Singles Rs80; doubles Rs100.

Sri Krishna Lodge, 68A Nellukkara St., (tel. 22831), west of Kamarajar St. Bright green, slightly dirty walls. Bring your own sheets. Squat toilets could be cleaner. Fans keep things cool. Padlocks on the doors. Funky purple faux-marble chairs perk up some rooms. Singles Rs70; doubles Rs110.

Sri Rama Lodge, 21 Nellukkara St. (tel. 22435 or 22436). Small canary-yellow rooms with soiled mattresses under the occasional sheet. Squat toilet, but at least it's tiled. No exterior windows. Singles Rs75; doubles Rs130.

Hotel Jaybala International, 504 Gandhi Rd. (tel. 22505). Slightly musty rooms have all the works including towels, soap, satellite TV, elevator access, marble tiles, room service, and a doctor on call. Both seat and squat toilets available. 24hr. check-in. Singles Rs120; doubles Rs275, with A/C Rs425. MC, Visa.

Hotel Baboo Surya, 85 E. Raja Veethi (tel. 22555 or 22556), near the Perumal Temple, about a 5min. walk from the bus stand. The poshest place around, Baboo Surya flaunts a glass-windowed elevator and circular driveway. You get what you pay for: immaculate rooms, seat toilets, and the morning paper. All rooms have Star TV. Singles Rs270, with A/C Rs375; doubles Rs320/450. MC, AmEx.

FOOD

Hotel Saravana Bhavan, 504 Gandhi Rd., inside Hotel Jaibala International. South Indian cuisine with a touch of class. Try the hot *masala dosa* (Rs13). Or cool off with chocolate ice cream (Rs20). Sweet, excellent *badam halwa* (Rs10) is also served. Open daily 9am-10:30pm. Meals available 10am-4pm and 7-10pm (Rs25-38).

Abirami, 109B Kamaraj St., across from the bus stand. Despite its somewhat run-down appearance, the *thali* receives good reviews from locals (Rs15). *Dosas* and *idli* can be had for pocket change. Food served on banana leaves set on metal trays. Wheel around on the wooden office chairs. Open daily 5:30am-10:30pm.

SIGHTS

In theory, a tour of Kanchipuram's major temples takes a few hours. However, to fully appreciate both the artistry and the spiritual importance of these sights, it's worthwhile to allow more time to visit them. Far more than historical relics, these constructions rank among the most sacred locales for present-day Hindus. Since the temples are fairly spread out, a walking tour may not be the best option. Auto-rickshaw drivers will ask for Rs150-200 for a tour, including "waiting charges"; bargain them down if you can. A happy medium might be to rent a bicycle for the day. Below, the temples are arranged in a roughly clockwise order.

Sri Kailasanatha Temple

Location: *1.5km out of town. Follow Nellukkara St. westward until it becomes Putteri St. Sri Kailasanatha is about on the right past a small lake.* **Hours:** *Open daily 8:30am-noon and 4-6pm.* **Admission:** *Free.* **Other:** *If you want to see much, plan to visit before sunset.*

Built by Rajasimba Pallava in the first quarter of the 8th century, the temple is the oldest construction in Kanchipuram. Its relatively modest size and the use of the soft amber sandstone are characteristic of Pallava temples; the famous shore temple at

Mahabalipuram was erected by the Pallavas at roughly the same time. The temple has a simple courtyard surrounding the sanctum sanctorum. The interior of the wall surrounding the shrine is marked by a row of 58 uncomfortably small meditation chambers, where *sadhus* of yore reflected in quiet solitude. In some of the small cubbyholes, traces of the temple's frescoes can still be glimpsed. On the sanctum's rear wall are carvings of Shiva performing the Urdhwa Tandava dance of destruction. The inner sanctum (closed to non-Hindus) houses a *linga* Vishnu is believed to have prayed to in order to help him defeat the demon Tripurantaka. To walk around the image, worshippers must first crawl on all fours through a hollow.

Sri Ekambaranathar Temple

Location: *Puthupalayam St. leads directly north to Sri Ekambarantha.* **Hours:** *Open daily 6am-12:30pm and 4-8pm.* **Admission:** *Free.* **Other:** *Camera fee Rs3.*

The magnificent white *gopuram* of the Sri Ekambaranathar Temple punctuates the skyline in the northern part of town, dwarfing all neighboring structures and mesmerizing visitors who pass through its regal doors. Beyond the *gopuram,* a grassy courtyard sprawls in all directions; straight ahead is the covered entrance to the *mandapa,* graced by an ornate (if lethargic) elephant and row upon row of sculpted pillars, which continue in the interior of the sanctum. *Yalis,* mythical half-lion, half-elephant beasts, stare from the stone columns. Above the *mandapa* is an intricate *vimana.*

The origins of the temple are recorded in the *sthalapurana,* which recounts an incident when Parvati jokingly covered the eyes of her consort, upsetting the process of creation and destruction. So angered was Shiva that he ordered Parvati to earth to expiate her wrongdoings. On earth, Parvati came to a mango tree on the banks of the river Kampa in Kanchipuram and fashioned a *lingam* out of sand. To test Parvati's devotion, Shiva placed before her all sorts of obstacles, which Parvati overcame. Finally, Shiva let flow the Ganga from his hair, hoping to inundate Kanchi and wash away the *linga.* Yet Parvati's devotion was such that she held tight, protecting the *linga* through the torrent. Shiva was pleased and took her once again as his consort.

Today, the inner sanctum still houses this *lingam,* one of five *linga* in Tamil Nadu devoted to the elements. A cavernous hallway surrounding the sanctum houses many *lingas* as well as statues of the 63 Alvar poet-saints. Also within the temple grounds is the mango tree under which Parvati knelt. Each of its four branches, which represent the four books of the Vedas and are supposedly 3500 years old, is said to produce a different type of leaf, as well as fruit of a different taste. Locals believe that eating the fruit cures women of infertility. The temple also houses a large bathing tank, a colorful *nandi* statue, and a famous image of Vishnu as Nilakanta, the blue-throated one.

Kamakshi Amman Temple

Location: *From W. Raja St., turn right onto Amman Koli St.* **Hours:** *Open daily 5am-12:30pm and 4-8:30pm.* **Admission:** *Free.* **Other:** *Photography not permitted.*

This temple, with *gopurams* cast in soft shades of yellow, green, and pink, and capped with tiny wooden spires, is dedicated to Kamakshi, the town's resident deity. A local incarnation of the goddess Devi, Kamakshi is said to have Lakshmi, Parvati, and Saraswati as her eyes. The temple is also one of the three sacred *shakti peeths* of India, devoted to the worship of the female element in creation. The inner sanctum (inaccessible to non-Hindus) is a squarish chamber with inscriptions on all sides. The image of Kamakshi faces southeast; *darshan* is possible only during prescribed *aarti* times. Outside, the *mandapa* is graced by a golden *vimana* which glows with a blinding brilliance under the South Indian sun. The temple grounds comprise a sizeable four acres. It is believed that the grounds were once filed with *champaka* trees, whose reddish blossoms exude a sweet scent. The sacred tank in the back is also entwined in legend; Vishnu sent two servants-turned-demons to bathe here to cleanse them of their evil ways. The temple also houses a shrine to **Sri Sankaracharya,** the first in a famous line of Hindu saints known as *acharyas.* A small gallery next to the *mandapa* bears the images of more recent holy men in this line. It is said that Sankaracharya appeased the goddess Kamakshi with prayer when she was causing trouble in town in the form of Kali. Kamakshi promised Sankaracharya that she would not go into town without his permission. Even today, when her image leaves the temple for the annual **Silver Car Festival** (Feb. or Mar.), a ceremonial stop is made before Sri Sankaracharya's shrine to symbolically request his permission to go.

Vaikunta Perumal Temple

Location: *From E. Raja St., turn right. The temple is several hundred meters ahead.* **Hours:** *Open daily 8am-noon and 4-8pm.* **Admission:** *Free.*

This temple, dedicated to Vishnu, is deserted, and its sculptures have been repaired with plaster by the Archaeological Survey of India. Legend holds that a Pallava king performed an elaborate *puja* at the Sri Kailasanatha Temple on the holiday of *Maha Shivratri.* Ancient texts proclaim that those who worship devotedly on *Maha Shivratri* will have sons who will be devotees of Vishnu. The courtyard surrounding the inner sanctum is lined with granite pillars and carvings that depict the Pallava kings, battle scenes, and musicians. Also visible is an image of the shore temple of Mahabalipuram. The well-preserved carvings are complemented with inscriptions in beautiful, ancient Pali script. The left corner at the back has a panel showing Hsuan Tsang, the Chinese Buddhist pilgrim who traveled all over India in the 7th century.

The inner sanctum (with its images of Vishnu) is generally locked, but generous *baksheesh* to the key-wielding guard can work wonders. The central spire houses three images of Vishnu, one on top of the other. On the ground floor he is seen sitting; on the second floor, reclining on the serpent *ananta;* on the top, standing in an ascetic pose. A small walkway around the *vimana* is filled with well-preserved panels of Vishnu and his consort, Lakshmi.

SHOPPING

The biggest and most reputed of Kanchi's silk *sari* shops is **Nalli Silks,** 54 Nellukkara St. You can also try **Srinivasan Silk House,** 17A T.K. Nambi St. Most owners will gladly take you to the back of the stores to show you silk yarn and the process of making *zari* (pure gold thread) designs onto *saris.* Turn right onto the road perpendicular to Sannadhi St. (outside Varadaraja Perumal Temple) and take a left at **Ammangar Street,** which teems with silk weavers who will willingly demonstrate their craft in the morning hours. In fact, weavers' cooperatives tend to cluster near temple entrances, so you'll probably be accosted by salesmen wielding business cards. Each *sari* is handwoven and takes fifteen days to a month to complete. Expect to pay at least Rs3000 for a good quality *sari* with a fair amount of *zari* and an intricately woven *pallu* (the part that drapes over the shoulder). Kanchipuram silks start at around Rs1000 and skyrocket into the tens of thousands for elaborate wedding *saris.*

■ Mahabalipuram மஹாபலிபுரம்

Officially and properly known as Mamallapuram, the village of Mahabalipuram seems an unassuming presence on the shores of the Bay of Bengal, some 60km south of Chennai. However, Mahabs (as it is unofficially and affectionately known) rises from its slumber into a whirlwind of frenzied activity during the tourist season (Oct.-Jan.) and during January's annual Dance Festival (Jan. 15-Feb. 15). As the foreigners flow in, the streets fill with the monotonous dinking of artists carving stone, and just about every door on East Raja St. seems to belong to a hotel, restaurant, or overzealous tour operator.

Long before travelers frolicked along the miles of unspoiled beach in resorts that extend north of town, Mahabalipuram was the main support of the Pallava kings, who ruled Kanchipuram from the 4th to 8th centuries. Aside from its splendid shores, the village is most famous for the architectural legacy of the prolific Pallavas, in the form of sculptural panels, caves, temples, and monolithic *rathas* (temples shaped like chariots), scattered along the edge of town.

ORIENTATION

Finding your way around in Mahabalipuram is a cinch. From the **inter-city bus stand,** it's a 500m walk due north along **East Raja Street** to the **tourist office,** which is next to the **post office** and a pungent outdoor fish market. On the way, you'll cross the two east-west streets. The first is the unmarked **Othavadai Road,** which leads east to a number of lodges and restaurants. A bit further north, **TKM Road** cuts across East Raja St. At the tourist office, East Raja St. becomes **Kovalam Road,** a long, solitary thoroughfare which stretches out of town, passing a bunch of hotels as it goes. **West Raja Street** runs parallel to East Raja St. The **beach** is a few hundred meters from the village: walk east from East Raja St. The road which runs east to the famous Shore Temple is called, appropriately enough, **Shore Temple Road.** To reach the caves, take Shore Temple Rd. west from the bus stand.

> **Warning:** The Bay of Bengal can be very dangerous, and every year many people drown. Before venturing into the water, ask at the tourist office and at your hotel about the advisability of swimming. Even if you are an experienced swimmer, don't underestimate the force of the undertow. If you have been drinking alcohol, don't even *look* at the water.

PRACTICAL INFORMATION

Bus: Bus Stand, E. Raja St. To: **Chengalpattu** (#212H and 108B, 40 per day, 45min., Rs 5.75); **Chennai** (#108B, 8 per day, 1½hr., Rs10), via **Kovalam** (#19c/119A, 24 per day, 2hr., Rs10), via **Thirupporur** (#118, 188, 188A, 22 per day, 1½hr., Rs10); and **Kanchipuram** (#212H, 212, 18 per day, 2½hr., Rs12.50). Buses to **Pondicherry** (#188A, 2½hr., 8 per day, Rs15) are invariably crowded and a nightmare if you have luggage. You'll be better off catching a bus to Pondy from Chengalpattu (every 30min.).

Local Transportation: Auto-rickshaws and **tourist taxis** wait outside the bus stand, but you won't need them in this small town unless you stay at one of the beach resorts outside Mahabalipuram proper. Many cycle shops rent 2-wheeled wonders. **Nathan Cycle Works,** opposite TTDC, has motorcycles (Rs200 per day) and bicycles (Rs20 per day). Open daily 8:30am-8pm. **Lakshmi Lodge** also rents bicycles.

Tourist Office: TTDC (tel. 42232), in a house at the northern end of E. Raja St., near Kovalam Rd., has good maps and bus schedules. Open daily 10am-6pm.

Budget Travel: Stores along E. Raja St. offer tourist taxis and trips to sites. None are government-approved since TTDC has its own tours to pitch. **G.G. Travels,** 102 E. Raja Street, at the Gazebo Restaurant, is reputable. **V.S. Travels,** opposite Tourist Office and many other travel agencies rub elbows an E. Raja St.

Currency Exchange: Indian Overseas Bank, 130 TKM Rd. (tel. 42222). Go north on E. Raja St. and turn left onto TKM. Open M-F 10am-2pm, Sa 10am-noon. Change AmEx, Thomas Cook, and Visa traveler's checks.

Pharmacy: Arafath Medical Store, 160 TKM Rd., next to Indian Overseas Bank. Some English spoken. Open daily 7am-11pm.

Hospital: Government Primary-Care Facility, adjacent to the Township Office, on E. Raja St., south of the tourist office. Has less than a dozen beds and is not a good option. In an emergency, the tourist office also recommends the private **Suradeep Hospital,** Thirukula St., (tel. 42389), but your best bet will be to get to Chennai.

Police: Vandavasi Police Station (tel. 42221), on Kovalam Rd., just north of town.

Post Office: E. Raja St., near the tourist office (tel. 42223). Open M-Sa 8am-4pm. Telegraph services attached. **Postal Code:** 603104.

Telephones: STD/ISD booths are on East Raja St. and Othavadai St. Booth at the intersection of Othavadai St. and East Raja St. open 24hr. **Telephone Code:** 04114.

ACCOMMODATIONS

Plenty of inexpensive lodgings have sprung up to cater to the droves of tourists who descend on Mahabalipuram during high season. The cheapest accommodations can be found on or near E. Raja Street or Othavadai St. For those with some extra cash, a number of resorts line Kovalam Rd., offering private beaches, extravagant buffet feasts, and oodles of services. During low season, some of these resorts are a superb bargain. If you do decide to stay out along Kovalam Rd., the town and its attractions are but a short, invigorating bike ride away.

In Town

Ramakrishna Lodge, 8 Othavadai St. (tel. 42331 or 42431). You'll recognize it by the shocking red paint job. Tastefully decorated, well-furnished, clean rooms (with hot water) are a fabulous bargain. Rooftop terrace offers tables to chat with fellow travelers—not to mention a soothing ocean view. Singles Rs100; doubles Rs150.

Lakshmi Lodge, 29/A2 Othavadai Street (tel. 42463), down the dirt road on the right at Tina Blue View Restaurant. Fancying itself an international meeting place, this sea-side lodge is crammed full of foreigners, and movie producers and agents frequent the lodge looking for foreign extras (free food, transport to site, and Rs500/day). Simple rooms open onto a small, busy courtyard. Most attached baths have squat toilets. Rooftop patio that overlooks the Bay of Bengal and Shore Temple. The helpful staff offers room service, boat (Rs250), bicycle (Rs25), and moped rental (Rs100/125), train tickets, telephone call-back, laundry, massage, and astrology readings. One single (Rs75); doubles Rs100-200.

Lunar Magic House, the yellow house two doors down from Lakshmi Lodge. Rooms vary considerably from a grimy ground-floor hole to the tiny penthouse "suite" with views of the Shore Temple. All attached baths have seat toilets and mosquito nets are provided, but bring a padlock. Nice garden in back, complete with a hammock. Unfortunately, the proximity of the shore necessitates stinging sea breezes, lots of mosquitoes, and a few bed bugs. Doubles Rs75-300. Negotiable.

Uma Lodge, 15 Othavadai St. (tel. 42322). Slightly grubby rooms have green doors, green walls, green curtains—aesthetic unity in a relatively quiet location. Seat and squat toilets available. Pachai school of yoga upstairs offers holistic massage. Restaurant open if there's sufficient demand. Singles with common bath Rs50, with attached bath Rs75; doubles Rs90; deluxe Rs130.

Hotel Tamil Nadu II: Camping Site (tel. 42287), on the road that veers south in the middle of Shore Temple Rd. You can't miss the billboard. This government-run hotel is a tad pricey, but its rolling gardens are immaculate and the site is serene (pitch a tent outside if you want). Rooms have modern wooden furnishings. Dorm beds Rs50; cluster cottage Rs250; sea-view cottage Rs300, with A/C Rs450.

Mamalla Bhavan Annexe, 104 E. Raja St. (tel. 42260). By far the most luxurious hotel in town, with an eager team of blue-uniformed employees. Spacious rooms have marble tiled floors with luxurious double beds, ceiling fans, and cable TV. Clean bathrooms with seat toilets and hot water heaters. The odor of moth balls and mildew suggests a recent flood. Attached A/C, veg. restaurant. Doubles Rs300, with A/C Rs475; deluxe Rs600. Additional 20% state luxury tax.

Sea Shore Restaurant, behind Lakshmi Lodge on beach (tel. 42074). Two upstairs rooms facing the Shore Temple, with double beds, fans, and seat toilets. In-season: Rs400. May, Jun., and Jul.: Rs300.

Surya Camping Site (tel. 42492 or 42292), on Thirukula St., the dirt road parallel to E. Raja St., off Othavadai St. 16 cottages spread across the grounds, surrounded by lush greenery and the sculptures of Mr. R. Natesan, owner and erstwhile archaeologist. The cottages front a tranquil lake, and upper-level rooms afford ocean views. Functional rooms have seat toilets and basic furnishings. Rooms Rs150-200, depending on view, with A/C Rs350. Singles Rs200/250; doubles Rs400/500.

On the Coastal (Kovalam) Road

Silversands (tel. 42283), about 2km north of town. Before there was Goa, or Kovalam, there was Silversands. India's first beach resort offers a wide variety of room configurations, all equipped with mosquito nets and splashes of character—colorful lanterns, couches smothered with pillows—that give the place a distinctively local feel. Local color continues with rusty roofs, and mosquitoes. Singles Rs400, with A/C Rs800; doubles Rs600/1100; deluxe Rs1600. Off-season (May-Sept.): Singles Rs300/600; doubles Rs400/900; deluxe Rs1300. High-season (Dec.-15 Feb. 15): singles Rs600/1000; doubles Rs800/1400; deluxe Rs2000. Add 20% luxury tax.

SOUTH INDIA

FOOD

In typical tourist-town fashion, Mahabalipuram overflows with restaurants proffering seafood as well as the typical Chinese-Indian-Continental *masala*. Some restaurants close between March and August.

Gazebo, E. Raja St., between Othavadai St. and the bus stand. Despite the Italian map on the wall, Gazebo serves Chinese and Continental. Its specialty is seafood (lobster Rs250, grilled fish Rs55-400). Open daily 8am-midnight.

Curiosity Restaurant, Othavadai St. Grilled fish *masala* and grilled prawns (Rs30) keep the tourists coming back. Four tables under a thatched roof enjoy evening sea breezes. Open daily 9am-9pm.

Mamalla Bhavan, opposite the bus stand on E. Raja St. A typical Indian eatery, with a battalion of fans whirring above and tons of locals below. Try *thalis* (Rs12) and spicy, non-pricy *masala dosas*. Open daily 8am-10pm.

Seashore Restaurant, behind Lakshmi Lodge, on the beach. Pick your barbecue live from the catch of the day, but beware! A platter of grilled tiger prawns can be more than Rs350. Enjoy lobster (Rs250 per ¼kg), jumbo prawns (Rs30-40 each), crabs (Rs150), and shark (price varies) while watching boats come in.

Golden Palace Restaurant, 104 E. Raja Street, inside Mamalla Bhavan Annex. Roses adorn the tables in this moderate-sized diner. During season, escape the stale pink A/C restaurant and take your meals on the "lawn" outside. *Masala dosai* (Rs18), *tandoori gobi* (Rs40), ice-cream sundaes (Rs30-65), and juice (Rs20-25). Open daily 11:30am-3pm and 7-10:30pm.

Silversands (tel. 33383), in the resort. You can't get any closer to the shore than this. Indian, Continental, Chinese, and seafood offerings under a thatched hut with hospitable service (Rs50-500). Board games available. Open 7-10am and 11am-11pm.

Moonrakers, Othavadai St. (tel. 42115), the six tables clustered beside a colorful painting of men raking a sandy shore in the moonlight. European breakfasts popular with tourists (muesli and yogurt Rs15), but travelers seem to linger here throughout the day. Lemon tea (Rs15), fish and chips with salad (Rs60), chicken in lime-mint sauce (Rs60), and honey pancakes (Rs20). Open daily 7:30am-11pm.

SIGHTS

While most of Mahabalipuram's magnificent rock carvings are weathered by the sun, sand, and surf, the town boasts an incredible concentration of intact top-quality sculpture. Each stone breathes with life and sings the glory of the Pallavas. It is believed that these rudimentary sculptures evolved into the more intricate figures at Kanchipuram. Little is known about life in the area when local sculptors produced the work they did, but scholars agree that most of these masterpieces were produced under the patronage of the 7th-century Pallava leader Narasimhavarman I, who went by the fearsome name Mamalla ("Great Wrestler"), hence the town's name. All of the sights are conveniently clustered near the southern part of town.

Shore Temple

Location: *1km east of the bus stand, jutting into the Bay of Bengal.* **Hours:** *Open daily 8am-6pm.* **Admission:** *Rs5.*

Dedicated to Shiva and Vishnu, the temple was built at the turn of the 8th century and is thought to have been the first South Indian temple built entirely of stone. The Pallavas' maritime activities diffused Pallava ideas and styles—echoes of the Shore Temple's lion carvings and stocky spires can be seen in subsequent South Asian temple architecture. Though the area around the temple boasts a profusion of sacred Nandi (bull) images, there has been speculation that the Shore Temple once served a more secular purpose as a lighthouse. The interior of the temple houses a flower-strewn image of Vishnu reclining on the serpent Ananta.

Arjuna's Penance
Location: *In town, just behind W. Raja St.*

This is claimed to be the world's largest *bas*-relief sculpture, measuring 9 by 27m. Particularly impressive is the elegant, witty depiction of animals and birds—look out for the delightfully out-sized renderings of an elephant family and the wry depiction of an ascetic, meditating cat surrounded by jolly dancing rats. While it is easy enough to admire all the frenetic visual splendor, scholars have had a hard time figuring out exactly what the sculpture represents. According to the widely accepted "Arjuna's Penance" theory, it depicts a well-loved story from the *Mahabharata*—the scrawny man standing on one leg is the archer Arjuna, who is gazing through a prism, doing penance, and imploring Shiva for the *pashupatashastra*, a powerful magic arrow. A handful of other historians believe that the images represent Rama's ancestor, Bhagiratha, begging the gods to give the Ganga river to the people of the world (see **Flashing Eyes, Floating Hair, Holy Dreds,** p. 163). The gods have agreed to comply with Bhagiratha's request, and the whole of creation—including the elephants—has turned out to watch the miracle of Ganga gushing down from the Himalaya.

Mandapas and Surrounding Monuments

The area to the west, from Koneri Rd. in the north to Dharmaraja Mandapa in the south, has an eerie, ashen ambience. The hilly area is strewn with massive boulders and 10 small **mandapas** (cave temples), which depict tales from Hindu mythology. Finding your way from *mandapa* to *mandapa* can be difficult, and making a systematic tour is tough. Still, getting a bit lost and stumbling upon *mandapas* can be lots of fun. Just around the corner to the northwest from the bas-relief is the **Ganesha Ratha,** a massive, free-standing monolith dedicated to the elephant-headed son of Shiva and Parvati. Two elaborate pillars mark the front, and a number of intricate columnar forms have been hewn from the stone. North of the *ratha* and off to the left is **Krishna's Butterball,** a massive, squarish-looking boulder precariously balanced on the side of a hill. The name comes from popular stories of Krishna's youth, which recount an incident when the baby Krishna was caught stealing solidified *ghee* from an urn. North of the Butterball, the **Trimurti Cave,** next to a Pallavan water tank, boasts shrines to Shiva, Vishnu, and Brahma, all with their right hands in the *abhya* pose, indicating a blessing. Up above, leaf-shaped windows have been cut from the stone. The **Kotikal Mandapa,** which dates from the turn of the 7th century and is regarded as the area's oldest *mandapa*, is down the hill to the left.

Heading south back toward the bas-relief, you first pass the 7th-century **Varaha Mandapa,** displaying four panels, the most impressive of which (on the left) shows Vishnu in the form of a boar with the goddess Bhudevi (Earth) seated in his lap. Another panel depicts the goddess of wealth, Lakshmi, accompanied by elephants. The trough in front of the *mandapa* was used by worshippers to wash their feet before entering the temple. From the Varaha Mandapa, walk 150m southeast to the exquisite **Krishna Mandapa,** a large mid-7th-century *bas*-relief which depicts Krishna raising up Mount Govardhana to protect his relatives from the god Indra. Other panels depict scenes from Krishna's life, including his play *(lila)* with the *gopis,* or milkmaids. A covered *mandapa* was added several centuries ago. The *mandapa* is also easily accessible from W. Raja St., just south of Arjuna's Penance.

Directly west of the Krishna Mandapa, up the steep hill, rests the decaying **Rayala Gopuram.** This uncompleted construction bears slender vertical panels that portray the 10 incarnations of Vishnu. Two pillars flank an elevated step, carved with an auspicious lotus symbol. From the Krishna Mandapa, it's a short walk south to the **Ramanuja Mandapa,** built in the mid-7th century. The panels are overflowing with Pali inscriptions, and two small chambers border the *mandapa* on the left and right. From there, the 100-year-old **New Lighthouse** is in view. Next to the New Lighthouse is the **Old Lighthouse**—a Shiva temple perched at an especially high elevation, used as a lighthouse with a bonfire on top until the turn of the century.

SOUTH INDIA

Five Rathas

About 1½km south of town along E. Raja St. is a collection of stunning monoliths carved during the reign of Narasimhavarman I Pallava. Known as the **Pancha Pandava Rathas,** these are full-size models of temples known to the Dravidian builders of the 7th century. The complex includes life-size depictions of animals as well as five temples influenced by Buddhist temple architecture and named for the five Pandava brothers, the heroes of the *Mahabharata.* The largest of the temples is the Dharmaraja Ratha, adorned with various carvings of demi-gods and Narasimhavarman. The Rs5 paid to see the Shore Temple gives you access to the Five Rathas and vice-versa.

Government College of Sculpture and Architecture

About 3km north of central Mahabalipuram along Kovalam Rd., hundreds of artisans learn their craft at this sprawling seaside complex. Though there are sculptors busying themselves with hammer and chisel throughout Mahabalipuram, the always-lively Government College can be a fun place; ask at the tourist office or contact the college directly (tel. 42261) to make an appointment and have a look around.

▓ Pondicherry பாண்டிச்சேரி

Many visitors to Pondicherry expect the one-time capital of French India to be a wholly unadulterated enclave of European culture, but the hype surrounding this coastal town is hyperbole: Pondicherry isn't Paris. It's a decidedly divided town, split geographically and culturally by a narrow canal. To the west, Pondicherry is Pondy, your basic, bustling mid-sized South Indian city. To the east of the canal, Pondicherry is *Pondichérie.* The streets here are relatively well-kept, the cops sport red *képis,* restaurants serve up hefty helpings of French food, and much of the architecture is typically European. Pondicherry is a promenader's paradise, its streets populated from early morning until late evening with magistrates in flowing robes, barefoot bourgeois joggers, and hip French wayfarers taking holidays in the sun.

Of course, things haven't always been like this. Two-thousand years ago, the area was dominated by a Roman trading outpost; in the 9th century, the site of present-day Pondicherry was a center of Sanskrit learning. Modern Pondicherry was established in 1673 by the Frenchman Francois Martin, who hoped to gain a commercial advantage for his country over the roving Dutch and English mercenaries. Over the next centuries, the French ruled their South Asian colonial enclaves from Pondicherry. In 1954, the French handed over their scattered territories to India, which gave them the status of semi-autonomous Union Territories and made Pondicherry their capital. Pondy has worked hard since then to preserve its distinctive heritage, luring tourists with a host of cultural and spiritual offerings.

Pondicherry's European heritage is also subtly intertwined in its newfound importance as home of the Aurobindo Ashram, established in 1926. A French artist, Mirra Alfassa (later known as "the Mother"), helped the Bengali mystic Sri Aurobindo Ghose popularize his spiritual teachings among thousands of devotees worldwide. The fruits of their efforts are apparent today: the ashram occupies a sizeable chunk of real estate in Pondy, and at the Mother's request, followers have established Auroville, an experimental community 12km north of the city. Like everything else in Pondicherry, the Aurobindo Ashram seems to have more than one side. For many locals, the Mother emerges as "The French God," complementing "The Muslim God," "The Hindu God," and other powers in the local pantheon. For the several thousand non-Indians who now call Pondicherry home, Auroville is a rural haven where The Mother's research into scientific yoga and the inner-cellular evolutionary passage to the next species can be continued. For many a tourist, the ashram and its devotees— Indian and non-Indian alike—seem stranded in the 1960s. Alongside the colonial buildings, the Sri Aurobindo legacy becomes an intriguing example of Western visions lost to the ravages of time.

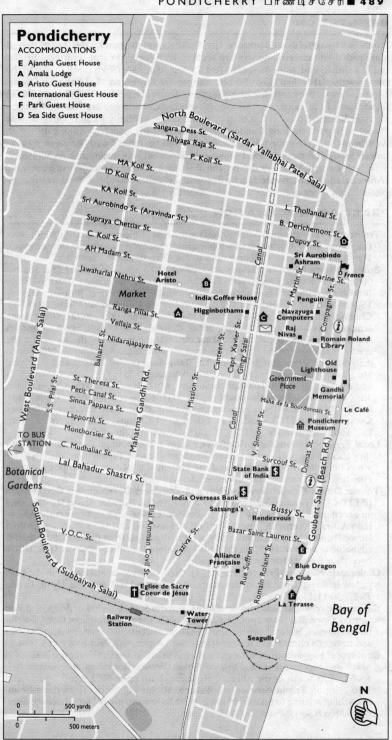

Pondicherry

ACCOMMODATIONS

E Ajantha Guest House
A Amala Lodge
B Aristo Guest House
C International Guest House
F Park Guest House
D Sea Side Guest House

North Boulevard (Sardar Vallabhai Patel Salai)

Sangara Dess St.
Thiyaga Raja St.
P. Koil St.

MA Koil St.
ID Koil St.
KA Koil St.
Sri Aurobindo St. (Aravindar St.)
Supraya Chettiar St.
C. Koil St.
AH Madam St.

Jawaharlal Nehru St.

L. Thollandal St.
B. Derichemont St.
Dupuy St.

Sri Aurobindo Ashram

Marine St.
France

Hotel Aristo

Market

Ranga Pillai St.
Vellaja St.
Nidarajapayer St.

Baharati St.

India Coffee House
Higginbothams

Penguin

Navayuga Computers

Raj Nivas

Romain Roland Library

Canteen St.
Capt. Xavier St.
Gingy Salai

Mission St.

F. Martin St.
Compagnie St.

St. Theresa St.
Petit Canal St.
Sinna Pappara St.
Lapporth St.
Monthorsier St.
C. Mudhaliar St.

S.S. Pilai St.

Mahatma Gandhi Rd.

Old Lighthouse

Government Place

Gandhi Memorial
Le Café

Mahe de la Bourdonnais St.

West Boulevard (Anna Salai)

TO BUS STATION

Lal Bahadur Shastri St.

Botanical Gardens

South Boulevard (Subbaiyah Salai)

V.O.C. St.

Elai Amman Covil St.

Cazivar St.

V. Simonel St.

Surcouf St.

Dumas St.

Goubert Salai (Beach Rd.)

Pondicherry Museum

State Bank of India

India Overseas Bank

Satsanga's

Bussy St.

Rendezvous

Bazar Saint Laurent St.

Alliance Française

Rue Suffren

Romain Roland St.

Blue Dragon
Le Club

La Terasse

Eglise de Sacre Coeur de Jésus

Railway Station

Water Tower

Seagulls

Bay of Bengal

N

0   500 yards
0   500 meters

SOUTH INDIA

ORIENTATION

Pondy is a remarkably well-planned city. Bordered on the east by the **Bay of Bengal** and divided into eastern and western sections by a covered **canal,** its streets are laid out in a simple grid. Important east-west thoroughfares are (from north to south) the busy **Jawaharlal Nehru (J.N.) Street, Rangapillai Street,** and **Lal Bahadur Shastri Street.** West of the canal, the major north-south avenue is **Mahatma Gandhi (M.G.) Road.** East of the canal, the major north-south thoroughfares are **Rue Suffren** and **Romain Roland Street** (both of which end at the centrally located **Government Place)** and a park, the long **Goubert Salai (Beach Road),** which runs along the shore. As it heads south, Goubert Salai hooks west and becomes **South Boulevard (Sub-baiyah Salai);** the rarely utilized **railway station** is off Subbaiyah Salai. As Subbaiyah Salai heads north, it passes the Botanical Gardens and becomes **West Boulevard (Anna Salai).** To the north, **North Boulevard (Sardar Vallabhai Patel Salai)** completes Pondy's circumference and links West Blvd. and Goubert Salai.

PRACTICAL INFORMATION

Trains: The **railway station** (tel. 36684) is a sleepy, little-used place on South Blvd. Four trains leave daily for nearby Villupuram (*Pondicherry-Villupuram Passenger,* 1hr., Rs7), with frequent connections to the Chennai-Rameswaram line.

Buses: Pondy's two **bus stations** are located 500m apart on Lal Bahadur Shastri, 600m west of Anna Salai. You'll get to know and love the massive U-shaped **State Bus Stand,** home to a number of indistinguishable local carriers. Buses leave every 15-30min. for **Chidambaram** (2½hr., Rs16) via **Cuddalore** (45min., Rs3.75), **Chennai** (4hr., Rs29), and every hr. to **Mahabalipuram** (2hr., Rs22). There is one semi-organized operation working out of this zoo: **Tamil Nadu State Transport Corporation (TSTC),** whose booking office at the far end of the station (at the center of the base of the U) reserves seats for some trips. Reservations office open daily 5am-12:30pm and 2-9:30pm. To: **Bangalore** (#450, 7:20am and 10:15pm, 8hr., Rs88); **Chennai** (every hr.); **Chidambaram** (#251, 9:35, and 9:49am, 3:23 and 8:20pm, 1½hr., Rs16); **Kanchipuram** (#302, 7:30, 11:25am, 3:40, 8:12pm, 3hr., Rs29); and **Tiruchirappalli** (#315, 4:45, 6:09, and 10:10am, 10pm, 5hr., Rs34). 500m east is the computerized-but-comatose **State Express Transport Corporation (SETC)** stand. SETC buses go to **Chennai** (#803, every hr., 4hr., Rs29) and **Coimbatore** (#842, 8, 9, and 9:45, 10pm, 12hr., Rs72).

Local Transportation: Auto-rickshaws line up at the stand on Capt. Xavier St., but they also wait in packs outside every major tourist spot. Pay no more than Rs20 for a trip between the bus stands and the French side of town. **Tempos** are overcrowded, often unsafe, and best avoided.

Tourist Office: Pondicherry Tourism and Transport Development Corporation (PTTDC), 40 Goubert Salai (tel. 39497), north of Lal Bahadur Shastri St., dispenses an excellent map of the city. They also conduct a 4hr. tour that covers the Aurobindo Ashram, Auroville, the Government Museum, and the Chunnambar Boat House. Tours (Rs42) begin promptly at 2pm, departing from the tourist office. It is advisable to reserve a seat on the tour bus before the office closes at 1pm. Office open daily 8:45am-1pm and 2-5pm.

Diplomatic Missions: France (tel. 34174), Compagnie St. at Marine St., in the light yellow building. Open for information and visas M and W 7:30am-12:45pm, Tu and Th-F 7:30-11:45am.

Currency Exchange: State Bank of India, Surcouf St. (tel. 36208 or 36730), at Rue Suffren. Open M-F 10am-2pm, Sa 10am-noon. On the western side of town, **Souvenir,** on Mission Street above the United Colors of Benneton, changes all currencies and traveler's checks (Rs5 fee per transaction). Open M-Sa 9am-1pm and 3-7pm.

Bookstore: Higginbothams, Gingy St. (tel. 33836), just north of Rangapillai St., is heavy on academic texts and low on fiction. **French Bookshop,** Rue Suffren (tel. 38062), just south of the Alliance Française. Both open M-Sa 9am-12:30pm and 3:30-7:30pm. **Sabda Ashram Bookstore,** Marine St., across from the ashram. Everything relating to Sri Aurobindo in most Indian and many European languages. Open M-Sa 8:30-11:45am and 2:45-5:15pm.

Cultural Centers: Alliance Française, 38 Rue Suffren (tel. 34351), has French classes and a French library. It also sponsors cultural events and houses periodic art displays in the gallery. Open M-F 8:30am-12:30pm and 2-8pm; Sa 8:30am-noon. Library open M-F 8:30-noon and 4-7pm. **Romain Roland** (a French Public Library), Rangapillai St. Open M-F 11am-6pm.

Pharmacy: National Medicals, J.N. St. (tel. 33073), east of M.G. Rd. Open daily 7am-10pm.

Hospital/Medical Services: The best place to go for medical concerns is **Jawaharlal Institute of Medical and Educational Research (JIMER)** (tel. 72389), a few km north of town; take National Highway 45 straight. **General Hospital,** Victor Simonel St. (tel. 36050), just south of Government Place.

Police: 14 Goubert Ave. (tel. 36790, **emergency:** 100).

Post Office: GPO, Rangapillai St. (tel. 33050). Open M-Sa 10am-7:30pm. Maintains a well-organized *Poste Restante* service. **Postal Code:** 605001.

Internet: Navayuga Computers, 29 (2nd Fl.) St. Louis St., (tel. 46382). Next to the Penguin Restaurant at the intersection of Nehru Street and St. Louis Street. Send email Rs25. Web browsing 1-9pm, Rs50 per 30min. Open M-Sa 7am-9pm.

Telephones: STD/ISD booths are located west of the canal, with particularly high concentrations on J.N. St. and M.G. Rd. They're harder to find on the French side. One is near **Le Club** restaurant on Dumas St. (open daily but irregularly 9am-10pm). There's a 24hr. STD/ISD/telegraph/fax communications **megaplex** next to the post office on Rangapillai St., just east of the canal. **Telephone Code:** 0413.

ACCOMMODATIONS

Apart from a couple over-priced "luxury" hotels, accommodations in Pondy fall into two basic categories: standard Indian lodges and ashram guest houses. Run by the followers of Sri Aurobindo, ostensibly for devotees, the three ashram guest houses offer serene, immaculate rooms, all on the French side of town. The guest houses abide by a 10pm curfew and prohibit smoking, drinking, and drug-taking.

Seaside Guest House, 14 Goubert Salai. (tel. 36494 or 21825), ½block south of A. Madam St. The homiest of the ashram guest houses, this aging, white-washed edifice's bare rooms have blinding white sheets and soothing sea breezes wafting through the quarters. Attached baths are scrubbed clean every morning. Often full, so call ahead. Four A/C and four non-A/C rooms Rs100-400.

International Guest House, 17 Gingy St. (tel. 36699). Modern establishment with a well-maintained garden and grassy courtyard, and its own set of rules. They prefer ashram devotees, but unless they're full they won't turn you away. Asceticism reigns: rooms have smallish, low-set beds, ceiling fans, and little else. Check-out noon. One single Rs60; doubles Rs70-90, with A/C Rs300-400. Suites Rs100-200.

Aristo Guest House, 50A Mission St. (tel. 36728), just north of J.N. St. Management offers "homely comforts" including spacious, Pepto-pink painted rooms and refreshing cleanliness. Green-and-white tiled baths large enough to bathe an entire family at once. Head over to their lush roof-top restaurant for a little air; the occasional exterior window offers an excellent brick wall view. Singles Rs100; doubles Rs150-250, with A/C Rs550.

Amala Lodge, 92 Rangapillai St. (tel. 38910), between M.G. Rd. and Mission St. Simple rooms with attached bath are reasonably clean, with yellow walls that sparkle amid the dinginess. Attached baths with squat toilets and showers—hot water by the bucket in the morning. Check-out 24hr. Singles Rs60; doubles Rs100.

Park Guest House, Goubert Salai (tel. 34412; email: parkgh@auroville.org.in). In the olive-green and white building at the south end of the street. Everything about this ashram guest house is calm, if not a bit cool. The receptionist may be reluctant to offer rooms to non-devotees, but this is the nicest place in town so be persistent. Rooms are cleaned daily and offer couches, ample desks, soothing beds, mosquito nets, and bureaus. Baths are attached with seat toilets, towels, soap, and shower heads. Enjoy the sunrise over the ocean from your balcony or the sea-side garden below. Complimentary filtered water and eerie portraits, too. Doubles Rs300.

Ajantha Guest House, 22 Goubert Salai (tel. 38898), south of the tourist office. Slightly musty rooms could use some brightening up. Attached baths have clean seat toilets. Prime location, but it suffers from the noise of evening promenades until about 10pm. Doubles Rs250, with A/C Rs350.

Hotel Mass, Maraimalai Adigal Salai (tel. 37221; fax 33654), immediately east of the state bus stand. The place to go if you're willing to splurge, or if you absolutely must stay near the bus stand. Posh rooms have central A/C and spacious baths. The hotel boasts 3 restaurants, a good bar, and a pastry shop. Check-out 24hr. Singles Rs620; doubles Rs770; deluxe suite Rs950.

FOOD

For those weary travelers who'd rather make a bodily sacrifice to Shiva than down another *dosa,* eating out in Pondicherry is a welcome change of pace. Pondy's colonial legacy includes a handful of impressive Continental restaurants featuring gourmet French fare and generous lists of drinks. Both sides of the canal also offer better-than-average Indian cuisine at inflated prices.

Hotel Aristo, 714 J.N. St., between Mission St. and M.G. Rd., west of the canal. A hot favorite, this rooftop restaurant will transplant you from the chaos of Nehru St. to a peaceful palace of culinary pleasure, where birds chirp and vines dangle overhead. *Naan* with sesame seeds (Rs12), fish curry (Rs45), and chicken corn soup (Rs14) are especially tasty. If you are craving a beer, the waiter will circumvent the Muslim management with a kettle of "special tea." Open daily 10am-10pm.

Satsanga's, 13 Bussy St., around the corner from Rendezvous Restaurant. This patio affair has a real artsy feel to it, with huge potted plants, columned archways, colorful canvases, and hand-made blue crockery. Try the all-organic Italian salad with home-made cheese (Rs45), pizza (Rs55-75), and *café au lait* (Rs10). While your meal is being prepared, check out the gallery. Restaurant open daily noon-2pm and 5-10pm. Tea salon open 8am-noon and 3-7pm. Breakfast 8am-noon. Closed Tu.

Blue Dragon Chinese Restaurant, 38 Dumas St., ½ block north of South Blvd. This tiny restaurant has five tables crammed downstairs, each illuminated by a Democlean lightbulb hanging precariously from above. Upstairs, you'll be serenaded by the sweet nothings of Tamil television. Good Chinese offerings, including soups (Rs20) and rice and noodle dishes (Rs27-38). Open daily 11am-10:30pm.

Le Club, 33 Dumas St. French open-terrace restaurant has a lush foyer leading to a simply beautiful decor and gracious service *en français ou anglais.* Try *brochette de crevettes* (grilled shrimp; Rs190), or one of the other seafood offerings. Tea served with scalded milk. European desserts include chocolate mousse and apple fritters (Rs70-85). Open daily 8-10am, noon-2pm and 7-10pm. Closed M. Excellent Continental Breakfasts (Rs100-150). AmEx, Visa.

Rendezvous, 30 Rue Suffren (tel. 39132), just south of Lal Bahadur Shastri St., east of the canal. Dine amid tuxedoed waiters, elegantly folded *serviettes,* and oddly appropriate rattan chairs. Rooftop dining available. Continental dishes are priced a bit higher than your Indian faves. A luscious bowl full of pasta doused in sauce costs Rs60-100. Prawn and mushroom quiche (Rs90). Open daily 8-10:30am, 11:30am-3pm, and 6-10:30pm. Closed Tu.

La Terasse, 5 South Blvd., a short jaunt westwards from the southern end of Goubert Salai. Eat in a small courtyard beneath a thatched roof as the musty scent of the wood-fire oven wafts into the dining area, as cardboard cut-outs dangling from above. Italian-style pizza (Rs50 and up) is a so-so imitation of the real thing. Plenty of Indian and seafood options. Open daily 8am-3pm, 6-10pm. Closed W.

Seagulls Restaurant, behind Park Guest House on South Blvd. A stream-lined terrace to rival any cruise ship sits near the ocean at the southeastern edge of town. Bow-tied waiters provide efficient service at this tourist-board-run establishment. Plenty of seafood (Rs50 and up), pizza (Rs40), Chinese noodles (Rs36-42), tandoori (Rs35-130), and desserts (Rs20-40). The *mutton nilgiri korma,* a spicy curry with flavor of mint, (Rs46) is recommended. Open daily 11am-11pm.

Ajantha Sea View Restaurant, 22 Goubert Salai, upstairs from the hotel of the same name. Although only a small handful of tables actually enjoy an ocean vista, this spacious restaurant remains immensely popular with locals and tourists alike—perhaps because of its copious drinks. Indian and Continental dishes Rs50-150. Beer Rs35-40. Open daily10am-11pm.

Le Café, on the Goubert Salai promenade. The ocean mist and a sea-salty scent pervade the small ring of tables that front the ocean. The food is average, but, with waves lapping at your feet, you won't get any closer to the water. Popular for a late-night drink or caffeine fix. Open daily 6am-10pm.

India Coffee House, on J.N. St., across from Hotel Aristo. The Pondy *avatar* of a national chain: steaming-hot *idlis* (Rs5) and *dosas* (Rs12). An army of servers deftly weaves between the densely packed tables and chairs. Open daily 9am-8pm.

Penguin Restaurant, (tel. 38598), 27 St. Louis St., off the eastern end of J.N. St., east of the canal. The Arctic climate and typical non-vegetarian selection are geared for tourists. Less atmosphere than its roof-top brethren, but at least you'll stay cool and insect-free. Tandoori, Continental, Seafood, and Chinese cuisine (Rs30-100.) Milkshakes Rs30. Accepts Visa and MC.

SIGHTS

Sri Aurobindo Ashram

Location: *Marine St.* **Hours:** *Open daily 8am-noon and 2-6pm.* **Admission:** *Free.* **Other:** *Photography allowed only with prior permission. No children under 8 permitted.*

Far and away Pondicherry's most popular attraction, the ashram teems with devotees from around the world. Sri Aurobindo Ghose was a Bengali mystic who evolved "internal yoga" as a way of mingling the principles of yoga with the findings of modern science. Sri Aurobindo was born in Calcutta in 1872, and at the age of seven he left for schooling in England, eventually earning a degree in Classics from King's College, Cambridge. As a young adult, he headed up an Indian nationalist newspaper, and his staunch opposition to British rule led to his incarceration in 1908. In the confines of the prison cell his spiritual evolution took place, and in 1910 he gave up political activities and headed for French-ruled Pondicherry. Here, Sri Aurobindo met "the Mother," who had come to India to further her spiritual development. The Mother gradually became involved in the activities of the ashram, and she was Sri Aurobindo's constant companion until his death in 1950. After he died, the Mother dominated the spiritual life of Pondicherry, lending her energy and charisma to "internal yoga" until her death in 1973. Under her leadership, the ashram witnessed remarkable growth, drawing about 2000 people to Pondicherry to work in this spiritual community. After her death, the ashram faced tumultuous times, as internal struggles developed over the direction the ashram would take—in particular, the fate of Auroville, the ashram's experimental community (see **Near Pondicherry**, p. 495).

These days, the ashram, which was founded in 1926, houses an exquisite rock garden and the flower-strewn *samadhis* (mausoleums) of Sri Aurobindo and the Mother. At any time of the day, devotees can be seen around the perimeter of the *samadhis,* bowing their heads in silent prayer. The building also houses a small bookstore.

Other Sights

Aside from the ashram, most of Pondicherry's attractions are clustered around **Goubert Salai,** the pleasant promenade where Pondicherriens go to see and be seen in the evening hours. During the day, the street is peacefully desolate, disturbed only by tourists and the occasional ice cream vendor. The 1500m rocky beach is pretty to look at but not safe for swimming. Along the beach is a 4m statue of a striding Mahatma Gandhi surrounded by eight elaborately sculpted monoliths, as well as some splendid French architecture, including a monument built in memory of Indians who died fighting on the French side during World War I.

About 1km north of the Alliance Française and just west of Goubert Salai is the pleasant park, **Government Place,** a grassy quadrangle that houses at its center a solemn, neo-Classical monument dating from the time of Napoleon III. On the northern edge of Government Place is the elegant, French-built **Raj Nivas,** once the home of

Tamil for Animals

Mice squeak, elephants trumpet, dogs bark—well, in English, anyway. Like any language worth its script, Tamil has its own set of words to describe the sounds our animal friends make. The following quiz lets you guage your own alacrity for Animal Tamil. Just match the sound with the animal who makes it:

1. கரைகிறது	*karaikerathu*	A. Rat
2. குரைகிறது	*duraikerathu*	B. Lizard, Mouse
3. பிளிறுகிறது	*pellerukerathu*	C. Dog
4. கீச்சிடுகிறது	*keechchedurathu*	D. Monkey
5. கதறுகிறது	*katharukerathu*	E. Crow
6. கீச்சிடுகின்றது	*keechchedukenrathu*	F. Elephant
7. குஅலப்புகின்றது	*alappukenrathu*	G. Cow

Answers: 1-D, 2-F, 3-B, 4-G, 5-A, 6-C, 7-E.

Governor Dupleix, now the plush residence of Pondicherry's Lieutenant Governor. At the southern edge of Government Place is the **Pondicherry Museum,** which displays dusty 19th-century French furniture and an assortment of pottery and other objects dug up at the nearby site of Arikamedu. *(Open Tu-Su10am-5pm. Admission Rs1.)* Among the museum's most interesting pieces are a small collection of Chola bronze sculpture and some remarkable Thanjaveur paintings. There is also an exhibition of vintage black and white photographs of colonial buildings in Pondicherry.

If shady pleasures and greener pastures are on your agenda, follow Goubert Salai to South Blvd., off which are the **Botanical Gardens,** planted by the French in 1826, home to exotic species from around the world. *(Open daily 9am-5:30pm.)* On your way to the gardens, have a peek at the absolutely mammoth Gothic **Eglise de Sacre Coeur de Jésus,** whose altar is flanked by three stunning stained-glass panels depicting the life of Christ.

Chunnamber Boat House, 10 km out of town on the backwaters of the Bay of Bengal offers boat rentals (kayak, paddle, sail, water scooter Rs10-75). Take in some murky green water and open sky, but don't go too far out or you'll find yourself in the ocean. From February to September it is also possible to take a **sea cruise** to watch dolphins. For more information, contact the tourist office (tel. 39497).

SHOPPING AND ENTERTAINMENT

Some of the best accommodations and restaurants are on the east side of the canal in the old French quarters, but be sure not to limit your stay in Pondicherry to the colonial haunts. Instead, take in the busy streets and tremendous shopping west of the canal. Pondicherry is a shopper's paradise: there are a variety of shops and not much else to do. The commercial centers are to be found along J.N. St. and M.G. Rd., where hundreds of hawkers sell export garment rejects for throwàway prices. There are also expensive silk shops, ritzy suit shops, and even a **United Colors of Benetton** (on Mission St. off of J.N. St.). **La Boutique d'Auroville,** 12 Jawarhalal Nehru St. (tel. 37264) has an assortment of clothing, postcards, books, jewelry, and handicrafts made by, for, or about the ashram. They also can provide information about visiting Auroville.

Since alcohol flows freely in this town, bars are relatively common in the French side. Most of the bars attached to hotels—including the **Ajantha Bar** and the **Bar Qualithé Hotel,** located on the southern edge of Government Place—are dominated by local men, and are not the most comfortable place for foreigners, especially women. Many tourists spend the evening at waterfront restaurants that serve alcohol, including the **Ajantha Sea View Restaurant, Blue Dragon,** and **Le Café,** but you wouldn't want to disregard the Mother, now would you?

■ Near Pondicherry: Auroville ஆரோவல்

Twelve kilometers north of Pondicherry, Auroville is an experiment in international living that arose from the vision of Sri Aurobindo and his disciple, the Mother. Soil from 126 countries was placed in an urn at the community's opening in 1968, and the town now consists of about 70 rural settlements inhabited by 500 families from all over the world, all living in bizarre, self-designed houses. The settlements are spread across Auroville's roughly circular area of land, with each focusing on one of the town's principal developmental goals. A large number are devoted to improvements in agricultural technology and methods. Another sector focuses on education and community development. Perhaps best-known are Auroville's industrial and entrepreneurial settlements, which include **Aurelec,** the town's very own computer company. It is hoped that as these settlements continue to grow, Auroville will inch toward its target population of 50,000.

Visits to Auroville are made difficult both by the inaccessibility of the town and by the discouragement of residents unappreciative of tourists who lack a sincere interest in Auroville and its fundamental purpose. If you're interested in a brief visit to Auroville, consider joining the **tour** (Rs42) sponsored by the tourist office in Pondicherry (see **Practical Information,** p. 490). As part of a group, you'll avoid the hassles of transportation and the bureaucracy of getting to see the Martimandir, Auroville's famed temple. To get to Auroville on your own, you can employ one of the many eager rickshaw-*wallahs* in Pondy (Rs100 plus waiting charges) or hitch a ride from a devotee with attached car. To get around Auroville, you'll need a **bike.** Some are available in Auroville, or you can rent one from the Park Guest House in Pondicherry and pedal the 12km to Auroville. One advantage to visiting the community on your own is that you'll have a better chance of actually meeting Aurovilians and seeing their interesting homes. The tour office's brief excursions are limited to the temple and visitors' office. More planning is required for **longer stays;** contact **La Boutique d'Auroville,** 12 Jawarhalal Nehru St., Pondicherry (tel. 37264), for more information. Alternatively, you can contact the **Visitor's Information Centre** (see below) in Auroville directly (tel. 62239; fax 62274; open daily 9:30am-5:30pm). If you'd like to plan your trip before you leave for India, contact **Auroville Guest Programme,** Visitor's Centre, Auroville 605101 (email guests@auroville.org.in). Information regarding **joining Auroville permanently** can be garnered from Entry Group, Auroville Secretariat, Bharat Nivas 605101. Auroville, Tamil Nadu, India (tel. 91-413-62191; fax 91-413-62274; email entry@auroville.org.in). Be advised however, that there is currently a housing shortage in Auroville for newcomers.

Accommodations for visitors to Auroville are limited to guest houses in each of the settlements, as well as to the **Centre Guest House,** which is unaffiliated ("requested contribution" for your stay ranges from under Rs100 to Rs400). Many of the accommodations include kitchen facilities, bath, laundry services, and/or breakfast. The Visitors' Information Centre will gladly provide a list and make arrangements.

Once you've actually gotten into Auroville, your first stop will be the Visitors' Information Centre, a tan brick building surrounded by carefully landscaped gardens. The Centre sells various brochures and displays photos and exhibits detailing Auroville's mission and development, including a model of the proposed town with its fractal-like design. An 11-minute video about the community is shown at 10:30am and 3:30pm every day except Sunday. Just across the way from the exhibits is a larger version of the Boutique d'Auroville (open M-Sa 9am-1pm and 2-5:30pm), selling all things New Age, and a cafeteria with fresh veggie offerings.

Before leaving the visitor's information centre, be sure to pick up a pass to see **Matrimandir,** the temple of Auroville (passes available 3:30-4:30pm; get there early, especially on weekends). Located 1km from the Centre, Matrimandir is the enormous geodesic dome, still under construction. The temple has been a source of tension in the striving-to-be-harmonious community, as some residents feel the considerable money and energy funneled into the project has been misdirected. Work is currently underway to drape the entire dome in a shimmering golden coat. At present, the structure remains an unfinished reminder of the 1960s and the Mother's unrealized vision of a world without religion, where all of humanity may do the Yoga of work and roam free around India's shores while evolving into the next species. Visitors are requested to remove their shoes before entering the Matrimandir single-file, in complete silence. (Open daily 4-4:45pm.) Some may find the rocky gravel path a bit tough on their bare feet, so wear socks. Inside, a winding ramp leads past the construction work to the other-worldly meditation chamber, which houses a large crystal ball surrounded by a ring of slender white columns. The crystal is illuminated by sunlight deflected from a mirror atop the dome; when the sky is overcast, lamps generated by solar power provide the necessary light. In fact, everything in the Matrimandir is powered by the sun, including the frigid A/C air of the meditation chamber (we told you to wear socks!). Surrounding the Matrimandir are elaborate gardens (open daily 8:30am-1pm and 2-5pm), and to its side is an amphitheater which allows any individual to address a crowd of 3000 without electronic amplification.

■ Chidambaram சிதம்பரம்

History has heaped affection on Chidambaram, entwining its past in legend and lore. According to Hindu belief, it is here that Shiva descended from the divine firmament as Nataraja ("King of Dance") and performed the *ananda tandavam* (Cosmic Dance). The forested clearing where Nataraja danced was tinged with holiness and the town which grew up around it was dubbed "Chit Ambaram," or "sky suffused with wisdom." Choosing Nataraja as their favored deity, the ascendant Cholas made Chidambaram their capital in 907AD and, from the time of Koluttanga (1070-1120AD), the history of the Cholas merged with that of Chidambaram. The Cholas built a grand temple, Sabhanayaka Nataraja, enlarging and embellishing it over the centuries. Today, the temple and its four resplendent *gopurams* dominate the center of town, drawing thousands of Shaivite and Vaishnavite pilgrims to its sacred grounds, one of the holiest sites in India. Every February, prominent dancers from throughout India converge on Chidambaram's temple for the Natyanjali Festival, presenting dance-offerings to Nataraja. Many tourists also feel compelled to visit the temple for its superb examples of pre-modern architecture and sculpture, but Chidambaram and its magnificent temple merit little more than a short trip from Pondicherry or Thanjavur. The bi-annual "car festivals" (when ritual chariots glide through the four streets bearing their names) attract revelers in mid-January and April, as does the Tamil New Year (April 13, 1999; April 14, 2000).

ORIENTATION

Chidambaram is small and easy to navigate. **North Car Street, East Car Street, South Car Street,** and **West Car Street** form a rectangular border around the temple. To reach them from the bus stand, turn right (north) as you exit; the main road directly ahead is South Car St. Follow it 500m west to the intersection with East Car St. Follow the north-south street that abuts the bus stand to its southern terminus, at Pillaiyar Koil St. Here, turn left (east) on Pillaiyar Koil and head past the hospital and over the **Khansahih Canal.** Just ahead, signs will point you to the **tourist office.**

PRACTICAL INFORMATION

Trains: The **railway station** is 200m south of the tourist office. Fares listed are 2nd/1st class. To: **Chennai** (*Rameswaram Exp.* 6102, 11:40pm; *Cholan Exp.* 6154, 11:20am, 7hr., Rs62/313); **Kumbakonam** (*Rameswaram Exp.* 6101, 2:25am; *Cholan Exp.* 6153, 3:20pm, 2hr., Rs27/140); **Rameswaram** (*Rameswaram Exp.* 6101, 2:25am, 11hr., Rs88/400); **Thanjavur** (*Rameswaram Exp.* 6101, 2:25am; *Cholan Exp.* 6153, 3:20pm, 2hr., Rs34/184); **Tiruchirappalli** (*Rameswaram Exp.* 6101, 2:25am, *Cholan Exp.* 6153, 3:20pm, 5hr., Rs47/223); **Tirupati** (*Madurai-Tirupati Exp.* 6800, 6:15pm, 10½hr., Rs82/410).
Buses: The typically chaotic **bus stand,** just off the eastern end of South Car St., is shared by the **Thiruvalluvar Transport Company (TTC)** and numerous local car-

riers. You're about as likely to find a beefy Big Mac in India as you are to see any information in English. Most local buses lack numbers, so that strategy is foiled too. TTC departs hourly for: **Chennai** (7hr., Rs42); **Madurai** (8hr., Rs65); **Pondicherry** (1½hr., Rs13). **State buses** run every 15-30min. to: **Pondicherry** (2hr., Rs12); **Thanjavur** (2hr., Rs20); **Tiruchirapalli** (3hr., Rs35).

Local Transportation: Rickshaws (auto and cycle) queue up just south of the bus stand, on Pillaiyar Koil St.

Tourist Office: TTDC (tel. 22738), just off Pilaiyar Koil St., next to Hotel Tamil Nadu on the way to the railway station. Open M-F 10am-5:45pm.

Currency Exchange: State Bank of India, 64 South Car St., just west of the intersection with East Car St., changes only cash. Open M-F 10am-2pm.

Hospital: The **Palanaswaminathan Hospital,** 80 South Car St. (tel. 23099), across from the State Bank of India. Open daily 8am-10pm. **Dr. Palani Swaminathan's Hospital** (tel. 23099), near the State Bank on South Car St. 24hr. **pharmacy.**

Police Station: The **Chidambaram Police Station** (tel. 22201) is open 24hr. The only sign in English reads "All Woman Police Station," which is next door.

Post Office: An inconspicuous light orange building on the western end of North Car St. Open M-F 10am-3pm. **Postal Code:** 608001.

Telephones: STD/ISD booths, most 24hr., opposite Shameer Lodge and Sri Murugan Lodge, at the corner of North and West Car Streets. **Telephone Code:** 04144.

ACCOMMODATIONS

Hotel Palace, Railway Station Rd. (tel. 22639). Not the royal dwelling it was 30 years ago, but clean and friendly. Blue-green rooms have attached bathrooms with squat toilets. Breezy patios off each hallway offer tables and chairs to sit and chat. Popular with students on their way to university. Hot water (Rs2/bucket). Padlocks on doors. Check-in 24hr. Singles Rs50; doubles Rs70.

Sri Murugan Lodge, 160 West Car St. (tel. 20419), north of the temple entrance. Clean rooms with comfortable beds, cavernous cabinets to store your grubby clothes, and squat toilets. Slightly nicer than others in its price range. Calm cream color scheme is a welcome change. Singles Rs50; doubles Rs100, with A/C Rs199; 5-bed family room a bargain at Rs180.

Star Lodge, 101-2 South Car St. (tel. 22743), near the intersection with East Car St., takes its star motif a little too far—wooden stars on the walls, star-shaped windows. Small, simple rooms, with curtains on the glassless windows. Bathrooms aren't as clean as they could be. Bring your own lock. Singles Rs50; doubles Rs70.

Hotel Tamil Nadu, Railway Station Rd. (tel. 20056), in the multi-level white building a few hundred meters north of the train depot. Slightly run-down rooms with choice of toilet, A/C, and TV. Nothing fancy, though the A/C doubles are a bit nicer. Attached restaurant. Singles Rs135; doubles Rs195/450.

Hotel Saradha Ram (tel. 21336), opposite the bus stand, is the most upmarket option in town. Neat rooms have TV, telephones, and attached seat toilet. Batik prints on the walls add a touch of class, while 22 cable channels provide entertainment. Singles Rs400; doubles Rs450-750. Accepts MC, Visa.

Hotal Akshaya, 17-18 East Car St. (tel 20191). This newer hotel has lots of potential. Basic attached bathrooms have either squat or seat toilets. All rooms have telephones. The rooftop terrace offers a spectacular aerial view of the temple. Singles Rs160; doubles Rs300, with A/C Rs480.

FOOD

Strangely, Chidambaram seems to offer more lodges and hotels than restaurants. However, if you want to do more than sleep, several hotels offer dining in tourist-oriented settings.

Hotel Saradharam, opposite the bus stand. The best food choices can be found here, where an efficient veg. restaurant, **Pallavi,** and the extremely popular **Annu Pallavi,** which serves an array of dishes, provide surprisingly tasty meals (Rs10-60). There is also an attached bar, weekend barbecue, and **Moon Shadow,** a late-night coffee house. Popular with both Indians and non-Indians. Open daily 8am-9pm.

Babu, in the Star Lodge. Babu continues the star-crazy motif—just check out the ceiling. Its banana-leaf *thalis* (Rs16) come with the requisite stainless steel cups. Open daily 6am-3pm and 7-10pm.

Aswani Restaurant, 17-18 East Car St., in the hotel Akshaya. Quiet dining in regal, cushioned chairs, with smooth soul and jazz music being piped in. Beyond the window, a few tropical fish frolic in a tank beneath a tropical tableau. Typical Indian and Chinese dishes (*thalis* Rs20-40). Open daily 7-10am, 11am-3pm, and 6-10pm.

SIGHTS

Sabhanayaka Nataraja Temple

Hours: *Open daily 6am-12:30pm and 4:45-10pm. Puja at 7, 9, 11am, noon, 6, 8, and 10pm.*

Covering more than 20 hectares, the Sabhanayaka Nataraja Temple dominates central Chidambaram. Though scholars believe that work on the temple began in the 10th century, local tradition holds that there has been a temple at this site for thousands of years. The modern Nataraja Temple, it is said, was built starting in the 6th century, when the Kashmiri monarch Simhavarman II (r. 550-575) made a pilgrimage to Chidambaram in the hope that bathing in the tank of the ancient Nataraja Temple would cure his leprosy. Speedily recovering after his bath, the king (thereafter known as Hiranyavarman, or the golden-bodied one) was overwhelmed with joy, and he ordered the temple enlarged and modernized. In addition, Hiranyavarman decreed that the holy entourage of 3000 *brahmin* priests (Dikshitars) who had accompanied him from Kashmir should remain behind at Chidambaram to serve the temple. Their descendants are still unique to Chidambaram. Dikshitars can be recognized by the knot of hair at the front of their heads. Regardless of the leper-king legend's veracity, it is built around at least a kernel of truth—the Nataraja Temple was not built all at once, but in stages; as such, its architecture mingles ancient and modern elements.

The Outermost Edge

Most visitors enter through either the eastern or western *gopuram* (gateway), where **guides** immediately accost any foreign-looking person. Their level of knowledge varies tremendously, so hiring one is something of a crapshoot. Make sure you negotiate a price beforehand. Also beware of English-speaking individuals who try to usher you to a priest to anoint you with *kumkum* for a "voluntary" donation.

The temple's four massive, pyramidal **gopurams,** painted in a rainbow of pastel tones, reflect the fragmented construction patterns characteristic of the entire complex. The western *gopuram,* whose interior is embellished with carvings of the 108 dance poses associated with *Bharat Natyam,* is said to date from the 13th century. The 42m northern *gopuram,* erected in the 14th century, nevertheless bears an inscription claiming that it was built by a 16th-century Vijayanagar king. Finally, the southern *gopuram,* raised in the 12th century, contains a set of impressive carvings of the goddess Lakshmi. Each of the four *gopurams* retains its original granite base, although the brick towers have been replaced numerous times, often falling victim to the winter monsoon. Across the front of each base are carvings of Shiva and Parvati.

After entering through the western gate, the **Shivaganga Tank** is diagonally to the left. This is where King Simhavarman bathed, emerging with golden-hued skin. Across from the tank is the **Shivakumasundari Temple,** dedicated to Shiva's consort Parvati. On the other side of the tank, in the northeast corner of the temple grounds, stands the 103m-long **Raja Sabha,** the temple's "1000-pillared corridor" where the victory processions of the Pandyas, Cholas, and other local powers were held. The corridor has only 999 pillars; Shiva's leg serves as the 1000th.

The Second Enclosure

The inner chambers are accessible from the west and east. On the eastern side of the enclosure, look out for the **Devasabha,** "Hall of the Gods," where images of the deities are stored when not being used in processions, and where temple administrators gather for meetings. In the southwest corner of the second enclosure is the **Nritta Sabha** (Dance Hall), which marks the spot where Shiva and Kali had their famous dance-duel. The hall is adorned with 56 pillars representing various dance poses. Apparently, Shiva was supposed to give *darshan* at this site, but the guardian goddess Kalika Devi would simply not be upstaged. The two agreed to a dance duel, the winner having undisputed possession of the forest of Tillai, now known as Chidambaram. At one point in the competition, Shiva dropped his earrings, but he made a characteristically smooth recovery. To put Kali away for good, Shiva raised his right foot above his head and replaced his earrings with deft toes, a move Kali could not match. The defeated goddess was relegated to a nearby shrine, which still stands a few blocks north of the Nataraja Temple.

The Inner Sanctum

The holy innermost chamber, accessed from the southern side of the second enclosure, is off-limits to non-Hindus. However, it is possible to get a glimpse of the gold-tiled **Chit Sabha** and **Kanaka Sabha** from the outside. Five silver-plated stone steps lead to the Chit Sabha; they are said to represent the five Sanskrit letters that comprise the famous Hindu Panchakshara mantra, "Nama Shivaya." The Chit Sabha houses a small image of Nataraja and Parvati. To the right, behind a string of vilva leaves, is the Chidambara Rahasyam, or "secret of Chidambaram"—the **Akasa Linga,** representing the elusive and invisible element *akasa* (ether). In the passageway leading to the sanctum sanctorum is a hallway which leads to the **Govindaraja Temple,** dedicated to Vishnu. This uncommon juxtaposition of the images of Vishnu and Shiva explains why both Vaishnavites and Shaivites worship at the Nataraja Temple.

■ Kumbakonam கும்பகோணம்

Situated on the banks of the Kaveri River, Kumbakonam has a profusion of temples, each a towering monument to the architectural and sculptural acumen of its Chola creators. Hindus from across India descend upon the town's Mahamakham Tank every 12 years, when the waters of nine sacred rivers are said to flow therein. When not inundated by pilgrims or sacred streams, Kumbakonam's religious importance takes a back seat to its role as an emerging center of silk production and small-scale industry, and crowded storefronts proudly display their nascent commercial efforts. The few tourists who journey here are primarily drawn by the impressive temples in the nearby towns of Darasuram and Gangaikondacholapuram.

What Goes Around...

The little image of Ganesh (also known as Vinayakar) on the east side of the Chidambaram Temple comes from a story in which Lord Shiva held a contest between his two sons, Ganesh and Kartikkeya. A delicious *mambazha* (mango) was to be given to the son who could go around the universe and return first. Kartikkeya immediately mounted his peacock and set off, confident of victory. The short, plump Ganesh had only a little mouse for a mount. He thought for a while and then rode around his parents, Shiva and Parvati. When Shiva asked his son what he was up to, the clever Ganesh replied: "Going around the supreme Lord Shiva and Goddess Parvati who create and contain the universe is equivalent to going around the universe." Shiva smiled in satisfaction, and presented the mango to his slow-footed but quick-thinking son.

ORIENTATION

Navigating Kumbakonam is quite confusing, with every street seeming to end at a temple gate. If you arrive at the train station or nearby bus park, it is probably best to pick a hotel and pay for a taxi or auto-rickshaw ride (1.5km) into town. Once in town, familiarize yourself with the three principal roads where you'll find food and lodging: the parallel east-west thoroughfares **TSR Big Street** and **Ayikulam Road,** and the north-south **Post Office Road,** which intersects Ayikulam Rd. to the north and runs into the famed **Mahamakham Tank** to the south. If you really want to walk into town from the railway station, take **Kamarajar Road** to HPO Rd.; turn right to reach Ayikulum Rd. From the bus stand, turn right (north) out of the western entrance, continue walking 150m, and you'll be at Ayikulum Rd. A left turn will take you to the center of town.

PRACTICAL INFORMATION

Trains: The **railway reservations counter** (tel. 20052 or 131) is open M-Sa 9am-noon and 2-6pm, Su 8am-2pm. Trains depart for: **Madurai** (*Tirupati Exp.* 6799, 3:20am; *Mahal Exp.* 6719, 1:45am, *Chennai-Madurai Exp.* 6737, 1:26pm, 6½hr., Rs57); **Chennai** (*Cholan Exp.* 6154, 9:40am, *Chennai Exp.* 6102, 9:50pm, 7½hr., Rs75); **Rameswaram** (*Sethu Exp.* 6713, 9:30pm, 9hr., Rs87); **Thanjavur** (*Thanjavur Passenger* 611, 7:10pm, 1hr., Rs15); **Tirupati** (*Tirupati Exp.* 6800, 4pm, 12½hr., Rs90); **Villupuram** (*Villupuram Passenger* 612, 5:10am, 6hr., Rs41).

Buses: Kumbakonam's **bus stand** has its departure bays labeled in Tamil. Buses leave from the northernmost row for **Thanjavur** (every 3min., 1hr., Rs8) and **Tiruchirapalli** (every 15min., 1½hr., Rs20). Buses also leave for **Chennai** (#303, every hr., 7am-9pm, 6hr., Rs52) and **Bangalore** (1 per day, Rs85).

Tourist Office: Friendly locals are the only source of tourist info you'll find here.

Currency Exchange: Thanjavur is the closest place to change money.

Hospital/Medical Services: KSR Medicals, located just east of the bus stand. Open daily 9am-10pm. **S.T. Hospital,** located on Head P.O. Rd., south of Ayikulam Rd.

Post Office: The **Head Post Office** is located farther south, on Head Post Office Rd., near PRV Lodge. Open M-F 8am-6pm and Sa 8am-6pm. **Postal Code:** 612001.

Telephones: STD/ISD booths are plentiful on TSR Big St. and Head Post Office Rd. Many open 24hr. **Telephone Code:** 043.

ACCOMMODATIONS

Femina Lodge, located in the red-tiled building across from the post office. Large beds dominate small, modest rooms, all with spotlessly tiled bathrooms (squat or seat toilets). A/C expected by summer 1999. Doubles Rs150; quads Rs250.

VPR Lodge, 32 HPO Rd. (tel. 421820), two doors down from the post office, near the bus stand and railway station. Older lodge offers functional accommodations and a downstairs restaurant. Most attached bathrooms have squat toilets. You may want to use your own padlock. Singles Rs70; doubles Rs110; triples Rs150. 5-bed family room with two showers and three fans, Rs360.

New Diamond Lodge, 93 Nageswaran Rd. (tel. 430870), just west of the intersection with Town Hall Rd. Cheap, though the green walls could use a good scrubbing, and the beds lack sheets. Still, one of the cleaner options in its price range. Squat toilets. Singles Rs50; doubles Rs75.

Hotel Athityaa (tel. 421794), south of Sarangapani Temple on the "Thanjavur" end of Ayikulam Rd. A breezy staircase with multi-colored glazed panels leads to well-furnished rooms complete with towels, televisions, and floor lighting. Seat and squat toilets available. Friendly management, attached restaurant and bar. Singles Rs325, with A/C Rs500; doubles Rs350/525.

Hotel Rayas, 28-29 HPO Rd. (tel. 423170), north of the post office and clock tower. Carved doors open on the nicest rooms in town. Attached baths have your choice of toilet, 24hr. hot water, and classy metal wash basins. Color TV and music channels provide evening entertainment and the downstairs **Sathars** restaurant supplies extravagant culinary options. Doubles Rs375-525, extra bed Rs75-100.

FOOD

Eating in Kumbakonam is about basic biological survival, not tastebud-titillation. The majority of local restaurants are fairly run-of-the mill and have dubious cleanliness. If you are dependent on Bisleri, be prepared to do without; try to buy mineral water with a plastic seal, add purification tablets, and pray for the best.

Arul, Sarangapani East Samadhi St. The sign hints at Chinese fare, but the only options here are straight from the Subcontinent. *Thalis* (Rs16) are served up on the dimly lit faux wood tables, with generous second-helpings of rice and ladle-fuls of rich *sambar*. Open daily 8am-10pm.

Pandiyar Hotel, across the street from Arul. Ground-floor cafeteria teems with hungry pilgrims. If you can find a seat, a banana leaf will be slapped down before you, and your *thali* (Rs15) will be constructed one heaping spoonful at a time. Open daily 6:30am-10pm.

Hotel Athityaa, 11/12 Thanjavur Rd. Offers many choices, with non-veg. options at **Aburva,** veg. staples at **Arogya,** fast food snacks concocted at **Abhinaya** in the back garden, and alcoholic delights dealt at the **Nattiya** permit room. You are sure to find *something* to eat between 6am-10pm in either outdoor or indoor surroundings. North and South Indian (and Chinese) dishes Rs15-60.

Sathars, inside Hotel Rayas on HPO Rd. Chicken, mutton, seafood, and beef dishes from across India (Rs30-100). Attached bar. Count on delicious *naan* (Rs8-15), *basamati* rice (Rs15), elaborate *thalis* (Rs25-36, 11am-3pm only), and excellent *dal* garnished with cilantro. Open daily 11am-11pm.

SIGHTS

Kumbeshwara Temple
Hours: *Open daily 6am-noon and 4:30-8pm.*

On the northern side of Ayikulam Rd., the Kumbeshwara Temple faces east, with its elaborately sculpted main *gopuram* rising to a height of 128 ft. Most people enter the shrine from the east, through a crowded market area. From the outer entrance, a hallway with painted columns leads to the portals of the main *gopuram.*

The *linga* enshrined in this temple is said to have been shaped by the hands of Shiva himself. According to legend, Lord Brahma placed a pot containing sacred nectar and the seed of creation atop Mount Meru. A potent flood carried the pot from the Himalaya to Kumbakonam, where it was discovered by Shiva, who was passing through disguised as a hunter. Shiva aimed an arrow at the pot and let loose, destroying the pot and spilling the nectar in all directions. Shiva then fashioned a *linga* from the pieces of the broken pot, or *kumba,* and the nectar eventually spread to the five locales within a 10-mile radius of Kumbakonam. It is said that modern pilgrims should visit these shrines before coming to Kumbeshwara. Some drops of nectar also trickled to the present day site of the Mahamakham Tank. The inner sanctum, which is closed to non-Hindus, opens with a figure of Nandi, Shiva's vehicle. The *prakarams,* (corridors) surrounding the sanctum sanctorum contain shrines to many lesser deities, as well as resplendent sculptures of the 63 Nayanmar poet-saints.

Sarangapani Temple
Location: *Off B.A. Rd.* **Hours:** *Open daily 6am-noon and 4:30-8pm.*

Sarangapani is one of the three most sacred shrines to Vishnu in India, along with Srirangam near **Tiruchirapalli** (see p. 506) and **Tirupati** in Andhra Pradesh (see p. 609). After passing through its 12-story slate gray *gopuram,* which is adorned with a profusion of deities and mythological figures, visitors arrive in a pillared hallway which connects with a smaller, though equally ornate, *gopuram.* Beyond the second *gopuram* lies a grassy courtyard. On the right, as you enter the courtyard, is a sacred shrine to Lakshmi, the goddess of prosperity. Legend holds that the Sage Hema discovered the goddess seated upon a thousand-petaled lotus in a tank (thereafter referred to as the Golden Lotus Tank) within the temple grounds. It was only later that Vishnu came to Kumbakonam to wed Lakshmi. It is customary for visitors to stop at the goddess' shrine before proceeding to the inner sanctum.

There are north and south entrances to the **inner sanctum.** During certain holidays, devotees are required to use the southern entrance, as it was from here that Vishnu and Lakshmi emerged after their marriage. The area around the sanctum is rather dark, and hence is best visited in the morning or early afternoon. It is believed that some drops of nectar from the pot broken by Shiva's arrow ended up at the **Golden Lotus Tank.** Devotees believe that bathing in the tank cleanses body and soul of any sins or ailments, leading to *moksha* after the next birth.

Nageshwara Temple
Location: *Off B.A. Rd.* **Hours:** *Open daily 6am-noon and 4:30-8pm.*

The Nageshwara Temple, dedicated to Shiva, was built sometime during the 10th century and temple is thought to be the oldest in Kumbakonam. The sculpted figures that adorn the *gopurams* are some of the best examples of early Chola workmanship. Some of the finest sculptures in the temple lie within the sanctum itself; surrounding the sanctum sanctorum are niches containing carvings of Shiva and Parvati. The temple has been constructed so that three times a year light passes through the opening in the *gopuram* and falls directly on the shrine image. It is believed that Lord Surya (the sun god) worships Shiva at these times.

Mahamakham Tank
Location: *At the southern end of HPI Rd.* **Hours:** *Open daily 6am-noon and 4:30-8pm.*

The sacred nectar of Brahma's *kumbh,* broken by Shiva, is said to have collected here at the Mahamakham Tank. Every 12 years, the tank's tranquility is disrupted by the **Kumbh Mela** (see p. 231), when thousands of pilgrims descend on Kumbakonam to bathe in the lime-green waters. It is said that when Jupiter passes Leo, the waters of the Ganga and eight other sacred Indian rivers (the Yamuna, Kaveri, Godavari, Narmada, Krishna, Saraswati, Sarayu, and Tungabhadra) flow into the tank, making it a *tirtha* (sacred river crossing), with all the deities in attendance. During the 1992 festival, over one million devotees came to Kumbakonam for a purification bath. During a chaotic stampede of people trying to see Jayalalitha take her purifying dip, 60 pilgrims were trampled to death. It is hoped that 2004 won't see a similar tragedy.

▩ Near Kumbakonam

■ Darasuram தாராசுரம்

A short 4km from Kumbakonam on the road to Thanjavur, Darasuram is known for its **Airavateshwara Temple,** a modestly sized but stunning example of 12th-century Chola architecture. The temple received its name from Airavata, the white elephant mount of Indira; the pious pachyderm apparently worshipped Shiva here.

At the entrance to the temple, two *dwarapalakas* (guardians), rich in anatomical detail, greet worshippers. Past the main *gopuram* lies a courtyard surrounded by colonnaded corridors. Near the base of the inside wall are some remarkably well-preserved carvings, among them some remarkably supple gymnasts, *Bharat Natyam* dancers, and even a woman giving birth. Fortunately, the carvings along the corridor, along with the fabulously intricate *vimana* (temple tower) with its miniature carvings, are being refurbished by the Archaeological Survey of India. To get to Darasuram, take a **bus** bound for Thanjavur and ask to be let off at Darasuram (Rs2).

■ Gangaikondacholapuram கங்கைகொண்டசோழபுரம்

The legacy of King Rajendra I (r. 1012-100) lives on at **Gangaikondacholapuram,** some 35km north of Kumbakonam. The town, whose name means "the city of the Chola who conquered the Ganga," was built by Rajendra when he defeated the kingdoms to the north. To commemorate his victory, the king had water from the Ganga transported south and dumped into the tank at this temple. As the temple is dedicated to Shiva, a sizeable Nandi guards the entrance, and among the most impressive carvings is a frieze that depicts Shiva and Parvati crowning King Rajendra. **Buses** from Kumbakonam regularly make the trip out here (Rs6-10). Never fear, eager bus attendants will be happy to help you out as you stumble through the name *Gangai-konda-chola-puram,* and, if you're lucky, they'll direct you to the correct bus.

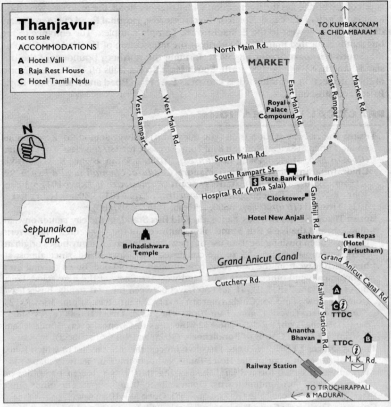

Thanjavur
not to scale
ACCOMMODATIONS
A Hotel Valli
B Raja Rest House
C Hotel Tamil Nadu

TO KUMBAKONAM & CHIDAMBARAM

North Main Rd.

MARKET

East Main Rd.

East Rampart

Market Rd.

West Rampart

West Main Rd.

Royal Palace Compound

N

South Main Rd.

South Rampart St.

State Bank of India

Hospital Rd. (Anna Salai)

Clocktower

Gandhiji Rd.

Hotel New Anjali

Seppunaikan Tank

Brihadishwara Temple

Sathars

Les Repas (Hotel Parisutham)

Grand Anicut Canal

Grand Anicut Canal Rd.

Cutchery Rd.

Railway Station Rd.

TTDC

Anantha Bhavan

TTDC

M. K. Rd.

Railway Station

TO TIRUCHIRAPPALI & MADURAI

SOUTH INDIA

■ Thanjavur (Tanjore) தஞ்சாவூர்

The small town of Thanjavur reached its pinnacle of political and cultural importance as capital of the Chola empire between the 10th and 14th centuries. The Chola bronzes, local handicrafts, and the grand Brihadishwara Temple, with its impressive *linga*, are the remnants of this golden era in the now dusty, unassuming, and primarily agricultural town. Though only an hour from the burgeoning urban center of Tiruchirappalli, Thanjavur remains laid back and provincial. The peak tourist season extends from October through March, gaining momentum in December and February. As in the case with any small town dominated by the tourist trade, locals seem to have mixed attitudes about the foreign parasites they periodically host. While some open their pharmacies, silk shops, and lodges willingly, others prefer to mind their own business. For the humble visitor, however, Thanjavur generally offers stretches of open space, fresh air to fill the lungs, and kind, hospitable people. And the spectacular architecture of the temple, along with the paintings and Chola bronzes on display at local museums, are sure to delight.

ORIENTATION

Thanjavur is divided into northern and southern sections by the **Grand Anicut Canal.** The **Thanjavur Junction Railway Station** is 600m south of the canal. From the station, **Railway Station Road** curves slightly as it heads north, passing a branch of the tourist office and several hotels before reaching the canal. As it crosses the canal, Railway Station Rd. becomes **Gandhiji Road,** which is dominated by silk shops. Just south of the bridge lies the intersection with **Kutchery Road,** the main east-west thoroughfare south of the canal. North of the **clocktower, Hospital Road** cuts across Gandhiji Rd., leading west to the **Brihadishwara Temple** complex. The entrance to the bus stands is located immediately north of the intersection of Hospital and Gandhiji Rd. **South Rampart Street** juts west, forming the northern boundary of the bus stands. Another 100m farther north, **South Main Street** trails off to the west. North of this intersection, Gandhiji Rd. is known as **East Main Road** and leads to the Royal Palace and Museum.

PRACTICAL INFORMATION

Trains: The **railway station** is on (you guessed it) Railway Station Rd. Reservations counter open M-Sa 9am-8pm, Su 8am-2pm. Fares are for 1st/2nd class. To: **Chennai** (*Cholan Exp.* 6154, 8:45am, *Cholan Exp.* 6102, 8:55pm, 8½hr., Rs79/395) via **Chidambaram** (3hr., Rs29/164); **Madurai** (*Madurai-Chennai Janata Exp.* 6799, 4:15am; 5½hr., Rs52/252); **Rameswaram** (*Rameswaram Exp.* 6101, 5:30am, 10hr., Rs74/357); **Tiruchirapalli** (*Rameswaram Exp.* 6101, 5:30am, 1½hr., Rs17/102); **Tirupati** (*Tirupati Exp.* 6800, 2:55pm, 15hr., Rs97/480).

Buses: Thanjavur has two bus stands: the **Old Bus Stand,** in the city center on Gandhiji Rd., and the **New Bus Stand,** 4km southwest of the city center. The government has been pushing locals to use the new stand by having many buses originate there, but most people stick to the congested downtown stand, since almost all buses that leave from the new stand pass through the old one. Buses arriving from Tiruchirapalli and other points south and west terminate at the new stand. Local buses #74, 74A, 74B, 74D, 41, and 60 travel between the two stands. Buses leave from the new stand to: **Chidambaram** (every 20min., 6am-10pm, 3hr., Rs12); **Kumbakonam** (every 15min., 6am-10pm, 1hr., Rs9); **Tiruchappalli** (every 5min., 5am-11:30pm, 1½hr., Rs12). The #323 bus runs to **Chennai** every 30min. (6am-2:30am, Rs65). **TTC** runs to **Pondicherry** (10am and 4pm, 5hr., Rs52).

Tourist Office: TTDC (tel. 30984) has two offices, the more useful of which is in a strip of stores in front of the Hotel Tamil Nadu complex on Railway Station Rd. Friendly and well-informed English-speaking staff. Has a decent pamphlet on Thanjavur and surrounding towns. Open daily 8:30am-8:30pm. The other office (tel. 23017) is opposite the GPO on M.K. Rd. Open M-F 10am-6pm.

Currency Exchange: State Bank of India (tel. 20082), on Hospital Rd. about 300m west of Gandhiji Rd. Open M-F 10am-2pm, Sa 10am-noon. If you're desperate, the **Hotel Parishutham,** on Grand Anicut Canal Rd. (just north of the canal) will gladly change currency for a less-than-favorable rate.

Local Transportation: Local **buses** circulate between the two bus stands. There is an **auto-rickshaw** stand right outside the railway station. A rickshaw ride between the railway station and the center of town should cost no more than Rs15-20.

Hospital: Thanjavur Medical College Hospital, Medical College Rd. (tel. 22459). A 15min. auto-rickshaw ride from the station to the southwest, approaching Tamil University. There are a few **private hospitals** on South Rampart St.

Police: East Police Station, Palace Complex, East Main St. (tel. 21450).

Post Office: M.K. Rd. (tel. 31022), off Railway Station Rd. in the southern part of town. Open M-Sa 7:30am-7pm, Su noon-4pm. **Postal Code:** 613001.

Telephones: There are 24hr. **STD/ISD booths** in the bus stand area and also right next to Hotel Tamil Nadu. **Telephone Code:** 04362.

ACCOMMODATIONS

Hotels in Thanjavur are evenly distributed along the main thoroughfares, from the railway station in the south to the bus stands in the north. Those south of the canal are likely to be more peaceful than those that overlook the bus stand.

Hotel Valli, 2948 M.K. Rd. (tel. 31580), on a small side street. From the railway station, take M.K. Rd. east, passing the tourist office. You'll soon see a sign on the left pointing to the hotel. Colorful old house, surrounded by lumbering trees and a variety of tropical plants, manages to stay cool. Rooms are slightly dusty and musty.

Attached baths (squat and seat toilets) and cable TV. Reasonably priced attached restaurant. Singles Rs165; doubles Rs195; with A/C Rs480.

Raja Rest House (tel. 30515), off Gandhiji Rd., just north of Hotel Tamil Nadu. A ring of rooms surrounds a desolate courtyard, its center overgrown with weeds. The dingy rooms have sullied walls and bare concrete squat toilets. The management is friendly, though, and these are some of the cheapest rooms in town. Hot water by the bucket (Rs4). Singles Rs60; doubles Rs100; triples Rs150.

Hotel Tamil Nadu (tel. 31421). In the large white complex on Gandhiji Rd. Rooms have Kashmiri wooden partitions, wall hangings, and neatly made, comfy beds. Rooms have attached bathrooms with seat toilets. Restaurant and bar downstairs. Check-out 24hr. Doubles Rs300, with TV Rs420, with A/C Rs600. Twelve-bed family room only Rs540!

FOOD

Unless you succumb to some hedonistic whim by dining at a swank hotel restaurant, most of the food in Thanjavur is uninspiring. There are hordes of seemingly indistinguishable vegetarian restaurants around the bus stand that cater to locals. Carnivores will find slim pickings in this conservative Hindu town, although there are several very good non-veg. restaurants in town.

Anantha Bhavan, Railway Station Rd., just north of the railway station. Along with the newer **Ganesh Bhavan** up the street, it serves good old-fashioned South Indian *thalis* (Rs15) on banana leaves. Not exactly tranquil, but at least you won't be lonely. Open daily 7-10am, noon-3pm, and 6-10pm.

Sathars Restaurant, 167 Gandhiji Rd., north of the canal. Woven reed matting encloses the romantic lower sitting area, while the upstairs terrace opens up to the stars above. Enjoy garnished chicken, mutton, beef, and seafood delicacies (Rs35-100). Open daily noon-11:30pm.

Hotel New Anjali, Gandhiji Rd., just north of the canal. One of the few non-veg. restaurants in town. Slightly cramped booths offer more privacy than neighboring restaurants. Hearty entrees run Rs35-70. Open daily 6:30am-11pm.

Les Repas, in Hotel Parisutham, north of the canal on Grand Anicut Canal Rd. Candlelight dining and place settings so meticulous that you're bound to feel a tinge of guilt disturbing them. The menu includes Continental entrees (steaks and sizzlers Rs75-175) and Indian standards (Rs30-60). Open daily 10am-2:30pm and 6-11pm.

Lingam Restaurant, inside Hotel Valli. Rice, *dosas*, and *channa masala* (Rs10-50) are always available at this slightly-better-than-average lodge diner. Popular spot for tea with hotel visitors; occasionally booked for conferences held in the upstairs meeting hall. Open 6-10am, noon-3pm, and 5-10pm.

SIGHTS

Brihadishwara Temple

Hours: *Open roughly 8am-1pm and 4-9pm.* **Admission:** *Free. Donations accepted in Temple office.* **Other:** *Fourth Maha Kumbaldishegam performed Su 7-30am. Museum open daily 9am-1pm and 4-8pm.*

Far and away Thanjavur's most impressive attraction is this absolutely spectacular temple, a serene example of Dravidian architecture. It was constructed over the course of 12 years by the Chola King Raja Raja I (r. 985-1013). Unable to find a cure for his leprosy, Raja Raja turned to his religious tutor for guidance, who promptly advised him to build a temple to Shiva using a *linga* from the Narmada River. Raja Raja rushed off to the river and pulled a *linga* from the water; as he pulled, the *linga* grew and grew and Raja Raja had no choice but to build a massive temple to enclose it. The temple *is* massive—its *vimana* (tower) is over 64m tall and is capped by a 73,700kg block of stone which was raised to the top by rolling it up a 7km ramp.

The entrance to the temple complex passes through two *gopurams,* each of which is carved with carefully wrought sculpted images. Through the *gopurams* is a spacious courtyard; just in front of the courtyard entrance stands a giant sculpture of

Nandi, the bull who guards and carries Shiva. This monolithic sculpture is 6m long, 2.6m wide, and 3.7m high, weighing in at 25 tons and making it the second largest Nandi in India.

The inside of the courtyard is lined with pleasantly shaded corridors, which are colonnaded and boast some decaying sculptures and frescoes, now being painstakingly restored. Fourteen stories tall and densely adorned with carvings, the granite **vimana** soars over the *gopurams* in an inversion of the traditional South Indian architectural order (*gopurams* are usually taller than *vimanas*). On the eastern face of the *vimana*, an exquisite carving depicts Shiva and Parvati atop a mountain in the Himalaya. On the eastern parapet is an image of the Buddha. The *vimana* is capped with an octagonal *stupa*, atop which a 4m golden *kalasa* juts skyward.

The interior of the *vimana* is accessed from steep, precarious staircases on the northern and southern sides. Inside, the **sanctum** is surrounded by three concentric hallways. The outer hallway dates from the 16th century and is always accessible. The innermost hallways contain frescoes that provide insight into the customs and beliefs of the Cholas and the Pandyas. The colorful paintings that adorn the walls and ceilings are currently being restored by the Archaeological Survey of India. The best of the **252 lingas** housed inside the temple can be found in the inner sanctum. The circumference of the *yoni* (base) is 16.5m, while the *linga* itself rises to a height of over 4m. Also in the temple compound is a small **museum** which has some interesting sculptures and copies of paintings. Next to the temple is the **Shivaganga tank** and garden, ideal for an evening or early-morning stroll.

Royal Palace Compound

Nearly 2km northeast of the temple, on East Main Rd., is the large **Royal Palace** built as a residence by the Nayaks in the 16th century and subsequently refurbished by the Marathas. These days, the palace has been colonized by a number of incongruous outfits, including a secondary school, an agricultural extension office, and a martial arts academy. If you are persistent, you might be able to locate the half-dozen museums enterprising entrepreneurs have carved out of the remains of the royal residence. Some of the more interesting museums include the **Durbar Hall Art Museum,** which displays an excellent collection of Chola bronzes and stone sculptures. *(Open daily 9am-1pm and 3-6pm. Admission Rs3.)*

Also inside the palace is the **Tamil University Museum** which displays antique musical instruments. *(Open M-F 10:30am-1pm and 2:30-5pm. Admission Rs1.)* Be sure to ask the curator to show you the wooden revolving chair—its maker would probably be shocked to see his design operating in modern office buildings.

The palace houses the **Saraswati Mahal Library,** famous for its collection of ancient palm leaf manuscripts. With 33,433 holdings (24,627 in Sanskrit, 953 in Marathi, 1206 in Tamil, 816 in Telugu, and 5831 others—we counted), the collection is considered one of the world's finest. While the stacks are not open to the public, a **museum** provides a sample of the collection. *(Open Th-Tu 10am-1pm and 2-5pm.)*

■ Tiruchirappalli திருச்சிராப்பள்ளி

For a growing industrial center of 700,000, Tiruchirappalli (commonly called Trichy or Tiruchi) is reasonably clean and relatively tranquil. The city has been continuously occupied for over 2000 years, ruled at various times by the Cholas, Pandyas, Pallavas, and Nayaks, who built the imposing Rock Fort. Since the late 19th century, when railroads brought industry to South India, Trichy has been ruled by manufacturing, and today's Tiruchirappalli is home to a working-class population center where *bidis* and costume jewelry are produced in staggering quantities. Trichy's greatest attraction is the massive temple-city complex at Srirangam, 4km north of town across the Kaveri River. For those en route to destinations farther south, Trichy is a convenient stopping point, with the railway station, bus stand, and a slew of hotels all within comfortable walking distance of each other.

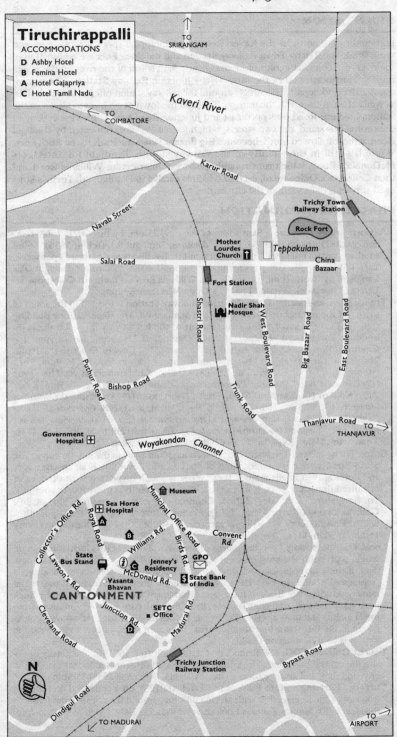

Tiruchirappalli

ACCOMMODATIONS

- **D** Ashby Hotel
- **B** Femina Hotel
- **A** Hotel Gajapriya
- **C** Hotel Tamil Nadu

TO SRIRANGAM

Kaveri River

TO COIMBATORE

Karur Road

Navab Street

Trichy Town Railway Station

Rock Fort

Salai Road

Mother Lourdes Church

Teppakulam

China Bazaar

Fort Station

Shastri Road

Nadir Shah Mosque

West Boulevard Road

Big Bazaar Road

East Boulevard Road

Purbur Road

Bishop Road

Trunk Road

Thanjavur Road

TO THANJAVUR

Government Hospital

Woyakondan Channel

Museum

Collector's Office Rd.

Sea Horse Hospital

Royal Road

Municipal Office Road

Williams Rd.

Birds Rd.

Convent Rd.

State Bus Stand

Jenney's Residency

GPO

Lawson's Rd.

McDonald Rd.

Vasanta Bhavan

State Bank of India

CANTONMENT

Junction Rd.

Madura Rd.

SETC Office

Cleveland Road

Trichy Junction Railway Station

Bypass Road

N

Dindigul Road

TO MADURAI

TO AIRPORT

SOUTH INDIA

ORIENTATION

Bordered to the north by the **Kaveri River**, Tiruchirappalli sprawls south, east, and west. While the **Trichy Town Railway Station** and the **Rock Fort** are within 1km of the river, the compact center of town is nearly 5km south of the river, in the neighborhood just northwest of the busy **Trichy Junction Railway Station**, where most trains arrive and depart. The streets around the railway station offer countless hotels, as well as banks, the GPO, the tourist office, and the town's two **bus stands.** From the station, **Madurai Road** runs northeast and **Junction Road** runs northwest directly to the central bus stand; the two streets, which form a "V," are connected by **Dindigul Road**, which, followed north, becomes **Big Bazaar Road** and leads to the **Rock Fort.** While it's still in the vicinity of the railway station, Dindigul Rd. intersects **McDonald's Road,** which runs roughly east-west, intersecting **Williams Road** and then **Collector's Office Road,** each of which is parallel to Dindigul Rd. Trichy's little-used **airport** is 8km south of the city center.

PRACTICAL INFORMATION

Airport: Trichy's airport is 8km south of the city, 25min. by bus (#K1, 7, 63, 63A, and 59; Rs2) or taxi (Rs175). **Indian Airlines,** Dindigul Rd. (tel. 463536), 500m southwest of its intersection with Junction Rd., has flights to Chennai (3 per week, 1hr., US$70). If you can pass for under 30, ask for the 25% youth discount. **Air Lanka,** in the Hotel Femina Complex on Williams Rd., has flights to **Colombo, Sri Lanka** (3 per week, 45min., US$111). Open M-Sa 9am-5:30pm.

Trains: The user-friendly **Trichy Junction Railway Station** is located in the south of town, off the intersection of Junction and Madurai Rd. The **Reservations Building** (tel. 1361) is the small white structure off to the left as you approach the main building. Fares listed are 2nd/1st class. Open M-Sa 7am-9pm, Su7am-5pm. To: **Chennai** (*Madurai-Chennai Exp.* 6738, 9:10am, 7hr.; *Cholan Exp.* 6154, 9:10am, 7hr.; *Chennai Passenger* 110, 4:30pm, 8½hr.; *Rockfort Exp.* 6878, 9pm, 7hr.; *Quilon Mail* 6106, 12:35am, 8½hr., Rs152/485); **Chidambaram** via **Thanjavur** (*Cholan Exp.* 6154, 7:05am; *Rameshwaram-Chennai Exp.* 6102, 7:25pm, Rs62/ 249); **Kollam** (*Quilon Mail* 6105, 1am, 12½hr., Rs161/515); **Madurai** (*Madurai Maha.* 6719, 5:55am; *Tirupati Exp.* 6799, 6:10am, Rs61/248; *Chennai-Madurai Exp.* 6737, 5:30pm); **Rameswaram** (*Rameswaram Exp.* 6101, 9:35am, 6½hr., Rs117/357); **Tirupati** (*Chennai-Tirupati Exp.* 6800, 6:10am, 15hr., Rs179/571) via **Thanjavur** (1½hr., Rs37/147) and **Chidambaram** (4hr., Rs62/249).

Buses: Trichy has two bus stands, located about 300m apart in the junction area. The **State Bus Stand** at the intersection of Rockins and Royal Rd., is an absolute zoo, and nothing is in English. Since they've pretty much dispensed with the idea of organized departure bays, it may take a while for you to actually locate your bus. To: **Bangalore** (4 per day, 22hr.); **Chennai** (every hr., 6am-9pm, 8hr., Rs86); **Coimbatore** via **Karur** (5hr., Rs35); **Madurai** (every 30min, 6am-10pm, 4hr., Rs27); **Pondicherry** via **Villupuram** (every 30min., Rs45); **Thanjavur** (every 15min., 5:30am-11pm, 1½hr., Rs10).

Local Transportation: Even the tourist office raves about Trichy's **local bus** system, which is probably the most efficient and modern in all of Tamil Nadu. A brand-new fleet of shiny silver buses, each equipped with a deafening sound system, shuttles passengers around the city. The **#1 bus** is every tourist's best friend. It passes the railway station, State Bank of India, and Head Post Office on the way to the Rock Fort (Rs1) and the Srirangam Temple (Rs2). Buses depart every few minutes from the State Bus Stand. As a result, Trichy has hordes of under-used **rickshaws** congregating in the bus stand/tourist office area. They aren't really necessary, unless the airport is your destination (Rs80).

Tourist Office: TTDC, 1 Williams Rd., Cantonment (tel. 460136), diagonally opposite the central bus stand. The knowledgeable staff dispenses a decent map of the city, and they will arrange tours to nearby sights. Open M-F 10am-5:45pm.

Currency Exchange: State Bank of India (tel. 460125), off a courtyard on Dindigul Rd., east of the intersection with McDonald's Rd., around the corner from Jenney's Residency. Exchanges Thomas Cook traveler's checks only. Open M-F 10am-2pm,

Sa 10am-noon. Many expensive hotels in the Trichy Junction area exchange foreign currencies. Try the **TTDC Hotel Tamil Nadu,** next to the tourist office.
Pharmacy: Jambu Medicals, near central bus stand. Open M-Sa 9am-9pm.
Hospital: Government Hospital, Puthur High Rd. (tel. 771465). The best private hospital is the 24hr. **Sea Horse Hospital,** 6 Royal Rd. (tel. 415660).
Post Office: Head Post Office, Dindigul St. (tel. 460575). Open M-Sa 10am-6pm. **Postal Code:** 620001.
Telephones: There are a number of 24hr. **STD/ISD** booths directly opposite the bus stand on McDonald's Rd. **Telephone Code:** 0431.

ACCOMMODATIONS

The Trichy Junction area has more hotels per square kilometer than there are crooked politicians in Bihar. All have 24-hour check-out.

Ashby Hotel, 17-A Junction Rd. (tel. 460652 or 460653), near the intersection with State Bank Rd. In a city of characterless hotels, this place bursts with personality. Aged paintings, a tank full of guppies, and wooden floorboards impart a homey feel. Rooms are dim but spacious, and the leafy courtyards keep things cool. Attached restaurant and bar. Singles Rs150, with A/C Rs420; doubles Rs270/570.

Hotel Tamil Nadu, McDonald's Rd. (tel. 414396), next to the tourist office. A step above most TTDC offerings, well-kept rooms are covered with amber tile and boast both gleaming white sheets and dark, billowy curtains. Singles with A/C Rs300; doubles Rs195, with A/C Rs400.

Railway Station Retiring Rooms, at Trichy Junction Railway Station. Basic accommodations are often full. Dorm beds Rs50. Doubles Rs150, with A/C Rs300.

Hotel Gajapriya, 2 Royal Rd. (tel. 414411). Look for the sign in the sky. Spacious rooms, with modern furnishings and TVs. Attached bathrooms have seat toilets, hot water, and smell of disinfectant. A laid-back place with an equally laid-back staff. Room service. Attached Chinese restaurant and bar. Singles Rs180, with A/C Rs400; doubles Rs300/500. 20% luxury tax. MC, Visa, Diners' Club.

Femina Hotel, 14-C Williams Rd., Cantonment (tel. 4145015). The cavernous lobby sparkles, and every inch of the rooms seethes decadence: plush carpets, a balcony view of the Rock Fort, and a bathtub to boot! Singles Rs225, with A/C Rs475; doubles Rs350/700.

FOOD

Trichy's restaurants fall squarely into two fabulously unoriginal categories: hotel restaurants and South Indian "meals" joints. On the bright side, you won't have to venture far to find food, and even the swankest hotel restaurants are reasonably priced.

Golden Rock (tel. 414501), in the Femina Hotel. With the window shades closed and the A/C in overdrive, this little cafe is guaranteed to help you chill out. South Indian standards: *idlis* (Rs9) and heavenly *masala dosas* (Rs22). Open 24hr.

Vasanta Bhavan, on the ground floor of Hotel Abhirami, opposite the bus stand. Enjoy a filling banana-leaf *thali* (Rs20) or take your pick of a number of typical options (just ask—there's no menu). Open daily 6am-11pm.

Peacocks Restaurant, in Ramyas Hotel. The menu offers an array of tasty veg. Indian and Chinese dishes (Rs40-50). You may have difficulty finding a seat at lunch time, when hotel guests and locals stream in. Open daily 6:30am-11:30pm. **Amaravathi,** the classier non-veg. restaurant downstairs, is open daily 11am-3pm and 7-11pm.

Jenney's Residency, 3/14 McDonald's Rd. (tel 414414). Recently bought out by the Park Sheraton group, this posh hotel is home to two restaurants. The South Indian restaurant, **Suvia,** has a breakfast buffet and serves a sumptuous lunchtime *thali* (Rs35). For a quick snack, munch on Jenney's Tidbits (Rs18). Open daily 7am-11pm. The **Peaks of Kunlun,** a Chinese and Continental restaurant, has good soups (Rs20-35) and rice and noodles (Rs30). Open daily 11am-3pm and 7-11pm.

SIGHTS AND ENTERTAINMENT

Trichy's most interesting sights cluster around the imposing **Rock Fort,** which lords over the flat landscape of the city from its 85m perch. *(Fort open daily 6am-8pm. Admission Rs1. Camera fee Rs10.)* The massive monolith upon which the fort stands is believed to be one of the planet's oldest geological specimens—3.8 billion years in the making. The site was developed as a citadel by the Pallavas and later by the Nayaks. Today, most people who reach the summit are Hindu pilgrims visiting the shrine there or camera-wielding tourists hoping to take in the unparalleled views. Four hundred numbered, rock-cut steps lead to the summit. At the foot of the staircase is a small shrine to Ganesha; remove your shoes as you pass through to the staircase. A little way up is the official entrance, where you can deposit your shoes. Most of the various shrines along the side of the staircase are off-limits to non-Hindus.

At the top (whew!) from the northwest corner of the rock, the *gopurams* of the Sri Ranganathaswamy and Jambukeshwara Temples are visible. One final crooked staircase leads to the whitewashed Vinayaka (Ganesh) temple at the Rock Fort's Summit. The temple is closed to non-Hindus.

The route from the nearest bus stop to the Rock Fort's entrance offers interesting diversions. To reach the Fort from the city, take bus #1 (Rs1) and get off when you see the towering **Saint John's Cathedral,** a Catholic church modeled after France's Lourdes Basilica. Heading due east from St. John's leads to the arched entrance of the **China Bazaar,** which is crammed with stalls selling flowers, *chappals*, silk fabrics, and locally produced handicrafts. If you follow the street eastwards, you'll reach the bright yellow sign that proclaims the entrance to the Rock Fort.

For a refreshing **swim,** head over to Jenney's Residency, where you can do laps in the not-quite-Olympic sized pool. *(Open daily 7am-7pm. Admission Rs125.)* Jenney's also houses the most original watering hole in town: the **Wild West Bar,** done up like an old-fashioned saloon, complete with swinging doors and an intoxicated cowboy clutching an economy-sized bottle of liquor. *(Open daily 11am-11pm.)*

If you fancy yourself an anthropologist and don't mind being a bit of a nuisance, head to the banks of the **Cauvrey River** in the morning. Each day, the Cauvrey, considered the Ganges of South India, witnesses a series of ceremonies and rituals, as pilgrims bathe for good fortune, priests pray for childbirth, and mourners spread fresh ashes. If you are serious about understanding the goings-on, hire a guide (see below).

▒ Near Tiruchirappalli

■ Srirangam ஸ்ரீரங்கம்

Board bus #1 for the half-hour ride to the **Sri Ranganathaswamy Temple** at Srirangam, 5km north of the city. (Temple open daily 6am-9pm.) The Vishnu temple, situated on a 600-acre island straddled by the Kaveri River and its tributary, the Kollidam, is by far the most fully developed of all the temples in South India. It was built over many centuries, starting in the 12th century, during the Pandya period, and was expanded greatly during the Vijayanagar period. Construction has continued into the modern era; the largest of the temple's 22 *gopurams*, rising to a height of 72m, was only just completed in 1987. The sheer expanse of the temple makes it unique; the seven concentric walls of the complex contain nearly 700 sq. km of land and an entire town.

The temple is entered from the south, where a gargantuan *gopuram* greets guests with its resplendent hues. Vendors in the courtyards hawk *puja* offerings such as fruit, coconuts, and sweet-smelling garlands, and all sorts of religious paraphernalia. Visitors need not remove their shoes until reaching the fourth wall, beyond which the oldest and most elaborate sculptures in the complex lie. On the eastern side of the fourth enclosure is a "1000-pillared hall" containing 936 columns carved in the shape of horsemen atop their rearing steeds. On the southern side of the courtyard, the famous sculptures of Krishna frolicking with *gopis* (milkmaids) in the Venugopala shrine are visible. The inner courtyards are inaccessible to non-Hindus.

It takes hours to traipse through the massive complex, but the sheer number of *gopurams,* the magnificent collection of jewels, and the stone pillars of this master-piece make the trek here rewarding. To get the best aerial view of the temple, be certain to take advantage of the staircase to the roof (Rs3), immediately inside on the left as you enter. Depending on your budget and time frame, you might also want to hire one of the government-licensed tour **guides** who make this temple their base. Contact S. Murai (tel. 431741), 77 A West Gate, Srirangam, who offers tours in French, Italian, and English. The **Vaikunta Ekadasi Festival** (Dec.-Jan.) draws thousands of pilgrims. During the festival, a procession of people proceed through a doorway called the "Gateway of Heaven," since doing so provides everlasting life in heaven. The sanctuary is closed to non-Hindus.

■ Tiruvanaikkaval திருவானைக்காவல்

Buses from the central bus stand drive to this submerged *linga* 2km east of Srirangam. The temple, one of the oldest and largest Shiva temples in Tamil Nadu, is named after a legendary elephant who worshipped the *linga.* The *linga,* fashioned by Parvati as an act of penance, is called Jambukeswara, after the holy *jambu* (blackberry) tree that shades the *linga.* The temple, with five enclosures, comprises an area of 765m by 460m. Among its outstanding features are an 800-pillar *mandapa* and a serene tank fed by a natural spring. Try to make it to the temple at noon, when a special ceremony is held. A priest, clad in a *sari* and crown, is said to represent the goddess Parvati. After offering *puja,* the priest proceeds to the goddess's sanctuary with an elephant in tow. (Temple open daily 7am-noon and 4-8pm.)

■ Madurai மதுரை

It's said that Shiva himself once stood over Madurai to dry his matted hair; the auspicious nectar that fell from his holy locks sopped the city and gave it its name, from the Tamil *madhuram* (sweetness). The sugar buzz is still going strong in modern Madurai, a temple town that is both holy and wholly modern, crazily chaotic but small enough to energize, not overwhelm, the thousands who visit it daily. Since its founding more than 2500 years ago, Madurai has been a cultural center, first flourishing as the capital of the ancient Pandya kingdom, which ruled central South India as far back as the 4th century BC. The powerful Vijayanagar Kingdom dominated throughout the 15th and early 16th centuries, during which time the temples and towers of Madurai's famous Meenakshi Amman Temple were built. From 1559 onward, Madurai was ruled by the Nayak dynasty, which built the showplaces of modern Madurai, the Teppakkulam, and the Raya Gopuram. The Nayak party came to a halt in 1736 when the East India Company bought and de-fortified the city, tearing down its walls and filling in its moat, where the Veli streets now run today.

Still damp from its original good-luck drenching, Madurai has survived to become an important commercial center with a population of 1.2 million. Huge electronic signboards illuminate the night sky, and large volumes of traffic (both automobile and bovine) surge in the streets, giving the town the feel of an ancient city entering the modern era in a whir of undirected enthusiasm. For all its vibrant clamor, though, Madurai still moves with the pulse of the temple's activities, and the festival season sees deities led around town followed by throngs of residents and visiting pilgrims.

ORIENTATION

Madurai sprawls north and south of the **Vaigai River.** South of the river, the city is bordered on the west and south by railway tracks and is dominated by the **Meenakshi Temple.** The **Central Bus Stand** and the busy **Madurai Junction Railway Station** are located off **West Veli Street,** 1km west of the temple. To reach the city center from the railway station, follow **Town Hall Road** east; from the **TTC Bus Stand,** follow **Dindigul Road.** In the vicinity of the temple, streets are arranged concentrically around the temple, forming an irregular grid. Closest to the temple are North, East, South, and West **Chittrai Streets.** A bit farther from the temple are North, East,

SOUTH INDIA

South, and West **Avani Moola Streets.** North, East, South, and West **Masi Streets** are encircled by North, East, South, and West **Veli Streets.** To cross the Vaigai River, head 1km northeast of the temple and across **Victor Bridge.** The road leading north from the bridge, **Alagar Koil Road,** is intersected by the east-west **Tamukkam Road.**

PRACTICAL INFORMATION

Airport: (tel. 25433) 15km south of the city center. A taxi into town will cost upwards of Rs170; alternatively, hourly buses leave near the exit. **Indian Airlines,** 7A W. Veli St. (tel. 741234, 741236), opposite the railway station. Open M-Sa 10am-1:15pm and 2-5pm. Flights to: **Chennai** (daily, 1hr., US$80) and **Mumbai** (4 per week, 2hr., US$170). 25% youth discount. Bookings can also be made with the Indian Airlines representative at **Hotel Supreme,** 110 West Perumal Maistry St. Open 24hr.

Trains: Madurai Junction Railway Station, W. Veli St. (tel. 135). Reservations counter open M-Sa 8am-1:30pm and 2-8pm, Su 8am-2pm. Fares listed are 2nd/1st class. To: **Bangalore** (*Bangalore Exp.* 6731, 8pm, Rs117/846); **Chennai** (*Madurai-Chennai Exp.* 6738, 6:25am, 9½hr.; *Mahal Exp.* 6720, 7:10pm, 9hr.; Rs102/511); **Chidambaram** via **Thanjavur** (*Madurai-Tirupati Exp.* 6800, 9:50am, 13hr., Rs74/357); **Coimbatore** (*Coimbatore Exp.* 6116, 9:50am, 6hr., Rs56/274); **Kanyakumari** (*Kanyakumari Exp.* 6721, 3:40am, 6hr., Rs32/293); **Rameswaram** (*Rameswaram Exp.* 6115, 6am, 5hr., Rs43/193); **Tiruchirappalli** (*Mahal Exp.* 6720, 7:10pm, 2½hr., Rs41/203); **Tirupati** (*Madurai-Tirupati Exp.* 6800, 9:50am, 18½hr., Rs135/672).

Buses: Madurai has a whopping 5 bus stands: one local bus stand and 4 inter-city bus stands. **TTC/RGTC Bus Stand,** West Veli St. (tel. 543754), just south of the state (local) bus stand, serves long-distance destinations in Tamil Nadu, Andhra Pradesh, Kerala, and Karnataka. To: **Bangalore** (11 per day, 8am-10:30pm, 9hr., Rs103); **Chennai** (every hr., 5:15am-9:30pm, 10hr., Rs92); **Mangalore** (2 per day, Rs170); **Pondicherry** (8:45pm, Rs60); **Thiruvanathapuram** (10:30pm, Rs57); **Tirupati** via **Vellore** (4 per day, 13hr., Rs104). **Arapalayam Bus Stand** (tel. 603740), 2km west of the city center, has frequent departures to cities to the north and west, including Coimbatore and Kodaikanal. To get to Arapalayam, take local bus #7A or an auto-rickshaw (Rs30). To: **Coimbatore** (every 30min., 6hr., Rs29); **Kodaikanal** (12 per day, 5:40am-5pm, 4hr., Rs18). **Anna Bus Stand** (tel. 533622), 4km north of downtown, services most of the temple-cities in northern Tamil Nadu— including Thanjavur, Chidambaram, and Kumbakonam—as well as Rameswaram. A number of buses, including bus #3, connect the Anna Bus Stand with the central bus stand (auto-rickshaw Rs30). To: **Rameswaram** (8 per day, 1:15am-7pm, 4hr., Rs26); **Thanjavur** (6 per day, 11am-10pm, 5hr., Rs30); **Tiruchirappalli** (every hr., 5:30am-9pm, 4hr., Rs21). Finally, buses from the **Palanganatham Bus Stand** (tel. 600935) run to destinations in southern Tamil Nadu and Kerala from its southern location in the city. Take bus #7 or a rickshaw to get there. To: **Kanyakumari** (every hr., 7hr., Rs47) and **Trivandrum** (every hr., 7am-8pm, 7hr., Rs57).

Local Transportation: Local buses leave from the **Periyar Bus Stand** on W. Veli St., a 2min. walk south from the railway station. The stand is so congested that a small overflow lot has been set up, east of the bus stand between W. Veli and W. Perumal Maistry St. **Auto-** and **cycle-rickshaws** are easily available; the main stand is right outside the railway station. A **pre-paid rickshaw** booth opens as trains arrive.

Tourist Office: Tamil Nadu Tourism Development Corporation (TTDC), 180 TB Complex, W. Veli St. (tel. 34757), south of the main bus stand. Friendly staff answers questions about the city and excursions from Madurai. Open M-F 10am-5:30pm. There are also offices at the airport (open irregularly) and railway station (tel. 542888; open daily 8am-8pm).

Currency Exchange: State Bank of India, 6 W. Veli St. (tel. 741650, foreign exchange tel. 742128), in Sangam Towers, north of the railway station and across the street. Exchanges AmEx traveler's checks in US$ and Thomas Cook traveler's checks in US$ and UK£. Open M-F 10am-2pm, Sa 10am-noon.

Bookstore: Malligai Book Centre, 11 W. Veli St. (tel. 740534), opposite the railway station. Open M-Sa 9am-1pm and 4-9pm.

SOUTH INDIA

Madurai

ACCOMMODATIONS

E Hotel Aarathy
D Hotel Alavai
A Hotel Keerthi
F Hotel Laxmi
C Hotel Ravi Towers
B Hotel Sentosh

Dr. SVK.S.Thangaraj Rd.

TO ALAGARKOIL

Alagarkoil Rd.

Tamukkum Rd.

Panagal Rd.

Central Telegraph Office

TO KODAIKANAL

Kalpaam Rd.

Victor Bridge

Workshop Rd.

Tamil Sangam Rd.

N. Masi St.

N. Veli St.

GPO

TO MADURAI BRIDGE STATION

Priya Surya

Madurai Railway Station

300 yards

300 meters

N

TO BODINAYAKKANUR

Tamukkam Palace

Anna Bus Stand

Anna Nagar Main Rd.

Kuruvikaran Salai

Kamarajar Rd.

New Ramanad Rd.

Vaigai River

Chairman Muthuramaiyer Rd.

East Madurai Railway Station

TO AIRPORT

Munichalai Rd.

E. Veli St.

E. Market St.

E. Masi St.

S. Masi St.

Palace Rd.

Old Kosavar Palayam Rd.

E. Avani Moola St.

E. Chittrai

N. Chittrai

S. Chittrai

W. Chittrai

Meenakshi Temple

Tirumalai Nayak Palace

Mariamman Teppakkulam

MADURAI MAIN MARKET

Hotel Mahal Rest.

Town Hall Rd.

Dindigul Rd.

W. Vadampokki St.

S. Veli St.

B C

A

Ruby

W. Perumal Maistry St.

W. Veli St.

Periyar Bus Stand

TTC/RGTC Bus Stand

TTDC

i

E A Kudal Azhagar Temple

F

S. Veli St.

T.P.K. Rd.

TO TUTICORIN AND KANYAKUMARI

Market: The chaotic **Central Market** on N. Avani Moola St. sells food. The government-run **Poompuhar Handicrafts Emporium,** 12 W. Veli St. (tel. 740517) has…handicrafts. Open M-Sa 10am-1pm and 3-8pm. Accepts Visa, MC.

Pharmacy: Suresh Medical, 63 Town Hall Rd. (tel. 541625). Open M-Sa 7:30am-10:30pm.

Hospital: Government Hospital, Panagal Rd. (tel. 43231), across the Vaigai River. The private **Jawahar Hospital,** 14 Main Rd., K.K. Nagar (tel. 650023 or 650024), also on the northern bank of Vaigai, is better. **Aravind Eye Hospital,** Anna Nagar Main Rd. (tel. 535434 or 532653) is renowned.

Police: The main station (tel. 538015) is on the north bank, on the road to Natham.

Post Office: Head Post Office (tel. 740756), on N. Veli St. The main entrance is around the corner on Scott St. *Poste Restante* at the corner entrance labeled Philatelic Bureau, M-Sa 10am-5pm. Main office open M-Sa 9am-7pm, Su 9am-4pm. **Postal Code:** 625001.

Telephones: Modern Tourism, 29 W. Perumal Maistry St., allows callbacks for a reasonable fee. **Telephone Code:** 0452.

ACCOMMODATIONS

The good news: nearly all of Madurai's hotels are within walking distance of the Meenakshi Temple and the city's transportation hubs. The bad news: in a Darwinian struggle for travelers' patronage, Madurai's mid-range hotels are slowly swankifying, leaving a sizeable gap at the center of the accommodations continuum. For now, good budget options still exist, but rooms under Rs150 are an endangered species.

Hotel Aarathy, 9 Perumal Koil, W. Mada St. (tel. 31571), down the small road on the right after W. Perumal Maistry St. as you walk east on S. Masi St. A well-maintained establishment. Room service. Attached restaurant. Pine-fresh attached bathrooms with seat or squat toilets. If you don't mind not having a balcony, take a room facing the temple and watch the sunrise. Check-out 24hr. Singles Rs195, with A/C Rs275; doubles Rs275/400.

Hotel Ravi Towers, 9 Town Hall Rd. (tel. 741961; fax 743405), 2 blocks east of W. Perumal Maistry St. Neat, tiled, cool rooms with clean sheets. Rooms have 24hr. hot water and reality-numbing TV (if you can hum the Star TV theme song, it's time to ask for help). In-room STD calls. Room service. Check-out 24hr. Singles with common bath Rs125, with A/C Rs175; doubles Rs165, with TV Rs195, with A/C Rs300.

Hotel Keerthi, 40 W. Perumal Maistry St. (tel. 741501), 1½ blocks north of Town Hall Rd. The whitewashed rooms are tiny, but the sheets are clean and all rooms have ample lighting, TVs, and telephones. Clean attached baths with tepid water and squat toilets. Avoid the enticingly painted elevator. Attached restaurant. Singles Rs175; doubles Rs220, with A/C Rs300. Additional 20% tax.

Hotel Laxmi, 36 Koodalagar Perumal Koil (tel. 628464). Follow S. Masi St. east past W. Perumal Maistry St. Take the first right down the dusty road along the side of the temple. Laxmi is at the end of the road, past Hotel Aarathy. Dark brown rooms with trial-size TVs. Clean attached baths with squat or seat toilets. Hot water by the bucket. Singles Rs100; doubles Rs150, with TV Rs225, with A/C Rs350.

Hotel Alavai, 86 W. Perumal Maistry St. (tel. 740551). Rooms are simple, offering the basic bed, plastic chair, and attached bathroom with squat toilet. Could use a cleaning, but it's cheap. Singles Rs60; doubles Rs100.

Hotel Sentosh, 7 Town Hall Rd. (tel. 743692). Dim corridors lead to rooms whose ascetic decor is contradicted by the massive TVs. The rooms all have attached baths with oft-scrubbed squat toilets. Doubles Rs100, with TV Rs160.

FOOD

The best restaurants in Madurai are in and around the hotels on West Perumal Maistry St. and Town Hall Rd. Many of the hotels offer rooftop dining, which usually means quiet surroundings, cool breezes, and, of course, great temple views.

(go down in history)

and use **AT&T Direct**^{SM} Service
to tell everyone about it.

It's all within **AT&T** your reach.

Before you go exploring lost cultures, get an

AT&T Direct^{SM} Service wallet guide.

It's a list of access numbers you need to call home fast and clear from

around the world, using an AT&T Calling Card or credit card.

What an amazing culture we live in.

For a list of **AT&T Access Numbers,**
take the attached wallet guide.

It's all within  your reach.

w w w . a t t . c o m / t r a v e l e r

For your
calling
convenience
tear off
and take
with you!

AT&T

AT&T Direct℠ Service

WALLET GUIDE

Inside you'll find simple instructions on how to use AT&T Direct Service to place calling card or collect calls from outside the U.S.

All you need are the AT&T Access Numbers when you travel outside the U.S., because you can access us quickly and easily from virtually anywhere in the world. And if you need any further help, there's always an AT&T English-speaking Operator available to assist you.

www.att.com/traveler

Calling From Specially Marked Telephones

Throughout the world, there are specially marked phones that connect you to AT&T Direct℠ Service. Simply look for the AT&T logo. In the following countries, access to AT&T Direct Service is *only* available from these phones: Ethiopia, Mongolia, Nigeria, Seychelles Islands.

Public phones in Europe displaying the red 3C symbol also give you quick and easy access to AT&T Direct Service. Just lift the handset and dial ✱60 (in France dial M60) and you'll be connected to AT&T.

Pay phones in the United Kingdom displaying the New World symbol provide easy access to AT&T. Simply lift the handset and press the pre-programmed button marked AT&T.

NEW WORLD

Customer Care

If you have any questions, call 800 331-1140, Ext. 707.

When outside the U.S., dial the AT&T Access Number for the country *you are in* and ask the AT&T Operator for Customer Care.

108-25   © AT&T 6/98

Printed in the U.S.A. on recycled paper.

To Call the U.S. and Other Countries Using Your AT&T Calling Card* or credit card,∞ Follow These Steps:

1. Make sure you have an outside line. (From a hotel room, follow the hotel's instructions to get an outside line, as if you were placing a local call.)

2. If you want to call a country other than the U.S., make sure the country *you are in* is highlighted in blue on the chart like this: ▢

3. Enter the AT&T Access Number listed in the chart for the country *you are in.*

4. When prompted, enter the telephone number you are calling as follows:
   • For calls to the U.S., dial the Area Code (no need to dial 1 before the Area Code) + 7-digit number.
   • For calls to other countries,† enter 01 + the Country Code, City Code, and Local Number.

5. After the tone, enter your AT&T Calling Card* or credit card number (not the international number). If you need help or wish to call the U.S. collect, hold for an AT&T Operator.

* You may also use your AT&T Corporate Card, AT&T Universal Card, or most U.S. local phone calling cards.
† The cost of calls to countries other than the U.S. consists of basic connection rates plus an additional charge based on the country you are calling.
∞ Credit card billing subject to availability.

Special Features

Just dial the AT&T Access Number for the country *you are in* and follow the instructions listed below.

● To call U.S. 800 numbers: Enter the 800 number you are calling. (Note: Based upon the 800 number dialed, calls may be toll-free or AT&T Direct℠ Service charges may apply for the duration of the call; some numbers may be restricted.)

● To set up conference calls: Dial AT&T TeleConference Services at 800 232-1234. (Note: One conferee must be in the U.S.)

● To access language interpreters: Dial AT&T Language Line® Services at 408 648-5871.

● To record and deliver messages: Dial #123 if you get a busy signal or no answer, or dial AT&T True Messages® Service at 800 562-6275.

Here's a time-saving tip for placing additional calls: When you finish your conversation, or if there is a busy signal or no answer, don't hang up – press # and wait for the voice prompt or an AT&T Operator.

AT&T

AT&T Access Numbers

(Refer to footnotes before dialing.) From the countries highlighted in blue below, like this ☐, you can make calls to virtually any location in the world; and from *all* the countries listed, you can make calls to the U.S.

AT&T — It's all within your reach.

Albania ●	00-800-0010
American Samoa	633 2-USA
Angola	0199
Anguilla + (Public Card Phones)	1-800-872-2881
Antigua + (Public Card Phones)	1-800-872-2881 / #1
Argentina	0-800-54-288
Armenia ✦ ▲	8✦0111
Aruba	800-8000
Australia	1-800-881-011
Austria ○	022-903-011
Bahamas	1-800-872-2881
Bahrain	800-001
Bahrain ↑	800-000
Barbados +	1-800-872-2881
Belarus ✕ —	8✦800101
Belgium ●	0-800-100-10
Belize ▲	811
(From Hotels Only)	555
Benin ●	102
Bermuda +	1-800-872-2881
Bolivia ●	0-800-1112
Bosnia ▲	00-800-0010
Brazil	000-8010
British V.I. +	1-800-872-2881
Brunei ●	800-1111
Bulgaria ■ ▲	00-800-0010
Cambodia ✱	#1
Canada	1 800 CALL ATT
Cape Verde Islands	112
Cayman Islands +	1-800-872-2881
Chile	800-800-311
(Easter Island)	800-800-311 or 800-800-288
China, PRC ▲	10811
Colombia	980-11-0010
Cook Island	09-111
Costa Rica	0-800-0-114-114
Croatia ●	99-385-0111
Cyprus ●	080-90010
Czech Rep. ▲	00-42-000-101
Denmark	8001-0010
Dominica +	1-800-872-2881
Dom. Rep. ★ □	1-800-872-2881
Ecuador ▽	999-119
Egypt ○ (Cairo)	510-0200
(Outside Cairo)	02-510-0200
El Salvador ○	800-1785
Estonia	800-12001
Fiji	004-890-1001
Finland ●	9800-100-10
France ●	0800 99 00 11
French Antilles	0800 99 0011
French Guiana	0800 99 00 11
Gabon ●	00●011
Gambia ●	00111
Georgia ▲	8✦0288
Germany ●	0130-0010
Ghana	0191
Gibraltar	8800
Greece ●	00-800-1311
Grenada +	1-800-872-2881
Guadeloupe + ✱ (Marie Galante)	0800 99 00 11
Guam	1 800 CALL ATT
Guantanamo Bay ✝ (Cuba)	935
Guatemala ○ ❋	99-99-190
Guyana ★	165
Haiti	183
Honduras	800-0-123
Hong Kong	800-96-1111
Hungary ●	00✦800-01111
Iceland ●	800 9001
India ✱ ➔	000-117
Indonesia ➔	001-801-10
Ireland ✓	1-800-550-000
Israel	1-800-94-94-949
Italy ●	172-1011
Ivory Coast ▲	00-111-11
Jamaica □	1-800-872-2881
Jamaica □	872
Japan IDC ▲	0066-55-111
Japan KDD ○	005-39-111
Kazakhstan ●	8✦800-121-4321
Korea ●	0072-911 or 0030-911
Korea ➔	550-HOME or 550-2USA
Kuwait	800-288
Latvia (Riga)	7007007
(Outside Riga)	8✦27007007
Lebanon ○ (Beirut)	426-801
(Outside Beirut)	01-426-801
Liechtenstein ●	0-800-89-0011
Lithuania ✱ —	8✦196
Luxembourg ✝	0-800-0111
Macao	0800-111
Macedonia, F.Y.R. of ✦ ○	99-800-4288
Malaysia ○	1800-80-0011
Malta	0800-890-110
Marshall Isl.	1 800 CALL ATT
Mauritius	01-111-11
Mexico ▽¹	01-800-288-2872
Micronesia	288
Monaco ●	800-90-288
Montserrat +	1-800-872-2881
Morocco	002-11-0011
Netherlands ●	0800-022-9111
Netherlands Antilles ✦	001-800-872-2881
New Zealand	000-911
Nicaragua	174
Norway ●	800-190-11
Pakistan +	00-800-01-001
Palau	02288
Panama	109
(Canal Zone)	281-0109
Papua New Guinea	0507-12880
Paraguay ■ ▲ (Asunción City)	008-11-800
Peru ●	0-800-50000
Philippines ●	105-11
Poland ✦	0✦0-800-111-1111
Portugal ▲	05017-1-288
Qatar	0800-011-77
Reunion Isl.	0800 99 0011
Romania ●	01-800-4288
Russia ● ✦ (Moscow)	755-5042
(Outside Moscow)	8-095-755-5042
Russia ● ✦ ▲ (St. Petersburg)	325-5042
(Outside St. Petersburg)	8-812-325-5042
St. Kitts/Nevis & St. Lucia +	1-800-872-2881
St. Pierre & Miquelon	0800 99 0011
St. Vincent △ ▲	1-800-872-2881
Saipan ▲	1 800 CALL ATT
San Marino ●	172-1011
Saudi Arabia ◇	1-800-10
Senegal	3072
Sierra Leone	1100
Singapore ●	800-0111-111
Slovakia ▲	00-42-100-101
Solomon Isl.	0811
So. Africa	0-800-99-0123
Spain	900-99-00-11
Sri Lanka ■	430-430
Sudan	800-001
Suriname △	156
Sweden	020-795-611
Switzerland ●	0-800-89011
Syria	0-801
Taiwan ●	0080-10288-0
Thailand ◁	001-999-111-11
Trinidad/Tob. ◁	1-800-872-2881
Turkey ●	00-800-12277
Turks & Caicos +	1-800-872-2881
Uganda	800-001
Ukraine ▲	8✦100-11
U.A. Emirates ●	800-121
U.K. ▲ ✦	0800-89-0011 or 0500-89-0011
Uruguay	000-410
Uzbekistan 8 ✦	641-7440010
U.S. ✓	1 800 CALL ATT
Venezuela	800-1111-0
Vietnam ●	1-201-0288
Yemen	00 800 101
Zambia	00-899
Zimbabwe ▲	110-98990

● Public phones require coin or card deposit. 2 Press red button. 2 Additional charges apply when calling outside of Moscow. ✱ AT&T Direct® calls cannot be placed to this country from outside the U.S. ✱ Available from pay phones in Phnom Penh and Siem Reap only. ✕ Not available from public phones.
✦ From St. Maarten or phones at Bobby's Marina, use 1-800-872-2881.

◇ From this country, AT&T Direct® calls terminate to designated countries only. — Not yet available from all areas. ✱ Select hotels. ▲ From U.S. Military Bases only. ➔ May not be available from every phone/public phone. † Collect calling from public phones. ✓ Available from phones with international calling capabilities or from most phones. ● Available from public phones only. ✦ Public phones and select hotels. ✓ From Northern Ireland use U.K. access code.

★ Collect calling only. ○ Public phones require local coin payment through the call duration. ◆ Await second dial tone. ▽ When calling from public phones, use phones marked "Ladatel." ✝ If call does not complete, use 001-800-462-4240. ● Available from public phones only. ■ Public phones and select hotels. ✓ When calling from public phones use phones marked Lenso.

□ Calling Card calls available from select hotels. ➔ Use phones allowing international access. ✦ Including Puerto Rico and the U.S. Virgin Islands. ✱ AT&T Direct® Service only from telephone calling centers in Hanoi and post offices in Da Nang, Ho Chi Minh City and Quang Ninh. ✝ If call does not complete, use 0800-013-0011.

Priya, in the Hotel Prem Nivas, 102W. Perumal Maistry St. Small eatery offers phenomenally cheap and yummy Indian dishes. A huge *masala dosa* can be had for a rock-bottom Rs8. Quick service. Open daily 6:30-10am and noon-10pm.

New Arya Bhavan, 241-A W. Masi St. (tel. 740345), at Dindigul Rd. A hot favorite among Madurai residents, despite the incessant rumble of buses barreling by. Try the *pakoras* (Rs10) and butter roast *dosa* (Rs12). The sweet shop has *jangri, ladoos,* and milk sweets, but *kalakand burfi* (Rs125 per kg) takes the cake.

Hotel Mahal, 13 Town Hall Rd. (742700), right next to the Taj Restaurant. Lots of options, including North Indian *thali* (Rs35), tandoori (Rs30-40), pasta (Rs65), and lamb (Rs60). Frequented by freaks like you. Open daily 8am-midnight.

Surya, 110 W. Perumal Maistry St. (tel. 743151), on the roof of Hotel Supreme, with a great view of Madurai and the *gopurams* of the Meenakshi Temple. Extensive veg. menu has Indian, Chinese, and Continental faves (most Rs30-40). If you can't take the great outdoors, head to the restaurant on the first floor (same menu). Restaurant open daily 6am-11pm. Rooftop open daily 5pm-midnight.

Taj Garden Retreat, Pasumalai Hill. The weekend evening buffet on the lawns at this swanky 5-star hotel (Rs150) is a good value for the money, but you'll also have to shell out Rs40 for the rickshaw ride.

Polly Want a Future?

In these modern times, the hand-cast horoscope is going the ill-starred way of, well, the dodo. Thanks to computers, one can now have one's *jadhagam* (horoscope) plotted just by specifying the date of birth, to be checked against a database of the stars' and planets' positions. The result is unceremoniously printed out in barely-legible dot matrix. In some parts of India, though, one's fortune can still be cast the old-fashioned way: by *kili josyam* (parrot astrology). The human astrologer has a number of cards with pictures of deities placed face down. To determine a customer's fortune, he releases a trained parrot from its cage, and the bird grabs one of the cards in its beak. Each deity corresponds to a chapter in the *Agastya Arudal,* an ancient treatise written by the sage Agastya. The astrologer then divines one's fortune from the designated chapter. The prognosticating polly is recaged, but the game continues, as the same astrologer is usually also a palmist and has myriad methods to clarify or elaborate upon the parrot's promise.

SIGHTS

Meenakshi Amman Temple

Location: *Entrance to the temple complex is generally made from E. Chitrai St., just south of the eastern gopuram.* **Hours:** *Open daily 5am–9:30pm. Sanctum closed 12:30-3pm.* **Admission:** *Free.* **Other:** *Camera fee Rs30. Museum open daily 8am-8pm. Admission Rs1. Camera fee Rs10.*

Though everyone has a personal favorite, the Meenakshi Amman Temple, which draws more than 10,000 tourists and devotees every day, is probably the most dazzling of Tamil Nadu's temple-cities. Aside from the vibrant hues of the 30 million sculptures adorning the complex, the Meenakshi Amman Temple is impressive simply for its sheer size; the complex covers an incredible 65,000 square meters and the tallest of the temple's twelve *gopurams* reaches 49m. Meenakshi Amman was originally built by the Pandyas as a humble shrine. Peace and prosperity gave the Vijayanagar kings the opportunity to embellish the temple. When the Nayaks came to power in the 16th century, they continued this work, further expanding the complex and building the temple's massive *gopurams.* In the 20th century, a boycott led by Mohandas Gandhi led to the temple being opened to Untouchables, and the Mahatma made a crucial visit here in 1946.

The temple is dedicated both to the goddess Meenakshi and to Shiva. According to legend, the Pandya King Malayadwaja was childless and desperately sought a male heir. The king appealed to the gods by performing a series of *yagnas* (fire sacrifices). To his great surprise, during one such ceremony, a three-year-old girl emerged from the sacred flames. Named Meenakshi, the "fish-eyed" goddess (fish-like eyes being considered a mark of beauty), the child was born with three breasts and a lot of divine attitude. The king was a bit troubled by his daughter's physical excesses, but a voice from above assured him that her third breast would disappear as soon as she met her future husband. After growing up to become a beautiful princess, Meenakshi set out to conquer the world, which she did promptly by defeating the other gods and demons, until only Shiva was left. When Meenakshi confronted Shiva (known in Madurai as Sundareswar, the "good-lookin' lord"), however, her heart turned to *ghee*, her third breast disappeared, and she was easily domesticated. It is said that Meenakshi and Sundareswar were wed in Madurai where they jointly ruled the Pandya kingdom. A grand festival called Meenakshi Kalyanam commemorates the wedding.

Visiting the Meenakshi Temple can be overwhelming, as painted ceilings, rows of hawkers, and blaring music assault the senses at every turn. Systematic tours are difficult and perhaps not desirable. The best way to see the complex is to wander about, watching the temple's activities unfold and lingering at places that catch your eye.

The E. Chitrai St., entrance leads directly to the **shrine** of Meenakshi. After entering, you'll be in the brightly painted **Ashta Shakti Mandapam,** where hawkers peddle postcards, curios, and *puja* offerings. The passageway receives its name from the eight manifestations of the goddess Shakti represented on its pillars. Other sculptures and painting depict some of the *tiruvilayadals* (miracles) of Shiva. Continuing westward, the spacious **Meenakshi Nayakkar Mandapam** has six rows of pillars, carved with images of the *yali,* mythological beasts with the body of a lion and the head of an elephant.

Going through another small *mandapam* and a narrow hallway leads to the northeast corner of the serene **Potramarai Kulam** (Golden Lotus tank). The corridors that surround the tank are often occupied by devotees, relaxing in the shade or taking in the spectacular view of the temple's southern *gopuram.* The tank itself is frequented by pilgrims seeking a purifying bath in its light green waters, following the tradition of Indra, who is said to have bathed here. In ancient times, the Tamil Sangam (Academy of Poets) met in the area around the tank. Locals claim that the Sangam judged the merit of literary works by tossing submissions into the tank. If a work sank, the aspiring writer's hopes went along with it. If the work did not sink, however, it was deemed worthy of the Sangam's attention. Should you find yourself in the temple after dark, be sure to take in the moonlight by the surreal waters of the pool.

The northwest corner of the tank leads directly to the Meenakshi shrine, which is closed to non-Hindus. The corridor outside the shrine is the **Kilikootu Mandapam** (Parrot Cage Corridor), where lucky green parrots (trained to repeat Meenakshi's name) were once kept in cages as offerings to the goddess. The *mandapam*'s 28 pillars are expertly carved with images from Hindu mythology. Adjacent is the 16th-century **Oonjal Manapam** (Swing Corridor), where on Fridays at about 5:30pm the golden images of Meenakshi and Sundareswar are carried in, placed on a swing, and sung to. The shrine's entrance is marked by a three-story *gopuram* and is guarded by two stern *dwarapalakas* (watchmen). The inner sanctum, filled with smoke from burning incense and ceremonial oil lamps, is supported by rectangular golden columns that bear the mark of a lotus. Along the perimeter of the chamber, black granite panels of Shiva and Meenakshi overlook the crowds of *darshan*-seekers. It is said that as a mother-fish need only look upon her spawn to bring them to life, worshippers' spirituality is stirred to life when the fish-eyed Meenakshi casts her gaze upon them.

North of the Meenakshi shrine, through brass-plated doors, is a shrine dedicated to Sundareswar, also closed to non-Hindus. Just inside the entrance is an eight-foot image of Ganesha (Mukkuruni Vinayakar), which was discovered in the 17th century when King Tirumalai Nayak began digging the Mariamman Theppakulam in the southeastern corner of the city. The outermost enclosure of the Sundareswar shrine is decorated with towering columns. The attention to detail here is remarkable. Even the iron gratings along the top of the outer walls, where a bit of sunlight filters in, have been fashioned in the shape of Nandi and a *linga.* In the northeast corner of the enclosure (accessible to non-Hindus) is the **Kambathadi Mandapam,** adorned with elegant pillars, each of which bears a sculpture of Meenakshi or Shiva. A gaggle of sculptures of Shiva and Kali trying to out-dance one another are pelted with small balls of *ghee* by devotees who hope to soothe the deities' competitiveness. The second enclosure houses shrines to various gods, including Durga and Siddhar. A sea of flickering votive lamps offered by devotees casts a magical glow through the otherwise-obscured corridor. The inner chamber contains the image of Sundareswar as well as an image of Nataraja, unique for having his *right* foot raised. Apparently, King Rajasekhara Pandya, a great devotee of Shiva, set out to learn the dance performed by Nataraja. While practicing, the king realized the great strain placed upon Nataraja's leg, and he felt a change was necessary.

Head east from Kambathadi Mandapam and you'll end up in the **Ayirakkal Mandapam** (Thousand Pillar Hall) which boasts 985 carved pillars (no word on the other 15) and has been converted into a small **museum** displaying paintings and sculptures The *mandapa* also has a set of pillars which plays seven notes when tapped.

Tamukkam Palace and Museums

Location: *Nearly 2km north of the river on Tamukkam Rd.* **Transportation:** *Local buses #1, 2, and 3.* **Gandhi Museum:** *Museum and adjoining library open Th-Tu 10am-1pm and 2-5:30pm. Free.* **Government Museum:** *Open Sa-Th 9am-5pm. Free.* **Other:** *Inter-religious prayers every Friday evening in front of the Gandhi Museum.*

While nearly every average-sized Indian city has a **Gandhi Museum,** Madurai's could well be the best. The museum, housed in the 17th-century palace of **Rani Mangammal,** chronicles the events of Gandhi's life and work and intelligently discusses their social context. Unapologetically anti-imperialist, though occasionally a bit too local in scope, the museum is an enjoyable history lesson. In 1921, during one of his visits to Madurai, Gandhi was moved by what he saw outside his train window as he pulled into the city: all along the Vaigai River, men bathed while hanging their one garment—a simple *dhoti*—out to dry. It was then that Gandhi decided to forsake expensive clothing and don the plain *dhoti* as a symbol of his unity with the common man of India. The highlight of the collection, kept behind bulletproof glass in a black-painted room, is the faintly blood-stained *dhoti* Gandhi was wearing when he was murdered. The exhibit also features a letter Gandhi wrote to Adolf Hitler in 1939. Other interesting artifacts include a replica of his modest home in Sevagram and a sample of his ashes.

The solid though not spectacular **Government Museum,** next to the Gandhi Museum complex, is full of things Tamil, including ancient weapons and colorful festival costumes.

Tirumalai Nayak Palace

Location: *1½km southeast of the Meenakshi Temple.* **Hours:** *Palace open daily 9am-1pm and 2-5pm. Sound and light show in English daily 6:45-7:30pm. Purchase tickets starting at 6:30pm.* **Admission:** *Palace, Rs1. Sound and light show, Rs2-5.*

What remains of Tirumalai's grand 17th-century palace is the cavernous **Swargavilasam** (Celestial Pavilion), an arcaded courtyard where the Nayak rulers held public audiences. Though heroic efforts are being made to renovate the courtyard, there will be no undoing the damage wrought by Tirumalai's grandson, who hauled off much of the palace to outfit the pad he was planning for himself at Tiruchirappalli. However, parts of the interior have been fully restored; the deep crimson hue, along with the cream carvings and figures in relief, hint at the palace's former grandeur. While the lighting is remarkably professional and the narration interesting and informative, the **sound and light show,** blaring out the story of Tirumala and of the Tamil epic *Shilappadigaram,* is sometimes hampered by poor tape quality.

Vandiyur Mariamman Teppakulam

On Kamarajar Rd., 5km southeast of the railway station (bus #4 or 4A), this squarish water tank has a tree-surrounded **shrine** in the center. The tank was built in 1646 by Tirumalai Nayak, who retired with his harem to the central shrine. These days, the tank is usually dry, and the only action to be seen is an occasional family picnic. The tank is filled with waters from the Vagai via an underground channel for a colorful float festival (Jan.-Feb.) and for the wedding of Meenakshi and Sundareswar in May, when the divine duo is tugged along the waters on a raft.

Thirupparankundram

Though not as tremendous as Meenakshi, Thirupparankundram is an impressive cave-temple. Located 8km south of town, the temple is dedicated to Lord Subramanya and houses several Sanskrit writing schools. The **inner sanctum** is carved right out of the rock in the side of a mountain. Guides will eagerly take you through the cavernous shrine (Rs30).

ENTERTAINMENT AND SHOPPING

There are a few **cinemas** near the Periyar Bus Stand. *The Hindu* has the latest listings for English-language films. Check with the tourist office for **cultural programs** in Lakshmi Sundaram Hall, Tallakulam (tel. 530858). **Boating** and indoor **roller skating** are possible at Vandiyur Karmoy Tourist Complex (tel. 42918).

Madurai is filled with **textile shops** and *sari* showrooms. You will undoubtedly be accosted by tailors who will offer to sew an exact copy of the pants you're wearing for a nominal cost. As always, beware of auto-rickshaw drivers who force you to check out a particular handicraft store—they're just after the commission. Even if you don't plan on buying anything, you may find yourself drinking a free 7-Up as crafty salesman try to convince you to buy outlandishly expensive handicrafts. Try to take your time and remember that it's your money to spend (or not spend) however you want. If you decide on the former, try the **Parameswari Stores,** 21 E. Chittrai St., just outside the southern *gopuram* of the Meenakshi Temple, for its well-known silk-cotton blends. **Cooptex Sales Emporium,** W. Chittrai St., sells fabrics as well as *saris.* **Khadi Emporium,** Town Hall Rd., is a good place to buy gifts and wooden carvings. Handicraft enthusiasts should visit the **Madurai Gallery,** Cottage Expo Crafts, 19 N. Chittrai St. (tel. 627851). The many tourist-oriented shops around the Meenakshi Temple are open daily (roughly 8:30am-10pm) and will usually take major credit cards, change traveler's checks, and mail your purchases back home.

▒ Rameswaram இராமேஸ்வரம்

A small island off the southeastern coast of India, Rameswaram is surrounded by the blue-green waters of the Bay of Bengal and the sweet smell of stale fish. The train ride to Rameswaram from the mainland is one of the most spectacular in all of India. Rameswaram is said to be the place where Rama, the hero of the *Ramayana,* launched his attack on Ravana's fortress in Lanka (see p. 94). According to a later myth, Rama, after defeating Ravana in their great cosmic battle, made a *linga* of sand here to honor Shiva and expiate the sin of killing Ravana. Rameswaram also marks the southern holy *dham* (abode), one of India's four sacred places marking the cardinal directions. (The others are Dwarka in the west, Badrinath in the north, and Puri in the east.) The Ramanathaswamy Temple is frequented by thousands of pilgrims who come to bathe in the various *tirthas* and build their own sand-*lingas,* which they toss into the sea after worshiping them. There are also a number of festivals held in Rameswaram, including Thai Amavasai (Jan.), Masi Sivarathiri (Feb.-Mar.), Thirkalyanam (July-Aug.), and Mahalaya Amavasai (Sept.).

ORIENTATION AND PRACTICAL INFORMATION Navigating Rameswaram is largely a matter of circling the four **Car Streets**—North, East, South, and West—which box in the **Ramanathaswamy Temple.** Most hotels, restaurants, and shops are located on these four streets and on **Sannadhi Street,** which runs east from the middle of E. Car St. to the Bay of Bengal. To reach the temple from the railway station, walk out the main entrance and follow the road for about 300m, as it curves slightly, then turn left (north) when you hit the principal north-south thoroughfare. Proceed north for 500m until you reach **Middle Street,** which leads east to the middle of W. Car St. and the western entrance of the temple. From the bus stand, silver-and-red local **buses** (Rs0.50) head to the northern end of E. Car St. The **tourist office,** 14 E.

Car St. (tel. 21371), is useful for their rudimentary map of Rameswaram (open M-F 10am-5:45pm). Traveler's checks can be exchanged at the **Indian Bank,** on the southern end of W. Car St. (tel. 21234; open M-F 10am-2pm, Sa 10am-noon). There is also a **Tourist Information Centre** inside the Railway station (tel. 21373) and a Temple Information Center inside Ramanathaswamy Temple.

Trains depart from the Rameswaram Station, 1km southwest of the temple (reservations counter open M-Sa 8am-2pm and 2:15-8pm, Su 8am-2pm). Tourists are encouraged to contact the Station Master directly for bookings. Fares listed are 2nd/1st class. Trains head to **Chennai** (*Rameswaram-Chennai Exp.* 6102, 12:40pm, 17½hr.,Rs176/642) and **Coimbatore** (*Rameswaram-Coimbatore Exp.* 6116, 4pm, 12hr., Rs84/388). The dusty **bus stand** is on Bazaar Rd., 2km west of the temple. Take an auto-rickshaw or a local bus (Rs1) to and from the temple. SETC runs buses to **Chennai** via **Tiruchirapalli** (4 and 5pm, 10hr., Rs100) and **Kanyakumari** (6am, 7am, 7pm, 8pm, up to 10 per day, 11hr., Rs75) and **Coimbatore** (8:15am and 7:15pm, 8hr., Rs71), both via **Madurai.** Local buses run every 30min. to Madurai via **Ramnathapuram** (4hr., Rs28). Unmetered auto-rickshaws circulate though Rameswaram, and local buses shuttle between the bus stand and E. Car St. (Rs1). **Bicycles** can be rented from shops on the Car Streets for about Rs20 per day.

Pharmacies, including **Shekhar Medical,** can be found on Bazaar St. (open M-F 9:30am-9pm). The **Government Hospital** (tel. 21233) is near the railway station; going toward the temple, take a left off Bazaar St. before the Township Office. You can also try the Temple Trust Ayurvedic Dispensary, near the temple police station. The **post office** has two branches: one on Middle St., toward the bus stand, and a smaller office on E. Car St. The **police station** (tel. 21227) is in a red faux-brick building at the junction of E. Car and N. Car St. **Telephone Code:** 04573.

ACCOMMODATIONS AND FOOD

Except for the TTDC Rest House, most hotels are located in the immediate vicinity of the Ramanathaswamy Temple. Accommodations are barest-of-bones, catering to pilgrims looking for a cheap place to crash for the night. Rameswaram's tapwater can be salty, and showers are extremely rare, so check the plumbing before checking in. Reservations are recommended during the pilgrimage season (Jul.-Aug.). The **Lodge Santhya,** W. Car St. (tel. 21329), near the intersection with S. Car St., has mosaic-floored rooms above street level, keeping the sound of bullock carts and seashell vendors at bay. Ask for rooms in their building across the way; these are fairly new and the bathrooms even have showers. (In-season: singles Rs100; doubles Rs125, with A/C Rs150/200. Off-season: Rs60/90/125/175.) The newest and poshest place in town is **Hotel Maharaja's,** 7 Middle St. (tel. 21271). All of its peachy rooms are well-maintained and have Star TV. The attached squat toilets are the cleanest you'll get in this town, and there's hot water on request. (Singles Rs120; doubles Rs195, with A/C Rs420.)

Dining options in Rameswaram are extremely limited. *Thali* restaurants are abundant in the streets around the temple. The best of these, **Hotel Abirami,** on Sannadhi St., piles up piping-hot *chapatis* and vegetable *sabjis* (open daily 6am-10pm). The **Hotel Tamil Nadu,** on the beachfront 2km from the railway station, has the town's only permit room. Those who crave a beer can sip it in a cane chair overlooking the sea as they contemplate the long walk back. Packed with pilgrims on day tours, especially at mid-day, they also serve meals (Rs20-40).

SIGHTS

At the heart of Rameswaram, the **Ramanathaswamy Temple** sees thousands of Hindu pilgrims pass through its *gopurams* every day. *(Temple gates open daily 4am-8pm. Admission Rs2. Sanctum closed noon-4pm.)* Its construction began in the 12th century under the direction of the architecturally prolific Chola empire; the temple was last altered significantly in the mid-18th century by the Raja of Ramnathapuram, Muthuramalinga Sethupathi. Despite its phenomenally filled coffers, construction has been slow; the eastern *gopuram* was just completed earlier this century.

The temple registers as one of the most sacred sites for Hindus, as it is believed the inner sanctum houses a *linga* fashioned out of sand by Rama. According to a later version of the *Ramayana,* after Rama killed Ravana in Lanka and rescued Sita, he returned to Rameswaram Island, only to discover that Ravana had been a *brahmin*—

and his murder thus a grave sin. Rama sent Hanuman to bring back a *linga* with which Rama could worship Shiva and expiate his guilt, but the monkey was late, and Rama had to make do with a *linga* of sand. When Hanuman finally returned, Rama suggested that they replace the sand *linga* with the new one, but when Hanuman tried to pull out the makeshift *linga,* it would not budge, so the new *linga* was installed to the left of Rama's. It was decreed that all pilgrims should worship Hanuman's installation first.

The inner sanctum of the temple (inaccessible to non-Hindus) houses both *lingas* in a smoky central chamber. Facing the main shrine is a huge sculpture of Nandi, Shiva's bull. Before having *darshan* of the resident deities, visitors normally bathe in the waters of 22 *tirthas* (tanks). To expedite the process, temple employees are on hand to dump buckets of holy water on the devotees. The entrance to the *tirthas* is just south of the temple's eastern entrance.

Aside from its spiritual importance, the Ramanathaswamy Temple is also famous for its sculpted pillars, which form corridors measuring 264m from east to west and 200m from north to south. The 1200 soft stone pillars in the outer corridor harmoniously unite form with function.

Located 20km along the precarious road towards Sri Lanka is the **Kothandaramar Temple.** *(Temple open daily 8am-5pm.)* Dedicated to Rama, the structure is said to mark the site where Ravana's brother Vibhishana was crowned king of Lanka after Ravana's death. A tremendous view of the sandy island terrain can be had at the **Gandamadana Paravtham,** 3km north of the Ramanathaswamy Temple. This simple, white-washed temple is set on the highest hill in town and houses an imprint of Lord Rama's feet. Cool off with a swig of coconut water from the vendors outside (Rs6-8).

The southeastern end of Rameswaram's island forms a great finger of sand pointing to Sri Lanka. Because the railway line to **Dhanushkodi,** at the tip, was destroyed by a cyclone in 1964, one must trudge 6km in the sand or hire a jeep (Rs500 from Ramanathaswamy Temple) to get there. Local buses also make the trip. There is no trace of human habitation on this stretch of sand, but those who make the chilly predawn trek are rewarded with a stunning sunrise.

■ Kanyakumari கன்னியாகுமாரி

Kanyakumari (Cape Comorin) marks the southernmost tip of the Indian Subcontinent. In keeping with the Hindu belief in the auspiciousness of physical confluence, this meeting place for three bodies of water—the Arabian Ocean, the Bay of Bengal, and the Indian Ocean—is a particularly holy site. Hindu pilgrims ranging from dredded *babus* to laughing families holding hands come in droves to sacred Kanyakumari. Legend has it that the goddess Kanya Devi—an incarnation of Parvati—did heavy penance here in order to win the hand of Lord Shiva in marriage. Finally consenting, Shiva set off for the midnight wedding ceremony. The other gods, however, wanted Kanya Devi to retain her divine *shakti* by remaining a virgin, and they schemed to make the wedding go awry. The sage Narada assumed the form of a rooster, crowing to make Shiva think that the dawn had come and he was too late. Shiva fell for it and went home, and the heartbroken Kanya Devi remained a perpetual virgin. The Kumari Amman Temple celebrates her penance and loss.

In the light of day, the glamor lent Kanyakumari by the myth fades, as vendors along the beach hawk cheap souvenirs and "shell art." The gaudy buildings that pockmark the southernmost tip of the city begin to come into view, and the place starts to seem less than chaste. At night, however, the booths light up, and the influx of people lends Kumari Amman a carnival air that somewhat mitigates the city's grimness.

ORIENTATION

Buses from Trivandrum and Madurai head south down **Main Road** past the **railway station.** You can hop off as they approach the sea or wait for the bus to turn west, pass the square-towered **lighthouse,** and stop at the **bus stand.** Main Rd. continues south past this junction to the **tourist office,** and peters out at the **Gandhi Memorial.** Main Rd. becomes **Beach Road** as it curves to the east along the shore. From the bus stand, the road continues east, crossing Main Rd., then **Sannadhi Street,** finally ending at the **ferry service station.** Sannadhi heads south through the souvenir stalls to the **Kumari Amman Temple.** Following the east shore north from the temple leads to a **hotel district** and the **railway station.**

PRACTICAL INFORMATION

Trains: The **railway station** is a 15min. walk north from the sea on Main Rd., on the left. Fares listed are 2nd/1st class. To: **Bangalore** (*Bangalore Exp.* 6525, 7:20am, 20hr., Rs169/821); **Chennai** (*Kanya Kumari-Chennai Exp.* 6722, 4pm, 17hr., Rs174/849); **Ernakulam** (5, 7:20am, 10hr., Rs79/113); **Mumbai** (*Kanya Kumari-Mumbai Exp.* 1082, 5am, 48hr., Rs396/1549); **Trivandrum** (5, 7:20am, 2½hr., Rs30).

Buses: The tidy bus stand has a schedule posted in English and a helpful information desk. The tourist office also has up-to-date bus schedules and rates. Buses are prone to last-minute cancellations. To: **Chennai** (11 per day, 10:15am-8:30pm, 16hr., Rs146); **Coimbatore** (7pm, 11hr., Rs97); **Ernakulam** (7:15 and 9:15am, 9hr., Rs89); **Kodaikanal** (8:45pm, 9hr., Rs82); **Kollam** (9:15am, 8hr., Rs25); **Kottayam** (7:15am, 8hr., Rs89); **Kovalam** (6:30, 7:05am, and 2pm, 2½hr., Rs19); **Madurai** (frequent, 8am-8:30pm, 6hr., Rs69); **Ooty** (6:30pm, 14½hr., Rs123); **Rameswaram** (4 per day, 7:30am-8pm, 10hr., Rs91). The **Tamil Nadu Government Express** service (tel. 71019) runs daily buses to Bangalore, Coimbatore, Kodaikanal, Madurai, Chennai, Ooty, Pondicherry, Rameswaram, and Tirupati.

Local Transportation: Kanyakumari is small enough to navigate on foot. Innumerable rickshaw-and taxi-*wallahs* will try to take you to Kovalam.

Tourist Office: Main Rd. (tel. 71276), north from the Gandhi Memorial, on the right. Knowledgeable staff doles out pamphlets, brochures, and info. Open M-F 10am-5:45pm. The **TTDC** (tel. 71276) can be contacted at Hotel Tamil Nadu.

Budget Travel: Many small offices sell private bus and train tickets; several are clustered north of the Kumari Amman Temple.

Currency Exchange: Canara Bank, Main Rd. A 5-10min. walk north of the intersection with the road leading to the bus stand, on the left. Changes AmEx and Thomas Cook traveler's checks. Open M-F 10am-2pm, Sa 10am-noon.

Bookstore: Shamus Book Centre, Sannadhi St., near Hotel Saravana. Carries travel maps and guides. Open M-W and F-Su 8:30am-8pm.

Pharmacy: Sastha Pharmacy, Main Rd. (tel. 71932), halfway between the railway station and the tourist office. Open daily 8:30am-9:30pm.

Hospital: Government Hospital, next to the police station. Since it has no phone, tourists needing assistance might have better luck contacting a private doctor: Dr. Arumugam (tel. 71349), Dr. Geetha (tel. 71267), Dr. Pandiyan (tel. 71261).

Police Station (tel. 71224), next to the GPO.

Emergency: Police, tel. 100; **Fire,** tel. 101; **Ambulance,** tel. 102.

Post Office: GPO, Main Rd., just south of Canara Bank. Stamps and *Poste Restante.* Open M-Sa 9am-1pm and 2-5pm. **Postal Code:** 629702.

Telephone Code: 04652.

ACCOMMODATIONS

The section of Kanyakumari closest to the temples seethes with ugly hotels. The hotels off Main Rd. are both prettier and more modern. In season (Aug.-Feb.), and particularly during peak season (Oct.-Feb.), the prices fly upward.

Hotel Sangam, Main Rd. (tel. 71351), across the street from the GPO. Clean, well-lit rooms with attached, spotless bathrooms with seat toilets. All rooms have sea views. Add the 24hr. room service from Restaurant Sangam, you may never leave your bed. Deluxe A/C rooms come with TVs. "Ordinary" rooms Rs270; "deluxe" Rs410; quads Rs620, with A/C Rs820. Prices double during peak season.

Hotel Maadhini, East Car St. (tel. 71787 or 71887; fax 71657), near the Sea Shore Restaurant. Brand new, with all the amenities of a Western hotel. Rooms are carpeted and brightly lit, with large disinfected bathrooms (soap and towels provided). Breathtaking views and Discovery Channel vie for your gaze. Running hot water 24hr. In-season: doubles Rs400, with A/C Rs900. Off-season: Rs300/800.

Manickam Tourist House, Car St. (tel. 71387 or 71687). Near Hotel Maadhini. With most of the amenities of Hotel Maadhini, but lacking the views and the higher prices. Tolerably tidy rooms with either seat or squat toilet. Buckets of hot water upon request. In-season: doubles Rs280-350; triples Rs450, with A/C Rs650 and up. Off-season: Rs180-250/Rs350/Rs550 and up.

Kerala House (tel. 71229). From the bus stand, turn left and look for the sign on the right. From the railway station, turn right onto the main road, then right onto the road past the lighthouse, then left into the driveway. Massive rooms have high ceilings, huge windows (some overlooking the ocean), dressing rooms, and attached baths with seat toilets. Singles Rs240; doubles Rs360. Additional beds Rs120.

Railway Station Retiring Rooms, upstairs in the railway station. The high-ceilinged rooms are spacious and have mosquito nets. Singles Rs50; doubles Rs80.

FOOD

Gastronomically, Kanyakumari is pretty much the pits—we dare you to find a single *gulab jamun.* Most of the food is vegetarian. The soon-to-be-mentioned establishments are virtually the only eateries of note. Surprisingly, none boast great sea views.

Hotel Saravana, Sannadhi St. The larger A/C branch is on the left heading up the hill from the temple. South Indian breakfasts, as well as Gujarati, Rajasthani, Punjabi, and South Indian veg. *thalis,* and Chinese eats. The veg. "Manjoorian" is particularly tasty, as is the giant, conical *masala dosa.* Open daily 6am-10pm.

Famili Restaurant, Sannadhi St. From the temple, walk north up the steps and watch for this tiny blue crevice of a restaurant. It doesn't look good until you glimpse the steam rising from a huge pot of fresh *idli,* or from the giant *dosa* griddle. Open daily 10am-3pm.

Hotel Sangam, Main Rd. Opposite the GPO. Your best chance of finding Chinese and non-veg. food. A wide range of slightly-misspelled tasties ("chow mine") are all theoretically available 24hr. Most dishes Rs25-70.

SIGHTS AND ENTERTAINMENT

At the seaward end of Main Rd., **Gandhi Mandapam**—an unusual interpretation of Orissan architectural style—overlooks the last bit of India. (*Open daily 4:30am-noon and 4-8pm.*) A black marble box marks the spot where the ashes of Mahatma Gandhi were stored briefly before being scattered seaward. The *mandapam* rises 79 ft. (23m), one for each year of Gandhi's life, and is engineered so that every year on his birthday, October 2, a ray of sunlight falls here at noon. The "guard" will spew the basic facts and then hit up guests for "something for a poor watchman." Nonetheless, it is worth taking his advice and climbing up the spires for inspirational photo-ops.

The seaside **Kumari Amman Temple** is a few hundred meters back from the tip of India, indelibly marked by the trademark red-and-white vertical temple stripes. (*Open daily 4am-noon and 4-8:30pm.*) Dedicated to Kanya Devi, the temple celebrates the penance she did in hopes of winning the hand of Shiva. All visitors must shed their shoes, and men must shed their shirts.

Accessible by ferry are two rocks, now swathed in concrete, which the Hindu reformer Swami Vivekananda swam to and meditated atop for several days in 1892 (see **Modern Hinduism,** p. 95). A glossy temple, the **Vivekananda Memorial,** commemorates the event. (*Ferries daily 7:45am-4pm, Rs6. Catch the ferry from the east coast 100m from Kumari Amman Temple.*) There's also a temple built around a footprint left by the goddess Parvati. Arrows mark the path around the island.

Although the sections of Kanyakumari near the temple and the cape overflow with cheap lacquered seashells, Ray-Ban-*wallahs,* and soulless hotels, the **village** on the east coast north of the hotel district has its charms, including bright, lavender and yellow houses, small church-shrines, and fishermen repairing nets while their wives weave new ones. The elegant and imposing **St. Mary's Church** towers over the southern edge of the village. While its facade is beautiful, the church's interior disappoints with bright plastic flowers and gaudy gold-foil-edged portraits of a milky-white Jesus and Mary. Expect to be befriended by an English-speaking local who will feed you a sob story and hit you up for a "gift."

Kanyakumari's **Pongal Festival** (Jan. 14-15) celebrates the end of the rice harvest with South India's beloved, sweet, rice-based bread. The **Cape Festival,** held in the last week of November, celebrates Tamil culture, especially Bharatanatyam dance. Finally, **World Tourism Day** (Sept. 27) is celebrated with free cultural shows, and free food and garlands for foreign tourists (see **Holidays and Festivals,** p. 805).

■ Near Kanyakumari

On the way to Trivandrum, 45km from Kanyakumari, is **Padmanabhapuram,** which was the capital of Travancore until 1798. Inside Padmanabhapuram's **fort** is a grand **palace** covering 2.5 hectares (open Tu-Su 9am-5pm; admission Rs6). Many tour buses from Trivandrum stop here on their way to Kanyakumari. A bit closer to Kanyakumari is the **Suchindram Temple,** 13km by rickshaw, taxi, or tour bus. This temple is dedicated to the holy trinity of Hinduism—Shiva, Vishnu, and Brahma—and contains many sculptural odds and ends, including India's only depiction of a female Ganesha. Also of note are a 2500-year-old tree and a limestone Nandi, which, according to local lore, is actually growing.

■ Kodaikanal கொடைக்கானல்

Though Kodaikanal, 2133m above sea level in the southern crest of the gentle Palani Hills, is among the most famous hill stations in Tamil Nadu, the town suffers little of the colonial hangover that characterizes its brethren. There are few architectural or cultural reminders that the British dominated local life for the century between the 1840s (when Kodai was founded as an antidote to the sweltering, malaria-infested plains) and the 1940s, when India pushed for independence. Today, hoteliers have turned the town into a tribute to the tastes of India's burgeoning leisure class. Yet unlike Ooty, Kodai remains relatively free of noise and pollution, and its surroundings are arguably the most beautiful of any hill station, with precipitous green mountainsides giving way to the lush plains of Coimbatore. Kodai can get a bit nippy, especially at night, and the daily high temperature is usually 10-20°C cooler than Chennai's.

ORIENTATION

Getting around in Kodai is a snap. Buses pull into a lot just south of **Anna Salai (Bazaar Road),** the town's major east-west thoroughfare. Anna Salai leads west to the Seven Road Junction, where (at last count) six roads meet at a traffic circle. At the junction, **Club Road** and the restaurant-laden **P.T. Road (Hospital Road)** head north. P.T. Rd. connects Anna Salai with **Law's Ghat Road,** which runs roughly parallel to it. Heading south from the junction takes you to **Bryant's Park** and **Coaker's Walk,** while west of the junction sits Kodai's artificial lake. **Observatory Road** leads west past the lake and out of town.

PRACTICAL INFORMATION

Trains: The nearest railway station is **Kodaikanal Road** (3hr. by bus), but it may be more convenient to catch a train from Madurai Junction (4hr. by bus). From Kodaikanal Rd. to: **Chennai** via **Tiruchirappalli** (*Madurai-Chennai Janata Exp.,* 5pm, 17hr.; *Madurai-Chennai Exp.* 6720, 11:06pm, 14hr.; Rs152/682); **Madurai** (*Chennai-Madurai Exp.* 6737, 10am; 1hr., Rs15/85); **Tirupati** (*Madurai-Tirupati Exp.* 6799, 2am, 17½hr., Rs123/547).

Buses: The **bus stand** is a dirt lot just off Anna Salai, on Wood Will Rd. To: **Bangalore** (6pm, 12hr., Rs169); **Chennai** (6:45pm, 12hr., Rs155); **Coimbatore** (8:30am and 4:30pm, 6hr., Rs35); **Kankyakumari** (9am, 9hr., Rs65); **Madurai** (9 per day, 7:30am-4:30pm, 4hr., Rs35); **Ooty** (via Kodaikanal, 11:40am, 3:40, and 4:15pm, 3hr., Rs65; via Palani and Coimbatore, 8:30am, 8hr., Rs35); **Trichy** (1:30 and 5:45pm, 5hr., Rs45). There are a number of **private bus** operators with daily departures to Chennai, Madurai, Ooty, and Coimbatore.

SOUTH INDIA

Local Transportation: There are no **rickshaws** in Kodaikanal. Their absence is both a blessing and a burden, since **taxis** (available outside the bus stand) charge an offensive Rs50 minimum. The best way to get around is to **walk.**

Tourist Office: On the northern side of Anna Salai (tel. 41675), a 2min. walk east of the bus stand (look for the glut of tourist vans). Open M-Sa 10am-5:45pm.

Travel Agent: For bus, train, and airline bookings, try the agent adjacent to the **Hilltop Towers Hotel,** Club Rd. Open M-Sa 9am-1pm and 2-5pm, Su 2-5pm.

Currency Exchange: State Bank of India (tel. 41068), next to the tourist office. Changes traveler's checks in US$ and UK£. Open M-F 10am-2pm, Sa 10am-noon.

Bookstore: CLS Bookstore (tel. 40465), opposite the tourist office. Miscellaneous books, some tourist information. Open M-Sa 9am-1pm and 2-6pm.

Market and Pharmacy: Kurunji Mini Super Market, next to the post office. Stock up on peanut butter, Kotex, and mineral water. Other pharmacies line Anna Salai.

Hospital: Government Hospital (tel. 41292). From the Seven Road Junction, follow P.T. Rd. north for about 250m. The hospital is on the right, before Law's Ghat Rd. **Van Allen** (tel. 41273) is a reputable private hospital near Coaker's Walk.

Police: Diagonally opposite the post office on Anna Salai (tel. 40262).

Post Office: A huge yellow building on Anna Salai (tel. 41267), opposite Snooze Inn. Open M-F 9am-5pm. *Poste Restante.* **Postal Code:** 624101.

Telephone Code: 04542.

ACCOMMODATIONS

At the current growth rate, hotels will soon occupy just about every square inch of land in Kodai. The cheapest lodgings are located right on Anna Salai; as you move away from the town center, quality and prices increase exponentially.

Snooze Inn, Anna Salai (tel. 40837). Cozy beds with cushioned headrests, surrounded by furry red carpets and token ethnic *objets d'art.* Pint-sized TVs in all the rooms. Ultra-clean bathrooms have marble tiles, seat toilets, and hot water. Jun.-Mar.: doubles Rs300; quads Rs650. Apr.-May: Rs395/600. Heater Rs30, extra blanket Rs7. Major credit cards accepted with prior approval.

Hotel Sangeeth, Wood Will Rd. (tel. 40456), opposite the bus stand. Thick wool blankets to keep you warm on chilly nights. Attached baths have 24hr. hot water. Apr.-June: doubles Rs400. July-Mar.: Rs200.

Lodge Everest, Anna Salai (tel. 40100). One of the many small lodges on the eastern end of Anna Salai, just before the road makes a steep descent down the side of the hill. Pleasant staff holds down the fort in the rustic, wood paneled lobby. The small rooms contain simple, well-kept furnishings that do the job. Dorm beds Rs30. Doubles Rs150. Prices go up in peak season.

Hilltop Towers, Club Rd. (tel. 40413), north of the Seven Road Junction, opposite the International School. This upper-range hotel may be worth investigating off season, when prices are slashed. Charming rooms are spacious, with pleasant views, huge beds, telephones, and TVs. Attached baths have seat toilets and fairly reliable hot water. In-season: doubles Rs725. Off-season: Rs475.

Greenlands Youth Hostel, St. Mary's Rd. (tel. 410899), near Coaker's Walk. From the Seven Road Junction, follow Club Rd. south, past the Kodaikanal Club, Van Allen Hospital, and down the lonely road. It's a hike, but the views are simply stunning—that is, when the whole complex isn't wrapped in a cloak of mist. Dorms escape the cell-block feel that nags most hostels. Equally cozy private rooms with attached baths (hot water!) and working fireplaces (hot fire!). In-season: dorm beds Rs55; doubles Rs180. Off-season: doubles Rs200.

MYH Youth Hostel, Post Office Rd. (tel. 40831). Climb the stone staircase immediately east (left) of the post office and continue straight ahead. Crowded dorm with plaid sheets. Rooms have dingy walls and nappy carpets. Attached baths are clean and have seat toilets and bucket hot water (Rs5) 24hr. In-season: dorm beds Rs60; doubles and cottages Rs250. Off-season: Rs40/150.

Hotel Astoria (tel. 40524), at the intersection of Wood Will and Anna Salai. Nice, upscale place with a popular restaurant downstairs. Ample beds, seat toilets, and satellite TV. Popular attached restaurant serves basic *thalis* (Rs21) and is open daily 7am-9:30pm. In-season: doubles Rs325. Off-season: Rs550.

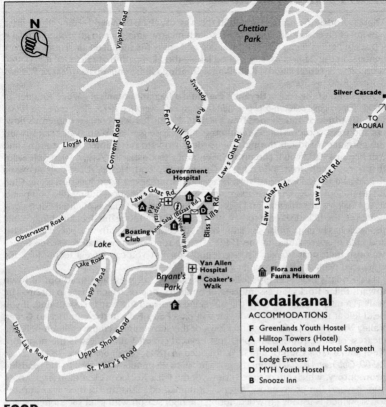

Kodaikanal
ACCOMMODATIONS

F Greenlands Youth Hostel
A Hilltop Towers (Hotel)
E Hotel Astoria and Hotel Sangeeth
C Lodge Everest
D MYH Youth Hostel
B Snooze Inn

FOOD

Kodaikanal's restaurant scene caters to the cosmopolitan culinary tastes of its visitors. If you don't leave town a kilogram or two heavier, then you've definitely missed out. Many of the best restaurants are on Hospital Rd., north of the Seven Road Junction.

Tibetan Brothers Restaurant, P.T. Rd., upstairs on the left. Near-authentic cuisine served up by the Tibetan family that owns the place. Juicy vegetable *momos* Rs35, lemon tea (Rs6), Tibetan bread Rs10. Open daily noon-4pm and 5:30-10pm.

Chef Master, Hospital Rd. (tel. 42073), just past Tibetan Brothers. Blue-and-white striped tablecloths, plastic placemats, and fake flowers scream kitsch, but the cuisine is infinitely more tasteful. Gratifyingly greaseless Chinese, Continental, and Keralan food draws locals and foreigners alike. Open daily 9am-10pm.

Hotel Punjab, Hospital Rd., just north of the Seven Road Junction. Lip-smackin' delicious tandoori fare is dished out in this classy upstairs restaurant. The windows provide a not-exactly-romantic view of P.T. Rd. Keep your attention focused on the menu (entrees Rs30 and up) and your voracious appetite for *naan,* chicken, and veg. dishes. Open daily 10am-10pm.

Hot Breads, Hospital Rd. (tel. 41169), past Chef Master. A popular franchise that serves pastries, pizza, hot dogs, and chips. A la carte array of breads, cakes, pastries, mini-pizzas, and cookies (Rs15); otherwise, have a seat and choose from the menu (entrees Rs20-35). Best selection in the morning. Open daily 9am-9pm.

Eco-Nut, upstairs from Hot Breads on Hospital Rd. A crunchy, health foods and natural products shop loaded with *neem* soap (Rs8), henna (Rs10), herbal cola, and fresh juices. Even if you don't plan to buy, come take a quick peek at the funky merchandise. Open daily 9:45am-6:30pm.

SIGHTS AND ENTERTAINMENT

Though Kodai doesn't offer much in the way of wham-bam sight-seeing, there are a handful of diversions and more than enough mellow ambience to go around. Kodai is a place where you can just keep walking and enjoy the mountain air. Tourist activity centers on the 24-hectare star-shaped **lake**—the 5km path that encircles it is dotted with bicycle rental stands. **Kodaikanal Boating Club** rents boats. *(Rentals 9:30am-5:30pm. Rs40 per 30min.).*

Just south of the lake is **Bryant's Park** and a fragrant **botanical garden** founded in 1902. *(Open daily 8:30am-6:15pm. Admission Rs5. Camera fee Rs25. Plant a tree Rs1000.)* Expertly trimmed and clipped by a a staff of 45, the gardens contain numerous flowers and trees, a cactus-filled greenhouse, and a rose garden. With your back toward the entrance, head left through the gardens (toward the painted tree stumps) and exit Bryant's Park; you'll end up at the entrance to **Coaker's Walk**, a 10-minute jaunt that traces an arc from Taj Lodge to Greenland's Youth Hostel. *(Open daily. Admission Rs2, camera fee Rs5.)* Alternatively, head south from Seven Road Junction along Club Rd. to the entrance. On clear mornings, the views of the surrounding hills and plains from Coaker's are amazing, and it is claimed you can see as far as Madurai. Most days, however, the hillside is covered by mist and it's tough to see much of anything. While the walk has been popular since the late 19th century, the path was paved and lights and railings were added in the 1980s. During renovations a small **telescope house** was also built near Coaker's western end—for Rs1 you can have a technologically enhanced peek at the surrounding countryside.

For Kodai's best scenery, follow Observatory Rd. west and head out of town toward **Pillar Rocks**, an assemblage of boulders, one of which soars to 122m. The walk is a mostly flat 8km from the bus stand area, and the way is easy to find. If you head left at the fork in the road, you will pass **Fairy Falls** to the entrance to **Green Valley View**, which allows grand views of the surrounding countryside on only the clearest of days. *(Open 8am-6pm.)* Just beyond Green Valley View is the nonprofit **Kodiakanal Golf Club** (tel 40323), founded in 1895. *(Open 8am-6pm. 18-hole course Rs500. Club rental Rs200.)* From the golf club it's a 25-minute walk west to the **roadside promontory**, which offers superb views of the Pillar Rocks on clear mornings. About 40m beyond the promontory, a series of unmarked paths thread their way into the forest, which is usually crowded during the high season with loud vacationers scampering about. No matter—the woods here are incredibly lush and there are many chances for seeing the hulking Pillar Rocks up close.

There are a couple of other interesting short excursions from Kodai. Three kilometers northeast of the bus-stand is **Chettiar Park**, a secluded spot which renews its fame every 12 years when the chronically shy *kurinji* plant springs into colorful bloom; blossoms are next scheduled for 2006. Don't blink twice if you see some flowers, since there are a few plants whose biological clocks are off kilter. Also in Chettiar Park is the **Kurinji Andavar Temple**, dedicated to Muruga, which commands a panoramic view. Follow Law's Ghat Rd. southeast and out of town for 3km to reach the **Flora and Fauna Museum**, on the grounds of the Sacred Heart College (open M-Sa 9:30am-noon and 3-6pm; Rs1), featuring a fine **orchid house**. About 800m past the museum is the mid-sized **Silver Cascade**, a waterfall along the road to Madurai—you may have caught a glimpse of it on your way into town.

■ Coimbatore கோயம்புத்தூர்

Coimbatore is a busy, commercial center with modern hotels, cybercafes, and wide streets. Although it has no real tourist attractions (aside from a handful of picturesque lakes), the city's bus and railway stations teem with travelers en route to or from Ooty, Kerala, or Karnataka. Like them, you will probably only spend the night, maybe check your email, and leave Coimbatore unexplored.

ORIENTATION AND PRACTICAL INFORMATION Though the Coimbatore city limits are expanding endlessly with the daily influx of new residents, the area of interest to travelers passing through is fairly self-contained. The north-south thoroughfare of

Bank Road holds a number of tourist services, including the **State Bank of India** (tel. 213251; open for your money-changing needs M-F 10am-2pm, Sa 10am-noon). Bank Rd. heads north from the bank; 200m before it hits **Mill Road** (called **Avinashi Road** farther east), it forks. The right fork feeds into Avinashi Rd., while the left fork ends when it hits Mill Rd. Its continuation on the northern side of Mill Rd. is **Dr. Nanjappa Road,** Coimbatore's chaotic main drag. **Coimbatore Junction Railway Station** (reservations tel. 131; open M-Sa 8am-2pm and 2:15-8pm, Su 8am-2pm) is located in the southern part of the city center on **Bank Road**. If you're headed to Ooty, take the *Nilgiri Express* 6606 (8:35am) for the hour-long ride to Mettupalayam, where you can change immediately to the *Blue Mountain Railway* that's standing by. Other trains lurch towards: **Bangalore** (*Kanniyamari* 6525, 8:50pm, 8½hr., Rs99/490); **Chennai** (*West Coast Express* 6028, 4:55am, 9hr.; *Cochin-Bilsapur Express* 7057, 2:30pm; *Nilgiri Express* 6606, 8:35pm, 9½hr.; *Cheran Express* 6674, 11:05pm, 9hr.; Rs107/531); **Delhi** (7:10pm, 20hr., Rs304/1823); **Kanyakumari** via **Trivandrum** (*Trivandrum Superfast* 2625, 7:10pm, Rs96/484); **Madurai** (11:25am, 6hr., Rs56/274); and **Mumbai** (*Mumbai Exp.* 1082, 6:05pm, 23hr., Rs332/1391).

Three of the city's four **bus stands** are located on the northern end of Dr. Nanjappa Rd., 1.5km (15min. walk) from the railway station. The northernmost is the **TSTC** and **Karnataka Regional Transport Corp. (KRTC)** stand, located on Cross Cut Rd. just east of the intersection with Bharatiyar Rd. Their busy reservations center (tel. 434969) is open daily from 7am until 10pm. Buses meander toward **Mysore** via **Ooty** (almost every hr. 5am-midnight, 6hr. and 3hr., Rs47/22) and **Chennai** (4 per day, 12hr., Rs128). There's also frequent service to **Madurai** (6hr.) and **Trichy** (5hr., Rs32). A five-minute walk south on Dr. Nanjappa Rd. will bring you to the shockingly organized **State Bus Stand**, with departures to **Mysore** (3 per day, 6hr., Rs29) and **Bangalore** (morning and evening departures, 9hr., Rs76). You can also catch the frequent buses to Ooty via Mettupalayam (every 30min., 3hr.). Diagonally across the street is the **Town Bus Stand** (known to locals as **Gandhipuram** for the neighborhood in which it is situated). From here you can catch bus #55 or 57, which shuttle between the bus stand area and the railway station. A fourth stand, **Ukkadam,** is located 1.5km south of its 3 northern brethren. This stand services smaller towns to the south; buses from Kerala and other southern destinations may arrive here. Take bus #38B from Ukkadam to the railway station. **Rickshaw-wallahs** seem to have decided that Rs30 is an acceptable amount to charge for this distance, but with some serious haggling you can bring them down to Rs15. Coimbatore's **airport** is located 10km northeast of the city center. Indian Airlines (tel. 309821) has flights to **Calicut, Chennai,** and **Mumbai.**

There are plenty of garden-variety **pharmacies** near the bus stands, or if your needs suit, come out and see the 24-hour **Ellen Hospital,** 284 Sathy Rd. (tel. 435920 or 435972), a few hundred meters further north. Coimbatore's **Head Post Office** is on Railway Feeder Rd.—from the intersection of Mill and Dr. Nanjappa Rd., head west and make the first left after Hotel Sri Thevar. (Open M-F 9am-5:30pm.) **Netserf,** 205-H Vivekananda Rd. (tel. 235983), up the stairs and around the corner from the big sign offers **Internet** access in cool blue surroundings (Rs60 for 30min., Rs120 per hr.). **Postal Code:** 641001. **Telephone Code:** 0422.

ACCOMMODATIONS AND FOOD Coimbatore's best hotels and restaurants are around the bus stands, but there's also a small enclave of hotels near the railway station. The best option for those who need to catch a train may be the **railway retiring rooms,** upstairs in the station building across from the computerized reservation area. Immaculate and often full, the freshly mapped blue rooms with attached baths are set along a shiny hallway (Rs250-300, with A/C Rs300-350). The only drawback is the noise. A small path directly across the street from the railway station entrance leads to a number of small hotels, including the **Hotel Anand Vihar** (tel. 230569). This friendly establishment has basic accommodations, attached baths, and squat toilets. (Singles Rs75; doubles Rs125.) The unusually opulent entrance of **Hotel Tamil Nadu,** down the street from the main bus terminals on Dr. Nanjappa Rd. (tel. 236311) leads to standard rooms. (Singles Rs195; doubles Rs275, with A/C Rs375/

425; TV Rs50 extra.) There are also plenty of high-rise hotels in the same price range on Nehru St. and Sastri Rd., opposite the central bus stand.

Dining options run the gamut from typically proletarian eateries to gourmet buffets. For the former, head to **Sree Annapoorna,** just south of the State Bus Stand on Dr. Nanjappa Rd. It'll seem like every itinerant traveler is in the house, slurping *sambar* by the bucket. (Open daily 7:30am-late.) **Cloud Nine** at the Hotel City Tower has an assortment of unusually good Indian, Chinese, and Continental dishes (Rs30-50). Western-style breakfasts are also available. (Open daily 8am-9pm.) The popular **Gayathri Restaurant,** between the hotels in Nehru St., opposite Hotel Blue Star, has an open air patio (meals Rs15-19).

■ Ooty (Udhagamandalam) ஊட்டி

Ooty (whose full name, Udhagamandalam, comes from the language of one of the pastoral tribes that inhabited the area) was "established" in 1821 by an enterprising collector with the East India Company, John Sullivan. Sullivan conceived Ooty as a hill station, offering Company officials harried by the heat and humidity of the plains a place to chill out. Maharajas followed suit, transforming hill station into hunting station, and solidifying Ooty's reputation as an exclusive getaway.

You can still visit the tombs of John Sullivan's wife, daughter, and son in the cemetery of St. Stephen's Church in Ooty, but Sullivan himself is buried in his mother England, where he probably spins in his grave, bemoaning the popularization of his verdant utopia. Since Independence, Ooty has become a summer migratory spot for hordes of Indian tourists as well as for the rich and famous. No longer the elite retreat Sullivan founded, Ooty is often condemned as a tourist trap where bus exhaust fouls the crisp mountain air, rubbish defiles the once-pristine valley, and the over-booming hotel and package-tour industries undermine Ooty's quaint charms.

Although it takes a little scouring to escape the jungle of hypercommerciality, such assiduity is well-rewarded: the locals are laid-back; the tea, potato, and carrot plantations make for some lush scenery; and at 2638m, Mt. Doddabetta is the closest you can get to heaven in South India. Ooty's season runs from April 1 to June 15; temperatures hover around a dry 25°C during the day, and nights can be chilly. Monsoon season runs from July to August, and September sees the return of dry weather. Ooty's cold, relatively dry winter stretches from November to March.

ORIENTATION

Because its streets snake about the valley and surrounding mountainsides, getting around in Ooty can be somewhat disorienting. No worries, though: the town is fairly small, and locals are accustomed to directing tourists. Ooty's sprawling **lake** is in the southwestern part of town, a 200m walk west from the **railway station** and the **bus stand** along **North Lake Road.** From the railway station, walk northeast along **Upper Bazaar Road** for 1½km and you'll reach **Charing Cross** in the town center. From the bus stand, you can reach Charing Cross by skirting the well-stocked fruit market via **Lower Bazaar Road,** which becomes **Commercial Road** 750m before hitting Charing Cross. From Charing Cross, follow **Garden Road** 1km north to reach the **Botanical Gardens.** Climb the hill 500m behind Charing Cross to reach **Town West Circle.** From there, **Hospital Road** makes a steep and lengthy westward descent back to the area near the railway station.

PRACTICAL INFORMATION

Trains: Railway Station, North Lake Rd. The Blue Mountain Railway (the "toy train") chugs through tea and potato plantations and past waterfalls and is, like much in Ooty, crowded. The steam-powered mini-trains head to **Mettupalayam** (2:50pm, return 7:50am, 4hr., Rs9/85) and **Coonoor** (9:30am and 6pm, return 8, 11am, and 3pm, Rs15/48). April 1-June 15, an extra train departs from Mettupalayam at 9:30am. Restricted service on Su. Reservations counter officially open daily 10am-2pm and 3:30-4:30pm, but often extends its hours. Fares listed are 2nd/1st class.

SOUTH INDIA

Ooty

ACCOMMODATIONS

B Hotel Mount View
E Nilgiri Woodlands
A Reflections Guest House
D Sabari Lodge
C Surya Holiday Inn
F YWCA

TO DODDABETTA

Kotagiri Road

Botanical Gardens

TO COIMBATORE

Wood House Road

Garden Road

Wildlife Warden's Office

Conoor Road

Elk Hill Road

Havelock Road

Archies

Etienes Road

TTDC ①

CHARING CROSS

Tandoor Mahal

State Bank of India

Commercial Road

Hospital Road

GPO

TOWN WEST CIRCLE

St. Stephen's Church

Shinkow's Chinese Rest.

Upper Bazaar Road

Lower Bazaar Road

Race Course

Butcher's Road

F

D

E

Railway Station

B

Westbury Road

Woodcock Road

A

Sigur Road

TO MUDUMALAI AND MYSORE

Ooty Lake

Boat Rental

North Lake Road

South Lake Road

Kamp Bazaar Road

0   300 yards

0   300 meters

N

Buses: The **bus stand** is 100m south of the railway station. Regular state buses and private carriers operate out of one dusty lot. Fortunately, the departure bays are labeled in English, and the buses actually use them most of the time. The **State Transport Company** reservations counter is open daily 9:30am-1pm and 1:30-5pm. Make reservations for long-distance buses 2 days in advance. To: **Bangalore** (11 per day, 6:30am-10:30pm, 8hr., Rs104); **Chennai** (4:30pm, 8hr., Rs94); **Gobi, Erode,** and **Salem** (4:30pm, 10hr., Rs153); **Kanyakumari** via **Coimbatore** and **Madurai** (12:45pm, 11hr., Rs123); **Mysore** (5 per day, 2½hr., Rs40); **Thanjavur** via **Coimbatore** and **Trichy** (6am and 6:15pm, 5½hr., Rs80); **Tirupati** (6pm, 12hr.). **Karnataka State Road Transport Corporation (KSRTC)** has a reservations counter open daily 6:30am-10:30pm. To: **Bangalore** (9am and 6:30pm) and **Mysore** (9am and 1:30pm). Local buses head to **Coimbatore** (every 30min. 5:30am-9pm, 2½hr., Rs27); **Coonoor** (every 10min., 5:30am-11pm, 30min., Rs5); **Mettupalayam** (every 15min. 5:30am-8:30pm, Rs11). Hordes of **private bus operators** run daily trips to Kodaikanal, Mysore, Bangalore, and Chennai in "luxury coaches." Keep in mind that "luxury" is a relative term, and the exorbitant costs may not be worth it.

Local Transportation: Unmetered **auto-rickshaws** charge at least Rs20 for a ride from the railway station to Charing Cross. **Taxis** are more expensive. **Kemp's,** on Etiennes Rd., 500m from Charing Cross, rents **motorcycles** (Rs50 per hr., Rs350 per day; Rs500 deposit). If you're really not up for the walk to Charing Cross, hop on the bus to Coonoor, which goes through downtown before leaving the city.

Tourist Office: TTDC, Commercial Rd. (tel. 43977), 200m from Charing Cross. Provides copious information and maps for the Nilgiri tourist. Open M-F 10am-5:45pm. For trekking information and reservations for government accommodations at **Mudumalai Wildlife Sanctuary** (see p. 533), contact the **Wildlife Warden** (tel. 44098), in the Mahalingam Building, a 10min. walk up Conoor Rd. from Charing Cross. Open M-F 10am-5:45pm.

Budget Travel: Tourist agencies are as numerous as *paan* stalls, and they all offer the same unimaginative tours of Ooty and its environs. **Thomson Tours and Travels** (tel. 43111), in the strip of stores at Hotel Charing Cross, books plane tickets. Open daily 9am-5:30pm.

Currency Exchange: State Bank of India, Town West Circle (tel. 43940). Changes AmEx and Thomas Cook traveler's checks in US$ and UK£. Open M-F 10am-2pm, Sa 10am-noon. If you're in a bind, **The Big Shop** on Commercial Rd. will exchange traveler's checks at bad rates.

Supermarket: K. Chellaram's, Commercial Rd., offers cheddar cheese, toilet paper, eucalyptus oil, and Nilgiri tea. Open daily 9:30am-1:30pm and 3-7:30pm.

Bookstore: Higginbothams, Oriental Building (tel. 42546), up the road toward St. Stephen's Church from Town West Circle. Stocked with *Hobson-Jobson's,* current paperbacks, and the latest installment of the *X-Files* reader. Open M-Sa 9am-1pm and 2-5:30pm.

Pharmacy: Commercial Rd. is lined with pharmacies, most of which close at 9pm.

Hospital: Government Hospital, Jail Hill, Hospital Rd. (tel. 42212). **Vijaya Hospital,** Etiennes Rd. (tel. 42500), behind Alankar Theatres, has a 24hr. ambulance.

Police: Town West Circle (tel. 43973) , near the collector's office.

Post/Telegraph Office: Town West Circle (tel. 42776). From the traffic circle, head northwest up the steep staircase on the side of the hill. Post office open M-F 9am-5pm. *Poste Restante* and special services M-F 9am-5pm, Sa 9am-2pm. Telegraph Office open M-F 8am-10pm. **Postal Code:** 643001.

Telephone Code: 0423.

ACCOMMODATIONS

Lodging in Ooty reflects India's socioeconomic strata: lots of undermaintained and overbooked hovels, a few overpriced luxury hotels, and not much in between. During season (Apr.-June) make reservations to avoid paying too much for too little.

The Reflections Guest House, North Lake Rd. (tel. 43834), 500m west of the bus stand. Soft beds and woolly flannel bedcovers, wildflowers, and a lakeview make this place sublime. Proprietress Mrs. Dique is legendary in backpacker circles. Scrumptious, home-cooked meals. Seat toilets, luggage storage, and laundry service. Heat in the winter; hot water 6-11am. Check-out noon. Apr.-June: rooms Rs300-350, Off-season: Rs199. Reserve 14 days ahead in season.

Sabari Lodge Upper Bazaar (tel. 42735). Trek through the complex to reach the reception. Simple but immaculate, dim rooms escape the noise of the restaurant downstairs. Attached baths (squat toilet), hot water in the morning. Curfew 10pm. Check-out 24hr. In-season: singles Rs80; doubles Rs180. Off-season: Rs150/250.

Surya Holiday Inn, Upper Bazaar (tel. 42567). One of the few decent hotels in the Bazaar/Commercial Rd. area. Rooms are colorful, bright, and clean. Common TV blares 24hr.; bucket hot water 7-9am. Squat toilets. Check-out noon. In season: singles Rs150; doubles Rs350. Off-season: Rs75/175.

YWCA, Etiennes Rd., 500m from the racetrack. Clean dorm beds, sparkling cottages, pleasant sitting rooms and dining hall with piano, TV, and library. Dorms have common baths with squat toilets; cottages have seat toilets. Dorm beds Rs50. Cottages and bungalows Rs160-530. Additional tax.

Nilgiri Woodlands, Etiennes Rd. (tel. 42551), on the southern side of the racetrack, perched on the hill. A mounted bull's head welcomes you to the reception area. Spacious, high-ceilinged rooms have soft carpets and antique furniture. Clean attached baths with seat toilets have 24hr. hot water. In season: rooms Rs450; cottages Rs850. Off-season: Rs300/550. Accepts major credit cards.

Hotel Mount View, Etiennes Rd. (tel. 44182 or 43307). Charming colonial house turned hotel. Enormous, clean rooms with seat toilets and hot water in the morning. Doubles Rs360.

FOOD

For a town that's sold its soul to the tourist deities, Ooty has surprisingly few top-notch restaurants. As in other towns, many of the better restaurants are attached to hotels and offer the same uninspiring array. Luckily, a number of small eateries have cropped up where tourists can refuel on inexpensive Western or Indian snacks.

Shinkow's Chinese Restaurant, 42 Commissioners Rd. (tel. 42811), across from the State Bank of India, Town West Circle. Serving stir-fry to locals and tourists since 1954. The ambience is consummately Chinese-restaurant, down to the fringed lamps. Sliced beef (shhhh!) with peanuts Rs60, veg. dishes around Rs50. Open daily 12:30-4pm and 6:30-10pm.

Tandoor Mahal, 69 Commercial Rd. (tel. 43054). Serves Indian (tandoori) and Chinese cuisine. The interior is classier than the generic yellow sign suggests. Efficient service. Perfectly polished silver pitchers, but don't drink the water. Veg. dishes (Rs20-40) and non-veg. (Rs50). Open daily 9:30am-3:30pm and 6:30pm-midnight.

Archies, Charing Cross. A hole in the wall (literally), near the intersection of Commerical and Coonoor Rd. Spicy "frankies" (chicken, mutton, or vegetable curries wrapped up in *parathas* Rs25), vegetable and mutton burgers, pizza (Rs25), and shakes (Rs15). A crowded juke joint, filled with Western tourists and Bettys and Jugheads from the nearby international school. Open daily F-W 10am-7:45pm.

King Star, The English Confectionery, Commerical Rd., a few hundred meters from Charing Cross. Absolutely mouth-watering. Sample the wide array of deliciously decadent options (the milk chocolate walnut is divine), including some uniquely Indian (read: mango-flavored) offerings. Open daily 10am-8pm.

SIGHTS

Commercial sightseeing in and around Ooty is not exactly a rejuvenating experience. Jam-packed maxicab tours (Rs100) will make you wish you'd wandered around the Nilgiris alone.

Ooty's **Botanical Gardens,** a 22-acre cosmopolitan oasis of flora for landscaper and layperson alike, were designed in 1847, spruced up in 1995, and 150 years after their inception are green as ever. *(Open daily 8:30am-6:30pm; admission Rs5, camera fee Rs25, video fee Rs500.)* With more than 2000 species on display, the gardens have come a long way from their original purpose of producing "English vegetables at reasonable cost." The vivids of the rose garden (India's largest) are complemented by the *saris* of women basking in the sun with somersaulting youngsters. Look for the map of India made out of plants (the Andaman and Nicobar Islands are a bit out of scale, but everything else seems to be in order). A **flower show** during the third week of May is a veritable carnival of flowers.

One kilometer west of the gardens, just up the road from Town West Circle, is the gothic **Saint Stephen's Church,** built in 1829 atop the remains of a tribal temple with lumber from Tipu Sultan's palace. Whether due to post-colonial angst or good old-fashioned Indian mismanagement, the church has fallen into disrepair. British colonialists are buried in the spooky, overgrown cemetery out back, under maudlin markers.

Just west of the railway station and bus stand is Ooty's **lake,** which was constructed in the 1820s by the ever-enterprising John Sullivan. Though packed with tourists and so polluted that parts could be called a swamp, the lake is undergoing de-silting, which should clear it up within the next two years. *(Rowboats and pedal boats Rs40 per 30min; boathouse admission Rs2; camera fee Rs5.)* Near the boat house is a miniature train (Rs5 for a whirl). Equestrian types can rent horses near the lake. They'll ask Rs100 per hour, but if you feign indifference they might come down to Rs50. On the way to the boathouse you'll pass a **children's playground** with jungle gyms and topiaries. *(Admission Rs1, camera fee Rs3.)* Perhaps more than anything, the playground is a testament to how overcommercialized Ooty has become. Where else in India can you have your picture taken next to a 6m bottle of Gold Spot?

ENTERTAINMENT AND SHOPPING

If occupied, most **bars** in Ooty have but a few men in the corner. A somewhat cheerful watering hole is the bar at **Hotel Charing Cross** (tel. 42487), where you can drain a Kingfisher for Rs40. (Open daily 11am-11pm.)

Atari era refugees might resort to one of several **arcades** along Commercial Rd. **Moodmaker's** (tel. 40397), near the Charing Cross Hotel, is open 10am-9:30pm. Look for the packs of young boys beyond the brandy shop. A bit further down the street, at 49 Commercial Rd., is the subterranean **Missing Link.** Denizens dish out Rs1 for 10 minutes of Pac-Man, Super Mario Bros., or Tetris. About 750m up from Moodmaker's on Garden Rd. is **Assembly Halls Movie Theater** (2 shows daily, 2:30 and 6:30pm, Rs1.90-11.75. Weekday shows 2:30 and 6pm, Sa 2:30, 6, and 8:30pm), which screens dated American flicks. Don't be surprised if you don't recognize the title, since most of the films have been renamed to suit the melodrama-hungry, Hindi-film-going audience. The **Race Course,** near the bus stand, is a 1¼-mile loop, where jodhpured jockeys test their horses to the delight of riotous but small-betting crowds. Races are run from April to June. **Wenlock Downs,** about 8km from the bus stand and rail station, has an 18-hole golf course spread over 100 sq. km.

Shopping in Ooty focuses upon locally made oils and textiles. **The Big Shop** (tel. 44136), equidistant between Charing Cross and the Lower Bazaar on Commercial Rd., sells Toda tribal shawls (Rs200-300), silver jewelry, and other handicrafts. They accept traveler's checks and major credit cards (open daily 10am-8:30pm). A **Tibetan Refugees' Market,** along Garden Rd. near the Botanical Gardens, sells mohair sweaters and the colorful wool blankets you'll need to brave Ooty's freezing winter nights. (Open daily 6am-8:30pm.)

■ Near Ooty

■ Coonoor குன்னூர்

Aside from the Botanical Gardens, the best things about Ooty are definitely outside Ooty. Skip the tour bus companies if possible, and hire private transport or take local buses in order to best imbibe the incredible scenery of the Nilgiris. Separated by only 18km from Ooty, getting to this sister hill station is a snap (see **Ooty: Practical Information,** p. 528)—it's getting to the sights that's a bit harder. The railway station and bus stand are in Lower Coonoor, the town's center of commerce (and traffic). There are a few inexpensive accommodations here, but most of the attractions are in the posher Upper Coonoor. Local buses go to most sights, but it might be easier to hire a taxi so you can take your time and not be at the mercy of mass transport.

Coonoor's response to Ooty's Botanical Gardens is **Sim's Park,** located high upon a hill on the road to Kotagiri, some 3km from the Coonoor bus stand. Set in a small ravine, the park displays a variety of flora, much of which is not found in Ooty due to the different altitude and climate. (Open daily 8am-6:30pm. Admission Rs5 for adults, Rs2 for children. Camera fee Rs5, video fee Rs25.) Eight and 12 kilometers, respectively, from Lower Coonoor are **Dolphin's Nose** and **Lamb's Rock.** The former is a rock formation resembling a you-know-what and affording views of a gaping, bewaterfalled gorge. The latter overlooks the Coimbatore plains, far below the shaky railings. Buses run to both spots from Coonoor (to Dolphin's Nose: 7 daily, 7am-4:15pm; to Lamb's Rock: 4:45 and 6:45pm). Travel around Coonoor invariably involves traversing tea plantations; for those with piqued pekoe passions, several area **tea factories** offer tours, and in January there's a week-long **Tea and Tourism Festival.** For more information, contact the Public Relations Dept. of the United Planters' Association of South India (tel. 32030), in Upper Coonoor.

■ Pykara பைகாரா

Twenty kilometers west of Ooty, the tranquil village of **Pykara** is a lush setting for those who crave sensory stimuli. A small boathouse on Pykara's lake rents out boats (Rs30-40 per 30min.) and sells snacks to munch on while floating on the placid water. Near the lake is the **Pykara Dam,** 2½km downstream, is an attractive series of rocky **waterfalls** which gush hardest in July and August. All buses to Gudalur from Ooty pass through Pykara (every 30min. 6:30am-9pm).

If you're up for the climb, the 9km hike up **Mt. Doddabetta** (trail open daily 8:30am-5:30pm) takes about 2 hours and offers Technicolor detail you'll miss from an aisle seat of a tour bus. And speaking of Technicolor, no visit to Ooty's surrounds would be complete without a **Filmy Chakkar** (Film Trip), a package tour of the scenic spots where countless romantic pairs have frolicked for Bollywood's cameras.

The Bandit Pandit

Covered in thick deciduous forest set upon rolling hills, **Mudumalai Wildlife Sanctuary** is home to nearly 800 wild elephants, 25 tigers, as well as panthers and leopards, bears and hyenas, parakeets and eagles—and one renegade, cop-killing gentleman-poacher, the infamous **Veerappan.** Although Mudumalai was officially closed for much of 1998 due to drought and monsoon, informed locals from Ooty to Bangalore gladly divulge the real story behind the sanctuary's closing.

Since childhood, Veerappan the Bandit is said to have roamed in the park, emerging as a poacher and sandalwood smuggler, and more recently as a well-connected criminal with a cadre of assistants. One of his favorite activities, when he and his crew aren't killing police officers sent to capture them, is hijacking tour buses. After commandeering a busload of nature-lovers, he serves everyone tea and biscuits (so that they can enjoy his hospitality), refuses any offers of jewelry or money, and releases most everyone, save any government officials. Needless to say, this tendency is rather irksome to law-and-order types, who have tried bargaining and arresting Veerappan's friends and relatives, to no avail.

Once Veerappan comes to justice (or at least stops nabbing tourists), Mudumalai will undoubtedly reopen. Contact the Wildlife Warden in Ooty (p. 528) for the latest on the park's closure. For the latest on Veerappan, just ask around. Anyone up on the gossip will gladly divulge his latest shenanigans.

SOUTH INDIA

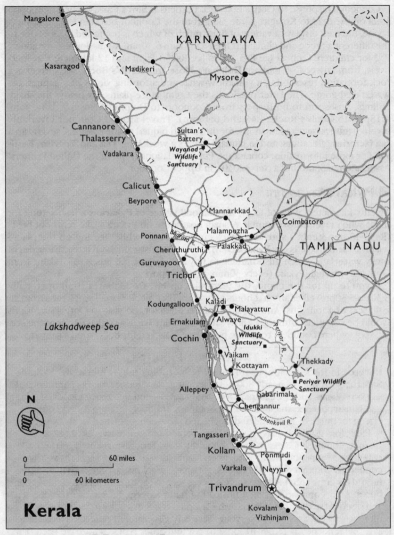

Mangalore

KARNATAKA

Kasaragod

Madikeri

Mysore

Cannanore
Thalasserry

Vadakara

Sultan's
Battery
*Wayanad
Wildlife
Sanctuary*

Calicut

Beypore

Mannarkkad

Coimbatore

Ponnani

Malampuzha

Cheruthuruthi

Palakkad

TAMIL NADU

Guruvayoor

Trichur

Kodungalloor

Kaladi

Malayattur

Ernakulam

Alwaye

Lakshadweep Sea

*Idukki
Wildlife
Sanctuary*

Cochin

Vaikam

Thekkady

Kottayam

Alleppey

Sabarimala

■ *Periyar Wildlife
Sanctuary*

Chengannur

Achankovil R.

N

Tangasseri

Kollam

Ponmudi

0   60 miles

Varkala

Neyyar

0   60 kilometers

Trivandrum ✪

Kerala

Kovalam
Vizhinjam

Kerala കേരളം

Kerala's heavy representation of religious minorities is the result of a complex, multi-
ethnic history. As early as the 3rd century BC, Egyptians, Phoenicians, Chinese, and
Babylonians had established trade relations with this center of maritime commerce.
In 52 AD, St. Thomas the Apostle purportedly arrived here, establishing strong Christian roots in India, and in 70 AD, Jews fleeing persecution in Palestine landed on Kerala's palm-lined shores. Beginning in the 8th century, Arabs dominated Keralan trade,
spreading Islam throughout the region, until the Portuguese landed at Calicut in 1498
and used their brutal diplomacy to gain exclusive trading rights. Meanwhile, rivalry
between the port cities of Cochin and Calicut weakened both, and the Dutch and

British ejected the Portuguese from their forts early in the 17th century. During the 18th century, Kerala came under the rule of the British Raj.

After Independence, the princely states of Cochin and Travancore were joined to form the state of Kerala, and, in 1956, Kerala's boundaries were redrawn along linguistic (Malayalam) lines. In 1957, Kerala's became the first electorate in the world to freely elect a Communist government. Despite a low per capita income, reforms have brought Kerala the most equitable land distribution in India. Kerala's literacy rate, at around 90%, is the highest in India and around twice the national average, making the state a breeding-ground for bureaucrats.

Kerala has more women than men, most likely due to low female infanticide and good health care, as well as to the exodus of Keralan men going to work in the Gulf states. The U.N. has commended the state for its exemplary women's rights record. The higher status of women is due in part to the existence of vestiges of ancient matrilineal, polyandrous systems, such as those still practiced by the Nayar caste.

The state has long been a haven for foreigners, and the presence of other cultural influences continues to contribute to Kerala's laid-back cultural montage. This attitude has made Kerala particularly amenable to tourism. Kerala has become second only to Goa in hoasting droves of certified sun-worshippers and bona fide beach bums. Forty lazy rivers run from the Western Ghats to the sea, channeled through canals and rice paddies and past islands of palm groves.

🏮 HIGHLIGHTS OF KERALA

- The cool **backwaters** of **Cochin** (p. 549) and **Alleppey** (p. 557), shrouded in greenery and plied by fishing boats, offer a look at Keralan life at its most idyllic.
- **Periyar Tiger Reserve** (p. 545), in Kerala's eastern hills, is home to laughing thrushes, flying squirrels, and a few very big, very shy cats.
- Kerala is home to the elaborate, gripping **Kathakali** dance form. The best places to see performances are **Cochin** (p. 518) and **Trivandrum** (p. 503).
- Sun-seekers from all over find solace if not solitude in sandy **Kovalam** (p. 540).

SOUTH INDIA

■ Trivandrum (Thiruvanathapuram)
തിരുവനന്തപുരം

While most foreign tourists consider Trivandrum a piddling stop-off on the way to the brackish beaches of Kovalam or the beckoning backwaters of Alleppey, the well-administered but laid-back capital of Kerala, offers a good glimpse into Keralan culture. Speckled with parks, palaces, monuments, and museums, Trivandrum is well-suited to exploring on foot. The city was the capital of Travancore State for two centuries and became the capital of Kerala when the state was formed in 1956. It still retains its trademark red-tiled and pagoda-roofed houses, winding streets, little cafes, and gardens. The city's Malayalam name means "the city of Anantha," the serpent holding the reclining form of Lord Vishnu (Lord Padmanabha) in the Shree Padmanabha Swami Temple. Though the inner temple is only open to *dhoti*-clad Hindus, the zoo and museums, set in the lovely public gardens, require neither specific religious allegiance nor costume. The great arts of Kerala are on display at the various schools of Kalarippayat (martial art), Kathakali (dance), and Kutiyattum (theatre). Overall, Trivandrum is an inviting, friendly, pleasant place to chill out at the start or finish of a journey through South India, or as a respite from beach-hopping.

ORIENTATION

The streets tangle over 74 sq. km of coastal hills, but if you stick to the few main drags, navigation is easy. **M.G. Road** broadly traverses the city center from north to south. At the northern end, M.G. Rd. dumps all its traffic onto **Museum Road,** forming an intersection like a capital "T." Farther south, M.G. Rd. cruises down a hill to a hectic intersection with the city's other main drag, **Central Station Road,** also known as Station Road. Left from M.G. Rd. onto Central Station Rd., then left at the Ambika Café, is **Manjalikulam Road,** the home of the budget hotel district. Further down Central Station Rd., the **long-distance bus stand** is on the left; a tiny bit further on the right is the **railway station,** a huge gray-and-yellow concrete and stone arched building on the right side. M.G. Rd. continues south of the intersection with Central Station Rd., which becomes **Overbridge Rd.,** to the **East Fort area,** the old part of the capital. A few blocks south, a great yellow gate marks the entrance to **Shree Padmanabha Swamy Temple.** Turning left off M.G. Rd. opposite the gate, the **local bus stand** features a herd of buses and a line of covered kiosks and fruit sellers. Here, **Chalai Bazaar Road** leads from behind the Gandhi statue through a bazaar area.

PRACTICAL INFORMATION

Transportation

Airport: Trivandrum's **international airport** is a few km outside town. Buses marked Shanumugham leave from the city bus stand at East Fort (south of the train tracks on M.G. Overbridge Rd.) every 30min. Auto-rickshaws cost around Rs50. and stop at the airport. Trivandrum is a convenient site for flights to and from **Male** in the Maldives (M, Tu, Th, and Sa, 1hr., US$75) and **Colombo,** Sri Lanka (1 per day, 1hr., US$75). **Indian Airlines Office,** Museum Rd. (tel. 436870), 1 block left from the intersection with M.G. Rd. **Jet Airways** (tel. 321018) also has flights. To: **Bangalore** (M, W, F, and Su, 1hr., US$105); **Chennai** (1-2 per day, 1½hr., US$105); **Delhi** (1 per day, 5hr., US$325); **Mumbai** (1 per day, 2hr., US$175).

Trains: The **railway station** is located on Station Rd., a few min. walk east of M.G. Rd. Reservations counter open M-Sa 8am-2pm and 2:15-8pm, Su 8am-2pm. To: **Alleppey** (4:30pm, 3hr., Rs43); **Bangalore** (10:30am, 15hr., sleeper Rs225); **Chennai** (1:30pm, 17½hr., sleeper Rs236); **Cochin** (several per day, 5am-9:45pm, 5hr., Rs61); **Delhi** (*Kerala Exp.* 2625, 9:40am, 55hr., sleeper Rs461); **Kanyakumari** (12:30 and 3:30pm, 2hr., Rs30); **Kollam** (several per day, 5am-9:45pm, 1½hr., Rs26); **Madurai** (8:40pm, 9½hr., Rs77); **Mumbai** (5am, 46hr., sleeper Rs369); **Varkala** (several per day, 6am-9:45pm, 30min., Rs21).

Buses: The **long-distance KSRTC bus station** is on Station Rd., almost directly across from the railway station. To: **Alleppey** (every 20min., 3½hr, Rs55.); **Cochin** (every 30min., 6hr., Rs65); **Kanyakumari** (12 per day, 2½hr., Rs29); **Kollam** (frequent, 1½hr., Rs25); **Mangalore** (1:30am, 18hr., Rs240). The **Tamil Nadu Transport Office** (tel. 327756), located at the far east end of the KSRTC bus station, runs buses to cities in Tamil Nadu. Open daily 7am-9pm. To: **Chennai** (9 per day, 17hr., Rs206); **Madurai** (10:30am and 10:30pm, 7hr., Rs88); **Pondicherry** (4pm, 16hr., Rs173). The **local bus station** is on M.G. Rd. a few min. walk south of the train tracks at East Fort. Buses from here (marked Shanmugham) leave frequently to **Kovalam** and the airport.

Local Transportation: Auto-rickshaws set their meters (Rs50 to Kovalam).

Tourist and Financial Services

Tourist Office: Tourist Facilitation Centre, Museum Rd. (tel. 321132; fax 322279), across from the big red entrance gate to the zoo and museums (from M.G. Rd., turn right). Equipped with maps, brochures, and knowledgeable staff. Open daily 10am-6pm. **KTDC Reception Centre,** Central Station Rd. (tel. 330031). Between the intersection with M.G. Rd. and the long-distance bus station. This office mainly promotes KTDC tours. Open M-Sa 6:30am-9:30pm. There are also smaller tourist offices at the **KSRTC Bus Stand** (tel. 327224) and the **train station** (tel. 334470). Both open M-Sa 9am-5pm.

Budget Travel: Travel Destinations, Chaitram Hotel lobby, Central Station Rd. (tel. 330702; fax 331346), between the intersection with M.G. Rd. and the long-distance bus station. Books flights, confirms airline tickets (Rs50), and makes train and private bus bookings. Open M-Sa 9am-9:30pm.

Immigration Office: Foreigners Registration Office, Office of the Commissioner of Police, Residency Rd. (tel. 321399). Take a rickshaw. Extensions for student and entry visas "with proper documents." The process should take about 2 weeks; it's

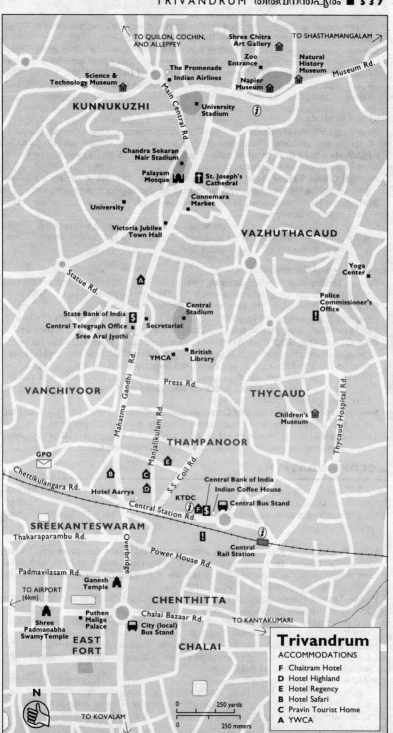

TO QUILON, COCHIN, AND ALLEPPEY

Shree Chitra Art Gallery

TO SHASTHAMANGALAM

Zoo Entrance

Natural History Museum

Museum Rd.

Science & Technology Museum

The Promenade
Indian Airlines

Napier Museum

KUNNUKUZHI

Main Central Rd.

University Stadium

Chandra Sekaran Nair Stadium

Palayam Mosque

St. Joseph's Cathedral

University

Connemara Market

VAZHUTHACAUD

Victoria Jubilee Town Hall

Statue Rd.

Yoga Center

Central Stadium

Police Commissioner's Office

State Bank of India
Central Telegraph Office
Sree Aral Jyothi

Secretariat

Mahatma Gandhi Rd.

YMCA

British Library

Press Rd.

VANCHIYOOR

THYCAUD

Manjalikulam Rd.

Children's Museum

Thycaud Hospital Rd.

THAMPANOOR

GPO

Chettikulangara Rd.

Hotel Aarrya

S.S. Coil Rd.

Central Bank of India
Indian Coffee House

Central Bus Stand

KTDC

Central Station Rd.

SREEKANTESWARAM

Thakaraparambu Rd.

Overbridge

Power House Rd.

Central Rail Station

Padmavilasam Rd.

TO AIRPORT (6km)

Ganesh Temple

CHENTHITTA

TO KANYAKUMARI

Shree Padmanabha Swamy Temple

EAST FORT

Puthen Maliga Palace

City (local) Bus Stand

Chalai Bazaar Rd.

CHALAI

N

TO KOVALAM

| 0 | | 250 yards |
| 0 | | 250 meters |

Trivandrum
ACCOMMODATIONS
F Chaitram Hotel
D Hotel Highland
E Hotel Regency
B Hotel Safari
C Pravin Tourist Home
A YWCA

not necessary to forfeit your passport during that time, but bring a copy of it. Open M-Sa 10am-1pm and 2-5pm; closed the 2nd Sa of each month.

Currency Exchange: Central Bank of India (tel. 330359) has an office in the Chaitram Hotel lobby. They exchange foreign currency and major traveler's checks. Open M-F 10am-2pm, Sa 10am-noon. **State Bank of India,** M.G. Rd., north of the Secretariat. Changes currency and traveler's checks (US$: AmEx, Barclay's, and Thomas Cook; UK£: Thomas Cook). Open M-F 10am-2pm, Sa 10am-noon.

Local Services

Pharmacy: Vishnu Medicals (tel. 449447). Across from the Cosmopolitan Hospital. Friendly and efficient. Open daily 8:30am-9:30pm. 1km farther north is **Janatha Medicals,** across from the medical college. Open 24hr. Both fill prescriptions written by European and American doctors.

Market: Chalai Bazaar Road, which intersects with M.G. Rd. at the local bus station, is choked with fruit-and-vegetable-*wallahs* and upper-crust jewelry stores.

Bookstore: Higginbothams, M.G. Rd., 10min. north of Station Rd. on the right. Open M-Sa 9:30am-7pm.

Library: The **British Library,** just off Manjalikulam Rd. where it swerves left, is officially open only to card-carrying members. But bat your lashes, and they will happily let you browse. Open Tu-Sa 11am-7pm.

Emergency and Communications

Police: Thampanoor Police Station, Station Rd. (tel. 326543), near the long-distance bus station. Outpost station inside the Museum Compound (tel. 315096).

Emergency: Police, tel. 100. **Fire,** tel. 101. **Ambulance,** tel. 102.

Hospital: Cosmopolitan Hospital (tel. 448182). In the northwest area of town, a Rs20 rickshaw from Station Rd. Considered the best private hospital in the city.

Post Office: The **GPO** does its best to elude detection. Follow Station Rd. west through the intersection with M.G. Rd.; at the next traffic circle (the 2nd intersection), make a hairpin turn to the right, and hope to see it on the left after a few blocks. Otherwise, ask for directions. *Poste Restante* is downstairs and can be claimed M-Sa 8am-4pm. **Poste Restante addressed to Kovalam tends to end up here.** Stamps are sold M-Sa 8am-8pm.

Internet: N.N. Computers and Communication Centre (tel. 321311), located off M.G. Rd., on the same street as the Hotel Regency. **Email** Rs20 per page.

Telephones: STD/ISD booths line M.G. Rd. The **Central Telegraph Office** (opposite the Secretariat) allows collect calls. Open 24hr. **Telephone Code:** 0471.

ACCOMMODATIONS

M.G. Rd. and Station Rd. offer plenty of large hotels, but Manjalikulam Rd. is the real budget hotel district. Turn right from the bus station or left from the railway station, walk a few minutes west on Station Rd., take the first right after the bus station, and bear left at the fork.

Hotel Regency (tel. 330377). Follow Manjalikulam Rd. to the first cross-street, then turn right. Fancier than the standard fare, with big clean rooms and TVs with satellite channels. Seat toilets and running hot water. Foreign exchange. Singles Rs250, with A/C Rs500; doubles Rs400/600. MC, Visa.

Pravin Tourist Home, Manjalikulam Rd. (tel. 330443). A 5min. walk north, on the left. Super-friendly proprietor. Rooms are fairly good-sized and have big windows and attached bathrooms (seat and squat toilets). TV in the lobby. Singles Rs86; doubles Rs149; triples Rs215; quads Rs258.

Hotel Highland, Manjalikulam Rd. (tel. 333200 or 333416). Near Station Rd., on the left. Standard hotel with big rooms. Seat toilets. A/C rooms have TV. Singles Rs190, with A/C Rs440; doubles Rs230/540.

YWCA (tel. 477308), opposite the Secretariat. Lovely, Lysol-christened rooms with attached bathrooms. Everything smells and looks deliciously clean. The root, perhaps, of the sterile comfort: no unmarried couples are allowed. Singles Rs150; doubles Rs200, with A/C Rs350; family room Rs300.

Hotel Safari, M.G. Rd. (tel. 477202), a few min. north of Central Station Rd. Standard, but the A/C rooms are cushy: bathtubs, hot water, and lots of space. Pleasant restaurant has city views. Women traveling alone may want to steer clear of the hotel's sketchy bar. Singles Rs185; doubles Rs250; triples Rs240. A/C Rs150 extra.

Chaitram Hotel, Central Station Rd. (tel. 330977). A 5min. walk west of the bus and railway stations. Turn right from the bus station or left from the railway station onto Central Station Rd. You pay for location, location, location. Nice big rooms with TVs. Singles Rs450; doubles Rs550; A/C Rs400 extra.

FOOD

It's difficult to find veritable Keralan food in Trivandrum, as most South Indian restaurants dish out a Tamil-influenced menu.

Indian Coffee House, facing the bus station, it's the red, spiraling building on the left. The coolest structure in Trivandrum, its Tower-of-Pisa grandeur must be seen to be believed. Standard *dosas*, and coffee available. Open daily 7:30am-10pm.

Hotel Aarrya, Station Rd., just before the junction with M.G. Rd.; look for the sign. This friendly hole-in-the-wall offers smashingly great, simple South Indian hotel fare. Good *masala dosas* (Rs10). Open daily 6:30am-10:30pm.

The Promenade, in the Mascot Hotel. From M.G. Rd., turn left onto Museum Rd. A cafe/snack bar that serves expensive treats (*masala dosa* Rs25, cheeseburgers Rs50, sundaes Rs40-60) to local businessmen and well-to-do dope fiends with post-*charas* munchies. Open 24hr.

Sree Aral Jyothi, directly opposite the Secretariat. Authentic Keralan "raw rice meals" are Rs19 in this crowded restaurant. Meals served daily 3-10pm.

SIGHTS AND ENTERTAINMENT

Hindu pilgrims flock to the **Shree Padmanabha Swamy Temple,** visible from M.G. Rd. and a short walk south of the train tracks. The entrance to the temple is marked by a large yellow gate. The foundations of the present *gopuram* were laid in 1566 and built up to the fifth story; the sixth and seventh lofty stories were added during the reign of Maharaja Rama Varma. The current structure was completed in 1733. The temple itself is intricately carved. While most of the designs are coated in a thick layer of soot and grime, seven small domes shine from atop the shrine. The temple features a six meter statue of Vishnu reclining—the whole of the god's body is visible only by opening three doors (one at the sacred head, one at the divine midsection, and one at the holy feet). Although the temple itself is open only to Hindus wearing *dhotis* or *saris,* non-Hindus may climb the steps and see the less sacred images.

On the way back along the temple lane, through a maze of handicraft hawkers, you'll see a vast green **tank,** used by bathing pilgrims. A new museum is on the right in the palace of Prince Swati Tirunal (also a famed musician and court composer). Every inch of the **Puthen Maliga Palace** or **"Horse Palace"** (so-named for the 122 galloping horse sculptures beneath its eaves) is intricately carved. *(Open Tu-Su 8:30am-12:30pm and 3-5:30pm. Admission Rs5.)* According to the tale, the beautiful carvings were completed in four years, and the insolent Swati Tirunal subsequently occupied it for only one year, leaving in a huff. The palace is now saddled with life-size Kathakali figures in full regalia, paintings of the rajas and ranis of Travancore, weaponry, a Bohemian crystal throne, and gifts to the maharajas from China, Italy, and France. The **Swati Music Festival** (late Feb.) presents evenings of classical music on the lawn. Tour guides who recruit on the street will expect a handsome donation to their pockets but their information is often worth it. The temple lane stretches from the temple straight across M.G. Rd. and leads past many **handloom stores** into the ancient **Chalai Bazaar,** hopping with fruit and vegetable sellers, upscale 22-karat gold jewellers, bauble-*wallahs,* and people carrying various large objects on their heads.

On the other side of Station Rd., a good 15-minute walk north up M.G. Rd., stands a bastion of purity, the white colonial **Secretariat** whose roadside lanes are constantly decorated by crowds of protesters and strikers. Behind the Secretariat and across from the back side of the British Library is the government-run **SMSM Institute,** where a wide array of handicrafts are sold at fixed prices. *(Open M-Sa 9am-8pm. Foreign currencies, AmEx, Visa, MC, and traveler's checks accepted.)* M.G. Rd. leads next to the **Connemara Market,** and then to the final intersection with Museum Rd. Bear right through the big red gate that is the entrance to the **zoo, public gardens, and museums.** *(Open Tu-Sa 9am-6:30pm. Admission Rs4, camera fee Rs5, video camera fee Rs250. Tickets must be purchased before 5pm.)* Many animals probably have better habitats than animals elsewhere in India, but some inhabit small cages that bear an odd resemblance to Indian hotel rooms.

Set in the lovely, 20-hectare public gardens dotted with moon-eyed couples, are the **Napier Museum,** the **Shree Chitra Art Gallery,** the **Paniker Gallery,** and the **Natural History Museum** *(Admission Rs5 for all four. Purchase tickets at the Natural History Museum. Galleries open Tu and Th-Su 10am-5pm, W 1-5pm.)* The Natural History Museum features dioramas of natural history, a model of a traditional wealthy house in Travancore (mid-pageant it seems, with Kathakali dancers—check out the skin color of the *brahmin* denizens), a collection of dolls wearing traditional costumes from all over India, and models of "tribal Indians," complete with laughable ethnographs.

To the right of the Natural History Museum squats the K.C.S. Paniker Gallery, which features paintings by the renowned 20th-century Indian artist. Sadly, the musty gallery does not do justice to the beautiful works. Better is the Shree Chitra Art Gallery, across from the Napier Museum, decked with Western-style portraits by the famed Raja Ravi Varma, Tibetan *thankas,* Japanese, Chinese, and Balinese paintings, 400-year-old Rajasthani miniatures, and modern Indian works. Dedicated to the last Maharaja of Travancore, the Gallery also boasts an authentic royal carriage.

Set in front of these three galleries is the Napier Museum. One might suspect one of Walt Disney's minions designed the gabled red-, black-, and pink- tiled building, fancifully striped on the inside in yellow, pink, red, and turquoise. In reality, Robert Fellowes Chisholm designed the building as a courageous experiment in the Indo-Saracenic style, simultaneously attempting to incorporate the Keralan style into colonial architecture. The museum houses sculptures, a wooden temple car, an array of gifts given to foreign rulers, and Javanese shadow-play figures.

A school at West Fort called **MARGI** (tel. 434066) performs free **Kathakali dance drama** and **Kutiyattum theater** (Keralan martial art) in the evenings. Follow M.G. Rd. south over the train tracks, turn right at the bright corner temple, walk 10 minutes into West Fort until the street comes to a final T, and turn right. MARGI is behind Fort High School. Look for a big banyan tree. The sign on the door is in Malayalam, but the delineation of a dancer gives it away. Performances are usually only twice a week; call for details. The **Nishagandhi Dance Festival** will take place in Trivandrum in February 1999, with outdoor classical performances. Contact the KTDC for a complete festival schedule.

Trivandrum boasts 18 **movie theaters. Sree Kumar** and **Sree Visakh** (both near the Chaitram Hotel), and **New Theatre** (walk east on Station Rd., turn left at Aristo Junction) show English-language films.

■ Kovalam കോവളം

The pounding of hammers and pouring of concrete have forever altered the calm landscape of Kovalam's black sands and turquoise waters. Since the arrival of hippie sun- and soul-searchers in the 60s, Kovalam has become Kerala's most popular beach resort, and one of the most popular in India. Restaurants play Pink Floyd and the Pixies, as though to make up for the lack of Goan psychedelia. Establishments built illegally close to the beach pay metaphorical *baksheesh* to the monsoon-swept seas that lap at their doorsteps. The hectic beachfront has been consumed by hotels, downcast but persistent touts, and thieves in the guise of tailors and handicraft sellers. Enjoy the carnival atmosphere—after all, it was created just for you. But in spite of it all, local fishing boats still traverse the bays, and beyond the explosion of tourists, life continues in the huts and peaceful rice paddies that predated them.

ORIENTATION

Kovalam Beach is composed of three coves divided by rocky promontories. A prominent lighthouse is the beacon of the southernmost **Lighthouse Beach.** From here, **Lighthouse Road,** crawling with seafood restaurants, leads down to the water and the budget hotels favored by Western tourists. North of the rocky promontory is the crescent called **Eve's Beach.** Here are pricier hotels, decent restaurants, and busloads of Eve-calling tourists. The northernmost beach is **Samudra Beach,** home of the chi-chi **Ashok Hotel,** also known as the Kovalam Hotel, but it's otherwise quite serene, with most visitors preferring the bustle of the two southern beaches.

A road leads up from the north part of Eve's Beach past several travel offices and more handicrafts and tailors to the **bus stand.** Taking a right turn leads to **Kovalam Junction,** 2km away, where a left turn at the fork brings you to the **post office** and **Central Bank.** Between Lighthouse Rd. and the road to the bus stand paths twist through rice paddies and past houses to quieter restaurants and hotels.

> **Warning:** The ocean in Kovalam can be dangerous. The undertow and ripcurrents here can be very strong, so follow the warnings of the signs, flags, and gesturing lifeguards with whistles. In addition, women should not wear revealing swimsuits. Public displays of female flesh are frowned upon, so women in swimsuits inevitably attract negative attention. Consider swimming in a *lungi*, or light pants and a t-shirt instead.

PRACTICAL INFORMATION

Buses: The **bus stand** is at the top of the road up from the north end of Eve's Beach. There is no ticket office, but the Tourist Facilitation Centre can give bus schedules. Purchase tickets on the bus. To: **Cochin** (7am, 5½hr., Rs65) via **Kollam** (2hr.) and **Alleppey** (4hr.); **Kanyakumari** via **Nagercoil** (4 per day, 9:30am-6:10pm, Rs30); **Trivandrum** (every 15min., 20min., Rs4.50).

Local Transportation: Rickshaws and **taxis** hover at the bottom of Lighthouse Rd., the bus stand, and Kovalam Junction. A ride to Trivandrum should cost Rs100.

Tourist Office: Tourist Facilitation Centre (tel. 480085). From the bus stand, follow the road to the Kovalam Hotel; the tourist office is on the left. Run by the Kerala Department of Tourism, the office has maps and general information about Kerala, as well as booking hotels all over India, and arranging tickets for the Kollam-Alleppey backwater tour (Rs150) and commission-free local backwater trips (Rs300). Open in season daily 10am-5pm.

Budget Travel: Western Travels (tel. 481307 or 481334; fax 481429), next to the bus stand. Energetic and helpful staff will confirm plane reservations for the price of the phone charge, and make plane, bus, hotel, and train reservations (Rs50 service charge). Taxis available for hire. They organize **sight-seeing tours,** including backwater trips in season (7:30am-9pm, 6hr., Rs550). Open in season daily 6:30am-12:30am, off-season 7am-9pm. MC, Visa, AmEx.

Currency Exchange: Some shops on the beach exchange money. The reception desks at **Wilson's Tourist Home,** behind Hotel Neelakanta (open daily 9:15am-5:30pm) and **Hotel Neptune,** on the southern edge of Lighthouse Beach (open 24hr.) both give bank rates. The **Central Bank of India** has a branch in the Kovalam Hotel shopping complex. Open M-Sa 10:30am-1:30pm.

Bookstore: Many shops on the beach sell musty used books. **Anjana Emporium,** in the Ashok Hotel, has more expensive English-language books, magazines, and postcards. Open daily 10am-8:30pm.

Library: Jungle Book Library (on the way to Lonely Planet Restaurant from Hotel Neptune) has books in English, French, German, and Dutch for rent or sale. Deposit required. Open daily 10am-1pm.

Hospital: Upasana Hospital (tel. 480632). On the road to Kovalam Junction, a 10min. walk from the bus stand, after the Hotel Raja. **Pharmacy** is open daily 9am-1pm and 4-8:30pm. In an emergency, you can call Dr. Chandrasenan (tel. 472357).

SOUTH INDIA

Police: (tel. 480255), on the road to Kovalam Junction, a 10min. walk up from the bus station on the left. In season, the **Tourist Aid Post** is on the beach.

Emergency: Police, tel. 100; **Fire,** tel. 101; **Ambulance,** tel. 102.

Post Office: The **GPO** can be reached by taking a left at Kovalam Junction. *Poste Restante.* Open M-Sa 9am-1pm and 1:30-5pm. **Poste Restante sent to Kovalam sometimes ends up at the Trivandrum GPO. Postal Code:** 695527.

Internet: Pournami Currency Exchange (tel. 48147), near Hotel Raja, expects to be on-line by October, 1998, with email (Rs30) and Internet access (Rs250 per hr.) **Telephone Code:** 0471.

ACCOMMODATIONS

Prices peak around December and January, when rates can increase by 1000%. During the monsoon, it's a buyer's market, so the rule is to bargain hard—don't let persistent touts determine where you will stay. Unless otherwise noted, all accommodations listed are on Lighthouse Beach.

Wilson's Tourist Home (tel. 480051 or 480052). Take a left at the Hotel Neelakanta on Lighthouse Beach and follow the signs. Wilson's is behind the beachfront restaurants. Rooms, arranged around a large courtyard, each have a balcony and massive beds. Friendly female staff is a draw, especially for single women travelers. Peak season: doubles Rs500. Off-season: Rs100. Visa.

Green Valley Cottages (tel. 480636). From the beach, walk straight past Hotel Neptune, and follow signs back to the paddies. Absconding from the beachfront has its advantages: lower prices, tranquil setting, and stunning views. Each immaculate room has a private balcony and lolling-around chairs. In-season: doubles Rs550-700. Off-season: Rs150. Reserve at least one month in advance in season.

Hotel Neptune (tel. 480222; fax 460187), on the southern tip of Lighthouse Beach. From the beach, follow the alley between Hotel Sunset and the tourist police post. It's on the right. Beginning to show signs of age, but the rooms are pleasant, some with seaviews. Rooftop restaurant. Off-season: singles Rs200; doubles Rs250. In-season: singles and doubles Rs550. Extra person Rs75. AmEx, MC, Visa.

FOOD

Starting at Lighthouse Rd., the beach-side restaurants spread in an almost uninterrupted sweep all the way to the road and the bus stand, in the hopes of trapping customers like so many fish. What little Indian food there is has been de-spiced to appease Western palates. Prices can be exorbitant, but compared to fresh seafood in most Western countries, it is still a reasonable treat. Alcohol is often served at beachfront establishments.

Achutha Restaurant (also confusingly called Leo Restaurant), next to Santana. Yummy mixed fruit pancakes (Rs25) and grilled seafood. Open daily 7am-10pm.

Santana. Makes great *masala* and tandoori seafood, and dessert-grade chocolate banana pancakes. Open 7am-5pm.

Garzia, on the northern end of the beach. Fresh pasta is a treat, although their version of mac 'n'cheese ain't so Kraft-y. Open daily 7am-10pm.

Lonely Planet Restaurant. Follow directions for Green Valley and take a left at the fork; look for the sign. Mostly Indian fare. No liquor allowed on the premises.

SIGHTS AND ENTERTAINMENT

If you're tired of watching the waves, jumping in the waves, and hearing the waves, wave good-bye to your aches and pains with an **ayurvedic massage.** Kerala is being touted as an ayurvedic haven, and the tourist office even promotes "rejuvenation" vacations during the ayurvedic-friendly monsoon months. In Kovalam, there are numerous establishments hawking these treatments. **Wilson's Tourist Home** (tel. 480051), has a female masseuse (no fellas; Rs150 per blissful hour; open M-Sa 9am-5pm). Peak season is **yoga** season in many hotels and private institutions. **Hotel Nep-**

Ayurvedic Medicine

The predominant medical tradition in Hindu culture is associated with the *Ayur-Veda*, which translates literally to the "the knowledge of long life." Practitioners of this wisdom are called *vaidyas*. Ayurvedic medicine takes a holistic approach to diagnosis—a broken heart is as much an ailment as a broken leg—and to treatment—a combination of herbal potions and life notions. The earliest known herbal prescriptions date back to the *Atharva Veda* (c. 1000 BC), which reveals the precocity of Indian medical thought. *Vaidyas* were performing surgery on external wounds long before their Western counterparts were doing so. Ayurvedic medicine, however, is primarily associated with maintaining a balance of the three bodily essences or *doshas: vatta* (wind), *pitta* (bile), and *kapha* (phlegm). *Vatta* represents kinetic energy and is associated with the nervous system and movement. *Kapha,* which opposes *vatta,* is potential energy and is associated with lymph and mucus. Finally, *pitta* mediates between these two forces, governing digestive and metabolic processes. Balance between the three *doshas* is essential to good health, but decadent *doshas* develop distortions.

---

tune, offers a week of twice-daily classes (Rs1200). Pirated **movies,** complete with laughter from the original audience, show nightly at several restaurants, such as **Hotel Flamingo** (tel. 480421) and **Hawah Beach Restaurant** (tel. 48431).

During high season, "cultural nights," often featuring **Keralan dance** (see **Kathakali, p. 557),** take place at the **Hotel Ashok** (Sa-Su, Rs100) and **Hotel Neptune** (M, W, and Sa, Rs75). The Tourist Facilitation Centre also arranges commission-free local **backwater tours.** The Rs300 fee covers transportation to the boat, two hours of cruising time, and the return trip back to Kovalam. Unlike the Alleppey-Kollam tour, the boat used in season is a traditional, non-motorized vessel with a rattan shade; off season, an uncovered boat is used. The tour circles an island 5km from Kovalam and stops for the requisite *coir*-making demonstration.

The small ramshackle village of **Vizhinjam** (VEER-in-yam) is a 20-minute walk south of Kovalam along the coast road. Formerly the capital of the Ay Kings, only ruins of some small shrines remain. Brightly painted fishing boats fill the harbor, which is crowned at the north end by a dizzying pink-and-yellow **mosque.**

■ Alleppey (Alappuzha) ആലപ്പുഴ

The two canals that carve out the center of Alleppey were once the heart of a great shipping center, but now only tangles of water plants survive. The bustle of the town is due mainly to the prodigious amount of *coir* (woven coconut fiber) products being shipped through here to Cochin, often on small boats propelled by pole. Several snakeboat races, especially the Nehru Trophy Boat Race on the second Saturday of August, attract attention and international tourists.

ORIENTATION AND PRACTICAL INFORMATION The village is sandwiched between two canals running east to west: the **North Canal** and the **South Canal,** only about 10 minutes apart. The streets in between the two canals are gridded in simple fashion. The **railway station** is several km outside the village near the beach. Trains chug to: **Ernakulam** (9 per day, 1½hr., Rs11/25); **Kollam** (*Trivandrum Exp.* 6324, 8pm, 2½hr., Rs30); **Mumbai** (*Mumbai Exp.* 6332, F, 7:30am, 44hr., Rs251/13911); and **Trivandrum** (*Guruvayar-Nagercoil Exp.* 6305, 12:50am; *Ernakulam-Trivandrum Exp.* 6341, 7:35am, 3hr., Rs43). The **KSRTC bus station** is at the east end of **Boat Jetty Road** (which runs along the southern bank of the north canal). Buses roll towards: **Cochin** (every 20min., 1½hr., Rs17); **Kollam** (frequent, 2hr., Rs26); **Kottayam** (several per day, 1½hr., Rs15); and **Trivandrum** (10 per day, 3½hr., Rs47). Tickets must be purchased on the bus, no coupons or reservations available. A little to the west, on Boat Jetty Rd., is the **District Tourism Promotion Council (DTPC)** (tel. 253308 or 251796), which has maps and sells tickets for boat rides and the Nehru Trophy Boat Race. (Open daily 9am-6pm.) Public and private boats depart from the jetties near here.

The large cross-street that bridges the North Canal is **Mullakal Road.** To the north over the canal it leads to the fruit and vegetable **market.** Immediately after crossing the canal, take a right and then a left to reach the new office of the **Alleppey Tourism Development Cooperative (ATDC)** (tel. 243462; fax 243462; open Apr.-Sept. daily 8am-8pm; Oct.-Mar. 24hr.). The next nameless cross-street to the east features a footbridge over the north canal; to the south the street leads to several landmarks: the South Canal, the **Central Telegraph Office** on the left corner; the **Indian Overseas Bank,** a few buildings down on the first floor, accepts only American Express and Thomas Cook traveler's checks in US$ and UK£ (open M-F 10am-2pm, Sa 10am-noon). Alleppey's **Medical College Hospital** (tel. 251641) is 1.5km south of the intersection of Boat Jetty and Mullakal Rds.; it houses a 24hr. **pharmacy.** To get to the **Head Post Office,** follow Mullakal Rd. south from the North Canal, turn right on Collan Rd., walk until crossing over a canal, then turn left. The HPO is huge and on the right. It has *Poste Restante* (M-Sa 9am-2:30pm) and sells stamps (M-Sa 8am-5:30pm). **Postal Code:** 68801. **Telephone Code:** 0477.

ACCOMMODATIONS AND FOOD Most hotels are just north of the canals, 10 minutes from the bus stand. To get to the **Komala Hotel** (tel. 243631), follow Mullakal Rd. north over the North Canal traffic bridge, turn right, then left; the hotel will be on the right. The attached baths (some seat and some squat toilets), have glowing white tiles. (Singles Rs97, with A/C Rs385; doubles Rs130/495; triples Rs165.) **Karthika Tourist Home** (tel. 245524) is also north over the North Canal traffic bridge; watch for the sign on Mullakal Rd. Pleasantly painted blue, this well-run building is set back from the road, with could-be-cleaner rooms but great prices. Attached baths with seat and squat toilets available. (Singles Rs50; doubles Rs100-150.) **Hotel Araam** (tel. 244460), a few kilometers by rickshaw from the Bus Station, has nice clean rooms (singles Rs110, with A/C Rs220; doubles Rs150/330).

Most of Alleppey's hotels have attached **restaurants.** There's also the **Indian Coffee House,** on Mullakal Rd. a few blocks south of the North Canal, where the standard ruffled waiters serve *masala dosas* (Rs6) and meals (Rs10). **Hotel Annapoorna,** Boat Jetty Rd. next to the bus station, serves standard South Indian vegetarian fare in an antiseptic environment (meals Rs14-18; open daily 7am-9:30pm).

SIGHTS AND ENTERTAINMENT The green backwaters that bring Alleppey its living as a passage for shipping *coir* rake in the international tourist dollars. The annual **Nehru Trophy Boat Race** is held on the second Saturday of August in the lake to the east of town. The 65m Snake Boats, traditional Keralan battle vessels, are maneuvered by hundreds of oarsmen. The first race was held "impromptu" in 1952, in honor of Prime Minister Jawaharlal Nehru. Nehru was so flattered and fascinated that he established the tradition of awarding a trophy to the winners. Tickets are available from the DTPC one month in advance up to the date of the race and range in price depending on location (Rs10-250). Other Snake Boat races are held during the year, among them the **Moolam Boat Race** at Champakulam in July. The ATDC arranges backwater boats there and back for Rs100.

For most of the year, daily **backwater cruises** run the green canals between **Alleppey and Kollam.** During the off-season in June and August, these trips are cancelled unless there happen to be 10 people interested on any particular day. The ATDC (private) and DTPC (government) both sponsor trips leaving Alleppey at 10:30am and arriving in Kollam at 6:30pm. Trips run in the reverse direction with the same timings. Arrive at either office before 10am. Make reservations at least one day in advance. Each trip makes several stops: the ATDC stops at an 11th-century statue of Buddha, a temple, a *coir* village, a swimming hole, and an ashram. Lunch is a traditional Keralan meal on a banana leaf. Both the ATDC and DTPC charge Rs150 for the trip, but DTPC gives a small discount to ISIC card holders and children under 12. The ATDC arranges shorter trips both on small motorized boats (Rs150 per hour) and big paddle-powered country boats, as well as stays on traditional shipping boats converted into **houseboats** with tiny bedrooms, bathrooms, and dining areas, and two guys to pole the boat around. *(Rs4200 for 2 people for a day-and-night stay, including food.)* A shorter, cheaper, but still pleasant, option is the public ferry ride to and from Kottayam. *(8 per day; 2hr. each way, Rs12.)*

▓ Periyar Tiger Reserve പെരിയാർ

Situated in 777 sq. km of lofty woodlands interspersed with grasslands on the border of Tamil Nadu, Periyar Tiger Reserve surrounds the artificial Periyar Lake. The forests around the lake were set aside as Reserved Forests in 1899, becoming the Nellikkampatty Sanctuary in 1934. Renamed and merged with the forest department in 1966, Periyar was incorporated into **Project Tiger** in 1979 (see p. 248). The reserve is home to a variety of animals including wild boar, monkeys, many species of birds and butterflies, Malabar giant squirrels, barking deer, and mongoose. People come to Periyar, however, to see its main attractions: wild elephants and the extremely elusive tiger. Unfortunately, the golden cats have been hunted to the brink of extinction and are a rare sight. Nonetheless, Periyar is a good place to relax, start short treks, or take that elephant ride. The best time to come is between November and May; in particular, April and May draw animals down to the lake to drink and make Periyar a cool respite from the muggy heat elsewhere. The crowds thin down to a trickle in those months, so discounts can be expected on accommodations.

ORIENTATION

Periyar encompasses the reserve and the town of **Thekkady,** which lies within the reserve itself. It has also come to refer to Kumily, the town bordering the reserve. **Thekkady Rd.** runs from the bus station on the border of Tamil Nadu on the one end of Kumily all the way to the boat jetty at the end of Thekkady. It is approximately 1.5km from the bus stand to the entrance to the reserve, and then another 3km to the boat jetty. Walking into the park is permitted, as long as you stay on the private road. Walking into the forest without an official guide, however, is prohibited.

PRACTICAL INFORMATION

With few exceptions, most tourist needs are met in Kumily rather than Thekkady. Unless otherwise noted, the following listings are for Kumily.

Buses: Kumily Bus Stand on the Tamil Nadu border. From Kumily to: **Ernakulam** (4 per day, 7am-3:30pm, 6hr., Rs75); **Kottayam** (every 30min. 2:10am-9:30pm, 4hr., Rs34); **Madurai** (every 30min., 3½hr., Rs30); **Munnar** (5 per day, 6-9:45am, 5hr., Rs27). From Thekkady to: **Emakulam** (6am and 2:45pm) and **Trivandrum** (8am and 3:30pm, 8hr., Rs75).

Local Transportation: Taxis, jeeps, and **auto-rickshaws** readily available from the Kumily bus stand to the boat jetty in Thekkady (Rs35). Also, there's a minibus that runs every 20-25min. into the Reserve, but it's infrequent off season (Rs2).

Tourist Office: The **Gov't of Kerala Tourist Office** (tel. 122620) is a 5min. walk from the bus station, in the direction of the reserve. It's on the left, up the stairs in a yellow building set back from the road. Kerala brochures, but little else. Open M-Sa 10am-5pm. For information on activities in Periyar, see the **Wildlife Information Centre** (tel. 22028) at the boat jetty in Thekkady. Open daily 7am-5pm.

Currency Exchange: The State Bank of Travancore exchanges foreign currency and AmEx and Thomas Cook traveler's checks. Open M-F 10am-5pm, Sa 10am-noon. Some hotels also exchange currency and traveler's checks.

Police: Just beyond the bus station on the main road heading toward the Tamil Nadu border. **Emergency: Police,** tel. 100; **Fire,** tel. 101; **Ambulance,** tel. 102

Hospital: Central Hospital, Thekkady Rd. (tel. 22045), a 10min. walk from the bus stand. English-speaking doctor who will see foreign patients, on call 24hr. On-site **pharmacy.** Other pharmacies can be found along the main road.

Post Office: The post office is located near the bus stand on the main road. Open M-F 9am-5pm (packages accepted until 3pm), Sa 9am-2pm. **Postal Code:** 585536.
Telephone: There are a number of **STD/ISD** booths along Thekkady Rd. **Telephone Code:** 04869 (will change to 04863 in 1999).

ACCOMMODATIONS

There are only three hotels inside the reserve, each run by the KTDC, so be prepared to spend more to stay there; otherwise, plan to shack up in Kumily.

Hotel Regent Tower (tel. 22570), 50m from the bus stand on the main road. You'll be sitting pretty-in-pink in these clean, new rooms. Attached bathrooms have hot and cold running water and seat toilets. Singles Rs150; doubles Rs253.
Muckumal Tourist Home (tel. 22070), a few doors down from the Regent. Run by the same folks, which explains the rosy motif. This is the older of the two hotels, and it shows, but the rooms are clean. Attached baths have 24hr. hot and cold water and seat toilets. Singles Rs107; doubles Rs150, with A/C Rs350-450.
Lake Queen Tourist Home (tel. 22084), 200m down the main road. Basic rooms. Attached bathrooms have seat toilets. Singles Rs107-215; doubles Rs161-268.
Hotel Ambaldi (tel. 22193), about 1km from the bus stand. Slightly dark cottages are an especially good deal, with nice rugs and furniture, and large attached baths with seat toilets and towels, blankets, and toilet paper provided. Cottages (sleep two) Rs380; rooms Rs650-900. Visa, MC.
Periyar House (tel. 22026), 1km inside the Reserve. If one simply *must* stay in the park, this is the cheapest and most modest choice. All have attached baths with seat toilets. Breakfast and dinner included. In-season: singles Rs500-1300; doubles Rs700-1500. Off-season: Rs300-750/Rs500-950. Visa, MC.

FOOD

Hotel Ambadi Restaurant is one of the best, offering the standard Indian-Chinese-Continental fare. The "Kerala meal" (Rs20) is delicious, but mashed potatoes (Rs40) and French onion soup (Rs30) are good too. Open daily 6:30am-10:30pm.
Sabala Restaurant, Karthika Tourist Home, near Central Hospital. Locally recommended for good, cheap South Indian food. *Thalis* Rs16-25. Open daily 7am-10pm.
Coffee Shop, near the Thekkady boat jetty, is the only place in the Reserve to eat besides hotel restaurants. The menu's limited to Indian food, but pre-packaged snacks can also be bought here. Open daily 8am-6pm.

SIGHTS AND ENTERTAINMENT

Warning: So-called "official" guides often approach tourists at the boat jetty offering jungle walks and jeep tours. Don't take them up on their offer—contracting them is illegal, and you may be fined.

Peryiyar Tiger Reserve
Hours: *Open daily 6am-6pm.* **Admission:** *Rs50 for 2 days for foreigners.* **Other:** *Boat Tours at 7, 9:30, 11:30am, 2 and 4pm. Purchase tickets a day ahead in season at the Wildlife Information Centre (Rs25) or the KTDC ticket booth at the boat jetty (top deck Rs50; lower Rs25). Jungle walks begin at 7:30am, 3hr., Rs10. Elephant rides 30min., Rs30.*

The two main ways to explore the Reserve are by boat tour and trekking. The best times to see the animals are 7:30am and 4pm, when temperatures are cooler. During the monsoon, jungle walking groups are small, but come prepared for leeches. At other times of the year, the group may have as many as a dozen people, so it might be wise to hire a private guide from the Centre. Elephant rides are purely for entertainment, so you probably won't see much. One of the best ways to see the wildlife is to spend a night in an **observation tower.** The Wildlife Information Centre handles the necessary reservations. The tower sleeps a maximum of two people, who must provide their own food, water, and bedding. The Centre will arrange drop-offs and pickups by boat (Rs100 plus boat fee Rs25).

■ Kollam (Quilon) കൊല്ലം

The appellation Quilon is giving way to the ancient name of the town, Kollam (Koy-LAM). Called Kaulam Mall by ancient Arabs, and Coilum by Marco Polo in the thir-teenth century, the port was the centre of the "heroic rebellion" led by Veluthambi Dalava against the British rule. Little of this former glory is visible in Kollam today. It is still an active industrial town and exporter of coconuts, but a shopping mall and modern storefronts have obliterated both ancient palaces and most of the village streets. Consequently, there is very little of interest to tourists in Kollam itself. The tourist office readily acknowledges this fact, and locals are prone to ask, "Where you are going? Alleppey? Varkala? Cochin?" since most foreigners stay only overnight.

ORIENTATION

The strange angles of the streets follow the bends of the canals. As a result, navigation can be a little confusing. **National Highway 47 (N.H. 47)** runs southeast to northwest through town to the **Clock Tower** at the intersection with **Tourist Bungalow Road. Main Road** also starts at this junction, running northwest of N.H. 47. The main road twists, in an overall northeast direction, past the **Post Office**, the sprawling **Bishop Jerome Nagar Shopping Centre,** then past the wild **Shrine of Our Lady of Velam-kanni.** The next junction is with **Jetty Road,** which leads to the right to the **KSRTC bus station** and the **ferry jetty.** To the left, this road goes past the **hospital** and then after about a 10-minute walk to the sprawling **fruit and vegetable market,** housed in small red-tile-roofed stores.

PRACTICAL INFORMATION

Trains: The **railway station** is on the main road southeast of the junction with Tour-ist Bungalow Rd.; take the flyover. Fares listed are for 2nd/1st class. To: **Alleppey** (*Intercity Exp.,* 5:50pm, 1½hr., Rs30/184); **Bangalore** (*Island Exp.,* 11:50pm, Rs228/1049); **Chennai** (*Chennai Mail,* 2:55pm, 16hr., Rs243/792); **Delhi** (*Kerala Exp.* 2625, 9:40am, 53hr., Rs487/2028); **Ernakulam** (*Intercity Exp.,* 5:50pm, 3hr., Rs47/249); **Kanyakumari** (2 per day, 10:30am, 1:35pm, 3½hr., Rs46/248); **Manga-lore** (*Parasuram Exp.,* 7:20am, 14hr., Rs190/623; *Malabar Exp.,* 7:15pm); **Mum-bai** (*Jayanthi Janatha,* 8:40am, 46hr., Rs384/1470); **Trivandrum** (several per day, 6:35am-8:30pm, 1½hr., Rs26/154); **Varkala** (several per day, 6:35am-8:30pm, ½hr., Rs18/125).

Buses: KRSTC bus station, follow N.H. 47 past the Shrine of Our Lady of Velam-kanni, turn right at the Jetty Rd. intersection, follow it down the hill toward the river and the boat jetty. To: **Alleppey** (every 30min., 2hr., Rs26/30 regular/express); **Ernakulam** (every 30min., 3½hr., Rs42); **Trivandrum** (every 10-30min., 2hr., Rs20/25 regular/express); **Varkala** (9 per day, 6:30am-8pm, 1hr., Rs10).

Tourist Office: District Tourism Promotion Council (DTPC) has outposts at the railway station (tel. 745625; open M-Sa 8am-6pm), bus station (open M-Sa 9am-5pm), and near the Tourist Bungalow (tel. 742558; open M-Sa 10am-5pm). Backwa-ter tour booking and hotel reservations. Expect heavy promotion of *their* backwa-ter tour (over the ATDC's version) and *their* hotel, Yatri Nivas.

Currency Exchange: PL Worldways (tel. 741096; fax 744823). From the gates of the post office, turn right onto N.H. 47, take an immediate sharp right; it will be on the right (look for the sign over the dentist's office). All brands of traveler's checks, all currencies. Open M-F 9:30am-5:30pm, Sa 9:30am-2:30pm.

Market: A fruit and vegetable market district occupies a few blocks of the road that leads from the boat jetty into town (15min. walk from the boat jetty).

Pharmacy: Kochappally Medicals, Tourist Bungalow Rd. (tel. 749286), just south-west of the main intersection with N.H. 47 and Main Rd. Open daily 8am-9pm.

Hospital: District Hospital (tel. 742004), on the road from the boat jetty into town, past the junction with the main road, on the left.

Police Station: (tel. 742072). Take a right out of the railway station; it's just before the flyover, next to a large temple. Nosy but ultimately amiable.

Emergency: Police, tel. 100. **Fire,** tel. 101. **Ambulance,** tel. 102.

Post Office: Head Post Office, on the main road, northeast of the intersection with Tourist Bungalow Rd. on the left. *Poste Restante* available. **Postal Code:** 691001.

Telegraph Office: on Tourist Bungalow Rd. (follow the main road southeast from the post office, take a left at the massive intersection). **Telephone Code:** 0474.

ACCOMMODATIONS

The Tourist Bungalow (Government Guest House), Tourist Bungalow Rd. (tel. 743620), a few km outside of town (take a rickshaw). In a beautiful old British mansion with a huge empty ballroom and enormous balconies occupied by pigeons, the few rooms have 3m ceilings and antique furniture. Attached bathrooms (seat toilet) with tubs and dressing rooms. Wonderfully romantic and almost always full. Singles Rs75; doubles Rs100. Student discounts. Reservations recommended.

Yatri Nivas (tel. 745538), directly across the river from the boat jetty—if you phone from the boat jetty, they will come pick you up in their speedboat (Rs10); otherwise hire a rickshaw. Clean rooms have attached baths. Singles Rs110; doubles Rs165. Extra person Rs50. Reservations recommended.

Iswarya Lodge (tel. 750214), Main Rd., a 5min. walk from the intersection with Tourist Bungalow Rd. and N.H. 47. With 62 large, clean rooms, there's a good chance of finding last-minute accommodations here. Singles Rs86; doubles Rs150.

FOOD

Jala Subhiksha, next to the boat jetty, is a floating restaurant in a lovely traditional *kettuvallam* (boat). Deliciously gorgeous Chinese and Indian dishes: *saiwoo* chicken Rs55, Manchurian tofu Rs45 (don't be surprised if the tofu bears a resemblance to *paneer*). Open daily 6pm-10pm.

Indian Coffee House, on Main Rd., near Iswarya Lodge. From the post office, turn right onto N.H. 47, then take the second right. Once a franchise, always a franchise. Rooms provided for women and families. Open daily 8am-8:30pm.

Supreme Bakers, from the post office, turn right onto N.H. 47, then take an immediate right; it will be on the left. Fresh cakes and breads are available in this spick-n-span, bustling bakery. Cold drinks and spicy snacks offer relief from the sugar overload. Open M-Sa 9am-8pm.

SIGHTS AND ENTERTAINMENT

The towering **Shrine of Our Lady of Velamkanni** rises above everything on N.H. 47 near Jetty Rd. Festooned with bright plastic flowers and tinsel, the shrine occupies a central place in Kollam's religious life. Although a mere 13 years old, the adolescent shrine has already gained a reputation for healing and granting miracles. Crowds line up inside, reciting rosaries and praying for hours. The path to the shrine is lined with beggars and peddlers, seeking not only grace but your money. *(Mass W at 8am, noon, and 5pm, later mass usually conducted in Malayaram.)*

The **market** area of town remains quaint. Narrow streets pass between buildings roofed in red tile and carts of fruits and vegetables stacked for perusal. Another market sits in front of the flyover in the center of town. Mangoes, butcher knives, and international editions of *Newsweek* are all available here.

The main attraction in Kollam is, of course, **backwater tours** to Alleppey. The boat can take both you and your luggage, making this a convenient and beautiful mode of transport north up the Keralan coast. Run by the District Tourism Promotion Council (DTPC). For more information, see p. 544. *(Tours leave at 10:30am from the DTPC office near the KSRTC bus stand and the boat jetty, arriving in Alleppey at 6:30pm. The reporting time is before 10am. Rs150.)*

■ Cochin (Kochi) കൊവ്വി

In 1341 torrential floods tore down from the Western Ghats and scoured out Lake Vembanad, Cochin's perfect harbor. Over the next few centuries, the quiet fishing village grew over a cluster of islands and narrow peninsulas, transforming itself into a wealthy, cosmopolitan port. First, Cochin attracted Arab and Syrian Christian settlers from the Middle East. Centuries later, Portuguese and Dutch sailors scrambled for access to the Malabar Coast and a lucrative spice trade; after 1500, Cochin was ruled first by the Portuguese and then the Dutch. Shortly afterward, the Raja of Cochin harbored Goan Jews, who were facing persecution from the Portuguese. Later, British magisterial types set up administrative shop, briefly ruling the Chennai Presidency from here. Throughout, the Europeans met with little resistance from the local monarchy who were content to be coddled by the visiting rulers.

Cochin's cultural grafts have thrived, and the part of the city known as "Fort Cochin" is renowned for its collection of different traditions, heritages, and architectures. Chinese fishing nets line the harbor's mouth, Dutch-style houses cram narrow streets, and Jew Town is a five-minute stroll from the Portuguese-built raja's palace, which is filled with murals depicting scenes from the Hindu epics. In contrast with the vaguely archaic European feel that Ft. Cochin has managed to preserve, Ernakulam plays the part of its modernized alter-ego. Developing, bustling, and polluted, Ernakulam provides every tourist amenity imaginable, except the peninsula's extraordinary sense of history.

ORIENTATION

Cochin is arranged around **Lake Vembanad,** encompassing **Ernakulam,** on the shore of the mainland, the peninsula of **Fort Cochin** and **Mattancherry, Vypeen Island,** and the smaller Willingdon, Vallarpadam, Gundy, and Bolghatty Islands. Along the eastern shore of Lake Vembanad, Ernakulam contains the central railway and bus stations and most of the hotels, but tourists generally devote their waking hours to the sight-filled peninsula on the other side of the lake.

Ernakulam's three main streets, **Park Avenue, Mahatma Gandhi (M.G.) Road,** and **Chitoor Road,** run north-south parallel to the shore. M.G. Rd. is divided into three areas corresponding to its main junctions with cross-streets leading to the lake shore. From **Shenoys Junction, Amman Kovil Road** leads east to the **central bus station.** Three blocks south of Shenoys Junction, **Hospital Road** runs east-west between M.G. Rd. and Park Ave. South of this is **Jos Junction,** crossed by **Durbar Hall (D.H.) Road.**

On the peninsula, **Princess Street,** at the northern tip, is Fort Cochin's main drag. It extends to the **shore,** skirted by **Calvathy Road. Mattancherry,** the site of the palace, and **Jew Town** are on the east side of the peninsula.

In the early 20th century, a mammoth dredging project created **Willingdon Island,** sandwiched between Ernakulam and the peninsula. The island lacks character, but the **airport** is here, 2km south of the Cochin Harbour Railway Station. With a 270° view of the harbor, the **Taj Malabar Hotel** sits at the northern tip of the island.

PRACTICAL INFORMATION

Airport: At the south end of Willingdon Island. **Indian Airlines,** D.H. Rd., Ernakulam (tel. 370242 or 37141), near the Park Ave. intersection. Open daily 10am-1pm and 1:45-5pm. To: **Bangalore** (1 per day, 1hr., US$60); **Chennai** (4 per week, 1hr., US$84); **Delhi** (1 per day, 4hr., US$256); **Mumbai** (1-2 per day, 2hr., US$135). **Jet Airways** (tel. 369423 or 369212) also has daily flights to Mumbai.

Trains: Cochin has 3 stations. **Ernakulam Junction Railway Station** is at the east end of D.H. Rd., and gets the most use. North 4km is the **Ernakulam Town Railway Station**—quite a distance from M.G. Rd., along Banerji Rd. **Cochin Harbour Railway Station,** on Willingdon Island, may be convenient if you have a flight to catch, but few trains service it. Fares listed are 2nd/1st class. From **Ernakulam Junction** to: **Alleppey** (7 per day, 6:30am-11:50pm, 1½hr., Rs30/95); **Mumbai (Kurla)** via **Madgaon** (*Netravati Exp.* 6636, 4:45am, 36hr., Rs314/1619); **Trivan-**

drum (8 per day, 4am-5:15pm, 4½hr., Rs60/280). From **Ernakulam Town** to: **Bangalore** (*Bangalore Exp.* 6525, 3:40pm, 13hr., Rs161/7920); **Calicut** (*Parsuram Exp.* 6349, 2am-11pm, 4½hr., Rs38/245).

Buses: The **KSRTC Bus Stand** is central to Ernakulam, at the end of Amman Kovil Rd. To: **Alleppey** (every 30min., 1½hr., Rs25); **Bangalore** (8 per day, 6am-9:15pm, 15hr., Rs190/220) via **Mysore** (10hr., Rs120); **Calicut** (every hr., 5hr., Rs75); **Coimbatore** (20 per day, 4½hr., Rs54); **Trivandrum** (over 50 per day, 4½hr., Rs80). **Private bus companies** also run long-distance buses from Cochin. Several agencies, including **Indira Travels** (tel. 360693), have offices near Jos Junction in Ernakulam. Many of their coaches depart from **Jos Junction**. Prices are for deluxe coaches to: **Bangalore** (14 per day, 12hr., Rs230); **Chennai** (4, 4:30, and 5pm, 15hr., Rs300); **Coimbatore** (13 per day, 2:30am-midnight, 4hr., Rs170).

Ferries: The best way to move from one island to another, commutes cost less than Rs2, are frequent, and run at least 6am-9pm (however, avoid the lunchtime lull—you may wait 90min. for a lift). **From Ernakulam: Main Jetty** (mid-town) to Willingdon Island and Fort Cochin—buy tickets at the SWTD counter to avoid being double-charged; **High Court Jetty** to Vypeen Island and to and from Bolghatty Island. **From Fort Cochin: Customs Jetty** to Willingdon Island's Terminus and Malabar Hotel Jetties (daily except Su), then on to Ernakulam's Main Jetty (last ferry 6:30pm); **Vypeen Island Jetty** (across from the bus stand) to Vypeen Island. **From Mattancherry** (the jetty is across from the Dutch Palace) to Willingdon Island. **From Willingdon Island: Embarkation Jetty** (northeast side) to Vypeen Island and Ernakulam; **Terminus Jetty** (southwest side) to Fort Cochin and Mattancherry. **From Vypeen Island:** to Fort Cochin, Willingdon Island's Embarkation Jetty, and Ernakulam's High Court Jetty.

Other Local Transportation: Local buses are cheap (under Rs4) and orderly, provided you avoid morning and evening rush hours. Around **Ernakulam,** local buses depart frequently from the KRSTC bus station or can easily be nabbed as they pass through town. Buses to Fort Cochin depart from the east side of M.G. Rd., south of Jos Junction. In **Fort Cochin,** local buses run from the bus stand across from the Vypeen Island ferry landing, across the bridge onto Willingdon Island, past the airport, across the bridge to Ernakulam, and up M.G. Rd. In Ernakulam, **taxis** and **auto-rickshaws** are plentiful during the day but scarce at night. They flock near jetties and bus and railway stations. In Fort Cochin, buses and taxis do not operate and even cycle- and auto-rickshaws can be difficult to find. Try the areas near the ferry landings. **Auto-rickshaws** are metered, but drivers often blatantly refuse to use them. The peninsula (once you get there) is easily navigable by foot.

Tourist Office: The privately-run **Tourist Desk** (tel. 371761) is in Ernakulam, at the dockside ticket office at the main jetty. Brimming with pamphlets and festival calendars, the staff bend over backwards to answer questions. In season the office posts a cultural events news board outside. Open daily 9am-6pm. For information on their **Backwater Cruises,** see p. 557. **KTDC Tourist Reception Centre,** Shanmugham Rd., Ernakulam (tel. 353234), next to the State Bank of India. The helpful staff can offer more than expensive tours. Open daily 8am-7pm.

Immigration Office: Police Commissioner's Office, Banerji Rd., Ernakulam. East of the High Court Jetty, on the corner of Shanmugham Rd., on the left. Visa extensions (student and entry visas only) take up to 10 days; it may be necessary to leave your passport for the duration but a photocopy might suffice. Open M-Sa 10:15am-1:15pm and 2-5:30pm. Closed holidays and 2nd Sa of each month.

Currency Exchange: Thomas Cook, M.G. Road, Ernakulam (tel. 373829), near the Air India building. Open M-Sa 9:30am-6pm. **South Indian Bank,** Fort Cochin (tel. 226824). Go south on Princess St., turn left at Elite Travels, and after a few blocks the bank will be on the right. All traveler's checks accepted. Open M-F 10am-2pm.

Market: In Fort Cochin, beach shacks sell fresh fish. At Jos Junction, in Ernakulam, are shops of every conceivable stripe. The area near the Boat Jetty features roadside hawkers, used-book kiosks, and fruit stands.

Bookstore: Idiom, Fort Cochin, across from the Pardesi Synagogue. Crusty classics and Indian fiction. Open daily 10am-6pm. **Bhavi Books,** Convent Rd., Ernakulam, just west of M.G. Rd. Everything from Larry McMurtry to Khalil Gibran. Open M-Sa 10am-7:30pm.

SOUTH INDIA

Elamkulam Rd.

TO TRIVANDRUM

Warriom Rd.

K.P. Vallon Rd.

Azad Rd.

KSRTC Bus Stand

Ernakulam Junction Railway Station

See India Foundation

Cochin Cultural Center

ERNAKULAM

Parambhilhara Rd.

Ernakulam Town Railway Station

Veekshanam Rd.

Chittoor Rd.

Amman Kovil Rd.

Ernakulam South Bus Stand

Buses to Fort Cochin

Manikath Rd.

Medical Trust Hospital

Mahatma Gandhi Rd.

Gopalaprabhu Rd.

Convent Rd.

Hospital Rd.

JUNCTION

Bimbi's/ Khyber

Durbar Hall Rd.

Church Landing Rd.

Hot Breads

Thomas Cook

Banerji Rd.

T.D. Rd.

Jews St.

Princess Room/ Sayanna

Fruit Garden

Indian Coffee House

Park Ave.

GPO

Foreshore Rd.

Matha Manjeran Rd.

Market Rd.

Broadway

Shanmugham Rd.

Indian Airlines

Police Commissioner's Office

Marine Dr. Walkway

High Court Jetties

Ancient Mariner

GCDA Shopping Centre

State Bank of India

KTDC Tourist Reception Center

Main Jetty (i)

Tourist Desk

Bolghatty Island

Vembanad Lake

Willingdon Island

TO AIRPORT

Bristow Rd.

Cochin Harbour Railway Station

Terminus Jetty

Milne Rd.

Indira Gandhi Rd.

Embarkation Jetty

Malabar Hotel Jetty

(i) ITDC

Mattancherry Jetty

Customs Jetty

Hotel Seagull Rest.

Synagogue

Dutch Palace

Moulana Azad Rd.

MATTANCHERRY

Bazaar Rd.

Jain Temple

Nehru Memorial Town Hall

Gundu Island

Padinara Mosque

Santo Gopalan Rd.

Vypeen Island

Vypeen Island Jetty

Calvathy Rd.

Palace Rd.

FORT COCHIN

Bastian St.

SEE FORT COCHIN MAP

Arabian Sea

N

Cannery Rd.

Napier St.

Beach Rd.

Cochin

ACCOMMODATIONS

A Bharat Tourist Home
B Hotel Aiswarya
C Hotel Sangeetha
D Woodlands Hotel

Hospital: Medical Trust Hospital, M.G. Rd., Ernakulam (tel. 371852), 3 blocks south of Jos Junction. The hospital is being renovated with U.S. equipment. Doctor's visits Rs75. **Pharmacy** inside is open 24hr. **Gautham Hospital** (tel. 223055; ambulance 227289), Fort Cochin. Difficult to find on your own; it's better to take a rickshaw or call an ambulance. The chief medical officer is Dr. K. R. Jayachandran.

Police: Police Commissioner, Banerji Rd., Ernakulam. East of the High Court Jetty, on the corner of Shanmugham Rd., on the left. The **police station** is north of the commissioner's office, on the left around the curve to the right. **Fort Cochin Police:** follow Rampart Rd. inland; the police office is on the left. **Tourist Police:** take Princess St. to the beach, turn right on Calvathy Rd.; it will be on the left.

Emergency: Police, tel. 100. **Fire,** tel. 101. **Ambulance,** tel. 102.

Post Office: The **Kochi Head Post Office** is located in Fort Cochin. All *Poste Restante* addressed to Cochin arrives here (open M-Sa 9am-5pm). Telegrams and stamps sold M-Sa 9am-5pm; parcels accepted M-F 9am-3pm, Sa 9am-2pm. Ernakulam's **GPO** is on Hospital Rd., midway between Park Ave. and M.G. Rd. Open M-F 8:30am-8pm, Sa 9:30am-2:30pm and 4-8pm, Su 10am-4pm. **Postal Code:** 682011.

Internet: Raiyan Communications (tel. 13513877), on M.G. Rd. at Padma Junction in Ernakulam, sends **email** for Rs25 per page.

Telephone Code: 0484.

ACCOMMODATIONS

Ernakulam

Hotel Luciya (tel. 354433). From the KRSTC bus station turn right, then take the first left. Hotel Luciya is immediately on the left. All doubles have balconies. Singles (squat toilet) Rs100, with A/C Rs225; doubles (seat toilet) Rs200, with A/C Rs350.

Hotel Aiswarya (tel. 364454), on Warrion Rd., near Jos Junction where Warrion bends up to meet D.H. Rd. This new establishment is a good deal. Cool marble floors and cooler bedspreads that are—alas!—whisked away once you check in. Hot and cold water in all rooms, as well as TV's. All rooms with attached baths and seat toilets. Singles Rs250, with A/C Rs400; doubles Rs350/450; deluxe Rs350/500.

Hotel Sangeetha (tel. 368487). From Jos Junction head east along D.H. Rd. towards the railway station and take the first left. Sangeetha is on the left. Smiling staff will escort you to a clean room with Star TV and soft, blanketed beds. The aroma of *sambar* from the restaurant entices (guests receive a complimentary breakfast). Singles Rs280, with A/C Rs500; doubles Rs400/600; extra person Rs110. Visa, MC.

Woodlands Hotel (tel. 381177), on M.G. Rd., 1 block north of Jos Junction. The gold bedcovers are faded, but diamond and jewelry expositions still take place in the back hall. Color TVs and carved furniture grace the rooms, and the marble bathrooms have running hot water. Singles Rs350, with A/C Rs525, extra person Rs75; doubles Rs475/700, extra person Rs100. Visa, MC, AmEx, traveler's checks.

Bharat Tourist Home (tel. 353501), on D.H. Rd. near its intersection with Foreshore Rd. Cooler than *kulfi*—guard, A/C lobby, sweets shop, seat toilets, and running hot water. Bilious green carpets and walls. Check-out noon. Singles Rs430, with A/C Rs600; doubles Rs500/750-850. Extra person Rs125, with A/C Rs250.

Fort Cochin

If you don't mind taking a ferry to the mainland, it's worth staying here: prices are reasonable and accommodations can be lovely.

Spencer's Tourist Home (tel. 225049). From Rose St., turn right onto Parade St. Spencer's is on the left. Run by friendly brothers. Large, clean rooms. Dorm beds in a large front room, which has cable TV, a couch, and reading materials. Clean bathrooms with seat toilets. Dorm beds Rs45. Doubles with bath Rs150-175.

Delight Tourist Resort, Rose St. (tel. 228658). Behind St. Francis Church, walk south. Delight is on the left before the end of the field; look for the blue balcony behind a whitewashed wall and coconut trees. Large rooms with attached baths, set in a rambling, lovely house with a large library. Un-groovy "foreigners only" rule. Singles Rs100; doubles Rs125-500.

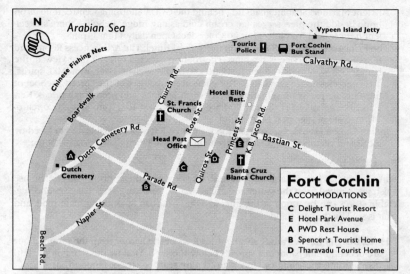

Fort Cochin

ACCOMMODATIONS

C Delight Tourist Resort
E Hotel Park Avenue
A PWD Rest House
B Spencer's Tourist Home
D Tharavadu Tourist Home

PWD Rest House (tel. 225797). Turn left from the gates of St. Francis Church, then right onto Dutch Cemetery Rd. Owned by the government. Palatial rooms, with high, sloping ceilings. The double fits at least 8. The garden fronts the beach, near the Chinese fishing nets. Staff can arrange backwater cruises and fishing trips. Doubles Rs100. Extra mattress Rs20.

Tharavadu Tourist Home (tel. 226897). From the south end of Princess St. turn right, then left onto Quirose St. Well-maintained, 400-year-old house has dim stairs leading to 8 fairly clean rooms, some with common bath (seat toilet and shower). Rooms Rs135-205, based on size and availability of the "Goofy" bedspread.

Hotel Park Avenue (tel. 22267), at the intersection of Princess and Bastion Streets. A new place with large, sparkling clean rooms, they give generous off-season discounts. All rooms have attached baths and 24hr. room service. Singles Rs200, with A/C Rs500; doubles Rs250/750. Off-season: knock off another Rs50-100.

FOOD

Ernakulam

Thriving on the comings and goings of ships, Ernakulam's eateries present the best in international mishmash, Indian-style. That said, make sure to sample local stuff like *appam* (a thick *dosa*), served with fish stew and coconut dishes.

Bimbi's, Jos Junction. A landmark, popular with locals and tourists alike. The chaos is incredible, the food good and cheap. Pay at the register on the side, get a receipt, then claim your chow at the appropriate counter. Excellent *masala dosa* Rs10. Huge selection of Indian and Western sweets at the front. Open daily 8am-9:30pm.

Khyber Restaurant, Jos Junction, upstairs from Bimbi's. Dimly lit, marble-floored, and more expensive than its downstairs neighbor, the A/C Khyber offers Chinese and Indian veg. and non-veg. food. Luscious *kadai* (ginger) *paneer* (Rs38), incredible garlic *naan* (Rs16), and smooth, creamy *lassis* (Rs12). Open daily 11am-11pm.

Hot Breads, Warriom Rd. Follow M.G. Rd. south from Jos Junction and turn right; Hot Breads is on the right. True to its name, this is Ernakulam's best spot for warm treats. Fresh pastries and cakes, including apricot croissants and chocolate doughnuts. Pizza, burgers, and sandwiches, too. Open daily 9am-9pm.

Fruit Garden, at the corner of M.G. Rd. and Convent Rd. Icy cold squeezin's of fruits both usual (orange) and exotic (pomegranate) are Rs10-25. Fruity milkshakes Rs10. Open daily 9:30am-10pm.

SOUTH INDIA

Ancient Mariner, Shanmugham Rd., behind the GCDA Shopping Centre. It floats on brine beside the pier, serves ice cream cold as any fridge. Behold—there's excellent *paneer,* and fruit juice, but no Coleridge. Open daily 11am-11pm.

The Princess Room and **Sayanna,** in the Sealord Hotel. The A/C Princess Room, 2nd fl., is lush, and service is fawning. The rooftop Sayanna offers a nice view of the harbor below, and its Golden Jug Bar is atypically well-lit. Beer, non-IMFL spirits, and even champagne available. The chefs are upholders of the "pretty" school of fine cuisine: pretty presentation, pretty small servings, and pretty high prices. Keralan dishes Rs65-95. Princess Room open daily 6am-10:45pm; Sayanna open 6-11pm; Golden Jug open 11am-11pm.

Indian Coffee House, across from the Main Boat Jetty. Dependable and beloved by locals and visitors alike, ICH is convenient and fast. Open daily 7:30am-8:30pm.

Fort Cochin

Fort Cochin has few restaurants, but in shacks down by the seafront you can choose a fish just yanked from the water and grilled before your very eyes. Bakeries and vegetable stores can be found at the intersection of Bastian St. and the main road, and fruit is sold by the bus stand.

Hotel Seagull Restaurant, Calvathy Rd. Views of the harbor from the ground floor are decent, but a panorama spreads below the 1st fl. (follow the stairs on the left, disregarding the Families Only sign). Enjoy seafood (fried, tandoori, or *masala* style) as boats and dolphins cruise below. Grilled squid Rs80; crab fry Rs40; mixed vegetable curry Rs25. Beer available to wash it all down. Open daily 8am-10pm.

Elite Hotel Restaurant, Princess St., on the ground floor of the infamous Elite Hotel. So popular you may have to settle for whatever's in the cabinet: usually *paratha, appam,* and *channa* curry, though they usually have a fresh seafood offering. *Dosas* appear after 6pm. Open daily 8am until the crowd trickles out (10 or 11pm).

SIGHTS

Fort Cochin

Fort Cochin fulfills the typical tourist fantasy of South India, with its grassy fields and massive churches glowing as the orange sun slips into the sea behind Chinese fishing nets. Needless to say, historic sites here are more common than cows (but not as common as goats).

The first European church in India, **St. Francis Church** (locally called the Vasco da Gama Church), was constructed by Portuguese Franciscan friars in 1503 and still stands near the northeast shore of the peninsula, among the houses built by British traders and Dutch farmers. *(Open M-F 9:30am-1pm and 2:30-5:30pm. English services Sun. 8am.)* When Vasco da Gama died in Cochin in 1524, his remains were buried under the church floor. After 14 years, the remains of the remains were transferred to Lisbon, but his tombstone remains embedded. The original wooden structure of the church was upgraded to stone during the mid-16th century. Cochin fell to the Dutch in 1663, and the church was Protestantized in 1779. Although the British occupied Cochin in 1795, the church remained a Dutch bastion, and the walls are lined with Dutch memorials. In 1864 the church finally became Anglican, and the Church of South India now fills the same stone walls with its faithful, who have dedicated the church to St. Francis.

Turn left from the gates of St. Francis Church, then right onto Dutch Cemetery Rd., to reach the **Dutch Cemetery,** where crumbling tombs disintegrate beside the beach. The cemetery has fallen into complete disrepair; the entire lot is overgrown with weeds. A driveway next to PWD Guest House leads to the **beach,** where the faraway crowd at the water's edge consists of fishermen, fish sellers, fish buyers, and fish. The nearby skeletal cantilevered **Chinese fishing nets** were brought to Kerala by Chinese traders in the 13th century. As massive cargo ships pass into the harbor, not so far away, fishermen return from the sea in long canoelike boats (propelled by sev-

Jews in Cochin

The first Jews are said to have come to Kerala in the 10th century BC, as traders from King Solomon's Israel. The destruction of the Second Temple in Jerusalem by the Romans in 70 AD led to the dispersion of the Jewish people, some of whom landed in Shingly (30km north of Cochin, now known as Cranganore) in 72 AD. Around 500 AD, a large group of Jews immigrated to Shingly from Iraq and Iran. In the 16th century the Portuguese began persecuting Jews, who then were expelled from Shingly. Legend has it that Joseph Azar, the last surviving Jewish prince, swam to Cochin with his wife on his shoulders. The Jewish Keralans placed themselves under the protection of the Raja of Cochin, who gave them a parcel of land next to his palace for a synagogue.

Emigration to Mumbai and Israel has pared Cochin's Jewish population down to about 18, but you'll still see menorahs in some windows. There has been no rabbi for several years, so the elders of the synagogue make decisions and conduct ceremonies. Happy to discuss their future with visitors, the remaining Jews seem unworried about the survival of their community. Eighty or so Jews remain in Kerala, and 4000-5000 in India as a whole, mostly in Mumbai.

Today you can still visit the **Pardesi Synagogue** (open to visitors Su-F 10am-noon and 3-5pm; requested donation Rs1) located in **Jew Town,** tucked away in an alleyway parallel to Bazaar Rd. The synagogue, which is the fifth-oldest in the world, is lit by colored 19th-century oil-burning chandeliers suspended over blue-and-white Cantonese tiles. The hand-painted tiles, which line the entire floor, number over 1600. The synagogue's Torah is written on sheepskin scrolls and stored in ornate metal canisters, one of which was a gift from the Raja of Cochin.

eral buzzing Evinrudes) with the day's catch. Crowds clamor on the beach to purchase fish, prawns, and crabs directly from the boats.

The **Santa Cruz Basilica** can be reached by following Princess St. south until it ends, then turning left onto Bastian St.; the basilica is on the right. *(English mass Su 4:30pm.)* A church was first built on this site in 1505, then replaced by a cathedral in 1558. This cathedral was consecrated in 1902.

Mattancherry

By following Bastian St. from the back of St. Francis Church until it ends, then turning right, a fast walker can reach the heart of Mattancherry in 30 minutes. Mattancherry can also be found by following Cavalthy Rd. directly from the Seagull Hotel. Lazy or tired tourists can hire a rickshaw for about Rs10. Along streets lined with export warehouses, the aroma of tea spills out from them and onto the streets.

The **Mattancherry Palace** (a.k.a. the **Dutch Palace**) on the right side of the road, was built by the Portuguese in 1557 for Raja Virakerala Varma as a "goodwill gesture" (probably in exchange for trading rights). During their occupation in 1665, the Dutch renovated and renamed the palace. Two **temples,** one dedicated to Krishna and one to Shiva, were also built on the palace grounds by the Portuguese, but today only Hindus may enter. Detailed **murals** cover nearly 300 square meters of the palace walls, depicting the faces of gods and goddesses in scenes from the *Ramayana* and the *Puranas* in distinct Keralite style. Downstairs in the queen's bedchamber, a number of less detailed paintings show scenes of a divinely sexual nature set in a beautiful forest (inspiration to produce a male heir?). In one, Krishna uses six hands and two feet to pleasure a group of admiring *gopis* (milkmaids) and two more hands to play the flute. An attached **museum** houses oil portraits of Cochin rajas and their *palanquins* (hand-carried chariots), robes, weapons, and umbrellas. *(Open Sa-Th 10am-5pm. No photography permitted.)*

Vypeen Island

Miles of ignored beaches roll along the Arabian Sea on Vypeen Island, passing a **lighthouse** at Ochanthuruth (open daily 3-5pm) and the early 16th-century **Palliport Fort** (open Th). The beaches are empty except for herds of sunbathing cows and a few fishing boats, until the foreigners arrive. Then men come running from the nearest village for the show. Women will be seen as more respectful swimming in a t-shirt and shorts or pants. **Cherai Beach** is more frequented by foreigners and is probably safer than the others for women without an accompanying "husband." Public buses (Rs2, 45min.) are available and frequent—tell the ticket man to let you know where the stop is—and the ride by auto-rickshaw is another 10min. Coconut quaffs can be sipped at a **toddy bar** on the right side of the main road about a 5min. walk from the Fort Cochin ferry landing. The bar closes around 9pm. The island is also a spectacular place to watch the sun set into the harbor. Ferries run between Vypeen Island and the High Court Jetty in Ernakulam (every 20min., 5:30am-10pm). The same is true of ferries to Fort Cochin, which depart from the launch across from the bus stand.

ENTERTAINMENT

For those with the disco itch, **Ice's** (at Ravipuram, near M.G. Rd.) serves up Western and Hindi hits, as well as Pepsi and ice cream (but no alcohol). There's an outdoor patio and an ancient dance floor. If that isn't your style, the resident band in the Princess Room at the **Sealord Hotel** cranks out a good "Mustang Sally," with ice cream *and* alcohol available. The band stops around 10pm each night, but the club doesn't close until 1 or 2am. The Sridar **movie theater,** near Vypeen Jetty across from GCDA Shopping Centre, screens English-language films in Dolby stereo and A/C comfort.

The **Cochin Cultural Centre** (tel. 353732) teaches dance, yoga, music, costume making, and more. The traditional Keralan martial art of Kalaripayatu, dating from Indian medieval times, is taught at the **ENS Kalari Centre** (tel. 809810). The school is about 9km from the city center; call for directions.

The **Kerala Ayurveda Pharmacy** (tel. 361202), on Warriom Rd., is one of many places offering **ayurvedic massage** in Cochin (see **Ayurvedic Medicine,** p. 543). **P.N.V.M. Santhigiri Ayurvedic Hospital** (tel. 348757), on Azad Rd., offers massage (Rs250) and consultations (Rs50). To get there, take one of the frequent buses running from Jos Junction to Palarvattom Junction, and then walk 10min. down Azad Rd. to the clinic. (Open daily 11am-6pm.) Ayurveda is an important part of Kathakali, so several dance centers also offer massage, including the Cochin Cultural Centre and **Kerala Kathakali Kendra** (tel. 740030). Appointments are necessary.

Dance

Cochin offers spectacular nightly performances of **Kathakali dance** (see p. 557). Geared toward tourists, these performances are usually prefaced by elaborate make-up demonstrations, an explanation of the music and hand-symbols, and a synopsis of the tale to be enacted. Performances last from one hour to 90 minutes.

Cochin Cultural Centre (tel. 366923 or 380366). From Jos Junction, follow M.G. Rd. south, turn left on South Overbridge Rd., right on Chittoor Rd., and then left onto Manikath Rd. A green Kathakali visage is painted on the center's wall. Make-up begins at 5:45pm; shows start at 6:45pm. Admission Rs100.

See India Foundation (tel. 369471). From M.G Rd., follow Warriom Rd. 2 blocks east; the Foundation will be on the right under the huge painted face of a Kathakali dancer. Director Devan has been performing here for 26 years. Make-up begins at 6pm; dance starts at 6:45pm. Admission Rs100.

Kerala Kathakali Centre, in the Cochin Aquatic Club near the Fort Cochin bus stand, features a young troupe of artists. Make-up begins at 5pm; dance starts at 6:30pm. Tickets for the small hall can be reserved at some hotels. Admission Rs70.

Kerala Kathakali Kendra (theater tel. 355003; office tel. 740030), in the Bolghatty Palace on Bolghatty Island near the ferry jetty. The palace was built by the Dutch in 1744. Make-up starts at 4pm; prayer, then dance at 6pm. Admission Rs100.

Art Kerala (tel. 366231). From Jos Junction, follow Durbar Hall Rd. toward the railway station; take 1st right onto Chittoor Rd., then the 1st left into Kannanthodath Ln.; hall is on the right. Elaborate make-up process precedes 6pm shows (Rs100).

BACKWATER CRUISES

Beyond the city are magical green fields, palms, and lazy backwaters—some of India's most remarkably green and beautiful landscapes. Kerala's tourist industry has capitalized on the verdance by offering backwater tours on non-motorized boats through the mazes of lagoons, lakes, canals, and streams. The privately run **Tourist Desk** charters tours daily, from 9am to 1:30pm and 2 to 6:30pm (Rs275; save Rs50 by booking directly at the Tourist Office). A guide paddles the vessel, which contains no more than six people, for several enchanting hours, stopping for a fresh coconut break and a stroll through the paddy fields. The flora and fauna are remarkable, as is the opportunity to see Keralan village life (although you'll still be hit up for pens by kids). In season, reserve at least one day in advance; off season, show up 30 minutes before departure. The Tourist Desk also conducts special **moonlight cruises** on full moon nights in-season. The Tourist Desk can arrange almost any of your Keralan fantasies—from fishing jaunts to visits to *coir* factories. The **KTDC** also provides backwater tours on country boats that leave daily at 8:30am and 2:30pm (Rs300). A **sunset tour** runs daily (5:30-7pm, Rs30); the Periyar Tiger Reserve tour leaves at 7:30am on Saturdays and returns Sunday at 8pm (Rs250, doesn't include accommodation).

Don't Make That Face or It'll Stick That Way

Kathakali, which means "story play," is one of India's four schools of classical dance. Transformed into gods and demons by the application of wildly colored make-up, massive golden headdresses, and skirts bright and full enough to put any ballerina to shame, the performers are traditionally men who have studied scripture, Kalaripayatu, Ayurvedic massage, and music for eight years beginning at the age of 10 or 12. Make-up is elaborate, and dancers require training lasting 4 years. Emphasis is given to proper lifestyle and the deep understanding of archetypes set out in the *Vedas*. The dancers communicate through the use of 24 *mudras*, hand gestures augmented by convulsive movements of the eyes and facial muscles and the pounding dancing of belled feet. By using combinations of these 24 *mudras* (signifying "love," "courage," "bee drinking from a lotus flower," etc.), stories from the *Ramayana* and *Mahabharata* are told. Ear-piercing drums and classical vocals narrate the story. Although traditional Kathakali was (and is on special holy days) performed as part of a temple ritual, the modern art of Kathakali has been truncated neo-colonial-style: now most shows last only one hour and are given in theaters filled with tourists hoping to "watch the Gods dance."

■ Near Cochin

In the village of **Kadalikad,** 55km southeast of Cochin, the 2.5-hectare **Haritha Farms** was established in 1962 as a rubber and coconut plantation. In 1990, the farm converted to sustainable farming, discontinuing the use of all pesticides. It continues to strive to be a model for "economically viable eco-farming," re-establishing *thodi*, an old Keralan system. Haritha Farms hosts a maximum of eight guests per day, offering traditional Keralan cooking, a tour of the spice garden with explanations of sustainable farming methods, and an exploration of the farm (by foot or by bicycle). The place is also great for short hikes and a swim in the clean river. Reservations are necessary: contact the Tourist Desk in Ernakulam or call the farm (tel. (0485) 260216; leave a message at (0484) 313621). Entry to the farm and food for the day is Rs450; plus overnight stay, Rs900 for a single or Rs1200 for double-occupancy. **KSRTC buses** from Ernakulam, Trivandrum, Kottayam, and Calicut stop in nearby Muvattupuzha, from whose private bus stand they run frequently to Thodupuzha, stopping in Kadalikad, 150m from the farm.

The hill station of **Munnar,** 4½hr. from Cochin, is situated at an elevation of 2000m, where three streams come together in a land of lush tea plantations. Popular with Indian tourists, especially Cochinites, the accommodations are often fully booked. Although the best time to visit is between November and May, Munnar's country setting beckons to the tired city dweller and harried tourist alike even in the monsoon months. The KTDC Tourist Office in Cochin recommends the following budget accommodations: **Munnar Tourist Home** (tel. 30736; doubles Rs250); **S.N. Lodge** (tel. 30212; doubles Rs350-400); **Hotel Ambat** (tel. 30661; doubles Rs150); and **Krishna Tourist House** (tel. 30669; doubles Rs150). A trek connects Munnar and Kodaikanal, and Ernakulam National Park is nearby (about 20km away). **Buses** run between **Munnar** and **Cochin** (5 per day, 4½hr.); **Kottayam** (7 per day, 5hr.); **Kumily** (4 per day, 4½hr.); **Madurai** (1 per day, 6hr.); and **Trivandrum** (5 per day, 8hr.).

■ Trichur (Thrissur) തൃശൂർ

With its high concentration of universities, museums, and temples, Trichur bills itself as the "cultural capital of Kerala," but most foreign visitors only come for the annual Puram Festival held in April and May. During Puram, deity-bearing revelers from neighboring villages, heralded by musicians and brightly bedecked elephants, descend on the tiny town, as hordes of tourists and locals cheer wildly. During the rest of the year, Trichur is rather unextraordinary, but serves as an adequate stopover. You won't find the usual tourist attractions, but by the same token, you won't *be* the usual tourist attraction in this workaday city.

ORIENTATION

Trichur is laid out like a wheel. The hubcap is the vast, green **Swaraj Round,** on which stands **Vadakkunathan Temple.** The major roads spoke off the Round: moving clockwise, these are **Mahatma Gandhi (M.G.), Shornur, Palace, College, High, Municipal Office, Kurrappam,** and **Marar Roads.** Most hotels and restaurants are clustered on these roads, near the Round. Following Mara Rd. 500m away from the Round leads to the **KSRTC bus stand** and farther down, the **railway station.**

PRACTICAL INFORMATION

Trains: The **railway station,** Mara Rd., is 1km from the Round. Trains to Goa and Maharashtra use the newly opened **Konkan Railway.** As of July, 1998 the line was still experiencing delays of up to 16hr. Fares are 2nd/1st class. To: **Bangalore** (*Bangalore Exp.* 6526, 11hr., 5:25pm, Rs189/604); **Calicut** (5 per day, 6am-6pm, 3hr., Rs36/180); **Chennai** (8:30am, 6, and 7:25pm, 15hr., Rs132/642); **Delhi** (*Kerala Exp.,* 4:10pm, 43hr., Rs431/1823); **Mangalore** (*Malabar Exp.* 6329, 12:25am; *Parasuram Exp.* 6349, 12:30pm, 10hr., Rs79/398); **Mumbai (Kurla)** (*Netravati Exp.* 6636, 6:20am, 24hr., Rs348/1309); **Madgaon** (*Parasuram Exp.* 6349, 12:30pm, 8hr.); **Trivandrum** (8 per day, 6hr., Rs73/361).

Buses: The **KSRTC bus stand** is on Marar Rd. To: **Alleppey** (frequent, 3½hr., Rs50); **Calicut** (frequent, 3hr., Rs45); **Ernakulam** (frequent, 2hr., Rs30); **Kottayam** (frequent, 3hr., Rs40); **Mangalore** (9pm, 8hr., Rs135); **Trivandrum** (frequent, 7hr., Rs105). **Sakthan Thampuran bus stand,** T.B. Rd., sends frequent private buses to Calicut, Guruvayoor, and Irinjalakuda.

Local Transportation: Most of Trichur's sights and accommodations are within walking distance. **Auto-rickshaws** are plentiful, however, and meters are the norm. Rs5 first km, Rs3 each subsequent km.

Tourist Office: The **KTDC** office, Yatri Nivas Hotel (tel. 332333), has, like Trichur, little to offer. Open 24hr. The **DTPC** office, Palace Rd. has decent maps and brochures, but the staff's English is lacking. Open M-Sa 9am-6pm.

Currency Exchange: State Bank of India, on the round near Palace Rd., exchanges foreign currency and traveler's checks. Open M-F 10am-2pm, Sa 10am-noon.

Bookstore: Current Books, M.G. Rd., off the Round. Large selection of highbrow reads (Camus, Naipaul) and juicy trashies. Random shelving system and Grisham galore. Open M-Sa 9am-8pm.

Hospital: West Fort Hospital (tel. 27822), W. Fort-Punkunnam Rd., off M.G. Rd.

Post Office: The **GPO** is near the Sakthan Thampuran bus station. *Poste Restante* is at the enquiry counter. Open M-Sa 10am-5pm. **Postal Code:** 680020.

Telephone Code: 0487.

ACCOMMODATIONS

During Puram, prices are triple or quadruple the rates listed below.

Yatri Nivas, Palace Rd. (tel. 332333), about 1½km from the Round (rickshaw Rs7). Trichur's best bargain is this KTDC-run operation, featuring big, clean rooms with printed bedspreads and large bathrooms (squat and seat toilets). Restaurant and beer parlor attached, but no room service. Doubles Rs150, with A/C Rs400.

Hotel Elite International (tel. 421033; fax 442057), on the Round, between Kuruppam and Municipal Office Rd. Cheap by local standards. Huge beds easily fit four. Phones and seat toilets all around. Attached restaurant serves up the usual. Check-out 24hr. Singles Rs210, with A/C and TV Rs410; doubles Rs260/480; quad Rs400.

FOOD

Trichur's eating scene is wholly unremarkable. Visitors choose between cheap South Indian coffee-house fare and overpriced hotel meals. There is one bright spot: fresh-fried banana chips are available on the road to the railway station.

Ming Palace, across from the Elite Hotel, on the 2nd floor. Yummy Chinese (Rs25-45) dished out by a courteous staff. Alcohol-free, but the red lanterns and chintzy furniture make for an intriguingly seedy air. Open daily 11am-10pm. Visa, MC.

Hotel Bharath Restaurant, behind the Elite Hotel, offers cheap veg. food (*idlis* Rs5). Pepsi is available and frosty-cold. Open daily 6:30am-10:30pm.

SIGHTS AND ENTERTAINMENT

Most tourists only know Trichur by its association with the **Puram Festival,** held annually each April and May. This festival features a multitude of elephants, masses of onlookers, and noisy bands—Indian pageantry at its very best. During this festival period, hotels fill up fast and charge extravagant rates, so plan well in advance. The festival is held on the grounds of the **Vadakkunathan Temple.** The main temple is dedicated to Shiva and sits on the site at which his bull, Nandi, is said to have rested. The temple is closed to non-Hindus.

The **Art Museum** and **Zoo** are in the northeast corner of Trichur, about 2km away from the Round. (*Museum open T-Sa 10am-5pm. Zoo open Tu-Sa 9am-5:15pm. Joint ticket Rs4. Camera fee Rs3.*) The zoo is typically pathetic, but the museum has a good collection of carvings, sculptures, and jewelry (one of Trichur's main industries). The **Archaeological Museum** is about 30m up the road, but is only worth seeing for its architecture (*Open Tu-Sa 9:30am-5pm. Free.*) Trichur's **gold jewelry industry** is renowned; excellent craftsmanship can be found in the several stores clustered around the Round, especially on Municipal Office Rd.

▨ Calicut (Kozhikode) കോഴിക്കോട

Calicut was once among India's best-celebrated seaports. As early as the 7th century, it was the harbor of choice for Chinese and Middle Eastern spice traders. In 1498, Malabar-man Vasco da Gama tread his first subcontinental steps just north of here, catalyzing a three centuries-long struggle between spiciers from various European countries, as well as a shorter one between Haider Ali and his son, Tipu Sultan. In 1792 Calicut was conquered by the British, who corrupted its Malayalam name of Kozhikode, coming up with the word "calico," a cotton fabric woven here. Present-day Calicut, however, hardly lives up to its vivid history. Those who imagine a city filled with ruined forts, wharfside temples, and cartloads of black pepper will be disappointed to find a dearth of potential Kodak moments in this small, bustling city which serves mostly as a stopover between Cochin and Mysore.

ORIENTATION

At the center of town is **Mananchira Park,** flanked on the right by **Bank Road,** which runs north-south and turns into **G.H. Road** as it heads south, and on the left by **Town Hall Road.** Following Bank Rd. north, **Mavoor Road (Indira Gandhi Road)** runs off to the right, leading to the **KSRTC Bus Station.** To the south, G.H. Rd. intersects with **M.M. Ali Road,** which leads east to an older part of the city. The **railway station** is on Town Hall Rd., southwest of the park. The **beach,** 2km west of town center, is not safe for visitors walking alone.

PRACTICAL INFORMATION

Airport: The airport is at Karippur, 23km from Calicut, accessible by taxi. **Air India** and **Indian Airlines** office, Bank Rd. (tel. 766243 or 755343). To: **Chennai** (1-2 per day, 2hr., US$80); **Coimbatore** (1 per day, 30min., US$35); **Mumbai** (1 per day, 1½hr., US$140). **Jet Airways** (tel. 356518) also has daily flights to Mumbai.

Trains: The **railway station** (tel. 703822) is about 1km south of the park; follow Town Hall Rd. Fares are 2nd/1st class. To: **Delhi** (*Mangala Exp.* 2617, 3:40pm, 40hr., Rs447/2312); **Ernakulam** (5 per day, 4½hr., Rs53/171); **Mangalore** (8 per day, 5hr., Rs61/229); **Mumbai** (*Netravati Exp.* 6636A 9:45am, 20hr., Rs176/349).

Buses: KSRTC Bus Stand (tel. 723796), near the intersection with Bank Rd. Slightly dirty and scary, but at this point in your travels, so are you. To: **Bangalore** (16 per day, 3:30-midnight, 8½hr., Rs122); **Cochin** (27 per day, 5½hr., Rs75); **Mangalore** (12:20 and 4:10am, 7hr., Rs92); **Mysore** (19 per day, 12:30am-8pm, 5½hr., Rs80); **Trivandrum** (15 per day, 10hr., Rs150). Cleaner and cheaper **private buses** run from the **new bus stand,** farther down Mavoor Rd. To: **Cochin** (16 per day, Rs45); **Devala,** near Ooty (2:15pm, 10hr., Rs40); **Mangalore** (5:45am, 8:30, 9:30, and 10:30pm, 6hr., Rs68); **Mysore** (6 and 8:30am, 6hr., Rs56).

Local Transportation: Auto-rickshaws are ready, willing, and metered (Rs5 per km). **Taxis** are unmetered and readily available. **Local buses** run around town and to the beach. Buses to Beypore run every 30min. from the new bus stand; most green buses run from Malabar Mansion to within walking distance of the museums.

Tourist Office: The **KTDC** office (tel. 721394 or 721395) is in the Malabar Mansion on the south side of the park. It is staffed by KTDC officials 9am-5pm, but maps and brochures are sold 24hr.

Budget Travel: PL Worldways, 3rd fl., Lakhotia Computer Centre (tel. 722564), at the intersection of Mavoor Rd. and Bank Rd. Books airline reservations and obtains foreign visas. Open M-F 9:30am-1pm and 2-5:30pm, Sa 9:30am-1:30pm.

Currency Exchange: State Bank of India (tel. 721321) changes foreign currency and traveler's checks. Open M-F 10am-2pm, Sa 10am-noon. **PL Worldways** (see above) also cashes traveler's checks.

Library: Kozhikode Public Library, on the right of Malabar Mansion. This A/C haven has a decent selection and an original painting by Keralan homeboy M.F. Hussain on the south wall. Open Tu-Su 2-8pm.

Market: An extensive fruit and vegetable market is on the left side of M.M. Ali Rd. Silver and gold jewelry-sellers are sequestered along this road, too.

Hospital: The best hospital in town is **National Hospital,** Mavoor Rd. (tel. 723066), near the KSRTC bus station. Its **pharmacy** is open 24hr.

Police Station: (tel. 703499), near the Railway Station.

Emergency: Police, tel. 100. **Fire,** tel. 101. **Ambulance,** tel. 102.

Post Office: On the west edge of the park. The impressive shiny marble-and-granite post office sells stamps M-Sa 8am-7:45pm, Su 2-4:45pm and mails parcels M-Sa 4-7:30pm, Su 2-4:30pm. **Postal Code:** 673001.

Telephone Code: 0495.

ACCOMMODATIONS

Sasthapuri Tourist Home (tel. 723281), further down M.M. Ali Rd., on the left. Makes you feel part of the shopping mall it's in, but the most interesting part of town is just outside. Singles Rs75, with bath Rs100; doubles Rs100/150.

Malabar Mansion (tel. 722391), on the south side of the park. KTDC-run, with a tourist reception desk, A/C restaurant and beer parlor. All rooms have TV, phone, and attached bath. A/C rooms are huge and well-outfitted. Singles Rs175, with A/C Rs360; doubles Rs225/400; quads Rs350. Extra person Rs60, in A/C rooms Rs120.

Metro Tourist Home (tel. 766029), at the junction of Mavoor and Bank Rd. Set in the whizzing, grinding heart of town, it's grimy but a goodie. Deluxe rooms have breathing room and seat toilets; non-deluxe rooms are tiny, and you'll have to squat. Singles Rs125; doubles Rs175; deluxe Rs225.

Kalpaka Tourist Home (tel. 720222), Town Hall Rd., just south of the park. Run by a cadre of alarmingly efficient women. Big beds with sheets and blankets. Hot water 24hr. Singles Rs115, with A/C Rs350; doubles Rs175/450. MC, Visa.

FOOD

Woodlands Restaurant, in the Hotel Whitelines on G.H. Rd. not far from the intersection with M.M. Ali Rd. Set in a groovy circular, maroon dining room, this restaurant feels more like a diner than a *dhaba,* but its excellent all-veg. food is the real thing. *Thalis* Rs24-35. Open daily 8am-10pm.

Kalpaka Restaurant, Kalpaka Tourist Home. No meat, but a variety of Indian, Chinese, and pseudo-Continental dishes (Rs15-35). Open daily 7am-10pm.

Casino Restaurant, across from the Metro Tourist Home. Standard Indian/Chinese menu in stunningly plush (for Calicut) environment. The South Indian all-you-can-eat lunch buffet (noon-3pm) is a mere Rs45. No smoking. Open daily noon-11pm.

Cochin Bakery, across from the State Bank of India. Spicy snacks, cold drinks, and scrumptious pastries. Open daily 9:30am-9pm.

The Nest, at Seaqueen Hotel, features a dimly lit, uninspired dining room, but its seafood is probably the best in town—and it's priced accordingly. Alcohol served. Open daily 7am-10pm.

SIGHTS AND ENTERTAINMENT

> **Warning:** The beachfront is known by locals to be home to illegal drug trafficking and a dangerous drug culture. Heed local cautions and avoid the beach after dark.

Tourist pamphlets blithely suggest **shopping** as the premier entertainment in Calicut: fancy clothing stores line "Sweet Meat Street" (S.M. St.) and Mavoor Rd., while jewelers pack into tiny shops on Palayam Rd., near the interesting gauntlets of the **fruit and vegetable market. The Sangam Movie Theatre** near the railway station features Hindi flicks and films of the John Woo *oeuvre.* Every evening at the park, a little guy in a box madly flips switches to manipulate a **Music Fountain** choreographed to Hindi pop. *(6:30pm, 2hr. Admission Rs3.)*

Walks on the **beach,** just 2km from the city center, are not as nice as they sound. A local tourist handbook reads, "two sea piers almost 125 years old are a speciality." (Translation: two old rotting piers extend into the sea from a slightly muddy beach—and is that sewage running into the ocean there?)

The **Pazhassiraja Museum,** East Hill, 5km from Calicut, has copies of ancient mural paintings, bronzes, old coins, dolmonoid cysts (for geology buffs only), and umbrella stones. Take a rickshaw or taxi, or a green bus from the front of Malabar Mansion (ask the driver to make sure the bus is going to West Hill—the distance to East Hill is walkable from there). Next door, the **Krishna Menon Museum** houses the personal belongings of the late Indian president (who was Keralan), and the **Art Gallery** has a collection of paintings by Raja Ravi Varma. *(Museums and gallery open Tu-Su 10am-5pm.)*

Although no one will confuse Calicut with a shopper's nirvana, the Comtrust Store on Town Hall offers a glimmer of *satori.* It's the outlet store for the factory next door that produces hand-loomed fabrics including damask tablecloths and towels. *(Open M-F 10am-1pm and 2:30-7:30pm.)*

Ten kilometers—and 100 years—away from Calicut is the ship-building town of **Beypole** (round-trip by taxi Rs200). Step back a century, and realize why power tools were invented. Under thatched roofs, but otherwise exposed to the elements, master woodworkers carve, scrape, and pound huge beams into barges without the benefit of metal or electricity. Each amazing ship takes approximately two years to complete.

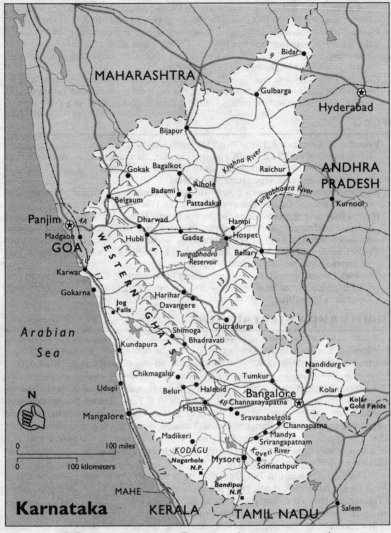

Karnataka ಕರ್ನಾಟಕ

Karnataka's coastline is dominated by the jagged Western Ghats, which shield the Deccan Plateau from the torrential monsoons of the coast. On the plateau, saffron rocks give way to verdant fields and narrow waterways. The area upland of the Ghats is forested with teak and sandalwood, and the rivers produce so much hydroelectric power that Karnataka used to sell its surplus energy to neighboring states. The boulder-filled terrain around the Ghats provided material for some of India's ancient architectural masterpieces: in the north, Chalukyan temples and the Vijayanagar ruins at Hampi; in the south, the florid temples at Belur, Halebid, and Somnathpur.

Despite the ancient monuments and residents as mild as the climate, the attitude here is neither overly traditional nor alarmingly cosmopolitan, and Karnataka is one of India's most progressive states. The British Raj had direct control of Mysore State for a relatively brief period, and the native maharajas who ruled the state under British protection until 1947 gave it a cohesive vision—they were hailed for their efforts to speed modernization. In 1956, Kannada-speaking regions in the north were added to the Mysore State, creating a Kannada-speaking state, renamed Karnataka in 1973.

🐘 HIGHLIGHTS OF KARNATAKA

- India's technology capital, **Bangalore** beckons with pubs, gardens, unbelievable shopping, and all things cyber (p. 563).
- The **Maharaja's Palace** (p. 578) is a fairytale vision set amidst the laid-back, sweet-smelling chaos of **Mysore** (p. 574).
- Hippie-tested and UNESCO-certified, **Hampi's** extensive and intricate **ruins** (p. 591) are nice enough to make you glad to be in the middle of nowhere.

■ Bangalore ಬೆಂಗಳೂರು

Bangalore is a strange place, where American executives and their Indian counterparts down *dosas* streetside, where local kids open cyber-cafes in their backyards and auto-rickshaws display web addresses in their rear windows. A city of direct satellite links and three-*lassi* lunches, of Hewlett-Packard and Microsoft, as well as Wipro Systems and other local players, Bangalore is ground zero for India's technological revolution. A sizeable chunk of the world's software is written here, and in the conference rooms along M.G. and Residency Roads, India's wired elite plans to sell the trappings of technology to the world's largest middle class—we're talking hundreds of millions of potential customers here. This is the wild West, Silicon Valley come to India.

When Kempegowda, a petty chieftain under the Vijayanagar Empire, founded Bangalore in 1537, his son built four watchtowers and decreed that the city should never spread beyond them. Four and a half centuries later, the towers still stand, but modern Bangalore gushes far beyond their limits, both physically and metaphorically. The growth of India's fifth largest city (pop. 4.5 million) has been accelerated by the influx of rural Karnatakans as well as Tamils, Keralites, and North Indians lured by Bangalore's mild climate and cosmopolitan feel, all looking for their big break.

Bangalore offers more for foreigners than just a place to check email, eat franchise fast-food, and check out some of India's best nightlife. There's a palpable excitement about the city, as the epidemic optimism of a nation's technological dreams spreads and shifts. Bangalore is changing fast, and it is unclear how long the city can maintain its upward trajectory—whatever happens here, it'll be quite a ride.

ORIENTATION

The hub of modern, international Bangalore is the intersection of **Mahatma Gandhi (M.G.) Road** and **Brigade Road.** South of and parallel to M.G. Rd. are **Church Street** and **Residency Road,** home of high-tech pubs, high-class hotels, and shops. North of M.G. Rd. is the aptly-named **Commercial Street,** whose shops lead west towards **Shivajinagar,** a bustling market district that is downtown for most locals. Most of the museums are in **Cubbon Park,** which stretches along **Kasturba Road** from **Kempegowda Road** to M.G. Rd. The **Majestic** area, near the **City Railway Station** and **bus stand,** is fertile ground for budget hotels. South of Majestic is the frenetic **City Market** area, with its unpaved narrow roads, bullock carts, temples, and mosques.

PRACTICAL INFORMATION

Transportation

Airport: southeast of the city, 8km from the M.G. Rd. area. A Rs30 auto-rickshaw ride from downtown. There's a 24hr. pre-paid taxi booth at the airport to get into town. Unless otherwise noted, airline offices are open M-F 9:30am-1pm and 2-5pm,

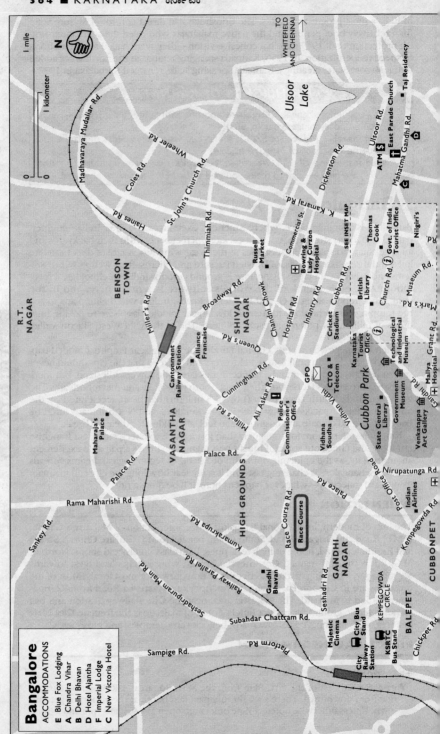

Bangalore

ACCOMMODATIONS

E Blue Fox Lodging
A Chandra Vihar
B Delhi Bhavan
D Hotel Ajantha
F Imperial Lodge
C New Victoria Hotel

N

1 mile
1 kilometer

TO
WHITEFIELD
AND CHENNAI

Ulsoor Lake

Taj Residency

Ulsoor Rd.
ATM
East Parade Church
Mahatma Gandhi Rd.

Dickenson Rd.

K. Kamaraj Rd.

SEE INSET MAP

Thomas Cook
Govt. of India Tourist Office
Niligiri's

Commercial St.

Russell Market

Bowring & Lady Curzon Hospital

Church Rd.
British Library

St. John's Church Rd.

Thimmiah Rd.

Broadway Rd.

Chandni Chowk

Hospital Rd.

Infantry Rd.

Cubbon Rd.

Mark's Rd.

Museum Rd.

Madhavaraya Mudaliar Rd.

Wheeler Rd.

Coles Rd.

Haines Rd.

Miller's Rd.

BENSON TOWN

R.T. NAGAR

Maharaja's Palace

Palace Rd.

Rama Maharishi Rd.

Sankey Rd.

Palace Rd.

VASANTHA NAGAR

SHIVAJI NAGAR

Queen's Rd.

Cunningham Rd.

Miller's Rd.

Ali Askar Rd.

Alliance Francaise

Cantonment Railway Station

Police Commissioner's Office

GPO

CTO & Telecom

Vidhana Soudha

Cricket Stadium

Karnataka Tourist Office

Technological and Industrial Museum

Government Museum

Venketappa Art Gallery

State Central Library

Cubbon Park

Vidhan Vidhi

HIGH GROUNDS

Palace Rd.

Race Course Rd.

Kumarakrupa Rd.

Race Course

Nirupatunga Rd.

Post Office Road

Indian Airlines

Mallya Grant Rd.
Hospital

Gandhi Rd.

Kempegowda Rd.

CUBBONPET

BALEPET

Chickpet Rd.

Seshadri Rd.

GANDHI NAGAR

KEMPEGOWDA CIRCLE

Gandhi Bhavan

Railway Parallel Rd.

Seshadripuram Main Rd.

Subahdar Chattram Rd.

Sampige Rd.

Platform Rd.

Majestic Cinema

City Bus Stand

KSRTC Bus Stand

City Railway Station

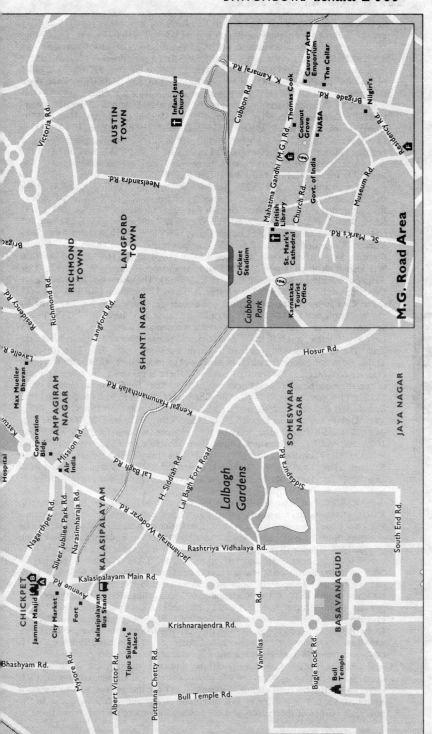

Sa 9:30am-1pm. **Domestic Airlines: Indian Airlines,** at the airport (tel. 526 6233, ext. 142) and Cauvery Bhavan, Kempegowda Rd. (tel. 526 6233, ext. 140), offers the most flights out of Bangalore. **NEPC,** 138A Brigade Gardens, Church St. (tel. 526 2842). **Sahara,** 1 Church St. (tel. 224 6435-9), on the corner of Church and Brigade St., opposite Hotel RRR. **Jet Airways,** 22 Ulsoor Rd. (tel. 227 6617), 1 block behind the Taj Residency. Open M-F 9:30am-5:30pm, Sa 9:30am-1pm. **East West Airlines,** 11A M.G. Rd. (tel. 558 8282), near St. Mark's Rd. Open daily 9:30am-5:30pm. To: **Ahmedabad** (3 per week, 2hr., US$200); **Calcutta** (2 per day, 2½hr., US$240); **Chennai** (5 per day, 45min., US$65); **Cochin** (1 per day, 1hr., US$70); **Coimbatore** (3 per week, 45min., US$55); **Delhi** (7 per day, 2½hr., US$230); **Goa** (4 per week, 1hr., US$95); **Hyderabad** (3 per day, 1hr., US$95); **Mangalore** (1-2 per day, 45min., US$70); **Mumbai** (9-11 per day, 1½hr., US$125); **Pune** (1-2 per day, 1½hr., US$130); **Trivandrum** (4 per week, 1hr., US$105). **International Airlines: Air India,** J.C. Rd., Unity Bldg. (tel. 227 7747), 1 block from Corporation Bldg. **Air France** (tel. 558 9397), **Kuwait Airways** (tel. 558 9021), and **Gulf Air** (tel. 558 4702) are all in Sunrise Chambers, 22 Ulsoor Rd., 1 block north of M.G. Rd., behind the Taj Residency. **British Airways,** St. Marks Rd. (tel. 227 1205). **KLM,** West End Hotel (tel. 226 8703, ext. 1362). **Lufthansa,** 42-2 Dickenson Rd. (tel. 558 8791), near Munipal Center. Open M-F 9am-5:30pm, Sa 9am-1pm. **Swissair,** 51 Richmond Rd. (tel. 221 1983), opposite BPL Plaza. Open M-F, 9:30am-5:30pm, Sa 9:30am-1:30pm. **Qantas,** 13 Cunningham Rd. (tel. 225 6611), near Wockhardt Hospital. Open M-F 9:15am-1pm and 2-5:30pm, Sa 9:30am-12:30pm. **Singapore Airlines,** Richmond Rd. (tel. 221 3833); **Thai Airways,** Imperial Court, Cunningham Rd. (tel. 226 7613); **United Airlines,** 12 Richmond Rd. (tel. 224462).

Trains: City Railway Station (arrival and departure information tel. 131, enquiry and reservations tel. 132), at the end of Race Course and Bhashyam Rd. The **reservations counter**, with special counters for women and foreigners, is in the building on your left as you face the station. Open M-Sa 8am-2pm and 2:15-8pm, Su 8am-2pm. The **enquiries** counters is in the main building. Open daily 7am-10:30pm. Trains from Bangalore are often booked weeks in advance. Go to the foreigner counter (counter 14) for regular booking; if there is no space available, you may get on the emergency quota. Prices are 2nd/1st class. To: **Calcutta** (*Howrah Exp.* 6512, F 11:50pm, 38hr., Rs344/1450); **Chennai** (*Lalbagh Exp.* 2608, 6:30am, 5hr.; *Brindavan Exp.* 2640, 2:30pm, 6hr.; *Chennai Mail* 6008, 10:15pm, 7hr., Rs82/334); **Delhi** (*Karnataka Exp.* 2627, 6:25pm, 42hr., Rs389/1672; *Rajdhani Exp.* 2429, W and F 6:45pm, 34hr., Rs422/1796); **Hospet** (*Saptagiri Exp.* 6057, 9:55pm, 10hr., Rs135/464); **Mangalore** (*Bangalore Tiruchi Exp.* 6532, 10:10pm, 26hr., Rs116/400); **Mumbai** (*Kurla Exp.* 1014, 12:10pm, 24hr.; *Udyan Exp.* 6530, 8:30pm, 24hr., Rs275/984); **Mysore** (*Kaveri Exp.* 6222, 7:15am, 3hr.; *Shatabdi Exp.* 2007, 10:55am, 2hr., Rs250; *Tippu Exp.* 6206, 2:25pm, 4hr.; *Chamundi Exp.* 6216, 6:30pm, 3hr., Rs50/190).

Buses: KSRTC Bus Stand, Bhashyam Rd. (tel 287 3377). Listed buses are with KSRTC (Karnataka Transport); other states' bus companies also service Bangalore—they have counters in the reservations office as well. Advanced reservations counters open 7-8am, 8:30am-4pm, and 4:30-11pm. To: **Badami** (5:30 and 9pm, 9hr., Rs134); **Bijapur** (8 per day, 4:30-10:15pm, 11hr., Rs154/183); **Chennai** (9 per day, 9:30-11:20am, 9, 9:30, and 10:30pm, 7hr., Rs75/112); **Cochin** (4 per day, 4-7:30pm, 12hr., Rs162/220); **Hassan** (every hr., 6am-11:40pm, 4hr., Rs48/65); **Hospet** (10 per day, 4:30pm-10:30pm, 8hr., Rs90/119); **Hyderabad** (5 per day, 4:30-10:30pm, 12hr., Rs174/219); **Kodaikanal** (9:15pm, 10hr., Rs133); **Mangalore** (20 per day, 8am-11:20pm, 8hr., Rs93/122); **Mumbai** (2 and 4pm, 24hr., Rs292/343); **Mysore** (frequent, 5:45-12am, 3hr., Rs48/63); **Panjim** (4:45pm, 11hr., Rs203); **Ooty** (8:30 and 10am, 10pm, 8hr., Rs103); **Trivandrum** (4pm, 16hr., Rs270). **Private buses** to Mumbai, Ooty, Mysore, and other destinations leave from the KSRTC bus stand area. Their agencies line the streets near the bus stand.

Local Transportation: Bangalore is diffuse, and even the hardiest walkers might need assistance at times. Don't be shy about insisting that **auto-rickshaws** use their meters—it's the law and common practice (Rs7 for the 1st km, Rs3.40 for each additional km). If you arrive by bus or rail, go to the auto-rickshaw queue in the northeast corner of the railway station parking lot—there's a policeman there to ensure meter use. From 10pm-6am, expect to pay around double the meter charge. Two kinds of local buses leave from the city bus stand—ordinary buses, and the swifter, more comfortable, and more expensive tan Pushpak buses. **Buses** to M.G. Rd. leave every few minutes (platforms 17 and 18 from 6:30am-10pm (Rs2/5). Route #7 serves the Corporation Building and M.G. Rd. (every 20min., Rs4). To Whitefield, take the #333e, 334 bus (Rs7, 1hr.). **U-Rent Services,** 19 RBDGT Bldg. (tel. 287 9760) rents **mopeds.** As you head out of the railway station, turn right and scan the sidewalk for their wooden sign (24hr. rental Rs200 plus Rs0.20 per km oil charge). Open daily 9am-6pm.

Oh Kannada!

Not everyone in Bangalore is pleased with the rapid Westernization that has accompanied the city's high-tech revolution. It wasn't too long ago that militant agrarians stormed and ransacked the KFC on Brigade Road, and attacks by vandals temporarily shut down Bangalore's Pizza Hut a few months after its 1996 opening. Western-bashing is not just relegated to the political fringe, though. In 1997 the Bangalore city council ruled that Karnataka's capital ought to do more to support Kannada, the state language. Thus it was decreed that all business signs must be primarily in Kannada. Today most of the shops in downtown Bangalore have large plastic Kannada placards placed above their original (English) signs. You can join in the fun by making a new cover for this book using the following Kannada text, which roughly translates to "let's go." *Navu boguvevu!*

ನಾವು ಹೂಗವನವು

Tourist and Financial Services

Tourist Offices: Government of India Tourist Office, 48 Church St. (tel. 558 5417). Turn on Church St. from Brigade Rd. The office is on the right (look for the sign—it's inside an office complex). Ask for a copy of *Bangalore This Fortnight.* Open M-F 9:30am-6pm, Sa 9am-1pm. **KSTDC,** 10/4 Kasturba Rd. (tel. 221 2901). Near the junction of Kasturba and M.G. Rd., opposite the Queen Victoria statue in Cubbon Park, 2 flights up in a big off-white building. Operates daily Bangalore bus tours (Rs75) and tours of far-off Karnataka cities like Belur and Halebid. This is also the place to book a night in one of KSTDC's myriad Mayura hotels. Open M-Sa 10am-5:30pm. Closed 2nd Sa.

Budget Travel: Scads of travel agencies line the streets near the railway and bus stations, but they focus on sight-seeing tours or private coaches to Mumbai, Mysore, Ooty, and other locales. For car rentals and bus, rail, air, and tour bookings, go to **Trade Wings,** 48 Lavelle Rd. (tel. 221 4595), across the street from the Airlines Hotel. Open M-F 9:30am-1pm and 2-5:30pm, Sa 9:30am-1pm.

Immigration Office: Foreigners Registration Office is at the **Office of the Commissioner of Police,** 1 Infantry Rd. (tel. 225 6242, ext. 251). Walk north along Cubbon Park past the GPO onto Queen's Rd. Take a left 1 block later onto Infantry. Open M-Sa 10am-5:30pm. To apply for visa extensions, head to Rm. 224 in Vidhana Soudha, the office of L. Shanmukha, Undersecretary to Government, Home and Transport Dept. (Passports and Foreigners). Open M-F 3:30-5:30pm.

Currency Exchange: Thomas Cook, 55 M.G. Rd. (tel. 558 6742), just before the intersection with Brigade Rd., is the fastest place to trade foreign cash or traveler's checks for rupees. Open M-Sa 9:30am-6pm. A 24hr. **ATM,** Municipal Center, 47 Dickenson Rd., outside the Hong Kong Bank (tel. 558 5444), accepts cards with Plus or Global Access logos. Walk east on M.G. Rd., 1 block past the parade grounds. Turn left on Dickenson Rd. at the East Parade Church. **Bank of Baroda,** Bluemoon Complex, 66 M.G. Rd., (tel. 559 6981) does cash advances on Visa and MC. 1% commission. Open M-F 10:30am-2:30pm, Sa 10:30-12:30.

Local Services

Bookstore: Gangaram's Book Bureau, 72 M.G. Rd. (tel. 558 6189). Horizontally and vertically immense with 3 floors of fiction, social sciences, stationery, postcards, and travel guidebooks for India and elsewhere. Open daily 10am-8pm. **Pre-**

mier **Bookshop,** 46/1 Church St. (tel. 558 8570), around the corner from Berry's Hotel. Stuffed with paperbacks, the shelves were either disposed of or obscured years ago. Open M-Sa 10am-1:30pm and 3-8pm.

Library: State Central Library, Cubbon Park (tel. 221 2128). Approach Cubbon Park from the Kasturba Rd. side, and follow Lavelle Rd. into the park. The library is a red building with green sills. Thousands of dusty tomes, although most patrons peruse the papers. Open Tu-Su 9am-7pm. **British Library,** 29 St. Mark's Rd. (tel. 221 3485), off M.G. Rd., near Koshy's. Technically, they don't allow nonmembers, but in practice they're not that stuffy. It's A/C. Membership Rs300 plus Rs20 for each book borrowed. Open Tu-Sa 10:30am-6:30pm.

Cultural Centers: Bharatiya Vidya Bhavan (tel. 226 7421), opposite the race course on Race Course Rd. The Bangalore branch of this all-India organization conducts cultural and literary activities. Library open M-F 10:30am-5:30pm, Sa 10:30am-1:30pm. **Max Mueller Bhavan,** 3 Lavelle Rd. (tel. 221 4964), at the end farthest from Kasturba Rd. German language courses. **Alliance Française** (tel. 225 8762), Thimmiah Rd., near Cantonment Railway Station and opposite the United News of India Bldg. Membership Rs300. French films and cultural programs. Library open M-F 9am-1pm and 4-7pm, Sa 9am-noon. For other **events,** check out the *Deccan Herald* (listings every day on p. 3; comprehensive listings M and F) or pick up a copy of *Bangalore This Fortnight* (free at the tourist office and in hotels and restaurants). Prices and times are not always accurate, but the magazine does provide a good sense of potential opportunities.

Market: Food World, 86 M.G. Rd. (tel. 559 1426), between St. Marks Rd. and Brigade Rd., is a full-on supermarket, complete with a packaged produce section and numerous fruit vendors outside. (Open M-Th 9:30am-9pm, F-Su 9:30am-10pm.) **Russell Market,** 2km north of M.G. Rd., off Cunningham St., Shivajinagar, is an indoor market selling fruit, flowers, veggies, and meat. The combined smells of raw fish and coriander make for a unique olfactory experience. Generally open M-Sa 9:30am-1:30pm, 4-8pm. **City Market,** 1½km southwest of City Railway Station, near Jamma Masjid, also sells food, and flowers indoors. Open from dawn to dusk.

Emergency and Communications

Pharmacy: Cash Pharmacy, 2 St. Mark's Rd. (tel. 221 0713). Open 24hr., **Al-Siddique Pharmaceutical Centre,** near City Market (tel. 605491).

Hospitals: The best-respected government hospital is **Bowring and Lady Curzon Hospital** (tel. 559 1362, ext. 244 for emergency), off Hospital Rd., 2km north of M.G. Rd. For private care, 3 modern hospitals are **Mallya Hospital,** 2 Vittal Mallya Rd. (tel. 227 7979), **Manipal Hospital,** 98 Rustumbagh Airport Rd., (tel. 526 6441) and **St. John's Medical College and Hospital,** Sarjapur Rd. (tel. 553 0724).

Emergency: tel. 100. **Fire,** tel. 101. **Ambulance,** tel. 102.

Police: Commissioner's Office, 1 Infantry Rd. (tel. 225 4501). From the intersection of M.G. and Kasturba Rd., walk northwest so that Cubbon Park is on your left; follow Queen's Rd. to Infantry Rd. and take a left. There is a branch in Cubbon Park (tel. 556 6242), next to the aquarium on Kasturba Rd. Headquarters (tel. 221 1803) are on Nirupatunga Rd., next to the YMCA.

Post Office: The **GPO** is a stone colossus on the corner of Raj Bhavan and Ambedkar Rd. in Cubbon Park. Several branches are convenient to M.G. Rd.: Brigade Rd., halfway between KFC and Wimpy's, across the street; and Museum Rd., at its intersection with St. Mark's Rd., which is a computerized post and telegraph office. All open M-Sa 10am-6pm. **Postal Code:** 560001.

Internet: You've come to the right place! **Cyber Café,** Windsor House, Brigade Rd. (tel. 555 0949). Rs60 buys you 30min. of online time plus a cup of coffee. Send and receive email, access the web, or use their software. Computers upstairs in the hipper cafe area are Rs100 for 45min. Open daily 7am-11pm. If you crave beer not coffee, opt for the **Cyber Pub** (see **Entertainment,** p. 572). Numerous other email centers abound in the M.G. Rd. area. The going rate is Rs60 per hour.

Telephones: The 24hr. **Central Telegraph Office** (tel. 286472) and **Public Telecom** (tel. 286 4019) are behind the GPO on Raj Bhavan Rd. **Telephone Code:** 080.

ACCOMMODATIONS

Even with a reservation, it's difficult to find a decently priced room in the hip, hi-tech, and happening **M.G. Road** area. The area around the city bus stand and city rail stations, with its innumerable high-rise hotels of sixty or more rooms, has plenty of cheap places to stay, but they are more impersonal and inconvenient to M.G. Rd.'s services (5km away). A string of hotels lines **Subahdar Chhatram Road (S.C. Road),** a five-minute walk from the City Railway Station. To get there, take the underground walkway (subway) toward the bus station, and the pedestrian overpass to the street, continuing for one block in the same direction. Hotels near the Corporation Building are equidistant from M.G. Rd. and the rail station. The lodges in **City Market** are cheap, but require residents to be adept at weaving through traffic and impervious to noise.

M.G. Road Area

Hotel Ajantha, 22 M.G. Rd. (tel. 558 4321). Clean, reasonably-priced rooms only a 10-minute walk from Brigade Rd. make Ajantha a rare find. Color TV, hot water 5-10am. Check-out 24hr. Singles Rs168; doubles Rs330, with A/C Rs562.

Hotel Imperial Lodge, 93-94 Residency Rd. (tel. 558 8391). Plain, entirely functional rooms. During the day, the place is quite cheery with its large windows and the bustle of the street below. Squat toilet, hot water in the morning. Attached restaurant. Check-out 24hr. Singles Rs170, doubles Rs300. Extra person Rs60.

Airlines Hotel, 4 Chennai Bank Rd. (tel. 227 3783), off Lavelle Rd. A 10min. walk from M.G. Rd. Hotel complex houses a travel agency, an STD/ISD/xerox booth, a supermarket, and a *sari* shop. Rooms aren't sparkling, but they're well-appointed: telephones, towels, seat toilets, and running hot water (until 10:30am). Check-out 24hr. Singles Rs600; doubles Rs800. Visa, AmEx. Reservations recommended.

New Victoria Hotel, 47-48 Residency Rd. (tel. 558 4076). Lost in trees and wildflowers, the New Victoria's bungalows were a British military canteen and library until about 1935. Attached baths have 24hr. hot water and seat toilets. Rooms are more average. Check-out 24hr. Singles Rs420, doubles Rs1050. Credit cards and traveler's checks accepted. Reservations recommended.

Blue Fox Lodging, 80 M.G. Rd. (tel. 558 3205). Between Food World and Brigade Rd. Two flights up from the neon-lit Blue Fox Restaurant and bar. Ten huge, pie-shaped if somewhat unpleasant-smelling rooms fixed around a spiral staircase. 24hr. hot water, telephones, and laundry service. Check-out noon. Doubles Rs460, with A/C Rs575, but try bargaining. Reservations couldn't hurt.

Near the Railway/Bus Stations

Royal Lodge, 251 S.C. Rd. (tel. 226 6951). Basic rooms in a strangely calm and welcoming atmosphere. Hot water 6:30-9am. Check out 24hr. Singles with bath Rs100. Doubles Rs140, with bath Rs205, with TV Rs253.

Sri Ramakrishna Lodge, S.C. Rd. (tel. 226 3041). Next to Kapali Theater. Rooms with extra-cushiony beds. Two attached restaurants (*thalis* Rs19), travel counter, and pharmacy. Each floor has a pleasant verandah. Squat toilets in immaculate bathrooms. Hot water 6:30-9:30am. Laundry and room service. Check-out 24hr. Singles 150-155; doubles 250-300.

Hotel Mahaveer, 8-1 Tankbund Rd. (tel. 287 3670). On the corner of Chickpet Rd. on the right outside the rail station exit. 66 modern, boxy-but-clean rooms have TVs, phones, and attached baths with seat toilets. Running hot water 5:30-9:30am, same-day laundry service, foreign exchange. Friendly management. Check-out 24hr. Singles Rs256; doubles Rs365, with A/C Rs500; triples Rs290. Visa, MC.

Hotel Adora, 47 S.C. Rd. (tel 220 0324). Very clean rooms have telephones but the barest of furnishings. Room service from the attached veg. restaurant, laundry, and travel services. Check-out 24hr. Singles Rs150; doubles Rs253.

City Market

Chandra Vihar, MRR Ln. (tel. 222 4146). Opposite the City Market Bldg., 1 block from Jamma Masjid. So typical, it's weird. Telephones and TV in all 50 rooms. Check-out 24hr. Singles Rs145; doubles Rs275. Extra bed Rs75.

Delhi Bhavan Lodge, Avenue Rd. (tel. 287 5045). Standard, clean rooms. Check-out 24hr., hot water 6-9am. Singles Rs100-120; doubles Rs150-180. Extra bed Rs30.

FOOD

Inundated by Wimpy's, Baskin-Robbins, and Pizza Hut, Bangalore's balkanized restaurant scene makes for some exciting dining. But whether you're into tandoori or KFC, burgers or *bhel puris*, lasagna or *lassi*, don't be afraid to exploit the culinary warfare—its fruits are almost uniformly good.

The Coconut Grove, 86 Church St., (tel. 559 6149), in the Spencer building. Reasonable prices and subdued tropical decor make this the place to come to discover the culinary gems of Kerala, Karnataka, and Tamil Nadu. Try the *kaikari kootu* (Rs45), a dish of lentils and grated coconut, or come during lunchtime for an unbeatable *thali* (Rs55 veg., 75 non-veg.). Seafood specialties Rs. 105-115. Pineapple-based *kaidachakka halwa* makes for a heavenly dessert. Open 12:30-4pm and 7-11pm.

Cafe Schorlemmer, Max Mueller Bhavan, 3 Lavelle Rd. Recently opened by a German expatriate, this rooftop cafe serves up the best apple strudel in all of South Asia (Rs20-30). Cheesecake Rs30, chocolate cake Rs15, *kugel* Rs20—as well as a full German lunch of the day (Rs50/90 veg./non), and sandwiches (Rs30-40). Loaves of brown bread and baguettes Rs30-60. Open M-Sa 9am-8pm.

Kamat, Unity Bldg., J.C. Rd. (tel. 222 4802). One of Bangalore's best-value Indian restaurants. Heaping *thalis* (noon-3pm) Rs30, Rs55 in the A/C section. Sweets counter. Open M-Sa 8am-11pm, Su 10am-3pm (snacks only) and 7-11pm.

Nilgiri's Café, 171 Brigade Rd. (tel. 558 8401), attracts a clientele so well-scrubbed that they look fresh from the dairy farm Nilgiri's founded in 1905. Into the mouths of babes go hefty grilled sandwiches and doughy cheese pizzas (Rs60-80). Hazelnut milkshakes (Rs30) bring customers to tears, as Lou Reed and the Cars croon away. Open daily 9am-11pm.

Karavalli, 66 Residency Rd. in the Gateway Hotel. Bangalore's most elegant Keralan coastal cuisine. *Appam* with fish or veg. stew is the specialty, but you shouldn't miss the coconutty curries. *Thalis* Rs215-250. French wine Rs90 per glass. Count on Rs300 for two people. Open daily 12:30-3:30pm and 7:30pm-midnight.

Casa Picolla, Devatha Plaza, 131 Residency Rd. (tel. 221 2907), a 10min. walk from the Brigade Rd. area, past Black Cadillac; half the Casa is underground. The food's not as ethereal as the decor, but it's cheap and cheesy (spinach lasagna Rs65). Steak Rs76. Save room for crepes, profiteroles, and cappuccino. Open daily 11:30am-10:30pm.

U.S. Pizza, 19 Church St. (tel. 559 9347). Remarkably good simulacra to be had: loads of cheese and toppings on a chewy crust. Free delivery within 3km. Rs55-70 for a 7-inch deep pan pizza. Garlic bread Rs25. Beer and wine available. Open daily 11am-11pm. Visa, MC, Diner's Club.

The Only Place, 158 Nota Royal Arcade, Brigade Rd. (tel. 558 8678). This restaurant has been serving beef burgers (Rs40), apple pie (Rs40), pancakes (Rs35), and lasagna (Rs75) for years. It's now a Bangalore institution, out-shouting its newer rivals. Open daily 11am-3pm and 6:30-11pm. MC, Visa, AmEx.

Shanbag Cafe, 92 Residency Rd., is the place for cheapish, pleasantly plump *dosas* (Rs17-23), cloud-like *puris* (Rs19), and *lassis* (Rs18). Service is mellow and conscientious—a rarity in Bangalore's restaurants. Open for *thalis* (Rs23-80) daily 11am-3:30pm and 7-10:30pm, for *chaat* 4-10:30pm.

The Rice Bowl, Lavelle Rd. (tel. 224 0216), in the basement of the Rama Hotel. Owned by the Dalai Lama's sister and niece, the 'Bowl represents the antithesis of all that is austere. The fried ravioli (Rs80) is indulgent and the date/banana pancake with ice cream blasphemously decadent. Open daily 11am-3:30pm and 7-11pm. Reservations recommended. Visa, MC.

Indian Coffee House, 78 M.G. Rd. (tel. 587088). Possibly the cheapest and smartest sit-down place on M.G. Rd. to grab a cup of joe (Rs4.50) and smoke a cigarette. The brew (black and unsugared, if you so desire) is served by festooned waiters. Peruse a newspaper over omelettes (Rs20) and toast (Rs6.50). Open daily 8:30am-8:30pm.

SIGHTS

Cubbon Park and Museums

Set aside in 1864 and named for the former chief commissioner Mark Cubbon, the Park consists of 132 hectares of lush greenery in the center of the city. The park extends from the corner of M.G. Rd. to the Corporation Building and provides much needed shade and escape from the buses, cars, and buildings that surround it. Cubbon Park houses the **K. Venkatappa Art Gallery and Government Museum** (tel. 286 4483). *(Open Tu-Su 10am-5pm. Admission Rs1.)* The former exhibits watercolor landscapes by K. Venkatappa, the Mysore court artist who painted much of the Maharaja's Palace in Mysore. The second floor displays works by contemporary Karnatakan artists. The Government Museum, now in its 112th year, is one of India's oldest. It houses Hoysalan sculptures and archaeological finds such as arrowheads from Mohenjo-Daro, pottery, coins, and megalithic bones. Next door is the **Visveswaraya Industrial and Technological Museum,** which celebrates Bangalore's industrial prowess from 1905, when City Market lit India's first light bulb, to Bangalore's current info-tech boom. *(Open daily 10am-5:30pm. Admission Rs10.)* Use your brain and muscle power to learn the inner workings of the pulley, the computer, and the nuclear bomb. Across the park lies the gothic **Attara Kachari,** which housed the 18 departments of the secretariat until 1956 (*attara* means "eighteen" in Hindi). It's now the turf of the High Court, where you can mingle with black-robed, wig-clad barristers. Across the road is the **Vidhana Soudha,** which now houses the Secretariat. In the early 1950s, members of a visiting Russian delegation quipped about the abundance of European architecture in Bangalore. Spurred to action by the Russians' remarks, the chief minister of Mysore state decided to construct this spectacular neo-Dravidian structure. The Vidhana Soudha became not only an affirmation of Indian sovereignty but also an assertion of Bangalore's new legislative power. It was built of pure Bangalore granite by craftsmen, most of whom were imported from Andhra Pradesh (one of Bangalore's largest slums was formed by the displaced masons' families). Atop the main entrance sits Emperor Ashoka's four-headed lion (the symbol of the Indian nation which can be seen in all rupee notes when they're held to the light). Statues of Jawaharlal Nehru and B. R. Ambedkar stand in the front lawn, gesticulating at each other beneath the self-congratulatory inscription proclaiming, "Government Work is God's Work." The building is not open to the public, but the wonderful exterior is flooded with light every Sunday night. Nearby, across from Raj Bhavan on T. Chowdiak Rd., is the eight-year-old **Jawaharlal Nehru Planetarium** (tel. 220 3234), built to commemorate the 100th birthday of the freedom fighter and prime minister who called Bangalore "India's city of the future." *(Open Tu-Su. Closed 2nd Tu. English shows at 4:30pm. Admission Rs10.)* Across the Golf Course (High Grounds), down Kumara Krupa Rd. from the five-star Windsor, sits the **Gandhi Picture Gallery** in **Gandhi Bhavan,** 2nd floor (tel. 226 1967). *(Open M-Sa 10:30am-1:30pm and 3-5pm. Free.)* It's a beautifully organized journey through the Mahatma's life, with grainy blown-up photographs, quotations full of Gandhian wisdom, as well as artifacts such as Gandhi's wooden *chappals* and clay drinking bowls. Glass-encased letters to Franklin Roosevelt, Tolstoy, Gokhale, and Nehru. Few visit this jewel; there's no permanent staff, and you'll need to ask to have the door unlocked. The library downstairs sells cheap copies of Gandhi's writings.

Lalbagh Gardens

Location: *2km south of Cubbon Park.* **Hours:** *Open daily dawn-dusk.* **Admission:** *Free.*

Haider Ali laid out Lalbagh Gardens in 1760. His son Tipu Sultan later extended the 16-hectare gardens to 96 hectares and added the mango grove. After Tipu's demise in 1799, the British took over Lalbagh, and Prince Albert Victor of Wales built the Glass House as homage to London's Crystal Palace in the late 1800s. The gardens are home to 150 different varieties of roses and 1000 kinds of tropical and subtropical flora and fauna, a giant floral clock, a lotus pond, and innumerable walkers, joggers, cyclists, and monkeys. One of the four watchtowers that Kempegowda built to mark Bangalore's city limits is here.

SOUTH INDIA

Take Me to Your Leader

With his expansive hairdo, saffron robes, and "What, me worry?" smile, Satya Sai Baba's photographic *avatars* decorate and bless restaurants, hotels, homes, and autos throughout India. Thought to be a divinely-sent miracle worker, and labelled "godman" by Western news services, he counts millions around the world as his faithful followers, who believe him to be a reincarnation of an early saint called Sai Baba—the prefix "Satya" means "truthful." Born in a small village, the young Satya first displayed his spiritual leanings at the age of 13. Stung by a scorpion, the boy fell into a trance and began chanting Sanskrit passages. His parents thought him possessed, and an exorcist was called in. When that failed, his father tried to beat the devil out of him, but Satya just infuriated him further by producing sweets out of thin air. Finally his father cried, "Who are you?" to which his son answered, "I am Sai Baba."

Since then, Satya Sai Baba has achieved renown through the usual methods: raising the dead, healing the sick, and producing diamonds out of thin air; however, he considers these "tricks" secondary to his main task of teaching spiritualism and spreading love. Thousands of Indians and foreigners flock to Sai Baba's ashrams in Andhra Pradesh and Karnataka, hoping to observe, learn, and bask in the aura of peacefulness that radiates, Afro-like, from the master.

Other Sights

Haider Ali also refurbished Bangalore's **fort,** opposite Vanivilas Hospital on Krishnarajendra Rd. It was originally built in mud and brick by Chikkadevaraga Wodeyar in the late 1600s as an extension of another of Kempegowda's forts, originally encompassing the area which now lies between the Corporation Offices and City Market. Though most of it was destroyed in the Anglo-Mysore War, the remains are beautifully preserved, with ornately carved Islamic-style arches and turrets, and an exquisite **Ganpati Temple** inside. Five-hundred meters south of the fort is **Tipu Sultan's Summer Palace,** which Tipu liked to call Lask-e-Jannat, "The Envy of Heaven," but which was really just a low-budget replica of Daria Daulat in Srirangapatnam. The palace took 10 years to complete because Haider Ali was killed during its construction and Tipu was busy avenging his death (you know how it goes). Most of the original wall paintings have been obscured by shiny brown paint. South of the Palace on Bull Temple Rd. is the **Bull Temple,** with a massive black Nandi over 500 years old. *(Open daily 8am-8pm.)* Legend has it that a raging bull used to torment local farmers by ravaging their fields at night. The frustrated farmers finally hired a night watchman who killed the bull with a crowbar. The next morning, they discovered that the carcass had transformed into a solid granite bull. Look closely, and you'll see the crowbar embedded in the poor beast's back.

Brindavan Ashram, 16km from Bangalore on Chennai Rd. in Whitefield, is Satya Sai Baba's Karnataka haunt, although he spends most of the year at his main ashram, Puttaparthi, in Andhra Pradesh. Sai Baba runs hospitals and schools, performs miracles, and enjoys quite a following. When he's in Whitefield, devotees and interested travelers can stay there for about Rs100 per night. For information call the ashram office (tel. 845 2233). City bus #333e, #334 (Rs7, 1hr.) runs to Whitefield, as do three trains (*Marikuppan* 256 and 254, 6:45am and 6:10pm; *Chennai Passenger* 96, 10:30am, 1hr., Rs4/65 for 2nd/1st class).

ENTERTAINMENT

Pubs and Bars

Though plagued by water shortages, Bangalore is never dry. Its burgeoning pub culture (second only to Mumbai's) has earned the city the title "Bar Galore." Most pubs are clustered around Brigade Rd., and they're frequented by regulars who greet the pubs' godfather-esque owners with hearty hugs and call the bartenders by their first names. Due to a recent city ordinance, pubs must close at 11pm. The police come by around midnight, suggesting that "good people sleep early," and stragglers exit quietly through the back door. Unless noted, pubs are open daily from 11am to 2:30pm and 5:30 to 11pm. Note that many pubs refuse admission to unaccompanied women.

The Cellar, 7 Curzon Ct., Brigade Rd. (tel. 555 0948), opposite the intersection with Church St. Woody decor and booths that encourage sinking into over a good conversation. The mellow afternoon may have been invented here. Proportionate representation of the sexes. Pitchers Rs136. Open daily 11am-3pm and 5-11pm.

The New Night Watchman, 4611 Church St. (tel. 558 8372), near Berry's Hotel. Caters to a largely North Indian crowd, which means it's one of the only pubs around that plays *bhangra*. The pub is shaped like a mini-stadium, with the bar in the center, in the surrounding audience. It's one big happy (if alcohol-induced) family. Happy Hour (11am-2:30pm) offers discounted drinks (pitchers Rs80, mugs Rs16, instead of Rs95/19). Visa, MC.

Peco's Pub, 34 Rest House Rd. (tel. 558 6047), one street south of Church St., off Brigade Rd. Hendrix, Marley, Joplin, and Zeppelin grace the walls as well as the stereo. Three floors packed with college-aged guzzlers imbibing mugfuls at Rs26. Rooftop has relaxing chairs. Open daily 10:30am-2:30pm and 5:30-10:30pm.

Cyber Pub, 2 Mohan Towers, 50 Residency Rd. Upstairs from The Black Cadillac. The most recent addition to both Bangalore's pub scene and info-tech scene combines the world of daytime with the world of night. Imbibe booze while chatting without inhibitions on-line, or sit in the regular bar section lighted by blue neon lights. Mug Rs25, pitcher Rs120. Internet 10am-10pm (Rs60 for 30min.).

The Pub World, 65 Residency St. (tel. 558 5206). Marginally more upscale than its neighbors, with oak banisters, lace curtains, and tapestried footstools. Well-lit, too, so you won't feel like a reprobate for pounding in the middle of the afternoon. Bartenders have honors degrees in chivalry. Mugs Rs35, pitchers Rs175.

The Black Cadillac, called "BC" by regulars, Mohan Towers, 50 Residency Rd. (tel. 221 6148). A few blocks west of Brigade Rd., with a red neon sign that is obscured so that all you can see from the street is a giant cursive "C." This is where Bangalore's fashionable elite go to see and be seen (model want-ads grace the walls). Sublimate in the sublime garden area. Mugs Rs22, pitchers Rs110.

NASA, 1/4 Church St. (tel. 558 6512). The walls are decorated with pictures of spaceships, astronauts, and everyone's favorite extra-terrestrial, Michael Jackson. The interior is correspondingly out of *Captain Eo.* The beer itself is pricey (mugs Rs30, pitcher Rs150), but atmosphere comes at a price, especially in space. Unaccompanied women not allowed.

Discos

Another much-loved city ordinance against late operation of discos prevents a full-fledged dancing scene from taking root. Still, a few clubs have managed to stay open. By far the most popular club is **The Club,** outside of town on Mysore Rd. (round-trip rickshaw will cost you Rs200-400). Unfortunately, lack of competition has meant that the club can play nonstop, overpoweringly loud techno music and be less than friendly to its patrons. What is surprising is the lack of energy and verve on the part of the rich and hip clientele. (Open M, W, F, Sa 9pm-5am; Rs300 per couple). Two other clubs in town draw significantly smaller crowds but therefore have more space for personal creative expression: **Orion,** on Residency Rd. (tel. 227 3546), above the Black Cadillac (open 9:30pm-2am W, F, and Sa) and **JJ's** (previously the Concorde Club) on Airport Rd., just before the airport. (Open W-Sa 10-2.) However, the party doesn't get started till past midnight. Don't miss Sunday **jazz night,** where patrons relax to groovy old rock and jazz.

Other Diversions

Several cinemas in the M.G. Rd. area play English-language flicks. **The Plaza,** 74 M.G. Rd. (tel. 558 7682), and **The Rex,** Brigade Rd. (tel 571350), show not-too-old American movies (admission Rs10-35). Try to buy tickets at least an hour in advance.

Nrityagram Dance Village (tel. 846 6313; fax 846 6312; http://www.allindia.com/nritya), 35km from Bangalore on Bangalore-Pune Highway, was established and is run by Protima Gauri, possibly the best Odissi dancer in India. Dancers from all over India come to train here and Gauri also conducts classes for children from neighboring villages. The village is open from September to May (closed M), and it's possible to arrange an hour-long lecture-demonstration of Odissi and Kathak dance, along with a tour of the architecturally-award-winning village, a lecture on Indian philosphy and culture, and an organically grown lunch. (Min. 4 people, Rs650 each; advance booking required. Casual tour Rs20 per person. Open 10am-5pm Tu-Su. Closed June and July.) **Buses** run regularly from Bangalore (#253, 253A, 253D from City Market) to Nrityagram, but the village is 5km from the bus stand and there aren't many auto-rickshaws around. It's easier to arrange a private **taxi** (about Rs500 round-trip) or book through Cosmopole Travels (tel. 228 1591) or Cox and Kings Travel (tel. 223 9258). In the first week of February, the dance village conducts an all-night dance and music festival, free of charge, with performances by Gauri and her students as well as musical heartthrobs Zakir Hussain and Amjad Ali Khan. Buses run directly to the village during the program and the amphitheater is packed with more than 25,000 people. Get there by 5:30pm if you don't want to stand all night.

The **Windsor Manor Sheraton,** 25 Sankey Rd. (tel. 226 9898), near the High Grounds, will let you use their outdoor swimming pool for Rs300 (open daily 7am-7pm). If you don't mind a much less luxurious atmosphere, go for a dip in the public **Kensington Swimming Pool** (tel. 536413), opposite Ulsoor Lake. (Membership fee Rs100, plus Rs3 per hr. Open daily 6am-5pm.)

SHOPPING

Even if you've spent all your money in Bangalore bars, you should still check out Bangalore's arts and crafts emporia: tables covered with handpainting or inlaid with precious gems, *saris* fit for a rani, and sandalwood Krishnas taller than people. The government-run **Cauvery Arts Emporium,** 45 M.G. Rd. (tel. 558 1118), near Brigade Rd., has fair prices and a decent selection, though the salespeople are practically comatose (open M-Sa 10am-1:30pm and 3-7:30pm). You probably can't afford much at **Artefacts,** 56 Residency Rd. (tel. 559 6843)—it's more like an art gallery than an emporium. The paintings and giant statues provoke sharp intakes of breath—just hold it there, because exhaling might mar the works. They accept major credit cards, so you can rue the purchase of that antique jade Buddha later (open M-Sa 9:30am-8:30pm). In general, the M.G. Rd. area is the emporiophile's paradise, with arts and handicrafts shops selling stuff from all over India. On **Commercial Street,** you'll find *salwar kameez* and *saris* in unthinkable permutations of style, color, and price. **Kempegowda Road (KG Rd.)** also offers a wide selection at slightly lower prices, as well as various household goods. Finally, to get an idea where all of Bangalore's software fortunes are spent, head out to the glitzy **Kemp Fort,** Airport Rd. (tel. 529 9555), the self-proclaimed largest toy store in the universe.

■ Mysore ಮೈಸೂರು

When tourist brochure writers dream, they dream of Mysore. Phrases like "surrounded by lush, verdant countryside" and "shady streets, where the scents of jasmine and sandalwood mingle" have been used and overused to describe countless cities south of the Himalayas. But in Mysore, the cliches actually ring true, and visitors are rewarded with one of the few places in India that are even better than the brochures make them sound.

Mysore was ruled by the Wodeyar dynasty from the 15th century all the way up to Independence in 1947, and as the former capital of a princely state, the city is strewn with grand old palaces and other maharaja ex-haunts, as well as mounments, temples, gardens, and parks. Mysore's strong sense of tradition explodes during the annual Dasara festival, a ten-day-long celebration in October.

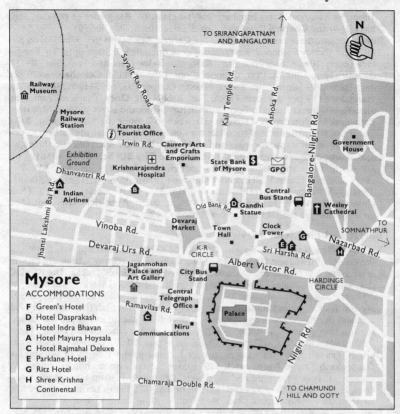

Mysore

ACCOMMODATIONS

F Green's Hotel
D Hotel Dasprakash
B Hotel Indra Bhavan
A Hotel Mayura Hoysala
C Hotel Rajmahal Deluxe
E Parklane Hotel
G Ritz Hotel
H Shree Krishna Continental

ORIENTATION

Although Mysore is dotted with rotaries and streaked with unforgiving twisty-turny roads, the city itself is quite compact. A visit to the summit of **Chamundi Hill,** southeast of the city, provides a surprising perspective on Mysore's tidy boundaries. Running north-south, **Sayajit Rao Road** bisects Mysore proper into roughly equal halves, cutting through **K-R Circle,** the true center of the city. The **City Bus Stand** is off the southeast quarter of K-R Circle. If you head east from K-R Circle, you'll walk along the outskirts of the gigantic **Maharaja's Palace.** About 300m north of K-R Circle, Sayajit Rao Rd. meets the east-west **Old Bank Road (Sardar Patel Road).** Old Bank Rd. leads east to a granite obelisk, a smaller rendition of Delhi's Gandhi Memorial: this is **Gandhi Square,** where you'll find a number of tourist accommodations. About 75m southeast is a tall **Clock Tower;** south of that, the road intersects Sri Harsha Road, which leads east to a north-south thoroughfare, **Bangalore-Nilgiri (B-N) Road.** North on B-N Rd., across from Wesley Cathedral, is the **Central Bus Stand,** and further north is **Irwin Road,** which leads west past the GPO, the State Bank of Mysore, and the tourist office. One block further west and set back from the road is the domed **railway station.**

PRACTICAL INFORMATION

Transportation

Trains: The **railway station** is at the intersection of Irwin and Jhansi Laxmi Bai Rd. The desks for enquiry (tel. 131) and reservations are open M-Sa 8am-2pm and 2:15-

10pm, Su 8am-2pm. Fares listed are 2nd/1st class. To: **Bangalore** (3 per day, 3hr., Rs41/170) and **Chennai** (*Shatabdi Exp.* 2008, 2:10pm, 7hr., Rs570).

Buses: Long-distance buses leave from the **Central Bus Stand** (tel. 520853), on B-N Rd., near Wesley Cathedral. Reservations desk open daily 7:30am-9pm. To: **Bangalore** (every 10min. 6am-9pm, 3hr., Rs36/48); **Belur** (7am and 1pm, 5hr., Rs41); **Bijapur** (1pm, 18hr., Rs183); **Chennai** (7pm, 12hr., Rs115); **Coimbatore** (20 per day, 7:15am-10:30pm, 5hr., Rs49); **Hassan** (22 per day, 6am-11pm, 3hr., Rs31); **Mangalore** (19 per day, 6am-11pm, 7hr., Rs68/100); **Ooty** (frequent, 7am-3pm, 5hr., Rs43). Direct buses to **Somnathpur** leave from the street in front of Wesley Cathedral, but you may first have to take a bus to **Bannur** (frequent, 30min., Rs7), 7km from Somnathpur, and then catch a bus from there. Near the cathedral, **private bus** companies vie for space and customers. Most are open late into the night.

Local Transportation: Local buses leave from the **City Bus Stand** (tel. 425819), off K-R Circle. Fares are Rs3-6. To: **Chamundi Hill** (Platform 6: #303, 304, 305, 306, every 20min., 40min.); **Brindavan Gardens** (Platform 8: #201, every 30min., 25min.); **Srirangapatnam** (Platform 6: #313, 316, every 20min., 45min.). **Taxis** cluster in Gandhi Sq. Fares are subject to negotiation. **Auto-rickshaws** *should* be metered (Rs7 for the 1st km, Rs6 per subsequent km).

Tourist and Financial Services

Tourist Office: Karnataka Tourist Office, Old Exhibition Building (tel. 22096), at the corner of Irwin and Diwan's Rd., 1 block east of the railway station. Indifferent service and few brochures. Open M-Sa 10am-5:30pm. Closed 2nd Sa. The **KSTDC** (tel. 423652), on Jhansi Laxmi Bai Rd., adjacent to the Hotel Mayura, will book you on hectic day tours of Mysore (Rs100, not including admission fees, express Rs50). Mysore Tour includes Somnathpur, Srirangapatnam, Chamundi Hill, Maharaja's Palace, and Brindavan Gardens (7:30am-8:30pm). It's a cheap, low-stress way of seeing the major sights. Tours of Belur, Halebid, and Javanabelagh (Tu, W, F, Su, 7:30am-9pm, Rs160) and Ooty (M, Th, Sa, 7am-9pm, Rs160). Open daily 6am-9pm.

Budget Travel: Many travel agencies are located in the vicinity of Gandhi Sq. **Dasprakash Travel Agency** (tel. 529949), in the eponymous hotel complex off Gandhi Sq., books tours, air and rail tickets. Open daily 6:30am-10pm. **Indian Airlines,** Hotel Mayura Complex (tel. 421846 or 426317), Jhansi Laxmi Bai Rd., 250m south of the railway station. Open M-Sa 10am-1:30pm and 2:15-5pm.

Foreigners Registration Office: Police Commissioner's Office (tel. 564242), 3km from Mysore center on Lalitha Mahal Rd. May grant free 3-month visa extensions, which take 1 week to process, but all too often a trek out to Bangalore is necessary.

Currency Exchange: The **State Bank of Mysore** (tel. 543502) has a foreign exchange branch at the junction of Sayajit Rao and Old Bank Rd. The **State Bank of India** (tel. 530826), K-R Circle, changes a number of currencies. Banks are open M-F 10:30am-2:30pm, Sa 10:30am-12:30pm.

Local Services

Luggage Storage: Railway Station, first day Rs3, second day Rs5, then Rs6 per day. Open daily 8am-10pm.

Bookstore: Ashok Book Centre (tel. 435553), on Dhanvantri Rd., near Sayajit Rao Rd. A post-colonial paradise, rife with the latest Rushdie, Mehta, and Ishigaro. Open M-Sa 9:30am-2pm and 3:30-8:30pm.

Library: Mysore City Central Library, at the intersection of Irwin and Sayajit Rao Rd. Full of musty books, but as airy as a library should be. Periodical room is packed. Open Tu-Su 8:30am-7:30pm.

Market: Devaraja Market, tucked behind the glitzy *sari* shops on Sayajit Rao Rd. and the sandalwood shops on Dhanvantri Rd., is one of South India's most memorable. Open daily dawn-dusk. Sells fresh vegetables and fruit, and color film. **Pick 'n' Pack Mini Supermarket** (tel. 425445), Hotel Luciya complex, Old Bank Rd., between Gandhi Sq. and Sayajit Rao Rd. Open M-Sa 9am-9pm, Su 9am-2pm.

Emergency and Communications

Pharmacy: Many are clustered near the hospital grounds, on Sayajit Rao and Dhanvantri Rd. **Sharada Medical and Optical Stores** (tel. 422472) quickly fills medical and optical prescriptions and has a giant stock of saline solution and contact lens cleaner. Open M-Sa 10am-9pm.

Hospital: K-R Hospital (tel. 420887 or 423300), at the corner of Sayajit Rao and Irwin Rd., is the main government hospital in Mysore. The private **Holdsworth Memorial (Mission) Hospital** (tel. 427716), on Sawday Rd., is nicer and cleaner.

Police: Branch offices across from the GPO and at the Central Bus Stand.

Post Office: GPO (tel. 22165), intersection of Ashoka and Irwin Rd., 750m east of the tourist office. Open M-Sa 10am-6pm. **Postal Code:** 570001.

Internet: Niru Communications (tel. 432359). Rs50 for 30min., or Rs2 per min. under 30min. Open daily 8am-11pm.

Telephones: 24hr. **STD/ISD** booths near Gandhi Sq. and at the **Central Telegraph Office,** south of KR Circle, before Ramavilas Rd. Callbacks Rs1 per min. **Telephone Code:** 0821.

ACCOMMODATIONS

Mysore is full of reasonably priced, centrally located hotels. Many have built devoted followings, so advance reservations (1 week in season, a few days otherwise) are key.

Parklane Hotel, 2720 Sri Harsha Rd. (tel. 30400). The doubles and singles are about the same small size, but they're clean. Extra pillows and blankets in each room. Hot water 6-8am; squat toilet on the ground floor, seat toilet on the first floor. Check-out 24hr. Singles Rs100 (ground-floor), Rs125 (1st floor); doubles Rs125/150; triples Rs200; quads Rs240. Extra person Rs40.

Green's Hotel, 2722/2 Sri Harsha Rd. (tel. 422415), next door to Parklane Hotel. Large corridors, great balcony, and high-ceilinged rooms whisper of the grand old past. Dirt-cheap prices also seem to have remained unchanged over the years. Mostly Indian clientele. Check-out 24hr. Attached restaurant and bar (open 10:30am-2:30pm and 5:30-11pm). Singles Rs50; doubles Rs65.

Hotel Dasprakash (tel. 442444), on the corner of Gandhi Sq. and Old Bank Rd. The many rooms are spacious and airy, and the location ideal. Palm-treed courtyard houses an ice cream parlor, an on-call astropalmist, and a travel agency. Hot water 5am-noon, towels and soap provided. Specify seat or squat toilet. Veg. restaurant. Check-out 24hr. Singles Rs125-155; doubles Rs275-365, with A/C Rs525.

Hotel Indra Bhavan (tel. 423933), on Dhanvantri Rd., on the SRRD side. Manned by cordial and sometimes downright sweet old men who are inflexible about 3 things: no alcohol, no meat, and no dirt. Rooms are well-lit and ugly in a cheerful sort of way. Attached baths. The restaurants downstairs are two of Mysore's best. Local tour info, newspapers, 24hr. STD/ISD service, and laundry available. Check-out 24hr. Singles Rs130; doubles Rs135-220; quads Rs240.

The Ritz Hotel, 5 B-N Rd. (tel. 422668), 100m south of the Central Bus Stand (on your right as you exit). Batik-decorated rooms lie off a patio with overgrown foliage. First and foremost one Mysore's best restaurant-bars, the Ritz doesn't skimp on the quality of its rooms, which are usually booked solid. Attached baths have seat toilets and 24hr. running hot water. Check-out noon. Doubles Rs300. Visa, MC.

The Hotel Rajmahal Deluxe, Lakshmirilasa Rd. (tel. 421196), to the right as you walk out of Jaganmohan Palace. Large, spotless rooms have huge windows; all have baths (seat toilets) and running hot water 6-8am. Some have TVs. Room service 24hr. Check-out 24hr. Singles Rs150; doubles Rs200; triples Rs250.

KSTDC Hotel Mayura Hoysala (tel. 425349), opposite Hotel Metropole. Next door to KSTDC's bland Hotel Mayura Yatrinivas is its ritzier cousin, with marble floors, oak-framed beds, and wicker-chaired balconies. Attached bathrooms have both seat and squat toilets, and running hot water 24hr. Thatch-roofed bar attached. Check-out noon. Singles Rs200, with A/C Rs550; doubles Rs350/650.

Shree Krishna Continental, 73 Nazarbad Main Rd. (tel. 37042 or 37044). A marble-floored lobby and staircase lead to 58 spacious, sparkling rooms overlooking a park (or if you're unlucky, a trash heap). All have seat toilets and hot water from 5-9am. Free laundry, restaurant with "*chaat* corner," travel counter, and 24hr. check-out. Singles Rs250; doubles Rs300-600; triples Rs800. Extra bed Rs50. Additional tax.

FOOD

Mysore's cheapest, most sumptuous, and most authentic food can be had at one of the myriad "meals" or "tiffins" cafes, whose dingy, painted signs proclaim "Meals Ready!" in Kannada and English. It's a minute for two *idlis* at Rs5 or a *thali* at Rs15. The cafes are pretty much devoid of tourists, who tend toward upscale venues.

Akshaya Vegetarian Restaurant, in the Hotel Dasprakash, serves brimming *thalis* (Rs20-35) to brimming crowds of locals and travelers. *Kheer* for dessert. Open daily noon-3pm and 7:45-10pm. Tiffin 6-10:30am and 4-10pm.

Samrat, Dhanvantri Rd., next door to Hotel Indra Bhavan. The North Indian veg. menu will satisfy your penchant for *paneer.* (16 varieties may well be a Mysore record!) North Indian *thali* Rs55. Open daily noon-3pm and 7-10:15pm.

Parklane Hotel, Sri Harsha Rd. (tel. 430400), near New Statue Circle. A little more hyper than the Ritz: its menu solemnly notes that "disposable vomit bags are available on request in case of need, and out of consideration for fellow diners." Secluded booths are ideal for twilight dining and boozing. Boneless chicken kebabs are out-of-this-world. Great *kadai paneer* (Rs50), tandoori items (60-150), and veg. *biryani* (Rs36), too. Beer starts at Rs41. Open daily 10am-11:15pm.

The Ritz Hotel, 5 B-N Rd. Serves the most attentively spiced and delicately crafted dishes in Mysore. The standard restaurant repertoire is uniformly delish. Popular with mellow clientele. Candle-lit dining and a patio to boot. Meals with drinks run at least Rs100. Open daily 7am-11pm. Bar open daily 11am-11pm.

Jewel Rock Restaurant, 2716 Sri Harsha Rd., at Hotel Maurya Palace. Serves delectable tandoori and *tikkas* and *ghee*-laden *biryanis.* Chintzy tablecloths, dim lighting, red carpet, and jazz muzak. Try the Jewel Special: a sampling of chicken, mutton, and fish kebabs (Rs75). Open daily 11am-3:30pm and 6:30-11pm.

Swathi, across the street from the Akshaya Vegetarian Restaurant, off Gandhi Sq. A tiny milk stall where *lassis* (Rs6) are manually frothed by a wooden stick rubbed at high speed between the wet palms of the proprietor. Open daily 6:30am-8pm.

Mylari Hotel, Door #738, Nazarbad Main Rd., past Shree Krishna Continental Hotel. Popular tiffin room is consistently packed with locals enjoying the two items on the menu: incredible *dosas* (Rs9) and *idlis* (Rs5). Open 7-11am and 4-7pm.

SIGHTS

The Maharaja's Palace

Location: *Purandara Dasa Rd.* **Hours:** *Open 10am-5:30pm.* **Admission:** *Rs10. Residential Palace Rs10.* **Other:** *Camel rides Rs15. Elephant rides Rs25.*

The home of the current maharaja and the psychological center of Mysore, the Maharaja's Palace (Amber Vilas) is impressive in ways a monument should be, namely girth (it's more than 3.5 sq. km, and 44m tall) and worth (it was completed at the cost of Rs4.2 million, which was a lot of money 100 years ago). In 1897, during the reign of Krishnaraja Wodeyar IV, who had been reinstated as ruler by the British 16 years earlier, the original wooden palace burnt to the ground. Immediately afterward, a bloke named Mr. Henry Irwin was commissioned to rebuild it, which took him and his Indian artisans 15 years. Durbar Hall is bannered with murals depicting scenes from the Dasara festival, complete with scores of cavalry in various stages of uniform. The museum is a must-see for those craving kitsch: gold chariots, slightly androgynous Wodeyar family portraits, a weapon room with scintillating scythes, Ganesh stained-glass windows, and a wax effigy of the maharaja. Built in the Indo-Saracenic style, the palace is visited by slow-moving streams of tourists each day. The **Maharaja's Residential Palace** is visible from the exit of the Palace. The home of Mysore's current maharaja is anticlimatic after the grandeur of the old glory: tarnished cutlery and shabby school uniforms fail to impress. But you don't have to go in to take a camel ride or elephant ride around the compound. On Sunday nights and government holidays, the palace is illuminated with 80,000 delightfully ostentatious light bulbs.

Other Downtown Sights

The **Jaganmohan Palace,** containing the **Jayachamarajendra Art Gallery** (2 blocks west of the Maharaja's Palace), is a jumble of ill-exhibited randomalia. *(Open daily 8am-5pm. Admission Rs8.)* Still, a few gems hang on the walls, including Raganendranath Tagore watercolors and Raja Ravi Varna oils; a collection of *tablas, sitars,* and *veenas;* a series of Buddhas carved on an elephant tusk; and ancient silk game boards.

The **Brindavan Gardens** and **Krishnarajendra Dam** are a popular picnicking spot for Mysorians, and throngs of local families relax there on the weekends. The dam was built across the Kaveri River at the turn of the century by Maharaja Krishnaraja Wodeyar Bahadur. Abutting the dam are the gardens, whose lack of flowers is supplanted by a barrage of fountains which let loose at night to the beat of Hindi and Kannada music, and a much talked-up **light show.** To get there, take city bus #201. *(Open M-F 7am-8:30pm, Sa-Su 7am-9:30pm. Admission Rs5, camera fee Rs25. Light show M-F 7-7:55pm, Sa-Su 7-8:55pm.)*

As Indian zoos go, the **Mysore Zoo,** which spreads over 250 green acres, is rather pleasant. *(Open W-M 8am-5pm. Admission Rs8.)* Plenty of tigers (including a white one) aimlessly and impotently prowl about their lush, enclosed grounds. Pure white peacocks, drag-queen-esque lemurs, ponderous pachyderms, and elegant emus eke out an existence here amidst expertly groomed topiary and gazing *Homo sapiens.* Efforts to couch animals in their most natural habitats led to the 1994 escape of two vagrant crocodiles into rural Karnataka.

Chamundi Hill

Location: *SE of town.* **Transportation:** *City bus #303, 304, 305, and 306, Rs4 each way. Taxis about Rs100.* **Hours:** *Chamundeswari Temple open 7:30am-2pm and 4-8pm. Shiva Temple open 7:30am-2pm and 3:30-9pm.*

Even if you're not into the *devi* scene, the ride up Chamundi Hill, 4km south of and 1km above the city center, can still be a religious experience. The view of the Deccan plain, with its squares of saffron and green, is divine. Other angles afford terrific views of Mysore City—even at a distance, you can see the Maharaja's Palace in all its splendor. At the top of the hill a 16m Mahishasura, the buffalo demon who plagued Mysore (and from whom Mysore takes its name) greets you at the car park in all his gaudiness. Chamundi (a form of Durga) was the goddess who smote Mahishasura and the **Sri Chamundeswari Temple** at the hill's summit, with a 40m *gopuram,* is devoted to her. The area is a bit of a madhouse (mind your shoes!), but the rest of the hill is quite peaceful.

Near the Mahishasura statue is the tiny **Godly Museum,** which is filled with dioramas depicting various stages of spiritual life. One exhibit delineates "Today's Problematic World," whose troubles all seem to stem from overpopulation (note the picture of a family of seven on one bicycle and the prophetic sketch of the crowded bus you'll take down the hill). This is also your source for holographic Om stickers.

Pilgrims climb the 1000 steps (or down) Chamundi Hill, a journey which takes at least two hours and have you exclaiming "My-sore feet!" at the end of it all. If you opt to foot it, however, don't miss the **Shiva Temple** one-third of the way up. The temple is protected by a corpulent granite statue of Nandi, Shiva's bull. Nandi has been protecting the temple for 300 years and it's whispered that each year he, like all of his stone brethen, grows an itsy-bitsy bit. It is expected that in 300 more years, Nandi will grow so large that he'll sit atop Mysore—but that may just be a lot of bull.

ENTERTAINMENT

Cinemas proliferate in the Gandhi Square area, and on Sundays they're crammed with movie fiends. The price of admission (Rs3-15) depends on where you sit. **Uma Talkies,** in Gandhi Square, screens English-language films, as does the farther-off **Sterling Cinema** in Vidyaranyapuram (near the government silk and oil factories). Take the bus (#3, 8, 11, 13, 14, and 44, every 10min., 15min) to Vidyaranyapuram. Probably the most popular pastime is going out to dinner and topping it off with a couple of drinks in one of the hotel bars (see **Food,** p. 578).

Royal Legacy, Nazarbad Main Rd. (tel. 36721), next to the Shree Krishna Continental, is a hip, happening club where you can get a mug of beer (Rs23) and chill in the dark (but innocuous) lounge. Otherwise, pay the cover charge (Rs50-100) to go upstairs, where the smooth DJ spins happy dance tunes and honors requests. (Open daily 11am-2pm and 5:30-11pm.) Mysore's only disco resides in a 5-star hotel, naturally. **XTC-Club,** Hotel Southern Star, Vinoba Rd. (tel. 438141 or 438784), sports a small dance-floor crowded with lively, good-natured locals. Unlike the more cosmopolitan clubs, the standard fare here is rap and Rs60 beers. (Couples only, Rs250. Open F and Sa 8pm-12:30am, but the party may last later.)

SHOPPING

Mysore produces half of India's **sandal oil** as well as massive quantities of **silks, sandalwood,** and **jewelry.** The state government's **Cauvery Emporium** (tel. 521258) on Sayajit Rao Rd., is a giant warehouse of such exotica. They accept major credit cards and traveler's checks, and will arrange packing and export. Cauvery has an open-air annex near the Palace (open M-Sa 10am-1:30pm and 3-7:30pm). Scores of private arts and crafts emporia cluster near the annex (generally open 9am-7pm). Cheaper mini-emporia with more malleable prices crowd Dhanvantri Rd., near its intersection with Sayajit Rao Rd. Farther down Sayajit Rao Rd., near K-R Circle, silk stores sell enough *saris* to wrap around Mother Earth. Many stores have tailors capable of whipping up a dress or shirt in an afternoon. The **Government Silk Weaving Factory** (tel. 521803), in Vidyaranyapuram, allows tours with prior permission. Here you can watch your silk being woven and buy it later at mill prices (open M-Sa 9:30am-4:30pm). Next door is the **Government Sandal Oil Factory** (tel. 521889), where, again with permission, you can schedule a rather smelly tour (open M-Sa 8am-5pm).

■ Near Mysore

■ Somnathpur ಸೋಮನಾಥಪುರ

A tiny village 38km east of Mysore, Somnathpur is home to the famous **Keshava Temple,** built in 1268 AD. The village was established, and the temple commissioned by Soma, a high officer under the Hoysala King Narasimha II, hence the name Somnathpur. Legend has it that when the temple was completed, it was so beautiful and grand (despite its minuscule height of 10m), that the gods thought it too good for this earth and wanted to transport it to heaven. The temple quaked and began to levitate, and the chief sculptor in his horror began to mutilate some of the images on the outside wall to avert such a catastrophe. The slightly disfigured temple came crashing back down to earth, which explains why the *garudagamba* (stone pillar depicting the god Garuda) is not exactly opposite the entrance, as is usual, but slightly skewed to the northeast. The Keshava Temple is swimming with carvings: six strata of friezes—elephants, scrolls, geese, scenes from the *Bhagavad Gita, Mahabharata,* and the *Puranas* border the exterior, while scores of deity images fill the interior. Of the 144 large images, 114 are female. The temple was carved out of supple soapstone in order to give sculptors a chance to flaunt their artistic prowess, and the temple is one of the most exuberantly carved around. It's very dark inside, but Indra and company were thoroughly justified in their covetousness—the temple *is* too beautiful for this earth. To get to Somnathpur, take a private bus from near Wesley Church, or hire a taxi. See **Buses,** p. 563. (Open daily 9am-5:30pm. Admission Rs2. Video fee Rs25.)

■ Srirangapatnam ಶ್ರೀರಂಗಪಟ್ಟಣ

Sixteen kilometers from Mysore, Srirangapatnam was the site of Tipu Sultan's island fort and the seat of his vast kingdom until the fourth Anglo-Mysore war in 1799. Tipu and his forces had made South India a living hell for the British for some time. Tipu's father, Haider Ali, defeated Mysore's Hindu raja in 1761. In 1782, Tipu inherited his dad's throne and his rivalries (with the Marathas, the French, and the British). He proved especially fearsome to the East India Company, to whom he dealt two sound defeats before the tide turned towards the colonialists. Tipu met his final defeat here in 1799, ending his subcontinental conquest and opening up the path for the East India Company's expansion in South India. Today, Srirangapatnam is a history buff's heaven—this is, after all, where the roguish ruler and warrior met his demise, in an series of legendary events. Barraged by redcoat bullets, Tipu toppled off his horse into a pile of the dead and dying. A grabby British soldier, catching a glimpse of Tipu's ostentatious gold belt buckle, tried to snatch it for booty. But the barely-breathing Tipu lanced the soldier with his ever-ready sword. Alas, the soldier was merely injured and was still sharp enough to lodge a bullet in Tipu's temple.

It is rumored that, in the depths of the Karnatakan night, the ghost of Tipu wanders around his former digs in search of his stolen belt buckle. This legend, along with the utter lack of hotels and restaurants in Srirangapatnam, explains why most visitors daytrip it. **Buses** from Mysore leave every hour (6am-8pm, Rs7); the last bus to Mysore leaves at 9pm. Turn left from the bus stand to reach the **Jumma Masjid,** the mosque Tipu built on the grounds of an old Hindu temple. Remnants of walls put up to keep the British out encircle the area (they're "protected ancient monuments," according to the Archaeological Survey of India, but local woman use them to dry cow-dung patties). **Daria Daulat,** Tipu's summer palace, is about 1km from the village. Tipu's main palace was dismembered in 1807 by Colonel Wellesley, and its timbers went to build, among other things, the maharaja's palace in Mysore and St. Stephen's Church in Ooty. Either take a **rickshaw** (Rs20) or walk (from the bus stand, make two rights and then turn left at the sign). The manicured lawns and splendid palace recall a bygone era of pomp and luxury; today, you'll share Tipu's old stomping grounds with busloads of tourists and vagrant Architectural Survey of India guides looking for work. The palace, built in 1784 in an Indo-Islamic style, is now a **museum** housing some marvelous murals of Tipu's battles and portraits of the entire Tipu Sultan clan, including a portrait of Tipu wearing his signature tiger stripes. (Open Sa-Th 9am-5pm.)

The hospital that housed Colonel Wellesley and company is also on the premises, as is an obelisk commemorating British lives lost in the siege, and the dungeons where Tipu held British soldiers. (Open Sa-Th 9am-5pm. Admission Rs2). Beyond Daria Daulat, another 1km down the road, lies **Gumbaz,** the mausoleum where Tipu and his father, Haider Ali, lie (at least during the day). The **Sri Ranganatha Temple,** the town's namesake, dates from the Hoysala age. (Open daily 8am-1pm and 4-8pm.)

▧ Hassan ಹಸನ

The busy, industrial city of Hassan, filled with goods carriers and plastics manufacturers, has little tourist appeal and no sights of its own, but its location has saved its complacent tourist industry. Hassan is situated about 40km from the temple villages of Halebid and Belur and, unlike these villages, Hassan has both railway and bus stations and an array of hotels that would cause either Belur or Halebid to explode into commercial convulsions. Though hardly engaging of its own accord, Hassan is a practical place to spend your nights and take care of business that demands more modern conveniences than either Belur or Halebid can provide.

ORIENTATION

It would take a supreme effort (or spiked *paan*) to get lost in this tidbit of a burg. Most hotels and lodges are within 500m of the **bus stand,** which is at the southwest corner of the aptly named **Bus Stand Road** (north-south) and **Church Road** (east-west). Running parallel to Bus Stand Rd. about 200m to the east is **Race Course Road.** It intersects the second east-west thoroughfare, **Bangalore-Mangalore (B-M) Road,** about 300m to the south. The city jumps around the bus stand and the intersection of Race Course and B-M Rd. Follow B-M Rd. 1km east to the **railway station.**

PRACTICAL INFORMATION

Trains: Hassan's **railway station,** 2km from the bus stand, currently only serves **Mysore** (#86 at 6am, #861 at 6:30pm, 3hr., Rs23) and **Arsikere** (#862, 11am, 1hr., Rs10). Both connect to Bangalore, but Mysore is faster.

Buses: The **bus stand** is on Church Rd., across from Maharaja's Park. Hordes of private bus companies offer Rs50 service to Bangalore. Government buses to: **Belur** (every 30min., 6am-8:30pm, 1½hr., Rs10); **Bangalore** (every 15min. 5:30am-7:45pm and midnight, 4hr., Rs48/58); **Halebid** (every 30min., 7:30am–7pm, 1hr., Rs8); **Mangalore** (20 per day, 6am-6:30pm, 3½hr., Rs35). To get to **Sravanabelagola,** first go to **Channarayapatna** (every 15min. 5:15am-7:45pm, 1hr., Rs10); from there, buses leave for Sravanabelagola (every 20min., 15min., Rs3.5). For **Hampi**—head to **Shimoga** (15 per day, 5:30am-8:15pm, 4hr., Rs45) and transfer. **Tempos** also service Belur and Halebid very frequently. From the bus stand make a left onto Church St. and take the first right and proceed for a few blocks.

Tourist Office: Regional Tourist Office, Vartha Bhavan, B-M Rd. (tel. 68862). From the bus stand, walk 1 block south, turn left onto B-M Rd., walk 300m, and it will be on the left. Friendly and helpful. Open M-Sa 10am-1:30pm and 2-5:30pm.

Immigration Office: Foreigners Registration Office (tel. 68000), at the Police Station, B-M Rd., in the women's grievances office. Open M-F 10am-5:30pm.

Currency Exchange: State Bank of Mysore, on the corner of Bus Stand and B-M Rd., changes US$, UK£, and traveler's checks in U.S., Canadian, British, German, and French currencies. Open M-F 10:30am-2:30pm, Sa 10:30am-12:30pm.

Market: On west side of the bus stand and Maharaja's Park. Pyramids of tangerines, grapes, apples, and mangoes alongside *chaat* carts, *chai* stalls, and omelette fryers.

Pharmacy: Gopal Medicines, across from Karnataka Bank. Open 9am-9:30pm.

Hospital: CSI Redfern Memorial Hospital, Race Course Rd. (tel. 67653), 1 block north of its intersection with Church Rd. **Mangala Nursing Home** (tel. 67236).

Emergency: Police, tel. 100. **Fire,** tel. 101. **Ambulance,** tel. 102.

Post Office: Opposite the bus stand on Bus Stand Rd. Open M-F 10:30am-5:30pm, Sa 10am-1pm. **Postal Code:** 573201.

Telephones: STD/ISD booths cluster near the bus stand. **Telephone Code:** 08172

ACCOMMODATIONS

Vaishnavi Lodging, Harsha Mahal Rd. (tel. 67413). Exit from the northeast corner of the bus stand, walk east on Church Rd., and turn left. Big rooms with triple-duty fans, clean sheets, fluffy pillows, telephones, and attached baths (squat, baby, squat). Hot water 6-9am. Check-out 24hr. Singles Rs100; doubles Rs145.

Hotel New Abiruchi, B-M Rd. (tel. 67852). From the bus stand, walk 2 blocks south on Bus Stand Rd. and take a right as soon as you pass the police station. Clean rooms and spotless bathrooms with seat details. Attached restaurant. Hot water 6-9am. Check-out 24hr. Singles Rs80, with TV Rs145; doubles Rs140/200.

Hotel Suvarna Regency, B-M Rd. (tel. 64006; fax 63822). From Bus Stand Rd. walk 1 block, turn right after the police station, and follow B-M Rd. to where it turns south; you can't miss the Suvarna Regency's towers. Star TV, telephones, your choice of toilet, travel services, currency exchange, fluffy towels. Check-out 24hr. Singles Rs308; doubles Rs448, with A/C Rs616; quads Rs728.

FOOD

Hotel Sanman, M-O Rd. From the bus stand, head south on Bus Stand Rd. and take the last road before hitting B-M Rd. The *puris* are consistently fresh—three steam-filled wonders almost reach eye-level when the plate is on the table. Open daily 6am-9:45pm. *Thalis* (Rs15, 11:30am-4pm and 7-9:45pm).

Suvarna Sagar, B-M Rd. Attached to Hotel Survarna. Dishes out competent if costly *thalis* (South Indian Rs18-36, North Indian Rs35-55) and *tiffins* in a tapestry-chaired, mega-friendly hall. They've scooped the competition when it comes to ice cream desserts. 15% surcharge to sit in the A/C section. Open daily 7am-10:30pm.

Hotel GRR, Bus Stand Rd., directly opposite the bus stand. This Andhran transplant focuses all of its culinary energy on its banana-leaf *thalis* (Rs15)—no sweets, *lassis,* or even tea or coffee. Ornate wooden chairs and stone kitchen make it an aesthetically pleasing place as well. Open daily 11:30am-4:30pm and 7:30-11pm.

ENTERTAINMENT

Hassan's happening nightspot for the well-to-do happens to be the new restaurant-bar **Golden Gate,** behind Suvarna Sagar. Great patio and Kebabs too (Rs50-70; open 10:30am-11:30pm). The bar at the **Malanika Restaurant,** atop Hotel Amblee Palika on Race Course and Hospital Rd., is lit with dim, colored lightbulbs. Hallucinogenically tinted windows complement the beer (mild Rs44; strong Rs48—look out!). Mind the mosquitoes on the rooftop garden. (Open daily noon-3pm and 7-11pm.) The **Prithvi Theater,** down B-M Rd. past the tourist office and before the railway station, screens three English-language flicks per day. **Picture Palace,** across from the GPO on Bus Stand Rd., does Indian (mostly Kannada) films.

∎ Near Hassan: Sravanabelagola ಶ್ರವಣಬೆಳಗೊಲ

The beatific smile of Bahabuli, who stands 17m in naked, monolithic glory, showers the tiny town of Sravanabelagola with serenity. The streets are clean and virtually pedestrian-free, the air is suffused with calm, and the touts are less aggressive than their postcard-pushing brethren in most temple towns. While the main attraction is, of course, the towering statue of Bahabuli (Gomateshvara), Sravanabelagola is also the site of important and even longer-standing Jain *bastis* (temples).

The **bus stand** sits on **Bangalore Road (C.R. Patna Road),** across from the Chandragiri Hilltop Jain *basti.* **Buses** leave for **Bangalore** (6:45, 8, and 10am, 3pm, 3hr., Rs38); **Chanayapatna** (every 15min. 6am-8:30pm, 15min., Rs3); **Hassan** (6, 7:45, and 8:30am, 1:45pm, 1½hr., Rs13); **Mysore** (7:15am, 2½hr., Rs24). Make a right from the station onto Bangalore Rd. and your first right will be **Kalyani Road,** which houses many small stores and cold-drink shops, and leads to **Temple Road.** The hill with all the *bastis* and Bahabuli looms to the right, and the KSTDC **tourist office** (tel. 57254; open M-Sa 10am-5:30pm) is at its base. The staff speaks little English, but one of the guides is sure to be helpful. Guides charge a minimum of Rs100 for a tour around Banubali. **Telephone Code:** 08176.

Most visitors make Sravanabelagola a daytrip, but the town is replete with accommodations, in part because of the dodecennial Mahamastakabhisheka ceremony which attracts thousands of Jain pilgrims from all over the country. Visitors should respect the Jain prohibitions of meat and alcohol. The Jain **lodging houses,** which must be reserved through the central **Accommodations Office** (tel. 57258), have quiet, clean doubles with attached baths (seat toilet) for Rs135. From the bus stand, turn left and you'll see them on your left. Farther down the street, **Yatri Nivas,** also reserved through the Jain Accommodations Office, has bigger, marginally more luxurious rooms (doubles Rs160; triples Rs210).

Tall, naked ascetics tend to get all the attention, and Bahabuli is no exception. However, the surrounding hills have been a Jain pilgrimage site since long before the statue was carved 1000 years ago. The *bastis,* built over many centuries, form a sort of architectural history book. Legend has it that Sravanabelagola (Naked Ascetic of the White Pond) was first alighted upon in 300 BC by the Mauryan emperor Chandragupta, who abdicated his throne up north to retire here as an ascetic. His guru Bhadrabahu came with him and attained a sacred state more rapidly than his pupil. Chandragupta (for whom the Chandragiri Hill is named) used to worship the footprints of Bhadrabahu in a cave on Chandragiri Hill; the feet still attract pilgrims today, as it is believed that the sight of the prints cures any illness.

Built around 980 AD, the **Bahabuli statue**—said to be the largest monolithic statue in the world—is a relatively recent fixture in Sravanabelagola's history. Bahabuli wears the smile of enlightenment, and not much else. Vines creep up his legs, snakes coil around his feet, and anthills fester at his ankles, all symbolizing Bahabuli's detachment from worldy worries. The 620 steps leading to the statue require about 15-20 minutes of dedicated climbing. Wear a pair of thick socks if your soles are not ascetically hardened to the touch of burning granite. Alternatively, a group of tired-looking old men will carry you up in a chair for Rs80. Every 12 years the Jain mega-festival **Mahamastakabhisheka** is held here. On the eve of the ceremony, scaffolding is erected behind the monument, and 1008 pots of sacred and colored water are placed in front of the statue. Priests (and wealthy devotees who have enough rupees to pay for a sacred anointing spot) drench Bahabuli with the water, chanting *mantras;* then they pour milk, dates, bananas, jaggery, curds, *ghee,* sugar, almonds, and gold and silver flowers over his head. The entire sticky process is watched by thousands in pindrop silence. The next Mahamastakabhisheka is scheduled for 2005. The temple housing the statue is open daily from sunrise to sunset. *Puja* is performed daily at 8am and 8pm. Visit in the morning to avoid the crowds and the heat (though the pesky monkeys are nearly always unavoidable).

■ Belur ಬೇಲುರು

Belur, a little town on the right bank of the Yagachi River, was the capital of the Hoysalan empire before it was moved to nearby Halebid. Seven hundred years and several dynasties later, Belur has become a blink-and-you'll-miss-it town, its two roads lined with dank eateries, tea stalls, and a few meager stores that give no hint of the town's gilded history. Only the Chennakshava Temple, set off from the town by its tall *gopuram*, reminds visitors of what once was. Although Belur is equipped with marginally more hotels and restaurants than Halebid, those wishing to get out of Hassan and spend the night in a temple town would no doubt enjoy Halebid's peaceful village feel more than Belur's small-town-but-getting-a-little-scuzzy vibe.

ORIENTATION AND PRACTICAL INFORMATION There are two roads in Belur. **Main Road** runs more or less perpendicular to **Temple Road,** which runs from the **bus stand** to the **Chennakeshava Temple. Buses** go to: **Arsikere** (every 30-60min., 6am-7pm, 1½hr., Rs13); **Halebid** (every 30-60min., 6am-8pm, 45min., Rs4/5); **Hassan** (every hr., 5:30am-11:30pm, 1hr., Rs10); **Mangalore** (every hr., 5:30am-11:30pm, 5hr., Rs58/68); and **Mysore** (every hr., 5:30am-6:45pm, 4hr., Rs35). Auto-rickshaws head to the temple (Rs5), or you can walk it in about seven minutes. Make a left from the bus stand onto Main Rd., and the **post office** will be a few blocks down on your left. (**Postal Code:** 573115.) On your way, you'll pass the **Karnataka Tourist Office,** located inside the Mayura Velapuri Hotel Complex (tel. 22209; open M-Sa 10:30am-5pm), but if no one's there, check inside the hotel or restaurant. Across the street you'll find more **pharmacies** than you'll ever need. Just past Hotel Mayura Velapuri is the unmarked **Government Hospital** (tel. 22333), and further down is the **State Bank of Mysore,** which no longer exchanges foreign currency (open M-F 10:30am-2:30pm, Sa 10:30am-12:30pm). **Telephone Code:** 08177.

ACCOMMODATIONS AND FOOD The limited lodging options in Belur run the gamut from cheap and functional to cheaper and less functional. No A/C or TVs here. At least you won't be watching roaches scuffle across the clean floor of **Hotel Mayura Velapuri** (tel. 22209), the most expensive (this is relative) hotel in town. Functional, dark rooms and a gregarious proprietor let you know you're livin' large (singles Rs75; doubles Rs100). A few minutes' walk down Temple Rd. brings you to **Swagath Tourist Home** (tel. 22159). Cheaper, cheerier, and more personal than its neighbors, the Swagath is owned by a mellow family who run the market down below. Pretty pink painted balconies overlook a tiny green courtyard. (Check-out 24hr.; doubles Rs60.) Best bets for eating are in the hotels. The **restaurant** at Hotel Mauryan Velapuri dishes up *thalis* (Rs25) and Continental snacks (open daily 7am-9pm). **Hotel Annapoorna** does a good *thali* (Rs15; open daily 7am-10pm).

SIGHTS Facing the **Chennakeshava Temple** at Belur is a statue of Garuda, Vishnu's eagle mount, with palms together, guarding the temple. *(Temple open daily from 8am to 8:30pm. Inner sanctum closed 1-3pm. Free. Rs1 fee for shoe storage.)* Perhaps it was the fearsome Garuda who protected Belur's Hoysala Temple from the extreme ransacking to which Halebid suffered. More likely, it was the fact that Belur simply didn't have much to plunder. Nevertheless, like the temple at Halebid, the Chennakeshava (*"chenna"* means beautiful, "Keshava" is an incarnation of Vishnu) Temple was never finished. Work on it began in 1117 and, for 103 years, three generations of sculptors devoted their lives to it. The Hoysala king Vishnuvardhana built the temple to commemorate his conversion from Jainism to Hinduism; along with the temples at Somnathpur and Halebid, this is considered one of the best examples of Hoysalan architecture. Like the temples at Halebid and Somnathpur, the temple base is covered with horizontal friezes alarming in their detail. To bear the weight of the temple, 644 stone elephants stand at the bottom; no two are alike. There are nine statues of Vishnu around the exterior. Also outside is the emblem of the Hoysalan empire: the boy **Sala** smiting a beast with the head of a tiger and the body of a lion. When Sala was a boy, he and his classmates were sitting under a tree with their guru when this ferocious animal appeared. The other boys skedaddled home but Sala stared down the tiger as his guru ordered him to **"Hoy, Sala"** ("Kill, Sala"). This episode launched the boy into history as the founder of the great Hoysalan Empire, which reigned over most of Karnataka and some of Tamil Nadu from the 10th through 14th centuries.

The temple is renowned for its 42 **bracket figures,** or *apsaras,* which line the interior ceilings and exterior walls. The detail of the bracket figures is awesome: voluptuous women carved out of a single stone, whose bangles and head pendants move; a lady wearing an expression of longing as she holds a letter to her far-away lover while a lusty monkey tugs at the edge of her *sari;* and the famed **Thribhanghi Nritya,** a classical dancer contorting her body so perfectly that a drop of water from her right hand would gloss off the tip of her nose, then her left breast, and then hit the thumb of her left hand, landing at the arch of her right foot. Supposedly, no real-life dancer has ever been able to attain this pose.

Inside the temple is a platform once used by the *devadasis* (temple dancers), a sitting area for the audience, as well as some fabulously carved and filigreed pillars, which were so heavy—about four tons—that they had to be turned by elephants while sculptors designed them. The Narasimha pillar at the center of the temple depicts, in miniature, all of the temple's carvings in the little squares. One square is left empty, perhaps as a challenge to a future artist or to indicate that despite the artists' earthly efforts, God cannot be truly depicted. Inside the sanctum are two images of Vishnu; a large, silver-plated image which is prayed to daily, and a smaller wooden sculpture which is used in temple processions. Non-Hindus may view the images, and *pujas* are performed at 9am and 7pm. On the wall in front of the images is carved a strange creature, a mishmash of animals, with a peacock's tail, boar's body, lion's feet, crocodile's mouth, monkey's eyes, elephant's trunk, and cow's ears. These are considered the best parts of each of the animals; the result is more perfect than any single animal, and hence, fit to guard Vishnu himself.

The temple's **gopuram** outside was originally constructed in 1397 by the Vijayanagar Dynasty, but it burned down and had to be rebuilt. On the bottom right-hand corner, as you exit the temple, are some particularly erotic engravings, and if you hire one of the ASI **guides** (Rs30 for a very well-done 1hr. tour; make sure you have an authorized guide—he'll have an official ASI nametag), he'll be sure to point them all out to you. You have to leave your shoes and your inhibitions at the door.

■ Halebid ಹಳೇಬೀಡು

It's difficult to imagine Halebid as "Dwarasamudram," the capital of the magnificent Hoysala Empire at its zenith in the 12th and 13th centuries. Halebid's current name means "Destroyed City," which is grimly fitting, as the village is presently home to more cows and goats than kings and sculptors. But the grandeur of Halebid's great temple fits well in this serene village of 6000—in the distance rise the Western Ghats, small children play games in the road, and old men gossip over *chai* in mud cottages. Halebid indulges all our romantic stereotypes of India's long-lost simplicity (or backwardness), and no matter how politically incorrect the vision is, it's at least temporarily entrancing. That is, until one of the sweet children morphs into a vehement postcard tout, lurching you back to reality—a little relieved that the world is not as cut-and-dried as the soapstone engravings of the Hoysalesvara Temple.

ORIENTATION AND PRACTICAL INFORMATION There are more 12th-century shrines in Halebid than there are banks, police stations, hospitals, and telephones combined. Across the street from the bus stand lies the **Hoysalesvara Temple.** It's the only star-shaped soapstone edifice with exuberant engravings and figures in town, it's hard to miss. To the right as you exit the bus stand is the village's sole hotel, **Tourist Cottages,** manned by Department of Tourism employees. There's a **Tourist Help Desk** here, manned by an enormously energetic, safari-suited employee who will supply you with information on every subject (open M-Sa 10am-5:30pm). Five hundred meters down the road is the **Jain Mandir (Bagadi Hall).** Make a left at the fork in the road. **Buses** leave Halebid's bus stand for **Arsikere** (10 per day, 3hr., Rs58); **Belur** (every 30min., 7am-6:30pm, 45min., Rs5); and **Hassan** (15 per day, 6:30am-7pm, 1hr., Rs8). You can also catch private **maxicabs** in front of the temple to go to Hassan and Belur (every 30min. to Hassan). If you take a left from the bus stand, you'll walk along Halebid's more (relatively, of course) commercial road, whose buildings include a Canara Bank (which doesn't do foreign exchange) and a **post office** (open M-F 9:30am-5:30pm, Sa 10am-1pm). **Postal Code:** 573121. **Telephone Code:** 08177.

ACCOMMODATION AND FOOD Halebid's **Tourist Cottages** (tel. 3224) are currently the only lodging in town. Carpeted rooms have attached baths with seat toilets and 24hr. running hot water. The dorm beds are not so nice—no carpet or wicker furniture and you'll need your own sheets and mosquito nets (singles Rs150; doubles Rs200; quads Rs250). The attached **restaurant** serves a vegetarian menu, but no cold drinks (*thalis* Rs20; open 7am-11pm). The bus stand also has a **restaurant,** open daily 6am-7pm, with *thalis* and good *dosas* (open 5:30am-8:30pm).

SIGHTS Set in vast, immaculate lawns, the **Hoysalesvara Temple** is the largest of the Hoysalan temples. Work started on it in 1121, but before it could be completed, town and temple were sacked by Malik Kafur and his Delhi Sultanate armies in 1311 and 1326. By India's Independence only 14 of the original 84 large statues remained, and only one of the "bracket figures" (the mini-statues for which Belur's temple is famed) was left. The rest were destroyed, vandalized, or stolen; perhaps not coincidentally, quite a few are on display in British museums. But the Hoysalesvara Temple is still awe-inspiring and readily recognizable for the genius and assiduity that created it. The detail, humor, and accuracy of the temple's engravings are striking. Though the grounds it sits on seem incongruous with the village's landscape, the temple's majesty is somehow right at home here. In 1952 the Archaeological Survey of India took over the temple to protect it from the elements and graffiti-writing vandals.

Hoysalan temples usually sit on star-shaped platforms: the temple at Somnathpur has three temples on one platform, while at Belur, there's only one. Here in Halebid, the temple is composed of two Shiva temples on one platform. Like all Hoysalan temples, the deities face east, towards the sunrise. Unlike the Belur temple, Hoysalesvara Temple has no *gopuram,* indicating that it's merely a monument and no longer a place of worship, although the images are still present. The larger of the two was commissioned by the Hoysala king Vishnuvardhana, the smaller one by his senior wife, the famed dancer Shantaladevi. Over 20,000 elaborate figures remain in and around the temple, and ASI-sanctioned **guides** will explain the best and brightest for Rs30 (for up to 5 people). The guides are surprisingly hip, funny, well-informed, and probably underfed, as most are freelance post-grads searching for a "real" job.

Six strata of **frieze work** border the base of the temple: elephants first, then lions, horsemen, scrolls, stories from the *Puranas* and epics, and geese. Meanwhile, larger, gorier engravings of gods and goddesses line the upper exterior walls: Shiva killing the elephant demon, somehow dismembering his trunk from his head, and then dancing in the pachyderm's stomach in celebration; Vishnu peeling off the face of a demon like you would peel a plantain; Bhima tossing elephants over his shoulders like so many tennis balls. The carvings have also provided scholars with ample anthropological and historical evidence; one scene, for example, shows a royal hoisting a surprisingly modern-looking telescope, peering into the heavens. Inside the temple are two *lingas* and a dancing platform for devotional dances no longer performed. Leave your shoes at the entrance (Rs1).

A (soap)stone's throw from the temple is the **Archaeological Museum,** which houses deity statues from the temples and nearby ruins. *(Open Sa-Th 10am-5pm. Free.)* Half of it is outdoors, and some of the statues—fortunately, they're labeled—sit in a pretty, fountained garden. It doesn't compare with the temple itself, but it's a turn-on to get face-to-face with Arjuna in good lighting.

About 500m from the temple (turn left as you exit) is the 12th-century **Jain Bastis,** built by King Vishnu Vardhevna before he converted to Hinduism. The architectural style is the same as the famous Hindu temples, though the images etched in soapstone tell the stories familiar to different faiths. The most prominent of these is the **Parswanathasmy Temple,** held up by twelve lathe-turned columns, so remarkably plain in comparison to the intricate designs of the later Hindu versions that they convey the serenity and meditation of worship. *(Open 10am-5:30pm. Puja 9am.)* You can see your own reflection in them, distorted differently in each pillar.

■ Mangalore ಮಂಗಳೂರು

An important trading port for centuries and a major shipbuilding center during the 18th century, modern Mangalore retains its mercantile feel but little of its erstwhile glory. Nowadays, Mangalore is hailed as India's major cashew-and-coffee processor and *bidi*-production center—it's little wonder that Mangalore isn't exactly a tourist magnet. Nevertheless, it's a modern, bustling city with a number of budget hotels and cheap restaurants. As a transport node along the west coast between Goa and Kerala, Mangalore is serviceable stopover, and its importance can only increase now that the Konkan Railway is finally completed.

ORIENTATION

Defying logic or easy grasp, the streets of Mangalore cross and converge at kaleidoscopic angles. It's not a bad idea to just hop in an auto-rickshaw and state your destination. On the other hand, visitors really only need to move around the area around the major artery, **K.S. Rao Road.** It runs north from a major **intersection** of six roads, past the **private bus stand,** and to the **KSRTC bus stand** 3km further. **Dr. U.P. Mallya Road** runs southeast from the intersection, past the **Town Hall.** Lighthouse Road moves uphill to the **lighthouse.** About 500m south is the **railway station.**

PRACTICAL INFORMATION

Airport: Bajpe Airport, 22km from town, can be reached by local buses #47A, 47b, and 22 or by taxi. **Indian Airlines** office (tel. 455259) is on Hat Hill (rickshaw Rs12 from Rao Rd.). To: **Bangalore** (4 per week, 1hr., US$50); **Chennai** (4 per week, 2hr., US$70); **Mumbai** (1 per day, 1hr., US$85). Open daily 9:30am-1pm and 1:45-4pm. **Jet Airways** (tel. 440694 or 752709) has flights to Bangalore and Mumbai.

Trains: The **railway station** is 500m south from the intersection of Rao and Lighthouse Rd. Reservation counter open M-Sa 8am-8pm, Su 8am-2pm. Fares listed are 2nd/1st class. To: **Calicut** (7 per day, 5hr., Rs76/319); **Chennai** (*Mangalore-Chennai Mail* 6602, 12:30pm, 18hr.; *West Coast Exp.* 6628, 7:45pm, 18hr., Rs253/830); **Ernakulam** (*Parsuram Exp.* 6350, 4:05am, 10hr.; *Malabar Exp.* 6030, 5:50pm, 10hr., Rs150/496); **Margao (Madgaon)** *Kurla Superfast* 2620, 9pm, 5hr., Rs124/450); **Mumbai** (*Kurla Superfast* 2620, 9pm, 15hr., Rs320/800); **Trivandrum** (*Malabar Exp.* 6030, 6pm, 19hr., Rs202/675).

Bus: Private buses run from the new bus stand located near the intersection of Maidan Rd. and Maidan Rd. West. Many companies, offering different services, have offices at the old bus stand in the alleyway near the intersection of Lighthouse Hill Rd. and K.S. Rao Rd. **Ganesh Travels** (tel. 422977) sends buses to: **Bangalore** (7 per day, 9hr., Rs150/180); **Mumbai** (7:30pm, 24hr., Rs350/400); **Cochin** (8:45pm, 10hr., Rs210); **Panjim** (9:15pm, 9hr., Rs150); **Mysore** (10pm, 8hr.,

Rs135). **KSRTC Bus Stand** plies to: **Bangalore** (7 per day, 9hr., Rs113/135); **Panjim** (3 per day, 10hr., Rs150); **Hassan** (every ½hr., 5hr., Rs54/65); **Mysore** (13 per day, 7hr., Rs135).

Local Transportation: Most **local buses** stop on Dr. U.P. Maliya Rd., near Town Hall. **Auto-rickshaws** are the easiest way to navigate. Most will use their meters (except those that hover around the bus and railway stations).

Tourist Office: Department of Tourism Information Office, Hotel Indraprastha, Lighthouse Hill Rd. (tel. 442926). No maps, but the friendly staff will answer questions and give directions. Open M-Sa 10am-1:30pm and 2:30-5:30pm.

Currency Exchange: State Bank of India, K.S. Rao Rd., exchanges cash and traveler's checks. Open M-F 10am-2pm and 2:30-3:30pm, Sa 10am-12:30pm.

Bookstore: Higginbothams, on Lighthouse Hill Rd., near the intersection with K.S. Rao Rd., has a small section of fiction and textbooks. Open M-Sa 9:30am-1:30pm and 3:30-7:30pm.

Hospital: Government-run **Wenlick Hospital** (tel. 425038) and **City Hospital** (tel. 217424). They are in the Kadri section of town; it's best to take a rickshaw.

Pharmacy: City Drug House (tel. 217357), next to City Hospital. Open 24hr.

Police: (tel. 426426). The main police station is across from the railway station.

Emergency: Police 100, **Fire** 101, **Ambulance** 102.

Post Office: Dr. U.P. Mallya Road, southwest from Town Hall, past the park, Shetty Circle, and a mosque. Open M-F 10am-6pm.

Telephones: STD/ISD booths are all over K.S. Rao Rd., many of which grind 24hr.; a few allow call-backs. The main **Telegraph Office,** Dr. U.P. Maliya Rd., next to the GPO, allows collect calls. **Telephone Code:** 0824.

ACCOMMODATIONS

Weary travelers need look no farther than K.S. Rao Rd., where the hotels are almost uniformly cheap, clean, and pleasant. Most own back-up generators, so you can lounge in well-fanned, Star TV'd bliss all day long. Hot water is only available 6 to 9am, though hot water buckets are available all day.

Hotel Naufal (tel. 428085). With the Town Hall on your left, follow Maidan Rd. to Mission St.; the hotel will be on your right. A so-so hotel at so-cheap prices. Smiling staff guide you to spartan rooms (no top sheets—just like in Sparta) and bathrooms with seat toilets. The waterfront is only a short walk away. Jasmine Restaurant downstairs serves basic foodstuffs. Singles Rs100; doubles Rs150; triples Rs200.

Hotel Shaan Plaza, K.S. Rao Rd. (tel. 440312). Large well-kept hotel that distinguishes itself by its staff, who bring unsolicited, extra towels, enquire after your meals, and generally anticipate your every unspoken need. Huge rooms have heavy-duty fans. Room service, telephones, seat toilets, and Star movies, too. Singles Rs270; doubles Rs350, with A/C Rs600. Extra person Rs75, with A/C Rs100.

Hotel Navaratna (tel. 440520) and **Navaratna Palace** (tel. 441104), K.S. Rao Road. The lobby of the Palace is snazzier, and the rooms a little nicer, but the Hotel is a close second at the same price. All rooms have Star TV, laundry, and room service. Singles Rs200; doubles Rs325, with A/C Rs650. Extra person Rs100.

FOOD

Pai Cafe, in Hotel Navaratna. An excellent veg. restaurant, with delectable *puri thalis* (Rs16), *chaat,* South Indian breakfasts, and Bengali sweets. Waiters are supernice, in spite of the bizarre uniforms. Open daily 6am-10pm.

Tai Chien, in Hotel Moti Mahal, Fahir Rd, near Milagres Church. An impeccable spread of silverware, porcelain, linens, sauces, and pickles is only vaguely discernible in the gilded light of paper lanterns, but the food is so good you don't need to see it. Szechuan pork ribs Rs75. Beer and liquor available. Open daily 7-10:30pm.

The Galley, in Manjuran Hotel (Rs10 by rickshaw from K.S. Rao Rd.). Pricey, but the food is scrumptious and the atmosphere is almost good enough to eat. Indian and Continental dishes on the menu, but the kitchen does requests. Enjoy the delicate Fish Almondine (Rs120) as you sway to the smooth sounds of Urdu love songs, performed live Sa and Su evenings. Frequent special *prix fixe* (Rs150). Open daily 12:30-3pm and 7:30-11pm.

Janatha Restaurant, in the Hotel Shaan Plaza. This bustling restaurant serves up Northern and Southern Indian dishes along with ice cream treats (Rs13-24). The mushroom *masala* is yummy and affordable at Rs26. Open daily 7am-10:30pm.

SIGHTS

The **Lighthouse** up on Lighthouse Hill Rd. is uniquely ugly (with an orange racing stripe), but it is surrounded by lovely gardens and serene hillside views. Further uphill is the Jesuit **St. Aloysius College Chapel,** with painted ceilings dating from 1899. *(Open daily 8:30-10am, noon-2pm, and 3:30-6pm, but ceiling ogling is not welcome during "divine service" Sa and Su mornings. English mass M-Sa 6:30 and 7am, Su 6:30 and 8am.)*

Five kilometers north of the city center, on the headlands of the old port, is **Sultan's Battery,** a fort constructed by Tipu Sultan. Take the #16 bus or a rickshaw (about Rs40 round-trip). The 10th-century **Manjunath Temple** stands 5km north of city center at the bottom of Kadri Hill (buses #19, 14, 14a, and 48; Rs25 round-trip by rickshaw). Once a center for the Shaiva and Tantric Natha-Pantha cult, the temple is noted for its bronze figures, including a seated Lokeshvara, considered among India's finest. The gabled, towered temple complex is surrounded by nine tanks. A path opposite the temple leads to several shrines, then to the **Shri Yogishwar Math,** whose Tantric *sadhus* contemplate Kala Bhairawa (a terrifying aspect of Shiva), Agni (the god of fire), and Durga.

■ Hospet ಹೊಸಪೇಟ್

The famed Vijayanagar king Krishnadevaraya built Hospet between 1509 and 1520 and it became one of his favorite haunts. Today, though, all traces of the Vijayanagar Empire have been eradicated, and Hospet is hum-drum Karnataka, treading the line between heavy industrialization (blaring, barreling trucks transporting the products of a burgeoning steel industry) and village life (pigs, roosters, and dogs sorting through the streetside trash). The only residues of the Vijayanagar ruins here are the regular buses to Hampi (12km northeast). Although rooms and grub can also be found in Hampi Bazaar, Hospet offers a modicum of luxury unavailable in Hampi and easy access to trains and frequent buses.

ORIENTATION

Life in Hospet revolves around **Station Road** (its new name is M.G. Rd., but no one calls it that); it runs more or less north to south from the **railway station,** past the **bus station,** and turns into **Main Bazaar Road** in Hospet's commercial area. It bridges two canals in the process, as well as the **Hampi Road** (which runs northeast) and the **Tungabhadra Dam Road,** which runs west and skirts the market area.

PRACTICAL INFORMATION

Trains: Hospet Junction Station (tel. 131), 750m from the bus stand at the end of Station Rd. Enquiry and reservation counters open daily 8am-8pm To: **Bangalore** (*Hampi Exp.* 6951, 8:30pm, 10½hr., Rs135/464); **Bijapur** (change at Gadag—get there on the *Hampi Exp.* 6592, 7:30am, or *Amaravati Exp.* 7225, 11am, 2hr., Rs30); **Hyderabad** (*Hampi Exp.* 7:30am, 12hr., Rs172/556). For connections to Delhi and Mumbai, take the *Hampi Exp.* to Guntakal.

Buses: The bus station (tel. 28802) is in the middle of town on Station Rd. across from Hotel Vishwa. Enquiry counter open 24hr. Reservation counters open daily 8am-noon and 3-6pm. Enquiry open 24hr. To: **Badami** (6:45, 9:30am, 1pm, Rs55); **Bangalore** (9 per day, 5:30am-2am, 8hr., Rs92/119); **Bijapur** (7 per day, 5:30am-1pm, Rs62); **Hassan** (10am, 11:30pm, 10hr., Rs90); **Hyderabad** (6 per day, 9:30am-12:30am, 11hr. Rs113); **Mangalore** (7:30pm, 12hr., Rs113); **Mumbai** (3pm, 24hr., Rs230); **Mysore** (6:30, 8, 8:30am, 7:30 and 10pm, Rs114).

Local Transportation: You really don't need anything but your feet in this tiny town. **Auto-rickshaws** are unmetered. You can also ride with a **cycle-rickshaw** ("bicycle tonga"), as the rickshaw-*wallah* smokes a *bidi* to reduce the strain of pulling your weight (Rs8 to railway station). To get to **Hampi** (12km), take a bus from platform 10 (every 30min. 6am-7:30pm, Rs3-4), catch an auto-rickshaw (Rs60-80), or rent a bike. **Bicycles** can be rented from **Khizer Cycle Market,** Station Rd., across from the turn off the Malligi Tourist Home (Rs3 per hr., Rs30 per day). Open daily 7am-8:30pm.

Tourist Office: Karnataka Dept. of Tourism and **KSTDC** (the commercial wing which organizes tours) share an office (tel. 58537), at the corner of College and Old Bus Stand Rd. Make a left onto Station Rd. from the bus station; take your first left onto College, then your first left onto Old Bus Stand Rd. You can book a bus tour of Hampi and the Tungabhadra Dam here (Rs60), get a decent map of Hampi, and learn about Karnataka's other hotspots. Dept. of Tourism open M-Sa 10am-5:30pm. Closed 2nd Sa. KSTDC open daily 7am-10pm.

Budget Travel: Monika Travels (tel. 27446). Make a left from the bus station onto Station Rd.; the office is on the left. Book air, rail, and bus tickets, and rent cars at Rs3.5 per km. Open M-Sa 9:30am-3pm and 6:30-9pm.

Currency Exchange: State Bank of India, Station Rd. (tel. 58470), a few steps north of Hotel Priyadarshini. Changes cold hard cash in US$ and UK£ only. Open M-F 10:30am-2:30pm. **Monika Travels** exchanges AmEx and Thomas Cook traveler's checks at slightly inflated rates.

Hospital: Government General Hospital (tel. 28199 or 28444). Go west on College Rd. past the Evangelical Church and Vijayanagar College, and turn left immediately. Cross a canal and continue; the hospital will be on your right. Recently refurbished and very clean. **Medinowa** is a new private hospital.

Police Station (tel. 54204). On the same block as the Tourist Office, 200m south.

Post Office, Station Rd. (tel. 28210), south of the bus station. Open M-Sa 8am-12:30pm and 2-5:30pm. **Postal Code:** 583201.

Telephones: Telegraph Office (tel. 58212), next door to the State Bank of India on Station Rd., has a 24hr. STD/ISD phone. **Telephone Code:** 08394.

ACCOMMODATIONS

Malligi Tourist Home, 6/143 J.N. Rd. (tel. 28101). From the bus stand, walk south 250m and turn left before the second intersection—Khizer Cycle Market will be on your right. Regular rooms are a good value; luxury complex digs are spectacular, down to the seat toilets. Newly built pool open Tu-Su 6am-7pm (Rs25 per hr. for non-deluxe room guests). Currency exchange for guests. Check-out 24hr. Singles Rs80; doubles Rs140-170; deluxe Rs350-2250.

Hotel Priyadarshini, V/45 Station Rd. (tel. 28838), 500m south of the railway station. The 82 rooms are spacious if dusty, with telephones, gung-ho fans, room service, and same-day laundry. Each has a balcony. Hot showers in the mornings. Great attached restaurant. Check-out 24hr. Singles Rs140; doubles Rs165; quads Rs220. A/C rooms Rs380-425. TV Rs100 extra.

Hotel Shalini (tel. 28910), 300m south of the railway station on Station Rd. With flowering trees outside its tiny pink facade, the place makes up in character what it lacks in convenience or cleanliness. Join the staff for *chai* in the central courtyard. Squat toilet and bucket hot water in the morning. Bring your own sheets. Check-out 24hr. Singles Rs50; doubles Rs80; triples Rs90; quads Rs150.

FOOD

Naivedyam Restaurant, attached to Hotel Priyadarshini. Dishes out consistently fresh huge portions. North and South Indian *thalis* (Rs17-35) with a choice of *chapati* or *puri. Alu* and *palak* prepared a million different ways. Open daily 7am-10:30pm, for *thalis* noon-3:15pm and 7-10:30pm.

Iceland Restaurant, College Rd. (tel. 27347), scoops sundaes (Rs10-20), near-solid milkshakes (Rs10-20), and North Indian cuisine. Open daily 10:30am-10pm.

Waves Restaurant, the new, ultra-slick restaurant at Mallisi Tourist Home overlooks the swimming pool and could just as easily be Bangalore's latest hot-spot. Expect to pay about Rs100 for a meal. Kashmiri *pulao* (Rs50) and chicken *tikka* (Rs55).

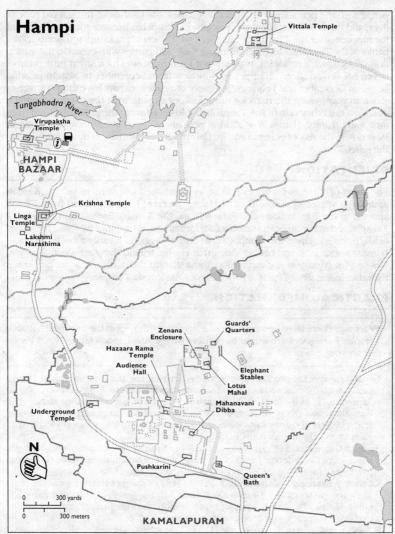

Hampi

- Vittala Temple
- Tungabhadra River
- Virupaksha Temple
- HAMPI BAZAAR
- Krishna Temple
- Linga Temple
- Lakshmi Narashima
- Guards' Quarters
- Zenana Enclosure
- Hazaara Rama Temple
- Audience Hall
- Elephant Stables
- Lotus Mahal
- Mahanavani Dibba
- Underground Temple
- Pushkarini
- Queen's Bath
- N
- 0   300 yards
- 0   300 meters
- KAMALAPURAM

■ Hampi ಹಂಪೆ

It is said that gold once rained down in Hampi, figuratively if not literally. The city was awash in rubies and diamonds, and wealth dripped from its corniced rooftops and flowed in its gutters, filling its sacred tanks. There was a time when Vijayanagar's king would distribute his weight in precious metals to the area's needy. But the king can only get so fat, and eventually riches beget ruin. Five dynasties ruled the resplendent kingdom and its capital from 1336 to 1565, building all manner of temples, pavilions, aqueducts, and palaces, but in 1565, a confederacy of Muslim sultans from the north annihilated the empire and sopped up Vijayanagar's wealth, leaving the once thriving capital dry and desolate.

Despite ongoing attempts by the Archaeological Survey of India (and UNESCO) to restore the Vijayanagar ruins to their 15th-century splendor, Hampi may never dispense with the pervading aura of decay: the desolate landscape; the languid pace of lives; and the utterly decadent tourist culture. Hampi has become the latest hang-out for hippies: after the Christmas raves in Goa, the crew packs up and heads to the banks of the Tungabhadra River, bringing their acid parties with them (to the frustration of the town's residents, who are not keen on seeing their town turned into a haven for drug-dealers). Hampi's season runs from September to March, peaking between December and February, but more than a few expats have turned a week's stay into years, using the ruins for drug dens, or eloping with Hampites and settling down on the other side of the Tungabhadra River to avoid the police. Isolated from time and urbanity, Hampi is an alluring permanent oasis for any traveler seeking to slow down; the risk of going to admire Hampi's history is that you might get mired in the ruins.

ORIENTATION

The ruins of Vijayanagar spread 26 sq km, and the bulk of them start at **Kamal-apuram,** a village 4km southeast of **Hampi Bazaar.** The paved road from Kamal-apuram to the Bazaar skirts the **Palace Area,** the **Zenana Enclosure,** the **Krishna Temple,** and many other shrines, boulder formations, coconut groves, and sugarcane fields, before reaching the Hampi Bazaar. Hampi Bazaar is actually a cluster of guest-houses, restaurants, and bauble shops that cluster around the **Virupaksha Temple,** whose 53m *gopuram* you can't miss. About 2km to the northeast of the bazaar lies the other major area of ruins, which includes the **Vittala Temple.**

PRACTICAL INFORMATION

> **Warning:** There have been reports of muggings and rapes in the area near Vittala Temple. **Foreigners are asked to register with the police at Hampi** when they first arrive in town.

Local Transportation: The "bus stand" is actually just the intersection of Hampi Bazaar with the road to Hospet and Kamalapuram. **Buses** to: **Hospet** (every 30min. 7am-8pm, 45min., Rs2). **Auto-rickshaws** shuttle between Hampi Bazaar and **Kamalapuram** (Rs5), or **Hospet** (Rs50). The best way to get around town is to rent a **bicycle** at Guru's Bicycle Shop, 50m behind the tourist office (Rs30 per day; Rs3 per hr.) Open daily 6am-7pm.

Tourist Office (tel. 51339), 100m towards the Virupaksha Temple from where the buses stop. Get a detailed map of the ruins and hire an approved guide (in-season: Rs100-500; off-season: Rs100). Open M-Sa 10am-5:30pm. Closed 2nd Sa.

Currency Exchange: Canara Bank (tel. 41243) exchanges traveler's checks only. They accept AmEx and Thomas Cook checks in US, British, and French currency. Open M, Tu, Th, and F 11am-2pm. In season, various private travel agencies exchange currency—try **Modi,** next to the tourist office.

Bookstore: Aspirations Store (tel. 41254). Open 9:30am-8pm.

Hospital: The nearest medical services are in Hospet.

Police (tel. 41241), inside the Virupaksha Temple, immediately to your right. Register here when you get in town—it will take all of 2 minutes. Open 24hr. (closed for breaks). There's also a branch in Kanakpuram (tel. 41240), east of the bus stand.

Post Office (tel. 41242), just outside the temple, beside the *gopuram. Poste Restante.* Open M-Sa 8:30am-1pm and 2-4:30pm. **Postal Code:** 583239.

Telephones: The bazaar's **STD/ISDs** are 24hr. in season. **Telephone Code:** 08394.

ACCOMMODATIONS

To 15th-century traveler Domingo Paes, the Hampi Bazaar was "a broad and beautiful street, full of rows of fine houses and mantapas…[where] you will find all sorts of rubies, and diamonds, and emeralds, and pearls and seed pearls, and every other sort of thing there is on earth that you wish to buy." To the 20th-century tourist, Hampi Bazaar, flanked by Virupaksha Temple's huge *gopuram* and the monolithic Nandi, is important not for its magnificent architecture, glimmering jewels, or vivid silks, but for its cheap rooms, pancakes and spaghetti, and stone(r)s of a different variety than in Paes' day. Staying in the guest houses of the Bazaar, most of which are portions of homes, usually requires a lack of concern for cleanliness and sprawling space, a fondness for squat toilets, and a tolerance for buggies, doggies, and froggies.

Shanthi Guest House (tel. 41568). From the bus stand, walk toward the Virupaksha Temple, turn right, and walk around the Sree Rama Lodge. Its enclosed garden, cheerful exterior, and clean common toilets (cold showers) make it a wellspring of tourist camaraderie. Check-out 10:30am. Jan.-Feb.: singles Rs100; doubles Rs120. Mar.-Dec.: Rs60/80).

Vicky Guest House (41694). 200m behind the tourist office, has huge beds, fans, and pretty-clean common baths. Rooms downstairs are super-modern (for Hampi) and a great bargain. Attached restaurant (in season). Check-out is at 11am. Cold bucket showers. Dec.-Feb.: singles Rs60; doubles Rs80; Mar.-Nov.: Rs140/150.

Hotel Mayura Bhuvaneswari, Kamalapuram (tel. 41574), 500m to the right (east) as you exit the Kamalapuram bus stand, or make a left coming from the bazaar. About 4km from Hampi. A big sign on the right marks a long, paved driveway that leads to the hotel. Spacious, spotless rooms are deserted in the off-season by all but frogs, lizards, and the doting waitstaff. Hot water 24hr. and seat toilets. Check-out noon. Singles Rs220, with A/C Rs363; doubles Rs264/424.

Lakshmi Guest House (tel. 41287), behind the tourist office, has common trough baths. The mattresses are hard, but the sheets are clean. Bring your own padlock. Check-out noon. Doubles are Rs30-50 depending on how far you can talk the manager down. Sleeping on the roof is free Oct.-Mar.

Sree Rama Lodge (tel. 41219). A good, clean bet for doubles, but look elsewhere for singles. Lighting is fickle at best, and dim even when it's on. Attached squat toilet and shower. Check-out 24hr. Singles Rs50; doubles Rs100.

FOOD

Open-air cafes line the main bazaar. These are probably the only places in Karnataka that serve hummus and "fal-fel." Hybrid Indian-Western food means fruit *parathas,* chocolate *lassis,* and *masala* macaroni. But don't get your hopes up—the sub-standard Western fare can leave you craving a fresh *thali,* which can be surprisingly difficult to find. Most rooftop restaurants are open in-season.

Hotel Mayura Bhuvaneswari, Kamalapuram. The only enclosed restaurant in the whole area. It has *thalis* on Sundays (Rs20-35) and toast, *dosas, chapatis,* and veg. and chicken curries all the time. Piles of vegetable *pakoras* go for Rs10. Open daily 6:30am-10pm.

Welcome Restaurant, Hampi Bazaar. Popular for its pasta (Rs30-35) and standard backpacker course of pancakes and hummus.

Om Shankar Restaurant, on the way to Vittala Temple, a few minutes from Hampi Bazaar. Unspectacular fare, but the view of the river is grand.

Gopi Restaurant. Open throughout the year. Good rice (Rs8) and decent if uninspired vegetable curry (Rs20).

SIGHTS

Vijayanagar Ruins

The ruins spread at least 26 sq. km; although it's impossible to see everything in a day or two, if you have stamina you can soak up the main sights in one foot-killing, back-aching, thigh-throbbing day. Renting a bicycle in Hospet, Kamalapuram, or Hampi Bazaar will help you see everything except the Vittala Temple area to the northeast (the path is too rocky for bikes). Either lock your bike and leave it with the tourist office or approach Vittala from the southeast, along the tour bus route. Be sure to watch out for your belongings; it is recommended that you carry only a few hundred rupees on your person. **Avoid walking along the river or behind the Vittala Temple alone** (though the path to the temple is considered safe).

At one end of the Hampi Bazaar is the imposing **Virupaksha Temple.** This was the king's personal temple; inside is a marriage hall and assembly hall. Toward the rear, you can enter a small room where a *camera obscura* of sorts throws an upside-down image of the *gopuram* on the wall. Walk back toward the *gopuram* and take a right before exiting. Hike up the stony hill, past the **Jain Temples** on your right (this is a great place to stop for a breather because of the beautiful views of Hampi), veer left, and you'll approach some boulder-caves where armies used to chill in the shade. The road down below leads to **Kamalapuram** and the ruins in the Palace Area. Before you see these, you will pass the **Krishna Temple** on your right. Just after that, make a right on the dirt path to reach the **Narasimha Lakshmi statue.** When Muslim sultans sacked the city, they sliced open Narasimha's belly to see if the 7m-high monolith had eaten any rubies or diamonds. They were disappointed, and Narasimha remains disfigured, but he still cuts one of Hampi's most striking figures. Around the back you can see the feminine hand of his consort Lakshmi, who was probably depicted sitting on Narasimha's thigh. The ASI is trying to restore Narasimha to his original wholeness, but this would·mean sacrificing his monolithic nature to mortar. Next to the state is the **Linga Temple,** distinguished by its huge *linga* (the second-largest in India).

Back on the main road, continue until you see a sign pointing to the left for the Lotus Mahal. On your right will be the **Underground Temple,** which, because of a collapsed roof, now fills up with rainwater and fish during monsoon season. Follow the signs to the Lotus Mahal at the end of the road. Make a left, walking away from the **Hazara Rama Temple** and past the pink Archaeological Camp House. Here you'll see the **Zenana Enclosure,** a stone wall within which the ladies of the court used to stay, unmolested by the eyes of the less fair sex. *(Open daily 6am-6pm. Admission Rs5.)* To the right is the pink stucco **Lotus Mahal,** a sweet little example of Indo-Saracenic architecture. Nearby is a **watchtower,** used to survey the terrain for enemies, or, according to some accounts, to provide a vantage point for the king's wives to watch the goings-on without being spotted. Across from the Lotus Mahal are the **Guard's Quarters,** with high arches and polished floors. To the east and through the stone walls are the 11 domed **Elephant Stables,** where the royal beasts (more than 15,000 of them during the 15th century) slept, rested, and ate a whole lot of elephant food. Backtrack to the sign pointing to the Mahanavami Dibba and take that road south; on your right will be the Hazara Rama Temple. The enclosure walls are carved with relief work on both the inside (scenes from the *Ramayana*) and the outside (a parade of horses, elephants, dancing girls, and soldiers). Inside the sanctum are two rare images of Vishnu as Buddha, his ninth incarnation. Continue on the road, and just as the path veers east (to your left), you will see a large platform, which was the **Audience Hall.** Next comes the **Mahanavami Dibba** (also on your right), crossed by ancient aqueducts and stone canals (all dry now), where the gala Dasara festival was held. *Dibba* means platform; this Dasara platform is one of the tallest and most ornate around. The Dasara throne, replete with gold and gems, was stored inside. Because, like most other Vijayanagar monuments, it was carved out of granite, the frieze work and detail are not that fine, but what it lacks in embellishment it makes up for in stature. South of the *dibba* is the recently excavated **Pushkarini,** a deep sacred water tank with mind-blowingly regular steps. Just before the dirt road joins back with the main paved road to Kamalapuram, on your left you will see the **Queen's Bath,** a giant stone enclosure surrounded by a moat. The inside has a huge swimming pool where the queen supposedly kicked back after a hard day.

Kamalapuram lies another 600m down the road. You can continue this way and ride on the paved road about 5km north to the **Vittala Temple,** or you can backtrack to Hampi Bazaar and walk the 2km along the river to the temple. Vittala looks unimpressive and small from the outside, but you'll know you're there from the cold-drink dealers and tourist buses. It sits on the south bank of the Tungabhadra River and was never finished or consecrated. According to the 20-odd inscriptions in and around the temple, the Vijayanagar King Krishnadevaraya began building it in 1513, and the work was probably halted by the city's destruction in 1565. Another bit of lore has it that Vittala, the incarnation of Vishnu to whom the temple is dedicated, came to look at the temple, found it too grand for him, and hightailed it back to his humbler home in Maharashtra. Indeed, the carvings here are certainly the most ornate around the ruins. Fifty-six musical pillars inside the temple each sound a different note when tapped with the knuckles. The best way to hear the reverberations is to put your ear to one pillar and have someone else do the tapping. Outside the temple is the massive stone chariot for Garuda, Vishnu's mythical bird, with stone wheels that actually rotate (this is harder than it looks).

Anegundi

The ancient cave temples at Anegundi are seldom visited by tourists. The Archaeological Survey of India isn't in charge here, and getting to the caves is an adventure in itself. Because there are no signs, it may be best to solicit the assistance of a certified guide at Hampi's tourist office (Rs100-500 in season, Rs100 off season). From the Vittala Temple, continue on the main paved road along the Tungabhadra River. Eventually the road deteriorates into a path leading to the river bank where two grass-basket boats shuttle people, bicycles, and (more perilously) motorcycles to and from Anegundi. Hop in and stay still—balance is key here. Once you reach the other side, walk straight up a small slope and you'll see the village. If not, just ask your boat-*wallah* ("Anegundi?"), and he'll point you in the right direction. A left turn at the first opportunity, and a subsequent left at the next fork in the road will lead you past the Andhra Bank and under a small gate. After the gate, turn left onto the paved road that cuts through rice paddies. A dirt path veers off to the left; take it and you'll be at the base of the rocky hill you need to climb. At the midpoint is a **Durga Temple,** thought to be the site at which Rama killed the monkey king Vali. The temple is still functioning and is especially favored by soldiers who perform *pujas* to gain strength. A *bidi*-smoking *swami* will offer you *chai* and (perhaps) other treats, and will point you past his shrine and up the hill to the **Laxmi Temple.** Here, purportedly, Sita prayed for Rama's forgiveness after he banished her, demonstrating her devotion to her doubting husband, as well as her purity of mind, body, and soul. The nearby **Pampasaro-vara Pond** is believed to be the site where Parvati prayed for a husband (quite successfully—the reward for her efforts was no less than Shiva). A small 7th-century temple marks **Hanuman Hill,** the monkey-god's birthplace. His simian descendants still scamper about and are irreverent enough to snatch cameras and lunches.

■ Badami ಬಾದಮಿ

This jumping little town in the middle of nowhere was the capital of the mighty Chalukyan Empire from 543 to 757. Locals live beside or inside the ancient cave temples and edifices that dot the landscape, and though they are friendly, few speak much English. The temples are situated high in the mountains surrounding an ancient Chalukyan tank, around which the thwacking and thumping of women doing the family laundry reverberates (in fact, the brilliant green hue of the tank's water is due to overabundant algae which thrives on detergent). Badami is also the closest town to Pattadkal (20km), where Chalukyan kings were crowned, and Aihole (47km), the first Chalukyan capital, on the Malaprabha River.

Together, these three towns are a fascinating study in the development of Indian temple architecture. Aihole is considered the birthplace of the style that came to characterize Indian temples: these structures were built up rather than carved out, as older cave temples were. The cave temples of Badami and the later temples at Pattadkal represent the evolution of an increasingly sophisticated style. Though they are less aesthetically impressive than what you'll find in Belur, Halebid, and Somnathpur, the Chalukyan temples served as a template for styles that would later emerge throughout the country.

ORIENTATION AND PRACTICAL INFORMATION Badami's main road is **Station Road,** probably the only straight path in the entire village. It runs from the **railway station** in the north to the **bus stand** (5km) and to the routes to Pattadkal and Aihole in the south. Most accommodations and cafes are around the bus stand. **College Road (Ramdurg Road)** is the other roadway in Badami—it runs east from Station Rd., south of the bus station, and winds around to reach the KSTDC hotel and **Tourist Information Center** (tel. 65414; open M-Sa 10:30am-5pm; closed second Sa), 1km later. The **Bhutanatha Temples** are north of **Agastya Lake. Buses** run to: **Aihole** (6 per day, 5:30am-3pm, 2hr., Rs11); **Bangalore** (5:30am, 5:30 and 8:30pm, 9hr., Rs150); **Bijapur** (5 per day, 6:45am-5pm, 5hr., Rs35); **Hospet** (5:30, 9am and 1:30pm, 5hr.); **Pattadakal** (every hr., 5:30am-9pm, 1hr., Rs7). The only **private bus** service in town goes to Bangalore (9:30pm, 9hr., Rs150); book through Hotel Mookambika Deluxe (tel. 65067). Private **maxicabs** are another way to reach Pattadakal. **Trains** run to **Bijapur** (5:15 and 11:30am, 4:50, 8:10, and 11:45pm, 4hr.) and **Gadag** (for connections to Hospet, 9hr. total).

There is no bank offering **currency exchange,** but Hotel Mookambika will exchange US and English currency for both hard cash and traveler's checks. The **police station** is opposite the bus stand. The **GPO** (open M-Sa 7-11am and 2-5pm) and (supposedly) 24hr. **Telegraph Office** (tel. 65030) are just north of the bus stand. **Postal Code:** 587201. **Telephone Code:** 08357.

ACCOMMODATIONS AND FOOD Compared to the sparse offerings at Aihole and Pattadkal, Badami's accommodations are downright plentiful. **Hotel Mookambika Deluxe** (tel. 65067), across from the bus stand in Badami, is the cheeriest and cleanest of the hotels near the bus stand. Screened windows look out upon the Chalukyan hills, and an in-house travel agency will help get you there. Don't be shy about bargaining off season. (Singles Rs150, with TV Rs300, with A/C Rs600; doubles Rs200/350/650.) The attached restaurant serves food made-to-order with selection and prices geared to tourists. The hotel's travel agency also runs the only tour of the temple sites (Rs150, 3 person minimum); otherwise you'll have to hire a cab (Rs450). Cheaper options include **Hotel Anand** (tel. 65074), across from Hotel Mookambika (singles Rs50, with bath Rs70; doubles Rs70/120, with air-cooling Rs160), and, across the street, the somewhat brighter **Hotel Satka** (tel. 65417; singles with bath Rs70; doubles Rs100-150). If proximity and *paise*-pinching are not your top priority, consider the **Hotel Mayura Chalukya,** College Rd. (tel. 65046). From the bus stand, turn right, walk 500m, and take the first right on the first paved road. Walk down this road 1km; the hotel is set back from the road on your right. This is monkey territory, but the rooms are huge, relatively clean, and look out onto overgrown gardens. Both seat and squat toilets are available, and hot water flows night and day. The attached restaurant does mediocre cuisine. (Check-out noon. Singles Rs168; doubles Rs200; triples Rs250). For cheaper food, try the stand-up, no-nonsense, clean **Geeta Darshini** (tel. 65234), where nothing on the menu costs more than Rs5 (open M-Sa 6:30am-9pm). If you want to sit down, head across the street to **Laxmi** for spicy *thalis* (Rs15), *dosas* (Rs8), and a variety of veg. side dishes.

SIGHTS A visit to the **cave temples** near Badami is a great way to scramble over rocks and see some ancient beauty while you're at it. *(Temples open 6am-9pm. Admission to cave temples Rs2. Guides Rs175 for 2-3hr. tour or Rs350 for a whole day.)* The **South Fort** cave temples, carved out of the red sandstone cliff and connected by steps, are some of the most important cave temples in India. To get from the bus stand to the cave temples, head right on Station Rd. past College Rd. You'll see a statue of Dr. Ambedkar; turn left on the road he faces and head up the 40 giant steps to the first cave and the three younger caves. These temples are Hindu, but the influences of Jainism and Buddhism are apparent. **Cave 1,** the oldest, is dedicated to Shiva in his different guises. On the right front wall is an 18-armed dancing Shiva. The is also a *lingam* in the back of the cave protected by granite cobras. **Cave 2** is dedicated to Vishnu, as is **Cave 3,** the largest and best-sculpted of the group, dating from 578 AD.

The 21m-long facade of Cave 3 is carved with figures of humans, gods, and dwarves, as are the pillars and the steps leading to the foundation. Check out the depiction of Vishnu reclined on a serpents lap; the asp's mouth looms over him, but the god remains mellow (divinity has its perks). The caves were once painted, but now the only traces of color are on the ceiling of Cave 3. The path up to Cave 3 leads past a natural cave which was once used as a Buddhist temple; the Buddha image inside has been defaced. **Cave 4,** which was probably the only cave here used as a Jain temple, overlooks the lake. The pillars in Cave 4 are held up by an assortment of creatures, including one which bears a startling resemblance to Yoda from *Star Wars*.

Across the lake from the cave temples, lie a plethora of other temples, including the Bhutanantha and Shivalaya temples. To reach these, as well as the **Archaeological Museum** (open Sa-Th 10am-5pm; free), head right from the bus stand and you'll find a sign, which leads you through a tiny neighborhood on narrow stone paths. The **Upper Shivalaya Temple** is one of the oldest of the group at Badami. Carvings on it depict scenes from the life of Krishna. The most spectacular of the temples is the **Malegetti Shivalaya,** with a pillared hallway flanked by Shiva on one side and Vishnu on the other. The temple perches precariously atop the hill, and the views of the village and the fields below are spectacular. The **Jambulinga Temple,** built in 699 by the Vijayanagars, is in town, by Agastya Tank near the rickshaw stand. The **Bhutanatha Temples** are on the opposite side of the Agastya Tank. Though it seems that virtually every temple is architecturally, historically, or religiously significant, they may seem to all blend together to unschooled Western eyes. Your best bet is to simply wander around and enjoy the interplay between the natural beauty of Badami's sandstone cliffs and the man-made beauty of the architecture.

■ Aihole ಐಹೊಳ

Forty-four kilometers northeast of Badami on the banks of the Malaprabha River, **Aihole** offers spectacular opportunities for temple viewing. And these aren't just any temples: the litter of beautiful half-finished temples are the playground of a civilization hell-bent on building the greatest architecture in the region. There are over 100 temples in Aihole, combining elements of both Dravidian and Northern Nagar styles—note that there are *gopurams* of both styles. The distinct Chalukyan architecture of the temples includes square pillars and flat roofs in the center that gently slope downwards on the periphery. The most impressive temple within the main compound is the **Durgigudi Temple,** dedicated to Vishnu, but so named because it is next to a fort (*durga*). The temple has Islamic-style perforated windows whose round shape betrays its influences drawn from Buddhist *chaitya* halls. The Jain **Meguti Temple** has a stone inscription in Old Kannada script dating to 634, making it one of the oldest dated temples in India. Just below is the relatively unadorned Buddhist temple. Also in the main compound is the **Ladh Khan Temple,** further south, named after a 19th-century Muslim who set up house in the sanctuary. Due to its similarity to megalithic caves, this temple was once thought to date from the 5th century, although now it is believed to have come from the early 8th century. The structure combines elements of Dravidian style with hints of typical Chalukyan architecture (such as a flat roof).

Outside the compound, but within walking distance, is the **Ravan Phadi** cave temple, a precursor to the more sophisticated cave temples of Badami. Also nearby is the **Jain Meguti Temple,** on top of a hill with a spectacular view of Aihole's temples interlaced with the less aesthetically pleasing ramshackle concrete abodes.

There's only one place in Aihole for non-locals to lay their weary heads at night: the **Tourist Home Aihole** (tel. 68041). The manager is gracious, the food cooked to order, and you can bet there are no postcard touts hanging around. Standard, clean rooms cost half of what they would in Badami. (Singles with common bath Rs35; doubles Rs45/60.) Otherwise, you can daytrip here; the bus back to Badami leaves at 10:30am and 4:30pm.

■ Pattadakal ಪಟ್ಟದಕಲ್

About 20km between Badami and Aihole, **Pattadakal** was the Chalukyan capital during the 7th and 8th centuries. Its temples are the most stylistically advanced in the region. Since there are no accommodations, travelers must stay in Badami or Aihole and daytrip here. **Buses** and private maxicabs make the 45 minute trek to Badami (every 45min., 6am-7pm, Rs5-7). Buses to Aihole leave at 7, 8, 9, 10am and 4pm.

Pattadakal's ancient temples are clustered at the base of a pink sandstone hill. (Temple compound open 6am-6pm. Admission Rs5. Guides Rs50—bargain for a shorter tour at a reduced cost.) The **Virupaksha (Lokeshvara) Temple** has a three-story spire with a chlorite stone Nandi sitting in front of it. Passages lead around the shrine to carvings depicting episodes from the *Ramayana* and *Mahabharata,* as well as scenes of Chalukyan triumphs on the battlefield. The **Virupaksha Temple** is one of the only active temples in the area. The other prominent temples in the compound are the **Mallikarjuna Temple** and the **Papanatha Temple.** About 1km south of the compound is the **Jain Temple,** which has an upper-story sanctuary accessible by a staircase, guarded by a gate carved with crocodiles. Climbing to the top leads to a lovely view of sunflower-filled fields.

Road Writing

The backsides of Indian motor vehicles make for interesting recreational reading. Even the most fume-filled of city drives can be brightened by a simple game of "guess-the-rickshaw-driver's-religion-from-his-bumper-stickers." Similarly, road trips offer the eye-candy of those humorously ominous warnings painted on the backs of lumbering Tatas and Ashok-Leylands. The most pervasive genre of this lorry literature is the proper-horn-use statement: "Soundhorn," "No Horn!," and the ubiquitously inane "Horn OK Please." The latter phrase finds its origins in the days when many Indian goods carriers had a centered, cyclopic brake light. The "Horn Please" directed drivers to signal if they wished to pass the larger, slower vehicle. If the truck driver saw fit to allow such a maneuver, he would tap his brake, and the center light, labelled "OK," would flash. Eventually the one taillight became two, but by then word order stayed. "Horn OK Please" was fixed in the mind and tailgate of Indian automotive consciousness.

Andhra Pradesh

Andhra Pradesh
ఆంధ్రదేశము

The state of Andhra Pradesh occupies a large portion of southeastern India, from the dry Deccan Plateau to the coast of the Bay of Bengal, where the Krishna and Godavari Rivers feed into rich, cyclone-drenched deltas. Inland lies Telangana, the poorer region of Andhra Pradesh. The state is named for the kingdom of the Andhras, also known as the Satavahanas, who ruled most of the Deccan from the 2nd century BC until the 3rd century AD. As part of Emperor Ashoka's vast kingdom, the region was also a major Buddhist center. Beginning in the 16th century, Andhra Pradesh was ruled by Muslims, first under the Golconda Sultanate, then as part of the Mughal Empire, and finally under the Nizams, who ruled from Hyderabad under British protection from 1723 until 1948.

Despite the state's diversity of inherited religious influences, the people of Andhra are linked by their language, Telugu. In 1956, Andhra Pradesh became the first state in India to have its boundaries drawn along linguistic lines. When India gained Independence in 1947, Nizam of Hyderabad refused to cede his lands to the new nation. After a year-long standoff, the Indian government forcibly annexed the territory, which was later merged with other Telugu-speaking areas to form Andhra Pradesh. Today, Andhra remains one of the least-touristed destinations in India, but the state is still home to a number of attractions including Hyderabad. The capital remains one of India's great centers of Islamic culture, and the richly endowed Hindu temple at Tirupati, which evokes a religious fervor unparalleled in South India.

🖐 HIGHLIGHTS OF ANDHRA PRADESH

- **Unpretentious Hyderabad's** bazaars and monuments (p. 607) are but a prelude to the serenely spooky ruins of **Golconda Fort** (p. 605), west of town.
- **Tirupati's** hilltop temple frenzy (p. 609) provides an interesting look at contemporary Hinduism, followed immediately by a harrowing plunge of a bus ride.

■ Hyderabad హైదరాబాదు

Let millions of men and women of all castes, creeds, and religions make it their abode, like fish in the ocean.
—Muhammad Quli Qutb Shah, upon laying Hyderabad's foundation

The story of Hyderabad's beginnings stands as a testament to the overwhelming power of love in a country that has endured centuries of religious strife. The city was founded in the late 16th century by Muhammad Quli Qutb Shah, Sultan of Golconda. Though he was to ascend to the throne of one of the greatest kingdoms in India, the young Muhammad had fallen in love too hard and too fast to heed religious and social barriers. His love, Bhagmati, was a simple but lovely Hindu dancer and singer. Muhammad risked his life and inheritance, making midnight horseback journeys from Golconda to a village on the banks of the Musi River to tryst with the beautiful Bhagmati. Upon discovering his son's smittenness, Muhammad's father capitulated and allowed Muhammad to marry the common Hindu girl. The boy became king and founded a new city on the banks of the Musi, which he christened Bhagnagar. Although the city was later renamed Hyderabad, and Golconda is now in shambles, the city's syncretist tendencies remain legendary.

Today, this metropolis of 5 million has the highest proportion of Muslims of any city in the south, yet was one of the few urban centers that did not erupt in riots following the 1992 destruction of the Babri Masjid in Ayodhya. The Muslim Nizam of Hyderabad ruled over a doting Hindu-majority state until his death in the 1950s. The city's architecture is striking not only for its grandeur (the last Nizam was reputedly the wealthiest man in the world, and liked to show it), but for its masterful embodiment of Indo-Saracenic character.

While past visitors noted Hyderabad's relatively clean streets and mellow pace, recent years have seen only increasing congestion and urbanization, with all the related benefits and problems. An immense new bus station and plans for an international airport have solidified the city's status as the travel and tourism hub of Andhra Pradesh—you won't need to take a midnight horseback ride to get here—but the increased traffic has quickened the tempers and dirtied the streets. Nevertheless, the beautiful Muslim monuments and traditional bazaars of the Old City rightly make Hyderabad a popular tourist destination.

ORIENTATION

The **Musi River** divides the **Old City**—land of the Charminar, Mecca Masjid, and bazaars—from the **New City** of government offices, glitzy downtown shops, and glimmering Birla-commissioned landmarks to the north. The **Abids** area forms the heart of the New City: it's about 1.5km south of the gargantuan, Gautama-guarded **Husain Sagar,** the artificial lake built during the Golconda empire, and it houses **Hyderabad (Nampally) Station,** one of the area's transport hubs. The other hub is in **Secunderabad,** to the northeast of Husain Sagar, where the **railway station** sends travelers in and out of the city.

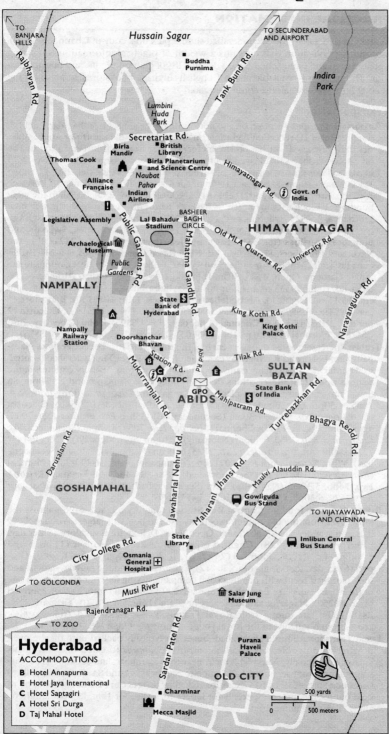

TO BANJARA HILLS

Rajbhavan Rd.

Hussain Sagar

TO SECUNDERABAD AND AIRPORT

Buddha Purnima

Tank Bund Rd.

Indira Park

Lumbini Huda Park

Secretariat Rd.

Birla Mandir

British Library

Thomas Cook

Birla Planetarium and Science Centre

Himayatnagar Rd.

Govt. of India

Alliance Française

Naubat Pahar

Indian Airlines

Legislative Assembly

Public Gardens Rd.

Lal Bahadur Stadium

BASHEER BAGH CIRCLE

HIMAYATNAGAR

Mahatma Gandhi Rd.

Old MLA Quarters Rd.

University Rd.

Archaeological Museum

Public Gardens

NAMPALLY

Narayanguda Rd.

State Bank of Hyderabad

King Kothi Rd.

King Kothi Palace

A

Nampally Railway Station

Doorshanchar Bhavan

Abid Rd.

D

Tilak Rd.

SULTAN BAZAR

B

Station Rd.

C

APTTDC

E

Mukarramjahi Rd.

GPO

ABIDS

Mahipatram Rd.

State Bank of India

Turrebazkhan Rd.

Bhagya Reddi Rd.

Darusalam Rd.

GOSHAMAHAL

Jawaharlal Nehru Rd.

Maharani Jhansi Rd.

Maulvi Alauddin Rd.

Gowliguda Bus Stand

TO VIJAYAWADA AND CHENNAI

City College Rd.

State Library

Imlibun Central Bus Stand

Osmania General Hospital

TO GOLCONDA

Musi River

Salar Jung Museum

TO ZOO

Rajendranagar Rd.

Sardar Patel Rd.

Purana Haveli Palace

N

Hyderabad

ACCOMMODATIONS

B Hotel Annapurna
E Hotel Jaya International
C Hotel Saptagiri
A Hotel Sri Durga
D Taj Mahal Hotel

OLD CITY

Charminar

0   500 yards
0   500 meters

Mecca Masjid

PRACTICAL INFORMATION

Visitors to Hyderabad and Secunderabad should pick up a copy of **Channel 6** (Rs10), a monthly publication that contains a wealth of practical information (including updated train and flight schedules), a detailed list of cultural events, and business listings. The booklet is available at most English-language bookstores and also on the Web at http: //www.allindia.com/channel6.

Transportation

Airport: Begumpet Airport, on the north side of Husain Sagar, off Sardar Patel Rd. (enquiry tel. 141, recorded flight information tel. 142), 8km north of Abids. Auto-rickshaws (Rs25-30—insist on the meter) sputter to the airport from town. The blue auto-rickshaws that leave from the airport to town charge a fixed rate of Rs75 to Abids. Taxis cost twice as much. **Airline offices: Air France** (tel. 230947), open M-F 9:30am-5:30pm, Sa10:30am-1:30pm; **Air Canada, Royal Jordanian, TWA** (tel. 230995); **Kuwait Airways** (tel. 234344); and **Gulf Air** (tel. 230697). All in the same building, 1 block (500m) north of Basheer Bagh, off the road, on the left side. **Lufthansa,** 3-5-823 Hyderguda Rd. (tel. 235537), to the right off Basheer Bagh Circle. Open M-F 9:30am-5:30pm, Sa 9:30am-1:30pm. **Delta Airlines, Swissair,** and **Singapore Airlines** (tel. 331 1144); and **Jet Airways** (tel. 330 1222), all in the Navbharet Chambers, Raj Bhavan Rd. **KLM Royal Dutch Airlines,** 3-6-284 Hyderguda Rd. (tel. 237358). **Air India,** 5-9-193 HACA Bhavan (tel. 211894), opposite the Public Gardens. Open M-Sa 9:30am-1pm and 1:45-5:30pm. **Indian Airlines,** Secretariat Rd. (tel. 599333 or 141), opposite Ravindra Bhavan. Open daily 10am-1pm and 2-5:15pm. Flights to: **Ahmedabad** (4 per week, 1½hr., US$150); **Bangalore** (3 per day, 1hr., US$95); **Bhubaneswar** (M, W, and F, 1½hr., US$145); **Calcutta** (2 per day, 2½hr., US$190); **Chennai** (3 per day, 1hr., US$95); **Delhi** (2 per day, 2hr., US$185); **Mumbai** (5 per day, 1hr., US$105); **Tirupati** (Tu and Th, 1hr., US$75).

Trains: There are tourist quotas at each of the three **stations: Secunderabad, Nampally** (in Abids), and **Kachiguda** (east side of Sultan Bazaar) in Hyderabad (centralized enquiry tel. 131). Many trains stop at multiple stations. Enquiry counters at the stations open 24hr. Reservations (tel. 135) open M-Sa 8am-2pm and 2:15-8pm, Su 8am-2pm. Fares are 2nd/1st class. To: **Bangalore** (*Kachiguda-Bangalore Exp.* 7685, 4:30pm (Kachiguda), 5pm (Secunderabad), 17hr., Rs102/540); **Calcutta** (*East Coast Exp.* 8046, 7:30am (Secunderabad), 35hr.; *Falaknuma Exp.* 7003, 4pm, 30hr.; Rs211/1149); **Chennai** (*Chennai Exp.* 7054, 4:15pm (Secunderabad); *Charminar Exp.* 7060, 6:40pm (Nampally), 7:10pm (Secunderabad); 12hr., Rs143/722); **Delhi** (*Andhra Pradesh Exp.* 2723, 6:45am (Nampally), 7:15am (Secunderabad), 37hr.; *Nizamuddin Exp.* 7021, 8pm (Nampally), 35hr.; Rs200/965); **Mumbai** (*Konark Exp.* 1020, 11am (Secunderabad), 18hr., Rs144/736); **Tirupati** (*Krishna Exp.* 7406, 5:30am (Nampally), 6am (Secunderabad), Rs145/700; *Rayalaseema Exp.* 7429, 5:30pm (Nampally); 16hr., Rs133/676).

Buses: The new **Imlibun Central Bus Station** (enquiry tel. 461 4406), across the Musi River from the old station, proclaims itself to be Asia's largest. You'll believe it as you wander the 73 platforms. Open 24hr. Deluxe to: **Bangalore** (5 per day, 8am-7pm, 12hr., Rs228); **Chennai** (4pm, 14hr., Rs249); **Hopset** (11am, 4 and 5:30pm, 8hr., Rs115); **Mumbai** (7 per day, 10:30am-9:30pm, 16hr., Rs285); **Tirupati** (6 per day, 2:30-8pm, 14hr., Rs212). The areas around the railway stations and the Charminar teem with private coach companies vying for your company on one of their daily trips. To: **Bangalore** (6pm, Rs200); **Chennai** (7pm, Rs240); **Mumbai** (4pm, Rs250); **Nagarjunakonda** (every hr., 7am-11pm, 5hr., Rs70); **Tirupati** (8pm, Rs180). Get fare quotes from **Royal Travels,** Public Garden Rd. (tel. 201983), across from Nampally, in the Royal Lodge complexes. Open M-Sa 9am-10pm.

Local Transportation: In Hyderabad, **buses** are typically packed until they're overflowing with people, and you'll need turbo-*chappals* to catch one. Terminals located at Nampally, Nurkhan Bazaar, near the Charminar, and Secunderabad Railway Station. From Secunderabad Station to Nampally: #2 and 8A. From Nampally to Golconda Fort: #119 and 142N. **Auto-rickshaw** drivers can be stubborn, but try to hold out for the meter, especially for longer trips (Rs6 for 1km, Rs3 per km thereafter). **Taxis** are unmetered.

Tourist and Financial Services

Tourist Office: Government of India Tourist Office, Sandozi Building, Himayatna-gar (tel. 763 0037). From Basheer Bagh, the office is 750m down the road, on the left, two flights up. A useful source for information and advice regarding travel throughout India. Good, free Hyderabad city map. Open M-F 9:30am-5:30pm.

Budget Travel: Sita World Travel, 3-5-874 Hyderguda Rd. (tel. 233628; fax 234223), next to Apollo Hospital. Coming from Abids Circle to Basheer Bagh, take a right. Open M-F 9:30am-6pm, Sa 9:30am-1:30pm. **Omega Travels,** 13 Buddha Bhavan Complex, M.G. Rd., Secunderabad (tel. 825111).

Immigration Office: Foreigners Regional Registration Office, Commissioner of Police, Purana Haveli Rd. (tel. 809715), 500m southeast of the Salar Jung Museum. Registration fee Rs150. No 3-month tourist visa extensions. Other extensions $US5-100. Open M-Sa 10am-5pm. Closed 2nd Sa.

Currency Exchange: State Bank of Hyderabad, M.G. Rd. (tel. 201978), 700m north of Abids Circle. Currency and traveler's checks. Open for exchange M-F 10:30am-2:30pm. In Secunderabad, **Synergy Forexpress,** 62 Sarojini Devi Rd. (tel. 780 6552), near Gangaram's. All currencies. No commission. Guaranteed 5min. exchange, or your money back. Open daily 9am-7:30pm. **Thomas Cook,** 6-1-57, Saifabad (tel. 596524), near the junction of Secretariat and Public Gardens Rd. Thirty currencies and traveler's checks changed here. Rs20 encashment charge. Open M-Sa 9:30am-5:30pm.

Local Services

Bookstore: A.A. Hussain & Co., 5-8-551 Arastu Trust Building, Abid Rd., Abids (tel. 203724). Decent paperback collection. Pick up a copy of *Channel 6* here. Open M-Sa 10am-8:30pm. **Walden,** 6-3-871 Greenlands Rd., Begumpet (tel. 331 3434), en route from Abids to the airport, in the Vivekananda Hospital complex. One of the best-stocked bookstores in South India. Open W-M 9am-8:30pm.

Library: State Central Library, Turrebaz Khan Rd. (tel. 500107), near Osmania General Hospital. Open M-W and F-Su 8am-8pm. **British Library,** 5-9-22 Sarovar Centre, Secretariat Rd. (tel. 230774). Members-only, but policy is don't ask/don't tell. Open Tu-Sa 11am-7pm. **Henry Martyn Institute of Islamic Studies Library,** Chirag Ali Lane (tel. 201134). Open M-F 9:30am-4:30pm.

Cultural Centers: Bharatiya Vindya Bhavati, 5-9-1105 King Kothi Rd. (tel. 237825), off Basheer Bagh circle. Holds classical and popular dance and music concerts, often for free. Check *Channel 6* for details. **Alliance Française,** Adarshnagar (tel. 236646), next to the Birla Science Centre. Two weekly movies, plus cultural events and short-term French courses. Open M-F 9am-1pm and 3-6pm, Sa 9am-1pm.

Emergency and Communications

Pharmacy: Apollo Pharmacy, in the Apollo Hospital Complex. Open daily 24hr. **Medwin Hospital Pharmacy** (tel. 202902), off Station Rd. in Chirag Ali Ln., in a building so tall it's visible from the Nampally Railway Station. The pharmacy is inside the lobby to your left. Open daily 24hr.

Hospital: Apollo Hospital Medical Center, Hyderguda Rd. tel. 231380), north of Abids. Open daily 24hr. **Gandhi Hospital** (tel. 770 2222), near Secunderabad R.S.

Police: Abids Circle Police Station (tel. 203531), to the right as you face the GPO.

Emergency: Police: tel. 100. **Ambulance:** tel. 102.

Post Office: GPO, Abids Circle (tel. 595978). *Poste Restante* in the back left corner of the main room. Stamps upstairs on the right. Open M-Sa 8am-8:30pm. *Poste Restante* M-F 10am-3pm, Sa 10am-1pm. **Postal Code:** 500001.

Internet: Zen Computerdrome, Bluechip Arcade, Himayangar (tel. 322 6631; email rajesh@hd1.vsnl.net.in), 100m east of the tourist office, on the right. Web browsing Rs80 per hr. Open daily 7:30am-10:30pm. There's also **dot.com** (tel. 237675; http://www.dotcom.india.com), near Birla Maudir. Follow the road to the left of the British Library, take the first right, and follow the signs. Web browsing (Rs60 per hr.) and espresso (Rs9). Open daily 9am-11pm.

Telephones: STD/ISD booths abound in Abids and elsewhere. **Telegraph Office,** Abids Circle, adjoins the GPO on the left. Open 24hr. **Telephone Code:** 040.

ACCOMMODATIONS

Budget dives are 10-paise-a-dozen in the Abids area. There are a few lodges around the Secunderabad Railway Station, but the area is grungy, and there's no reason to stay there unless you have a morning train to catch.

Abids

Hotel Jaya International, 4-1-37/A&B Reddy Hostel Rd. (tel. 475 2929). Facing the GPO in Abids Circle, walk left along Mahipatram Rd. for 50m; make a left at the Dhanalakshmi Bank. Clean rooms in good condition, with direct-dial phones, TVs, and large windows. Seat toilets and showers. Free South Indian breakfast buffet. Check-out 24hr. Singles Rs185, with A/C Rs400; doubles Rs265/500.

Taj Mahal Hotel, 4-1-999 King Kothi Rd. (tel. 237988). Walk away from the GPO in Abids Circle and veer right after 200m. One of Hyderabad's most popular hotels. Large, well-kept rooms with gleaming mirrors and polished floors. TVs, direct-dial phones, seat or squat toilets, 24hr. hot water. Check-out 24hr. Singles Rs275, with A/C Rs400; doubles Rs400/550.

Hotel Saptagiri, 5-4-651 Nampally Station Rd. (tel. 460 3601). Turn left as you head out of the Abids Circle GPO and walk 200m before turning left down a narrow dirt road opposite the CLS Bookshop. Scrubbed and polished through and through. Balconies, telephones. A/C rooms have carpets, TVs, and seat toilets. Check-out 24hr. Singles Rs150; doubles Rs195, with A/C Rs375. Reservations recommended.

Hotel Annapurna, 5-4-730 Nampally Station Rd. (tel. 473 2612), one block past Hotel Saptagiri, set off from the street, directly across from the collector's office. Overwhelmingly pink (but otherwise unexciting) place has TVs, direct-dial phones, and towels. Deluxe rooms have seat toilets and a sitting room. Check-out 24hr. Singles Rs180; deluxe Rs205; doubles Rs260/290, with A/C Rs480.

Hotel Sri Durga, Public Garden Rd. (tel. 202286), on the left corner of the street across from the rail station. Cheap, and it shows, but rooms are clean. Squat toilets. Hot water 6-9am. Check-out 24hr. Singles Rs100; doubles Rs150.

Secunderabad

Hotel Sitara, 7-1-2, SPG Church Complex (tel. 770 0308). From the Secunderabad station, veer diagonally left. By far the cleanest and friendliest hotel in the area. Broad, well-lit hallways, tiled bathrooms with flush squat toilets, balconies, and spacious rooms. Running hot water 6-9am. Singles Rs100; doubles Rs200, with air-cooling Rs270.

National Lodge, 9-4-48 Syed Abdulla St. (tel. 770 5572), opposite the Secunderabad station. As basic as they get: narrow beds, tube lighting, no hot water. But rooms and bathrooms are relatively clean, and the management polite. Check-out 24hr. Singles Rs80; doubles with bath Rs130.

FOOD

Traditional Andhra cuisine demands iron taste buds or stubborn stoicism. Either way, you'll never have clogged sinuses in Hyderabad. To ease your pain, delve into one of the ubiquitous bakeries that have popped up in the past few years. Irani hotels serve *biryani, kheemal* (ground mutton curry), mutton chops, along with pastries and *faloodas* for dessert. Hyderabad offers less-spicy South Indian cuisine too, but even the chutney here seems a little wicked. For real gorging, try one of the ritzy hotels on the west side of Husain Sagar—some do five buffets a day.

Taj Mahal, off M.G. Rd. on King Kothi Rd., is a Hyderabad institution for good reason: it's cheap, comfortable, and doles out large portions of South Indian favorites. *Masala dosas* Rs12 in the regular section, Rs18 in the cush, hygienic A/C section. North Indian dishes (all veg.) 11am-3:30pm and 7-10:30pm. Tiffins 7am-9:30pm. No smoking or alcohol.

Palace Heights, Triveni Complex, Abid Rd. (tel. 242540). About 500m north of the GPO, 8th fl., just before King Kothi Rd. Look for the blue neon sign. Fabulous city views, especially of the Abids area, through huge polished windows. Funky decor. Entrees Rs70-125. Open daily 11:30am-3pm and 7-11pm.

Chinese Garden, 6-3-349 Rd. No. 1, Banjara Hills (tel. 332 6978), above Midway's Bakery. One of the few Chinese restaurants around with more Chinese than Andhra influence, despite the gaudy decor. Entrees Rs77-97. Buffet lunch (Rs90) is an excellent deal. Open daily 12:30-3:30pm and 7-11pm.

Minerva Coffee Shop, 3-6-199/1 Himayat Nagar (tel. 322 0448), on the right, if you're coming from M.G. Rd. Upscale veg. joint, where *dosa*s come in *avatar*s such as veg. cheese (Rs23). Huge *puri*s (Rs18). Prompt servers weave between the rows of potted plants as locals gossip away. The Minerva Special Ice Cream (Rs40) is guaranteed to please. Open daily 7am-11pm; *thali*s 11am-2:30pm and 7-9:30pm.

SIGHTS

Golconda Fort

Location: *8km west of the city.* **Hours:** *Open daily 7am-8pm.* **Admission:** *Sa-Th Rs2. F free.* **Other:** *Video fee Rs25. Sound and light show every evening March-Oct. 7pm; Nov.-Feb. 6:30pm; 1 hr., adults Rs20, children Rs15. English show on W, Sa, and Su.*

The erstwhile headquarters of the Qutb Shahi kingdom from 1512 to 1687, the fort is Hyderabad's most popular attraction. In its heyday, the Golconda empire stretched to the Bay of Bengal; now the circumference of the fort is a mere 7km. Crushed and annexed after two sieges by the Mughal emperor Aurangzeb, the kingdom was, during its zenith, a center for arts and learning, as well as a symbol of religious tolerance. At dusk, the crumbling ruins, shrieking bats, and sheer, unguardrailed drops marking the path to **Durbar Hall** cause you to look over your shoulder, expecting to see specters of the Qutb Shahi Kings. Durbar Hall is supposedly a 1000-step climb, but it takes only 30min., and that time is a good investment. From the top there is a panoramic view of the ramparts below and Hyderabad's other landmarks: the Birla Mandir and the Charminar can be seen in the distance to the east, near the horizon (squint hard).

The fort is best toured in a roughly circular manner. On the way up, visitors follow the path used by everyday citizens during the fort's heyday; the descent leads down the steep route once used exclusively by the king and his pallbearers. Visitors first pass through the heavily studded **Balahisar Gate,** which served as the first line of defense from invaders. Just ahead, past some small exhibits, lies the **Grand Portico,** where guides are constantly clapping to demonstrate the fort's acoustics: Golconda was engineered so that a clap at the summit of Durbar Hall would reverberate at 5 places along the inside perimeter of the fortress wall. A clap at the center of the Grand Portico can be heard at the summit, 1km away. This built-in communication system was used to notify the king of any visitors and detect standing ovations while they were still far off. Continuing straight ahead leads to the covered **body guard barracks.** Exiting ahead and to the right leads to the **Nagina Bagh,** a royal garden.

From the gardens, a stone staircase begins the ascent to the summit. At the foot of the steps, on the right, one can see the 12m deep **water tank,** one of three within the fort. The water originated from a natural spring and was transported by a sophisticated system of limestone pipes, the stumps of which can still be seen today.

Durbar Hall at the summit commands spectacular views of Hyderabad and Secunderabad. Unfortunately, much of the interior has been defaced by visitors who have carved their names into the slowly decaying walls. The summit is also home to the Hindu **Sri Jagadamba Temple,** built in the 12th century (the garish paint is a more recent addition). From Durbar Hall, one must descend the king's staircase almost entirely before reaching the next sight. At the foot of the hill is a water tank, and around the corner are the **Rani Mahals,** a series of buildings once occupied by the king's harem and their bodyguards. A somewhat functional fountain graces the central courtyard, where the daily sound and light show is held. Once upon a time, these buildings were decorated with curtains, mirrored glass, and jewels. Now, a colony of bats occupies the main building, and the once-lush gardens have been overtaken by weeds. Passing through the Rani Mahals takes you by the **Taramati Mosque** to the 3-

Little. Slimy. Different. Better.

Every year in early June, thousands of asthmatics flock to the outskirts of Hydera-bad to the home of the Battina Gowd brothers. The reason: an ancient ayurvedic cure that involves ingesting a live fish wrapped in herbs. According to a loose interpretation of Vedic texts, the live fish squirms around inside the body, clearing up the breathing passages. But there's an added benefit: the fish is thought to be a heat-generating agent, which is a good preventive measure for the coughs and colds that accompany the beginning of the monsoon in early June. Despite the lack of any hard scientific evidence, crowds continue to line up to have the slimy little sucker shoved down their throats. The Indian government has even arranged extra trains to Hyderabad during the times the fish camp is scheduled. It's difficult to gauge the fish's effectiveness, but many patients have been coming back for several years and report a decrease in attacks. The treatment is free, so if there's the slightest chance of a cure, the masses will continue to come.

story arched **arsenal.** There are only a few dusty guns and cannonballs inside, but authorities are in the process of converting the building into a museum that will doubtless feature, well, dusty guns and cannonballs.

Qutb Shahi Tombs

Location: *1km north of Golconda Fort.* **Hours:** *Open dawn-dusk.* **Admission:** *Free.*
Other: *Museum open Sa-Th 9am-4:30pm. Admission Rs2. Camera fee Rs5. Video fee Rs25.*

Housing the remains of seven of the dynasty's patriarchs (each of whom supervised his own tomb's construction), the Qutb Shahi tombs play an undeserved second fiddle to the oft-visited Golconda Fort. They are magnificent architectural specimens nonetheless, and, perhaps due to the relative paucity of visitors, remain in startlingly good condition. Each is built on a square base with an Islamic-style onion dome, but adorned with Hindu motifs like lotus friezes and leaves, a testament to the empire's religious tolerance and cultural syncretism. The cenotaph in the center of the tomb, draped in a sheer cloth, covers the real crypt below.

Since the tombs are somewhat haphazardly arranged, the best approach is simply to wander about the meticulously maintained gardens and explore the tombs as you happen upon them. Each is labeled in English, describing the history of the king interred therein and some of the structural attributes of his tomb. Though the tombs have a similar shape, each bears the distinctive traces of its designer. The grandest tomb is certainly that of **Muhammed Quli Qutb Shah,** which is surrounded by gardens criss-crossed by waterways. Farthest from the entrance, the tall, thin tomb of **Jamshid Qutb Sham** commands views of Golconda and other, as-yet undeveloped ruins from its terrace. The complex also contains a mortuary bath, where bodies were ritually cleansed before being buried. Next door, a small **museum** contains a variety of artifacts from Qutb Shahi times: ceramics, weapons, and beautiful hand-written texts. The portraits of the Qutb Shahi kings allow you to finally place a name with the face.

Charminar and Mecca Masjid

The four-minaret **Charminar** is Hyderabad's most enduring and ubiquitous landmark. The edifice, built by Muhammed Quli Qutb Shah in 1591 to celebrate the end of an epidemic plaguing the city, adorns patches on school uniforms, is immortalized in miniature statuettes in kitsch shops throughout the state, and most famously, graces every packet of Charminar cigarettes. (It's said that the last Nizam of Hyderabad refused to smoke any other brand.) There's not much to see in the building, since you're no longer allowed to climb the 149 steps to the small mosque on top, but a prime bazaar area surrounds it. **Mecca Masjid** is 100m south along Sardar Patel Rd. Like the Charminar, it was built during the sultanate of Muhammad Quli Qutb Shah, but after Golconda's fall, completion of the mosque was left to Aurangzeb. It is claimed that 1400 bullocks were needed to haul the granite slabs that form the colonnaded entrance from a quarry 11km away. Named for the few bricks from Mecca embedded in its central arch, the mosque is the largest in Hyderabad, accommodating up to 10,000 faithful at Friday prayers. Before entering the Mecca Masjid, chuck your *chappals* at the podium on the left (Rs5) and walk through a pavilion containing the tombs of the various *nizams* to preside over Hyderabad.

Salar Jung Museum

Location: *C.L. Badari Malakpet, south of the Musi River.* **Phone:** *523211.* **Hours:** *Open Sa-Th 10am-5pm.* **Admission:** *Rs6.*

The imposing white Salar Jung Museum is touted as one of the world's largest one-man collections, but is actually the work of three generations of Salar Jungs, each of whom served as the Nizam's *wazir* (prime minister). The museum is huge and well-stocked. Everything from gorgeous Chola sculptures to mediocre European oil paintings can be found here. Check out Room 14, the Ivory Room, with a solid ivory chair given to Tipu Sultan by Louis XV. Room 17 has some marvelous modern paintings by premier Indian artists (Ravi Varma, Abanindranath Tagore, K. Hebbar); in Room 18, next door, you can trace the chronological and regional evolution of Indian miniature painting. Free guided tours depart from the office (which also has handy maps of the layout) on your right as you enter.

Old City

It's worth the time to explore the back streets of the Old City, which is arguably the most "Hyderabadi" part of Hyderabad, with a distinctly Muslim flavor. Nestled discretely among these streets are some of the most sacred pilgrimmage sites for Shi'a Muslims, each housing a revered *alam,* or heavy banner in which gold, gemstones, and precious objects are woven. Ask a local to show you to the **Biha ka alawa,** which protects a bright green shrine within its whitewashed walls. The *alam* is said to contain pieces of a wooden plank upon which the Prophet Muhammad's daughter bathed. Not far away is the **Sar tauq ka alawa,** which houses an *alam* containing portions of the shackles and chains in which the fourth *imam* was bound.

All Things Birla

The **B.M. Birla Science Centre and Archaeological Museum,** atop Naubat Pahar hill (tel. 235081) is more like a children's playground, but the archaeological section downstairs is more interesting, with excavations from Vaddamanu dated 100 BC to 200 AD, wood and stone sculptures, and miniature paintings. *(Open daily 10:30am-8:15pm, closed last Tu of every month. Admission Rs7.)* It's air-conditioned and well laid out. Exit to the right and climb the stairs leading to the domed **Birla Planetarium** (tel. 241067), where you can learn all about stars and aliens. *(Four shows per day. Closed last Th of every month. Admission Rs10.)* On the opposite hill from the planetarium is **Birla Mandir,** dedicated to Lord Venkateshwara. *(Open daily 7am-noon and 3-9pm.)* Commissioned by the industrial kings of India and built over 10 years, it affords awesome views of Hyderabad and Secunderabad. The elevation and the pure white Rajasthani marble of the temple set against the blue of Husain Sagar are sublime, and the serenity is unmarred by shoe-touts or alms-driven priests. At night, the whole structure is illuminated.

Husain Sagar

Visitors to Hyderabad will spend much time within view of Husain Sagar, the 6.5km by 800m artificial tank whose blue water decorates the city's vistas. Pragmatists say that the tank was constructed during the Golconda Empire, but some believe that the tank's origin is far less mundane. Legend has it that the tank was promised hundreds of years ago by a *sadhu* who collected large sums of money from the thirsty population. Weeks passed and no construction had begun, prompting the people to confront the *sadhu,* who promised to undertake the project or return their money. The next morning, the shimmering tank was in place, and the *sadhu* had disappeared. The magic continued in the 1980s, when a monolithic **Buddha statue** was hyped,

---

The Third Sex

India has an entire subculture of *hijras,* which translates very roughly as "those between" or "shifters." Some *hijras* are hermaphrodites, others eunuchs, while the rest have functioning male organs. They wear *saris* and live with other *hijras* in modern-day *zenanas.* Because of their ambiguous "sexual orientation" and their dabbling in prostitution, *hijras* have little status in Indian society, and most Indians are reluctant or unable to explain who and what the *hijras* are to Westerners. However, when a baby is born, a group of *hijras* will show up at the hospital, where the proud parents welcome their raucous, bawdy blessing (which involves singing, dancing, and often, throwing the baby in the air) with mounds of *baksheesh,* for it is considered quite auspicious.

---

built, and then placed on a barge for transport across the artificial lake. It promptly sank into the water, taking seven people with it. Several years ago, the statue was retrieved from the bottom intact, no damage having been inflicted by the water.

The only real park on the lake is **Lumbini Huda Park,** just off Secretariat Rd., near Public Gardens Rd. *(Open Tu-Sa 9am-9pm. Admission Rs2. Boats available Tu-Su 9am-6pm. 4-person motorboat with driver Rs70; paddleboats Rs10.)* It may be small, but it is nicely landscaped and well-maintained. Boats are available for tours or do-it-yourself jaunts.

ENTERTAINMENT AND SHOPPING

The bazaar areas around the Charminar in the Old City are the best places to hone your bargaining skills. The **Laad Bazaar,** which extends west from the Charminar, is renowned for its bangles and exquisite wedding fashions. Step into a shop and take a look at the heavily embroidered *kamdani* dresses for women or the regal, sultanesque caps for men. People from all over India visit this street for pre-wedding purchases. If you're not into buying jewelry (strands of imperfect pearls for Rs100-500), armfuls of bangles, and bidriware, then just stroll around and look into the stalls where craftsmen hand-pound sheets of silver foil. Most of the shops in the Old City are open from 10am to 7pm; some observe Friday as a holiday. Emporia line the roads in the Abids area. **Kalanjali Arts and Crafts,** Hill Fort Rd. (tel. 231147), across from the Air India office, is swanky and not eye-bulgingly expensive. The store has a wide selection of just about everything but jewelry. Open daily 9:30am-8:30pm.

Hyderabad is justly proud of its myriad cultural events, including dance programs, *ghazal* sessions, and plays. **Ravindra Bharati** (tel. 233672), in the Public Gardens, stages about four events per week at 6pm. Hyderabad unofficially claims more than 100 **cinemas.** The best English theatres are **Sangeet,** 23 Sardar Patel Rd., Secunderabad (tel. 770 3864), and **Skyline,** 3-6-64 Basheer Bagh Rd., Hyderabad (tel. 231633). There are generally three shows per day and balcony seats cost Rs25. Tickets for sold-out shows can often be purchased from scalpers roving the parking lot. **The Alliance Française** (tel. 236646) screens two flicks per week: one French, the other German or English. The **Hyderabad Film Club** (tel. 290265) has weekly screenings at the Sarathi Studio Preview Theatre in Ameerpet, north of Banjara Hills. *Channel 6* is the best source of information for upcoming events.

As Hyberabad only recently repealed its prohibition law, the **bar scene** is just getting off the ground. **My Choice** (tel. 320 4060) in the Residency on Public Garden Rd. is fairly popular, and many other five-stars are planning their own watering holes.

For a different kind of liquid refreshment, try the **Ritz Hotel,** Hill Fort St., Basheer Bagh (tel. 233570), where you can swim in the same **pool** as the Nizam's privileged guests (open daily 3-7pm, Rs60 per hr.). If you can't handle the sultry mid-mornings, there is the **Taj Residency,** Rd. No.1, Banjara Hills (tel. 339 9999), open daily from 7am to 7pm. Time-efficient pleasure-intake is key here: rates are Rs150 per hr.

■ Nagarjunakonda నాగార్జునకొండ

The ruins of one of the largest Buddhist monasteries and learning centers in South India lie 150km southeast of Hyderabad and about 20m underwater. Excavations in 1926 first revealed evidence of *stupas*, *chaityas*, and other artifacts dating back to the 2nd century BC. However, not much work was done until the 1950s, when plans to build a dam on the Krishna River adjacent to the site spurred government archaeologists to resume digging. The most important ruins were evacuated brick-by-brick to a nearby hill before the dam was finished in 1966. Today, a lake engulfs the original site, except for Nagarjunakonda, now an island supporting both the rebuilt structures and a museum. Nagarjuna himself, a Buddhist scholar of the 1st century AD, would have had no problem meditating in the surrounding village, and neither will you, but don't expect to find much else to do. The **museum** and reconstructed **ruins** are the biggest draws. Visitors typically head straight to the former from the ferry. The museum features a range of sculpture, friezes, and other artifacts, all with detailed description in several languages. (Open Sa-Th 9am-4pm.) The rebuilt ruins are somewhat anticlimactic, but each has a sign describing the purpose of the original structure. You can see the ruins and the nearby **Ethipothala Waterfall** in one day on the **APTTCH** (tel. 501519) **guided tour** (6:30am-9:30pm, Rs190) from Hyderabad.

The **Nagarjunasagar Dam** is the axis around which the village revolves. The lake is to the west, and the **Krishna River** continues to the east. To the north lies **Hill Colony,** home to the better tourist hotels and the **bus stand.** Buses depart to **Hyderabad** (every hr., 4hr., Rs60); **Tirupati** (2pm, 13hr., Rs150); and **Vijaywada** (5am, 9am, 3pm, 10pm, 4hr., Rs60). You'll find the APPTDC **tourist office** (tel. 76634; open Sa-Th 9am-6pm) opposite the bus stand in Project House (Sagara Paryataka Vihar). The **police station** (tel. 76533) and **post office** are nearby. **Postal Code:** 508202. The nearest **train station** is Macherla, 13km east of the dam, but Vijaywada is better serviced. About 6km south of Hill Colony, just before the dam, is **Pylon Colony,** with a number of **STD/ISD** booths. The **boat launch** is on the opposite end of the dam at Vijayapuri South (ferries Sa-Th 9:30am and 1:30pm, 45min., Rs20; returns 12:15 and 4:15pm). **Auto-rickshaws** are hard to spot and are unmetered, so buses are your best bet to get back to Hill Colony. **Telephone Code:** 08680.

The best rooms in town are in Hill Colony and are run by the APTTDC. **Project House** (tel. 76540) has uninspiring but clean double rooms with seat toilets (Rs125-150; check-out noon). The **Vijay Vihar** complex (tel. 76633), 2km north, has more spacious doubles with A/C, attached baths, and seat toilets (Rs300). Dining halls at both lodges and snack stands near the bus stops are the only food options.

■ Tirupati తిరుపతి and Tirumala తిరుమల

Red rock hills covered by lush greenery form the backdrop for the temple of the Sri Venkateshwara at Tirumala, the most popular pilgrimage site in South India. Built in the 11th century by the founder of the Sri Vaishnava sect, the place constantly swarms with thousands upon thousands of Hindu pilgrims, each of whom must be housed, fed, and herded around. Thus exists Tirupati, the town located 20km down the hill, where all economic activity derives from its divine neighbor. Shops sell flowers and trinkets, and lodges and restaurants compete for customers.

Although Sri Venkateshwara is one of the few temples in India that allows non-Hindus into the inner sanctum, few foreigners visit it. Aside from the temple, there's little to do or see, and battling the crowds for *darshan* of the image can be nerve-racking and physically exhausting. If you're not a devout Hindu, make your trip on a weekday, preferably Tuesday, in order to escape the weekend rush and avoid the months of June and September and any public holidays.

ORIENTATION AND PRACTICAL INFORMATION Visitors come here to see the temple at Tirumala, but Tirupati provides accommodations, as well as the railway station, bus station, and all the restaurants and services. The **APSRTC bus station** is 500m from the center of Tirupati. Buses run to: **Bangalore** (9 per day, Rs167); **Chen-**

SOUTH INDIA

nai (every hr. until 11pm, 4hr., Rs71); **Hyderabad** (4 per day, 10hr., Rs170); **Nagarjunakonda** (6pm, 13hr., Rs165); **Pondicherry** (3pm, 7hr., Rs137); and **Vijayawada** (4 per day, Rs142). Near the bus stand is the **tourist office** (tel. 23208), which offers daily tours of the area (Rs200, does not include admission fees). The **railway station** (enquiry tel. 131) is in the heart of town, near the **Govindaraja Temple.** (Reservations counter, across from the station, next to bus stand, open M-Sa 8am-2pm and 2:15-8pm, Su 8am-2pm.) Fares listed for 2nd/1st class. To: **Chennai** (*Tirupati-Madras Exp.* 6054, 10am; *Saptagiri Exp.* 6058, 5:30pm; 3hr., Rs61/176); **Chidambaram** (*Tirupati-Madurai Exp.* 6799, 3:40pm, 10hr., Rs77/354); **Hyderabad** (*Rayalaseema Exp.* 7430, 3:30pm, 16½hr., Rs211/972); **Madurai** (*Tirupati-Madurai Exp.* 6799, 3:40pm, 18hr., Rs126/574); **Mumbai** (*Tirupati-Mumbai Exp.* 7494, Th and Su, 9:40pm, 24hr., Rs297/1382); **Thanjavur** (*Tirupati-Madurai Exp.* 6799, 3:40pm, 12½hr., Rs97/436); **Tiruchirappalli** (*Tirupati-Madurai Exp.* 6799, 3:40pm, 14hr., Rs103/470). The **Tirumala bus stand,** 250m from the railway station, sends a constant stream of buses up holy hilltop (Rs15), along **Alipiri Road.** Be prepared for a long, long wait, and buy a round-trip ticket to avoid a wait on the way back. The bus ride to Tirumala takes 45 minutes on curvy roads (57 hairpin turns) with insane driving. You might consider taking a taxi (Rs50 if you share). Tirupati's **airport** is located 12km from the city. **Indian Airlines** (tel. 22349), in the Hotel Vishnupriya complex opposite the Tirumala bus stand, flies to **Chennai** (Tu and Th, 2:40pm, 20min., US$35) and **Hyderabad** (Tu and Th, 11:50am, 1hr., US$65). For **currency exchange,** head to the first floor of the **State Bank of India** (tel. 20699; open for exchange M-F 10am-2pm, Sa 10am-noon), which also accepts major traveler's checks. Follow the road opposite the Bhimas Deluxe Hotel, and take the first right. **Gandhi Road** is home to the **police station** (tel. 20301), and the **post office** (tel. 22103; open M-F 10am-5pm, Sa 10am-5pm). **Telephone Code:** 08574.

ACCOMMODATIONS AND FOOD

All of the good hotels are in Tirupati. The only option in Tirumala are the Devasthanam dormitory rooms, which offer the barest minimum: rooms are free but usually full. Otherwise, careen back to town. The **Bhimas Hotel,** 42 G. Car St. (tel. 25744), about a block from the railway station, is everpopular with Indian pilgrims, given its reasonable price and prime location. The rooms aren't spectacular, but fans make sure things stay cool in the dry Andhra heat, and the place is pretty clean. The attached baths have thoroughly disinfected squat toilets (singles Rs150; doubles Rs275, with A/C Rs475). Across the street from its humbler namesake is the **Bhimas Deluxe Hotel** (tel. 25521). When the owners of Bhimas Hotel made it big, they decided to go upscale. The result: comfortable rooms, inviting beds, and shiny baths with seat toilets. After waiting in line at Tirumala for several hours, you may want the frigid A/C and Star TV (doubles Rs575-675; 24hr. check-out).

Aside from some grubby *dhabas*, the best restaurants are attached to hotels in Tirupati. Dining in Tirumala is only for those eager to wait in line with thousands of others to eat quasi-hygienic (but free) food slapped onto a banana leaf. In Tirupati, the **Bhimas Deluxe** has a popular, subterranean restaurant that offers the usual North and South Indian fare. It remains open at odd hours to accommodate pilgrims returning from Tirumala. **Surya,** Hotel Mayura's vegetarian restaurant, serves fresh North and South Indian food (Rs20-45) and chutneys (open daily 9am-10pm).

SIGHTS

Tirumala is seemingly in the middle of nowhere, but all roads lead the faithful here. Taking the *darshan* of Lord Venkateshwara (Balaji) at the **Sri Venkateshwara Temple** in Tirumala is an experience that most devout Hindus hope to have at least once during their lifetime. It is believed that any wish made at the temple will be granted by Lord Venkateshwara. For this reason, pilgrims flock here by the thousands each day, many expending their scant resources for the lengthy trip to this tiny town.

Visits to the temple begin in Tirupati, where buses shuttle passengers along a winding mountainside road to Tirumala and deposit them at the top of the hill; you'll have to follow the crowds past vendor stalls, bathing areas, and pilgrims' quarters to reach the vicinity of the temple. Don't be surprised to find a large number of people with shaved heads, as pilgrims to Tirupati commonly make a sort of barber-barter agreement with God: hair in exchange for some favor. If you're willing to lose your locks, tonsuring stations will gladly do the job in assembly-line fashion. (It comes as no surprise that the area around Tirupati is home to a flourishing wig industry.)

Near the temple grounds, large billboards proclaim the different types of *darshan* available. Regular *darshan* comes at no cost, but often entails waits of 12 hours or more. The "special *darshan*" queue (Rs30) will reduce your waiting time to 2-4 hours, depending on the crowds; follow the signs for **Sarvadarshanam.** There are a number of other, more expensive *darshans* which must be arranged with temple authorities in advance. Do not rely on middlemen to purchase your tickets, as scams are common; head directly to the appropriate temple office. Before entering the temple grounds, you'll have to leave your shoes with a shopowner, who will watch them for a few rupees.

The wait to enter the temple—even in the "special *darshan*" line—involves passing through a network of narrow wire cages. You'll be pressed into constricted passageways with hundreds of other pilgrims as little boys offer cold drinks for sale, and countless beggars implore the trapped masses for spare change. Once you've entered the line, you'll have little idea of where you're going or how much farther you have to inch along. Just rest assured that a few hours later, you'll round the corner to the home stretch, and the entrance to the temple won't be far ahead.

Although it's hard to appreciate the temple's structural attributes while you're being jostled on all sides, the interior contains some impressive sculpted columns. The *vimana* is fully covered with gold, and its dazzling brilliance is testimony to the wealth of the temple. After all the waiting in line, *darshan* is generally very short and you will be shoved by temple workers yelling at you in Telugu as they yank your arm to force your exit. If they recognize you as a (wealthy) foreigner, the workers may pull you aside, giving you extra *darshan* time in exchange for *baksheesh.* The image is impressive: the mask of Vishnu drawn clearly on its forehead, wearing a gold crown and covered with flowers so that not much else is visible. After eyeing the inner sanctum, worshippers pass through a corridor where temple employees can be seen counting piles of money. The last leg of the visit takes you to the *prasad* line, where workers dish out free food consecrated by Lord Venkateshwara. *(Temple open daily 24hr.)* Opposite the temple is a small, unremarkable **museum.** *(Open M-F 8am-8pm. Admission Rs3.)* If, after all the waiting in line, you feel like an amusement park patron, the roller-coaster bus descent will not disappoint. There's no need to fear for loss of life or limb, though—after all, you've got Lord Venkateshwara on your side.

How the West Was Worn

While many Indians currently seek to adopt ever more Western forms of dress, a number of supposedly Western fashion concepts came from the subcontinent in the first place (and we're not just talking Madras cotton or Nehru Jackets here). What goes around comes around—call it clothing karma.

calico [Western corruption of "Calicut"; see p. 559]: Cotton cloth with prints (in the U.S.) or without (in the UK). Also an epithet for splotchy cats.

cashmere [from Kashmir; see p. 367]: See "shawl," below.

dungarees [from Hindi *dungri*]: Pants made of coarse calico.

jodhpurs [from Jodhpur in Rajasthan; see p. 301]: Pants for horseback riding, tight at the ankles.

khaki [from Urdu for "dusty"]: Everyone's favorite junglewear.

pajamas [from Urdu *pay jamah,* or "leg garment"]: Europeans in India and thereabouts copied the silk pants worn all around them, but only nocturnally.

seersucker [Indian corruption of Persian *shir o shakkar,* or "milk and honey"]: A striped and puckered fabric, and the most evocative word in this box.

shawl [from Persian *shal*]: Originally made in Kashmir from the wool of the highland shawl-goat *(Capra lanigera).*

Maharashtra महाराष्ट्र

Maharashtra straddles the Subcontinent, from the tropical coast to the arid Deccan Plateau, from the fringes of the hot and hectic Gangetic plain to the palmier, balmier, more easy-going south, and from isolated villages to metropolitan Mumbai. From the Hindu devotees immersing themselves en masse in the sacred Godavari at Nasik to the giddy red-robed, Birkenstock-wearing acolytes of the Osho Commune to the businessmen and billboards of Mumbai, the state encompasses both the sacred and the profane. Over half of India's foreign trade and roughly 50% of its tax revenue flow from the state, yet almost two-thirds of Maharashtra's population still survives on near-subsistence agriculture. The state also has a formidable tradition of martial independence embodied by the warrior-king and folk-hero Shivaji and the Shiv Sena (literally, "Shivaji's Army") party, which, in coalition with the similarly right-wing BJP, grips the state government in a vise of Hindu nationalism. While most Indian states can be fairly described as *mirch masala* amalgams, however, what distinguishes Maharashtra is the bold intensity that binds the massive state together. Only by visiting can you truly come to understand the dizzying diversity of Maharashtra.

HIGHLIGHTS OF MAHARASHTRA

- The intricately carved **cave temples** at **Ajanta** (p. 649) and **Ellora** (p. 648) are among the world's architectural wonders.
- Bombay by any other name smells as sweet—well, maybe not, but **Mumbai** (below) impresses with its sights, sounds, nightlife, and ceaseless energy.
- Peaceful **Pune** (p. 636) is home to the stubbornly famous **Osho Commune**, whose red-robed enlightenment-seekers mingle with vacationing Mumbaiites.

Mumbai (Bombay) मुंबई

In attitude as well as population, Mumbai is India's largest city, uniting all of the country's languages, religions, ethnicities, castes, and classes in one heaving, seething sizzler of a metropolis. Mumbai blends myriad traditions and innovations from each region, city, and village in India and beyond, offering everything from *bhel puri* to bell bottoms. The city accounts for 50% of India's imports and exports and its densest concentration of industry, as well as the nation's largest stock exchange. Rupee and dollar billionaires, film stars, models, and politicians flock to frolic at the many opulent hotels, expensive discos, and ritzy restaurants. But Mumbai also harbors more of the desperate poor than any other Indian city; the endless shanties at Dharavi have expanded into Asia's (and perhaps the world's) largest slum. As many as half of Mumbai's 15 million residents live in shacks or on the street. Still, scores of laborers from the countryside flood into Mumbai daily to seek their fortunes.

The unimaginable press of people, combined with arcane rent control provisions prohibiting the conversion of industrial to residential property, has driven real estate prices beyond those of New York or Tokyo—in a country whose yearly per capita income is just US$350. Right-wing and sectarian politicians stoked this pressure-cooker of economic disappointment, inconceivable crowding, wretched sanitation, hopeless congestion, choking pollution, and religious tension until it exploded into riots and bomb blasts in 1992-93. Recently, internal conflicts have quieted somewhat as Indians redirect their energy to denouncing U.S.-imposed sanctions protesting the BJP-led government's nuclear tests in June 1998. American tourists need not be concerned, however. You and your money are still very welcome.

This urban extravaganza began modestly. Artifacts found in the suburb of Kandivli prove that the original seven islands which make up the city have been inhabited since the Stone Age. Successive Indian dynasties ignored Mumbai's potential as a port, but when the Portuguese acquired the islands in 1534, they called them Bom

ORISSA

Bay of Bengal

MADHYA PRADESH

ANDHRA PRADESH

Ramtek

Taroba National Park

Nagpur

Pauna

Wardha
Sevagram

6

Vijayawada

Krishna R.

Amaravati

Nizamabad

7

Hyderabad

Akola

Nanded

Gulbarga

Ajanta

Jalna

Godavari R.

Pakthan

Bid

Solapur

9

Bijapur

13

KARNATAKA

Jalgaon

Daulatabad

Aurangabad

Ahmadnagar

Ellora

6

Dhule

Malegaon

Pandharpur

Belgaum

Manmad

50

Nasik

WESTERN GHATS

Sangli

Kolhapur

Bharuch

Trimbak

Karle

Pune

Satara

4

17

18

Lonavla

Mahabaleshwar

Surat

GUJARAT

Gulf of Cambay

Daman

DADRA AND NAGAR HAVELI

Vasai

Thane

Matheran

Bhaja

Raigarh

Murud

Ratnagiri

GOA

Mumbai (Bombay)

Arabian Sea

Maharashtra

WEST INDIA

N

100 miles

100 kilometers

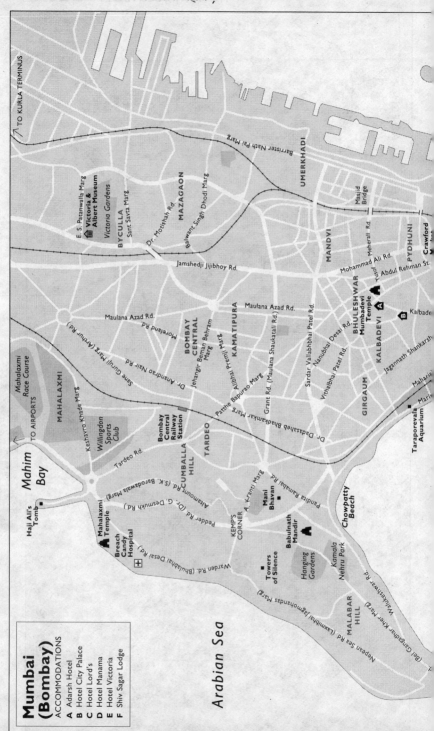

TO KURLA TERMINUS

Barrister Nath Pai Marg

UMERKHADI

E. S. Patanwalla Marg

Victoria & Albert Museum

Victoria Gardens

Sant Savta Marg

MAZAGAON

BYCULLA

Dr. Motishah Rd.

Balwant Singh Dhod Marg

Masjid Bridge

MANDVI

PYDHUNI

Jamshedji Jijibhoy Rd.

Mohammad Ali Rd.

Yusof Meherali Rd.

Abdul Rehman St.

Crawford

Maulana Azad Rd.

Maulana Azad Rd.

Moreland Rd.

Sane Guruji Marg (Arthur Rd.)

KAMATIPURA

Sardar Vallabhbhai Patel Rd.

BHULESHWAR
Temple

Mumbadevi

Kalbade

BOMBAY
CENTRAL

Jehangir Beman Behram Marg

Nanubhai Desai Rd.

KALBADEVI

B

Dr. Anandrao Nair Rd.

Patthe Bapurao Marg

Grant Rd. (Maulana Shaukatali Rd.)

Vithalbhai Patel Rd.

Jagannath Shankarsh

Mahalaxmi
Race Course

MAHALAXMI

Keshavrao Khade Marg

Willingdon
Sports
Club

Tardeo Rd.

TO AIRPORTS

Bombay
Central
Railway
Station

CUMBALLA
HILL

TARDEO

Dr. Dadasaheb Bhadkamkar Marg

GIRGAUM

Taraporevala
Aquarium

Mari

Maharis

Mahim
Bay

Haji Ali's
Tomb

Mahalaxmi
Temple

Breach
Candy
Hospital

Altamount Rd. (S.K. Barodawala Marg)

Pedder Rd. (Dr. G. Deshmukh Rd.)

A. K. Marg

Mani
Bhavan

Pandita Ramabai Rd.

KEMPS
CORNER

Babulnath
Mandir

Chowpatty
Beach

Warden Rd. (Bhulabhai Desai Rd.)

Towers
of Silence

Hanging
Gardens

Kamala
Nehru Park

Bel Gangadhar Kher Marg

MALABAR
HILL

Nepean Sea Rd. (Laxmibhai Jagmohandas Marg)

Walkeshwar Rd.

Arabian Sea

Mumbai (Bombay)

ACCOMMODATIONS

A Adarsh Hotel
B Hotel City Palace
C Hotel Lord's
D Hotel Manama
E Hotel Victoria
F Shiv Sagar Lodge

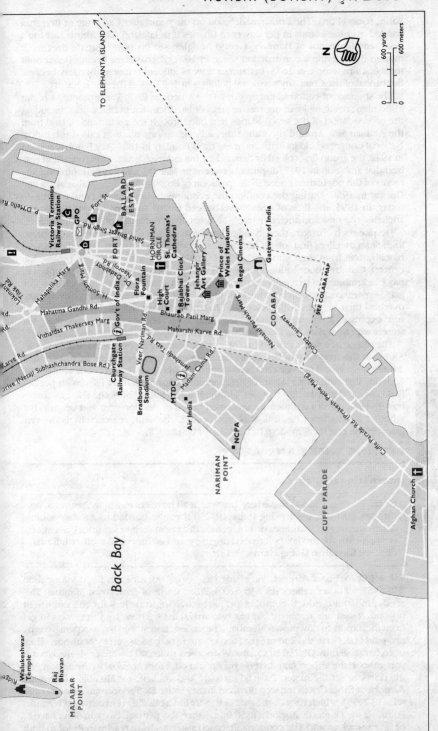

TO ELEPHANTA ISLAND

N

600 yards
600 meters
0

P. D'Mello Rd.

Fort St.

Victoria Terminus Railway Station

GPO

BALLARD ESTATE

Sahid Bhagat Singh Rd.

FORT

HORNIMAN CIRCLE

D. Naoroji Rd.

St. Thomas's Cathedral

Dadabhoy Naoroji Rd.

H. Somani Marg

Mahapalika Marg

Lokmanya Tilak Rd.

Flora Fountain

High Court

Rajabhai Clock Tower

Jehangir Art Gallery

Prince of Wales Museum

Regal Cinema

Gateway of India

Mahatma Gandhi Rd.

Vithaldas Thakersey Marg

Bhaurao Patil Marg

Nathalal Parekh Marg

COLABA

SEE COLABA MAP

Karve Rd.

Rd.

Govt. of India

Veer Nariman Rd.

Maharshi Karve Rd.

Colaba Causeway

Drive (Netaji Subhashchandra Bose Rd.)

Churchgate Railway Station

Bradbourne Stadium

Jamshedji Tata Rd.

Madam Cama Rd.

MTDC

Air India

NCPA

NARIMAN POINT

Cuffe Parade Rd. (Prakesh Pethe Marg)

CUFFE PARADE

Afghan Church

Back Bay

Walukeshwar Temple

Raj Bhavan

Ridge

MALABAR POINT

Bahia, (Good Port). The British made good on the name after Catherine of Braganza handed over the islands in her dowry to Charles II of England. The fourth East India Company Governor of Bombay, Gerald Aungier, set his pomegranate dreams in motion by ordering a construction spree in 1672. Zoroastrians fleeing Persia built their first fire temple in 1675, initiating a flow of affluent refugees. Bombay became the capital of the Company's regional holdings in 1687—and the rest is history.

The shortage of cotton in Britain due to the American Civil War prompted a boom in Bombay, resulting in an impressive array of late-Victorian public works, including the consolidation of the seven islands into one through the reclaiming of land from the Arabian Sea. Around the same time, a fledgling organization called the Indian National Congress held its inaugural meeting in Bombay in 1885. At a Bombay session in 1942, the group first voiced its demand for full independence. After the nation realized that ambition in 1947, disputes between the Marathi- and Gujarati-speaking segments of the population ended in the partition of Bombay State into Maharashtra and Gujarat in 1960. During the conflict, the economy boomed, as it continues to do today. In 1995, the flick of a Shiv Sena-backed politician's pen gave the new and ancient city a new and ancient name—Mumbai, from the local goddess Mumbadevi.

Despite such changes, the city once known as Bombay remains wholly irrepressible. Slum-dwellers find jobs if not houses, so they can blast the latest Bollywood blockbusters from their imported VCRs (Mumbai is India's largest film production center). Cellular phone-toting "puppies" (Punjabi yuppies) jump off their mopeds to pay black money to sign-painters for massive advertising blow-ups for Levi's or Colgate. Eve-teasers (cat-callers) whistle at miniskirted teens, while lunch delivery men overload their bicycles with pickles and *papads* for businessmen. Even the architecture expresses a uniquely urban schizophrenia: Victorian-Gothic vestiges share the streets with high rises, Art Deco apartments, Hindu shrines, and bamboo lean-to's.

The plague of tourists gawking at the city's insane extremes causes hardly a ripple. Although the array of standard sights hardly overwhelms, the manic mix of London double-deckers and bullock carts, *sadhus* and stockbrokers, and constant shuffle will floor any first-time visitor. Mumbai defies expectations of an India filled with pot-bellied cows and ramshackle temples, although it has plenty of both. The city forces travelers to confront a hitherto unimagined fusion of development and despair. But whether it delights or disgusts, this unexpected, ebullient, eclectic city is the vanguard of the emerging modern India. *Salaam* Bombay, indeed.

GETTING THERE AND AWAY

International Flights

> **Note:** There is a Rs500 **departure tax** which all travelers must pay before going through customs and leaving India. (Rs250 if you're headed to another South Asian country). Most airlines do not include this tax in their ticket prices. Set aside enough cash for the tax before exchanging your last rupees. For other information, see **Customs: Going Home,** p. 11.

Sahar International Airport, Ville Parle (tel. 836 6700; Air India flight information 836 6767; all other airlines tel. 836 6200), 20km north of downtown Mumbai. This seedy, mosquito-ridden complex prepares arriving travelers for the continent beyond. It's all one terminal, but has two arrival halls. There are three ways to get from the airport to downtown Mumbai. The easiest, fastest, and most expensive is by **pre-paid taxi.** Go to the 2nd pre-paid taxi counter you pass as you exit customs. They overcharge slightly (Rs250 to Colaba as opposed to Rs200 by meter, 1½hr.), but if you go solo, the airport taxi drivers will rip you off. From Mumbai to the airport, get the driver to set the meter. Pre-paid taxis are also available for Mumbai's **Domestic Airport,** at Santa Cruz. One step down in luxury is the **Ex-Serviceman's Coach** (info tel. 618 2995), which runs from Sahar to the Air India building downtown at Nariman Point, via the Domestic Airport. (Rs50 from Sahar; Rs5 per bag. No, you don't have to be an ex-serviceman.) The comfortable coach also runs from **Nariman Point** to both airports (12:30am, 1½hr., longer during rush hours). Finally, the rock bottom method of getting into town is to take **Bus 321 Ltd.** to Vile Park Station (Rs2) and then a commuter train to Churchgate (Rs4), but this route is confusing, tiresome, and chest-crushingly crowded at rush-hour.

International Airlines: Air India, Air India Building, Marine Drive, Nariman Point (tel. 202 4142 or 287 4156). Open M-Sa 9:15am-6pm, Su 9:15am-5:15pm. **Air Lanka,** Mittal Tower, "C" Wing, Nariman Point (tel. 282 3288 or 284 4156). Open M-F 9:30am-5:30pm, Sa 9am-4pm. **Bangladesh Biman,** Airline Hotel Building, 199 J. Tata Rd., #32, Churchgate (tel. 282 4580). Open M-F 9am-5:30pm, Sa 9am-3pm. **British Airways,** 202-B Vulcan Insurance Building, Veer Nariman Rd., Churchgate (tel. 282 0888). Open M-F 9:45am-6pm, Sa 9:30am-5:30pm. **Cathay Pacific,** Taj Mahal Hotel, Apollo Bunder, Colaba (tel. 202 9113). Open M-Sa 9:30am-1pm and 1:45-5:30pm. **Delta,** Taj Mahal Hotel, Apollo Bunder, Colaba (tel. 288 3274 or 288 5652). Open M-Sa 9am-1pm and 1:30-5:30pm. **Emirates,** Mittal Chambers, 288 Nariman Point (tel. 287 1649 or 287 1650). Open M-Sa 9am-5:30pm. **Lufthansa,** Express Towers, Nariman Point (tel. 202 3430 or 287 5264). Open M-F 9am-1pm and 1:45-5:45pm, Sa 9am-1pm. **Pakistan International Airlines,** Mittal Towers, Nariman Point (tel. 202 1598). Open M-Sa 9am-1pm and 2-5:30pm. **Royal Jordanian,** Jollymaker Chamber #2, Nariman Point, 4th fl. (tel. 202 2779). Open M-F 9am-1pm and 2-5:30pm, Sa 9am-3pm. **Royal Nepal,** 222 Maker Chamber V, Nariman Point (tel. 283 6197 or 283 5489). Open M-F 10am-6pm, Sa 10am-2pm. **Singapore Airlines,** Taj Mahal Hotel, Apollo Bunder, Colaba (tel. 202 3316 or 202 2747). Open M-Sa 9:15am-5:30pm. **Thai Air,** World Trade Center, Shop 15, Ground Floor, Cuffe Parade (tel. 218 5426). Open M-F 9:30am-5:30pm.

Domestic Flights

Santa Cruz Airport, 20km northeast of downtown, 3km from Sahar International Airport. The new Terminal 1A is for Indian Airlines and 1B is for all private carriers; free shuttle buses connect the two (every 15min., 4am-midnight). The **Ex-Serviceman's Coach** (info tel. 618 2995), runs from Santa Cruz to the Air India building downtown at Nariman Point (Rs40, Rs5 per bag). Free shuttle buses also depart from both terminals to the international airport (hourly, 24hr.). No pre-paid taxis, but the ones at the stand outside should follow the meter one-way (Rs200 to downtown; less than Rs75 to Sahar International Airport). **Domestic Airlines: Indian Airlines,** Air India Building, 1st fl., Marine Drive, Nariman Point (enquiry tel. 140; reservations tel. 289 6161). Open M-Sa 8:30am-5:30pm, Su 10am-5:30pm; open 24hr. at the Domestic Airport for ticketing. **Jet Airways,** Amarchand Mansion, Madam Cama Rd. (tel. 287 5086 or 287 5087). Open M-Sa 10am-5:30pm. **Skyline NEPC,** Lyka Labs Building, 77 Nehru Rd., Ville Parle (E) (tel. 610 7356). Open M-Sa 10am-6pm.

Indian Airlines flies to: **Ahmedabad** (2 per day, 1hr., US$75); **Aurangabad** (1 per day, 1hr., US$65); **Bangalore** (3 per day, 1½hr., US$125); **Bhopal** (1 per day, 2hr., US$115); **Bunbaneshwar** (4 per week, 3hr., US$225); **Calcutta** (2 per day, 2½hr., US$205); **Calicut** (1 per day, 1½hr., US$140); **Chennai (Madras)** (2 per day, 2hr., US$145); **Cochin** (1 per day, 2hr., US$150); **Coimbatore** (1 per day, 2hr., US$135); **Delhi** (4 per day, 2hr., US$155); **Goa** (1 per day, 1hr., US$75); **Hyderabad** (3 per day, 1½hr., US$105); **Indore** (1 per day, 1½hr., US$80); **Jaipur** (1 per day, 1½hr., US$140); **Mangalore** (1 per day, 1½hr., US$115); **Trivandrum** (1 per day, 2hr., US$175); **Udaipur** (1 per day, 1-2hr., US$110); and **Varanasi** (2 per week, 3hr., US$120).

Trains

The Western Railways connect the city to Gujarat, Rajasthan, and Delhi, while the Central Railways also serve Delhi and other destinations. You must go to the correct booking office to reserve tickets. **Central Railways,** Reservation Office, Victoria Terminus (enquiry tel. 135 or 269 5959; automated arrivals and departures tel. 265 6565; arrivals from south tel. 136, from north tel. 137, from Pune tel. 138). This A/C office, adjacent to the long-haul platforms, becomes less confusing if you head straight for **Window 8,** the Foreign Tourist Guide (open M-Sa 9am-1pm and 1:30-4pm). They sell tickets for rupees if you have an encashment certificate, or for dollars or pounds sterling otherwise. They release the tourist quota the day before departure only, unless you hold an Indrail Pass (which they also sell). The following trains leave from **Victoria Terminus (V.T.)**, officially known as **Chhatrapati Shivaji Terminus (CST)**. Fares given are for 2nd/1st class. To: **Agra** (*Punjab Mail* 2137, 7:10pm, 22hr., Rs191/1009); **Aurangabad** (*Tapovan Exp.* 7617, 6:10am, 10hr.; *Devgiri Exp.* 1003, 9:20pm, 7hr., Rs94/470); **Bangalore** (*Udyan Exp.* 6529, 8am, 24hr., Rs184/952); **Bhopal** (*Punjab Mail* 2137, 7:10pm, 14hr., Rs150/737); **Calcutta** (*Gitanjali Exp.* 2859, 6am, 35hr., Rs235/1385; *Howrah Mail* 8001, 8:15pm, 35hr., Rs235/1385); **Chennai (Madras)** (*Mumbai-Chennai Exp.* 6011, 2pm, 27hr., Rs191/1009); **Hyderabad** (*Hyderabad Exp.* 7031, 12:35pm, 18hr.; *Hussain Sagar Exp.* 7001, 9:55pm, 15½hr., Rs144/736); **Madgaon** (*Goa Exp.,* 10:30pm, 8½hr., Rs1050/231); **Miraj** (*Mahalaxmi Exp.* 1011, 8:20pm, 12hr., Rs100/500); **Pune** (*Deccan Exp.* 1007, 6:40am, 4hr.; *Deccan Queen* 2123, 5pm, 4hr., Rs48/239); **Trivandrum** (*Kanyakumari Exp.* 1081, 3:40pm, 48hr., Rs272/1709). One Central Railways train departs from the **Kurla Terminus** (15km northeast of downtown) to **Earnakulam** (*Netravathi Exp.* 6635, 4:40pm, 26hr., Rs1680/352).

Western Railways, Churchgate Reservation Office, Maharishi Karve Rd., Churchgate (enquiry tel. 131; booking information tel. 209 5959; arrivals from Delhi tel. 132, from Gujarat tel. 133). Opposite Churchgate Station, in the same building as the Government of India Tourist Office. To get to the **Foreign Tourist Counter,** ignore the first reservation office you see, walk past the entrance to the tourist office, and enter the next door on your left. Tourist quota tickets are available only the day before; dollars, pounds sterling, and rupees (with encashment certificate) are accepted. The Foreign Tourist Center is open M-F 9:30am-1:30pm and 2-4:30pm, Sa 9:30am-2:30pm. The following trains leave from **Mumbai Central,** which can be reached from downtown Mumbai (see **Public Transportation,** below). To: **Ahmedabad** (*Shatabdi Exp.* 2009, 6:25am, 7hr., A/C chair Rs1150); **Delhi** (*Rajdhani Exp.* 2951, 16½hr., A/C sleeper Rs1320, A/C chair Rs1095); and **Jaipur** (*Jaipur Exp.* 2955, 7pm, 18½hr., A/C sleeper Rs798, non-A/C Rs317).

Buses

State Transport Terminal, J.B. Behran Marg (tel. 307 4272 or 307 6622), just opposite Central Railway Station, next door to the Maratha Mandir Cinema. **Maharashtra State Road Transport Corporation** runs relatively quiet, comfortable buses to the major tourist destinations in the state, although services are cut back during monsoon. To: **Aurangabad** (8:15 and 9:15am, 10hr., Rs104/146) and **Mahabaleshwar** (6 and 7am, 9:30pm, 7hr., Rs78/142). For other destinations in Maharashtra, travelers must book at the ASIAD office (tel. 413 6835) in Dadar, or at an MTDC luxury service office, although trains are likely to be quicker and more convenient. **Goa State Transport** (Kadamba) runs a daily luxury bus to **Panjim** (5pm, 15hr., Rs241). **Gujarat's State Transport** lays on at least 3 services daily to **Ahmedabad** (6, 7, and 8pm, 12hr., Rs114). Karnataka's company runs a service for the truly intrepid to **Bangalore** (10:30am, 2:30, and 7pm, 24hr., Rs272). **MTDC,** CDO Hutments, Madam Cama Rd. (tel. 202 6713). Check with them to see what routes they offer, as their destinations keep changing. Currently, they go to **Mahabaleshwar** (6:30am, 7hr., Rs160) and **Nasik** (6am, 6hr., Rs90).

GETTING AROUND

Just watching the local transport in Mumbai evokes surges of pity and fear in the average bystander; riding it tends to deaden the senses and sap emotions. Still, while the local trains and buses may shatter your worldview and your collarbone, they leave your finances largely intact.

Local Buses

Buses are slightly easier to deal with than trains and, for most tourists, more useful. Try to learn the Hindi numbers so you can recognize the bus as it approaches. (The English number and destination is written only down on the side—often visible too late to secure footing before the bus roars off again.) Red numbers indicate "limited" services, which supposedly stop less frequently and certainly cost marginally less, but no fare in the city should exceed Rs3, limited or otherwise. Climb in the rear door only (the front is for exiting), be ready to name a destination for the conductor, and buy your ticket on the bus as the conductor approaches with a click. Keep hold of your ticket because there are frequent inspections. All this sounds quite easy, but at rush hour, when masses of commuters stampede through and fling themselves at the narrow metal door of a moving bus, you may feel more hesitant. Don't lose heart: outside the peak hours and on less traveled routes, buses are a convenience most tourists don't have the gumption to utilize.

Bus #	Hindi #	Route and Destination
1 ltd.	१	Colaba-Regal-Flora-V.T.-Crawford Market-Mahim
3	३	Afghan Church-Colaba-Regal-Flora-V.T.
62	६२	Flora-Metro-Marine Lines-Mumbai Central-Dadar Station
61	६१	Regal-Metro-Opera House-Mumbai Central-Dadar Station
81 ltd.	८१	V.T.-Kemp's Corner-Breach Candy and Haji Ali-Nehru Planetarium
91	९१	Mumbai Central-Dardar-Kurla
106	१०६	Afghan Church-Colaba-Regal-Chowpatty-Kamala Nehru Park
108	१०८	V.T.-Regal-Chowpatty-Kamala Nehru Park
132	१३२	Regal-Churchgate-Breach Candy and Haji Ali
188 ltd.	१८८	Borivli (E)-Sanjay Gandhi NP-Kanheri Caves
231	२३१	Santa Cruz (W)-Juhu Beach
321 ltd.	३२१	Airport-Ville Parle (E)
343	३४३	Goregaon (E)-Film City

Local Trains

Mumbai's commuter rail system is even more complicated than its bifurcated long-haul cousin—and 10 times more crowded. **Western Railways** runs one line, from Churchgate through Mumbai Central, Dadar, Bandra, Santa Cruz (for Juhu), and Ville Parle (for the airports) to Borivli (Sanjay Gandhi NP) and beyond. One-way tickets, sold at windows in each station, cost Rs5-11 for 2nd class (depending on the distance traveled), and about 10 times as much for 1st class. The difference between 1st and 2nd class is slight. First class has marginally cushier seats (but you're unlikely to get one) and is more civilized, though not less crowded, during rush hour. When boarding a train, make sure it's heading to the right destination by checking the digital display. It will read a letter code, then a time, and then F or S. The first code indicates the destination: A for Andheri, Bo for Borivli, C for Churchgate, D for Dadar, etc., depending on which line you're on. The time is the scheduled departure (trains usually leave every 10min.). Finally, F stands for fast and S for slow. Fast trains skip the stations whose names are illuminated on the board below. That's right, the names that are lit up brightly by the train are the places it does **not** go. There are special, less crowded cars for women only (striped and stamped with a stencil of a damsel in a *sari*) on all trains. Keep hold of your ticket and be on the lookout for your stop since the platform side varies. If you can keep all of this in mind with one foot on the ground and the other out the open doorway, with hundreds of commuters pressed up against you, with the summer sun beating down on the little metal *tandoor* oven you're riding in, and with your clothes torn by the crush and your bag ripped off your shoulder by the pressure of the mob, you should be fine. Otherwise, travel out of town in the morning, and return well after noon. The same rules apply to the **Central Railways** lines that run out of V.T., which are of less use to the traveler. Byculla, for the Victoria and Albert Museum, and Kurla, for certain long-distance trains, are served by Central Railways.

Taxis

Taxis rule Mumbai, since auto-rickshaws aren't allowed in the downtown area and public transport is so crowded. Luckily, they are plentiful and the drivers only healthily argumentative. Set the meter and go—this shouldn't be the struggle it is elsewhere unless it's very late or the weather's very bad. You pay roughly 11 times what the meter shows—for the precise figure, consult the chart that the taxi driver should carry. He may deny it at first, but an imperious "chart *de*" usually works.

Auto-Rickshaws

These only roam the suburbs, but the taxi fare rule applies. The conversion rate is just about 7 times the amount shown.

ORIENTATION

Mumbai is shaped like a vast lobster claw clutching out into the Arabian Sea. The long pincer, **Colaba,** home to most of the budget hotels, faces the shorter, residential neighborhood of **Malabar Hill,** across the choppy waters of **Back Bay.** North of these two are piled successively the business and financial district, the bazaar district, the old mill areas, and then the endless suburbs, stretching all the way to the end of Bombay Island, 50km north of the city center.

Most tourists only catch a fleeting, jet-lagged glimpse of these areas on their way to or from the international and domestic airports in the suburbs of **Ville Parle** and **Santa Cruz,** 20km from downtown. Instead, the Colaba district, centering on **Colaba Causeway (Shahid Bhagat Singh Marg)** claims most of their time. The Causeway ends at **Wellington Circle,** universally known as **Regal** after the movie theater that presides over it. From Regal, **Madam Cama Road** runs west (left) to **Nariman Point,** Mumbai's Wall Street, which houses the offices of many international banks, airlines, and even a few consulates. North of Regal runs **Mahatma Gandhi Marg (M.G. Rd.)** past the Prince of Wales Museum, the high court, and the University to **Flora Fountain (Hutatma Chowk).** From here, **Veer Nariman (V.N.) Road** leads left to **Churchgate Station** and **Marine Drive,** and right to the heart of **Fort,** Mumbai's oldest neighborhood. **Dr. Dadabhoy Naoroji (Dr. D.N.) Road** proceeds north from Flora to **Victoria Terminus (V.T.),** also called **Chhatrapati Shivaji Terminus (CST),** the colonial colossus from which many of Mumbai's long-distance trains depart. Beyond V.T., Dr. D.N. Rd. comes to a halt at **Crawford Market,** the beginning of the **bazaar district.** Marine Drive follows the bay from Nariman Point all the way to **Chowpatty Beach.** A 10-minute ride north lies **Mumbai Central,** another major railway station and the terminus for state-run buses.

Potato, Potahto: The Politics of Name Changes

Most tourists spin or stroll down Netaji Subhas Chandra Bose Rd. in Mumbai several times without even realizing it. They, like all the city's residents, know this street by its colonial name, Marine Drive. No matter how civic-minded or patriotic the new designations selected by the municipal corporation, latter-day Mumbaiites rebel against today's authorities by refusing to relinquish the monikers of past oppressors. Nepean Sea Rd. is never Laxmibhai Jagmohandas Marg; even the bus conductors say Ridge Rd. for Bal Gangadhar Kher Marg; Shahid Bhagat Singh Marg evinces blank stares from taxi drivers—but everyone recognizes Colaba Causeway. On the rare occasions when the populace accepts the new names, they inevitably abbreviate them beyond recognition: heedless city-dwellers compress Sir Pherozeshah Mehta Rd. into P.M. Rd.; Doctor Dadabhoy Naoroji barely escapes as Dr. D.N., and even the nation's Great Soul gets squashed to M.G.

Bombay's name game developed from small-scale civil disobedience to big-time politics, as the Hindu nationalist Shiv Sena party, senior partners in the state's coalition government, has decided that streets by any other name would smell more sweet. In 1995 the Sena dropped their biggest bomb—literally. They renamed the whole city Mumbai, in line with its perceived "traditional" Marathi name (Madras followed suit in 1996, switching its name to the hardly homophonic Chennai). But the struggle continues, as urbanites now wryly refer to the city as "Slumbai."

PRACTICAL INFORMATION

Tourist and Financial Services

Tourist Office: Government of India Tourist Office, 123 Maharishi Karve Rd. (tel. 203 3144 or 203 3145). About 100m along the road running down the right-hand side of Churchgate Station as you face it. The place looks a lot like a travel agency, but those printers are churning out computerized tourist information for all of India. The friendly staff has a few non-electronic brochures and can answer questions about Mumbai, but their map supply tends to dry up. Open M-F 8:30am-6pm, Sa 8:30am-2pm. Also at **Sahar International Airport** (tel. 832 5331, open 24hr.) and at Santa Cruz Domestic Airport (tel. 614 9200, open at flight arrival times). **Maharashtra Tourism Development Corporation (MTDC),** CDO Hutments, Madam Cama Rd. (tel. 202 6713). From the Air India building, walk away from Marine drive on Madam Cama Rd. The MTDC is on the left, after the giant Nehru statue. The staff sells maps, but are little more than glorified booking agents for MTDC tours and hotels. Open M-F 9:30am-6pm, Sa 9:30am-2pm. Main office located at Express Towers, 9th fl., Nariman Point. Other offices at Santa Cruz airport, **Sahar International Airport,** Churchgate Station, and the Gateway of India.

Help Line: Ask Me (tel. 888 8888). Questions about Mumbai, from the esoteric to the inane (but not including the lewd), will be answered by the helpful staff.

Diplomatic Missions: Australia, Maker Towers, 16th fl., E. Block, Cuffe Parade (tel. 218 1071). Replacement passport AUS$106 (2 working days). Open M-F 9am-5pm. **Canada,** 41/42 Maker Chambers VI, Nariman Point (tel. 287 6027). Replacement passport Rs1500. Open M-F 9am-5:30pm. **Ireland,** Royal Mumbai Yacht Club, Apollo Bunder, Colaba (tel. 202 4607). Open M-F 10am-noon. **Netherlands,** International Bldg., Marine Lines Cross Rd. #1, Churchgate (tel. 201 6750). Replacement passport 55 guilders. Open M-F 9am-3:30pm. **South Africa,** Gandhi Museum, Altamount Rd., near Kemp's Corner (tel. 389 3725). Open M-F 9am-12:45pm. **Sri Lanka,** Sri Lanka House, 34 Homi Modi St., Fort (tel. 204 5861 or 204 8303). Most visas obtainable on arrival in Sri Lanka. Open for visas M-F 9:30-11:30am. **Thailand,** Krishnabad, 2nd fl., 43 Bhulabhai Desai Rd., Breach Candy (tel. 363 1404). Two-month visa Rs400. Many nationalities can enter for under 2 months without a visa. Open M-F 9am-noon. (For more information, see **Surrounding Countries,** p. 8.) **U.K.,** Maker Chambers IV, 1st fl., Nariman Point (tel. 283 3602 or 283 0517). Replacement passport Rs1100. Open M-F 8am-1pm and 2-4pm. **U.S.,** Lincoln House, 78 Bhulabhai Desai Rd., Breach Candy (tel. 363 3611 or 363 3617). Registers U.S. citizens and issues travel advisories and lists of doctors and dentists. Replacement passport US$65. Open M-F 9am-12:30pm and 2-3:45pm.

Currency Exchange: Hong Kong Bank, 52160 M.G. Rd., Flora Fountain (tel. 267 4921). Cash advances on Visa and Mastercard (up to Rs6000). On-site **ATM** is connected to the Plus network. Open M-F 10:30am-3:30pm, Sa 10:30am-1:30pm. **Standard Chartered,** 81 Ismail Bldg., Dr. D.N. Rd. (tel. 204 5056), near Flora. On the right-hand side as you walk from Flora to V.T. 24hr. **ATM** connects to the Plus and Cirrus systems. **Thomas Cook,** Thomas Cook Bldg., Dr. D.N. Rd., Fort (tel. 204 8556). On the left-hand side about 2 blocks up as you walk from Flora to V.T., with the bright red sign. They cash their own traveler's checks for free but charge Rs20 per transaction for other brands. Open M-Sa 9:30am-6pm. **American Express** Regal Cinema Bldg., Shivaji Marg, Colaba (tel. 204 6361), on Wellington Circle. Inside this A/C haven, AmEx card or traveler's check holders can collect their mail (held for 1 month) or have it forwarded. The office changes its own traveler's checks without a commission, but charges 1% for most other brands. They also make travel arrangements and will cash a cardholder's check for up to US$1000. Open M-Sa 9:30am-6:30pm.

Local Services

Luggage Storage: Cloak Room at V.T. Inside the station building, near platform 13. Bags must be locked closed (including the unlockable portion of backpacks). Whatever you do, don't lose the receipt. The facility sometimes runs out of room, at which point people sit around mournfully, waiting for space. Each bag is Rs5 for the first day, Rs6 for the second, and Rs7 per day thereafter. 31-day max. deposit. Open daily 12:30-7:30am, 8am-3:30pm, and 4pm-midnight.

Bookstore: Crossword Bookstore, Mahalaxmi Chambers, 1st. fl., 22 Bhulabhai Desai Rd., Breach Candy (tel. 492 0253). Look up for the yellow sign in the window. Inside, Mumbai's best collection of English-language fiction bursts from the bookshelves. Indian, British, and American magazines, music, games, and office supplies. Open daily 10am-6pm. **Nalanda Bookstore,** Taj Mahal Hotel (tel. 202 2514). In the back of the modern wing. The most convenient bookstore to Colaba proffers paperback novels and Indian and Western music, all at distinctly non-Taj prices. Open daily 8am-midnight. **Used book stands** along Veer Mariman Rd. west of Flora, have various well-worn novels and travel guides at highly negotiable prices.

Library: American Center Library, 4 New Marine Lines, Churchgate (tel. 262 4590). The barricaded building on the right-hand side as you walk from Churchgate. The library caters to Mumbaiites more than expatriates, but for Rs15 per day, nonmembers may lounge in the A/C calm and read dated U.S. papers or indulge in the library's reasonable American fiction collection. Open M-Tu and Th-Sa 10am-6pm. **British Council,** A Wing, Mittal Towers, 1st fl., Nariman Point (tel. 282 3530). Although short-term visitors cannot join the library, they are suffered to glance through the British papers. Open Tu-F 10am-5:45pm, Sa 9am-4:45pm. **Alliance Française,** Theosophy Hall, 40 New Marine Lines, Churchgate (tel. 201 6202). Directly opposite the American Center. Again, in theory, nonmembers have few rights, although they can *je'ttent un coup d'oeil* at the temporary exhibits and peruse the papers. Some even worm their way into a movie, depending on the pressure of numbers. Open M-F 9:30am-1pm and 2-5:30pm, Sa 9:30am-1pm. **Max Mueller Bhavan,** Prince of Wales Annex, Kalaghoda (tel. 202 7542). Behind the Prince of Wales Museum, next door to the Jehangir Art Gallery. German newspapers and books, and occasional cultural events. Open M-F 9:30am-5:30pm.

Market: M Phule Market, Dr. D.N. Rd. Universally known as **Crawford Market,** despite the best efforts of several governments. This huge warren of fruit, vegetable, meat, and dry goods at the north end of D.N. Rd. furnishes flora and fauna you have never seen before. Open M-Sa 6am-6pm.

Emergency and Communications

Pharmacy: New Marine Lines is lined with late night chemists, such as **Mumbai Chemists,** 39-40 Kakad Arcade, New Marine Lines, Churchgate (tel. 200 1173), right next to Mumbai Hospital. Open 24hr. **Kemp & Co.,** Taj Market, Apollo Bunder, Colaba (tel. 202 3519), in the old hotel, at the beginning of the connecting corridor. Sells cheap pills and cheap thrills: chocolate, massage oil, and Indian Barbie dolls. Open daily 7am-11pm.

Hospital: Mumbai Hospital, New Marine Lines (tel. 206 7676). Modern, established, and centrally located. Open 24hr. **Breach Candy Hospital,** 60 Bhulabhai Desai Rd., Breach Candy (tel. 363 3651), on the sea-side of Warden Rd., just past the American Consulate and the Breach Candy Swimming Club. Farther from Colaba, but one of the most modern hospitals in Mumbai. Open 24hr.

Emergency: Police, tel. 100. **Fire,** tel. 101. **Ambulance,** tel. 102.

Police: Police Commissioner's Office, Dr. D.N. Rd., Crawford Market (tel. 100). Opposite the market building behind an iron fence. You can report thefts at this head office, but expect an endless bureaucratic nightmare.

Post Office: GPO, W. Hirachand Marg (tel. 262 0956). The huge stone building right next door to V.T., off Nagar Chowk. Tiny, individualized counters, with specialized functions detectable only by use of an out-dated wall chart, line this cavern of communication. **Poste Restante** is at counter 2 (not counter 93, as posted), on the left as you enter the main hall. For parcels *poste restante*, retrieve your claim form at counter 2, then head to the New Building, ground floor, directly to the right of the GPO. The parcel delivery counter is to the left behind the elevator. Open M-Sa 9am-6pm, Su 10am-3pm. Counters 80-89 proffer stamps M-Sa 9am-8pm, Su 10am-5:30pm. To mail letters abroad, head to counter 4 where they will be postmarked and (hopefully) whisked away to their destinations. **EMS Speed Post** resides at counters 8-12, in the apse on the left of the main hall. Open M-Sa 9am-7pm, Su 9am-

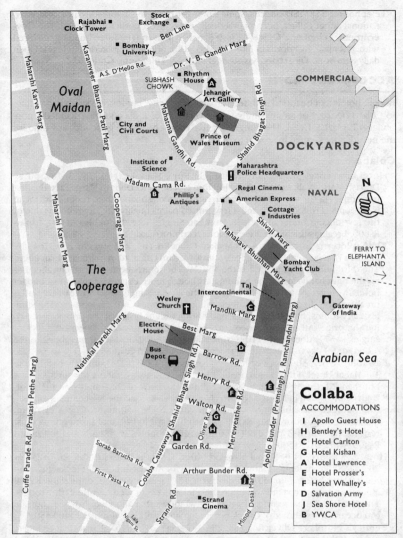

The following labels appear on the map:

Rajabhai Clock Tower
Stock Exchange
Ben Lane
Bombay University
Karamveer Bhaurao Patil Marg
A.S. D'Mello Rd.
Dr. V. B. Gandhi Marg
Rhythm House
SUBHASH CHOWK
Jehangir Art Gallery
COMMERCIAL
Maharshi Karve Marg
Oval Maidan
City and Civil Courts
Mahatma Gandhi Rd.
Prince of Wales Museum
Shahid Bhagat Singh Rd.
DOCKYARDS
Institute of Science
Madam Cama Rd.
Maharashtra Police Headquarters
Phillip's Antiques
Regal Cinema
American Express
NAVAL
N
Cooperage Marg
Cottage Industries
Shivaji Marg
Mahakavi Bhushan Marg
FERRY TO ELEPHANTA ISLAND
Maharshi Karve Marg
The Cooperage
Bombay Yacht Club
Taj Intercontinental
Wesley Church
Mandlik Marg
Gateway of India
Nathalal Parekh Marg
Electric House
Best Marg
Barrow Rd.
Apollo Bunder (Premsingh J. Ramchandni Marg)
Arabian Sea
Bus Depot
Henry Rd.
Cuffe Parade Rd. (Prakash Pethe Marg)
Walton Rd.
Mereweather Rd.
Oliver Rd.
Sorab Barucha Rd.
Garden Rd.
First Pasta Ln.
Arthur Bunder Rd.
Colaba Causeway (Shahid Bhagat Singh Rd.)
Strand Rd.
Jaia Nigam Sc.
Strand Cinema
Minod Desai Marg

Colaba
ACCOMMODATIONS
I Apollo Guest House
H Bentley's Hotel
C Hotel Carlton
G Hotel Kishan
A Hotel Lawrence
E Hotel Prosser's
F Hotel Whalley's
D Salvation Army
J Sea Shore Hotel
B YWCA

WEST INDIA

3pm. Parcels begin their journey from window 39, in Bicentennial Hall, up the stairs at the back of the mail hall. Open M-Sa 10am-4pm, Su 10am-2pm. The whole building is open M-Sa 9am-8pm, Su 10am-5:30pm. **Postal Code:** 400001.

Internet: Internet Cyber Cafe, Modi and Modi Bldg, 74 Nagindas Master Rd., Fort (tel. 267 1331 or 267 1525; fax 267 1756; email mahendra@indiayellow-pages.com). From Flora, walk south, to the left of Hong Kong Bank, about 250m. Quiet, A/C, convenient to Colaba. Web browsing Rs120 per hr. Open M-Sa 10am-8:30pm. **Asiatic Shopping Center** (tel. 283 4526), on Veer Nariman Rd. across from Churchgate Station. Eight PC's tucked into a cool but cramped compartment on the right side of the building. Web browsing Rs120 per hr. Open M-Sa 10am-8:30pm. **Net Express Cybercafe** (tel. 284 6278), Express Towers, Nariman Point. From Madam Cama Rd., walk to the left of the Air India Building, and head up the stairs of what seems to be the back entrance to the Towers. Web browsing Rs160; noon-7pm: Rs200; students Rs80/100. Open M-Sa 8am-10pm.

Telephones: STD/ISD booths, some open 24hr., for local, long-distance, and international direct calling, occupy practically every street corner in Mumbai. The **Government Telephone Office,** Videsh Sanchar Bhavan (the huge building, covered with antennae, just north of Flora on M.G. Rd.), offers telegrams and telexes. Open daily 8am-8pm. **Directory Assistance:** tel. 197. **Telephone Code:** 022.

ACCOMMODATIONS

Budget hotels can be found in different parts of the city, but tourists seem to gravitate to Colaba because of its proximity to the Gateway of India and the (decidedly non-budget) Taj Mahal Hotel. The congestion makes reservations a good idea any time for the best deals, essential in season (Nov.-Feb.).

Colaba

Hotel Lawrence, 3rd fl., ITTS House, 33 Rope Walk Ln. (tel. 284 3618), off K. Dubash Marg. Walk to the right of Rhythm House on K. Dubash Marg. Take the first left, and go in the second door on the right. Ten reasonably sized rooms with clean bathrooms, a friendly staff, and a few potted palms qualify the Lawrence as one of the few decent budget hotels in Mumbai. Singles Rs300; doubles Rs400; triples Rs600. Breakfast included. Reservations recommended.

YWCA International Centre, 18 Madam Cama Rd. (tel. 202 5053 or 202 9161; fax 202 0445), near Regal. From Regal, follow Madam Cama Rd. toward Nariman Point. The third building on the left is the YWCA. The International Centre entrance lies on the right-hand side of the building. Although more expensive than most budget hotels, you get your money's worth at the Y: rates include all-you-can-eat buffet breakfast and dinner, daily room cleaning, telephones, and TV lounges. The spotless, airy rooms, breezy balconies, and florid curtains brighten the prospect of paying the price. All have attached bathrooms. Check-out noon. Dorm beds Rs521; singles Rs571; doubles Rs1102; triples Rs1603. Additional Rs60 membership fee (good for 90 days). Reservations essential 1-2 weeks in advance.

Salvation Army, 30 Mereweather Rd., Colaba (tel. 284 1824), directly behind the Taj Mahal Hotel. From Regal, head down the Causeway, take a left on Mahakavi Bhushan Rd. (by Mondegar's) and a right at the back of the Taj; it's on the right. High ceilings, dim lighting, and pistachio-green walls lend the big complex an institutional feel. Passable dorms and large, nondescript doubles. Check-in 10am, check-out 9am. Dorm beds Rs100, with full board Rs140, and dorm guests must rent lockers for Rs3 per day (Rs50 deposit). Doubles with bath and full board Rs400, with A/C Rs500.

Hotel Sea Shore, 1139 Kamal Mansion (4th fl.), Minod Desai Rd. (tel. 287 4237 or 287 4238). From Regal, follow the Causeway to Arthur Bunder, 9 blocks down on the left. Just before Minod Desai meets the sea, an alley runs off to the right. Kamal Mansion's entrance stands on the right. Pink-stuccoed, tiled corridors, tiny rooms. The "sea" in the name refers to the few windows that allow you to "see" outside (no ocean views, though). Check-out noon. Singles Rs300; doubles Rs400-450.

Bentley's Hotel, 17 Oliver Rd., (tel. 284 1474; fax 287 1846). A real treat—vintage rooms with hardwood floors, whitewashed balconies, and mosaic tiling. Breakfast included in price. Rooms priced according to their size (Rs550-875). A/C Rs200 extra. Visa, MC, AmEx accepted.

Hotel Carlton, Florence House, 12 Mereweather Rd., (tel. 202 0642 or 202 0259). One block before the Salvation Army, behind the Taj. The guest house's balconies, equipped with tiny tables and red plastic chairs, allow residents to escape their cramped quarters. Common baths. All rooms have TV's. Check-out noon. Singles Rs275; doubles Rs400-500, with attached bath and A/C Rs900; triples Rs600.

Whalley's, Jaiji Mansion, 41 Mereweather Rd., Apollo Bunder (tel. 282 1802 or 283 4206). A renovated, big, breezy villa surrounded by greenery, where the birds make more noise than the traffic. Breakfast included. Check-out noon. Singles Rs550, with shower Rs650; doubles Rs750/950, with A/C Rs1200.

Hotel Prosser's, Curzon House, 2-4 Henry Rd., Apollo Rd., (tel. 284 1715 or 283 4937). Where Henry Rd. (the 6th left off the Causeway from Regal) meets the sea. High ceilings make the spacious rooms look like corridors temporarily filled with metal beds and dusty mattresses. Check-out noon. No "visitors" after 11pm. Singles and doubles with common bath Rs350. Extra person Rs100. Sea view Rs550.

Apollo Guest House, 1st fl., 43/44 Mathuradas Estate Building, Colaba Causeway, (tel. 204 1302). On the left-hand side of the road as you walk away from Regal, on the same block as Leopold's. Follow the signs through what looks like a shoe shop. Beyond the plush lobby are tiny, box-like rooms off a cramped, noisy warren. Single Rs350; doubles Rs450.

Hotel Kishan, Shirin Manzil, Walton Rd., (tel. 202 1534 or 283 3886). Walton Rd. is the 7th left off Colaba Causeway from Regal. Hotel Kishan is on the right. A/C doubles feature attached bath, Arabic graffiti, stained tiles, and peeling paint for Rs560.

Aga Begs Guest House, run through Hotel Kishan, offers spacious, drab doubles with slightly tatty beds for Rs360.

Beyond Colaba

Hotel Manama, 221-5 P. D'Mello Rd. (tel. 261 3412). Walk past the GPO on Hirachand Marg, take a left on D'Mello Rd.; Manama is on the right. This crowded, middle-class Indian hotel is a good value. Bellhops in the lobby and TVs in all the rooms. Doubles with attached bath and shower Rs500, with A/C Rs600.

Hotel City Palace, 121 City Terrace, W Hirachand Marg (tel. 261 5515). Opposite V.T. Most of the rooms cost more than they're worth, but the ground floor A/C cubicles with common bath are a cheap Rs400. Other rooms have attached baths: singles Rs650, with A/C Rs950; doubles Rs800/950; triples Rs950/1100.

Shiv Sagar Lodge, 144/146 Kalbadevi Rd. (tel. 201 4753 or 205 3938), about 1km north of the Metro Cinema, opposite the Cotton Exchange. Nestled in the densely packed garment district of Bhuleshwar, the Shiv Sagar offers clean, well-appointed rooms, all with TV, telephone and attached bath. A good location for seeing the city's less touristy side. Check-out 8am. Singles Rs400, with A/C Rs600; doubles Rs500/700. Extra person Rs125.

Adarsh Hotel, Kalbadevi Rd. (tel. 208 4989 or 208 4960), at P.H. Purohit Marg, about 250m south of Shiv Sagar Lodge. Opulent marble hallway leads to smallish, well-kept rooms with telephones and squat toilets. Check-out 8am. Prices climb with TV, A/C, and attached bath. Singles Rs250-450; doubles Rs390-700; triples Rs700-950. Extra person Rs150.

Hotel Lord's, 301 Adi Marzban Path (Mangalore St.) (tel. 261 0077 or 261 8311), off Shahid Bhagat Singh Rd., Fort. At the intersection of Mangalore and SBS Rd., 4 blocks down from Hirachand Marg and the GPO. It's downhill all the way from the grandiose reception desk, but elaborate stucco ceilings distract attention from the cracked linoleum and the broken windows. Check-out noon. Singles Rs200; doubles Rs250, with attached bath Rs300, with A/C Rs400.

Hotel Highway Inn Part One, Vishal Shopping Centre, Andheri-Kurla Rd., Andheri (E) (tel. 830 1494). 3km from the airport. From Andheri Station, exit on the east side, turn left and then right at the intersection with Sir Mathurdas Vananji Rd. (Andheri-Kurla Rd.). Vishal Shopping Centre is 500m on the left. One small, grubby double available at Rs550. Others with TV, bathroom, and fridge Rs950-110.

FOOD

Food in Mumbai runs the gamut from gastronomical delight to gastrointestinal distress—the stupefying street food is a constant temptation, while the city's restaurants beckon with not only every type of Indian cuisine, but also the best approximations of foreign food to be found in India.

Colaba

Trishna, 7 Rope Walk Ln. (tel. 267 2176 or 265 9644). Follow Dr. V.B. Gandhi Marg past Rhythm House, turn left at the first intersection (Rope Walk Ln.), and walk 2 blocks; it will be on your right. Trishna started out as a food-stall and through word of mouth became Mumbai's trendiest seafood restaurant. Serves freakishly sized shellfish at a fraction of their would-be Western price. Medium prawns (since the big ones are 15cm long, these are pretty big) with butter, pepper, and garlic are worth every paise of the Rs160, as are the pomfret (big enough for two, Rs250) and

---

Street Eats in Mumbai—How Brave Are You?

Life in the streets is tough in Mumbai—you need an iron constitution just to eat there. But a streetwise stomach unlocks some of the city's greatest culinary pleasures. At every major intersection, several food stalls vie for the attention of passersby. One sidewalk staple, **pao bhaji,** consists of battered and fried balls of potato and chilies, served on a white roll. Other vendors proffer veggie sandwiches, spread with butter and grasshopper-green chutney, and stuffed beyond bursting with potatoes, cucumber, tomato, onion, and an optional slice of beetroot. But the most popular pavement peddling is the **puri.** This innocent-looking dried pastry shell appears in both flat, disk-like, and hollow, spherical *avatars.* The disk form serves to scoop up a sticky mixture of green chutney, tamarind sauce, chili paste, fried vermicelli, puffed rice, potato, tomato, onion, green mango, and coriander called **bhel puri.** As **sev puri,** the crunchy little frisbees act as platters for the same vegetable mix, without the starch. Other *chaat-wallahs,* as the snack merchants are known, fill the spherical *puris* with a thin sauce or a spiced curd to create **pani puri** and **dahi puri** respectively. Vendors also sell roasted peanuts, chickpeas, and **Bombay Mix** in Rs1 servings. Round off a full meal with a plate of assorted fresh fruit, or, by request, with straight mango, papaya, or pineapple. Tender **coconut water, nimbu pani** (lemonade), and (if you're into typhoid roulette) **sugarcane juice** help to wash it all down—and at Rs6 per portion, you'll have money left over for medicine, should the unfortunate happen.

---

calamari (crisp, Rs100). Ignore the Chinese and Indian selections. Reservations essential at night. Open M-Sa noon-4pm and 6pm-midnight, Su 7pm-midnight.

Ling's Pavilion, 19/21 K.C. College Hostel Bldg., Mahakavi Bhushan Rd., (tel. 285 0023). From the Causeway, turn right on the lane before Mondegar's; Ling's is on the right. Ultra-swank, Ling's serves Chinese fare free of mutation *a la masala.* Cantonese dishes include *dim sum* platter for two (Rs100) and sweet-and-sour vegetables in a pineapple boat (Rs110). Mao would be proud but for the decidedly non-prole digs—check out the iridescent fish frolicking in the purple pond. Open M noon-3pm and 6-11:30pm, Tu-Su noon-11:30pm.

Leopold's, Colaba Causeway. On the left in the 3rd block down from Regal. Passable, swiftly prepared food (decent *biriyani* Rs65, omelette Rs30), but Leo's (both downstairs and up, see **Entertainment,** below) remains Mondegar's rival in attracting a lively crowd of Indians and tourists to drink away the day under slowly rotating fans. Beer Rs50, pitchers Rs200. Open daily 8am-midnight.

Cafe Mondegar, Metro House, Colaba Causeway. The first corner on the left after Regal. Cartoon murals of dining hilarity provide distraction while you eat breakfast (Rs40-55) or a Continental meal (Rs35-80). Beer (Rs70 per bottle). Popular with tourists and locals alike, thanks in part to the CD jukebox. Open daily 8am-11pm.

Khyber Restaurant, 145 M.G. Rd. (tel. 267 3227). On the far side of the parking lot behind the Prince of Wales Museum. The sumptuous antiques-and-mirrors decoration, the mural by India's most famous modern artist, MF Hussain, the intimate, multi-storied nooks and crannies, and, above all, the excellent, rich, tender, Mughlai cuisine all conspire to make this Mumbai's most popular restaurant. The chicken *makhanwala* swims in a thick, tangy tomato sauce (Rs260). The *maa ki dal* undulates with creamy intensity (Rs150). The subtle flavoring of the chicken *badami* sends a *frisson* through your taste buds (Rs250). Open daily 12:30-3:45pm and 7:30-11:45pm. Reservations essential.

Delhi Darbar, Holland House, Colaba Causeway (tel. 202 0235). On the right-hand side, about 100m from Regal. Upmarket A/C joint for businessmen and families offers good North Indian cuisine to the faint, encouraging tones of Flashdance. Not a hint of alcohol, but the overzealous use of *ghee* provides debauchery enough. Try the Parsi specialty *dhansak* (Rs65). Entrees Rs60-80. Open daily noon-midnight.

Majestic, Colaba Causeway. Opposite Mondegar's, up a few stairs. This huge hall of low tables under whirring fans furnishes only basic *thalis*—at an unbeatable Rs25. And you thought there was no budget in Mumbai. Open daily 6:30am-10:30pm.

Edward VIII, 113/A Colaba Causeway. Next to the gas station at the corner of Garden Rd., 1 block before Arthur Bunder. Quiet booths provide a discrete spot for breakfast (Rs25-60), beefless burgers, sandwiches (Rs20-40), or a delicious fresh juice or shake (Rs15-35). Gaze at the larger-than-life-sized portrait of Marilyn Monroe as you slurp your *mosambi* juice. Open M-Sa 9am-9pm.

Madras Lunch and Coffee House, 56 Dr. V.B. Gandhi Marg (tel. 270 1479). Down the street to the left of Rhythm House, at the first intersection. The simple, clean office-*wallahs* breakfast and lunch joint offers authentic South Indian snacks. *Sada, rava, masala,* and *paper dosas* all for Rs12-25. Also *upma, utthapams, idlis* and *vadais,* Rs10-18. Open M-Sa 8am-8pm.

Beyond Colaba

Cafe Naaz, B.G. Kher Rd. (Ridge Rd.), Malabar Hill (tel. 367 2969). Opposite the Hanging Gardens (or Sir P.M Gardens), just beyond Kamala Nehru Park. Perched on the tip of schmancy Malabar Hill, this open-air cafe commands unparalleled views of all of Mumbai, from Chowpatty to Nariman Point and Colaba. The Irani meals (Rs35-80) are tasty, but most come here for a beer (Rs70 per bottle, Rs50 per draft), ice cream, juices, shakes, and sundaes (Rs20-50) after a stroll in the nearby parks. Open M-Sa noon-10pm.

Under the Over, 36 Altamount Rd., Kemp's Corner (tel. 386 1393). Actually just beyond the flyover at Kemp's Corner. For tourists homesick for European and American food, this place imitates it better than any other in Mumbai. Barbecued chicken, with fries and cornbread (Rs185) and chicken chimichangas (Rs175) all taste sort of like the real thing. Brownies (Rs85) or cheesecake (Rs110) to wind up. Open daily 12:30-3:30pm and 7:30-11:30pm.

Samrat, Prem Court, J. Tata Rd., Churchgate. On the left side of the road that leads to the right of Eros from Churchgate. Fancy pure veg. restaurant specializes in the slightly sweet Gujarati *thalis* (Rs80). Unlike more down-to-earth *thali* joints, you can wash down the plateloads of all-you-can-eat *chapatis, dal,* and vegetables with a bottle of beer (Rs85). Open daily noon-10:30pm.

Bachelor's, opposite Thacker's Restaurant along the Chowpatty Seaface. No address, no telephone, in fact, no actual building, just two glorified street stands straddling the pavement and serving up the best fresh fruit juices (Rs15-40), *kulfi* (Rs30), and cream desserts (Rs40) in Mumbai. Open late (daily 8am-2am).

Gaylord's, V.N. Rd., Churchgate (tel. 282 1259). On the left as you walk from Churchgate to Marine Drive. The sidewalk cafe, barricaded by potted plants, offers a pleasant compromise between indoors and out. The indoor restaurant is overpriced; their menu of drinks and snacks is cheaper. Pastries Rs50, grilled sandwiches Rs70-85. Open daily 9:30am-11pm.

The Pizzeria, 143 Marine Drive, Churchgate (tel. 285 6115). Where V.N. Rd. meets Marine Drive. The cool bay breeze and the red brick and straw blinds that help keep it out lend the joint a Mediterranean feel. The pizza itself is as close to authentic as Mumbai can muster. Choices include the Margherita (8in. Rs90, 12in. Rs150) and the stuffed-crust mixed seafood Fisherman's Wharf (Rs165), as well as pasta dishes (Rs135-190). Open daily noon-11:30pm.

Rajdhani (tel. 342 6919), opposite Mangaldas Market, in the warren of bazaars near Crawford Market. From Crawford, look down the crowded lanes opposite D.N. Rd.; Radjhani is on the right of the lane that reveals a many-turreted white building at the far end. Offers Mumbai's best, richest, most filling Gujarati *thali* at lunch (Rs85). At dinner, they switch to Maharashtrian, Kathiawadi, and Rajasthani *thalis,* but the quality is just as high. Open daily noon-3:30pm and 7-11pm.

SIGHTS

Fort and Colaba

The Raj may have ended over half a century ago, but the most British-influenced area continues to dominate the sight-seeing scene in modern Mumbai, for better or for worse. A good starting point from which to lose yourself in the endless metropolis is the **Gateway of India.** Built to commemorate the visit of King George V and Queen Mary in 1911, this Indianized triumphal arch stands guard over the harbor next to the

Taj Mahal Hotel. With a cosmopolitan nonchalance typical of Mumbai, the gateway combines carved brackets derived from Gujarati temple architecture with Islamic motifs such as the minaret-like finials in a purely European building type. Especially in the evening, the gateway plays host to strolling couples, camera-happy tourists, peanut vendors, snake charmers, and touts pushing do-it-yourself embroidery kits with which to make your very own velour rendition of the celebrated archway.

In the small nearby park stands an imposing equestrian statue of the great 17th-century Maratha leader **Shivaji Bhonsle** (see p. 641). The reputation of this historical king and legendary hero has been hijacked by the right-wing Maharashtrian party, Shiv Sena, which decks out the unwitting image in marigold garlands and saffron flags.

The modern tower of the **Taj Mahal Hotel** just behind dwarfs Shivaji, and the building's older wing really catches the tourist's attention. Jamshedji Tata, one of India's first industrialists, founded this luxurious Mumbai landmark in 1899 in retaliation against the Europeans-only policies of Raj-era hotels. Like all the other Tata enterprises, which dominate today's Indian economy, the Taj soared to success, monopolizing both the hotel industry and the city's early skyline. A self-assured expression wins even grubby backpackers access to the echoing air-conditioned corridors.

Colaba Causeway begins at Willingdon Circle, more popularly known as Regal Circle after the grand old movie theater which faces it. Opposite the cinema stands the **Prince of Wales Museum** (tel. 284 4484). *(Open Tu-Su 10:15am-6pm. Admission Rs5.)* The intervening gardens provide a buffer between the newly restored domed gallery and the breakneck traffic outside. Within, cluttered displays feature everything from exquisite Mughal miniatures to stuffed animals and fourth-rate oil paintings. The first hall houses an amazing trove of archaeological treasures dating back to the Indus Valley Civilization. They include exquisitely preserved stone tools and home burial urns from both Harappa and Mohenjo-Daro. Another highlight is the collection of 16th- to 18th-century metal deities, including a depiction of Shiva as Natraj, the king of dancers. By far the most impressive exhibit, more than enough reason alone to visit the museum, is the collection of **miniature paintings** from the 16th to 18th centuries. These painstakingly detailed works showcase the various Rajasthani, Deccani, and Mughal schools in scenes of palace life, Hindu mythology, and animals.

The **Jehangir Art Gallery** (tel. 204 8212), just behind the Prince of Wales Museum, hosts temporary art exhibits. *(Open daily 11am-7pm.)* The displays focus on contemporary Indian painting, providing a fascinating counterpoint to the miniatures next door. The quality of the art here is mixed, but it's free and air-conditioned.

Down at the southernmost end of the Causeway stands the 19th-century **Afghan Church,** built to commemorate the soldiers who died to keep the Khyber Pass British, as well as an old colonial cemetery, and the now-defunct **Colaba lighthouse.** But the meat of Mumbai's sight-seeing lies north of Regal. The buildings of **Mumbai University** and the **High Court** line the left side of M.G. Rd. from the Prince of Wales Museum to Flora Fountain—their finest facades face the Oval Maidan, one block to the west. These Victorian-Gothic extravaganzas, centering on the 85m **Rajabhai Clock Tower** (open daily 11am-5pm), used to occupy the seafront until the Art Deco neighborhood opposite was built on reclaimed land in the 20s and 30s.

Another area of attractions stretches north from **Flora Fountain,** now renamed Hutatma Chowk (Martyrs' Square) in honor of the protesters who died agitating for a separate Marathi-speaking state in the 1960s. Flora is lined by still more detailed Raj-era Gothic buildings; now foreign banks have seized control, separated by frequent ramparts of offset printers and STD booths. In the midst of the commercial hubbub, **Horniman Circle** strikes a calm, dignified note. The elegant Neoclassical colonnade faces the early 19th-century **Asiatic Society Library** (originally the Town Hall) over a small park complete with fountain. The neighboring **Mint and Customs House** also dates from the early 1800s. But Mumbai's oldest English building is **St. Thomas's Cathedral,** on the southwest corner of the Circle. Although begun by East India Company Governor Gerald Aungier in 1672, when Surat was still the capital of the Bombay Presidency, St. Thomas languished incomplete until 1718. The architects must have hoped to intimidate the local populace into conversion with the gratuitous flying buttresses. The interior reveals a fascinating slice of colonial life with its *punkahs* (hand-operated cloth fans) and endless marble memorials to stiff-upper-lipped Englishmen lost in battle, to disease, or at sea, during the struggle to "civilize" the natives. *(Open daily 6:30am-6pm.)*

At the northern edge of the Fort area stand the grand colonial edifices of the GPO and **Victoria Terminus.** Opposite V.T., the **Bombay Municipal Corporation Building** comes as close to scraping the sky as any Victorian building. The 76m dome can be viewed from the interior during office hours. A quick stroll up Dr. D.N. Rd. from V.T., past the huge Times of India building and the Mumbai School of Art, **Crawford Market** sends a lesser, if equally architecturally improbable spire into the sky. Lockwood Kipling, Rudyard's father, designed the rather condescending sculptures on the exterior during his tenure at the nearby art school.

The Grrls of Mumbai

The Koli fisherwomen of Mumbai swear, spit, scream, and will seek retribution if you dare turn up your nose at them, let alone hold it as you walk by. In Marathi, Koli means "contentious woman." If you want icons of women's liberation, skip the bourgeois short-skirted babes of Breach Candy and extol these authentic anti-chicks instead. Utterly unrefined (every conversation starts with a profanity and sounds like a cat fight) and completely self-sufficient, Koli women will douse with reeking fish water those passersby who note, under their breath, the Kolis' putrid stench. They rise at dawn, head to the wharf to purchase the day's catch, return home after the entire load is sold, only to be greeted by a slew of domestic duties. Indeed, amid the cosmopolitan chaos of Mumbai, these "traditional" types perform, with superior agility, the working woman's balancing act. Then again, most of Mumbai's *Femina*-flaunting females are too busy holding their noses to notice.

Churchgate and Back Bay Coast

The pink-and-white wedding cake of **Eros Cinema** in the middle of this period-piece area exemplifies Mumbai's unparalleled wealth of interwar architecture. Some of the surrounding buildings, on the same square as Churchgate Station, have been restored to their original waxy, zig-zag glory—but most have suffered from damp, salty air and landlords constrained by rent control. Visitors strolling down the side of the maidan from Churchgate will find it hard to believe that these dilapidated apartments fetch millions of dollars on the rare occasions when they come up for sale. From the maidan, Maharishi Karve Rd. merges with Cuffe Parade Rd., where an abrupt gap in the land reclamation schemes has left a small bay between the towers of Nariman Point and the Cuffe Parade Extension. A fishing village, still populated by the original inhabitants of Mumbai, the **Kolis,** lines the shore here (see **The Grrls of Mumbai,** p. 629). The incongruous juxtaposition of the carved wooden boats and waterless, powerless shanties of the village with the high-rises of the multinationals next door strikes even the most hardened tourist.

In the opposite direction from Churchgate, **Marine Drive** stretches all the way from Nariman Point around Back Bay to Chowpatty Beach at the foot of Malabar Hill. At sunset, Mumbaiites love to stroll, powerwalk, and jog along the seaface, chatting, buying snacks, and treating their children to rides on toy cars and makeshift merry-go-rounds. During the monsoons, tremendous waves crash down on the street and its roasted-corn hawkers as buses and cars whiz by, unperturbed. As the natural light fades, the neon ads and the string of streetlights seize the limelight and transform the seaside strip into what was once known as the **Queen's Necklace.**

Beyond the beach rises **Malabar Hill,** home to Mumbai's wealthiest jet-setters. The **Walukeshwar Temple** hides in one of the many old back streets lined with bright flower stalls and renegade chickens that wind through Malabar. In local legend, the area hosted the banished hero of the epic *Ramayana*, Rama, and his brother and companion, Lakshmana, as they traveled south to free Sita, Rama's wife, from captivity in Ravana's kingdom. In order for Rama to perform his daily worship, Lakshmana had to bring a *linga* from far off Varanasi. He was late one day, prompting Rama to create his own from the only material he had—*waluk* (sand), hence creating a *walukeshwar* (sand god). The temple's massive gray *shikhara* sits at the head of **Banganga Tank,** a huge rectangular pool of greenish water surrounded by jagged lines of rundown settlements and as full of legend as it is of bathers and *dhobis*. The thirsty Rama created the tank by shooting his arrow into the ground, at which point water began to gush forth to relieve the parched deity. What was once a celestial drinking fountain is now a glorified sink. Just behind the temple, the maze of *dhobi ghats* along the shore is crowded with row upon row of half-dressed washermen crouched low on the rocks, rhythmically beating the washables of everyone else in the city. While the city boasts even more impressive *dhobi ghats* near the Mahalaxmi race course, these are less accessible to most tourists.

The seven massive **Parsi Towers of Silence,** upon which Zoroastrians set out their dead for vultures to eat, crown Malabar Hill. The whole complex is screened from sight by artful landscaping, but the funeral customs of the Parsis nonetheless received close scrutiny a few years ago when the vultures threatened to contaminate the city's water supply by dropping leftover luncheon morsels in the nearby reservoirs.

The city's two most famous gardens are also located at the top of Malabar Hill. **Sir Pherozeshah Mehta Garden,** locally known as the **Hanging Garden,** sits right at the terminus of buses #106 and 108. *(Open daily 5am-9pm. Free.)* Along with the **Kamala Nehru Children's Park** across the street, it entices visitors with a topiary, penguin-shaped trash cans, a life-sized reproduction of the shoe in which the old lady lived, and stunning views of the city. In both parks, frolicking children and their parental chaperones face down the hordes of surreptitious smoochers, supposedly hidden from public eye by the single branch hanging over them.

The entrance to **Babulnath Mandir** on Babulnath Mandir Rd. is an unassuming set of three connected small stone arches, seemingly held up by the throngs of flower sellers, holy men, and worshippers around their base. The gates open up to a world far removed from the jams of Marutis below, where a dense concert of blaring bells and voices reciting *aarti* blankets the path up the stone stepped hill. The temple itself, with its small shrine, is loudly alive during worship times. As your ears ring on the way back down, don't be surprised to find lines of women squatting beside baskets of coiled cobras asking for money to feed milk to their serpents—feeding them on certain days of the week is considered an auspicious tribute to Shiva.

As the site of the first meeting of the Indian National Congress, it is only fitting that Mumbai pay tribute to the Father of the Nation and onetime citizen of the city—Mahatma Gandhi. The Mahatma stayed at **Mani Bhavan,** 19 Laburnum Rd. (a quiet, leafy, lane in the streets behind the temple), during his frequent political visits to Mumbai. *(Open Tu-Su 9:30am-6pm. Admission Rs5.)* The building now houses a **museum** to the great man, with a huge research library on Indian history, Gandhi, and Independence. Along with a film archive, the museum includes a small collection of old photos and a "look-and-see" diorama version of the great moments in Gandhi's life and the struggle for Independence.

North past the flyover-ed shopping hub of Kemp's Corner lies **Mahalaxmi Temple,** near the sea on Warden Rd. (Bhulabhai Desai Rd.). The goddess (like Mumbai) devotes herself to wealth and beauty, making this *mandir* the city's most popular. In addition to Lakshmi riding a tiger (normally Durga's vehicle), the temple contains images of Kali and Saraswati, two other major goddesses of the Hindu pantheon.

Just beyond Mahalaxmi, on an island in the middle of the Arabian Sea, the shrine of the Sufi saint **Haji Ali** battles the waves daily. The bright white building stands out against the pacific blue or stormy gray of the ocean like a beacon for all camera owners. The narrow causeway to the island disappears at high tide and during the monsoon storms, but at other times, even non-Muslims can stride past the expectant rows of beggars as far as the outer chambers. It's better from a distance. On dry ground next to Haji Ali, the **Mahalaxmi racecourse** cuts a green gash through the gray cityscape. The races (and betting) run on weekends from December to May.

Farther north still, on the edges of the upmarket neighborhood of Worli, the **Nehru Centre** showcases Indian history, culture, and scientific achievement. The theater offers both Indian and Western performing arts (see **Entertainment,** p. 632). The **Nehru Science Museum** (tel. 494676), whose park is dotted with animal rides and old train cars, seems mostly geared to children, but contains an exhibit on Indian contributions to science, from ancient ayurvedic medicine and the dawn of mathematics to current genetic discoveries by H.G. Khorana. *(Open daily 11am-5pm.)*

Central and Northern Mumbai

West of Crawford stretches an endless string of bazaars—first **Zaveri (Silversmiths) Bazaar,** then **Bhuleshwar Market,** near the Mumbadevi Temple for produce and housewares, and finally **Chor (Thieves) Bazaar,** northward by Johar Chowk. Strolling and shopping here provides a more traditionally Indian commercial foil to the faxes and stock-options of Nariman Point.

North again from Johar Chowk along Sir J.J. Rd., in the neighborhood of Byculla, the **Victoria and Albert Museum** (now Veermata Jijabhai) receives relatively few foreign tourists. *(Open Th-Tu 9:30am-5pm. Admission Rs2.)* The exhibits on Mumbai's history include the carved stone elephant that gave Elephanta Island its name. For the real McCoy, head next door to **Mumbai's Zoo,** where mangy animals subsist in depressing surroundings. The adjacent **Botanical Gardens** provide a more salubrious setting for a stroll. *(Open Th-Tu 10:30am-4:30pm. Admission Rs2.)*

Finally, the distant northern suburb of Borivli offers two diametrically opposed attractions. The same railway stop (Borivli) caters to both the **Sanjay Gandhi National Park,** with its rock-cut caves, and Esselworld, the larger of Mumbai's two amusement parks. **Kanheri** features over 100 caves, although few of them amount to more than holes in the wall. *(Open daily 9am-5:30pm. Admission Rs2.)* Nonetheless, those planning to hit Ajanta, Ellora, or Karla and Bhaja can come here for a quick prep course, while others can visit as consolation. Cave 3, a *chaitya* hall guarded by two huge standing Buddhas, makes for the most interesting exploration.

For **Esselworld** (tel. 492 0891 or 807 7321), head to Govai Creek (Borivli-W) where free ferries whisk eager children and beleaguered parents to the 35-ride complex on Corao Island. *(Open daily 11am-7pm; ferries 10:30am-7:30pm. Admission Rs150; children Rs128.)* Your ticket also grants admission to the neighboring **Water Sports Complex.** Interesting for sociological as well as recreational purposes, Esselworld exhibits middle-class urbanite life at its most packaged and plastic for ruin-weary travelers.

ENTERTAINMENT

Unlike most cities in India, Mumbai has a nightlife, complete with bars, clubs, and Western performing arts. Barbaric backpackers will be pleased to discover nary a hint of culture at the city's many pubs and discos. But beware the pervasive (if sporadically enforced) "couples only" policies on busy nights and the occasional refusal of t-shirted or sandaled sybarites. Check the *Bombay Times* in the *Times of India* for the weekly bulletin of the latest concerts and plays at the **Tata Theater,** the **Nehru Centre,** and a host of smaller venues.

Bars and Clubs

The Ghetto, 30 Bhulabhai Desai Rd., Breach Candy (tel. 492 1556), in an alley on the seaward side of the road, just before Mahalaxmi. Mumbai's most happening bar seethes with yuppie kids every night. When the police close the front door, regulars slip in the side entrance. Beers Rs50, spirits Rs50 and up. Open daily 7pm-until they get shut down—usually Su-W about 2am, Th-Sa about 4am.

Leopold Cafe, Colaba Causeway, Colaba (tel. 202 0131), about three blocks down from Regal, on the left side. Tourists and Indians mingle here to eat, drink, and party. The dim A/C section upstairs hosts the most serious drinkers amid a black and white check decor, punctuated by psychedelic drawings. Beers Rs58. Pitchers Rs200. Open daily 1pm-1am. Downstairs open daily 8am-midnight.

Three Flights Up, Shivaji Marg, Colaba (tel. 282 9934), next to the Cottage Industries. The latest and techno-heaviest disco in Mumbai, this phat farm boasts the longest bar (40m) in the city. Beer Rs75, pitcher Rs200. Open F-Su 7pm-12:30am.

The Other Room at Sundance Cafe, Eros Building, 42 Maharishi Karve Rd., Churchgate (tel. 202 3583), opposite Churchgate Station. The entrance to The Other Room (not to be confused with the main Sundance Cafe) lies in an alley down the left-hand side of the building. This cool, secluded spot provides the perfect venue for a quiet daytime drink, disturbed only by the lilting cadences of the VJs who interminably grin down from the idiot box. Draft beers Rs40-45; tasty snacks Rs40-105. Open daily 11am-11pm.

Voodoo, Arthur Bunder Rd., Colaba, 4 doors up on the left from the seafront. Mumbai's only above-ground gay bar attracts fashion designers and filmmakers, especially on Saturday nights. India's most famous gay rights activist, Ashok Rao Kavi, is a regular. Cover charge Rs110. Beers Rs55. Open daily 7pm-12:30am.

The Pub at Rasna, J.Tata Rd., Churchgate (tel. 283 6243), on the left on the road that leads to the right of Eros from Churchgate, just after the small circle. Futuristic—if the future hinges on tall metal chairs, neon lights, streamlined decor, and a confusing floor plan. Late on weekend nights, the children of Mumbai's jet-set jam up against the aerodynamic bar, leaving breathing space only on the small dance floor. Beers Rs45. Open daily 7pm-1am.

The Cellar, Oberoi Towers, Marine Drive, Nariman Point (tel. 202 4343). Inside India's most expensive hotel, the Rs175 cover seems like a bargain. The faux stone booths and dance floor look more like a cheesy Italian restaurant than a disco—but the crowd boogies away unconcerned to the boppy dance tunes. Beers Rs55. Open Su-Th 10:30pm-12:30am, F-Sa 10:30pm-4am.

Copa Cabana, 8 Dariya Vihar, 39B Chowpatty Seaface, Marine Drive, opposite Chowpatty Beach on Marine Drive, below the restaurant Revival. Music and passion are always in fashion at this hot spot north of Colaba. Open daily 7pm-1am.

Performance Centers

Nehru Centre, Dr. Annie Besant Rd., Worli (tel. 492 8192 or 492 6042). In the same complex as the Nehru Planetarium, on the right side just past Mahalaxmi racecourse. Lots of Indian and Western classical music as well as some theatre.

Tata Theatre, Marine Drive, Nariman Point (tel. 282 4567). At the very tip of Nariman Point, just beyond the Oberoi. The compound houses a main theatre, an experimental theatre, and a third venue scheduled to open soon. More European and American offerings than at the Nehru, but good Indian music and theatre, too.

Prithvi Theatre, Janki-Kutir, Juhu-Church Rd. (tel. 614 9546; fax 493 9071). Along a lane that juts off the main road leading to the Juhu bus station. The theatre hall here is appropriately among Mumbai's most popular, with performances in many languages. Tickets Rs60. English-language shows Sa-Su, 6 and 9pm.

SHOPPING

Like some enormous, quasi-tropical Mall of India, Mumbai can fulfill every material need and wanton consumer desire in every price range. A two-minute walk north from Flora Fountain leads to a part of M.G. Rd. known as **Fashion Street,** an endless chain of street stalls selling cheap, disorientingly similar merchandise. The hawk-eyed hawkers of hackneyed, Western designer cast-offs can spot naive tourists from miles away—bargain without shame. If the "salesperson" is being difficult, keep in mind that farther down the street is a more soulful seller. (Open daily 10am-8pm.)

For those who need a hiatus from haggling, **Cottage Industries,** Shivaji Marg, offers a government **fixed-price** alternative. Though it's unabashedly geared toward tourists and, compared to the chaos of the streets outside, rather sterile, you're guaranteed good quality and reasonably fair prices. The emporium is also a pathetically convenient one-stop souvenir shop, proffering such wares as batik fabrics, handmade silk Nehru jackets and scarves, and all things sandalwood. Cottage Industries accepts major credit cards and exchanges money. (Open M-Sa 11am-7pm.)

The more upscale **Mumbai Store** (tel. 288 5048; fax 287 3478) burrows along Sir P.M Rd. in Fort. Formerly known as the Mumbai Swadeshi Store, the gleaming glass cases and polished hardwood shelves bear little resemblance to the *swadeshi* movement's spinning wheels and simple, homemade cloth. Like a department store specializing in "ethnic" merchandise, this is sterile, spoon-fed shopping, but the quality and selection is commendable and reliable, and the store is A/C. (Open M-Sa 10:30am-8:30pm, Su 11am-7pm. Major credit cards accepted.)

Finally, travelers whose wallets are feeling particularly fat should head over to **Warden Road** (Bhulabhai Desai Rd.) near Kemp's Corner. The line of stores is the place to go to match, thread for thread, the clothing donned by Mumbai's hipsters.

■ Near Mumbai: Elephanta Island

About 10km northeast of the Gateway of India, the island of Elephanta, in Bombay Harbor, offers travelers a fleeting glimpse of a quaint Indian fishing village in its heyday. Then it delivers a full-barreled assault—Elephanta is what happens to the quaint village when more tourists than gilled wildlife are dragged in from the water. Elephanta's 8th-century cave temples have lured in thousands of visitors, and locals haven't hesitated to capitalize. Point your Nikon at picturesque fisherwomen draped in emerald, magenta, and lime *saris*, only at the risk of repercussions—they will chase you, squawking demands for *baksheesh* (without upsetting the silver *mutkas* balanced on their heads). Also be prepared for free-roaming monkeys who readily strip tourists of chips, Frootis, and bananas.

In spite of its hassles (the ferry ride itself is an adventure), Elephanta remains best known for its truly extraordinary cave temples. At the end of a 125-step climb up the mountainside, the cave itself covers over 5000 square meters, many of which are filled with moss and bats. The main chamber has a cross-like arrangement of massive pillars with no functional purpose. The image of Shiva as the cosmic dancer Nataraja is carved in detail near the entrance; the damage is due to the Portuguese who reportedly used it for target practice when they occupied the island in the 1800s. A weathered and beaten-up panel of Lakulisha, a saint considered to be an incarnation of Shiva, stands opposite. The main **Linga Shrine** in the center of the cave is accessed by entrances on all four sides, each flanked by a pair of **dwarapalas,** guardians who are at least as vicious as the fisherwomen. The other attractions in the cave are the elaborate **wall panels** depicting assorted scenes from Shiva mythology in remarkable detail. On the north side is a lively panel depicting Shiva as Bhairava killing the demon Andhaka, who was attempting to steal a divine tree. The three panels on the south side of the temple are the caves' central attraction. The 6m bust of Shiva as the three-faced Trimurti, Lord of the Universe, is formidable. To the sides, the Descent of the Ganga and Shiva as Ardhanarishvara are shown, while near another entrance is a detailed panel showing Ravana's attempt to uproot Mount Kailasa.

Elephanta is accessible by boat from the Gateway of India. Ordinary boats make the one-hour trip for Rs50. Luxury boats with tour guides do the same for Rs70. It is not unheard of for these slow-moving ferries to ram into each other. Only luxury boats run in the monsoon months, and then only when waters are navigable (enquiry tel. 202 6364). Both ordinary and luxury boats leave every half-hour from 9am to 2:30pm and return after four hours.

▒ Matheran मथेरान

Formerly an exclusive retreat for Raj-era White Men weary of toting their onerous Burdens, today the hill station of Matheran (95km east of Mumbai) swarms every weekend from September to June, shutting down when the monsoon rains arrive. For frazzled Bombayites, the posh and overpriced full-board resorts, the absence of motor vehicles, and networks of foliage-canopied red clay paths are just the ticket for an idle weekend. Other travelers, though, may find that there's a whole subcontinent full of better retreats than Matheran.

ORIENTATION AND PRACTICAL INFORMATION The access point for Matheran is the small town of **Neral,** at the base of the hill station. From Mumbai V.T. Station, local trains to **Karjat** stop at Neral Junction, as do some on the Mumbai-Pune route (every hr., 6am-11pm, 3hr., Rs14). Express trains (*Deccan Exp.,* 6:40am; *Koyana*

Exp., 8:45am, 2½hr., Rs28). From Neral, Matheran is 6.5km up the hill, but the trip up is hardly as easy as the distance suggests. The **miniature train** that runs to Matheran (8:40 and 11am, and 5pm, 2½ hr., Rs21/140) and back (5:45am, 1:10, and 2:35pm) forms an integral, if unpleasant part of the hill station's experience. During the monsoon, service is sporadic and may be cancelled entirely. Those who find the tiny train tiresome opt for **shared taxis** (Rs40 per person; Rs160 solo) on the way back.

Matheran is roughly lined along the north-south **Mahatma Gandhi Marg,** which becomes **Shivaji Marg** further south. The **Matheran Railway Station,** where the miniature train arrives, marks the center of town. If you enter Matheran by other means, you'll be dropped off 2.5km north of the railway station at the **taxi stand,** the point closest to the center of the hill station that motor vehicles are allowed. From the taxi stand it's a 30-minute walk to town. A **horse ride** into town is rocky but fun (Rs80). **Cycle-rickshaws** are also available (Rs120). Adding insult to injury, Matheran levies a **cover charge** (adults Rs7, children Rs4).

The **tourist office** is opposite the railway station and has town maps (open M-Sa 9:30am-5:30pm). Moving south down Mahatma Gandhi Marg, the **GPO** is on the left. Past the GPO, a fork to the right passes the **police station** before continuing on to **Charlotte Lake. Currency exchange** is only available in the top hotels, generally for guests only. The **telephone code** is 02148.

ACCOMMODATIONS AND FOOD During high season weekends there are no bargains in Matheran, only varying levels of extortion. Reservations are required in season. In the off season, many hotels close down or offer substantial discounts. Midweek in Matheran, rates are generally negotiable but no one offers single rates, and most family resorts will turn away solo travelers. Check-out times are drastically early (7am is standard), and hotels will gladly bill you for another half-day if you sleep in. **Hope Hall Hotel,** M.G. Rd. (tel. 30253), is a family-run place with average-sized, spotlessly clean rooms, and cheerful attached baths. (Check-out 10am. In-season: doubles Rs350. Off-season: Rs175.) **Gujarat Bhavan Hotel,** Maulana Azad Rd. (tel. 278, in Mumbai (022) 388 1998), is more resorty with 24hr. room service (check-out 10am; rooms Rs350 per person, Rs450 with TV). The **Hotel Prasanna** (tel. 30258) across from the train station has tidier-than-usual bathrooms. Hardly a bargain at Rs200 per night during the high season and weekends, it's still among the cheapest in town. Since most hotels offer full- or half-board, the outside dining scene is sparse. Some hotels allow non-guests to eat there, or will do so for the right price, but you're otherwise restricted to basic snacky eateries along M.G. Rd. Tooth enamel trembles at the mention of *chikki,* a sweet, sticky, crunchy peanut brittle vended everywhere. **Kwality Restaurant**, M.G. Road, lets you sample their many varieties, as well as another local "delicacy," mango fudge, which tastes much better than it sounds, or looks, for that matter (open daily 10am-10pm).

SIGHTS The only sights in Matheran are the numerous viewpoints which mark the borders of the hill station. All offer views of the surrounding valleys from sheer cliff outcrops. Those on the western side, including **Porcupine and Louisa Points,** have views of Neral in the distance. The viewpoints at sunset and sunrise would be romantic but for the mobs of clutching, touching honeymooners. Women are advised not to explore the more remote viewpoints alone at night. **Panorama Point,** to the far north, has breathtaking views. Also popular are **Monkey Point** to the north, which includes **Porcupine** and **Louisa Points,** and **Alexandra Point** to the south.

■ Nasik नाशिक

Blackened bursts of diesel fumes, swirls of red and orange *kum kum* powder, and clouds of dust kicked up by thousands of bare feet all come together in Nasik, along the banks of the sacred Godavari River. Nasik is believed to be the site where Ravana abducted Rama's wife Sita, igniting one of the greatest metaphysical match-ups in Hindu religious lore (see **The Ramayana,** p. 94). Just as Sita's chastity became suspect after she spent so much time in Ravana's lair, Nasik's purity today seems to be threatened by the deluge of industrial plants growing along the riverbanks. The jingle of temple bells and the humming of the meditative syllable *om* combine discordantly with the chug and spit of smokestacks and exhaust pipes. Nevertheless, every year thousands of devotees head to Nasik to trek the same pathways that their gods and goddesses once did. Every 12 years, Nasik is host to the Kumbh Mela festival (see p. 231). During the Mela, one of the most auspicious moments in the Hindu calendar, millions of Hindus flock to Nasik to take a purifying dip in the waters of the Godavari.

ORIENTATION

Nasik basks along the banks of the **Godavari River,** 565m above sea level. The city's most important landmark is the **Central Bus Stand (CBS),** which stands in the middle of the metropolis, at the intersection of **Sharanpur** and **Old Agra Roads.** Running parallel to and north of Sharanpur Rd. is **Gangapur Road.** To the south is **Trimbak Road. M.G. Road**—from which one can access the river area in the city's northwest corner—is off Old Agra Rd. to the north. The **Nasik Road Railway Station** is 8km southeast of CBS and is preceded by chaotic **Dwarka Circle.**

PRACTICAL INFORMATION

Trains: The **railway station** (tel. 561274) is 8km from the city center. As you leave the platforms, the booking office is to the left. Fares listed are 2nd/1st class. To: **Japalpur** (*Kurla-Varanasi Exp.* 1065, 9am, 14hr., Rs144/736); **Mumbai** (*Pancharati Exp.* 1402, 6:54am, 4hr.; *Tapovan Exp.* 7618, 6:22pm, 4hr., Rs48/238); **Nagpur** (*Mumbai-Howrah Mail,* 12:20am, 11hr., Rs124/620).
Buses: Central Bus Stand, Sharanpur Rd. (tel. 572854). To: **Ahmedabad** (6 per day, Rs112); **Aurangabad** (8 per day, Rs78); **Mumbai** (frequent, Rs70); **Nagpur** (frequent, 8pm-9am, Rs268); **Pune** (every hr., Rs83). Buses from Mumbai end up at **Mahamarga Bus Stand,** 7km away.
Tourist Office: MTDC, T-1, Golf Club, Old Agra (tel. 570059). From the State Bank near CBS, head left, then turn right at the 2nd major intersection. After 5min., the MTDC's red and white Marathi sign will be visible. Train and bus schedules, and a few pamphlets about other places. Open M-F, first and third Sa 10am-5:30pm.
Currency Exchange: State Bank of India, Old Agra Rd. Walk right from CBS; it's 200m after the intersection on the left. Open M-F 11am-3pm, Sa 11am-1pm.
Local Transportation: Auto-rickshaws rule the road but are subject to meters.
Hospital: Lifeline, Canada Corner (tel. 578418), near the police station. Nasik's best.
Police: Sharanpur Rd. (tel. 100).
Emergency: Fire, tel. 101. **Ambulance,** tel. 102 or 576106.
Post Office: GPO, Trimbak Rd. (tel. 72141). *Poste Restante* should be addressed to the Postmaster. Open M-Sa 11am-6pm, Su 10am-2pm. **Postal Code:** 42001.
Telephones: Directory enquiry, tel. 197. **Telephone Code:** 0253.

ACCOMMODATIONS

Budget hotels congregate near CBS on Shivaji and Old Agra Rd., or along Dwarka Circle. During the Mela, finding a room is almost impossible. Check-out is usually noon.

Hotel Basera, Shivaji Rd. (tel. 575610). From CBS, head right to the opposite side of the intersection. The reception is through the small alleyway on the left. Institutional rooms, but bathrooms are outfitted with tubs. Corridors circle an open space that reveals the building's bowels and restaurant fumes. Singles Rs190, with A/C Rs350; doubles Rs300/450; triples Rs375; quads Rs475.
Raj Mahal Lodge, Sharanpur Rd. (tel. 580501; fax 571096), across from CBS. Basic rooms, unbeatable location, and relatively cheap rates conspire to fill the Raj's rooms early, so act fast. 24hr. STD/ISD in the lobby. Singles Rs160; doubles Rs220, with bath Rs320; triples with bath Rs390; quads with bath Rs450.
Hotel Siddharth, Nasik-Pune Rd. (tel. 55376 or 554280; fax 554288), near the Nasardi Bridge, 2km past Dwarka Circle, on the right. Dark halls lead to sunny rooms with sparkling white walls. An expansive, well-maintained lawn in the back is ideal for evening lounging. Singles Rs300, with A/C Rs400; doubles Rs400/500.

FOOD

Samrat Restaurant, Hotel Samrat, Old Agra Rd. Across from the State Bank. Pure veg., Gujarati *thalis* are a diner's dream and popular with locals (Rs55). Ambience is decidedly canteen-like but in step with the bus stand hullabaloo outside. Open daily 11am-3pm and 7-10:30pm.

Nandinee Woodlands Restaurant, Nasik-Pune Rd., in the plaza across from Hotel Siddharth. Sleek decor gives no hint of the taste explosion provided by the South Indian dishes (Rs14-39). Also serves Western snacks (pizza Rs50, french fries Rs22). All-you-can-eat breakfast buffet, Rs50 (9-11am). Open daily 9am-11pm.

Hotel Surici, Shivaji Rd. (tel. 573347), right below the Hotel Basera. Cheap, cheap, cheap. South Indian snacks (Rs9-13), Punjabi entrees including *pilaf* and curry (Rs3-18). You have to squeeze in at peak meal-times. Open daily 6:30am-10:30pm.

Panchavati group of hotels, 3 on M.G. Rd. in Vakil Wadi and 1 at the intersection of Thimbak and Boys Town Rd., has a collection of great *thali* restaurants.

SIGHTS

The widely worshipped **Godavari River** is most easily accessed via the narrow, meandering alleys that shoot down from M.G. Rd. The downsloping pathways quickly swap thick traffic fumes for the clatter of candy, *kurta,* and cloth vendors, and end at a Nasik strikingly dissimilar to the industrial city center. Upon emerging from the Old Quarter's streets, shallow squares in murky water are visible to the far right, next to the **Santar Gardhi Mahara Bridge.** Most mornings they are merely a gathering place for hundreds of *dhobi-wallahs* percussively pursuing their clothes-cleaning trade. Every 12 years, however, these *ghats* experience the onslaught of thousands of Hindu devotees who flood Nasik during the **Kumbh Mela.** Nasik's next Mela is scheduled for the year 2003, but it's not impossible to imagine the fervent cacophony that ensues at this time—one glance at the sprawling **market** directly behind the *ghats* will give you an idea. Rickety wooden stalls provide row upon cluttered row of religious paraphernalia, as well as a gleaming glut of fruits, vegetables, nuts, lentils, and less perishable steel jewelry, carved statuettes, and bronze vessels.

Immersed within the market, across from the **Ram Sita Footbridge,** are sites steeped in mythology. Nasik's religious focal point, several meters to the left of the footbridge, is the **Ram Kund** (tank). Thousands of Hindus immerse themselves here in order to purify themselves of their sins. The waters are reputed to have the unusual ability to dissolve bones. The remains of several celebrities and top politicians (from members of the Nehru-Gandhi dynasty to Rama's father, King Dasharatha), are rumored to languish here in the **Astivilaya Tirth** ("Bone Immersion Tank").

Up the hill from Ram Kund is the **Kala Ram Mandir,** a temple at the site where Rama's brother, Laxman, sliced off the nose (in Sanskrit, *nasika*) of Ravana's monstrous sister, Shurparnakha. The *mandir* boasts slick ebony images of the myth's main protagonists: Ram, Sita, and Laxman. Sita's cave, or **Gumpha,** is the site where the Hindu goddess languished, waiting for her boys to come home, and from where she was snatched by the lascivious demon Ravana.

■ Pune पुणे

As Mumbai becomes increasingly congested and cosmopolitan, the drip-drip of daily commuters between Mumbai and Pune (POO-nay) has deluged into a mini-exodus for the cooler, more relaxed Pune—a four-hour, 190km climb up the Deccan Plateau. Birthplace of the Maratha hero, Shivaji, capital of his successors, and almost purely Marathi-speaking, Pune lays a much more credible claim to son-of-the-soil status than its upstart cousin on the coast. Some of Mumbai's urban sophistication has migrated to Pune, due to its many internationally respected colleges and strategic position on road and rail routes. The biggest dose of internationalism, though, springs from Pune's infamous ashram, the Osho Commune International of the late export guru Rajneesh. The Birkenstock-clad clientele (known as Sannyasins) converge from all

Pune

ACCOMMODATIONS

E Central Lodge
B Green Hotel
D Hotel Alankar
C Hotel Milan
A National Hotel
F Sardar Lodge

Race Course

KOREGAON PARK

Osho International Commune

Koregaon Rd.

Bund Gardens Rd.
Boat Club Rd.

Mula River

Connaught Rd.

Sassoon Rd.

Pune Railway Station

GPO

Moledina Rd.

East St.
M.G. Rd.

PUNE CANTONMENT (CAMP)

Thomas Cook

S. Dorabji Padamji Rd.

Jawaharlal Nehru Rd.

Sans Rd.

Shankar Shet Rd.

Sangam Bridge

Motilal Rd.

Dr. B.R. Ambedkar Rd.

Dengle Bridge

Shivaji Bridge

Shaniwar Wada

Badge Rd.

Phule Market

Swargate Bus Station

Shivajinagar Station

TO MUMBAI

Mumbai-Pune Hwy.

Laxmi Rd.

Tilak Rd.

Nehru Stadium

Saras Bagh

Shinde Bridge

Jangli Maharaj Rd.

Pataleshwar Temple

SHIVAJI NAGAR

Sambhaji Park

Apte Rd.

City Bus Stand

Sambhaji Bridge

Lal Bahadur Shastri Rd.

Parvati Mandir

Bus Stand

Ganeshkind Rd.

Fergusson College Rd.

Bhandarkar Rd.

DECCAN GYMKHANA

Prabhat Rd.

Railway Booking Office

Mhatre Bridge

Mutha River

TO PUNE UNIVERSITY

Fergusson Hill

BMCC Rd.

Kamala Nehru Park

Law College Rd.

ERANDWANA

Karve Rd.

Pune Telecom Office

GANESH NAGAR

Connaught Rd.

Railway Station

A B F

C E

D

MTDC

Byramji Rd.

MPL Rd.

GOKHALE NAGAR

Law College Hill

Film Institute of India

Dash Bhuja Ganapati Temple

TO SHOLAPUR

SEE INSET

WEST INDIA

over the world in red robes and wooden beads to undergo Osho's famous laughter therapy, while their antics provide another kind of laughter therapy for skeptical locals and tourists alike.

Despite its vast reserves of intellect, discipline, and "religiosity," Pune's biggest selling point is its citizens' unreserved demeanor. Punenites offer warm smiles, advice, or stories while chomping *chaat* under the cooling shade of a large palm frond or sweltering in interminable queues for train tickets. Although Pune's attractions may not be as renowned as its ashram, there are enough friendly people and engaging things to do to make any stay interesting.

ORIENTATION

Although Pune seems quiet by comparison to Mumbai, its population of three million sprawls over two major sections: the **Camp** side and **Old Town**. The railway station and a major bus stand rub shoulders between **Sassoon Road** to the north and **MPL Road** to the south. A 10-minute rickshaw ride west of here is the Old Town, where traditional *wadas* (extended family houses) surround the **Swargate Bus Terminal,** the **Raja Kelkar Museum, Phule Market,** and the ruined **Shaniwar Wada Palace.** Across the Mutha River, the middle class neighborhood of Deccan Gymkhana stretches to Fergusson College Rd., where Pune's students hobnob in a string of restaurants and cafes. A third segment of town, occupying its own, distinctive space physically (and psychologically), can be identified by the Koregaon Park suburb to the east of Camp, home to the indefatigable **Osho Commune.**

PRACTICAL INFORMATION

Airport: Pune Nagar Rd. (tel. 667538), 10km from the city center. An Ex-Servicemen's bus leaves every hour from outside the GPO (Rs20). **Indian Airlines,** Dr. Ambedkar Rd. (tel. 141 or 142), near the Sangam Bridge, in Camp. **Skyline NEPC,** 17 M.C. Rd. (tel. 637441 or 633125), in Camp. **Spar Aviation,** Vishnu Darshan 113213, Fergusson College Rd., Deccan Gymkhana (tel. 352478 or 354481). To: **Bangalore** (M, W, F, and Su, 2hr., US$115); **Mumbai** (daily, 30min., US$65); **Delhi** (daily, 2hr., US$165); **Goa** (in-season: daily, 1hr., US$85; off-season: Tu, Th, and Sa-Su); **Madras** (daily, 3hr., US$132).

Trains: Railway Station, Sassoon Rd. Sparkling new booking office, on your left as you face the station, has separate sections for local tickets and reservations. Prices listed are 2nd/1st class. To: **Bangalore** (*Udyar Exp.* 6529, 12:20pm, 20hr., Rs171/845); **Hyderabad** (*Hyderabad Exp.* 7031, 5:15pm, Rs117/581); **Miraj** (for Goa) (*Sahyadri Exp.* 7303, 5:45pm, *Mahalaxmi Exp.* 1101, 1am, *Konya Exp.* 7307, 1:50pm, Rs65/321); **Mumbai** (*Deccan Queen* 2124, 7:15am, 3½hr., Rs48/238; *Indrayani Exp.* 1022, 6:30pm Rs48/238).

Buses: Pune has 3 main state stations and many private carriers. The most convenient station for tourists is right next to the railway station. Reserved deluxe buses to Mumbai depart from the counter around the corner and to the right. To: **Mumbai** (every hr., 5am-10pm, 4hr., Rs30/91); **Mahabaleshwar** (6 per day, 4hr., Rs50/70); **Panjim** (7 per day, 4:30am-7pm, 12hr., Rs200). For **Aurangabad,** head to **Shivajinagar Station** in Deccan Gymkhana (10 per day, 6hr., Rs100).

Local Transportation: Auto-rickshaws are the best means of getting around in Pune. The conversion rate for auto-rickshaws is roughly 4 times the meter reading; ask to see a chart. **Buses,** while cheaper, are stifling and don't cater to English-speakers. Local bus #4 (४) goes to Deccan Gymkhana, while #5 (५), 6 (६), and 31 (३१) go south towards Swargate bus station and the old town.

Tourist Office: MTDC, Central Building, I Block (tel. 626867 or 628169; fax 628189), in Camp. Left along the main road from the railway station, and right at the first roundabout. The MTDC is about 3min. down on the right, in a low office behind the massive stone Central Building. Bland brochures and MTDC hotel reservations. Open M-F 10:30am-4pm. **Railway Station Office:** (tel. 625342).

Budget Travel: Apple Travels, Amir Hotel, Connaught Rd. (tel. 628185 or 632325; fax 625421), in Camp. At the junction of Sassoon and Connaught Rd. Arranges domestic and international air travel. Open M-Sa 9:30am-6pm.

Currency Exchange: Central Bank of India, M.G. Rd. (tel. 631413 or 631415), in Camp, about 5min. south of Moledina Rd. Up to US$500 cash advance on Visa or MasterCard. Open M-F 11am-1:30pm. **Thomas Cook:** ground floor, 13 Thacker House, 2418 General Thinimaya Rd. (tel. 646171 or 643026), in Camp. A 10min. walk down M.G. Rd. from Moledina Rd., turn left down the sidewalk next to the villa labelled M. Nusserwanji. They cash their own checks for free, and others Rs20 per transaction. Open M-Sa 10am-5pm.

Bookstore: Manney's Bookstore, 7 Moledina Rd., Clover Centre (tel. 631683), in Camp. English books galore, travel guides and maps of major Indian cities (Rs30). The best source for Pune maps. Open M-Sa 9:30am-1pm and 4-8pm.

Pharmacy/Hospital: Pune Medical Foundation, Ruby Hall Clinic, 40 Sassoon Rd. (tel. 623391), in Camp. From MPL, turn left on Connaught Rd., cross the railroad tracks and turn right. The clinic is on the left. Pharmacy open 24hr.

Police: Bund Garden Station, Byraniji Rd. (tel. 62202 or 100). From the railway station head south along Connaught Rd. and make your first left on to Byraniji. The station will be on the left. Open 24hr.

Post Office: Connaught Rd., in Camp. A 5min. walk to the left away from the railroad lines (south) from the intersection with MPL Rd. On the right, in a Victorian domed stone building. *Poste Restante* at the Enquiries counter. Open M-Sa 10am-4pm. Stamps sold M-Sa 10am-6pm. **Postal Code:** 411001.

Internet: ICE, 113 Ashoka Mall, Bund Garden Rd. (tel. 636611), opposite the Holiday Inn. Surf the web Rs75 per hr., Rs25/15 to send/receive email. Open Tu-Su 8am-6pm. **Weikfield Computer Academy,** 45 Sassoon Rd. (tel. 623341 or 625331), at Bund Garden Rd. Web browsing Rs200 per hr. Open M-Sa 10am-4pm.

Telephones: STD/ISD booths abound along Sassoon Rd. **Telephone Code:** 0212.

ACCOMMODATIONS

The overwhelming majority of budget hotels in Pune cluster within the square-shaped **Wilson Garden** area. Though most of these buildings were once opulent personal *wadas* (mansions), they now stand in dilapidated decadence. To reach any of the Wilson Garden Hotels, take the small lane to the left of the National Hotel and turn right at the corner.

National Hotel (tel. 625054), opposite the railway station. Vast verandahs seem to sprout from the well-tended gardens. Earthy, spacious in-house rooms were recently renovated to include TV and A/C. Bright yellow cottages in the back are a bit smaller, providing sumptuous serenity. All rooms except singles have attached bath. Check-out noon. Doubles Rs300-350, triples 350-400, quads 400-450.

Green Hotel, 16 Wilson Garden (tel. 625229). The sensational decor—replete with stained glass, wood finish, wrought iron, and old furniture—makes the Green the most unique budget dive in Pune. Check-out 5pm. Singles Rs150; doubles Rs175, with shower Rs200, with full bath Rs250; triples Rs350-375; quads Rs400-425.

Hotel Alankar, 14 Wilson Circle (tel. 620484). A frieze of female musicians enlivens the otherwise simple rooms (some with balconies) lined along long, quiet, corridors. Check-out 24hr. Singles Rs325; triples Rs375. Add 4% tax.

Hotel Milan, 19 Wilson Garden (tel. 622024). One of the cheaper places with TVs and telephones—unfortunately, such frills don't defuse basic shortcomings like stained linen, dim rooms, and partitions between bedrooms and bathrooms that don't reach the ceiling. Singles Rs150, with bath Rs210-255, with TV and bath Rs275-305; doubles Rs190/305/355; triples Rs250/350/420. Four, five, and six-bed rooms are also available.

Central Lodge, Wilson Garden. The mattresses here could be improved, the common bathrooms (no showers, squat toilets) don't quite glisten, and the dorm beds located in a nook to the right of the front desk are exposed to the chatter of auto traffic outside and human traffic inside the hotel. This place won't beckon to the soul of a weary traveler, but it does assuage the moneybelt. Check-out 24hr. Dorm beds Rs50; doubles Rs125; triples Rs150; quads Rs200. Rs100 deposit required.

Sardar Lodge, Wilson Garden (tel. 625662). Resplendent in happy hues, this establishment looks as though a child from the park across the street had a field day with his crayon box. Baby blue steps wind toward rooms that are better maintained and offer more amenities (TV, attached bath) than their downstairs counterparts. Only semi-dingy bathrooms detract from the Sardar's perfectly palatable palette. Check-out 24hr. Doubles Rs125, with bath Rs200, on second floor Rs225, with TV Rs300; triples with bath Rs180, with bath and TV Rs400.

FOOD

Lieutenant Colonel Tarapore Marg, which crosses Connaught Rd. a block before Moledina Rd., serves as a huge open air cafe in the afternoons and evenings. Count-less drink and *chaat* stalls lure revelers into streetside seats (or squats) to gossip and people-watch. Also, the area between the bus stand and the railway booking office is full of fruit carts, providing perfect provisions for a peelable early-morning breakfast.

The Place: Touché the Sizzler, 7 Moledina Rd. (tel. 634632), in Camp. A trendy, 2-tier A/C hotspot; the dimmed lights and Tudor interior pack in Pune's carnivorous yuppies for "sizzlers"—iron skillets filled with mixed vegetables, fries, and a choice of entrée (veg. Rs90, meats Rs110-175). Traditional tandoori dishes also available (Rs70-125). Open daily 11am-3:30pm and 7-11pm.

Woodlands Restaurant, Woodland Hotel, Byraniji Rd. (tel. 661111), in Camp. Head south along Connaught Rd. and turn right at the first intersection. The comforting canopy of the Woodland and its unearthly entrees are welcome reprieves from sun or rain. Punjabi, Mughali, and Chinese dishes Rs50-75. South Indian fare, like the magnificent Mysore *dosa* (Rs30), however, tickles the taste buds and leaves the pocketbook unfazed. Open daily 7-11am, 12:30-3pm and 7-11pm.

Coffee House, 2 Moledina Rd. (tel. 630716), in Camp. This A/C hang-out's name belies its scope: an array of Chinese and Indian dishes are available (Rs30-55) along-side caffeinated quaffs. Tables are jammed with locals at peak hours; don't be sur-prised to be seated at a table already occupied with other diners. College students and locals contribute to the general hullabaloo. Menu touts this place as "the exclu-sive rendezvous." Indeed. Open daily 8am-11:30pm.

The German Bakery, North Koregaon Park Rd. (tel. 636532). From the Osho ashram, walk north (to the right from the Gateless Gate) to the end of the road and turn left; it's on the right. Homesick Sannyasins spill crumbs from Gouda or feta rolls (Rs16), apple crumble (Rs22), or cinnamon rolls (Rs16) on their red robes. The apple pie may not be as good as Mom's, but for Rs22 it pays frugal homage to her oven. More upbeat devotees pick up their co-religionists with a cappuccino (Rs16) or a slurp of "sterilized" pineapple juice, all the while pondering the merits of the acupuncture, *tai chi,* and Tao healing lessons advertised colorfully around them. Open daily 7am-11:30pm.

Shabree, Hotel Parichay, Fergusson College Rd. (tel. 321551). At the corner of Shola Rd. opposite Deendayal Hospital. One option—the ultimate, unlimited *thali* (Rs50)—is served up by a line of majestically uniformed waiters, each responsible for one portion of the entree. Earthen walls, mirrorwork-adorned arches, and patchwork ceilings recreate (in ornate fashion) a genuine *ghara* (Maharashtrian home). Open daily 11am-11pm.

Sagar Restaurant, Hotel Dreamland; look for the gold letters over the door (tel. 626452). A few hundred meters across the street and to the left of the railway sta-tion. This place offers South Indian snacks (paper *masala dosa* Rs22, *upma* Rs9) as well as a few Western breakfast items (toast with butter Rs12, juices Rs17-23) and mushroom pizza (Rs32). A section for women and families to the right has cushier booths, but minimalism is the dominant motif here. Open daily 7am-11pm.

Domino's Pizza, Grafikon Arcade, Sassoon Rd. (tel. 633022 or 657585), across from Ruby Hall clinic. An undeniable symbol of Pune's increasing worldliness (for better or worse), this Domino's will serve up the same well-manufactured pie you get at home (plain Rs80, large Rs155, toppings Rs20-45). And yes, they deliver within 30min. (within the 3km delivery area), or it's Rs30 off. Open daily 11am-11pm.

SIGHTS

Upwardly mobile meditators worldwide flock to Pune's **Osho Commune International,** 17 Koregaon Park (tel. 628561; http://www.osho.org), in Camp. *(Visitors' Center open daily 9:30am-1pm and 2-4pm. Daily guided tours 10:30am and 2:30pm, 1hr., Rs70, advance ticket purchase recommended.)* From the station, cough up for a rickshaw or face a 30-minute walk down Sassoon Rd. to Koregaon Rd., then left over the railroad tracks. Double back on your right to the road that runs parallel to the tracks, and take the first left. The commune is the huge complex on the right. Here, followers of the late guru Osho (also known as Bhagwan Rajneesh Vashwari) gather to practice his New Age meditation techniques alone or en masse, but always among the lush tropical plants and simple marble structures of the park. Then, it's off to the jacuzzi, *"zen-nis courts,"* or vegetarian canteens of "Club Med-itation" for a slightly more conventional vacation. A longer stay requires an HIV test (Rs125), two passport photographs, various colored robes, and Rs100 per day to use the facilities. Apart from six daily meditations—which encourage you to "become an empty vessel" or engage in the cathartic explosion of "shouting wildly the mantra 'Hoo!'"—all courses, food, and other services cost extra.

Raja Kelkar Museum, Baji Rao Rd., Deccan Gymkhana. *(Open M-Sa 8:30am-6pm; Rs5, children Rs1, foreigners Rs30.)* The packrat passion of the late Dr. D.G. Kelkar, the museum's founder, has resulted in a vast collection that is both eclectic and exceptional. Enthusiastic guides wander the three floors' galleries highlighting unique exhibits and their special peculiarities: an elephant-shaped foot scrubber; eight images of Lord Ganesh carved on a bean; a brass scorpion which, if you pull the tail, reveals a secret lock. More than a melange of bric-a-brac, the exhibits delightfully articulate the diversity of India's cultures throughout the centuries in a spunky, subtle voice that is often missing in more esoteric *objets d'art.*

Shivaji

By the time of Shivaji Bhonsle's birth in 1630, Muslims had dominated the Subcontinent for 400 years. The last significant Hindu-ruled kingdom, at Vijayanagar, collapsed a century earlier, and many Muslim rulers persecuted their Hindu subjects. Against this backdrop of oppression, the 16-year-old nobleman from the landholding Hindu Bhonsle family of the Maratha region of the Bijapur Sultanate declared his divine mission: the violent restoration of religious tolerance.

In 1647, Shivaji began seizing some of the smaller outposts of Bijapur. By 1659, his daring attacks so incensed the Sultan that he sent an army of 20,000 to quash the uprising. Shivaji lured the Muslim general, Afzal Khan, into a discussion, then embraced him closely and ripped out his innards with his *wagh nakh,* or metal "tiger claws." Meanwhile, his troops ambushed and destroyed the Bijapuri army.

Shivaji's victory aroused the anger of the ardently Muslim Mughal emperor, Aurangzeb. Despite an overwhelming advantage in manpower and resources, Aurangzeb never overcame Shivaji's cunning and courage. In 1666, the Maratha gave himself up at Agra, only to smuggle himself out of house arrest in a basket of candy. On another occasion, he captured the sheer-walled fort of Simhagad (near Pune) by training lizards to carry ropes up the cliff face.

Shivaji's huge popularity among Hindus and Muslims alike helped fend off the Mughal colossus. He ruled with religious impartiality, recruiting officers from both faiths. Even after Shivaji died in 1680, the Maratha Confederacy he founded prospered. The British eventually subdued the Marathas, though, and Shivaji faded to a folk hero until the 1950s, when Balasahek (Bal) Thackeray, a journalist-turned-cartoonist, founded a political party in Maharashtra named Shiv Sena in his honor. The party, though, does not share Shivaji's tolerance, opting instead for a general Hindu nationalism hostile to Muslims. When the Sena gained power in the state in 1995, they changed the name of Aurangabad (Aurangzeb's capital) to Sambhajinagar (after Shivaji's son, Sambhaji).

WEST INDIA

The **Gandhi National Memorial,** Aga Khan Palace, Pune-Nagar Rd. (on the way to the airport,) is unfortunately neglected. *(Open daily 9am-5:45pm. Requested donation Rs5, children Rs2.)* The elegant architecture of the Aga Khan Palace, where Gandhi was imprisoned at one time, fades behind the crumbling paint and stained floors as you approach. A timeline, in similar condition, of Gandhi's life leads you through a few rooms and, outside, to the *samadhis* containing the ashes of Gandhi's wife.

ENTERTAINMENT

One of the few discos around to cater to Mumbai wanna-bes is the **Black Cadillac,** Grafikon Arcade, Sassoon Rd., Camp (tel. 626500). Opposite the Ruby Hall Clinic, behind Domino's Pizza. Flat beer (Rs60) but a bubbling scene as the student-dominated crowd, long repressed in single-sex secondary schools, grinds away to the glory of their newfound un-chaperoned liberty. (Open daily 11am-3pm and 7:30-midnight.) **Alankar Cinema,** Connaught Rd., and **West End Cinema,** next to **Touché the Sizzler** on Modedina Rd., both show Bollywood flicks to huge crowds, afternoon and night. **The Film Institute of India,** Law College Rd., offers more substantial movies, but (at least in theory) you have to be a member. **Nehru Memorial Hall,** in Camp, and **Bal Gandharva Theater,** Jangli Maharaj Rd., stage performances of Indian drama, music and dance. For more detailed listings and schedules, see the "Pune Plus" section in the *Times of India.*

■ Near Pune: Lonavla लोनावला

Lonavla is a popular destination for both foreign and Indian tourists, easily accessible by train and bus on the Mumbai-Pune routes. It's the best place to drop your bag while you visit the Buddhist caves at Karla and Bhaja. Lonavla lies between **National Highway 4 (NH4)** and the Bombay-Pune rail line, 60km west of Pune. From the **train station,** the center of town is up the stairs and to the right on the **pedestrian bridge,** down the last set of stairs, and to the right (around the field). Trains to **Mumbai** (3hr., Rs34/160) and Pune (1½hr., Rs21/99) depart frequently. Lonavla's **bus station** is at the intersection of Shivaji Road and NH4 (reservation office open M-Sa 8am-2pm and 2:30-8pm, Su 8am-2pm). Buses head to Pune (every 30min., 1½hr., Rs36) and Mumbai (every 30min., 3hr., Rs53), and to the Karla and Bhaja caves (see below). Both **Shivaji Rd.** and NH4 are dotted with more **STD/ISD booths** than you'll ever need (**telephone code:** 02114).

Most of the tourists in Lonavla are families from Mumbai and Pune looking to splurge on resort-style, hill station living. For this reason, budget travelers have few viable accommodation options, especially during the high season, from April until June. About 100m down from the bus station on Shivaji Rd., the **Hotel Chandralok** (tel. 72294 or 72921), has clean rooms (Rs325) and great *thalis* (Rs55). Opposite Shivaji Rd. on the highway, up the pink-walled driveway left of the garden building, is **Madhu's Resort** (tel. 72657), a traditional Maharashtrian villa with simple wooden rooms (Rs150 per person). A couple of bona fide restaurants exist to break the hotel-*dhaba* monotony. Eat your fill at **The Mehfil** (tel. 73960), around the corner and to the right from the bus stand. This A/C restaurant has exceptional Chinese dishes (vegetable fried rice Rs70). Cheaper food can be found near the bus stand at **Sagar Snacks** (tel. 2279), where basic Indian and some Continental snack foods are available (*samosas* Rs25).

Most foreign tourists to Lonavla distract themselves with the exquisite first-century B.C. cave architecture at nearby **Karla** and **Bhaja.** Thirteen buses per day shuttle 12km from Lonavla's railway station to Karla (Rs2). At Karla, a steep staircase leads up from the drink stalls to the outcrop high above the plain where the main cave is located. A Hindu shrine and pillar capped by four lions obscure the entrance to the *chaitya* hall. The *pipal*-tree-shaped window, which signifies learning, illuminates the Buddhist *stupa.* The capitals of the interior columns each depict two kneeling elephants carrying a couple—perhaps stylized donors in the construction of the cave. (Open daily 8am-6pm. Admission Rs0.50.) Unless you locate a rickshaw, a non-taxing 5km walk beckons to would-be **Bhaja**-goers. Cross the main road and go up the gentle incline over the Malouvil Station tracks to the cold drinks stall at the edge of the tiny Bhaja village. Another staircase leads up to 18 caves which date from the second century BC. The *chaitya*s and *vihara*s feature some lovely sculpture, including a celebrated relief of a war elephant tearing up trees in its path. (Caves open dawn-dusk. Free).

Looming in and out of the monsoon mists, or baking in the sunshine hundreds of meters above the caves, the **Lohagad** and **Visapur Forts,** from the Maratha era, cater to the strong of leg. About 4km south of the Lonavla train station is Lonavla's most popular in-town attraction during the monsoons: the **Bhushi Dam,** which has stone steps carved along its face. At the peak of the rainy season cascades of white, foamy water spill down these stairs. Both *salwaar-kameez-* and shorts-sporting tourists sit happily upon these steps, getting doused in the natural jacuzzi action.

■ Aurangabad (Sambhajinagar) औरंगाबाद

Cradled within the crags of the desiccated Deccan Plateau and named after the orthodox Mughal ruler, Aurangzeb, Aurangabad (pop. 1,000,000) is tinged with a distinctive Persian aura. Square stone homes with smooth edges line the street in some small sections of town. Nightlife and entertainment may be dry, but two things—foreigners and politics—still stir up a little sand in the city. Thousands of travelers tromp to Aurangabad, using it as a base for exploring the caves at nearby Ajanta and Ellora. As a result of this constant influx, the tourist infrastructure is better developed in this city than in most throughout the state. Politically, far-right Shiv Sena city councilors, meeting in the shadow of Mughal monuments, recently voted to rename Aurangzeb's capital in honor of Shivaji's son and Maratha Hindu hero in his own right, Sambhaji. Few use the new name, Sambhajinagar, and the city's Muslim flavor endures amid the tourist boom and the economic development typical of Mumbai's hinterland.

ORIENTATION

Tourist facilities can be found along **Station Road,** which has two branches: the western half runs north from the railway station to the bus stand, and the eastern branch runs northeast past several hotels and restaurants to **Kranti Chowk,** home to the State Bank of India. From Kranti Chowk, **Jalna Road** runs east to airline offices and the airport, while **Dr. Rajendra Prasad Marg** cuts back to Station Rd. W. North of this intersection, Station Rd. becomes **Dr. Ambedkar Marg** near the bus stand and proceeds past the turn off for Panchakki on the left and the **GPO** on the right. Its terminus on the north end of town lies near the Bibi-Ka-Maqbara and the Aurangabad Caves.

PRACTICAL INFORMATION

Airport: Located at Chikalthana, Jalna Rd. (P. Nehru Marg), 8km from city center. Buses run to and from the railway station (Rs5). **Indian Airlines** (tel. 485421 or 482421), next to Rama International Hotel, Jalna Rd. Open daily 10am-1:15pm and 2-5pm. To: **Delhi** (daily, 3½ hr., US$150); **Jaipur** (M, Tu, Th, and Sa, 2½hr., US$125); **Mumbai** (2 per day, 50min., US$65); **Udaipur** (daily, 1hr., US$105).

Trains: Railway station, Station Rd. (tel. 331015). Fares are 2nd/1st class. To: **Bhopal/Agra/Delhi** (*Nanded-Amritsar Exp.* 7612, 12:50pm, 15/24/28 hr., 2nd class Rs163/230/250, 1st class Rs435/1032/1126); **Mumbai** (*Tapovan Exp.* 7618, 3:10pm; *Nanded-Mumbai Exp.* 1004, 9:40pm, 10hr., Rs119/497); **Pune** (passenger 1322, 7:45am, 9hr.).

Buses: Bus station, Dr. Ambedkar Rd. (tel. 331217). About 2km north of the railway station along the continuation of Station Rd. W. To: **Ahmedabad** (9pm, Rs171); **Mumbai** (8am, Rs155); **Hyderabad** (3pm, Rs205); **Jalgaon** (10 per day, 7am-9pm, Rs55); **Pune** (5:30am, 11:45pm, Rs90). Frequent local buses head to **Daulatabad** (Rs4), **Ellora** (Rs8), and **Ajanta** (Rs48).

Bicycle Rental: At the **Railway Station,** Station Rd.

Tourist Office: Government of India Tourist Office, Krishna Vilas, Station Rd. (tel. 331217). On the right-hand side of the main (western) branch of Station Rd., about

250m from the station. Helpful staff provides a range of city and regional maps, brochures, and general information, as well as guides for both MTDC and MSRTC tours (given in Hindi or English, no tours M). Open M-F 8:30am-6pm, Sa 8:30am-1pm. **MTDC,** MTDC Holiday Resort, Station Rd. E. (tel. 331198). Offers daily tours of Ajanta (Tu-Su 8am-5:30pm, Rs150); Ellora, Daulatabad, and Aurangabad (9:30am-5:30pm, Rs110); Paithan (3:30-9:30pm, Rs100). Open daily 7am-9pm. **MSRTC** (tel. 331647) also offers tours to Ellora, Daulatabad, and Aurangabad (Tu-Su 8am-4:30pm, Rs50), and Ajanta (Tu-Su 8am-6pm, Rs133, including guides but not entrance tickets). MSRTC tours depart from the Central Bus Stand.

Budget Travel: Classic Travel, MTDC Holiday Resort, Station Rd. (tel. 335598 or 337788; fax 338556). Inside the lobby near reception. Can arrange bus, train, and air travel. Open daily 7am-9pm. Also located in the Hotel Ajanta Ambassador, Airport Rd. (tel. 486399 or 485211; fax 484367).

Currency Exchange: State Bank of India, Dr. Rajendra Prasad Marg, Kranti Chowk, on the left, right on the square. Foreign exchange upstairs to the right. Open M-F 10:30am-2:30pm, Sa 10:30am-12:30pm.

Market: To the right along Jalna Rd. about 2km before reaching the airport. In good weather one can purchase anything from potatoes to papayas.

Hospital: Kamalnayar Bajaj Hospital, past Kranti Chowk on a lane 100m to the left (tel. 331448 or 334447), has a **24hr. pharmacy.**

Police: Kranti Chowk (tel. 331773 or 100).

Post Office: GPO, Juna Bazaar Chowk, Bazaar District. *Poste Restante* at Counter 1. Open M-Sa 10am-5pm. **Postal Code:** 431005.

Telephone Code: 0240.

ACCOMMODATIONS

Hotels cluster in the areas immediately surrounding the three major transportation hubs: the railway station, Central Bus Stand, and airport. Budget hotels are more readily found near the railroad and the bus stand while the airport area boasts many five-star, resort-style accommodations.

Youth Hostel (HI), Station Rd. W (tel. 334892), one km from the station, just before the intersection with Dr. Rajendra Prasad Marg, on the right. Spotless, gender-segregated student hostel with cheap, mosquito-netted dorm beds and cafeteria (breakfast Rs9, lunch and dinner Rs15). Three-night max. stay unless an extension is granted by the warden. Check-in 7-11am and 4-8pm. Check-out 9am. Curfew 10pm. Dorm beds Rs20, nonmembers Rs40; doubles Rs100, extra bed Rs50. One-time linen charge Rs5.

Hotel Great Punjab, Station Rd. E. (tel. 336482 or 338735), on the left, 100m from the station gates. Stained walls and a susceptibility to mosquito swarms, but helpful staff. Rooms include satellite TV, balconies, squat toilets, soap, towels, and a daily paper. Check-out 24hr. Singles Rs195; doubles Rs275, with A/C Rs375.

Hotel Natraj, Station Rd. W, 100m north of the station on the right. The two Sharma brothers from Gujarat have run this place since 1938. The responsibility has bent their frames over the years, but left their spirits, tea-making talents, and quiet, lime-green, single-story hotel intact. Singles Rs80; doubles Rs100; triples Rs135.

Hotel Shree Maya, Bharuka Complex (tel. 333093 or 333094; fax 331043). Walking north on Station Rd. from the Government Tourist Office, take the first two right turns; it's 100m on the right. Off the main road but still easily accessible, Shree Maya beckons with marble halls and attractive rooms with spacious attached baths. Check-out 24hr. Singles Rs100; doubles Rs150, with TV Rs350. Extra bed Rs40.

Hotel Shangrila (tel. 336481 or 329917), across from the Central Bus Stand, next to the Modi Samrat. Red carpets, golden carvings on the lobby's ceiling, and posters of the white Goan sands are the closest it gets to its namesake, but still a comfortable haven with clean bathrooms. Check-out 24hr. Singles Rs50, with attached bath Rs80; doubles Rs80/125, with A/C Rs250.

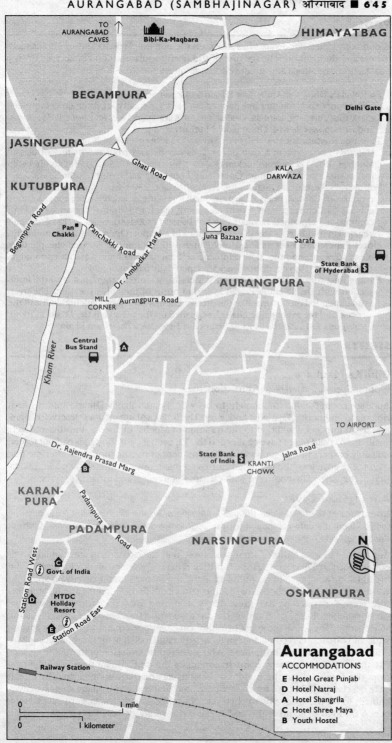

TO
AURANGABAD
CAVES

Bibi-Ka-Maqbara

HIMAYATBAG

BEGAMPURA

Delhi Gate

JASINGPURA

Ghati Road

KALA
DARWAZA

KUTUBPURA

Begumpura Road

Pan Chakki

Panchakki Road

GPO
Juna Bazaar

Sarafa

State Bank
of Hyderabad

Dr. Ambedkar Marg

AURANGPURA

MILL
CORNER

Aurangpura Road

Central
Bus Stand

Kham River

TO AIRPORT

Dr. Rajendra Prasad Marg

State Bank
of India

Jalna Road

KRANTI
CHOWK

KARAN-
PURA

Padampura Road

PADAMPURA

NARSINGPURA

N

Station Road West

Govt. of India

OSMANPURA

MTDC
Holiday
Resort

Station Road East

Railway Station

0   1 mile
0   1 kilometer

WEST INDIA

Aurangabad
ACCOMMODATIONS

E Hotel Great Punjab
D Hotel Natraj
A Hotel Shangrila
C Hotel Shree Maya
B Youth Hostel

FOOD

A company called Foodwala's has a lock on the non-hotel restaurants in Aurangabad. To escape their monopoly, try one of the ever-popular garden restaurants or buy snacks from the shops and street vendors along Station Rd. E.

Foodwala's Bhoj, Dr. Ambedkar Rd., in a big building 200m south of the bus stand, 1 floor up. Classy touches like painted fan blades, a small rock fountain centerpiece mark this pure veg. joint as a hideaway for Aurangabad's elite. *Thalis* Rs35, *dosas,* and *utthapams* Rs9-14. Open daily 11am-11pm.

Tandoor Restaurant (tel. 352144), Shyam Chambers, Barsilal Nagar, Station Rd. E. (tel. 28482). Egyptian kitsch decor does not detract from the quality of classic Mughlai (Rs65) or butter chicken (Rs90). Chinese, too (Rs40-60). Yet another subject of the Foodwala Empire. Open daily 11am-4pm and 6:30-11:30pm.

Foodlovers Restaurant, Station Rd. E., on the right, 250m from the station. This cavernous, dirt-floored, open-air thatched hall forms the most concrete proof of Aurangabad's garden restaurant fetish. Mammoth menu (353 items) features a table of contents to help diners navigate chicken dishes (Rs80-100), Chinese (Rs42-65), and vegetarian numbers (Rs28-48). Beer comes in a teapot. Open daily 11am-midnight.

Hotel Panchavati Restaurant, Hotel Panchavati, Station Rd. W. This cheapie doubles as a watering hole, with canteen-like benches and bare walls an extra edge. *Utthapams* Rs10, veg. dishes Rs15-35. Open daily 6am-midnight.

Patang Restaurant, Hotel Printravel, Station Rd. W., on the right, just after the intersection with Dr. Rajendra Prasad Rd., 1km north of the railway station. The overhead expended on features like the groovy circular doorway, pink highlights in the alcoves, and the avant-garde chairs has pushed up the prices a little. *Dosas* Rs10-30, *utthapams* Rs18-22, *thalis* Rs40. Beers Rs42-45. Open daily 7am-11pm.

SIGHTS

Bibi-Ka-Maqbara

Hours: *Open daily dawn-dusk.* **Admission:** *Rs2.*

Aurangzeb's milk-white monument to his wife, Begum Rabi'a Durani, suffers much ridicule as an inferior Taj Mahal knock-off. The Bibi-Ka-Maqbara does deserve recognition as an important addition to the tradition of Mughal mausolea, but the relatively small tomb could never have challenged the Taj even if cash shortages had not forced ungainly corner-cutting, such as the abandonment of marble for plaster after the first meter. Nevertheless, the building remains an ingenious compression and simplification of the Taj's plan, complete with elegant floral reliefs and ornate *jali* screens.

Aurangabad Caves

Location: *In the hills behind the Bibi-Ka-Maqbara, up the dirt road that leads past the tomb; 20min. by auto-rickshaw.* **Hours:** *Open dawn-dusk.* **Admission:** *Free.* **Other:** *Bring a flashlight—the caves are not artificially lit.*

Aurangabad's caves temples often get forgotten in the excitement surrounding their counterparts at Ellora and Ajanta, but they remain a wonderful introduction to the breathtaking sculpture to be found all along the Maharashtrian cave trail. Split into western and eastern sections, these important examples of Buddhist art and architecture were excavated by two great dynasties during the 6th century. The western caves, numbers 1 through 5, are off the dirt road atop a treacherous climb on winding stone steps. The third and most beautiful cave, supported and guarded by several wide and ornately carved pillars, is a *vihara,* or residence hall for the wandering Buddhist *bikshus* (monks) of the time, who gathered in monastic communities' caves like these around the state. Some fragments of the original paintings depict stories from the *Jataka* about the Buddha's previous incarnations upon earth. The fourth cave is a *chaitya* hall, used for congregation and prayer. Even ordinary speech echoes enough to fill the space with a rhythmic chant-like sound. The eastern caves, numbers 6 through 9, lie up at the end of the dirt road about 1km farther, affording an incredible view of the surrounding landscape and the silhouette of Bibi-Ka-Maqbara against the city in the distance. The seventh cave greets visitors with lotus-framed *apsaras* (celestial dancers) at the entrance to the crypt. The shadowed Buddha sits peacefully within the sanctuary surrounded by the frozen faces of intent listeners at his mammoth feet. Try the caves early in the morning when few tourists are there. Beware of the packs of slumbering bats who find the caves as wonderfully isolated and peaceful as tourists do.

Panchakki

Location: *Dr. Ambedkar Rd., near the center of the city.* **Admission:** *Rs2.*

The Mughal water mill at Panchakki is a good stopover on the return trip from the caves or Bibi-Ka-Maqbara. Although the mill's facade is not in itself awe-inspiring, the concept behind it is noteworthy and thus attracts thousands of tourists each year. Constructed by the Baba Shah Musafir to provide enough grain for hundreds of orphans, *fakirs,* and paupers who were his devotees, the mill's water reserve is located 6km from the actual grindstone. The water gushes through earthen pipes to eventually be raised by a siphon and dropped with intense force upon the blades of the water wheel. The result, in the Panchakki's heyday, was almost four tons of finely ground grain. Now, Panchakki's seems a mere breeding ground for hawkers and crafts shops selling the city's special *himroo* fabric, as well as polished-stone neck-laces, wood-carved boxes, and *bidri* jewelry.

■ Near Aurangabad: Khuldabad खुल्दबाद and Daulatabad दौलताबाद

Buses pass through several important sights on the road between Aurangabad and Ellora. The Emperor Aurangzeb finally found rest from the struggle to subjugate Maharashtra in **Khuldabad,** or Rauza, a small, strongly Muslim town just over the ridge from Ellora. In a departure from the grandiose mausolea that housed all his Mughal forbearers, Aurangzeb chose a modest grave funded by the proceeds from his own transcription of the Qur'an. The shrines of various Sufi saints nearby far out-shadow it.

Farther along the road, 13km from Aurangabad, the **Daulatabad** fortress crowns a tall hill. A series of sadistic despots have endowed this formidable complex with a col-orful history. In the 14th century, Muhammad Tughluq, the Sultan of Delhi, decided it was just the spot for a capital city. Rather than leave the development of a thriving city to chance, the not-so-savvy sultan decided to march the entire population of Delhi 1000km across India to people his new metropolis. Needless to say, the small proportion of the deportees who did not die on the way greeted life in the Deccan with a sullen resentment unconducive to prosperity. The Sultan abandoned his brain-child after only 17 years and marched the few survivors back home.

Through the first gates, spiked as usual to prevent elephant attacks, a huge, ruined city awaits the visitor. The **Chand Minar** victory tower, built in 1435, rises over a mosque cobbled together with columns pillaged from temples and a water tank from Daulatabad's advanced hydraulic system. Beyond, a series of steps leads up the hill past ruined palaces to the Chini Mahal, with its trace blue tiles, where the unfortu-nate King Abdul Hassan Tara Shah met his end. On top of the small tower next door, a cannon called Qila Shikan (Fort Breaker) points menacingly at the horizon. From here, the defenses begin in earnest, with the crossing of the moat to enter the sheer-walled citadel. A flashlight will guide you through the pitch black maze of passages excavated from the inside of the hill. Endless stairs lead ever upwards, re-emerging into daylight and a further series of palaces coating the slope to its summit. From the top, magnificent views reveal Aurangabad and the surrounding country through the Deccan dust. (Open daily dawn-dusk. Free.)

■ Ellora इलोरा

Ellora's Buddhist, Hindu, and Jain "caves" are, along with similar structures at Ajanta, Maharashtra's most notable tourist attraction. Generations of India's most skilled artisans chiseled a series of temples and residence halls from the solid rock of the hills. They are still referred to as caves, even though they are man-made architectural and sculptural wonders. **The caves are closed on Mondays.** (Cave 16 open Tu-Su 6am-6pm. Admission Rs5, under 15 free; video fee Rs25, exterior only. All other caves free.)

A mere 29km from Aurangabad (frequent buses via Daulatabad, 6am-6pm, 45min., Rs8), Ellora usually gets relegated to daytrip status. The main road, which runs west from the bus stand by the site entrance, conceals one budget hotel amid the trinket and cold drink stands 250m down on the right. Hard core ruin-lovers can stay at **Hotel Natraj** (tel. 41043; in-season: dorm beds Rs50, singles Rs100, doubles with bath Rs150). Another option is the MTDC's **Kailas Hotel** (tel. 41043 or 41067, singles Rs150, doubles Rs250-400; attached restaurant: breakfast Rs70, main dishes Rs45-80, open daily 7am-9:30pm). Short of this hotel and the sodas and unsanitary *pakoras* from the street stands, hungry sightseers are caught depending upon **Foodwala's Ellora Restaurant** (tel. 41041; *samosas* Rs15, main dishes Rs40-65; open daily 8am-6pm) for their culinary needs. Many hotels and restaurants in Aurangabad offer packed lunches. Ellora's **telephone code** is 02437.

Of the 32 caves, numbers 1 through 16 give the clearest impression of Ellora's development over the centuries, culminating in the masterpiece of the Kailasa Temple (number 16). Starting at the southernmost cave (right as you face the caves, number 1 according to the Architectural Survey of India's reckoning) allows for a roughly chronological sequence. Caves 1-12 date from Buddhist India's twilight in the 6th to 8th centuries (see **Trade and Buddhism,** p. 77). The caves in this group grow increasingly elaborate and ornate in an attempt to stave off the popular revival of Hinduism evidenced by the neighboring Shiva temples whose construction began in the 7th century. Of the first nine **vihara** (monastery caves), individual cells and statues of the Buddha and *bodhisattvas,* **Cave 5** stands out. The flat, low ridges in the floor probably served as benches to make a community dining hall. The stern Vajrapani (the *bodhisattva* who holds a thunderbolt) and the more forgiving Padmapani (flower-power in the form of a lotus-totin' *bodhisattva*) preside over the meals from the sides of the central shrine.

Cave 10, Ellora's only *chaitya* hall, echoes earlier structures at **Ajanta** (p. 649), **Karla** (p. 642), and elsewhere in the state. Octagonal pillars flank the walls and create an ambulatory around the *stupa,* while a window and balcony above provide illumination and a vantage from which to appreciate it. The carved beams in the ceiling imitate wooden rafters from Karla and presumably earlier free-standing halls.

The last Buddhist gasp at Ellora, **Cave 12,** contains some beautiful sculpture on the third level. *Bodhisattvas* line the side walls, while the seven previous incarnations of the Buddha flank the main shrine. A different type of tree shades each Buddha, on the left, identifying them iconographically according to a symbology developed at Sanchi in Madhya Pradesh and other early Buddhist monuments. Traces of paint in the sanctum and chamber hint at the once bright decoration of the caves.

Caves 13-29 date from Ellora's Hindu era, which lasted late into the 9th century. These more elaborate, densely sculptured temples share many motifs: Shiva appears most often on Mount Kailasa playing dice with his wife Parvati while a demon tries frantically but futilely to dislodge him; at other times he dances with both legs bent like Nataraja, whose gyrations shook the world into being and will one day destroy it. Vishnu crops up as Narasimha, the man-lion, Varaha, the boar, and most commonly as a sleeper in the coils of a serpent, floating on the cosmic sea. From his navel grows a lotus, out of which Brahma emerges to create the world. The image of the Seven Mothers, buxom goddesses with children, flanked by Kala and Kali, also appears regularly. All of these sculptures appear in **Caves 14** and **15.** The latter also houses a depiction of Shiva emerging from a *linga,* while Brahma and Vishnu kneel before him—testimony to Shiva-worship among Ellora's patrons.

Ellora's Hindu epoch, and Maharashtrian rock-cut temples in general, reach their apogee in **Cave 16,** the **Kailasa Temple.** This massive 8th- and 9th-century building was excavated from the top down by several generations of impeccably skilled craftsmen. The sheer scale of this vast replica of Shiva's home in the Himalaya begs belief even before you consider the technical challenge of slicing it from solid rock from the elegant *shikhara* on down. Traces of plaster and paint bear witness to further decorative complexity on top of the elaborate sculpture and architecture.

The paved road by Foodwala's restaurant leads to the remaining caves—don't let the stairs up to the left fool you. **Cave 21** repeats Cave 14's iconographic scheme, while **Cave 29** contains perhaps the only mooner protected under UNESCO world heritage provisions: in another panel of Shiva ignoring Ravana's ruckus, you'll notice a dwarf baring his ass. **Caves 30-34** date from Ellora's third and final phase of construction under Jain patrons during the 9th and 10th centuries. **Cave 32** depicts the *tirthankara* Gomatesvara so deep in meditation that he has not noticed the vines growing on his limbs or the animals surrounding him.

■ Ajanta अजन्ता

Ajanta remains as remote today as it was in the 2nd century BC, when it was a Buddhist retreat. The builders chose a sheer cliff-face above a horseshoe shaped valley in the Waghora River to render their contemplative spiritual visions in painting and sculpture. During the 7th century AD, the monks abandoned their 29 *chaityas* and *viharas* (and the astonishingly life-like art with which they had filled them) to an even greater obscurity. Only the local tribespeople knew of the masterpieces, prowled by tigers and overrun with creepers, until one of those red-coated hunting parties that infested the forests of imperial India spied Cave 10 from the opposite ridge in 1819.

Would-be visitors no longer have to beat back the brush but they do have to suffer through long, hot, jolting **bus** rides to get here. Otherwise, many **buses** stop at Ajanta between Jalgaon and Aurangabad, starting early in the morning and ending at 5:30pm in Aurangabad and 6:30pm in Jalgaon. You can come from one town, leave your bags to be guarded at the entrance to the caves (Rs10) while sightseeing, and proceed to the next in the evening. However, most visit en route between Aurangabad (108km south) and Jalgaon (58km north) on the main **railway** line. **Telephone Code:** 02438.

The MTDC, naturally, runs the **hotel** and **restaurant** at the caves themselves (tel. 4226). Their rooms are clean but spare, with balconies and common bathrooms. (Singles Rs125; doubles Rs200. Attached restaurant: entrees Rs40-50; open daily 9am-5:30pm.) For reservations call the regional MTDC manager in Aurangabad (tel. (0240) 331198 or 331513). The cold drink stands furnish the only other refreshment while the **Forest Guest House** 500m up the road offers cluttered, air-cooled rooms with a wicker-furnished and flowerful veranda for those who book in advance at the Divisional Forest Officer, Opp. Government, Engineering College, Osmanpura, Aurangabad (tel. (0240) 334701; Rs15 per person).

The **caves** are located up the steps behind the drinks stands and over the rise. The guided tours, although interesting, rely primarily on gimmicks: "See the expression of the Buddha change when I move the light" and "see the earliest known bangs in hairdo history." On the other hand, they do guarantee decent lighting while you visit. **The caves are closed on Monday.** (Caves open Tu-Su 9am-5:30pm. Admission Rs5, additional Rs5 fee for 1, 2, 16, and 17. Video fee Rs25, exterior only.)

Cave 1, which dates from the 5th century AD, contains some of Ajanta's most naturalistic paintings. As with all of Ajanta's art, the life-like jewelry, clothing, and domestic life materials matter more than the story here. On the left-hand wall, a king, converted to Buddhism, abandons earthly pleasures for a life of meditation. Just to the left of the rear shrine, a painting depicts the elegant Padmapani (the lotus-holding *bodhisattva*), while Vajrapani stands sentry to his right with his thunderbolt. On several capitals on the right-hand side of the hall, four deer sharing a single head gaze out contentedly at the tourists.

WEST INDIA

In **Cave 2,** paintings to the left show the dream of a six-tusked elephant which foretold the Buddha's conception, and his miraculous birth directly into the arms of his mother. In the right-hand rear corner, a sculptural frieze of a classroom depicts an ill-behaved student pulling the hair of the girl in front. Above to the right, the demon Hariti dances furiously while, on the left, his teachings have lulled a princess into a peaceful repose.

The *chaitya* hall in **Cave 9** dates from the Theravada era, during which the Buddha was not directly depicted. Instead, the *pipal*-tree-shaped window in the facade signifies learning, while the huge *stupa* in the apse symbolizes (somewhat more literally) the relics of the Buddha. The same goes for **Cave 10,** which dates from the 2nd century BC, although here millennia of sunlight and the scratchings of graffiti artists have obscured most of the symbolic paintings. In **Cave 16,** the most celebrated fresco shows yet another princess swooning in distress as her husband throws in the worldly towel. *Jataka* stories about the Buddha's earlier incarnations fill the walls of **Cave 17.** In the *vishavantara,* on the left-hand wall, a well-intentioned prince gives away his father's magic elephant, his cart and possessions, and even his wife and children, renouncing all earthly ties before entering into the final life-phase of hermitage. On the opposite wall, confusing tales of seductive beauties and bloodthirsty demons revel in surprisingly accurate anatomical detail. The tour guides love to show off the 3-D effect created by shining their flashlights on the pearls of the princess in the upper-right-hand corner of the right wall.

The elaborate interior and exterior sculpture of **Cave 19** indicates the Buddhist response to the Hindu renaissance of the 6th century AD. A columned *chaitya* hall, Cave 19 dates from the Mahayana period, during which depictions of the Buddha were permitted. The most splendid example of this freedom reclines along the left-hand wall of **Cave 26:** Buddha on the verge of attaining *nirvana,* surrounded by disciples.

The path behind Cave 26 leads down the hill to a bridge. From here, intrepid visitors can climb to a **viewpoint** to relive the astonishment of the British in 1819. A second path along the river will guide the less historically minded to a waterfall and washing pool for villagers in the rainy season.

■ Nagpur नागपुर

Located smack dab in the center of India, Nagpur is the hub for virtually every major road and rail route. But it certainly doesn't *feel* like the entire Subcontinent rotates around this city of 2 million. Here you'll find streets filled with tattered *tongas* and auto-rickshaws rather than taxis and aggressive Tata two-tonners. The seat of the state legislature alternates between Nagpur and Mumbai, but Nagpur lacks the skyscrapers and concrete that characterize other cities of its size. In fact, Nagpur is the second-greenest cosmopolitan area in India, with numerous parks and playgrounds. Most of its visitors are corporate types here to attend conferences (or convert to Buddhism, as a few hundred thousand of Dr. B. R. Ambedkar's Untouchable followers did here in 1956), but for tourists who find themselves at the center of things, Nagpur is subtle, sweet, and a good starting point for excursions into national parks nearby.

ORIENTATION AND PRACTICAL INFORMATION The pulse of Nagpur originates at the **railway station** (enquiry tel. 131 or 521455) on **Central Avenue Road,** whose north-south tracks split the city into eastern and western halves. Trains (fares are 2nd/1st class) chug to almost anywhere in India, including: **Calcutta** (*Howrah Mail* 8001, 11:30am, 17hr.; *Gitangali Exp.* 2859, 8:15pm, 17hr., Rs184/982); **Chennai** (*Tamil Nadu Exp.* 2622, 2:35pm, 19hr., Rs151/737); **Delhi** (*Tamil Nadu Exp.* 2621, 2pm, 14hr., Rs187/930); **Hyderabad** (*Andhra Pradesh Exp.* 2724, 10:25am, 10hr., *Hyderabad Exp.* 7022, 6pm, 11hr., Rs114/574); and **Mumbai** (*Gitanjali Exp.* 2860, 7:45am, 14hr., Rs151/737). Near the railway station is **Mayo Hospital** (tel. 726127). **Wardha Road (NH7)** runs parallel to the train tracks and leads to the **airport** (tel. 260348), 8km from the city center. The **State Bus Stand,** 1.5km south of the railway station, has buses to Hyderabad (2 per day, Rs250), Indore (1 per day, Rs195), Jabalpur (4 per day, Rs130), and Pune (2 per day, Rs320).

All other areas of tourist interest are in the western half of the city. **Central Avenue Rd.** becomes **Kingsway Road** after the railway station, where you'll also find the **State Bank of India** (tel. 521847; open M-F 10:30am-2pm). You can exchange currency and cash traveler's checks at the **foreign exchange office** in the center of the left-hand building. Running parallel to and south of Kingsway is **Palm Road,** home of the **GPO** (open M-Sa 10am-6pm) and **Indian Airlines office** (tel. 523069; open M-Sa 10am-1pm and 2-5pm), which runs flights to: **Calcutta** (3 per week, 3hr., US$150); **Delhi** (1 per day, 1½hr., US$135); **Hyderabad** (3 per week, 1hr., US$95); and **Mumbai** (2 per day, 1½hr., US$115). Farther south is the tourist center, **Sitabuldi,** with shining shops and a smattering of cheap hotels. North and west of Sitabuldi lies the **Civil Lines** area. **MTOC tourist office** (tel. 533325), on Dr. Munje Rd., off Buty Rd., can provide information on area parks and lakes (open M-F and 1st and 3rd Sa of the month 10am-5:45pm). **Postal code:** 440001. **Telephone Code:** 0712.

ACCOMMODATIONS AND FOOD The plethora of business travelers to Nagpur sustains an explosion of accommodations. The thickest tangle of budget (and disorientingly similar) hotels is on **Central Avenue Road** and its arteries. **Hotel Blue Diamond,** 113 Central Ave., Dosar Chowk (tel. 727461), is good, if you can handle a huge, psychedelic honeycomb. Rooms with common baths are cheap (singles Rs55-250; doubles Rs90-350). Nearby, **Hotel Midland** (tel. 726131) has tidy rooms, slickly disinfected marble bathrooms, and funky-smellin' hallways. (Singles Rs190-275; doubles Rs325-525.) The cluster of cheapies in **Sitabuldi,** in the heart of Nagpur's market district, are less consistent in terms of quality but are well-suited to those inclined to explore. Head east on Mahatma Gandhi Rd. from his statue and take the third left to reach **Hotel Amrta,** Madi No. 3 (tel. 543762; fax 553123). Even the "regular rooms" in this aqua oasis put other dwellings to shame. (Check-out 24hr. Singles Rs300-475; doubles Rs350-550. Visa, MC, AmEx.) In Nagpur, fine food is the dear domain of the five-star luxury hotels, but a few other establishments challenge their authority. **Nanking,** Mount Rd., Sardar (tel. 531850), is the best-known, best-value establishment for a Far East feast. (Non-veg dishes Rs65-90. Veg. fare Rs45-80. Open Tu-Su noon-3pm and 6-11pm.)

ENTERTAINMENT The **Hotel Centre Point,** 24 Central Bazaar Rd. (tel. 520910), boasts the most pulsating pub-cum-discotheque in town: **The Zodiac** (open for "jam sessions" W 2-5pm and Sa 9-11pm) is popular with locals. For those seeking to see rather than be seen, **Liberty Cinema,** Residency Rd. in Sardar, shows fairly recent English-language films (daily 10:30pm, Sa-M 11am). Finally, **Ambajhari Lake and Garden,** on the western outskirts of Nagpur, is ideal for early morning or evening strolls (open daily 5:30am-9pm).

WEST INDIA

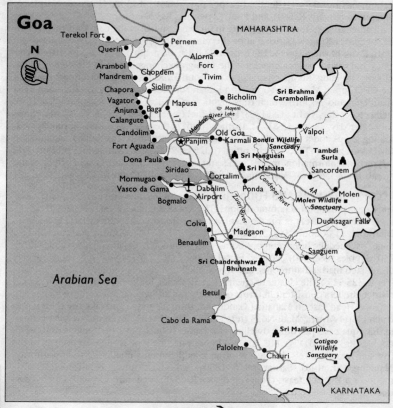

Goa

Goa गोवा

In the minds of travelers, Goa looms so large that the legend alone intrigues and entrances. Goa's siren call takes myriad forms, from the lullabies crooned by luxurious resorts and the steady drone of waves, to the macho roar of Enfield motorcycles cruising the beaches for full-moon technofixes, to the carnivalesque cacophony of Anjuna's flea market. Tourists in turn recreate the Myth of Goa, which reverberates across the Internet and radio waves. The homes of Goans have become their guest houses; restaurants, whose chefs have mastered the art of banana pancakes, surface from the sand; and five-star hotels have transformed pristine beaches into capitalist megaplexes. These newer institutions sit alongside moss-covered Baroque churches, leafy coconut groves, and soft-sanded shorelines strewn with fishing nets.

This destination of dreams first captured the imagination of the West in 1498, when the Portuguese explorer Vasco da Gama landed on the Keralan coast in search of spices. For business purposes, Portugal needed a foothold on India's west coast, and in 1510 Goa ended up becoming a Portuguese colony. In the 16th century, Goa became a prosperous trading city where Portuguese soldiers and adventurers mixed with the locals, many of whom converted to Catholicism and married Europeans. Through the guidance of the Jesuits and the terror of the Inquisition, Goa also developed into a stronghold of Christianity in India. Portugal prevented Goa's absorption into the British Raj and held on until 1961, when Indian troops annexed the region, making Goa both the first piece of Subcontinental soil clutched by European coloniz-ers and the last let free. Goa became a Union Territory, and, in 1987, an official state.

According to some, the invasion of hippies and posher tourists in search of para-dise has made Goa a colony all over again, but indulging in its pleasures need not be an exploitative venture. After five centuries of Portuguese rule, Goa is unique among Indian states: you are as likely to meet a Portuguese-speaking Roman Catholic dressed in jeans and a muscle shirt as a *lungi*-clad fisherman shouldering his day's catch. About 30% of Goa's inhabitants are Christian, and the state has one of India's highest literacy and income levels. Goa is small enough to explore thoroughly, and the locals are usually eager to share their Eden with visitors.

⊚ HIGHLIGHTS OF GOA

- India's most legendary (and decadent) nightlife raves the winter away at the northern beaches of **Anjuna** (p. 668) and **Calangute** (p. 664).
- Time stands still in **Old Goa** (p. 661), home to Portuguese monuments, cathe-drals, and the interred remains of **St. Francis Xavier** (p. 662).
- **South Goa** (p. 674), particularly the beach towns of **Benaulim** (p. 677) and **Palolem** (p. 678), offers sandy respite from the Northern tourist frenzy.

WHEN TO GO

Goa's northern beaches are hopping from early November to late March when near perfect weather (sunny, hot, and cloudless) brings sun-lovers in droves. Beach fever is intense in the weeks before and after Goa's psychedelic Christmas; the months of December and January are considered peak season. Practically everything closes down during the monsoon (June-Sept.), and guest house prices bottom out, while Westerners move out, traditionally heading for Manali. The monsoon cools Goa and fills its wells, but the showers often cease for long sunny stretches. Other holidays well worth the trip are the Carnival, Panjim's pre-Lent Bacchic revelry (Feb. 14-16, 1999; Mar. 5-7, 2000), and the more solemn Festivities for Goa's Favorite Saint, Fran-cis Xavier, in Old Goa on December 3 every year.

GETTING THERE AND AWAY

Most travelers reach Goa from Mumbai, 600km to the north.

Domestic Flights
Dabolim Airport, (info tel. (0854) 512644), 29km south of Panjim, serves mostly domestic flights. Indian Airlines and Jet Airways both offer flights to and from: **Banga-lore** (3 per week, Tu, Th, and Su, 1hr., US$100); **Delhi** (1 per day, 2½hr., US$150); **Mumbai** (1 per day, 1hr., US$50). There is also a Rs750 airport tax for all flights. Dur-ing Goa's peak season, seats on the Mumbai-Goa flight are difficult to procure. Reserv-ing months ahead for Christmas week is common practice.

Dabolim's prepaid taxi counter, outside the airport's main doors, will shove new-comers off most anywhere in Goa. A board to the left of the ticket counter lists fares (to Panjim Rs300). Off season (May-Sept.), when the resorts are empty, touts clutter the main exit, threatening to whisk you off to a plush hotel you've never heard of.

Trains
After years of waiting and wondering, the **Konkan Railway** is complete. Now, travel to the south from Mumbai is speedier, more comfortable, and incredibly beautiful as the tracks wind through lush tropical forests, over more than one hundred bridges, and through over 150 tunnels. The only drawback is that the tracks were laid some 15 to 20km outside city stations, so the railway only skirts major towns. Mumbai-Mad-gaon express trains to **Mumbai** stop at three stations in Goa: **Tivim,** in the north, 20km due east of Vagator beach (KR0112, 7:30pm, 11hr.); the centrally located **Kar-mali,** 12km due east of Panjim (KR0112, 7:05pm, 11½hr.); and **Madgao,** in the south, about 5km outside the city (KR0111, 10:30pm, 12hr.). All Mumbai fares Rs231 for

Don't Mess With Goa

Goa's tourist boom has speckled its coast with huge resorts and small guest houses, all of which consume a hefty share of resources. The flood of thirsty (and dirty) travelers depletes Goa's freshwater resources so much that village wells run dry or are contaminated by salty seawater. Hotels drilling private wells and filling superfluous Olympic-sized swimming pools deserve most of the blame for water waste. But backpackers too can have an effect. There are ways to conserve water, however, like taking bucket baths, or turning off the shower while soaping, and bringing your clothes to a *dhobi* instead of washing them in your room.

Beaches once imprinted only by the feet of fishermen are now littered with Bisleri bottles, plastic bags, and light bulbs. Fishermen still fish here, and people (including you) still eat the fish they catch. But now, in addition to fish, the ocean is violently belching up tourist trash—take the hint and don't litter.

If you are considering a long stay, volunteering for one of Goa's Non-Governmental Organizations (NGOs) allow you to help on a local level. ECOFORUM in Mapusa publishes a book, *Fish Curry & Rice* (Rs200), which lists Goa's activist groups. For more information, see **Environmentally Responsible Tourism,** p. 69.

non-A/C sleeper, Rs597 for 3-tier A/C with blanket and pillow. Other trains continue down, eventually connecting Mumbai with Mangalore, Bangalore, and the tip of the sub-continent, Konyakumari. Trains for **Delhi** leave daily from **Vasco da Gama,** on the coast, near the airport (*Goa Exp.* 2779, 4pm, 12hr., Rs425/1515).

Note: Expect delays of one to five hours, especially in the monsoon season. Even the mighty Konkan must yield to Mother Nature.

Catamarans

Frank Shipping runs a catamaran service between Panjim and Mumbai. Prices are only slightly cheaper than flying, and since the boat generally sails over 10 mi. from the shoreline, it's hardly scenic. The service operates between September and April.

Arrivals: From **Mumbai** to Panjim (Tu and Th, 10am, F-Su 10:30pm, 7hr., Rs1400/1600). In late December, reserve a seat several weeks in advance; at other times, 3-5 days is sufficient. Frank's Mumbai office (tel. (022) 3743737) is in Colaba (open year-round). The catamaran leaves Mumbai from the dock along P. D'Mello Rd., 3km north of Victoria Terminus.

Departures: The Catamaran heads from **Panjim** to Mumbai at 10am (M, W, and F-Su). Frank's Panjim office (tel. (0832) 228711) is opposite the Hotel Mandovi on the Mandovi River, but this branch is only open during months of operation. (Open M-F 9am-5pm, Su 10am-6pm.)

Buses

For travelers on a budget, buses are currently the best way to reach Goa from: **Bangalore** (16hr.; see p. 563); **Mangalore** (10hr.; see p. 587); **Miraj** (7hr.); **Mumbai** (17hr., see p. 612); **Mysore** (16hr.; see p. 574); **Pune** (15hr.; see p. 636). In most cities, you can buy the tickets at the bus, which offers a chance to check out the goods first hand. Alternately, intrastate buses careen to and from the **Kadamba Bus Terminals** in the transport hubs of Panjim, Mapusa, and Madgaon. **Private carriers** offer more extensive services, and their coaches are generally more comfortable (except for the infamous "Video Coaches"). Book private coaches through travel agencies or from the shacks surrounding the bus terminals in Goa. For details on interstate bus travel, see the listings for **Panjim** (p. 658), **Mapusa** (p. 663), and **Madgaon** (p. 674).

ORIENTATION

Goa is roughly divided into two regions: North Goa and South Goa. The state capital, **Panjim,** is right in the middle but is considered part of North Goa. The town of **Mapusa,** 11km north of Panjim along National Highway 17, is a smaller center for North Goa and a transport hub for most northern beaches. **Madgaon,** 30km southwest of Panjim, is a hub for the south. Goa's train line from Karnataka passes through Madgaon on its way to Vasco da Gama.

The sandy turf you stake on Goa's beaches, also divided into northern and southern strips, may be the biggest factor in molding your Goa experience, from the type of accommodations you choose, to the food and drink you consume, to the travelers and locals you meet. Some beaches feature five-star resorts, others brim with homey guest houses, while still others are filled with palm leaf shacks as transient as the backpackers who construct them. In general, the North packs more crowds and nightlife than the South, and package and luxury tourism give way to backpackers as you head north from Candolim to Arambol.

The southernmost of the northern beaches, resort-filled **Candolim,** is on the north bank of the River Mandovi, across from Panjim, stretching from Fort Aguada north along **Sinquerim** beach. Near the ruined fort, the Taj Group runs a five-star complex, and the posh package-tourist atmosphere seeps onto the nearby the beaches. For most backpackers, Goa's northern beaches begin farther up the coast. From **Calangute** all the way to **Arambol,** 70km northeast of Panjim, backpacker culture has, over the past 30 years, inscribed the sandy terrain with its exploits. In the 1960s, tsunamis of hippies, soul-searchers, and surf-snorkelers crashed onto the pure sandy stretches of **Calangute.** They soon expanded into nearby **Baga,** where a steep hill temporarily stopped the party from exploding right into **Anjuna,** now home to a madcap flea market and Goa's famous **rave scene**. Calangute and Baga have since become more developed, and backpackers have migrated ever northward in search of beaches more removed from the attentions of other tourists and police. Long-termers love **Vagator,** which has beautiful, increasingly crowded beaches, and its sister village **Chapora,** essentially a short street with a good cafe scene. To reach the beach of **Arambol,** beyond the remote, hippified Chapora river, one must take a ferry from the small town of **Siolem** to **Chopdem** northeast of Chapora.

The beaches of South Goa are either highly developed resorts or completely undeveloped sand sanctuaries, stretching all the way to Karnataka. Slightly south, and easily reached from Madgaon, are **Colva** and **Benaulim,** similar to the northern beaches in the mixed package tour/backpacker clientele, but far cheaper and more sedate at night. South of Benaulim is a desolate strip of beach fronts, before the landscape succumbs to Holiday Inn Hell at **Cavelossim** and **Mobor.** The beachcombers pay heed to picture-perfect **Palolem** before heading south to **Gokarn,** in Karnataka.

LOCAL TRANSPORTATION

Traveling by bus through Goa's narrow roads is not as stomach-wrenching as in other parts of the country; the popular routes are generally packed, though mercifully short. Local **buses** run extensively, frequently, and cheaply. **Express buses,** available only for certain routes, are the fastest—others halt in every village and paddy as locals hop on and off. There are few real bus stops in the state, and most locals simply flag down non-express buses as they pass by.

Tourist vehicles (expensive minivans) and **taxis** are available for short jaunts or longer-term rentals (40km or 4hr., Rs250-300). **Auto-rickshaws,** disinclined to set their meters, are readily found zipping between beaches or herding passengers in at rickshaw stands in town. Their fares tend to be a little more than half of what taxis charge. During the off season and when heading to more remote areas, all require return fares even if you're not coming back. The distinctly Goan **motorcycle-rickshaws** or **pilot taxis** (painted yellow and black), whose licensed drivers tote tourists on the bike's back seat, are theoretically cheaper than either, though luggage larger than a medium-sized backpack might present problems.

The simplest, riskiest, and sexiest transportation method employed by many visitors is an automatic Enfield, Honda Kinetic, or Yamaha **motorcycle,** which can be rented by the day or month through most hotels and guest houses in virtually every town and beach. **Motorcycles are convenient and exciting but also dangerous,** and an Indian or international driver's license is officially required (see **Driving Permits,** p. 13). Goan police have been known to enjoy busting unlicensed bikers in the cities

(Panjim, Mapusa, Madgaon), although license enforcement on the beaches is notoriously lax (except in Anjuna during Wednesday's flea market). If you are pulled over by a police officer, and you do not have a valid license, keep your cool and remember that a little *baksheesh* might go a long way. **Helmets** are not compulsory, but there's nothing worse than cracking your skull on the way to that hot rave. With prodding, most bike rental places can drum up a helmet.

Short distances, lack of direct buses and overabundance of motorcycles make hitching an attractive proposition, although riding with a stranger is inherently dangerous and *Let's Go* does not recommend it. **Bicycles** (Rs3-5 per hr., Rs30-50 per day) are a non-polluting alternative and can be rented through hotels and guest houses. You can pedal along the entirety of Colva Beach when the tide is out. Plan to get wet and bring plastic bags for cameras and valuables.

Hard Drugs and Naked Flesh

No, that polite man in Anjuna inquiring "smoke?" isn't bumming a cigarette, he's trying to sell you **hashish.** And if you purchase one of the "Christmas presents" touted in some Vagator cafe, you'll get a mild dose of acid instead of the expected ribbons and tinsel. Goa's drug culture flourishes in Anjuna and Vagator. But despite all evidence to the contrary, **drugs are illegal** in Goa, and though enforcement waxes and wanes, even exorbitant *baksheesh* might not dissuade the more incorruptible officers of the Goan police force.

Another frequently indulged-in no-no in Goa is **public nudity.** Ambling about in your birthday suit, no matter how free and easy it feels, is a good way to get time behind bars. Women who bathe topless, while not technically breaking the law, will offend the sensibilities of most Goans, as well as Indian and American tourists, and will inevitably attract unwanted leers.

FOOD AND DRINK

Four centuries of European customs and customers have made Goa an oasis for carnivores in the desert of Indian vegetarianism. The quintessential Goan dish, fish curry, is self-explanatory and spicy, while *vindaloo* dishes are vinegary and mild. And so long as you're putting your arteries through their paces, a slice of rich, layered **bebinca** cake brings any Goan meal to a satisfying, seam-splitting conclusion.

Beer and spirits are cheap and easy to find in Goa. Along with the ubiquitous **Kingfisher,** the more robust **Arlem** and **King's** are widely available, while the locally brewed **Belo,** widely available in the South, tends to be overpriced. Western spirits abound, too. Finally, ordering a peg of **feni,** the potent spirit distilled from twice-fermented coconut or cashew sap, will win the respect of any waiter or bartender.

NORTH GOA

■ Panjim (Panaji) पणजी

Mellow and small for a state capital, the city of Panjim (pop. 100,000) covers the south bank of the Mandovi River. Its Portuguese past is most visibly displayed in the porticoed mansions that dominate the narrow streets of the Fountainhas area, fulfilling the romantic, colonialist dream of a quaint miniature Europe transplanted to the East. Panjim effectively became the capital of Goa in 1759, when the viceroy moved from Old Goa to reside in Yusuf Adil Shah's old palace in Panjim (today's Secretariat), and it continued to grow, officially becoming the capital in 1843. Relative to the rest of the state, Panjim positively bustles, but there's a politeness in the "taxi, friend?" of the rickshaw-*wallah* that's rare in urban India.

Mandovi Bridge

TO MAPUSA

Ribandar Causeway

TO OLD GOA AND PONDA

PATTO

TO MERCES

Fishing Jetty

Kadamba Bus Terminal

Patto Bridge

GTDC

i

Panjim

ACCOMMODATIONS

C Hotel Venite
B Hotel Vihar
D Mandovi Pearl Guest House
E Orav's Guest House
G Panjim Inn
F Park Lane Lodge
A Tourist Hotel

Ferry for Mapusa Buses

Dom João Castro

Ourem Rd.

GPO

Foot-bridge

Ourem River

Avenida

31st January Rd.

G.P. Rd.

Ourem Rd.

A

C B

D

E

Emidio Gracia Rd.

C.A. Rd.

Armada Portugesa Rd.

F

FOUNTAIN-HAS

G

TO AIRPORT AND MARGAO

Mandovi River

Abbé de Faria Statue

Secretariat

Karnataka Tourist Office

Dr. R.S. Rd.

Church of the Immaculate Conception

School

Chapel of St. Sebastian

Customs House

Cunha Rivara Rd.

i

Municipal Gardens

Rangoli

CHURCH SQ.

Govt. of India Tourist Office

i

Pe Agnelo

A Pastelaria

Avenida

Frank Shipping Ferry Terminal

State Bank of India

Hotel Mandovi

Sher-e-Punjab

Ormuz Rd.

Cine National

Phone Office

Central Telegraph Office

Dr. Dada Vaidya Rd.

Goenchin

Mahalaxmi Temple

Dr. Pisurleka Rd.

Azad Maidan

Dr. P. Shiragaonkar Rd.

Ferry Ramp

Malaca Rd.

Central Library

Mahatma Gandhi Rd.

Swami Vivekananda Rd.

National Parks Office

Ashok and Samrat Cinemas

18th June Rd.

Borkar Rd.

Dr. Atmaram Borkar Rd.

Dr. Gama Pinto Rd.

Gen. Costa Alvares Rd.

Dayanand Bandodkar Marg

Heliodoro Salgado Rd.

Indian Airlines

Municipal Market

Gen. Bernardo Guedes Rd.

Museum

TO TALEIGAO

Dr. Brazanga Pereira Rd.

200 yards

200 meters

N

Children's Park

Dayanand Bandodkar Marg

TO DONA PAULA, MORMUGAO, AND MIRAMAR

ORIENTATION

Situated on the south bank of the **Mandovi River,** Panjim can be easily navigated on foot. The **Ourem River** joins the Mandovi at Panjim; on the east bank of the Ourem is the **Patto** area, enclosing the chaotic **bus terminal. Emidio Gracia Road** leads west uphill from the Ourem to **Church Square,** dominated by the white facade of the **Immaculate Conception Church.** Here, the **Municipal Gardens** stretch northward almost all the way to the Mandovi River and the **Secretariat.** Past the Secretariat runs **Dayanand Bandodkar (D.B.) Marg (Avenida Dom Joao Castro),** which follows the bank of the Mandovi River. **18th June Road,** featuring a panorama of hotels, eateries, and shops, leads southwest from Church Sq.

PRACTICAL INFORMATION

Airlines: Air India, 18th June Rd. (tel. 231101 or 231104), next to Hotel Fidalgo. Open M-F 9:30am-1pm and 2-5pm, Sa 9:30-1pm. **Skyline NEPC,** B.G. Rd. (tel. 229234), behind the Hotel Delman. Open daily 9am-6pm. **Indian Airlines,** D.B. Marg (tel. 224067). Open M-F 10am-1pm and 2-5pm. **Jet Airways, Air France, TWA, Gulf Air, Air Canada,** 102 Rizvi Chambers (tel. 221472). Open M-F 9am-5:30pm, Sa 9:30am-1:30pm. **British Airways,** M.G. Rd. (tel. 224336). Open M-F 9am-5:30pm, Sa 9:30am-1:30pm. **Thakkers Travel Service,** 2nd Mahalaxmi Chambers (tel. 226678), is an agent for KLM. Open M-F 9:30am-1pm and 2-5:30pm.

Buses: Kadamba Bus Terminal, Patto. Dual prices are for regular/deluxe service. **Interstate buses** to: **Bangalore** (6 and 7pm, 14hr., Rs223); **Bijapur** (8am, 9hr., Rs107); **Mangalore** (11:15pm, 10hr., Rs118/145); **Miraj** (10:30am, 7hr., Rs99); **Mumbai** (4 and 6:30pm, 18hr., Rs277); **Pune** (7pm, 15hr., Rs156/223). Advance reservations are recommended and can be made at the booking office. Most counters are open from 9am-6pm, but try to show up before 4pm, as some close early. **Private buses** departing for the same destinations can also be booked at myriad hotels and travel agents, or just show up at the bus stand (north of Kadamba under the overpass) along the river, and look for the sign with your destination. **Intrastate buses** zip to destinations throughout Goa 6am-8pm. To: **Calangute** (every 15min., 45min., Rs5); **Mapusa** (every 15min., 6am-8pm, express 20min., regular 40min., Rs3); **Madgaon** (every 30min., 1hr., Rs10); **Siolem** (every 30min., 2hr., Rs5).

Local Transportation: Taxis hover in front of the Hotel Mandovi. **Auto-rickshaws** line up near the market and the Municipal Gardens. When the weather's fair, budding capitalists hawk **motorbikes** across the street from the GPO. It's inadvisable to rent in Panjim without an international driver's license. **Bikes** are available at Daud M. Aga (tel. 222670), across from the Cinema National entrance (Rs2 per day). Open M-Sa 9am-1pm and 2-7pm, Su 9am-1pm.

Tourist Office: Government of India Tourist Office, Communidade Building, Church Sq. (tel. 223412). Disappointing brochure selection, but you can browse their booklets for hours just to stay in the A/C. Open M-F 9:30am-1pm and 2-6pm, Sa 9:30am-1pm. **Goa Tourism,** Patto Tourist Home, Dr. Alvares Cross Rd. (tel. 225715; fax 223926), between the traffic bridge and the footbridge on the bank of the Ourem River. Arranges tours and sunset kitsch cruises on the river. Open 24hr.

Currency Exchange: State Bank of India, D.B. Marg (tel. 42132), across from the Hotel Mandovi. Open for exchange only M-F 10am-2pm and 3-4pm, Sa 10am-noon. **Thomas Cook,** D.B. Marg (tel. 221312), exchanges cash and all traveler's checks at better-than-bank rates. Open Oct.-Mar. M-Sa 9:30am-6pm, Su 10am-5pm.

Pharmacy: Hindu Pharmacy, Cunha Rivara Rd. (tel. 223176), to the left of the Hotel Aroma and next to the Municipal Gardens. Open daily 9am-1pm and 3-8pm.

Bookstore: Hotel Mandovi has a passable bookstore, with travel guides, novels, language books, and, as if defying you to explain their existence, decade-old back issues of *Mad* magazine. Open M-Sa 9am-9pm, Su 9am-6pm.

Police: Police Headquarters (tel. 223124), 2 streets to the left of the Hotel Mandovi. Visa extensions are available here, but they take a while.

Emergency: Police, tel. 100. **Fire,** tel. 101.

Hospital: Dr. Bhandare Hospital, Fountainhas (tel. 224966). Go south on 31st January Rd., passing the Panjim Inn; bear left where the road forks and continue to the gates of the hospital. Walk-ins admitted. **Ambulance** (tel. 224096).

Post Office: From the traffic bridge at the Ourem River, continue along the road into Panjim. The **GPO** is on the left behind a garden. The desk to the left as you enter franks stamps and handles *Poste Restante* (M-Sa 9am-6pm), and the counters in the right wing hawk stamps (8am-noon and 1-4pm). **Postal Code:** 403001.

Internet: NetMagic, 7 Shanta Bldg., 18th June Rd. (tel. 224106), behind Don Bosco High School, past the petrol station; go right onto 18th June. NetMagic is five shops down on the left. Web access (Rs100 per hr.) Open M-Sa 9am-1pm and 3:30-6pm.

Telephones: Panjim has recently switched from 5-to 6-digit phone numbers. Replace the leading 4 with 22 in any 5-digit numbers you may stumble across. **Telephone Code:** 0832.

ACCOMMODATIONS

Guest houses and swanky hotels do a brisk business, but since most folks only stay a night or two before heading beachward, same-day accommodations can be easily arranged. Standards (and, sadly, prices) are high for the region, and tariffs often double around Christmas. Two options for dirt-cheap dormitory lodging will console penny-pinchers: the **Patio Tourist Home** (tel. 225715), between the bus terminal and the Ourem (packed to the rafters Dec.-Jan. Rs50; off-season Rs40), and the remote, less crowded **Youth Hostel** (tel. 22533) in suburban Miramar, a 30-minute walk from the town center along D.B. Marg (dorm beds Rs40; check-out 8am).

Panjim Inn, 31st January Rd., Fountainhas (tel. 226523; fax 228136; email Panjimin @bom2.vsnl.net.in), on the left when walking south from Emidio Gracia Rd. Set in a 17th century mansion, the Inn, with an accommodating staff, vine-covered veranda, and antique furniture, quickly becomes home. Internet service. Hot showers, all in attached baths. Check-out 9am. In-season: singles Rs495; doubles Rs630; suites Rs720; A/C Rs225 extra. Off-season: Rs360/585/140. Rooms at the equally beautiful adjacent annex, **Pousada,** are about 20% cheaper, but call well in advance for a reservation. Check-out 9am. MC, Visa.

Park Lane Lodge, Fountainhas (tel. 227154 or 220238), near St. Sebastian Chapel. Head north along 31st January Rd.; it's visible from the main road. Cozy common TV room/study and a terrace. Rooms with common bath are far more spacious than those with attached bath. Lockers. Check-out 8am. In-season: singles with common baths Rs360; doubles with attached baths Rs300. Off-season: Rs160/180.

Tourist Hotel, Dr. Alvares Costa Rd. (tel. 227103), a few blocks northwest after crossing Patto Bridge. GTDC institutionality breeds cleanliness, but also sterility—even the welcome mats in the rooms are government-issue. Rooms have attached baths, fans, clean sheets and towels, and telephones; some have TVs. Noon checkout coddles layabouts of all nationalities. In-season: doubles Rs320; with A/C Rs600. Peak season: 10% increase. Off-season: Rs250/550.

Mandovi Pearl Guest House, (tel. 223928), just scamper up the hill behind the Tourist Hotel. Large rooms with a unique blend of carpet and furnishings, but well-kept. All have attached baths, some with seat toilets. Hot water Rs5 per bucket. Check-out 9am. In-season: singles Rs350; doubles Rs450. Off-season: Rs150/175.

Orav's Guest House, 31st January Rd., (tel. 226128). A family-run spot with rooms of widely varying quality. The more expensive ones facing the front are a much better value than the cramped interior rooms. Check-out 9am. In-season: doubles Rs150-300; family room Rs400-700. Off-season: Rs100-250/400.

FOOD

Panjim's myriad top-drawer eateries may be the best reason to stay in the city longer than it takes to hail a beach-bound taxi. Visitors pick from chow mein, lasagna, South Indian snacks, Gujarati *thalis,* Punjabi *dal,* and Goan fish curry.

Rangoli, Ormuz Rd., near Cine National. A large, colorful sign painted on the wall directs diners to a shady staircase at the back of the building. Waiters provide endless fresh *chapatis,* along with curries, chutneys, pickles, peppers, and curd. Marvelous pure-veg. Gujarati *thali* Rs40. Open daily 11am-3pm and 7-10pm.

Sher-e-Punjab (tel. 225657), on the 1st fl. of Hotel Aroma, on the west edge of the Municipal Gardens. The delicacies that emerge from the restaurant's well-known tandoor (entrees Rs75) will remind you why you eat meat in the first place. Open daily noon-3:30pm and 7-11:30pm.

Hotel Vihar (tel. 225744), around the corner north of Hotel Venite. Enormously popular, this stainless steel and formica greasy spoon serves up meal-sized *dosa* and *samosas* (Rs11) masquerading as snacks. Veg. *thali* Rs19. Open daily 7-9am, 11am-3pm, and 6:30-9pm.

Goenchin, Dr. Dada Vaidya Rd. (tel. 227614), on the left if you're coming from Church Sq. The delicious Chinese food is only slightly Indianesque (you can even request chopsticks), and the ambience is swank. Most entrees go for Rs80-90; veg. Rs60-70. Open daily 12:30-3pm and 7:30-11pm.

Hotel Venite (tel. 225537). Turn north from Emidio Gracia Rd. at the bright orange and blue Quench Corner, then head north towards the Mandovi River. A sign will direct you up a narrow staircase. Self-pitying Westerners eat macaroni and cheese (Rs60), but Venite's fish curry (Rs60), and nightly specials (Rs60-100) are what really bring in the crowds. Have a beer or a *feni* (coconut or cashew Rs20), or try the artery-clogging *bebinca.* Open M-Sa 8am-3pm and 7-11pm.

A Pastelaria, Dr. Dada Vaidya Rd. (tel. 225718). On the left side of Dr. Dada Vaidya Rd. heading toward the Mahalaxmi Temple from Church Sq. Another haunt for the homesick, with sweet bakery delights (Rs12-18). Discount 15% during Happy Hour (7:30-8:30pm). Open M-Sa 9am-8:30pm, Su 9am-1pm.

SIGHTS

Not even the tourist offices pretend that there are any honest-to-goodness sights in Panjim. Still, it's a pleasant place for idle meandering, particularly the Fountainhas area on the west bank of the Ourem.

The bright white **Chapel of St. Sebastian,** dating from the 1880s, stands at the end of a short street opening off 31st January Rd. *(Open daily 6:30-8am.)* The life-sized crucifix that used to hang in the Palace of the Inquisition in Old Goa hangs here now, open-eyed and head unbowed. In Church Sq. stands the **Mary Immaculate Conception Church (Igreja Maria Immaculada Conceicao),** the top tier of a stack of white and blue criss-crossing staircases. *(Open Su and Holy Days of Obligation 10:30am-1pm and 6:15-7pm, other days 9am-1pm and 3:30-6pm.)* The outside of the church is usually crowded with playful school kids in their starched uniforms. The original chapel, consecrated in 1541, was the first stop for Portuguese sailors thanking God for a safe voyage. The chapel was renovated in the 17th century. This is the main place of worship for local Christians, and its musty dark interior is heavy with silence and prayer.

The **Secretariat** sits on the banks of the River Mandovi. The grand white building was constructed in the 16th century as a palace and fortress for Yusuf Adil Shah of Bijapur. The Portuguese rebuilt it in 1615, and in 1759 it became the palace of the Portuguese viceroy. A bit farther downstream lies Panjim's most auspicious monument—a dark statue of a man hypnotizing a buxom lady. The man is Abbé José de Faria, an expatriate Goan priest who gained fame (and eventually infamy) as a hypnotist in 19th-century Paris. Faria was ruined by rumors that he took undue liberties with his female groupies, rumors that the monument does little to dispel. The **Mahalaxmi Temple,** with a large open marble sacred space, can be reached by following Dr. Dada Vaidya Rd. southwest from Church Sq.

ENTERTAINMENT

Panjim provides generously for the age-old entertainment of consuming alcohol. Local brews are sold in small shops, and tiny bars lurk throughout the city, especially in Fountainhas. Try **Kwality Bar & Restaurant,** Church Sq., a place where Chinese flavor, wicker lanterns, Stevie Wonder tunes, and Goan hipsters all come together.

Government and private companies still organize **evening cruises** on the Mandovi River. The cruises feature traditional dancing—*denki, fijddi,* Portuguese, and *corredmino* dances—and, depending on the time, a stunning view of the sunset at sea. Book at any GTDC office, or just show up at the pier and look for the boat. (Daily shows at 6 and 7:15pm. Rs60.) Check an English-language newspaper to find what's showing at Panjim's three **cinemas:** the **Samrat** and the **Ashok** (which shows the dregs of English and American cinema), are in the same building on 18th June Rd., and the **Cine National** is behind the Hotel Aroma on Ormuz Rd.

■ Old Goa ओल्ड गोवा

Tourists who won't venture inland from the beaches might think European fascination with Goa began in 1970s Calangute. Old Goa, 9km east of Panjim along the Mandovi River, gives the lie to this myth, evoking the 16th-century glory days of Portuguese rule, when the city of 200,000 was hailed as the "Rome of the Orient." The euphoria began in 1510, when Alfonso de Albuquerque, the original Portuguese man-o'-war, trounced the Bijapur Sultan and seized the capital on the Mandovi, then known as Ela. Regional control gave the Portuguese a valuable monopoly, allowing the city to attract wealth, sailors, and the epic debauchery such elements inevitably create. Galvanized by the tales of sin, the Jesuits arrived shortly thereafter, targeting hedonists and heathens with the proselytizing zeal that culminated in the horrors of the Inquisition. As Portuguese fortunes declined, so did Portuguese India. Old Goa's demise was hastened by malaria epidemics and silting in the Mandovi—by the 17th century the party had ended for good, and the seat of government moved to Panjim. Today's viceroys are not aristocratic *hidalgos,* but the Archaeological Survey of India, plastering the churches to keep them from crumbling in the monsoon.

At the center of Old Goa, along the main road from Panjim, the yellow **Cathedral of St. Catherine da Sé** looms to the left from an expanse of the green trimmed lawn. Erected by the viceroy in 1564, the vast, three-naved cathedral was 80 years in the building. One of the cathedral's twin towers was destroyed by lightning in 1775, and the other houses the mellow-toned **Sino du Ouro (Golden Bell),** said to be the largest bell in Asia. Scenes from the life of St. Catherine are carved into the grand golden altar; and fourteen smaller ones are set within the cavernous church. Large pillars and somber silences may inspire, but try not to vocalize your reactions too loudly; this is still an active place of worship. Also in the Cathedral complex is the former **Convent and Church of St. Francis of Assisi.** Tread softly upon the church floor—it is paved with coats of arms marking family graves that date back as far as the 16th century. Gold ornamentation and oil paintings adorn the walls, holding fast against the advancing orange water stains. Mary and Jesus are depicted with dark hair and complexions, similar to the dark-skinned cherubs in the Sé Cathedral. The attached convent is now the **Archaeological Museum,** which displays portraits of the viceroys, currency from "India Portuguesa," Christian icons, and sculpture from Goan Hindu temples. *(Open Sa-Th 10am-5pm.)*

Across the road, the **Basilica de Bom Jesus,** (Cathedral of the Baby Jesus), with its dark orange stone walls, may be Old Goa's most legendary site. *(Open M-Sa 9am-6:30pm, Su 10:30am-6:30pm.)* The Basilica was built between 1594 and 1605 to house the remains of St. Francis Xavier. Its interior is an explosion of gold, attesting to the former wealth of the Goans in India. At the far end of the nave, above the altar, is a painting of St. Francis Xavier embracing Christ on the cross. The saint's mausoleum is set off to the right of the altar behind a curtain of stars. Inside the windowed silver casket, a lightbulb shines on St. Francis' slightly shriveled body, which was "donated" by Cosimo III de Medici in exchange for a pillow on which the saint's head rested. A doorway to the left of the mausoleum leads to a small room with historical "tidbits" and photographs of the relic at different stages. Stairs lead to an **art gallery** with trippy modern religious works, scenes from the life of Goa's favorite do-gooder, and an aerial view of the casket. *(Open Sa-Th 9:30am-12:30am and 2-5:30pm).*

Divine Dismemberment, Part Two

When he was 36, Spanish saint Francis Xavier was dispatched to Goa by the king of Portugal, who was worried by reports of the hedonism practiced by his Portuguese subjects there. Although Xavier engaged in social work among Continental sybarites for several months, he found his forte among Subcontinentals: Xavier is said to have won converts by the thousands in India, and whole villages would embrace Christianity mere days after his arrival. Undoubtedly, part of his appeal lay in his aptitude for curing the dying, raising the dead, and performing other mundane feats. God and duty called Xavier on missions to the rest of Asia until his death at the age of 46 in 1552, on the Malaysian coast, where he was buried.

But this was only the beginning for Francis Xavier, known as *Goench Sahib* (Lord of Goa), who performed some of his greatest miracles as a corpse. When, after five months, his body was disinterred to bring the bones back to Goa, it was found to be "fresh as on the day it was buried." Jesuit priests in Goa plunged their fingers into a hole in Xavier's chest and examined the blood for hokey preservatives, but the blood was "smelt and found to be absolutely untainted." Soon everyone wanted a piece of the soon-to-be-canonized Xavier. When the saint's body was installed in the Basilica of Bom Jesus, the Pope got his right arm and parts of his intestines were dispatched to southeast Asia, while Japan cashed in on Xavier's hand. An enshrined fingernail still sits in the Braganza-Perriera mansion in Chandor. Most infamously, during an exposition of the body in 1634, an ecstatic devotee bit off St. Francis' big toe, which gushed blood from her mouth all the way home. Since the canonization in 1622, St. Francis Xavier's relics (minus a few) have been housed in the Basilica de Bom Jesus, where a marble pedestal and a fence restrain the overzealous from swarming the corpse. An exposition is held every ten years (the next is in 2004), during which the wilted body is placed on view in the Sé Cathedral.

To the west of the Sé Cathedral, the **Church of St. Cajetan,** was, according to local lore, built atop an ancient Hindu temple by Italian friars of the Order of Theatines in the 17th century. Today it's known for its unique dome (modeled after St. Peter's in Rome) and the elaborate woodwork of the interior. Here, the ruined gate to Yusuf Adil Shah's collapsed palace rises in a forlorn tribute to pre-Portuguese Goa. Up the road toward the Mandovi River, the **Viceroy's Arch** patiently waits to receive another incoming Portuguese viceroy, who would be handed the keys to the capital as he ceremoniously passed under the arch. There is an inscription on the arch left by Governor Francisco da Gama (r. 1597-1600) in memory of his great-grandfather Vasco. Up the hill to the west of the Basilica de Bom Jesus are the ruins of the **Church of St. Augustine.** The 46m tower has stood stubbornly since 1602. Gravestones line the floor, and the knobby alcoves have hints of carvings. Across the street, at the **Church and Convent of St. Monica Christon,** the "miracle cross" probably won't open its eyes, bleed from its wounds, and try to speak, as it did for patrons in 1636, but a peek couldn't hurt. *(Churches open daily 8am-5:30pm, but may close for a 12:30-3pm siesta.)*

Auto-rickshaws (Rs50), **motorcycles,** and **bicycles** easily make the scenic, 9km trip along the Mandovi riverbank from Panjim to Old Goa. **Buses** also shuttle from Panjim's bus terminal (every 15min. 7am-7pm, 20min., Rs3). Unofficial guides, frequenting the churches for earthly reasons, are chock full of history and legends, and they expect to be tipped. For eats, *dhabas* serve snacks (Rs10-20).

■ Near Old Goa

A handful of Hindu temples lurk deceptively near the Portugese ruins of Old Goa, on NH4 and between Panjim and Ponda. Although far from India's finest, they provide daytrippers with an interesting glimpse of the Hindu majority behind coastal Goa's Portuguese facade. As active (and sometimes hyperactive) places of worship, they provide a refreshing contrast to beachfront hedonism.

Six temples hide near NH4, conveniently becoming less interesting the closer one gets to drab **Ponda**. Thus, for visitors who tire of the temples, it's a simple matter of hopping a bus back to **Panjim** (every 30 min. 7am-8pm, 1hr.; Rs10). Disembarking at **Mangeshi** (also called Priol) village, a colorful arch highlights the walkway to the **Sri Manguesh** temple. Like most of the temples in this area, it was built in the 18th century to house deities smuggled inland in the 16th century from the Inquisition-ravaged coast. Just a 15-minute walk south leads to the more sedately decorated **Sri Mahalsa**, acclaimed for the wood carvings on the facades of its *mandapa* (sloping roof). Veering right off NH4, 10 minutes farther south, the paved road winds west to **Vingua** village. As the town square with its cement shine looms into view, a gate and steps lead south to the **Sri Laxmi Narcenha**. The interior is closed to non-believers, but heathens can gawk at the temple's lovely water tank. From here, it's best to hop a bus or thumb a ride on the 4km stretch to the Farmagudi junction, where an equestrian statue of Shivaji points down a narrow back road through **Nageshi** village to the **Sri Naguesh** temple. Colorful woodcarvings in the entrance hall depict scenes from the **Ramayana** (see p. 94), though it's difficult to piece together the narrative. Lumbering down the road another 20 minutes (keep right), hordes of buses indicate you've arrived at **Sri Shantadurga**, notable for its size, Western influences, and tourist multitudes. As long as you're here, the ornate silver screen at the **Sri Ramnath** (10min. up the road to your left as you exit Shantadurga) is worth a peek.

■ Mapusa म्हापुसा

Mapusa (MAP-sa) clings to a hillside about 30km north of Panjim and about 10km inland from the hopping beaches at Anjuna, Calangute, and Baga. As the main population center for North Goa, Mapusa is of interest to travelers for its bus terminal. Most beach-cravers coming from Mumbai or Bangalore jump off the bus at Mapusa and head straight for the sand.

ORIENTATION AND PRACTICAL INFORMATION Mapusa's dismal, but at least it's easy to leave; throngs of buses shuttle frequently from the **Kadamba Bus Terminal** to the North Goa beaches, Panjim, and Madgaon. Buses run from 6am to 8:15pm and travel to: **Anjuna** (every 20min., 45min., Rs3.50); **Arambol** (8, 10am, and 1pm, 1hr., Rs10); **Baga and Calangute** (every 20min., 30min., Rs4); **Madgaon** (every hr., 1½hr., Rs17); **Panjim** (every 15min., express 20min., local 40min., Rs4); and **Siolim** (every 30min., Rs3). **Motorcycle rentals** are hard to come by, due to Mapusa's police crackdown on foreigners without papers; would-be easy-riders rent in the resort villages. If you're heading to Mumbai, Bangalore, or Pune, there's no reason to go to Panjim to book and catch a bus. The area around Kadamba teems with private coach operators. The state-run bus stand's long distance booking office is conveniently located opposite bus stall 8 (open daily 9am-noon and 2-5:30pm.) Buses run to: **Hubli** (11:30am, Rs57, 5hr.); **Miraj** (10:45am, Rs91, 5hr.); **Mumbai** (3:30, 4, 4:30, and 7pm, 17hr., Rs277); and **Pune** (regular 6:30am, deluxe 7:30pm, 14hr., Rs138/223).

For currency exchange, the **State Bank of India** is to the right as you exit the front of the bus terminal (open M-F 10am-2pm, Sa 10am-noon.) Two blocks west are the police station (tel. 262231) and the **GPO**. Though the post office is open for *Poste Restante* (M-Sa 9am-noon and 3-6pm), the offices in tourist-saturated Anjuna and Calangute are more efficient. **Postal Code:** 403507.

ACCOMMODATIONS AND FOOD Finding lodging in Mapusa presents a catch-22: if you've planned ahead, there shouldn't be any need to stay here; if you haven't, you're unlikely to find any vacancies. In an emergency, taking a taxi to Calangute or Panjim might be more productive than trying to find a good place on short notice in Mapusa. If it is necessary to stay overnight in Mapusa, the **Tourist Hostel** (tel. 262694), visible from the roundabout where the buses stop, will make you feel more like the just-off-the-bus tourist that you are (check-out noon; doubles Rs250; quads Rs320; off-season: Rs200/260). To the left of the Tourist Hostel at the next roundabout stands the **Hotel**

Satya Heera (tel. 262849), with spacious rooms, spectacular views (on the upper floors), and even an antiquated TV (check-out 9am; doubles Rs300, with A/C Rs600; triples Rs400/700; MC,Visa). **Ruchira,** the hotel's rooftop restaurant, serves Goan, Chinese, and pan-Indian dishes Rs10-60 (open daily 7-11am and 11:30am-10:45pm). Myriad food stalls around the bus terminal serve delicious, grimy fare, and every Friday, Mapusa's **market**, southeast of the bus terminal, cooks up a more authentically Indian version of the Anjuna flea market (open early morning-late afternoon).

■ Calangute कालांगुद and Baga बागा

Once winter hangouts of the backpacker set, Calangute and Baga have largely sold out to the security of package tourism. Calangute is more densely commercialized—if you drop a rupee, it's apt to land on a guest house, restaurant, or Kashmiri rug shop. Wizened locals, ex-pats, and travel guides tantalize newcomers with tales of Calangute in its late-70s hedonistic heyday, full of free drugs, free love, and (for the voyeuristic Indian gawkers who came in droves) a free peep show. Today, it's difficult to see what all the fuss was about. Certainly, the *laissez-faire* attitude is gone. Police strictly enforce the beaches' "no nudity" ordinance and frequently shut down the rickety shacks fronting the beach on the slightest suspicion of drug-peddling. Rampant (by Goan standards) development has further narrowed what was never an expansive beach with resorts and seafood shacks that stretch all the way to Baga village, 2.5km north. Today, while the sunsets are rarely enhanced with anything stronger than an ice-cold Kingfisher, Calangute and Baga still provide sun and a brief escape to an impressive number of people.

ORIENTATION

Most **buses** from out of town plod into Calangute **market** at the base of the main road heading west to the **beach.** Proceed straight along this road for about 1km and make a right at the **roundabout** (before the beach) and onto the Calangute-Baga strip, where most budget accommodations are found. There are two main roads in Calangute and Baga, an east-west road leading from the **market** west to the **beach,** around which clutter the hotels and restaurants of Calangute proper, and a north-south road which intersects it at the roundabout before heading 2km north to Baga.

PRACTICAL INFORMATION

Buses: Buses stop at the stand at Calangute market before rolling some 800m to the beach, halting just before the sea. From there, some continue to Baga. Buses on the Panjim-Calangute-Mapusa route stop at the market, the roundabout, and just before the beach. The slightly-less-frequent buses that also head to Baga stop at the market, the roundabout, and in Baga village (Rs3).

Local Transportation: Tourist taxis will take you between Calangute and Baga for around Rs40-50. **Rickshaws** and **motorbikes** will do the same for about Rs30-40 (to Panjim Rs150, to Anjuna Rs100). All three types of vehicles hover near the Calangute bus stand. **Motorcycle Rental:** signs appear everywhere in season. Otherwise, ask taxi drivers or around the gas station west of the market. **Bicycle Rental:** Look for the signs, or try **Jay-Jay's,** on the road between Baga and Calangute. Open daily 8am-7pm.

Budget Travel: MGM Travels (tel. 276073), on the Calangute roundabout, handles plane and catamaran tickets, and has fax and **STD/ISD** telephone services. In season: open daily 9am-7pm. Off-season: M-Sa 9:30am-6pm.

Currency Exchange: State Bank of India, located past the roundabout heading away from the beach, on the left. Open M-F 10am-2pm, Sa 10am-noon. **Prince Santosh** (tel. 276417), on the inland side of the Calangute-Baga road, exchanges all major traveler's checks and currencies. Open daily 9am-10pm.

Bookstore: Rama Books & Jewelry, at the roundabout, right before the Tourist Hostel, swaps English, German, and French books. Open daily 9am-7pm.

Pharmacy: Calangute Medical Stores, Shop #B-11 of the beachfront "Tourist Complex" stocks its shelves with over-the-counter goodies. Open daily 9am-7pm.

Post Office: Located in a cute pink building south of the market and to the left. Open 9am-1pm and 2-5pm.

Internet: The Computer Spot at Shivam Xerox (tel. 276290) has Web access. Rs150 per hr. Open M-Sa 9am-1:30pm and 2:30-6:30pm.

Telephone Code: 0832.

ACCOMMODATIONS

Accommodations swarm around the main villages and the road between them, offering attached doubles for under Rs200. In general, the ones close to Baga offer more pleasant surroundings, though most places between the villages are far from the beach. Haggling can be profitable until around mid-December. Unless otherwise indicated, expect prices to double during peak season (Dec. 20-Jan. 5). Try to show up before then or call ahead to reserve rooms at better rates. Flats and houses for longer stays, the more desirable ones being just north of Baga, are still available in early December. Watch for signs and ask around.

Venar Holiday Home (tel. 276867), halfway between Calangute and Baga on the inland side of the road. Run by the world's nicest family, who rents several rooms in a large house and several more in separate cottages. All have fans and 24hr. running water; hot water is available by the bucket. Check-out noon. Sometimes closed off season. In-season: singles Rs225, with attached bath Rs250; doubles Rs250-300. Extra bed Rs25. Off-season: prices go down about Rs100.

Albenjoh (tel. 276422), just north of Calangute on the inland side. Resort-style whitewash, terraces, and lovely gardens at guest house prices. In-season: Rs400. Off-season: Rs100-150.

Alidia Cottages (tel. 27901 or 276835), farther along the road to Baga, behind a white church on the left. Another friendly, family-run establishment. Best of all, wander through the back gate, past the tiny fishing village and right to the blissful beach. Check-out noon. In October, rates begin an upward climb, reaching Rs700 by winter. Off-season: doubles Rs150. Discounts for long-term singles.

Joaquin (tel. 276969—the home of the proprietress' sister), just off the east-west road that leads to Tito's. From the main north-south road, head east between the Sunshine Beach and Miranda Resorts and looks for signs on your right. Beautiful rooms with sparkling attached baths. Guests savor the thatched roof patio. Check-out noon. In-season: Rs400-500. Off-season: Rs300.

Four Seasons (formerly Lucky Bar & Restaurant), along the main road in Baga. Rents rooms in a building near the beach or in brightly painted cottages with attached

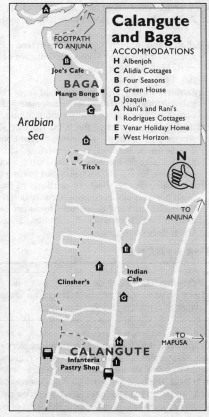

Calangute and Baga
ACCOMMODATIONS
H Albenjoh
C Alidia Cottages
B Four Seasons
G Green House
D Joaquin
A Nani's and Rani's
I Rodrigues Cottages
E Venar Holiday Home
F West Horizon

WEST INDIA

bath and 24hr. running water. In-season: doubles Rs300, with hot water Rs350; triples Rs400/450; cottage doubles Rs250. Off-season: rooms Rs100-150.

Nani's and Rani's, (tel. 276313), north of Baga, across the river—you can't miss it. The cream of the northern crop. The splendid doubles (all attached) clutter around the house's popular restaurant. Singles with common bath Rs150; doubles with fan Rs250. One A/C room Rs.400.

Rodrigues Cottages (tel. 276538), across from the Calangute Association building. Basic rooms strung around a courtyard, all with attached bath. Proprietress is amenable to further discounts for "poor" travelers. Rooms Rs100-150.

West Horizon, (tel. 276489). From the main north-south road, turn seaward at the sign for Hotel Carey's, and follow the road as it becomes sand and ends at the Beach Queen Guest House. Then turn due left—it's 100m away through the pines. A ramshackle hut with some brightly painted concrete rooms added on for guests. Bathroom fixtures are relatively new and clean, and the place gets bonus points for beach proximity. In-season: doubles Rs200. Off-season: Rs100.

Green House (tel. 277434), inland on the main north-south road. The smallest single may be the cheapest in town. Common baths. Clean enough, especially considering what you're paying. Rooms Rs100-150.

FOOD

You can't please all of the people all of the time, but that doesn't stop the throngs of touristy seafood shacks here from trying. Copycat menus proffer mediocre renditions of regional delights and favorites from home, whether that's in Beijing, Boston, or Bologna. Still, the seafood is good, and if you're just craving a good spot to meet fellow travelers over a cold beer and a sunset, try the popular and serviceable **Britto's** or **St. Anthony's,** side by side on the Baga beachfront.

Indian Cafe, midway between Calangute and Baga. Look for the sign on the main north-south road. A curious combination of currency exchange and cafe. Excellent *masala dosa* (Rs18). An excellent lunchtime retreat. Open daily 8am-6pm. Closed Jun. 1-Sept. 31.

Infanteria Pastry Shop, to the right from the roundabout, by the church. Pastries galore, doughnuts (plain Rs7, chocolate Rs10), pizzas, and fresh soups. Open daily 8am-9pm. Table service stops about 30min. before closing.

Clinsher's, just west of the West Horizon Guest House, or follow the large, fish-shaped sign, from the Calangute tourist complex along the beach. Excellent, moderately priced seafood, in surroundings so tranquil you can hear the waves lapping in the distance. Friendly and attentive wait-staff tout the restaurant's brush with greatness: John Malkovich stopped in for a drink in 1997. Closed Jun. 1-Aug. 31.

Joe's Cafe, on the southern outskirts of Baga, serves cheap, tasty breakfasts and fresh juice on tables cunningly constructed of curvy brick pillars. Omelettes Rs20. For health nuts and those needing to dry out, a variety of fresh juices combos are available, with or without spirulina, an algae with reputed healing properties. Open daily 8am-6pm.

THE BEACHES

> **Warning:** The water on some beaches is off limits during the monsoon season because of rough waves and dangerous undertow. Ask before taking a dip and be aware of boulders and steep drop-outs.

The strip between Calangute and Baga is good, if not great, as Goan beaches go. Despite the development, the sands are very quiet in the morning, and the water is incredibly calm. Toward noon, however, crowds of daytrippers and package tourists begin to come steadily trickle in from the village to the beach. As the beach bleeds into Baga, the beaches get wider while crowds grow thinner and bodies get younger and buffer, as backpackers strive to work up a credible tan before heading north. South of the Baga end of the beach, a strip of beach is designated as the area for water sports. **Goan Bananas** (tel. 276362) has a fleet of boats that run the gamut of tourist watersports. (Water-skiing Rs450 for 15min. Parasailing Rs1000 for 15min. Being dragged behind the boat on a giant inflatable banana Rs200 for 15min. Ubiquitous Goa puns free.) Next door, **Atlantis** rents windsurfers (Rs250 per hr.). **Fishing boats,** chartered by numerous companies in season, make the wet and wild journey to the Anjuna flea market every Wednesday, and offer dolphin, crocodile, and mud-soaked hippie-spotting tours at similar rates (Rs200-500 per day).

ENTERTAINMENT AND NIGHTLIFE

Despite a raucous past, nightlife in today's Calangute and Baga tends to wind up early, and errs on the side of resort-area hokeyness. The more upscale hotels pack their bar-restaurants with the sort of live "musicians" who'd be confined to street-performing back home, though there are worse places to begin or wind up a night of drunken revelry. Aside from surf-splashing and beer-swilling, there's little to do here—but isn't that why you came in the first place?

For nightlife without the schmaltz, the reggae-themed **Mango Bongo** bar—a beach shack transplanted onto the main Baga road—plays red, black, and green tunes, and serves until as late as 1am during the season. But even their bartenders acknowledge that there's only one after-hours game in town—**Tito's,** a bar-restaurant on the Baga beach that serves expensive drinks, accompanied by a dance floor and boomin' hi-fi, often until the break of dawn. Outside the village proper, the **West End,** a somewhat tame party venue on the road between Calangute and Panjim, hosts parties as often as twice a week in December and January. Watch for their flyers, or ask area bartenders and taxi-*wallahs* eager to take you there (Rs50-150). Calangute isn't well-connected to the party scene farther north, but closer to Baga you're more likely to catch word of happenings in Anjuna or Vagator.

■ Near Calangute: Fort Aguada and Candolim

Mocked and scorned by scenesters farther north, the resort-packed village of **Candolim** is largely the preserve of well-off, older package tourists. But the hillside south of the Taj hides the impressive 17th-century **Aguada Fort,** which guards the mouth of the Mandovi. Follow the Candolim road south past the Taj, and keep right as it winds 3km uphill. The citadel commands an excellent view of the Mandovi and the southern coast, but if you can find someone to let you in the oddly shaped lighthouse the view is even better.

Between the citadel and the river lurks the **Central Aguada Jail,** filled with native and imported drug offenders. From the citadel, follow the road east as it curves downhill and southwest. Charitable folks eager to conduct works of mercy (or pretenders hungry for juicy conversation) can show up (Tu and F 9am-noon and 3-5pm) to chat with inmates who don't have another monthly visit scheduled.

Goa Trance

At least one aspect of Goa's party scene has transcended international borders. **Goa trance music,** also known as "psychedelic" or "psyche" trance (because of its supposed psychoactive effects), has emerged as one of the most popular forms of techno music around the world. Relying on multi-layered, harmonic synthesizer patterns rather than thick, pounding bass pulses, Goa trance is said by fans to represent the merging of technology with tribalism and spiritualism. Don't be fooled—there's absolutely nothing Indian about this music, except for the occasional Sanskrit chant or catch-phrase ("Bom Shankar!" "Aum Shiva!") sampled over the sound. Instead, Goa trance emerged from the subculture of travelers to India, making it possible for partiers in Tokyo, Tel Aviv, and the rest of the world to taste the Goa freak scene without ever leaving home.

■ Anjuna आंजुना

October through March, Anjuna hustles with beach raves, full-moon parties, jungle boogies, and all the accompanying psychedelic mayhem. Seaside restaurants and low cottages with red roofs run along the shore to the hill in the distance. For many a bud-get hedonist, the Goan ideal—idyllic beachside days, wild, raving nights, and a liberal dose of cheap drugs to smooth the transition between the two—is realized only in Anjuna. The village's charms (or vices, for in Anjuna, they're one and the same) have been more resistant to police crackdowns than those of its southern neighbors. Anjuna continues its wonderful way of marking time—a beautiful sunset tags each day, each week brings psychedelic mayhem in the form of Anjuna's famous flea mar-ket (unfortunately closed during the off season), and the world-renowned full-moon raves mark the months. As Christmas approaches the parties escalate in intensity and frequency. Despite attempts to tame its wild side, Anjuna still plays host to a crazy cast of characters from freaks to fishermen, package tourists to smacksters, Euro-yup-pies to Kashmiri handicraft hawkers—which are you?

> **Warning: Theft happens frequently in Anjuna,** particularly on party nights. Carry important documents and valuables on you, or lock them somewhere safe.

ORIENTATION

From Anjuna's main intersection (crowned by the Starro Restaurant), roads lead west to the beachfront and bus stand, east to Mapusa and most banking facilities, south to the fleamarket grounds and restaurants, and north to Vagator and some of the main party venues.

PRACTICAL INFORMATION

Buses: Buses stop at the end of the road above the beach and at several places along the road away from the beach To: **Calangute** and **Baga** (20min., Rs50); **Mapusa** (20min., Rs50); **Panjim** (30min., Rs100); **Vagator** (10min., Rs30).

Local Transportation: Taxis and **auto-rickshaws** loiter near the bus stand. **Motor-cycles and bicycles** can also be rented along the main road at standard rates.

Currency Exchange: The exchange at **Orchard Food Stores** stocks exotic goodies like Pringles, Marmite, and ketchup. Open daily 9am-9pm, shorter hours in the off season. Visa encashments can be had at the **Bank of Baroda** (tel. 274460), but their hours are short and wildly various. Open daily 9:30am-1:30pm and 2:30-6pm; closed Su off season. Show up at around 11am on a weekday and wish hard, or just head down the road to the Mapusa branch, closer to the beach.

Budget Travel: MGM Travels (tel. 274317) deals with plane tickets, reconfirma-tions, and car rentals. In-season: open M-Sa 9am-6pm. Off-season: 9:30am-6pm.

Bookstore: Johnson's Library and **The South Anjuna Information** are both on Anjuna's main drag.

Police: On the road away from the beach, on the left.

Post Office: Sub-post office, 2km up the road from the beach, on the right, has *Poste Restante.* Open M-Sa 9:30am-noon and 2:30-4:30pm. **Postal Code:** 403509.

Telephones: Nehal Communications, across from the bus stand, boasts a 24hr. **STD/ISD** facility. **Telephone Code:** 0832.

ACCOMMODATIONS

Anjuna has acquired a somewhat undeserved reputation as a difficult place to find a bed, particularly during the peak season. A lack of phones in most guest houses rules out reservations, but those who show up are generally rewarded with a room. Addi-tionally, because of the large number of long-termers, houses here aren't as prone to the insane Yuletide price fluctuations of their southern counterparts. Guest houses hug the beachfront and the Mapusa Road. South of the flea market grounds lies a ver-itable tourist colony for long-stayers, a good place to look for bare-bones house or room lodgings for stays ranging from a week to several months. In-season prices are listed. As a rule, bargaining is the way to go at other times of the year.

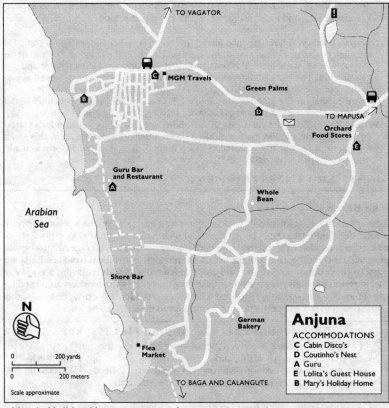

Guru Bar and Restaurant

Arabian Sea

Shore Bar

N

0   200 yards
0   200 meters

Scale approximate

TO VAGATOR

MGM Travels

Green Palms

TO MAPUSA

Orchard Food Stores

Whole Bean

German Bakery

Flea Market

TO BAGA AND CALANGUTE

Anjuna
ACCOMMODATIONS
C Cabin Disco's
D Coutinho's Nest
A Guru
E Lolita's Guest House
B Mary's Holiday Home

Mary's Holiday Home (tel. 273216), directly behind the Sea Rock Restaurant. A number of attached doubles, close to the beachfront action, but the rooms face inland, providing quiet, communal tranquility. Satisfied customers sing the praises of the showers. Doubles Rs175-250.

Coutinho's Nest (tel. 274386), a 15min. walk down the main road. An excellent, affable place to tuck your head under your wing after a hard day of beachcombing. Doubles with shared (but shiny and convenient) bathroom Rs150.

Cabin Disco's, on the south side of the road, about 1km from the sea. Cool clientele boogie-oogie-oogie their way into comfy tasteful rooms after a mellow evening in the groovy bar-restaurant. Fortunately, the mattresses refrain from doing the bump. Doubles Rs200, with attached bath Rs250.

Guru Bar-Restaurant and Guest House. Bare rooms are airy and serviceable, but outdoor common shower is a bit muddy. For better or worse, the bar is a hub of the beachfront dope scene. Singles Rs100; doubles Rs150. Off-season: a few rooms available for Rs100.

Lolita's Guest House, just north of the Orchard Store, a 30min. walk from the beach. The homey, freshly painted bungalows are an excellent place for a rendezvous with the nymphet of your dreams. The immaculate doubles, stocked with a fridge and a sound system, may prove to be the light of your life. Doubles Rs350.

FOOD

Anjuna seaside fare is fast, cheap, greasy, and plentiful. Those not blessed with stomachs of steel will be better off at the restaurants lining the road that curves away from the **Shore Bar,** which pack more variety and flavor than their sea-side brethren. On Wednesday, an abundance of foodstalls materialize out of the ether to make the **flea**

market Anjuna's premier spot for lunch or early dinner—the atmosphere is unbeatable. These places, and those listed below, are closed off season.

German Bakery. Follow the road inland from the Shore Bar and watch carefully for the sign. Not to be confused with the German Bakery at the Paradise Restaurant on the main road. Batik-printed hippie boys and angst-ridden babes lounge and sip cappuccino. The laid-back atmosphere comes complete with savory baked goods in the morning, veg. North Indian chow at night. Open daily 7am-midnight.

Green Palms, on the Mapusa road about 1.5km inland. Enjoy the delicious falafel sandwich (Rs40) and a banana milkshake (Rs20). Open M-Sa noon-10:30pm.

Whole Bean, along the road east of the Shore Bar. For every vegan who's stared enviously while a fellow patron slurped down a delicious banana *lassi*, this small tofu shop pours out soy milkshakes in a variety of flavors (Rs30-40). Homemade tofu and tempeh sandwiches (Rs60). Open M-Sa 9:30am-5:30pm.

SIGHTS AND ENTERTAINMENT

The Beach

Perhaps the most stereotypically Goan of the state's beaches, Anjuna's postcard-pretty shores draw understandably large crowds, and tanned, toned ravers in various states of inebriation crash all along the strip. Perhaps the sloth of the average Anjuna beach-goer accounts for the variety of the beach's annoyingly convenient hawkers. It's quite easy to slurp down cold drinks and tropical fruit all day, while having a good ear cleaning and full body massage—practically the only things the hawkers aren't selling are tranquility and solitude. Thronged with tourists, particularly on Wednesdays, this is the beach to sea and be scene, but for peace and quiet, look elsewhere.

> ### Technomics 101: the Anjuna Flea Market
>
> Every Wednesday since time immemorial, or at least since the mid-70s, the invisible hand sparks a joint over the market grounds in southern Anjuna and hordes of rational and irrational economic actors partake in one of the world's freest interplays of market forces (but only in season). Some key terms:
>
> **Demand:** Throngs of tourists of every stripe. Funneled into Anjuna by every form of conveyance in the state, their only common denominator being pockets packed with red hot rupees.
>
> **Supply:** Anyone with a good, service, freaky talent, or disfigurement. In addition to the usual rigmarole of hawkers, ear cleaners and henna painters offer image enhancements while elaborately decorated bulls and prepubescent tightrope walkers clamor for Kodak moments (for a fee, of course).
>
> **Goods:** They ain't greats. Unfortunately, the market is packed with the same stuff you've been refusing all through India, usually at double the price. For the true finds, look for the hawkers from Kashmir or Karnataka, Tibetans with intricate prayer wheels, and Westerners who subsidize their own permanent vacations (or try to scrap together a free home) by selling handcrafted leather goods, trance and dub mixes, and rave gear (including psychedelic pants that would make Jimmy Page blush).
>
> **Price:** Those Kashmiris are itching for revenge after being rebuffed for so long. To avoid paying for the undeniably heady atmosphere, haggle hard.

The Raves

Anjuna's sloping hills have gained international renown as a **rave** venue. The monthly coming of the full moon summons the werewolf lurking within many of Goa's tourists, transforming them from placid beach-chillers into wild, snarling party-beasts, especially during Goa's peak season. New Year's Eve and Christmas Eve are the biggest nights, but things slow only somewhat during the intervening evenings. Roads are rife with people cycling from party to party, and huge fields are deluged with ravers. Good domestic and European DJs broadcast the rave's techno soundtrack to a core of gyrating dancers, themselves surrounded by crowds of people resting and chilling, even as the Goan minions serve them tea, omelettes, chocolate, and smack (not recommended—seaside raves are often sponsored by local drug-dealers, who are willing to shell out the cash for a sound system in order to boost their trade). Understandably, many locals bemoan these monthly debauches, and participants should be considerate, responsible, and, of course, careful.

Other Nightlife

If there isn't any scheduled action, most of the crowd heads to the **Shore Bar,** right in the middle of the beach. The terraced steps leading down to the beach throng with beer guzzling sunbathers or stargazers, depending on the hour. Upstairs, the requisite black lights flicker and imported DJs of varying acumen pilot the gargantuan sound system, as techno ravers go for broke on the small sandy dance floor. Hours vary wildly by season. The **Sea Rock Restaurant,** just south of the bus stand, is another popular hangout, especially for Westerners. Don't worry if you're not hungry since only fractions of the packed restaurants occupants are dining at any one time; the rest are having coffee, tea, or juice, scoping each other out, or sneaking a joint. Farther south, the **Guru Bar** serves tall cold ones late into the night, with a much laxer drug policy. Its southerly neighbor, **Francis Bar and Restaurant** occasionally catches the Saturday night fever, stacks up the tables and chairs, and hires a DJ and sound system for a night of techno and dancing, but don't hold your breath.

■ Vagator वागातोर

Of all the northern beach towns, Vagator strikes the superlative balance between hotspot and hideaway. Popular, but not over-populated, sceney but not seedy, Vagator suns all day and raves all night without losing its cheerful, down-home vibe. A shortage of guest houses makes the town home to mostly longtime dwellers, but the regulars here are less jaundiced than their southern counterparts, probably because the rigors of the tourism boom have yet to sap Vagator's easy, jubilant grace. Provided you can find a place to spend the nights, it's a prime place to while away your days.

ORIENTATION AND PRACTICAL INFORMATION Most resources for the budget traveler in Vagator cluster on the east-west street running inland from Big Vagator Beach. **The Primrose Bar and Restaurant** (heading inland, it's the first right past the See Green Restaurant) besides being a nighttime hot-spot, does **currency exchange** into the wee hours of the morning. **Su Jata Travels** (tel. 273308), just inland from the big beach, handles bookings and reconfirmations (open M-Sa 9am-6pm). About 1km inland, **buses** stop at the crossroads every half-hour, shuttling between **Mapusa** and **Chapora** (a 7min. walk to the north; buses start at 6am; last bus for Mapusa leaves Chapora around 6pm; last bus to Chapora leaves Mapusa around 7pm; Rs5). Hourly buses also shuttle between Anjuna, Chapora and Vagator (Rs3).

Roseland Auto Center, just off the big road, rents and repairs Kinetic and Yamaha **motorcycles** at good rates (rentals Rs3500 per month). Look for the signs; the proprietors live behind the shop and will offer emergency help until 11:30pm nightly. Tours along the road from Ozran (Little Vagator) Beach also hawk bikes at similar rates. This area is also a good place to ask about **bicycle rental. Taxis** cluster behind Big Vagator Beach. Rates are almost identical. During peak season, this is a good place to get a taxi to the north (Rs150, to Mapusa Rs150, to Anjuna Rs50, between Vagator and Chapora Rs40). The nearest **post office** is in Anjuna.

ACCOMMODATIONS AND FOOD Vagator housing still caters primarily to folks here for the long haul. Follow the yellow signs north of Big Vagator Road to **Dolrina** (tel. 273382), a large and popular guest house run by a friendly family. (In-season: doubles Rs200, with attached bath Rs250; book in advance. Off-season: Rs50-100.) **Balbina's** has its own set of signs north of the road. The ballyhooed "fort view" is a bit overrated, but the lush valley this small guest house overlooks is easy on the eyes (doubles with toilet and common shower Rs200). As the paved Big Vagator road curves in front of the beach and narrows to a dirt path, **Yellow House** is on the right, with airy, sparsely furnished doubles (in-season: Rs150) and clean common toilets and showers. The **Blue Bird Cafe,** near the seashore along the Ozran Beach road, is particularly mellow and cozy, even by Vagator standards. Patrons play backgammon under the thatched roof and over delicious, reasonably priced veg. and non-veg. Indian cuisine. (Open 8am until the last diner leaves.) The attached guest house has serviceable rooms at decent rates (in-season: attached doubles Rs250; off-season: Rs150). **Abu John's,** Big Vagator Road, sports an open kitchen and a jovial, well-dressed crowd that make this joint a popular dinner spot for tandoori and barbecue dishes (Rs80-90; open daily 8am-noon and 6pm-midnight; closed during monsoon season). Next door, the **Garden Villa** offers slightly better prices and food, and nightly bootlegged American movies on the TV (open daily 8am-11pm; movies 7:30pm).

SIGHTS Ozran Beach (Little or Small Vagator) reigns as Vagator's mellowest, most picturesque strip of sand—something like Anjuna in miniature, minus the vendors and the daytrippers. Farther north, Vagator's distinctive grassy, gently shelving hills lead, like giant steps, to the shore at **Middle Vagator** beach, a rocky bit of nothing, remarkable only for the large, grassy field separating it from the hills—the best place in the north for a seaside picnic. **Big Vagator,** just north past the hills, is the longest expanse of fine white grains around, though occasionally cramped by the big crowds it draws from **Sterling Vagator Resort** and the nearby bus stand.

Towering over the whole scene to the northeast are the ruins of the 17th-century **Portuguese Fort** which separates Chapora from Vagator. Today the ruins only shelter the occasional errant cow or enterprising cold drinks salesman, but the quick clamber up to the fort rewards with a smashing panoramic sampling of the whole scene—beach blanket bingo to the south, fishermen hauling in their nets to the east, and the desolate, unspoiled territory looming across the Chapora River to the north.

NIGHTLIFE Vagator's bars remain lively all night in December and January. Proprietors will pour beer until no one's standing upright to drink it. **The Primrose Restaurant and Bar** is the local answer to Anjuna's Shore Bar, with late nights, black lights, and techno DJs with varying levels of skill. The Primrose is also your source for information about upcoming full moon parties, raves, and other debauches. A new rival has recently sprung up—the **Loot Discotheque** at the Alcove Restaurant overlooking Ozran Beach (signs are everywhere), but the beats aren't as thumpin', and the crowd is rarely as hyped. Parties often break out between Vagator and Anjuna, with would-be partiers commuting back and forth in search of the sweetest scene.

■ Near Vagator: Chapora चापोरा

Separated from Vagator by a ruined fort and a few hundred meters, Chapora isn't graced with anything resembling Vagator's beachside charm, or anything resembling a beach, but that's the secret of its entropic appeal. The abundance of bars and restaurants crowding its main drag fill daily with cats anxious to eat, drink, and unwind away from the beachside bustle. The languor even affects the usually industrious **taxi drivers,** who huddle under the banyan tree, playing cards on Chapora's main street instead of hustling for fares to Panjim and Mapusa (Rs150), Anjuna (Rs50), and Vagator (Rs40). Chapora's short-term accommodations are limited to a few overpriced, under-impressive guest houses along the main road. Commuting from Anjuna, Baga, or Calangute until something long-term pops up would be a better move, but if you're hot to stay here, **private rooms** (inquire at the restaurants) are a good alternative; two can sleep well for under Rs100 per night. In the eats department, **Priyanka,** off the main Chapora road, exudes atmosphere, with tablecloths, colored lampshades, and sweet 70s rock. The food's no slouch either—cheap, no-nonsense Indian, Continental, and Chinese victuals, and a Rs30 veg. *thali.* (Open daily 7am-late.) **Scarlet Cold Drinks,** on the main road, just past the taxi stand, provides a choice place to sip a fresh, cold milkshake as you watch the world saunter by. If their two tables are full, neighboring **Sai Ganesh Cafe** provides comparable smoothness (both open daily 8am-11pm).

▓ Arambol (Harmal) आरामबोल

In the Beatles-esque nomenclature used by backpackers to categorize North Goan beaches, Arambol is "the remote one." Though a bridge over the Chapora river slowly (*very* slowly) nears completion, the city is currently only accessible by ferry. Thus, Arambol's proximity to pristine beaches, a freshwater lake, and scenic vistas just outside the clutches of the long arms of the law and the package tour trade continue to appeal to rugged souls looking to get away from it all. Remote, however, is relative. During peak season, some 50-odd seaside cafes and bars swarm with daytrippers and fortnighters seeking solitude and driving the die-hard sociopaths south to Mandrem, north to Querim Beach, or into the trees. North of the main beach, along a rocky path negotiable only on foot lies the smaller, more secluded **Paradise Beach,** backed with a lovely aquamarine **freshwater lagoon.** Further inland from the lake (about a 15min. walk into the forest), the wafting odors of *cheeba* and the plaintive lowing of *digeridoos* alert wanderers to the presence of even more weirdness, this time in the form of a small colony of back-to-the-earthers holding court under the sheltering branches of a great banyan tree.

ORIENTATION AND PRACTICAL INFORMATION Buses roll into Arambol Junction from Chopdem in the south. From the junction, backtrack south and take the first right, where the narrow road winds about 400m. to the beach. The road heads north to the region's only **petrol station.** Gas up here before heading north to Querim or Terekol; there may be folks in the Querim village willing to sell you water bottles full of petrol, but don't bet on it. To reach Arambol from south of the Chapora River, journey to Siolem—there are **buses** from Mapusa (every 30min.), and it's a quick 8km along the riverside from Chapora by bike—and take the **river ferry** to Chopdem (every 15min, 6am-10pm, 10min, Rs4). From the ferry dock, buses shuttle at least hourly between Arambol and Chopdem (15min., Rs3). If you're self-propelled, just veer right from the dock and take a left at the first intersection (following the signs to Harmal). Three daily buses run directly from Mapusa to Arambol (8am,10am, 1pm; 1hr.; Rs10). **Boats** from Baga make the popular day trip to Arambol every morning (Rs200 round-trip) and the **Welcome Restaurant** near the beach sends boats to Anjuna for the flea market every Wednesday morning (Rs150 round-trip). **Taxis** in Vagator, Chapora, Mapusa, and Siolem happily carry you to Arambol, though outside of December and January you'll have to pay for a round-trip (at most Rs400), even if you're only going one-way. **Tara Travels,** just north of the junction, handles the transport bookings and reconfirmations and does **currency exchange.** Just south of the beach road, the tiny **post office** has *Poste Restante* (open M-Sa 10am-1pm and 2-5:30pm).

ACCOMMODATIONS AND FOOD Most visitors here return year after year and rent houses for several months. A few new guest houses are available for short-term stays, and even during peak season, accommodations can be arranged with a little legwork. During the monsoon, most lodges and restaurants are simply closed. **Houses** may be rented for Rs100-150 per night, or Rs2000-5000 per month. Sizes and facilities vary as widely as the prices: many houses have no toilets or running water, only access to nearby bushes and wells, respectively. **The Ganesh Bar** (tel. 297307) has double rooms, situated on the cliffs midway between the two beaches, that excel for three reasons—location, location, location (rooms Rs200). **Tara Travels** also rents a few rooms which are farther from the surf, but fill up more slowly. Even in season you can bargain a double with attached bath down to Rs125.

Where the road intersects the beach, the **Sea Horse Restaurant** serves up Goan, Continental, and Chinese cuisine to a packed house (Rs20-90; open daily 9am-11pm). Just south of Paradise Beach, **Lake Paradise** has fresh *hummus* (Rs50), milkshakes (Rs15), a paperback exchange and, in season, puppies! (Open daily 7am-10pm.) The Ganesh Bar and the rasta-themed **Jah Kingdom,** on the southern end of the main beach, offer food and drink, and the dozen-or-so bars along the main road pour fizzies to fuzz your mind. All of these restaurants are closed off season.

WEST INDIA

■ Near Arambol: Mandrem मांड्रेम

Over-endowed (even by Goan standards) with palm trees and white sand and over-looked by backpackers on their northward push to Arambol, Mandrem stakes its claim as Goa's Next Big Thing. Residents, perennially confident that the popularity and propriety that have graced Anjuna, Vagator, and even Arambol are only a season away, furiously tout their beachside shack restaurants and signpost the town's humble amenities grandly. Long-staying tourists hope that they're wrong, enjoying the unparalleled solitude while it lasts.

"Beach" is a bit of a misnomer for Mandrem's seafront landscape. It's more like someone placed a smallish desert conveniently near the water. Vast expanses of sand stretch over 100 unspoiled meters inland at their widest, and it's rare to see more than a dozen beachcombers sauntering about, even on the busiest days. Mandrem village lies on a short stretch of road branching off of the main thoroughfare between Arambol and Chopdem; if you pass the Sunshine Restaurant's ambitious sign, you've gone too far. Travel amenities are still scarce, however. For currency exchange, buses, or even rickshaws, denizens must schlep 5km or so up the road to Arambol. Accommodations, both short and long-term, are more plentiful, and the first offer for a double with bath during peak season shouldn't top Rs200. Restaurant-affiliated "guest houses" are basically rallying points where eager villagers will whisk you from home to home until you find something to your liking. Mandrem's most upscale option is the **Villa Riverrat** (tel. 297303), a newly whitewashed house with one single (Rs350) and eight spacious and clean doubles (Rs400, with bath and hot water Rs500). The **Villa's Miau** restaurant is as close as Mandrem gets to gourmet dining (open daily 7am-11am and 5-10pm), although a handful of shacks line the beach, mainly serving drinks and snacks. **Molly Malone's Irish Pub,** on the southern end of the beach is about as Irish as yoga, but the guys who run it personally catch the prawns (alive, alive, oh!) in the prawn curry rice (Rs60).

■ Querim खेरीम Beach and Terekol तेराखोल Fort

North of Arambol junction, virtually all traces of backpacker culture vanish. Beyond the pale of hippie settlement, though, a couple of spots stand out. The first is Querim Beach, a fir-backed strip of the white stuff where you can vegetate from Noel to New Year's and see nary a Kodak or dreadlock. Querim (Keri) Beach is a long (2hr.) walk north from Paradise Beach in Arambol, or you can head north from the Arambol junction, following the signs to Keri (about 10km). Faint white writing on the road will point you to the beach, which is also known as Terekol Beach. Nowadays, **Terekol Fort,** as if tired of living a lie, has given up trying to look anything like an impressive 400-year-old fort, and is now a spruced-up, overpriced hotel and restaurant. Buses make the long trip from Panjim, but getting there is all the fun. The journey north to Terekol has some spectacular scenery, but it isn't worth the trip if you don't have your own bike. **Ferries** cross the Terekol from Querim (every 30min., daily 6am-10pm, 5min., Rs3). From there it's just a few kilometers west to the fort.

SOUTH GOA

■ Madgaon (Margao) मारगांव

The town of Madgaon is South Goa's transportation hub and the capital of Salcete Province. Madgaon is known to most travelers only as the gateway to the southern beaches, and few stop here except to catch a bus or train. Colva and Benaulim are very close, so there's no need to stay overnight in this bleak spot. Madgaon is centered on the rectangular **Municipal Gardens,** which are brushed on their west side by **National Highway 17**. West of the Municipal Gardens is the **State Bank of India** (open M-F 10am-2pm, Sa10am-noon), and to the north is the **police station** (tel.

722175) and the **GPO** (open Su-Sa 7am-6:30pm). *Poste Restante* can be received at an office nearby: from the GPO hang a right, then the third left (open M-Sa 8-10:30am and 3-4:30pm; **postal code:** 403601). For a more high-tech form of communication, head directly up the road from the Tourist Hotel 50m to the Rangavi Complex shopping center on the left. **Internet** access is available in shop #9 on the ground floor at **Cyberlink** (tel. 73444; Rs200 per hr.; open M-Sa 8am-8pm). **Telephone code:** 0834.

Trains leave from Madgaon Railway Station, 4km southeast of the municipal gardens on Station Rd. The Konkan Railway's major station has trains to: **Mumbai** (*Mumbai-Madgaon Exp.* KRO112, daily, 7:25pm, 11hr., Rs231 for non-A/C sleeper, Rs597 for 3-tier A/C with pillow and blanket) and **Mangalore** (*Madgaon-Mangalore Exp.* KR0021, daily, 8:20am, 6hr; *Madgaon Mangalore Passr.* KR1, 2:10pm, 7hr., Rs114). **Buses** leave from the **Kadamba Bus Stand,** 2km north along the road to Panjim to: **Hubli** (6:30, 8:45, 10:15am, 1:15pm; 6hr.; Rs50); **Mangalore** (7:15am; 10hr.; Rs122); **Mumbai** (2:30pm; 16hr.; Rs287); and **Pune** (5pm; 14hr.; Rs227). Travel agents around the tourist hostels book frequent **private buses** to the same destinations. **Intrastate buses** chug to: **Colva** via **Benaulim** (every 30min. 7am-8pm, 30min., Rs4); **Chaudi** (every hr. 8am-8pm; 1hr; Rs10); and **Panjim** (frequent; 6am-9:15pm; Rs12). Buses to and from Colva and Benaulim also stop on the side of the Municipal Gardens, while those heading to other interstate destinations stop on the western side.

Few foreigners eat or sleep in Madgaon; those who do find that the budget dives sit between the market and railway station along Station Rd. generally fill up by morning's end. The **Tourist Hotel** (tel. 721966), just south of the Municipal Gardens, is overpriced but dependably institutional. All rooms have attached baths. (In-season: singles Rs200; doubles Rs250, with A/C Rs350. Off-season: Rs150/200/300.) **Longuinhos** (tel. 721038), across the street from the Tourist Hotel, dishes up cheap, Goan delights and copious cocktails (open daily 8am-10:45pm). The god-fearing **Crislene Café,** west of the GPO, beats the heat with cold treats (open 7:30am-8pm).

The most interesting things to see in Madgaon aren't actually in Madgaon at all, but in smaller towns to the east, quickly and easily accessible by bus. In **Rachol** (7km from Madgaon, buses every 30min., 25min., Rs3), the **Museum of Christian Art**, at the Rachol Seminary, provides an elegant overview of Goan Christianity. The treasures include an 18th-century palanquin used to carry around ecclesiastical highrollers, a portable altar for mobile missionaries, and an enormous, kingfisher-shaped silver and wood monstrosity looted from the Sé Cathedral in Old Goa. (Open daily 9am-1pm and 2-5pm. Rs5.) On the kitschier side, **Ancestral Goa** in **Loutilim** (10km east of Madgaon, buses every hr., 30min., Rs4) provides an eclectic presentation of Goan village life in ye olde days, the Limca World Record Book's longest laterite sculpture, a garden full of edible foliage, and a tour to tie these widely disparate elements together. (Open daily 9am-6pm; Rs20.) A number of stately old **Portuguese villas** also grace Loutilim, but to see these, you've got to make an appointment through the GTDC.

■ Colva कोल्वा

If first impressions told the whole story, any self-respecting backpacker would tuck tail and run after being dumped at Colva's beachfront roundabout. Bollywood's finest minds couldn't design a more perfectly overdeveloped resort scene. Colva's beachfront heart is an unsightly mass of concrete pavement, garish resorts, and skeletal construction sights. But the town puts its worst foot forward, and this facade of cement mixers run amok is just that. Moving away from the beachfront in any direction, the concrete jungle quickly recedes and camera-clicking Mumbaiites and extortionist scarf sellers fade away like extras after a shot's been wrapped. Though far and away the south's most touristed beach, Colva has far less traffic than you'll find in the north, and its mellow crowd of youngsters of all ages sun and fun less frantically.

ORIENTATION AND PRACTICAL INFORMATION The Madgaon road winds westward, forming Colva's main strip. The road then passes through **Colva Village,** a crossroads leading south to Benaulim and north to Vasco da Gama, and peters out 1km away at a beachfront **roundabout. Buses** from Madgaon stop at the crossroads and at the roundabout, plying to Benaulim from the crossroads (every 30min., Rs3). For other destinations in Goa it is necessary to travel first to Madgaon. **Auto-rickshaws** frequent the beach roundabout and the main road to take you to Benaulim (Rs35) or Palolem (Rs175). **Taxis** charge about double these rates. **Bicycles** and **motorbikes** can be rented at many shops and resorts, including **Maria Joanna Cycle Shop,** just east of the Rice Bowl.

West of the church in the village is the **Bank of Baroda,** which gives cash advances on Visa cards (open M-Tu and Th-F 9am-1pm, Sa 9am-11am). Any resort with an ounce of pretension will do **currency exchange,** but rates are less than ideal. Trashy paperbacks in many tongues can be bought or swapped at **Damodar's Books,** north of the roundabout (open daily 10:30am-9:30pm). Just east of Damodar's is the **tourist police** and their crack detective squad (open daily 8:30am-8pm). *Poste Restante* is available from the **sub post office,** just southeast of the church (open 9:30am-noon and 2:30-4pm; **postal code:** 403708.) **STD/ISD** booths are scattered along the main road. **World Linkers** booth, east of the Rice Bowl on the main road, is open 24 hours.

ACCOMMODATIONS Transients holing up in Colva after a tour of duty in the North will be pleasantly surprised by the area's digs. Although facilities vary as widely as they do elsewhere, prices are little more than half what you'd pay for comparable rooms north of Panjim. Additionally, outside of Christmas week, only the hyper-popular lodges fill up, and bargaining can pay off big, particularly for loners and those taking long stays. A dense thicket of budget guest houses nestles in the **4th ward** area, due northwest of the crossroads; from there, head west and then north when you reach cluster of signs. **Ronnie's Cottages** (tel. 721926) is the best bargain. Six well-kept concrete blocks with attached baths sit in a particularly remote, relaxed neighborhood, about 500m off the road, down a winding sandy path. (Doubles Rs100.) **Joema Tour's Home,** 4th Ward, next door to Garden Cottages, is one of the ward's brighter, newer establishments, complete with mosquito netting to keep out the creepy crawlies. (In-season: doubles Rs200. Off-season: negotiable.)

The small road leading north from the beachfront roundabout heads towards the **Hotel Colmar** (tel. 721253), a happening place providing high-value resorty perks. The relatively posh rooms sequestered in a lush garden are cool and airy. (In-season: doubles Rs400. Off-season: Rs100.) The pasta dishes (Rs35-70) at the attached **Pasta Hut** supersede standard Indo-Italian fare. The restaurant's attached bar serves as a popular watering hole. (Open daily 8am-11pm.) North of the Colmar are **The Fisherman's Cottages** (tel. 734323), with a freshly whitewashed facade in view of the rolling surf and 24-hour running water. True to its name, the place is operated by local fishermen, who occasionally leave their nets in the hall. (In-season: doubles Rs200. Off-season: Rs100). **Lucky Star** (tel. 730069), just north of Fisherman's, isn't as well-kept as its competitor, but it's cheaper. Six second-story attached doubles, above the eponymous bar and restaurant (In-season: Rs150. Off-season: Rs100). Backpackers flock to the **Tourist Nest Hotel** (tel 723944), north of the crossroad, and left at "La Touche." This 200-year-old Portuguese mansion is a tangled grove shelters a guest house in the old Goan tradition—light on price and amenities, heavy on hospitable vibe. Out back are two cottages with attached baths, one with a kitchen. (Doubles Rs80, with bath Rs85. Cottages Rs300 per night, Rs5000 per month). **The Sea Pearl,** north on the first road east of the roundabout, draws a huge crowd for seafood specials (Rs60-175) so fresh, they ought to be slapped. (Open daily 8:30am-2pm and 6-11pm; last orders 10pm). To round off the cosmopolitan selection, the **Rice Bowl** (tel. 711151), east of the beachfront, whips up above par Chinese food (Rs30-65) to delighted Indian tourists (open daily 10am -11pm).

BEACHES AND NIGHTLIFE As far as globetrotting budgeteers are concerned, the southern beaches begin at **Colva beach,** but the village actually lies midway along the states' longest beach. Decked out in sparkling white and emerald blue 26km from tip to tail, the sheer length of the strip makes bicycles a feasible and desirable mode of waterfront locomotion. At high tide, it's possible to wheel on wet, packed sand along the beach's entirety. Although the sand may seem crowded around Colva, solitude awaits those willing to venture a kilometer north or south. Between Colva and Benaulim, the water is relatively quiet and very swimmable. Balmy breezes and mildly rippin' tubes make **boogie boarding** and **windsurfing** fairly popular here, and shacks south of Colva beach lease the appropriate equipment (Rs30/200 per hr.).

Nocturnal Colva never slams, and outside Christmas week, rarely works up more than a dull thudding. The beach bars south of the roundabout host most of the action, and some stay open after midnight. The homogeneity of the beach bar scene has barmen wracking their brains to come up with contrived amusements, from star gazing to beach volleyball. Beware—**Splash's** touted "fire party" rarely amounts to more than a few baby boomers busting the White Man's Overbite on the dance floor, but they pull in a lively crowd. Nearby **Ziggy's** is also popular, albeit nondescript.

▓ Benaulim बेनावलीम

Just a 20-minute walk south of Colva, Benaulim (been-AH-li) serves largely as a "suburb" to its larger sister village. It provides the same beach access without all the resort area climate and bustle. Denizens have to commute back to Colva for anything resembling nightlife. In the southern fashion, the accommodation Benaulim offers is cheap, plentiful, popular, and only slightly bland. Although a few gaudy resorts and construction sites dot the village-scape, they fail to disrupt the hamlet-like tranquility.

ORIENTATION AND PRACTICAL INFORMATION Two parallel north-south roads—the heart of Benaulim Village—intersects the east-west Madgaon road's inevitable march towards the beach. **Buses** stop at the eastern (Marin Hall) crossroads. Benaulim is on both the Madgaon-Mobor and Madgaon-Colva lines (every 30min. 8am-8pm) to: **Colva** (10min., Rs3); **Madgaon** (25min., Rs4); and **Varca** (10min., Rs3). **Taxis** and auto-rickshaws wait at the drop spot to whisk you off to the shimmering sands 2km away (Rs20), or to Madgaon (Rs70) and Colva (Rs60). **Auto-rickshaws** ply to all corners of Goa as well, and cost marginally less. Benaulim is a 50-minute taxi ride from Dabolim **airport** (Rs250). At the western crossroads, the north-south road packs the majority of the village's numerous guest houses and is cluttered with signs and entrepreneurs touting **motorcycle** (Rs125-200) and **bicycle** rentals (Rs50). The **Bank of Baroda** is located right at the Marin Hall crossroads in town (open M-Tu and Th-F 9am-1pm, Sa 9-11am), but only does cash advances on Visa cards, leaving **currency exchange** to the travel agents lining the western crossroads (some open 24hr.). The **Benaulim Medical Store** is situated right beside the Bank of Baroda and features all sorts of medications as well as toiletries and cheap film developing (open M-Sa 9am-1pm and 4-9pm, Su 9am-1pm). Benaulim's **post office** and telegraph south of Marin Hall and west just past the Holy Trinity Church (in Trinity Hall) sell stamps (open M-Sa 10am-noon and 2-4pm).

ACCOMMODATIONS AND FOOD For those who don't fancy fashioning themselves a palm-leaf hut, cheap comfortable guest houses line the Madgaon road and the two north-south streets. Those listed below can be reached by heading south from the western crossroads and watching for signs. **Diogo Con** (tel. 733749), 100m east of the Meridian Restaurant on a dirt road, is one of Benaulim's best kept secrets, with freshly painted, petite rooms with shiny tiled attached baths (singles Rs150; doubles Rs200). **Kenkre Tourist Cottages** (tel. 737944), on the east side of the western north-south road (confused yet?), offers six rooms in a house, all doubles, with attached bath and running water. Many guests stay for months. (In season: Rs80-85. Off-season: Rs50.) **Casa De Caji Cottages** (tel. 722937), in an idyllic spot west of the western north-south road (watch for the sign), has a location, proprietress, and rooms which all radiate a charm unique in Benaulim. Calling them "common" does the spotless toilets and bath a disservice. (Doubles Rs125, with balcony Rs150.) On the beach front, **Johney's Restaurant** distances itself from the competitors with late hours, excellent values, and a dandy name. The prawns *amotik,* prepared with fiery chilies and whole cloves of garlic, is unsubtle and undeniably tasty. (Open daily 8am-midnight. Closed intermittently during monsoon season.)

■ Palolem पालोलेम

When overworked desk jockeys daydream of telling the boss to shove it, quitting the rat race, and starting life anew in a tropical paradise, they envision Palolem. Strolling along its kilometer-long crescent of sand, it's hard to shake the feeling that you've unwittingly walked into a Jimmy Buffett song. The tiny cove, flanked by forested hillocks and black rocks, gives the not-so-disheartening impression that this is the only place on earth, while the bathing beauties strolling the sand raise hopes that sweet-but-fleeting tropical romance is only a couple of fruity cocktails away. Hammocks strung between densely packed palm trees shelter guitar-strumming hippies, and for a touch of the exotic, the tide recedes to connect the northern end of the beach with an island "peopled" with black-faced monkeys. The only tropical beach virtue Palolem doesn't exemplify is quiescence, but the crowds, under the beach's spell, are mellower, more content, and happier than most. You'll be too, if you don't mind sharing—Palolem has plenty of paradise to go around.

The road from Chaudi (33km south of Madgaon) zigzags 4km northwest to Palolem, drawing parallel to the beach midway along, and intersecting the 100m beach road at the northern end of the sand. During peak season, **buses** run to Madgaon (7 and 9:30am, noon, and 2:30pm, 2hr., Rs12), but service is less frequent at other times. Fortunately, most guest house owners double as accurate bus timetables. If you miss the direct services, the bus from Chaudi to Madgaon (every hr. until 6:30pm, 1½hr., Rs10) is a viable option. You can also take a **rickshaw** (Rs30) or **taxi** (Rs50), or you can take a hike—about 4km. Signs on the Chaudi road also tout **bike** (Rs3 per hr.) and **motorcycle rental.** In a pinch, some restaurants (including the Sun 'n' Moon) will **exchange currency,** but their rates will have you wishing you'd brought enough cash. The nearest **post office** is in Chaudi.

Compared to Colva and Benaulim, Palolem's accommodations are overpriced and underkept—expect to pay Rs200 in season for the privilege of crashing in a cramped, charmless double and using an outhouse. Staying in one of the colonies of straw huts on the beach front provides a more photogenic alternative. Midway down the beach, on the low end of the scale, the **Deena Bar and Restaurant** (tel. 643449) rents simple huts with light bulb, bed, and chair; the common toilet is squat, the shower is bucket, and there's a safe for valuables (Rs150). **Cocohuts** offers relatively (for a hut) posher digs, up off the ground on stilts, with lockers, electric fans, and a more sophisticated common toilet (doubles Rs300). Those who like to make a wild rumpus behind closed doors should bear in mind that the thin layer of dried vegetation offers very little privacy. The sole bright blip on Palolem's otherwise dreary restaurant radar is the **Sun 'n' Moon,** which serves delicious sizzlers (Rs50-75) to a lively, chatty, cards-and-board game playing crowd (open daily 8am-10:30pm). When it closes, folks can be found blowin' in the wind to **Dylan's** on the beach. Late at night, the rest of the town is Desolation Row.

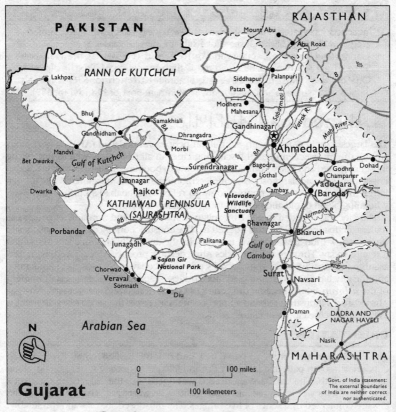

Gujarat

Gujarat ગુજરાત

One of India's richest industrial regions, Gujarat has much to offer, in part because it sees fewer travelers than its neighbors Rajasthan and Maharashtra. Gujarat is also one of the safest places to travel for two reasons; prohibition and the lack of mass tourism. The former makes it far safer for women to travel alone, even at night, and the latter keeps tourists from feeling victimized by locals.

Originally settled by the Indus Valley people in 2500 BC, Gujarat prospered under several empires including the Solanki dynasty in the 11th and 12th centuries AD, which left its culture a blend of Jain and Hindu influences. In 1299 the area was conquered by Muslims, who formed the Sultanate of Gujarat in 1407. In the 16th century, the Portuguese stormed onto the scene in Gujarat with the capture of the ports of Diu and Daman. During India's independence struggle, Gujarat gained acclaim as the birthplace and operational base of Mahatma Gandhi. But Gujarat was also home to M.A. Jinnah, architect of Pakistan, which shares Gujarat's northwest frontier.

Gujarat can be geographically divided into three vastly different regions. The eastern region, containing the capital Gandhinagar, the metropolis Ahmedabad, and the commercial cities of the mainland strip, is characterized by its modern industrialization. The northwestern quasi-island of Kutchch, a dry, isolated area, sits peacefully content with its traditional village lifestyle. The Kathiawad Peninsula (also known as Saurashtra), is known for lush land, rich temples, forts, palaces, and all things Gandhi.

■ Ahmedabad અમદાવાદ

The largest city in Gujarat with 3.6 million people, Ahmedabad (AHM-da-vad) ranks among the most eccentric and fascinating cities in all of Asia, as well as one of the most congested and noisy. Ahmedabad is home to booming industries and businesses enveloping spectacular mosques, temples, monuments, and museums. While it's definitely not a place where people come to relax, Ahmedabad's curious and overwhelming blend of old and new has intrigued many a traveler.

The city was founded in 1411 by Sultan Ahmed Shah, and it rapidly expanded as traders, craftsmen, and artisans flocked in. The construction of countless mosques in the then-new Indo-Saracenic style lent the city the decidedly Muslim character which it retains today. Through the centuries Ahmedebad's prosperity see-sawed, with devastating famines. Initially, Ahmedabad's prominence lay in textiles and handicrafts, and the city has always encouraged those trades—especially since the establishment of the *ashram* which became the center of Gandhi's *swadeshi* movement. Now, as Ahmedabad's industries expand and broaden their scope, the sense of excitement is as palpable as the clouds of factory smoke.

ORIENTATION

The city is separated into two parts, new and old, by the **Sabarmati River,** which cuts a north-south path that is usually dry and filled with grazing water buffalo, along its entire width. The **Lal Darwaja (Red Gate)** opens into the old city on the river's east side; the newer industrial and urban centers lie westward. The two parts of the city are connected by a series of five bridges. The most used are **Ellis** and (preferably, for the sake of safety) **Nehru,** which connect the centers of the old and new cities.

East of the old city, the **Ahmedabad Railway Station** is connected to Lal Darwaja by **Relief Road** (officially known as **Tilak Road**) and **Gandhi Road,** both running through the heart of the old city. The **local bus stand** is located in Lal Darwaja near the end of Gandhi Rd. The **Central Bus Stand** is south of town near the end of **Sardar Patel Road,** which leads southeast from Ellis Bridge to **Astodia Darwaja.** Vivekanand Road leads from Astodia Darwaja to the railway station. **Ashram Road (R.C. Rd.)** is a major commercial center conveniently lined with banks and big stores. **Gujarat College** and the **Law Gardens** are off Ashram Rd. just north of Ellis Bridge.

Most of Ahmedabad's modern facilities are to be found in the ever-expanding **new city,** to the west of Sabarmati. Ashram Rd., **Panchwati Circle,** and **C.G. Road** are bustling areas with helpful services, but they are far away from the traditional old city of primary interest to tourists.

As Easy as Ek, Be, Tran...

Bus numbers and auto-rickshaw fare cards in Ahmedabad are usually printed in **Gujarati numerals.** Save countless time and rupees (and impress your friends) by learning to count in Guju. 1 ૧, 2 ૨, 3 ૩, 4 ૪, 5 ૫, 6 ૬, 7 ૭, 8 ૮, 9 ૯, and 0 ૦.

Ahmedabad

ACCOMMODATIONS

F A-One Hotel
A Gandhi Ashram Guest House
C Hotel Arif
B Hotel Diamond
D Hotel Natraj
E Hotel Paramount
G Hotel Shakunt

TO GANDHINAGAR

TO GANDHINAGAR

Sabarmati (Gandhi) Ashram

Subhash Bridge

SHAHIBAG

Ashram Rd.

Vadaj Low Level Bridge

DUDHESWAR

Calico Museum of Textiles

Civil Hospital

Sabarmati River

Police Commissioner's Office

City Rd.

HARIPURA

Balvantri Mehta Rd.

Mehta Rd.

Dada Hari Vav

Gandhi Bridge

Hatheesingh Temple

Kasturba Gandhi Rd.

Shahpur Darwaja

Delhi Darwaja

Dariapur Darwaja

Lady Vidyagauri Rd.

Rani Rupmati's Mosque

Kalupur Darwaja

Khanpur Darwaja

Dr. Tankara Rd.

Dr. Bapisa Rd.

Ahmedabad Railway Station

MITHAKALI

Indian Airlines

Swaminarayan Temple

F

Ramanlal Sheh Rd.

GPO

Tilak (Relief) Rd.

G

Nehru Bridge

Sidi Saiyad's Mosque

LAL DARWAJA

KHAS BAZAAR

Peer Mohammedshah Rd.

Chetna Dining Hall

Arjun Lala Rd.

Panchkuva Darwaja

Shaking Minarets & Sidi Bashir's Mosque

R.C. Rd.

Kalapi

Central Telegraph Office

E

Gandhi Rd.

Local Bus Stand

SBI

B

Law Gardens

Ellis Bridge

SEWA

C

D

Teen Darwaja

Akhandanand Rd.

Jumma Masjid

K.T. Desai Rd.

Sarangpur Darwaja

Ahmed Shah's Mosque

Victoria Garden

Anandshankar Dhruv Rd.

Vivekananda Rd.

Gopi Dining Hall

V.S. Hospital

Bhadra Fort & Azamkhan's Palace

R.M. Rd.

Sardar Patel Rd.

Rani Sipri's Mosque

RAIPUR DARWAJA

Mehta Museum of Miniatures

Sardar Bridge

Astodia Darwaja

Central Bus Stand

Dayanand Rd.

PALDI

TO VISHALLA

Jamalpur Rd.

Jagannathji Rd.

JAMALPUR

Kankaria Lake

Zoo

Nehru Kids Park

BEHRAMPURA

0   400 yards

0   400 meters

N

WEST INDIA

PRACTICAL INFORMATION

Transportation

Airport: Ahmedabad International Airport, 10km northeast of the city center (tel. 6425633). Taxis into the city cost Rs150-200, auto-rickshaws Rs60-75, and buses run to Lal Darwaja Bus Stand (every 30min., Rs4). **Air India** (tel. 6585633 or 6585644; fax 6585900), behind the High Court off Ashram Rd., west of the Gandhi statue. Open M-F 10am-1:15pm and 2-5:15pm, Sa 10am-1:30pm. **Indian Airlines,** Lal Darwaja (tel. 5503061; fax 6585900), near the east end of Nehru Bridge. Open daily 10am-1:15pm and 2:15-5:15pm. **Jet Airways,** Ashram Rd. (tel. 467886), 1km north of Gujarat Tourism. Open M-F 10am-7pm, Sa-Su 10am-5:30pm. The *Times of India* Ahmedabad edition has updated flight and train information on the second page. To: **Amritsar** (3 per week, 1½hr., US$155); **Bangalore** (3 per week, 1½hr., US$180); **Calcutta** (1 per day, 2½hr., US$200); **Chandigarh** (3 per week, 3hr., US$155); **Chennai** (1 per day, 2½hr., US$200); **Delhi** (3 per day, 1½hr., US$105); **Goa** (3 per week, 1½hr., US$130); **Hyderabad** (2 per week, 1½hr., US$135); **Jaipur** (3 per week, 1½hr., US$80); **Mumbai** (5 per day, 1hr., US$65).

Trains: Ahmedabad Railway Station (tel. 131 or 1331), on the east side of town. The **Reservation Office** (tel. 135), in the station, is open M-Sa 8am-8pm, Su 8am-2pm. Fares listed are 2nd class/2nd class A/C. To: **Abu Road** (*Delhi Mail* 9105, 8:30am, 4½hr., Rs61/387); **Bhopal** (*Rajkot-Bhopal Exp.* 1269, 7pm, 14hr., Rs187/855); **Calcutta** (*Howrah Exp.* 8033, 9am, 43hr., Rs349/1765); **Chennai** (*Navajivan Exp.* 6045, 6:35am, 22½hr., Rs335/1664); **Delhi** (*Delhi Mail* 9105, 8:30am, 8hr., Rs239/1051; *Sarvodaya Express* 2473, Tu, W, and Sa, noon, 17hr., Rs267/668); **Dwarka** (*Saurashtra Mail* 9005, 6am, 10hr., Rs154/688); **Jaipur** (*Delhi Mail* 9105, 8:30am, 14hr., Rs187/851); **Junagadh** (*Girnar Exp.* 9946, 9pm, 9hr., Rs131/598; *Sommath Mail* 9924, 11pm, 10hr., Rs131/598); **Mumbai** (*Gujarat Exp.* 9012, 7am, 9hr., Rs112/323; *Shatabdi Exp.* 2010, 2:45pm, 9hr., Rs475 A/C only; *Gujarat Mail* 9102, 10pm, 9hr., Rs157/399); **Rajkot** (*Saurashtra Exp.* 9215, 8pm, 5hr., Rs95/449); **Udaipur** (*Udaipur Exp.* 9944, 11pm, 9hr., Rs110/503); **Varanasi** (*Sabarmati Exp.* 9165, 8pm, 42hr., Rs286/1175); **Veraval** (*Girnar Exp.* 9946, 9pm, 11hr; *Sommath Mail* 9924, 11pm, 12hr., Rs151/665).

Buses: The **Central Bus Stand** (tel. 214764) is for intercity buses. **Government buses** are great in number but low in quality; private buses are much more comfortable. To: **Abu Road** (every 30min., 5am-midnight, 4 deluxe per day, 5hr., Rs42/50); **Bhuj** (11 per day, deluxe 1:30pm, 9hr., Rs62/71); **Bikaner** (5:30pm, 17hr., Rs196); **Chittaurgarh** (9 and 10pm, 11hr., Rs100); **Diu and Una** (3 per day, 11hr., Rs73); **Dwarka** (6 per day, 11hr., Rs81); **Jaipur** (3 per day, 15hr., Rs150/230); **Jaisalmer** (7pm, 12hr., Rs140); **Mt. Abu** (8 per day, Rs52/60 for regular/deluxe); **Mumbai** (3 per day, 12hr., Rs100); **Rajkot** (express every 15min., deluxe every hr., 5hr., Rs40/46); **Ranakpur** (6:30am, 8hr., Rs90); **Udaipur** (16 per day, 6hr., Rs64/83); **Veraval** (8 per day, 11hr., Rs72). Opposite the Central Bus Stand are dozens of **private bus** company stalls but most are ticket agents only; most private buses depart from the main company office. The best companies are **Punjab Travels,** Embassy Market (tel. 6589200; fax 6573155), off Ashram Rd., a bit north of Gujarat Tourism (open daily 6am-10:30pm), and **Shrinath Travels,** Shahi Bhag (tel. 5625351; fax 5625599), near the police commissioner's office (open daily 6am-midnight).

Local Transportation: Auto-rickshaws create most of the city's chaos but they are convenient. Insist on the meter, and ask to see the fare card. **Local buses** are extensive, inexpensive, and at least as dangerous as auto-rickshaws. The **Lal Darwaja Bus Stand** (tel. 5507739) is the local bus stand. Some useful routes: #82 (૮૨) and 84 (૮૪) cross the river and run north up Ashram Rd.; #32 (૩૨) runs to the Central Bus Stand and southeast to Kankaria Lake; #102 (૧૦૨) runs to the airport; #34 (૩૪) and 112 (૧૧૨) run past the Civil Hospital; and #131 (૧૩૧) and 133-135 (૧૩૩, ૧૩૪, and ૧૩૫) run to the railway station. Fares are less than Rs4. A/C Ambassador **taxis** can be found at the two bus stands at the airport, at the railway station, at V.S. Hospital, and lining Lal Darwaja (Rs200 to cross the city).

Tourist and Financial Services

Tourist Office: Tourist Information Bureau (Gujarat Tourism), H.K. House (tel. 6859683; fax 6582183), off Ashram Rd., down a side-street opposite the South Indian Bank between Gandhi and Nehru Bridges. Ask rickshaw drivers for H.K. House. A helpful staff with an assortment of brochures. City maps Rs4, Gujarat maps Rs20. Open M-Sa 10:30am-1:30pm and 2-6pm; closed 2nd and 4th Sa. The **tourist counter** at the airport (tel. 785608) has limited information. **City tours** depart from the tourist window at the Lal Darwaja Bus Stand (9:30am and 3pm, 4hr., Rs40, A/C Rs60).

Immigration Office: Foreigners Registration Office, Commissioner of Police, Dr. Tankeria Rd. (tel. 5620990; fax 5624526), in Shahi Bagh 3km north of Lal Darwaja. Come at least 15 days before visa expiration. Open M-Sa 10:30am-2pm and 3:30-6pm. Closed 2nd and 4th Sa.

Currency Exchange: State Bank of India, Lal Darwaja (tel. 5506116), near Lal Darwaja bus stand. **Bank of Baroda,** Ashram Rd. (tel. 5684292, 6580362; fax 6585175), south of the Gandhi statue, gives cash advance by credit card (1% service charge). **Dena Bank,** Ashram Rd. (tel. 5684292; fax 6588613), north of Nehru Bridge, wires money for Rs250. All exchange currency and cash traveler's checks. All open M-F 11am-3pm. State Bank of India is also open Sa 11am-1pm.

Local Services

Luggage Storage: The railway station offers luggage storage (Rs3 per item for first 24hr., Rs5 for the second, and Rs6 per additional 24hr).

Bookstore: Crossword, Sri Krishna Shopping Centre, Mithakali (tel. 402238; fax 444180). West of Ashram Rd. and south of Nehru Bridge. Books of all types, plus magazines, newspapers, stationery, computer games, and a cafe. Open daily 10:30am-8:30pm. **Sastu Kitab Dhar,** Relief Rd. (tel. 5351785). Gracious staff and good selection of paperbacks. Open M-Sa 9:30am-6:45pm. Lots of **book stalls** with smaller collections line the west end of Relief Rd.

Library: British Library, Bhaikaka Bhawan (tel. 6560693; fax 6449493), near the Law Garden. Extensive book and periodical collection. Nonmembers are allowed to browse for a Rs100 fee, but cannot check out books. Open Tu-F 10:30am-6:30pm, Sa 11:30am-7:30pm. **M.J. Public Library** (tel. 6578513) at Ellis Bridge and Ashram Rd. Decent English collection. Open daily 7:30am-7pm.

Cultural Centers: See *Times of India* for notices. **British Library,** Bhaikaka Bhawan (tel. 6560693; fax 6449493), near the Law Garden. Organizes lectures and video shows. **Alliance Française,** opposite Gujarat College (tel. 6441551; fax 6560211). Small library with French books and newspapers. Organizes cultural activities and exhibitions. Open M-F 10:30am-6:30pm, Sa 11am-5pm. The **Gymkana Club,** next to the British Library, has a luncheon series.

Market: Relief Rd., Gandhi Rd., Sardar Patel Rd., Khas Bazaar, and **Ashram Rd.** are the main commercial areas. Most stores open daily 9am-9:30pm.

Emergency and Communications

Pharmacy: Pharmacies are especially numerous around the 3 main hospitals (see below). Most open daily 9am-7pm, but in every cluster a few are open 24hr.

Hospital: New Civil Hospital, Shahibagh (tel. 2123721), off Khandubhai Desai Rd., 3km north of the railway station. **Sheth Vadilal Sarabhai Hospital** (tel. 6577621), south of the intersection of Ashram Rd. and Ellis Bridge. Both are government hospitals. The best private hospital is **Chaturbhuj Lajpatrai Hospital,** also known as **Rajasthan Hospital,** Dr. Tankerin Rd. (tel. 7866311), south of the police commissioner's office. English-speaking, modern, efficient. All open 24hr.

Emergency: Police: tel. 100. **Fire:** tel. 101. **Ambulance:** tel. 102.

Police: Major police stations are **Karanj,** in Teen Darwaja; **Shaherkotada,** opposite the railway station; and **Ellis Bridge,** at the intersection with Ashram Rd.

Post Office: GPO (tel. 5500977). *Poste Restante.* Large and efficient. Open M-Sa 8am-7:30pm, Su 10:30am-1:30pm. Branch offices at the airport, Gandhi Ashram, and opposite the railway station. Open M-Sa 10am-5pm. **Postal Code:** 380001.

Internet: Interactive Technologies, C.G. Rd., Mardia Plaza, above Tomatoes Restaurant. Five terminals with fast connections. Open daily 9am-9pm. **Random Access,**

Panchwati Circle, Agarwal Arcade, Ambavadi Rd. The city's first real cyber-cafe, featuring great coffee and super-fast computers. Open daily 10am-midnight.

Telephones: Many STD/ISD booths offer fax services and are open 24hr. **Central Telegraph Office,** Lal Darwaja (tel. 5502139; fax 5500066), offers telex and telegraph services. Open 24hr. **Telephone Code:** 079.

ACCOMMODATIONS

Hotels in the city center are noisy; those on the east side, near the railway station, are mostly insufferable. The best budget hotels are conveniently scattered around the west half of the city center. If these are too grimy to bear, luxury hotels cluster between the Gandhi and Nehru Bridges on the east side of the river, around Khanpur Darwaja. All hotels in Gujarat are subject to a 10% luxury tax.

Hotel Natraj (tel. 5506048), next to Ahmed Shah's Mosque south of the local bus stand. If you're lucky enough to get a room with balcony overlooking the gardens of the mosque next door, you've got the best view in the city proper. Otherwise, rooms are large but boring. Attached baths all around. Check-out 24hr. Singles Rs100; doubles Rs170.; triples Rs240. Extra bed Rs30.

Gandhi Ashram Guest House (tel. 7483742), opposite Gandhi Ashram. Located away from the city, this guest house catches some of the peaceful vibes exuded by the ashram across the street. Room decor ranges from Grecian busts to abstract art. Run by Gujarat Tourism—the staff is well-informed about the city. Good veg. restaurant. Check-out 9am. Singles Rs200, with A/C Rs550; doubles Rs350/400.

Hotel Alif International, Khanpur (tel. 5501270; fax 5500540). Cheap for the Khanpur luxury cluster. Modern rooms with TVs, telephones, attached baths, and coordinated corporate furniture. Check-out 9am. Singles Rs295, with A/C Rs350-460; doubles Rs340/475-600. Extra bed Rs125.

Hotel Shakunt (tel. 2144615 or 2144500), opposite Railway Station. This is your best bet if you want to be near the Railway Station. A modern hotel with a pleasant terrace garden and friendly staff. Rooms are large and have TV, telephone, and attached bath. Check-out 24hr. Singles Rs200, deluxe Rs240, with A/C Rs450; doubles Rs230/275/400; triples Rs300. Extra bed Rs80.

Hotel Diamond, Khanpur (tel. 5503699; fax 5505330). A good deal for the facilities. Well-kept rooms with attached baths, TVs, telephones, spotty red carpet, and bland beige bedspreads. Check-out 24hr. Singles Rs140, with A/C Rs250; doubles Rs200/300; triples Rs270/350. Extra bed Rs60.

A-One Hotel (tel. 2149823), opposite the railway station. The undecorated, unfurnished, nondescript and slightly grungy rooms are barely larger than the beds. Check-out 24hr. Dorm beds (men only) Rs50. Singles Rs80; doubles Rs130, with TV and attached bath Rs200; triples Rs170/275.

FOOD

Ahmedabad is home to every type of restaurant fathomable. It's well worth sampling a Gujarati *thali*, which conveniently blends several local specialties in a delightful, often sweet, mix. For quick and spicy stall food, **Khas Bazaar** can't be beat.

Gopi Dining Hall, near V.S. Hospital on west side of river—look for the sign above the building. Excellent, enormous Gujarati *thalis* (Rs40) served in a packed-solid den of fine stainless steel dining. Come early, or be prepared to wait. The service here is unbeatable, and the price is right. Open daily 10:30am-3pm and 6-11pm.

Kalapi Restaurant, near Advance Cinema, Lal Darwaja. Dim, A/C, and one of the best bargains in town. All veg., no smoking. The food is excellent, well-presented, and cheap. Madrasi specialties Rs20. Open daily 9am-11pm.

Tomatoes Restaurant, C.G. Rd., in the new city. If you miss Western food, this pizzeria/steakhouse is your chance to splurge and sate your cravings (entrees Rs75-200. Open daily 10am-10pm.

Hotel Paramount, near Khas Bazaar. Bland, vinyl-booth atmosphere, but dim lights and A/C make it comfortable. Good seafood dishes for under Rs45, veg. entrees under Rs40. Open daily 9:30am-11:30pm.

Chetna Dining Hall, Relief Rd. Almost directly north of the Jumma Masjid. Your standard *thali* house—stainless steel everywhere and waiters rushing from packed table to packed table with pots of steaming vegetables. South Indian dishes downstairs; substantial *thalis* (Rs50) upstairs. Open daily 10:30am-3pm and 6:30-10pm.

SIGHTS

Calico Museum of Textiles

Location: *Shahi Bagh, 3km north of Delhi Gate.* **Phone:** *786 8172.* **Bus:** *Local bus #101 (૧૦૧), 102 (૧૦૨), or 106 (૧૦૬).* **Hours:** *Open Th-Tu.* **Admission:** *Free.* **Other:** *Guided tours at 10:30am and 2:45pm, 2hr. Photography only allowed in the gardens.*

Creatively set up in the *haveli* of the city's richest family, India's premier textile museum is split into two sections surrounded by peacock- and fountain-filled gardens. The first half displays non-religious textiles and features an enormous collection of textiles made from every possible fabric, in every possible style, for every possible purpose, from every part of India. The white-on-white translucent shadowwork is remarkable, as are the lavish silk embroideries. Other highlights include beautiful *saris* (Rs80,000 and up) made by a complicated procedure in which one mistake means beginning entirely anew, and clothes so heavily laden with gold lace that their weight reaches over 9kg. The second half of the museum displays textiles for religious use and features an exquisite 8m-long pictorial scroll, a multitude of old tapestries, and a series of rooms explaining the methods in minute detail—every knot, stitch, thread type, dye, bead, and mirror technique imaginable.

Sabarmati (Gandhi) Ashram

Location: *Ashram Rd., north of the Gandhi Bridge.* **Phone:** *748 3742.* **Bus:** *Local bus #81 (૮૧), 82 (૮૨), 83 (૮૩), 84 (૮૪), 86 (૮૬), 87 (૮૭), 200 (૨૦૦), or 300 (૩૦૦).* **Hours:** *Open daily April-Sept. 8:30am-7pm; Oct.-Mar. 8:30am-6:30pm. Closed during monsoon.* **Admission:** *Free.* **Other:** *Sound and light show is shown on Su, W, and F at 8:30pm; Rs5.*

The ashram was Gandhi's base of operations from 1917 until 1930. His simple living quarters are here, as is an impressive display of his biography, philosophy, paintings, photographs, quotes, political cartoons, and stamps. The focus is on the revitalization of the Ahmedabad textile industry, which he effected. It is common to see people studying or meditating among the reddish buildings and lush gardens.

Mosques and Temples

Even in the city proper, under its incredible noise and industry, there are a number of extraordinary sights to captivate visitors. Most prominent in Ahmedabad are the dozens of mosques, found about every 500m in every part of the city. The **Jumma Masjid** (Friday Mosque), on Gandhi Rd., is a good place to start. Built in 1424 by Sultan Ahmed Shah I, Jumma Masjid opens into a large marble courtyard. A small reflecting pool surrounded by devotees stands in the center. The structure's 15 domes are supported by 256 pillars, whose detailed carvings are predominantly Hindu. The curious black slab by the main massive archway is said to be an inverted Jain image. Through the left gate of the courtyard are the **Tomb of Ahmed Shah** and the **Rani-ka-hazira,** the tomb of his queens. The cenotaphs, in vast pillared chambers, are covered with fancy gold-laced cloths. A guard can lift one for you to reveal some fine stonework. Women are prohibited from entering the chambers holding the tombs of the male members of the family.

Sidi Saiyad's Mosque, in Lal Darwaja, was constructed by one of Ahmed Shah's slaves in 1573 and now graces half of Gujarat Tourism's literature. The interior of the mosque is impressive, with elaborately carved ceilings and domes, but the highlight is the delicate latticework on the screens lining the upper walls. Most are floral or arboreal in nature, with windy threads of marble meandering through one another. Women are not allowed to enter, but can enjoy the screens from the gardens.

Near the railway station, on Sardar Patel Rd., is **Rani Sipri's Mosque,** also known as **Masjid-e-Nagira** (Jewel of a Mosque), built in 1519. The central grave holds Rani

Sipri, who ordered the mosque built after her son was executed for a petty crime. The mosque is known for its exquisite latticework. The tomb itself is surrounded by 12 pillars under a single stylish dome. Near Sarangpur Darwaja are the famous **Shaking Minarets** and **Sidi Bashir's Mosque.** A huge arch supporting two 21m minarets explains half the name. These are balanced such that if one shakes, the other will move to counteract the tremor, allowing the mosque to survive jostles by earthquake and colonialist alike. Unfortunately, shaking the minarets is now prohibited.

The **Swaminarayan Temple** on the north side of the city is a Hindu temple dedicated to Vishnu and Lakshmi, built in 1850. It's a barrage of rainbow and metallic colors, dramatically contrasting with Ahmedabad's stonework. The temple features fine woodwork and detailed bright painting rivaling the mosques in intricacy. The **Hatheesing Temple,** north of Delhi Lake, is one of a few Jain temples in the city. *(Open to non-Jains daily 10am-noon and 4-7:30pm.)* It was built in 1848 of white marble and dedicated to the 15th *tirthankara,* Dharamarath. The temple's design is typically Jain, with detailed carvings of dancers and floral patterns.

Let's Go: Fly a Kite

For three nights in January, the skies of Ahmedabad are speckled with kites of all styles, colors, and sizes. Enthusiasts from all over the world descend upon the city for the International Kite Festival, the largest kite-related happening in the world. For weeks before, shops and stalls sell huge assortments of kites and kite equipment, as experts roam the streets offering lessons on the finer points of the craft. The festival itself has competitions for kite size, originality, and beauty, and it is accompanied by dancing, singing, shows, parades, and general merriment. At night the skies light up as kites are adorned with lights attached to the tails. The festival ends with a highly competitive contest in which kite strings are coated with adhesive and ground glass, turning them into razor-sharp lines. Kites are then sent flying into one another, slashing each other's lines until one emerges victorious. In 1999, the festival runs January 15-17.

Museums

The **Mehta Museum of Miniatures** (tel. 463324), southwest of the river in Paldi, has a large collection of miniature paintings, most of them modern, from throughout India. *(Open Tu-Su 11am-noon and 3-5pm. Free.)* The **Shreyas Folk Museum** (tel. 411338), west of the city, displays folk work—costumes, handicrafts, and textiles—from all over Gujarat. *(Open Tu-Su 10am-5pm. Free.)* Much of its collection is being moved to the **L.D. Institute of Indology** (tel. 442463), off Ashram Rd. near the Gandhi statue. *(Open M-Sa 10am-5:30pm. Free.)* Buses #34 (૩૪), 35 (૩૫), 41 (૪૧), and 200 (૨૦૦) serve both sites. The **Tribal Research and Training Museum** (tel. 446146), north of Ashram Rd., showcases similar crafts from regional tribal peoples and explains their customs. *(Open M-Sa 10:30am-2pm. Free.)*

■ Near Ahmedabad

Nineteen kilometers north off the road to Gandhinagar, the step-well **Adalaj Vav** ranks among the most impressive in the state. Built in 1499 by Rani Rudabai as a summer retreat, it now serves mainly as a popular relaxation spot for locals. The gardens around are pleasant enough, but the carvings on the well are the main attraction. The walls, pillars, and platforms of the 5-story well are adorned with intricate lattices and detailed carvings of mythological scenes. The best time to visit is just before noon, when the sunlight illuminates the stonework all the way to the bottom. Buses going to Mehsama Kalol from the Central Bus Stand pass Adlaj Vav (every 15min., 30min., Rs3). Shared jeeps cost Rs8-32, depending on how many people are sharing.

Eight kilometers southwest of the city sits **Sarkhej,** the erstwhile summer retreat of Gujarati sultans and present-day suburb, whose pacific atmosphere makes it seem much more removed than it physically is. Set on one side of an artificial lake is the tomb of Sheikh Ahmed Khattu Ganj Buksh, the spiritual mentor and unofficial advisor of Ahmed Shah. It is the largest mausoleum in the state, with a huge central dome supported by pillars and decorated with exemplary marble, brass, and wood ornamentation. Sultan Muhammed Beghada's mausoleum and that of his wife Rajabai are interesting as well. It was Sultan Beghada who vastly transformed Sarkhej in the 1500s, adding palaces, gardens, fountains, and courtyards to the previously solemn complex. It has declined over the years, but it is still an attractive place about which to wander peacefully. Bus #31 (3₹) from Lal Darwaja makes the trip here.

The site of **Lothal,** around 90km southwest of Ahmedabad, shook the archaeological community when it was discovered in 1945. Lothal is what remains of a city of the ancient Indus Valley Civilization dating from 2400 to 1900 BC. Lying in ruin are old roads, a bathhouse, a sewer, houses, shops, and a dock, suggesting Lothal was a major port city. A **museum** showcases the findings of years of excavation. Of particular historical interest are the pots and toys made from red pottery, which suggest that an even older civilization once inhabited Lothal, before 4000 BC. (Open M-Sa 10am-5pm.) To reach Lothal, take the bus to Bhavnagar, get off at Dholka, and take a frequent bus from there.

The unassuming town of **Modhera,** 100km northwest of Ahmedabad, is home to an extraordinary Jain-influenced **Sun Temple,** built in 1026 by the Solanki King Bhimdev I. As per Sun Temple norms, the temple was constructed and positioned so that at the time of the equinoxes, sunlight falls directly on the image of Surya, the sun god, in the sanctuary—many worshippers come at these times. The main pillared entry hall is adorned on the sides with 12 *adityas* representing the sun's phases through the year. (Open daily 10am-6pm.) Buses frequently run to Modhera from the Central Bus Stand (3hr., Rs40) and from Mehsana, which is connected to Ahmedabad by rail.

Thirty-two kilometers northeast of Ahmedabad is **Gandhinagar,** the capital of Gujarat and the second state capital in India planned and constructed after Independence. Designed by Le Corbusier, who also laid out Chandigarh (see p. 321), the city is rather boring with its symmetry and numbered sectors. Buses run to Gandhinagar every 30 minutes. (State buses from the Central Bus Stand cost Rs7; city buses can be caught at Lal Darwaja and along Ashram Rd. for Rs4.)

The artificially constructed Gujarati village of **Vishalla,** 4km south of Ahmedabad, offers a night of earthy village dining, as weavers and potters work in mud-and-thatch huts. Eat plentiful, spicy food from leaf plates and drink from clay cups as dressed-up villagers fan insect-repelling scented smoke in your face and musicians play. There's a museum with a collection of household objects. Dinner is an expensive Rs175-250, but snacks are also available. (Open daily 7-11pm.) Buses #31 (3₹) and 90 (₹0) run to Vasama, from which Vishalla is 15 minutes by foot or Rs25 by auto-rickshaw.

■ Rajkot રાજકોટ

Rajkot is of interest to travelers primarily as a gateway to the Kathiawar Peninsula, but it is also a clean, relaxed, typical Gujarati town. Founded in the 16th century, it was the capital of Saurashtra state and an important administrative center for the Raj. It is also famous for its connection to Mahatma Gandhi, who spent much of his youth here. In Rajkot, Gandhi went to school, married, and received permission from his mother to go to England—the rest, of course, is history.

ORIENTATION

Everything of interest in Rajkot is sandwiched between the **railway station** in the north and the **bus stand** in the south. The bus stand is on **Dhebar Road,** which darts north to **Trikonbaug,** a major circle that marks the city center. East of the circle is **Lakhajiraj Road;** west is an intersection at the eastern edge of the **Playing Fields.** Toward the left, **Dr. Yagnik Road** heads south and circles the fields, and at the right, **Jawahar Road** runs north past Jubilee Gardens to the Civil Hospital and **Junction Road.** A right at Junction Rd. and a left onto **Station Road** takes you to the railway station. From the Civil Hospital, **Kasturbai Road** leads southwest to the **race course** west of the Playing Fields.

PRACTICAL INFORMATION

Airport: Rajkot Airport (tel. 454533), 4km northwest of town. **Indian Airlines,** Dhebar Rd. (tel. 234122; fax 233329), near the circle. Open daily 8:30am-1pm and 2-6:30pm. **Gujarat Airways,** Jawahar Rd. (tel. 222866; fax 224590), Sterling Apartments, south of Jubilee Gardens. Open daily 9am-1pm and 3-7pm. To: **Delhi** (3 per week, 3hr., US$105); **Jaipur** (3 per week, 2½hr., US$80); **Mumbai** (1-3 per day, 1hr., US$75); **Udaipur** (3 per week, 1½hr., US$65).

Trains: Rajkot Railway Station (tel. 131). Reservation office (tel. 135) open M-Sa 8am-8pm, Su 8am-2pm. Fares listed are 2nd/1st class. To: **Ahmedabad** (5 per day, including *Bhopal Exp.* 1269, 2:35pm, 5hr., Rs100/300); **Dwarka** (*Saurashtra Mail* 9005, 10am, 5hr., Rs60/280); **Junagadh** (4 per day, including *Veraval Mail* 9838, 11am, 3hr., Rs31/61); **Veraval** (*Veraval Mail* 9838, 11am, 6hr., Rs51/242).

Buses: Main Bus Stand (tel. 235025). To: **Ahmedabad** (every 15min., 4hr., Rs.40); **Diu** (2 per day, 6hr., Rs38); **Dwarka** (12 per day, 5:30am-11pm, 5½hr., Rs51); **Junagadh** (every 30min., 2am-midnight, 2hr., Rs20/23); **Veraval** and **Somnath** (14 per day, 6am-midnight, 4½hr., Rs36/40). **Private bus companies** line the road opposite the bus stand, serving many cities in Gujarat and Rajasthan. **Eagle Travel Agency,** Moti Tonki (tel. 450300) is recommended. Open daily 6am-midnight.

Local Transportation: Unmetered **auto-rickshaws** buzz to the airport (Rs20). **Local buses** head anywhere in the city for Rs3 or less. Ask the locals for help in determining the right bus for your destination. **Chakka-rickshaws** (tempo-motorcycle hybrids) charge Rs5-10 between various points in the city.

Tourist Office: Tourist Information Bureau (tel. 234507), behind State Bank of Saurashtra at the southern end of Jawahar Rd. in a yellow brick building, on the second floor. Moderately helpful staff sells maps of Gujarat (Rs20) but none of Rajkot. Open M-Sa 10:30am-6:10pm.

Currency Exchange: State Bank of India, Jawahar Rd. (tel. 226416-7; fax 223439). Just north of Jubilee Gardens, on the opposite side of the road. Changes cash and traveler's checks. Open M-F 11am-3pm, Sa 11am-1pm.

Market: The main commercial areas are in the old city, on Lakhajiraj Rd., and along the Dharbar-Jawahar Rd. stretch. Most stores open M-Sa 9am-1pm and 3-10pm.

Pharmacy: There are a few on every major road. Most open daily 9am-8pm.

Hospital: Civil Hospital (tel. 440298; fax 445868). Clean. English-speaking staff.

Police: Police Commissioner's Office (tel. 444288), opposite the racecourse next to Galaxy Cinema. **Control room** (tel. 444288) open 24hr.

Emergency: Police, tel. 100. **Fire,** tel. 101. **Ambulance,** tel. 102.

Post Office: GPO (tel. 228611), west of Jawahar Rd., opposite Jubilee Gardens. Open M-Sa 8am-7pm. **Postal Code:** 360001.

Internet: Wesphil C.C. (tel. 237290), 2nd floor of Galaxy Building, just below the hotel. Surf the web for Rs30 per hr.

Telephones: Telegraph Office, Jawahar Rd. (tel. 227592; fax 221452) opposite Jubilee Gardens. STD/ISD, fax, telegraph. Open 24hr. **Telephone Code:** 0281.

ACCOMMODATIONS

Cheap hotels cluster near the railway station and on Lakhajiraj Rd. Business hotels surround the Playing Fields. There are plenty of both types behind the bus stand.

Galaxy (tel. 222904), in the Galaxy Building overlooking the Playing Fields. If you can spend a little more, you can enjoy the largest singles in town with nice bathrooms, room service, and laundry. Singles Rs300-400.

Himalaya Guest House, Lakhajiraj Rd. (tel. 213736). Enter through the shopping complex below, from the side street. Spacious, bland, clean rooms with attached bath. Check-out noon. Singles Rs100; doubles Rs150; triples Rs300; quads Rs400.

Hotel Moon Guest House (tel. 225522), behind the bus stand. The best budget hotel in the cluster. Clean, sparsely decorated rooms, clean bathrooms, and great terrace views of the city's commotion. Room service 24hr. Check-out noon. Singles and doubles Rs100, with attached bath Rs200.

FOOD

Rajkot's eateries serve a blend of traditional and modern Indian cuisine. *Thali* lovers will surely be appeased here, but all kinds of food is available. Many restaurants also specialize in ice cream and have yummy joints lining Race Course Rd., which are popular hang-outs for youths and couples.

Havmor Restaurant, Jawahar Rd., just south of Jubilee Garden. Revel in Punjabi, Chinese, and Continental entrees in the A/C, mirrored, and marbled dining room. Havmor is renowned here, but when they're busy, the service flags. Veg. dishes Rs30-50, non-veg. Rs40-60. Open daily 9am-11pm.

Lord's Banquet Restaurant, Kasturbai Rd. Gaudy chandeliers, A/C, huge, soft, semi-circular booths, and an enormous selection of Chinese, Continental, and Indian veg. specialties (Rs30-60). Open daily 11am-3pm and 7:30-11:30pm.

Rainbow Restaurant, Lakhajiraj Rd., under the Himalaya Guest House. Cheap, with a range of veg. South Indian snacks and Punjabi and Chinese dishes, plus novelty-named ice cream confections. A/C upstairs. Open daily 10am-11pm.

SIGHTS

In the heart of the promenade lies Jubilee Gardens—worthy but unspectacular, save for the **Watson Museum,** flanked by stone lions and curiously dedicated to Colonel John Watson, a 19th-century British political agent. The museum houses Indus Valley Civilization artifacts, exquisite miniature paintings, and Rajasthani brass- and silver-work. Most peculiar is an 1899 statue of a grim Queen Victoria surrounded by portraits of Gujarati rulers. *(Open M-Sa 10am-2pm and 2:30-6pm. Closed 2nd and 4th Sa. Admission Rs1.)* **Kaba Gandhi no Delo,** on Ghitaka Rd., was the residence of the Gandhi family when they moved here in 1881. It now features a small collection of photographs and memorabilia. *(Open M-Sa 9am-noon and 3-6pm.)* The Playing Fields (or **maidan**) host concerts a few nights a week—check local listings.

■ Diu ઼િ઼

Life on the small island of Diu (DEE-ooh on the island and Dew on the mainland) off the southern coast of Gujarat, revolves around the twin pleasures of fish and alcohol. Diu was a Portuguese colony and important trade outpost until 1961, when India repossessed it, so it is considered part of a Union Territory rather than a part of Gujarat. Since Gujarat's prohibition laws don't apply in Diu, Gujaratis invade Diu by the thousands every weekend for mass debauchery. Many tourists also come to Diu to take a break from their travels: colorful buildings, an impressive fort, and marvelous beaches serve to cheer up hung-over revelers.

ORIENTATION

Diu Island is roughly 12km long from east to west and 3km wide. One enters Diu via the port town of **Una** in Saurashtra, past the **railway station** in the town of **Delwada,** and through the little island of **Goghla,** off the northeastern tip of Diu Island. **Diu Town** occupies the eastern tip of the island. From there, roads head west through the island past **Chakratirth Beach** and **Sunset Point** and, on the southside, the village of **Fudam, Diu Airport,** and the famous **Nagoa Beach,** before ending at the western tip of the island in Varakbara. Diu Town itself is defined by a wall running north-south across the eastern tip. Most people enter through the northern gate near the **main bus stand** along **Burden Road,** which runs south through the city past the **local bus stand** and the **Public Gardens** before bending and dead-ending into **Diu Fort,** which marks the extreme east tip of the town and island. Entry into Diu Town through the middle **Jampa Gate** inevitably results in disorientation among the tiny, winding streets of the old city. The southern entry into the city is along **Jallandhar Beach,** bending up past St. Francis' Hospital and St. Thomas' Church to meet Burden Rd.

PRACTICAL INFORMATION

Airport: Diu Airport, 5km west of Diu Town, north of Nagoa Beach (auto-rickshaw Rs50). **Gujarat Airways,** off Burden Rd. next to the GPO, flies daily to **Mumbai** (50min., US$80). Departures are irregular; expect delays and cancellations.

Trains: Delwada Railway Station, between Una and Goghla, 8km from Diu Town (auto-rickshaw Rs70). To: **Junagadh** (*Rail Bus* 1, 1:30pm, 7hr., Rs17) via **Sasan Gir** (5hr., Rs13) and **Veraval** (*Veraval Local,* 6am, 4½hr., Rs14).

Buses: Main Bus Stand, outside city walls, near the bridge to the mainland. Most buses leave between 6 and 8am or noon and 3pm. To: **Ahmedabad** (1 per day, 7am, 8½hr., Rs75); **Mumbai** (evening, 22hr., Rs250); **Rajkot** (3 per day, 6½hr., Rs50); **Una** (every ½hr., 6am-8pm, 40min., Rs7); **Veraval** (3 per day, 2½hr., Rs22). The **Una Bus Stand** runs buses to: **Ahmedabad** (every 2hr., 7am-8pm, 8hr., Rs69); **Junagadh** (every 1½hr., 6am-10pm, 5hr., Rs35); **Rajkot** (every 2hr., 7am-10pm, 6hr., Rs43); **Veraval** (every hr., 6am-11pm, 2hr., Rs18). **Private bus companies** surround the Main Sq. in Diu Town. **Gayatri Travels,** next to the State Bank of Saurashtra near the Main Sq., is recommended. Open daily 6am-midnight. **Avoid Sunday night buses out of Diu, which are inevitably filled with drunken Gujaratis.**

Local Transportation: Auto-rickshaws are ubiquitous in Diu. Rs5 gets you around town, Rs30 to Nagoa Beach, and Rs70 to Una. Add Rs20 for night travel out of Diu Town. **Local buses** leave from the **local bus stand,** west of the Main Sq., to Nagoa Beach (every 1½hr., 7am-4:30pm, Rs2) and Delwada (every hr., 6am-11pm, Rs3). **Bicycles** can be rented from Abdul Cycle Store in Main Sq. (Rs15 per day). **Mopeds** can be rented from Alpama Hotel, on Burden Rd. past the vegetable market (Rs100 per day; Rs150 for an auto-start—highly recommended).

Tourist Office: Tourist Information Bureau, Burden Rd. (tel. 52653), near Main Sq., has maps and travel information, and can make camping arrangements. Open M-F 9:30am-1pm and 3-6pm, Sa 9:30am-1pm.

Currency Exchange: State Bank of Saurashtra, around the corner behind the GPO. Open M-F 11am-3pm, Sa 11am-1pm.

Market: Most markets and stores open daily 9am-9pm; many are closed Su and between 1-3pm. Behind Main Sq. is the **Fish Market,** while the **Vegetable Market** is farther down Burden Rd., 200m toward the fort past Main Sq.

Pharmacy: Many shops near Main Sq. sell basic medicines and toiletries. Most open daily 10am-6pm.

Hospital: Government Hospital, in St. Francis of Assisi Church, 200m north of Jallandhar Beach (tel. 102). English spoken. Pharmacy for patients. Open 24hr. for emergencies; open 9am-1pm and 3-6pm for consultations.

Police: Main Police Station, Burden Rd. Past Public Gardens on the left. Open 24hr.

Emergency: Police, tel. 100. **Fire,** tel. 101. **Ambulance,** tel. 102.

Post Office: GPO, Burden Rd. in Main Sq. *Poste Restante.* Open M-F 10am-12:30pm and 1:30-5pm, Sa 10am-12:30pm. **Postal Code:** 362520.

Telephones: STD/ISD booths line Burden Rd. and the inner city. Most open daily 8am-10pm. **Telephone Code:** 02875.

ACCOMMODATIONS AND FOOD

Considering that most visitors to Diu are only looking for a place to black out after a night of drinking, hotels in Diu have no incentive to be spectacular, but they are generally adequate. Off-season discounts are substantial, but you'll need to bargain. Most restaurants in Diu provide only the minimum amount of food required to serve alcohol, since free-standing bars are prohibited. A few restaurants have good seafood between November and April. If you don't mind going a little out of your way to Fudam, Diu's only luxury hotel, **Kohinoor** (tel. 52209), has a good restaurant called **Rio** that serves Indian and Chinese delicacies for Rs40-70. In general, hotels are your best bet for decent food.

Diu Town

Jay Shankar's Guest House, Jallandhar Beach (tel. 52424). Catering to backpacking foreigners, Jay has a social guest house, diner, and bar rolled into one. Small, clean, homey rooms. The restaurant has Indian and Western dishes of all sorts—try the French toast anytime!—but the seafood makes it stellar. Check-out noon. Singles Rs70; doubles Rs125-250. Note: the water in the attached baths is seawater.

Hotel Sanman, Burden Rd. (tel. 52273). A Portuguese mansion that changes its name every few years. Big rooms with local hand-made furnishings and views of the northern shore. Limited room service but a good rooftop restaurant and bar. Check-out 10am. Singles with bath Rs100; doubles Rs150-200, with A/C Rs300.

Hotel Mozambique, Burden Rd. (tel. 52223). A distinctly Portuguese building in the heart of the vegetable market. Rooms are big and draw in a nice breeze through the balconies with seaside (or market) views, but they're not especially clean. Good restaurant with cheap seafood. Check-out noon. Singles Rs75, with bath Rs100-125; doubles with bath Rs200-275.

Nagoa Beach

In season, younger crowds like to camp on Nagoa Beach. **Oasis Camping Site,** run by the tourist office, has campgrounds with equipment for rent (tents Rs200 per night). Camping outside of these authorized sites is strictly prohibited.

Ganga Sagar Rest House, Nagoa Beach (tel. 52249). Rooms are small and undecorated, but clean, and the location on the beach is unbeatable. The outer courtyard faces the sea directly and is very relaxed. Limited room service, decent restaurant and bar. Check-out 8am. Singles Rs150; doubles Rs225.

SIGHTS AND ENTERTAINMENT

Wandering through the labyrinthine streets is the best way to see Diu Town, especially after a few drinks at the countless bars (or countless drinks at a few bars). The old inner city is filled with painted Portuguese-style buildings and villas that make it almost impossible to believe you're in India. **Nagar Seth's Haveli** (ask for directions once you're in the old city) is considered the most impressive and distinctively Portuguese of the lot. Toward the fort are Diu's three churches, also very European in architecture. **St. Paul's** is badly weathered, but it has grand ceilings and arches, excellent paintings, and a beautiful organ. Mass is still held here each Sunday. **St. Thomas'** is nearby, holding the **Diu Museum** and its religious paintings and Catholic statues. To the east, past the police station, is the **Diu Fort,** the most impressive structure on the island. Built in 1591, the fort is immense, guarded by a tidal moat. There's little to do there except to wander among dozens of cannonballs and a few cannons. The views of the sea and town are beautiful, especially at sunset. The fort also doubles as the island jail. *(Fort open daily 9am-6pm. Photography very loosely prohibited inside.)*

Travelers sick of (or from) drinking might enjoy Diu's excellent beaches. On the south side of Diu Town, **Jallandhar Beach** is rocky but great for wading. **Chakratirth Beach** is better for swimming. The nearby **Sunset Point** is a favorite local hangout. But Diu's longest and most famous (but filthy) beach is at **Nagoa,** 7km west of town. Across the bridge in **Goghla** is another long beach that's great for swimming, with fewer palms but fewer tourists than Nagoa. Auto-rickshaws shuttle from the Bazaar to Jallandhar Beach and Chakratirth (Rs15), Goghla Beach (Rs20), and Nagoa (Rs30).

■ Veraval and Somnath વેરાવળ સોમનાથ

The busy city of Veraval is the most important port in Saurashtra, home to over 1000 boats and a hand-built wooden *dhow* industry. While the docks no doubt provide for an intriguing but smelly stroll, Veraval is more interesting as a stepping stone to nearby Somnath, 5km away. Known for its once-magnificent temple, Somnath is a popular and convenient religious vacation spot for many Gujaratis.

ORIENTATION AND PRACTICAL INFORMATION Veraval's main **bus stand** (tel. 21666) is on the main town thoroughfare, which runs roughly northwest-southeast and dead-ends at the port. The center of town is the intersection marked by the **Clock Tower,** towards the port from the bus stand. STD/ISD **telephone** booths are

WEST INDIA

concentrated here (**telephone code:** 02876). At the Clock Tower, the left road heads northeast, passing the **GPO** (tel. 21255; open M-Sa 10am-6pm; **postal code:** 362266) down the first street on the left, and forks just past the **State Bank of India** (no foreign exchange facilities). The fork's left tine leads to the **Veraval Railway Station** (tel. 20444, 23426). Trains (fares listed are 2nd/1st class) run to: **Ahmedabad** (*Girnar Exp.* 9945, 7:30pm, 10hr., Rs151/445); **Junagadh** (4 per day, 2hr., Rs85/126); and **Rajkot** (*Saurashtra Mail* 9837, 11:25am, 5hr., Rs82/213). From the station, the road leads to another that bends around Veraval Harbor, ending up in Somnath. Its **bus stand** and the **Temple of Somnath** are about 100m apart. Buses run to: **Ahmedabad** (8, 11am, and 7:30pm, 10hr., Rs85); **Diu** (7:30, 9:30am, and 4:30pm, 3hr., Rs20); **Dwarka** (6, noon, 12:45, and 2:15pm, 6hr., Rs50); **Junagadh** (every hr., 8am-7:30pm, 2hr., Rs17); and **Rajkot** (every hr., 7am-10pm, 4hr., Rs32). From the Clock Tower, **local buses** run from Veraval to Somnath and back (every 30min., 6am-11pm, Rs3). **Auto-rickshaws** make the same trip for Rs25. The **State Bank of Saurashtra,** on Shubash Rd., past the clock tower and toward the port, changes currency and traveler's checks (open M-F 11am-3pm, Sa 11am-1pm). The **police station** is to the right of the tower (tel. 20003; open 24hr.).

ACCOMMODATIONS AND FOOD Hotels in Veraval congregate along the route between the bus stand and the railway station. Although staying in Veraval is convenient, the two hotels in Somnath are cheaper and far more peaceful, but more spartan. Most restaurants in Veraval are between the bus stand and Clock Tower, but there are stalls and *dhabas* all over the city. Somnath has many such quasi-eateries, but no full-fledged restaurants.

The **Mayuram Hotel** (tel. 20286), near Somnath bus stand, has big, spotless and spartan rooms (singles and doubles Rs200; triples Rs300; quads Rs350; off-season: Rs125/175/250). The bedcovers grow on you, and mosquitoes are surprisingly absent. Attached baths and noon check-out round out the pretty picture—and you'll wake to the soft chanting of hymns from the nearby temple. The **Chetna Rest House** (tel. 20688) has clean rooms surrounding a debris-riddled courtyard. Don't let the rubbish scare you away—it's an excellent value. (Check-out 1pm. Dorm beds Rs35; singles Rs50, with attached bath Rs70; doubles Rs95/125.) **Hotel Ajanta,** on the left as you walk out of the Veraval bus stand, has more luxurious and expensive rooms than the Chetna (singles Rs100-150, with A/C Rs300; doubles Rs150-200/350; triples Rs200; quads Rs250; extra bed Rs50), but it's still a good deal, with travel, laundry, and 24-hour room service (noon check-out). **Jill Restaurant** (tel. 20713), about halfway between the bus stand and the Clock Tower in Veraval, has an A/C dining hall with tall cushioned booths and greasy food. (Veg. Punjabi, South Indian, Chinese, and Continental dishes Rs20-40. Open daily 8am-11pm.) Note: Even though Veraval is a fishing town, pious Gujarati culture keeps seafood confined to a handful of hotels and Muslim restaurants. Don't even *think* about meat in Sommath.

SIGHTS Somnath is renowned throughout Gujarat for its **Temple of Somnath,** also known as **Prabhas Patan Mandir,** which faces the sea. The history of the temple is actually more interesting than the temple itself. According to popular myth, the site of the temple was dedicated to a hallucinogenic ritual plant called *soma* which appears often in the *Vedas* (see **The Vedas and Upanishads,** p. 92). Legend has it that the temple was built first of pure gold by Samraj the moon god, then of silver by Ravana the sun god, then of wood by Krishna, and finally of stone by the Pandava brother Bhima (of *Mahabharata* fame). Historians insist that the temple was built in the early 10th century AD and are quite adamant that the temple has always been made of stone. At one time, however, the temple was so rich that its coffers were stuffed with gold and jewelry, and its full-time staff included hundreds of dancers and musicians. The notorious Mahmud of Ghazni raided and destroyed it in the early 11th century, effectively starting a cycle of sacking and rebuilding that persisted until Aurangzeb's final plundering and restoration in 1706. In 1950, the temple's reconstruction was funded by Sardar Patel, who is commemorated with a statue outside the temple. Very little of the original temple remains. Nonetheless, it is still very grand, and the stonework is quite elaborate in places, although the bitter sea winds seem to have gotten the better of the stone on the ocean side. Thousands of devotees flock here, and there are enthusiastic *pujas* at 7am, noon, and 7pm.

Near the temple is the **Somnath Museum,** which holds the eclectic remains of previous temple glories, including paintings, latticework, stone sculptures, and pottery. *(Open M-Sa 9am-noon and 3-6pm, closed 2nd and 4th Sa. Admission Rs0.50.)*

■ Junagadh જૂનાગઢ

Less than 100km north of Diu, the lively town of Junagadh, also known as Junagarh, is refreshingly untainted and un-Westernized. Nestled at the base of Mount Girnar, the town is filled with temples, *havelis,* mosques, and vibrant bazaars. In the 4th century BC, Junagadh was the capital of Gujarat under the emperor Ashoka. After Ashoka's death, the city passed through several hands before falling under Muslim rule, where it remained until Independence. The ruler of Junagadh at the time wanted to pass it on to Pakistan, but the Hindu majority in town promptly exiled him, and Junagadh joined the Indian Union. While Junagadh is a fascinating city to visit at any time, the pilgrimage site of Mount Girnar ensures that during the Shivaratri Festival, February through March, it turns into a wild, nine-day party.

ORIENTATION AND PRACTICAL INFORMATION Due to its nonsensical layout, Junagadh is a rather difficult city to navigate, but it's so small that it's hard to get too lost. The **long distance bus stand** (tel. 30303) is on the west side of town, off **Dhal Road,** the main, vaguely east-west thoroughfare. **Station Road** crosses Dhal Rd. just east of the bus stand; going north on Station Rd. takes you to **Junagadh Railway Station** (tel. 131). From the bus stand, Dhal Rd. runs east, crossing the railroad tracks on the way to **Chittakhana Chowk,** the central bazaar area, and eventually to **Uperkot Fort.** At Chittakhana Chowk, **Mahatma Gandhi Road** branches south and runs down to **Kalwa Chowk,** another market area, passing the **Government Hospital** (tel. 20652; open 24hr.), the **local bus stand,** the **GPO** (open M-Sa 9:30am-5pm; **postal code:** 362001), the main **police station** (tel. 27001), the **public library,** and the **Bank of Baroda** (open M-F 11am-3pm, Sa 11am-1pm), which exchanges money much more quickly than the State Bank. Roughly halfway between Chittakhana Chowk and Uperkot Fork, **Jhalorapa Road** branches south off Dhal Rd. through Diwan Chowk, near the **State Bank of India** (open M-F 11am-3pm, Sa 11am-1pm).

Trains (fares listed are 2nd/1st class) run to: **Ahmedabad** (2 per day, 6hr., Rs83/434); **Rajkot** (3 per day, 3hr., Rs28/156); and **Veraval** (5 per day, 3hr., Rs25/139). **Buses** go to: **Ahmedabad** (express every hr., 5:30am-12:30am, 7hr., Rs60); **Bhuj** (5:40am and 7:50pm, 6hr., Rs50); **Dwarka** (5:30am, 5hr., Rs40); **Rajkot** (every 15min., 5:30am-2am, 2hr., Rs20/23); and **Veraval** (every hr., 5:30am-12:30am, 2hr., Rs22). **Private bus companies** reside along Dhal Rd. and run comfortable minibuses and buses to towns in Gujarat and to Bombay.

Most of the city's many **STD/ISD** telephone booths are open daily from 8am to 10pm (**telephone code:** 0285). **Pharmacies** can be found in Kalwa Chowk and Chittakhana Chowk near the General Hospital. **Shree Medical Stores,** Dhal Rd. (tel. 31820), just west of the railway crossing, is open 24 hours. **Auto-rickshaws** are everywhere; Rs20 gets you around town, Rs35 to Mt. Girnar. **Local buses** run to Mt. Girnar from the local bus stand (every hr., 6am-5pm, Rs2). **Bicycles** can be rented from several locations around Chittakhana Chowk for Rs3 per hour or Rs25 per day.

ACCOMMODATIONS AND FOOD During Shivaratri, all hotels are fully booked; be sure to reserve well in advance. Most hotels are in Kalwa Chowk and along Dhal Rd. west of Chittakhana Chowk. There are also a few near the main bus stand and the railway station. **Hotel Relief,** Chittakhana Chowk (tel. 20280), is popular mainly because it has assumed the role of the city's unofficial tourist information center. The rooms (singles Rs100; doubles Rs200; with A/C both Rs440) are average-sized and tastefully decorated, and have attached baths. The hotel has 24-hour room service, travel services, and a decent restaurant. (Check-out 10am.) The spartan **Hotel National,** Kalwa Chowk (tel. 27891), is a gem in its environs. Rooms (singles Rs100, with bathtub and A/C Rs440; doubles Rs200/550) are spotless, carpeted, well-decorated, and even a bit romantic. All rooms have attached bath, and the restaurant is another bargain. (Check-out 10am.) **Hotel Somnath** (tel. 24645), near the railway station, is far from town but near the sights, offering clean, well-furnished rooms (singles Rs100, with TV Rs165, with A/C Rs400; doubles Rs150/200/550; extra bed Rs60, with A/C Rs80).

Food in Junagadh is unspectacular. Although a number of food stalls and *dhabas* fill Chittakhana and Kalwa Chowk, you'll find better food at hotels. **Sagar Restaurant** (tel. 23939), near Kalwa Chowk, has a dim A/C dining room and the best food in town. (Entrees Rs20-40. Open daily 9am-3pm and 5-10:45pm.) **Santoor Restaurant,** M. Gandhi Rd. (tel. 25090), near Kalwa Chowk, has a somewhat shabby exterior and a popular A/C eatery inside. Indian vegetarian dishes are artfully presented. (Open daily 9:45am-3pm and 5-10:30pm.)

SIGHTS The impressive **Uperkot Fort,** stoutly sitting atop its mini-plateau in the middle of the town, ranks among the best in the state. Built in 319 BC, it was ignored for 1300 years until its rediscovery in 976. It was then besieged a whopping 16 times over an 800-year period; one unsuccessful siege lasted 12 years. A high stone *tripolia* gate marks the entrance to the fort and the start of the twisty cobblestone path that meanders first to the **Jumma Masjid,** built on top of a Hindu temple. It must have been quite amazing at one time, with 140 pillars supporting its high ceiling; now, however, the lack of maintenance shows. If you fancy spelunking, check out the **Babupyana Caves,** south of the fort, and the **Khapra Kodia Caves,** north of the fort. The fort also holds two *vavs* (step-wells). The **Adi Chadi Vav** has 170 steps descending into dimness below, while the extraordinary **Navghan Kuva** has a unique 11th-century circular staircase that winds over 50m down the well. *(Open daily 9am-6:30pm. Admission Rs2.)* Near Diwan Chowk outside the fort is the **Durbar Hall Museum.** The collection is extensive, but pretty standard as fort city museums go. *(Open Th-Tu 9am-12:30pm and 3:30-6:30pm. Admission Rs3.)*

On the road to Mt. Girnar, west of the railway station, is the dazzling **Baha-ud-din-Bhar Muqbara,** with spiraling minarets, curved grand arches, and numerous domes. The architecture throughout is intricate and smooth, providing for a *muqbara* unique in Gujarat. The opulent interior has carved silver doors. Also on the way to Mt. Girnar is the granite boulder inscribed with the **Ashokan edicts** (named for their author, Emperor Ashoka). Dating from the 3rd century BC, these edicts teach assorted moral lessons of *dharma*, tolerance, equality, love, harmony, and peace. The Sanskritic inscriptions were added later by other rulers and refer to flooding in nearby areas.

The extinct 1100m volcano **Mount Girnar** is about 4km east of Junagadh and has been sacred to several religions since 300 BC. Nearly 5000 steps wind their way up to the summit through forests alternating with sun-scorched stone outcrops. Start your climb before 7am to avoid the heat and stop frequently at the drink stalls lining the ascent. One and a half hot hours later, you'll come upon a cluster of fine Jain temples. The marble **Neminath Temple,** dedicated to the 22nd *tirthankara* who, according to legend, died on Mount Girnar, houses a black marble image of the ascetic and features typical richly detailed Jain temple carvings along pillars, domes, and arches. The colorful mosaic-work in several locations is unusual in Jain temples, but still congruous with the latticework. At this point, the suggestion of another 2000 steps to the peak may be laughable, but it's worth the struggle, if only to engrave your name with chalk in the rocks along the side. At the top, the small **Amba Mata Temple** sees as many newlyweds as do some hill stations because a visit is said to guarantee a happy marriage. Tinier shrines also dot the peak. The view is breathtaking.

■ Near Junagadh: Sasan Gir National Park સાસાણ ગીર

Sasan Gir, 54km from Junagadh, is the last stronghold of the Asiatic lion. The Indian edition is almost nine feet in length, and can be distinguished from its African cousin by its bigger tail tassel, bushy elbow tufts, larger belly folds, and smaller mane. Long ago, these big cats lived in forests and grasslands from Greece to Bengal, but by the 20th century, there were only 239 left on the planet. In 1900, the Nawab of Junagadh invited Lord Curzon, then Viceroy of India, on a lion hunt, and the two met a firestorm of criticism for further endangering an endangered species. Lord Curzon cancelled the hunt and advised the Nawab to protect the lions on his land, the only place outside the African continent that lions can be found in the wild.

The forest became a wildlife sanctuary in 1969, and it now covers over 250 square kilometers. Lions number more than 300 and are proliferating. The forests and grasslands of the park also harbor peacocks, hyenas, panthers, and many varieties of deer. Sasan Gir is open October 16 to June 15. Admission is Rs70 for foreigners (camera fee Rs8). The park is accessible by train (*Delwara Local* 352, 6:15am, 3hr, Rs13) and bus (every hr., 7am-1pm, 2hr., Rs26) from Junagadh. Shared jeeps are required to tour the park (Rs3.5 per km per person; departures at 8:30am and 3:30pm). Jeep and entry fees total about Rs80. The average trip takes about 45 minutes, and at least one lion sighting is probable, though you shouldn't be disappointed if all the beasts do is stare at you and lick their chops. The **Mane Land Lodge** is a decent guest house with ubiquitous lion motifs (singles Rs70; doubles Rs100).

■ Dwarka દ્વારકા

Most Hindu legends are in agreement on the subject of Dwarka's holiness. One story holds that Krishna set up his capital here, on the westernmost point on the Kathiawar peninsula, after being forced to flee Mathura in Uttar Pradesh. Vishnu is said to have descended as a fish and battled demons here, while the 9th-century saint Shankara established a monastery, marking Dwarka as the westernmost point of India, corresponding to other monasteries in the north, east, and south. Few tourists come here, but those who do ascribe their satisfaction to the town's mystical remoteness and the pious sense of peace that the sea and the temple inspire in the place and its people.

ORIENTATION AND PRACTICAL INFORMATION Dwarka is small enough to wander about on foot, even though **auto-rickshaws** are available (Rs10 to the railway station). The main entry road into the city bends right as it joins the road between the main gate into the **old city** and the **railway station** (tel. 34044), about 2km away. Just before reaching the **main gate,** it turns right, skirting a huge empty field, then bending left. After the bend is a set of three arches—the second gate into the old city—on the right. Going straight leads to a road that runs along the coast, and the main road bends left, passing the **main bus stand** (tel. 34204) and a small building that serves as the **GPO (postal code: 361335),** on its way to Okha, the port for Bet Dwarka. The old city is a maze of tiny streets, so the easiest way to navigate is to ask locals. The old city is centered around **Dwarkadish Temple,** with the main **police station** (tel. 34523) next door; **Dwarka Lighthouse** marks the old city's sweep back to the coast. **Navajyot Hospital** (tel. 34419; open daily 9am-1pm and 4:30-8:30pm for consultations, 24hr. for emergencies), the best hospital in town, is on a street 400m toward the coast from the main gate. **STD/ISD** booths are usually open daily 9am-1pm and 4-9pm **(telephone code: 02892).**

Trains (fares are 2nd/1st class) run to: **Ahmedabad** (*Saurashtra Mail* 9006, noon, 10hr. Rs100/500); **Mumbai** (*Saurashtra Mail* 9006, noon, 20hr., Rs225/820); and **Rajkot** (3 per day, 5-7hr., Rs90/60). The reservations office is open daily 9:30am-12:30pm. **Intercity buses** run to: **Ahmedabad** (7 per day, 10hr., Rs82/92 regular/deluxe); **Bhuj** (7:30am, 9hr., Rs73); **Junagadh** (9:30, 11am, and 2pm, 7hr., Rs45); **Rajkot** (14 per day, 5am-9pm, 5hr., Rs50/60; **Veraval** (8 per day, 6am-6pm, 6hr., Rs50/60). **Local buses** shuttle to **Okha** (every 15min., 4am-10pm, 45min., Rs7).

ACCOMMODATIONS AND FOOD Most lodgings in Dwarka cater to pilgrims, so spartan living standards are the norm, but the rooms are clean and well-maintained, with attached bathrooms. **Hotel Meera** (tel. 34031), near the main gate into the old city, boasts spotless whitewashed rooms (singles Rs100, Rs200 with A/C; doubles Rs175/250), and a familial staff. The **Meera Dining Hall** makes it a great stay, with delicious bottomless *thalis* for Rs25. (Open daily 11am-3pm and 7-11pm.) **Radhika** (tel. 34063) is a stone's throw from the S.T. bus stand and has rooms as nice as those at Meera for the exact same prices. The **Toran Tourist Guest House** (tel. 34013), near the coast, is another good choice. Run by Gujarat Tourism, it features big, well-kept rooms and a knowledgeable staff. Mosquito nets are provided. (Check-out 9am. Dorm beds Rs30. Doubles Rs200; triples Rs250. Discount 50% July-Sept.) **Guru-prenna** (tel. 34512), on the way to the temple from the bus station, features an A/C garden restaurant and outdoor fast food joint offering dirt-cheap and tasty *thalis*, as well as Punjabi and Chinese dishes (Rs20-40).

SIGHTS Dwarka's principal attraction is the staggering **Dwarkadish Temple,** marking the center of town with its 6-story, 50m-high main spire. The impressive, weathered exterior stonework is dominated by spiky motifs. Sixty columns support the main structure, which houses a black marble Krishna image in a silver-plated chamber. Smaller shrines decorate the edges of the complex. *(Temple open daily 7am-1pm and 5-9:30pm, to Hindus only; non-Hindus may sign a release form to obtain entrance.)* The **Dwarka Lighthouse** is open to visitors daily 4:30pm until sunset, and offers spectacular views of the sun setting over the Arabian Sea *(Admission Rs1)*. Nearby is a long, clean beach that is rarely crowded, except on Sunday, and is great for wading and wandering past the small beach temples. Leave early from Dwarka—around 8am—as standing in line in the hot sun can ruin this trip for even the most pious pilgrim.

No pilgrimage to Dwarka is complete without a visit to the tiny island of **Bet Dwarka,** at the tip of the peninsula. The island is accessible by the port at Okha, an hour north of Dwarka. From the port, pile onto overloaded, unbalanced, pink and blue wooden boats that make the 30-minute crossing (every 20min., Rs2). The island has a number of architecturally uninspired temples dedicated to Krishna, where devotees come for *prasad* and *puja*. The main temple has a central well that brings up supposedly sweet-tasting water, although it apparently draws from the surrounding salty ocean. It marks the spot of Krishna's death, according to legend. The main appeal of Bet Dwarka is its remote solitude and mysticism, eerily enhanced by the silence, broken only by howling dogs and chanting old women.

KUTCHCH કચ્છ

One of the most isolated regions in India, Kutchch (also spelled Kachch, Kuchch, or Kachchha), is surrounded by the Gulf of Kutchch and the Arabian Sea to the west and north, and east by the Rann of Kutchch, a marsh that is part of the Thar desert and home to pink flamingos and the rare wild ass. During the monsoon, the Rann of Kutchch floods, cutting Kutchch off from its neighbors Saurashtra (Gujarat) and Sindh (Pakistan) and causing varying degrees of damage but leaving the Rann scenic and well-hydrated the rest of the year.

The Muslim Sultans who ruled Gujarat tried repeatedly to cross into Kutchch, but it remained separate, developing its own customs, laws, and a thriving maritime trade with Muscat, Malabar, and the African coast. Kutchch was absorbed into the Indian Union in 1948. Northern Kutchch is semi-desert and inhospitable to farming, but the southern district of Banni used to be one of India's most fertile regions and, though drier, still produces cotton, castor-oil plants, sunflowers, and wheat. Because farming couldn't bring Kutchchis their livelihood, they turned to handicrafts. In Kutchch you'll find mirrorwork, embroidery with beads, gold and silver jewelry, leatherwork (mostly in the villages of Dhordo, Khavda, and Hodko), woodcarving (in Dhordo), silver engraving (in Bhuj), and *bandhani* cloth, practiced in most villages but concentrated in Mandvi and Anjar.

> **Warning:** In June 1998 one of the century's worst cyclonic storms slammed into Gujarat from the Arabian sea. Low-lying Kutchch was hardest hit—communication and transport lines were severed, and thousands of salt-pan workers were drowned in the flooding that ensued. The region will be long in rebuilding, and much of the practical information listed in this section is subject to change.

■ Bhuj ભુજ

Bhuj was founded in the 16th century as the capital of the Kutchch by Rao Khengarji, a Jadeja Rajput, and it remained the center of economic activity in the region until the establishment of Gandhidam and the port of Kandla to the east. Today, the city, with its labyrinthine old city bazaars, is a wonderful place to take a stroll and serves as a base for exploring outlying villages as well.

ORIENTATION

Bhuj's main bus stand is on **S.T. Road,** which runs roughly east-west along the southern edge of the old city. At **Mahadev Gate** at the west end of S.T. Rd., **Uplipar Road** runs north along the eastern edge of **Hamirsar Tank** past Swaminarayan Temple and the walled complex that contains **Prag Mahal** and **Aina Mahal,** while **College Road** runs south past the Kutchch Museum, the main police station, and the Folk Art Museum. Going straight at Mahadev Gate takes you along the southern edge of Hamirsar Tank on **Museum Road,** which bends north at **Sharad Bagh.** At the eastern end of S.T. Rd., **Waniawad Road** leads north to old city's **Shroff Bazaar.** Just east of the intersection of S.T. and Waniawad Rd., **Station Road** runs north along the east side of the old city. From the northern edge of the old city, roads lead to the **railway station** and the **airport,** 6km north.

PRACTICAL INFORMATION

Airport: Bhuj Airport, 6km north of town (auto-rickshaw Rs50, taxi Rs150). **Indian Airlines,** Station Rd. (tel. 50204). Open daily 10am-5:30pm. **Gujarat Airways,** S.T. Rd. (tel. 52285). Open M, W, and F 7:30am-1pm and 3-7pm; Tu, Th, and Sa 9am-1pm and 3-7pm. To **Mumbai** (5 per week, 1½hr., US$100).

Trains: **Bhuj Railway Station** (tel. 20950), 1km north of town (auto-rickshaw Rs20). Reservations office (tel. 131 or 132). Open M-Sa 9am-9pm, Su 9am-2pm. Prices listed 2nd/1st class. To: **Gandhidam** (4 per day, 2hr., Rs9/40) for trains to Ahmedabad and Rajkot; **Jodhpur** (*Jodhpur Passenger* 658, 8pm, 14hr., Rs107/400).

Buses: S.T. Bus Stand, S.T. Rd. (tel. 20002). To: **Ahmedabad** (18 per day, 5am-10:30pm, 8hr., Rs80); **Dwarka** (10:45am, 11hr., Rs75); **Jaisalmer** (2pm, 16hr., Rs210); **Junagadh** (6 per day, 9hr., Rs70); **Mandvi** (24 per day, 1½hr., Rs11); **Rajkot** (18 per day, 5am-10pm, 6hr., Rs44). **Private bus companies** line S.T. Rd. **Shree Shajanand Travels** (tel. 22437), west of the bus stand, is recommended.

Local Transportation: Auto-rickshaws are unmetered. **Taxis,** found opposite the bus stand will take you to villages around Bhuj for Rs3 per km (min. Rs150).

Tourist Office: Tourist Information Office (tel. 20004), in Aina Mahal, sells maps of Bhuj (Rs3) and Gujarat (Rs15), books about the tribes and history of Kutchch, and great postcards. The staff is very helpful and knowledgeable about other parts of Kutchch. Open Su-F 9am-noon and 3-6pm.

Currency Exchange: State Bank of India, Station Rd. (tel. 21274; fax 50162), changes cash and traveler's checks. **Bank of Baroda,** Station Road (tel. 20553), gives cash advances for MC. Both open M-F 11am-3pm, Sa 11am-1pm.

Market: S.T. Rd. and **Shroff Bazaar** are the main market areas. The old city swells with shops. Most open M-Sa 9am-9pm; many close for 2-3hr. in the early afternoon.

Pharmacy: Hospital Rd., which heads south from an intersection just east of the GPO, is lined with pharmacies. There are also a number along Station Rd. and a few in the old city. Most open daily 8am-1pm and 2-9pm.

Hospital: Seth Gophandas Khetsey Hospital (tel. 22850), to the left at the south end of Hospital Rd., is clean and modern, and has English-speaking doctors.

Police: The main **police station** (tel. 20050), on the east side of College Rd., has English-speaking officers. To get a permit to visit villages in the sensitive border area north of Bhuj, go to the **District Superintendent of Police,** east of the south end of College Rd., with 2 copies of your passport and visa. The office will give you forms, which you must take to the Collectors office for issuing.

Post Office: GPO (tel. 222592) off Station Rd., south of S.T. Rd. Open M-Sa 10am-6pm. **Postal Code:** 370001.

Telephones: The **Central Telegraph Office** on Station Rd. also has **STD/ISD,** fax, and telex services. Open 24hr. **Telephone Code:** 02832.

ACCOMMODATIONS AND FOOD

Hotel Jahtaghar, S.T. Rd. (tel. 20222; fax 37145). Austere rooms are quite clean. The A/C dining hall serves Gujarati *thalis* for Rs30. Check-out 5pm. Singles Rs40, with attached bath Rs60; doubles Rs60/100; triples Rs80/150; quads Rs100/200.

Hotel Abha, S.T. Rd. (tel. 24451; fax 20428). An upscale hotel just east of the bus stand. All rooms have attached baths and TVs. Check-out 24hr. Singles Rs150-200, with A/C Rs450; doubles Rs250-300/600; triples Rs300. The hotel's excellent **Resoi Restaurant** offers Punjabi, Chinese, and Continental food. Most entrees Rs30-50. Open daily 11am-3pm and 7-10pm.

Hotel Lake View (tel. 20422), south of Hamirsar Tank. A luxury hotel far from the noise of S.T. Rd. Rooms have TVs, spotless attached baths, and padded wooden furniture. The swimming pool is open to non-guests (Rs10 per 45min., free for guests). Check-out noon. Singles Rs450; doubles Rs500-800.

Hotel Amam Dining Hall, S.T. Rd. (tel. 23397), near the intersection with Station Rd. A very popular *thali* joint with black-and-white wildlife pictures all over the walls. Gujarati *thalis* Rs40. Open daily 11am-3pm and 7-10pm.

SIGHTS

Bhuj's museums are an excellent place to learn about the culture and history of Kutchch before heading off to the villages. The **Kutchch Museum,** College Rd., is filled with eclectic exhibits covering tribal life. *(Open Th-Tu 9am-noon and 2:45-5:45pm. Admission Rs1. Camera fee Rs2 per shot.)* The beautifully designed **Maharao Madansinji Museum,** in Aina Mahal, is filled with artifacts and memorabilia from the reign of Maharao Lakhad, known as Lakhpatji. *(Open Su-F 9am-noon and 3-6pm. Admission Rs5. Photography prohibited.)*

Prag Mahal (tel. 20878) is a beautiful red sandstone building built in 1816, now given over to hunting trophies. The marble stairs ascend to the main hall beneath wavy arches and gray sandstone columns. The main hall is a macabre monument to death, with the heads of lions, tigers, leopards, sambar, deer, and wild cows covering the floor. A spiral staircase leads to the top of the belltower, where fantastic views await. *(Open M-Sa 9-11:45am and 3-5:45pm. Admission Rs5. Camera fee Rs15.)* At the southwestern corner of Hamirsar Tank is the beautifully kept **Sharad Bagh Museum,** the residence of the last Maharao of Kutchch until his death in 1991. Near the entrance is a small greenhouse flanked by two stone lions and a small bamboo forest. The museum is pretty much as the Maharao left it, and his TV and VCR nestle amid the hunting trophies and Chinese vases. *(Open Sa-Th 9am-noon and 4-7pm. Admission Rs5. Camera fee Rs10, video fee Rs50.)*

South of Hamirsar Tank are the eerie **Memorial Chattris,** commemorating some of the previous Maharaos of Kutchch and their wives who committed *sati.* The largest is a red sandstone memorial to Maharao Shri Lalehpatjo (1710-1761) and his 15 wives. It is surrounded by the ruins of other *chattris* in the middle of a deserted, sandy plain.

■ Mandvi માંડવી

As a once-important port city, Mandvi was the center of trade between the Middle East and Kutchch and Rajasthan. The influence of Arab and European sailors and merchants is still visible along the miniature, winding streets of the old city. Today, the pace of life is considerably more relaxed. Pushcarts and auto-rickshaws wander slowly as if pushed by the breeze, and handbuilt wooden *dhows* lean lazily against the docks, beached by the low tide. Shopowners sit quietly in the nooks and crannies of old buildings while sawmills, blacksmiths, and welders send dust, sparks, and blue light into the salty evening air.

ORIENTATION AND PRACTICAL INFORMATION Buses run to **Ahmedabad** (6:45, 9am, 7, and 7:15pm, 12hr., Rs77); **Bhuj** (20 per day, 6:15am-8:30pm, 1½hr., Rs13); **Dwarka** (9:30am, 11hr., Rs93); **Junagadh** (7:15am, 11hr., Rs90); **Rajkot** (6:15, 8am, 2:10, and 8:45pm, 7hr., Rs57). The unnamed **bridge** across the salt flats leads directly to **New Station Road,** which runs north-south along the western edge of the estuary. From **Mandvi Gate** at the end of the bridge, turning right takes you along the northern city wall and eventually to the **GPO,** about 1km away (tel. 20266; open M-F 8am-5pm, Sa 8am-1pm). Straight ahead is the **Kutchch Cardyka Hospital,** a very clean, modern facility (tel. 20558; open daily 9am-1pm and 5-9pm for consultations, 24hr. for emergencies). Another right takes you down New Station Rd. past the **main police station** (tel. 20008; open 24hr.), opposite **Sadaya Gate,** which opens onto the salt flat and the **main bus stand** (tel. 20004). It then curves westward and joins **Bandar Road,** which leads past the **State Bank of India** (tel. 20031; foreign exchange open M-F 11am-3pm, Sa 11am-1pm) to the port at the southern end of the city. All roads to the right lead into the **old city.** Bandar Rd. runs north behind the petrol station, past several sawmills, to the southern end of **Bhid Chowk,** the central market area of the city. The road that runs north of the State Bank of India twists and turns through the old city, through **Gilla Gate,** past the clock tower which marks the center of the city, and through Bhid Gate to the southeastern corner of Bhid Chowk. **Telephone Code:** 02834.

ACCOMMODATIONS AND FOOD **Sahara Guest House,** Bhid Chowk (tel. 20272), south of the market, is isolated from the noise of hawkers and sawmills. The beds are soft, and the attached baths are spotless. (Check-out noon. Singles Rs125, with A/C Rs350; doubles Rs200/450.) More expensive lodgings are available at the maharaja's guest house **Vijay Vilas Palace** (tel. 20043), 9km west of town, but you must reserve in advance and it's not exactly budget (Rs350-600). The sweet, proprietary caretaker serves a delicious vegetarian *thali* for dinner in the formal dining room (order in advance; Rs70).

Hundreds of stalls in Bhid Chowk and along New Station Rd. serve imagination-defying snacks. **Zorba the Buddha,** in the market, dishes unlimited *thalis* (Rs20). **Hotel Krishna,** Bhid Chowk (tel. 21365), has excellent vegetarian food and a friendly staff. (Entrees Rs20-30, *thalis* Rs30-40. Open daily 10am-3pm and 6:30-11pm.)

SIGHTS The town shelters many beautiful haunts: the old city walls; the port with its wooden ships perched on the salt flats; the canyon-like streets with stone mansions; and the temples and mosques that crowd the eastern side of the salt flats.

Nine kilometers west of Mandvi, down the road past the GPO, is the **Vijay Vilas Palace,** a domed, latticed mansion set on 692 acres, built in 1927 as a summer home for the Maharao of Kutchch. *(Open daily 9am-1pm and 2-6pm. Admission Rs5, camera fee Rs30. Vehicle charges: bicycle Rs2, scooter Rs4, others Rs6-10.)* Inside are spotless marble floors and walls, with delicate inlaid flowers, and decadently gorgeous furniture of carved rosewood and teak. There are two remarkable courtyards with sandstone jungles carved on the walls. On the third floor, a rusting spiral staircase leads to a domed terrace with a view of the Arabian Sea, as well as the coconut trees and windmills on the flat, green Kutchch. Visitors are also allowed to use the private **beach,** 1km away.

NEPAL नेपाल

From the daunting peaks of the Himalaya to the green valleys, Nepal is a country molded by its geography. Ridges and rivers split the land into small pockets of tillable earth, connected to one another by tenuous roads, often impassable for parts of the year. Wedged between India and China, Nepal is located on the frontier of several civilizations, its landscape giving expression to their many cultures, all of which come together in the country's political and social center, the Kathmandu Valley. A closed kingdom until 1951, Nepal now greets travelers with a rapidly developing tourism industry and the ubiquitous welcoming gesture of *namaste*.

ESSENTIALS

■ Money

IRs100=Rs160	Rs100=IRs63.1
US$1=Rs67	Rs100=US$1.49
CDN$1=Rs45.7	Rs100=CDN$2.33
UK£1=Rs109	Rs100=UK£0.91
IR£1=Rs93.7	Rs100=IR£1.07
AUS$1=Rs39.5	Rs100=AUS$2.63
NZ$1=Rs32.7	Rs100=NZ$3.06
SAR=Rs10.5	Rs100=SAR9.55

Currency is measured in rupees (Rs) which are divided into 100 paise (p.). Rupees appear in one and ten-rupee coins and 1, 2, 5, 10, 20, 25, 50, 100, 500, and 1000 rupee notes. Check all bank notes carefully; ripped bills will be refused by many merchants (although banks will exchange them for new ones).

The cost of living and traveling in Nepal is very low, and budget tourists in Kathmandu tend to get by on about Rs500-800 (US$10-15) per day, and when you're trekking you'll have a hard time spending more than Rs300 (US$5) a day. It is always a good idea to take an extra few hundred dollars to Nepal with you in case of emergencies. Also, remember to budget for tips to trekking guides and porters.

■ Hours and Holidays

Although five different **calendars** are in use in Nepal, the official one used in newspapers, government offices, and on historical displays in museums is the Bikram Sambat (or Vikram Sambat) calendar, named after the legendary King Vikramaditya. Day one of this calendar was February 23, 57 BC. The year 2055 BS began on April 12, 1998. For more information, see **Holidays and Festivals,** p. 805.

Government offices are typically open from 10am to 5pm Sunday through Thursday, closing at 3pm on Fridays, and at 4pm on weekdays in the winter (mid-Nov. to mid-Jan.). **Banks** are open from 10am to 2pm Sunday through Thursday, closing at noon on Fridays. Most businesses are closed on Saturdays but keep longer hours than government offices; only embassies and international offices take Sunday off. They are usually open from 9am to 5pm Monday through Friday.

Nepal is 15 minutes ahead of Indian Standard Time, which puts Nepalese Time at 5hr. 45min. ahead of GMT, 10hr. 45 min. ahead of North American Eastern Standard Time, and 4hr. 15min. behind Australian Eastern Standard Time. No Summer Time or Daylight Saving Time is used in Nepal, so in summer Nepal is only 4hr. 45min.

ahead of British time, and 9hr. 45min. ahead of North American Eastern Daylight Saving Time.

LIFE AND TIMES

■ Geography

Snow-peaked heights, emerald-stepped valleys, cascading glacial rivers, river-rent gorges, thick tropical jungles—all are part of the terrain of the tiny, landlocked Kingdom of Nepal, nestled between India and Tibet on the southern slopes of the Himalaya. With eight of the world's ten highest peaks packed within its 140,797-square-kilometer area, nearly 75% of Nepal is mountain. Yet its entire surface was once submerged beneath an ancient sea. All of that changed, though, with the tectonic collision of India and Asia some 50-60 million years ago, Nepal began to be pushed upward in a mound of breathtaking geological wreckage. Over subsequent millennia, continued continental crunch gave rise to the mountain systems defining the region today. And the mountains continue to grow (at a rate of a few centimeters per year).

Nepal is customarily divided into geographical belts running east-west across the country. The **Terai,** adjacent to the Indian border, is the northernmost reach of the Indo-Gangetic Plain and encompasses 17% of Nepal's total land. Fertile, low-lying (200m elevation), hot, and humid, the Terai once was covered with dense, malarial forest that supported wildlife but few humans. Recently deforested, the region today teems with Nepal's mobile, growing population. Rising abruptly from the Terai plain to altitudes between 1300m and 1800m, the forested **Chure** or Siwalik hill chain runs parallel to its neighbor further north, the 3000m Mahabharat Range. Dry climate and poor soil keeps the Chure hills sparsely populated. Intermittently separating the Chure and Mahabharat ranges are broad spindled valleys referred to as the **Inner Terai.** At altitudes of 700-1000m, the Inner Terai harbors tropical deciduous forests and wildlife similar to that once found in the Terai, although it too is quickly succumbing to development. With steep escarpments to the south offering natural fortification, the **Mahabharat** is moderately settled (despite its steep slopes, the range is endowed with water-retentive soils amenable to terrace cultivation), but excepting its passes, it is cut off from human traffic. The region is a transverse zone for much of Nepal's water, cut by the deep, north-south river gorges of Nepal's three major river systems, the Karnali, Narayani, and Kosi.

Between the Mahabharat and the Himalaya resides the **Pahar** zone. At altitudes of 500-2000m, the region holds flat fertile valleys, including the Kathmandu, Banepa, and Pokhara Valleys. With accommodating climate and good crop-bearing conditions, the Pahar has been inhabited and cultivated for centuries, and today supports nearly 40% of Nepal's population. Last but not least, the **Himalaya** are inhabited only in scattered mountain pockets, valleys, and elevated plateaus. Human settlement gives way by 4000m, where pervasive mist and clouds inhibit any crop cultivation. Above 4000m, dense forest yields to alpine pasture, which yields in turn, at 4900m, to snowline, beyond which nothing but mountains grow. Ten Nepalese peaks rise higher than 8000m, including Mt. Everest, at 8848m, the highest point on earth. Beyond these peaks is a high desert plateau known as the **Trans-Himalaya.**

■ People

Described in its constitution as a multilingual, multi-ethnic nation, the Hindu Kingdom of Nepal represents a population of 20.6 million people and over 60 ethnic, linguistic, and caste groups. Nepal owes much of its cultural heterogeneity to its rugged and sometimes impassable terrain, which kept different pockets of the country isolated. Only over the past few centuries has the word "Nepal" come to represent the country as a whole (formerly, a "Nepali" was an inhabitant of the Kathmandu Valley), and it is

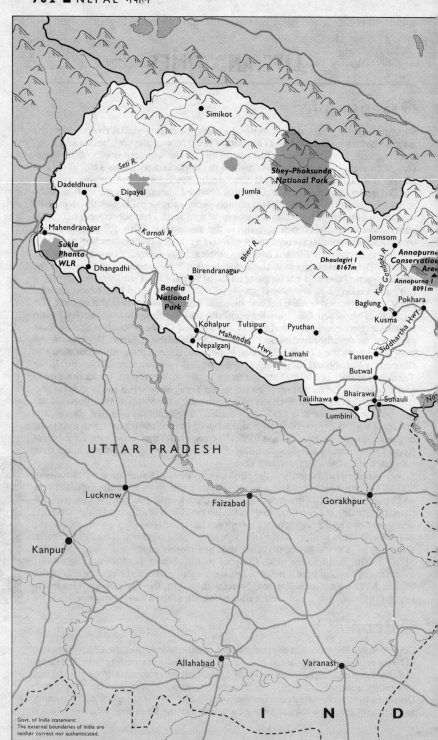

Govt. of India statement:
The external boundaries of India are
neither correct nor authenticated.

Nepal

still customary among people who retain strong regional affiliations to identify themselves as *pahari, madeshi,* or *bhotia* (hills, plains, or northern border dwellers).

While most Nepalis are Hindu, speak Sanskrit-derived languages (such as Nepali),
and trace Indo-Aryan ancestry, many are equally affected by Buddhist tradition. The
Newaris, the earliest known arrivals to Nepal and the original settlers of the Kathmandu Valley, practice a unique synthesis of Buddhism and Hinduism. Today
accounting for only 4% of the population, they produce some of the country's most
celebrated art. The Eastern mid-hills are inhabited by **Rais, Limbus,** and **Sunwars.** The
Terai is populated by **Tharus, Yadavas, Safars, Rajvanshis,** and **Dhimals.** In west-cen-
tral Nepal, the **Gurungs** and **Magars** are also thought to be among Nepal's earliest
inhabitants. Although of Mongolian stock, they developed a Sanskritized language.
Relatively more recent large-scale migrations from Tibet and the east brought Tibeto-
Burmese languages and Tibetan Buddhist culture to Nepal, today accounting for 45%
of the population. While Indo-Aryans settled mostly in southern regions and lower
altitudes, where Hindus are a majority (although there are also populations of Muslims and aboriginal tribes), the Tibeto-Burmese settled mostly in higher altitudes in
the north, where Buddhist culture predominates. The highlands and northern border
peoples retain much in common with Tibetans, influenced not only by Tibetan
Mahayana Buddhism, but also by Bön, the early religion of Tibet prior to Buddhism.
Among the most recent immigrants from Tibet are the **Tamangs,** the most populous
of Tibeto-Burmese ethnic groups, and the **Sherpas,** some of the northernmost inhabitants of the Himalaya. Other Tibeto-Nepalese groups include the Limbus of the far
eastern hills, and the Sunwar and Rai of the mid-eastern hills. **Tibetan refugees** continue to seek asylum in Nepal, perpetuating the influence of Tibetan culture on modern Nepal. Ethnic conflicts in Bhutan have resulted in an influx of tens of thousands
of ethnic Nepali Bhutanese into eastern Nepal.

Forming a nation of villages, about 90% of Nepalis live in small market centers and
rural settlements. Under a predominantly agricultural economy, with most people
dependent on subsistence farming, population density is a function of agricultural
productivity. The fertile Terai supports Nepal's highest population density, and has
become not only the country's bread-basket but also a booming industrial region. The
highlands and trans-Himalayan valleys, with less than 1% of land under cultivation,
remain sparsely populated, with people leading a nomadic way of life.

■ Language

The official language of Nepal is **Nepali,** which is the mother tongue of 50% of the
population and is spoken and understood by just about everyone. Formerly the language of the high-caste elite, Nepali was introduced by Prithvi Narayan Shah as a *lingua franca* for his new kingdom. It is an Indic language, descended from Sanskrit like
the languages of North India, and it uses the same Devanagari script that Hindi uses.

Other languages abound but each has only a small number of speakers. In the
Terai, varieties of Hindi such as Mathili and Bhojpuri are the biggest groups, while in
the hills small pockets of various Tibeto-Burmese languages are found. The Newari
spoken in the Kathmandu Valley is of Tibetan origin, although it has borrowed its
Devanagari script and half of its vocabulary from Sanskrit. In contemporary Nepal
you'll also encounter Tibetan, which uses a Sanskrit-based script in spite of its foreign
origin. English is widely taught in Nepalese schools nowadays too, so it's not difficult
to get around knowing no more Nepali than the greeting, *namaste,* a Sanskrit-derived
term that translates literally as "I salute the God in you." For basic Nepali vocabulary,
see the **Phrasebook,** p. 811.

■ History

Despite being wedged neatly between India and China, Nepal has produced a history
and culture that differ greatly from its neighbors and is as diverse as the land itself (see
Geography, p. 701). The country's insularity is inversely proportional to the accessibility of specific regions. Thus, the Terai lowlands were influenced by Indian culture

and history. The central hills and the muffin-tray of mountain valleys, including Kathmandu, have tended towards independence but not isolation, and in the heart of the mountains, life has progressed without much outside influence at all.

Origins and Early Dynasties (200,000 BC-1200 AD)

Much of Nepal's early history is shrouded in myth and mystery. Stone Age settlers probably arrived around 200,000 BC, but things get hazy after that. In 543 BC, **Siddhartha Gautama,** the man who would be Buddha, was born in the Terai. Three hundred years later, the Buddhist emperor **Ashoka** came to the land that spawned the man who spawned his faith, installing one of his famed pillars at Lumbini (see p. 784) and leaving behind a daughter, Charumati, to found the village of Chabahil, in the **Kathmandu Valley.** It is that valley which is the historical heartland of Nepal and the source of its greatest cultural traditions. Most of what is known of Nepal's early history comes from the Kathmandu Valley, and the name "Nepal" originally referred only to the Valley. The early kingdoms of Nepal never expanded far, however, content to guard their strategic position and control the closest adjacent lands.

The **Kiratis,** a dynasty of northern Mongol ancestry, may have ruled the Kathmandu Valley during the first millennium BC and introduced Buddhism to the area. Between the 4th and 5th century AD, the **Licchavis,** Nepal's first dynasty from the Indian plains, took over. The Licchavis brought with them Hinduism, establishing a long-standing pattern of a Hindu upper class ruling over Buddhist commoners. Under the Licchavis the Kathmandu Valley enjoyed an era of prosperous trade, which continued despite the petty wars and poor administration of the **Thakuris,** who rose to power in the 9th century. The city of Kathmandu was founded around this time.

The Malla Kingdoms (1200-1742)

A new dynasty emerged from the Kathmandu Valley in 1200 when the **Mallas** came to power. Despite shaky beginnings, they ushered in the best years of Kathmandu Valley culture and ruled for over 500 years. Unlike earlier Hindu kings the Mallas imposed Hindu laws on the valley, dividing the Buddhist Newaris into 64 occupational castes. After Yaksha Malla, the greatest of the Malla kings, died in 1482, the kingdom he had ruled from Bhaktapur was split among his three children. Kathmandu, Patan, and Bhaktapur became rival city-states, and internal competition sharpened the Malla family's political acumen. In spite of constant feuding over trade with Tibet, all three kingdoms reached new heights in urban planning and art—the great wooden-screened temples and cobbled Durbar Squares of the valley date from this time.

Unification (1742-1816)

The Mallas were unprepared for the force that would hit them in the 18th century and expand their dominion into a proper Kingdom of Nepal. The small hill-state of Gorkha, 50km west of Kathmandu, was under the rule of the **Shahs,** the most ambitious of the many immigrant Rajput clans that had come to western and southern Nepal between the 14th and 16th centuries, driven out of India by Muslim invaders. In 1742 King Prithvi Narayan Shah ascended the throne of Gorkha, and within two years he set out to conquer Nepal's richest region, the Kathmandu Valley. After a 25-year war of attrition, in 1768-69 the three cities of Kathmandu, Patan, and Bhaktapur surrendered. When Prithvi Narayan Shah invaded Kathmandu, King Jaya Prakash Malla asked the English East India Company for help. If the company had acquiesced, the British might have ruled Nepal. Instead, the victorious Shah became the founder of the modern nation of Nepal. He did not stop after conquering the Kathmandu Valley. Lusting for land, his Gorkha army proceeded to conquer the eastern Terai and hills. Soon Prithvi Narayan implemented the closed-door policy that would keep Nepal isolated until the 1950s. An astute ruler, he set up an exemplary government. Speaking of his kingdom as a "garden of many flowers," he respected the country's local institutions and rewarded his officials according to their merit. After his death in 1775, however, Prithvi Narayan's kingdom deteriorated. The throne passed to a series of infant Shahs, and members of the nobility battled one another to act as regent. Peasants were taxed more and more harshly.

Eventually a cunning chief minister named **Bhim Sen Thapa** took control, finding that he could get Nepalese to work together by launching a war. Nepal struck out to the west, annexing the Garwhal and Kumaon regions which are now part of India's Uttar Pradesh state, as well as Himachal Pradesh. But Nepal mishandled its new lands and got into trouble with foreign powers. From 1788-92 it fought a war with Tibet and China, and in 1814 its expansion in the Terai provoked the calculated hostility of the British East India Company.

Although Nepal could not defeat Britain, the Anglo-Nepalese War was not the easy victory the British expected. In spite of superior numbers and weaponry, the British were routed by Nepalese soldiers, who held their hilltop forts and charged with *khukuri* knives. It took the British two years to break through and defeat Nepal. The **Treaty of Segauli** they imposed in 1816 stripped Nepal of Himachal Pradesh, Garhwal, Kumaon, and the Terai lands and fixed its eastern and western borders where they remain today. But the impression the Nepalese made on the British counted much more. Britain didn't like the prospect of fighting Nepal again, and thus Nepal became the only South Asian kingdom to remain independent in the 19th century. Eventually, the British began recruiting Nepalese soldiers for their new **Gorkha** (or Gurkha) regiments.

Stagnation and Coup d'Etat (1816-46)

The years following the war with Britain saw little progress. Prime Minister Bhim Sen Thapa kept the country stable by building up the army, but chaos ensued when he fell from grace in 1837. Various palace factions struggled for power. Finally, on the night of September 14, 1846, a powerful minister was murdered. When the queen assembled the entire royal court in the Kot (the army headquarters courtyard) to find the culprit, the personal guards of **General Jung Bahadur,** the cabinet minister for the army, surrounded the Kot and opened fire, killing thirty-two of Kathmandu's most powerful nobles. During the next few hours, after a secret agreement, the queen appointed Jung Bahadur prime minister.

The Rana Regime (1846-1951)

Jung Bahadur took the title of **Rana,** and under this name his family would keep an iron grip on Nepal for 105 years. Jung Bahadur usurped the king, Rajendra, and took total control for himself. He started a process of reform, encouraged by a visit to London in 1850 during which he saw the efficacy of Britain's institutions (as well as the glamour of its neo-Classical architecture). Upon his return Jung began to thoroughly bureaucratize the Nepalese government (though paradoxically he also all but quarantined his nation, severely restricting western access to Nepal). He did away with patronage and kept strict track of spending. In a victory for the common peasants, land tenure was registered, and landlords could no longer arbitrarily evict their tenants. Some of Jung's other decisions hurt many people, but this made little difference to a man who was by now absolute dictator of Nepal. In 1856, Jung Bahadur had himself raised to the title of super-Minister as well as "Maharaja of Kaski and Lamjung," with the power to overrule the king. The position was made hereditary in his family, and the Shah dynasty remained only as a figurehead.

The Indian **Mutiny of 1857** was a chance for Nepal to flex its muscles and also win British support. Jung Bahadur sent 10,000 men to aid the British, and in return the British gave back the Terai lands they had taken in 1816. The British befriended Nepal, and especially the Rana regime, trying to give Nepal "guidance" on its foreign policy, but Nepal remained independent, scoffing at British demands for trading rights and limiting British Gorkha recruitment.

The Rana prime ministers were at least as interested in advancing their family fortunes, however, as they were in helping the country. Jung Bahadur Rana ruled Nepal until his death in 1877. During the second half of his reign he continued his pursuit of personal power and wrapped up his family business ventures in state policy. Jung Bahadur's successors turned out to be just as venal and iron-willed but less competent. The end of the 19th century saw a plethora of halfhearted public works projects, especially bridges, whose main purpose was to impress the British.

Chandra Shamsher Rana, who ruled from 1901-29, was a better administrator than the other Ranas, but he remains a figure of some controversy: the question remains whether the famous leader was motivated less by his social conscience than by his desire for political immortality. Either way, his place in Nepal's history seems secure. He began his reign by building the enormous Singha Durbar palace for himself, consuming all of the national public works budget for the first three years of his rule. Some changes came with the First World War, since Chandra Shamsher knew he would have to do something to please the 100,000 Nepalese Gorkha soldiers who had gone to fight for the British overseas or in India and would return to their villages with new ideas from around the world. Chandra Shamsher responded by instituting major infrastructural changes—including the introduction of a mechanized system of transportation—and social reforms, and the banning of slavery and *sati*. In 1918 Tri Chandra College, Nepal's first college, was founded, and in 1923 tenant farmers were made the owners of the lands they had rented for centuries. Another major accomplishment of 1923 was the Treaty of Friendship with Britain, which formally recognized Nepal's independence. Meanwhile, however, the lowering of trade restrictions made Nepal more economically dependent on imported British and Japanese goods. Prime Minister Judha Shamsher Rana (r.1932-45) went back to ruling Nepal in military fashion, and dissatisfaction became rampant. Not even the great earthquake of 1934 shook Kathmandu like Judha's widely protested execution of four would-be revolutionaries in 1940.

Indian Independence in 1947 gave Nepal a new neighbor to deal with, and Prime Minister Jawaharlal Nehru disapproved of the Rana regime. In 1947 the **Nepali Congress** was formed in the tradition of the Congress that had led India to freedom. The Ranas didn't know how to deal with these new forces. Some family members who favored democratization went to India and joined the growing anti-Rana resistance. The turning point came in 1950 when **King Tribhuvan,** a palace figurehead since 1911, also fled to India. By this time, he had captured popular support. The king, the prime minister, and Congress leaders met in Delhi where Nehru engineered the **Delhi Compromise of 1951.** The Rana regime was over. The king would now preside over a government of Ranas as well as popularly elected leaders.

Nepal after the Ranas (1951-1990)

Major changes came to Nepal in the years after the Rana defeat. Nepal's doors were opened to foreigners, and vast improvements took place in the government's social policies. The Delhi Compromise was replaced in 1959 by a new constitution which called for a democratically elected assembly. The Nepali Congress won a large majority in the elections, and its leader, **B.P. Koirala,** became prime minister. But this state of affairs was fragile. King Tribhuvan had died in 1955, and his son **Mahendra,** who came to the throne, was less enthusiastic about political reforms, believing Nepal wasn't developed enough to handle them. He dismissed the Congress government almost as soon as it took power and threw its leaders in jail. In 1962 a new constitution replaced the national assembly with a system of *panchayats* (village councils) which elected members to district councils which elected a National Panchayat. Political parties were banned, and the new system, which was supposed to be a form of democracy especially suited to Nepalese traditions, was effectively a return to absolute monarchy. Mahendra opened Nepal to foreign aid, however, and started the long controversial process of development that is transforming Nepal today.

King Birendra, who came to power in 1972 (although for astrological reasons he wasn't crowned until 1975) fully supported the *panchayat* system. Early in his career Birendra declared Nepal a "Zone of Peace" (a declaration of neutrality which angered India) and tightened visa restrictions for foreigners. The *panchayat* system was highly contested, however, and resistance came to a head in 1979 with riots in Kathmandu and Patan. In response, Birendra called a referendum to let the people choose between *panchayats* and multiparty democracy. The *panchayats* won by the feeble margin of 55 to 45 percent, and the king's system hung on for ten more years, assisted by censorship and police brutality.

NEPAL

Democracy Restored (1991-present)

Inspired by the previous year's revolutions in Eastern Europe, and provoked by an economic blockade by India, the outlawed opposition parties banded together in 1990 to demand democracy. Protests filled the streets of Kathmandu, and when King Birendra realized his riot police and mass arrests would not quell the uprising, he gave in, lifting the ban on political parties on April 8. A week later the major parties formed an interim government and wrote a new constitution. A parliamentary system of democracy came into effect, and Birendra became a constitutional monarch.

The May 1991 elections gave a majority to the Nepali Congress, which had led the democracy movement. The **Communist Party of Nepal-United Marxist-Leninist (CPN-UML)** became the main opposition. The prime minister was now **G.P. Koirala,** the brother of the late B.P. Koirala. Although G.P. Koirala's government stabilized Nepal's democracy, most people were disappointed by his leadership. Rising inflation caused general discontent, and an agreement with India over the Mahakali dam project on Nepal's western frontier brought accusations of selling out to India. Unimaginative and stubborn, Koirala alienated much of his own party, and he was forced to resign in 1994 when a large chunk of the Congress backed out on him.

The ensuing elections brought the Communists to power in a minority government. Prime Minister **Man Mohan Adhikary** quickly launched a series of populist schemes, including the "build-your-own-village" program, which gave large cash grants to local governments to spend as they pleased. Adhikary then resigned, hoping to improve his government's standing through another election. While the king, trying hard not to meddle, approved Adhikary's call for elections, the Supreme Court ruled in 1995 against this maneuver. No elections were held, and the Congress party took power by allying itself with the right-wing **National Democratic Party (NDP).**

New Congress Prime Minister **Sher Bahadur Deuba's** efforts to bolster ties with the NDP were waylaid by a rift within the smaller party. He could muster only 101 of 103 votes needed to defeat a no-confidence motion in March 1997, deserted by the NDP faction led by **Lokendra Bahadur Chand.** Seizing on the Supreme Court precedent, Chand formed a coalition government with the CPN-UML, pushing Nepal into a new era of instability. Although democracy appears fairly well-entrenched, several years of little or no substantial legislation has resulted in the *panchayat* system, once reviled by the pro-democracy mass movement, being viewed by some with new respect, and frustration is said to be brewing in extremist groups. For his part, King Birendra has played his role as a constitutional monarch admirably, refraining from interfering with politics.

■ This Year's News

Guerillas from the Communist Party of Nepal-Maoist continued a program protest directed against development organizations they purport to be mishandling funds; this tactic has turned violent with the slaying of some Non-government Organization (NGO) employees. The Maoists also cut off phone service in all of the Eastern Terai for nearly three weeks in July of 1998. The assassination of opposition-party Parliament member in July 1998 has brought on a sea of political unrest and nationwide strikes to protest the already-unstable government's inaction following the assassination. Kathmandu was brought to a standstill in April as shopkeepers held a general strike to protest the introduction of a new Value-Added Tax (VAT). Smaller strikes and large-scale resentment continue. And finally, tourism continued to expand unchecked, as facilities are improved to grease the wheels of Nepal's greatest income machine.

■ Government and Politics

Nepal is a constitutional monarchy with a parliamentary system of government. The power of the sovereign, a position held since 1972 by King Birendra Bir Bikram Shah, is limited, although His Majesty is still said to wield some influence on His Government. Real executive power is in the hands of the prime minister (currently Girija

Prasad Koirala) who is chosen by a majority in the 205-member House of Representatives. Members of the House of Representatives are elected by universal suffrage for a term of up to five years. An upper house, the 60-seat National Assembly, comprises appointed and elected positions. Nepal's judiciary appears to be politically impartial.

The main political parties in Nepal are the moderate Nepali Congress (NC), the Communist Party of Nepal-United Marxist-Leninist (CPN-UML), and the younger rightwing National Democratic Party (NDP). Though the NDP lacks the wide base of support of the NC and the Communists, it has played kingmaker in the nation's coalition politics. Also on the scene is the Nepal Sadhbhavana Party (NSP), a regionalist party from the Terai.

■ Economics

With 90% of its population depending on subsistence agriculture, Nepal ranks as one of the poorest countries in the world by Western standards. Farmers cut terraces into hillsides, facing down landslides, erosion, and leeched soil. In the Terai, where farming is potentially more lucrative, high population growth makes even subsistence farming difficult. The geography of Nepal presents two hurdles to economic development. A lack of mineral resources below ground is matched by the difficulty of establishing an infrastructure over the rugged terrain above. The pearl in the economic oyster is the hydroelectric potential of Nepal's raging rivers, but its development stands at odds with the bankable tourist appeal of pristine valleys for rafting and hiking. Roads are expensive to build and maintain, while the Indian border is the only easily negotiable channel of trade. Large industry is therefore concentrated in the Terai. Most manufactured goods and machinery are imported from India.

Woolen rugs and garments are Nepal's biggest export, but an important chunk of foreign cash reaches Nepal through foreign aid. This well-meaning boost to Nepal's economy over the past four decades has in fact produced a plethora of complications. Donors have often introduced unsuitable technology and programs due to their ignorance of local climate conditions or customs. Development aid has also been unevenly allotted, lavishing the central hills around Kathmandu while neglecting the poor mountainous regions of the far west. Grants often get siphoned back to contracting companies in the donor countries. Small-scale rural NGOs (non-governmental organizations) are a good idea in theory, but they are unregulated and often rife with corruption. Some assistance comes with a price: China and India both give aid to Nepal for blatantly political ends. And environmental destruction raises the question of whether industrial "development" is a good idea at all in a country which has maintained a way of life that need not be sustained by floods of consumer goods.

■ Religion

Nepal's religious mixture reflects its position as a cultural crossroads between India and Tibet. By the numbers, Nepal is 89.5 percent Hindu, 5.3 percent Buddhist, 2.7 percent Muslim, 0.23 percent Christians and others, and 0.1 percent Jain, with the remainder of the pop. Strict divisions do not belie the syncretism which characterizes the nation's faith—although theirs is the only country in the world with Hinduism as its state religion, most Nepalis follow some mixture of Hinduism and Buddhism, with plenty of local traditions thrown in for good measure. Asked if they are Hindu or Buddhist, many Nepalis will say they don't know or that they're "both." The fact that the Nepalese can at once follow a religion of 33 million gods and a religion that originally recognized no gods at all baffles many visitors, but it seems to work nonetheless.

In general, the mountainous northern regions of Nepal close to Tibet tend to be Buddhist, while the Terai lands close to India are Hindu. The hilly areas in between (including the Kathmandu Valley) have gone the furthest in synthesizing the two.

HINDUISM

For a more elaborate introduction to **Hinduism,** see p. 91. Hinduism first came to the Kathmandu Valley and other parts of the Nepalese hills around the 4th-5th centuries AD, with the advent of the Licchavi dynasty. (The Terai has always been a part of the Ganga Valley world and has even older connections to Hinduism.) Because Hinduism was introduced to the hills by conquerors, it has long been Nepal's religion of status; **brahmins** (the priestly caste) and **chhetris** (Nepalese *kshatriyas*) have long been at the top of the social hierarchy. Various Nepali Hindu legal reforms long ago tried to work the lower-class Buddhists into an occupational caste system; the practice has taken hold socially, although few Buddhists truly recognize the legitimacy of a caste system.

Shiva is perhaps the most popular Hindu god in Nepal; he is a fitting lord for this mountainous land, since he began his career as a Himalayan wanderer. He commonly appears in Nepal as Bhairava or "Bhairab," a terrible ghoulish figure who chases away demons, but he is also referred to as the compassionate Mahadev and worshipped out of love and devotion. In his form as Pashupatinath, the benevolent Lord of Animals, Shiva is Nepal's patron deity, and Nepal is often referred to as Pashupatinath Bhumi ("Land of Pashupatinath"). The temple of Pashupatinath near Kathmandu is the most important Hindu site in Nepal (see p. 740).

The god **Vishnu** is also the object of a large devotional cult. A cosmic "preserver," Vishnu has repeatedly stepped in to save the universe from calamity. In Nepal he is often called Narayan; this name of Vishnu comes from his role in the Hindu creation myth, in which he sleeps on the cosmic ocean while the creator god, Brahma, sprouts from his navel. As in India, the goddesses are also worshipped in Nepal, and Nepal's grandest festival, Dasain, is held in honor of **Durga.** Nepal also holds a special place for **Annapurna,** goddess of abundance and distributor of food and grain. The goddesses are all considered separate individuals but also consorts of the male deities, embodying the female aspect *(shakti)* of each god. Due to the Tantric influence in Nepal, this *shakti* is often considered to be the more powerful and active force in the cosmos.

BUDDHISM

Lumbini, where the Buddha was born about 560 BC, is within the borders of present-day Nepal. Although Siddhartha Gautama left Lumbini and spent most of his time in India, his doctrines eventually returned to the land of his birth, spreading much further in the country than the Terai area where he was born. For a detailed description of the doctrines of Nepal's foremost son, see **India's Life and Times: Religion,** p. 97.

Buddhists in Nepal follow the **Mahayana** (Great Vehicle) school, which differs in many ways from the **Theravada** (Doctrine of the Elders) school. The Mahayana school developed as a popular new sect around the first century AD and came to predominate in India, Tibet, China, and other parts of East Asia. The more orthodox Theravada school persisted in Sri Lanka and most of Southeast Asia. While Buddhism in India was subsumed by Hinduism, a particularly Indian-influenced Mahayana Buddhism remained in Nepal, which is what is practiced today. The northern mountainous areas of Nepal have the strongest Buddhist traditions, while in the hills a Hindu-Buddhist synthesis is more common.

Mahayana Buddhism initially developed after a disagreement over the *vinaya* (monastic rules) in the Buddhist communities. The Mahayana doctrines de-emphasized the individual quest for *nirvana* and instead stressed the need for acquiring compassion for all beings. One of these doctrines was the Prajnaparamita, or Perfection of Wisdom. Furthermore, the Buddha became no longer just an enlightened human being in the Mahayana tradition; instead, he became a cosmic *bodhisattva* having many incarnations or emanations. A *bodhisattva* is one who vows to put off his enlightenment for the sake of saving all sentient beings, a concept which plays an important role in the Mahayana tradition (unlike Theravada, which emphasizes the individual attainment of *nirvana*). A number of *bodhisattvas* are worshipped along with the Buddha in Mahayana Buddhism.

TIBETAN BUDDHISM

A unique form of Buddhism developed in Tibet, where Mahayana and Vajrayana (Thunderbolt Vehicle) Buddhist traditions were mixed with the indigenous religion, Bön. Even though Buddhism was brought to Tibet through Nepal, the Tibetan tradition has in turn influenced Nepal, and due to the occupation of Tibet by China there are many actual Tibetan Buddhists around as well. Prayer wheels and prayer flags, blow the mantra *Om Mani Padme Hum* ("Hail to the jewel in the lotus") over the mountaintops. The beliefs of Tibetan Buddhism are not very different from those of standard Mahayana Buddhism, though different rituals and imagery are used. The Buddha is divided into five "aspects": the *dhyani* (meditating Buddhas), reflected in each of the five elements (earth, water, air, fire, and space). Tibetan Buddhism is also noted for its monastic tradition; it is estimated that before the Chinese invasion, 25% of Tibetans belonged to some religious order. Of the 6,000 Tibetan monasteries that were once in Tibet, only about five remain. The rest were destroyed in the Chinese occupation. **Tibetan monasteries** are headed by teachers called *lamas,* addressed by the title *rimpoche* (precious one), who are believed to have cultivated wisdom over many lifetimes, transmitting their realization to each reincarnation. The reincarnation of a *lama* is usually identified through of astrology, consulting the Tibetan oracle, and having the young candidates identify the former *lama*'s possessions.

TANTRA

Some forms of Tibetan Buddhism are classified as Vajrayana (Thunderbolt Vehicle), another sect apart from the Mahayana and Theravada schools. The major symbols of Vajrayana are the *vajra* or *dorje* (thunderbolt) and the *ghanti* (bell), representing the male element of compassion and the female element of wisdom. Vajrayana has inherited much of its cosmology from the tradition of Tantra, a medieval cult in eastern India that relished the female power of *shakti.* The Hindu Tantric tradition espoused a non-dualistic philosophy and used specific methods to help people go beyond dualistic thought. Polar opposites were no longer seen as external objects opposed to one another. They were seen as the dual manifestations of consciousness. In this light, the true nature of desire and the mind could be realized by transcending opposites. Thus, in the Tantric tradition in India, there were rituals which prescribed the usually proscribed eating of meat, fish and parched grain, the drinking of alcohol, and the enjoyment of sexual intercourse as means of transcending dualities. The rituals of Tantra also involve the releasing and harnessing of different energies in the body. This is where the Tantric association with sex, so popularly known in the West, comes from. In Tibetan Buddhism especially, the conscious release of bodily energy is prominent and heavily ritualized, especially in visualization-meditations upon female goddess figures.

There is much that Tantra has in common with the Hindu traditions of *shakti* and yoga. From the 7th through the 9th centuries in India, Tantra became quite popular throughout India as a part of both Hinduism and Buddhism. It eventually died out in India, but its influence can be seen in Tibetan Buddhism. In line with its thunderbolt-and-bell symbolism, sacred gestures, patterns, and mantras, Vajrayana Buddhism couples the *dhyani* Buddhas and the major *bodhisattvas* with *taras,* female consorts who have much more power and strength. These figures are often depicted engaged in sexual intercourse, symbolic of the harnessing and reconciliation of dual energies.

INDIGENOUS TRADITIONS

Aside from the great religions of Hinduism and Buddhism, Nepal has its own collection of indigenous deities. Both Hindus and Buddhists worship these local heroes, regardless of the religion they claim to follow. In the Kathmandu Valley a unique practice persists in the worship of the **Kumari,** a young girl recognized as an incarnation of the Hindu goddess Durga. The chosen living goddess stays secluded in a palace for her entire childhood until she reaches puberty or sheds blood, when she reverts to the status of a mortal. The Newaris also worship Macchendranath, the god born of a fish identified both with Lokesvara, Shiva's form as "Lord of the World," and Avalokitesvara, a *bodhisattva*. Macchendranath's towering chariot makes his festivals pretty conspicuous. The Newari craftsmen of the Kathmandu Valley have also turned the hero Bhima (or Bhimsen) from the *Mahabharata* epic into their patron deity. Also prominent in the valley is Manjushri, the valley's creator god, who is associated with the Hindu goddess of learning, Saraswati. Manjushri used his sword to cut into the valley wall and drain out its primordial lake; he continues to use it to slice through ignorance.

Outside the Kathmandu Valley various ethnic groups preserve many of their local beliefs in spite of the arrival of Buddhism and Hinduism. In general, these larger religions have taken charge of good and evil, right and wrong, and other such concerns, while local gods are worshiped in order to ask for good harvests and healthy children. Animal sacrifices to the gods are common. The leaders of many of Nepal's local religions are shamans, who mediate between the human and supernatural world.

Climb (Almost) Every Mountain

Since large-scale mountaineering came to Nepal in the 1950s, many climbers have halted within sight of the summit of certain mountains and returned to the bottom without actually standing on top, in deference to local custom, since many peaks of the Himalaya are considered sacred. Looming over the land, the Himalaya provide water and tremendous beauty while remaining a near-impassable barrier. It's not difficult to understand how they came to be seen as the abode of the gods. The mythical Mt. Meru, believed by Hindus to be the center of the universe and the axis of all power, is located in the Himalaya. Mt. Kailash in Tibet is considered Shiva's stomping ground, and many other mountains are homes to other gods. In fact, the deified Himalaya was the father of Shiva's wife Parvati. Many mountains in Nepal such as Gauri-Shankar and Annapurna are named after gods and share their holiness, while others with more mundane names (such as Macchapuchare and Kanchenjunga) are sacred nonetheless.

■ The Arts

In art, as in many things, Nepal has long been at the intersection of various influences, often trading artwork with India and Tibet, absorbing their styles in the process. But whatever Nepal has taken from other countries it has adapted into styles of its own. The Newari artisan castes of the Kathmandu Valley are largely responsible for this. Art in the Terai has been very closely connected to India. The Kathmandu Valley, however, has produced one of South Asia's greatest regional styles. Unfortunately, many older works of art in the Kathmandu Valley have disappeared because they were made of wood and other short-lived materials. But many of the valley's masterpieces nevertheless remain, still found in their original setting. Much like Indian art, Nepalese art has generally been inspired by religion, executed by anonymous craftsmen, and paid for by kings. In Hindu temples especially, originality was not the point; a temple was meant to approximate a cosmic ideal.

THE VISUAL ARTS

Architecture

The oldest remaining structures in the Kathmandu Valley are **stupas,** sacred mounds of earth layered with plaster through the ages. *Stupas* usually mark Buddhist holy places or enclose relics, but being large hemispherical bumps, they are not very interesting architecturally (but they're very durable). Nepalese *stupas*, typified by the Kathmandu Valley's gargantuan Boudha Stupa, have distinctive symbolism on the square, golden spire at their top; these **chakus** are usually painted with the eyes of Buddha, surveying the four cardinal directions, and a number one (?) to represent the unity of all things. *Stupas* are usually accompanied by **chaityas,** small stone shrines that contain mantras or pieces of scripture.

The Kathmandu Valley's greatest architectural achievements have been the wood and brick **pagodas,** which may have evolved from elaborated *chakus* found in *stupa* architecture. Nepal is viewed as the birthplace of the pagoda; a 13th-century architect named Arniko is said to have exported the pagoda to Kublai Khan's China, where the rest of Asia adopted it. Most of Nepal's pagodas are Hindu temples, built around a central sanctum housing the temple's deity. This sanctum is made of brick, with intricately carved wooden doors, window frames, and pillars. The pillars and struts on the outside support the tiered, sloping square clay-tile roof. The upper portions of the temple are not separate stories; they are left deliberately empty, since nothing (except the roof) should be above the deity. The whole structure usually sits on a multi-level stone base with terraces, often resembling a step pyramid.

The Newaris also planned and built **bahals,** blocks of rooms around rectangular courtyards. These compact community units formed monasteries or blocks of houses in the cities. *Bahals* are designed to be perfectly symmetrical, with identical windows on the right and left sides; the main doors and windows usually appear along the central axis of the group.

Despite their xenophobic foreign policy, the Rana prime ministers, who reigned from 1846 to 1951, developed a fetish for the European Neoclassical look; parts of Kathmandu's Durbar Square seem like they belong in Trafalgar Square. The Ranas never made this style of building popular, but with their change of taste they cut off patronage for many of the Kathmandu Valley's traditional crafts, causing their decline. Modern architecture in Nepal consists of utilitarian brick and concrete block.

Sculpture

Early sculpture in the Kathmandu Valley was highly influenced by North Indian stone sculpture. Newari artisans of the Licchavi period made devotional images of Vishnu and the Buddha that strongly resembled the work of the Mathura school, although they gave it a distinctly Nepalese rhythm. Written accounts indicate that wood sculpture flourished at this time, but none of it has survived.

Stone sculpture in Nepal reached its zenith in the 7th, 8th, and 9th centuries, but virtually disappeared after the 10th century. Metal became the medium of choice for medieval Nepalese sculpture, under the influence of eastern and southern India. In the 17th and 18th centuries, Tibet began to influence Nepalese sculpture. Newari artisans made bronze images of Tantric aspects of the Buddha; these were exported to Tibetan monasteries, and many bronze sculptures usually identified as "Tibetan" were actually made in Nepal. Nepalese artists of the Malla period also created fantastic wood sculptures, usually as architectural ornaments. Wood carving was used in temple roof struts and spectacularly ornate wooden window grilles, which often depict plant and animal forms.

In the last two centuries the crafts of bronze casting and woodcarving in Nepal have declined due to lack of patronage. Foreign-funded restoration projects have recently given the sculptors some business, however. Tourism has created some demand as well, although it encourages the mass production of cheap, low quality works rather than the creation of masterpieces.

Painting

The earliest paintings from the Kathmandu Valley appear on palm leaf manuscripts; a few of these have survived from as far back as the 10th century, but most have decayed. More common in Nepal today are Tibetan **thankas** (intricate scroll-paintings of deities) and **mandalas** (meditation aids that represent theological ideas and must follow rigid patterns). During the medieval period a Newari style of *thanka* emerged, called a *paubha,* painted on coarser cloth than a Tibetan *thanka* and without the landscape background that *thankas* borrowed from Chinese art. Later paintings in Nepal were heavily influenced by the detailed miniatures of the Indian Mughal and Rajasthani styles.

NEPAL

MUSIC

Nepalese music is not simply relegated to professional performances and cultural festivals; it flourishes as much or even more in everyday life. Styles and occasions for performance are as numerous as ethnic, religious, regional, and tribal identities. Some sounds are as culturally and regionally grounded as the rice-transplanting songs of women in the fields, while reflecting an exchange with India or Tibetan musical cultures. Hindu and Buddhist religious traditions provide inspiration and performance occasions for many styles of music. The ritualistic music of the Sherpas and other Bhotiyas derives much of its character from the ancient rituals of Tibetan Buddhism, with ceremonies and rites sounding drums and blowing horns preserved from ancient times. Newari Buddhist priests chant ancient Tantric verses as part of meditation exercises, and on sacred occasions such hymns often accompany monks performing esoteric ritual dances. **Bhajan** (devotional hymn singing), like a musical *puja*, is a layman version of sacred music.

The continued presence and influence of **Indian classical music** harkens back to the days when it was the rage in the courts of Malla kings. The Rana prime ministers were such zestful patrons of Indian classical musicians that they banned Nepalese folk performers from their courts.

Music of the traditional and ubiquitous *panchai baja* (five-instrument) ensembles provide jubilant accompaniment to weddings, processions, and temple rituals. The **Gaines,** a caste of musician-storytellers, once actively wandered the hills and dales, accompanying themselves on the *sarangi* (four-stringed fiddle), spreading news between villages.

Several traditional hill styles of music still exist. Most popular is the *maadal*-based (double-sided drum held horizontally) *jhyaure* music of the western hills. The Jyapu farming caste developed an upbeat rhythmic style involving many percussion instruments, including the *dhime* (large two-sided drum) and the use of woodwinds to accompany nasal singing. The *selo* style, originayed by the Tamangs but happily shared by others, keeps the rythmn with the *damphu* (flat one-sided drum).

DANCE

Nepalese dance, be it folk or classical, usually concerns the dramatic retelling of sacred stories from Buddhism and Hinduism. The Newaris of the Kathmandu Valley are the chief exponents of classical dance, with elaborate festive masked dances. Newari performers enter into a trance to become vessels for the embodiment of gods. Sporting elaborate costumes and ornately painted *papier mâché* masks, they gyrate and gesture with emotion and precision. On the tenth day of the Dasain festival in September or October, *nawa* Durga dancers of Bhaktapur perform the vigorous dance-drama of the goddess Durga's victory over the buffalo demon.

The ritualistic pulse of Tibetan Buddhism also engages music, dance, and dramatic forms in festivals, ceremonies, and sacred rites. Performances often involve intricate hand gestures, ritual objects, and the contributions of many unusual and symbolic musical instruments. *Cham* is a dance-drama specific to Tibetans and Bhotiyas, in which monks don mask and costume to enact various Buddhist victory stories.

THE MEDIA

Nepal's English media is nowhere near as developed as India's. *The Rising Nepal* and the *Kathmandu Post* are daily **newspapers** published in English. *The Rising Nepal* is essentially a government mouthpiece that comes out in a Nepali edition as well. The *Post* is independent and focuses more on business, and *The Independent* is a weekly newspaper. The monthly magazine *Himal* covers South Asian issues intelligently and thoroughly. The *International Herald-Tribune, Time,* and *Newsweek* are widely available in English-language bookshops in Kathmandu, as are several Indian papers.

Nepal has been infected with the same **satellite TV** craze currently ravaging India. Star TV beams in the BBC and/or CNN, along with rock videos, Hindi films, and American drivel. Nepal has one brand new FM **radio** station, 100 FM, which broadcasts mostly English (classic and modern rock) and a little Nepalese and Hindi music from 7am to midnight.

■ Food and Drink

Dal bhat tarkari (lentils, rice, and vegetables) is the staple food for most Nepalis as it is for people in large parts of North India. Indeed, *bhat,* the word for cooked rice, is often used as a synonym for *khana* (food). Food in Nepal differs little from Indian food, with the exception of some Tibetan dishes which have made their way onto the Nepalese dining table. Ravioli-like *momo* and *thukpa,* a soup made with noodles, are popular dishes. Newari food is based largely on buffalo meat and radishes. *Choy-ala* is buffalo fried with spices and vegetables.

The most popular breads in Nepal are *chapati,* identical to their Indian counterpart. Western food is also commonly served in tourist restaurants in Nepal. Nepalis don't really eat breakfast, but again tourist restaurants and hotels take care of this. As in India, vegetarians should have no trouble finding delicacies to their taste. Due to Hindu religious beliefs, buffalo meat is commonly served instead of beef.

Milk, or *dudh,* is an important staple of the Nepalese diet that is often served hot—handy, because it is safe to drink once it has been boiled. Yogurt *(dahi)* is popular and forms the basis for *lassis,* which are the same as in India, and for the Newari delicacy *juju,* made from yogurt, cardamom, and cinnamon. Most sweets are milk-based, including *burfi* and *peda* (thick, sweet, spicy milk pastes).

Chiya (tea) is served hot with milk and lots of sugar. Fruit juices are yummy if overpriced and "cold drinks" (soft drinks) are a widely available alternative to tap water. **Alcohol** is consumed in Nepal primarily in the form of beer, which is locally produced and quite tasty (especially when cold) and *chang,* a homemade Himalayan brew. *Raksi* is a stronger version of *chang* that bears a resemblance to tequila in both taste and potency. *Tong-ba* is a Tibetan alcoholic brew made from fermented millet and drunk through a straw.

Just Add Water

Nepal's tea industry is the economic wave of the future given the current trend toward tea cash-cropping. In Eastern Nepal, visiting tea estates is the thing to do when you need a break from mountain gazing. An estate employee will likely give you an impromptu tour in exchange for a tip of about Rs10.

First off, the two types of black teas grown in Nepal and India are known as **orthodox** (or leaf) **tea** grown in the highlands of the Ilam tea estate and **Cut-Tear-Curl (CTC) tea** grown in the lowlands of the Jhapa district. They differ from Japanese **green teas** in that they are allowed to ferment. The strongly flavored and inexpensive **lowland tea** is used in *chiya,* the omnipresent milk tea, because it is much less valuable. The **highland teas** are hailed as top notch for their lighter orange-colored liquors and flavorful aroma. The high altitudes ensure slower growth, which limits production but enhances the quality. **Tea estates** function as plantation communities overseeing everything from the lodging, medical care, and maternity leave of their 1000 employees to the maintenance of the factory and the plucking of tea. Green leaves are **withered** for 16 hours to extract moisture. Next, the dried leaves are **rolled** for 45 minutes on a large rolling machine. **Fermentation** follows for a couple hours as the rolled leaves are laid out on aluminum trays or ceramic tiles. Then comes the **drying** step for over 20 minutes at 220°F in a large oven. Finally, they are sorted according to grade and the stalks are removed.

Making sense of the acronyms inherited from Britain's hand in establishing tea industries in its Empire can be really confusing. Strictly speaking, there are four grades of black tea. First grade is denoted as **FTGFOP** for Fine Tippy Golden Flowery Orange Pekoe; second is **TGBOP** for Tippy Golden Broken Orange Pekoe. The third and fourth grades are dust-like and used in tea bags (like Lipton) for speedier brewing: **GOF** for Golden Orange Fannings and **PD** for Pekoe Dust.

■ Further Sources

General

Nepal: Profile of a Himalayan Kingdom, by Leo E. Rose and John T. Scholz (1980). A country study of Nepal covering history, politics, culture, and economics. Very sensibly written, if somewhat out of date.

Culture Shock! Nepal, by Jon Burbank (1992). A guide to Nepali customs and etiquette especially aimed at those planning to live and work in Nepal. Advice for all sorts of social situations and business hassles.

Travel and Culture

Video Night in Kathmandu, by Pico Iyer (1988). A fascinating if somewhat single-minded account of the impact of western culture on Asia by the *Time* regular. Although only Kathmandu made it to the title, there are also extensive chapters on India as well as other regions of Asia.

Trekking in the Nepal Himalaya, by Stan Armington (1994). The most comprehensive trekking guidebook available. It includes maps, day-by-day descriptions, and altitudes charts for the most popular treks.

The Snow Leopard, by Peter Mathiessen (1978). Travelogue interspersed with contemplations of the existential variety. Sold ubiquitously in Nepal, The Snow Leopard sums up a lot of the soul-searching and nature-gazing that draw many to Nepal.

History and Politics

Nepal: Growth of a Nation, by Ludwig Stiller (1993). An account of the period from the unification of Nepal until 1950. One of the few histories of Nepal that doesn't slobber all over the Shah dynasty.

Politics in Nepal: 1980-1990, by Rishikesh Shah (1990). Once banned by the government, these essays take a look at the country's more recent political history.

Religion

Short Description of Gods, Goddesses, and Ritual Objects of Buddhism and Hinduism in Nepal. Published by the Handicraft Association of Nepal, this short but comprehensive book includes illustrations and is a valuable (and portable) reference. Available in Kathmandu bookstores (Rs80-100).

The Festivals of Nepal, by Mary M. Anderson (1988). A month-by-month description of the legends and practices surrounding Nepal's major festivals; you'll be in the right place at the right time.

Literature

Himalayan Voices: An Introduction to Modern Nepali Literature, by Michael Hutt (1991). The best of the limited number of English translations of Nepali poetry and prose.

Nepali Visions, Nepali Dreams: The Poetry of Laxmiprasad Davkota, translated by David Rubin (1980). A good introduction to the work of Nepal's most prominent modern poet.

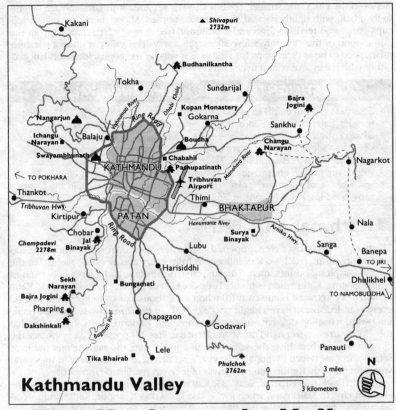

Kathmandu Valley

The Kathmandu Valley

He may have been a goofy-looking brute with a staggering case of halitosis, but Prithvi Narayan Shah knew a good thing when he saw it. So enamored was he with the Kathmandu Valley's green and rust-colored slopes, the two-step of light on the rough edges of its terraces, and its aura of sanctity, that he bid so long to the fun-loving maidens of Gorkha and lived out of his rucksack for ten long years, channeling his waxing libido into the conquest of the Malla trinity that ruled the impressive basin. By naming Kathmandu the capital of his hard-earned amalgamation of states, Shah chose a valley whose variety of economies and cultures was matched only by that of the new kingdom itself. And, as the valley has absorbed the activities of a flourishing country, it has only continued to diversify. Bovines yield to exhaust-belching autos, and structures of concrete and neon push fields farther uphill, as more and more people seek long-term refuge in the swelling valley.

While Nepal's veteran tourists will lament the changes wrought upon their erstwhile Eden-at-1300m, and though many newer visitors will stay only as long as it takes to get a trekking permit, the hills that surround Kathmandu enclose a helluva lot, including seven UNESCO World Heritage Sites, complemented by the backdrop of verdant hills and awe-inspiring peaks of the Himalaya. Kathmandu, Patan, and Bhaktapur, once individual city-states vying for control of the valley, each boast a Durbar Square filled with brick-and-wood temples and unrivaled metalwork crafted by the indigenous Newari people, who are among South Asia's foremost artisans.

Between the cities, the smaller, red-brick towns set amid lush farmland are surprisingly urban, with tightly packed, multi-storied houses. Above them, the valley's hilltops command terrific views and a pollution-free serenity far removed from the commotion of the city only a few kilometers away. The valley is quite a package, guaranteed to be as captivating for visitors as it was for the pugnacious Gorkhali godfather who fell in love with it over a century ago.

HIGHLIGHTS OF THE KATHMANDU VALLEY

- Countless cities in Nepal have a **Durbar Square,** but **Patan's** (p. 733), with its temples, palaces, and pavilions, is the one by which all others are judged.
- **Bhaktapur's** cobbled streets and restored temples (p. 751) give a glimpse of what the valley was like in an era before backpackers and brownie sundaes.
- The great stupa at **Boudha** (p. 748) graces so many postcards for a reason—a visit to the monument provides a glimpse of Tibetan Buddhism in Nepal.
- Some of Nepal's greatest **treks** are within 20 miles of the valley, in the **Langtang** and **Helambu** regions (p. 762).

■ Kathmandu काठमाण्डु

Thirty-eight years after Nepal opened its borders to the world, Kathmandu has become a pulsing patchwork of influences from every corner of the globe. For the Newaris, aspiring businessmen, Tibetan refugees, *sadhus*, and a large collection of ethnic groups, Kathmandu is home. Four decades of tourism have also made Kathmandu a Westernized home-away-from-home for thousands of trekkers and tourists every year. Exasperated, you might cry, *"Kenny G in the Himalayas!?"* But the honking buses, whistling rickshaw-*wallahs*, casinos, and Khukuri shops shout back that this city is *alive*—never mind the World Heritage Sites. It's possible to experience the city like a local: breathing the same foul air and dodging the same manic traffic. A sense of humor tinged by humility is what's needed here: all the savvy in the world won't prepare you for the pungent smells of incense, marijuana, and garbage.

Founded as Manju-Patan around 723, Kathmandu was not always the valley's preeminent city. In Malla days, when it was also known as Kantipur, Kathmandu stood on par with Patan and Bhaktapur, although it was more successful than the others at controlling trade with Tibet. King Prithvi Narayan Shah made Kathmandu his capital when he unified Nepal in the 18th century, and it has been the hub of the Kathmandu Valley ever since. Bursting into the 1990s as the fast-growing capital of a very poor country, present-day Kathmandu bears the scars and trophies of economic growth and rapid Westernization. The trophies include an array of imported goods, arts, and institutions; a plethora of diplomatic missions and foreign aid agencies; and of course, the tourists. But in spite of such bounty, and the optimism inspired here by the 1990 movement for democracy, Kathmandu faces many problems. The city suffers from oppressive pollution, resource shortage, and a lack of infrastructure, as it despairs under corrupt politicians.

Even so, Kathmandu is a fascinating old city, where pagodas crowd the traffic into narrow cobbled lanes, and women gaze from their carved-wood balconies at ancient courtyards as neighborhood boys kick soccer balls around dusty stone shrines. As in the other cities of the Kathmandu Valley, myth and history mingle at every corner, in the forms of glazed-over Ganesh shrines and old shops that have sunk into the street as the ground level has risen. However, not everything in Kathmandu is remote or mysterious; much of it is very mundane, and some of it smells very bad. But it's all part of the package—one which is guaranteed to leave jaws gaping, eyes bugging, and neurons stinging. Grin and let it overwhelm you.

GETTING THERE AND AWAY

International and Domestic Flights

If you're flying into Kathmandu from the east, try to sit on the right side of the plane to get a good view of the mountains. Flights land at **Tribhuvan International Airport,** 5km east of the center of town. The airport has a restaurant, a tea stall, and a communication center from which international calls can be made. Because planes are small and the number of passengers limited, formalities like check-in and security are much faster. However, facilities are so basic that **even slightly bad weather invariably delays flights,** so bring a book. The cheapest way into town is by **bus.** The bus stop is right down the hill. Buses to Ratna Park (#1, frequent, 30min., Rs3) can be prohibitively crowded if you're carrying luggage. To get to Thamel from Ratna Park, turn right after exiting the bus park, walk north along Durbar Marg all the way to the end, turn left and walk three blocks. The walk takes 15 minutes without luggage. Alternatively, **pre-paid taxis** (to Thamel, Rs200) can be arranged at a counter just before the exit or at a booth outside.

Visas are issued upon arrival to those with a passport and hard currency (available from the exchange counter). For more information, see **Visas: Nepal,** p. 8. Flying out, there is a **departure tax** of Rs600 to South Asian countries and Rs700 to all others. **RNAC** and **Indian Airlines** fly to **India.** International flights to: **Calcutta** (1 per day, 1hr., US$96); **Delhi** (3-4 per day, 1½hr., US$142); **Mumbai** (W, 2hr., US$257); **Varanasi** (1 per day, 40min., US$71). If you're under 30, you can get a 25% discount on international flight tickets purchased in Kathmandu.

Fares on domestic flights are virtually identical across airlines. To: **Bharatpur** (3-4 per day, 30min., US$40); **Bhadrapur** (W and Sa, 1hr., US$99); **Biratnagar** (10 per day, 1hr., US$77); **Janakpur** (1 per day. 35min., US$55); **Jomsom** (4 per day, 55min., US$101); **Lukla** (1-15 per day in-season, 40min., US$83); **Nepalganj** (1 per day, 1½ hr., US$99); **Pokhara** (15 per day, 30min., US$61). Mountain-viewing flights from Kathmandu cost US$99.

Airline Offices: RNAC, Kantipath (tel. 220757 or 214640), at New Rd. Open daily 9:30am-1pm and 2-5pm. **Necon Air,** Khicha Pokhari (tel. 480565 for reservations, 242507 to reach main office), south of New Rd., offers 25% student discounts. Open daily 9am-1:30pm and 2-5pm.

Buses

Most buses to locations outside the Kathmandu Valley leave from the Japanese-built **New Bus Park** on Ring Rd. in Gongabu, quite far from central Kathmandu. Almost all city buses make a stop at the New Bus Park; bus #23 from Ratna Park takes one of the most direct routes; it also stops along Kantipath north of Rani Pokhari (every 5min., 5am-8pm, 30min., Rs3-6). You can also take a taxi (Rs58 from Thamel or Rs65 from New Rd.). In the departure area, a flood of ticket counter signs will confuse anyone not proficient in Nepali, so ask around. There is a 24-hour "Police Room" in the departure area. The police can direct you to the right counter, and most of the people selling tickets speak passable English.

There are no express/deluxe distinctions here, and even tourist buses have been known to pick up locals along the way. Buses that leave after noon are night buses—for these you should book 1-2 days in advance. Unless otherwise noted, prices are for morning/night buses. To: **Bhairawa** (frequent, 6am-7pm, 10hr., Rs128/155); **Birganj** (7 per day, 6-8pm, 8hr., Rs120/150); **Butwal** (all buses to Bhairawa and Lumbini, 9hr.); **Dharan** (10 per day, 16hr., Rs298); **Hetauda** (direct 7am, others until 12:25pm, 7hr., Rs100/125; all buses to Birganj, Dharan, Janakpur, and Kakarbhitta pass through); **Janakpur** (4 per day, 12hr., Rs157/206); **Kakarbhitta** (10 per day, 3-5pm, 16hr., Rs337); **Lumbini** (7pm, 11hr., Rs162); **Pokhara** (every 30min., 6am-4pm, 7hr., Rs93/113); **Narayanghat** (frequent, 6:30am-2:10pm, 6hr., Rs80); **Tansen** (5:30pm, 12hr., Rs170); **Tardi Bazaar** (for Sauraha, frequent,7:45am-1:45pm, 6-7hr., Rs90).

Sajha, the government bus corporation, runs daytime buses, which should be booked 2 days in advance. Blue Sajha buses are 5% cheaper and a little faster than other buses. To: **Birganj** (3 per day, 9hr., Rs114); **Bhairawa** (7, 7:45, and 9am, 9hr.,

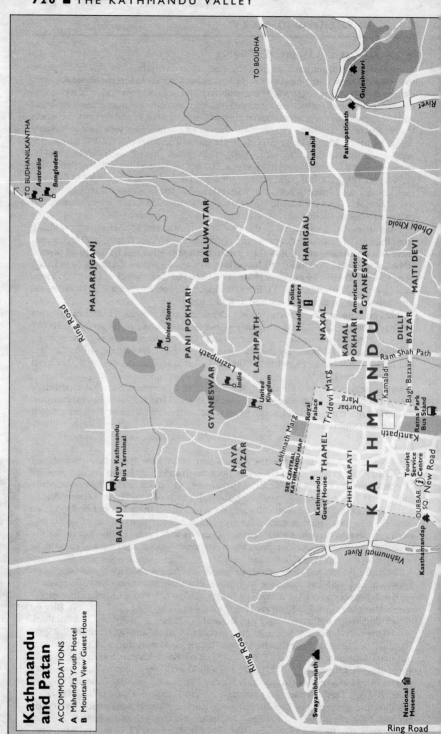

Kathmandu and Patan

ACCOMMODATIONS

A Mahendra Youth Hostel
B Mountain View Guest House

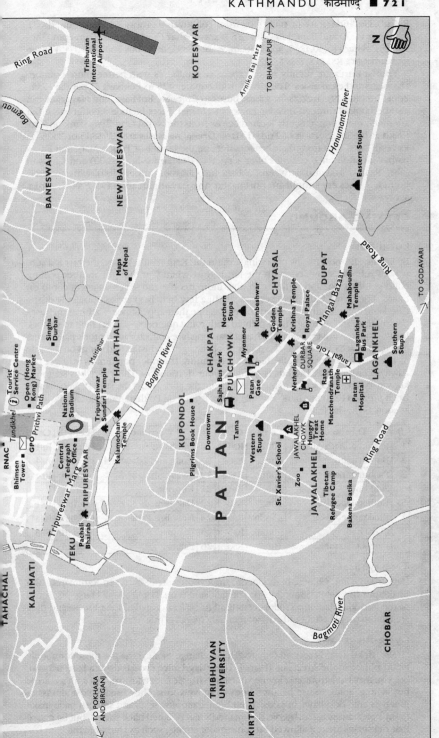

Rs148); **Hetauda** (must be picked up from Tribhuvan Highway Rd., 7am, 6hr., Rs67); **Janakpur** (6:30 and 7am, 9hr., Rs158); **Narayanghat** (5 per day, 6:30am-2pm, 5hr., Rs68); **Pokhara** (6:30, 6:45, and 7:30am, 7½hr., Rs93; night bus 7pm, Rs107); **Tansen** (7:30am, 9hr., Rs131).

Tourist buses are slightly more expensive minibuses with better, more comfortable seats and clear aisles. They leave from counter #25 to **Pokhara** (7 per day, 7am-2pm, 7hr., Rs119). Tickets for tourist buses to **Chitwan, Pokhara,** and **Nagarkot** can also be booked through travel agencies in Thamel. Fares include a commission but are much more conveniently located across from the Nepal Grindlay's Bank on Kantipath at the intersection of Tridevi Marg. **Greenline Buses** (tel. 253885 or 257544) leave at 7 and 8am from their headquarters on the corner of Trideri Marg and Kantipath. Air-conditioned coaches offer service to **Pokhara** (9hr., Rs600) and **Chitwan** (5hr., Rs480), and also between Pokhara and Chitwan (5hr., Rs480), with breakfast included. Tickets should be purchased one day in advance (MC, Visa, AmEx accepted).

GETTING AROUND

Local Buses

By far the cheapest means of getting around the Kathmandu Valley, the bus is a sure way of rubbing shoulders with the locals. Just when you thought another wailing child couldn't possibly squeeze in, five more people and seven roosters climb on board. The buses and minibuses (vans with a few benches) are astoundingly dilapidated and come in all shapes and colors. Despite their appearance, Kathmandu buses do function, and many are now painted with route numbers—a great help to visitors. In addition to a driver, every bus has at least one fare collector who prods passengers into tight spaces and directs the driver in a language of whistles and bangs on the side of the bus. If he hasn't collected the fare during the ride, pay him as you get off. **Always confirm that the bus is going to your destination.** The valley bus station is known as **Ratna Park** (the name is taken from the park across the street); Nepalis also call it *purano* (old) bus park. Bus #23 leaves from Rani Pokhari. Buses generally leave as soon as they're full.

#	Destination	Length	Cost	#	Destination	Length	Cost
1	Pashupatinath Airport	40min.	Rs4	12	Dhulikhel	2hr.	Rs15
2	Boudhanath	1hr.	Rs6	14	Patan and Jawlakhel	20min.	Rs4
2	Pashupatinath	30min.	Rs4	19	Swavpamblau	45min.	Rs4
4	Sankhu	2hr.	Rs10	21	Kirtipur	1hr.	Rs4
5	Budhanilkantha	1hr.	Rs6	22	Dakshinkali	1½hr.	Rs12
7	Bhaktapur	45min.	Rs6	23	New Bus Park	30min.	Rs3
9	Old Thimi	30min.	Rs5	23	Balaju	30min.	Rs3
9	Bahaka Bazaar	1hr.	Rs6	26	Patan	30min.	Rs4

Trolleybuses

Haggard-looking, Chinese-built electric trolleybuses creak between Kathmandu and Bhaktapur (frequent, 45min., Rs5). The first stop is on **Tripureswar Marg,** just south of the National Stadium. Trolleybuses tend to be less crowded than buses, and they are a far more pleasant (and environmentally friendly) ride.

Cycle-Rickshaws

"Hello, rickshaw?" is second only to "Hello, change money?" as the most commonly heard phrase in the streets of Thamel. These aggressive cyclists drive a hard bargain, but you may have trouble bringing yourself to haggle over a few rupees with a man or boy who is going to use his own body to move yours. They usually cost almost as much as auto-rickshaws or taxis. Their high, canopied seats and smooth pace make them a pleasant way to observe Kathmandu's less polluted back streets, but be aware that rickshaws are not allowed on some major streets, such as Durbar Marg.

NEPAL

Tempos

Larger, sturdier versions of auto-rickshaws, these blue vehicles seat 10 (though you'd never guess from the outside) and run along a prescribed route. Flag them down anywhere along their routes; to request a stop, bang on the metal ceiling. Tempos use the same route numbers as buses but leave from different places. Some leave from **Sundhara,** just outside the GPO: #2 to **Boudhanath** via **Pashupatinath** (30min., Rs6). Others gather just north of **Rani Pokhari:** #5 to **Budhanilkantha** via **Lazimpath** (45min., Rs6) and #23 to **Balaju** (40min., Rs3).

Auto-Rickshaws

These are the same black-canopied, three-wheeled contraptions that sputter and beep their way through India. If you can persuade the driver to use his outdated meter, auto-rickshaws are cheaper than taxis. If he refuses to use the meter, take a taxi. Auto-rickshaw-*wallahs* tend to be stubborn bargainers. The exhaust that these glorified lawn mowers spew is particularly noxious, and their semi-open construction won't keep out other vehicles' fumes. However, auto-rickshaws are great at maneuvering through narrow lanes and are fine for short jaunts.

Taxis

Shiny new red, green, or yellow taxis are all metered, as are the older ones (identifiable by their black license plates), but it may take some persuasion to get your driver to lift the rag he's casually draped over the meter. You shouldn't have to haggle over the price unless you're desperate (i.e., if it's the only cab around or you're going somewhere weird at a late hour). If the driver refuses to use the meter, get out and find another taxi. Have the fare ready as soon as you arrive, or the driver might let the meter jump a notch while you rummage for change. Rates typically start at Rs5 or Rs7 and go up in increments. Fares within the city should be less than Rs150; Rani Pokhari to Swayambhu or Pashupathi runs about Rs75; shorter jaunts like Thamel to New Road will cost around Rs40. An all-day sight-seeing tour around the valley costs about Rs600. Round up to the nearest rupee but don't tip. At night, rates go up by over 50%, and drivers may be unwilling to go to some destinations. Taxis queue on Tridevi Marg near the entrance to Thamel.

Bicycles

Bicycles can be rented from numerous little shops in Thamel, especially around Thamel Chowk. While mountain bikes (Rs150 per day) are better for trips outside the city, heavier one-speeders (Rs60 per day), equipped with bells, may be more suitable for getting around the city. Cycling is an excellent way of touring the Kathmandu Valley if you can stand the polluted air. Renting a motorbike or a moped (Rs500 per day, passport must be deposited) is a great way to contribute your own bit of exhaust.

ORIENTATION

Kathmandu's Newari citizens once tried to keep the city compact in order to maximize farmland, but today the city splays out past its old boundaries. For visitors, a dearth of street names renders the unregulated sprawl even more unruly. Nevertheless, Kathmandu is still rather small; neighborhoods, major temples, and main thoroughfares make navigation pretty straightforward. The shrines of **Swayambhunath** and **Pashupatinath** anchor the western and eastern edges of the city. Almost exactly halfway between them, the two main roads of **Kantipath** and **Durbar Marg** run parallel to each other, north-south. Kantipath, on the west, has the post office and a good collection of banks; Durbar Marg, on the east, has its share of airline offices, trekking agencies, luxury hotels, and restaurants, as well as the **Royal Palace** at its north end. Between the two streets farther south is the **Tundikhel** parade ground, a very flat landmark. Kantipath and Durbar Marg become one-way streets near this grassy rectangle as traffic moves clockwise around it.

Kantipath and Durbar Marg divide Kathmandu into two halves—west of Kantipath are the older, more interesting parts of the city, while the area east of Durbar Marg consists mainly of new neighborhoods. The year-round tourist carnival that is **Thamel** is west of Kantipath, at the northwestern end of town. Thamel is joined to Kantipath and Durbar Marg by the wide **Tridevi Marg.** The area just south of Thamel is **Chhetrapati,** centered on a six-way crossing with a bandstand in the middle.

Kathmandu's old center, **Durbar Square,** filled with magnificent architecture, is also west of Kantipath, south of Thamel and Chhetrapati, and close to the banks of the **Vishnumati River. New Road,** which was built in 1934 out of the rubble of a great earthquake, runs east from Durbar Square to Kantipath. New Rd. is the city's top commercial district, with rows of jewelers and electronics sellers. A nameless narrow lane that sprouts northeast from Durbar Square used to be the main trading center. It cuts through **Indra Chowk,** one of Kathmandu's most interesting neighborhoods, and **Asan Tole,** the seething center of Kathmandu's main bazaar.

Tripureswar Marg is the biggest road in the southern half of town, running east-west and leading to the **Patan Bridge.** Kathmandu's twin city, Patan, lies across the **Bagmati River,** which is the southern limit of Kathmandu. A wide **Ring Road** now encircles both Kathmandu and Patan, grouping them together with the new suburbs that have grown around them.

PRACTICAL INFORMATION

Tourist and Financial Services

Tourist Office: There are 2 government-run **Tourist Information Centers:** one at Basantapur Square on New Rd. (tel. 220818), and at Tribhuvan Airport (tel. 470537). Both open Su-Th 9am-6pm, F 9am-4pm. **Tourist Service Center** (tel. 256232 or 256230; fax 227281; email tourism@mos.com.np), south of Ratna Bus Park, just east of Durbar Marg. The room on the immediate left at the front entrance is staffed by a friendly English-speaking tourism representative. Open Su-Th 10am-5pm, F 10am-3pm.

Trekking Information: Himalayan Rescue Association (HRA), P.O Box 4944 (tel. 262746; email hra@aidpost.mos.com.np), Thamel Mall at Jyatha-Thamel. Focuses on mountain safety, providing information on altitude sickness, a message board for trekkers looking for companions, and free safety talks in the Spring and Fall, Su-F 2pm. HRA also runs 2 clinics in Manang (Annapurna circuit) and Pheriche (Everest trek); they appreciate donations of leftover medicine as well as monetary contributions. **Kathmandu Environmental Education Project (KEEP),** P.O. Box 9178 (tel. 259275 or 259567; fax 411533; email tour@keep.wlink.com.np), Thamel Mall, in the same building as HRA. While KEEP's primary aim is environmental education, its office is a virtual trekker's lounge, selling books, maps, t-shirts, biodegradable soap, as well as serving tea and coffee in a cushy reading room. Slide show presentations twice a week at 3pm Sept.-Nov. and Feb.-Mar. Both have small libraries, plenty of pamphlets, log books of trekkers' advice, mineral water (1L Rs10), and helpful staff. **Fill out an embassy registration form at one of these offices (or at your embassy) before you go trekking.** Both open Su-F 10am-5pm. Thamel is the place to look for **trekking supplies,** both new and used, to buy or rent. Watch out for phony North Face or Gore-Tex labels. Bring boots and other essentials from home, but heavy items like sleeping bags, Gore-Tex backpacks, and jackets can be rented, though most places would rather sell backpacks than rent them.

Budget Travel: Every other shopfront in Thamel seems to be a ticket-booking, trekking, rafting, or travel agency. Some are helpful, but others are shady and disappear quickly. Ask other travelers for recommendations or visit one of the well-established agencies on Durbar Marg **(Annapurna Travels, Everest Express,** or **Yeti Travels).** For bookings on tourist buses to places like Pokhara and Chitwan, most agencies offer comparable prices—check out a few to make sure you're getting the going rate. For plane tickets, go directly to the airline office; travel agencies might take a commission on flights (see **Getting There and Away,** p. 719).

Diplomatic Missions: Australia, Bansbari (tel. 371466 or 371678; fax 371533), on Maharajgunj, just past Ring Rd. Open M-Th 8:30am-5pm, F 8:30am-1:15pm. Consular services M-Th 10am-12:30pm. **Bangladesh,** Maharajgunj (tel. 372843; fax 373265), on Chakrapath near Hotel Karnali. Open Su-Th 9am-5pm. Apply for visa

TO LAINCHAUR
AND LAZIMPATH

SEE THAMEL MAP

Royal
Palace

PAKNAJOL

Pilgrims
Book House

Kaiser Library

TO NAXAL

K.C.'s

Kathmandu
Guest House

THAMEL

Department of
Immigration

Tridevi Marg

SAARC

Tridevi Marg

Greenline
Bus

Yak and Yeti
Hotel

ANZ
Grindlays
Bank

CIWEC
Clinic

Baan Thai Rest.

British
Council

Durbar Marg

Koto Japanese
Rest.

Nirula's

JYATHA

Everest Steak House

Delicatessen
Center

CHHETRAPATI

American
Express

Mangalore
Coffee
House

TO SWAYAMBHUNATH

THAHITY

Ikhapokhari

National
Theatre

Kamaladi

Bhanchha
Ghar

Kathesimbhu

KAMALACHHI

Tempo
Stand

Rani
Pokhari

Clock
Tower

BANGEMUDHA

ASAN

BHOTAHITI

Bagh
Bazaar

Nardevi
Temple

KILAGAL

Annapurna
Temple

Ratna
Park

Bhaktapur
Bus Stand

Itum Bahal

KEL
TOLE

Seto
Macchendranath

Ratna Park
Bus Stand

Akash
Bhairab

INDRA
CHOWK

Bir
Hospital

TO SWAYAMBHUNATH

MAKHAN

Shukra Path

Kala
Bhairab

Taleju
Temple

New
Road
Gate

DURBAR
SQUARE

Maju
Dewal

Hanuman
Dhoka

Tourist
Service
Centre

Om Pharmacy

New Road

RNAC

Angan

Kasthamandap

BASANTPUR
SQUARE

Photo Concern

Nepal
Bank

Tundikhel

Kumari
Bahal

Dharma Path

Little
Garden

Jhocche Tole
(Freak St.)

JHOCCHE

Khicha Pokhari

Kantipath

Bhimsen Tower

GPO

Baghdurbar

Martyrs'
Gate

N

NEPAL

Central Kathmandu

ACCOMMODATIONS

D Annapurna Lodge
B Century Lodge
C Himalaya's Guest House
A Hotel Sugat
E Journeyman Hotel
F Singapore Guest House

Su-Th 9:30-noon and pick it up the next day after 4pm. Two photographs and US$45 in Nepali currency required for Americans seeking a 15-day tourist/transit visa. **Canada,** Lazimpath (tel. 415193), down the lane opposite Navin Books stationery shop. Open M-F 8:30am-4:30pm. **China,** Baluwatar (tel. 411740, visa services tel. 419053). Visas Rs2000 for U.S. citizens. Allow 4 days for processing. Bring passport and 1 photo. Visas to **Tibet** available only to organized groups of 5 or more (although individuals can enter with a group and then go it alone, risking the wrath of Chinese officials). Ready in 4 days. Open M-F 10am-5pm. Visa dept. open M, W, and F 10-11:30am. **India,** Lainchaur (tel. 410900; fax 413132). Walk north up Lazimpth and veer left before Hotel Ambassador. Put yourself through the potentially **week-long visa ordeal** M-F. Telex forms issued at counter B 9:30-11am, accepted 9:30am-noon. Return a week later, check the board near counter B for your name, surrender your receipt at counter B in exchange for your approval slip. Bring the slip along with your passport, a completed visa application (available at the office behind counter B, where you may also have to negotiate if you want a multiple entry visa) and one photo to counter A. Pay your visa fee (3 months Rs1200, 6 months Rs2300; additional Rs1220 for U.S. citizens. Free for citizens of South Africa). Return the same day between 4:45 and 5:15pm to pick up your passport and visa. Check to make sure you got the visa for which you applied. Whew! Feel proud for having survived your first brush with Indian bureaucracy. For transit visas, bring 1 photo and Rs300 directly to counter A, M-F 9:30am-noon. Transit visas are valid for 15 days from date of issue and are ready the same day after 4:30pm. **Malaysia,** visas to Malaysia are administered through the U.K.'s consular services (tel. 410583). A 3-month tourist visa (Rs2400) can be approved in 2 days, provided you bring in 2 photographs, traveler's checks, plane ticket, and a hotel reservation slip. **Myanmar** (Burma), Chakupat, Patan (tel. 521788; fax 523402), near Patan Gate. Visas M-F 9:30am-1pm and 2-4:30pm. Apply in the morning and pick up one hr. later. Three photos required. Tourist visa US$10. **Pakistan,** Chakrapath (tel. 374024; fax 374012), near the intersection of Ring Rd. and Maharajgunj, northwest quadrant. Passports and 2 photos necessary for visa applications collected M-F 10-11am. Visas can be picked up the following day 10am-noon. Rs3543 for 3-month tourist visa for US citizens. **Sri Lanka,** Baluwatar (tel. 413623), near the Russian embassy. Visa applications Su-F 9am-12:30pm. **Thailand,** Bansbari (tel. 371410; fax 371408 or 371409). Turn east just north of the Australian Embassy. Visa applications M-F 9:30am-12:30pm. Visas ready in 24hr. Two photos required. One-month tourist visa Rs450, 2-month Rs700. **U.K.,** Lainchaur (tel. 414588; fax 411789). Open M-F 8:15am-12:30pm and 1:30-5pm. Consular services 9am-noon. **U.S.,** Pani Pokhari, Maharajgunj (tel. 411179; fax 419963). Open M-F 8am-5pm.

Immigration Office: Department of Immigration (tel. 412337 or 418573), on the north side of Tridevi Marg where it narrows and enters Thamel. **Trekking permits** for Kanchenjunga and Dolpa (US$10 per week for the 1st month, US$20 per week thereafter); Mustang and Upper Dolpa (US$700 for the first ten days, US$70 per day thereafter); Manaslu (Sept.-Nov. US$90 per week, Dec.-Aug. US$75 per week); Humla (US$90 for the 1st week, US$15 per day thereafter); for all other areas (US$5 per week for the 1st 4 weeks, US$10 per week thereafter). Two photos and passport required for trekking permits. Apply Su-Th 10am-2pm, pick-up 1-5pm; or F 10am-noon, pick-up noon-3pm. Payment accepted in rupees only. You can complete the process in 1 day, but at the height of the trekking season, long lines can extend the process to 2 or even 3 days—get there early. The office closes for a couple of days during the Dasain holiday in late-September. Permit officials have been known to make a fuss if all the members of the group seeking permits aren't present. There's an additional fee for treks entering a national park or a conservation area: Rs1000 for conservation areas and Makalu-Baran National Park, Rs650 for other national parks. Entry fees are collected at, well, the **Entry Fee Collection Centre** (tel. 233088, ext. 363), is across the street in the basement of the Himalayan Bank Building, to the right as you walk down a permanently stationary escalator. The process takes a few minutes. Open Su-Th 10am-5pm, F 10am-3pm.

Currency Exchange: Legally, currency can only be exchanged at banks or government-registered agencies. Ask for encashment receipts, which are necessary to exchange leftover rupees at the airport and could be requested if you apply for a visa extension of over 3 months. Illegally, traveler's checks and cash can be exchanged on the **black market.** It's better to walk into a carpet shop (most of which do exchange on the side) than to be brought in by a "change money?" tout. Ask around about going rates—they may be as much as 10% better than at banks. Big, crisp bills are favored. Be aware that many hotels require an encashment certificate—proof of legitimate exchange—in order to accept your rupees. **Nepal Bank Ltd.,** New Rd. (tel. 221185), offers the lowest commission around for cashing traveler's checks (0.5%). You must show your Nepalese visa as well as your traveler's check purchase agreement. Open daily 8am-1pm and 1:30-6pm. **ANZ Grindlays** on Kantipath, just south of Tridevi Marg, does cash advances and sells MC, Visa, and AmEx traveler's checks. The foreign exchange department, around the back of the building, is open Su-Th 9:45am-3:30pm, F 9:45am-12:45pm. The several official exchange counters with long hours around Thamel generally charge about 2% commission. **Western Union** is at Annapurna Travel and Tours, Durbar Marg (tel. 222339 or 223763; fax 222966), on the east side of the street, where it becomes one-way. Money can be wired here within 10min. Open daily 9:30am-7pm. **American Express: Yeti Travels,** Hotel Mayalu, Jamal, P.O. Box 76 (tel. 226172 or 227635; fax 226152 or 226153). Mail and faxes held for traveler's check and card holders. Checks and cards replaced, and card holders can buy traveler's checks. Open Su-Th 10am-1pm and 2-5pm, F 10am-1pm and 2-4:45pm.

Local Services

Luggage Storage: Available at most guest houses for free or a few rupees per day.
Laundry Service: Almost all guest houses have laundry service, but free-standing establishments often charge less. **The Laundry Service,** across from Pumpernickel Bakery in Thamel, has low rates for same-day machine-wash service (double for 3hr. service). Open daily 8am-8pm.
Market: You'll never be far from a fruit stand in any neighborhood. For fresh fruits and vegetables, try **Asan Tole,** in front of the Annapurna Temple. **Open Market** (also called Hong Kong Market), south of Ratna bus park down the stairs, is a large tarpaulin congregation of shoe sellers and "Levi's" hawkers popular with locals. Picnic and trekking supplies can be found in Thamel at the **Best Shopping Centre,** Tridevi Marg (tel. 410986), right where it narrows into Thamel. Open daily 8am-8pm. AmEx accepted. For the best simulation of a Western supermarket and its prices, head for a branch of **Bluebird Supermarket.** Open daily 10am-8pm.
Library: Kaiser Library, Ministry of Education compound (tel. 411318), on the corner of Tridevi Marg and Kantipath. 35,000-volume, non-circulating library housed in a charmingly decrepit Rana palace. Open Su-Th 10am-5pm, F 10am-3pm. Closed on government holidays. **American Center,** Gyaneswar (tel. 415845). Read *The New Yorker* and *Rolling Stone* in A/C comfort. Open M-F 11am-6pm.
Bookstore: Thamel is dotted with good used book shops. **Pilgrims Book House,** Thamel (tel. 424942; fax 424943; http://www.gfas.com/pilgrims), houses a big selection. Great restaurant near the used books in the rear. Open daily 8am-10pm.

Emergency and Communications

Pharmacy: Om Pharmacy, New Rd. (tel. 244658 or 222644), across from RNAC, is recommended by local medical experts. Open daily 8am-9pm. It may be difficult to find an English-speaker here. Several other pharmacies across from Bir Hospital. Clinics stock many common pharmaceuticals; medicines such as ciprofloxacin, and oral rehydration salts are also available in some convenience marts.
Hospital/Medical Services: Kathmandu has numerous reliable **clinics** geared toward Westerners. In case of illness, visit one of these first. If you are too ill to go to a clinic, ask your guest house to arrange a house call. If you need more care than the clinic physician can provide, you'll be sent to the appropriate hospital. The following clinics have the best reputations: **CIWEC Clinic,** off Durbar Marg (tel. 228531 or 241732), behind the Yak and Yeti sign, to the right. Staffed by Western doctors who charge Western prices. US$40 per consultation. Open M-F 9am-noon and 1-3:30pm. Open Sa-Su for emergencies and vaccines. Call 24hr. in an emergency. Accepts MC and Visa. **Nepal International Clinic** (tel. 412842), across from the Royal Palace, a 3min. walk east of the main gates, down a lane to the right. West-

ern-educated Nepalese doctors. Consultation US$35. Open Su-F 9:30am-1pm and 2-5pm, Sa 3-5pm. On-call 24hr. for emergencies. Accepts MC, Visa, and Amex. **Himalayan Internal Clinic,** Jyatha-Thamel (tel. 225455; fax 226980). Western-educated doctors. Consultation US$20 (US$40 for housecall), follow-up US$10. Discounts available for students with financial need. Open Su-F 9am-5pm, Sa 9am-1pm. **Patan Hospital,** Lagankhel, Patan (tel. 522295), has a better reputation than the government hospital in Kathmandu proper, **Bir Hospital.** The **Teaching Hospital,** Maharganj is also said to be good. However, calling hospitals can be useless—if someone answers, chances are they'll speak poor English.

Police: tel. 100 or 226999. **Tourist Police,** Basantapur Tourist Information Center (tel. 220818).

Emergency: Fire, tel. 101. **Ambulance,** tel. 228094 (Red Cross). No English spoken at any of these numbers. **In a medical emergency, call a clinic to find an English speaker. CIWEC** (tel. 228531 or 241732) has 24hr. emergency service.

Post Office: GPO, near Bhimsen Tower, entrance just off Kantipath. Self-service *Poste Restante* is behind the counter on the left. Open Su-Th 10:30am-4pm (winter 10:30am-3pm), F 10:30am-2pm. Rifle through the cubby-holes yourself; check for your first and last names, since letters are sometimes misfiled. A clerk may or may not ask for your passport before you make off with your mail. Stamps sold and cancelled Su-F 7am-6pm, Sa 11am-3pm. Letters to be mailed should be brought to the stamp cancellation window #1. Many guest houses and communications centers will post your letters for a small commission. In Thamel, Pilgrims Book House is a reliable place to bring your mail. **Express Mail Service (EMS),** at the GPO, delivers within 3 days to Australia, New Zealand, Canada, Denmark, Italy, Germany, and the United States as well as to most Asian countries. Open Su-Th 10am-5pm, F 10am-3pm. The entrance to the **Foreign Parcel Office** is around the corner on Kantipath. Bring your open parcel to be checked by customs, then properly sewn up and sealed by the packagers who wait outside. Open Su-Th 10:15am-1:30pm. **DHL** (US$40 to U.S.) can be problematic. The more reliable **FedEx, UPS,** and **Airborne Express** are offered by many shops in Thamel.

Internet: Most internet offices offer phone services. See **telephones,** below.

Telephones: Central Telegraph Office, on Kantipath, west of the National Stadium, has the best international rates and free callback. Open 24hr. Domestic and international calls and faxes available at the numerous STD/ISD booths sprinkled throughout the city. Most offer the same rates on outgoing calls but have different deals on callbacks—shop around. **Easy Link Cybercafe** (tel. 425933; email easylink@visitnepal.com), 2 blocks north of Tridevi Marg on Thahity-Thamel on the left, has good phone rates, and their electronic fax service (Rs70 per page) is the cheapest deal around. Email send/receive Rs10 per kb. During "Happy Hour" (8-10pm) internet access (Rs7 per min.) comes with a free cold drink. Open Su-Th 9am-10pm, Sa noon-10pm. **Global Communications,** Tridevi Marg (tel. 228143; fax 220143; email glocom@mos.com.np), in the shopping center across from Immigration, has the most experience and also offers good rates and charges a flat Rs25 for callbacks, which you receive in a quiet booth. Local calls Rs4 per 3min. Also offers fax and post. Email send/receive Rs10 per kb; web access Rs7 per min. Open Su-F 8am-8pm, Sa 11am-5pm. International phone and fax facilities in the **GPO** (fax 225145). Open Su-Th 10am-5pm, F 10am-3pm. This is a very cheap place to make local calls (Rs4) and receive faxes (Rs10 per page). **Directory Assistance:** 197. **Telephone Code:** 01.

ACCOMMODATIONS

Any mention of tourist facilities in Kathmandu must begin with **Thamel,** and that goes double for accommodations. Staying in the Thamel area is like hanging out in a mall—everything is within easy reach, but the experience won't broaden your horizons. Use its proliferation of pizza, bootleg cassettes, and enlightenment paraphernalia, but don't let it use you. Get out into the rest of Kathmandu every once in a while. Despite the ease of Thamel, the rest of the city is less of a hassle—it won't surround you with constant appeals to change money, buy hashish, or ride in a rickshaw.

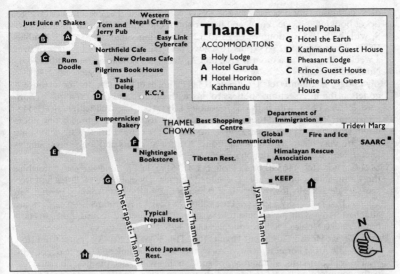

Accommodations in Thamel are climbing in price, but there are still many budget choices. The prices listed are for high season, but these are usually negotiable, depending on the season and the length of your stay. Ask for **student discounts;** many establishments will at least discount the 10% tax. **Don't let anyone lead you to his "friend's hotel"**— his commission (as high as 50%) will be tacked onto your bill.

Freak Street is Kathmandu's original tourist district, which peaked in the 70s. Freak St. is less hectic than Thamel; most of its hotels have been around for the last 25 years, growing musty watching lodges in Thamel steal all their business. **Sundhara,** south of Bhimsen Tower, lacks the in-your-face quality of the tourist ghettos—it's just a neighborhood where some hotels happened to appear. Popular with Indian tourists, its accommodations—cheap, unassuming, and conveniently located just south of New Rd.—are not quite the bargains found in Thamel, but they are wise selections if you want to "find" the city before it finds you. The places below, unless otherwise noted, have hot water, seat toilets, laundry service, luggage storage, and a noon check-out time, but no towels or toilet paper.

Thamel

Hotel Potala (tel. 419159; fax 416680), across from K.C.'s. Located in the center of Thamel, this place is a real find. Clean showers and toilets on each floor. Well-ventilated rooms allow for easy eavesdropping, like it or not. Clean rooms (some with fans) have shared balconies that create a nice neighborhood feel. Hang out among plants on the roof terrace or in the lobby. Singles Rs125; doubles Rs175-250.

Hotel The Earth, Chhetrapati-Thamel (tel. 260039 or 260312). South of Kathmandu Guest House on the west side of the street. Large, clean, generously furnished rooms with big windows, fans, and phones achieve a balance between luxury and economy. Towels and toilet paper provided. Discounts for students, volunteers, and long-term guests. Singles Rs150, with bath US$6; doubles Rs250/US$10.

Hotel Horizon Kathmandu, Chhetrapati-Thamel (tel. 220904 or 220927), down the first lane to the right, heading south from Kathmandu Guest House. Set back from the street, with a nice courtyard. Some of the large rooms have bathtubs. Carpets, fans, and plenty of furniture make for a comfortable stay. Student discounts up to 25%. Singles Rs150, with bath US$6; doubles Rs250, with bath US$10-20. MC, Visa.

Kathmandu Guest House (tel. 413632 or 418733; fax 417133; email kgh@thamel.mos.com.mp). Since all directions in Thamel are given in relation to this place, you'd better figure out where Kathmandu's original "budget hotel" is. The singles in the old wing are the cheapest way to get at the Guest House's amenities: communication center, swank lobby with satellite TV, currency exchange, ticket booking, bicycle rental, and barber shop. Old wing: Singles with sink US$6-8, with bath US$10; doubles US$8-10/12. New wing: Singles US$17-25; doubles US$20-30; triples US$25-35 (plus 10% govt. tax). Discount of 10% for stays of over a week, 30% for over a month. Visa, MC, AmEx. Reservations recommended Sept.-Nov. and Feb.-Apr.

Holy Lodge, Satghumti (tel. 416265 or 413441), north of Kathmandu Guest House—go left at the intersection. Spotless rooms with phones and fans off a quiet courtyard. Singles US$3, with bath US$7; doubles US$5/10; triples (all with bath) US$15.

Kathmandu View Guest House, Chhetrapati (tel. 260624 or 257482), a few doors down from the Everest Steak House. Rooms with exposed brick walls and stone inlay are very clean. Discounts of up to 20% for students and long stays. Singles Rs200, with bath Rs250; doubles Rs250/350.

Hotel Garuda (tel. 416340 or 414766; fax 413614), just around the curve north of the Kathmandu Guest House. The gilded Garuda has elaborate facilities and five-star service at really low prices. It also boasts one of the few "rooftop gardens" in Thamel that is actually a garden. Free callbacks (24hr.). All rooms have carpets and attached baths with towels and toilet paper. 25% student discount. Add 10% government tax. Singles US$9-20; doubles US$13-25. MC,Visa,AmEx.

Prince Guest House, Satghumti-Thamel (tel. 414456; fax 220143), across from Holy Lodge. The Artist Formerly Known As would Die 4 this pink and purple decor with wall-to-wall carpeting. Brand-new, pristine rooms with fans, phones, and attached baths complete with seat toilets and shower curtains. Rooftop garden and restaurant. Room service, safe deposit. Singles US$8; doubles US$10.

Hotel Tashi Dhele, Thahity-Thamel (tel. 224509 or 228491), south of Thamel Chowk through a driveway to the west. Clean rooms with desks, chairs, and screened windows. Most rooms have attached baths. Patio pleasantly distant from the dusty street. Fans and room service round out the amenities. In season: singles US$10; doubles US$15-25. Off-season: US$6-8/10.

Hotel White Lotus, Jyatha Thamel (tel. 249842; fax 220143). Sits beside the parking lot just south of Tridevi Marg, opposite the immigration office, but it must be entered through a lane leading east off Jyatha (follow the signs). Rooms vary in amenities and price, but all are clean. A dizzying spiral staircase leads to the roof garden; every floor has a balcony with rattan furniture. Towels provided. ISD service. Safe deposit. 20% student discount in-season. Singles US$3-4, with bath US$10; doubles US$6-8, with bath US$14; triples US$8, with bath US$17.

Pheasant Lodge, (tel. 417415), down a short alleyway off Chhetrapati-Thamel just south of Pub Maya. Cheap and smack dab in the middle of things. Basic rooms from the folks who brought you the Restaurant at the End of the Universe (see p. 759). Bamboo walls, clean sheets, and a choice of common toilets—squat or sit as you please. Showers are standing room only. The hotel is often full—try right at the noon check-out time. Singles Rs100; doubles Rs150.

Freak Street

Hotel Sugat, Basantapur, Durbar Sq. (tel. 246454; fax 221824), along the southern edge of Basantapur Sq. (facing the royal palace). A few wrinkles and age-spots suggest that this place weathered Freak Street's turbulent adolescence, but its location, prices, and mellow demeanor more than compensate for a lack of dazzle. Large, carpeted rooms overlook Durbar Sq.; some have tubs and balconies. Fans, toilet paper, towels provided. Long-term, off-season, and student discounts. Singles Rs110, with bath Rs300; doubles Rs300/350-400.

Annapurna Lodge (tel. 247684), on the right, walking from Durbar Sq. Angled stairway leads to quiet, basic rooms off a balcony. Seat toilets in attached baths; squat and seat toilets in common bath. Attached restaurant shows movies. Singles Rs125, with bath Rs175; doubles Rs200/275.

Himalaya's Guest House, Basantapur, Jhochhen (tel. 246555). From Durbar Square, head down a quiet lane filled with butcher shops on the right off of Freak St. Rooms are bright and clean, with fans, TV's (Rs30 extra), and free international callbacks. Discounts for long stays. Singles Rs150; doubles Rs250, with bath Rs300.

Century Lodge, Freak St., a minute's walk from Basantapur Square. Diminutive quarters, diminutive price. The place has a remarkable *Alice in Wonderland* feel. Petite rooms furnished conventionally, well-worn but not neglected. Squat toilet on each floor; two hot showers on ground floor courtyard. Singles Rs85; doubles with attached bath Rs250, with private garden balcony Rs275; quads Rs300.

Sundhara

Journeyman Hotel, Ganabahal, Pipalbot (tel. 253438; fax 22644). Walk along the paved road that leads southwest of Bhimsen Tower. Continue west past the *pipal* tree; the hotel is up ahead on your right. Large, carpeted rooms with phones and fans are old but well-maintained. Friendly and accommodating management. Attached restaurant. TV's upon request (Rs100 extra). Student and group discounts for longer stays. Singles Rs150, with bath Rs250; doubles Rs250/350.

Singapore Guest House, Baghdurbar (tel. 244105), directly south of Bhimsen Tower, towards the end of the street on the left. Large, quiet rooms with carpets and fans. Attached restaurant. Some nicer and more expensive rooms in the building across the street. All but one room with attached bath. Singles Rs225; doubles Rs250; triple Rs450. Credit cards accepted.

FOOD

Kathmandu has achieved mythic status as an oasis of displaced delicacies, from the 1954 founding of Kathmandu's first luxury hotel by a charismatic Russian entrepreneur who had chandeliers and fresh fish carried in by porters, to the advent of "Pie Alley," where 1960s overlanders gathered for apple pie and hash brownies. Today, steaks, pizza, enchiladas, french fries, and sundaes are de rigueur on tourist menus. Much of this fare tastes blandly similar, borrowing most of its flavor from the *ghee* in which it was baptized. The Japanese, Thai, Tibetan, and Indian restaurants that elbow for room in neighborhoods frequented by foreigners and wealthy Nepalis generally offer more appetizing and less contrived fare. "So what about Nepalese food?" asks the open-minded traveler who didn't come halfway around the world to meet with shoddy American simulacra. The best bet is to get yourself invited to someone's home for a meal.

Thamel

Typical Nepali Restaurant, Chhetrapati-Thamel (tel. 244378), south of Kathmandu Guest House down an alley on the left. Singing servers persistently refill clay bowls of *raksi* (rice wine), while live Nepali music plays. Complimentary bananas and popcorn provided while you look at the menu of all-you-can eat regional plates (Rs80-130), including *dal bhat taraari, roti, momos,* and *achaar.* MC, Visa, Amex. Open daily 7am-10pm.

Tibetan Restaurant, Thahity-Thamel, one floor up, just beside the sandwich shop with the Hebrew lettering. It's hard to spend more than Rs35 on this array of Chinese and Tibetan dishes (Rs13-35). Open daily 9am-9:30pm.

Fire and Ice (tel. 250210), in the shopping center on Tridevi Marg across from the Immigration Office. Wafting pizzeria smells will lure you in and the opera music and yummy food will keep you (and plenty of other tourists) there. Fantastic pizza (Rs160-270), minestrone (Rs110), salad, delicate crepes (Rs65-110), and imported soft-serve ice cream (Rs50-90) provide a little taste of Naples right here in Nepal. With wine at Rs160 a glass, how can you go wrong?

Pumpernickel Bakery, across from KC's. A Thamel institution. At breakfast time, the line to order freshly baked croissants, cakes, and cinnamon rolls (Rs8-25) spills onto the street. The pleasant garden patio and wicker furniture in the back make it a nice place to linger and watch the tourists. Open daily 8am-6pm.

Just Juice 'n' Shakes, down a little lane to the right, just after Redrock Restaurant, north of the Kathmandu Guest House. These friendly folk have made quite a reputation for themselves with their cold, thick frozen smoothies and shakes (Rs40-90), hot espresso (Rs30), cappuccino (Rs50), and yummy cakes (Rs30). Check out the amusing visitors' log. Open daily 6am-11pm.

Everest Steak House, Chhetrapati (tel. 260471). Carnivores delight in real, juicy, succulent steaks (Rs175-250). Stab into generous portions of beef *(shhh!)* or select from a menu that includes virtually everything but Nepalese cuisine—Tibetan, Mexican, pizzas, pastas, schnitzel, and burgers (Rs175). The Pokhara branch is a popular *après*-trek destination for the iron-depleted. Open daily 8am-10pm.

Koto Japanese Restaurant, Chhetrapati-Thamel (tel. 256449), next to Greenleaves Restaurant, near the Chhetrapati intersection (with another branch in Durbar Marg). The meal may begin with a hot washcloth, but this ain't no transatlantic flight. Impeccable service compliments the austere simplicity of the bamboo-furnishings. Refills and *yakis* will enliven the pizza-weary. Noodles, soups, meat, fish and Japanese curries (Rs150-350). Add 10% tax. Open daily 11am-9pm.

New Orleans Cafe, just north of the Kathmandu Guest House. Deliver yourself to the bayou in the bustling but low-key candlelit patio as you enjoy jambalaya, creole chicken, and other Deltan delicacies. Vegetable dishes Rs80-165; meat dishes Rs80-250. Live jazz on the outdoor patio Sa 6-9pm. Open daily 6:30am-midnight.

The Northfield Cafe (tel. 424884), a few doors north of Pilgrims Book House. This offspring of the legendary Mike's Breakfast is great for homesick gringos to munch tortilla chips and salsa (Rs90) and gnaw on spicy chicken wings (Rs100). After appetizers and huge burritos (Rs110–125), quesadillas (Rs120), and meat dishes (up to Rs205), the ubiquitous Eden-like green and the blaring classical, jazz, and blues will likely entice you to stay for dessert (brownie sundaes, Rs100). The breakfast menu is almost identical to Mike's in Naxal, but the pancakes with butter and syrup are better here. Open daily 7am-10pm.

KC's, Tridevi Marg (tel. 414387), across the street from the Maya Cocktail Bar. The third floor terrace is especially lovely in the candlelit evening. Vegetable rice, pasta, and meat dishes (Rs65-250). Open daily 7am-10pm. MC.

Durbar Marg

Mangalore Coffee House, Jamal Tole (tel. 231990), just off Durbar Marg above American Express. South Indian cheap eats; *masala dosa* (Rs30), *thalis* (Rs80). *Momos* and chow mein (Rs25-65) available too. Open daily 11am-9pm.

Bhanchha Ghar, Kamaladi (tel. 225172). Coming from Durbar Marg, turn left at the clocktower; the restaurant is on the right. The name of the restaurant, which is set in an elegantly restored Rana house, is Nepali for "kitchen," but there's no *dal bhat* here—this is Nepalese *haute cuisine.* Specialties (Rs140-200) include wild boar and curried high-altitude mushrooms. The enormous set menu is priced to match (Rs640), but you can spend half that and get plenty by ordering a la carte. Add 10% tax. Open daily noon-10pm. MC, Visa, Amex.

Baan Thai Restaurant (tel. 243271). Authentic Thai food in a swank, A/C setting. Watch Durbar Marg through lace curtains while you enjoy main dishes around Rs175, *pad thai* (Rs130-150), and seafood (Rs325-395). Open daily noon-3pm and 6-9:30pm. AmEx, Visa, MC.

Nirula's (tel. 225836). Hang here with Nepal's teenage elite if you think you're hip enough. This Indian-imported ice cream parlor/fast food joint serves 21 flavors of ice cream (Rs27-50) and "hot numbers" like pizzas and "mahaburgers" (Rs55-72). The fast food is well, fast food (read: greasy), but the ice cream is divine. Open daily 9am-10:30pm.

Kantipath

Delicatessen Center (tel. 247900) stocks an awesome variety of imported cheeses and meats, sold by the ounce. The bakery produces an equally impressive array of breads and pastries which you can take home or eat at high tables overlooking Kantipath. Hot dishes (for which grease is a common denominator) include goulash (Rs95), onion rings (Rs35), and fish and chips (Rs120). Open daily 9am-9pm.

New Road

Little Garden, Khicha Pokhari. From New Rd., walk south down Kicha Pokhari; the restaurant is down the second lane to the right, behind the Little Home Supermarket. The tiger and tall grass painted on sky blue walls are the only frivolities you'll find here. Ample portions of cheap and tasty stand-bys: *momos, thukpa, pakauda,* and chow mein (Rs25-50); burger and fries (Rs35-55). Open daily 8:30am-8:30pm.

Angan Sweet Namkeens and Vegetarian Fast Food, at the intersection of New Rd. and Dharma Path. Serves ice cream (Rs30-45), Indian sweets, *dosas* (Rs25-50), and other veg. treats (Rs12-50) to Nepalis on the go. Pay in front and shoulder your way into the back room to find a table. Free mineral water. Open daily 8:30am-9pm.

Naxal

Mike's Breakfast, (tel. 424303), near the police headquarters. From Thamel, walk east along Tridevi Marg and veer left after Nag Pokhari. Though diminished since its relocation to far-off Naxal, Mike's is still the mecca of Kathmandu breakfasts. Muffins, pancakes, and waffles are excellent; breakfast specials like *huevos rancheros* and Nepali omelettes cost around Rs170. For true decadence, try the epic brownie sundae (Rs90). Pizza (Rs120-180) Tu and F 5-9pm. Open daily 7am-10pm.

SIGHTS

Kathmandu is not a huge city but it's packed with things to see. There are so many temples that the word "templescape" has been coined to describe the city's skyline. If your time in the city is limited, use it to wander from **Durbar Square** through **Indra Chowk** and **Asan Tole.** A walk from Central Kathmandu along the **Vishnumati** and over to **Swayambhunath** is less glamorous but equally impressive. For **temple-gazing,** Boudhanath and Pashupatinath, and Dakshinkali (if you can visit on Tuesday or Saturday mornings) are among the valley's most active worship sites. What follows is a rundown of the highlights. The best way to tour Kathmandu is on **foot,** because many obscure and wonderful places are too easily missed in a car or on a bike.

Durbar Square

Durbar (Palace) Square is the heart of the old city. The royal family is gone from the palace here, having moved late last century to the north end of town, but that hasn't diminished Durbar Square's religious, social, or commercial importance. Many of Kathmandu's most interesting temples and historic buildings are located here, and the wide open space is infused with a bustling energy.

An appropriate place to start exploring the square is the southwest corner at the **Kasthamandap,** from which Kathmandu is said to have taken its name. This wooden pavilion (supposedly built from the wood of a single tree) may be Kathmandu's oldest existing building, dating from the 14th century at the latest, though it has been substantially altered. Originally a *dharamshala*, it was made into a temple, but a feeling of transience remains, and a bevy of loitering porters gives the place a train-platform feel. The Kasthamandap is sacred space, with a central image of Gorakhnath, the deified Hindu saint who watches over the Shah dynasty. Small Ganesh shrines sit in each corner; at one, a golden mouse points its nose at another Ganesh shrine, in its own metal-flagged enclosure. This **Maru Ganesh** (also known as **Ashok Binayak**) is frequently worshipped—as the remover of obstacles, Ganesh is a good god to visit before traveling.

The Story of the Kathmandu Valley

According to local mythology, the Kathmandu Valley was once a huge lake inhabited by snakes called *nagas*. A lotus grew out of the lake and was called *swayambhu*, or "self-created." When the *bodhisattva* of knowledge, Manjushri, went on a pilgrimage to the lotus, he was dismayed to find it swarming with snakes and thus inaccessible to human pilgrims. He sliced his sword into the valley, creating Chobar Gorge, from which the lake water gushed, taking the *nagas* with it. Then, to appease the *naga* king Krakatoa Manjushri allowed him to live in Taudaha Lake as guardian of the monsoon. The fertile valley was now ready for its first civilization, and a shrine, the *stupa* of Swayambhunath, was built on the hill from which the lotus had grown. According to geology, the valley was at one time filled with water, Swayambhu was an island, and the Chobar Gorge was created by an earthquake—but there's no mention of snakes.

From Maru Ganesh, a right turn leads past the row of stalls that make up the ground floor of Vishnu's **Trailokya Mohan Temple.** Unsurprisingly, a dusty-black statue of Garuda, Vishnu's man-bird vehicle, kneels before it. On the other side of the temple, great white columns bear down on the square. Prime Minister Chandra Shamsher Rana added this wing to the main royal palace in 1908. The Rana prime ministers were infatuated with the European Neoclassical style; in the end the notion of bigness seems to have won out over beauty.

On the right, across from this facade with its fancy lamp posts, stands a much more traditional-looking 18th-century Kathmandu palace, with beautiful carved window frames (some shaped like peacocks), the central one covered in gold. This is the **Kumari Bahal,** where the living, earthly, human goddess of Kathmandu, the **Kumari,** flutters, sometimes appearing at one of the windows in the courtyard. If she doesn't appear, plenty of touts in the square will offer their services in getting her to appear. Soft drinks and film are sold inside the Kumari's courtyard, though photography is forbidden.

The **Maju Dewal** Shiva temple takes up the prime location in the main Durbar Square, towering over everything on its great step-pyramid. The temple was built in 1690 and it makes a well-placed observation deck for Durbar Sq.—its height, however, does nothing to isolate it from the fray below. You could sit here for hours watching the square, but you're bound to be hassled by "guides," "English students," and kids asking, "Do you have one coin from your country?"

Beside the Maju Dewal, the **Temple of Shiva and Parvati** rests on a skewed platform. The divine couple waves from the window above the door. On the left is the **Big Bell,** which rings for worship in the Degutaleju Temple east of Durbar Square. All three valley cities (Kathmandu, Patan, and Bhaktapur) have big bells like this one.

The road widens ahead at the column of King Pratap Malla, the brains behind the buildings in this area. His statue prays at the top of the column toward his personal shrine in the **Degutaleju Temple.** Close to the temple is a wooden screen, behind which sits the figure of **Sweta Bhairab** (White Bhairab), whose big fanged face is actually golden. At the Indra Jatra festival (which falls between August and September), the screen comes off and beer pours from the mouth of this fearsome form of Shiva as devotees crowd in for a drink. On Pratap Malla's left is the **Jagannath Temple.** This is the oldest temple in the northern part of the square, dating from 1563.

Hanuman Dhoka Durbar

Location: *Durbar Square, near the Jagannath Temple.* **Hours:** *Open Sa-M and W-Th 10:30am-4pm; winter 3pm, F year-round 10:30-2pm.* **Admission:** *Foreigners Rs250.* **Other:** *Cameras prohibited.*

The old royal palace takes its name from the statue (guarding the entrance) of Hanuman lounging under a parasol; the monkey-god's face is disfigured by all the *sindur* rubbed on it. The royal family has not lived in this palace for over a century, but it is still used for royal ceremonies, such as King Birendra's coronation in 1975. Although the building has evolved steadily since the time of the Licchavi kings, prior to 1200, its art and architecture were influenced mainly by the patronage of King Pratap Malla (r. 1641-74). No Licchavi buildings remain, though, and the palace now has plenty of Shah-era whitewashing. Just inside the entrance is **Nasal Chowk,** a courtyard where the nobles of the kingdom used to assemble. It was here that in 1673 Pratap Malla danced in a costume of Narasimha, Vishnu's man-lion incarnation. Afraid that Vishnu would be angry about the stunt, he installed a Narasimha statue just inside the palace out of remorse. The main section of the palace open to the public is the **Tribhuvan Memorial Museum.** King Tribhuvan (r. 1911-55), who overthrew the Rana regime in 1951 and restored Nepal's monarchy, is eulogized here in a display of personal belongings. Touring through these cases full of ceremonial outfits, newspaper clippings, watches, even Tribhuvan's desk and fishtank, makes you feel like you know the guy. The museum continues around Nasal Chowk to the **Basantapur Tower** at the southern end. This nine-story lookout, erected by Prithvi Narayan Shah after he conquered the valley, is open for those who want to view Durbar Sq. from above.

The circuit around Nasal Chowk next leads to the **Mahendra Memorial Museum,** which isn't quite as impressive as Tribhuvan's, but does include a walk-through diorama simulating one of the king's hunts. Outside the palace, along the wall past the Hanuman statue, is a **stone inscription** by Pratap Malla, which uses words from 15 different languages (including English and French). It's said that if anyone manages to read the whole text (a poem dedicated to the goddess Kali), milk will gush from the spout.

North of the palace, the **Taleju Temple's** three-tiered golden pagoda towers over everything else in the square. King Mahendra Malla built the temple in 1564 to honor Taleju, his dynasty's patron goddess. At 37m, the Taleju Temple was, for a long time, the tallest building in Kathmandu, a distinction enforced by building codes; but eager-to "modernize" Kathmandu has dispensed with this tradition. The temple is open only to the king and a few priests. On the ninth day of the Dasain festival, the door is opened to ordinary Hindus, but non-Hindus are never allowed inside. Across the street from the Taleju temple, the **Mahendreshwar Temple,** a popular Shiva temple, is much more accessible.

The police compound west of this area doesn't have anything special to see, but it's worth noting for its history, as this is the site of the **Kot Massacre,** where Jung Bahadur Rana murdered most of Nepal's nobility in 1846, inaugurating 105 years of Rana rule (see **History,** p. 704). Back down the road to the main square stands the huge, garish monolith of **Kala Bhairab** (Black Bhairab). Anyone who tells a lie in front of this raging destroyer of evil will supposedly vomit blood and die (we dare you!). Just beyond Mr. Bhairab sits the octagonal **Krishna Temple,** in which Pratap Malla had placed images of Krishna and two goddesses that bear a curious resemblance to him and his wives.

North of Durbar Square

Kathmandu's most interesting street runs northeast from Durbar Sq., disrupting the whole grid system around it. Without a name of its own, this funny diagonal street takes the title of whatever area it's running through. In earlier times, it was the beginning of the trade route from Kathmandu to Tibet, and it was Kathmandu's main commercial area until New Rd. was built after the earthquake of 1934. The road is still a fascinating bazaar, where trays full of mangoes are jostled by passing bicycles, and old women crouch next to the piles of cheap clothes they're peddling. The first crossroads on the street, walking away from Durbar Sq., is called **Indra Chowk.** On the left side at this corner is the second-story temple of **Akash Bhairab,** a garish temple. Admire its metal gargoyles from across the street if you're not a Hindu, since the usual restrictions apply. Akash Bhairab's image, a large silver mask, is barely visible. During the Indra Jatra festival it is displayed in the middle of the chowk, along with a *lingam* specially erected next to it.

The next crossing is Kel Tole, marked by a short pillar capped with a meditating Buddha on the left. Enter the passageway behind it to approach the **Temple of Seto Machhendranath,** one of the most widely revered shrines in the valley. Hindus and

---

"Next Year, in Kathmandu."

With 95% of Nepal's 20 million citizens claiming Hinduism, Buddhism, or both, as their religion, you'd hardly expect Kathmandu to host the largest *seder* (ritual Jewish Passover meal) in the world. In some ways it seems fitting that this Hindu Kingdom which has taken religious syncretism to such impressive heights should augment its unique melding of ethnicities and languages with a tribute to another of the world's oldest religions. Each year the Israeli Embassy houses a *seder* for over 1000 young Jews who find themselves in Nepal during the week of Passover. Most of them have come to roam the Nepali wilderness following completion of their national military service, but at the *seder,* the trekking diaspora ditches *chapatis* and *dal bhat* in favor of *matzos* and *maror,* in remembrance of the ancient Israelite exodus from Egypt. In 1999, Passover is April 1-2; in 2000, April 21-22. For more information, contact the Israeli Embassy (tel. 411811).

Buddhists pay homage to Machhendra, the Valley's guardian and the most compassionate of the gods. The white-faced image is paraded around during the Machhendranath festival (to be held the first week of April in 1999). The pagoda in the middle of Kel Tole is dedicated to **Lunchun Lun Bun Ajima.** This goddess's bathroom-tiled sanctuary is now sunk beneath street level because the road has been repaved so many times. At **Asan Tole,** the next crossing, the road widens and is lined with stacks of vegetables. The **Temple of Annapurna** is on the right, draped with broad brass ribbons. The goddess of plentiful food, Annapurna's image here is simply a silver pot.

The diagonal road breaks out of its claustrophobia onto Kantipath across from the **Rani Pokhari** tank. King Pratap Malla built this pool and the temple in its center to console his wife over the death of their son. Unfortunately the green-and-yellow fence around it is locked all year except on Diwali (Nov. 7, 1999; Oct. 26, 2000).

The crossing known as **Bangemudha** is near the diagonal road, west of Asan Tole. Its name means "twisted wood"—in one of the southern corners is a twisted lump of wood stuck to the wall, with an armor of coins nailed into it. The wood is dedicated to the god of toothaches, Vaisya Dev, and nailing a coin here is supposed to relieve dental pain. On the road north from Bangemudha you'll be greeted by jawfuls of grinning teeth. This is the dentists' quarter, and their signs bear this happy symbol. On the left side of this road a lane leads to **Kathesimbhu,** a miniature model of the Swayambhunath *stupa* west of Kathmandu. Kathesimbhu is said to have been built with leftover earth from Swayambhunath, so it shares some of Swayambhunath's power. The elderly, or any who are too weak to climb the hill to Swayambhunath, can obtain an equal blessing here. Children seem to be the most devoted visitors to Kathesimbhu, however, holding endless soccer games around its *chaityas.* The current **Royal Palace,** at the top of Durbar Marg, is hard to miss. Built in the 1960s, its pagoda roof caps the grand mansion. The building is only open to the public on the 10th day of Dasain, when the king and queen offer blessings to their subjects.

South of Durbar Square

These sights are somewhat diffuse. On the lane that runs southwest of the Kasthamandap is the **Bhimsen Temple,** dedicated to the hero-god of Newari craftsmen. Its bottom floor has been entirely taken over by shops. Next to it is a *hiti* (water-tap) in a cellar-like depression, where jugs are filled from an elephant-shaped spout.

The **Jaisi Dewal Temple** is another of the step-pyramid sort. To get to it, continue to the end of the road from the Bhimsen Temple, then turn left and go up the hill. The Shiva temple is painted with flowers and leopard-skin patterns, and a smooth figure of Nandi (Shiva's bull) flicks his tail at the base of the steps. Across the street from the entrance, a 2m tall, uncarved *linga* rises up from a *yoni.*

At a crossroads in southern Kathmandu, close to Kantipath, the 59m **Bhimsen Tower** is a useful landmark. It looks like a lighthouse with portholes, though Bhim Sen Thapa, the prime minister who built it in 1832, was probably trying to imitate the Ochterlony Monument in Calcutta (ironic, since the British erected that monument to commemorate their defeat of Nepal in 1816). The tower is closed to the public.

On the other side of Kantipath is the **Tundikhel,** or parade ground, occasionally used for military marches and equestrian displays (the Ghora Jatra Horse Festival in late March, 1999 is prime time for this). Kathmandu's newer neighborhoods are located to the east of the Tundikhel. **Martyrs' Gate,** a monument to four accused conspirators who were executed after a 1940 coup attempt, sits on a circle in the middle of the road to the south of the Tundikhel.

Singha Durbar, which is to the east of the Tundikhel, was once the greatest of the Rana palaces; alas, most of it was burned down in a mysterious fire one night in July 1974. The buttery-white building, which was meant to rival the palaces of Europe, was put up in a few frantic years from 1901-04 by Prime Minister Chandra Shamsher Jung Bahadur Rana—his monogram is on all the railings. The prime minister's household and his entire administration fit into this complex, which, with its 1700 rooms, claimed to be the largest building in Asia. Ministries and departments are lodged in what's left of the palace, but their offices are off-limits to the public.

The Living Goddess: Kumari

A Newari Buddhist girl considered to be the living embodiment of the Hindu goddess Durga, the Kumari is a perfect example of the mixing of religions in the Kathmandu Valley. Kathmandu's Kumari, the most important of the 11 in the valley, is selected at the age of four or five from the Buddhist clan of the Newari *shakya* (goldsmith) caste. The Kumari-to-be must satisfy 32 physical requirements, such as thighs like a deer's, chest like a lion's, eyelashes like a cow's, and a body shaped like a banyan tree. She must remain calm in a dark room full of buffalo heads, frightening masks, and loud noises. Finally, her astrological chart must not conflict with the king's. If all these conditions are met, the Kumari is installed in the Kumari Bahal in Durbar Square, where she leads the privileged, secluded life of a goddess until she reaches puberty. Several times a year she is paraded about on a palanquin (the Kumari's feet must not touch the ground). As soon as the Kumari menstruates, or sheds blood any other way, her goddess-spirit is said to leave her body, and she must return to her parents' home, where the transition to mere mortality can be difficult. Former goddesses often have difficulty finding a husband, since men who marry them are said to die young.

Another cluster of temples are on the other side of Tripureswar Marg by the banks of the Bagmati River. The area is wet and dirty, and the wind whips past some of Kathmandu's worst slums—not a walk for the weak of stomach, but very interesting nonetheless. The **Kalamochan Temple** is visible from Tripureswar Marg, close to the Patan Bridge. It has a big onion dome like a Mughal mausoleum, but the dragons and doorways are Nepali, and, on the exterior, Jung Bahadur Rana's figure rises from a shaft protruding from a turtle's back. This Macchiavellian prime minister built the temple in the mid-19th century. The ashes of the 32 noblemen he slaughtered in the Kot Massacre are supposed to be buried in the foundations. The shrine of **Pachali Bhairab** is farther downstream from these temples, just before the footbridge across the river; it's slightly inland. Music from the nearby monastery jangles down into Bhairab's courtyard, where a golden human figure lies peacefully dead: this is a *betal*—a representation of death meant to guard against death. The image of Bhairab is beside it, garlanded with coins, under the spreading roots of a great *pipal* tree.

The junction of the Bagmati and Vishnumati Rivers, at **Teku** in the city's southwest corner, is a sacred place often used for cremations. The wailing of families echoes around the temples and *chaityas;* be sensitive about photography. A tall brick *shikhara* stands over the confluence. The riverbanks might look romantic, with buffalo munching hay in the shade, but look closely and you'll see the faded paper packages clogging the river and realize that the buffalo are in fact here to be slaughtered.

West of the City

The west bank of the Vishnumati River is beyond Kathmandu's traditional city limits, but it's been brought into the metropolis by the Ring Rd. around Kathmandu and Patan. Its most prominent feature is the hilltop *stupa* of **Swayambhunath,** over 2000 years old and 3km from the city. Swayambhunath is the holiest place for Newari Buddhists, and it is the seat of the Kathmandu Valley's creation myth (see **The Story of the Kathmandu Valley,** p. 733). The road from Kathmandu to Swayambhunath (a 30min. walk) certainly has a bit of a red-carpet feel to it, with the shrine looming on the hilltop ahead (bus #19 leaves from Ratna Park and stops along Ring Rd. just west of Swayambhunath). At the base of the hill is a large rectangular gateway, and after that the long crooked steps start to work their way through the trees and Buddha-icons to the top. You'll be catching your breath, but right at the top of the steps is an enormous *vajra,* the Tibetan thunderbolt symbol. And then there's the **stupa,** which is white-washed and flattened on top like other Nepali *stupas. (Admission Rs50.)* From the golden cube on top of the stupa, the Buddha's all-seeing eyes gaze out in each direction. What looks like a nose is actually a number "1" representing the unity of all things. Swayambhunath affords great views across the valley on clear days.

Nine golden shrines surround the *stupa,* four of them at the cardinal points of the compass, plus one at an angle. They enclose images of the *dhyani* Buddhas, who represent the Buddha's different aspects through the elements of earth, water, fire, air, and space. The four cardinal *dhyani* Buddhas also have female elements *(taras)* who occupy the shrines at the secondary points. Rhesus macaques slide down the dome of the *stupa* using the fallen prayer flag as a tie-line.

There's a **Buddhist Museum** on the platform west of the *stupa;* it's small and dark, but has a good assortment of Buddhist and Hindu images in its sculpture collection. *(Open W-F and Su-M 10am-5pm. Free.)* Next to the museum is a small monastery that will welcome visitors and their donations. The small temple in front of the monastery is dedicated to Harati, the goddess of smallpox, who can either protect or infect. It's not clear what she does now that smallpox is eradicated, although she is generally responsible for looking after children.

Following the motor road down the hill to the south of Swayambhunath brings you to the **Natural History Museum** (tel. 271899). *(Open Su-F 10am-4p. Admission Rs10; camera fee Rs10).* The museum houses a 14,000-piece collection of high-altitude flora and fauna. About 1km south of Swayambhunath, on a road that comes up from the riverside, is Nepal's **National Museum.** *(Open W-Th and Sa-M 10:30am-4pm, winter 10:30am-3pm, F 10:30am-2:30pm. Tickets sold 10:30am-2pm. Rs50, camera fee Rs100.)* The Art Gallery has a good collection of wood, stone, and metalwork. Equally excellent carvings can be seen in their places on the Kathmandu Valley's houses and temples, but the museum allows for a closer look. The Historical Museum Building is at least as interesting as (and certainly more eclectic than) the Art Gallery. Its natural history section sports the pelt of a two-headed calf, a set of mandibular bones from a blue whale, and an unusual abundance of stuffed deer heads, probably from some Rana palace. The Nepalese history section is an amusing tribute to rulers and their playthings; it includes early Nepalese cannons and machine guns, the personal weapons of Prithvi Narayan Shah and several Mallas, and typically droll portraits of all of Nepal's kings. The museum grounds are pleasant, and the roof terrace of the Art Gallery is a good viewpoint for the surrounding valley.

ENTERTAINMENT

When it comes to nightlife in Nepal, Kathmandu is where it's at—but that's not saying much. You'll have a choice of bars that close by 10 or 11pm, tourist-oriented cultural shows, and several casinos, some of which are open 24 hours. Thamel's bar scene caters to a foreign crowd, although twentysomething Nepalis dig it, too. These places are great for swapping stories with other travelers, if you can hear over the music. In addition to the following, try the **New Orleans Café** (see p. 732).

The Rum Doodle 40,000½-Feet Bar and Restaurant, Thamel (tel. 414336). Follow the turn in the road north of the Kathmandu Guest House, on the left. The namesake of this bar is a 1956 spoof about a mountaineering expedition. The book is for sale at the bar, along with exotic cocktails and expensive beer (Rs140). Large helpings of bland Continental food (Rs110-210) are served in the shady garden, roof terrace, floor-cushioned seating area, or cavernous dining room. Save room for dessert—hunks of warm apple pie (Rs60). Open daily 10am-10pm. MC, Visa.

Jesse James Bar, Thamel, at the Northfield Café, just north of the Pilgrims Book House. Mellow and devoid of hopeful Nepali teens armed with last year's one-liners. During Happy Hour (5-8pm), beer is only Rs100, and chips and salsa are free. On occasion, a band jams in the garden. Open daily 2:30-10:30pm.

Maya Cocktail Bar and **Maya Pub,** Thamel. The cocktail bar is upstairs from the Pumpernickel Bakery; the pub is at the intersection. Both offer free popcorn, loud pop music, and 2-for-1 cocktails 4-7pm. The dark, eccentrically decorated pub is just strange enough to be interesting; the cocktail bar is bigger and more swinging. Both bars open daily 3-midnight.

Tom and Jerry Pub, Thamel, just across from the Northfield Café, upstairs. The most bar-like of Thamel's bars, with pool tables and sports on TV. During Happy Hour (5-8pm), Rs10 discount on drinks, Thursday 10% discount for ladies, and free popcorn (actually tasty). Open daily 4-11pm.

Cultural Programs

In Nepal, as elsewhere, "cultural program" is something of an oxymoron. There's no substitute for catching a festival or watching morning or evening worship at a temple; however, the following traditional Nepalese songs and dances, staged for a tourist audience, are certainly entertaining.

Hotel de l'Annapurna, Durbar Marg (tel. 228787). Daily dance shows, 7pm, Rs250.

New Himachali Cultural Group, Durbar Marg (tel. 415280). Daily shows at 6:30pm, Rs300. Call for reservations.

Hotel Sherpa, Durbar Marg (tel. 227000). Cultural show in the restaurant Tu-Su; no charge for the show, but you're expected to eat—and it ain't cheap.

Pilgrims Book House hosts classical concerts—*sitar, tabla,* and *sarangi*—Su, Tu, and F. Posters in the store advertise details. Rs200.

Sports

The public **swimming pool,** at the end of the road that curves around the south end of the National Stadium, is open daily 10am-12:30pm and 1:30-4pm. (Admission Rs40 for women, Rs45 for men. M is ladies only.) Posh hotels on **Durbar Marg** (tel. 220123) allow non-guests to dip in their pools. The cheapest are Woodlands Hotel (Rs250 per day) and Hotel Sherpa (tel. 227000, Rs300 per day). Strokes of another sort are to be had at the **Royal Nepal Golf Course** (tel. 472836), near the airport (Rs1250). The **tennis** court at Hotel de l'Annapurna (tel. 122 1711) can be used by non-guests for Rs440 per hour (balls and rackets, too).

Casinos

Kathmandu now boasts the only four casinos on the Indian Subcontinent. Each is at a luxury hotel: **Casino Royal** at the Yak & Yeti; **Casino Everest** at Hotel Everest; **Casino Anna** at Hotel de l'Annapurna; and the **Royal Nepal Casino** at the Soaltee Holiday Inn. Some casinos may have special deals for new arrivals. Bring your plane ticket for free coupons or snacks. All but the Casino Royal are open 24 hours a day.

Movies

At least half a dozen restaurants—**Lotus Restaurant, Margarita Restaurant, Everest Steakhouse,** and **Paradise Pizzeria,** to name a few—in Thamel keep afloat selling the same ol' menu by showing videos of surprisingly recent releases. The quality is often sub-par, but it can make for a diverting couple of hours.

Volunteer Opportunities

Expat prisoners in the dismal central jail at **Sundhara,** near the GPO, appreciate visitors who'll talk to them for a little while. If you're so moved, newspapers, fruits, and books make nice gifts. Ask at the **Marco Polo Guest House** for more information.

SHOPPING

If you stand still for more than 10 seconds in Thamel or Durbar Square, you're sure to be approached by a roving merchant offering jewelry, flutes, chess sets, Tiger Balm, or knives—Swiss Army copies or *khukuri* style. The sheer volume of tourist trash can be off-putting, and you may be tempted to ignore it all, but there are also nice gifts and unique souvenirs to be found.

Prices are almost always negotiable. Try to bargain good-naturedly, and hope that the merchant does the same. Asking a price is interpreted as intent to buy, but you can get away with just asking if you're trying to shop around. Once you start bargaining, however, be prepared to buy if your price is accepted. Prices and quality vary greatly, so check out a few shops, especially for expensive souvenirs. With most products, from wool sweaters to *thankas,* you'll be able to see the difference in quality after a little practice. Antiques, jewelry, and gems require more expertise. Many things claimed to be old are not, and travelers should be very wary of buying gems unless they really know what they're doing; scam-artists are everywhere.

Although just about anything made in Nepal can be bought in Kathmandu, certain crafts can be found more cheaply and from a better selection in their places of origin. For **woodcarving and pottery,** head for Bhaktapur; for **papier mâché masks and puppets,** Thimi; for **metalwork,** Patan; and for **Tibetan crafts** like *thankas,* Boudha. A lot of Indian crafts are sold in Kathmandu too, such as Kashmiri *papier mâché* boxes. They're more expensive than in India, but still cheaper than in the West. In Thamel, you'll also find much Western-style hippie clothing. Embroidered shirts are a Thamel specialty—skilled tailors will embroider any design you wish. Hand-knit woolens are also a good deal here.

One shop in Thamel that deserves special mention is the **Khukuri House,** at the zig-zag north of the Kathmandu Guest House, near Rum Doodle's. This well-reputed knife shop is owned by a former Gorkha officer. (Open Su-F 10am-7pm.) **Western Nepal Crafts,** on Thahity-Thamel, has a wide selection of handmade paper products with fixed prices (about US$3-5 for stationery, US$10-20 for photo albums). **Didi's Boutique** and **Didi-daju,** both on Chhetrapati, east of Everest Steak House, carry a wide selection of distinctive items, most of which are produced by the Janakpur Women's Development Centre. (Open daily 10am-9pm. Visa, MC.) More serious and much more expensive antique shops are located on Durbar Marg.

For ready-made Indian and Nepali-style threads, head for **Bagh Bazaar.** *Saris* and cloth can be found north of Indra Chowk, and the chowk's bead bazaar is worth a gander just to see the stalls of multicolored, twinkling strands of glass beads. These are the beads that married Nepali women wear, often with an ornate gold clasp.

Moneyed Indians and Nepalis do their shopping on **New Road.** The street is lined with jewelry and ready-made clothing shops. Just inside the New Rd. gate is the government-run **Cottage Industry and Handicrafts Emporium,** which, in addition to its large selection of metal and woodwork, has some of the cheapest **postcards** in town (Rs6; open Su-F 10am-7pm, 6pm from Nov.-Feb.). **Photo Concern** (tel. 224092), on New Rd., east of Dharma Path, is the town's most reliable place for film development (B/W, slides, and prints) and camera repair. It also stocks a wide variety of cameras, accessories, and film. (Open Su-F 9am-8pm.)

If you're looking for maps, swing by **Maps of Nepal,** a five-minute walk, just before the Everest Hotel in Baneswar on the road to the airport. It's a bit out of the way (take the trolleybus or the bus to the airport) but has a larger selection and much lower prices than you'll find in Thamel. Nepalese land-planning and political maps can make great souvenirs. (Open Su-F 10am-7:30pm.)

■ Near Kathmandu: Pashupatinath पशुपती नाथ

The temple complex of Pashupatinath, east of Kathmandu, is the holiest Hindu site in Nepal. It is dedicated to Shiva's incarnation as Pashupati, the kind and gentle Lord of Animals and the guardian deity of Nepal. All the regular business of a Hindu pilgrimage site goes on here: there are monasteries, hospices for the dying, cremation grounds, and narrow roads clogged with devotees who offer flowers to Shiva and rice to the beggars. Pashupatinath is the heart of Nepali Hinduism—the king himself often comes to worship here. At the Shivaratri festival, which occurs in February or March, thousands come here to bathe and celebrate the deity's birthday in late February. Full-moon nights and the eleventh day after them are also auspicious times for a blessing from the sacred Bagmati River.

The **Pashupati Temple,** built in 1696, is located right on the Bagmati. A road leads directly up to it, though non-Hindus won't get any closer than the gate. The backside of the brontosaural brass Nandi is visible through the entrance, but the rest of the temple is obscured. Other viewpoints in the area afford peeks over the wall at the wood and marble pagoda.

There are more temples are downstream from the Pashupati Temple, but there's no direct access along the river here for non-Hindus. The only recourse is to backtrack away from the river, turn left and left again, until another, bigger road leads back to the river. On the right side of this road is a group of five temples known as

Panch Dewal, whose compound has become a social welfare center. **Biddha Ashram,** operated here by Mother Teresa's Missionaries of Charity, welcomes walk-in volunteers. Ahead, stone walls and *ghats* squeeze the river, making it look like a canal. Two footbridges are laid across it, and right between them on the near (west) bank is the 6th-century **Bacchareswari Temple.** The ghats downstream are used for cremations. If there are any cremations in progress, respect the mourning families' grief and don't take pictures.

Across the footbridges on the east bank of the Bagmati are a row of 11 boxy Shiva shrines. From here it's possible to see into the entire Pashupati Temple compound. The *ghats* immediately below it are sometimes used for VIP cremations, such as those of members of the royal family. There are a series of benches just above the shrine. The steps up the hill on the east bank of the river eventually level out at a small wooded village of Shiva temples; Nandi figures line the main street. At the end of it is a temple of Gorakhnath, an 11th-century saint who is revered as a form of Shiva. The steps continue downhill to the **Gujeshwari Temple,** which is locally considered to be the place where the goddess Sati's *yoni* fell when she was cut into pieces by Vishnu (the Kamakhya Temple in Guwahati, India is more widely recognized as this site—see **Divine Dismemberment,** p. 418). Buddhist lore interprets the sacred well housed in the temple in a different way, as a bottomless hollow left by the root of the lotus which blossomed atop Swayambhu and inspired the creation of the Kathmandu Valley (see **The Story of the Kathmandu Valley,** p. 733). Non-Hindus may not enter. The road downstream in front of the temple leads to a bridge, on the other side of which is a crossroads. To the left, a set of broken stone steps leads over the hill and back to the Pashupati Temple. The road to the right heads to **Boudha,** a pleasant 45-minute walk north through fields and small neighborhoods.

Pashupatinath is only nominally outside of Kathmandu and it's simple to get there by **bike**—follow Tridevi Marg away from Thamel, then turn right at the first road after Durbar Marg. When you see the Marco Polo Business Hotel, turn left, and follow the zig-zagging road east across a bridge. Eventually, signs will appear showing maps of Pashupatinath. The **#1 bus** from Ratna Park (frequent, 45min., Rs3) stops along Ring Rd. at the turnoff to Pashupathi; follow the signs from there. The **#2 tempo** from Sundhara (via Rani Pokhari) stops across the street, just inside Ring Rd. (frequent, 30min., Rs6). **Taxis** from Thamel cost about Rs50.

■ Patan पाटन

Patan (PAT-in), Kathmandu's temple-dotted neighbor to the south, certainly lives up to its old name, Lalitpur, or "City of Beauty." But the intricacies of its local culture can be more impressive than its prominent architecture. Patan has long been the center of Newari craftsmanship, and its back streets are filled with the clanging and hammering of tourist paraphernalia production. In the background, its lanes are littered with small *stupas, shikaras,* and onion-domed temples. While some of these crumbling shrines languish in disuse, weeds growing from their roofs, many still host daily *puja* for the residents of the alleys and courtyards that they decorate. Patan is also home to an increasing number of foreign aid agencies and, thanks to the Tibetan Refugee Camp in Jawalakhel, a major sector of the Tibetan carpet industry.

With only the Bagmati River lying between Kathmandu and Patan, the two cities have practically merged. However, their histories as independent kingdoms is evident. For locals and visitors alike, Patan is discernably more laid-back than the capital. Pedestrians dominate over vehicles, and there are no in-your-face souvenir salesmen or touts. Even shopping is less of a hassle in Patan, home to a collection of fixed-price handicrafts cooperatives whose proceeds usually benefit local causes.

ORIENTATION

Patan is linked to Kathmandu by a bridge over the **Bagmati River** and bounded to the south by the same **Ring Road** that encircles Kathmandu. Patan's main road, which

NEPAL

runs from Kathmandu, goes by the name of whatever neighborhood it is passing through: from the bridge south to the Ring Rd. it is called **Kopundol,** then **Pulchowk,** and finally **Jawalakhel.** The **old city,** east of the main road, is loosely bounded by four **stupas** (purportedly built by Ashok in the 3rd century BC), one in each direction. The eastern *stupa* lies beyond Ring Rd.; the western *stupa* sits along the main road, across from the turn-off to **Durbar Square,** the center of the oldest part of town. Several branches lead east from the main road. From north to south, the first leads to **Patan Dhoka** (Patan Gate), which is north of Durbar Sq. The second becomes **Mangal Bazaar,** the road that runs along the south end of Durbar Sq. Finally, at **Jawalakhel Chowk,** the road leads toward **Lagankhel** and the **bus park.**

PRACTICAL INFORMATION

Local Transportation: Bus #14 runs frequently from Ratna Park in Kathmandu along the main road to the bus park in Lagankhel (30min., Rs3). Buses leave for Kathmandu from Patan Gate. **Tempos** (frequent, 20min., Rs4) start at the GPO. Most head to Jawalakhel and then Lagankhel, but some go to Mangal Bazaar—ask the driver. Tempos leave for **Kathmandu** from Durbar Square on Mangal Bazaar. **Taxis** from Thamel to Patan's Durbar Sq. should cost about Rs75.

Currency Exchange: Nepal Grindlays, Jawalakhel Chowk (tel. 522490) charges a 1% commission on traveler's checks. Open Su-Th 9:45am-3pm, F 9:45am-12:30pm.

Bookstore: Pilgrims Book House (tel. 521159) has a huge branch along the main road in Kopundole. Open daily 9am-8pm. Visa, MC.

Market: Look for fruit, spices, and cheap fabric in Lagankhel near the bus park; a huge vegetable market is just south of the bus park. **Namaste Supermarket** (tel. 520026), along the main road in Pulchowk, caters to tourists. Open daily 9am-8pm.

Pharmacy: Many can be found on Mangal Bazaar, right below Durbar Sq. **Alka Pharmacy** (tel. 535146), on the main road in Jawalakhel, north of St. Xavier's School, hosts a variety of specialist clinics and can arrange housecalls. Open 7am-10pm.

Hospital: Patan Hospital, Lagankhel (tel. 522295) has a good reputation.

Post Office: Outside Patan Gate, on the west side. Open Su-F 10:30am-2:30pm.

Internet: Available at several STD booths around Jawalakhel Chowk.

Telephones: STD/ISD booths abound around Durbar Square. **Telephone Code:** 01.

ACCOMMODATIONS

None of Patan's few budget accommodations are centrally located, but this may be their greatest virtue. Hash dealers won't bid you good night at the door of your hotel, and you won't awaken to the screeching cacophony of *Resam Phiriri* rendered at five different cadences by four different people selling fiddles.

Mountain View Guest House, Kumaripati (tel. 538168). From Lagankhel bus park, a 10min. walk west, on the right, behind the Campion Academy. A little removed from the older section of town. Behind a stained-glass door, above the restaurant, these new rooms are still pretty pristine. STD/ISD available. Singles Rs200; doubles Rs300, with attached bath Rs350.

Café de Patan, Mangal Bazaar (tel. 537599), just southwest of Durbar Square. Clean, comfortable, and quiet rooms are available above this restaurant. Balconies, abundant furnishings, and spotless tiled bathrooms with seat toilets. Doubles Rs300, with bath Rs500.

Hungry Treat Home (tel. 534792 or 533568), a few minutes' walk east of Jawalakhel Chowk. The sizable rooms with large windows, fans, and Astroturf carpeting aren't winning prizes for aesthetics, but they are clean and equipped with all the necessities. Tiled bathrooms with seat toilets and toilet paper. Attached restaurant. Doubles Rs200, with bath Rs290; triples Rs270.

Mahendra Youth Hostel, Pulchowk Rd. (tel. 521003). North of Jawalakhel Chowk, down the second lane to the right, next to the Dept. of Irrigation, across from St. Xaviers. No smoking or hot water. Check-in daily 6am-10pm. Check-out noon. Dorm beds Rs50-75; doubles with attached bath Rs200. Additional 10% tax, 10% discounts for IYHF and HI members.

FOOD

While the selection doesn't compare to that in Kathmandu, there's plenty to eat in Patan. Fast-food tandoori joints line the main road. More expensive tourist places serve the same fare in more aesthetic settings. Jawalakhel Chowk is home to such esteemed chains as **Hot Breads** and **The Bakery Café.** For extra-yummy baked goods, however, head for the **German Bakery,** north of Jawalakhel Chowk, for cake and loaves of bread (Rs25-30).

Tama Restaurant and Bar, Pulchowk, across the street and south of the Sajha bus garage, set back from the road. Cheap Indian menu (Rs50-190) and pricier Japanese entrees (Rs155-300) in tidy, peaceful dining area. Open daily 11am-9:30pm.

Downtown Restaurant, Pulchowk (tel. 522451). Lace curtains screen the sights but not the sounds of the busy street. Deservedly popular with the expat community for its extensive menu and low prices. Chicken *tikka masala* (Rs75) is rich and flavorful, and *naan* (Rs12) sops the sauce nicely. Open Su-F 10am-9pm.

Café de Patan, Mangal Bazaar (tel. 537599), southwest of Durbar Square. Walk through the souvenir/music shop to the ground floor dining area or the garden rooftop. Cheap, authentic Newari menu (M-Sa, snacks Rs10-40, meals Rs70-90) supplements the usual ho-hum stuff. Open daily 8am-9pm.

Bakena Batika, Jawalakhel (tel. 523998), just inside Ring Rd., south of the Tibetan Refugee Camp. Beautifully renovated Nepali house and tranquil courtyard make the perfect setting for light meals (Rs70-100), traditional Nepali courses (Rs150-190), and *risotto* (Rs190). Open daily noon-8:30pm.

The Third World Restaurant, Durbar Square (tel. 522187), opposite the Patan Museum, directly upstairs from the craft boutique. The food has that canned-mushroom flavor of imitation cuisine, but this is the closest non-Hindus can get to the upper floors of Krishna Mandir. Terrace dining available. Sandwiches (Rs40-70), Continental dishes (Rs60-100), and rice or noodles (Rs40-55). Open daily 8am-9pm.

SIGHTS

As in the other cities of the valley, Durbar Square is sight-seeing central. Exhaustive renovations have made it the perfect place to indulge in quixotic visions of kingdoms past. Just a few minutes walk from the square in any direction, Patan's narrow streets offer intricate glimpses of daily life that will coax you back into the present.

Durbar Square

One tactic for exploring Durbar Square is to start at the southern end of the **Royal Palace,** which makes up the eastern side of the square, then continue north and circle around counter-clockwise. The southern courtyard, **Sundari Chowk** is not open to the public, but **Mul Chowk,** dating from the mid-17th century, can be entered between two stone lions. On the southern wall, gilded statues of the Indian river goddesses **Ganga** (on a tortoise) and **Yamuna** (on a *makara,* a mythical snouted sea creature) stand on either side of the locked doorway to the **Taleju Shrine.** Dedicated to the patron goddess of Nepal's royal families, the shrine is open to Hindus one day per year during the Dasain festival. The other pagodas that rise around Mul Chowk are the **Taleju Bhawani Mandir,** the octagonal tower in the northeast corner, and the **Degu Talle Temple** on the north side, which is the tallest in the square.

The new **Patan Museum** is housed in **Keshav Narayan Chowk,** the northernmost section of the palace; the entrance is through an elaborate golden doorway. *(Museum open W-M 10:30am-4:30pm. Admission Rs120 for foreigners.)* The whitewashed shrine inside is dedicated to Narayan. Beautifully restored with the help of the Austrian government and the Smithsonian Institution, the museum houses metal, wood, and stone sculptures with extensive and informative labels. Wide, cushioned window seats provide lookouts onto the square below, and a cafe in the manicured courtyard serves snacks. Around the corner from the palace to the north is the sunken water tank known as **Manga Hiti,** whose mythical crocodile-like statues have been spouting water since the 6th century. The northern adjacent pavilion, **Mani Mandap,** was once used for coronations.

NEPAL

Diagonally across the way, the northernmost temple in the square is the three-tiered **Bhimsen Mandir,** with a lion-topped pillar facing its recent marble facade. Merchants toss coins onto the older, gilded, first floor of this temple, dedicated to the god of trade. The next temple to the left is the **Vishwanath Mandir,** a double-roofed Shiva temple, guarded by two stone elephants and originally dating from 1627. The temple collapsed in 1990, but it has since been restored. The *linga* inside is said to replicate the Vishwanath *linga* in **Varanasi** (see p. 232). A Nandi faces the other side of the temple. Continuing south, the next temple is the stone, Indian *shikhara*-style **Krishna Mandir.** This temple stands out because of its foreign design and because it is one of the few temples in Durbar Square in active use. In the evenings, devotees set the building aglow with oil lamps. The upper floors—carved with friezes depicting scenes from the *Mahabharata* and *Ramayana*—are closed to non-Hindus.

Vishnu is the chief god of the next temple, the **Jagan Narayan Mandir.** Stone lions flank the front of this more Nepalese pagoda-style temple, complete with wildly erotic roof struts. The Jagan Narayan Temple is the square's oldest, built in 1565. The **Bhai Deval Mandir** squats in the southwest corner of the square, and, continuing around clockwise you'll pass a fountain before arriving at the octagonal stone **Chya-sin Deval,** which, like the other Krishna temple in the square, is built in an Indian style. Its construction is linked with the death of one of the Malla kings, but whether it spontaneously appeared, or was built to honor his eight wives who committed *sati* is now a matter of controversy. The **Taleju Bell** next door was the first of the valley's three big bells, cast in 1736. The next temple to the north is the **Hari Shankar Mandir,** an elaborately carved three-tiered pagoda from the 18th century. The temple is jointly dedicated to Vishnu (called Hari here) and Shiva (Shankar). Circling back into the square, the stone pillar topped by a golden statue of **King Yoganarendra Malla** has its own legends. The king kneels under the protection of a cobra's hood, and it is said that as long as the figure of a bird perched on the cobra's head remains there, the king may return. A door and window to his palace remain open, and his *hookah* waits inside. If the bird flies away, the elephants that guard the Vishwanath Mandir will leave their posts to drink from the Manga Hiti.

South of Durbar Square

Continuing along Mangal Bazaar, east of Durbar Square, you'll see signs for the **Mahaboudha Temple**—the right-hand turn-off is a short walk from the square. Inside the courtyard that houses this "temple of a thousand Buddhas," painted arrows point the way to walk around it, and even the prayer wheels are labeled. The temple's architect was inspired by the Mahabodhi Temple in **Bodh Gaya,** India, where the **Buddha** achieved enlightenment (see p. 456). The foreign influence is obvious: the *shikhara*-style temple is covered with terra-cotta tiles, each of which carries an image of the Buddha. Turning right from the Mahaboudha, the **Uka Bahal (Rudravarna Mahabihar)** the oldest monastery in Patan, is on the left at the next intersection. A pair of stone lions guards the former Buddhist monastery, while an ark full of brass beasts stands watch in the courtyard.

Tinker Street is on the left as you exit Uka Bahal. The sound of metal being hammered into form fills the street, which ends at the wide market street that runs south from Durbar Square. At the intersection of the two streets stands the **Ibaha Bahal,** a recently renovated monastery dating from 1427. Further south along the same street, but on the other side, behind a water tank, is the **Minnath Mandir** with its garishly painted details. Minnath is often called *sanno* (little) Machhendranath, in reference to the deity who inhabits the temple down a short lane across the street. This, the **Rato Machhendranath Mandir,** a 17th-century pagoda with an intricate, colorful three-tiered roof, stands in the center of a big, grassy compound. A collection of brass animals, each of which represents a month of the Tibetan calendar, is perched on posts facing the temple. The *rato* (red) image of Machhendranath gets to ride in a towering chariot that makes its rounds of Patan in late April. Machhendranath is a multi-purpose deity: he's the *bodhisattva* of compassion; as a Newari god he controls the rains; and he's revered as the guru of a 7th-century saint.

North of Durbar Square

The **Golden Temple,** one of Patan's most famous structures, is a five-minute walk up the first northern lane west of Durbar Square. *(Admission Rs25 for foreigners.)* Also known as **Hiranyavarna Mahavihar,** this ornate, gilded temple makes up the west side of the **Kwa Bahal,** a 12th-century Buddhist monastery whose courtyard is decorated by a golden shrine. **No leather is allowed beyond the walkway around the edge of the courtyard.** The temple's facade is elaborately worked in *repoussé* with images of Buddhas, *taras,* and mythological creatures. Gods are supposed to be able to slide down the *patakas,* the golden belts that hang from the roofs. Upstairs, in the northeast corner of the *bahal,* are Tibetan-style murals. A pair of stone tortoises stands on the south side of the courtyard; you can also look for real ones shuffling around the temple.

Continuing another minute north, the five-tiered pagoda of the **Kumbeshwar Mahadev** comes into view. The oldest temple in Patan, it only had two tiers when it was built in 1392. The three stories added later have made it one of two free-standing five-roofed pagodas in the Kathmandu Valley (the other is the Nyatapola Temple in Bhaktapur). The deity-in-residence is Shiva, as indicated by the Nandi outside the temple. The water tank next to the temple inside the compound is believed to be connected to the holy Himalayan lake of Gosainkund. A pilgrim is said to have dropped a *kumbh* (pot) in the lake, which then emerged in the tank in Patan, giving the temple its name. Thousands of devotees come to bathe in the tank during the Jana Purnima festival (to be held the first week of August in 1999), when high-caste Hindus change their sacred threads. One block east of the temple, the road to the right leads straight back to the northern end of Durbar Square.

Jawalakhel

The Jawalakhel neighborhood is notable for its foreign residents—both expats working for aid organizations and Tibetan refugees. Just west of Jawalakhel Chowk is the **Central Zoo.** *(Open Tu-Su 10am-6pm. Tickets sold until 5pm. Admission Rs50 for foreigners. Camera fee Rs10, video camera Rs50.)* The admission fee goes toward renovations. There's a pond in the middle of the nicely landscaped grounds, and you can see that tiger (as well as the showcased guinea pigs) that eluded you at Chitwan.

A five- to 10-minute walk south of the Jawalakhel Chowk, past the *pipal* tree, is the **Jawalakhel Handicraft Centre** (tel. 521305), part of the **Tibetan Refugee Camp.** *(Open Su-F 8am-5pm.)* Established by the Red Cross and the Nepalese government in 1960, the center employs Tibetans who fled their country after 1959. Visitors can wander freely, watching the carpet-making processes, and there is no pressure to buy anything. Proceeds from the souvenir shop go to the workers.

SHOPPING

Patan is less hopping than Kathmandu, but there's plenty of shopping to be done. Aside from carpets, metalwork makes an appropriate local souvenir. Wooden toys are also a Patan specialty: auto-rickshaws and Tata trucks make funky mementos. The **Educational Toys Centre,** on the main road in Pulchowk (tel. 537385), is a good place to look (open Su-F 10am-7pm). Patan is full of non-profit craft outlets that sell crafts from all over the country. Many of them benefit underprivileged workers (especially women) and ensure fair wages. There's one in the old Royal Palace on Durbar Sq. and several in Kopundol, on the main road. **Sana Hastakala** (tel. 522628), opposite the Hotel Himalaya, has a particularly good selection sponsored by UNICEF (open Su-F 9:30am-6pm, Sa 10am-5pm; MC, Visa, AmEx). The original **Khukuri House** is south of Jawalakhel Chowk, before you reach the Tibetan Refugee Camp.

■ Near Patan: Godawari गोदावरी

From Langankhel bus park, buses #13 and 14 continue up the hills, to Godawari (1hr., Rs4), with spellbinding, misty views of rice paddies along the way. A horticultural haven, Godawari is home to the peaceful, expertly landscaped **Royal Botanical**

Garden, the **National Herbarium,** as well as a bee-keeping workshop, the marble quarry, and the nurseries providing flowers to florists in Patan. The Botanical Garden is a 10-minute walk from the bus park, which is the last stop; continue until the paved road terminates at the garden's entrance. The quarry, five minutes up the hill past St. Xavier's School from the bus park, offers an interesting eye-witness view of the mining and polishing of the marble, and marble chunks picked up along the way make neat souvenirs. A **Jesuit ashram** (tel. 522219 or 290558; fax 535620;email: supreg@njs.mos.com.np), just beyond the bus park will provide pleasant lodgings for guests given a week's notice ($8 per day requested for stays under 5 days; includes 3 veg. meals and 2 teas). Basic **restaurants** can be found near the Botanical Garden.

■ Kirtipur कितीपुर

The citizens of Kirtipur are proud of their gallant 18th-century stand against Prithvi Narayan Shah's encroaching Gorkha forces (see **History,** p. 704). When Shah first attacked in 1757, citizens from all around the valley came to Kirtipur's aid and handily defeated Shah's army. During a second battle in 1764, Shah's brother was shot in the eye with an arrow, and the Gorkhas again retreated. But the Gorkhas' superior weaponry turned the tide two years later, when, after a six-month siege of the town, Kirtipur lay down their sickles and anvils. The Gorkhas punished the city's men by slicing off their noses, ears, and lips so that throughout the country folks would recognize them as troublemakers from Kirtipur. Kirtipur is home to Nepal's largest university, **Tribhuvan University,** whose campus lies below the town on land once cultivated by Kirtipur farmers.

ORIENTATION AND PRACTICAL INFORMATION Perched on twin hills about 8 km southwest of Kathmandu, Kirtipur is a typical Newari town with its maze of narrow streets lined by tightly packed rows of brick houses. To reach Kirtipur from Kathmandu, take a **taxi** (Rs20), **tempo** (Rs4), or **bus #21** (frequent departures, 40min, Rs3) from the Ratna Park bus station (ask to make sure it's headed to Kirtipur). Stay on the bus until it stops at the bus park just down the hill from Kirtipur. From the bus park, the town square, **Naya Bazaar** (New Market) and temples are on top of the ridge to the right, outside of Kirtipur. From the bus park, the town square and temples are on top of the ridge to the right. The bazaar is a collection of outdoor stalls and shops selling **fruits, vegetables,** and **Fanta.** The town square has **STD** and **Internet** facilities. Up the paved path from the bus park is a large **city map. Chilandeo Stupa** is up the hill to the left; beyond it to the left is the Queen's Palace and the ornate **Bagh Bhairav Mandir.** The narrow walkways and twisting paths make getting lost easy. Your best bet is to befriend a student studying English and have him (invariably him) point you in the right direction, usually up a steep hill.

SIGHTS An immaculately kept Thai Buddhist Temple is down a couple flights of stairs from the town square. Called **Shree Kirti Vihara,** it was built in 1975 and is tended by saffron-robe-wearing Buddhist monks. The red-, yellow-, and green-roofed temple houses gilded statues of Buddha. On the side is a building encasing a larger-than-life sized Buddha in parinirvana guarded by a series of lion statues. The site is also a good overlook of Patan. Turn right before the Desktop Publishing banner and Ratna's Beauty Parlor up the hill to reach the 1400-year-old **Chilandeo Stupa** (also called Chilanchu Vihara) and the mandalas in front of it. To the left is a path leading to **Bagh Bhairab Mandir.** The temple is dedicated to Shiva the destroyer (Bhairab) in the form of a *bagh* (tiger), but it is significant to Hindus and Buddhists alike. Look for the Gorkhali swords and uniform mounted on the upper facade, commemorating Kirtipur's defeat by the Gorkhas. Worshippers and musicians visit Bagh Bhairab every morning and evening, and there's a chicken or buffalo sacrifice on Tuesdays and Saturdays. Observe, but avoid, the religious marijuana smokers congregated there. Bagh Bhairab is also the center of Kirtipur's December festival for the goddess Indrani, an offshoot of Kathmandu's Indrani festival. A separate monument commemorates Rama's birth as Brahma, Vishnu, and Shiva look on.

Uphill and west of the town square are a gateway and steep steps that lead to the **Uma-Maheshwar Mandir.** Children play among the legs and trunks of the two stone elephants that guard the temple, but the pachyderms' spiked backs keep the kids from climbing higher. The deities residing here are Shiva and his consort Parvati, housed in remarkably carved wood. The couple is especially important to married people. More noteworthy than the temple itself is its 1435m panorama: to the southwest looms one of the highest points of the Kathmandu Valley's rim; to the northeast sprawls Kathmandu (look for Swayambhunath, the Monkey Temple, and Bhimsen Tower for orientation); and on a clear day, Mt. Everest is visible.

■ Chobar चोभार

The long staircase leading up to the village of Chobar rewards climbers with the quirky **Adinath Lokeshwar Mandir,** a half-Hindu, half-Buddhist temple whose facade is covered with pots and pans (contributions of kitchenware to the temple are said to enhance the culinary skills of new brides). Below the town, the Bhagmati River flows through **Chobar Gorge,** the legendary scar left by Manjushri's sword when he drained the lake that once filled the Kathmandu Valley (see **The Story of the Kathmandu Valley,** p. 733). Test your mettle by inching across the narrow **suspension bridge,** manufactured in Scotland and assembled here in 1903, that spans the gorge. Just south of the bridge on the banks of the river sits the three-tiered **Jal Binayak,** a temple dedicated to Ganesh, represented here in the form of a large rock protruding from the back of the temple. Around the temple a stylized **Shiva's penis** and Parvati dance before a rabbit statue.

Bus #22 (Rs3) heads from Ratna Park in Kathmandu to Chobar. Get off when it turns west into the gates of Tribhuvan University. Chobar is south along the road, past the **Himalayan Bee Concern** on the right, and a **cold store** on the left. (Since this is the last cold store for a while if you're heading to Patan, it's a good idea to stock up here for water.) Go up the stone stairs at the base of the hill on the right. From Kirtipur, Chobar is about a 30-minute walk. Walk down the hill away from the Kiritpur's center and turn right at the pavilion used to cremate the dead. Through fields and past a schoolhouse is a path that leads into Chobar. Turn left when the path meets the road and continue heading up the hill up the stairs past the cold store on the right to reach the temple.

The path to Patan heads down the hillside, along terraced fields and further down, a wide dirt road. The walk from Chobar down to the gorge gets significantly less pleasant since the landscape is dominated by a smoke-spewing cement factory. However, this bastard child of development serves two purposes for the traveler. First, its perpetual emission, visible from almost any high point in the valley, is a reliable landmark. Second, lambasting it will immediately endear you to most Nepalis you meet.

■ Nagarjun नागार्जुन and Balaju बालाजु

Many believe that the Buddha once meditated atop Nagarjun; others maintain that the first *bodhisattva,* Viswapa, stood on the peak to throw the lotus seed that would blossom into *swayambhu* (see **The Story of the Kathmandu Valley,** p. 733). After you complete the strenuous two-hour walk to the summit and look out over the valley, you will see that both claims are tenable. Crowned by an old *stupa* draped in a virtual canopy of colored prayer flags, Nagarjun (also called "Jamacho") is convincingly holy. As the closest summit to Kathmandu, it offers a tremendous panorama of the valley in clear weather (Rs5 entry fee). Camping permitted (Rs90 per tent), but finding a place to camp is problematic.

The **#23 tempo** (every 30min., Rs4) leaves from Rani Pokhari and stops just short of **Balaju Water Garden** (on the left; open daily 7am-7:30pm; admission Rs3, camera fee Rs2). The water garden is marked by the ticket window and gate with turnstiles.

One of the few manicured public spaces in the area, Balaju sports fountains, painstak-ingly-pruned hedges, and shaded benches, all unified by a pastel color scheme. During festivals, worshippers take ritual baths in the water coursing from the 22 carved crocodiles of the **Baais Dhara,** to the right. Midway through the park on the right is the small **Bala Nilkantha,** a 7th-century contemporary of the more elaborate sleeping Vishnu, located northeast of the valley in Budhanilkantha. The **swimming pool** within the garden is a big, raucous place to keep cool. (Open daily 9am-12:30pm and 1-4pm. Thursdays are women-only. Admission Rs35; students Rs30.)

To reach Nagarjun, turn left after exiting the water garden and continue north for about 30 minutes. Nagarjun sits in the **Rani Ban** (also called Nagarjun Royal Forest), a sizeable chunk of forest protected by the government. The Rani Ban entrance is on the left as you walk up the hill. If you continue a few meters past the entrance, you will come to a short dirt trail on the left leading up to a 15m-long cave that holds a shrine to Buddha. Bring a flashlight. A natural stone image of Buddha was supposedly found near the back of the cave, and a man-made image sits near the front on the left.

If you walk back down the road and enter the Rani Ban, you'll find a well-marked trail on your right to Nagarjun's summit (5km, 2hr.). Winding through the forest preserve, the walk is steep and secluded. At the top is the Buddhist shrine **Jamacho.** Though rarely visited on ordinary days, Jamacho is the center of April's full moon festival, **Balaju Jatra.** During this festival, worshippers hold an all-night vigil at the summit and descend to Balaju the next day for a ritual bath in Baais Dhara.

■ Boudha (Boudhanath) बौद्धनाथ

Dominated by the whitewashed dome of Nepal's largest *stupa* and dotted with *gom-pas* representing all four sects of Tibetan Buddhism (Nyingma, Kagyupu, Sakyapa, and Gelupa), Boudha is one of the best places outside Tibet to get some exposure to Buddhist culture. Nearly everyone who circumambulates Boudha's massive *stupa* claims origins elsewhere. Many have fled Tibet since the Chinese crackdown in 1959; others have migrated from Nepal's northern peaks, either to spend years or just to wait out the winter; and others are Buddhists from the rest of the world who have cashed in their life savings to make the pilgrimage to the *stupa*. The monasteries that surround it offer not only schooling for children and training for monks, but also respite for an increasing number of Westerners. A prevailing attitude of celebration and contemplation, informed by worldly realism, reflects the faith that is a common denominator for this complex community. For the casual visitor, Boudha's atmosphere is a proper tonic for the frenetic business of travel, and the simplicity of its *stupa* cleanses eyes weary of jumbled alleys and carved temple struts.

ORIENTATION

While Boudha has expanded far beyond the confines of the **stupa compound,** the *stupa* remains its symbolic center and is the reference point for all other geographical directions. Five kilometers east of Kathmandu, the *stupa* compound is entered through a **gate** on the north side of the main, east-west road. Directions to places on the **main road** are given locally as either "right" (west) or "left" (east) of the gate. The sprawling community north of the *stupa*, where you will find most of Boudha's monasteries, is accessed by two parallel lanes leading north out of the *stupa* compound. One, referred to here as the **northern lane,** begins directly north of the *stupa*, just beside **The Original Stupa View Restaurant.** Small east-west lanes connect these two. **Always walk clockwise around the stupa!**

PRACTICAL INFORMATION

Buses: Bus #2 from Ratna Park (about every 30min., 35min., Rs3) is crowded. Be alert for pickpockets! The bus will drop you off a few yards before the gate. Blue **tempos** (#2, Rs6) leave from Rani Pokhari. **Taxis** from Thamel cost a reasonable Rs80.

Local Transportation: Mountain bikes can be rented from a small stand on the left hand side of the main lane (Rs60 per day).

Currency Exchange: Mandala Money Changer, just inside the southern gates on the left, uses bank rates, charges 1% commission for traveler's checks, 2% commission for cash. Open Su-F 8am-6pm and Sa 8am-noon.

Market: Fruit sellers gather on the main road to the left of the *stupa* gate and in the lanes north of the *stupa*. Across the main road, a few minutes' walk to the left, the **Gemini Grocer** (tel. 471370) is well-stocked with Western treats and toiletries and takes credit cards. Open daily 8am-8pm. Within the *stupa* compound is **Khashyor Bazaar,** which has shelves of packaged goodies. Open daily 8:30am-8:30pm.

Internet: High Himalaya (tel. 472051), in the *stupa,* has **STD/ISD** with private booths and good rates, email (Rs10 per Kb to send or receive) and internet services (Rs10 per min.), and **fax** services (Rs120 per min.). Open daily 7am-9:30pm.

ACCOMMODATIONS

Most visitors to Boudha spend either a few hours or a few months, but considering the clean and peaceful lodgings available, you may want to stay a few nights. There are a few cheap places on the main road, but the ones in the back lanes are sheltered from exhaust and only slightly harder to find. Be warned that the neighboring *gompas* begin clanging and nagging at 4:30am. Check-out is noon at all guest houses.

Lotus Guest House (tel. 472432 or 472320). Beside the colorful Dobsang Monastery. Twenty large rooms enclose a well-tended garden with courtyard cats. Several clean baths with solar-heated water on each of the two floors. Attached kitchen offers breakfast. Reservations recommended Oct.-Nov., especially for longer stays; reservation requests faxed to any local STD will be brought to the Lotus. Singles Rs220, with bath Rs260; doubles Rs300, with bath Rs350.

Dragon Guest House (tel./fax 479562). A 10min. walk down the *other* northern lane. Follow the signs past the large Khentse monastery. Remote, but clean with sparkling bathrooms and a meticulously groomed garden. Free 7am tea, a small library, plastic slippers, laundry service, luggage storage, local personal phone calls, and attached veg. **restaurant** (open daily 7am-10pm; breakfast Rs20-60, entrees Rs15-60). Singles Rs220; doubles Rs340, with kitchenette Rs440; quads Rs150. Discounts for longer stays.

Kailash Guest House (tel. 480741). Five min. down the main lane, on the right, upstairs from the one-room **clinic.** Simple rooms furnished with mirrored bureau. Pleasant terraces on each floor. Airy, calm rooftop patio is a great place to orient your mental map of the surrounding *gompas*. Hot water, seat toilets, laundry, luggage storage, safe water, and discounts for students and longer stays. In-season: singles Rs200; doubles Rs250, with bath Rs300. Off-season: Rs50 and under.

Peace Guest House, just inside the southern *stupa* gates on the right, has a double, a triple, and a quad, all filled for Rs80 per bed. Austere but friendly communal feel. Padlocks with shared keys. Large rooms have carpet and fans, but no hot water. Check-in 7:30am-9pm. Attached restaurant has separate Chinese and German menus. Guess which one's cheaper. Open daily 7:30am-9pm.

FOOD

The Original Stupa View Restaurant (tel. 470 9044), next to the *stupa* where the northern lane begins. Beside a restaurant of a similar name, the Original Stupa View boasts an original menu melding together local and Middle Eastern flavors. Small, but appetizing selection of veg. entrees Rs120-200.

Om Shanti Restaurant and Cafe (tel. 479709), on the western side of the *stupa*. This enthusiastically decorated place seats you right next to the *stupa,* plays good music, and serves up Tibetan specialties (Rs35-50) and Indian food (Rs25-80) at unbeatable prices. Open daily 7am-9pm.

Tashi Delek Restaurant, on the corner of the *stupa* compound where the main lane begins. A blue-and-white curtain marks this 3-table, low-profile eatery. Wide selection of entrees, Rs15-70. The portions aren't huge, but they're yummy, and at Rs15 a plate, you can afford seconds. Open daily 6am-8pm.

Double Dorjee Restaurant (tel. 488947), just past the Karmapa Service Society Nepal on the right off the main lane. A favorite with monks and expats. Low tables, floral upholstery, paper lanterns, and "inspirational" posters. Blackboard menu offers Tibetan, Chinese, Japanese,. and Continental. A Tibetan family provides slow and friendly service, so you'll have plenty of time to chat with the regulars while you wait for your food. Entrees Rs40-110. Open daily 7:30am-9:30pm.

SIGHTS

Boudha's is not only Nepal's most imposing **stupa,** but also one of the world's largest. Various legends detail the *stupa's* origins, and the 5th-century date assigned by historians is only a guess. A Tibetan myth tells of a poultry-farmer's daughter who wanted to build a *stupa*. The king granted her the area that could be covered by a buffalo skin. Not content to build so small a *stupa*, the girl cut the skin into enough strips to trace the perimeter of the huge lot on which the *stupa* now stands. The Newari version relates a story of a king who constructed taps from which no water would flow. Convinced that only the sacrifice of a great man would bring water, he tricked his son into patricide by ordering him to go to the spouts and behead the shrouded man he found lying there. This, of course, turned out to be the king, and, horrified by his deed, the remorseful prince built the *stupa* in the hope of redeeming himself.

Whatever its origins, the *stupa* has inspired awe and reverence since ancient times, when its location along the Kathmandu-Lhasa trade route made it a popular pilgrimage site (people still pray at Boudha for safe passage through the Himalaya). Each segment of its structure is said to correspond to one of the five elements: the three-leveled *mandala*-shaped base represents earth; the dome, water; the spire (with its 13 steps corresponding to the 13 steps to *nirvana*), fire; the parasol, air; and the pinnacle, ether. The red-rimmed blue Buddha-eyes that gaze out from each of the four sides of the golden spire are unique to Nepali *stupas,* and the "nose" in between them is actually the number one in Nepali script. The *stupa* is whitewashed and splashed with stripes of rust-colored wash to resemble the lotus shape. Its wall is inset with niches containing prayer wheels and 108 Buddha images. At the entrance to the *stupa* itself is a shrine to the Newari goddess Ajima, protectress of children and goddess of smallpox. The *stupa* affords a view punctuated by prayer flags and the golden roofs of *gompas.*

The year's largest celebrations happen in February. Thousands come to Boudha and reunite with friends and family for **Losar,** the Tibetan New Year. The **Festival of Lights,** held the night of February's full moon, is a more sober occasion commemorating the historic completion of the *stupa* hundreds of years ago. Beginning at dusk, worshippers circle the *stupa*, praying and chanting in penance and thanksgiving.

Visitors are usually welcome in the **gompas**—there is one right off the *stupa* compound and many more farther afield—as long as they observe the necessary **etiquette.** Dress modestly, take your shoes off before entering the *lhakang* (main hall), walk around clockwise inside, and always ask before taking photos. As monasteries have traditionally relied on contributions from visitors and pilgrims passing through, donations are greatly appreciated. If you visit a lama, present him with a white *khata* (prayer scarf). These are inexpensive and available at many shops around Boudha, where someone can show you how to fold them properly. In the *lhakang*, you'll find intricate wall paintings in overwhelmingly vivid colors. Gold statues of the Buddha, other *bodhisattvas,* or the *gompa* sect's founder are surrounded by offerings of food, incense, and butter-lamps.

The *stupa* is surrounded by shops. You don't need to come all the way to Boudha to buy some of the standard tourist junk, but it is *the* place for Tibetan antiques, as well as cheap souvenirs like as Tibetan head- and foot-gear and Buddhist prayer flags.

STUDY AND VOLUNTEER OPPORTUNITIES

The **Ka-Nying Shedrup Ling Monastery** (tel. 470993), known as the white monastery or *seto gompa*, is located between the two northern lanes and is particularly accessible to Westerners (tel. 470993). Its charming and charismatic leader, Chyoki Nyima Rinpoche, meets with visitors daily from 10am to noon and holds a teaching session in English every Saturday morning from 10am to noon. To speak to him, walk around to the right of the main hall and climb the stairs to the top floor. **Kopan Monastery** (tel. 481268; fax 481267), located atop a hill 2km north of Boudha, offers several meditation courses throughout the year and welcomes volunteers to work in their **library** (Su-F 1-3pm) or clinic. It offers accommodations throughout the year and welcomes visitors for meditation and discussion sessions in English (Su-F 10am). Rooms are Rs190 per bed with attached bath, or Rs80 per dorm bed; breakfast is included. Kopan is a 45-minute walk from Boudha. From the northern lane, head northwest from the *stupa* and turn right onto the taxi road that leads north and winds up the hill. A large map sits just inside Kopan's entrance, and a shop on the left sells refreshments and postcards. The reception is behind you as you face the map. (Office open daily 9am-noon and 1-5pm.) Finally, the **Vajra Center** (tel. 481562 or 478978); is a great place for English-speakers to teach Tibetans English for either short or long-term periods. Tibetan classes are offered in exchange. (Classes run from 7:30-9:30am and 3:30-5:30pm.) The Center is up the *other* northern lane on the right from the *stupa*, a minute's walk before the white monastery.

■ Bhaktapur भक्तपुर

Handing over Rs300 at the gate in exchange for a colorful brochure and admission into a neatly-bricked pedestrian-only area suggests entry into a theme park, but Bhaktapur is more than a show put on for Westerners. It's actually a living, breathing city where Nepalis like to spend their vacations, too. The countless souvenir shops and the many children who approach with stares and requests do their part in reminding you how comparatively prosperous you are, but the museums were built with two audiences in mind: you and the Hindus and Buddhists to whom these artifacts are religiously significant—unlike in the congested streets of Kathmandu, you won't be the only one photographing temples. They were reconstructed after a disastrous 1934 earthquake to honor Nepal's history and inspire pride in local craftsmanship. A five-minute detour from the main sights bursts any illusion of timelessness and shows Bhaktapur to be a city that is well-maintained but not at all embalmed. While it boasts some of the valley's finest medieval architecture, Bhaktapur's allure lies not only in its magnificent pagodas but also in the way that civic life continues around them.

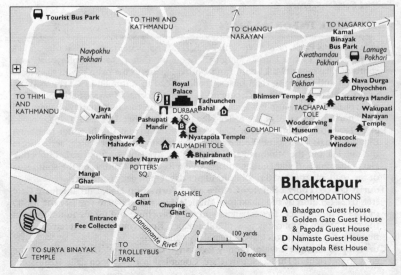

Bhaktapur

ACCOMMODATIONS

A   Bhadgaon Guest House
B   Golden Gate Guest House
    & Pagoda Guest House
D   Namaste Guest House
C   Nyatapola Rest House

NEPAL

Founded in the 9th century, Bhaktapur (also called Bhadgaon) was the capital of the Kathmandu Valley until its division into three kingdoms in 1482. Its prominence faded when the Gorkhas conquered it in 1768 and established the capital in Kathmandu (see **History,** p. 704). Many of its structures are reconstructed versions of temples built in the 15th-17th centuries. Restoration and rebuilding continue, encouraged by a German development project in the 1970s. The municipality is aware of the value of the treasures it possesses and charges foreign visitors an admission fee that funds ongoing preservation efforts.

> **Warning:** Tourists visiting Bhaktapur alone will be followed, tirelessly, by boys who claim to be practicing their English. While they are extremely well-informed about Bhaktapur's history, they will inevitably ask for money directly, relentlessly promote a *thanka* painting shop, or beg you buy them a school book or school clothes. These they will later return to the store for a portion of the price.

ORIENTATION

Bhaktapur is bordered to the north and south by main paved roads running to and from Kathmandu, 14km to the east. In the southern half of the city are residential streets, fields, and multiple *ghats* (platforms for religious worship) along the **Hanumante River.** Bhaktapur's main sights are in the northern half of the city, in three squares strung together by a curving main street. Anchoring the city's northwest edge, **Durbar Square** is connected in its southeast corner to **Taumadhi Tole** by a short lane. From the northeast corner of Taumadhi Tole, the connecting street widens into Bhaktapur's commercial area, **Sukuldhoka,** and takes a right-angle turn about a quarter of the way to **Tachapal Tole** (also called **Dattatraya Square**), which is about 10 minutes away by foot. Alleyways tangle and twist north and south of this main artery. Minibuses from Kathmandu arrive in an area that is a five-minute walk west of Durbar Square, near a large water tank called **Navpokhu Pokhari**—to the left coming from Durbar Square Gate. The **trolleybus** stop sits at the southern edge of town, a 15-minute walk south of Durbar Square.

Tourists must relieve themselves of Rs300 or US$5 at **Durbar Square Gate** or at any of the other checkpoints that secure access to the city. If you get into town by another route and avoid these booths, you may still be asked for your ticket once inside. The ticket can be used for multiple entries and days as long as you notify the **Tourist Service Centre.**

PRACTICAL INFORMATION

Buses: Minibus Park, near Navpokhu Pokhari (a large water tank). To: Kathmandu's **Bagh Bazaar,** east of Durbar Marg (#7, frequent, 45min., Rs6). **Trolleybus Park,** south of Bhaktapur. Walk south from Durbar Square to the main paved road. Less crowded and polluting than buses, **trollies** head to Kathmandu's **Tripureswar,** near the **National Stadium,** (frequent, 1hr., Rs4). **Kamal Binayak,** in the northeast edge of Bhaktapur. Turn left after the pottery square east of Dattatraya Square and head north to the edge of town. To: **Nagarkot** (every hr., 1½hr., Rs10-25).

Local Transportation: Buses: #7 bus skirts town from the hospital to Kamal Binayak. **Taxis** wait at the **Tourist Bus Park** beyond the Post Office, across from the cinema and the Minibus Park. **Bicycles** are available on the road connecting Navpokhu Pokhari and Durbar Square. **Cycle Repairing Center,** on the south side of the road, charges Rs10 per hr., Rs50 per day. Open daily 6am-7pm.

Tourist Office: Tourist Service Centre and Information Hall, Durbar Square Gate (tel. 612249). Run by the Bhaktapur Municipality, this is where you pay the Rs300 or US$5 entrance fee. In exchange, you get a brochure and use of an umbrella in the case of rain. Public toilets with toilet paper. Keep your ticket and have it certified to get in again if you leave. Open daily 6am-8pm.

Currency Exchange: Layaku Money Exchange Counter (tel. 612208), down the alley to the right of Durbar Square Gate. Commission 1.5%. Open daily 10am-5pm.

Market: Sukuldhoka, the main street that connects Tamadhi Tole and Tachapal Tole. Fruits, vegetables, and material sellers line the street from roughly 6:30am-10pm.

Police: (tel. 612204). District Police (tel. 100), just inside Durbar Square gates on the left, all the way in the rear of the disheveled courtyard. Manned daily 24hr.

Pharmacy: Several across from the hospital, including **Sewa Medicine Store** (tel. 613773). Open daily; 24hr. pharmacist. The 24hr. government **Hospital Pharmacy** (tel. 613218), across the street, is cheaper, but staffed by non-English speakers.

Hospital: Government Hospital (tel 610676), west of the Navpokhu Pokhari Minibus Park, on the north side of the street. A little decrepit. Staffed by specialists 9am-2pm; physicians and paramedic on call 24hr.

Post Office: Across from the Navpokhu Pokhari Minibus Park. No *Poste Restante*. No English, either. Open Su-Th 10am-5pm, F 10am-3pm.

Internet: Dhaubhadel Handicraft and Communication Center. (tel. 611320; fax 612780). Bahatal, connecting Durbar Square to Taumadhi Tole, across the street from Marco Polo Restaurant. **Email** (dhaubdel@mos.com.np) for Rs30/Kb and web access. Open daily 8am-6pm.

Telephones: STD/ISD offices dot the town. **Laiku Worldwide Communications,** near the corner on the right, facing the outside of Durbar Square Gate. Free callbacks for local calls. Private booth (tel. and fax 610258). Open daily 7am-7pm. **World Wide Hello Service** (tel. 613342 or 613473; fax 612607), Tibukchhen, just past Namaste Guest House on the left, heading towards Dattatraya Square. Rs10 per min. callbacks, but might negotiate to Rs5. Open daily 8am-8:30pm.

ACCOMMODATIONS

For many visitors to the Kathmandu Valley, Bhaktapur is just a daytrip from the 'Du. But Bhaktapur is worthy of more than an afternoon visit—it's also a very cool place to spend the night. Bhaktapur's guest houses fall into two categories: very nice or very cheap. But even the most luxurious hotels are moderately priced, and all accommodations have hot showers, laundry, convenient temple-side locations, ultra-accommodating owners, and rooftop gardens with magnificent views. Once you determine your price range, deciding which temple you want outside your window might be your greatest dilemma. Rates are always negotiable, especially for groups, students, and longer stays. Off-season (May-Aug.), bargain hard. Reservations recommended in high season. Noon check-out everywhere. Most places lock up at 10pm.

Namaste Guest House (tel. 610500), Sakotha Tole, on the corner where Tibukchhen meets Sakotha, leading into the northeast corner of Durbar Square. A great combination of economy and luxury. Clean, spacious rooms, some with attached bath. Guests receive a 14% discount at the affiliated **Sunny Restaurant** (see below) Singles Rs200; doubles Rs350-400. Off-season: Rs150/Rs250. MC, Visa.

Pagoda Guest House (tel. 613248; fax 612685), Taumadhi Tole, right behind the Nyatapola temple, to the left. Clean guest house offers all the extras: fans, heaters, towels, fuzzy slippers, and yappy dog! Rooms are practically *on top* of the 5-story temple. One seat-toilet bath on the second floor. Squat toilet bath on the cheaper ground floor. Rooftop restaurant (meals Rs110-150). Doubles only, but those staying alone get a single's rate. In-season: singles US$5-20; doubles US$6-12, with bath US$15-25. Off-season: singles Rs150-250, doubles Rs400. MC, Visa.

Bhadgaon Guest House (tel. 610488; fax 610481), Taumadhi Tole, on the left just as you enter Taumadhi Tole from Potters' Square, before Cafe Nyatapola. Marble stairs and carefully kept garden courtyard make the Bhadgaon Bhaktapur's poshest hotel. Rooftop restaurant with terrific views (entrees Rs100-180). Nine rooms, all with attached bath—toilet paper, towels, and slippers, too. In-season: singles Rs900; doubles Rs1000/US$20. Off-season: Rs400/500/US$12.

Nyatapola Rest House (tel. 612415), Taumadhi Tole, behind the Nyatapola pagoda, to the right. Four basic (but secure) rooms. A little shabby, but serviceable. Bathrooms across the courtyard. In-house restaurant (entrees Rs35-125). Singles Rs100-120, doubles Rs300. Off-season: negotiable!

Golden Gate Guest House (tel. 610534; fax 611081). Bahatal. On the left side of the street as you approach Taumadhi Tole from Durbar Square. Duck through the

NEPAL

doorway to reach the Golden Gate, two courtyards removed from Durbar Square. rooms, 9 with common bath, 6 with attached bath. Views and brightness improve with the stairs. Attached restaurant. In-season: singles Rs150; doubles Rs200-300. Off-season: Rs100/150-200. MC, Visa, AmEx.

FOOD

Despite its prime location and shameless advertising, **Cafe Nyatapola** still manages to leave a bad taste in your mouth (figuratively, at least). While none of Bhaktapur's tourist restaurants merit special mention based on their cuisine—they all offer up the usual mish-mash of Nepali-Continental-Indian-Chinese—several do stand out because of their settings. (Many guest houses have rooftop restaurants whose elevation is more alluring than their copycat menus.) Less-tourist-oriented restaurants provide Nepali cuisine for half the price and twice the excitement. They are not loudly advertised, but they *do* exist: most any place with tables, benches, and a stove will make a mean *dal bhat* for under a buck. One local treat, *ju dhau* (king of curds), a creamy, sweet yogurt, can be found wherever food's for sale.

Sunny Restaurant (tel. 612004), Taumadhi Tole, located in a typical old house, just to the right facing Nyatapola Temple. Sunny's clay floors, low ceilings, canvas-painted walls, knee-high tables, and rooftop kitchen give the basic dishes a flare appreciated by locals, too. Continental (Rs100-150), Newari (Rs55-95), and Nepali (Rs95-200) meals. Beer (Rs85-110) about as cheap as you'll find.

Marco Polo Restaurant (tel. 610955), Taumadhi Tole immediately to the left facing Nyatapola Temple. With its green shutters and plaid tablecloths, Marco Polo is a less sexy, but cheaper, alternative to other tourist restaurants. Rub elbows, shoulders, and knees with other budget travelers on the tiny balcony overlooking the northwest corner of the square. Fairly extensive menu with dishes (lasagna, burgers, Indian, and Nepali) from Rs45-90. Open daily 7am-8pm.

Cafe de Temple Town Restaurant (tel. 612432), Durbar Square. Walking from Durbar Square Gate, turn right. A small garden screens the patio tables from the noise of the square without obscuring the sights. Enjoy familiar fare during the day, or come in the evening to hang with the locals over grilled chicken, goat, and water buffalo. Vegetable dishes Rs60-65, main dishes Rs55-180. Open daily 8am-9pm.

Cafe de Peacock and Somo Bar (tel. 610684), Tachapal Tole. Facing Dattatraya Temple, Cafe de Peacock is up a floor on the left. With indoor and outdoor seating, it's a great place to people-watch. Mexican, Italian, chicken, and Nepalese plates (Rs120-300). Hard liquors (Rs20-30) and beer (Rs80-120). MC, Visa, AmEx. 10% European Traveler's Network discount. Open daily 9am-9pm.

SIGHTS

Durbar Square

Bhaktapur's is the oldest and least cluttered Durbar Square in the valley. Thinned out by a 1934 earthquake, it is a wide-open pedestrian area whose architectural feats number just enough to be majestic but not overwhelming. The **Royal Palace** encloses the north side of the square, and like the square itself, is only a shadow of what it once was. (*Open W-Th and Sa-M 10:15am-4:30pm, F 10am-2:30pm. Admission Rs20. No cameras allowed inside. English information pamphlet available.*) The current buildings date from the 16th and 17th centuries when, under Malla rule, Bhaktapur was the center of valley life. Paintings, statues, and tapestries from this era still decorate the west wing of the palace, which now houses the **National Art Gallery.** The gallery mostly displays incredibly intricate Newari *paubha* and Tibetan *thanka* paintings; its oldest objects are stone sculptures from as early as the 11th century. The gallery also affords the best glimpses of the palace's courtyards, most of which are closed to visitors. Next door is the acclaimed, Garuda-topped **Golden Gate,** built in the early 18th century by King Bhupatindra Malla, whose image is cast atop a stone pillar facing the gate. To the east of the larger palace building sits the **Palace of 55 Windows.** The craftsmanship of the carved wooden windows is less flashy but more

Thankas for the Memories

Traditional *thankas* (pronounced THANG-ka, meaning "something rolled up" in Tibetan) are religious paintings on cloth that serve as aids for meditation, usually in temples or family altars. Colorful and finely detailed, they are painted in accordance with strict rules that dictate style and subject matter. *Thankas* may represent the Buddha surrounded by scenes from his life, *bodhisattvas,* saints, or lamas. Other forms include the wheel of life and *mandalas,* which illustrate the steps to enlightenment. A good *thanka* can take anywhere from a week to six months to create. *Thankas* are made by stretching cotton cloth on a wooden frame and priming it with *gesso.* The cloth is then rubbed smooth with a stone or shell. The outlines of the images are drawn, then colors are added in layers. If a *thanka* is made in a workshop, layers are added by increasingly skilled artists: first large blocks of color, then the setting, then any gold details, and finally the faces of the figures. The painting is then mounted on a frame of three colors of brocade silk, with a rod at the top for hanging and rolling. A *thanka* cannot be used, however, until it has been consecrated by a lama, who will make an inscription on the back. Most *thankas* you will see for sale have not been consecrated (although some of the same artists still make *thankas* for religious use) and many do not comply with traditional guidelines. For example, the "detailed *mandala*" form with its minute details is a style created to meet the tastes of tourists. If you are interested in buying a *thanka,* shop around first. As with any fine art, the enormous range in prices (from Rs100-10,000) reflects the range of quality available, though a high price does not necessarily mean high quality.

impressive than that of the gate itself—each window took a craftsman about 100 days to construct.

Like the palace, Durbar Square's temples betray the remarkable craftsmanship of the Malla era. The westernmost temple in the Square, **Bansi Narayan,** is dedicated to Krishna, and its roof struts depict various incarnations of Vishnu. Behind the king's pillar is the elephant-flanked stone **Vatsala Durga Temple.** Built in the mid-18th century in the *shikhara* style, this temple boasts an impressive mixture of stone carving, metalwork, and wood carving. To the left is the **Chyasilin Mandap** (Eight-Cornered Pavilion), a 1990 reconstruction incorporating fragments of the 18th-century original. Using a 100-year old photograph of the *mandap,* the German Agency for Technical Cooperation and local craftsmen pieced the ruins back to its present grandeur. They incorporated a central steel structure to protect against future earthquakes. The upstairs serves as a lookout point for tourists and a hang-out for local teenagers. In the eastern section of the square, around the corner of the palace, are several more temples and temple foundations, the most interesting of which is the 17th-century stone **Siddhi Lakshmi Temple,** with its procession of animals and people on either side of the stairs. The souvenir shops that surround this part of the square were once *dharamshalas* (pilgrims' resthouses). Back in the southeast corner of the main part of the square, the **Pashupatinath Mandir** contains a 17th-century reproduction of the *linga* at Pashupatinath and is the most active of the Durbar Square temples. Check out the especially creative contortions of the couples on the roof struts, the only parts of the building that survive from the original 15th-century structure.

Taumadhi Tole

Connected to Durbar Square by a short, shop-lined street, Taumadhi Tole is Bhaktapur at its best, where architectural masterpieces and religious ceremony mingle with daily life. Taumadhi Tole hosts musicians and worshippers every morning and evening, and it is a focal point of **Bisket Jatra,** Bhaktapur's renowned celebration of the new year in April. Nepal's tallest pagoda, **Nyatapola Temple,** dominates the square and all of Bhaktapur. The newly-renovated red, five-story pagoda was originally built in 1702 by King Bhupatindra Malla. Five pairs of stone creatures flank the stairs to the temple. Each pair of guardians is said to be ten times stronger than the one below, starting with a tremendous pair of Malla wrestlers who themselves are ten times more powerful than the average man. Next are a pair of elephants, followed by lions, giraffes, and finally the goddesses Bahini (the Tigress) and Singhini (the Lioness). The image of the goddess **Siddhi Lakshmi,** to whom the temple is devoted, is locked inside the temple and accessible only to priests. The shaded upper level is a favorite local napping spot.

The eastern side of the square is dominated by the comparably solid **Bhairavnath Mandir,** which was built as a single-story temple in the 18th century. A second story was added during the 18th century, and the entire structure was rebuilt with the existing three stories after the 1934 earthquake. The golden image that peers down from the third story of the temple is that of Lord Bhairav, god of Terror, whose head is supposedly locked inside. A doorway in the building at the south side of the square leads to a courtyard filled by the **Til Mahadev Narayan Mandir,** a 17th-century temple (on an 11th-century temple site) reminiscent of Changu Narayan with its pillar-mounted golden Garuda, *chakra,* and *sankha.*

Tachapal Tole (Dattatraya Square)

A wide, curving street of shops catering to locals rather than tourists (although some of their wares make great souvenirs) links Taumadhi Tole to Bhaktapur's oldest square, Tachapal Tole. The wooden buildings that enclose the square were once *maths* (priests' residences). The **Dattatraya Mandir** presides over the square from the eastern end. Built in 1427, it is the oldest surviving building in Bhaktapur, and like other famous structures in the Kathmandu Valley, it is said to have been built from the trunk of just one tree—from the looks of it, one *mammoth* tree. A pair of Malla wrestlers, gaudily painted during festivals, guard the entrance in jarring multi-colored contrast to the monochromatic temple, whose beauty is in its detailed wood carvings. Dattatraya appeals to both Hindus and Buddhists since he is considered an incarnation of Vishnu, a guru of Shiva and a cousin of the Buddha. At the opposite end of the square is the rectangular **Bhimsen Temple,** which honors the favorite god of Newari merchants.

Behind the Dattatraya Temple are two museums housed in *maths.* To the left, the **Brass and Bronze Museum** displays a collection of 300-year-old, functional objects such as lamps, cooking pots, hookahs, spittoons, and intricately carved ritual paraphernalia. Opposite in **Pujari Math** is the **National Art Gallery Woodcarving Museum,** worth visiting more for its magnificent courtyard than for its minutely labeled objects. Get an intimate look at wooden windows and other carvings, such as temple roof struts up close. *(Admission to any one of the three museums allows entry to the other two. Open Sa-M and W-Th 10am-5pm, F 10am-3pm. Rs 20 to enter. Camera fee Rs20.)* Halfway down the street around the corner from to the Woodcarving Museum is the (inexplicably) famous **Peacock Window,** dating from the 17th century.

Other Sights

It is a pleasure to wander through Bhaktapur. Look for craftspeople at work—the squares just east and south of Taumadhi Tole are both known as **Potters' Square,** and you can see hundreds of pots lined up to dry in the sun or stacked up to be sold. Stroll south toward the river to see *ghats,* fields, and temples which, in contrast to the ones to their north, are more functional than they are grand. Most importantly, boldly lose yourself in Bhaktapur's alleys. A meander through Kamal Binayak is worthwhile if only to see market life completely independent of tourism. Even if you trip over playing children or fall victim to the refuse that is sometimes hurled from the windows, the experience may well be the highlight (comic or otherwise) of your visit.

SHOPPING

Bhaktapur is known for its **pottery** (best purchased at the **Potters' Square**) and for Newari **metal and wooden handicrafts.** Metalwork is available in countless shops that line the main streets, and woodcarvings are sold in Durbar and Tachapal Squares. The painted wooden toys like trucks and auto-rickshaws are actually made in Patan, but the miniature carved windows are all produced in Bhaktapur. You'll also see papier maché masks and marionettes—any of the handmade paper products are made at the UNICEF factory in Bhaktapur. Check the street between Tachapal and Taumadhi Squares for less touristy souvenirs like topis (traditional Nepalese men's hats) and saris. The black-and-red *saris* the local Newari Jyapu (farmer) caste women wear cost Rs400-1,000, depending on the quality.

■ Changu Narayan चाँगु नारायण

Sitting 7km north of Bhaktapur on the "shaking hill" of Changu, the temple of Changu Narayan is Nepal's oldest and most sacred. The two-tiered temple itself, eclectically patched and elaborated over 17 centuries, is delightfully intricate but physically unimposing. More impressive are the large sculptures and polished black relief panels that cluster around it—works that are considered among Nepal's greatest treasures. Astounding, finally, is the knowledge that worshippers have visited, adorned, restored, and revered the Vishnu shrine on this site since the 4th century. However, the temple is not the town's only draw; a mere two-hour walk from Bhaktapur, the town is a peaceful respite replete with breathtaking panoramic views.

ORIENTATION AND PRACTICAL INFORMATION Three roads lead north out of Bhaktapur to Changu Narayan; all start along the east-west road that runs along Bhaktapur's northern edge. The easternmost road is paved and clearly marked; buses depart from the bus park near the hospital (every hr., 30min., Rs5, last bus to Bhaktapur at 6pm). You can also bike along this road and reach Changu Narayan in about an hour, but the last 2km are very steep. The next two roads to the west of the paved road are shorter footpaths that converge north of Bhaktapur, making for a two-hour hike. Changu Narayan is a two-hour hike from the mountain viewpoint of Nagarkot to the east. Getting off the Nagarkot bus at Telkot (bus #7, 30min., Rs5) and walking straight along the ridge will get you there in about 1½ hr. Another approach is from the north side, off the road between Boudha and Sankhu, but it is trekkable only in the dry season when the Manohara River is low enough to be forded.

When you enter Changu, go to the tourist information center (tel. 290890; open daily 9am-5pm; off-season 10am-4pm), which sits in a hovel on the right. A volunteer staff (university students self-consciously clad in Newari dress) will ask you to sign a visitor log before they offer you a number of services: information pamphlets, maps, postcards (Rs150), a guide (Rs100/hr.), and even medicines. The temple is up the steps past the tourist center.

ACCOMMODATIONS AND FOOD Walking from Nagarkot, it's hard to miss the bright red and peacock-blue Changu Narayan New Hill Resort and Restaurant (tel. 290891) about ten minutes down the hill east of Changu village. The view from the balcony is worth the price of a cold drink or two. Instant noodles (Rs35) and *pilau* (Rs40-50), as well as more exotic dishes are available. (Open daily 8am-5pm.) The "resort" also offers very basic (almost harsh) accommodations if you're tempted to spend the night (doubles with common bath Rs200). In the village of Changu, which dribbles down from the temple, are a couple of other restaurants. The Lovely Coffee House (tel. 290958), right next to the bus parking lot, is not nearly as lovely as its view, but it does serve up reasonably priced tourist fare as well as shade while you wait for your bus. (Open daily noon-7pm.)

SIGHTS Entering Changu Narayan's courtyard from town puts you behind the temple, with two stone griffins facing you. Stone lions guard the front of the temple, and a spreading copper doorway embossed with flower designs frames the entrance. The 7th-century golden image of Vishnu inside is visible only to high priests; the temple is open only to Brahmins. On either side of the temple, pillars stand like big candlesticks, bearing Vishnu's symbols: a life-wheel and a stone staff on the left representing, respectively, Brahmins and Chettris, and a conch shell and lotus flower on the right representing the occupational and business castes. The inscription at the base of the pillar is the oldest stone inscription in the valley, dating from 454 A.D. and

NEPAL

relating the victories of King Manadeva. The excellent statue of Vishnu's man-bird vehicle, Garuda, who bows before the door wearing a cobra for a scarf, was carved at about the same time. His human face is said to be a likeness of King Manadeva himself, who reputedly remarked that he, like the Garuda, was a vehicle for Vishnu. In the birdcage over Garuda's shoulder are two more recent figures, Bupathindra Malla and Bubana Lakshmi, the 17th-century king and queen of Bhaktapur who introduced metalwork to the temple by financing the ornate copper doorway.

The best **sculptures** are beside the main temple, past the right pillar, on the brick pavilion of the **Lakshmi Narayan Temple** (the one with black wooden columns). In the central relief, Vishnu as Narasimha, half-man and half-lion, tears a hole in the chest of a demon. To the left of this, a relief shows the story of Vishnu as Vikrantha, the dwarf who grew to celestial size and stepped across the earth and the heavens in three steps. The heavens swirl around him and people clutch at his toes, while his legs span the whole scene. On the platform next to the Lakshmi Narayan Temple is an image of Vishnu as Narayan, sleeping on a knotted snake. The ten-headed, ten-armed figure above Narayan depicts the universal face of Vishnu, showing each of his ten incarnations. On the opposite side of the courtyard is the sculpture of Vishnu riding Garuda that appears on 10 Rupee notes. All of these sculptures date from the Licchavi period, before the Mallas took over in 1200, when stone sculpture in the valley was at its height (see **Nepal: History,** p. 704).

■ Dhulikhel धुलिखेल

Surrounded by mountains and valleys, this biker's and hiker's paradise sits at 1550m, bursting with mountain views rivalling Nagarkot's. Unlike Nagarkot, however, there was actually a town of Dhulikhel before tourists came along. The multitude of signs written only in Nepali script belies Dhulikhel's local importance as an important market town on the Nepal-China trade route. Himalayan sunrises, terraced farmland, and elaborately carved wooden doorways and windows are long-standing trademarks of this Newari town. But Dhulikhel is not merely a throwback to the past; as the district headquarters, it is home to several basic civic institutions.

ORIENTATION

Dhulikhel is just off the Arniko Highway, 32km southeast of Kathmandu. From Kathmandu, take the #12 **bus** (every 20min., 90min., Rs15). The road to Dhulikel runs southeast from the Dhulikhel **bus park.** To the right is a sign for Dhulikhel's new **hospital.** The road then curves past the **Rastriya Banijya Bank,** on the right and uphill to the **town center,** where a bust of King Mahendra stands next to a water tank. To the right of the king, the road leads northwest into the main square and the old town.

PRACTICAL INFORMATION

Buses: From Kathmandu, take the #12 bus (every 20min., 90min. Rs15) which also makes stops near Bhaktapur's trolleybus park and Banepa's bus park.

Currency Exchange: Rastriya Banijya Bank charges a 1.5% commission. Open Su-Th 10:30am-2:30pm, F 10:30am-noon.

Pharmacy: In the old town—follow the road and look to your left. Open daily 7am-8pm. Another pharmacy, whose staff speaks better English, is down the road to the southeast. Open Su-F 7am-7pm, Sa 7am-1pm.

Hospital: (tel. 61497 or 61237), 10min. away from the bus park—follow the sign. Amazingly well-kept. General practitioners staff the hospital daily 8am-5pm (on call after 5pm), except for Wednesdays and Saturday, when it offers emergency care only. In-house **pharmacy** opens 9am.

Post Office: Open Su-Th 10am-5pm, F 10am-3pm.

Internet: Sunrise Travels (tel. 62025; fax 64014), across the street and down the hill from Raju's Store, after the Nawa Ranga, provide provides email access (Rs30/Kb). Open daily 7am-9pm.

Telephones: Raju's Store (tel. 61472), past the post office and volleyball courts, has **STD/ISD.** Cheap callbacks. Open Su-F 7am-6pm. **Telephone Code:** 011.

ACCOMMODATIONS

Dhulikhel Lodge (tel. 61753), down the hill and to the right of the bus park. More like a high-rise than a lodge: 20 large rooms, all with common bath. Restaurant with low seating offers Nepali and Italian meals (Rs120/60-90) and a 10% student discount. In-season: singles Rs200; doubles Rs300. Off-season: singles Rs150; doubles Rs250. Credit cards accepted.

The Royal East Inn (tel. 64097), beside the bus park. Nice garden area and upscale restaurant serving continental dishes (Rs120-180). In-season: singles Rs200; doubles Rs300, with bath Rs500. Off-season: negotiable. 25% student discount. Reservations recommended.

Nawaranga Guest House (tel. 61226), a five-minute walk up the road. This backpacker haven has been in business for 25 years, offering rooms with low ceilings, concrete floors, and good rooftop views. Clean, common squat toilets. Hot water Rs10 per bucket. Dorm beds Rs60; singles Rs100; doubles Rs150-200.

Panorama View Lodge (tel. 62085), near Kali Mandir. Follow the road to the left of the Mahendra statue to the lodge's sign at the base of the hill (about 15min.), then take the road that veers right up the hill. The deeply eroded shortcuts are a steeper but much quicker way to the top. New brick building houses large doubles, and balconies. Clean bathrooms have hot showers and seat toilets. In season: doubles Rs300, with bath US$15. Rates negotiable; student (10-15%) and off-season discounts are available. Reservations recommended. Major credit cards accepted.

FOOD

Most of the restaurants in town are attached to guest houses. The restaurants at **The Royal East Inn** and the **Nawaranga Guest House** are an especially good pick. In a pinch, you can also sate your appetite at one of the **cold stores** in town. The **Yadagar Restaurant,** on the way up to the Panorama View Lodge, serves standard fare: *biryani* (Rs50-90) and curries (Rs25-60). (Open daily 8am-9pm.)

SIGHTS

The **mountains** are the featured attraction in Dhulikhel, but the cobblestoned town is worth a wander as well. In the main square, two temples honor two different forms of Vishnu: the small, brightly tiled temple is dedicated to Harisiddhi, and the even smaller one opposite it, to Narayan. They are guarded by two Garudas. Further northwest, at the high point of the town, the pagoda-like **Bhagwati Mandir** is of more interest as a lookout than as a temple. The most popular point from which to watch the sun rise over the Himalaya is the **Kali Shrine** at the top of the southeastern hill. Walk to the Panorama View Lodge and keep going. The shrine is about 45 minutes from town. **Namobuddha**, a 90-minute walk southeast of Kali Mandir, is another popular Buddhist pilgrimage—and day trek—destination. Pick up a sketched map from the Dhulikhel lodge (see above). The **monastery** at Namobuddha offers lodging for a reasonable donation (around Rs150).

■ Nagarkot नगरकोट

Teetering at 2175m on the eastern rim of the Kathmandu Valley, 32km from the capital, Nagarkot is the popular Himalayan viewpoint from which, in clear weather, one can see Mt. Everest. Originally a military base, tourism has spurred the creation of Nagarkot, the town. Daytrippers (actually, more like one-nighters) come to any of the dozen guest houses to catch the Himalayan sunrise. There are several day treks down to neighboring mountain villages, which can offer glimpses of Nepalese village life you'll never see in foreigner-packed Nagarkot. On the bus ride up, if you can muster a peek out of the window as the bus careens around a hairpin turn, you'll see patterned rice and corn plots etched into the hillside beside uncultivated hills draped in lush green vegetation. Monsoon season is exactly the wrong time to visit unless you're seeking coolness, not views. Nagarkot gets quite chilly at night; bring warm clothes.

NEPAL

ORIENTATION

Nagarkot consists of an ever-thickening growth of guest houses along a verdant **ridge.** The road from Bhaktapur continues north past the bus stop and forks at the base of a hill, where a large **map** on the left charts Nagarkot's guest houses. The road that curves to the right leads to **The Tea House** and **Club Himalaya,** both of which sit on top of the hill. The road that curves north around the left side of the hill leads to the bank, the rest of Nagarkot's guest houses, and the high point on the ridge, marked by the tiny **Mahakal Shrine.**

PRACTICAL INFORMATION

Local Transportation: Local buses are supposed to leave from the Kamal Binayak bus stop in the northeast of Bhaktapur every hour, but they are sometimes less frequent—ask around for the next departure time (1hr., Rs10). The last bus leaves Nagarkot at 5pm. **Tourist buses** leave from Kantipath in Kathmandu (1:30pm, 2½hr., Rs80) and return from Nagarkot the next morning (10am, 2½hr., Rs80). Tickets can be booked in advance from any agency in Thamel. **Jeeps** also leave from the Kamal Binayak bus stop in Bhaktapur for as little as Rs20 per person after some negotiating. **Taxis** from Bhaktapur to Nagarkot costs Rs400.

Currency Exchange: Himalayan Bank Ltd. (tel. 290885), just below the Tea House. Service charge of Rs150 or 1.5%. Open Su-Th 10am-2pm, F 10am-noon.

Hospital: The nearest is in Bhaktapur; stock up on meds before going to Nagarkot.

Internet: Club Himalaya (tel. 290883) has email for Rs22 per kb, internet services for Rs22 per min., and international telephone services with free callbacks.

ACCOMMODATIONS

As the hotel strip above the clouds expands, true budget lodges are becoming an endangered species. Prices are negotiable (especially in low season) so with a little friendly haggling bargains still exist. Most hotel managers are amenable to giving student discounts up to 15%. The following hotels cling to the ridge below the Mahakal Shrine.

The Resort at the End of the Universe (tel. 290709) is one of Nagarkot's originals. Rustic, wooded, and remote, the brick and bamboo bungalows are simple, but comfortable. Singles Rs250; doubles with bath Rs350. Students receive a 10-15% discount on food and lodging. Reservations, recommended in the high season, can be taken at the New Orleans Cafe in Thamel, or phoned in directly.

The Hotel Madhuban Village (tel. 290709) is a collection of A-frame bamboo cottages with big windows and not much room for anything but 2 single beds and a common squat toilet (no hot water). The glassed-in dining room (curries Rs120-200) affords good views. Doubles Rs250, with bath Rs600. Student discount 30%.

The Peaceful Cottage (tel. 290877), on the same turn-off, resembles a temple but is a skyscraper by Nagarkot standards, with a 360° view from the roof. Doubles with tub US$30, with shower US$20; singles with common bath and nice views, $5. 10% student discounts. Discounts negotiable. Major credit cards are accepted.

FOOD

The Tea House (tel. 290880), just below the **Club Himalaya,** is Nagarkot's most elegant, with tablecloths and plate-glass windows with terrific views on all sides. Uniformed waiters serve Continental (Rs125-250) and Indian and Nepali dishes (Rs60-150). A super-clean place to get some fresh air after the bus ride.

The Restaurant at the End of the Universe (290709), attached to the similarly titled resort, and named after the science fiction novel. The usual fare in a pleasant, dining space with cushioned platform seating. Burgers, chicken, rice Rs50-200.

Café du Mont (tel. 290877), attached to The Peaceful Cottage, serves veg. (Rs70-150) and non-veg. (Rs90-200) meals.

NEPAL

SIGHTS

The hip thing to do in Nagarkot is watch the sun rise above the hills and set behind the valley, washing the mountain peaks in pink light. While all guest houses have great views, you can also walk up to the **Mahakal Shrine,** right next to the **End of the Universe,** or find out if the **lookout tower,** an hour's easy walk south from the bus stop past the army base, is open. It is also fun to explore the surrounding hillsides; lodge owners enthusiastically offer directions for walks to **Changu Narayan** (2hr.), **Sankhu** (2hr.), **Dhulikel** (5hr.), and **Shivapuri** (2-3 days). Whether from a pitched tent or a guest house, guests are often seduced by Nagarkot into enjoying sunrises from bed, sunsets over dinner, and ardent loafing in between.

Getting Soused in Shangri-La

Sure, you can stick to imported liquors or settle for whatever brand of red wine the Western supermarket happens to have in stock—neither of these practices will violently pillage your booze budget. But braver, stingier souls consume domestic beer. The price (Rs60-90 for 650mL) is guaranteed to please, but the libations themselves are of varying quality. **Turborg** is tasty, while **Star** is palatable only if chilled to absolute zero. If your buck stops at the local brewery, though, you are missing a fantastic opportunity to indulge in the fruits of the venerable but vanishing art of moonshining. **Chang** is your basic rice- or millet-based home brew, enjoyed by the masses but appreciated most by lamas in the high mountains. Perhaps the most elusive brew for foreigners is **tong-ba,** a Tibetan millet concoction that is by far the most mellow member of the alcoholic trinity. Begin with fermented millet in the bottom of your vessel. Add hot water (make sure it's been boiled!), let it steep, and sip from a special straw that catches the grains. Kick back and enjoy the refills—the grains are good through several servings. Finally, **raksi** (rhymes with foxy) is Nepal's proudest and most potent offering. A distilled alcohol that resembles tequila, it's a sweet, smooth swallow that packs a serious punch. *Raksi* figures prominently in essential drinking vocabulary: *"malaai raksi laagyo"* literally means, "I am stricken by alcohol." Not an excuse, exactly, but sometimes it's better than nothing.

■ Sankhu साँखु

Sankhu sits at the end of the eastern road from Boudha, surrounded by farmland. Though an apt dayhike from Nagarkot, the disheveled, dumpy town is worth only a brisk walk through to reach the path up to **Bajra Jogini Mandir** (Vajra Yogini). The 17th-century temple is built on an ancient Buddhist holy site. The two-kilometer walk from town starts through the cement archway to the left of the bus stop. The dirt road leads through town; about halfway to the temple, it continues to the right, while a stone-paved footpath leads straight ahead. The two meet up again at the base of the long, steep stairway to the top of the hill. From the base of the stairs, it's a 15-minute walk to the top. Giving Swayambunath a run for its money, the stairs to the temple are swarming with outgoing monkeys—don't leave your possessions unattended, as our primate cousins are light-fingered.

Nothing better illustrates Nepal's fusion of Hinduism and Buddhism than Sankhu's shrine to Bajra Jogini. Buddhists have long revered the goddess as a protectress. Some say Bajra Jogini convinced Manjushri to drain the water-filled Kathmandu Valley. Another legend suggests that she requested the construction of the Boudhanath *stupa* and sent a white crane to select its location. She has since been adopted as a Tantric goddess, representing for Newari Buddhists the powerful female characteristics of Buddha, while Hindus in the valley worship her as a form of Durga. The temple has three gilded roofs and an elaborate door shielding the goddess's image from the public. The small two-tiered temple enshrines a replica of the Swayambhunath *stupa*.

Bus #4 (1½hr., Rs10) departs Ratna Park in Kathmandu as soon as it is full. It also stops east of Boudha: take the **#2 tempo** to the end of its route (Rs6) and walk down the hill (Bus #4, 75min., Rs5). Sankhu can also be reached by **bicycle** (the road from Kathmandu is flat and, beyond Boudha, fairly pollution-free) or by **foot,** down from Nagarkot along a northwest trail. It is also possible to walk between Sankhu and Changu Narayan in the dry season. A couple of **cold stores** are along the way.

■ Dakshinkali दक्षिण काली

While its open-air shrine is unimpressive by itself, the massive sacrificial scene that Dakshinkali hosts Tuesday and Saturday mornings is truly spectacular. For those who can stomach the slaughter, this temple to the Dakshin form of the mother-goddess Durga is one of the valley's most memorable destinations. Brightly clad women, men with roosters, goats, and sheep stand in a long, slow-moving line to the shrine. At the western end of the compound sits a small black image of Kali perched in victory atop a corpse. King Pratap Malla installed the statue here in the 17th century, purportedly on the orders of the goddess herself, but the site entertained worship to the mother goddess long before that. The small image is hardly visible to tourists, who are allowed only on the walkways above, but the explosion of activity that surrounds the shrine is quite enough to keep you stimulated. Devotees wash their feet and animal offerings (always male, incidentally) in a muddy pool before proceeding to the shrine itself. It is believed that animals killed in sacrifice will enjoy the reward of higher incarnation. Those offered during the eighth and ninth days of the festival of **Dasain**, the October celebration of the triumph of good over evil, are relieved from burdensome animal life altogether and reincarnated as humans. When man and beast reach the image of Kali, the animal's throat is cut, and its blood is used to drench the placated goddess. The animal's head is often given as payment to the butchers. The body is considered *prasad* (blessed) and becomes the main course for a family picnic in the surrounding hills.

Bus #22 from Ratna Park in Kathmandu (every 30min., 2hr., Rs10) heads to Dakshinkali; the journey can also be made with a half-day taxi rental (Rs500). Either way, the winding ride up the hillside through unassuming homes and fields offers with tremendous views of the valley. Stay on the bus past Pharping, past the deceptive Dakshinkali Cold Store, past the "Welcome to Dakshinkali" sign. Wait until the bus turns in to a parking lot filled with about 100 motorcycles and other sundry vehicles. When the beleaguered busload of folks and fowl get off, you know you've arrived. Stands selling snacks, garlands, bangles, and *sindur* line the walkway to the staircase down to the temple, which sits in a valley at the junction of two muddy streams.

■ The Langtang and Helambu Treks

Legend has it that the Langtang Valley was discovered by a lama who stumbled into it while chasing a renegade yak. This story may be true, but another oft-repeated bit of mountain lore—that Annapurna and Everest are Nepal's only real treks—is certainly not. The Langtang trek, the Helambu circuit, and the Gosainkund trek represent some of the best year-round trekking Nepal has to offer. The first expedition to the Langtang region was led by Major H.W. Tilman in 1949; the area was declared Nepal's first Himalayan National Park in 1971. Situated in the central Himalaya, it is the closest national park to Kathmandu, bordering Tibet to the north and east, while its southern border lies 20 mi. to the north of Kathmandu. Whether undertaken separately, or combined to make a lengthier and more challenging route, the experience these treks offer is flexible, diverse, and rich. Moreover, their accessibility from Kathmandu and their multiple permutations make them very convenient.

GETTING THERE

The **bus** from Kathmandu to **Dhunche,** the classic trailhead for Langtang, leaves from the New Bus Park north of Kathmandu (7 and 7:45am, 9hr., Rs100). Tickets go on sale at 8am the day before. The 7am bus continues on to **Syaprubensi** (10hr., Rs135), a day's walk past Dhunche. Starting from Syaprubensi will take a day off your trek but the bus ride there from Dhunche may take a few years off your life. The trip from Kathmandu to Trisuli (4hr.) is on a paved road, but from Trisuli to Dhunche, the road disintegrates into gravel. Past Dhunche, the road to Syaprubensi is often torturous and not always passable, even in a bus. Many trekkers choose to start from Dhunche and depart from Syaprubensi after their trek. On the way back, tickets can be purchased a day in advance from the counter at the Thakali Hotel in Dhunche.

Sundarijal, the starting point for the Helambu trek, is only 10km from Kathmandu. From Ratna Park in Kathmandu, **buses** leave for Sundarijal (every hr. 6am-6:30pm, 1½hr., Rs12). The bus makes frequent stops along the way. No tickets are required. From the bus park in Sundarijal, buses leave for Kathmandu (every hr. 5am-6pm, Rs12). **Taxis** also make the trip from Thamel to Sundarijal; bargain until the driver agrees to a fare of Rs550.

To cross the Ganja La Pass or go through Gosainkund to Thadepati (or vice versa), you will need a guide. **Sections of the Langtang trek can't be undertaken by unguided trekkers.** However, the Helambu circuit, the conventional Langtang trek, and the trek to Gosainkund from Dhunche can be done on your own. If you plan to go guide-less, you will have to spend several days in Kathmandu planning and getting the right equipment. For more information, see **Planning a Trek** (p. 59).

PRACTICAL INFORMATION

Let's Go: India and Nepal is not a detailed trekking guide. Most trekking guidebooks offer extensive information about the Langtang and Helambu regions: look for *Trekking in Nepal* by Stephen Bezruchka and *Trekking in the Nepal Himalaya* by Stan Armington in Kathmandu's new and used bookstores. Detailed **maps,** also available in Kathmandu, are useful supplements to these guides. Austrian Alpine Club maps, available from Pilgrim's Book House, are also helpful. The **KEEP trekkers' log books,** which are separated by region, are the most up-to-date way to get advice about lodging and which guidebook advice to disregard, so as to avoid AMS.

Trekking permits are available for US$5 per week from the Immigration Office in Kathmandu. Park permits (Rs650), which are necessary to enter Langtang National Park, are available across the street from the Immigration Office or at park entrances.

The only places with **electricity** in the Langtang and Helambu regions are Dhunche, Malemchi, and Sundarijal. The only **bank** is in Dhunche; it changes U.S. dollars, but not traveler's checks. Most lodges along the way will accept U.S. dollars. Remember to take small change on the trek, because the **tea houses** won't have change for large denominations. In addition to the **police posts** in Dhunche, Syabru, and Taramarang, **army posts** in the park can be contacted for help. Since the only **medical facility** besides local health posts is the Himalayan Rescue Association facility in Dhunche, it is a good idea to have a first aid kit with you. The trekking season lasts from September to November and February to May. Lodges and other establishments are often closed in December and January.

The price of food and lodging in Langtang National Park is fixed by the park administration (the Helambu region is not part of the park). Park regulations forbid the use of firewood. If you plan to camp out on your own, take a stove and sufficient fuel with you. For more information, see **Responsible Trekking** (p. 63).

THE LANGTANG TREK लाङटान

Because of its physical proximity to both Kathmandu and the Himalaya, the Langtang Trek combines two worlds. The region it traverses is sparsely inhabited but culturally and geographically diverse. The huge fluctuations in altitude within the Langtang region make for a great variety of vegetation. The conventional Langtang trek is comparable in difficulty to the Annapurna trek. Except for the sidetrips around **Kyanjin Gompa,** none of it is over 4000m, and because the ascent to Kyanjin Gompa is gradual, few people have altitude adjustment problems. Unlike the Helambu circuit, the Langtang trek takes you through mountains and glaciers and offers great views of the

NEPAL

Himalaya (except during the monsoon). The Langtang valley is surrounded by peaks such as Dorje Lokpa (6966m), Gang Chhenpo (6388m), Lantang Lirung (7246m), and Naya Kargri (5846m). Langtang village (3429m) has a distinctly Tibetan character.

The trek normally starts at Dhunche (1982m), the headquarters of **Langtang National Park** and a day's bus ride from Kathmandu over a rough road. Information about the park and the trek is available at the park entrance at Dhunche, where your Rs650 park fee will be collected if you haven't already paid it. The classic Langtang trek begins at Dhunche, with nights spent at Thulo Syabu (2120m) or Lama Hotel (2480m), though most people prefer to stay at the **Sunshine Evening View** in Rimche (2250m), then the Ghoda Tabela (3000m), followed by two nights spent acclimating in Langtang Village (3420m), before moving on to Kyangjin (3900m). A safe ascent should take a minimum of six days, averaging five hours of walking per day, with the return trip to Dhunche taking an additional two to four days.

THE HELAMBU TREK हेलम्बु

The Helambu trek is becoming increasingly popular because it's close to Kathmandu, stays below 3500m (no heavy clothing or bulky winter gear), is possible all year, and can be done in a week. The Helambu trek is fairly easy, but it doesn't have the views of the Everest, Annapurna, or Langtang treks (no *yeti* sightings either). But it does give trekkers a glimpse of the village life of the Yolmo and Tamang people, especially during the Tibetan New Year. Part of the trek takes you through the Shivapuri Watershed Reserve, for which you must pay an additional fee. A bus ride (1½hr.) or a shorter taxi ride to **Sundarijal,** gets you to the starting point of the Helambu trek. There are many tea houses open year-round, so you don't need a tent or your own food; heed the low-impact dining guidelines to minimize fuel use. For more information, see **Responsible Trekking** (p. 63).

Starting at Sundarijal (1400m), 21km northeast of Kathmandu, the trek goes through **Pati Bhanjyang** (1170m) and **Khutumsang,** (2470m), begins a clockwise loop at **Thadepati** (3630m), continuing on to **Malemchigaon** (2560m) and **Tarke Gyang** (2480m). From Tarke Gyang, there are two ways to proceed. The **Helambu circuit** proceeds to Taramarang through Kakani, Thimbu, Kiul, and Mahenkal to **Taramarang.** The loop is completed by passing through Batache and Thakani en route to **Pati Bhanjyang** (1770m). From there, you can backtrack for the first time, retracing the first day of your trek, and returning to Kathmandu through Sundarijal in one day. The circuit normally requires six nights, with stays at Pati Bhanjyang on the first and sixth nights. A popular alternative Helambu trek leaves the circuit at **Tarkeghyang** and continues on to **Shermathang** (2600m)—a day's walk. From Shermathang you can catch the gorgeous views going through Malemchi Pul, to reach the Arniko Highway (the road that connects Kathmandu to Tibet) at **Panchkhal.** Here you can find a bus back to Kathmandu. Otherwise, there are lodges where you can spend the night in Melanchi. Few people have problems with **altitude sickness** on the Helambu trek, so unless you choose to go slowly, you should be able to do this alternate route in five or six nights. Other, less common bookends for the circuit include Sankhu, Nagarkot, and Panchkhal.

THE GOSAINKUND TREK गोशाईकूण्ड

A variation of the classic Langtang trek is the trek to **Gosainkund Lake,** which is believed to have been created by Lord Shiva. This lake is holy to both Hindus and Buddhists, attracting pilgrims from all over the Subcontinent. A Hindu pilgrimage here during the festival of Janai Purnima in August was attended by 15,000 pilgrims in 1995. The trek to Gosainkund requires some steep climbing and is more difficult than the Langtang or the Annapurna treks. The trail rises from **Dhunche** (1960m) to **Gosainkund** (4380m) in four days, including a day to acclimate at Sing Gompa (3300m). **AMS** can be a problem here too, so take precautions. For more information, see **Health and Safety** (p. 62).

Dhunche is a day-long bus ride from Kathmandu. The first day's trek, involving steep climbing at times, will take you to **Sing Gompa** at **Chandan Bari** (3300m). The second day should be spent acclimating and exploring the forest. From here you can reach **Laurinbinayak** (3900m), where there is a good view of the Himalaya. **Heavy winter snowfall makes the trip from Sing Gompa to Gosainkund difficult if not impossible.** People have been killed in the snows here, so don't take unnecessary risks. Consider hiring a local guide or a porter. Several **lodges** are open on the trail to Gosainkund, except during the monsoon and the winter.

From Gosainkund, you can either walk back to Dhunche in two days and catch a bus to Kathmandu, or you can walk on to Thadepati to connect the Gosainkund trek with the Helambu trek. The trail from Gosainkund to Thadepati requires some steep climbing in some sections and crosses the 4610m **Lauribina Pass.** This route takes two days; most people stop at **Ghopte** for the night. There are a few lodges between Gosainkund and Thadepati. Here the trail becomes confusing, and a **guide** is very helpful. Even a little snow makes some sections of the trail very risky, if not outright impossible. If you plan to go from Gosainkund to **Thadepati**, it is best to consult a trekking agency in Thamel. You also must take precautions against AMS (see **Health and Safety**, p. 62). **Several people have died on this route, so be particularly cautious.** If you have guides or porters with you while crossing the Lauribina Pass, make sure they, too, are properly clothed and equipped.

From Thadepati, you can continue on with the **Helambu circuit,** making a loop through Melamchighyang. Another option is to walk straight to Sundarijal through Kutumsana and Pati Bhanjyang.

THE GANJA LA PASS

The Langtang and Helambu treks are connected by the Ganja La Pass (5106m), one of the most difficult passes in Nepal. Many trekkers have run into life-threatening situations and some have died trying to cross. Before attempting it, you should prepare for a much more difficult journey than the Helambu and Langtang treks. **A guide is essential.** Even a little snow or bad weather makes the Pass very difficult, if not impossible, and the route is effectively closed from December to March. The pass can be crossed in either direction, from **Kyangjin Gompa** to **Tarkeghyang.** You will have to carry your tents and food for the four-day crossing; you will also have to acclimatize before proceeding. **If you are considering crossing the pass, get in touch with a trekking agency in Kathmandu.** Again, for your sake and theirs, make sure your guides and porters are properly clothed and equipped.

The Western Hills

Modern-day Nepal was conceived in the hills west of Kathmandu, where 250 years ago King Prithvi Narayan Shah of Gorkha had a vision of a unified country. The central Himalaya, dominated by the Macchapuchhre and the Annapurna range, provide a magnificent backdrop, making this part of Nepal one of the country's most popular regions for tourism.

👏 HIGHLIGHTS OF THE WESTERN HILLS

- Nepal's second-most visited city, lakeside **Pokhara** (p. 770) serves as a base for the country's best trekking areas, including the legendary **Annapurna trek** (p. 777).
- Though often used as mere transit hubs, the hill towns of **Tansen** (p. 767) and **Gorkha** (below) offer scenic respite from Nepal's main tourist stream.

NEPAL

■ Gorkha गोर्खा

Perched on a hill facing the stunning mountains, Gorkha was under the control of many small kingdom-states until its favorite son, Prithvi Narayan Shah, direct ancestor to the present King of Nepal, united these kingdoms, eventually giving rise to modern Nepal. In 1744, Prithvi Narayan set off to conquer the Kathmandu Valley; he succeeded in 1768, later adding the eastern Terai to his realm. Prithvi Narayan's mighty soldiers were given the name "Gorkha." Later, all Nepalese soldiers became known as Gorkhas (or Gurkhas), and were recruited by the British as one of the "martial races" with whom they stocked their army. Gorkha preserves its history in the hilltop Gorkha Durbar, the former palace of the Shah dynasty, and in a new museum housed in the 19th-century Tallo Dubar Palace. As the terminus of a paved road to the Kathmandu-Pokhara highway, Gorkha is now the link between many villages and the outside world, and a starting point for treks to Annapurna and Manaslu.

ORIENTATION

Gorkha has evolved into three distinct sections. The newest part of town, only 15 years old, centers down and around the **bus park,** at the end of the paved road. The second part, which dates back about 100 years, winds uphill on a road toward a set of stone steps past three small shrines. The oldest part lies at the end of the stone stairway, at the very top of the hill where the **Gorkha Durbar** stands at attention.

PRACTICAL INFORMATION

Buses: Prithi Rajmarga Bus Syndicate, at the bus park, marked by a red sign. Open daily 5am-6pm. To: **Bhairawa/Sunauli** (7am, 6hr., Rs108); **Birganj** (4 per day, 6:30-11:20am, 6hr., Rs103); **Kathmandu** (8 per day, 6:15am-2:30pm, 6hr., Rs102; 7:30am, Rs66); **Khaireni** (4 per day, 4:10-6pm, Rs22); **Narayanghat** (7 per day, 8:45am-3:40pm, 3hr., Rs54); **Pokhara** (6 and 9:15am, 5hr., Rs60); and **Tandi,** for **Chitwan National Park** (3:10 and 3:40pm, 4hr., Rs44).

Hospital: (tel. 20208). Walk 5min. downhill on the main road from the bus park; pass the police station, take a left at the first paved road, and walk uphill for 5min. The road turns into a dirt road. The **hospital** is yellow with red lines. Outpatient care Su-F 10am-2pm; emergency open 24hr. There are several **medical stores** (marked with a Red Cross sign) along the road to the bus park, including the **Gorkha Medical Center,** across from Hotel Gorkha Prince.

Currency Exchange: Rastriya Banijya Bank (tel. 20155), almost at the end of the older part of town, is the only bank in Gorkha. Walk to the end of the narrow street just below the post office. Exchanges cash and traveler's checks in CDN$, US$, and UK£. Open Su-Th 10:30am-3pm, F 10:30am-12:30pm.

Police: To get to the **police station** (tel. 20199) from the bus park, walk downhill for 5min., turn right at the blue sign down the unpaved road, and take another right; the police station is the white building straight ahead.

Post Office: (tel. 20112). A white-walled, rock, 2-story building at the end of the older section of Gorkha. Walk right through the narrow street, past 3 stone water taps. No *Poste Restante.* Open Su-Th 10am-5pm, F 10am-3pm.

Telephones: Hello Gorkha, 50m on main road from bus park (tel. 20226), has good rates, free callbacks, and—coming soon—**email** service. Open daily 6:30am-8:30pm. **Hotel Gorkha Prince** has free callbacks, too. **Telephone Code:** 064.

ACCOMMODATIONS AND FOOD

Hotel Gorkha Prince (tel. 20131). Walk down from the bus park 100m; the hotel, marked by a red sign board, is on the left. Friendly staff provides spacious rooms around a courtyard, STD/ISD service, a tidy common room with 24hr. Star TV, and a rooftop restaurant. Fans, and extra bed are free. Common squat toilets. Check-out noon. In-season: doubles Rs200-300, with bath Rs300. Off-season: Rs100-200/200.

Hotel Gorkha Bisauni (tel. 20107), down the main road 100m past Hotel Gorkha Prince. Look for the large red sign on the left. Follow the dirt road at the sign around to the hotel. Quiet hillside balconies and brightly tiled bathrooms with hot showers provide comfort and repose. Check-out noon. In-season: doubles with bath Rs400, with seat toilet Rs500, extra bed Rs100. Off-season: discount 25-40%.

Hill Top Restaurant, at the bus park. Sit at an outdoor table under an umbrella, sip beer, and watch the bus park hubbub. Hearty breakfasts Rs50-80; Chinese, Italian, Tibetan, and Indian entrees Rs30-70. Open daily 6:30am-9:30pm.

Gorkha Prince Rooftop Restaurant. The Himalayan view has been known to inspire conquest. Declare war on Chinese veg. chow mein (Rs30), raid Tibetan chicken *thukpa* (Rs50), or pillage *dal bhat tarkari* (Rs70). Continental, Italian, and Indian foes too. Open daily 5:30am-10:30pm.

Fulpati Restaurant, Gurkha Inn, about 120m down the main road from the bus park. Probably the most beautiful garden in Gorkha; watch the sun set on the terrace, or sit in the dining room for good Nepalese, Indian, and Chinese cuisine (Rs20-90). They also serve continental breakfast. Open daily 6:30am-10pm.

SIGHTS

An hour's walk through the older section of Gorkha and up the stone stairway will take you to the **Gorkha Durbar,** where Prithvi Narayan Shah was born in 1722 and crowned in 1742. *(Open daily 6am-6pm.)* After the Gorkhali army set out from Durbar to capture the Kathmandu Valley and eventually unify Nepal, Prithvi Narayan never returned to Gorkha. Instead, he established his capital city in Nuwakot in 1744 before moving it to Kathmandu after his final victory in 1768. The palace is actually thought to have been built eight generations earlier, in 1609.

Gorkha was ignored by the Shah Dynasty until 1958, when King Mahendra, father of the present King Birendra, returned here. In the more than 200 years of royal absence, the same families of Hindu priests had continued to perform religious functions at the temples in the Durbar, and the palace's present priests are direct descendants of those who served during and before Prithvi Narayan's rule. **Cameras and leather articles— that includes belts and shoes—are not allowed inside the palace compound.** There is no repository for these items, so leave them behind in Gorkha. Most of the compound is open to the public, but some parts are restricted to Hindus; ask the policeman on duty where exactly you can wander. The main temple and palace aren't open to the public, but Prithvi Narayan's **throne** can be seen through a tiny window.

The Himalayas dominate the horizon from the palace's vantage point, and you see more of the mountains than you can from Pokhara, but there's an even better view from the antennae-topped hill another half hour along the stone stairway. If there are no clouds, you'll be lucky enough to experience exactly the same view that inspired one farsighted Gorkhali conqueror more than two and a half centuries ago.

A hundred meters uphill from the bus park is a terrace with a sunken pool (the **Rani Pokhari** or "Queen's Pond") and an elevated statue of Prithvi Pati Shah, Prithvi Narayan's father. The three temples on the right of the pond honor Mahadev, Vishnu, and Ganesh. Continuing on the stone road past the temple leads to an open square. On the left is the Bhimsen Mandir temple which draws crowds of pilgrims for the Janai Purnima festival in August. Directly across the square is the brown gateway to the **Tallo Durbar Palace,** built between 1835 and 1839 by King Rajendra in a failed attempt to lure his older son away from Kathmandu and succession to the throne. A museum park honoring Prithvi Narayan is presently under construction, but should be open by early 1999.

▓ Tansen (Palpa) तानसेन

It is hard to believe that such a charmingly beautiful place like Tansen can remain fairly untouched by the traffic between Pokhara and Sunauli. Perched at 1370m in the Mahabarat range, this sleepy town of near-perfect clime, steep cobblestone streets, small storefronts, and delicate architecture sees few Westerners. Beginning its growth under the 16th-century Sen kings, the mighty Kingdom of Palpa is said to have extended from Mustang to the Terai. From its assimilation into the kingdom of

Nepal in the early 19th century until the fall of the Ranas of 1951, Tansen served as an honorable exile for troublesome, power-hungry royal relatives; more recently, foreign-aid organizations have funded a new rash of development-inspired castles on the terraced hillsides. As a result, Tansen is one of Nepal's tidiest and most endearing hill villages. Views of the fields below and the green Chure hills further south are possible at almost any spot in town, creating a sense that one is walking on clouds.

ORIENTATION AND PRACTICAL INFORMATION The **bus park** is just south of Tansen; a walled **Durbar Square** sits roughly in the center of town. The **old bazaar** area, east of the square, is bounded by **Amar Narayan Temple** to the northeast and the large, grassy **Tundikhel** to the southeast. The newer part of town sprawls west of Durbar Sq. Just north of the Square, Tansen's major roads intersect at a chowk marked by the gazebo-esque **Shital Pati**. The paved road running north from here leads to **Srinagar**, a 1500m viewpoint. The road west of the chowk circles the newer part of town, curving south and then east back to the bus park. A steep flagstone road runs east from the chowk and downhill to the temple. Finally, heading south from Shital Pati, **Bank Road** runs along the eastern edge of Durbar Sq.

Just north of the bus park is the oft-closed **tourist information center.** More helpful are the English-speaking proprietors of any of the hotels listed below, who will provide travel information and offer **jeeps** for hire (rides to the top of Srinagar Rs100-125). Most services are found on Bank Rd. **Nepal Bank** (tel. 20130) exchanges traveler's checks (Su-F 10:15am-2pm). Most hotels can provide an accurate and much-needed map of Tansen. Gauri Shankar Guest House (see below) rents **motorbikes** (Rs100 per hr. and Rs500 all day). A counter at the northeast corner of the bus park sells **bus** tickets to **Butwal** (every 30min., 2hr., Rs24), **Pokhara** (6 and 9am, 6hr., Rs70), and **Kathmandu** (day bus 6am, 9hr., Rs135; night bus 5:30pm, 11hr., Rs170). **Sajha** buses also do the 'Du (6:15am, Rs131). The ticket office is southwest of the telegraph office. Nearby, **Sajha Swasta Sewa pharmacy** (tel. 20464) has a pharmacist on call 24hr. (Open daily 8am-7pm.) There is a district hospital just west of Tansen, but the **United Mission to Nepal Hospital** (tel. 20111), a short walk northeast of town, has a better reputation (**ambulance** tel. 20600). There is a **police** box (tel. 20255) at the western edge of the bus park. The **post office** is at the southern end of Bank Rd. (open Su-Th 10am-5pm, F 10am-1pm). Walk west from the **post office,** take the first right continuing a up the dirt lane, and turn right; the gated **telegraph office** at the end of the lane has the cheapest of Tansen's **STD/ISD/fax** services, and offers free call-backs (open daily 7am-7pm). **Telephone Code:** 075.

ACCOMMODATIONS AND FOOD Like the town itself, Tansen's comfortable lodges wait patiently for tourists to discover them. **Gauri Shankar Guest House,** Silkhan Tole (tel. 20150), is one of the best deals. Walk north from the bus park and turn left, continuing past the university campus (10min.); Gauri Shankar is on the right. The bright rooms are clean and conscientiously maintained; baths have hot water and toilet paper. (Singles Rs125, with bath, Rs250; doubles Rs175/350-400; triples Rs250/400.) The attached restaurant serves Nepali, Indian, Chinese, and some Continental items (Rs50-100), and is open daily 7am-10pm. **Hotel the White Lake** (tel. 20291; fax 20467) offers fancier rooms with carpeting, fans, and thick beds. All rooms have attached baths with seat toilets, towels, and toilet paper. (Singles US$12; doubles US$16. Student discount 25%. If you can get the Nepali rate of Rs400/600, this becomes an even better deal.) The adjacent restaurant serves one of the largest menus in town, with set breakfasts (Rs50-100), pizzas (Rs75-110), and Continental meat dishes (Rs100-140) supplementing the usual fare (open daily 7am-10pm). White Lake also runs a more basic facility (doubles with common bath Rs150) just northwest of town; it is often occupied by Peace Corps volunteers, so inquire at the hotel. **Hotel the Bajra,** just north of the bus park, is a bit older, but its linoleum-floored rooms with large windows are clean, cheap, with attached baths. Hot water buckets and a restaurant round out the pretty picture. (Dorm beds Rs50; singles, Rs200; doubles Rs250-320.)

NEPAL

Tansen's restaurant scene is significantly more dismal. Despite rumors of greater things in store, the only present option beside the hotels and *dal bhat* diners (the cleanliness of the latter appears to vary in direct proportion to their distance from the bus park) is the very new **Naglo West Restaurant** (tel. 20184), located in Shital Pati, which offers goodies from their bakery along with a fairly-priced but limited menu (Rs35-8) that includes burgers and something intriguingly called "duck chilly." In addition to the hotels above, **Hotel Srinagar** (tel. 20045; fax 20467), northwest of town, serves the standard tourist fare (Rs30-180). Meals are a little more expensive here, but on a clear day it's money well spent: the patio dining area, perched on the ridge just west of Srinagar peak, allows excellent views of himals to the north and ter-raced hills to the south (open daily 7am-8:30pm).

SIGHTS Tansen is billed as a "miniature Kathmandu" and indeed there is something familiar about the temple architecture and building style here. Located at its physical and communal center is Tansen's **Durbar Square,** entered from Shital Pati through **Baggi Dhoka,** a large whitewashed gate built by Palpa's first and most prolific exile, Khadga Shumshere, who came here in 1891. Said to be the largest gate in Nepal, it was reputedly built to be tall enough that Shumshere wouldn't have to dismount his elephant in order to enter it. Shumshere also erected the square's first palace, but the present blue-and-pumpkin-colored gingerbread structure was built by General Pratap Shumshere in 1927. The sixty-five room **Tansen Durbar** presently houses Palpa's dis-trict secretariat. Just northwest of the palace is the **Bhagwati Temple** (not to be con-fused with the heinously modern **Bal Mandir,** which has laid siege to the plot of ground directly north of the palace), which commemorates an 1815 victory over the British. The temple is the center of Tansen's largest festival, **Bhagwati Jatra,** held in late August. An all-night celebration precedes the festival; in the morning, a chariot holding an image of Bhagwati is led through town, reminding everyone that even imperial powers don't win all the time.

Exiting Durbar Sq. through Baggi Dhoka, turn right and follow a steep flagstone lane down through the old bazaar to one of Tansen's oldest structures, the **Amar Narayan Temple.** After annexing the city in 1804, Amar Singh Thapa imported Newari craftsmen and artisans and began to craft Tansen in the capital's image. The grandest of his accomplishments, the Amar Narayan complex encloses an image of Vishnu; it is surrounded by the one-meter-wide **Great Wall of Palpa** (only slightly less famous than its Chinese counterpart), a water tank with spouts fed by a natural spring, and a garden that receives a daily migration of bats that outnumbers even the crowds that visit for morning and evening worship. A few minutes south of Amar Narayan, the **Tundikhel** marks the southeast edge of town. Though this large plot of grass is in constant and spirited use, the rose-filled **Birendra Park** that sits nearby suf-fers the sense of enclosure that afflicts most of Nepal's "parks."

Several less-conspicuous temples sit around town—ask for a map at your hotel or (more enjoyably) stumble upon them while wandering around. Of special note are the **Mahachaitya Bihar** and the **Ganesh Temple,** which sit across from each other about five minutes' walk west of Shital Pati.

The road running directly north of Shital Pati leads to another Ganesh temple, set into the hillside about a 15-minute walk north of town. A short–but-steep flagstone path leads to the small red and white temple, which affords good views of the city below. (The minarets of Tansen's **Jama Masjid** are visible just south of the temple.) From the Ganesh temple, the flagstone path continues up the hill to **Srinagar,** Tansen's vigorously promoted viewpoint. The hilltop is a 15-minute walk past the temple, an easier 20-minute walk along the ridge from Hotel Srinagar, northwest of town, or a 10-minute ride up the road. Apart from a few ruins and a campsite, the pleasant hilltop park commands one of the longest mountain views in Nepal, from India's peaks to those of Tibet, including the Dhaulagiri range, Annapurna's Maccha-puchre, and Ganesh Himalt. The park gets its biggest workout on Saturdays when Tansen denizens make the trek up to enjoy a bit of familial quality-time. Sunrises and sunsets during the week are usually visited by a small handful of people.

NEPAL

Shopping is certainly not the reason to visit Tansen, but a few locally produced goods deserve special mention. Palpa's Newari craftsmen employ the lost wax method in their remarkable metalworks; the *Palpali kuruwa*, a bronze water jar, is well-known. *Palpali Dhaka*, woven by women in Tansen and the surrounding hills, is equally noteworthy; several handicraft associations in town (especially along Bank Rd.) sell shawls, *topis* (hats), and handbags produced from this cloth.

■ Pokhara पोखरा

Pokhara, Nepal's biggest tourist destination outside the Kathmandu Valley, is sunk in a subtropical valley surrounded by lofty peaks which yield some of the world's most staggering vistas. Nowhere else in Nepal is there such an abrupt change in altitude—from Pokhara to the tip of Annapurna I (the world's 10th highest mountain), a horizontal distance of only 48km, the land rises up to nearly 7200m. The sky, cracked into white fragments in the north, is enough to make travelers blink a few times and question their depth perception. Pokhara's name derives from the Nepali word for pond (*pokhari*); Pokhara Valley, like Kathmandu Valley, once collected the region's rain. Today, only three small lakes—Phewa, Begnas, and Rupa—remain.

The Gurungs, the true "natives" of the region, lived on the hilltops surrounding the valley. Only when Newari traders settled in Pokhara, trafficking salt between Kathmandu, Bandipur, and Dhankuta, did a city begin to rise on the banks of the Seti (Milk) River. These traders built the Bindyabasini Temple in the 16th century, and it's by far the oldest structure in Pokhara.

Development began with the construction of two highways in the 1970s—one connecting Pokhara to Kathmandu, the other linking it to India. Pokhara remained largely hidden from outsiders until first foreigners and then Nepalis rolled in on the new highways. Word of the "discovery" reached Kathmandu and spread quickly. Now rooftop restaurants and souvenir shops edge the banks of Phewa Tal, Nepal's second-largest lake, and colored signs compete with the mountains for attention. An important commercial and administrative center, Pokhara is the starting point for some of Nepal's most popular treks and is quickly becoming the heart of river rafting in Nepal. In season the tourist section is buzzing with activity, but it is also worth a visit off season (May-Sept.), when Pokhara seems more like a small town. It is easy to recuperate from traveling trauma in this cafe atmosphere where everyone is recognizable after a couple of days.

ORIENTATION

Phewa Tal (the lake) and **Pardi** (the dam) are the two major points of orientation for the small Pokhara. Just about all travelers' needs can be met in **Lakeside (Baidam)** or **Damside (Pardi)**. The residential section of town is higher up and away from the lake. The **Siddhartha Highway,** linking Pokhara to India, forms a great north-south arc through the city. It meets the **Prithvi Highway** from Kathmandu at **Prithvi Chowk,** the city center, where you'll also find the **bus station.** Farther north, the main road comes to the **Mahendra Pul** area, the historical heart of the city and the center of the **Pokhara Bazaar.**

Lakeside now overshadows **Damside** both in size and popularity. Lakeside's two main sections extend south from the campground to the Hotel Hungry-Eye, and east from the Royal Palace to Fish Tail Lodge—it's a 20-minute walk from one end to the other. Damside reaches south from the intersection with the main Lakeside thoroughfare along **Pardi Road.** The **maps** posted at some of Pokhara's *chowks* and intersections make navigation a little easier.

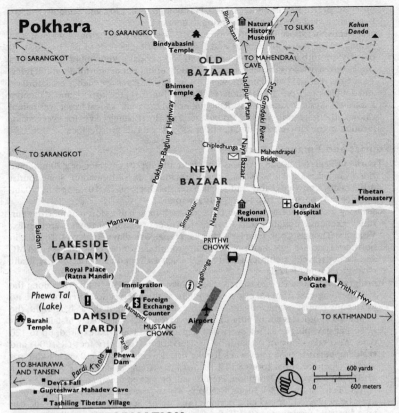

Pokhara

TO SARANGKOT

Bindyabasini
Temple

OLD
BAZAAR

TO SARANGKOT

TO SILKIS

Kahun
Danda

Natural
History
Museum

TO MAHENDRA
CAVE

Bhim Bazaar

Bhimsen
Temple

Nadipur Patan

Seti Gandaki River

TO SARANGKOT

Chipledhunga

NEW
BAZAAR

Naya Bazaar

Mahendrapul
Bridge

Manswara

Simalchaur

New Proy

Regional
Museum

Gandaki
Hospital

Tibetan
Monastery

Baidam

LAKESIDE
(BAIDAM)

Royal Palace
(Ratna Mandir)

Immigration

Foreign
Exchange
Counter

PRITHVI
CHOWK

Naghunga

Ratnapur

Pokhara
Gate

Prithvi Hwy.

Phewa Tal
(Lake)

Barahi
Temple

DAMSIDE
(PARDI)

MUSTANG
CHOWK

Airport

TO KATHMANDU

Pardi

Pardi Khola

Phewa
Dam

TO BHAIRAWA
AND TANSEN

Devi's Fall
Gupteshwar Mahadev Cave

Tashiling Tibetan Village

N

0   600 yards
0   600 meters

PRACTICAL INFORMATION

Transportation

Airport: The **airport** is between the bus park and the section of the lake where subtropical tourist jungles grow. Taxi fares from the airport to Lakeside are fixed
(Rs80-100), but rides to the airport cost Rs40-50, and bargaining is expected. The
airport has minimal facilities. Lumbini Air, Necon Air, Nepal Airways, and RNAC
have daily flights. To: **Kathmandu** (10 per day, 8:30am-3:15pm, US$61); **Jomsom**
(3 per day, 6:30 and 7:50am, US$50-55); **Manang** (in-season: 2 per week, 7:30am,
US$50). Flights are added or canceled according to demand.

Buses: The **bus park** is a soup of mud, garbage, fauna, and recycled water from the
Bay of Bengal. From the bus park, it's a 20-25min. bike ride to the city (taxi Rs60-
100). There are separate offices for day and night buses; the **day bus office** (tel.
20272) is in the center of the muck, consisting of a blue window and a red window. Open daily 5am-6:30pm. The **night bus office,** facing into the bus park, is on
the right and up a set of stairs under a white sign with a flag on it. Open daily
8:30am-8:30pm. **Day buses** to: **Birganj** (5 per day, 5:40-10:20am, 8hr., Rs120);
Gorkha (7 and 9am, 4hr., Rs60); **Kathmandu** (8 per day, 5:15-11:25am, 8hr.,
Rs100); **Narayanghat** (11 per day, 9:50am-2:30pm, 5hr., Rs65); **Sunauli/Bhairawa**
(7 per day, 5-9:25am, 8hr., Rs126); **Tansen** (7am, 7hr., Rs70). **Night buses** to: **Birganj** (6:30 and 7:30pm, 8hr., Rs140); **Butwal** (7pm, 8hr., Rs102); **Kathmandu** (10
per night, 6:30-8:45pm, 8hr., Rs113); **Narayanghat** (5pm, 5hr., Rs75); **Sunauli/
Bhairawa** (6, 7:45, and 8pm, 8½hr., Rs150). The travel agencies at Lakeside/Dam-
side operate pricier and more comfortable coaches from hotels. From 6 to 10am,

buses depart for **Kathmandu** (Rs300), **Narayanghat** (Rs170), and **Sunauli** (Rs250). Buses are added or canceled according to demand.

Local Transportation: Bikes are probably the best way to get around when it isn't raining. Many shops in Lakeside and Damside rent bikes (Rs8-15 per hr., Rs30-50 per day; motorbikes Rs150 per hr., Rs350-500 per day). Remember that Pokhara slopes down towards the lake, making for ugly uphill but delightful downhill rides. **Taxi** fares rise and bargaining power falls in season. Fares are higher on Saturdays and double after 7pm. Destinations such as the bus park, the airport, and Mahendra Pul from Lakeside/Damside cost Rs60 full or Rs12 shared. A **local bus** leaves Bahrai Chowk, the huge tree next to Moondance and Hotel Hungry-Eye, for every major location in the city (every 30min., under Rs5). Ask locals for specifics.

Tourist and Financial Services

Tourist Office: (tel. 20028). A short walk from the airport entrance or a 20min. bike ride from Lakeside. Free Pokhara maps, brochures, and information. Some tourist officers are knowledgeable and speak English. Open Su-Th 10am-5pm, F 10am-3pm; Nov.-Feb.: Su-Th 10am-4pm, F 10am-3pm.

Currency Exchange: Lakeside and Damside each have half a dozen authorized currency exchange counters and a bank. Most accept major currencies and AmEx, Visa, and Thomas Cook traveler's checks. **Nepal Grindlays Bank** (tel. 20102), in northern Lakeside, just south of the campground. Advances cash on Visa and MC and cashes traveler's checks. Open Su-F 9:45am-4:15pm; in summer they typically close at 1:15pm on Fridays.

Immigration Office: (tel. 21167). A 20min. bike ride or Rs30-40 taxi ride along the road heading east from Lakeside. Go straight at the intersection after there are no longer any tourist establishments. At the next intersection, make a sharp right; the immigration office is about 50m to the left. Extends visas in 30-day installments at US$1 per day, plus US$1 for every day elapsed since your visa expired, up to 120 days. Also takes care of Annapurna Conservation Area entry fees (Rs1000) and **trekking permits** (US$5 per week for the first 4 weeks and US$10 each additional week). Open for applications Su-Th 10am-1pm, F 10am-noon; Nov. 17-Feb. 13: Su-Th 10am-12:30pm, F 10am-noon. Permits can be picked up Su-Th 4-5pm, F 2-3pm; Nov.17-Feb.13: Su-Th 3-4:30pm, F 2-3pm. A passport and 2 passport-size photos must be deposited for trekking permit applications. Several shops in Lakeside can take "instant" visa photos (Rs125 for 4 photos). A photo booth outside the immigration office offers similar prices.

Budget Travel: Local **trekking agencies** can arrange **visa extensions** (service charge Rs100) and **trekking permits** (service charge Rs200). For same-day service go to the agencies before 9am. Some agencies will attempt to "expedite" the process; for Rs250-350 you might succeed in procuring a permit by noon.

Trekking Information: Annapurna Conservation Area Project (ACAP) (tel. 21102), located in the Natural History Museum on the Prithvi Varayan Campus in north Pokhara, is the most authoritative source of information on treks in the Annapurna region. Provides free and impartial information on ACAP and general advice on trekking. Cool maps and books for sale and several free pamphlets. Open Su-F 9am-12:30pm and 1:30-5pm.

Local Services

Luggage Storage: Most hotels and lodges offer luggage storage for Rs5-10 and safe box storage free of charge. The **Butterfly Lodge** (see below) will store luggage for free, even in the tourist season.

Market: The Lakeside/Damside area offers clothes, trekking equipment, pharmaceuticals, and souvenirs. Locals shop at the less expensive **Mahendra Pul** area.

Bookstore: Lakeside bookshops differ in size but not much in price. Most will let you trade books as well.

Emergency and Communications

Pharmacy: The half-dozen small pharmacies in Lakeside and Damside carry first-aid material for trekking; many have doctors on call.

Hospital: Most hotels and lodges can recommend a doctor or clinic. **Barahi Medical Hall** (tel. 22862), in the center of Lakeside, has a doctor in-season 4-6pm; he stays on call off-season. Open daily 7am-9pm. **Manish Medical Hall** (tel. 25650), damside, a few doors down from the Hotel Salinas, has Dr. Prakash Mishra (in-season W-M 4-5pm); he's on call the rest of the time. Open daily 7am-9:30pm. **Gandaki Hospital** (tel. 20066), a 15min., Rs100 taxi ride from Lakeside, has Western doctors.

Police: The **police station** (tel. 21087) is a 10min. bike ride from the center of Lakeside. After Hotel Kantipur, take a right at the blue sign board. The station is the white building about 100m down the unpaved road. The small **police post** at the entrance of the camping grounds at the end of Lakeside is open 24hr. in season. There is also a "Tourist Police" booth located in front of Moondance open 24hr.

Post Office: The **main post office** (tel. 22014) is on the main street in Mahendra Pul, a 40min. bike ride or a Rs50-60 taxi ride from Lakeside/Damside. Ask locals for directions to this single-story, white and red house marked Western Regional Postal Directorate. *Poste Restante* available. One-room post office at the beginning of Lakeside offers registered mail services. Come out of Lakeside, make a left turn at the first major intersection (Hotel Saino sign), and walk 200m to the stone house marked Pardi Bandh Area Post Office. Both offices open Su-Th 10am-5pm, F 10am-3pm; registered mail Su-Th 10am-2:30pm, F 10am-12:30pm. Most **bookstores** in Lakeside and Damside sell stamps and post letters.

Telephones: Just about every hotel and lodge has international calling facilities; Lakeside and Damside teem with **"communication" shops,** many which double as travel agents, that charge less. Prices are proportional to the facility's fanciness. There are many places to get plugged in. Sending **email** costs Rs15-30 per kilobyte. **Padma Shree Tours** (tel 28105) in central Lakeside offers the cheapest rates. Most facilities are open 8am-11pm. **Telephone Code:** 061.

ACCOMMODATIONS

Recent development has transformed Lakeside into a haven for travel agents, bookstores, money changers, souvenir stores, cool restaurants, and entertainment—not to mention the glorious lake. Damside, a half-hour walk away, is quieter, smaller, and less of a tourist jungle. In season, this may be a welcome escape from the throngs of trekkers and tourists, but off season Lakeside mellows out and Damside dries up.

When you get off the bus or come out at the airport, you will undoubtedly be the object of a bidding competition between young men peddling hotels. Ignore them, get into a cab, and go toward Damside or Lakeside. All hotels listed have luggage storage, laundry service, fans, 24hr. hot and cold water, STD/ISD, and mosquito coils on request. Attached bath all are with seat toilets, common baths have seat toilets. Check-out noon. Expect off-season discounts of up to 50%.

Lakeside

Pushpa Guest House (tel. 20332), not to be confused with the "Pushkar," behind Once Upon a Time at the center of Lakeside. This yellow-painted establishment is well-furnished—carpets, closets, window screens, and mirrors. Clean toilets and the not-on-the-street-but-very-close location makes this guest house a good value for money. Singles Rs200, with bath Rs300; doubles Rs250/400; triples Rs300/500.

Butterfly Lodge (tel. 22892). Heading north away from Damside, turn right at Pyramid Restaurant, then continue 100m on the right. Quiet garden lodge has lots of open space. The breeze breathes right into the rooms. Pristine rooftop views of the lake and mountains. Kitchen and laundry area. Ask for student and long-term discounts. Doubles Rs150, with bath Rs200-300; triples with bath Rs500.

Hotel Avocado (tel. 23617), also behind Once Upon a Time. In the center of Lakeside, but away from the noisy street. The views from the rooftop make for a great photo shoot. Friendly staff and well-furnished rooms. Doubles Rs200, with bath Rs250, with good views Rs500.

Hotel the Trans Himalaya (tel. 20917), on the same road as the Butterfly Lodge, but closer to the main street. Breezy courtyard construction makes the Trans Himalaya a haven for the heat-craven. Rooms are carpeted and spacious. The common squat toilet is spotless, and the shower has strong water pressure. Singles Rs200, with bath Rs400; doubles Rs300/500; triples with bath Rs600.

Alka Guest House (tel. 23357), in the center of Lakeside. Admire Alka's aesthetics: bright and clean building with fancy wooden handrails and marbled features. STD/ISD phones in the rooms, and internet too (email: Rs25/kb and Rs10 to get online). Walk up to the 3rd floor terrace for terrific views. No smoking. Foreigners must pay in "convertible currency." Singles US$5, with bath US$8; doubles US$8/12, extra bed US$4. Accepts Visa, MC.

Camping Ground (tel. 21688). At the north end of Lakeside, make a left turn and proceed 50m. It's on the right, past the police outpost. Bordering the lake, and with unobstructed mountain views, Pokhara's only campground is ideal in dry weather, but sloppy during the monsoon. Squat toilets. Bring a flashlight. Checkout 6pm. Hot showers Rs50, cold showers Rs30. Tents Rs40.

Damside

Hotel Salinas (tel. 24031), on the main road of Damside. Serene lodgings with a great view, green plants, and generous furnishings make this guest house a good value. Singles with bath US$4; doubles US$3, with bath US$8.

Hotel Himali (tel 25385), on the main road of Damside across from Hotel Salinas. A little older than Hotel Salinas, but rooms are still in good shape and well-kept. What they lack in great views, they make up for in price. Singles Rs150, with bath Rs200; doubles Rs180/250; extra bed Rs50.

Hotel Super Lodge (tel. 21861), left off the main road in Damside. The name says it all; nine super, blue rooms. Singles Rs150, with bath Rs250; doubles Rs300.

Hotel Cosmos (tel. 21964), behind the main road in Damside. If you're hell-bent on being on the water, this small hotel is a good option if you can get one of the 3 rooms with a view. Not so posh as the Hotel Mona Lisa next door, but at half the price, you'll still smile. All rooms with attached bath. In-season: singles US$10; doubles US$15. Off-season: discount 30-40%.

FOOD

In Lake/Damside, you are captive to the vices of the tourist food trade—but with German cinnamon buns, Swiss chocolate, garlic pizza, and steak *au poivre*, who's the spoilsport whining for *dal bhat*? If local cuisine is your bag, a few restaurants will scare up a mean lentil *thali*. **Bars** are prominent along the main drags and they have successfully cross-bred with international restaurants, engendering a fusion of tasty victuals, laid-back lounging, and people- and nature-gazing. **Musical entertainment** has also entered the fray, from choreographed Nepali dancers to quasi-karaoke Indian pop bands; there's even a piano bar. Food prices remain high all year, and it is easy to while away the hours in the numerous relaxing restaurants sucking down coffee *lassis* (Rs50), which indeed give a jolt when the bill arrives.

Once Upon A Time (tel. 22240), central Lakeside. Among the most popular restaurants in Lakeside. Sit upstairs under the bamboo hut and among bamboo furniture, or sit downstairs behind bamboo curtains. Entrees Rs75-110; beer Rs95; cocktails Rs85-150. Happy hour (5-8pm) includes yummy prawn chips with each beer order. Open daily 8:30am-10pm.

Maya Pub, central Lakeside. Tourists flock here, packing it to capacity even during low season. They play your requests—loudly—and serve 2-for-1 cocktails during Happy Hour (5-9pm). Continental dishes are good, but tasty Mexican food is better. Beer Rs90-95, cocktails Rs125. Open daily 7am-10pm.

Moondance, central Lakeside, next to Hotel Hungry-Eye. Named for the Van Morrison song, Moondance is reputed to play the best and most diverse music in Lakeside—they'll honor your requests. The setting is comfortable, dim, and *au naturel,* from the hay roof to the decorative yak tails. Scrabble, chess, and backgammon in the afternoons. Concoct your own pizza or take on an enchilada. Most entrees Rs85-160, most side dishes Rs45-70. Beer available. Open daily 8am-11pm.

Boomerang, central Lakeside. Probably the premier restaurant in Lakeside, Boomerang enhances its varied main courses with an attached German bakery (great for breakfast) and prime lakefront seating in private pagodas from where one can watch the water buffalo play in the lake. Down *mousaka* (Rs95), chicken tacos (Rs120), and grilled lake fish (Rs180). Open daily 7am-10pm.

Nirula's (tel. 20779), central Lakeside; look for the sign. This is *the* "fast food" joint in Lakeside—most dishes are ready in less than 10min. Serving pizzas (Rs70-100), burgers (Rs55-100), foot-long sandwiches, sundaes, and 21 flavors of ice cream, this Indian chain is great for a cheap bite. Open daily 10am-10pm.

Rodee Restaurant (tel. 21706), on the main road in Damside. Continental, Italian, Mexican, Chinese, and large Indian and Japanese selections. Off-season: chicken *cordon bleu* Rs130, chicken enchiladas Rs95, tandoori veg. *kofta* curry Rs85. In-season: prices increase up to 30%. Open daily 6:15am-10pm.

SIGHTS

Most sight-seeing in Pokhara is reserved for the mountains. The city itself has very few cultural attractions; it's not Kathmandu, and it doesn't try to be. A large portion of the old bazaar of Pokhara burned down in 1949 in a fire that spread from a *puja* at Bindyabasini Temple, so most of the architecture is very recent. Secluded on an island right in the middle of the lake is the **Barahi Temple**—hire one of the colorful boats from Barahi Ghat near central lakeside to get there. *(Rs120 for the first hour, Rs150 for 2hr., Rs200 for 4hr; with guide Rs150 per hr., Rs250 for 2hr.; sailboat Rs250 per hr.)* Across the lake, the Peace Pagoda (currently under construction) is perched atop the hill. Row to the large pink Hotel Fewa and take the trail behind it to the top (a 1hr. hike). Of course, just renting a boat for a couple of hours to paddle to the middle of the lake for a refreshing swim can be the highlight of a hot day. The water is cleaner further from the buffalo on the shore, and it is also easier to escape inquisitive eyes.

The lake's water flows out at the south end into the Pardi Khola, a stream which suddenly shoots down into a hole at **Devi's Fall,** 1km out of Pokhara down the road toward the Indian border. Devi's Fall is a 25min. bike or a Rs100 round-trip taxi ride from Lakeside. *(Open daily 9am-6pm. Admission Rs5.)* Rainbows are guaranteed if the sun is shining, since a powerful mist comes jumping out of the hole. Around to the left and behind the falls, there is a pool suitable for pre-monsoon swimming. Women beware, however, because groups of young men will insist on following. Across the road, the refugees at the **Tashling Tibetan Village** sell their usual array of jewelry and souvenirs. Farther into the village there is a shed where wool is dyed and spun for carpets, as well as a Tibetan Children's Village for orphaned Tibetan children in Nepal. Also across the street from Devi's Fall is the **Gupteshwor Mahadev Cave.** *(Cave open daily 6am-6pm. No photos.)* Only recently discovered in 1992 (reportedly first seen in a vision), this cave houses many ancient carvings and extends 3km into the earth. It takes 8-10 hours to explore the entire cave, and this is only possible in March. It is filled with water the rest of the year, but it's still worth the Rs20 to walk down to the mouth of the cave, in which a large *lingam* stands under an umbrella of cobra heads. The statue is old, the cobras not. Walk down behind the shrine and check out the large carved snake head above the mouth of the cave.

To the right on the road between Prithvi Chowk and Mahendra Pul is the farmhouse-like **Regional Museum** (tel. 20413), with an unimpressive collection of photographs, old weapons, and Nepali ornaments. *(Open M-Th 10am-5pm, F 10am-3pm;. Admission Rs5, camera fee Rs10.)* From Lakeside, take a taxi (Rs60) or a bicycle (35min.). If you follow the road to the museum, turn right at Mahendrapul Bridge, and cross the Seti Gandaki River, you'll reach the hilltop **Tibetan Monastery,** which has good views of the valley. Below the bridge, the river rushes through the 46m-deep Seti gorge. The monastery is a 1hr. bike ride and a Rs80 one-way taxi ride from Lakeside; ask for it by its Tibetan name, "Madepani Gompa."

The **Natural History Museum,** at the north end of Pokhara on the Prithvi Narayan Campus, has drawers and drawers full of all kinds of bugs, especially butterflies—the best collection anywhere of Nepal's *lepidoptera*. *(Open Su-F 10am-12:30pm,1:30-5pm; Sept.-Feb. 10am-12:30pm and 1:30-4pm. Free.)* A park, at the north end of town on the highway to Baglung, has a long flight of steps leading up to **Bindyabasini Temple,** built in the 16th century by Newari traders just settled in the Pokhara Valley. The fire that engulfed Pokhara in 1949 ignited here. The main shrine, dedicated to Kali, is accompanied by a new Shiva temple. The small Buddhist monastery at the base of the steps hints at the Nepali synthesis between Buddhism and Hinduism. Taxis charge Rs90 from Lakeside; cycling requires an hour of steady uphill pedaling.

North of Pokhara, outside city limits, is a cave called **Mahendra Gupha** *(Admission Rs10)*. Several tunnels inside the cave make for a half-hour of happy exploration; some parts of the cave have electricity, but take a flashlight anyway. Take a taxi (Rs150), or make the trip on a cycle.

Taxis will take you on a three-hour tour of all sights within Pokhara for Rs450-650. Contact any travel agent or inquire with a taxi operator.

ENTERTAINMENT

Entertainment in Pokhara primarily consists of eating, drinking, listening to music, and taking in the views in Lakeside restaurants. Engulfing elaborate entrees is entertainment in its own right after the monotony of simple trekking foods. Many restaurants feature Nepali cultural shows or movies during the evenings. Look for announcements posted on their signboards daily.

Pokhara has a few good places to hear music, imbibe, and dance. **Club Amsterdam** in central Lakeside has live music in the evenings, food, booze, a pool table, and an outdoor sitting area. (Open daily noon to 11pm or later if the crowd is jumpin'.)

For those wishing to catch a glimpse of Pokhara's hippie days or just a piece of small town USA that re-emerged in Pokhara, head to **Old Blue's Night Pub,** at the center of Lakeside. Pool tables, dart boards, TV sports, wall-space shared by Marilyn Monroe, U2, Jimi Hendrix, and the Beatles, and a yak head on a wall make for a very un-Nepali place to meet young Nepalis and tourists. Old Blue serves only beverages. (Soft drinks Rs15-25, beer Rs90-100. Open in season only.)

The Joker Dance Place, a 100m walk from the right turn at Nirula's, is the only place where you can bust a move amid the cool disco lights, a slightly sunken dance floor, and a bar. Several restaurants across the lake (catch a boat there and back for Rs40-70) also have **special parties,** advertised around town on hard-to-miss signs. Most begin around 10pm and rage until the wee hours of the morning.

RAFTING AND TREKKING

More than 40 travel agencies are based in Lakeside and Damside, many of which are associated with hotels and lodges. Agents usually specialize in rafting or trekking. Most accept major credit cards.

The established rafting companies include **Himalayan Encounters, Ultimate Descents,** north of Hotel Hungry-Eye in Lakeside, **Equator Expeditions,** Lakeside (open daily 9am-8pm), and **Sisne Rover Trekking** (tel. 20893; open daily 8am-8pm), Lakeside. The first two are only open Sept.-May. All three operate in the US$35-60 per person per day price range. Rates usually include river and camping equipment rental, guides, instruction, food, and transportation. A rafting permit fee (Rs80 for a 2-day trip) may be extra, but the company will pay it. Some companies, including Ultimate Descents, and Equator Expeditions, provide one or two safety kayakers who accompany every trip. Other companies have cheaper packages; check to find out their reputations before signing up. Routes on the challenging **Kaligandaki** (Class 4) and manic **Marsyangdi** (Class 5) only run in season—monsoon rains make them unmanageable. The **Seti Khola** and **Trisuli** are more fun during the high water levels of June to August (Class 3-4). Some companies combine a Trisuli trip to **Chitwan National Park** with excursions within the park.

Trekking agencies provide everything from equipment rental to individual guides to fully planned treks. Expect to pay US$12-15 per day for an English-speaking guide. Reputable agents include Equator Expeditions, Sisne Rover, the Korean-managed **Sa-Rang San Tours** (tel. 23513; fax 21595; open daily 8am-8pm), low Lakeside, and **Pokhara Tours and Travels,** near the airport. For suggested short and longer treks, see **The Annapurna Trek** (p. 777). **The Annapurna Conservation Area Project,** at the Natural History Museum in the north side of town, has an information center with literature on ecotourism. It's a Rs90 taxi ride or an hour uphill on a bike—stick to the road past Mahendra Pul until the Prithvi Narayan Campus sign appears on the right.

■ Near Pokhara

Phewa, Begnas, and **Rupa Lakes** were all part of the body of water that once filled the Pokhara Valley. Phewa is garlanded by the tourism-created Lakeside, but Begnas and Rupa remain untouched. Begnas Lake, 15km from Mahendra Pul, is serviced by Tal buses (every hr. 7am-6pm, 1hr., Rs7). The two-and-a-half hour cycle to Begnas will certainly loosen up your legs before the trek. Taxis charge Rs500-600 round-trip and will wait for your return. By renting a boat (Rs200 per hr.) and rowing to the other end of Begnas, one can then pick up the trail Rupa, a 20-minute hike over a mountain shoulder from Begnas.

Sarangkot (1592m) is one of the best places to view the mountains around Pokhara and the lakes below. The three-hour walk to Sarangkot is beautiful when there are clear views of Phewa Lake. Stay over in a tea house to witness the sunrise on the mountains. If you're feeling lazy, take a cab there for Rs500-600 round-trip (plus Rs100 per hr. waiting time) and walk up another half hour.

■ The Annapurna Trek अन्नपूर्ण

The Annapurna trek is by far the most popular in Nepal, and many consider it to be one of the most rewarding treks in the world. During trekking season (Mar.-May and late Sept.-Nov.), a United Nations of adventurers passes through the trekking routes and tea houses along the way, soaking up the scenery of the magnificent Himalaya, the "abode of the Gods." The terrain ranges from magnificent snow-covered peaks to lush valleys, barren land to river-fed tropical lowlands. Even during the snow-clad winter and monsoon-pounded summer, trekkers make their way up to or around Mt. Annapurna, named for the Hindu goddess of the harvest.

TREKKING ROUTES

Due to its greater number of trekkers, villages, and checkpoints, the Annapurna trek is safer than the Everest or Langtang treks. There are three main treks in the Annapurna region. The **Annapurna Sanctuary** goes to the base camps of Machhapu-chhre and Annapurna, surrounding trekkers with white peaks that appear within touching distance. The **Annapurna Circuit** takes hikers around these central Hima-layan mountains, into a desert-like land, and across the Thorang La Pass, the highest point (5416m) and most challenging part of these three treks. The easiest of the three, the **Jomsom Trek,** reverses the last week of the Annapurna Circuit; it marches up the Kali Gandaki Valley, through Jomsom, to the Hindu temple of Muktinath.

The Annapurna Sanctuary trek normally takes 11 days, the Jomsom trek 7 or 13 days, depending on whether you fly or walk back from Jomsom, and the Annapurna Circuit 18 to 21 days. Rest days, daytrips, and variations of the route can lengthen the trek. Treks can range in duration from three hours to a month. Many variations are possible; contact a tourist office or trekking agent for more extensive information.

If you don't have the time or energy to do one of the long treks, consider a **short trek** from Pokhara that either explores new routes or goes through select villages on the main treks.

GETTING THERE

Pokhara is the base city for these treks. Nayapul/Birethanti and Phedi, the starting points for the Jomsom and Annapurna Sanctuary treks, respectively, are on the road from Pokhara to Baglung. Both are easily accessible by bus and taxi from Pokhara. The main starting point for the Annapurna Circuit trek is Besi Sahar, north of Dumre on the road between Kathmandu and Pokhara. One does not need to go to Pokhara to start the Circuit trek, but Dumre is close to Pokhara, so a day or two in the city can be good preparation time.

Many flights and buses reach Pokhara from Kathmandu (see **Kathmandu: Getting There and Away,** p. 742). To get to **Nayapul (Birethanti)** or **Phedi,** take a taxi from Pokhara or the bus from Baglung bus stop (every hr., 2hr., Rs26). Cabs go from Lakeside in Pokhara to: **Baglung bus stop** (Rs60-70); **Nayapul** (2hr., Rs800-1000); and **Phedi** (30min., Rs300-400). The Baglung road is in fairly good condition. Once you arrive in Nayapul, head downhill and across the bridge (30min.) to reach the Birethanti checkpoint, where the treks officially begin.

All buses from Pokhara to Kathmandu or Narayanghat stop at **Dumre,** 78km east of Pokhara (9 buses per day, 5:50am-noon, 3hr., Rs34); from there, buses go on to **Besi Sahar,** the beginning of the Annapurna Circuit. There is also a direct bus from Pokhara to Besi Sahar that leaves at 7:25am and a mini-bus at 9:30am (Rs100). The 42km "road" that buses use was once a hiking trail, and bus passage depends on numerous streams and rivers being low enough to ford.

During the monsoon, when rivers are high, the road becomes an extremely hazardous mud trap. There are two ways to avoid this very real risk. One is to **hike** the 42km from Dumre to Besi Sahar, which can be done in two-three days and adds about two days to the Circuit trek. The other option is to depart for Besi Sahar from Gorkha rather than Dumre. Three days will take you to Tarkughat on the Marsyangdi's east bank; another day along the east bank will take you to Phalenkangu, where you can cross the bridge to the main road on the west bank or continue on the east side another 5km to Besi Sahar. However, these two routes are less clearly marked than the main road, are less traveled, and provide fewer facilities for meals and shelter. If you choose motorized transport (4-5hr.) from Dumre to Besi Sahar, jeeps and "public carrier" transport trucks (Rs200) are more dependable than buses (Rs100). For buses to Gorkha, see Kathmandu's and Pokhara's **Practical Information** sections.

PRACTICAL INFORMATION

> **Warning:** Women should think twice before trekking alone, particularly during low-season when the trails are less crowded. There have been occasional reports of robberies and rapes on the trails.

Let's Go: India & Nepal is not a detailed trekking guide. Please supplement it with another reference. A very good source for treks in the Annapurna region is Bryn Thomas' *Trekking in the Annapurna Region* (Trailblazer Publications, U.K., 1996; £9); it comes complete with copious route maps. If you left home without it, it crops up in second-hand bookstores in Kathmandu and Pokhara and in the second-hand hotel collections on the trail. A basic topographical map for many treks is *Round Annapurna,* widely available in Pokhara and Kathmandu (Rs50-150). For more information, see **Trekking** (p. 58).

Tea houses offering food and lodging can appear as often as every hour on the well-established routes of the Annapurna treks (note that tea and water prices increase with altitude). Although agencies do offer organized treks, they are not at all necessary or even advantageous. Trekking independently, you still have the option of hiring a guide or porter. Most people, especially in the trekking season, do Annapurna with only a map and trekking guidebook. This allows for flexibility and minimal cost—without mishap, you may spend Rs300-600 per day on the trail. There are rudimentary **health posts, post offices,** and **police check posts** in many of the villages on all three treks. The larger villages have radios which can be used to call for help in emergencies. There is **electricity** in Besi Sahar, Chame, Dhampus, Ghandruk, Jomsom, Ghorepani, and Tatopani. Ghandruk has weekly **postal service** and the region's only **ISD** availability (Rs200 per minute to the U.S., callbacks Rs20 per minute). There are **banks** in Besi Sahar, Chame, and Tatopani. Many lodges along the way **exchange U.S. dollars,** but rates are better in Pokhara and Kathmandu. There are elementary **hospitals** in Jomsom and Besi Sahar. Scheduled flights for Pokhara leave the airfield at Jomsom daily and the one at Manang in high season. There is a free **message board** in Equator Expeditions office in Lakeside, Pokhara.

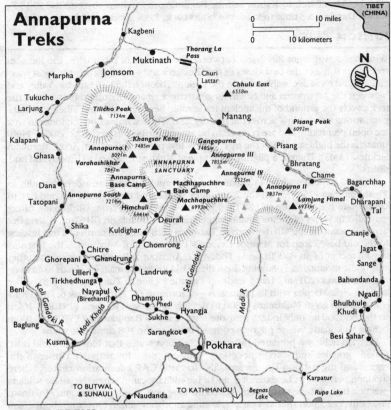

Annapurna Treks

TIBET (CHINA)

0   10 miles
0   10 kilometers

N

Kagbeni
Muktinath
Thorang La Pass
Jomsom
Marpha
Churi Lattar
Chhulu East 6558m
Tukuche
Larjung
Tilicho Peak 7134m
Manang
Kalapani
Pisang Peak 6092m
Khangsar Kang 7485m
Ghasa
Annapurna I 8091m
Gangapurna 7485m
Annapurna III 7855m
Pisang
Varahashikhar 7847m
ANNAPURNA SANCTUARY
Bhratang
Dana
Annapurna Base Camp
Machhapuchhre Base Camp
Annapurna IV 7525m
Annapurna II 7937m
Chame
Bagarchhap
Tatopani
Annapurna South 7219m
Himchuli 6441m
Machhapuchhre 6993m
Lamjung Himal 6931m
Dharapani
Tal
Shika
Kuldighar
Deurali
Chanje
Jagat
Chitre
Chomrong
Sange
Ghorepani
Ghandrung
Seti Gandaki R.
Bahundanda
Ulleri
Landrung
Tirkhedhunga
Ngadi
Beni
Nayapul (Birethanti)
Madi R.
Bhulbhule
Khudi
Dhampus
Phedi
Hyangja
Baglung
Sukhe
Sarangkot
Besi Sahar
Kusma
Kali Gandaki R.
Modi Khola
Pokhara
Karpatur
TO BUTWAL & SUNAULI
Naudanda
TO KATHMANDU
Begnas Lake
Rupa Lake

SHORT TREKS

One option is the 4- to 5-day loop from Pokhara to Ghorepani to Ghandruk (Ghandrung) and back, which crosses from the lower Jomsom trail to the lower Sanctuary trail. This trek actually begins with a four-hour bus ride to **Nayapul** (or taxi, 1¼hr. Rs600), a hike from there to **Ulleri** (6hr.), and then on to **Ghorepani** (5hr.) the next day; the return route takes you through Tadapani (5hr.) for the 3rd night, **Ghandruk** the 4th night, then to Nayapul. There are some superb Himlayan views at **Poon Hill,** near Ghorepani. The trek to Panchase, due west of Pokhara, also takes 5 days, but because the trail can be difficult to navigate and lacks facilities, it is wise to hire a guide. Trekkers head from **Khare** to **Bhumdi** (4hr.) for the first night. **Panchase** is reachable on the second night (5-6hr. hike). **Bhadauri** is four to five hours away, and is a good place to stop for the third night. The trail then goes to **Sarangkot** (7hr.) for the last night and a spectacular sunrise. Pokhara is a 3-hour downhill trek from there. The 6-night **Annapurna Skyline** trek, a ramble along the Bijaypur and Madi rivers east of Pokhara, is named for its views of the Annapurna Himal and Begnas and Rupa lakes. It requires trekkers to carry their own food and tent. Shorter options include the 2- to 3-night **Royal Trek,** so named because the Prince of Wales completed it. This hike follows part of the Annapurna Skyline trek, but since you remain in the low-altitude regions east of Pokhara, it is a worthy option for families with small children. The Royal Trek begins in **Kahun Khola,** a Rs150 taxi ride out of Pokhara, and progresses through **Arba** to Kalikasthan for the first night. **Majhthana** (4hr. away) is the second night's stop; **Syalung** is the third night resting place (5hr. away). The final day involves a hike to **Begnas Lake,** then on to **Sisuwa** for a bus back to Pokhara. There is

NEPAL

also the 3-hour trek to Kahun Danda. Beginning in Phulbari (by taxi Rs130-150), **Kahun Danda** is a 3-hour trek away, 4 hours back. Taxis are easy to hire in Phulbari.

JOMSOM जोमसोम

Winding its way from Birethanti between three groups of mountains, the Jomsom trek offers some of the best views of the Himalaya and is far and away the most spectacular (and most accessible) trek in the region. Through the Kali Gandaki Valley and between the Annapurna and Nilgiri ranges to the east and Dhaulagiri to the west, the trek covers the ground of the ancient trade route between India and Tibet. Past Kalapani, strong winds blow across the flat, dry land. The tea houses on the Jomsom trek are open year-round and are reputed to be among the best in Nepal. At 3800m, **Muktinath** is the highest point of the trek, so very few people suffer from Acute Mountain Sickness (AMS). There is a pilgrimage temple at Muktinath, sacred to Hindus and Buddhists.

It takes 7 days to walk up to Muktinath from Nayapul. The route ascends steadily to **Tirkhedhunga** (1525m) on the Bhurungdi Khola, and through the second day to **Ghorepani** (2844m). **Poon Hill** (3193m), an hour's climb from Ghorepani, offers magnificent views of the mountain range, including Dhaulagiri (8167m). A long but gentle descent on the 4th day leads to **Tatopani** (1189m), 1km north of a trail leading to the old base camp for Maurice Herzog's 1950 ascent of Annapurna, the first successful ascent of an 8000m peak. Today, the Annapurna Base Camp is on the other side of the mountains. Following the Kaligandaki River, the main trail leads to an overnight in **Ghasa** (2013m). Day 5 leads up a gentle incline to **Tukuche** (2591m) before arriving—via Marpha with its monastery—at **Jomsom** (2713m) on Day 6. From Jomsom you can go to **Muktinath** (3800m) directly or through **Kagbeni** (2810m), 10km to the north. The only lodges near the temple are in **Ranipauwaw** (3701m), 100m before Muktinath, where pilgrims come to bathe by the 108 stone-water taps.

Past Tukuche, be prepared for strong afternoon winds that blow sand and dust, making goggles and scarves necessary. Jomsom, the administrative center of the region and the last non-Tibetan area, also has an **ACAP information center,** where trekking permits can be extended, and a big military camp where Nepalese soldiers practice high-altitude maneuvers. Trails continue north from Jomsom and Muktinath and converge 35km later at **Tsarang,** leading another 15km to **Mustang,** about 20km from the Chinese border. With a normal trekking permit, however, northward progress is permitted only as far as Kagbeni.

From Muktinath you can either walk back to Jomsom in a day and wait (sometimes a day or more because of delays) for a flight back to Pokhara or spend (at most) another five days hiking to **Beni** where buses to Pokhara await (frequent, 4hr., Rs70). After 11am, strong winds make it impossible for planes to operate at Jomsom airport, so leave yourself a few days for delays if you're planning to fly out.

ANNAPURNA SANCTUARY

The Annapurna Sanctuary trek probes the divine circle of Himchuli (6441m), Annapurna South (7219m), Varahashikhar (7647m), Annapurna I (8019m), Khangsar Kang (7485m), Tarke Kang (7193m), Gangapurna (7455m), Annapurna III (7555m), Gandravachuli (6249m), and Machhapuchhre (6993m). Few hikes in the world boast such a majestic enclosure accessible to amateurs in a short time.

Avalanches are a concern on this trail, and during the winter, most inns beyond Dobang (which is reached on Day 4) are closed. Talk to locals below Dobang to find out what's open—some proprietors may return north to open in anticipation of your party. ACAP has also arranged for at least one tea house to be open at every point throughout the year. The only time that this trek is "closed" is when an avalanche blocks the approach to the base camps—a rare occurrence. If an avalanche does hit, trekkers may have to wait on the trail or at a base camp for a few days until the snow clears. The potential for **AMS** is greatest around Bagar (3900m), just before the Machhapuchhre Base Camp. Trekkers usually acclimatize well by spending two days

NEPAL

between Chomrong and the base camp (be sure to stay hydrated). Less severe but still unpleasant are the many leeches, particularly in monsoon season, which are most numerous north of Dobang. Bring salt or cut tobacco to get rid of them.

The trek can take anywhere from 8 days to 2 weeks. The Phedi path ascends on the east bank of Modi Khola, and the Birethanti trail follows the west bank, but they converge by Day 2 at **Chhomrong.** The bulk of traffic will probably be on the Phedi side since it's a shorter bus ride from Pokhara. Chhomrong has many good hotels, an ACAP office, a kerosene depot (with kerosene, cans, and stoves), provision shops, and even some rental stores. But don't wait until you get to Chhomrong to rent your equipment, as there is limited selection.

Dhampus is the scene of panoramic views, but also of rampant **theft.** Be especially careful if camping, as thieves have been known to cut tents at night and steal from slumbering hikers. Try not to walk alone, and if staying in a lodge, be sure to lock all windows and doors. For accommodation on Day 5, there are tea houses in the pseudo-town of **Himalaya** before Hinko Cave. **Deorali,** about a half-hour farther on from Hinko, is better insulated. By the time you pass Hinko Cave, the famous double-peaked fish tail of Machhapuchhre should be clearly visible. However, at the end of the day, from **Machhapuchhre Base Camp (MBC)** (3480m), the mountain is barely recognizable. It's a 2-hour push up to **Annapurna Base Camp (ABC)** (3900m).

Potential avalanche territory starts after Hinko. After Bagar, you "enter" the sanctuary, and, as you walk farther on to MBC and over snow to ABC, the mountains surround you completely. ABC has lots of snow and icy cold rivers for bathing. Wake up early to see the first rays of sun hit the mountains—it's a truly amazing sight.

The return trip is much easier, though the descent is taxing on the knees. From Chhomrong, you can either retrace your steps back through Landruk to Phedi, where there is transportation to Pokhara, or you can go to hike to Tadapani, then on to Ghorepani the next day, and continue on with the **Jomsom Trek.** From Ghandrung (1940m), you can go to Birethanti and catch the bus back to Pokhara from Nayapul, or hike to Ghorepani via Tadapani, then on to Birethanti stopping in Ulleri or Tirkhendhunga for the night; this latter route is particularly confusing, however, so ask locals for the correct trail. Gandruk is the second biggest Gurung village in Nepal (after Sikles, northeast of Pokhara) and has many lodges, some of them quite good.

ANNAPURNA CIRCUIT

The Annapurna Circuit is one of the most popular treks in Nepal. The Circuit crosses the Thorang La Pass (5416m), the highest altitude most trekkers reach in their lifetime, then winds behind the Himalayan range into the Tibetan Plateau-like desert. Apart from the elation of elevation, there's an enduring high to be had in circumnavigating something as sublimely massive as the Annapurna Himal.

The Circuit trek can be done in a span of 18 to 22 days. Although it's theoretically possible to do the Circuit clockwise—crossing Thorang La Pass west to east—it is much easier to cross it east to west. Without a single tea house between Thorung Phedi and Muktinath, the west-east passage is nearly impossible to complete without camping in the wild for a night. Aside from this stretch, there are tea houses all along the trail. The Circuit trek is usually closed from mid-December to mid-April when the **Thorang La Pass** (5414m) is covered in snow. As the pass is so high, there is significant danger of **AMS.** Trekkers spend the night at Thorung Phedi (4420m), cross the pass the next morning, and then settle down for the night on the other side in Ranipauwaw (Muktinath). The ascent is nearly 1000m between Thorung Phedi and Thorang La Pass. If symptoms of AMS develop, immediately return to Thorung Phedi. Try again the next day; this should be adequate time for acclimatization. Sudden bad weather can also make the pass impassable and compel trekkers back to Dumre.

A reliable place for a rest in Besi Sahar is **Hotel Tukuche Peak,** which has small rooms, clean common squat toilets and shower, and a good restaurant. (Singles Rs30-50; doubles Rs60-100; triples Rs90-150, depending on the season.) On a clear evening, the 30-minute walk (taking your first left heading past Hotel Tukuche Peak) up to Saraswati Temple rewards with a hilltop view of the serrated Lamjung Peak

(6931m). If you leave Besi Sahar in the morning, you may reach Bhulbhule by lunch time—head to the **Manang Guest House** for veggie *momos* (Rs50). Should you be at the end of your energy supply, there are rooms here.

The trail continues on the east bank of the Marsyangdi to Bahundanda, at the top of a fairly steep section. Watch for the **Mountain View Hotel,** which falsely claims "only 50 more steps," but is worth the climb for the view. Beds cost Rs30-60 per night. The shower and squat toilets are in a nearby building, and the hotel serves food.

Common overnight spots beyond Bahundanda are Chanje (1433m), Dharapani (1945m), and Chame (2713m), an administrative center for the Manang district. Chame has many facilities as well as great views of the eastern flank of Annapurna II. From Chame, continue through Pisang (3185m) and Braga (3475m) to reach Manang (3351m). Most people spend a day acclimatizing in Manang. There is an **ACAP infor-mation center** and a huge waterfall here, and from March to May and September to October, the **Himalayan Rescue Association** post provides a daily talk at 3pm on AMS and other issues of concern to trekkers. From Manang, the trail goes through **Churi Lattar** (4250m) to **Thorang Phedi** (4420m). As Thorang Phedi has only one lodge, it gets quite crowded in the trekking season, especially when snow has blocked the pass and a backlog of trekkers cram into the hotel. From Thorang Phedi, it is a long (8-10hr.) and difficult hike to **Muktinath,** crossing the Thorang La Pass. Consider staying at Phedi for a day or even retreating to **Lathar.** Thorang La Pass itself isn't a remarkable piece of ground at all—bare and ordinary, but with magnificent views. Most hikers rise at 4am to cross the Pass before the sun emerges, as the heat, coupled with the high altitude, makes climbing very difficult. From Muktinath, go to Jomsom for a morning flight to Pokhara, or walk the Jomsom trek in reverse to Bire-thanti. From Ghorepani, you can also go to Ghandrung and on to the Annapurna Sanctuary trek. If you need to exit from the Besi Sahar side, a bus shuttles to **Pokhara** (7:30am, 4hr., Rs120) and **Kathmandu** (8am, 5hr., Rs150), weather permitting.

The Terai तराई

The most maligned of Nepal's geographic regions, the Terai is noted by visitors for its well-developed roadways and its striking contrast to the majestic and mercifully cool hills and himals to the north. After a few hours in transit in the Terai, northern desti-nations are even more anticipated and agreeable. For Nepalis, however, these fertile flatlands are much more than a tedious passage. As Nepal's food basket, the Terai pro-duces the vast majority of the country's rice and hosts most of its industry, construc-tion, and transportation infrastructure. The Terai was covered with impregnable malarial jungle until the 1950s and 1960s; eradication efforts prompted a massive migration of people from Nepal's hills and the bordering Indian states. Fortunately, large chunks of land like the Royal Chitwan National Park have been set aside to pre-serve some of the original super-abundance of flora and fauna. Yet there continues to be conflict between wildlife needs, the demands of a growing population, and now, a burgeoning tourism industry. The neighboring towns of Narayanghat and Bharatpur form the gateway from the hills. Hetauda is an important transportation hub to the east and Butwal plays a similar function to the west. The Mahendra Rajmarg Highway, running east-west from one corner of Nepal to another, connects these cities and the whole Terai. Lumbini in the near-west and Janakpur in the near-east are two of Nepal's main religious sites.

⊛ *HIGHLIGHTS OF THE TERAI*

- The jungles, swamps, and plains of **Chitwan National Park** (p. 787) are proof that even the flat parts of Nepal can be pretty darn beautiful.
- **Janakpur's** temples (p.793) offer a look at heavily Indian-influenced culture and architecture, without the headache of a **border crossing** (p.783, 792, and 796)

■ Bhairawa (Siddharthanagar) भैरहवा

Bhairawa is on the road that connects Lumbini and Sunauli. As a destination, the town is entirely unremarkable, but its comparatively pleasant accommodations make it a popular overnight stop for daytrips to Lumbini or journeys across the border. The **Siddhartha Ramjarg Highway** passes north-south through town. **Bank Road** heads west from **Bus Chowk** (the main square) to the main bazaar. A 15-minute walk north of Bus Chowk toward Butwal is **Lumbini Chowk,** where the Lumbini road splits from the highway and heads west, leading to the **airport** 2km farther.

Several airlines have daily flights to **Kathmandu**. The **Necon Air** office (tel. 21244; open daily 6am-7pm), just north of Bus Chowk has daily flights to the capital (11:10am and 5:35pm, 40min., US$72). The **bus counter** is at Bus Chowk (tel. 20350; open daily 4am-8:30pm). Buses to **Sunauli** (frequent, 10min., Rs3) leave from Bus Chowk; buses to **Lumbini** (every 25min., 6:40am-6:30pm, 1¼hr., Rs12) leave from Lumbini Chowk. A **rickshaw** from Lumbini Chowk to Bus Chowk costs Rs10; to Sunauli Rs20. **Private jeeps** haul passengers to the **airport** (Rs100), **Sunauli** (Rs60), **Lumbini** (Rs300-500 round-trip, depending on waiting time), and **Butwal** (Rs300), and can be rented at Bus Chowk from 4am to 9pm. There are frequent **public jeeps** to Sunauli (Rs3), but passengers must wait until these fill up. The **hospital,** Bank Rd. (tel. 20193), 130m from Bus Chowk, is surrounded by medical stores. **Siddhartha Medical Hall** (tel. 22707), just east of the westernmost entrance to the hospital, is open 24 hours. There is a blue **police** booth at Bus Chowk. There are communication shops with **STD/ISD/fax** services along Bank Rd. (**telephone code:** 071).

New hotels, some relatively posh, are appearing faster than you can say "quality tourism." **Sayapatri Guest House** (tel. 21236), on the left of Bank Rd., is the best deal. Rooms are small but clean and bright, and they have fans. (Singles Rs100, with bath Rs250; doubles Rs250/300; triples Rs300.) **Hotel Yeti** (tel. 20551), at Bus Chowk, is relatively expensive (singles US$20, with A/C US$30; doubles US$25/35), but provides travel information and gives substantial off-season discounts. A few minutes' walk past these hotels walking towards the hospital on Bank Road, signs indicate a turnoff for **Kasturi Restaurant** (tel. 21580), which serves inexpensive and extremely palatable Indian food at dark wooden tables surrounded by comfy throne-like chairs. (Entrees Rs10-48. Open daily 8am-9pm.)

■ Sunauli सुनौली

The most generous thing one can say about Sunauli is that it isn't as miserable as the other hypertrophied bus stops that link India and Nepal. The second most popular entry point to Nepal (after Tribhuvan International Airport in Kathmandu), Sunauli has all of the grime, frowns, and touts that typically fester at the border, but it is far less hassle than Birganj and significantly less dismal than Kakarbhitta. Its central location recommends it as well (3hr. by bus to Gorakhpur, India; 10hr. to Pokhara; 12hr. to Kathmandu; and 10min. to the comparatively enchanting transit town of Bhairawa). This is the place to change foreign currency or traveler's checks, as there are no such spots in Bhairawa. All of Sunauli's limited facilities are in the budget range. While services on the Nepali side are better than those on the Indian side, they are not nearly as glamorous as the explosion of English billboards that welcomes travelers would suggest; the signs may be new, but the facilities are consistently decrepit.

ORIENTATION AND PRACTICAL INFORMATION The **bus park** on the Indian side is at the southern end of Indian Sunauli. There is no ticket counter, but tickets are purchased on board. Ask for the bus going to your destination. Regular and deluxe buses leave frequently for **Delhi** (all day, 24hr., IRs261/275) via **Allahabad** (15hr., IRs130/150); **Gorakhpur** (4am-8pm, 2-3hr., IRs30/34); **Kanpur** (12hr., IRs105/130); **Lucknow** (9hr., IRs90/105); and **Varanasi** (5am-8pm, 9hr., IRs95/105). The **bus park** (main ticket counter tel. 20194) on the Nepal side is about 100m from the border. Buses run to: **Kathmandu** (6 per day, 4:30-10:30am, 11hr., NRs125-128; 4 per night,

5-8pm, 11hr., NRs160); **Pokhara** (night buses 5-8pm, NRs128); **Bhairawa** (frequent, 5am-7pm, 10min., NRs3). The Kathmandu and Pokhara buses pass through **Butwal,** where there are connections to other Nepalese destinations. You can walk across the border or, if your luggage looms large, you can take a **rickshaw** (NRs30). The requisite stops at both Indian and Nepali customs and immigration should take under an hour. Nepalese visas can be obtained on the spot, but citizens of any country other than India or Nepal will need to have a visa already in order to enter India. The border, as well as both Nepalese and Indian immigration offices, are open 24 hours.

The Nepali **tourist office** (tel. 20304), between the Immigration Office and the border, has free brochures about the main tourist attractions of Nepal. (Open Su-Th 10am-5pm, F 10am-3pm.) The **tourist information center** on the Indian side is located in **Hotel Niranjana** (open M-Sa 10am-5pm; 7am-7pm in season). Several authorized **currency exchangers** on the Nepal side deal with major foreign currencies and traveler's checks (most open 7am-8pm; 1% commission for traveler's checks, 2% for cash.) The only bank on the Indian side does not change foreign currencies. STD/ISD **telephone** booths cluster on both sides of the border (**telephone codes:** Indian Sunauli 05522; Nepali Sunauli 071).

ACCOMMODATIONS AND FOOD The best place to stay in Sunauli is the government-run **Hotel Niranjana** (tel. 38201), on the Indian side, just north of the bus park. It's the impossible-to-miss white fort-like structure with a garden and multi-colored flags. Immaculate, well-furnished rooms have balconies, attached bath, and hot water. (Dorm beds IRs35. Singles with air-cooling, IRs200-250, with A/C IRs300; doubles IRs225-275/350.) Although there are many hotels and guest houses on the Nepali side of Sunauli, most are inadequate. The only recommendable place is **Hotel Paradise** (tel. 22777), 70m from the border. The large, clean rooms with thick beds and tiled attached baths are leagues above the others offered in Sunauli. (Dorm beds NRs100. Singles NRs250, with air-cooling NRs300; doubles NRs150-350/400; triples NRs200.) Off-season discounts can usually be negotiated. Their **restaurant** (open 5am-noon) is cleaner and slightly more expensive than most in Sunauli. They dish up Indian and Chinese standards (Rs12-55) as well as pizza and kebabs (Rs45-105). The **restaurant in Hotel Niranjana** (open 6am-11:30pm) is the best on the Indian side and serves Indian, Continental, Chinese, and Japanese dishes at a wide range of prices (*thali* IRs28; other entrees as high as IRs175). **Mandro,** 120m from the border on the Nepal side, serves typical but tasty Indian and Chinese food (Rs 30-90) as well as burgers (Rs30-40) and pizzas (Rs55-100) on a dimly lit patio (open daily 5am-10pm).

■ Lumbini लुम्बीनी

When, according to legend, Siddhartha Gautama, a prince in the Sakya royal family, was born at Lumbini in 623 BC, the site was merely a forest grove near a water tank. Siddhartha's mother, Mayadevi, was apparently on her way back from her husband's palace when she stopped for a bath in the water tank and then gave birth, holding the branch of a *sal* tree for support. As soon as the newborn baby emerged from between Mayadevi's ribs, he spoke, saying, "I am the foremost of all the creatures to cross the riddle of the ocean of existence. I have come to the world to show the path of emancipation. This is my last birth and hereafter I will not be born again." This precocious boy would come to be known as the Buddha. Today, the Sacred Garden marks the spot of this event; it also contains the pillar erected by the Indian Emperor Ashoka as a token of his visit to Lumbini and as a boundary marker. The pillar cites Lumbini as Buddha's birthplace, lending legitimacy to the location if not the natal particulars. Further evidence comes from remains of monasteries and *stupas* that date from as far back as the 3rd century BC and from accounts of two Chinese travelers who visited Lumbini in the 5th and 7th centuries. Khasa King Ripu Malla of Jumla made the last recorded visit to Lumbini in the 14th century before the town's sacredness was forgotten. Lumbini's significance was rediscovered in 1896 by a party led by Khadga Samsher and the German archaeologist R.A. Fuhrer.

Since 1985, the Lumbini Development Trust has been working on an ambitious plan to turn Lumbini into an international center for Buddhist pilgrimage and research. The Japanese architect Kenzo Tanze designed the plan, which will cost, by 1989 estimates, US$54 million. Progress has been very slow, so for the moment, Lumbini has minimal facilities and looks more like a construction site than an important pilgrimage site. Even with its scaffolding and mounds of rubble, however, Lumbini's tranquility is unmistakable. The area is filled with grass, singing birds, foxes, young *sal* trees, and very few humans. Current renovations to the Sacred Garden are intended to recreate the environment of Buddha's birthplace.

ORIENTATION AND PRACTICAL INFORMATION The **Sacred Garden** is a ten-minute walk from the **bus stop.** Walk west past the tourist information booth and make a left at the bunch of sign posts. The Garden appears on the right; to the east are monasteries, temples, a pilgrim rest house, and bathrooms. This is the southern-most section of the proposed complex. To the north is the **Eternal Flame** (a 10min. walk), the half-completed monasteries and temples of the various Buddhist countries (1-3km away), and, farther north across the main east-west road from Bhairawa, Lumbini's only **tourist accommodations.** There is no local transportation in Lumbini, making it a difficult place to get around.

Although the **information desk,** near the bus stop, is purportedly open daily from 7am to 6pm, it is often unoccupied. Information is also available from the **Lumbini Development Trust** (tel. 80200). The closest **airport** is in Bhairawa. Irregular **buses** to that town (every hr., 7am-7pm, 1¼hr., Rs12) stop across the street from the tourist information booth. The buses are generally over-crowded and slow, so hiring a jeep is a much better option. Rs500 will buy roundtrip transportation and three-hour waiting time—plenty for even the most devout. Less waiting time can bring the cost down to Rs300. There is a very basic, free **first aid clinic** in the pilgrims' home across from the Sacred Garden; contact the staff for assistance. Go to Bhairawa for anything serious. The **police station** (tel. 80171) is a few minutes' walk southwest of the Sacred Garden. The few hotels in Lumbini have **STD/ISD** facilities (**telephone code:** 071).

ACCOMMODATIONS AND FOOD The accommodations scene in Lumbini is grim. Most tourists make daytrips to Lumbini and then head back to hotels in Bhairawa. Lumbini's best option is **Sri Lanka Pilgrims Rest** (tel. 80109), a 3km (45min.) walk north of the Sacred Garden (rickshaw, when available, Rs50). Walk either way around the Eternal Flame, continue past all the temples and the Korean-funded research center, make a left on the main road, and take the next right. Built for Sri Lankan pilgrims, the rest house accommodates 196 people in peaceful rooms with 2-10 beds and communal bathrooms. Dorm beds cost US$6 for non-SAARC citizens (Rs77 on the ground floor and Rs143 on the 1st floor for SAARC citizens). The building's circular, communal design is centered around the dining hall (open 7am-10pm; 24hr. service available for guests), which isn't fancy but serves good Chinese, Continental, and Indian food (entrees Rs30-75). The monastery complex across from the Sacred Garden provides austere but conveniently located accommodations. The white building is a **pilgrims' rest house** (tel. 80172), whose rooms are little more than empty cubicles with hard straw mats, no bedding, and a single light bulb. The outside toilets and (cold water) shower room suffer from neglect. There is no fixed price, but donations are appropriate (Rs50-200 per night). Small **food stands** just west of the monastery serve snacks and basic Nepali meals. Once completed, Lumbini's new monasteries will likely offer accommodation as well. Lumbini's only restaurant proper, **Lumbini Garden Restaurant,** on the main road south of the turn to the Sacred Garden, serves good food at far-from-compassionate prices. The wide selection of Chinese, Indian, Nepali, and Continental entrees ranges in price from Rs100-205 (open daily 7am-10pm).

SIGHTS Lumbini's **Sacred Garden** is fronted by the **Mayadevi Temple,** which is currently under renovation and, for now, swathed in an unsightly tarp. The main **May-adevi sculpture** (3rd-4th century), which has long been worshipped as a

NEPAL

representation of a fertility goddess by Hindus in the area, was moved to the building at the entrance of the garden three years ago and will not be moved back to the temple until renovations are complete. The sculpture has been worn down from centuries of devoted caresses to the point that the figures are barely recognizable. There is another statue beside it with a detailed depiction of the Buddha's birth. Behind the Mayadevi Temple is Nepal's oldest monument, the **Ashokan Pillar,** erected in 249 BC when Ashoka came to Lumbini to mark the 20th anniversary of his coronation. The emperor himself is believed to have written the script at the bottom.

South of the Ashokan Pillar is the sacred **water tank** where Mayadevi bathed before giving birth to Siddhartha. To the southeast of the Ashokan Pillar are red baked-brick remains of monasteries, temples, and *stupas* dating from the 3rd century BC to the 9th century AD. By the huge tree next to the water tank, the sleeping Buddha and child Buddha statues bear the red and yellow colors of traditional Hindu worship. The large yellow temple opposite the Sacred Garden was constructed by King Mahendra in 1953 and contains statues from Burma, Thailand, and Nepal, including a large, gold Buddha at the main altar. Wall paintings depict the wheel of life, four *bodhisattvas,* and the major Hindu gods welcoming Siddhartha back to Nepal after he had become the Enlightened One.

About ten minutes' walk north of the Sacred Garden, the **Eternal Flame** commemorates the 1986 International Year of Peace. The road forks here; each branch continues north (enclosing what will eventually be a reflecting pool) to temples and monasteries currently being built by the 15 member nations of the International Lumbini Development Committee. Each country plans to send monks to live at its temple and represent its particular approach to Buddhism. Although there are many small vendors set up around the complex, most sell souvenirs available anywhere in Nepal. Of special note, however, are the *sal* wood *malas* (Buddhist rosaries).

▓ Narayanghat नारायणगढ़ and Bharatpur भरतपुर

The twin cities of Narayanghat and Bharatpur, located on the Mahendra Rajmarg highway in the center of Nepal, together constitute one of the nation's largest urban areas. Narayanghat hosts most of the area's businesses, shops, hotels, and tourists, most of whom are drawn by its bus park. The semi-rural Bharatpur is a 15-minute walk on the Mahendra Highway away from the river. Although there is little to recommend Narayanghat as a destination, it makes the dusty, grungy presence of the bus park more bearable. An hour's walk up the Narayani River from Narayanghat is the *sadhu* community of sacred and sublime Devghat, where the Kali Gandaki and Trisuli rivers meet to form the Narayani.

ORIENTATION

Narayanghat revolves around the junction of the Narayanghat-Mugling Highway and the Mahendra Rajmarg Highway. **Pulchowk Bus Park** sits at the intersection. **Sangam Chowk** is the central square of Narayanghat and lies about 120m away from Pulchowk Bus Park on the Mahendra Highway towards Bharatpur. Further northeast along the road to Mugling—about fifteen minutes' walk from Pulchowk—the **Pokhara Bus Park** hosts buses to and from Pokhara and Devghat.

PRACTICAL INFORMATION

Tourist Office: Chitwan Sauraha Tours and Travels (tel. 21890), at the southwest edge of the bus park at Pulchowk, provides information. Open daily 7am-10pm.

Currency Exchange: Nepal Bank (tel. 20170), 500m northeast of Pulchowk on the road to Mugling, changes major foreign currencies and traveler's checks. Open Su-Th 10am-3pm, F 10am-1pm.

Airport: RNAC (tel. 20326) is in front of the airport and is open daily 8am-5pm. To: **Kathmandu** (11:30am, 1 and 1:30pm, US$50).

Buses: Long distance bus tickets are available at box-like counters in the **Pulchowk** area. Buses to **Kathmandu** (every 30min., day buses 7am-1pm; night buses 7:30pm-4am, 5hr., Rs75-85) leave from north of the Pulchowk bus park. **Pokhara** buses (day buses, 5hr., 5am-2:30pm, Rs60-65; night buses every 30min., 5hr., 9pm-1am, Rs75-80) ply from Pulchowk proper.

Local Transportation: Minibuses to Tardi Bazaar (every 10min., 25min., 6am-7pm, Rs7) leave from the Sangham Chowk area. **Rickshaws** charge about Rs20 between Narayanghat and Bharatpur and Rs10 between the two bus parks. **Tempos** also leave from west of Sangam Chowk for Bharatpur (Rs5).

Hospital: (tel. 20111) north of the main square in Bharatpur. Sangam Chowk is home to about half a dozen **medical stores,** most open 6am-8pm.

Post office: From Pulchowk Bus Park, the post office is on the road to Mugling just a few minutes walk before the Pokhara Bus Park. Open Su-F 10:15am-2pm.

Internet: Hello Chitwan, Shaheed Chowk, across from the medical supply stores. Email (Rs20 per kb) and web access (Rs25 per min.). Open daily 7am-8pm.

Telephones: Hotels and booths alike offer **STD/ISD** service. **Telephone Code:** 056.

ACCOMMODATIONS AND FOOD

If an overnight stay is necessary, there are accommodations in Narayanghat that are clean and affordable, most within a stone's throw of the noisy Pulchowk Bus Park. Most hotels have their own restaurants. **City Centre Restaurant and Bar,** tucked in a small alley in Sangham Chowk, is one of the few places with an extensive menu (open daily 11am-10pm).

Regal Rest House (tel. 20755), directly across from the Gulf gas station at Pulchowk Bus Station. Clean rooms with fans. The ones with attached bathrooms also have hot water and air-cooling. Doubles Rs150, with bath Rs300. Triples with bath Rs350.

Quality Guest House (tel. 20939), behind Pulchowk Bus Park. Cheap, fairly clean rooms. Bathrooms have seat toilets and hot water. Single travelers may wish to choose the less-isolated Regal. Singles Rs100, with bath Rs150; doubles Rs150/250; triples with bath Rs300.

SIGHTS

The only real reason to spend more time in the Narayanghat area than a chai stop is lovely **Devghat,** a short taxi ride through towering forests, towards Mugling. *(20min. round-trip, plus 1hr. waiting time, Rs250.)* Devghat is the community on both sides of the Trisuli River. Don't miss the 4m pink statue of the monkey king Hanuman. Across the bridge there are many shrines set up for various deities and saints, most prominently Madevi and Durga. Non-Hindus should refrain from entering the small temples. In the early morning worshippers come to bathe in the confluence of the Trisuli and Kali Gandaki Rivers. The annual pilgrimage to this site is held around January 15, when thousands come to be purified in the holy waters.

■ Chitwan National Park चिटवान

Until recently, Chitwan was the playground for Nepal's elite—and the sport was large-game hunting. Any Nepalese history book is bound to have photos of Rana kings and foreign royalty posing on elephants behind the day's kill—tigers, black bears, and deer. Since 1846, hunting rights in Chitwan were reserved for royalty and their guests. Things have changed considerably, though. Royal Chitwan National Park is now the most protected wildlife reserve in Nepal, so visitors point cameras, not guns, at the large range of wildlife inhabiting the park. After malaria was eradicated in Chitwan in the 1950s, many people from the hills moved here and cleared land for farming, resulting in a rapid loss of wildlife habitat. People living in Chitwan began to be resettled in 1964, and the area was declared a national park in 1973. Eleven years later, UNESCO designated Royal Chitwan National Park a Natural World Heritage Site.

NEPAL

Though under strict regulation, Chitwan still provides a convincing jungle experience, catering to tourists of all budgets. Guests at the more expensive hotels inside Chitwan are submerged in the jungle, led through a standard two- or three-day safari program and treated to facilities and services that strive (often successfully) to provide luxury in a natural setting. Outside the park, the most popular and most developed tourist base is Sauraha. Forty-six lodges with varying facilities and prices have planted themselves here just outside the entrance to the park. Regardless of where you stay or how much you pay, herds of tourists don't obscure the wildlife, although in season, demand exceeds supply of jungle-related activities. If you can handle the wet and the sweat, consider visiting between May and October. Although the monsoon causes rivers to rise, humidity to soar, Chitwan and Sauraha to slumber, prices to drop and some places to close, but the animals don't leave.

ORIENTATION

Chitwan National Park is at the center of Nepal, bordering India to the south. Narayanghat and Bharatpur form the gateway area. The **Mahendra Rajmarg Highway** runs almost parallel to the northern boundary of the park. Roads head south to each of the park hotels and to the few outside-park villages that have hotels. **Tardi Bazaar,** 35 minutes east of Narayanghat on the highway, is the closest bus stop to Sauraha and the entrance to the park, both of which are 7km away from Tardi. Those without package deal transportation can take a **jeep** from Tardi to Sauraha in season. Off-season, it may be difficult to find transportation from Tardi to Sauraha. It is advisable to call ahead and make reservations at least for the first night, although this doesn't guarantee the hotel will come get you in Tardi for free, but at least they can arrange for transportation to meet you there. Typical cost is Rs300 for a jeep. Otherwise you may be stuck waiting for a random jeep to come along, and you will still have to pay the same price. The river does not flow all the way to Chitwan, so rafters must get off at Narayanghat and take a minibus to Tardi Bazaar.

It is a 15-minute walk from one end of Sauraha to the entrance of the park; **Sauraha Bazaar** sits at the center. There are two ways to the park entrance from Sauraha Bazaar. One is to follow the main gravel road past the **Tharu Village** and make two right turns. The other is to go right and loop along the banks of the river. At the park entrance, visitors pay entry fees, arrange elephant tours, and see exhibits on Chitwan's history and wildlife. Canoes depart from the riverbank next to the entrance.

PRACTICAL INFORMATION

Tourist Office: The **ticket office** is at the park entrance. Open daily 6-10am and 1:30-4pm; elephant ride hours are 6-7am and 1:30-3:30pm. The National Park **entry fee** (Rs650, valid for 2 full days) covers general entry and river canoeing rights. **Steep fines** await those caught in the park without a valid permit. **No one may enter the Park at night.** In season, the wait to get park entry permits can be 3-4hr. For an additional Rs50-100, a tout may get the permit for you.

Currency Exchange: Nepal Bank (tel. 60210), in Tardi, well-hidden 300m east on the highway. Changes major currencies and traveler's checks. Open S-Th 10am-3pm, F 10:30am-1pm. Some hotels in Sauraha exchange currency at terrible rates.

Buses: The **bus counter** (tel. 60134) in Tardi, 15m east of the turn to Sauraha, marked Prithivi Rajmarg Bus Syndicate. Open daily 7am-9:30pm. **Tourist buses** run to **Kathmandu** (10 and 11am, 5hr., Rs100-150) and **Pokhara** (9 and 10am, 5hr., Rs100-150). Prices may vary with service charges. A/C **Green Line buses** (US$10 to Kathmandu or Pokhara) and can be arranged through any of the travel agents in Tardi (try Baba Travel tel. 60245, daily 6am-5pm) or hotels in Sauraha. Cheap buses to main Nepalese destinations leave from Tardi.

Local Transportation: A **local bus** goes from Tardi to Narayanghat, where there are connections to many destinations. **Jeeps** between Sauraha and Tardi cost Rs300 to reserve and Rs30 with 10 passengers. Cars from Narayanghat to Tardi can be reserved through travel agents for around Rs400. In season, ancient **bicycles** can be hired from three rental shops on the main road (Rs10 per hr.). Better bicycles can are available in Sauraha at similar rates.

Pharmacy: There are several pharmacies in Tardi. About 100m to the east, look for a Red Cross sign. Open 6am-10pm. Doctor available 3-6pm.

Police: The **main police station** is a 20min. walk from Sauraha. For the police station in Tardi, walk 300m east on the main highway from the turn to Sauraha.

Internet: Hello Chitwan (tel. 29368), in Sauraha on the road to the Tharu village, has email (Rs50 per kb, send only). Open daily 7am-9pm.

Telephones: Several STD/ISD booths on the main road. **Telephone Code:** 056.

ACCOMMODATIONS

As soon as travelers step off the bus in Tardi, they are smothered by dozens of guides eager to earn the commissions hotels pay them. A wave of the receipt from a pre-arranged package deal (available from travel agents in Kathmandu or Pokhara for as little as US$60-80) is enough to disperse the guides while a jeep from the appropriate hotel takes over. If you have not purchased a package deal but have already decided on a hotel of choice, the appropriate jeep, if currently in Tardi, will take you to Sauraha for free. Otherwise, choose the least aggressive guide to take you to Sauraha. The jeep ride is free if you stay at the hotel they take you to, and Rs300 per car (Rs30 per person if the jeep is full) if you decide to leave.

All hotels offer basically the same jungle activities: everyone walks the same paths, drives in the same jeeps, and, most importantly, sees the same wildlife. Cheaper places have fewer jeeps, so their guests have to walk more often. Some hotels will give rides on private elephants and pawn them off as park rides. Keep in mind that only government elephants are allowed in Chitwan, so ask to see your park permit.

Most hotels will offer the standard 3-day, 2-night package consisting of a Jeep or elephant ride, half-day jungle walk, canoe-trip, stick dance, lodgings, meals, and bus transportation from Kathmandu or Pokhara to any return city in Nepal. Arrangements can be made from Kathmandu or Pokhara, but most hotels also offer walk-in package deals, usually US$60-70 for a 2-night deal. Prices plummet off season; bargain hard.

Hotel Wildlife Camp (tel. 29363—messages only), north of Sauraha Bazaar. The garden is almost as pretty as the campfire, which blazes from a permanent embankment. The attractive brick houses have well-furnished rooms. All bathrooms have hot water. In-season: doubles with bath Rs400-500. Off-season: Rs200-400.

Chitwan Resort Camp, (tel. 29363—messages only), on the main road north of Sauraha Bazaar. Rooms are fairly large and well-furnished; the newer ones are more attractive and have good bathrooms. The dining room stands out for quality and the menu for quantity. In-season: rooms Rs400-600. Off-season: Rs200-400.

Jungle Tourist Camp (tel. 29363—messages only), north of Sauraha Bazaar. Mud houses with mud floors and thatched roof. Bathrooms have hot water (make more mud!). Restaurant open 6am-8pm. Rooms Rs200-450.

Eden Guest House (tel. 29371), at the end of Sauraha, a 10min. walk east from the park entrance. While the walk to Sauraha may be a hassle, the isolation here makes it worthwhile, especially in season. The beds and lighting are better in the newer huts, which have clean attached bathrooms; the older mud houses have doubles with common bath. Attached restaurant. Rooms Rs100-500.

Royal Park Hotel (tel. 29361), located south of Sauraha Bazaar on the left overlooking the river, has a nice camping area with exceptionally clean common baths (seat and squat toilets) for US$2/person. However, for a real splurge, a night in one of their brand-spanking new cottages will soothe a haggard traveler's psyche. The rooms are all large and beautifully-appointed with comfortable beds and are handicap-accessible. Bathrooms can make a tired traveller cry with joy. Skip the overpriced package breakfast. In-season: rooms US$20-25. Off-season: US$15. 2-night package to walk-in tourists a pricey US$115.

FOOD

Restaurants in Chitwan take care of food and entertainment simultaneously. Hotels in Sauraha Bazaar, are run by owners who often disregard the closing time in favor of more singing, drinking, and dancing, and many eateries have campfires during the winter. Food here is expensive because much of it is trucked in. Sauraha's main road leads to the river where at sunset tourists gather to eat, drink, and swap stories.

Jungle View Restaurant and Bar, Sauraha Bazaar. Currently the most popular Bazaar hangout. Specializes in Italian food, with exceptional lasagna. Gorgeous rooftop views of the river, especially in the evenings. During Happy Hour (4-8pm), beer and snacks cost Rs80-90. Also serves breakfast, Indian food, and some Chinese food. Most entrees Rs80-110. Open daily 6:30am-10pm.

K.C.'s Restaurant and Bar, Sauraha Bazaar. The bamboo hut rooftop has good views and a decent selection of English music. The menu is among the most extensive in Sauraha, with Continental, Chinese, Indian, and Italian dishes. Goodies from a "German bakery" and a wide variety of cocktails are also available. The staff is friendly and knowledgeable about getting budget deals in jungle activities. Happy Hour (4-8pm) beer and snacks Rs80-90. Entrees Rs90-130. Open daily 6am-11pm.

SIGHTS

> **Warning:** Due to the risk posed by 1300 different animal species, particularly the rhinos, visitors to Chitwan National Park must be accompanied by a guide at all times. **Let's Go does not recommend being bitten, gored, or trampled.**

Chitwan National Park offers protection to 56 species of mammals including the one-horned rhinoceros, Bengal tiger, leopard, sloth bear, and wild bison. There are estimated to be 470 species of mammals, over 500 species of birds, nine species of amphibians, 126 species of fish, 150 species of butterflies, and 47 species of reptiles in the park. A 1995 study estimates that 107 of Nepal's 300 tigers are in Chitwan.

There are several ways to arrange for guides and organize activities in Chitwan. **Package tours** organize everything from jungle activities to return transportation to anywhere in Nepal (see above). One money-saving alternative is to arrange individualized itineraries by booking activities through a hotel and paying by the item (plus a service charge of about Rs300-400). Those who do not book through a hotel may endure more hassle, especially during high season, when hotel guests get priority in space-limited activities. **Guide companies** provide guides for every activity in Chitwan and generally charge less than hotels for bookings. On the other hand, hotel services are more reliable (especially for jungle walks) because they can't just pack up and leave if there is a problem. The recently formed **United Jungle Guide Service,**

> ### Chitwan's Ponderous Pachyderms
>
> Just about every elephant in Chitwan is from India, where wild elephants still roam despite a millennium-old trade of capturing and training them. With elephant stomping grounds receding and the art of elephant capture losing appeal, elephant prices have skyrocketed—some cost up to one million Indian rupees. Chitwan has responded with the Elephant Breeding Centre, established in 1987. Starting with 16 elephants, the park now has 64. At the age of two, elephants begin training with both human and elephant "teachers." Each elephant has three caretakers; most caretakers are Tharu, the indigenous people of Chitwan, so commands are given in the Tharu language. The elephants establish relationships with these individuals, particularly the *mahout*, the main driver. Some elephants even play polo with their caretakers during the winter. The elephant stables, which hold between 17 and 22 elephants throughout the year, are a 10-minute walk east from the park entrance. At feeding time (which is most of the time), the elephants hint at their favorite dinner balls by throwing grass and pointing their trunks.

located under K.C.'s Restaurant in the **Jungle Guide Office**, is an association of guides who have left their hotel overlords to go into business for themselves. *(Open daily 7am-9pm.)* While this may play on unionist sympathies, it is best with all guide companies to ask other tourists for referrals to the better guides and companies. The number of years of experience a guide has had is stated on the guide's permit certificate. Guides' fixed salaries are quite low, so if you are happy with a guide, remember that what would be an embarrassingly small tip in the West goes a long way here.

Elephant Rides

Times: *7:30am and 4:30pm.* **Duration:** *About 1hr.* **Cost:** *Rs650 plus Rs50-100 service charge.* **Tickets:** *Make arrangements through a guide company or hotel, or queue up a couple of hours before the park's opening times (6am-10:30pm and 1:30-4pm).*

Elephant rides are the most popular activity at Chitwan. If it is important to you to actually ride in the park, make this clear to the hotel or guide service. No more than eight elephants ever enter the jungle at one time.

Jungle Drives

Times: *7am and 1:30pm.* **Duration:** *4-5hr.* **Cost:** *Rs350-650, depending on season.*

The **jungle drive** is a close second to the elephant ride in popularity. Because jeep rides are quite long, they cover more of the jungle, including Kasara palace and the Gharial Conservation Project. But jeeps, unlike elephants, can't leave the road to follow animals or go through tall grass. More animals can be seen in the evening ride, but rhino sightings are practically guaranteed on any jungle drive. As the grass grows tall from June to the annual grass-cutting in January or February, animal sightings become increasingly difficult.

Canoe Rides

Times: *8am and 2pm.* **Duration:** *3-4hr.* **Cost:** *Rs300-350 per person. Add Rs50-100 service charge for hotel or agency booking.*

Most canoe rides involve an hour of floating down the river followed by a two- to three-hour guided walk back. The canoe ride and walk may be billed separately, but should be part of the same package.

Jungle Walks

Times: *6-7am.* **Duration:** *½ day 3hr., full-day 7hr.* **Cost:** *½ day Rs250, full-day Rs500.*

Jungle walks are ideal for jungle immersion, photography, and animal sightings, but since walkers are unarmed and have no easy getaway, they can be dangerous. A guide takes a maximum of eight people. There is only one walking path in some sections of the jungle, so they can become crowded during season.

Other Excursions

There is a two-day jungle walk to **Kasara,** the park headquarters and the location of the museum and the Gharial Conservation Project. From Kasara, walk back to Sauraha or get a ride via Bharatpur. Guides charge about Rs500 per person, with discounts for large groups. Some guides offer one- to two-hour bird watches (Rs100 per person), but much of that time is spent walking to and from the lookouts.

Another option is a one-hour **bicycle ride** to **Bis Hajaar Tal** (Twenty Thousand Lakes), outside the park to the northwest of Sauraha. *(Guides charge Rs200-300.)* The best time to leave is very early in the morning, arriving in time to see gharials, birds, and rhinos at the lakes. Bicycles need to be reserved the night before.

The **Tharus,** the indigenous people of Chitwan, are presented as another "attraction." A **guided walk** through the Tharu village along the road to the park entrance covers the culture, history, and religion of the people. *(Rs100 per person.)* The walk takes nearly two hours, but less than an hour is actually spent inside the village. Tharu stick dances are exuberant and easy to participate in. Tharu dance troupes perform regularly at hotels and nightly at the Tharu Culture Program on the left past the Hotel Wildlife Camp a couple of minutes by foot, walking away from Sauraha. *(Programs 7:30pm in-season, 8:30pm off-season, Rs50 per person.)*

■ Hetauda हेटौडा

Hetauda is a home to industries—cement, leather, beer, mineral water, you name it—and the first stop for cargo shuttling between Kathmandu and the Terai. Temporary host to buses and trucks heading to and from the Indian border at Birganj, the town is treated by travelers as a half-hour pit stop. This is a mistake. Among hills bordered by the Rapti River, and along uncongested tree-lined streets, there are pleasant strolls to be had. **Makwanpur Gudi** offers superb views if you have time to make the three-hour hike.

The north-south **Tribhuvan Highway** cuts right through town; Mahendra Vira Vikram Shah's **statue** marks the intersection with the town's main east-west street. The **bus park** is southwest of the statue, along an east-west road just south of the main street. All Birganj buses pass through Hetauda, and other frequent buses and trucks run between the two (2hr., Rs25). The pink **post office** is readily recognizable by the red letterbox in front and is located five minutes down the western branch from the intersection (open Su-F 10am-2:30pm). The **police** headquarters is next door. Across the street is the entrance to the **hospital** (tel. 20305). Out-patient care is available, as is a **pharmacy** (open Su-Th noon, F 9-11am), 24-hour **emergency** care, and Red Cross ambulance service. **Community Health Center** is well-stocked and open daily 7am to 7pm. **Nepal Bank,** along the highway, south of the statue, will exchange traveler's checks (open Su-F 10am-3pm). The only English that marks the bank is an "NB" on the gates; look for a three-story building a few doors south of Hotel Seema. **STD/ISD** service (Rs200 per min.) is offered at little shops in the town center, as well as most hotels. **Telephone Code:** 057.

As always, off-season rates in Hetauda are highly negotiable. **Motel Avocado** (tel. 20429) is on the highway, just north of town, a ten-minute walk from the bus park. All rooms have attached baths with towels and toilet paper, screened windows, fans, and mosquito mats. The most expensive rooms have A/C, color TV, and phones. (Singles Rs350-1500; doubles Rs550-2000. Student discounts up to 25%. Attached restaurant: entrees Rs35-125). The **Ho Lido Inn** (tel. 20937, fax 20655), on the highway south of Hotel Seema, is new and clean. All rooms have attached baths (with towels and toilet paper), TVs, fans, and thick, firm beds. (Singles Rs350-450; doubles Rs450-600.) The restaurant offers a large selection of curry and chow mein options, all Rs80 or less. **Hotel Seema** (tel. 20191; fax 20137), a two-minute walk east of the bus park, sits along the highway one block south of the statue. Rooms have fans and so-so common bathrooms with cold water and squat toilets. (Singles Rs150, with bath Rs350-1500; doubles Rs300/550-2000. Attached restaurant: entrees Rs20-80.)

■ Birganj बिरगञ्ज

> **Warning:** Crossing the border from Nepal to India requires four stops (see p. 463). Also remember that although the Indian immigration office is always open, **Indian visas are not available at the border.** The Indian embassy in Kathmandu is the only place in Nepal that issues them. The Nepali immigration office at the border is open daily from 4am to 10pm. If you don't already have a Nepalese visa when you arrive at the border (from India), you'll need a photo and at least US$15 in cash. All currencies are accepted except Indian and Nepali. **There are no exchange facilities at the border giving out U.S. dollars.** For more information see **Visas**, p. 6.

Birganj is the funnel through which traffic to India passes, narrowing at the border into a pot-holed, exhaust-filled passageway clogged with trucks, rickshaws, bullock-carts, and tongas. Nepalis are the first to declare that "Birgrunge" is a miserable place for tourists; the only reason to come is to cross the border. If you're heading to India, Birganj will relieve any separation anxiety and make you glad to leave Nepal. If you're coming from India, perhaps you'll appreciate that Birganj is at least a little more bearable than **Raxaul** (see p. 463), the town on the Indian side of the border.

ORIENTATION AND PRACTICAL INFORMATION Birganj clumps for miles along the main road that leads over the Indian border. The main landmark, at the north end of town, is a **clock tower**. Buses bypass the main road and stop at the **bus park** directly east of the clock tower. **Buses** mercifully run from Birganj to virtually every major city in the Terai; day buses (6-8am, 8hr., NRs150) and night buses (6-8pm, 8hr., NRs150) head to Kathmandu. **Local transport** consists of rickshaws and tongas. Both cross the border into India, but only rickshaws will wait while you stop at immigration. A rickshaw from Birganj to Raxaul takes from 40 minutes to two hours, depending on the extent of the perpetual traffic conjestion (NRs35 for foreigners). Settle a price with the driver before you get in the rickshaw, otherwise he will likely demand an exorbitant tourist price once you have arrived. There is a subtly marked **Tourist Information Centre** (tel. 22083) on the west side of the main road, well south of the clock tower. The office is tucked in a courtyard, up a flight of stairs. The staff is amiable and will happily dust off some brochures if you ask, but they don't seem to know anything more than a hotel manager might (open Su-F 10am-5pm). The **Nepal Rastriya Bank,** southwest of the clock, will exchange traveler's checks and dollars (open daily 10am-4pm; Sa only Indian and Nepali currency exchanged.) The hotels will also change money and accept Indian rupees. **Pharmacies** are plentiful along the main street at the southern end of town. **Telephone Code:** 051.

ACCOMMODATIONS AND FOOD The two best places to stay are next door to each other, along the north-south road, one block west of the main road, well south of the clock tower. The **Hotel Kailash** (tel. 22410) has a range of rooms, concrete but clean. The most basic have fans and mosquito nets; the more expensive have private baths, A/C, and TVs, but no hot water (singles NRs100, with bath NRs200; doubles Rs430/600; triples Rs265/430). The **Hotel Diyalo** (tel. 22370; fax 25375) is more expensive, and no less dank or old than the Kailash, but it has more perks—a 24-hour international communications center, a rooftop beer garden, and rooms with attached bath, TVs, phones, and mosquito nets. Cheaper rooms have fans and cold water; more expensive rooms have A/C and hot water. (Singles NRs400-1200; doubles NRs500-1500.) Both hotels have dimly lit North Indian restaurants with most entrees priced under NRs100. Around the corner from the hotels, on the street to the north that leads back to the main road, is **Kanccha Sweets,** with its fly-free display cases of Indian sweets and stand-up counter at which you can partake of South Indian snacks like *masala dosa* (NRs20). (Open daily 8am-9:30pm.)

■ Janakpur (Janakpurdham) जनकपुर

Visiting Janakpur coming from other regions of Nepal is like entering a new country: India. Janakpur shows just how distinct Nepali culture really is. The local Mithila people are largely of Aryan descent, and vehicles are displaced by roaming bovines and goats. Nearly all of the tourists here are Indians making their pilgrimage to the birthplace of the famous *Ramayana* heroine Sita. Westerners are often referred to as *rusin*, thanks to the presence of a Russian-initiated cigarette factory in Janakpur. The Mithila Kingdom, of which Janakpur was the capital, stretched into northern India from the 10th to 3rd centuries BC. Despite the ancient associations, however, none of the buildings are particularly old. The cityscape is dominated by the flaking onion domes and triangular roofs of its many *kuti* (pilgrims' hostels) and is broken up by *sagars* (artificial ponds) used for ritual baths. The pastel colors of sacred and secular buildings glow at dawn and dusk, when the sounds of cymbals and drums from the temples fill the air. The city truly comes to life during festivals, particularly Vivaha Panchami (Nov.-Dec.), which features a re-enactment of Rama and Sita's wedding.

ORIENTATION AND PRACTICAL INFORMATION Janakpur's network of curving alleyways makes it easy to get disoriented and end up walking in circles. Fortunately, the city is small enough that a recognizable landmark is never far away. The **railway station** sits at the northeast corner of town. Janakpur's main thoroughfare, **Station**

Road, runs southwest from the railway station through **Bhanu Chowk** (named for the Nepalese poet whose bust tops a pillar in the middle of the intersection) and then bears south past **Danush Sagar** and **Kuna Village.** The road continues south to the **airport,** 2km from town. Necon runs **flights** to Kathmandu (1pm, 30min., US$55). Their office (tel. 21900) is south of Bhanu Chowk on Station Rd. (open daily 8am-6pm). **Bus** tickets are sold at the bus park, but using one of the several English-speaking agents who cluster just south of the railway station may be less of a hassle; the bus park is difficult to navigate, and many ticket-sellers charge foreigners the same commission that booking agents do. Night and day buses are available to numerous destinations, including **Kathmandu** (7am-9pm, 10-12hr., Rs140), but catching a local bus from a major intersection—Dhalkebar to Janakpur from Hetauda, or Itahari to Dharan, Hile, and other points north—is often the best way to get where you're going. There are **cycle-rickshaws**—you shouldn't ever pay more than Rs30—but you can get around easily on foot. Across from Danush Sagar, on the west side of Station Rd., **Ram Mandir** is another useful landmark. The road that runs northeast of the Mandir leads through Janakpur's old bazaar area to **Janaki Mandir.** The major road that heads west (and then southwest), south of Ram Mandir, leads to the **bus park,** which sits at the southwest corner of town, just south of a tall telecommunications **tower.** The **tourist office,** Station Rd. (tel. 20755), north of Bhanu Chowk, has a friendly staff and offers a marginally helpful pamphlet (open Su-Th 10am-5pm, F 10am-3pm). The **Nepal Rastraya Bank,** on Station Rd., is open Su-F 10am-5pm. There is a **hospital** just west of the Janaki Mandir, and **pharmacies** along Station Rd. **Fruit stands** cluster near the southern end of Station Rd. and west of the Janaki Mandir. The **haat bazaar** (Su and W) is held west of Ram Mandir. The **post office,** southwest of Danush Sagar, is difficult to find, so ask for directions or take a rickshaw (open Su-Th 10am-4:30pm, F 10am-2pm). **Telephone Code:** 041.

ACCOMMODATIONS AND FOOD Janakpur's budget accommodations are a little shabby. The **Kathmandu Guest House** (tel. 21753), right at Bhanu Chowk, is a friendly and simple place that gets the job done, with open atriums, screened windows, ceiling fans, and mosquito nets, along with attached bathrooms with squat toilets. (Singles Rs150; doubles Rs250; triples Rs350.) A few minutes walk up the road heading northwest from Bhanu Chowk is the **Hotel Rama** (tel. 20059; fax 20798). Rooms in the old building are dim and dank, with ceiling fans and attached bathrooms with squat toilets; swanky rooms with attached baths and seat toilets in the new building are nicer. (Singles Rs90-700; doubles Rs140-1000; additional 10% tax.) At the north end of Station Rd., near the railway station, is the **Aanand Hotel** (tel. 20562; fax 20196), which features crowded rooms with good ceiling fans, mosquito nets, and attached baths with hot water. This place, run by a throng of young men, may make single female travelers uncomfortable. (Singles Rs100, with bath Rs150; doubles with bath, air-cooling, and TV Rs250.) **Hotel Welcome,** Station Rd. (tel. 20646; fax 20922), northeast of Danush Sagar, has bright rooms that run the amenities gamut. Private baths have hot water and squat toilets. (Singles Rs50, with bath Rs75, and A/C Rs600; doubles Rs150/300/1000-1500. Additional 10% tax.) The restaurant below, thanks to friendly proprietors, is the town's most popular, serving North Indian food (veg. Rs20-50; non-veg. Rs70-90).

As for the rest of Janakpur's dining scene, it's North Indian, North Indian, or North Indian, but some of it is so tasty that you'll hardly notice that there's no other choice. **Ramilo Restaurant** and **Eight Restaurant,** located just southwest of Bhanu Chowk, are both good and cheap, serving almost identical menus, though Ramilo has more of a sports bar atmosphere, while Eight feels like a tavern.

SIGHTS None of Janakpur's temples are very old, but all are very much in use. The **Janaki Mandir,** a huge wedding cake of a construction, was built in 1911 on the spot where an image of Sita was found in 1657, and where the infant Sita is said to have been discovered by her father. The silver image of Sita is revealed twice a day, once in the early morning and again in the evening. Next door is the **Ram Janaki Vivaha**

Mithila Painting

Maithili women (women from the area of southern Nepal and Northern India that was once the Mithila kingdom) have developed a painting tradition that has been passed from mother to daughter for generations. The art form originated with the bright designs that women paint on the walls of their houses (usually made of mud-covered bamboo, with thatched roofs) and has come to be known as Madhu-bani. These paintings often serve a ritual purpose, as part of a festival or wedding: a woman may create paintings for her future husband as part of their courtship, for instance. Stylistically, the paintings are characterized by bold outlines filled in with bright colors. Subjects vary from abstract geometric designs to scenes from daily life. Certain images have different symbolic significance; pregnant elephants, parrots, bamboo, turtles and fish represent fertility and marriage, while peacocks and (non-pregnant) elephants are good luck symbols. Traditionally, the process and the purpose of the paintings are more important than the product, which may be destroyed. Nowadays, they're also sold to tourists at hefty prices.

Mandap, built a decade ago to mark the place where Rama and Sita were married. (*Admission Rs5. Camera fee Rs1.*) This is a special kind of kitsch. Life-sized statues of the heroic couple sit inside the glass-walled pagoda, while other equally laughable statues reside in little houses surrounding it. During the Vivaha Panchami festival in December, *sadhus* and Brahman priests re-enact the wedding ceremony of Ram and Sita. Southeast of the Janaki Mandir is the **Ram Mandir,** Janakpur's oldest (built in 1882) and most typically Nepalese-style temple. Built under a big banyan tree, the temple is host to the Ram Navami festival the first week of April, celebrating Ram's incarnation on earth and subsequent destruction of evil demons. To the east of the Ram Mandir, Janakpur's largest and holiest ponds, **Dhanush Sagar** and **Ganga Sagar,** sit side by side. Across from Ramanand Chowk on the main highway is a brick path that leads to one of the most peaceful tanks in Janakpur, **Bihara Kund.** Surrounded by temples, it's actually possible to sit here for some time before attracting an audience. South of Ramanand Chowk on the main highway is **Hanuman Durbar,** a small temple which until recently housed the world's largest monkey, thought to be an incarnation of Hanuman and known to be a victim of stomach cancer. There are chained and caged monkeys for pilgrims to taunt.

There are a few other things to do in Janakpur aside from temple-hopping. The **Janakpur Women's Development Centre** (tel. 21080) is a delight for anyone interested in art or economic development. (*Open Su-Th 10am-5pm, F 10am-4pm.*) Located almost an hour's walk south of Janakpur, the center is best reached by rickshaw (Rs25) from the main road; ask to be taken to the "development store." Signs along the road to the airport indicate an eastern turnoff into the village of Kuwa. From a temple at the western edge of Kuwa, a 10-minute walk southeast leads to the center. Wandering back through the village, you'll see Mithila paintings in place on the walls of the houses. The artists use the traditional motifs of Mithila paintings on handmade paper, papier-mâché, ceramics, and textiles (see above). The center also trains women in literacy, mathematics, and business management. The center's products are for sale there and at various non-profit outlets in Kathmandu and Patan.

Janakpur's other anomaly, Nepal's only steam **railway,** is a good way to see the surrounding countryside. Trains to Bijalpur, to the west, take one hour, and leave at 7am and 3pm. **Get off the train before it reaches the border; you may have trouble leaving and re-entering Nepal.**

■ Dharan धरान

At the point where the landscape changes from plains to hills sits the bazaar town of Dharan, where people from the hills come to buy everything from cloth to electronics. Despite efforts to increase tourism, the few visitors who come here tend not to stay for long. While Dharan is a far more pleasant overnight than many of the Terai's transportation hubs, there isn't much to do unless you head for the surrounding hills. Chatara, where river rafters on the Sun Kosi finish, is 15km west. Hile and Basantapur, are trekking trailheads to the north. Once home to one of the British Army's Gurkha training camps, Dharan still hosts a number of Nepal's *khukuri*-smiths who make more knives for tourists than for mercenaries.

The center of town is along the main north-south road **Bhanu Chowk,** marked by a bust of the Nepalese poet Bhanu. **Buses** to and from the north stop to the right of the intersection, while those to and from the south stop off to the left. Two long blocks uphill from Bhanu Chowk, the major intersection of **Chata Chowk** roughly marks the center of town. The main street hosts numerous **travel agencies** and **STD/ISD** and **Internet** providers. **Nepal Bank Ltd.** (tel. 20084) is just north of Chata Chowk (open Su-Th 10am-3pm, F 10am-noon). The closest **airport** is in Biratnagar; Necon Air, and RNAC all have several daily flights to Kathmandu. **Buses** head north to **Hile** (every 30min., 4hr., Rs62) via **Dhankuta** and go on to **Basantapur** (Rs97) and **Biratnagar** (frequent, 2hr., Rs20). A daily night bus also goes to **Kathmandu** (4pm, 17hr., Rs300). Other bus connections can be made at **Itahari** (frequent, 30min., Rs11) at the junction of the area's two highways. The **market** to the left of Bhanu Chowk sells big mounds of fruit. **Telephone Code:** 025.

Shisti Guest House (tel. 20569) is a minute's walk down Chantra Line, left from Chata Chowk. Large rooms are well-maintained and have fans (singles Rs125; doubles Rs150, with bath Rs250). The grubbier **Bamboo House** (tel. 21309), just east of Bhanu Chowk, on the left, serves veg. (Rs20-50) and non-veg. (Rs35-65) curries in a dark setting (open daily 7am-9:30pm). Check out the **supermarket** next door for packaged food (open daily 7am-9:30pm).

■ Kakarbhitta काकर भित्ता

Kakarbhitta is a small trading town on the India-Nepal border that, good-humored as it is, offers little of distinction from either country. Located on the flood plains of the Mechi River, there is more or less free traffic across its **bridge.** Kakarbhitta is essentially a large, dusty bazaar centered around the **bus station,** which sits about 100m from the border on the northern side of the **east-west highway.** Many of Kakarbhitta's establishments—hotels, restaurants, and banks—line the highway east of the bus station. From the west side of the bus station, alleys that run parallel to the highway constitute the **market area** where Kakarbhitta's cheapest goods are to be found. Many shops will accept Indian currency.

Several buses leave for Kathmandu (1:40-6:40pm, NRs340). **Rickshaws** run from the border to Panitanki in India (IRs5/NRs8), where there are buses to **Siliguri** (1hr., IRs8, IRs30 for taxi). The **tourist office** (tel. 29035) is on the northern side of the highway, to the right of Hotel Kathmandu. The staff is knowledgeable, disseminating bus information and guiding you to interesting places (open Su-Th 10am-5pm, F 10am-2pm, closes 1hr. earlier in winter). **Travel agencies,** many of which double as **STD/ISD booths,** encircle the bus station. They charge about NRs30 commission on tickets, which can be avoiding by purchasing tickets at the white building that sits near the center of the bus park. At the border crossing, a Nepali visa is available to those with a passport photo and U.S. dollars (US$15 for 15 days, US$25 for 30 days, US$60 for 60 days). Nepali **immigration** is open daily 6am-6pm. Indian immigration is open 24hr. **Entry visas,** however, must be obtained from the Indian embassy in Kathmandu. **Nepal Rastra Bank,** across the highway from the tourist information center, buys foreign currency and traveler's checks at 1% commission and sells Indian and Nepali rupees. (Open daily 7:30am-6pm for foreign exchange). **Telephone Code:** 023.

A slew of **hotels** surrounds the bus station; with a few exceptions, most of them share its aesthetic and sanitary standards. At the far left corner of the bus park is the **Hotel Rajat** (tel. 29033), which has the cleanest dining area in town. Old rooms are clean, with fans, mosquito nets, and common squat toilets across the yard. Rooms in the new building are painted pink and have very clean attached baths with seat toilets (some have tubs), fans, TVs, phones, and mosquito mats (deluxe room has A/C). All rooms have hot water. Discounts available. (Old rooms: singles Rs100; doubles Rs150. New rooms: singles IRs400, with A/C IRs1000; doubles IRs600/1500; triples IRs800. Add 10% service charge). The attached garden restaurant—sporting the only grass in Kakarbhitta—serves an impressive array of entrees (Rs25-90; open daily 7am-9pm). The somewhat dingier **ABC Lodge** (tel. 29025), down the second alley north of the highway from the bus station, next to the vegetable market, has bright rooms with ceiling fans, mosquito mats, and common bath with squat toilets (singles IRs100; doubles IRs120).

The Eastern Hills

Eastern Nepal's immodest peaks are no place for mere mortals, but don't let that deter you. These mammoths are merciless, and visitors grow to love them for it. Broadcasting its preeminence from almost 9km above sea level, Everest instills an ass-kicking awe in even the most experienced mountaineers. The more obscure land-scape further east, which includes some of Nepal's most jagged and otherworldly peaks, similarly pulls no punches. Casual trekkers, marveling at the space-time con-tortions that brought them before these icy altars and baptized them in their own insignificance, usually stagger back to Kathmandu with wise and satisfied Cheshire grins, not to mention tauter leg muscles.

But a trip to the east is not all fireworks and adrenaline. While the mountains are shocking, the hills are sublime. If the pinnacles are imperious, the humble rolling landscape below is amiable and accommodating. And both the hills and the giants, the oft-trodden Everest and the infrequently visited far east, greet guests with a casual and forthcoming self-presentation as refreshing as it is unforgettable.

🕮 HIGHLIGHTS OF THE EASTERN HILLS

- The region's premier trek circles the world's premier peak. You may not make it to the top, but the **Everest Trek** (below) is pretty impressive nonetheless.
- Steeped in cool mists, the hills and tea fields of **Ilam** (p.802) are resplendent and serene, offering a little-touristed option for trekkers uninterested in Everest.

■ The Everest Trek

Forget that it's a tiring, humbling, messy undertaking. You are walking to the base camp of the mountain Sagarmatha, which is the highest point on earth and the pride of the Nepalese people—a feat that will elicit admiration from everyone back home. The Everest trek is practically a pilgrimage, and the mountain's famous name seems to be its main lure. This is not to say that the Everest trek is a bad choice. The Solu Khumbu area on the way to Everest offers unique terrain and a close encounter with the varied and dynamic cultures of the Tamangs, Rais, Limbus, and Sherpas who inhabit the area. Along the routes, monasteries offer year-round solace; countless fes-tivals (especially in October) create an atmosphere of relaxed reverence; and Satur-day markets draw people from far and wide to engage in spirited haggling. Closer to the giant peak, where the air is thinner, the trekkers seem to float along wide trails carved into green hills, skip through pine forests, and tremble across long, rickety wooden bridges that span stunning river valleys.

The Everest Trek has historically been more dangerous than the Annapurna Trek; it's steeper, longer, more difficult, and less crowded, reaching higher altitudes and heightening the risk of getting altitude sickness. However, this should by no means deter careful, fit, properly equipped, and guided beginners from setting off on a jour-ney that approaches the top of the world.

NEPAL

TREKKING ROUTES

The length and conditions of the trek to Everest allow for many variations, but the most popular approaches are from **Jiri,** the closest roadhead, and **Lukla,** the closest airstrip. The walk from Jiri to **Kala Pattar** (5545m) and **base camp** (which is about 5km northeast of Kala Pattar) takes 28 days and covers about 300km. If you fly to Lukla (2800m), walk up to the base camp, and walk back to Lukla to catch a flight to Kathmandu, the trek takes only about 14 days. Many travelers fly one way.

From Jiri, the walk begins with Nepal's trademark no-altitude-gain ascents and descents through pastures and rhododendron forests. Four days past Jiri is the 3500m **Lamjura Pass;** after two more days the trail descends and joins the **Dudh Kosi River** just before the village of **Jubing.** From Jubing, it's a two day walk along the river through the entrance to **Sagarmatha National Park** and on to **Namche Bazaar** (3440m). Kala Pattar is about five days past Namche. En route, you'll see brilliant views from Tengboche Monastery, the *yeti* skull at Pangboche, and the Khumbu glacier terrain, highlighted by the glacial lake at Gorak Shep, just south of Kala Pattar. The first base camp is a day's walk northwest of Gorak Shep (requiring a little backtracking from Kala Pattar). Lukla is a two days walk south of Namche Bazaar; treks follow the same route described above.

An alternative destination is **Gokyo** (4750m), a summer yak pasture and nearby lake, situated just east of Ngozampa Glacier. Four days walk past Namche, Gokyo affords tremendous views that take in the whole eastern range, from Cho Oyu to Makalu and beyond. The nearby peak of **Gokyo Ri** (5350m), a two hour ascent from Gokyo, offers the best vistas. From Gokyo, you can cross the **Nama Gawa Pass** and join the trail to Kala Pattar (about five days past Gokyo) or return to Lukla.

While most trekkers begin from Jiri or Lukla, the roadhead of **Hile** (see p. 801), the airports at **Phaplu** and, in-season, **Tumlingtar** are also appropriate starting points. These routes demand more planning, since neither has been pounded into submission by the boots of fellow trekkers. Both routes start at altitudes low enough to offer excellent preparation for high altitudes.

If you have less than a week to trek, the Everest region is a good place for a short jaunt. Flying to Lukla, walking north for a few days, and returning makes an enjoyable trek. The round-trip from Lukla to Namche affords a look at Everest and can take as few as four days from Kathmandu.

GETTING THERE

The **bus** or **airplane** rides that begin the Everest trek are adventures in themselves, and getting the tickets might be the biggest headache of the entire trek. The bus to Jiri is one of the few that still leaves from Kathmandu's old bus station in Ratna Park (5:30, 6:30, 8, and 9:30am, 11hr., Rs145; express 7am, 8hr., Rs170). Buy your ticket a day in advance and show up a half-hour early to load your bags.

Lumbini flies between Kathmandu (Tu, Th, Sa, and Su, 6:30 and 10:10am) and Lukla (8:05 and 11:45am). **RNAC** flies twice a day (45min., US$83) out of Kathmandu (7 and 7:15am) and Lukla (8:35 and 8:50am). Chartered **helicopters** and a rudimentary plane service can be booked for the 25-minute flight to Jiri. In season, flights are added to and from Lukla according to demand. Due to the weather demon, which has apparently made Lukla its home, you will be extremely lucky if your flight to or from Lukla leaves only a couple of hours late; in fact, you're lucky if your flight leaves on the scheduled day at all. In season, you might be bumped off your seat due to excess demand, while flights are sometimes canceled due to insufficient demand off season. Visit the airport or call your travel agent persistently to make sure your name is on the waiting list and that your flight hasn't been canceled.

Everest Treks

TIBET (CHINA)

Gauri Shankar 7134m

Melungtse 7181m

KHUMBU

SAGARMATHA NATIONAL PARK

Cho Oyo 8201m

Gyachungkang 7952m

Everest (Sagarmatha) 8848m

Lhotse 8516m

Nuptse 7879m

Pumori 7145m

Everest Base Camp

Kala Pattar 5545m

Gorak Shep

Kang Taiga 6685m

Pangboche

Tengboche

Pheriche

Gokyo

Gokyo Peak 5483m

Namche Bazaar

Dudh Kosi

SOLU

Karyolang 6511m

Beni Khola

Numbur 6959m

Pigpherago 6730m

Chukyimago 6259m

Likhu Khola

Junbesi

Sete

Kenja

Bhandar

Khimti Khola

Jiri

Charikot

Barabise

Tambo Kosi

Kodari

Tatapani

Lamosangu

Lukla

Jubing

Phaplu

TO HILE

TO KATHMANDU

N

0 5 miles
0 5 kilometers

NEPAL

PRACTICAL INFORMATION

Let's Go: India and Nepal is not a detailed trekking guide. It is important to consult another resource. Trekking maps of the area are also sold in Kathmandu; the **information center** in Lukla will probably have them in stock, along with a few other informational pamphlets. With a guidebook and a map, a hired guide is not necessary: trails are wide and well-worn, and lodges with English-speaking proprietors are numerous. If you need a porter (Rs300-500 per day), ask your lodge owner.

Trekking permits for the area (US$5 per week) are available at the Kathmandu Immigration office. If you plan to visit **Sagarmatha National Park** (tel. (038) 21114), it is also necessary to obtain a park **permit** (Rs650), either at the Immigration Office in Kathmandu or at the park entrance. **Currency exchange** (U.S. currency and traveler's checks only) is available in Lukla and Namche, but it's best to change money in Kathmandu. Bring plenty of small bills and remember that torn banknotes are often refused. Many lodges along the way accept U.S. currency. **Electricity,** available in larger towns such as Jiri, Junbesi, Lukla, Namche, and Tengboche, is increasingly common, but it's still a good idea to bring candles. There are **telephones** in Jiri, Namche, and Tengboche. Jiri, Namche, Tengboche, Pheriche, Lobuche, and Salari have **radio facilities.** Most of the **police posts,** in Jiri, Kinja, Lukla, Namche, and Tengboche, double as **post offices.** While **health posts** in several villages can provide minimal first aid, the best medical care is available at **Kunde Hospital** (tel. (038) 21113), built by Sir Edmund Hillary in Namche, and the **Himalayan Rescue Association Hospital** in Pheriche, which also provides helicopter evacuation for emergencies.

The best selection of **equipment** is in Kathmandu, but there are also rental stores in Lukla and Namche. During the trekking season, **food** can be found all the way to Gorak Shep, the location of the highest lodge. There are no lodges in Kala Pattar or at the base camp. **Fuel** is also a limited commodity. The selection of food rivals that in Kathmandu; choose from the standard and eclectic Chinese/Nepali/Continental menu or try yak delicacies found nowhere else. Many lodges close off season, and finding food and accommodation beyond Namche may be difficult. Ask lodge owners and returning trekkers at Namche before you proceed north.

■ Jiri जीरी

The one-road town of Jiri (1935m), the main trailhead for the Everest trek, provides travelers the beds and sustenance necessary for their recovery from the seemingly interminable ride from Kathmandu. **Buses** leave **Kathmandu** (5:30, 6:30, 8, and 9:30am, 11hr., Rs145) from the Old Ratna bus park in the rear of the lot. Tickets for assigned seats—be sure to get a window—must be purchased at the window beside the bus the day before the morning of your departure. There will soon be express bus service to Kathmandu as well.

The only **telephone** in Jiri is outside **Cherdung Lodge** (tel. (049) 20190; open daily 6am-8pm). From here, you can place calls to Kathmandu (Rs7 per min.) or to other countries (Rs500-700 for first 3min., Rs150 each additional minute; free callbacks). **Jiri Medical Mall,** at the bus park, has limited pharmaceuticals and no doctor (open daily 5:30am-7pm). The poorly marked **hospital** is a five-minute walk from the bus park on the unpaved path (open for outpatient care daily 9am-2:30pm). The Jiri Helminth Project, just down the hill from Naya Bazaar, is partially funded by the N.I.H. to study the parasitic worms that disproportionately affect Jiri castes. Staffed by two doctors, they administer free services and drugs (when available) They also have ambulance service to Kathmandu. (Open M, Tu, Th, and F, 8:30am-noon.) The **police station** is 4km away on the road to Kathmandu. On Saturdays, a **market** is held on the hilltop of **Naya Bazaar,** a 30-minute walk from the bus park.

Most lodges and restaurants are within 100m of the bus park. The following are helpful, clean, and government-registered: **Cherdung Lodge** (doubles Rs110; triples Rs150); **Sagarmatha Guide Lodge** (doubles Rs60; triples Rs100); and **Hotel Jin View** (doubles Rs100; triples Rs150). **Hotel Gauri Himal** has a decent rooftop restaurant and a great view of the Jiri Valley, as well as the cleanest bathrooms in all of Nepal.

■ Hile हीले

Perched above the Arun Valley at a cool, misty 1900m, with its spectacular mountain views and ethnic mix of Bhotiyas, Rais, Newaris, and Indians, Hile has a distinctly Nepalese feel to it. A trailhead for treks into the world's deepest valley, Hile hosts a colorful, bustling market, but the countless layers of terraced villages visible below counteract the bartering frenzy. Hile consists of a row of shops boasting stacks of shiny plastic buckets and heaps of flip-flops and salt. Piles of *doka* (the conical, head-strapped baskets that porters use) wait to be filled and carried off into the hills. Most of Hile's visitors are headed for higher ground, but the town merits a visit even for non-trekkers. There are several small *gompas* and a tea estate on the way up to Basantapur, but the most exciting thing to see is the Himalaya. There are great views from the hilltop north of town, a 45-minute walk. Less spectacular but still impressive is the view from the small hills that mark the north and the south ends of town.

The **bus stand** is at the northern end of town facing south. Tickets are sold at a small booth removed from the left side of the street. Buses to and from Dharan leave every hour (4hr., Rs62), and there is a direct night bus to **Kathmandu** (1pm, 18hr., Rs335). South of the bus stop sit several good trekking-style lodges to choose from. All of the following have electricity, shower rooms, hot water by request, and restaurants that serve Nepali and Tibetan, and *tongba* (see **Getting Soused in Shangri-La,** p. 761). **Himali Hotel** (tel. 20340), a few minutes south of the bus stop on the left, has large, bright rooms (singles Rs50; doubles Rs80; triples Rs120; attached restaurant: entrees Rs20-45; open daily 7am-10pm). A minute north of Himali, **Hotel Gajur** (tel. 20339) has **international phone** service and a nice garden and restaurant out back (singles Rs55; doubles Rs100; triples Rs150). The friendly **Doma Hotel** (tel. 20574), across from Himali, has cheaper, but still pleasant, accommodations (doubles Rs60; triples Rs80). The **post office** is down the hill from Hotel Doma on the same side of the street. It isn't marked—ask around or find a letterbox on the wall. A few **STD/ISD** services and **pharmacies** are along the main road. **Telephone Code:** 026.

■ Basantapur बसन्तपुर

Looking down from an elevation of about 2200m, Basantapur's beauty is mitigated only by impertinent diesel roosters intent on rousing slumberers from 4am. For such buses, this is the end of the road, but it's only the beginning for trekkers in the Eastern Hills. The town has accepted its role as temporary host with friendly panache. The **bus ride** (every hr., 2hr., Rs35) from Hile terminates at Basantapur's southern tip, near the **police post.** A five-minute walk along the rough, rutted road brings you to the other end of town, where the road continues east to **Therathum** and, in clear weather, great mountain views. All of Basasntapur's lodges offer similar tea-house style accommodation: beds in wooden rooms, common squat-toilets, and cozy restaurants where you can spend the evening sipping on cheap *tongba* (Rs10-20) and watching people stare at you. **Hotel Yak** (tel. 69047), a few minutes past the bus park along the main road, has the most cheerful appearance and a few other extras: toilets on upper floors, electricity, a shower room with hot water, and **STD/ISD** service, also available to non-guests from 7am to 10pm. (Singles Rs55; doubles Rs100; triples Rs130; quads Rs150; attached restaurant open daily 7am-10pm). **Laxmi Hotel** (tel. 69022), just past the bus park, provides less aesthetically pleasing accommodations at lower prices. No showers here, but the rooms have electricity, and the restaurant, equipped with a TV and bountiful array of chocolates, hosts most of Basantapur's after-dark action. (Singles Rs35; doubles Rs70; triples Rs80.) Across the street from the Laxmi, **Birat Hotel and Lodge** (tel. 69043) is the only place around to devour *dal bhat* under the watchful eyes of V.I. Lenin. Birat does not have electricity, but there is a shower facility, and rooms are tidy. (Singles Rs40; doubles Rs60; quads Rs120.) Basantapur's **post office** is just past Hotel Yak (toward Therathum). It isn't marked in English, so look for a red and white sign and stairs leading to a letter box. (Open Su-F 10am-5pm, Sa 10am-1pm.) **Telephone code**: 026.

NEPAL

■ Ilam ईलाम

Ilam would be as touristed as Pokhara were it closer to Kathmandu. Its few stalwart visitors are rewarded for their bus stamina with the exhilarating sense of calm provided by cool air, strolls among tea hills, and amazing views of lush hillsides and valleys. Getting a seat on the bus that winds its way up to Ilam can be difficult. Chances are best from Birtamod, accessible by local bus from Kakarbhitta (frequent, 25min., Rs9). Night buses from Kathmandu reach Birtamod (every hr. 6:30-11:30am) and continue to Ilam (4hr., Rs80). There is a ticket office alongside the line-up of westbound buses. The bumpy last hour of the ride is touch-and-go. The Ilam bus park is at the bottom of the hill, a short walk from the town square. Lodges and **pharmacies** cluster along the main street, from the bus park up to the **town square,** which is marked by the ubiquitous bust-of-watchful-king. **Mechi Tours and Travels** (tel. 20113 or 20367; fax 20365), on the left side of the square, provides bus and domestic plane tickets, private vehicles and drivers, **STD/ISD** and **fax** service, and **currency exchange** (no travelers checks accepted yet). The accommodating proprietor is also a good source of information about Ilam and surrounding areas (open Su-F 9am-5pm, Sa 9am-1pm). Two lanes diverge from the square opposite the main street. The one to the right leads to the **post office** (open Su-Th 10am-5pm, F 10am-3pm) and the **haat bazaar** (open Sa and Th). The rudimentary **hospital** is at the end of the path. Buses leave for **Charali** and **Birtamod** in the morning (every hr., Rs80) and for **Kathmandu** (noon, 24hr., Rs340). Private jeeps and lorries can be entreated to take passengers south. **Telephone Code:** 027.

While visitors lament Ilam's scarcity of guest houses, the lodgings aren't bad. All are budget lodges offering similar rooms and restaurants with the menu you've grown to love. One decent option is **Bhattarai Hotel and Lodge** (tel. 20139), next to the bus park. It compensates for the noise with electricity and large, clean rooms, some with attached baths with squat toilets and cold showers (doubles Rs80-100, with bath Rs150). The **Himalayan Restaurant** downstairs is, along with a few other hotel restaurants, one of the few places to eat.

One notable place to visit is Ilam's **tea estate,** which stretches over the hills above the bus park. Curious tourists can have an unintelligible (but well-meaning) impromptu guided tour of the tea factory. Watch the harvest, wander among vast expanses of thick crops, or, in the late evening, catch a glimpse of Ilam's illicit teen dating scene. The **haat bazaar** held outside the town square by the post office every Sunday may be less risque, but it promises some action. Ilam is also one starting point for treks through the Kanchenjunga region. For those with less time or wanderlust, daytrips in the surrounding countryside can be just as rewarding. The four- to six-hour walk to the pilgrimage site of **Mai Pokhari,** 12km to the north, leads through tea gardens and forests to the top of a ridge crowned by a temple and sacred lake. To the northwest, a three-hour walk leads to the bazaar town of **Mangalbare.** Descending to the scenic **Mai Khola** is another rewarding journey that takes just a few hours on foot.

■ Far Eastern Treks

Among Nepal's least publicized trekking destinations, the hills and peaks east of Everest are quiet wonders. A trip to eastern Nepal entails sacrificing the logistical ease and the lemming-like camaraderie enjoyed on Annapurna treks. Likewise, eastern trekkers won't receive the whistles and bewildered stares that greet those coming back from Everest with photos and used moleskin in hand. For those willing to forego these dubious honors, however, far eastern treks offer an opportunity to casually but soundly acquaint themselves with Nepal, and to do so at their own unhurried pace. Accommodation is available, and treks through valleys and over ridges provide just enough altitude: you get views and cool breezes, but no nausea or nosebleeds. Finally, having left behind the droves of other tourists, eastern trekkers walk alongside locals who depend on the trails for transportation. Craggy, sparsely populated peaks loom over Nepal's fertile tea hills. Four hours west of the border lie the bazaar towns Dharan and Hile, gateways to the Anun Valley for trekkers and goods alike. In between, austere peeks tower over grassy ridges, alpine patches, forests, moss-and-vine-decked jungles, and rich, cultivated hillsides, making for breathtaking strolls.

TREKKING ROUTES

Sitting along the border of Nepal and Sikkim at about 8590m, **Kanchenjunga Massif** is unquestionably the sexiest destination in the east. Courting this bad boy—the world's third highest mountain—is no easy task, requiring at least three weeks and a lot of heavy breathing. Kanchenjunga was not opened to casual trekkers until 1988, and it remains protected by a shroud of bureaucracy: trekkers pay US$10 per week to visit the area and are technically required to travel in groups. (This prohibition against solo travel, applied also to trekkers in Dolpa, is seldom enforced. Even if you're not with a trekking agency, try your luck at Immigration; they will likely approve your permit.) These logistical obstacles, numerous but surmountable, add to the mystique of a pristine and snowy wilderness prowled by musk deer, snow leopards, blue sheep, and very few tourists. The mountainscape, highlighted by Everest, Makalu, and Kanchenjunga, is spectacular, and rolling hills below afford a unique look at Limbu culture. Kanchenjunga has a northern and a southern **base camp,** both difficult but feasible three-week destinations. The challenging hike between base camps, however, requires at least one more week.

Roughly halfway between the giants of Kanchenjunga and Everest, the **Arun Valley** is another underrated eastern destination. Sitting on the border of Nepal and Tibet, **Mount Makalu,** the world's fifth highest peak (8463m), crowns the region. The Arun River, born in Tibet and nursed by snowmelt from the northern flanks of Everest and Kanchenjunga, cuts through the Himalayan chain only 35km east of Mt. Makalu. Flowing all the way to the Terai, its waters irrigate fertile lowlands, rolling out a green carpet to the mountains in the north. Trekkers ascend through luxuriant farmland to ridges covered with pastures and age-old forests. Paths rise above clouds, affording magnificent vistas and the kind of visions you only thought possible in fantasy literature. Further north, about a nine days' walk past **Hile,** mountain passes, alpine woods, and turquoise lakes decorate an equally magnificent but vastly different high-altitude landscape. Depending on your starting point, **Makalu base camp** is between ten and fifteen days from the hill towns to the south. Descending is fast: the round-trip can be accomplished in as few as 18 days.

Of course there's no need to struggle all the way to either base camp. If you have less time, you can abbreviate either of these routes, walking a few days toward Makalu or Kanchenjunga and then returning. Since the area's airports and roadheads are fairly far south, however, most satisfying treks take at least a week. A particularly pleasant Kanchenjunga approach begins from **Hile** or **Basantapur** and ascends through rhododendron forests and along a grassy ridge to **Gupha Pokhari** (2930m), a high-altitude lake with beautiful mountain views. Gupha Pokhari is only two days from Basantapur; continuing on toward Kanchenjunga, and then southeast toward **Phidim** and **Ilam,** or returning to Basantapur.

GETTING THERE

The **Taplejung airport** offers the quickest access to the Kanchenjunga region. Early morning flights from Kathmandu or Biratnagar will bring you within ten days walk of Kanchenjunga's south base camp. Approaching from one of several roadheads takes a little longer, but the slow ascent through terraced fields and luxuriant forests can be as quietly dazzling as the Himalayan destination itself. The road starting from Charali in the far east goes through Ilam to Phidim, both of which make excellent starting points. Beginning from Hile or Basantapur—each is well-equipped to send trekkers packing—is also a good option. Arun Valley treks start from the Tumlingtar airport or the roadheads of Hile or Basantapur.

NEPAL

PRACTICAL INFORMATION

Let's Go: India & Nepal **is not a detailed trekking guide.** It is very important to seek supplementary information. As the far eastern hills are relatively less traveled, no trekking guides presently offer exhaustive coverage. *Trekking in the Nepal Himalaya,* by Stan Armington, offers some information, and small handbooks for the region may be found in Kathmandu's larger new and used bookstores. Maps of the region are plentiful in Kathmandu. While the area's trails endure heavy local traffic, they are not widely touristed, and getting around is more difficult than it is in more popular regions. You may want to consider hiring a guide or going with an organized trek, especially if you plan to ascend to high altitudes in the Kanchenjunga region. Another option is to hire a dependable porter who knows the trails. Ask around at any of the trailheads. Lodge owners can usually find someone reliable.

Trekking permits are necessary for any journey past a roadhead. They are available at the Immigration Office in Kathmandu and cost US$10 per week for Kanchenjunga and US$5 per week for other areas. You have about as much chance of seeing the *yeti* as you do of finding a place to **exchange currency.** Bring fat wads of small, unripped bills from Kathmandu, as proprietors sometimes cannot make change and often balk at torn banknotes. **Electricity** is also relatively rare in the area, so candles are useful. **International calls** can be made from the trailheads (Hile, Basantapur, Ilam, and Phidim). **Radio service** is available in Chianpur, Khandari, Taplejung, Phidim, Bhojpur, Therathum, Dhankuta, Ilam, and Chandra-gadhi. Government **health posts** at the trailheads and in other large villages will provide basic primary care, but **bring first aid supplies** for higher altitudes. For serious medical problems, try to contact doctors or hospitals in Kathmandu or Dharan for assistance.

Food and accommodations are sparse in Kanchenjunga's higher altitudes, where the population is small. Trekkers should take tents, food, and ample supplies. In lower altitudes, however, tea houses and *dal bhat* are plentiful. There are slightly more elaborate lodges at the trailheads and at popular destinations like Gupha Pokhari. If you have difficulty finding a place to eat, ask at a house along the trial; many people will be happy to provide *dal bhat* for Rs25-40. You can also inquire about lodging at local houses, which won't cost more than Rs40.

APPENDIX

■ Holidays and Festivals

Hindu, Sikh, Buddhist, and Jain festivals correspond to the Indian lunar calendar, so the dates vary from year to year with respect to the Gregorian calendar. Islamic festivals are determined by the Islamic lunar calendar, whose years are equal to 12 lunar cycles, meaning that festivals rotate throughout the solar year, so the dates given are approximate. There are also a number of secular holidays—in India these are dated according to the Gregorian calendar, and in Nepal they follow the official Vikram Sambat (or Bikram Sambat) calendar. The dates given here are for 1999; dates for the year 2000 are in parentheses.

Date	Holidays and Festivals
January	**Pongal festival,** celebrates the end of the South Indian harvest in Tamil Nadu.
January 1	**New Year's Day** of the Gregorian calendar, celebrated in both India and Nepal.
January 11	**Prithvi Narayan Shah's Birthday,** honors the king who united Nepal.
January 26	**Republic Day,** one of India's four national public holidays; highlighted by a military parade in New Delhi.
February	**Lhosar,** the Tibetan New Year, is a three-day festival celebrated by thousands of Tibetans and Sherpas who flock to Boudhanath Stupa in Nepal and to Dharmasala.
February	**Shiva Ratri,** an all-day, all-night Hindu festival dedicated to Shiva, whose creation dance took place on this day.
February 1	**Vassant Panchami,** honors Saraswati, the Hindu goddess of learning.
March 2	**Holi,** a rowdy Hindu festival during which revelers from both India and Nepal throw colored water and powder at each other.
March 28	**Eid-ul-Zuha,** when Muslims commemorate Abraham's intended sacrifice of his son Issac, celebrated with the slaughtering of sheep for feasts (March 17, 2000).
April 24	**Ramanavami** celebrates Rama's birth with readings of the *Ramayana* in Hindu temples all over India and Nepal (April 12, 2000).
April 28	**Mahavira Jayanti,** the major Jain festival of the year that celebrates the birthday of the religion's founder (April 16, 2000).
April	**New Year's Day** of the Vikram Sambat Year 2056, celebrated in Nepal.
April 14	**Vaisaki,** the Sikh festival celebrating the day Guru Gobind Singh founded the Khalsa; features readings of the Guru Granth Sahib and major feasting.
April 27	**Muharram** commemorates the martyrdom of the Prophet Muhammad's grandson; especially important for Lucknow Muslims (April 15, 2000).
April/May	**Budda Jayanti** honors the Buddha's birthday and his subsequent attainment of *nirvana.*; varies according to the full moon.
April/May	**Machhendranath Rath Yatra,** a popular festival during which a massive chariot holding Lokeswar, a patron deity of Kathmandu, is pulled through the streets of Nepal by hundreds of worshippers.
May	**Meenakshi Kalyanam** celebrates the goddess Meenakshi with festivities in Madurai.
July 14	**Rath Yatra,** commemorates the journey Krishna made to Mathura; Hindus party at the Jaganath Temple in Puri and cities in the South (July 2, 2000).
June 26	**Milad-un-Nabi (Eid ul Mulad),** the Prophet Muhammad's birthday.
August	**Raksha Bandhan** celebrates the Hindu sea god Varuna; the holiday is associated with brother and sisters.
August 15	**Independence Day,** India's biggest national holiday.

August 22	**Zoroastrian New Year's Day,** celebrated by Parsis in India.
Late August	**Ganesh Chaturthi** is when Hindus venerate the god of obstacles with spectacular processions, especially in Bombay and Rajasthan.
September	**Dussehra,** a 10-day festival, celebrates the vanquishing of demons and honors Durga, the demon-slaying goddess. Known as **Dasain** in Nepal and **Durga Puja** in West Bengal.
September/ October	**Indra Jatra,** when Kathmandu celebrates the capture of the King of Gods, Indra, in the Kathmandu Valley; processions and the annual blessing of the King of Nepal by the Living Goddess Kumari.
September/ October	**Daisan,** the most important hoilday in Nepal, commemorating the victory of Durga over the evil demon Mahisasura. Offices and stores are closed for most of this 11-day celebration.
October/ November	**Tihar,** the Festival of Lights, an important five-day holiday in Nepal.
November	**Pushcar Camel Fair,** one of India's most famous camel fairs held at the sacred lake at Pushkar, Rajasthan.
November 7	**Diwali** (Deepvali), a 5-day festival of lights celebrating Rama and Sita's homecoming as per the *Ramayana* (October 26, 2000).
November 23	**Guru Nanak Jayanti,** the founder of Sikhism's birthday (November 11, 2000).
December 11	**Ramadan,** a 28-day period when Muslims fast, a celebration ending with **Eid-ul-Fitr,** a three-day feast celebrating the Prophet's recording of the word of God in the Holy Quar'an.
December 25	**Christmas Day** is celebrated by Christians in India, particularly in the South.
December 25	**Guru Gobind Singh's Birthday,** celebrated by Sikhs everywhere, particularly important in the Punjab.
December 28	**King's Birthday,** a Nepalese public holiday declared by the monarch.

▨ Telephone Codes

DOMESTIC

Agra: 0562	**Delhi:** 011	**Patna:** 0612
Ahmedabad: 029	**Dharamsala:** 01892	**Panjim:** 0832
Amritsar: 0183	**Guwahati:** 0361	**Shimla:** 0177
Bangalore: 080	**Hyderabad:** 040	**Trivandrum:** 0471
Bhopal: 0755	**Jaipur:** 0141	**Varanasi:** 0542
Bhubaneswar: 0674	**Khajuraho:** 07686	
Calcutta: 033	**Leh:** 01982	**Kathmandu:** 01
Chandigarh: 0172	**Manali:** 01902	**Chitwan:** 056
Chennai: 044	**Mumbai:** 022	**Pokhara:** 061

INTERNATIONAL

Australia	61	**Ireland**	353	**South Africa**	27
Canada	1	**Nepal**	977	**U.K.**	44
India	91	**New Zealand**	64	**USA**	1

▨ Time Zones

India is 5½ hours ahead of GMT, 4½ hours behind Australian Eastern Standard Time, and 10½ hours ahead of North America's Eastern Standard Time. Summer time puts the northern countries an hour closer to India. India is 15 minutes behind Nepal.

■ Phrasebook

English	Hindi	English	Hindi
Hello.	Namaste.	How are you?	Kaisehain?
Sorry/Forgive me.	Maaf kijiyega.	Yes/No	Ha/Na.
Thank you.	Shukriya.	No thanks.	Nahin, shukriya.
Good-bye.	Phir milenge.	No problem.	Koi baat nahin.
When (what time)?	Kab?	What?	Kya?
OK.	Thik hai.	Why?	Kyon?
Who?	Kaun?	Help!	Bachad!
How much does this cost?	Iska kya daamhain?	Go away/Leave me alone.	Chod dijiya/Tang na karo.
Stop/enough.	Bas.	Is...available?	Yaha...milta hai?
Please speak slowly.	Zara dhire boliye.	What's this called in Hindi?	Hindi mein ise kya kehte hain?
My country is...	Mera desh...hai.		
I don't understand.	Samajha nahin.	Please repeat.	Phir se kahiye.
What is your name?	Apka nam kya nai?	My name is...	Mera nam...hai.
I like...	Mujhe...acha lagta hai.	I don't like...	Mujhe acha nahin lagta.

Directions

English	Hindi	English	Hindi
(to the) right	dayne hath	(to the) left	bayan hath
How do I get to...?	...ka rasta kya hai?	How far is...?	Kitna dur hai...?
near	pas mein	far	dur
Where is...?	...kahaan?		

Numbers

English	Hindi	English	Hindi
one	ek	ten	das
two	do	eleven	gyaarah
three	teen	twelve	baarah
four	char	fifteen	pandraah
five	panch	twenty	bees
six	chei	twenty-five	pachees
seven	saat	fifty	pachaas
eight	aath	one hundred	ek sau
nine	naun	one thousand	ek hazar

Food and Drink

English	Hindi	English	Hindi
bread	dabal roti	rice	chawal
meat	naans	water	pani
vegetables	sabzi	sweets	mitthai

Times and Hours

English	Hindi	English	Hindi
open	khula	closed	band
What time is it?	Kitne baje hain?	morning	subah
afternoon	dopahar	evening	shaam
night	raat	yesterday	kal
today	aaj	tomorrow	kal

Other Words

English	Hindi	English	Hindi
alone	akela	friend	dost
good	accha	bad	bura
hot	garam	cold	thanda
medicine	dawaii	doctor	daaktar

English	Bengali	English	Bengali
Hello.	Namashkar.	How are you?	Kemon achhen?
Sorry/Forgive me.	Mapf korben.	No problem.	Oshubidha ney.
Thank you.	Dhonnobad.	Yes/No.	Ha/Na.
Good-bye.	Abar dekha habe.	OK.	Achha/Thik.
Why?	Kano?	When(what time)?	Kata?
Who?	Ke?	What?	Ki?
What is your name?	Apnar nam ki?	Stop/enough.	Bas.
How much does this cost?	Koto taka?	Go away/leave me alone.	Chede bin/Birakt korben na.
Is...available?	...ase?	What's this called in Bengali?	Banglay eta ke ki bole?
Help!	Sahajjo!		
My name is...	Amar nam...	Please speak slowly	Aste aste bolun.
I like...	Amar...bhalo lage.	I don't like...	Amar...bhalo lage na.
I don't understand.	Bujhi na.	Please repeat.	Aabar bolun.

Directions

English	Bengali	English	Bengali
(to the) right	dan dike	(to the) left	bam dike
How do I get to...?	...jabar rasta?	How far is...?	...koto door?
near	pashe	far	door
Where is...?	...kothai?		

English	Bengali	English	Bengali
one	ak	twenty	bish
two	dui	thirty	tirish
three	tin	forty	chollish
four	char	fifty	ponchash
five	panch	sixty	saat
six	choi	seventy	sattar
seven	shat	eighty	aashi
eight	at	ninety	nabbai
nine	noi	one hundred	ek sho
ten	dosh	one thousand	ek hajar

Food

English	Bengali	English	Bengali
bread	paoruti	rice	bhat
meat	mansho	water	jol/pani
vegetables	shobji	fish	maachh

Times and Hours

English	Bengali	English	Bengali
open	khozla	closed	bandho
What time is it?	Koita baje?	morning	shokal
afternoon	dupur	evening	sondhya
night	rat	yesterday	kal
today	aj	tomorrow	kal

Other Words

English	Bengali	English	Bengali
alone	eka	friend (M/F)	bandhu/banhobi
good	bhalo	bad	kharap
happy	khushi	sad	dukhi/mon kharab
hot	gorom	cold	thandha

English	Tamil	English	Tamil
Hello.	Namaskaram.	How are you?	Yep padi irukkai?
Sorry/Forgive me.	Mannichuko.	No problem.	Kavalai, illai.
Thank you.	Nanri.	No thanks.	Illai, véndam.
Yes/No.	Amam/Illai.	OK.	Se ri.
Good-bye.	Poittu Varén.	When(what time)?	Yepo?
Why?	Yén?	What?	Enna?
Who?	Yaru?	Is...available?	Trukka?
How much does this cost?	Yenna vélai?	Go away/leave me alone.	Enna vidu.
Please speak slowly.	Médhoova pésùngo.	What's this called in Tamil?	Tamille Enna?
I don't understand.	Puriyailai.	Help!	Kapathu!
Please repeat.	Thiruppi.	Stop/enough.	Porum.
I like...	Ennaku ... pidikkum.	I don't like...	Ennaku ... pidikkaath.
What is your name?	Unga péyar ennai?	My name is...	En peyar...

Directions

English	Tamil	English	Tamil
(to the) right	valadu pakkam	(to the) left	idadhu pakkam
How do I get to...?	...eppadi pôradu?	How far is...?	...evvalavu dooram?
near	pakkam	far	dooram

Numbers

English	Tamil	English	Tamil
one	onrru	twenty	erupathu
two	eranndu	thirty	muppathu
three	moonrru	forty	naarrpathu
four	naanku	fifty	iympathu
five	iynthu	sixty	arrupathu
six	aarru	seventy	azhupathu
seven	aezhu	eighty	annpathu
eight	addu	ninety	thonnorru
nine	onpathu	one hundred	noorru
ten	paththu	one thousand	aayeram

Food

English	Tamil	English	Tamil
vegetables	kari kai	rice	saadam
meat	maamsam	water	thanni
mango	maampazham	bread	rodde

Times and Hours

English	Tamil	English	Tamil
open	tharandhu	closed	moodi
What time is it?	Enna néram?	morning	kaathaalai
afternoon	madyaanam	evening	saayankaalam
night	raatri	yesterday	nethikki
today	innikki	tomorrow	nazhaikki

Other Words

English	Tamil	English	Tamil
alone	thaniya	friend	nanban
good	nalladhu	bad	kéttadhu
hot	soodu	cold	aarinadhu
temple	kohyel	doctor	maruthuvar
beach	kadarrkarai	town	pattenam

English	Marathi	English	Marathi
Hello.	Namaste/Namaskaar.	How are you?	Kasa kaya aahey?
Sorry/Forgive me.	Maaf karaa.	OK.	Achha/thik Aahey.
Thank you.	Dhanyawad.	No thanks.	Nako.
Who?	Kuon?	When(what time)?	Kehva?/Kadhi?
Why?	Kaa?	What?	Kaaya?
I don't understand.	Mala samasta hani.	Yes/No.	Ho/Naahi.
Please speak slowly.	Sowkash bolaa.	Is...available?	...aahey kaa?
What's this called in Marathi?	Maratheet?	Please repeat.	Parat Sangaa.
		Help!	Madat laraa!
Go away/Leave me alone.	Ikerdun zaa.	How much does this cost?	Hey kiti aahey?
My name is...	Maaza nau...aahey.	My country is...	Maza gay...ahey.
I like...	Mala...awarta aahey.	I don't like...	Mala...awardat naahi.

Directions

English	Marathi	English	Marathi
(to the) right	uz ni kar dey	(to the) left	daa vi kar dey
How do I get to...?	Mala kaa zaitsa...?	How far is...?	Kiti dur...?
near	zawal	far	dur

Numbers

English	Marathi	English	Marathi
one	ek	twenty	vis
two	don	thirty	tis
three	tin	forty	chalis
four	char	fifty	pannas
five	pach	sixty	sath
six	saha	seventy	sattar
seven	sat	eighty	ainsi
eight	ath	ninety	navvad
nine	nau	one hundred	sambhar
ten	daha	one thousand	ek hajar

Food

English	Marathi	English	Marathi
bread	chapati/bhakri	rice	bhat
vegetables	bhaji	water	pani
meat	mans	fruit	phal

Times and Hours

English	Marathi	English	Marathi
What time is it?	Kiti waazle?	closed	band
night	ratri	morning	sakarli
today	kal	yesterday	kal
tomorrow	aazudya	open	ughad

Other Words

English	Marathi	English	Marathi
alone	ekta	friend (M/F)	mitra/maitrin
hot	garam	cold	thandha
good	changla	bad	vait
medicine	ausadh	doctor	vaidya
road	rasta	restaurant	upahagrha
museum	padarthasangrahalay	cockroach	jhural

English	Nepali	English	Nepali
Hello.	Namaste/Namaskar.	How are you?	Kasto chha?
Sorry/Forgive me.	Sorry (maph garnus).	No problem./I'm fine.	Thik chha.
Thank you.	Danyabad.	No thanks.	Pardaina, danyabad.
Yes/No.	Ho/Hoina.	Good-bye.	Namaste.
When(what time)?	Kahile?	What?	Ke?
Who?	Ko?	Is...available?	...paincha?
Why?	Kina?	OK.	Huncha./La.
How much does this cost?	Kati ho?	Go away. (polite/ impolite)	Tapai januus ta./Jau!
I don't understand.	Bujina.	Please repeat.	Feri bhannus.
Please speak slowly.	Bistarai bolnus.	What's this called in Nepali?	Nepali ma ke bhanchha?
Stop/enough.	Pugyo.		
What is your name?	Tapai ko naam ke ho?	My name is...	Mero naam...ho.
Help!	Guhar!	My country is...	Mero desh...ho.
I like...	... man parcha.	I don't like...	... mar par dai na.

Directions

English	Nepali	English	Nepali
(to the) right	daya, dahurie.	(to the) left	baya, debre.
How do I get to...?	...kosari janne?	How far is...?	...kati tada cha?
near	najik	far	tada
east	purba	west	paschima

Numbers

English	Nepali	English	Nepali
one	ek	twenty	biss
two	dui	thirty	tees
three	teen	forty	chaliss
four	char	fifty	pachass
five	panch	sixty	saathi
six	chha	seventy	sattari
seven	saat	eighty	asi
eight	aathh	ninety	nabbe
nine	nau	one hundred	ek saya

Food

English	Nepali	English	Nepali
bread	pauroti	rice	bhat
meat	masu	water	pani
vegetables	tarkari	food/meal	khana

Times and Hours

English	Nepali	English	Nepali
open	khulcha	closed	bandha
What time is it?	Kati bajyo?	morning	bihana
afternoon	diooso	evening	sanjha
night	rati	yesterday	hijo
today	aaja	tomorrow	bholi

Other Words

English	Nepali	English	Nepali
alone	eklai	friend	sathi
good	ramro	bad	naramro
happy	kushi	sad	dukhi
hot	garmi (weather)/tato	cold	jaado (weather)/chiso

English	Gujarati	English	Gujarati
Hello.	Namaste.	How are you?	Kem cho?
Sorry/Forgive me.	Maaf karo.	Yes/No.	Ha/Na.
Thank you.	Aabhar.	I am fine.	Hu majama chu.
Good-bye.	Avjo.	No problem.	Kaso vando nahi.
When?	Kyare?	I like...	Mane...gameche.
Is...available?	...maleche?	Stop/enough.	Bas.
What is your name?	Tamaru nam su che?	Help!	Bachao!
My name is...	Maru nam...che.	My country is...	Maro desh...che.
Go away/Leave me alone.	Jatore.	I don't like...	Mane...gamtu nathi.

Directions

English	Gujarati	English	Gujarati
to the right	jamani baju	to the left	dabi baju
How do I get to...?	...no rasto kayo che?	How far is...?	...ketlu dur che?

Numbers

English	Gujarati	English	Gujarati
one	ek	six	chah
two	be	seven	sat
three	tran	eight	aath
four	char	nine	nav
five	pach	ten	das

Times and Hours

English	Gujarati	English	Gujarati
open	khulu	closed	band
night	raat	yesterday	kale (gay kale)
today	aaje	tomorrow	kale (avti kale)

English	Kannada	English	Kannada
Hello.	Ain samachar.	Good-bye.	Namaskara.
What is your name?	Ni nna he sa ru?	My name is...	Na nna he sa ru...
Please excuse me.	Da ya ma di na nna ksha mi si ri.	How much is this?	...nsu he ge?
		Give me...	Ardha...

Numbers

English	Kannada	English	Kannada
one	ondu	twenty	ippaththu
two	eradu	thirty	muvaththu
three	muru	forty	naluvaththu
four	nalku	fifty	ivaththu
five	aidu	sixty	aruvaththu
six	aru	seventy	eppaththu
seven	elu	eighty	embaththu
eight	entu	ninety	thombaththu
nine	ombathu	one hundred	nuru
ten	haththu	one thousand	savira

Food

English	Kannada	English	Kannada
bread	rotti	rice	akki
meat	mamsa	fruit	hannu
vegetables	tharakarl	water	niru
curd	mosaru	dal	thovve

English	Malayalam	English	Malayalam
Hello.	Namaste.	How are you?	Enngane irikkunnu?
Sorry/Forgive me.	Kshemikkuga.	Yes/No	Ade/alla
Thank you.	Valara upakaram.	No thanks.	Véndá.
Good-bye.	Pogetté.	No problem.	Sárawilla.
When/What time?	Eppoýá/eppam?	What?	Endo?
Who?	Árá?	Why?	Endá?
Go away/Leave me alone.	Pó, salyappadade.	Stop/enough.	Madi.
		OK.	Seri.
I don't understand.	Samajha nahin.	Please repeat.	Phir se kahiye.
What is your name?	Ninngade pér endá?	Help!	Onnu saháyikkámó?
My name is...	Enda péru ...	My country is...	Enda támassam ... ilá.
I like...	Enikka ... istamá.	Use the meter!	Míteru kanakkáyitta!

Directions

English	Malayalam	English	Malayalam
How do I get to...?	... édu vazhiyá?	How far is...?	... ettara dúramá?
Where is...?	Ewidá?		

Food and Drink

English	Malayalam	English	Malayalam
bread	rotti	rice	córa
meat	eracci	water	vellam

Times and Hours

English	Malayalam	English	Malayalam
open	torannu	closed	adaccu
What time is it?	Ettara maniyá?	yesterday	innala
today	innu	tomorrow	nále

English	Telugu	English	Telugu
Hello.	Emandi	How are you?	Meeru ela unnaru?
Sorry/Forgive me .	Kshaminchandi.	No problem.	Paravaledu.
Thank you.	Krithagnatalu	No thanks.	Vaddandi.
Yes/No.	Avunu/Kaadu	OK.	Sare.
Good-bye.	Poyesta.	When(what time)?	Eppudu (time entha)?
What is your name?	Mee peru emiti?	My name is...	Naa peru ...

Directions

English	Telugu	English	Telugu
How do I get to...?	... ki poye daniki dari	How far is...?	... entha duramu?
near	daggara	far	dooramu

Numbers

English	Telugu	English	Telugu
one	okati	six	aaru
two	rendu	seven	eedu
three	moodu	eight	enimidi
four	naalugu	nine	tommidi
five	aidu	ten	padi

Food

English	Telugu	English	Telugu
vegetables	kooragayalu	rice	annamu
meat	mamsamu	water	neeru

Times and Hours

English	Telugu	English	Telugu
open	terachu	closed	moosiveyabadinadi
What time is it?	Time enthandi?	yesterday	ninna
today	nedu	tomorrow	repu

APPENDIX

■ Glossary

General Terms

aarti: Hindu floating lights ceremony

adivasi: aboriginal, tribal people of India

Agni: Hindu god of fire, messenger of the gods

ahimsa: non-violence

AIADMK: All-India Anna Dravida Munntra Kazhagam, regional party in Tamil Nadu

AIR: All-India Radio

air-cooling: low-budget air-conditioning—a fan blows air over the surface of water

Allah: literally, "the God," to Muslims

AMS: Acute Mountain Sickness

artha: material wealth, one of the four goals of Hindu life

ashram: hermitage for Hindu sages and their students

ASI: Archaeological Survey of India

atman: Hindu concept of individual soul, the breath of Brahman

attar: alcohol-free perfume

auto-rickshaw: three-wheeled, semi-enclosed vehicle with the engine of a scooter

Avalokitesvara: the popular *boddhisattva* of compassion

avatar: descent of a Hindu god (usually Vishnu) to earth; an incarnation

ayurveda: ancient Indian system of medicine

azan: Muslim call to prayer, usually given from a minaret

bahal: Newari houses or monasteries forming a quadrangle with a central courtyard

baksheesh: tip, donation, bribe, or all of these at once

bagh: garden

ban: forest

bandh: general strike; usually involves shop closings and transportation difficulties

basti: Jain temple

bazaar: market area of a town

betel: red nut with mild narcotic properties when chewed; key ingredient in *paan.*

Bhagavad Gita: Hindu philosophical scripture sung to the hero Arjuna by the god Krishna

bhajan: Hindu devotional song

bhakti: personal, emotional devotion to a Hindu deity

bhang: dried leaves and shoots of the male cannabis plant

bhangra: Punjabi folk music often used in modern Indian-techno-pop remixes

Bharat: the Sanskrit word for India

bhavan: office or building

bidi: small cigarette made from a rolled-up tobacco leaf

bindi: forehead mark, worn mostly (but not exclusively) by Hindu women; symbolizes the third, all-seeing eye

BJP: Bharatiya Janata Party (Indian People's Party); the major Hindu nationalist party, symbolized by a lotus

bodhisattva: would-be Buddha who postpones his own enlightenment to help others

Bön: pre-Buddhist, animist religion of Tibet

Brahma: creator god in the Hindu "trinity," no longer commonly worshiped

Brahman: the universal soul or spirit, embodied by Brahma

brahmin: member of the hereditary priesthood; highest of the four Hindu *varnas*

Buddha: Enlightened One

bugyal: high meadow, above the treeline

cantonment: former British military district in a city

caste: Hindu group that practices a hereditary occupation, has a definite ritual status, and marries within the group

chador: shawl

chaitya: Buddhist prayer hall or miniature *stupa*

chakra: Wheel of the Law in Buddhism; Vishnu's discus weapon in Hinduism

chalo: let's go

chappals: leather sandals

charbagh: traditional Mughal garden form, used particularly in tombs.

chauk (chowk): market area or square

chhattri: cenotaph; cremation monument

chillum: mouthpiece of a *hookah,* or a pipe use to smoke *ganja*

chorten: Tibetan Buddhist memorial shrine

chowkidar: watchman

coir: woven coconut fibers

communalism: religious prejudice, especially between Hindus and Muslims

Congress (I): party that grew from Indian National Congress that pushed for Indian Independence; party of Jawaharlal Nehru, Indira Gandhi; "I" is for "Indira"

CPM; CPI(M): Communist Party of India (Marxist), based in West Bengal, symbolized by a hammer and sickle

CPN-UML: Communist Party of Nepal-United Marxist-Leninist, symbolized by a sun

crore: ten million, written 1,00,00,000

dacoit: armed bandit

Dalit: currently preferred term for former "Untouchables"

darshan: "seeing" a Hindu deity through his or her image

deodar: tall Indian cedar tree

dham: place, often a sacred site

dharamshala: resthouse for Hindu pilgrims

dharma: it refers to one's duty and station in life, and also to a system of morality and a way of life or religion (Hindu or Buddhist)

dhobi: washerman or -woman

dhoti: *lungi* with the cloth then pulled up between the wearer's legs

dhow: boat of Arab origins

diwan-i-am: hall of public audience

diwan-i-khas: hall of private audience

DMK: Dravida Munnetra Kazhagam; regional party in Tamil Nadu

dorje: Tibetan Buddhist thunderbolt symbol

dowry: money or gifts given by a bride's parents to the son-in-law's as part of a marriage agreement; officially illegal but widely practiced

durbar: royal palace or court

Durga: Hindu goddess who slayed the buffalo demon Mahisha

dun: valley

dupatta: scarf warn as part of the *salwar-kameez* costume.

durbar: royal court

Eve-teasing: cat-calling, sexual harassment

export guru: spiritual leader whose teachings are marketed towards Westerners, often with financial as well as philanthropic motives

fakir: ascetic (usually Muslim)

FRO: Foreigners' Registration Office

ganj: market

ganja: dried leaves and flowering tops of female cannabis plant, used for smoking

garh: fort

Garuda: Vishnu's half-man, half-bird vehicle

ghat: riverbank used for bathing, often paved with steps; also the name of the ranges of hills on the east and west coasts of the Indian peninsula

ghazal: Urdu love song

godown: factory warehouse

gompa: Tibetan Buddhist monastery

gopis: Krishna's milkmaids

gopuram: trapezoidal entrance tower of a South Indian Hindu temple

GPO: General Post Office

guru: religious teacher; in Sikhism, one of the ten founding leaders of the Sikh faith

gurudwara: Sikh temple

Guru Granth Sahib: Sikh holy book

Haj: the pilgrimage to Mecca that all Muslims are required to make once in their lifetime if physically and financially able

Hanuman: monkey god, helper of Rama in the *Ramayana*

harmonium: air-powered keyboard instrument

harijan: literally, "child of God"; Mahatma Gandhi's name for the Untouchables

hartal: general strike

haveli: Rajasthani mansion, traditionally painted with murals

hijra: eunuch; transvestite

hiti: Newari water-spout

hookah: elaborate smoking apparatus in which the smoke is drawn through a long pipe and a container of water

howdah: seat for an elephant rider

imam: prayer leader of mosque, or Shi'a Muslim leader descended from Muhammad

imambara: tomb of a Shi'a Muslim imam, or a replica of one

Indo-Saracenic: architecture merging Indian styles with "Islamic" styles from the Middle East

Indra: early Hindu god of thunder, king of the Vedic gods

jagamohana: audience hall or "porch" of a Hindu temple

jali: geometric latticework pattern in Islamic architecture

Janata Dal: political party based largely in Uttar Pradesh and Bihar, supported by low-caste Hindus, symbolized by a wheel

Jat: large North Indian agricultural case

jati: sub-division within the four Hindu castes

jauhar: Rajput custom of mass *sati* (self-immolation)

-ji: suffix added to names as a mark of respect

JKLF: Jammu and Kashmir Liberation Front; militant group seeking independence for Kashmir

juggernaut: bastardation of the deity Junnagadh's name; refers to large ceremonial carts used to transport the deity

Kali: Hindu goddess of black skin and lolling tongue who wears snakes and skulls

kama: physical love, one of the four goals of a Hindu's life; when capitalized, "Kama" is the Hindu god of love

kameez: loose-fitting woman's shirt

karma: what goes around comes around, man

kata: silk prayer shawl, usually presented to a lama when visiting a monastery

khadi: homespun, handwoven cotton cloth

Khalistan: "Land of the Pure"; name of independent Punjab desired by Sikh separatists

khalsa: Punjabi "pure"; a Sikh who has been "baptized"

khukuri: machete-like Nepalese "Gurkha" knife

Krishna: Hindu god who plays flute and frolics with milkmaids; Arjuna's charioteer in *Mahabharata* who sang *Bhagavad Gita;* considered an *avatar* of Vishnu

kshatriya: member of the warrior/ruler caste, second highest of the four *varnas* of the Hindu caste system

kumbh: pitcher or pot

kurta: long men's shirt

lakh: one hundred thousand (usually rupees or people), written 1,00,000

Lakshmi: Goddess of fortune and wealth, often considered the consort of Vishnu

lama: Tibetan-Buddhist priest or holy man

lila: Hindu concept of divine "play:" a god (usually Krishna) sporting with human worshipers, or theatrical production depicting a myth (usually *Ramayana*).

linga: also *lingam;* stone shaft that symbolizes Shiva; while originally a phallic symbol, it has lost that meaning for most Hindus

Lok Sabha: lower house of the Indian parliament

lungi: sarong tied around a man's waist

Macchendranath: Newari god associated with rain

maha: great

Mahabharata: long, long, Sanksrit epic telling the story of the five Pandava brothers' struggle to regain their kingdom

mahal: palace

mahout: elephant trainer

mandala: circle symbolizing universe in Hindu and Buddhist art, used in meditation

mandapam: colonnaded hall leading up to a Hindu or Jain temple sanctum

mandir: Hindu or Jain temple

mantra: sacred word or chant used by Hindus and Buddhists to aid in meditation

marg: road

masjid: mosque; Muslim place of worship

math: residence for Hindu priests or sadhus

maya: Hinduism's illusory world of everyday life

mela: fair or festival

mendi: painting of intricate, semi-perminant henna designs on the hands or feet

moksha: Hindu salvation; liberation from *samsara*

monsoon: season of extremely heavy rains, usually from June to September

muezzin: crier who calls Muslims to prayer from the minaret of a mosque

mullah: Muslim scholar or leader

nadi: river

naga: Hindu aquatic snake deity

nagar: city

Nandi: Shiva's bull vehicle

Narayan: Vishnu, especially when sleeping on the cosmic ocean

nawab: Muslim governor or landowner

NDP: National Democratic Party, right-wing party in Nepal

neem: plant-derived product used as an insecticide

Nepali Congress: centrist party that led the movement for democracy in Nepal, symbolized by a tree

nirvana: nothingness, a blissful void, the goal of Buddhists

Om: ༀ; sacred invocation; mantra used by Hindus and Buddhists.

paise: 1/100 of a rupee

pajama: men's baggy pants

pagoda: Nepali Hindu temple, usually with stepped roofs

panchayat: traditional five-member village council

palanquin: hand-carried carriage

pandit: honored or wise person; Hindu priest

Parsi: "Persian"; Zoroastrians who migrated to India after Muslim conversion of Iran

Partition: 1947 division of British India along religious lines to create India and Pakistan

Parvati: mountain goddess; consort of Shiva through whom his power is expressed

peon: low-level worker

pipal: bodhi tree

pitha: Hindu holy place associated with the goddess Sati

prasad: food consecrated by a Hindu deity and given out to worshipers

puja: prayers and offerings of food and flowers to a Hindu deity

pujari: Hindu priest conducting ceremonies in a temple

pukkah: finished, ripe, complete

pur: city

Puranas: "Old stories"; Hindu mythological poems

purdah: the Muslim (and sometimes Hindu) practice of secluding women

qawwali: Sufi devotional or love song

qila: fort

Qur'an: Muslim holy book containing Muhammad's Arabic divine revelations

Radha: milkmaid consort of Krishna

raga: melodic structure used as a base for lengthy musical improvisations

raj: government or sovereignty; when capitalized, usually refers to the British Empire in India

raja: king

Rajputs: medieval Hindu warrior-princes of central India and Rajasthan

Rama: Hindu hero-god of the epic *Ramayana* who defeats the demon Ravana; considered an *avatar* of Vishnu

Ramadan: holiest month in the Islamic calendar, when Muslims are required to fast between dawn and dusk

Ramayana: epic telling the story of Rama's rescue of his wife Sita from Ravana

rani: queen

rath: cart, particularly one used in Hindu religious festivals

Ravana: villain of the epic *Ramayana*

RNAC: Royal Nepal Airlines Corporation

RSS: Rashtriya Swayamsevak Sangh (National Volunteer Corps), Hindu nationalist paramilitary organization

sadhu: ascetic Hindu holy man

sagar: sea or lake

sahib: "master," title given to English colonial bosses and still used for Europeans

salwar: women's baggy pants worn with kameez

sambar: large, dark brown deer; South Indian curry sauce

samsara: the endless cycle of life, death and rebirth in Buddhism and Hinduism

sangam: meeting point of two rivers; also name of early gatherings of Tamil poets

sankha: Vishnu's conch shell

sannyasin: "renouncer." Hindu ascetic wanderer who has given up worldly life

sant: saint, holy man

sari: six (sometimes nine) yards of cloth, usually silk or cotton, draped gracefully around a woman's body and worn with a matching blouse

Sati: Hindu goddess who landed in pieces all over India, forming *shakti* pithas; considered a consort of Shiva

sati: custom that widows burned themselves on their husbands' funeral pyres

satyagraha: "soul/truth force" Mahatma Gandhi's protest by non-violent non-cooperation

scheduled castes: official name for the former "Untouchable" groups, whose castes are listed in a "schedule" in Indian law

scheduled tribes: aboriginal groups recognized under India law

sepoy: Indian serving in British Indian army under the Raj

Shaiva: follower of Shiva

shakti: divine feminine power in Hinduism

Shankara: Shiva

shanti: peace

Shi'a: Muslim sect which split from the Sunnis in the 8th century AD in a succession dispute; Shi'as look to imams in Iran as their spiritual leaders

shikhara: pyramid-shaped spire on a Hindu temple

Shitala: "cool" goddess of smallpox and other fever diseases in North India

Shiva: one of great gods of Hinduism, known as the Destroyer in the Hindu "trinity," though he has other roles as well; usually depicted as an ascetic holy man

Shiv Sena: regional Hindu nationalist party in Maharashtra

shudra: member of the laborer caste, lowest of the four Hindu *varnas*

sindur: vermillion paste used as an offering to Hindu deities

Sita: Rama's wife in the *Ramayana*, she is kidnapped by Ravana leading to the battle between Rama and Ravana

sitar: 20-stringed instrument made from a gourd with a teakwood bridge

Sri: title of respect and veneration

STD/ISD: standard trunk dialing/international subscriber dialing

stupa: large hemispherical mound of earth, usually containing a Buddhist relic

Sufi: member of Islamic devotional, mystical movement

Sunni: largest Muslim sect; believes in elected leaders for the Islamic community

swadeshi: domestic goods; the Indian freedom movement called for their use rather than British imports

swaraj: self-rule; what the Indian freedom movement demanded

sweeper: low-caste or Untouchable Hindu whose vocation is sweeping streets or cleaning latrines

tabla: two-piece drum set

tal: lake

tara: Tantric female companion to a *dhyani* Buddha

Terai: foothills near the base of the Himalaya

tempo: three-wheeled motor vehicle meant to carry about six people

thanka: Tibetan scroll-painting of a *mandala*, used as an aid in meditation

tirtha: "crossing" between earth and heaven in Hinduism; while this usually means a holy place, it can also mean a holy man, *mantra*, etc.

tirthankara: one of 24 Jain "crossing-makers," a series of saints culminating with Mahavira, the founder of Jainism

tonga: two-wheeled carriage drawn by a horse or pony

topi: cap worn by Nepali men

trek: organized hike through the countryside in mountain regions

trichul: trident; symbol of Shiva and originally a symbol of the Goddess

Untouchables: casteless Hindus, formerly shunned by high-caste Hindus because their touch was considered polluting. Now known as scheduled castes, Dalits, or harijans

Upanishads: speculative, philosophical Sankrit Hindu hymns composed around 800 BC

Vaishnava: follower of Vishnu

vaishya: member of the merchant caste, third-highest of the four Hindu *varnas*

vajra: Nepali word for *dorje*, the Tibetan Buddhist thunderbolt symbol

varna: broad group of Hindu castes; *brahmins, kshatriyas, vaishyas,* and *shudras* are the four *varnas*

Vedas: sacred hymns in Sanskrit composed between 1500 and 800 BC, forming the basis of the Hindu religion

Vishnu: one of the Great Gods of Hinduism, known as the "Preserver" in the Hindu trinity; frequently appears on earth as an *avatar* to save earth from demons

VHP: Vishwa Hindu Parishad (World Hindu Society); Hindu nationalist organization.

wallah: occupational suffix: e.g. rickshaw-*wallah*

yaksha: early Hindu nature deity

yakshi: female *yaksha*

Yama: early Hindu god of death

zakat: obligatory almsgiving required of Muslims

zamindar: tax collecter or landlord in Mughal India

Food and Drink

alu: potato

am: mango

appam: South Indian rice pancake

arrak: drink made from brewed, fermented barley

badam: almond

baingan: eggplant

barfi: milk-and sugar-based Indian sweet

bhaji: vegetables dipped in batter and fried

bhat: cooked rice

bhindi: okra (lady's fingers)

biryani: rice cooked with spices and vegetables or meat

capsicum: bell pepper

chai (chiya): tea, generally boiled with milk and sugar

channa: chickpeas

chang: Himalayan rice wine

chapati: unleavened, griddle-cooked bread

chaat: snack

cheeni: sugar

chikki: peanut brittle

cold drink: carbonated drink

cutlet: patty-shaped food unit, can contain meat and/or vegetables

dahi: yogurt

dal: lentil soup; staple dish eaten with rice

dhaba: roadside food stand

doplaza: with two onions

dosa: South Indian rice-flour pancake

dudh: milk

dum: steamed

feni: Goan drink made from fermented coconuts or cashews

garam: hot

ghee: clarified butter

gosht: mutton or goat

gulab jamun: dry milk balls in sweet syrup

halal: food prepared according to Islamic dietary rules

idli: South Indian steamed rice-flour cakes

jelaibis: deep fried, orange-colored, syrup-filled sweet

kaju: cashew nut

kheer: rice cooked in sweetened milk, raisins, and almonds

kofta: meat- or vegetable-balls

korma: creamy curry

kulfi: thick pistachio-flavored ice cream

lassi: yogurt and ice-water drink

machli: fish

masala: a mix of spices, usually containing cumin, coriander, and cardomom

methi: cooked with fenugreek leaves and spices

mirch: hot pepper

momo: Tibetan stuffed pastry similar to wontons or ravioli

murgh: chicken

mutter: green peas

naan: unleavened bread cooked in a tandoor

naryal: coconut

pakoras: cheese or other foods deep-fried in chick-pea batter

palak: spinich

paneer: homemade cheese

pani: water

papadam: crispy lentil wafer

paratha: multi-layered whole-wheat bread cooked on a griddle

paan: betel leaf stuffed with areca nut for chewing

permit room: (in Tamil Nadu) establishment with a liquor license; bar

phal: fruit

pongal: rice item garnished with black peppers and chillies

prapad: crunchy chick-pea cracker; like a tortilla chip

pulao: fried rice with nuts or fruit

puri: small deep-fried bread

raita: spicy salad of vegetables and yogurt

raksi: strong Himalayan liquor

roti: bread

saag: pureed spinach or other green vegetables

sabjiv: vegetables

sambar: South Indian lentil soup

samosa: deep-fried pastry pyramid containing vegetables or meat

tandoor: clay oven shaped like an inverted cone

thali: complete meal served on steel plate with small dishes of condiments

thukpa: Tibetan noodle soup

tiffin: snack or light meal

toddy: unrefined coconut liquor

tong-ba: Nepali grain liquor, drunk through a straw

utthapam: thick dosa made with onion

vadai: doughnut-shaped rice cake soaked in curd or sambar

vindaloo: very hot South Indian curry

Index

Researcher-Writers

Asbury P. Jones, Jr.   *M.P., Bihar, Orissa*
Always the professional, Asbury charted an epic journey across the center of India for Let's Go. From the beautiful *stupa* at Sanchi to the Valley of the Shadow of Bihar and (thankfully) farther still, to the placid Orissan coast, Asbury continually amazed us with his casual wit and clear social conscience. Making friends and sharpening his Hindi skills as he went, Asbury kept us posted on the tourist scene with his concise, clear copy, and those much-needed phone calls.

Keith Lee   *U.P. Plains, Northern M.P., Goa*
Keith's long-awaited return to India was indeed triumphant. Whether sculpting new coverage of the Konkan Railway, sniffing out cybercafes, or uncovering colonial scandals, Keith laid on the southern charm, and sent us the beautifully written copy that ensued. Keith gave us all the dirt on U.P.'s Mughal tombs and holy cities, and in monsoonal Goa he found a sort of sultry tropical languor reminiscent of his native Louisiana. All in all, his unflagging optimism sustained him through good times and, well, better times.

Andrew E. Nieland   *Goa*
Known (mostly to himself) as "T-bone," Andrew is something of a Let's Go legend. Having broken the cycle of office *samsara*, this former *Let's Go: London* editor headed East for the winter, and he capped off his career in grand style—with a jaunt to Goa in peak season. Andrew reported on all the food (some of it still crawling), folks (some of them living in trees), and fun (much of it chemically-enhanced) the state had to offer. Anjuna, Calangute, and Vagator, and the 60s will never be the same.

Abena Dove Agyepoma Osseo-Asare   *Tamil Nadu*
Who better to send to Gangaikondacholapuram? Abena is a woman with a long name and a long history of traveling and living around the world: Ghana, Japan, and now India. Firmly committed to the process of deconstructing colonialism, Abena updated our coverage of Tamil Nadu with skill and sensitivity. This daughter of a professional chef put her picky palate to work sampling everything from *dal bhat* to *brochette de crevettes* and closed her journey dodging bandits and honeymooners alike in the cool Nilgiri Hills.

Kishan Kumar Putta   *Gujarat, Rajasthan*
Kishan never lost his cool, even after a massive cyclone left him stranded in a disaster zone. Twenty-foot waves and undertow be damned, daredevil Kishan even went for a swim in the Arabian Sea (though he did wait thirty minutes after eating, to avoid cramping his style). Emerging unscathed in spite of freak weather and hungry mosquitoes, Kishan went on to cover romantic Rajasthan, sending back stories of valiant horses, holy rats, and budget deals.

Elizabeth Tova Russo   *Kathmandu Valley, Eastern Nepal*
So conscientious she corrected her own copy twice before she even sent it in, linguistically versatile Elizabeth was an editor's dream. With little use for public transportation, she made the seven-hour uphill hike from Dhulikhel to

Nagarkot on foot—*pole pole ndiyo mwendo!* Throughout her trip, Elizabeth's business-card collection and beautiful photos reminded us just how good a time she was having—so good a time, in fact, that she stayed longer, and covered more, than either she or we expected.

Adam Rzepka
Punjab, Haryana, H.P., Kashmir, Andaman Islands

It reads like the script of an adventure movie: start in the seedy bazaars of a third-world capital, move on to mystic religious centers, forbidden cities, and stunning mountains. Add a few bus chases, a two-day hike across washed-out roads and glaciers, and closing scenes on a lush, tropical isle—then watch the credits roll. Our leading man, Adam wowed us with his down-to-earth manner, and rock-solid journalistic skill, and impeccable sense of the historical and the hysterical. We can't wait to see the sequel.

Tim Santry
Maharashtra, Andhra Pradesh

Making Mumbai (if not street-stall food) safe for the novice traveler, Tim set out for Maharashtra with water-proof pen-in-hand and Marathi on his mind. His graphic design skills came in especially handy in his drawings of Indian advertisements for Viagra and Wino Brand Detergent. Whether he was dodging traffic in Hyderabad, touring the temple at Tirumala, or scanning Star TV for yet another showing of *Seven*, Tim kept his sense of humor intact. It was an auspicious beginning for a long and happy relationship with India.

Shlomtzion Shaham
U.P. Hills, Delhi, Karnataka

Shlomtzi put her years of Third World experience to use discovering India. Popular with editors and locals alike, Shlomtzi combined a cheerful attitude with maturity and insight. After a warm-up in the hill stations of Garhwal and Kumaon, she dove straight into Delhi, revamping Let's Go's coverage from top to bottom. With her social conscience and eye for detail in full effect, she closed her epic stint with a trip down south to Karnataka. In fact, she loved India so much, she decided to stay a little longer. We wish her luck during her upcoming year of travel.

Vivek Waglé
West Bengal, Sikkim, Northeast States

Insurgent tribals, monsoonal deluges, and vacationing students all conspired to hinder Vivek's coverage of India's beautiful Northeast, but in spite of the obstacles, our former *Let's Go: Southeast Asia* editor completed top-notch research in record time. Whether expanding our coverage of India's hilly postage-stamp states, reviewing nationalist graffiti in Meghalaya, pounding the pavement in Calcutta, or typing Hindi for the good of many, Vivek unswervingly and unceasingly exceeded our expectations. Then he was off to Chicago and Michigan to do the same for *Let's Go: USA.*

Katarina Wong
Western Nepal, Kerala

After doing time in the Terai ("this place is hotter than the surface of the sun!"), Katarina was eager to take a dip in the green mountain surrounds of Pokhara. Calm, collected, and a bit cooler, Katarina hopped a plane for South India, stalking big cats at Periyar Tiger Reserve, and sending back prose even more amazing than the stationary on which it was written. Katarina ended her (mostly) perfect trip at the very tip of India: sitting on the beach writing toddies and sipping copy, er, you know what we mean.

Acknowledgments

Thanks to Heath Ritchie, Maryanthe Malliaris, Eben Kenah, Adam Rzepka, Vivek Waglé, Keith Lee, Elizabeth Russo, and Angma Jhala for office help; to Sharmila Sohoni and Derek McKee for advice and regional knowledge; to M. Ranjit Matthews and Balaji Gadhiraju for Malayalam and Telugu aid; to team Southeast Asia for picking up the phone and putting up with the noise; to Nic for endless copy edits; to Mapland for manning the compass, the Managing Editors for sleeping with the cell phone, and Caroline-*cum*-Anna for running the show; and, of course, to Abena, Adam, Andrew, Asbury, Elizabeth, Katarina, Keith, Kishan, Shlomtzi, Tim, and Vivek, who collectively went the distance and lived to write about it. **Team I&N**

Thanks first to Bina and Daley for all your dedication and hard work. This book wouldn't be here without you (you too, Pooja and Derek). Thanks also to everyone else in the office—never has so much work been so much fun. Kudos to the Movienite regulars, and of course Doug and Ben; *gracias* to Adriana for the late-night food. Thanks to my whole family. And, more than any other thing, *asante Mungu*. **NHB**

Thanks to Bashir, Ryan, Rebecca, Pooja for sticking around Boston and to my far-flung girlies whose hilarious group emails were almost as good as real-live chillin: you were all like a bloody mary for my college hangover. Thanks Naté for your patience, Daley for your sense of humor, and Babu *(il n'est pas buste)*. Finally, thanks to my parents, for supporting me in this (and every) endeavor, and for all the exposure to a culture with which I have fallen completely in love. Clem, Randi, Lisa: meet you in India! **BG**

Thanks BG. Thanks to CPP and NAB because it's not easy. Thanks to JHM for comin' a knockin'. Thanks to YLC and SMB for transferring in. Thanks to AKB and VM for not transferring out. Thanks to NAS for letting me call him by his name. Thanks to GWW for agreeing. Thanks to AD for the Tacareia Airlift. Thanks to NCM for staying in our house for free and eating our food. Thanks Mom, Dad, Devon, Max, and Babu. **DCH**

Editor	Nate Barksdale
Associate Editor	Bina Gogineni
Associate Editor	Daley Haggar
Managing Editor	Nicolas R. Rapold
Publishing Director	Caroline R. Sherman
Publishing Director	Anna C. Portnoy
Production Manager	Dan Visel
AssociateProduction Manager	Maryanthe Malliaris
Cartography Manager	Derek McKee
Design Manager	Bentsion Harder
Editorial Manager	M. Allison Arwady
Editorial Manager	Lisa M. Nosal
Financial Manager	Monica Eileen Eav
Personnel Manager	Nicolas R. Rapold
Publicity Manager	Alexander Z. Speier
New Media Manager	Måns O. Larsson
Map Editors	Matthew R. Daniels, Daniel J. Luskin
Production Associate	Heath Ritchie
Office Coordinators	Tom Moore, Eliza Harrington, Jodie Kirshner
Director of Advertising Sales	Gene Plotkin
Associate Sales Executives	Colleen Gaard, Mateo Jaramillo, Alexandra Price
President	Catherine J. Turco
General Manager	Richard Olken
Assistant General Manager	Anne E. Chisholm

Thanks to Our Readers...

Mano Aaron, CA; Jean-Marc Abela, CAN; George Adams, NH; Bob & Susan Adams, GA; Deborah Adeyanju, NY; Rita Alexander, MI; Shani Amory-Claxton, NY; Kate Anderson, AUS; Lindsey Anderson, ENG; Viki Anderson, NY; Ray Andrews, JPN; Robin J. Andrus, NJ; L. Asurmendi, CA; Anthony Atkinson, ENG; Deborah Bacek, GA; Jeffrey Bagdade, MI; Mark Baker, UK; Mary Baker, TN; Jeff Barkoff, PA; Regina Barsanti, NY; Ethan Beeler, MA; Damao Bell, CA; Rya Ben-Shir, IL; Susan Bennerstrom, WA; Marla Benton, CAN; Matthew Berenson, OR; Walter Bergstrom, OR; Caryl Bird, ENG; Charlotte Blanc, NY; Jeremy Boley, EL SAL; Oliver Bradley, GER; A.Braurstein, CO; Philip R. Brazil, WA; Henrik Brockdorff, DMK; Tony Bronco, NJ; Eileen Brouillard, SC; Mary Brown, ENG; Tom Brown, CA; Elizabeth Buckius, CO; Sue Buckley, UK; Christine Burer, SWITZ; Norman Butler, MO; Brett Carroll, WA; Susan Caswell, ISR; Carlos Cersosimo, ITA; Barbara Crary Chase, WA; Stella Cherry Carbost, SCOT; Oi Ling Cheung, HK; Simon Chinn, ENG; Charles Cho, AUS; Carolyn R. Christie, AUS; Emma Church, ENG; Kelley Coblentz, IN; Cathy Cohan, PA; Phyllis Cole, TX; Karina Collins, SWITZ; Michael Cox, CA; Mike Craig, MD; Rene Crusto, LA; Claudine D'Anjou, CAN; Lizz Daniels, CAN; Simon Davies, SCOT; Samantha Davis, AUS; Leah Davis, TX; Stephanie Dickman, MN; Philipp Dittrich,GER; Tim Donovan, NH; Reed Drew, OR; Wendy Duncan, SCOT; Melissa Dunlap, VA; P.A. Emery, UK; GCL Emery, SAF; Louise Evans, AUS; Christine Farr, AUS; David Fattel, NJ; Vivian Feen, MD; David Ferraro, SPN; Sue Ferrick, CO; Philip Fielden, UK; Nancy Fintel, FL; Jody Finver, FL; D. Ross Fisher, CAN; Abigail Flack, IL; Elizabeth Foster, NY; Bonnie Fritz, CAN; J. Fuson, OR; Michael K. Gasuad, NV; Raad German, TX; Mark Gilbert, NY; Betsy Gilliland, CA; Ana Goshko, NY; Patrick Goyenneche, CAN; David Greene, NY; Jennifer Griffin, ENG; Janet & Jeremy Griffith, ENG; Nanci Guartofierro, NY; Denise Guillemette, MA; Ilona Haayer, HON; Joseph Habboushe, PA; John Haddon, CA; Ladislav Hanka, MI; Michael Hanke, CA; Avital Harari, TX; Channing Hardy, KY; Patrick Harris, CA; Denise Hasher, PA; Jackie Hattori, UK; Guthrie Hebenstreit, ROM; Therase Hill, AUS; Denise Hines, NJ; Cheryl Horne, ENG; Julie Howell, IL; Naomi Hsu, NJ; Mark Hudgkinson, ENG; Brenda Humphrey, NC; Kelly Hunt, NY; Daman Irby, AUT; Bill Irwin, NY; Andrea B. Jackson, PA; John Jacobsen, FL; Pat Johanson, MD; Russell Jones, FL; J. Jones, AUS; Sharon Jones, MI; Craig Jones, CA; Wayne Jones, ENG; Jamie Kagan, NJ; Mirko Kaiser, GER; Scott Kauffman, NY; John Keanie, NIRE; Barbara Keary, FL; Jamie Kehoe, AUS; Alistair Kernick, SAF; Daihi Kielle, SWITZ; John Knutsen, CA; Rebecca Koepke, NY; Jeannine Kolb, ME; Elze Kollen, NETH; Lorne Korman, CAN; Robin Kortright, CAN; Isel Krinsky, CAN; George Landers, ENG; Jodie Lanthois, AUS; Roger Latzgo, PA; A. Lavery, AZ; Joan Lea, ENG; Lorraine Lee, NY; Phoebe Leed, MA; Tammy Leeper, CA; Paul Lejeune, ENG; Yee-Leng Leong, CA; Sam Levene, CAN; Robin Levin, PA; Christianna Lewis, PA; Ernesto Licata, ITA; Wolfgang Lischtansky, AUT; Michelle Little, CAN; Dee Littrell, CA; Maria Lobosco, UK; Netii Ross, ITA; Didier Look, CAN; Alice Lorenzotti, MA; David Love, PA; Briege Mac Donagh, IRE; Brooke Madigan, NY; Helen Maltby, FL; Shyama Marchesi, ITA; Domenico Maria, ITA; Natasha Markovic, AUS; Edward Marshall, ECU; Rachel Marshall, TX; Kate Maynard, UK; Agnes McCann, IRE; Susan McGowan, NY; Brandi McGunigal, CAN; Neville McLean, NZ; Marty McLendon, MS; Matthew Melko, OH; Barry Mendelson, CA; Eric Middendorf, OH; Nancy Mike, AZ; Coren Milbury, NH; Margaret Mill, NY; David H. Miller, TX; Ralph Miller, NV; Susan Miller, CO; Larry Moeller, MI; Richard Moore, ENG; Anne & Andrea Mosher, MA; J. L. Mourne, TX; Athanassios Moustakas, GER; Laurel Naversen, ENG; Suzanne Neil, IA; Deborah Nickles, PA; Pieter & Agnes Noels, BEL; Werner Norr, GER; Ruth J. Nye, ENG; Heidi O'Brien, WA; Sherry O'Cain, SC; Aibhan O'Connor, IRE; Kevin O'Connor, CA; Margaret O'Rielly, IRE; Daniel O'Rourke, CA; Krissy Oechslin, OH; Johan Oelofse, SAF; Quinn Okamoto, CA; Juan Ramon Olaizola, SPN; Laura Onorato, NM; Bill Orkin, IL; K. Owusu-Agyenang, UK; Anne Paananen, SWD; Jenine Padget, AUS; Frank Pado, TX; G. Pajkich, Washington, DC; J. Parker, CA; Marian Parnat, AUS; Sandra Swift Parrino, NY; Iris Patten, NY; M. Pavini, CT; David Pawielski, MN; Jenny Pawson, ENG; Colin Peak, AUS; Marius Penderis, ENG; Jo-an Peters, AZ; Barbara Phillips, NY; Romain Picard, Washington, DC; Pati Pike, ENG; Mark Pollock, SWITZ; Minnie Adele Potter, FL; Martin Potter, ENG; Claudia Praetel, ENG; Bill Press, Washington, DC; David Prince, NC; Andrea Pronko, OH; C. Robert Pryor, OH; Phu Quy, VTNM; Adrian Rainbow, ENG; John Raven, AUS; Lynn Reddringer, VA; John Rennie, NZ; Ruth B.Robinson, FL; John & Adelaida Romagnoli, CA; Eva Romano, FRA; Mark A. Roscoe, NETH; Yolanda & Jason Ross, CAN; Sharee Rowe, ENG; W. Suzanne Rowell, NY; Vic Roych, AZ; John Russell, ENG; Jennifer Ruth, OK; William Sabino, NJ; Hideki Saito, JPN; Frank Schaer, HUN; Jeff Schultz, WI; Floretta Seeland-Connally, IL; Colette Shoulders, FRA; Shireen Sills, ITA; Virginia Simon, AUS; Beth Simon, NY; Gary Simpson, AUS; Barbara & Allen Sisarsky, GA; Alon Siton, ISR; Kathy Skeie, CA; Robyn Skillecorn, AUS; Erik & Kathy Skon, MN; Stine Skorpen, NOR; Philip Smart, CAN; Colin Smit, ENG; Kenneth Smith, DE; Caleb Smith, CA; Geoffrey Smith, TX; John Snyder, NC; Kathrin Speidel, GER; Lani Steele, PHIL; Julie Stelbracht, PA; Margaret Stires, TN; Donald Stumpf, NY; Samuel Suffern, TN; Michael Swerdlow, ENG; Brian Talley, TX; Serene-Marie Terrell, NY; B. Larry Thilson, CAN; J. Pelham Thomas, NC; Wright Thompson, ITA; Christine Timm, NY; Melinda Tong, HK; M. Tritica, AUS; Melanie Tritz, CAN; Mark Trop, FL; Chris Troxel, AZ; Rozana Tsiknaki, GRC; Lois Turner, NZ; Nicole Virgil, IL; Blondie Vucich, CO; Wendy Wan, SAF; Carrie & Simon Wedgwood, ENG; Frederick Weibgen, NJ; Richard Weil, MN; Alan Weissberg, OH; Ryan Wells, OH; Jill Wester, GER; Clinton White, AL; Gael White, CAN; Melanie Whitfield, SCOT; Bryn Williams, CAN; Amanda Williams, CAN; Wendy Willis, CAN; Sasha Wilson, NY; Kendra Wilson, CA; Olivia Wiseman, ENG; Gerry Wood, CAN; Kelly Wooten, ENG; Robert Worsley, ENG; C.A.Wright, ENG; Caroline Wright, ENG; Mary H. Yuhasz, CO; Margaret Zimmerman, WA.

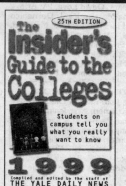

★Let's Go 1999 Reader Questionnaire★

Please fill this out and return it to **Let's Go, St. Martin's Press,** 175 Fifth Ave., New York, NY 10010-7848. All respondents will receive a free subscription to **The Yellowjacket,** the Let's Go Newsletter. You can find a more extensive version of this survey on the web at http://www.letsgo.com.

Name: _____

Address: _____

City: _____ **State:** _____ **Zip/Postal Code:** _____

Email: _____ **Which book(s) did you use?** _____

How old are you? under 19   19-24   25-34   35-44   45-54   55 or over

Are you (circle one)   in high school   in college   in graduate school   employed   retired   between jobs

Have you used Let's Go before? yes no **Would you use it again?** yes no

How did you first hear about Let's Go? friend   store clerk   television   bookstore display   advertisement/promotion   review   other

Why did you choose Let's Go (circle up to two)? reputation budget focus   price   writing style   annual updating   other: _____

Which other guides have you used, if any? Fodor's Footprint Handbooks   Frommer's $-a-day Lonely Planet Moon Guides Rick Steve's   Rough Guides   UpClose   other: _____

Which guide do you prefer? _____

Please rank each of the following parts of Let's Go 1 to 5 (1=needs improvement, 5=perfect). packaging/cover practical information   accommodations   food   cultural introduction   sights   practical introduction ("Essentials")   directions   entertainment   gay/lesbian information   maps   other: _____

How would you like to see the books improved? (continue on separate page, if necessary) _____

_____

How long was your trip?   one week   two weeks   three weeks   one month   two months or more

Which countries did you visit? _____

What was your average daily budget, not including flights? _____

Have you traveled extensively before? yes no

Do you buy a separate map when you visit a foreign city? yes no

Have you used a Let's Go Map Guide? yes no

If you have, would you recommend them to others? yes no

Have you visited Let's Go's website? yes no

What would you like to see included on Let's Go's website? _____

_____

What percentage of your trip planning did you do on the Web? _____

Would you use a Let's Go: recreational (e.g. skiing) guide gay/lesbian guide   adventure/trekking guide   phrasebook   general travel information guide

Which of the following destinations do you hope to visit in the next three to five years (circle one)? Canada Argentina Perú Kenya Middle East   Caribbean   Scandinavia   other: _____

Where did you buy your guidebook?   Internet   independent bookstore   chain bookstore   college bookstore   travel store   other: _____